Rudolph Valentino the Silent Idol: His Life in Photographs

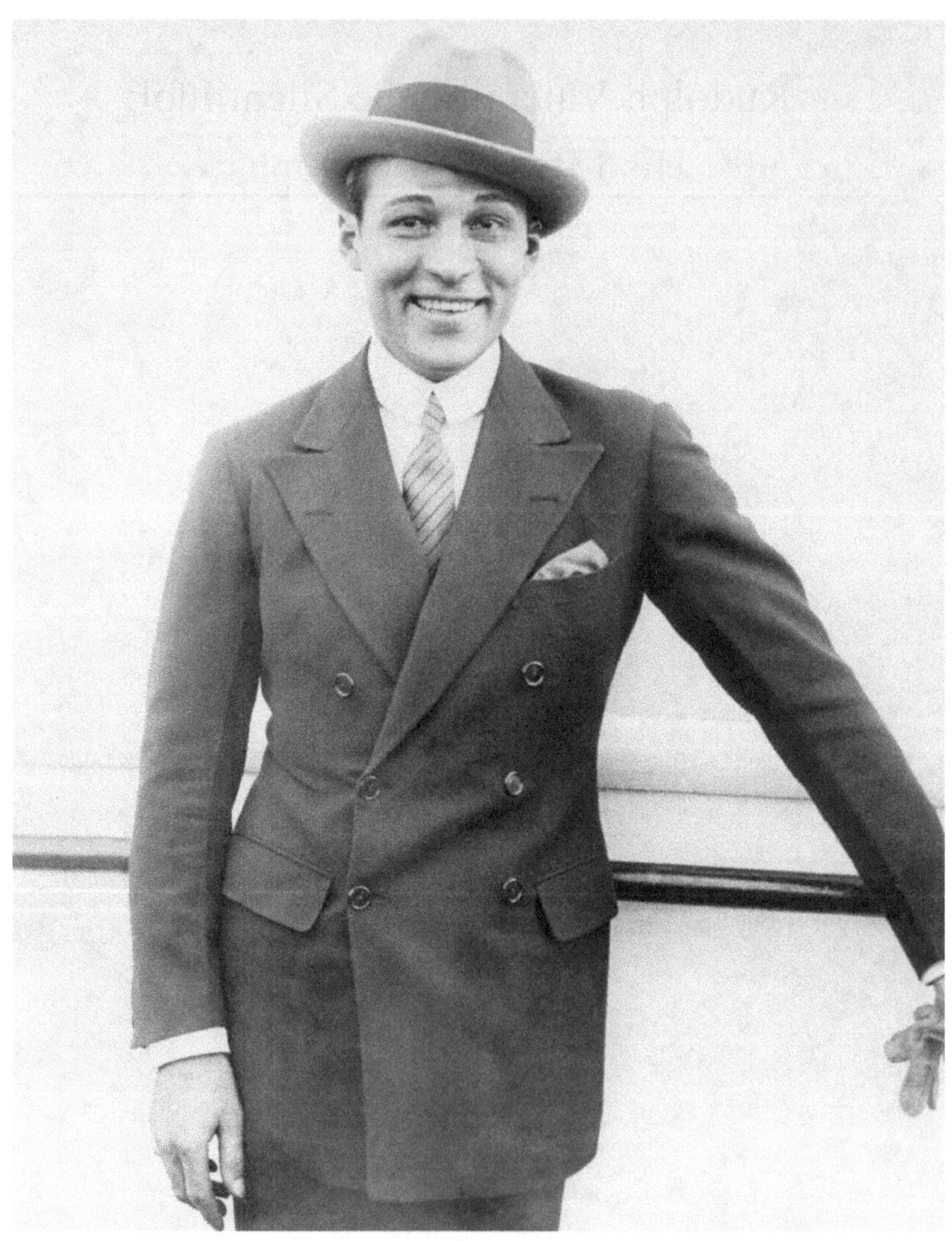

Women are not in love with me but the picture of me on the screen.
I am merely the canvas on which women paint their dreams.

-Rudolph Valentino 1923

Rudolph Valentino the Silent Idol: His Life in Photographs

Donna L. Hill

Foreword by Emily W. Leider

RVG

2019

First Printing: 2010
Revised Edition: 2019

ISBN 978-0-578-47224-9

Library of Congress Control Number: 2019936041

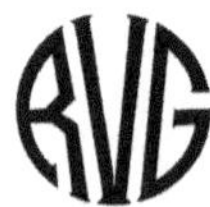

RVG Books
San Francisco, CA 94109

www.rudolph-valentino.com

Dedication

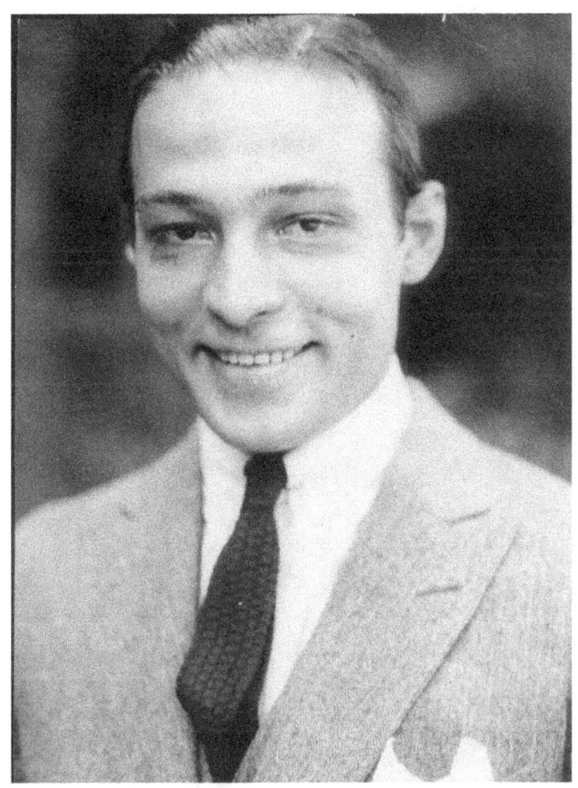

In memory of Rudolph Valentino,
who provided endless inspiration;
and to all my friends,
who provided endless support
and encouragement

Contents

It is rare that any project of this nature is completed due to the efforts of one person, and this book is certainly no exception. While my name is on the cover, I had a great deal of assistance and my debts are numerous and heavy. To everyone who provided support, friendship, and help with material, the following somewhat perfunctory acknowledgements and thanks are but a smidgen of the deep and sincere gratitude I feel. Their belief and encouragement for this project kept me going.

First, I must thank the late Nikki Shacklett, who used much blue pencil to edit my poor prose down to the most effective use of the English language.

In addition, I must thank my reviewers who helped fact-check and make the words flow. Joan Myers, Jeanine Villalobos, Emily Leider, Rebecca Eash, Tracy Terhune, Toni Lopopolo, and Caroline Rupprecht all did yeoman service.

Grateful thanks to Jennie Sloan who created the beautiful cover art for the first edition. Christy Pascoe did the cover art for this new edition. Her patience with me as I nitpicked over it was beyond the pale. I could not be happier, it's perfect. I must also thank Dana Grae Kane for translating portions of Robert Florey's recollections and Gloria Bowman for translating portions of Jeanne de Recqueville's 1978 biography *Rudolph Valentino*.

Fellow collectors and connoisseurs of fine vintage photographs freely provided rare material along with their good wishes and generous spirit: Michael and Virginia Back, the late Robert S. Birchard, Gloria Bowman, Manoah Bowman (Independent Visions), Kevin Brownlow (Photoplay Productions Archive), Jeff Carrier, Dansmuseet (Stockholm, Sweden), Sandra Davidson, Allan Ellenberger, Brad Frick, Tracey Goessel, Michael Hawks, Dr. Paula Hinton, Kristen Burkhart Hua, Sylvia Valentino Huber, Francis Lacassin, Paul Lamastra, Robert Lanier, Emily Leider, Craig MacPherson, the late Fr. Michael Morris, John Neil, David Price, Caroline Rupprecht, Tonia Salom, Dian Sharma, Suzanne Stadler Snowden, Tony Susnick, Tracy Terhune, Jeffrey Vance, Jeanette Valentino Villalobos, Jeanine Villalobos, Marc Wanamaker (Bison Archives), Mark Vieira, Suzanne Weakley, and Linda Wulfstieg. Their generosity cannot be underestimated and I am exceedingly grateful.

I truly had an embarrassment of riches to choose from. In the prior edition of the book I was limited by the number of pages I could use in the manuscript. Sadly, in the effort to conserve space and to not be repetitive, some of the images shared with me were not used. In this edition I had no such restrictions. I have greedily utilized all the space I could, and then some.

Over the years as this project morphed from a complete biography to a book of photographs, many friends and authors shared research material on Valentino. Even casual visitors to my Rudolph Valentino website at http://www.rudolph-valentino.com sent articles to me. Although much of that material was not germane to this book, I thank each and every person who generously sent me information. Rest assured, all that material will be utilized in my next Valentino project, nothing ever goes to waste.

I must thank the individuals below for their invaluable help: Kevin Brownlow, Chris Connelly, the late Sally Dumaux, Paula Duryea (who provided access to the Baroness de Beckendorff diaries), Rebecca Eash, Thomas Gladysz, Tracey Goessel, Stella Grace, Emily Leider, Annette D'Agostino Lloyd, Mary Mallory, Graceann MacLeod, Joan Myers, R. Tina

Porta, Caroline Rupprecht, Chris Snowden, Tracy Terhune, Arlene K. Witt, and Joe Yranski all shared material or tipped me off to a good source or story.

I spent countless hours sifting through news clippings in scrapbooks, on microfilm and via newspaperarchive.com and other online news sources, but I cannot match the sheer bull-dog tenacity of Rebecca Eash. Were it not for her single-minded efforts in researching the stops and tour dates of the 1923 Mineralava Tour, this volume would be far less informative about this interesting period of the Valentino's short and amazing life. I only regret I was not able to do full justice to the tour in this book. Saying "thank you" conveys little of my high regard and thanks for Rebecca's assistance and friendship over the years. For friendship's sake, and for the memory of Rudy and Natacha, she shared all her hard work and material with me.

I regret I did not travel the world in search of photos in the literal sense—I did so virtually. Thank goodness for archives, libraries and the Internet. Because of these many resources, I had available at my fingertips a vast amount of material. This all added to the quality of the images used herein. Grateful thanks to the librarians and archivists of the world. We live in a wonderful age!

I could not have completed this book without the wise counsel of the late Robert Cushman of the Academy of Motion Picture Arts & Sciences. The collection of images maintained at the Margaret Herrick Library is incredible, and so much of the credit for that is due to Robert Cushman. I deeply mourn the fact that Robert is not here to see the finished project. I hope that he would have been pleased with the results.

Manoah Bowman of Independent Visions offered fantastic advice and helped me obtain many rare photographs, candids and stills, from *Uncharted Seas* and *Moran of the Lady Letty*. He also performed digital magic on images that needed tender loving care, so that they could be seen at their very best. He is an artist and a man of delicate taste and sensibilities when it comes to choosing exactly the right photograph. He also taught me a few tricks of the trade, for which I am extremely grateful. I hope to continue applying this knowledge on future projects.

I obtained a long-sought photograph thanks to Dorinda Hartmann, Assistant Archivist Film and Photo Archive at the Wisconsin Historical Center. I found a wealth of photos at the San Francisco Public Library in the San Francisco History Center. I must also thank various dealers in memorabilia as well as fellow collectors for images I purchased for my collection: Marty Kearns, Danny Schwartz, Mike Hawks, John and Helen Hunt, John Hillman and Marcelo Coronado, the late Erik Stogo, and Mack Dennard. The eBay sellers (and several eBay adversaries) who helped reduce my savings account and who provided wonderful photos shall have to remain blameless and nameless. I crossed paths and swords with far too many of them to remember their monikers.

I am a vintage photograph geek. It sounds dramatic, sometimes I do gasp with joy when I have the opportunity to examine a particularly rare pristine vintage print. For most of these images, I have done very little retouching unless it was necessary to preserve the original luminosity and contrast. Happily, many images required only minor cosmetic repair, such as scratch removal and brightness/contrast adjustment.

Other photos suffered the ravages of time which had not been gentle with them. Ripped, stained, color washed, bent—other hands had treated beautiful photos as if they were trash. I am indebted to a few friends who hold magical knowledge of digital repair. We tried to be both deft and considerate, using Photoshop to repair the wear and tear of time, but not add or subtract to the original images.

Kevin and Susan Elder did a great deal of work on photos I thought would be utterly hopeless. They proved me wrong, and their work is amazing. The time and effort they spent was an act of kindness I will not soon forget. Caroline Rupprecht attacked each project handed to her with gusto, and I am grateful for all the work she dedicated to my project. I could not have done this without her assistance. In the blink of an eye, Manoah Bowman performed death-defying feats of digital magic on images. Practice really does make perfect. It was truly an awesome display. For the new edition of this book Tony Susnick helped me out and worked some incredible magic.

The late Dian Sharma who was one of my nearest and dearest friends for decades. It was our common interest in Valentino that began our friendship. Her unerring eye for a truly great photograph added so much to our combined collection of Valentino photos. She had the knack for finding amazing shots. Without her, some of the best photos would not have been included.

Tracy Terhune provided encouragement throughout the long years this project took to incubate. Well before one word had been etched on paper, he was behind the scenes constantly pushing and encouraging me. He also offered carte blanche to use photos from his impressive collection of Valentino memorabilia. His friendship and encouragement got me through many a dark day when I thought I would never finish.

My friend, Toni Lopopolo, who offered sage advice all along the way and offered to represent me, could not have been more supportive and helpful. It had to have been arduous for her, but she always displayed humor and grace, and I thank her for believing in me and in Valentino's continuing appeal.

Emily Leider graciously offered to write the foreword to this book and I gratefully accepted. She also shared copies of photographs not used in her biography entitled*, Dark Lover: The Life and Death of Rudolph Valentino*. I appreciate her generosity and words of advice and support. It's an honor to have her name attached to this project.

Joan Myers, Rebecca Eash, and Caroline Rupprecht have proven to be great friends and tremendous boosters throughout this process. I cannot thank them enough for getting me through the dark days of staring at the virtual blank pages on the monitor.

No good deed goes unpunished, so they say. All my friends and acquaintances, as well as co-workers and employers, who put up with me during this lengthy process deserve the lion's share of kudos. Most of them did not have to witness the horrid spectacle of me writhing on the floor trying to put words on a blank canvas or struggling while deciding which photos to keep and which to discard. Nonetheless, they had to endure my endless prattle and musings on Valentino for years and years. I am happy to say they survived the ordeal and I hope they have forgiven me my excesses and I can still call them friends.

Deborah Anderson, the late Michael Back and his wife Virginia, Thomas Blount, Gloria Bowman, Kelly Brown, Kevin Brownlow, Lisa Cone, Braddoc deCaires, Liz McCann di Norma, B. Joan Donovan, Kevin and Susan Elder, Kim Ray Flanagan, Thomas Gladysz, Tracey Goessel, Eve Golden, Stella Grace, Greg Higgins, Kristen Burkhart Hua, Sylvia Valentino Huber, Jeffrey Karceski, Dana Grae Kane, Gail Lang, Robert Lashmore, Annette D'Agostino Lloyd, Bill and Emily Leider, Graceann MacLeod, Christian Meinke, Michael Morris, Joan Myers, Jesse Obstbaum, Christy Pascoe, Tonia Salom, Dian Sharma, Steven F. Shorb, Greg and Jennifer Sloan, Patrick Stanbury, Tracy Terhune, Patricia Tobias, Jeanine

Villalobos, Wendy Warwick White, Arlene K. Witt, Joe Yranski, and, it goes without saying, my friends not named here who comprise the Daughters of Naldi and the Lounge of Tomorrow.

Two of my friends are not here to see this project come to fruition. I miss them very much. Their encouragement was profoundly appreciated: the late Penny Barkin and my fellow founding Daughter of Naldi, the late Sally Dumaux. I'm sorry this project took so very long.

Rudolph Valentino, gone so many years, still has many friends. I have made the effort during the lengthy gestation process to keep good records on who helped and who provided encouragement and support. God forbid I have left anyone off this long list. If by some horrible mischance your name is not here, please forgive me and remember that your name is inscribed on my heart.

The story of Rudolph Valentino's short, sad and dramatic life has been told many times before, but never as authentically as in *Rudolph Valentino – The Silent Idol: His Life in Photographs*, a unique assemblage of more than 400 photographs, many of them here published for the first time. The Donna Hill collection spans his entire biography, from Rudolfo Guglielmi's late nineteenth century beginnings as the rebellious son of a middle-class family in an obscure town in Puglia, Italy to his tumultuous New York funeral and solemn Los Angeles farewell in 1926, reported in newspapers and newsreels worldwide.

A collector, webmaster (www.rudolph-valentino.com), silent film buff and recognized Valentino authority, Donna Hill has been accumulating Valentino photographs and memorabilia for more than thirty years. Although she doesn't overlook the thousands of film stills and publicity pictures that document Valentino's influential, decade-shaping movie career, she has particularly sought out the private man captured in family photographs, candid shots and behind-the-scenes images.

The pictures tell us that long before he appeared in films, Valentino displayed a love of finery, a propensity for posing before the camera and a preoccupation with his own image. An actor in life before he become one professionally, as an underemployed immigrant he would don a tuxedo and spend money he didn't have on a New York studio photographer in order to be able to send home a likeness of himself that looked prosperous, upper class and elegant. In his Hollywood heyday he relished donning period costumes, military uniforms, the robes and turban of a sheik, an ornate brocade matador suit; but he'd dress as a cowboy just to go riding on his own. Alone with his friends he'd take up the straw hat and cane of a music hall dancer, or spar in the shorts, tank top and boxing gloves of a fighter. He was justly proud of his toned, muscular physique.

Valentino often shared the frame with a car, a camera, a fellow actor or film crewmember, a dance partner, a male buddy, a horse, or one of his beloved dogs. The few shots of him with children disclose an easy rapport and ready warmth. Nowhere does he appear more relaxed and content than when he rests his head on the breast of wife-to-be Natacha Rambova on the set of *Camille*. The shot of him and Rambova as they embark for Europe after the battle with Paramount and the exhausting Mineralava tour tells a different story. They both look weary and under great strain. Valentino's hair is thinning and there are shadows under his eyes. Although he was only thirty-one when he died a few years later, the last images of him are not portraits of a young man.

To his legions of fans, Rudolph Valentino's arresting face has always conjured mystery. "Who am I?" his asymmetrical eyes seem to ask. Donna Hill's splendid parade of images helps us finally crack the code.

Emily W. Leider, May 2010

Preface

The present volume is an updated and expanded edition of *Rudolph Valentino the Silent Idol – His Life in Photographs* originally published in 2010.

This edition allows me to increase the size of the book and provide full-page photographs without the limitations of the earlier edition. The scope of Valentino's life story was expanded by including many new photographs—photographs that either did not make the cut in the first edition or have been added to my personal collection in the time since. The revision allowed me to correct textual errors, including inadvertent photo misidentifications.

While it would have been preferable to publish this edition in full color as the original; the pricing for a full color book was prohibitive. The increased size and number of the images, will enable the reader to appreciate the greater detail that can now be seen and will make up for the lack of color images.

It is my hope that this expanded edition of *Rudolph Valentino The Silent Idol: His Life in Photographs* will help readers more understand the story of Rudolph Valentino the man hidden behind the myth. May this visual biography please Valentino fans old and new for many years to come.

Donna Hill
May, 2019

Introduction

After their brief meeting in 1926, the American writer and keen cultural observer H.L. Mencken aptly described the film star Rudolph Valentino as "one who was catnip to women." Even today, the name evokes an aura of romance, a melancholy whisper of days gone by, an intangible dream.

"Rudolph Valentino" brings to mind many images: a Latin lover, a ravishing sheik, a dashing hero, a tragic figure. During his lifetime, the real Valentino—the man—was scarcely known to the general public. His fans were interested in the shadow figure on the screen and the fantasy it personified, not the man himself. In fact, Rudolph Valentino was nothing like the image he is most remembered for today, the cruel, dangerous, and exotic Arab sheik.

Young Rodolfo Guglielmi emigrated from Italy to the United States of America in 1913, alive with the spirit of adventure. In a brief span of only thirteen years, the unknown immigrant Rodolfo Guglielmi transformed into an icon: Rudolph Valentino. Wildly famous and widely reported on during his stardom and his untimely passing at the age of 31 only increased the hunger for stories about him. Over thirty biographies have been published to date about Valentino, but none of them has yet told the complete story of his life[1]. What follows is not a biography in the strict sense. It is a photographic account of the public and private Rudolph Valentino.

I discovered Valentino in the "dark ages" before the easy availability of VHS tapes and DVDs. The opportunity to see a film starring Valentino, or any other silent star, was a rare pleasure, and often a challenge. My first exposure to him was in the 1922 film *Blood and Sand*. I was twelve years old and utterly bewitched by the leading man. His performance as the doomed matador Gallardo revealed depth and charisma. I was intrigued by Valentino and sought to learn more about him.

Always an avid reader, I was also a budding student of film - in less fancy words, a "movie buff." I read everything I could get my hands on relating to film. My interest, happily, coincided with a boom in film history publishing. Many biographies, autobiographies, and other excellent film history books appeared at the same time my interest in the subject developed. One such book that I can say truly changed my life was Kevin Brownlow's epic history of the pioneers of the silent era, *The Parade's Gone By*, compulsory reading for any student of film history. Any student should also read the other volumes of what I call "Brownlow's Trilogy": *The War, the West and the Wilderness* and *Behind the Mask of Innocence*. As I studied silent film and learned more about the era, Rudolph Valentino remained an enigmatic figure. The biographies available to me told wildly different stories.

My real quest to learn about Valentino, however, was not sparked by seeing him on film or in reading books. It was a single, unassuming photograph that caught my attention and fired my interest. Contrary to what I had read, this photograph seemed to encapsulate the real Valentino. I asked myself, "Who is this young man who seems so serious, so unexotic, so normal?"

[1] One hopes that Valentino's great grand niece will complete and publish her manuscript on her famous relative.

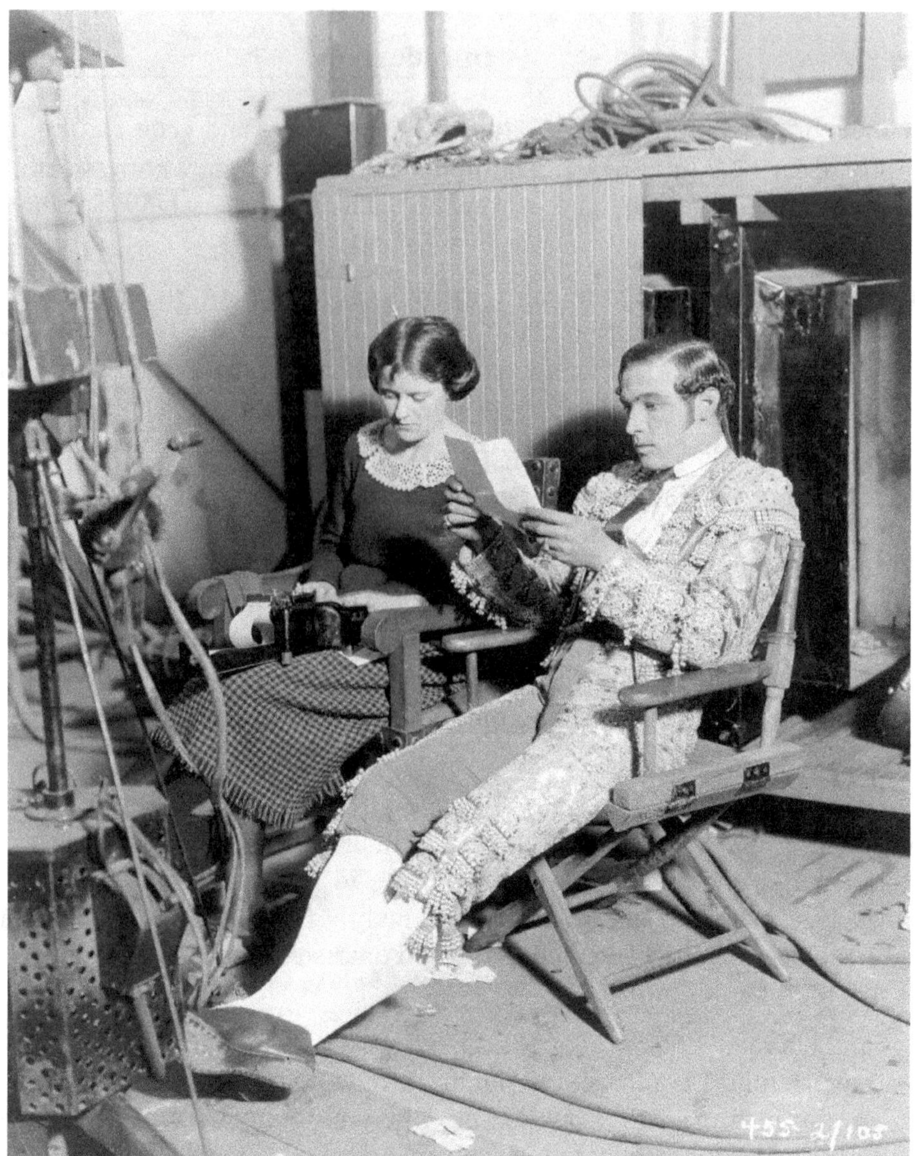

This was the photo that sparked my fascination and set me on the path of discovery wondering who was the man behind the screen image.
Valentino with his secretary Margaret Neff
on the set of the 1922 film *Blood and Sand.*
(Bison Archives)

This was not Sheik Ahmed Ben Hassan, nor was it a "lounge lizard," the persona that seemed to adhere to Valentino. It was my first glimpse of Rudolph Valentino, the person. This photograph set me on a journey of discovery. A dear friend suggested that I one day do a book on Valentino, using candid and unpublished photographs. That suggestion remained with me for years and has now come to fruition with the publication of this volume.

Rudolph Valentino lived and worked at a time before radio or television became popular media outlets. Because silent film was one of the first "mass media," the power of silent film cannot be exaggerated or underestimated. The great publicity machines created and perfected in the silent era did their best to keep names and faces before the public. They used every tool available: newspapers, magazines, movies, newsreels, and later radio for those with a crystal set. Valentino's popularity was enormous, equaling that of his fellow superstars Charles Chaplin, Douglas Fairbanks, and Mary Pickford. They truly were household names, and household names throughout the world.

Silent films died in the autumn of 1927, but Rudolph Valentino is still relevant. His name is familiar to even the most novice film buff, and he is one of the very few silent era stars who is recognizable by people who are not film buffs. Mary Pickford was America's sweetheart, Douglas Fairbanks was every boy's hero, but today both are all but forgotten by the general public[2]. It is unfortunate, but they and so many others from the era are footnotes in the consciousness of the modern filmgoer.

Though Valentino has been dead for over 90 years, his name and his image are still familiar. Modern viewers are fortunate that so many of his starring films are extant and available for home viewing. But what of his cinematic legacy? Was Valentino a great actor? The answer is, under the right circumstances and with the right director, he could be. More often than not he was hampered by poor scenarios, lackluster direction, and cheap production values. But a cinematic legacy is not necessarily a function of thespian craftsmanship. Rudolph Valentino was--indubitably--a star.

Valentino was fortunate that his breakout role in *The Four Horsemen of the Apocalypse* was a great part. Great part or not, he came to the table with abundant natural talent, and under the tutelage, guidance, and nurturing of June Mathis and Rex Ingram, he turned in a performance that is as moving today as it was in 1921.

It was *The Sheik*, however, that rocketed him from featured player to superstar. Working under a more pedestrian director, George Melford, in a low-budget production based on a scenario that had been neutered, Valentino mugged, overacting grandly and shamelessly. His triumph in that role is due to sheer star power.

In sharp contrast, *Moran of the Lady Letty* is a sleeper. *Moran of the Lady Letty* was also helmed by Melford, but this time the results were very different. Cast as a San Francisco socialite who is shanghaied, Valentino gave a relaxed and virile performance in a "small film."

He really came into his own in his last two films, *The Eagle* and *The Son of the Sheik.* Both films are timeless Hollywood fantasy romance, but both have the light touch of comedy, at which he excelled. Directed by Clarence Brown in *The Eagle* and George Fitzmaurice in *The Son of the Sheik*, Valentino's sex appeal and easy manner on screen are still vivid today. He was reluctant to make *The Son of the Sheik* but he nonetheless took pride in it, believing it a job well done. His charm and magnetism are undeniable. He smoldered through the rape scene without so much as touching Vilma Banky. The scene is not the least pornographic—all Valentino does is remove is his jeweled belt, smoke a cigarette, and move, catlike, toward his victim . . . fade out, and the women in the audience swoon. If *The Son of the Sheik* were Valentino's only extant film, it alone would be sufficient to confirm for modern audiences the magnitude of his appeal in the 1920s.

What could Valentino have accomplished had he lived to see the dawn of sound? We can only speculate. He knew his screen life as a romantic ideal was short-lived, and he longed to work behind the camera. One role that would have been surprisingly suitable in the racier pre-

[2] Eight years from the time this introduction was originally penned, times they are changing. Douglas Fairbanks has been the subject of a towering biography by Tracey Goessel, *The First King of Hollywood: The Life of Douglas Fairbanks* (Chicago Review Press). Fairbanks' films are being restored and released on DVD/Blu-Ray to great acclaim. Mary Pickford's legacy is being championed by The Mary Pickford Foundation with her films being restored and released on DVD/Blu-Ray through Flicker Alley.

Code era would have been Bram Stoker's *Dracula*. Valentino's penetrating gaze, panther-like grace, suave manner, and incredible sex appeal could have made *his* Count Dracula a block-buster and a career breaker (in perhaps the same way it was for Bela Lugosi). By 1935 Valentino would have been 40 years of age and at the peak of his physical beauty. At that time, however, the foreign lover was completely out of fashion on screen. With Alexander D'Arcy and Erik Rhodes, this character was more of a buffoon in the Depression-era films. Valentino's career in front of the camera may not have lasted too far beyond the dawn of sound. This is a question that can never be truly answered.

Valentino sometimes made terrible choices, in his life and in his career. There is no reason to assume he wouldn't have continued making poor choices in both areas. All he could do with money was spend it—if he'd saved, or had any real business sense, he might have been as formidable a United Artists partner as were founders Pickford and Fairbanks. When he had intelligent guidance behind the camera, from mentors such as Rex Ingram, June Mathis, or Clarence Brown, everything went well for him. If he had heeded the financial advice of Joseph Schenck he might well have come out ahead. He was a stubborn man and was, unfortunately, willing to listen to people who weren't any better at choices than he was.

Co-star Alice Terry once surmised that the best thing Valentino did was to die. There is some truth in that statement. Valentino died unexpectedly, in his prime and at the apex of his career. His early death caused speculation from the tabloid press of the day whether or not he was murdered. As studios re-released his earlier films to cash in, there were lines around the block in cities worldwide for his final film, *The Son of the Sheik*. United Artists considered shelving it but were surprised by the rabid, morbid curiosity of the fans. They put the film into general release and it was a smash hit. The demand for Valentino did not lessen with the passage of time. It has been over 90 years since Rudolph Valentino breathed his last on that abysmally hot and muggy August day in 1926. Silent film, the art form in which he shot to fame, died not long after. Even so, Valentino is remembered and revered to this day. Hundreds, if not thousands, of people visit his grave every year. His films, when shown at festivals and revival houses, always draw large crowds. It is my sincere hope that what follows will help illuminate the appeal and the charisma of the man named Rudolph Valentino.

A Note on the Photographs

Rudolph Valentino was a photographed personality. It was a rare issue of Photoplay, Motion Picture, Movie Weekly, or Motion Picture Classic between 1921 and 1926 that did not bear an article, interview, or at least a mention or photograph of Rudolph Valentino. Wherever he went, he was news, and he was photographed. These photographs were taken by design, for use as publicity material, or by news photographers, or by friends. Many have not been used in previous books on Valentino: the candid shots, the "behind the scenes" shots, the more relaxed images. Today, these are the most intriguing and sought-after images of Valentino. As I began collecting, they told me far more about him than what I'd read in books. That collection was eventually to form the skeleton for this book. For most of these, the photographers were anonymous. I have tried to identify the photographer whenever possible.

Valentino himself was an avid photographer and a collector of expensive camera gear. Two of the earliest unpublished photos of Valentino in this volume originate, most likely, from his own camera. As Valentino traveled around the United States in the early years, he carried a camera and often posed with his friends.

As stated above, while many of the photographs used in this book are from my own collection, I am indebted to many fellow collectors and archives for their generous loan of rare photos used in this book. Without their assistance and generosity, this book could not have come to be.

Donna Hill, 2019

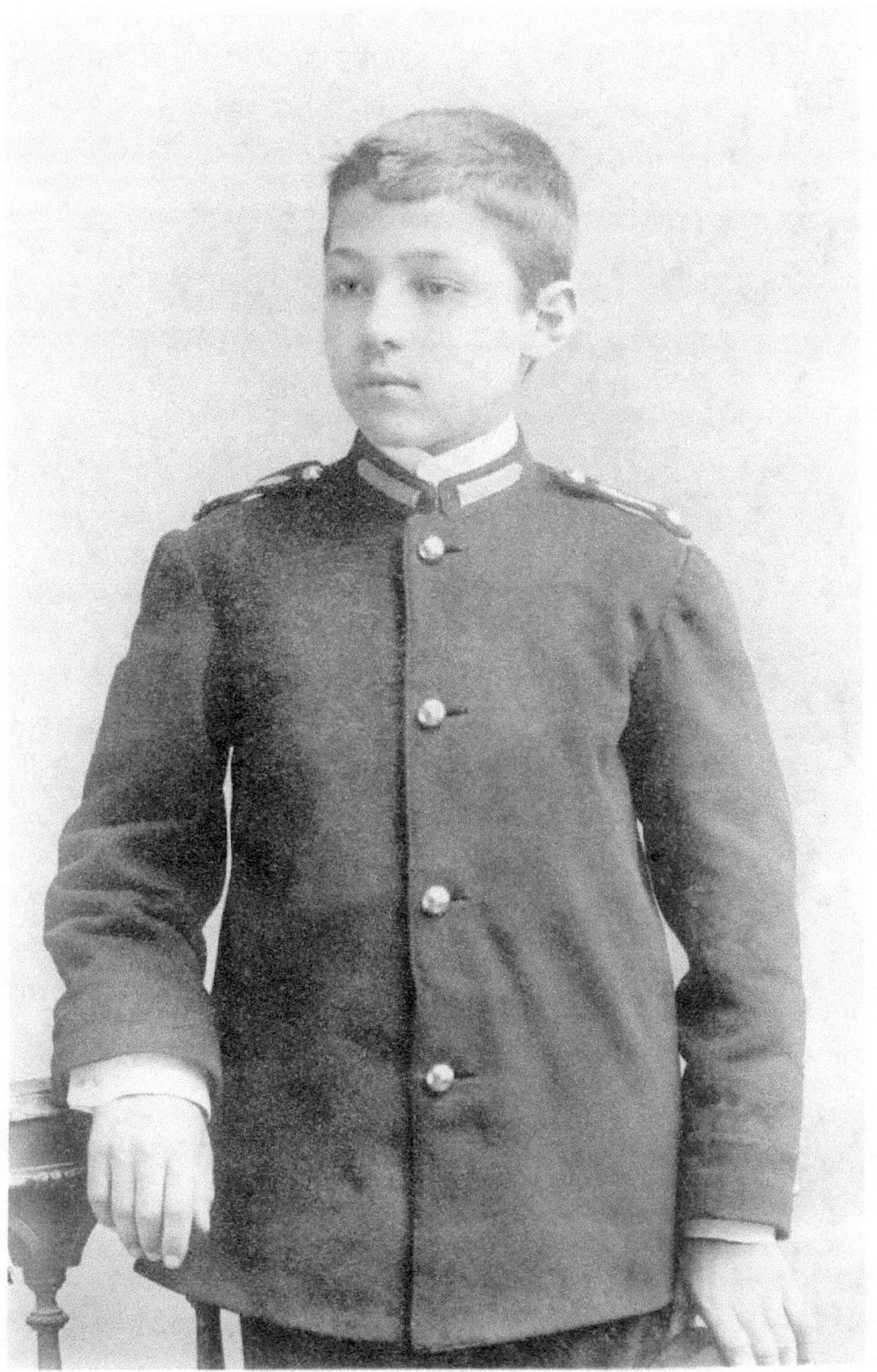

He always said Italy is too small for me.
—Alberto Valentino

Rodolfo Pietro Filiberto Raffaello Guglielmi was born in Castellaneta, Italy on May 6, 1895. Rodolfo was the third of four children born to Giovanni and Gabriella Guglielmi (*neè* Barbin). Eldest sister Grazia Bice Maria Teresa Amalia (b. June 1, 1890) barely survived infancy and died at 14 months. Alberto Pasquale Filiberto Alfonso (b. April 5, 1892) and Maria Grazia Martina Anna (b. September 1, 1897) rounded out the family.

The Guglielmi family was solidly middle class and lived in a pleasant home on a quiet street named Via Commercio. Giovanni Guglielmi was a veterinarian in the Italian military and a respected member of the community. Mother Gabriella was a devout French-born woman who doted on her children, and by all accounts she was a loving and indulgent mother. She was skilled with the needle and skilled in handling her headstrong and sometimes unruly middle child, and Rodolfo grew up worshiping her as the ideal maternal figure. Both parents were strict disciplinarians; while Gabriella's hand was velvet-gloved, Giovanni did not spare the rod when the occasion required it. Young Rodolfo certainly earned his share of correction. Older brother Alberto was a stoic, disciplined student and Giovanni's favorite. Younger sister Maria was the occasional foil and tomboy pal to her elder brother, Rodolfo. The Guglielmi household included a cook and a wet nurse.

Young Rodolfo loved adventure and make-believe, either of his own devising or acting out fairy tales of days gone by. He was an indifferent student, usually far too restless to apply himself to his studies. He did apply himself, however, to the art of penmanship; his handwriting, even at a young age, was a beautiful and distinct script.

In 1905, Giovanni Guglielmi uprooted his family and moved south to Taranto in order to advance his career in the field of biological research. In 1906 Giovanni contracted malaria—the disease he was studying. As he lay dying, Gabriella kept vigil while his two sons received their last counsel from their father, "Love your mother and above all, love your country." Both young men carried this maxim with them to their dying days. Giovanni's death was a terrific blow to the family: the loss of the patriarch and the family breadwinner. As a result of her husband's passing, Gabriella was forced to support herself and her children on a small widow's pension and the modest savings that she and Giovanni had accumulated by the time of his death.

Rodolfo grieved for his father, but the loss did not change his wild behavior. His school grades suffered and his restless behavior tried his mother's already tested affection. He was soon packed off to the Collegio-Convitto per gli Orfani dei Sanitari Italiani, a boarding school for orphans of the medical professionals in Perugia, in the vain hope that he'd bow to the discipline meted out by the schoolmasters. While in attendance his strongest subject was history, but he also did well in civics, geography, and written Italian. Mathematics bored him, and he cut classes whenever he could. He loved sports, soccer in particular. Repeated disciplinary actions did not tame him, however, and he left before threats of expulsion were carried out.

With his mother's help, Rodolfo applied for naval training in Venice. In later life, Valentino bitterly recalled being rejected for the naval training school. He had, surprisingly, passed the written test, but failed the physical examination. This humiliation spurred him to a lifelong pursuit of physical fitness—in fact, his only real vice was chain-smoking. Rumors persist to this day regarding other troubles in Venice, especially those surrounding his attraction to the ladies.

He was next sent to the Istituto di Agraria de Sant'Illario in Nervi, near Genoa. The institute boasted a technical curriculum that he found to his liking and more suited to his temperament. The quasi-military training included fencing, wrestling, and equestrian instruction, along with animal husbandry courses. He also nursed a romance with the school cook's daughter, which he later alluded to with fondness in the magazine series The Story of My Trip Abroad later published in book form as My Private Diary. In 1912 he returned home to Taranto, a graduate at last—but with no prospect of a job.

At age 17 Rodolfo was restless and unsettled, and quickly fell into unacceptable behavior. He spent less and less time in respectable circles and more time seeking friends from the stage, cafés, and other undesirable groups. Taranto was too small and too restrictive, he thought. What could he do? Desperately longing for adventure, he persuaded Gabriella to finance a trip to Paris—the dazzling French capital known for its fashionable women and bustling nightlife.

In a biography ghostwritten by Herbert Howe and published in Photoplay in 1923, Valentino recalled: "I was a little vain in my social successes—until my money was gone. Then vanity was handed the truth. I pleaded for money from home, dashed away to Monte Carlo to retrieve my fortunes, and a few weeks later enacted that perennial tragedy, The Return of the Prodigal." In My Private Diary, he said: "I came home feeling more stifled than ever. My experience in Paris had only whetted my appetite for foreign lands and other scenes. Even though they were scenes of trial—which God knows they were. I wanted to get away. There were no opportunities, no horizons."

He relapsed into his old ways upon returning to Taranto, and it did not take long for the family to send Rodolfo out on his own, to succeed or fail away from the family hearth. He later admitted that he helped the family arrive at this decision, "Before the decision was reached to send me on my desired way, I had plenty of time to prove to everyone concerned that something had better be done about me." In December 1913, the young and adventurous Rodolfo Guglielmi sailed to America, toward an uncertain future.

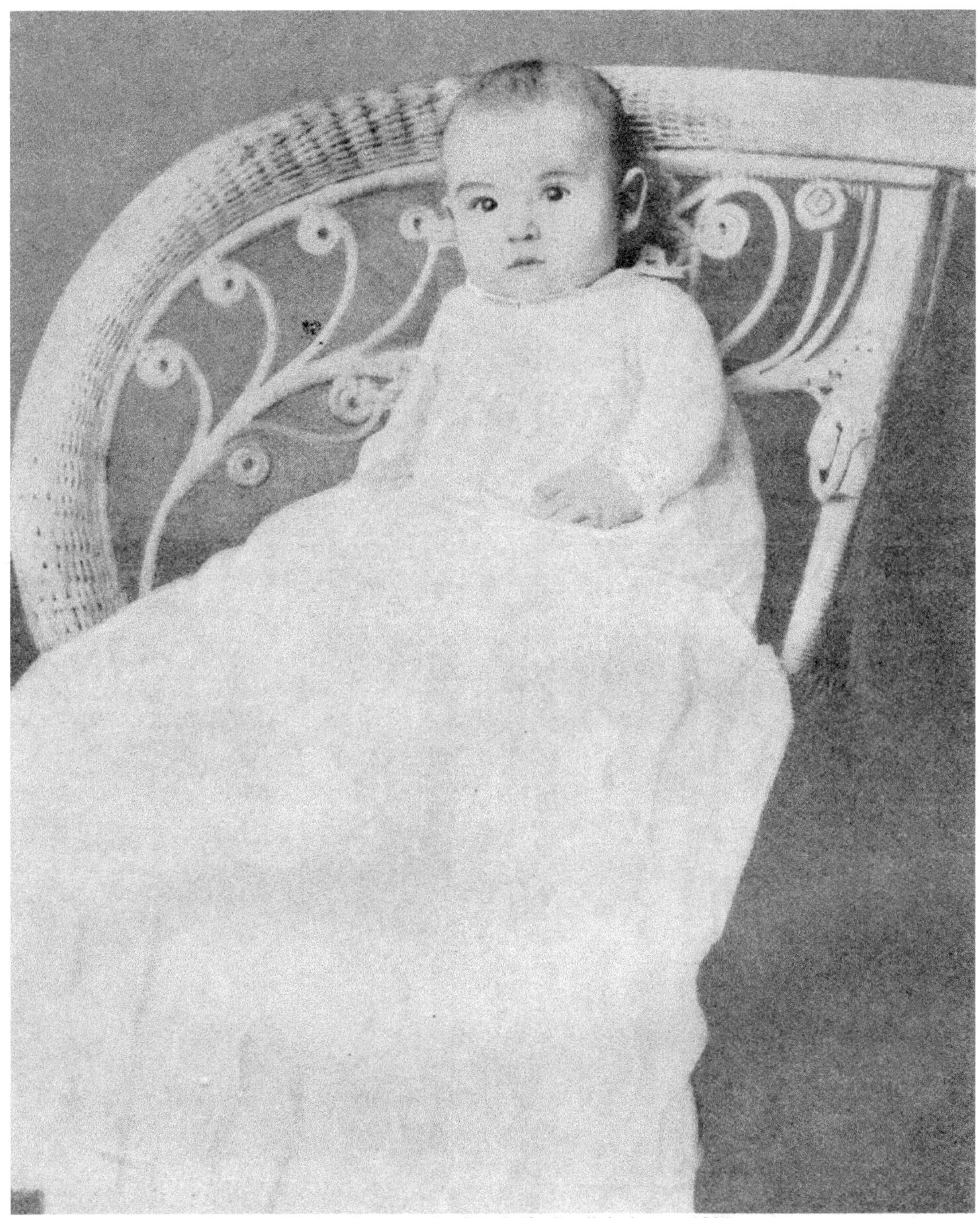

Purported baby photograph of Rodolfo Guglielmi *circa* 1895
(Author's Collection)

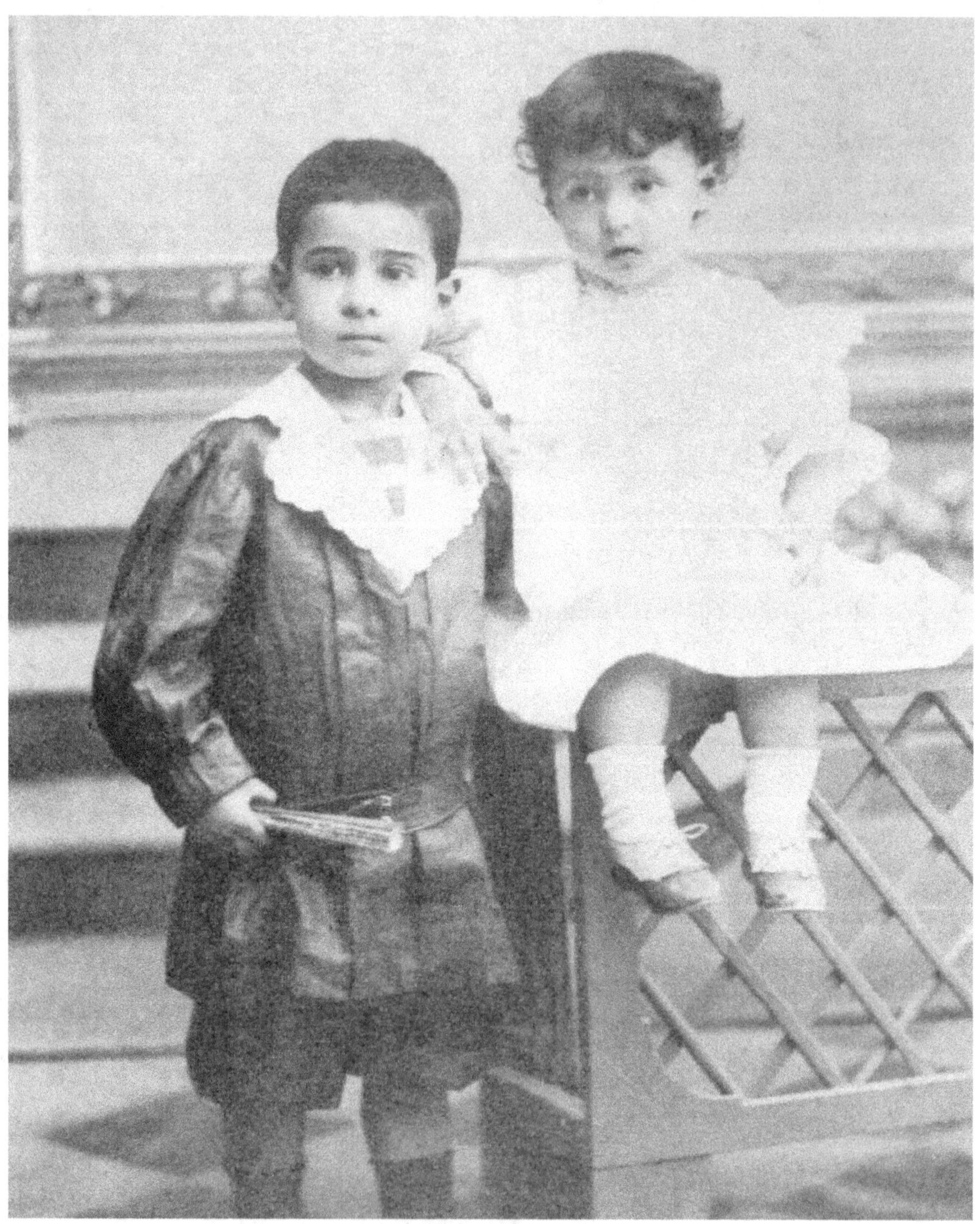

Alberto Guglielmi alongside his younger sibling Rodolfo *circa* 1897.
(Author's Collection)

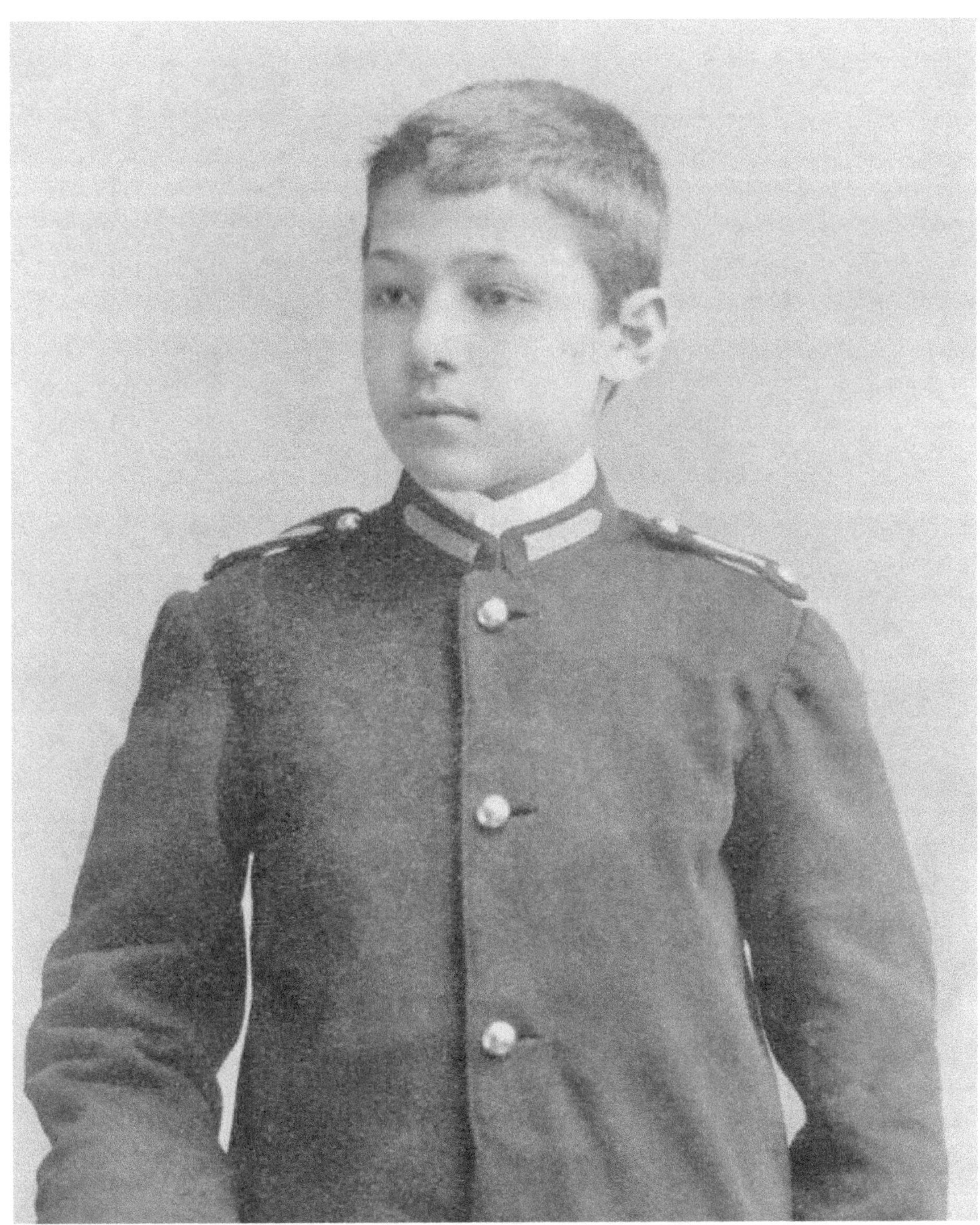

Rodolfo in his school uniform *circa* 1907,
Perugia Collegio-Convitto per gli Orfani dei Sanitari Italiani. (Author's Collection)

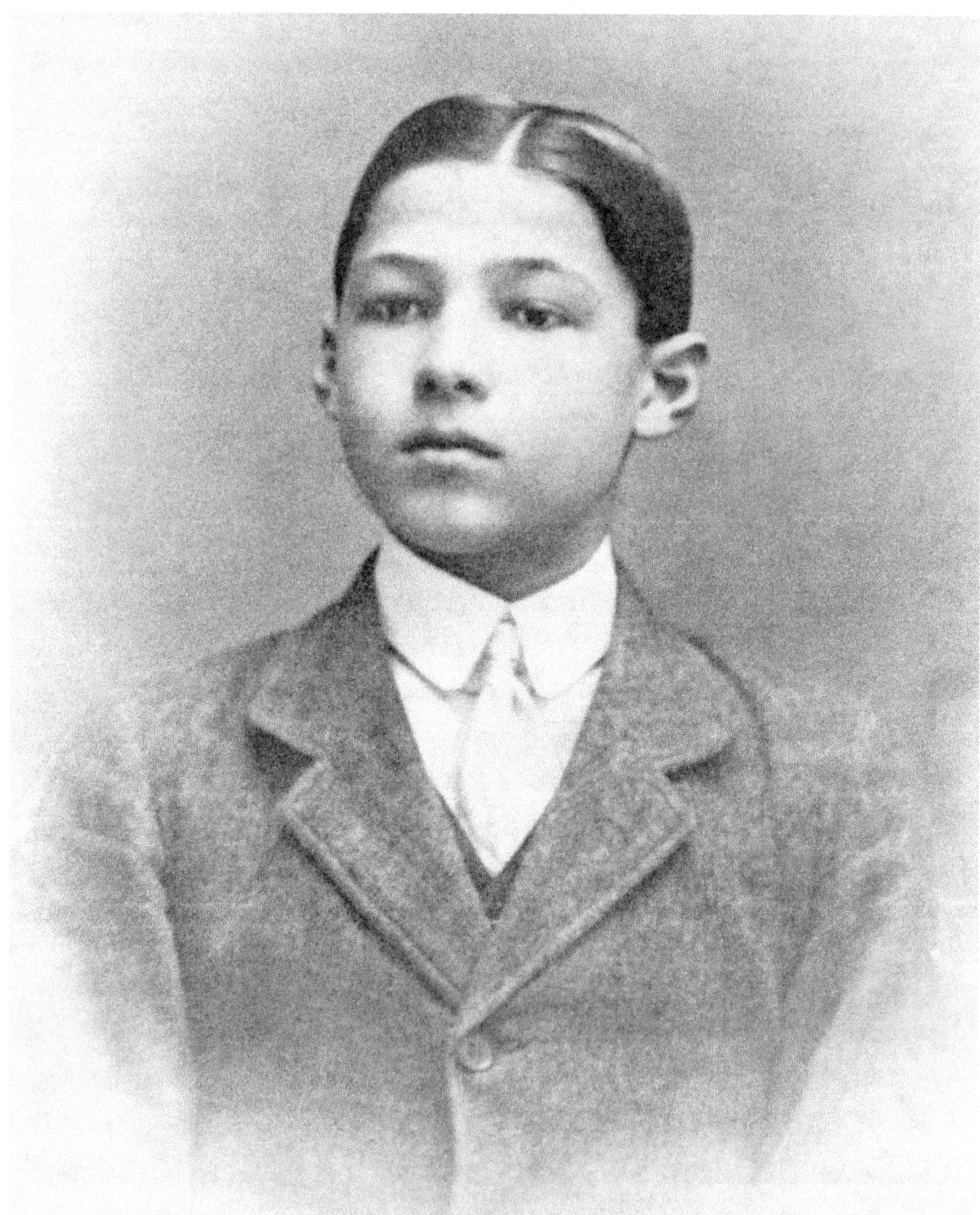

Rodolfo Guglielmi *circa* 1908 (Author's Collection)

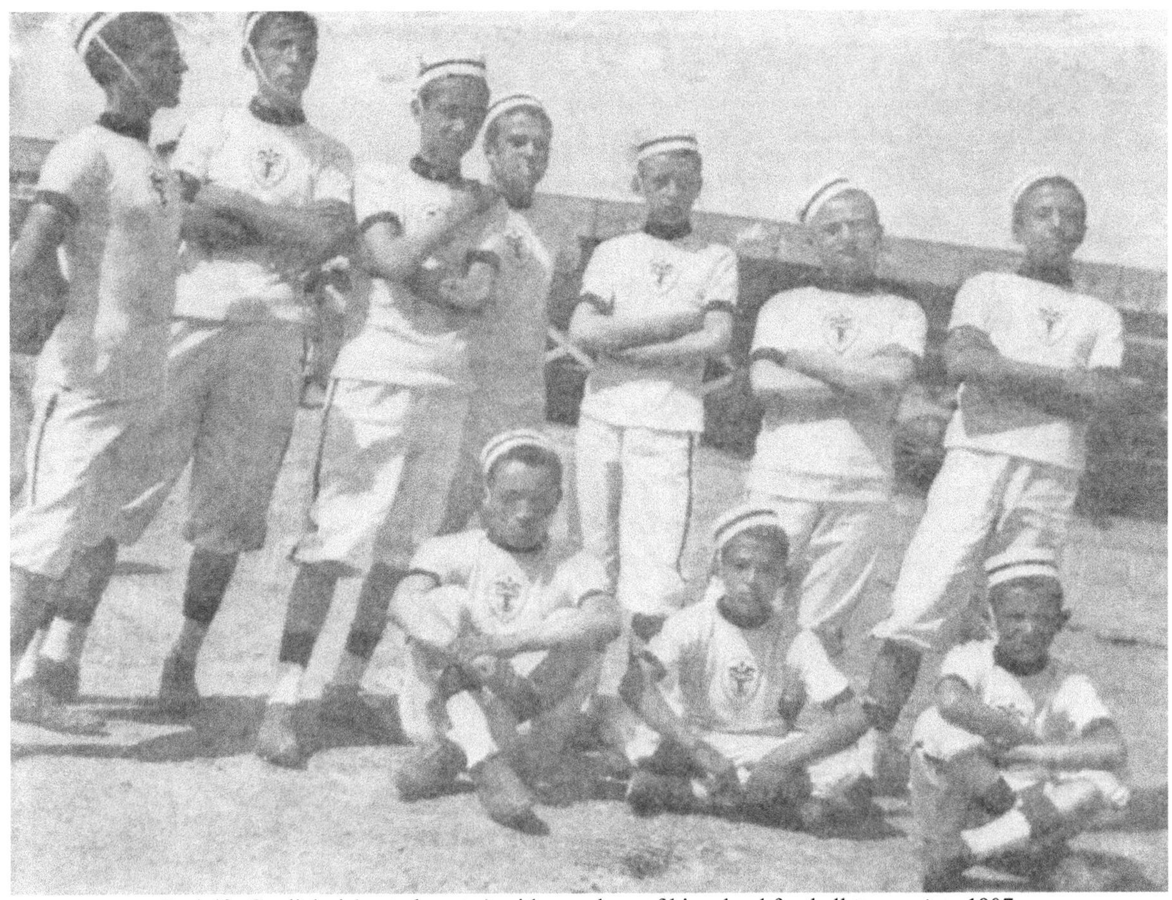

Rodolfo Guglielmi (seated center) with members of his school football team, *circa* 1907.
(Author's Collection)

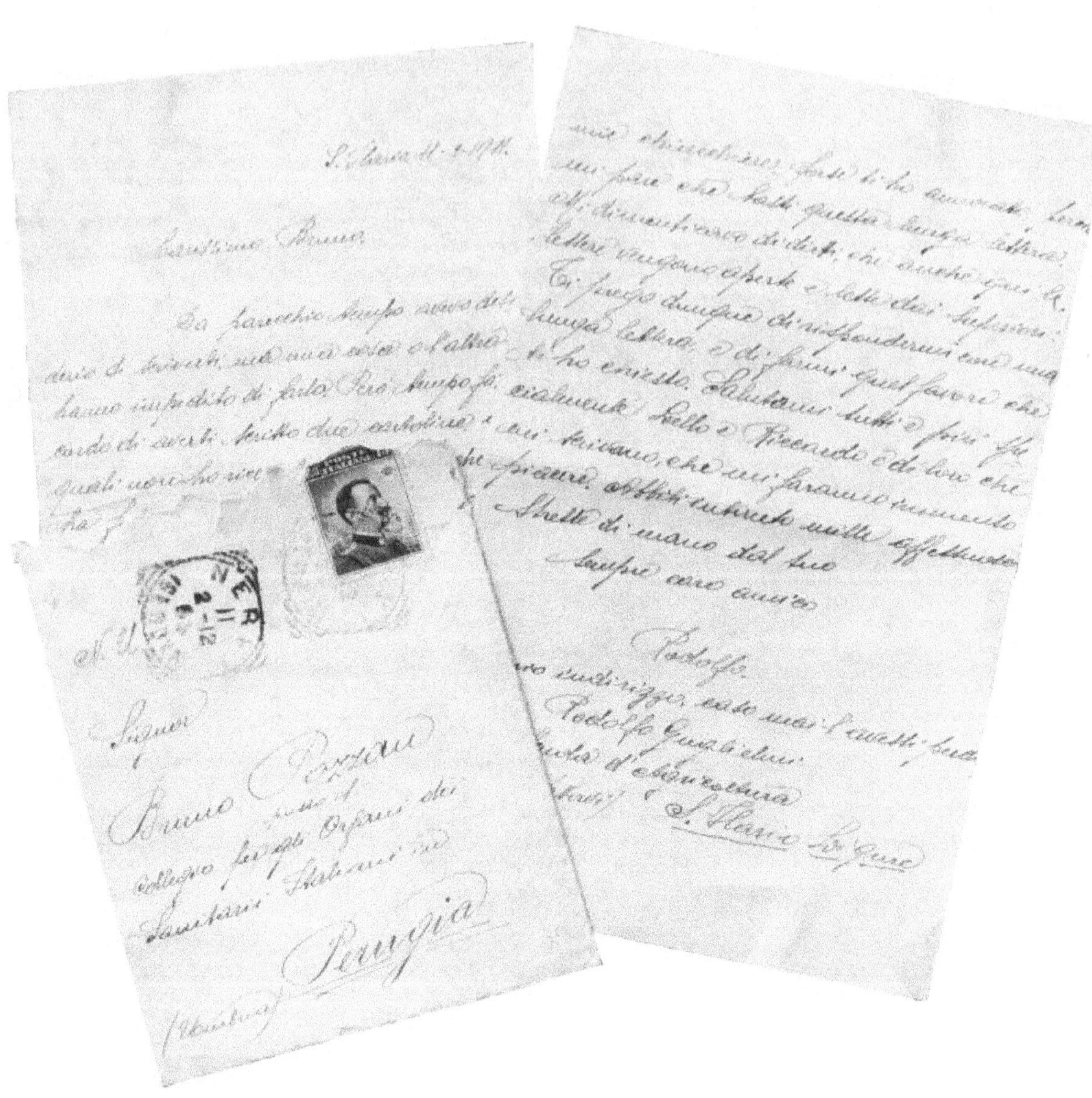

Rodolfo, not scholarly by nature or inclination, received one of his few high marks in school for his penmanship. Letter to his childhood friend Bruno Pozzan 1911.
(Author's Collection)

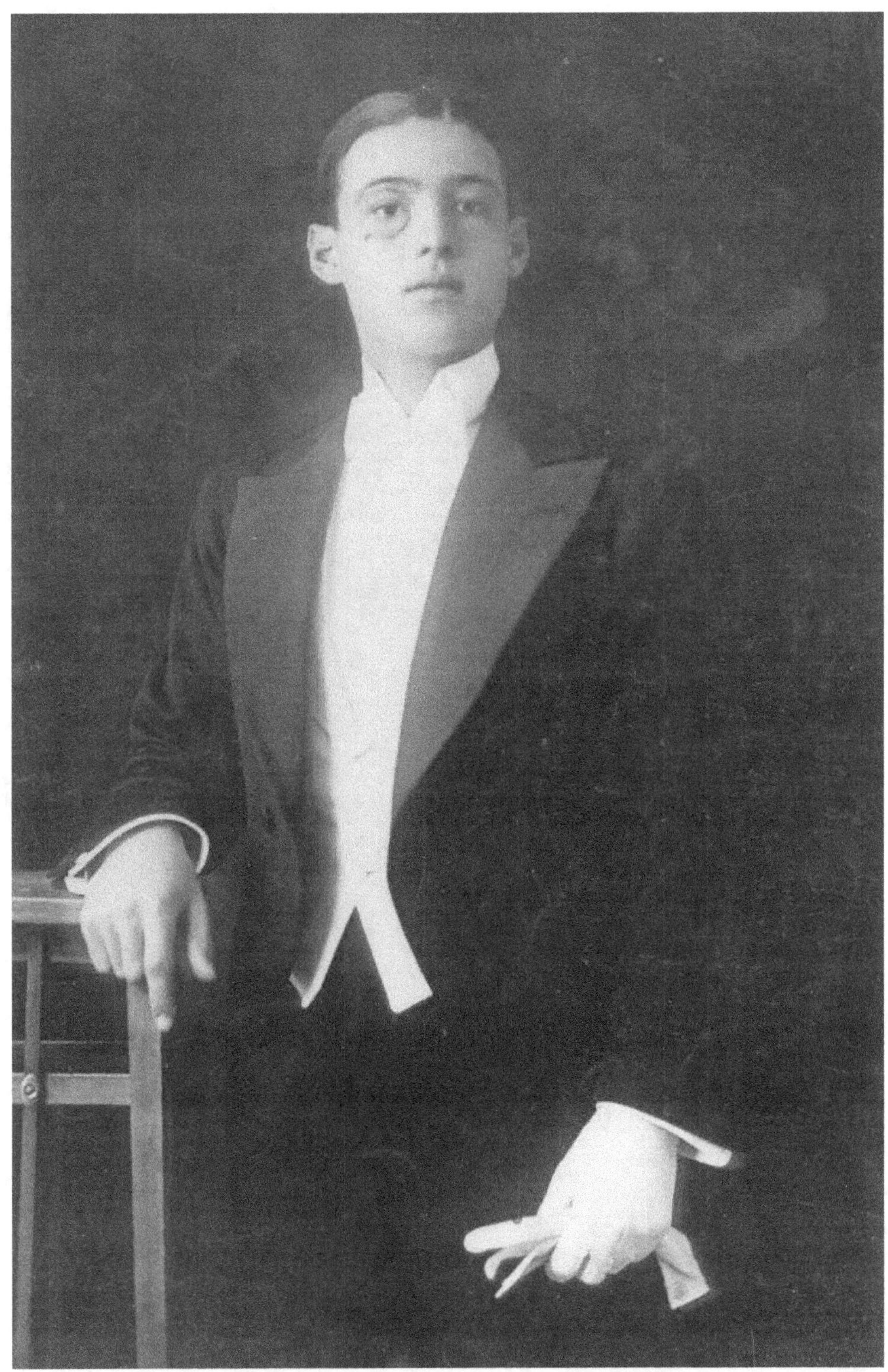

Ever the dandy, Rodolfo Guglielmi, Taranto 1913.
His last formal portrait before embarking to America.
(Michael and Virginia Back collection)

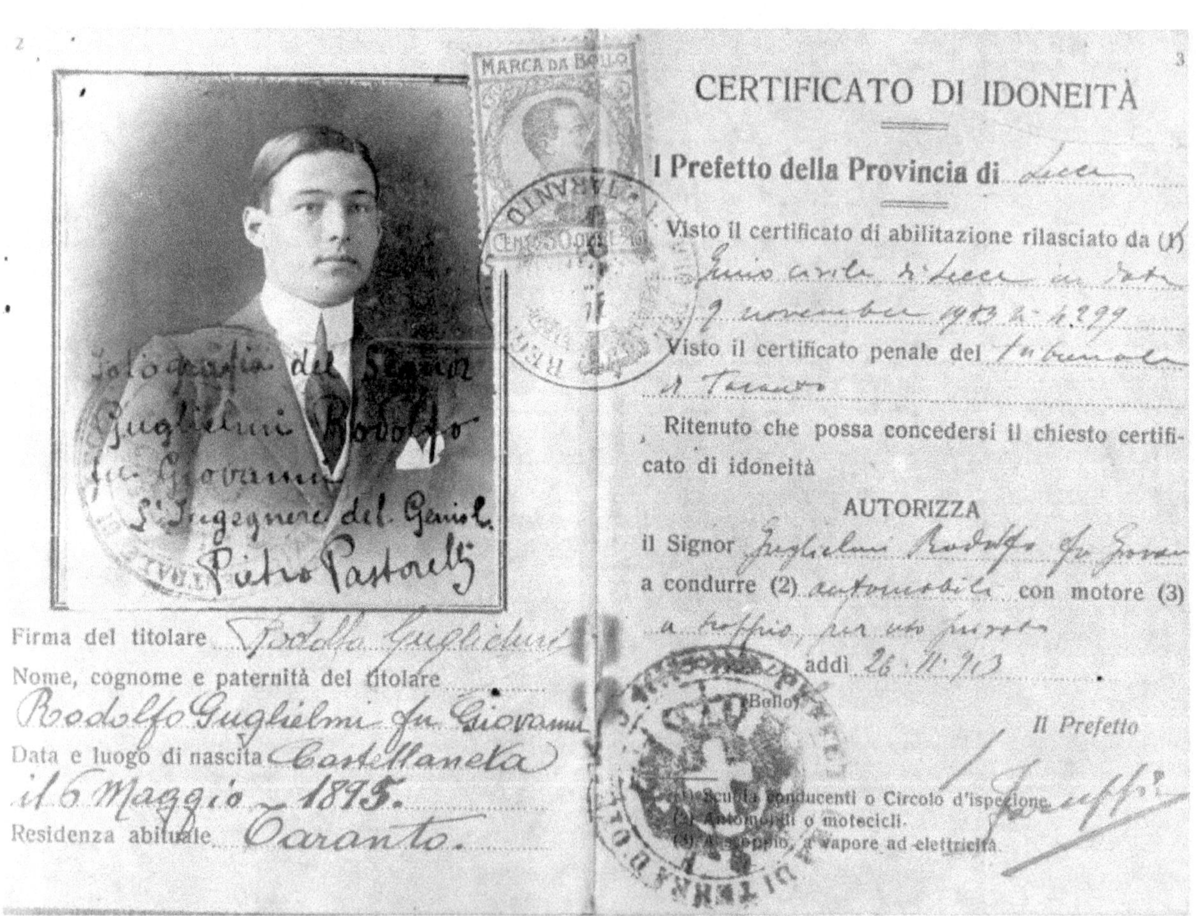

2

MARCA DA BOLLO

Firma del titolare Rodolfo Guglielmi

Nome, cognome e paternità del titolare

Rodolfo Guglielmi fu Giovanni

Data e luogo di nascita Castellaneta

il 6 Maggio 1895.

Residenza abituale Taranto.

3

CERTIFICATO DI IDONEITÀ

Il Prefetto della Provincia di Lecce

Visto il certificato di abilitazione rilasciato da (1) Genio civile di Lecce in data 9 novembre 1913 n. 1299

Visto il certificato penale del tribunale di Taranto

Ritenuto che possa concedersi il chiesto certificato di idoneità

AUTORIZZA

il Signor Guglielmi Rodolfo fu Giovanni

a condurre (2) automobili con motore (3) a scoppio, per uso privato

addì 26-11-913

(Bollo)

Il Prefetto

(1) Scuola conducenti o Circolo d'ispezione.
(2) Automobili o motocicli.
(3) A scoppio, a vapore ad elettricità.

Rodolfo Guglielmi's Italian identification card from 1913.
(Tracy Terhune Collection)

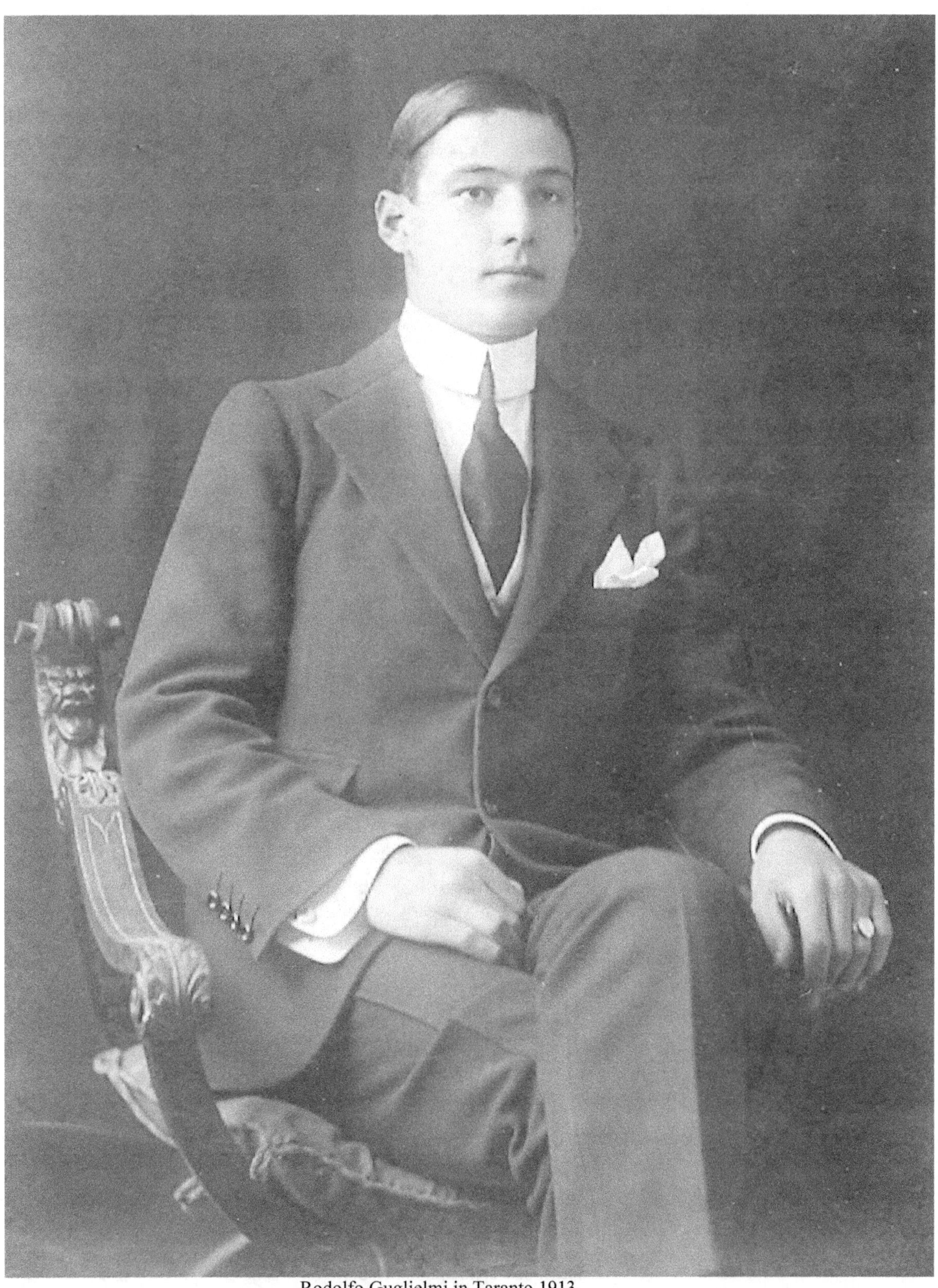

Rodolfo Guglielmi in Taranto 1913.
Anxious and ready for his adventure in America.
(Valentino Family collection)

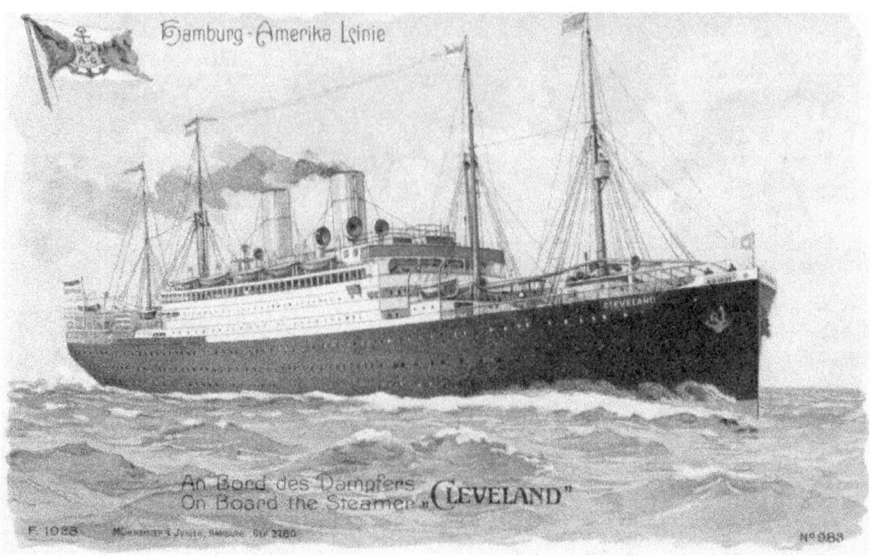

Hamburg America Liner SS Cleveland on which Valentino sailed to the United States.
(Author's Collection)

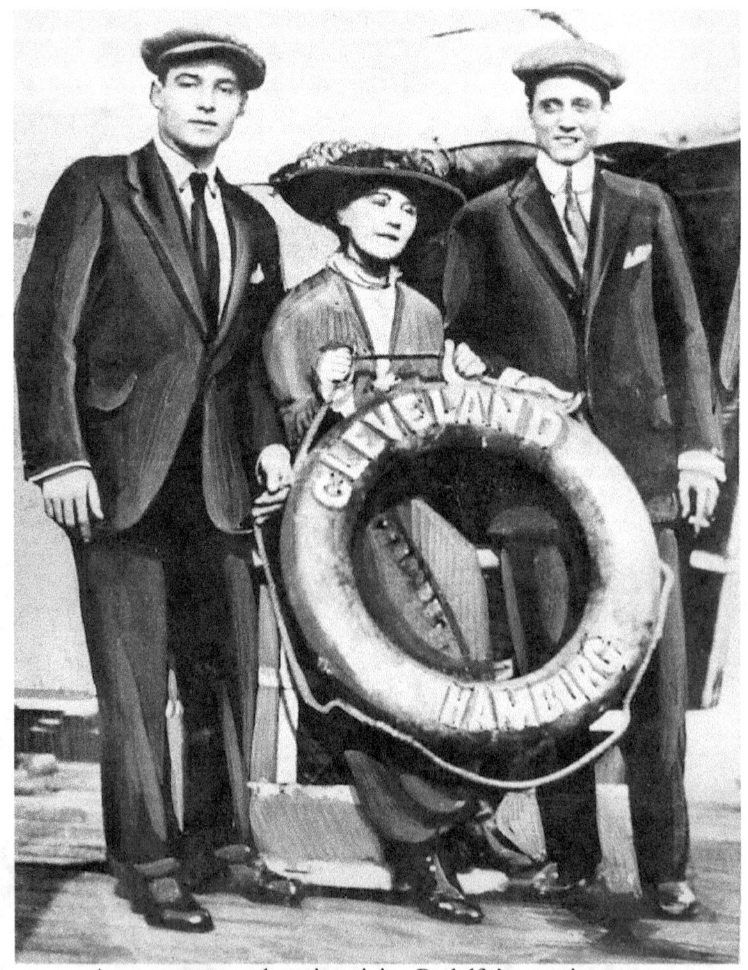

A newspaper mock-up imagining Rodolfo's crossing.
This image was utilized later on illustrating Valentino's studio biography.
(Author's Collection)

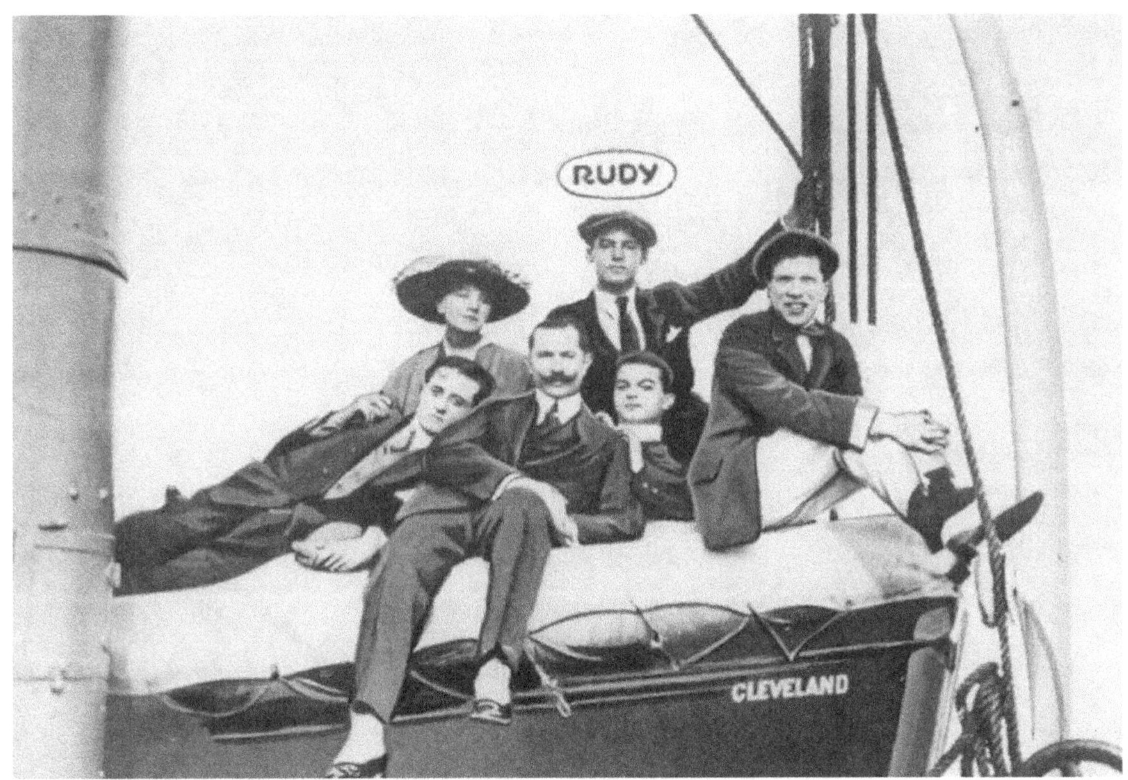

Another example of a mock up imagining Rodolfo and his new friends on board the SS Cleveland
(Author's Collection)

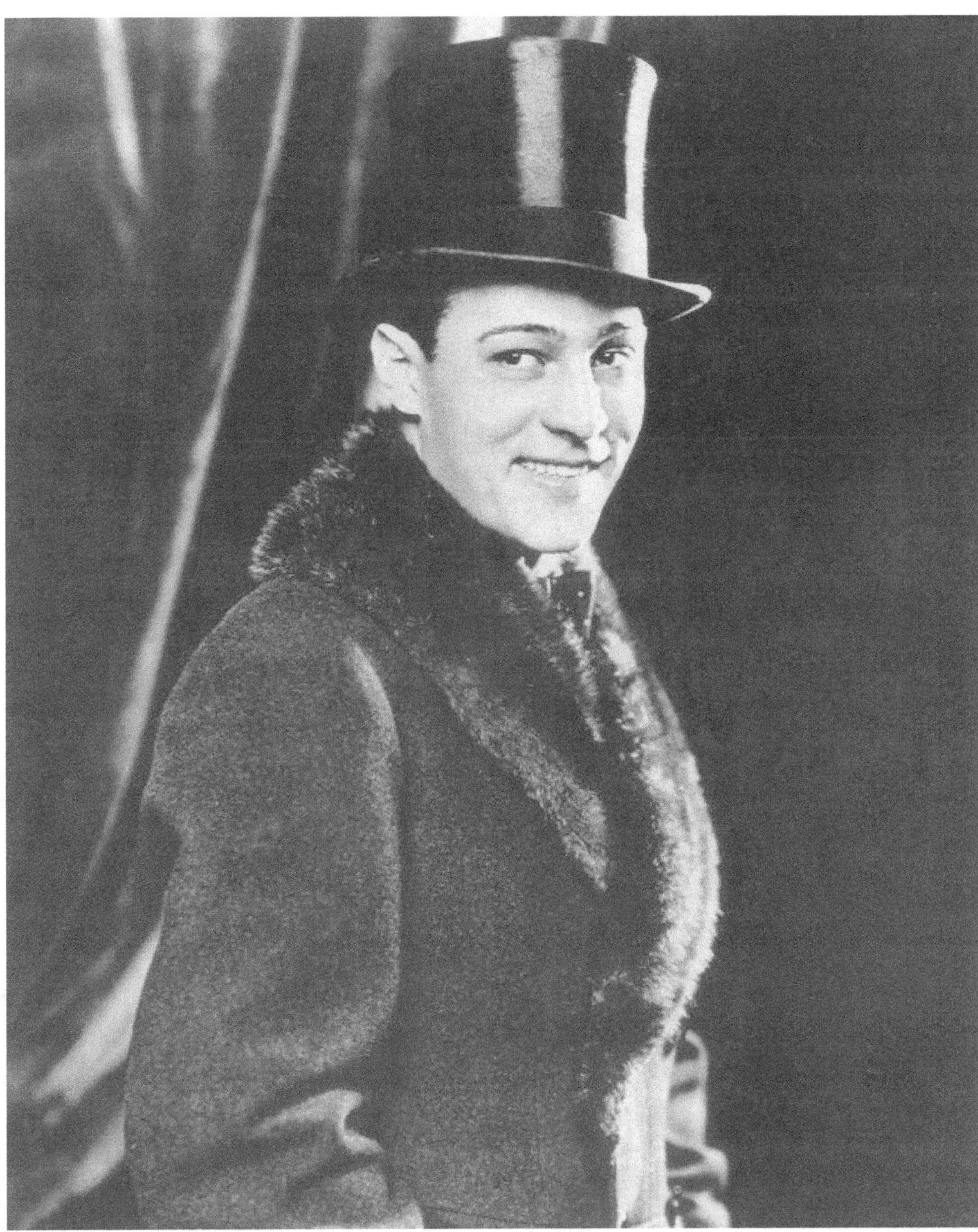

And so, I finally approached America, flaming with zeal, vehement with ambition, eager to take the land and wrest its secrets from it.

—Rudolph Valentino

Shortly after embarking on the SS Cleveland from Naples, spendthrift Rodolfo upgraded his second-class cabin and proceeded to enjoy the trans-Atlantic crossing in first-class accommodations. Handsome, charming, and friendly, Rodolfo spent the 15-day trip pursuing the American girls in first class. He also made friends with other, more experienced Italians whose advice he sought on life in New York. On December 23, 1913, the ship docked in Brooklyn, New York, and Rodolfo made his way into Manhattan. His Italian friends advised him to head to Giolito's, a modest Italian hostelry, for room and board. Instead, he dined at the fashionable uptown eatery, Rector's. At the rate he was spending, his nest egg would not last long.

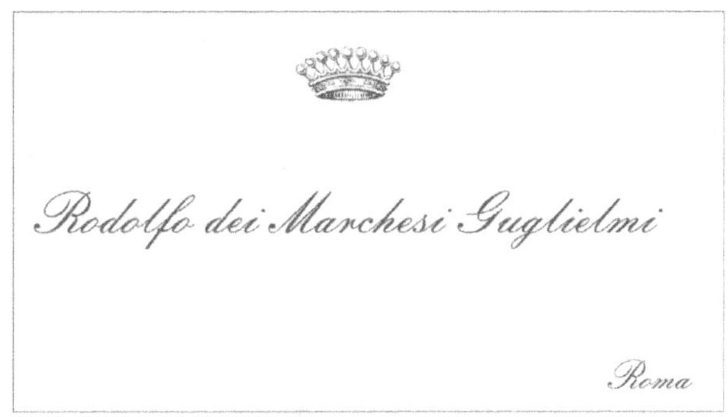

Rodolfo's rather pretentious calling card.
(Author's Collection)

Young Rodolfo's English was far from perfect, so he made friends with waiters at Italian and French cafes and restaurants. He moved into a boarding house where English was the only language spoken, and as his money dwindled, he made an effort to seek gainful employment. He presented his agricultural diploma and a letter of introduction to the Commissioner of Immigration, who secured for him a position with a prominent banker, Cornelius Bliss. He was employed to design an Italian garden for Mr. Bliss's Long Island estate; sadly, Mrs. Bliss changed her mind about the Italian garden, and Rodolfo was reduced to menial jobs. This was not to his liking, so he returned to Manhattan with no money and a little too much pride.

He walked the streets seeking employment, but found nothing. With no money for lodging, he occasionally slept on benches in Central Park. With no money for food, he ate free lunches at bars and saloons, scurrying out before the bartender could demand a nickel for a glass of beer. He later admitted that he was evicted from many boarding houses for nonpayment.

He posed for photographers in his topcoat and top hat for portraits to send home, and wrote letters to his mother on Hotel Astor stationery to support the charade that all was going well in America. The letters his family sent back told him all was not well. Gabriella was ailing, money was short, and the Great War was raging in Europe. Gabriella and Maria had moved from Taranto to Gabriella's native France for the duration of the war. In New York, Italian citizens under the age of 40 were required to enlist. Rodolfo tried to do so but was rejected for his poor eyesight. He later called this period of his life "my real Gethsemane." He was at rock bottom—there was no place to go but up.

The headwaiter at Bustanoby's Cafe de la Paix, a popular restaurant and dance club, advised Rodolfo to try his luck at the Café Maxim, on 38th Street. This advice proved to be the turn of his fortunes. He was engaged at Maxim's as a dancer-for-hire (a "taxi dancer"). There was no salary, but the dancers worked for tips from the ladies they partnered. They were also provided with rooms in the dance studio above the restaurant, where they could give private dancing lessons. Real money could be made and social connections forged.

Rodolfo was adept at charming his clients, and he danced with the grace and agility of a cat. When not dancing at Maxim's, he danced and partied at other clubs, late into the evening. He haunted the Broadway theaters to make connections and went to gatherings attended by actresses and socialites. Aimee (Crocker) Gouraud held one salon he frequented; there he met and danced with popular actresses such as Gaby Deslys and Gertrude Orr (the future Baroness de Beckendorff). In her unpublished diaries, the Baroness recalled that Gaby Deslys[3] introduced Rodolfo to her glowingly: "one day he will be Europe's premier dancer." She also credited him as the man who introduced her to her future husband, Baron Andre de Beckendorff. After her marriage, she recalled a visit from the "perennially broke" Rodolfo. She suggested that he try his luck at acting, "since he was dancing but not setting the world on fire." She, Andre, and Rodolfo traveled to Philadelphia, where she introduced Rodolfo to producer Sigmund Lubin in the hope of securing work in a play or films. Nothing came of this association, although she claimed Lubin requested photographs of Rodolfo. The Baroness would meet the more successful Valentino some time later at the Alexandria Hotel in Los Angeles. She recounted in her diary they spent a happy afternoon recalling the not so distant and not always so good "good old days."

His nights were spent dancing, but during the day Rodolfo sought work as a film extra. His first confirmed screen appearance is in the 1916 film, *Seventeen*, starring Jack Pickford. In it, Rodolfo can be seen as a smiling extra, positively towering over the diminutive Jack Pickford.

He met and befriended the Ziegfeld Follies dancer Mae Murray, a friendship that would later serve him well in Hollywood. It is believed that another new friend, Norman Kaiser (later known as the actor Norman Kerry), introduced Rodolfo to the popular exhibition dancer Bonnie Glass. Glass had recently fallen out with her dancing partner, Clifton Webb, and was in need of a new one. Rodolfo was hired, and as "Monsieur Rudolph" he danced professionally with Glass in vaudeville as well as in exhibitions on the stage. Later, when Glass opened her own club, Chez Fysher, he was billed as "Signor Rodolfo." The engagement with Glass was a prestigious step up, but it resulted in a reduction in pay. In June 1916, Glass married the artist Ben Ali Haggin and shortly thereafter retired. Rodolfo once again found himself unemployed.

Valentino's "official" biography of 1923 skipped over two major events in his life: his association with Chilean heiress Blanca de Saulles, and his arrest on vice-related charges in September 1916. Valentino was still dancing with Glass when he first met the wealthy and beautiful Blanca Elena Errazuriz de Saulles. They both spoke Spanish and shared a love of dancing. How deep their friendship went can only be speculated upon. What is known is that

[3] In 1923, Variety mysteriously reported that Valentino had appeared with Gaby Deslys in London in 1914 in her stage show *Rosey Rapture*. When asked about this later, Valentino denied reports he was in the play. There is no record of him returning to Europe prior to 1923. Valentino hardly had the means for lunch, let alone the fare for crossing in 1914.

Blanca was unhappily married and Rodolfo's friendship provided solace, on the dance floor and, presumably, off.

Joan Sawyer, another popular exhibition dancer with a taste for exotic-looking men, was in need of a new partner and hired Rodolfo in the summer of 1916. The two toured the B.F. Keith circuit[4] and, as Valentino later proudly recounted, danced an exhibition before President Woodrow Wilson at a 1916 banquet. Later that summer Blanca de Saulles sued her husband, Jack, for divorce, alleging indiscretions with Rodolfo's dance partner, Joan Sawyer. Rodolfo testified on Blanca's behalf in November 1916, upon which Joan Sawyer immediately fired him. He was unemployed and at loose ends . . . and his situation soon became dramatically worse.

On September 5, 1916, "Marquis" Rudolfo Guglielmi was arrested in a vice squad raid. Unable to raise the $10,000 bail, he sat in jail for three days. The bail was later reduced and Rodolfo was eventually released. Where he obtained the bail money is unknown, and the police file on the case has long since disappeared[5]. It was rumored that Jack de Saulles arranged the arrest, and that Rodolfo Guglielmi had become a thief, a blackmailer, and a white slaver. Whatever the circumstances were, to his dying day Valentino denied any wrongdoing.

With his name besmirched and his reputation ruined, Rodolfo had a difficult time obtaining work. Cafe society was no longer open to him. He picked up film work in the serial drama *Patria*[6], starring Irene Castle and Milton Sills. His stint on the picture could not have lasted more than a few days at the most. No doubt it provided some much-needed pocket change. Still, it was clear that he would have to "get out of Dodge" if he wanted to earn a living on the stage. Fortunately, in the spring of 1917 he was cast as a featured dancer with the touring company for *The Masked Model*. Interestingly, he was billed in the show as Mons Rudolph, his stage name with Joan Sawyer and Bonnie Glass. He was not exactly traveling incognito.

The company traveled by a special train and stopped in Pittsburg, Omaha, Denver, Ogden and finally played San Francisco in May 1917. It appears that Rodolfo did not appear in the San Francisco run at the Cort Theater. His name is not mentioned in any of the local newspaper stories on the show. How and why he left the show is not recorded.

He remained in San Francisco and took an apartment on Bush Street[7] just off Union Square and plied his terpsichorean trade at clubs around town. While dancing at Tait's Café, Rodolfo made a social connection with the wealthy Spreckels family and, through the Spreckels, with A. P. Giannini of the Bank of Italy (later the Bank of America). He tried to secure a loan through Giannini for a nebulous agriculture enterprise, but the banker denied the loan, advising him to save his money. It was good advice, but saving money was virtually impossible for Rodolfo. He took a job selling insurance bonds, a job at which (he later admitted) he was an abject failure. His money again dwindled. It was then that Valentino crossed paths

[4] Joan Sawyer and Signor Rudolph famously toured with her "Persian Garden Orchestra" which comprised only African-American musicians on the B.F. Keith circuit in 1916. Future film comedian, Harry Langdon and his wife, also shared the same bill in Pittsburgh.

[5] The movie studios, their press agents and their lawyers wielded much power during the Hollywood golden age. Negative stories were quashed, people were paid off and police records mysteriously disappeared. While there is no factual evidence to support this theory, it is assumed that this arrest record went missing and was destroyed soon after Valentino rose to stardom.

[6] *Patria* is extant, at least in part. Valentino can be seen briefly in the third episode of the serial dancing in the background. The total number of episodes in which he appeared is not known.

[7] His apartment was at 1776 Bush Street, the building is still standing. Valentino did not stay long in San Francisco and had no listing in the 1917 San Francisco telephone directory.

with Norman Kerry who suggested that Rodolfo make his way to Hollywood and try his luck in films.

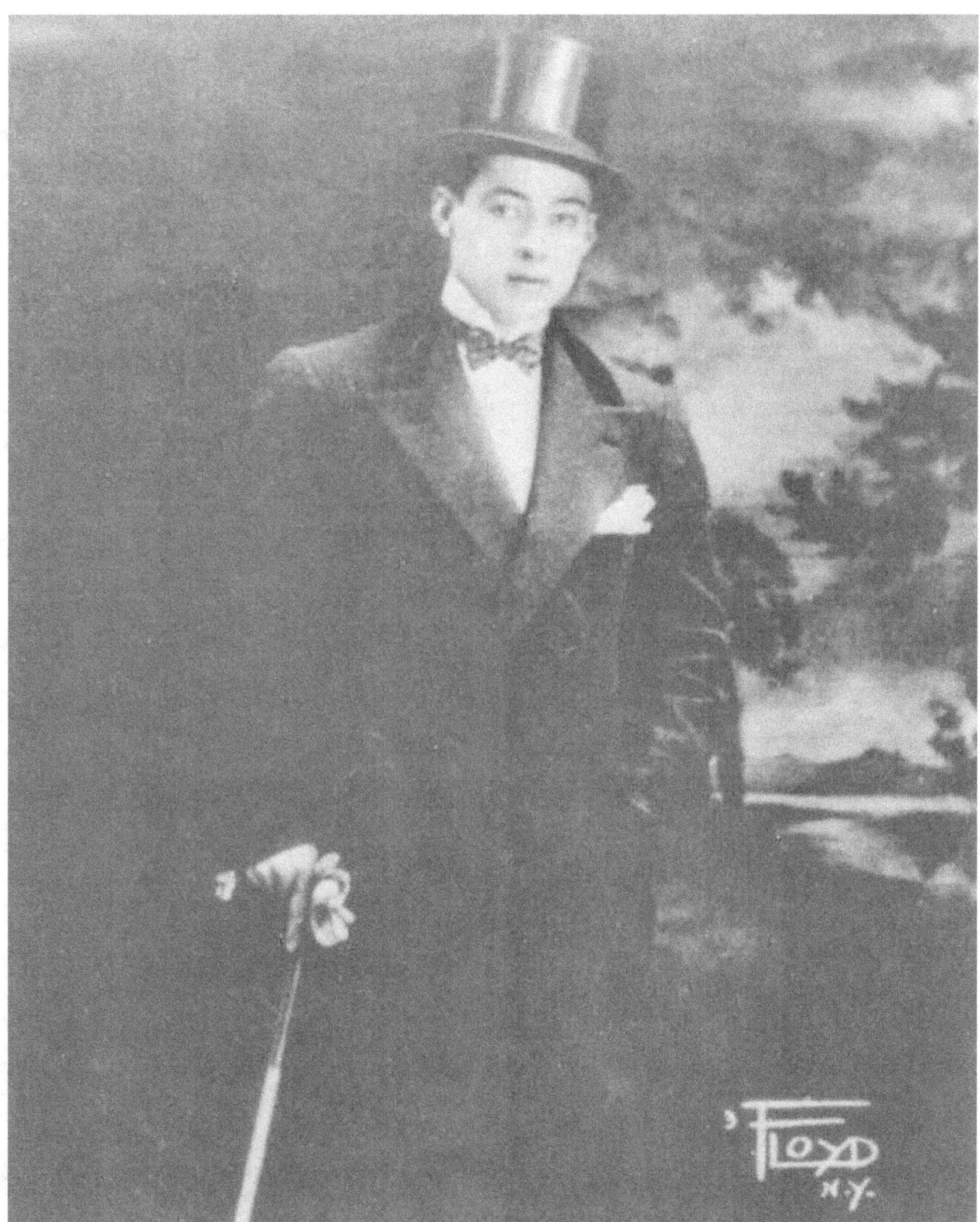

Rodolfo Guglielmi in New York 1915.
(Kristen Burkhart Collection)

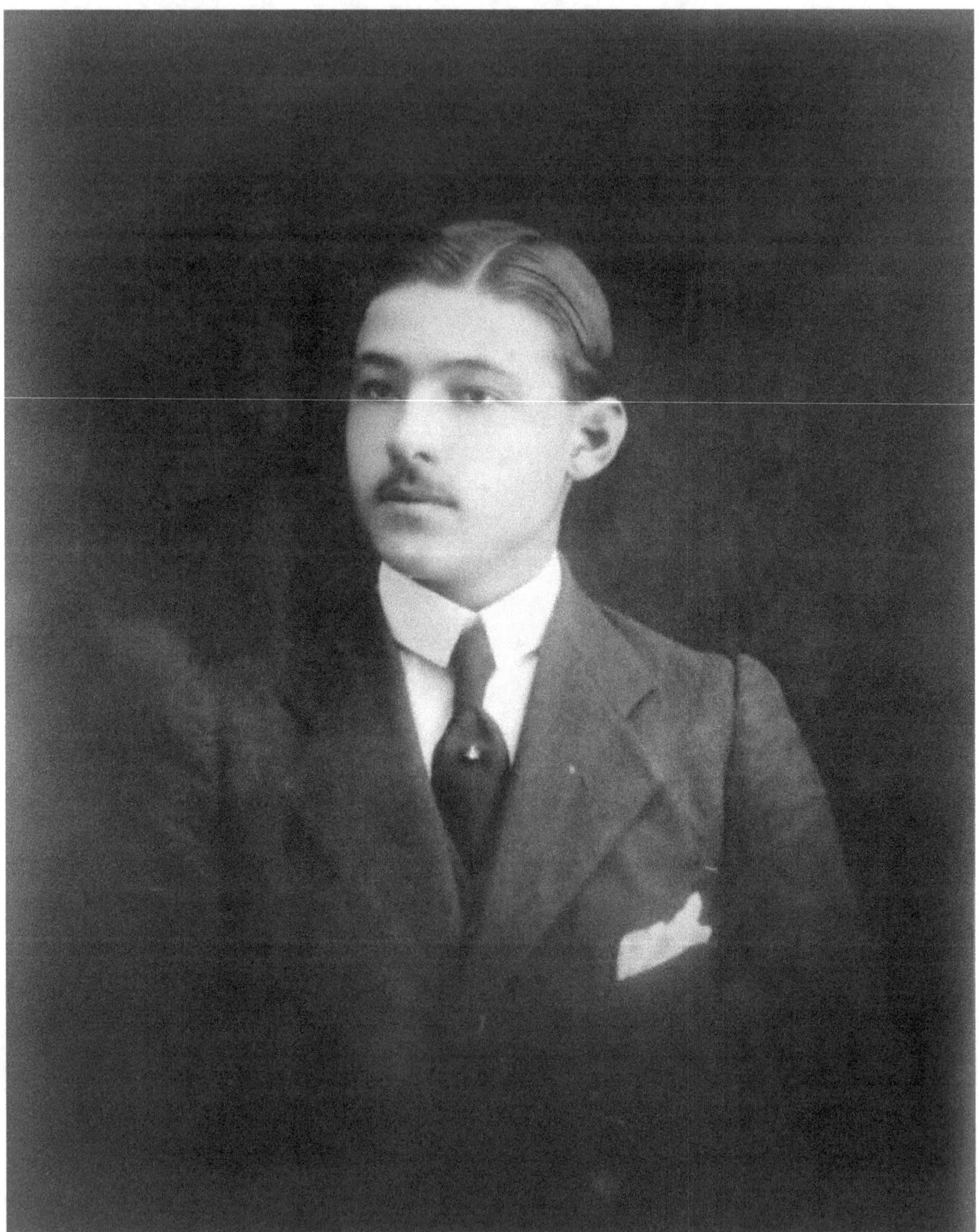

Rodolfo Valentino *circa* 1915, portrait taken in New York.
(Author's collection)

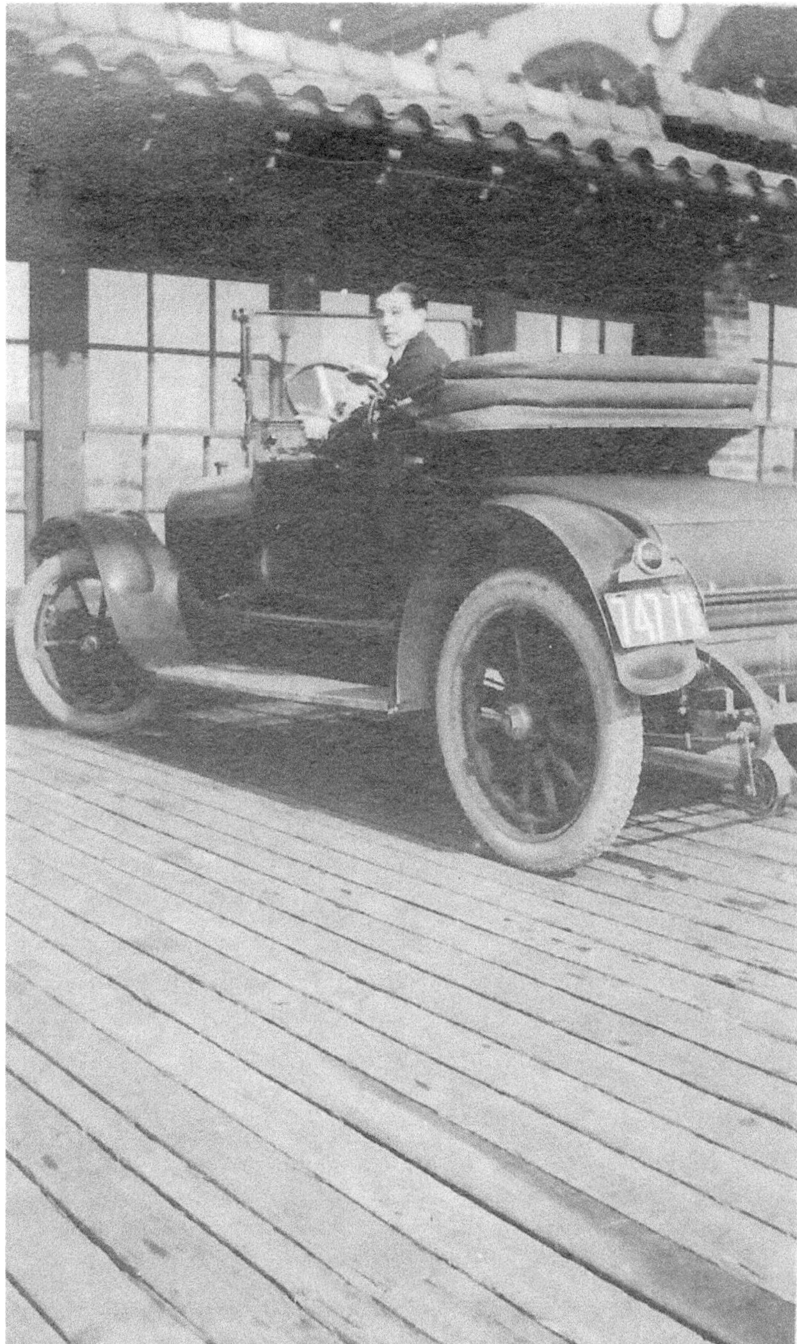

Rodolfo Guglielmi poses at the Garden Pier in Atlantic City, NJ, *circa* 1915.
He was a car aficionado from an early age.
(Valentino Family Collection)

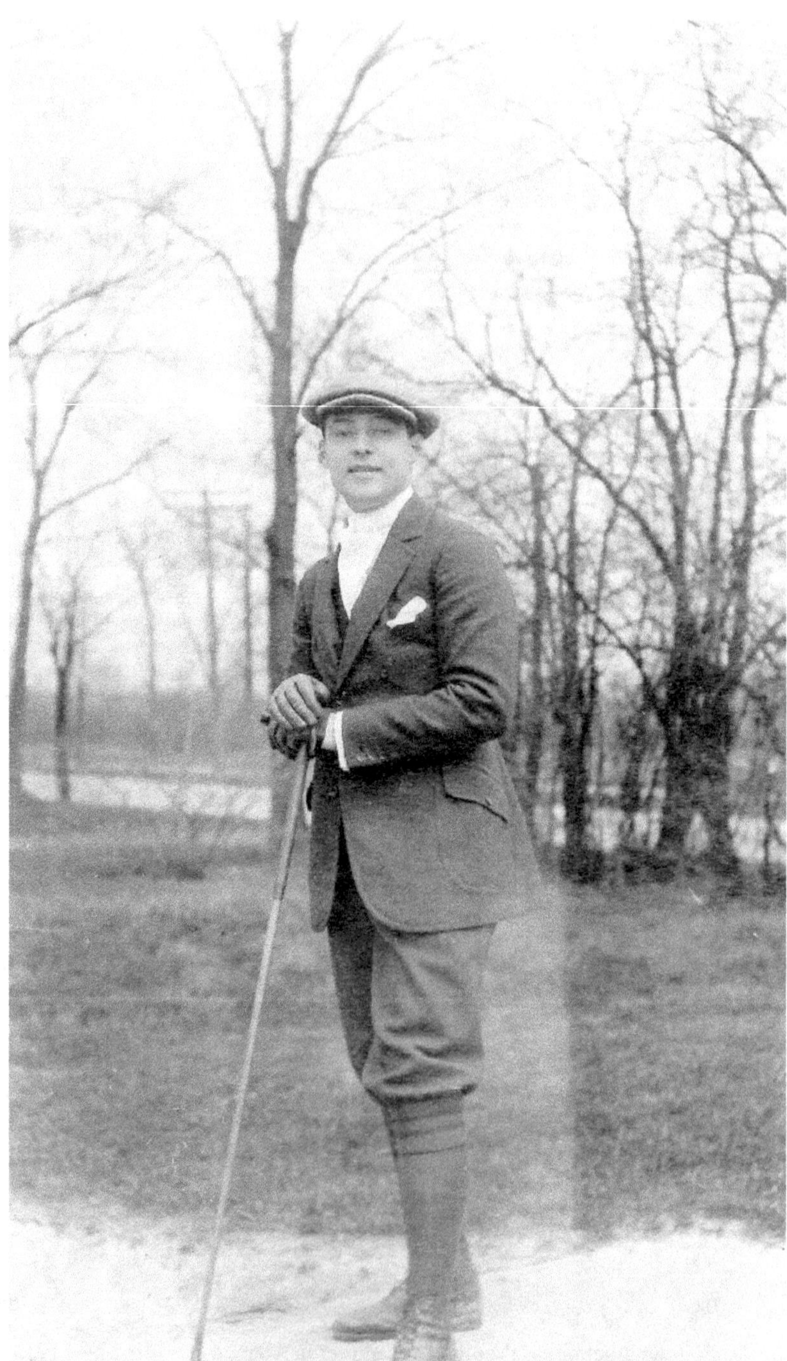

Snapshot of Rodolfo Valentino taking a walkabout *circa* 1915-1916.
Presumed New York or New Jersey. (Valentino Family Collection)

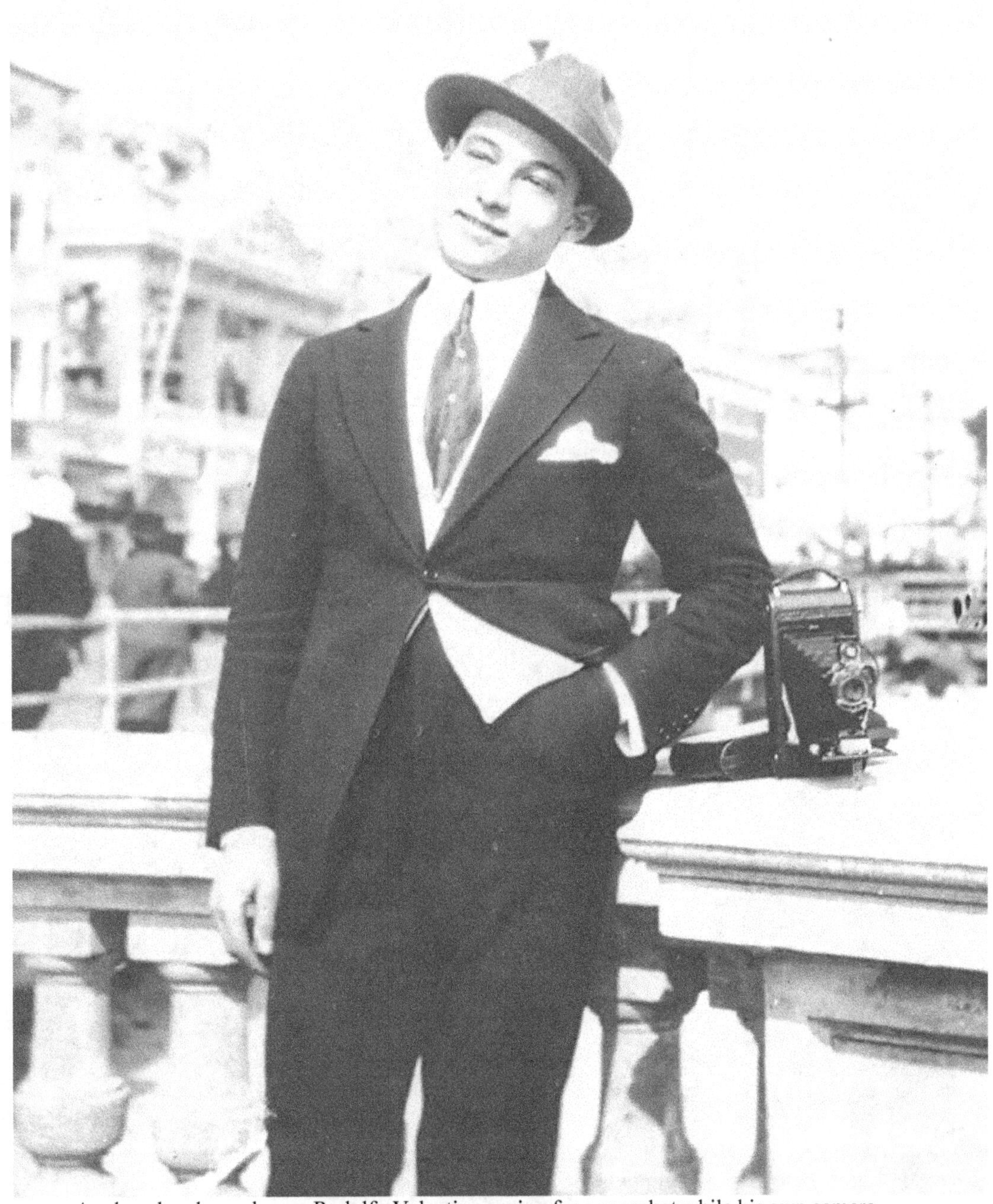

A relaxed and very happy Rodolfo Valentino posing for a snapshot while his own camera rests on the balustrade. The exact location is uncertain, possibly in New York. (Valentino Family collection)

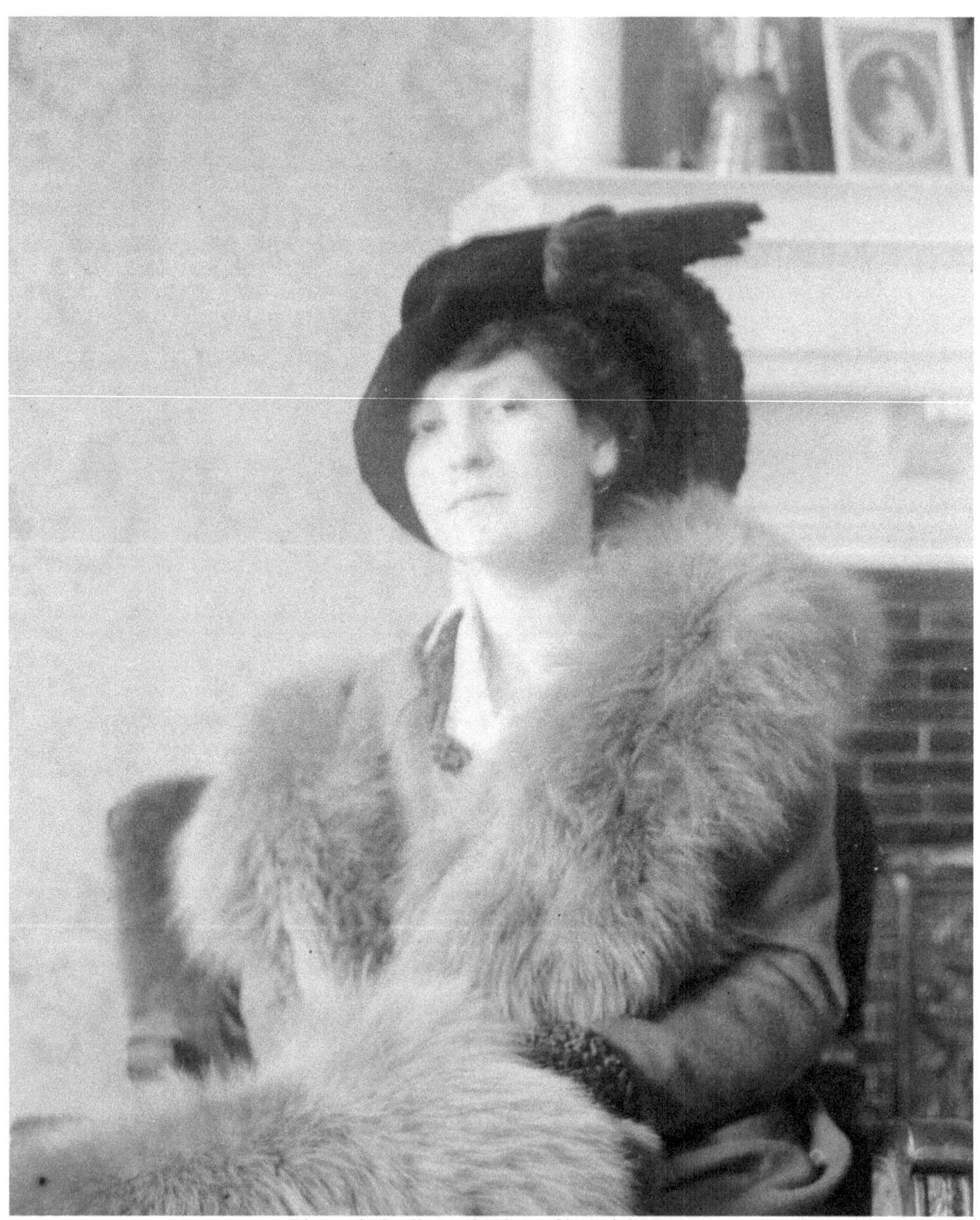

Blanca de Saulles at the time of her trial.
Detail from a Bain News Service photo *circa* 1917.
(Library of Congress)

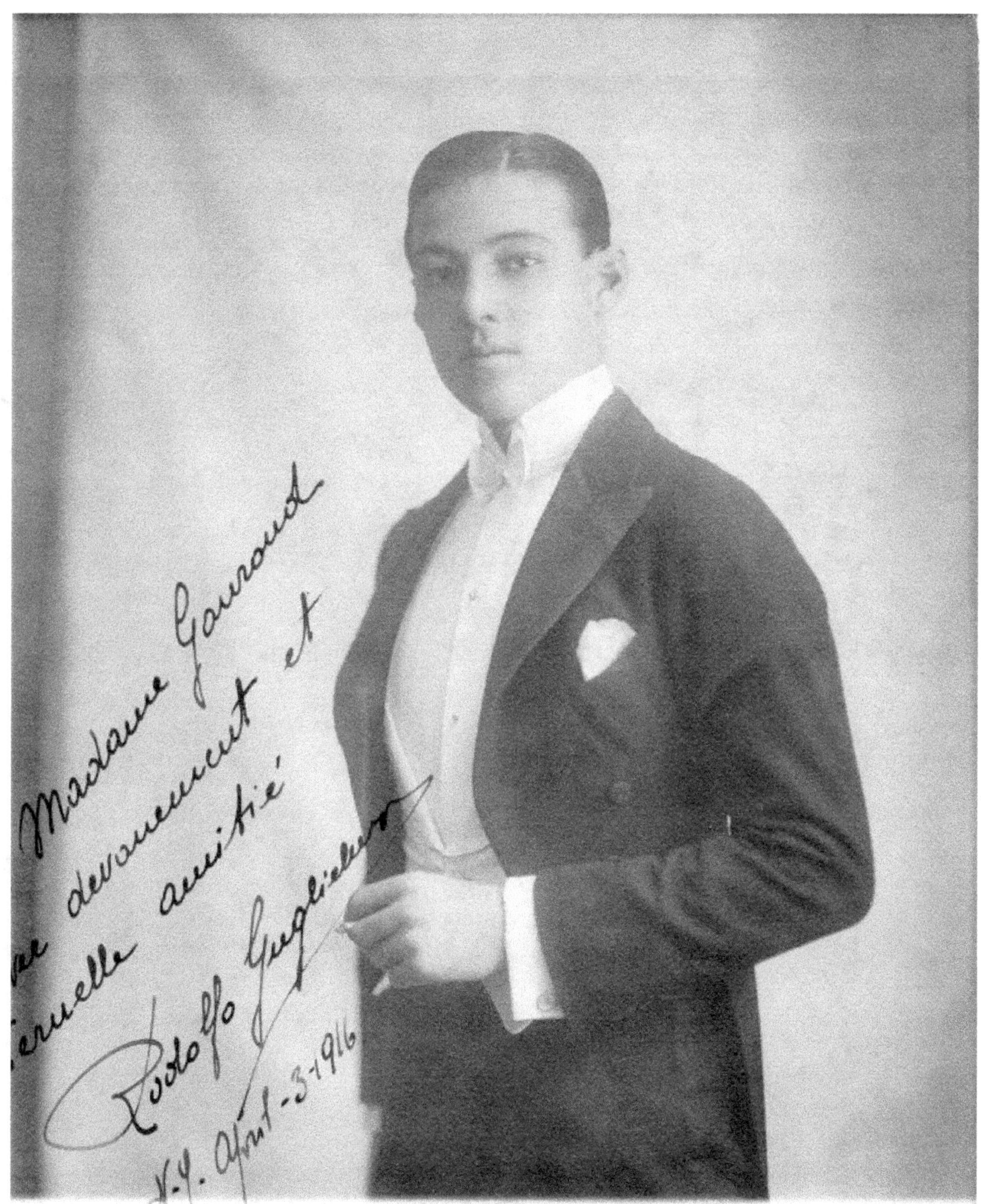

Rodolfo Guglielmi, now a dancer at Maxim's in New York, 1916.
This portrait inscribed to Socialite Mrs. Aimee (Crocker) Gouraud using his real name.
At 21 years old in 1916, still very much the coltish and sophisticated youngster.
(Tracy Terhune Collection)

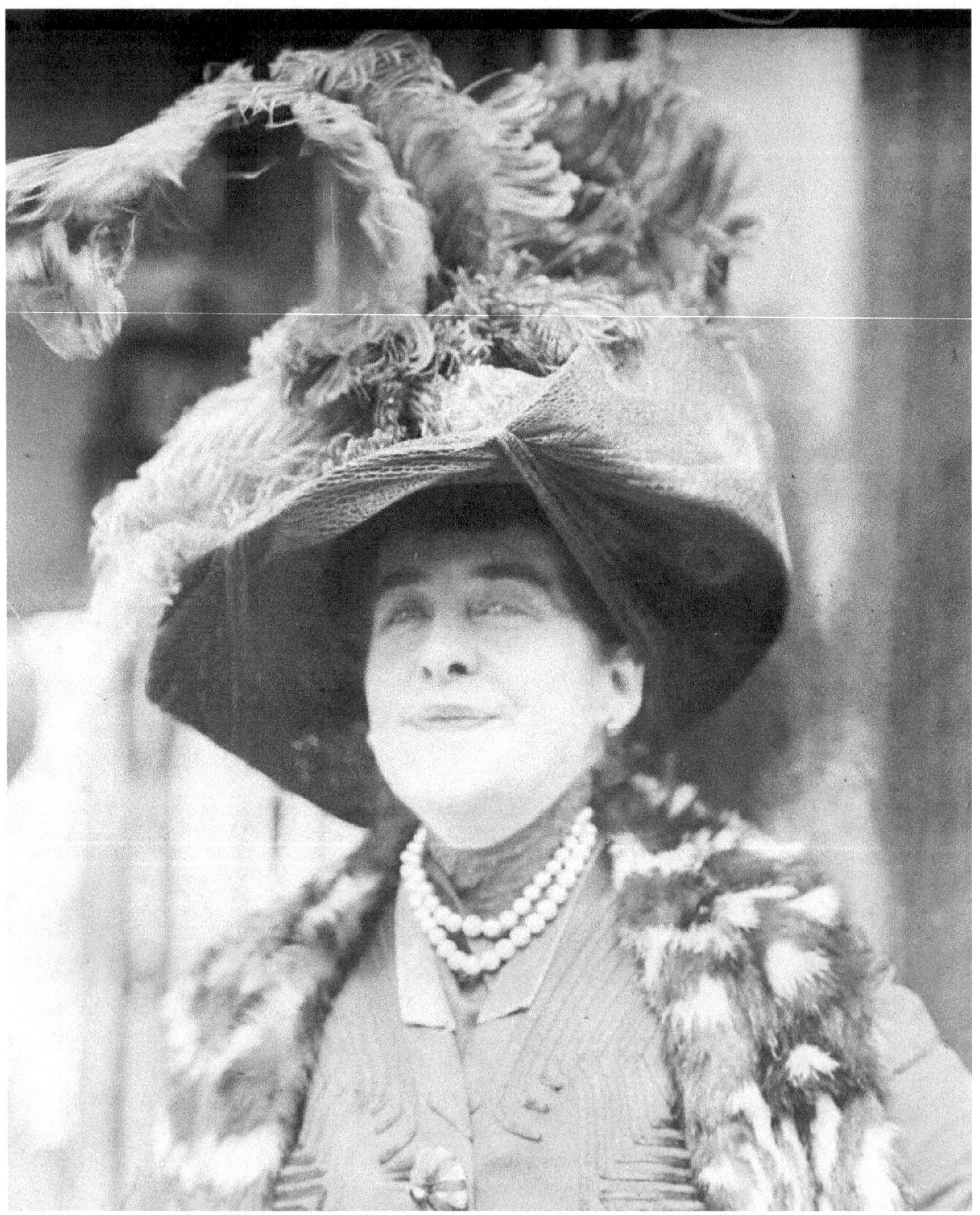

Socialite Aimee Crocker Gouraud in 1911. (Library of Congress)

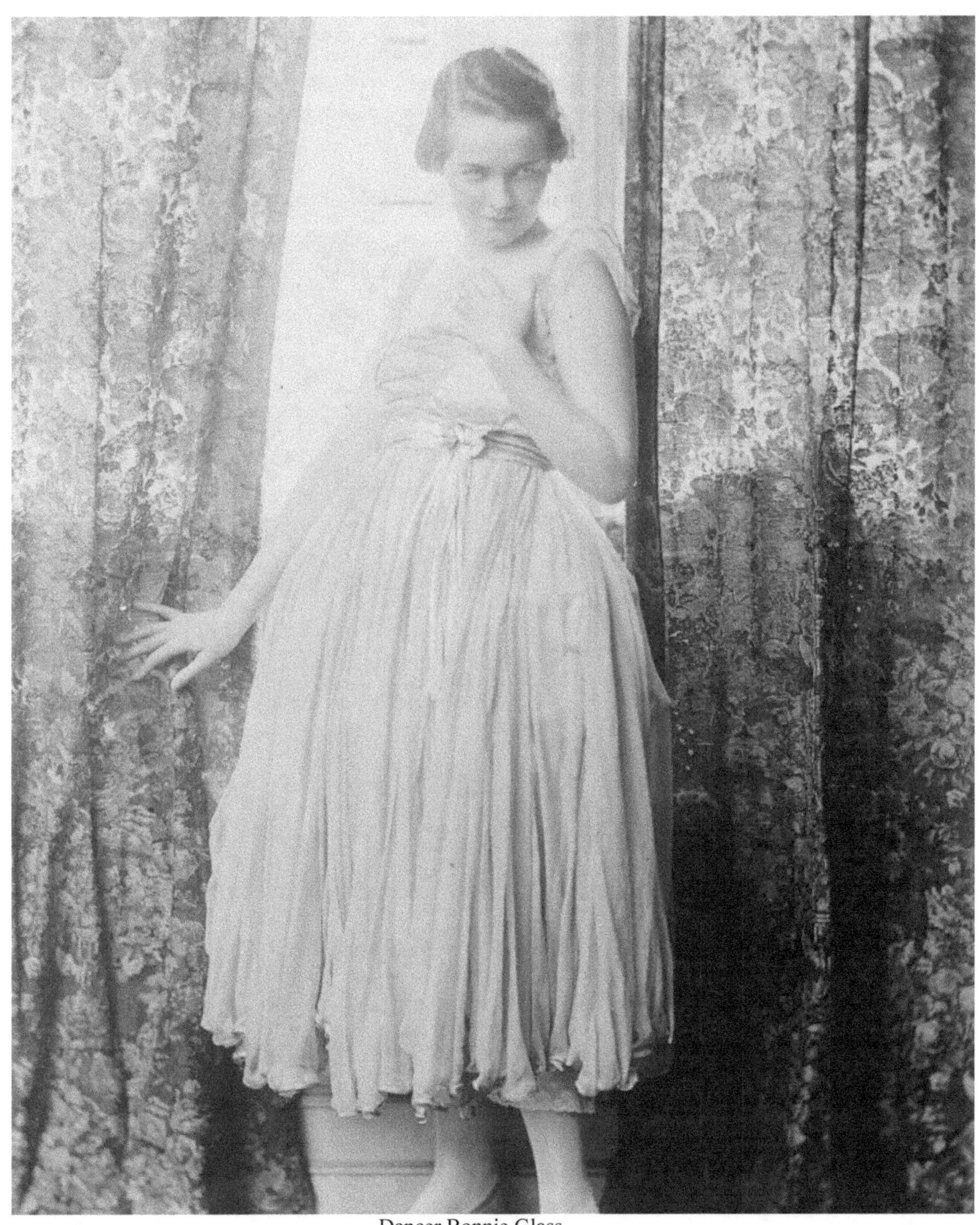

Dancer Bonnie Glass
(Library of Congress)

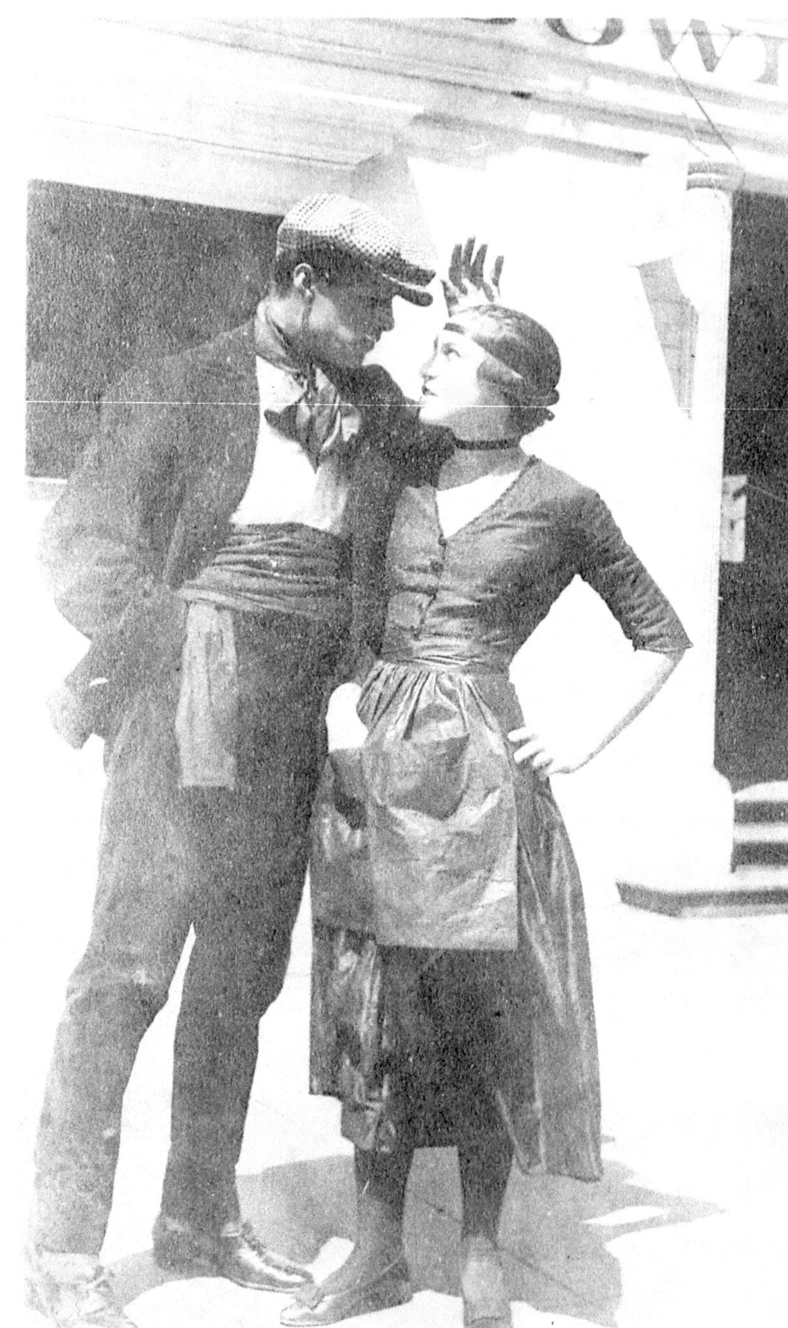

Mons. Rudolph and Bonnie Glass in costume for an Apache Dance circa 1915.
(Valentino Family collection)

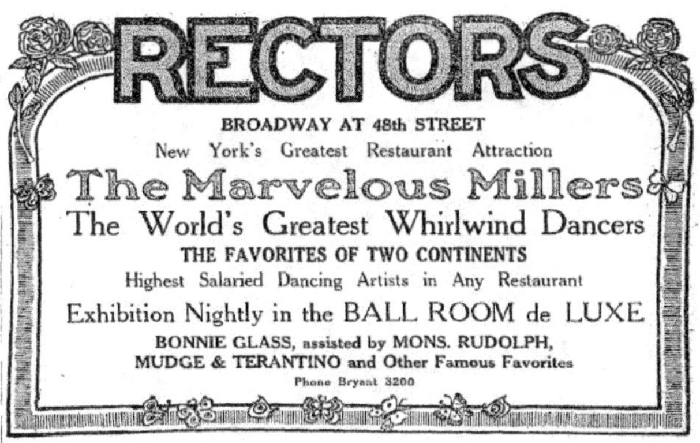

BONNIE GLASS
ASSISTED BY
SIGNOR RODOLFO
Returned to Vaudeville and scored at B. F. Keith's Palace Theatre last week
Dancing at the Smartest Restaurant in Town---CHEZ FYSHER
Direction M. S. BENTHAM

CAFE BOULEVARD
Broadway and 41st Street Telephone, 4220 Bryant.
The Best of Food and Service
Dinner $1.00 Luncheon 60c
Famous Hungarian Orchestra
DANCING AT DINNER AND AFTER THEATRE IN THE GRILLE.
Exhibition Dances by BONNIE GLASS Assisted by RUDOLPH.

B.F. KEITH'S
"WHERE THE NATION'S GREATEST LAUGH AT VAUDEVILLE."
Twice Daily & Sunday. Mats., 25c. Eves., 25c to $1. Buy Today
Beginning Tomorrow Matinee and Ending Next Sunday Night
GALA SPRING FESTIVAL BILL OF AUGMENTED SIZE AND SPLENDOR
JOAN SAWYER
America's Own Waltz Queen. Assisted by Signor Rudolph
"The Lady With the R. S. V. P. Eyes, the Face of an Angel and the Back of a Duchess."
Accompanied by Her Own Orchestra from the Persian Gardens
EXTRA ADDED | WM. GAXTON & CO. "A Regular Business Man." | BEATRICE MORRELLE'S GRAND OPERA SEXTET
SPECIAL STELLAR FEATURE—Kaufman Brothers in "Tuneful Originalities." Tony Hunting & Corinne Frances. Palfrey, Hall & Brown. Ameta, Deiro, Morin Sisters. Pipe Organ Recitals. Pathe.
TODAY 3 & 8:15 —NORA BAYES Geo. Nash & Julia Hay Paul Morton & Naomi Glass.
Orth & Dooley, Leo. Beers, and All Last Week's Stars and Hits.
APRIL 3 WEEK—ADELE ROWLAND, OF "KATINKA," AND FINE BILL

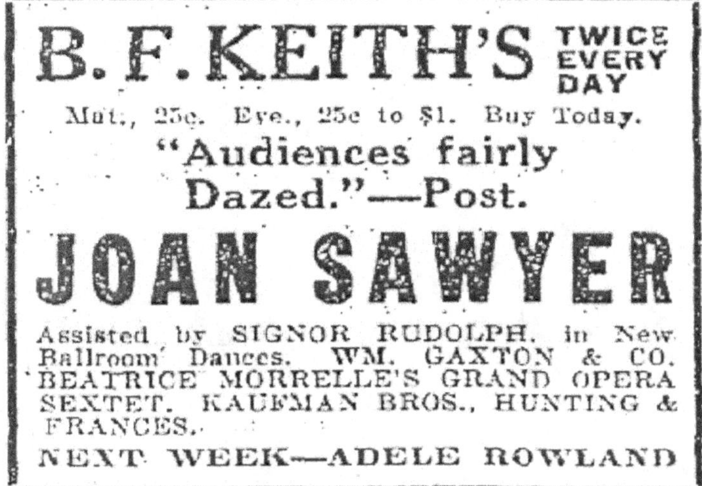

Newspaper advertisements are all that remain chronicling Valentino's early dancing career on the East Coast with Bonnie Glass and Joan Sawyer. No publicity photos of Valentino and Joan Sawyer have come to light.

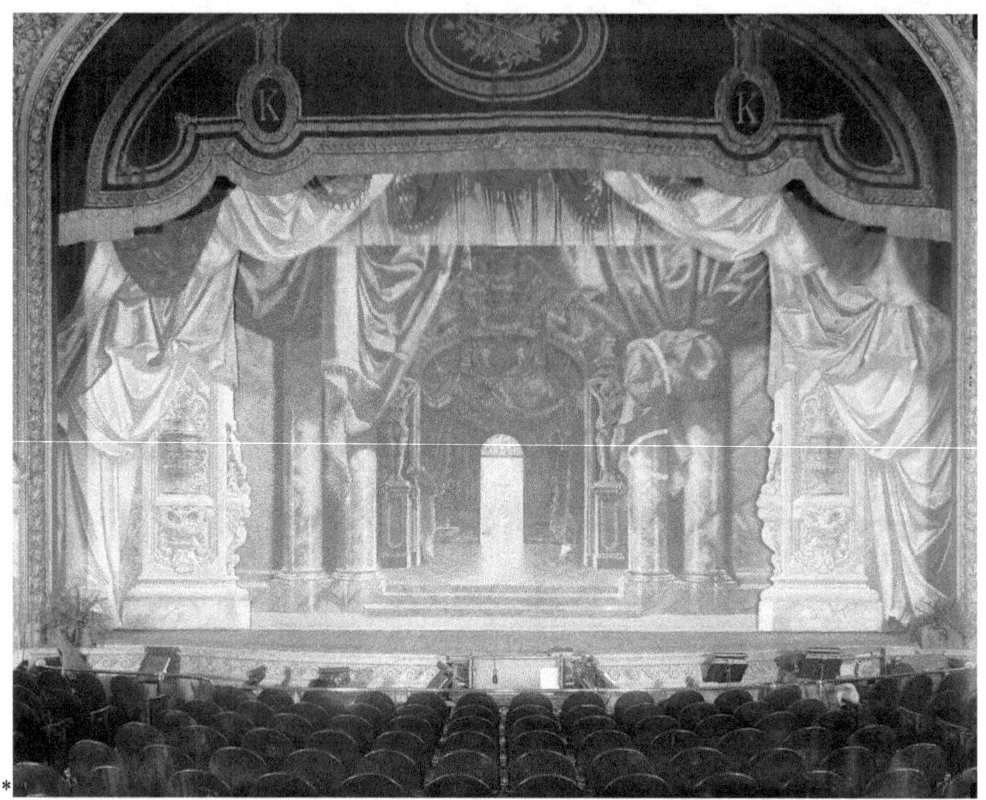

*
Proscenium, orchestra pit and the beautiful painted fire curtain at B.F. Keith's Theatre[8], Washington, D.C. where Joan Sawyer and Signor Rudolph danced in 1916.
(Library of Congress)

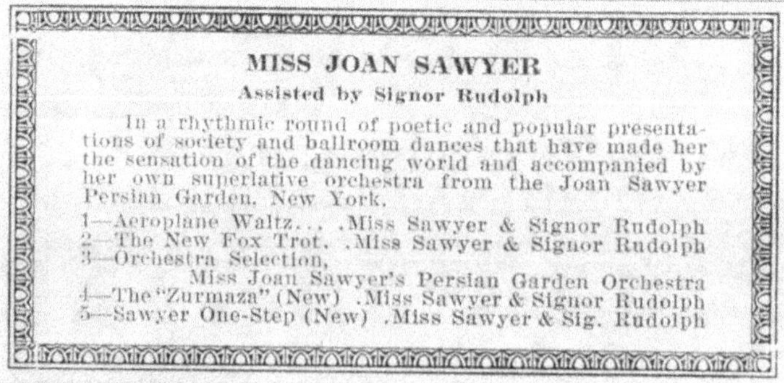

MISS JOAN SAWYER

Assisted by Signor Rudolph

In a rhythmic round of poetic and popular presentations of society and ballroom dances that have made her the sensation of the dancing world and accompanied by her own superlative orchestra from the Joan Sawyer Persian Garden, New York.

1—Aeroplane Waltz... .Miss Sawyer & Signor Rudolph
2—The New Fox Trot. .Miss Sawyer & Signor Rudolph
3—Orchestra Selection,
Miss Joan Sawyer's Persian Garden Orchestra
4—The "Zurmaza" (New) .Miss Sawyer & Signor Rudolph
5—Sawyer One-Step (New) .Miss Sawyer & Sig. Rudolph

Detail from the program page at B.F. Keith's Theatre in 1916.[9]
(Author's collection)

[8] The Theatre building was demolished in 1978.

[9] Joan Sawyer and Signor Rudolph were the "Next to Closing" act which was *the* coveted spot reserved for the starring act on the bill. The film or act that followed was considered a "chaser" to get the audience out of the theater and cleared for the next show.

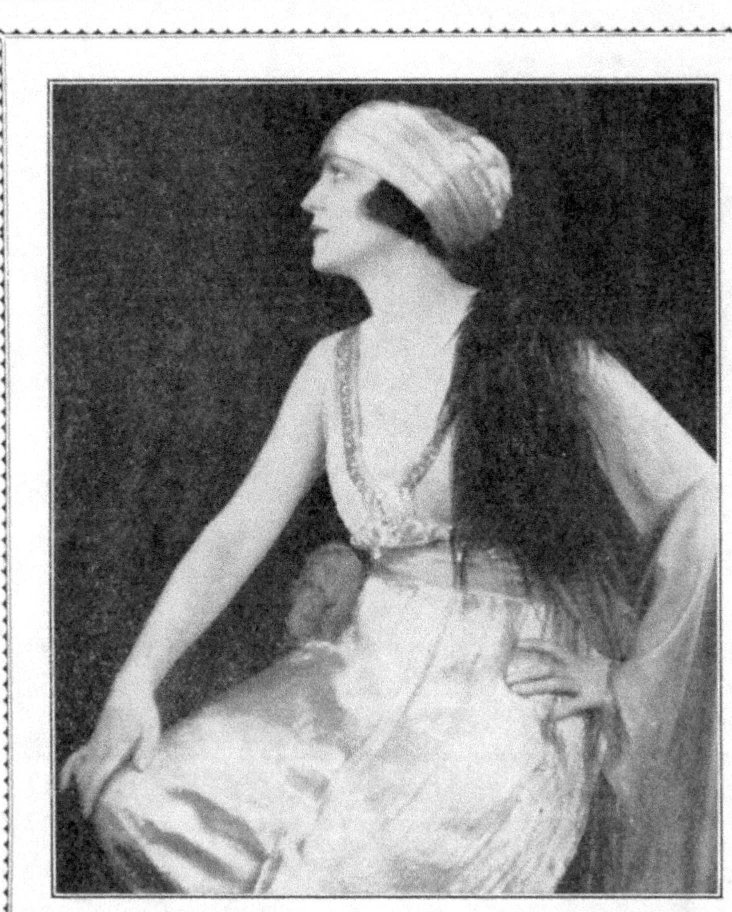

Miss Joan Sawyer is not only an able exponent of Terpsichore, but a woman of marvelous charm and personality. She also is widely followed in dress fashions by society women throughout the country. On her recent return she brought with her some exquisite examples of the fashions of the French capitol and her ability to grace these costumes would make the little mannikin of the fashion stage, look to her laurels.

Joan Sawyer in 1921, Broadway Brevities Magazine, April 1921.
(Internet Archive)

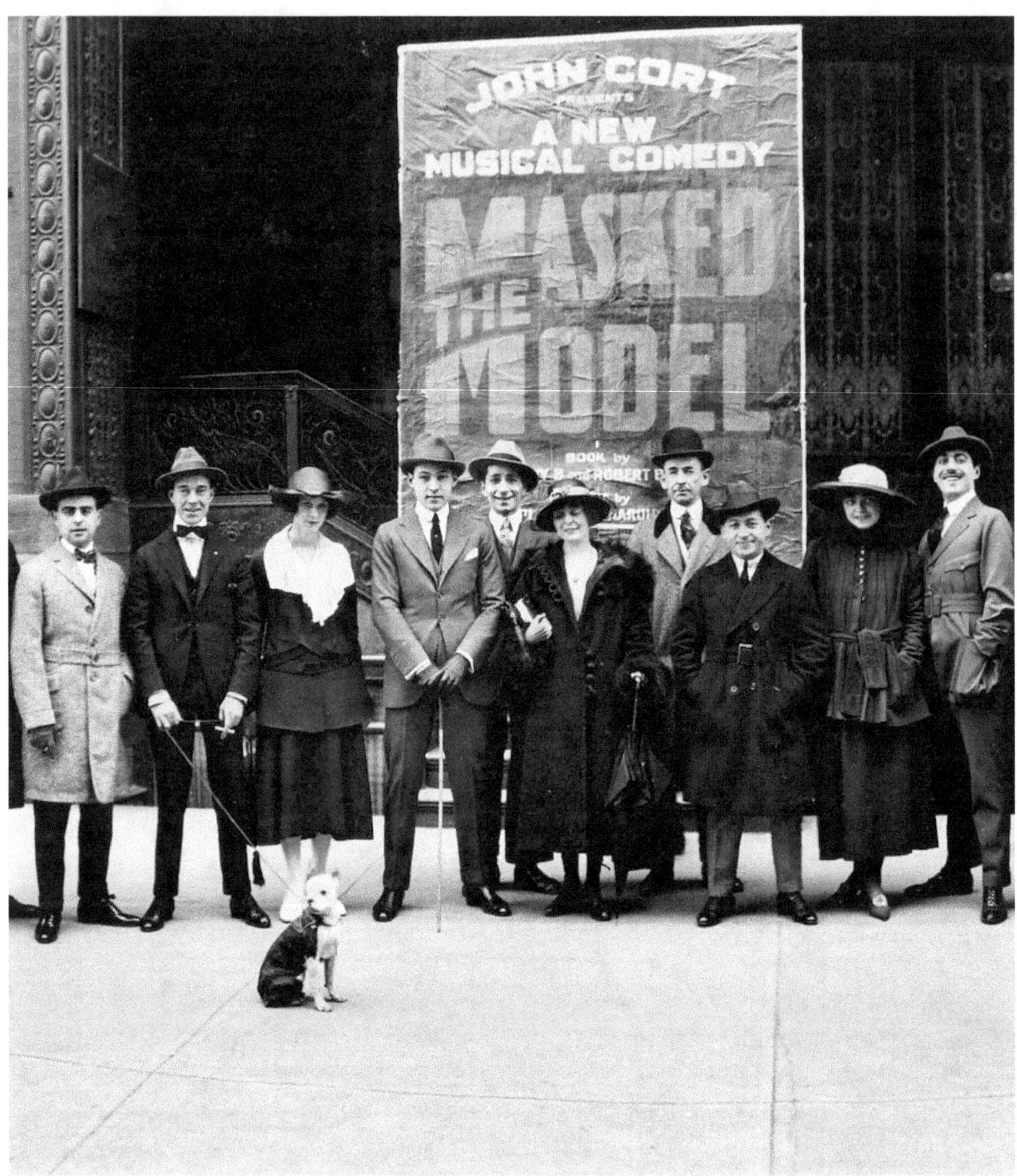

Rudolph Valentino and some fellow cast members of *The Masked Model* pose in front of The Broadway Theater, Denver, CO, May 1917.[10]
(The Denver Public Library, Western History Collection Z-1122; detail of original image)

[10] The original image by the Rocky Mountain Photo Company is much too large for this volume. To view the original "yard long" photograph, it can be accessed at the following link: http://digital.denverlibrary.org/cdm/singleitem/collection/p15330coll22/id/87192/rec/1

CORT'S NEW MUSICAL COMEDY

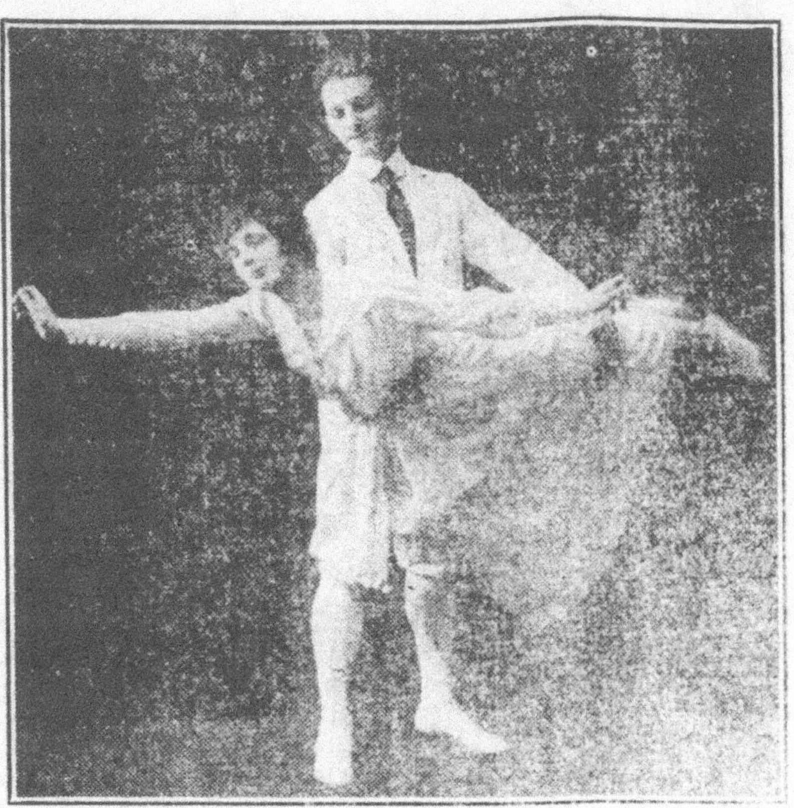

MONS RUDOLPH AND DOLLY BEST, DANCERS WITH "THE MASKED MODEL"

A large chorus, many clever dancing acts and scenes and an abundance of new songs are featured in "The Masked Model," John Cort's newest production, which will be shown at the Majestic Saturday afternoon and evening, affording lovers of musical comedy an opportunity to see one of the big ones.

The songs are said to be nicely welded into the love story told by the play and they include a large number of waltzes which largely predominate in the musical program. Among others they include: "The Girl That Wins My Heart," "Wonderful World," "Chat, Chat, Chatter," "When Fortune Smiles," "The Road to the Girl You Love," "Meet Me in Havana," "We Should Care," "Caravan Land," "Where Do They Come From," "Marionettes" and "Little Women." In the cast of principals will be found: Lew Hearn, Joseph Lertora, Irene Audrey, Roydon Keith, Roy Purviance, W. L. Romaine, Thos. B. Handers, Arthur G. Millis, Edna Pendleton, Dale Turner, Mons Rudolph and Edith Mason.

As *The Masked Model* toured across the country, Rudolph was billed as he was when dancing with Bonnie Glass "Mons Rudolph." This caption on the photograph published in the Reno Gazette-Journal is spectacularly wrong. (newspapers.com)

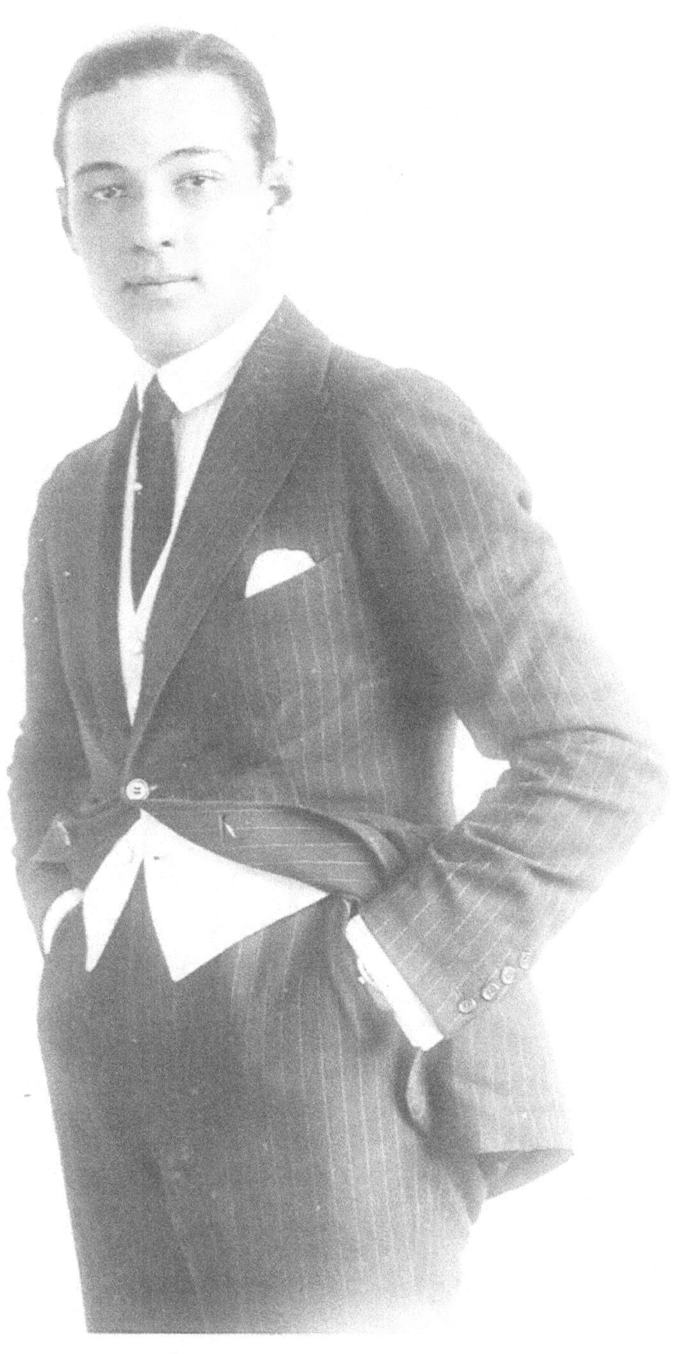

I was utterly unknown in Hollywood. I was a beginner like thousands of others. Don't think that people exclaimed upon meeting me "Here is wonderful find!" No one hailed me for photographic qualities, for personality or for anything else.

—Rudolph Valentino 1923

Rudolph Valentino arrived in Los Angeles in the summer of 1917. He and Norman Kerry took rooms at the Alexandria Hotel; the favored residence for Hollywood's power elite, hoping to make connections and be seen. He joined the hopefuls hanging around various studios, looking for day work as an extra. He quickly learned that being distinctive got him more work, and he was soon well known to the cowboys, pirates, vamps, and other extras for his attention-grabbing dress. He later said, "Even when I was not called in, I arrived early in the morning. I adopted a conspicuous outfit: riding pants, boots, open collared shirt, and riding crop. I greeted the world smiling."

Money was in short supply, and although he disliked the idea of exhibition dancing for a living, he had no choice. Extra work was not steady, and no directors were knocking on his door. He went to work at the raucous Watts Tavern, partnering Marjorie Tain, for $35 dollars a week. This engagement led to dancing with Katherine "Kitty" Phelps at 'the prestigious Hotel Maryland in Pasadena[11], a genteel and wealthy Los Angeles suburb. Happily, the Maryland also provided room and board in exchange for his dancing services. In 1918 he was hired for his first major film role (using the stage name Rodolpho di Valentina) for Joseph Maxwell's silent melodrama *The Married Virgin*, but legal troubles caused the film to remain unreleased until 1922.

After his engagement at the Hotel Maryland ended, he returned to Los Angeles in time for a crushing personal blow. His mother, Gabriella Guglielmi, who had been in failing health, died on January 18, 1918. He learned of the sad news over a month later in a letter from his sister Maria, and he was inconsolable. He had been in America for five years, and one of his great desires was for her to see her son as a successful man.

Universal Studios soon cast him in two five-reel comedies starring 18-year-old Carmel Myers. The first, *A Society Sensation*, he played a wealthy society playboy who falls in love with a poor fisherman's daughter, played by Myers. In the second, *All Night*, inexplicably featured the ethnic-looking Valentino as Myers' all-American boyfriend "Dick Bradley."

While at Universal, Valentino met actor Douglas Gerrard, who would become one of his closest friends and confidants. Gerrard was an outgoing Irishman who started as a director but spent most of his time doing small parts and extra work. He encouraged the still grieving and morose Valentino to resume his social life.

After a bout with the Spanish flu, Valentino reconnected with his old friend from New York, Mae Murray, who was by then married to the director Robert Z. Leonard. His next big break came when he co-starred with Murray in *The Big Little Person* and *The Delicious Little Devil*.

In 1919 Valentino appeared in a D.W. Griffith–supervised, Elmer Clifton directed, comedy starring Dorothy Gish, entitled *Out of Luck.* While he once more played a cad, working with Dorothy Gish was a really good chance for more visibility. Dorothy Gish later recalled

[11] Valentino saved clippings from this appearance and others in a scrapbook he maintained from 1917 to 1920. He meticulously indexed the clippings; which newspaper and the dates of each in his own hand up to the time of the release of *The Four Horsemen of the Apocalypse* in the scrapbook that survives.

that Valentino would often come to the Gish home and cook spaghetti for the family, "… it was *so* good!"[12] Hoping to be cast by Griffith for *Broken Blossoms*, he posed for portraits dressed in Chinese costume. Griffith, if he saw the photographs, was unimpressed. Alla Nazimova's protégée, Richard Barthelmess, in the coveted role. To Valentino's chagrin, Griffith instead hired him to dance in the stage prologue to *The Greatest Thing in Life*, partnering Carol Dempster.

At a party at the home of actress Pauline Frederick, Valentino met a pretty young actress named Jean Acker. He and Acker shared similar interests—in particular, a love of horseback riding—and immediately hit it off. He later said that he had been unbearably lonely and "longed for the sympathy and understanding of a woman." On one of their shared moonlit horseback rides, a smitten Valentino proposed marriage. To his delight, Acker accepted.

Jean Acker of Metro Weds

Almost duplicating the romance of the character she enacted in "Lombardi, Ltd." the Screen Classics, Inc., production starring Bert Lytell, Jean Acker, who was seen in the picture as "Daisy, a Model," one of the sextette of beauty mannequins, married Rudolpho Valentino, an Italian dancer and leading man of the screen, at Hollywood, Cal., at midnight, November 5.

The wedding came suddenly after two months of courtship.

Their nuptials were announced in Motion Picture News.
At this time, it was Acker's career that was the more successful.
This would soon change, dramatically.

Their courtship was brief and their marriage was hasty. The ceremony took place on November 5, 1919, at the Hollywood home of Metro Pictures' treasurer, Joseph Engel. After the wedding festivities, the newly married couple retired to Acker's room at the Hotel Hollywood, whereupon the ardent Valentino found himself locked out of the room and barred from the marriage bed. After pleading with his bride to let him in, he returned to his apartment, alone.

Jean Acker, who identified as a lesbian and/or bisexual, had not told her husband about her sexual orientation. Valentino, it appears, was further confused by her mixed signals. The lovesick bridegroom penned ardent inscriptions on several portraits dedicated to Acker, and he pursued her by telephone, mail, and telegram. Acker continued to keep him guessing, indicating one day her affection, the next her desire to have nothing further to do with him. She soon departed for location work, leaving Valentino and the marriage in limbo.

At another dance, he met Helen Troubetskoy, who was married to the artist and exiled Russian prince Paulo Troubetskoy. Troubetskoy later sculpted Valentino's right hand and gifted it to him. It is speculated that Valentino modeled for Troubetskoy's sculpture The Flag Bearer. She introduced Valentino to what would become one of his favorite spots to retreat

[12] Kevin Brownlow interview with Dorothy Gish, New York, 1964.

from Hollywood and the tribulations of stardom, Palm Springs. During a spur-of-the-moment trip to the desert city, she had second thoughts on the propriety of their sharing living quarters, since both were married. She arranged for Valentino to bunk with her neighbor and friend Paul Ivano. This inauspicious meeting began one of Valentino's staunchest male friendships.

At the end of 1919, his personal life was in shambles, but his career was on the upswing. His breakthrough performance came when he was cast as a lecherous heavy in Clara Kimball Young's *Eyes of Youth.* Valentino played Clarence Morgan, "a cabaret parasite" hired to entrap Young into a compromising position. It was a small role, but Valentino imbued the character with physical grace and more than a hint of menace. His performance caught the eye of a woman who would be his most important connection in Hollywood: June Mathis.

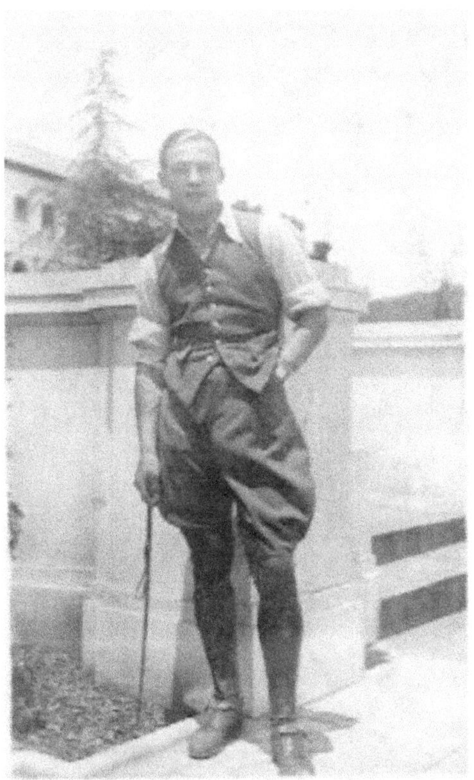

Valentino in Los Angeles
circa 1918.
(Private collection)

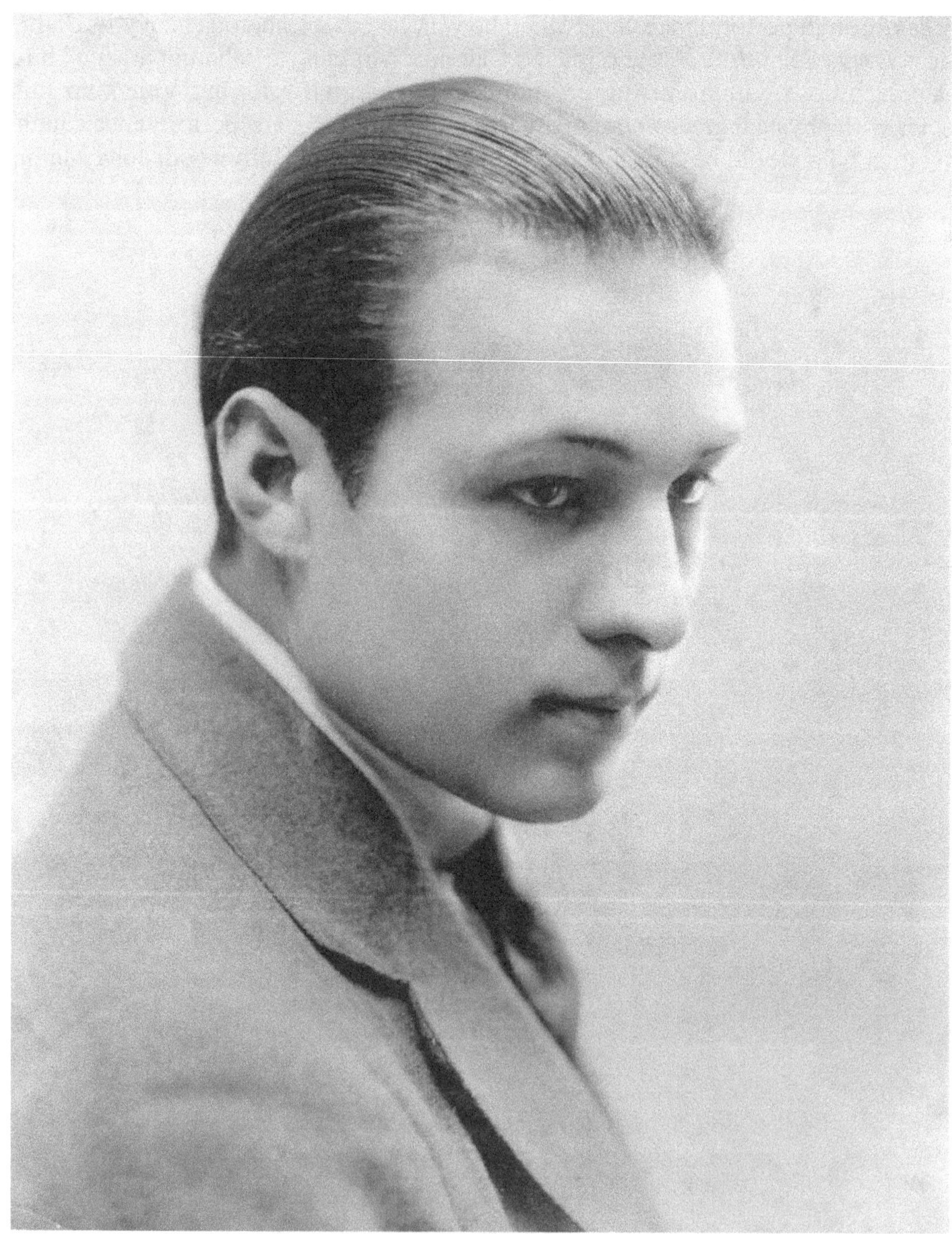

One of Rudolph Valentino's first official publicity portraits by Witzel Studios.
(Author's Collection)

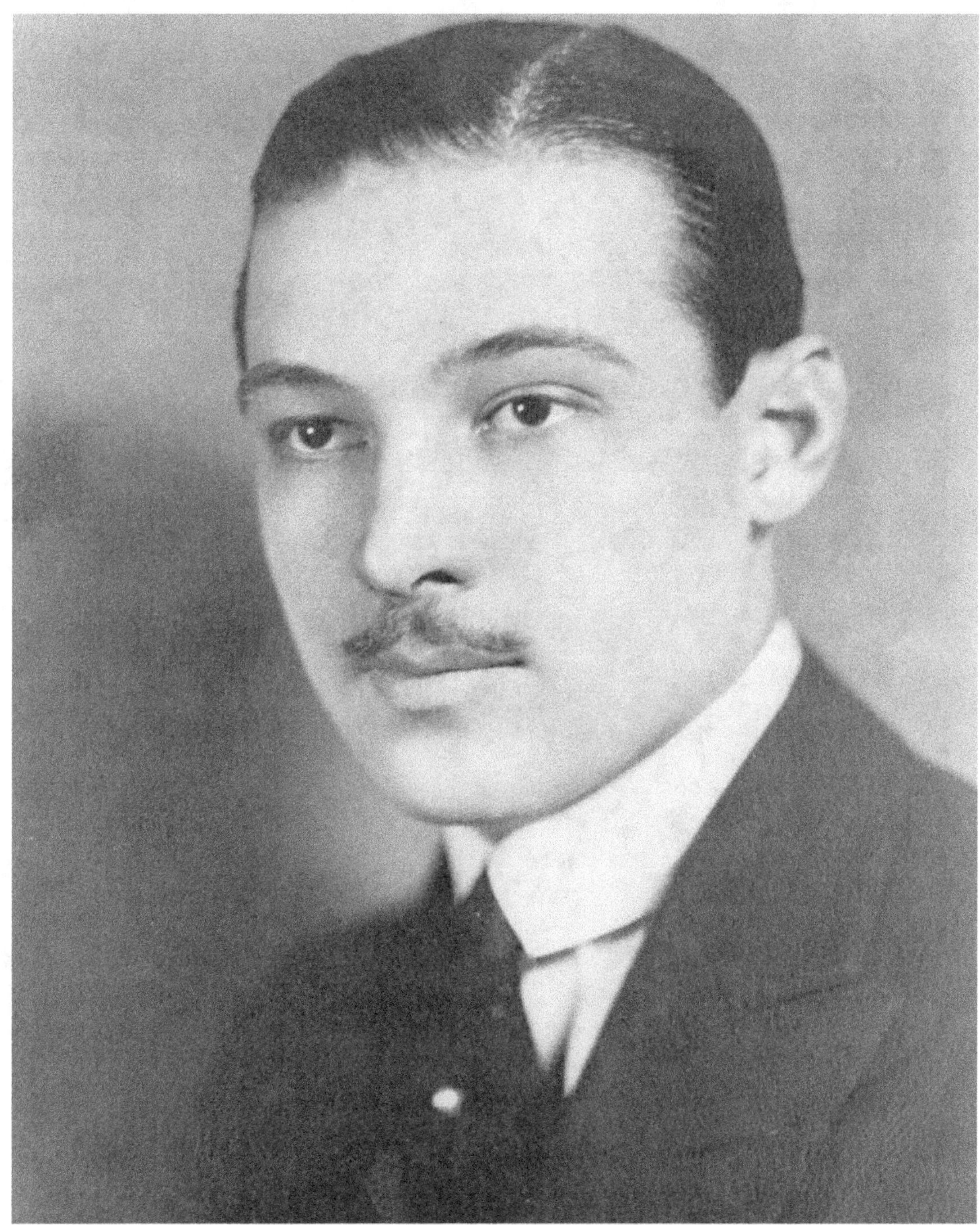

Rudolph Valentino sporting a snazzy moustache *circa* 1918, portrait by Murillo.
(Author's Collection)

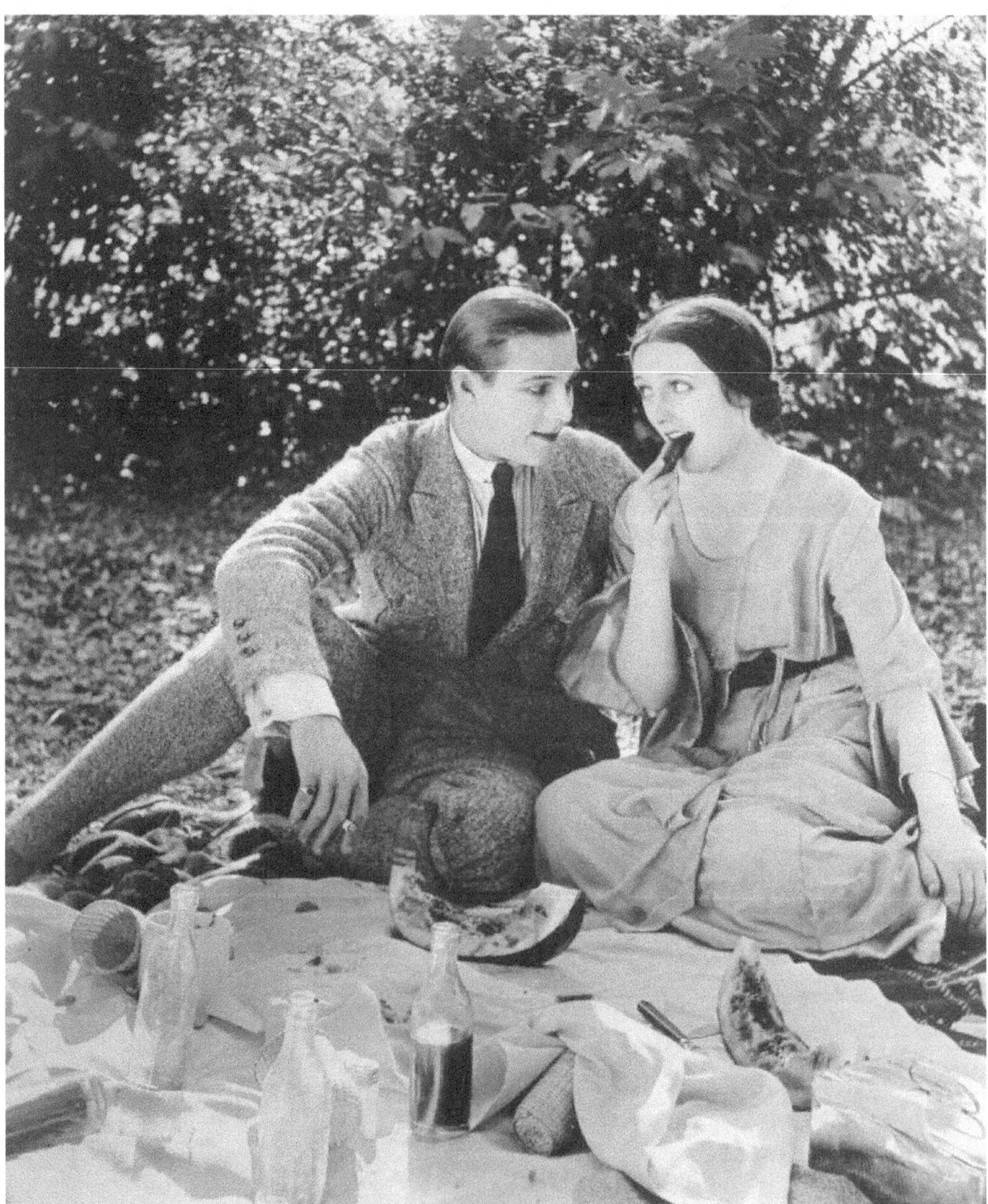

Valentino with Carmel Myers in *A Society Sensation* 1918. (Tracy Terhune collection)

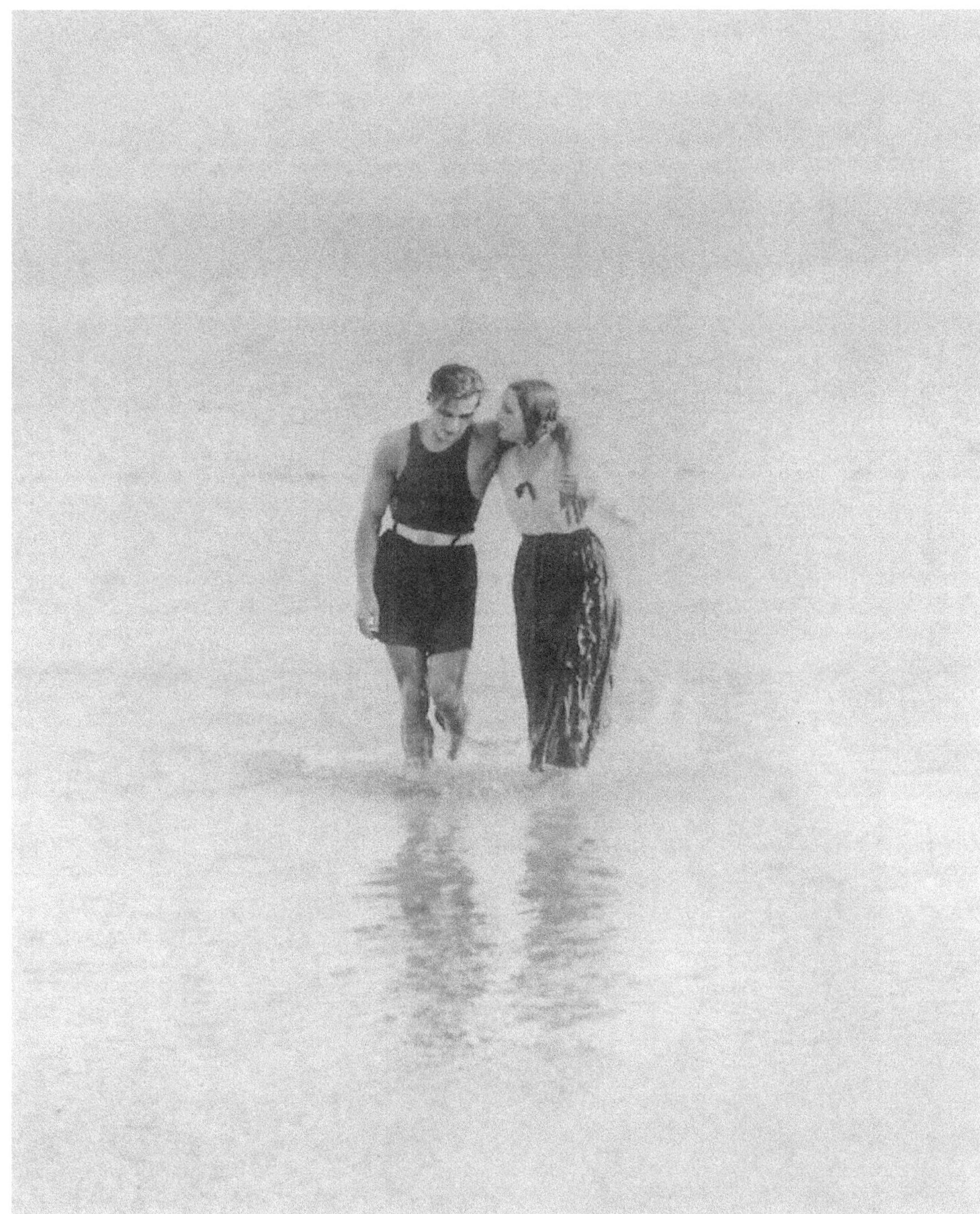

Carmel Myers rescues Valentino in *A Society Sensation*, 1918. (Brad Frick collection)

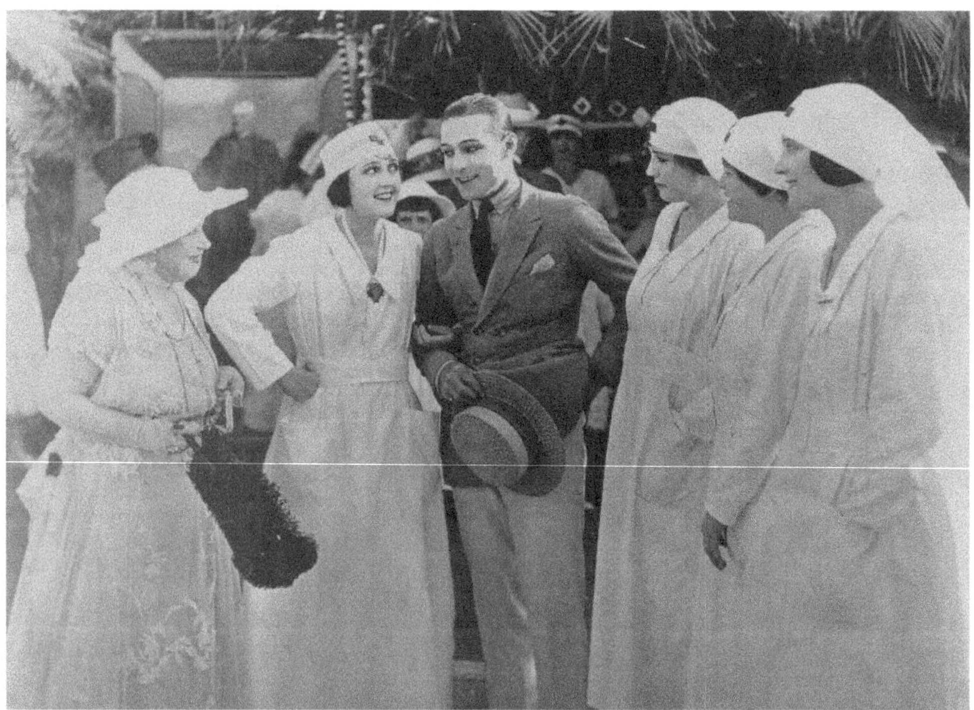

Valentino charms the ladies in *A Society Sensation*, 1918. (Independent Visions collection)

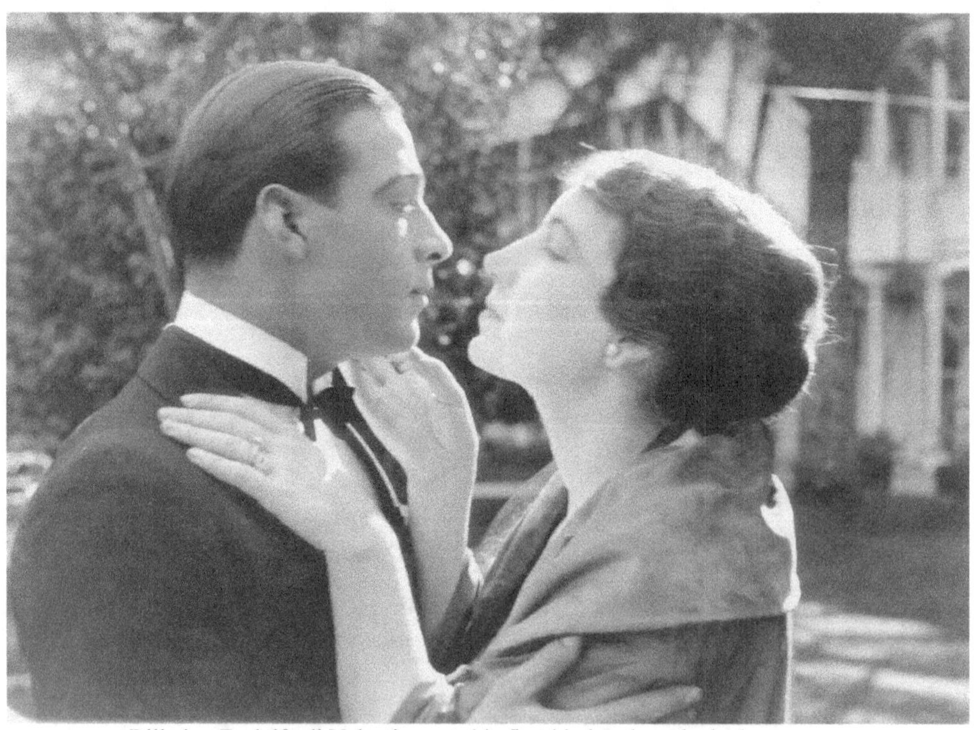

Billed as Rodolfo di Valentina gets his first big break as the bad guy
opposite Kathleen Kirkham
in Joseph Maxwell's *The Married Virgin*, 1917.
(Michael and Virginia Back collection)

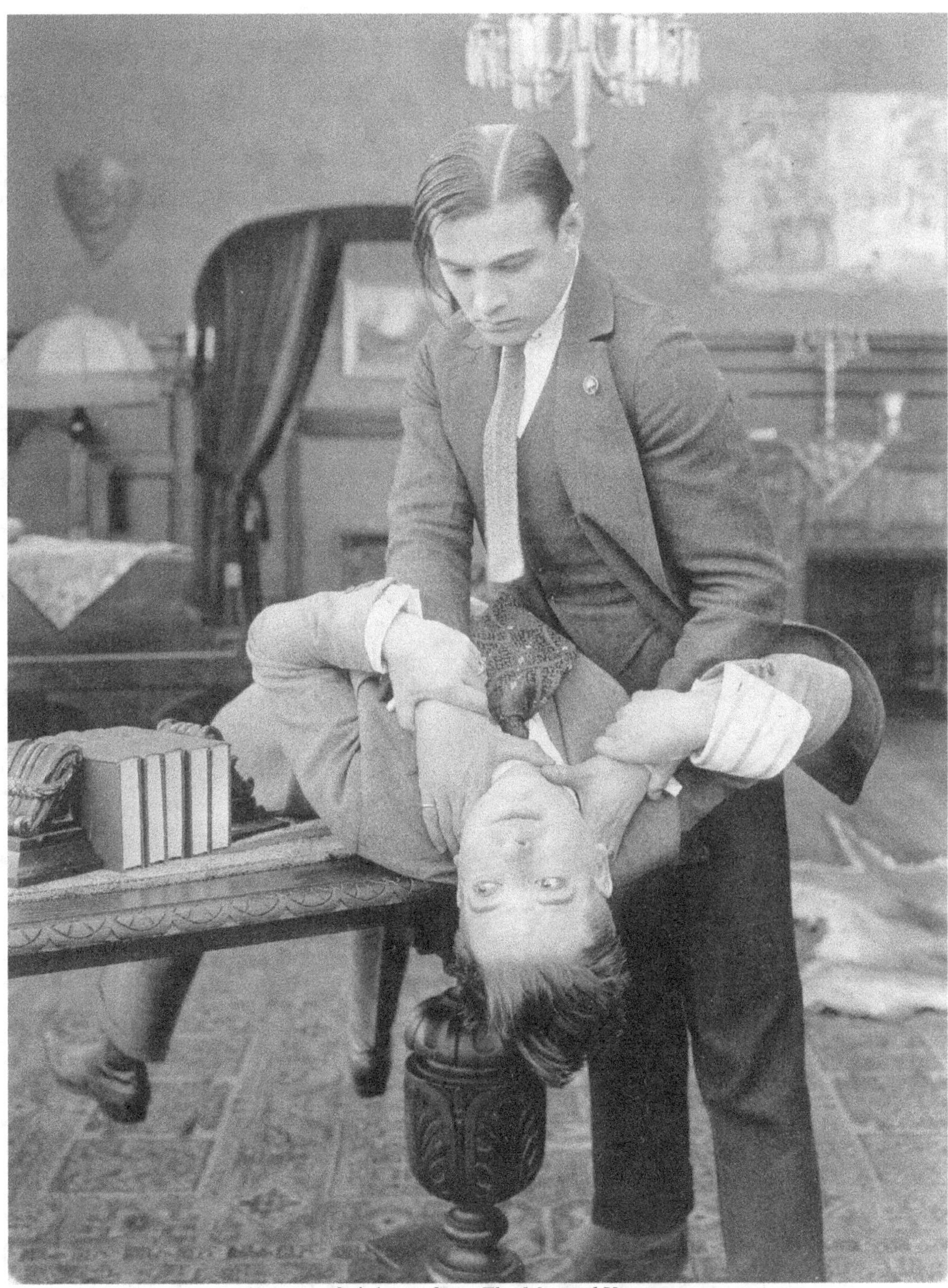

A scene of violence from *The Married Virgin*,
with Frank Newberg.
(Michael and Virginia Back collection)

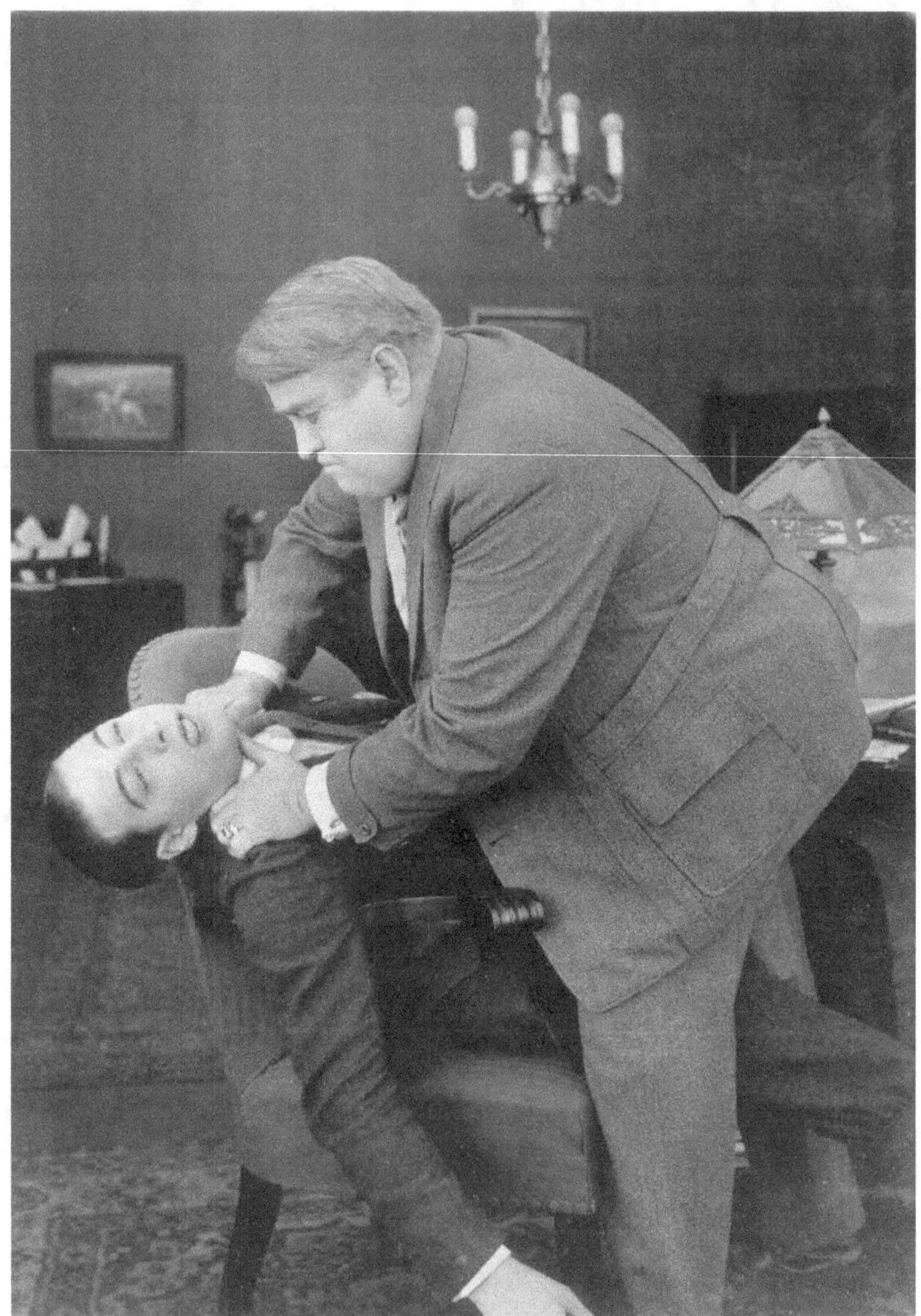

Edward Jobson metes out some justice, *The Married Virgin.*
(Michael and Virginia Back collection)

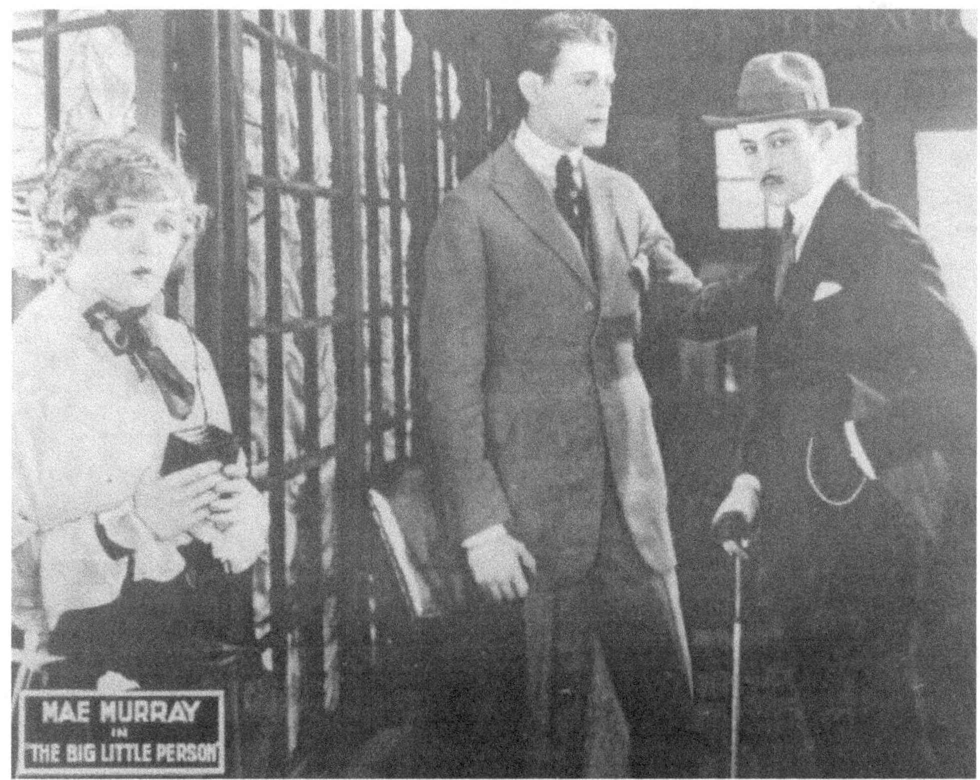

Mae Murray, Allan Seers and Rudolpho di Valentina in *The Big Little Person.*
This was a step upward in Valentino's career trajectory.
(Author's collection)

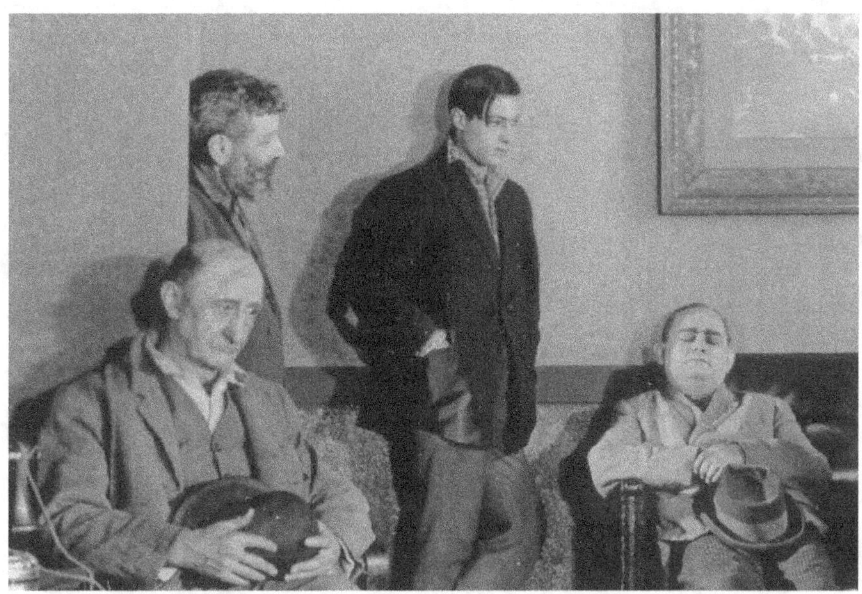

Valentino, back to bit parts, temporarily. Here an extra, in his friend
Norman Kerry's 1919 film *Virtuous Sinners.*
(Margaret Herrick Library; Academy of Motion Picture Arts and Sciences)

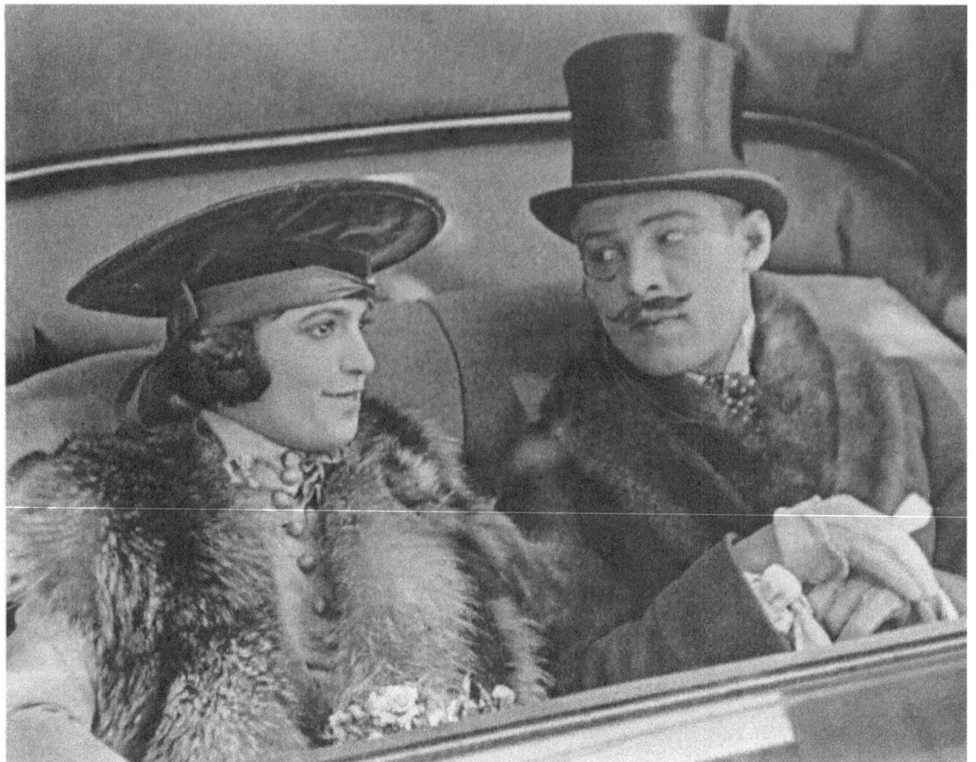

Valentino was cast along with Virginia Rappe in *An Adventuress*.
The film had a torturous path with three separate releases, three different titles and it failed each time.
Not to be attributed to either Valentino or Rappe's truncated performances.
(Author's Collection)

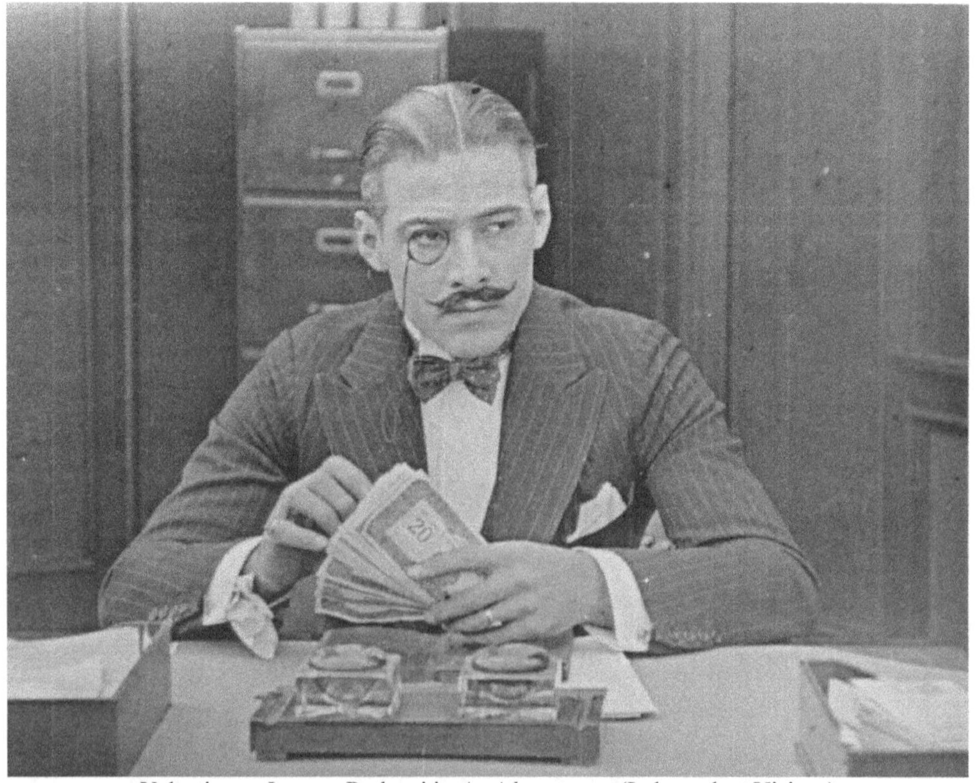

Valentino as Jacques Rudanyi in *An Adventuress*. (Independent Visions)

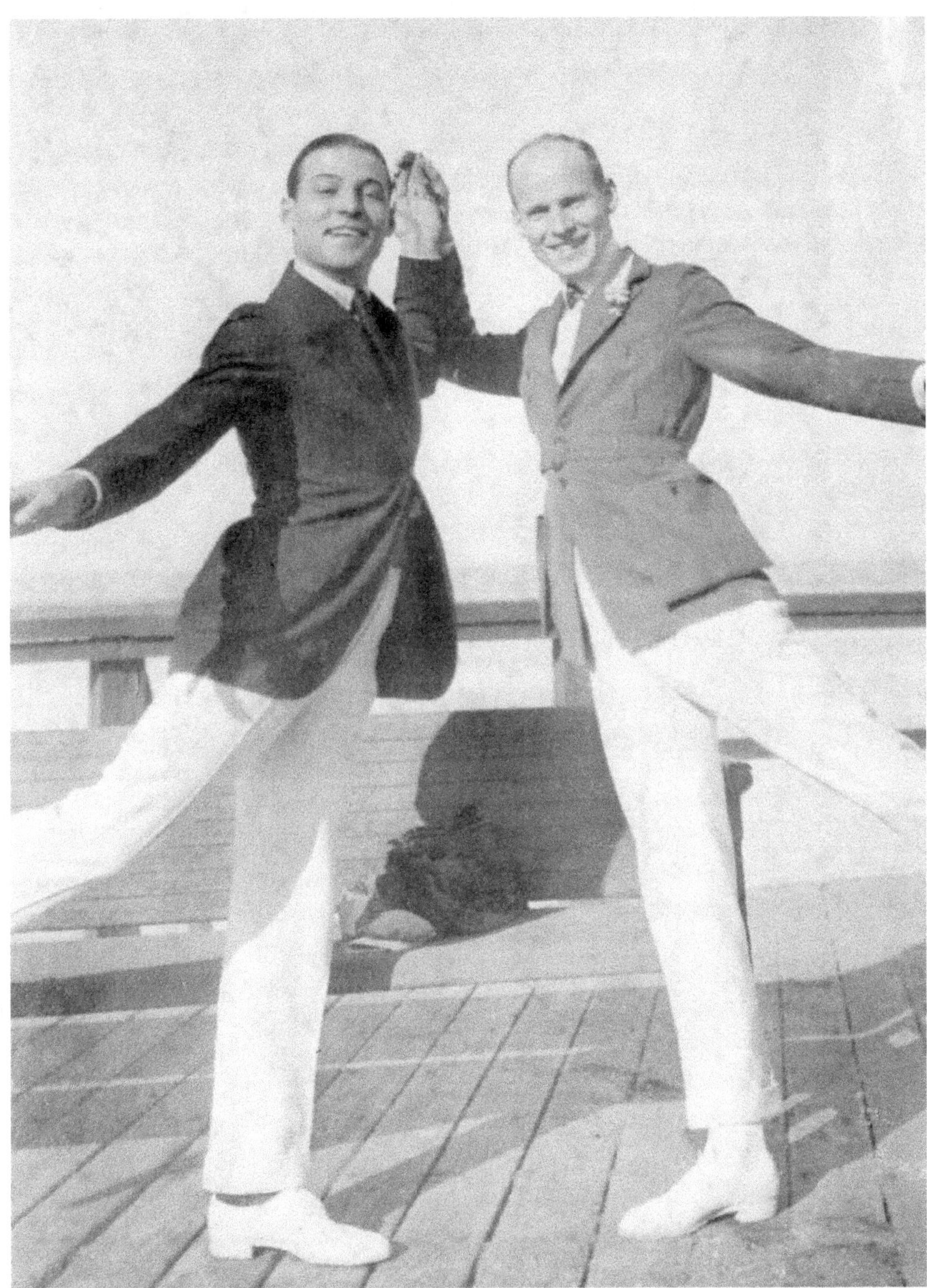
Valentino clowning with an unknown friend *circa* 1918. (Author's Collection)

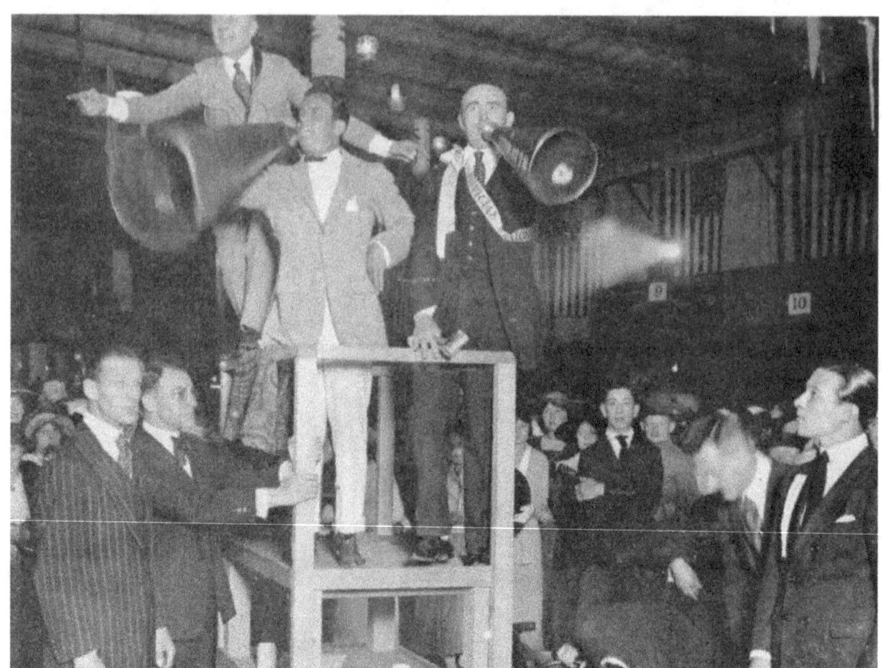

Rudolph Valentino, far right foreground, attends a Liberty Bond Rally in 1918.
On the makeshift podium are Douglas Fairbanks and Donald Crisp.
(Tracy Terhune collection)

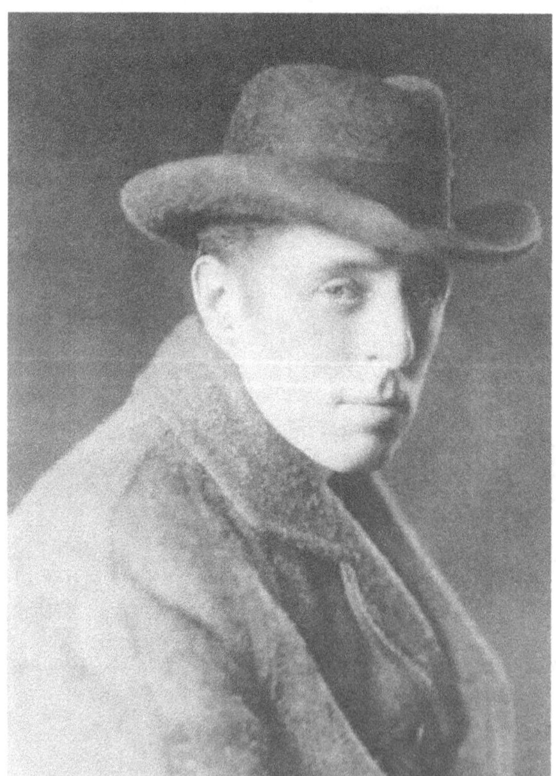

Never let it be said Valentino did not aim high.
he wanted to work with D.W. Griffith
in the worst way. Griffith, by all accounts, was blind
to Valentino's appeal and talent. (Author's Collection)

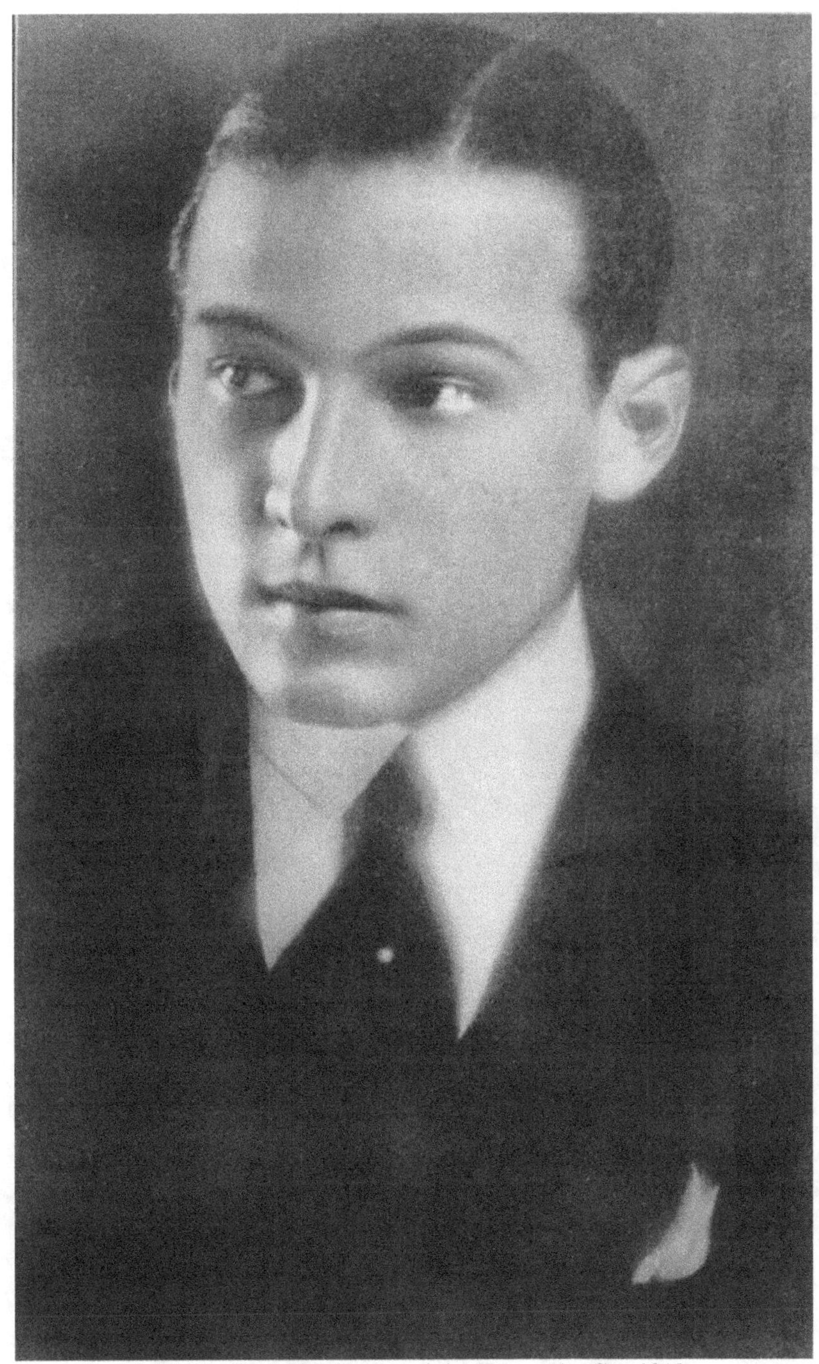

Rudolph Valentino publicity portrait by Hoover Art Co., 1918.
(Author's Collection)

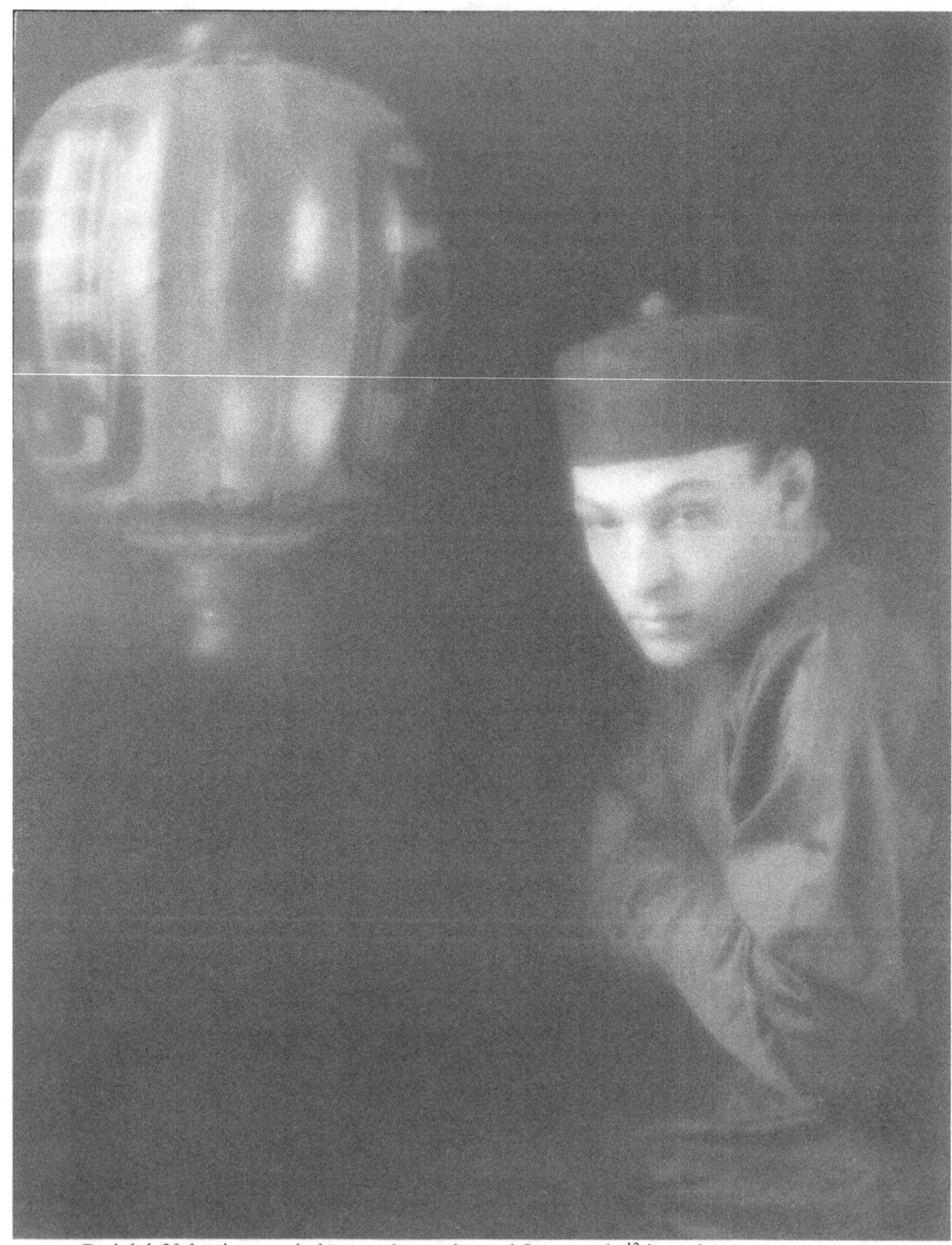

Rudolph Valentino sought better roles, and posed for portraits[13] in various costumes.
This in the vain hope of winning the attention of D.W. Griffith.
He longed to star in the plum role opposite Lillian Gish in *Broken Blossoms*.
Griffith, if he saw the portraits, he took no notice of Valentino. (Michael and Virginia Back collection)

[13] The original photographs from this series are hand tinted. The tinted images can be seen in the first edition of *Rudolph Valentino The Silent Idol* (blurb books 2010).

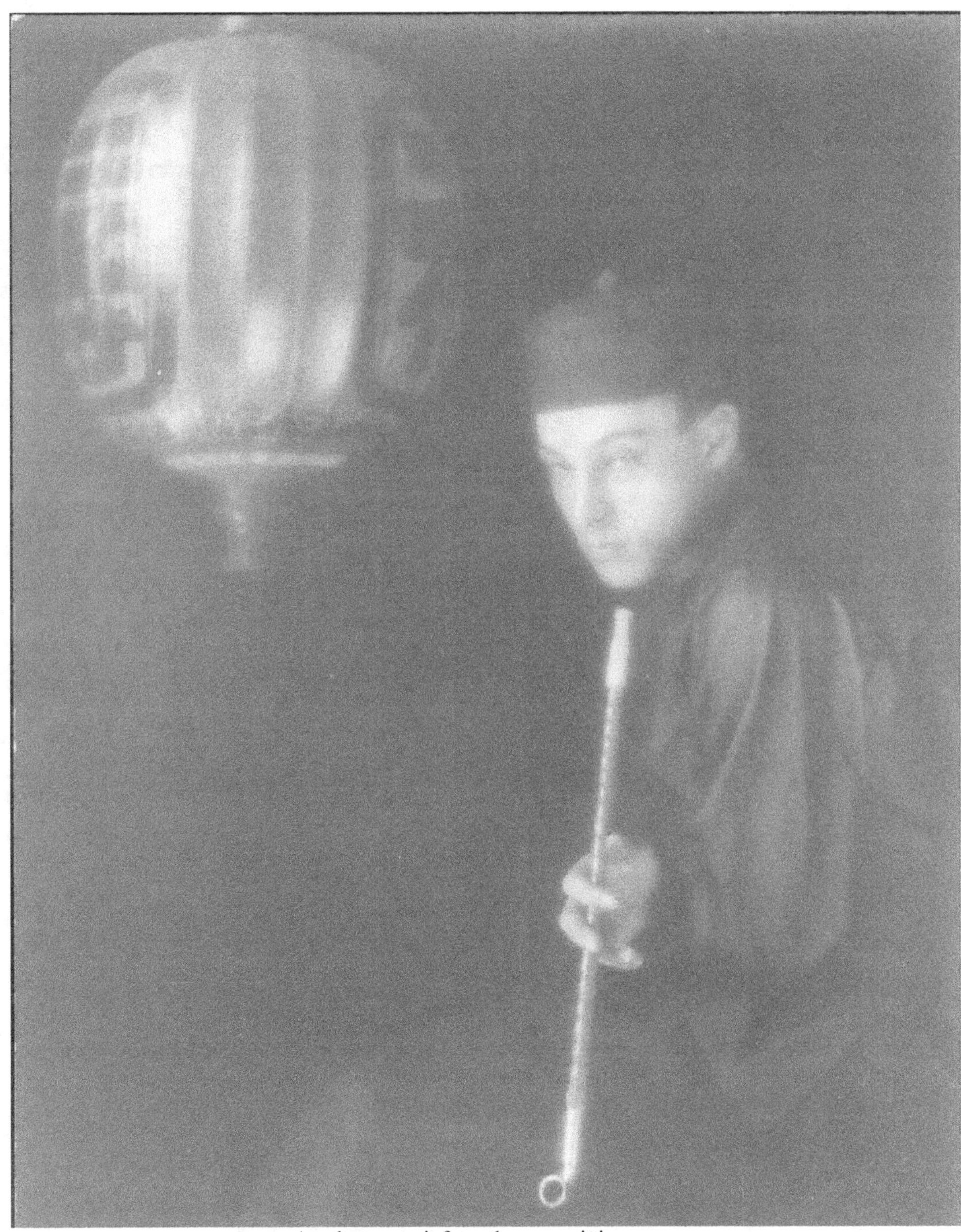

Another portrait from the same sitting.
This is a perfect illustration of the fluidity of Valentino's features, which would suit him well later on.
(Michael and Virginia Back collection)

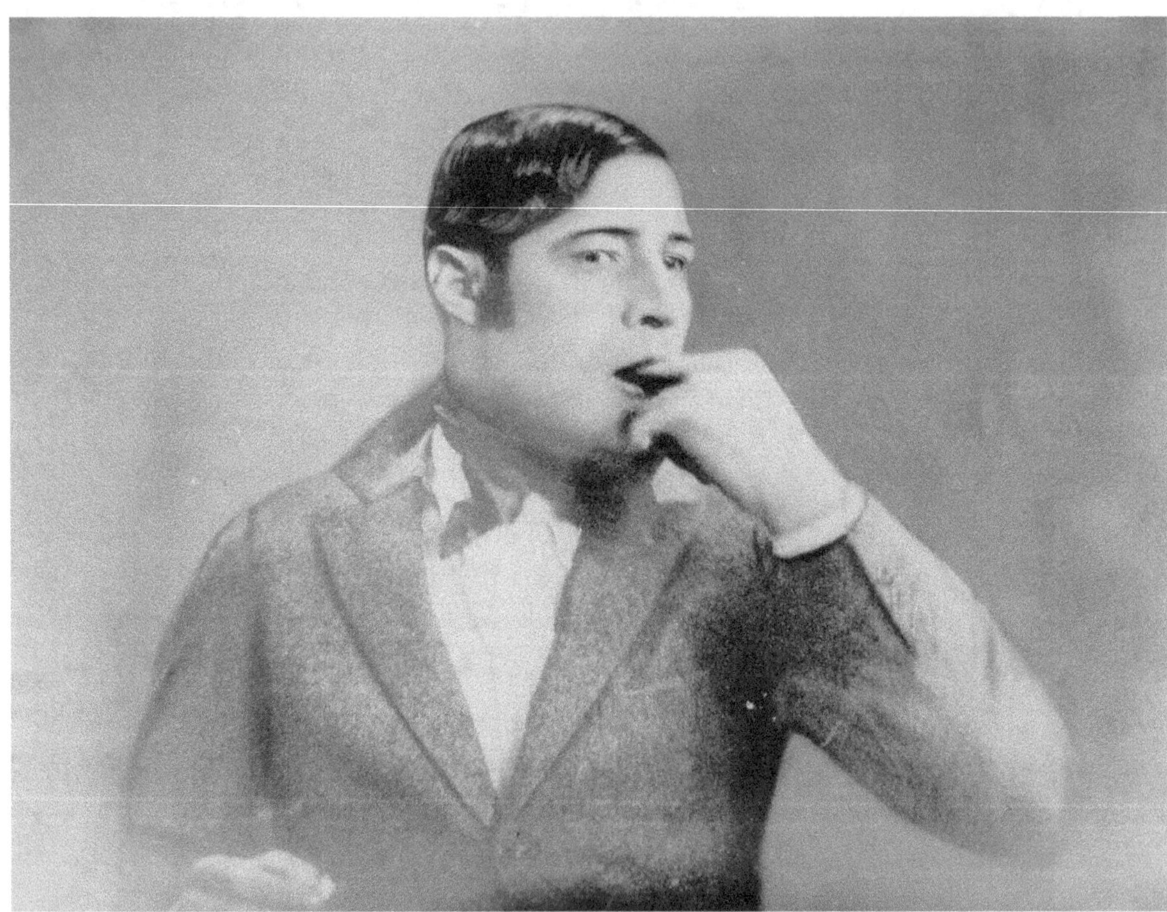

Whistling for his moll. Here playing yet another in a lengthening line of thugs in *A Rogue's Romance*.
(Author's collection)

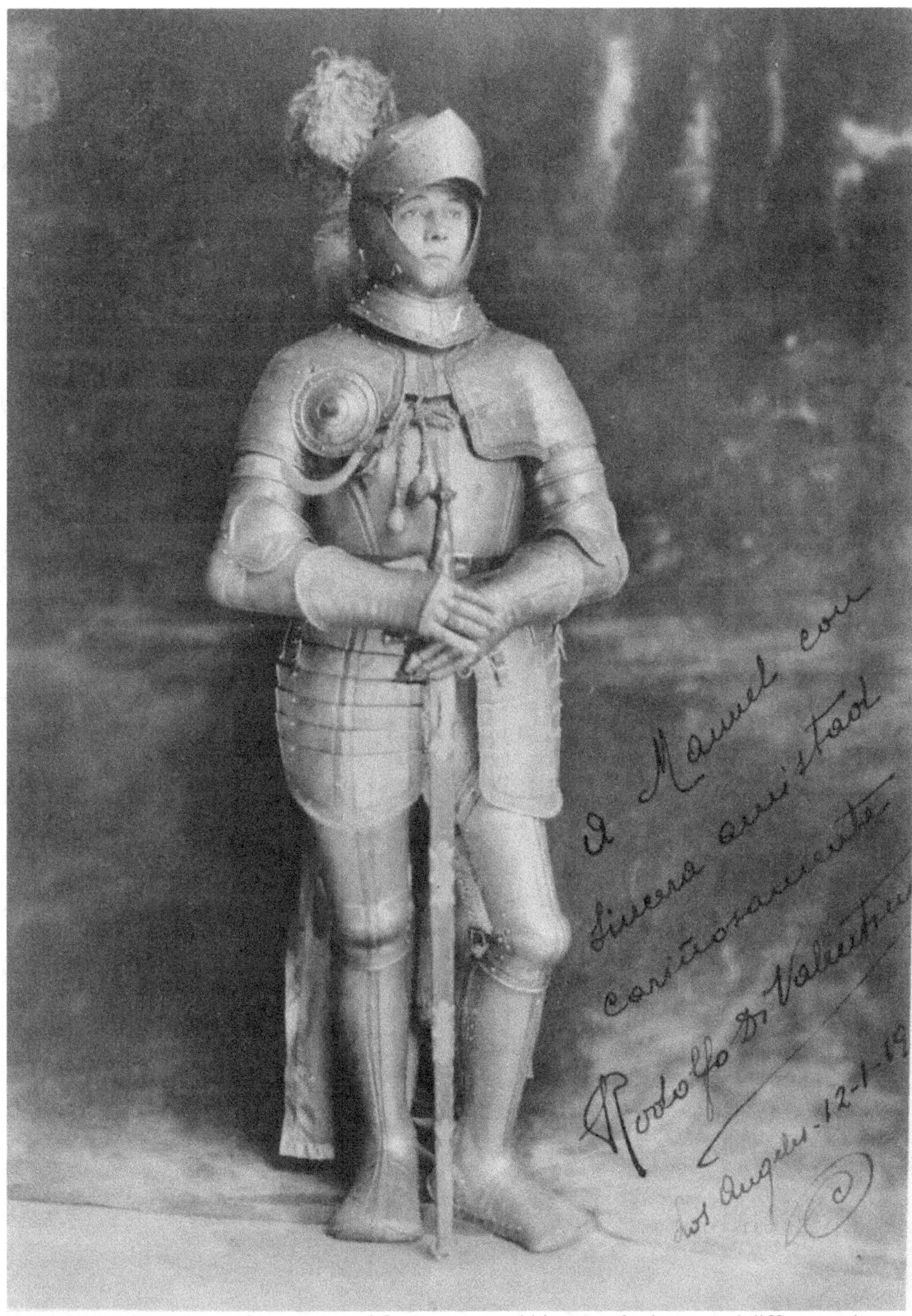

Rudolph Valentino's love of costume and fantasy spurred his quest for better and different roles.
This portrait was inscribed to his good friend Manuel Reachi.
(Margaret Herrick Library; Academy of Motion Picture Arts and Sciences)

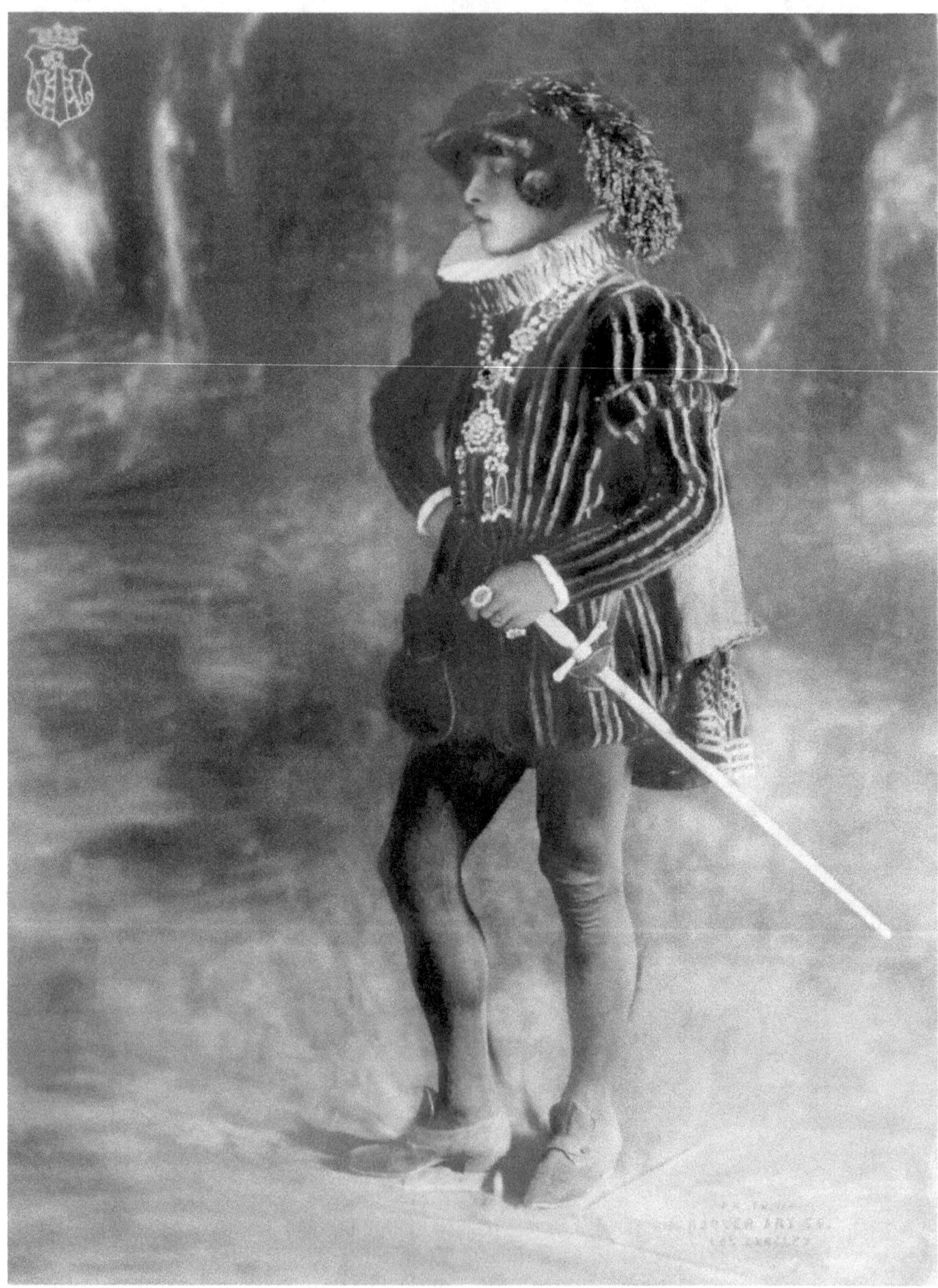

Rudolph Valentino's love of Italy and the Renaissance is evident in this portrait study.
Sadly, none of these photos resulted in his being cast other than a villain, usually American or Irish.
(Kristen Burkhardt collection)

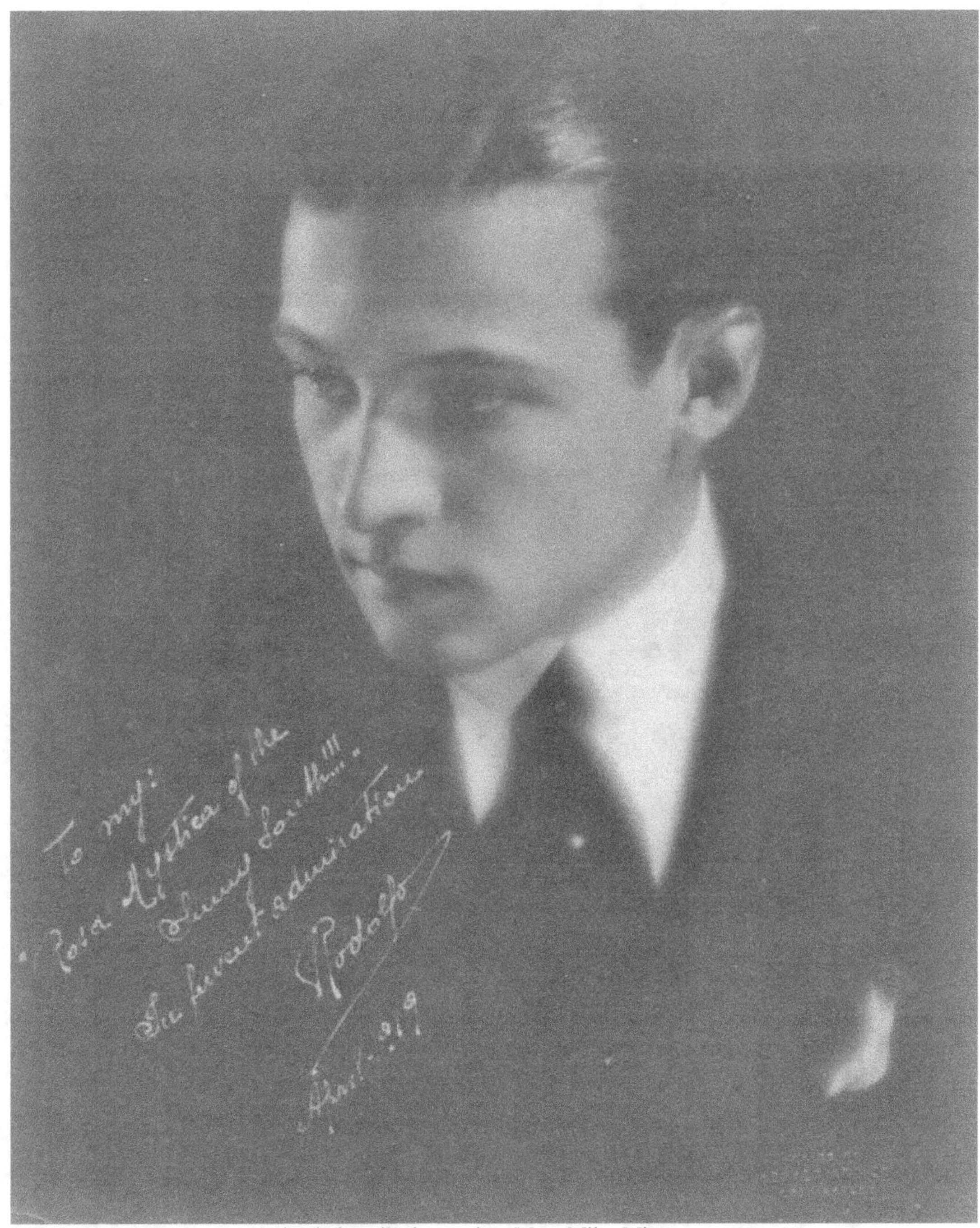

Ardently inscribed portrait to Mary Miles Minter,
"To my Rosa Mistica from the Sunny South!!! In Fervent Admiration, Rodolfo, April 1919."
(Author's collection)

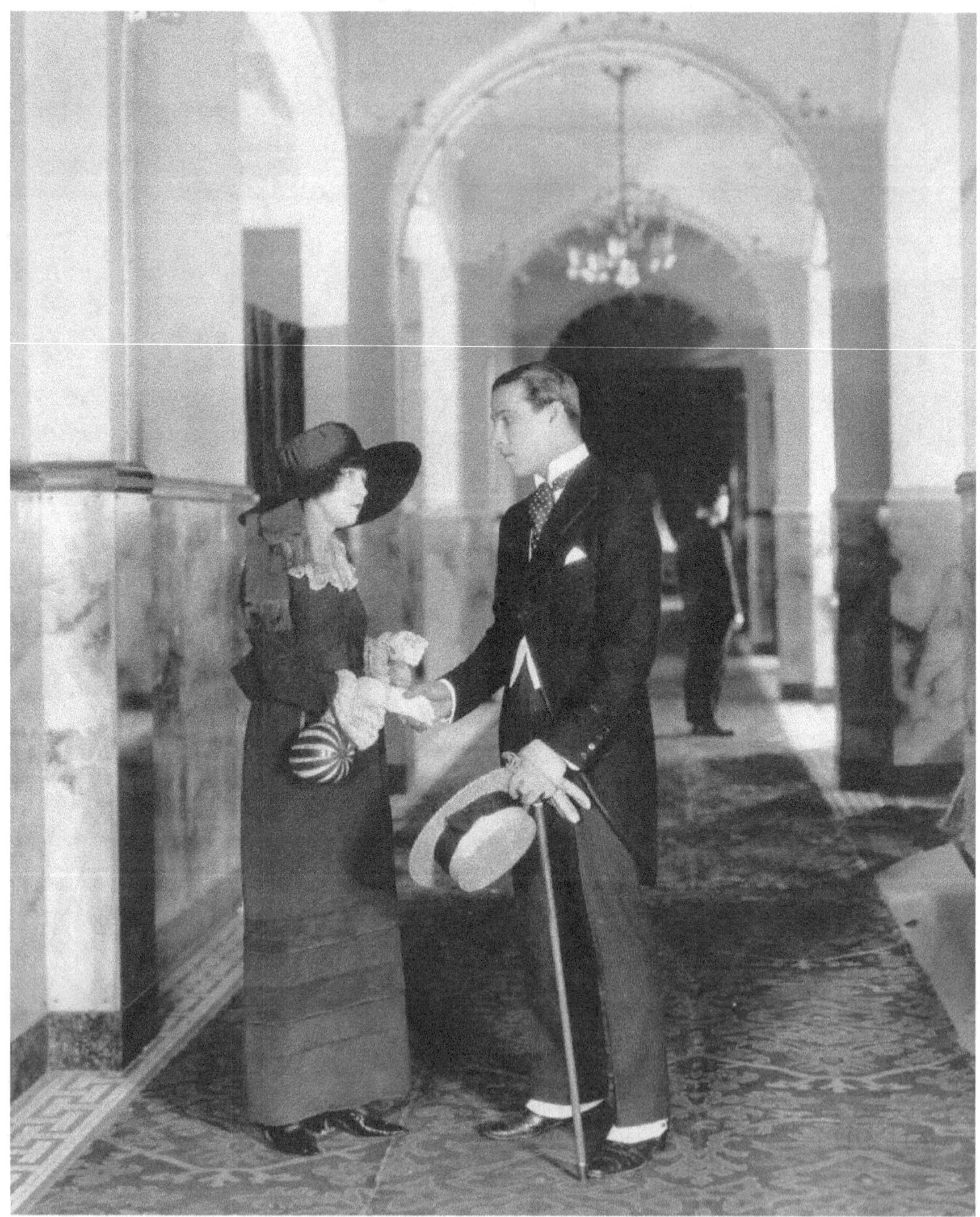

D.W. Griffith could not recognize Rudolph Valentino's talent and screen appeal, Dorothy Gish did.
Cast once more as a baddie, Valentino did have a chance to show his vulnerability and romance in *Out of Luck*.
Filmed on location at The Hotel Green in Pasadena. (Author's collection)

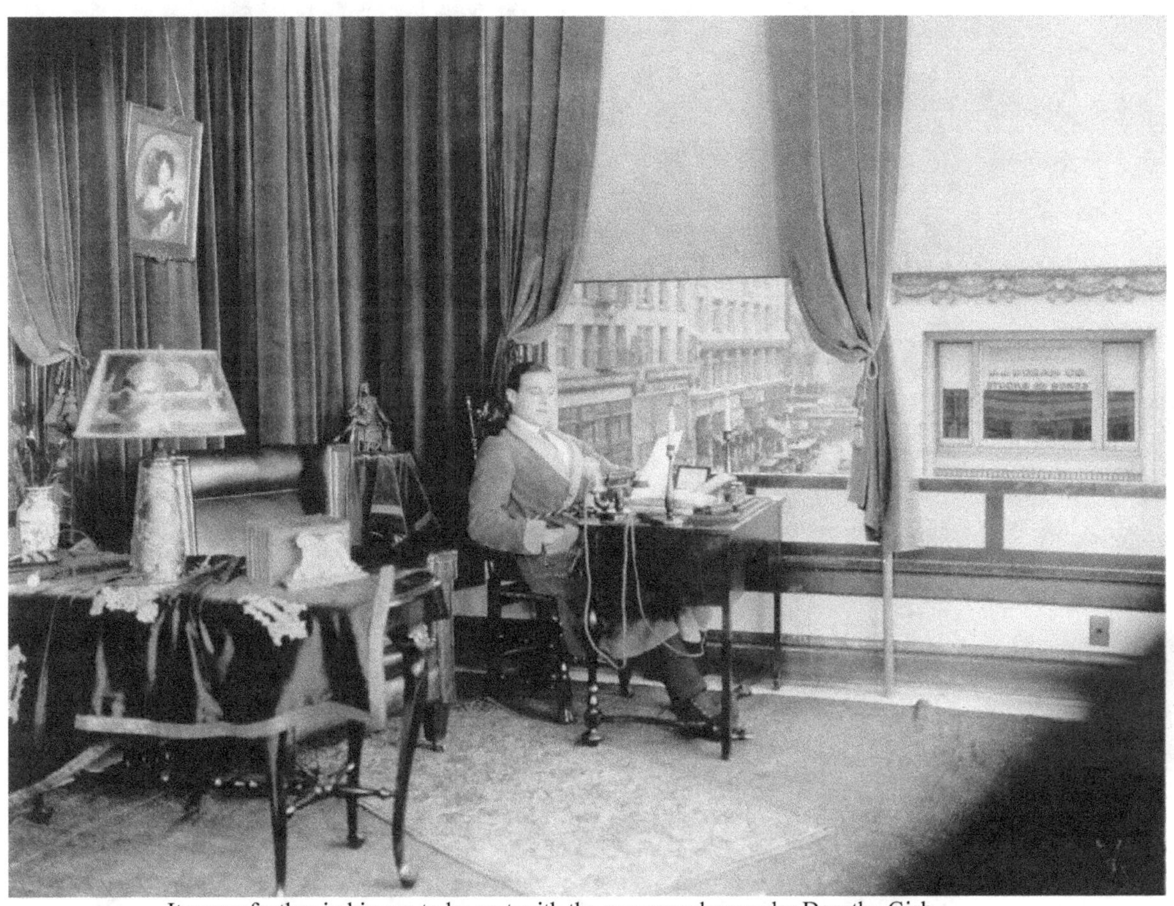

It was a feather in his cap to be cast with the enormously popular Dorothy Gish in *Out of Luck*. He was still playing a cad, but, this time in a comedy. (Robert S. Birchard collection)

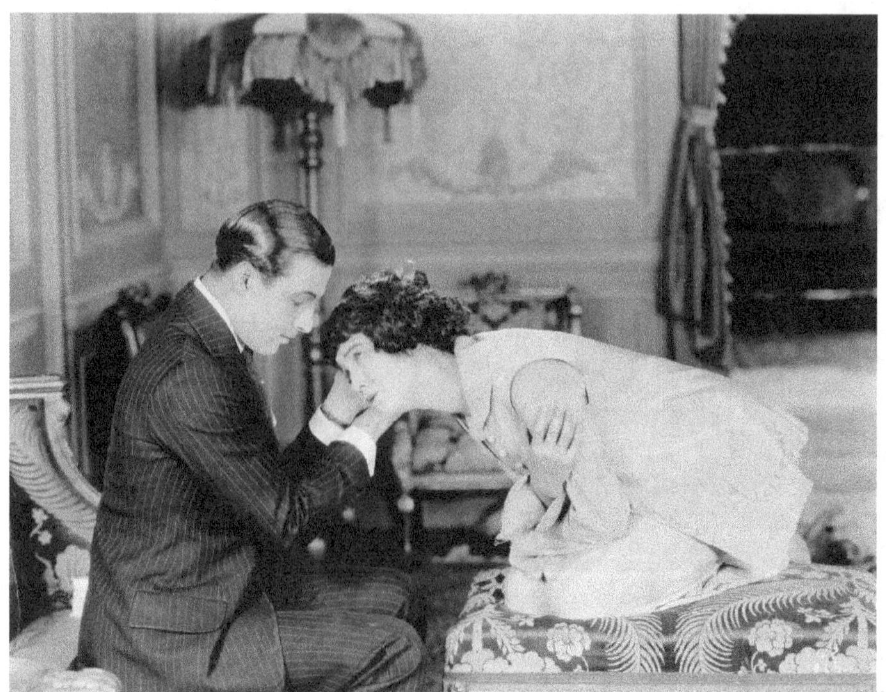

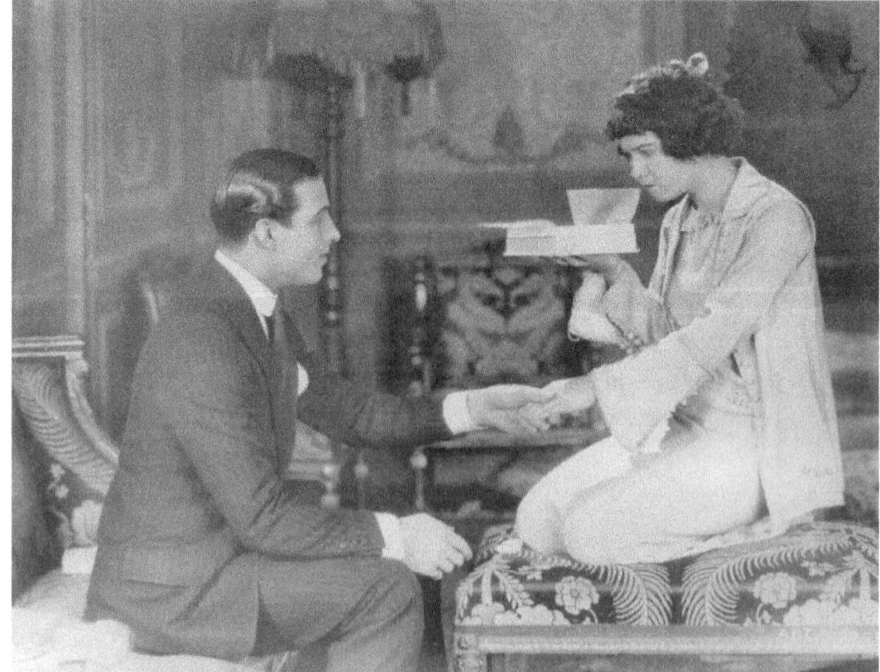

Two stills from *Out of Luck* with Dorothy Gish. (Author's collection)

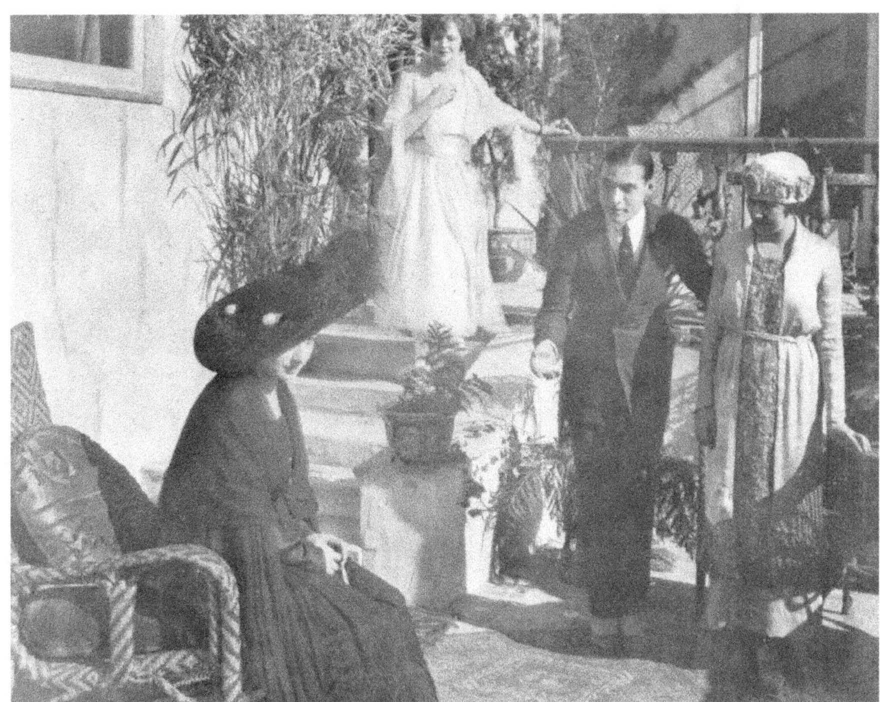

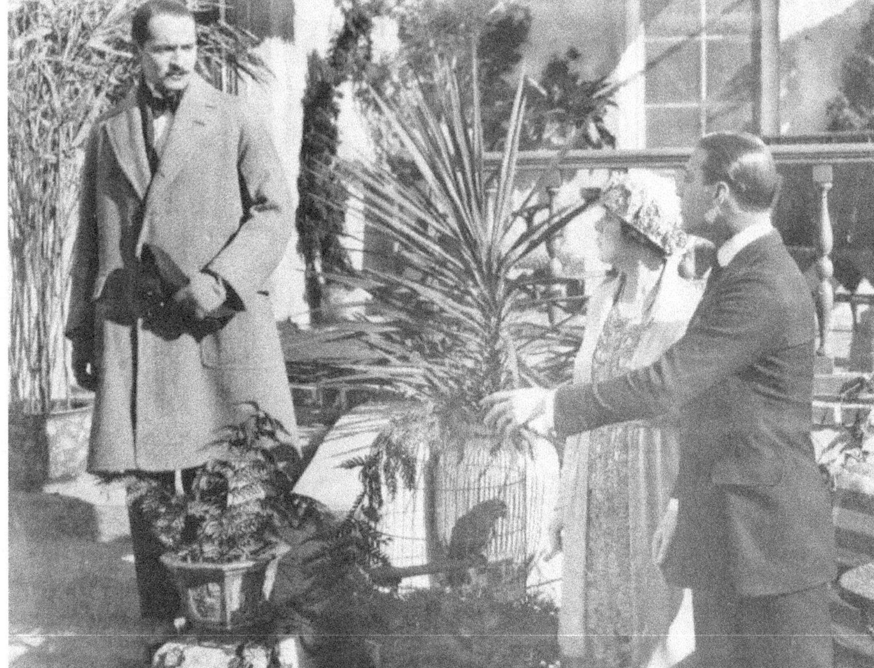

Two stills from *Passion's Playground* with Norman Kerry and Katherine MacDonald.
(Tracy Terhune collection)

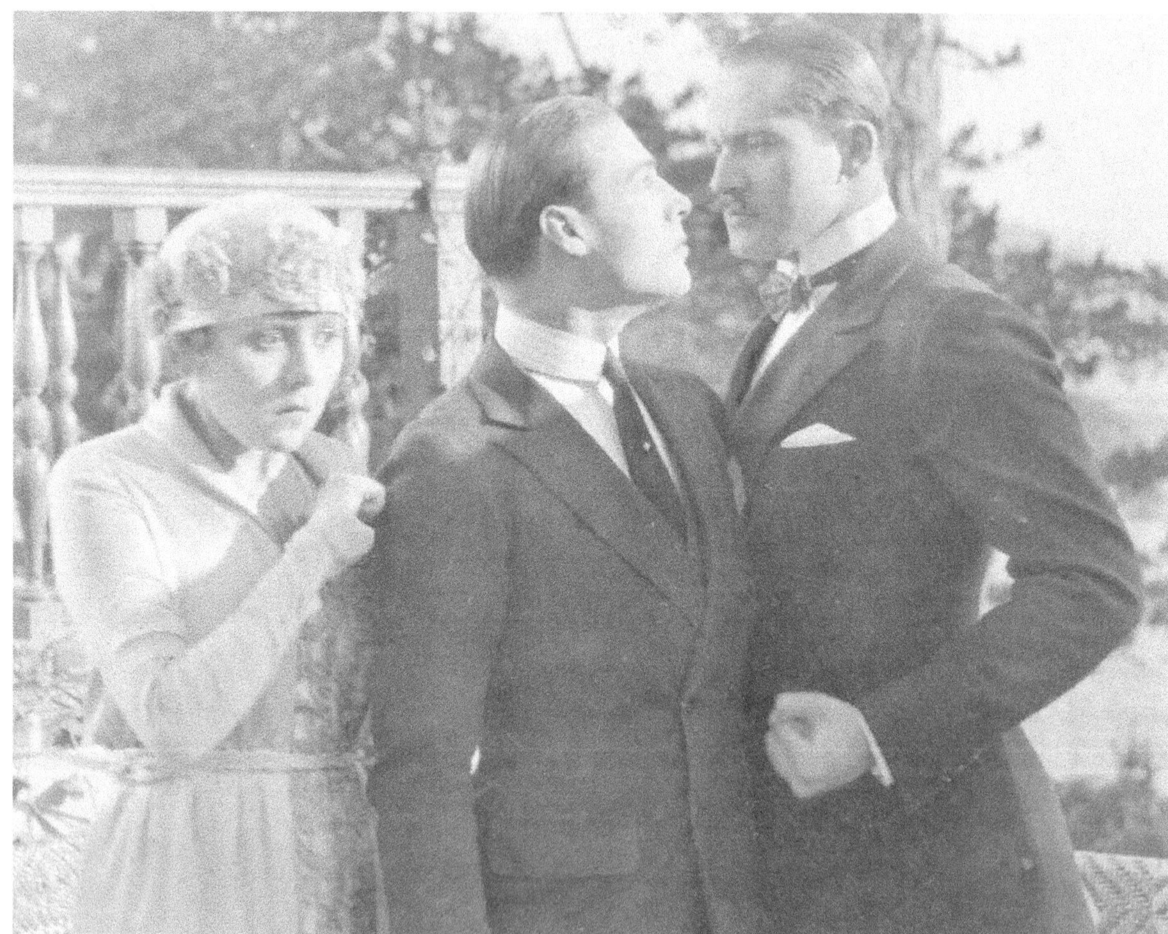

Katherine MacDonald and Norman Kerry in *Passion's Playground.*
(Author's collection)

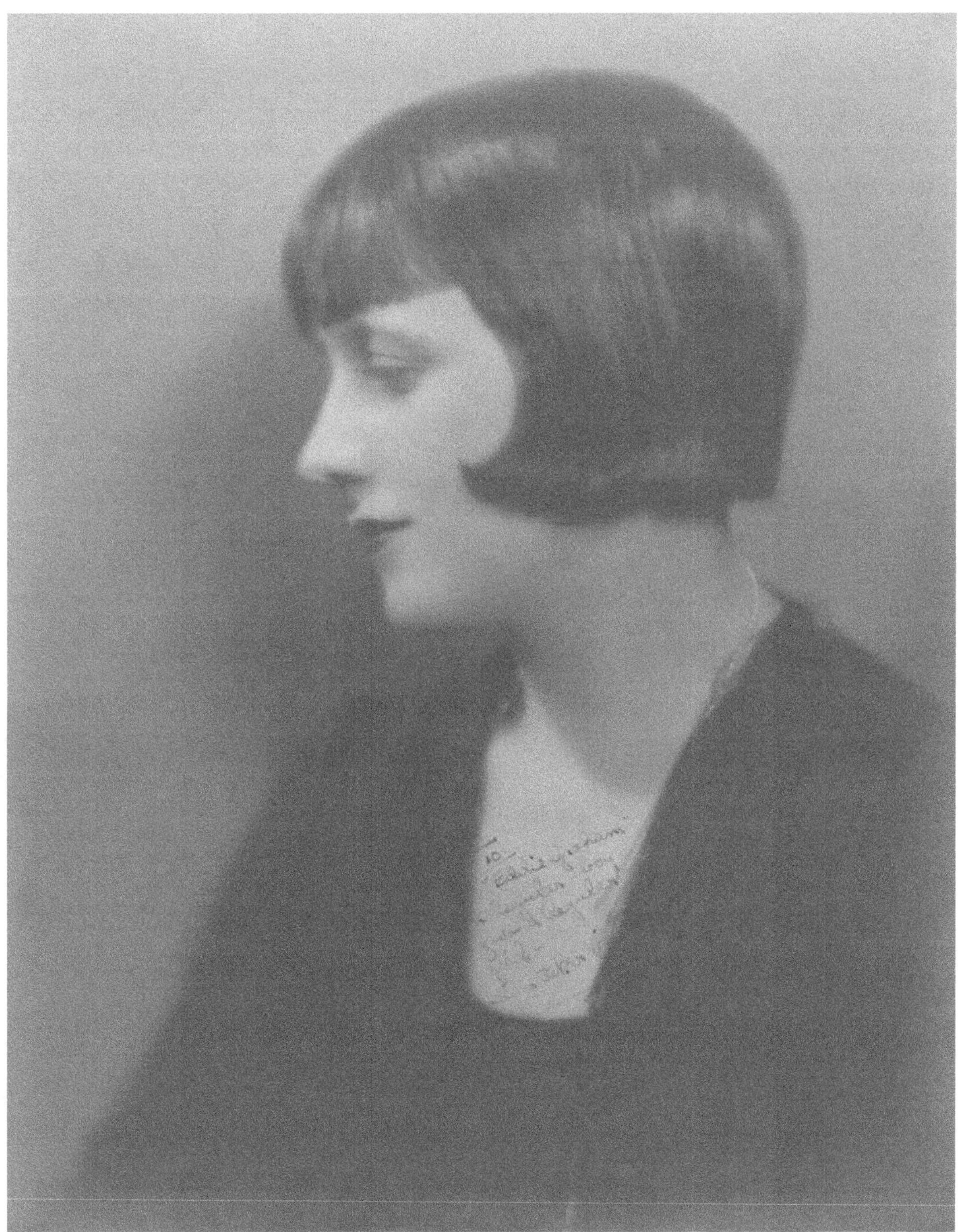

Jean Acker *circa* 1922 (Author's collection)

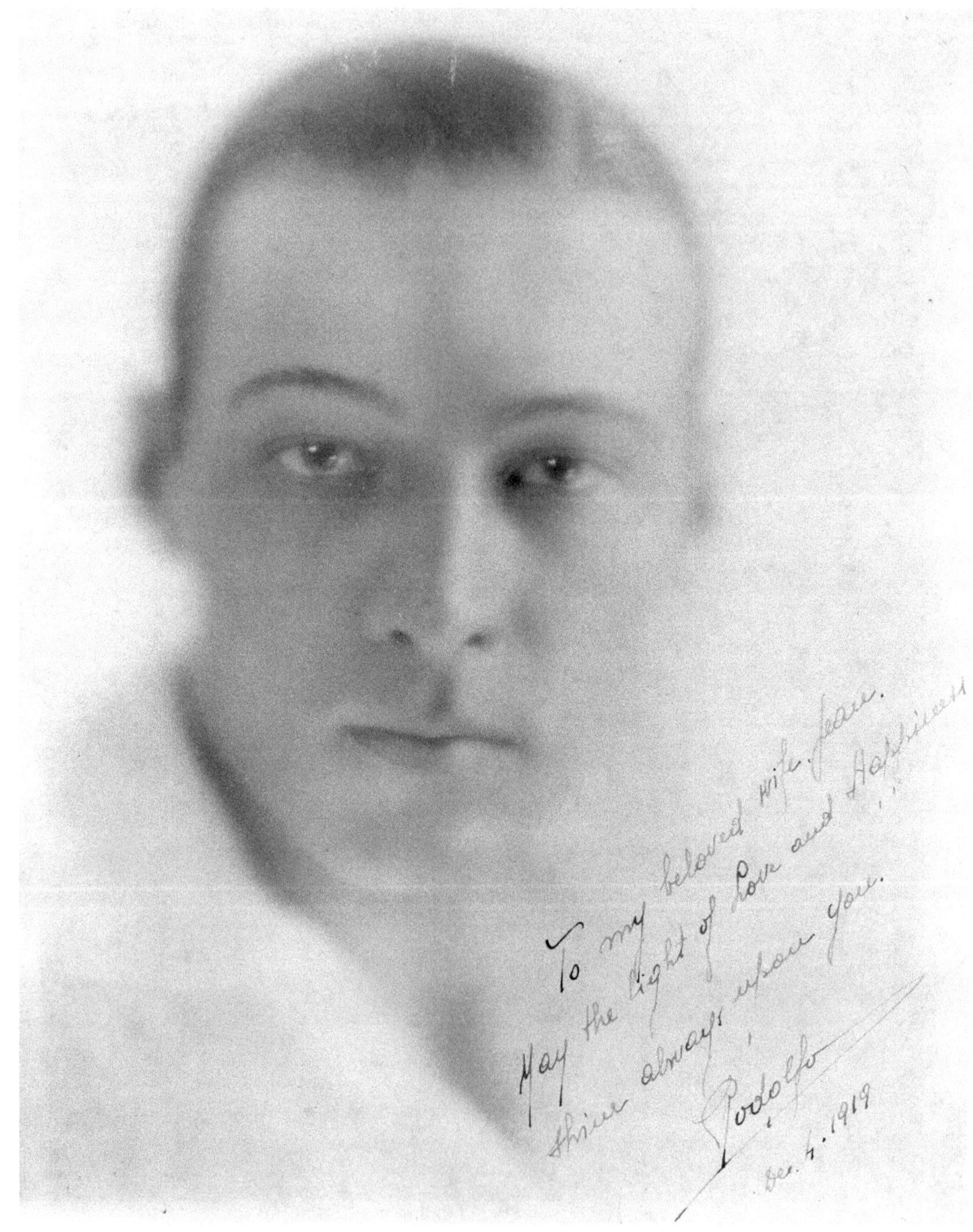

This portrait inscribed to his wife, Jean Acker.
It is clear he was in love with her despite the mixed signals she was sending.
(Author's collection)

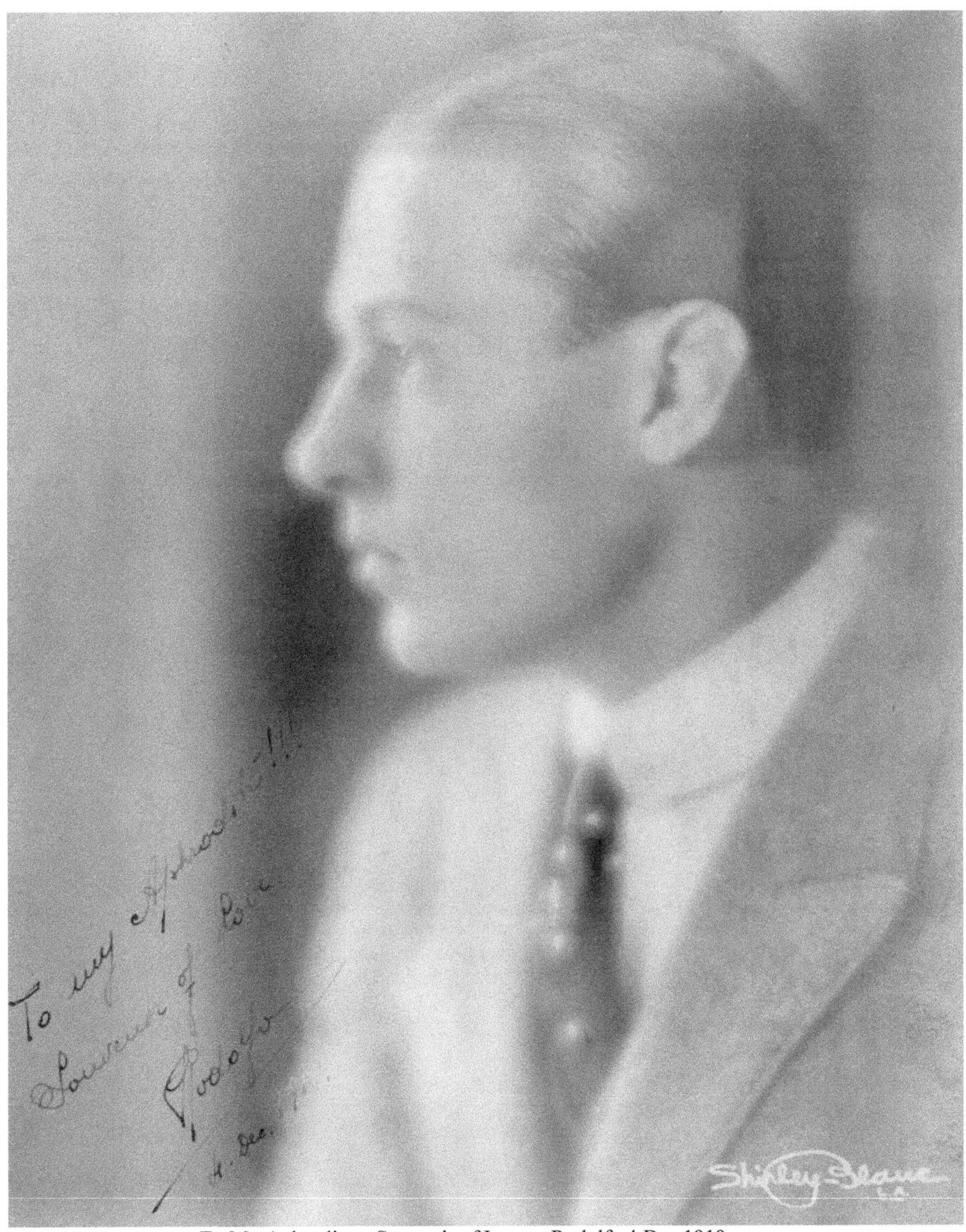

To My Aphrodite – Souvenir of Love – Rodolfo 4 Dec 1919
(Author's collection)

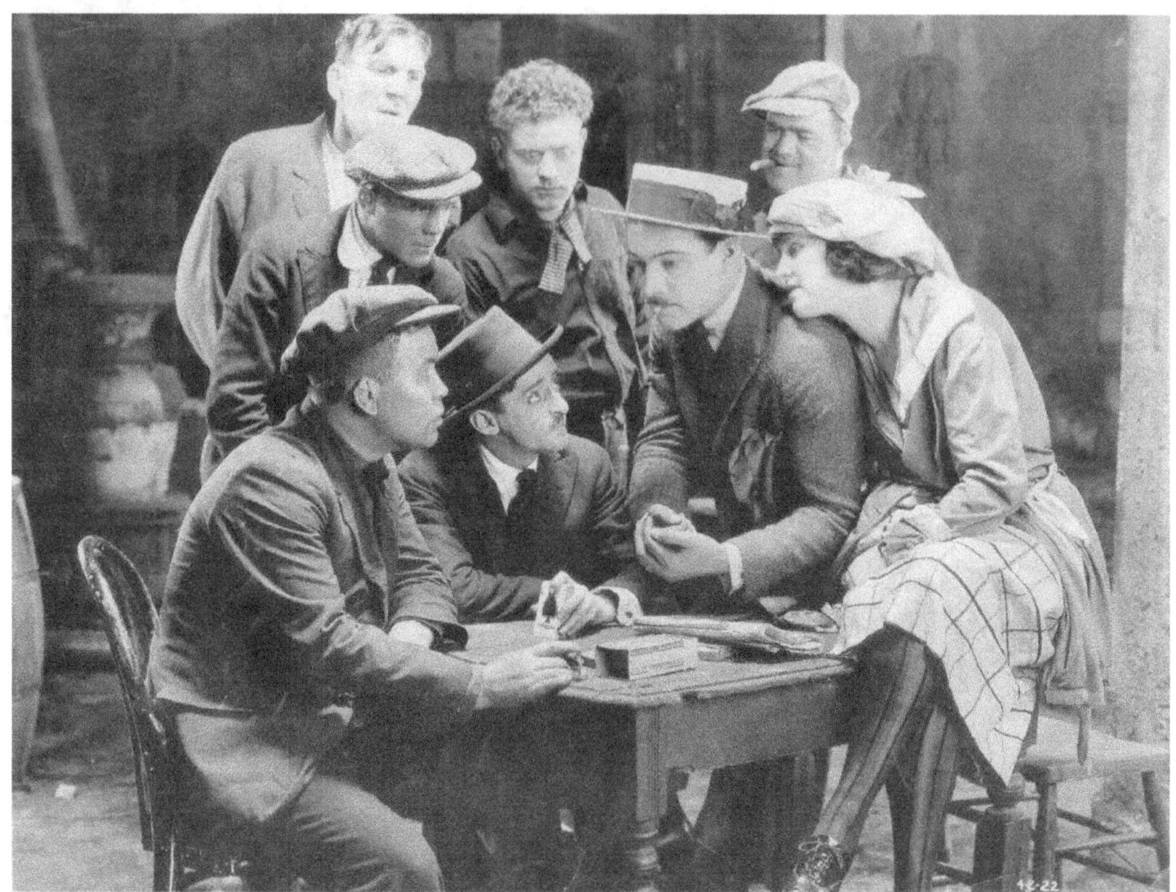

In *The Wonderful Chance*, Valentino cast again as a villain, Joe Klingsby.
At this time there was no outcry over his moustache. That would come later.
(Linda Wulfstieg collection)

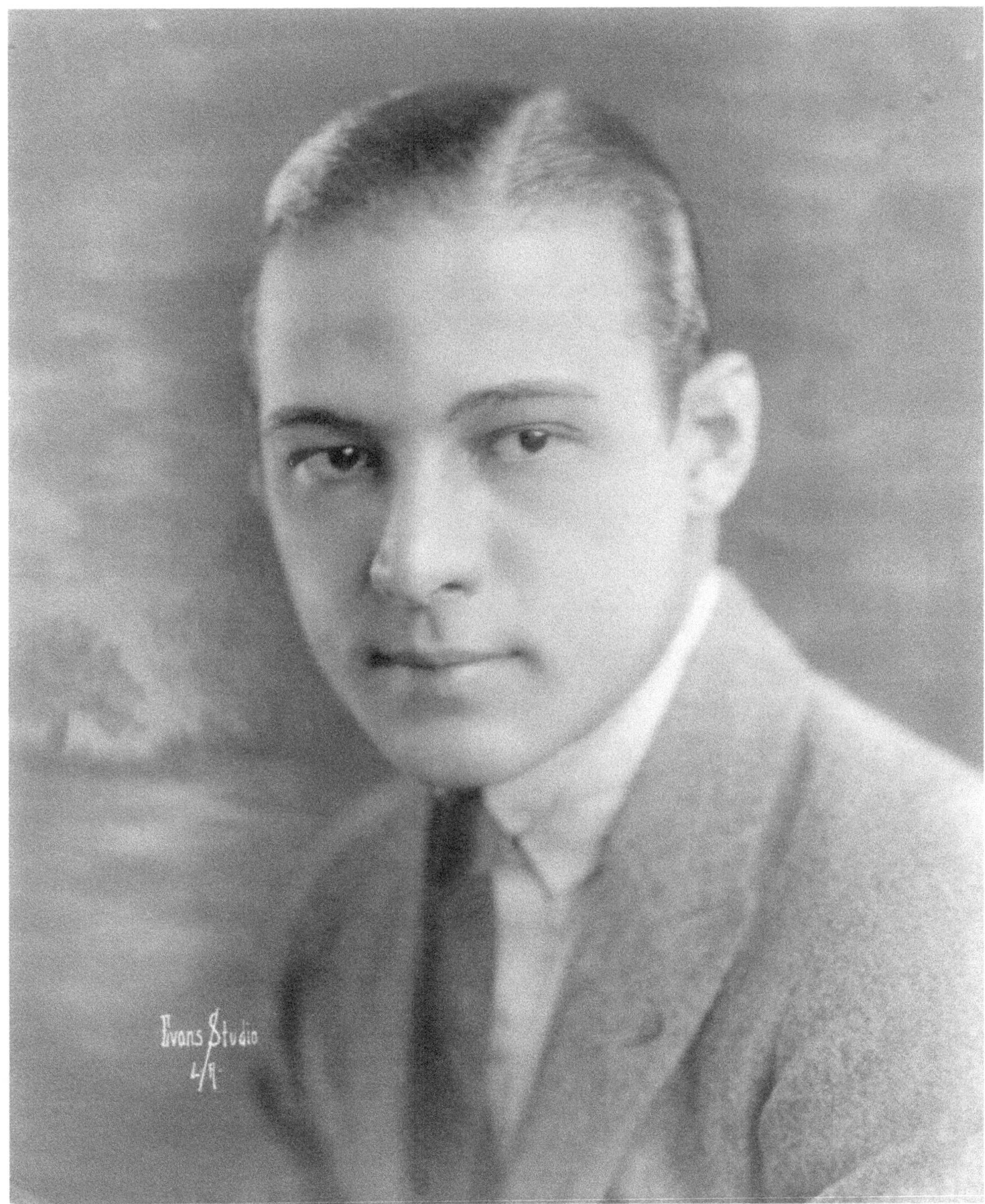

Looking hopeful in advance if his big break, publicity portrait by Evans Studio circa 1919-1920
(Author's collection)

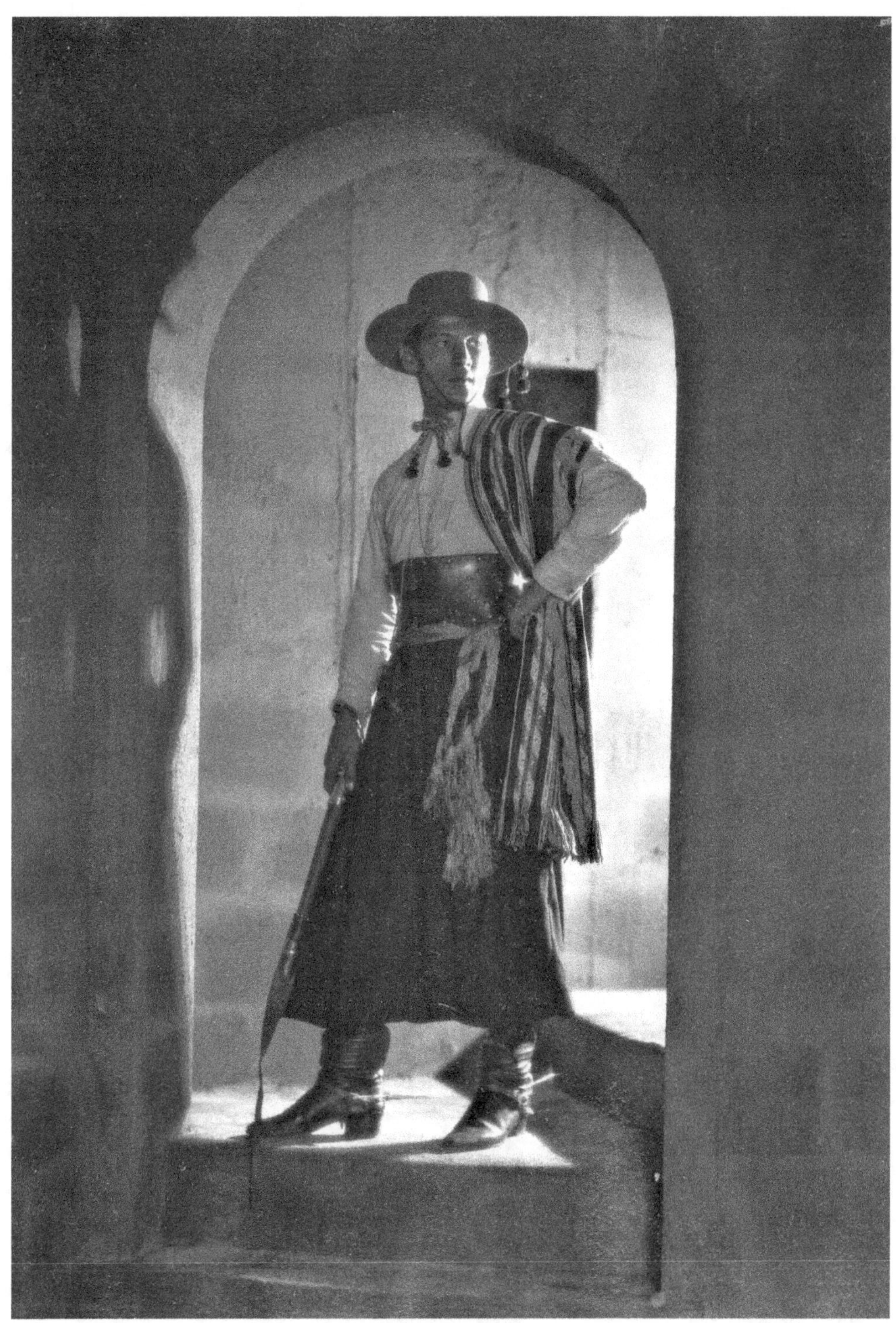

During the running of the film not a sound could be heard. About the middle of the picture Rudy took hold of my hand, which he held tightly in his own until the end. When it was over, there was a moment of hushed silence, and then tremendous applause.

—Natacha Rambova, 1926

In early 1920, Valentino was as yet unaware of June Mathis's interest. His marriage was a mess, his career path was still uncertain, and money was always a problem. He traveled to the East Coast, where he was offered supporting roles, once again playing the heavy in both *The Wonderful Chance* and *Stolen Moments*. While still in New York, he met with Metro Pictures' general manager, Maxwell Karger, who introduced him to Mathis. Mathis had just written the scenario for Metro's upcoming film based on Vicente Blasco Ibáñez's best-selling novel *The Four Horsemen of the Apocalypse*; she thought Valentino would be perfect for the role of the tragic hero, Julio Desnoyers. It was through her he was hired for the part.

The Four Horsemen of the Apocalypse was an ambitious and expensive project for Metro. Studio favorite Rex Ingram had been tapped to direct, and Ingram's future wife, actress Alice Terry, had been cast as the female lead. As the screenwriter, June Mathis oversaw almost every aspect of the shoot, but everyone at Metro knew that their investment was riding on the performance of a relative unknown, and for Valentino it was a make-or-break role. Mathis provided him with support, counsel, and encouragement and he worked hard to prove that he was worthy. His new friend Paul Ivano was hired as a technical consultant on the film, and Ivano also shot hundreds of behind-the-scenes production photographs during the six-month shoot.

Upon viewing the daily rushes Metro executives soon realized they had a hot property on their hands. After the *Four Horsemen* shoot was completed, they rushed Valentino into *Uncharted Seas*, with Alice Lake, filmed partially on location in Flagstaff, Arizona. While working on *Uncharted Seas*, Valentino was summoned before the imperious Russian actress, Alla Nazimova, and her art director, Natacha Rambova. The two were considering casting Valentino as the male lead in Nazimova's next film, *Camille*. Nazimova, had an eye for talent.

Valentino was instantly attracted to Natacha Rambova, but her first reaction to him was not at all favorable. He arrived at the interview covered in sweat, wearing a heavy parka and a dazzling smile. Natacha was initially unmoved, but after he won the part and she got to know him better, she began to thaw. She described him as a young and eager boy—a prankster and joker. Soon his performance as an ardent lover was being replayed off-screen—he was thoroughly smitten with the distant and aloof Rambova. She was beautiful, intelligent, well-connected, artistic, and outside of his grasp. Her coldness towards him seemed only to spur Valentino to further pursuit; eventually her feelings toward him softened, and the two fell in love. As romance blossomed off-screen, Valentino sizzled on-screen, a fact that did not escape Nazimova. The diva was not about to be upstaged by the newcomer, and much of his performance as Armand ended up on the cutting room floor. This did not affect their friendship—Nazimova joined the long list of people who loaned Valentino money when times were tight. Although still legally married to Jean Acker, Valentino soon moved into Natacha's Sunset Boulevard bungalow. The two shared many interests, foremost of which was a love for animals. The bungalow included a menagerie featuring dogs, birds, a monkey, a snake, and a lion cub named Zela.

Another interest they shared was spiritualism. Natacha had been interested in the spiritual arts from a young age. Valentino was not a practicing Catholic and had a curiosity about the afterlife and a belief in reincarnation. Attending séances with June Mathis and later with Cora McGeachy, Valentino was thought to have a natural flair for "automatic writing." Both also communicated with personal spirit guides; Natacha's was an Egyptian named Meselope and Valentino's an American Indian named Black Feather. Natacha later related that some of their most important business or personal decisions were guided by their spirit friends.

The Four Horsemen of the Apocalypse was released in March 1921 and Valentino and Rambova attended the very public Los Angeles premiere together. Natacha later recalled that Valentino grasped her hand during the film and that both wept at the conclusion. Audience reaction was uniformly positive with regard to Valentino. Metro had an unqualified smash hit and Valentino was suddenly a star.

Hoping that lightning would strike again, Metro quickly cast Valentino in another Ingram/Mathis picture, *The Conquering Power*, a modern-dress version of Honore de Balzac's *Eugénie Grandet*. Valentino was once again teamed with Alice Terry, but by this point his relationship with Metro Pictures had become strained. His value to the studio had increased with the success of *The Four Horsemen of the Apocalypse*, but Metro Pictures refused his modest request for a corresponding raise in salary. Disagreements occurred during the filming of *The Conquering Power* that also strained his previously friendly relationship with Rex Ingram. After the completion of *The Conquering Power*, Valentino's agent brokered a two-picture deal with the Famous Players-Lasky Corporation at $500 a week. Jesse Lasky also had an option to extend the contract further. The raise in salary was not a huge improvement over what he was making with Metro Pictures in the begining, but he felt it was time to make a jump.

The first film scheduled under his new contract was a film version of the hottest novel of the year, E.M. Hull's bodice-ripper, *The Sheik*. Lasky felt the role of Sheik Ahmed Ben Hassan was tailor-made for Valentino, and he reported to Adolph Zukor (not without some glee) that Valentino had signed at a low salary, which would reduce the cost of production. Neither Natacha Rambova nor Paul Ivano were happy with Valentino's decision to accept the role or with the studio's choice of material, but Valentino enjoyed the shoot and the physical demands the role made on him.

The Sheik was shot partially on location in Oxnard, California, where the Pacific Ocean beach substituted for the sand dunes of the Sahara Desert. Valentino's rapport with his co-star Agnes Ayres and director George Melford made for a happy set. When the location work was finished, the cast and crew returned to Hollywood to finish the picture. Valentino returned home to the bungalow and to Natacha. With Valentino's salary secured, the couple decided to purchase a home in the stylish Whitley Heights celebrity enclave above Hollywood Boulevard. Decorated by Natacha in her favored black lacquer and filled with Chinese-inspired furnishings, the house became a home befitting a star of Valentino's upwardly moving magnitude.

Valentino's next picture was based on the Frank Norris novel *Moran of the Lady Letty*, a rough-and-tumble tale of cargo ships and shanghaied crews. He starred with Dorothy Dalton as the eponymous heroine and Walter Long as the villainous sea captain. The film was helmed again by George Melford and shot on location in San Francisco. Paul Ivano was again present on the set, and the two shared digs at the posh St. Francis Hotel. Both enjoyed San Francisco's nightlife, and during his time there Valentino reconnected with old friends. In the middle of filming, Natacha arrived in San Francisco, ostensibly to visit her mother and stepfather.

Presumably it was Natacha who introduced Valentino to Helen MacGregor, a photographer with a studio not far from Union Square. During the filming of *Moran of the Lady Letty*, and at Natacha's insistence, Valentino posed for several erotic and balletic photos, painted and costumed as the faun from dancer Vaslav Nijinksy's 1912 ballet *L'après-midi d'un faune*. While both Valentino and Natacha loved these images and had framed prints hanging in their home in Whitley Heights, the "photographic studies" would later prove to be a very public embarrassment when they were entered as evidence in the divorce trial from Jean Acker and reported in the newspapers.

In 1919, when they married, Valentino had been unsuccessful in Hollywood and Jean Acker had the more prominent career. By 1921, however, their positions were reversed. Rudolph Valentino was a star and Jean Acker's career was on the skids. Their brief time together as a couple hardly constituted a marriage, except in the eyes of the law. Jean Acker wanted a seat on the gravy train and the divorce trial proved to be ugly. At the same time, Jesse Lasky was feeding publicity stories to the newspapers and fan magazines to ensure Valentino was constantly in the news. On March 13, 1923, Jean Acker was granted her divorce and $175 a month in alimony.

When *The Sheik* was released in late October 1921, Rudolph Valentino's life was forever changed. E.M. Hull's scandalous, naughty novel had flown off the shelves, selling out multiple print runs, and the film surpassed it. The combination of Rudolph Valentino's appeal and the subject matter made this modestly produced film one of Paramount's highest grossing films of the year. Rudolph Valentino was now the hottest, most sought-after romantic star in Hollywood. His female fans were suddenly legion. The studio mailroom was filled with sacks of fan mail requesting his autograph and photographs. As a result, his private life suddenly became public. He could not walk from his house in Whitley Heights down to Hollywood Boulevard with his dogs or stop for an informal chat with the waiters at Musso and Frank's Grill without being chased by fans. Valentino enjoyed the stardom, was courteous to his fans, and still longed for the obscurity and dusty trails in Palm Springs as his retreat from the hurly-burly of stardom.

At the end of 1921, Valentino signed a new contract with Jesse Lasky that included a salary increase of $1,000 a week and the award of a new picture, to be based on the Vicente Blasco Ibáñez novel *Blood and Sand*. His good friend and mentor, June Mathis, had moved from Metro to Famous Players-Lasky and would fashion the scenario. While Mathis was penning *Blood and Sand*, Valentino traveled to Catalina Island, about 20 miles from Los Angeles, to co-star with one of Hollywood's most popular actresses, Gloria Swanson, in *Beyond the Rocks*, based on Elinor Glyn's best-selling novel. Glyn's novels were just as scandalous as E.M. Hull's. Glyn herself was more scandalous than her own novels.

The year ended with Valentino and Natacha enjoying their first Christmas in their new home. Natacha later recalled it fondly as one of their happiest moments together. Much to Natacha's delight, Valentino surprised her with a tiny Pekingese puppy she christened "Chuckie."

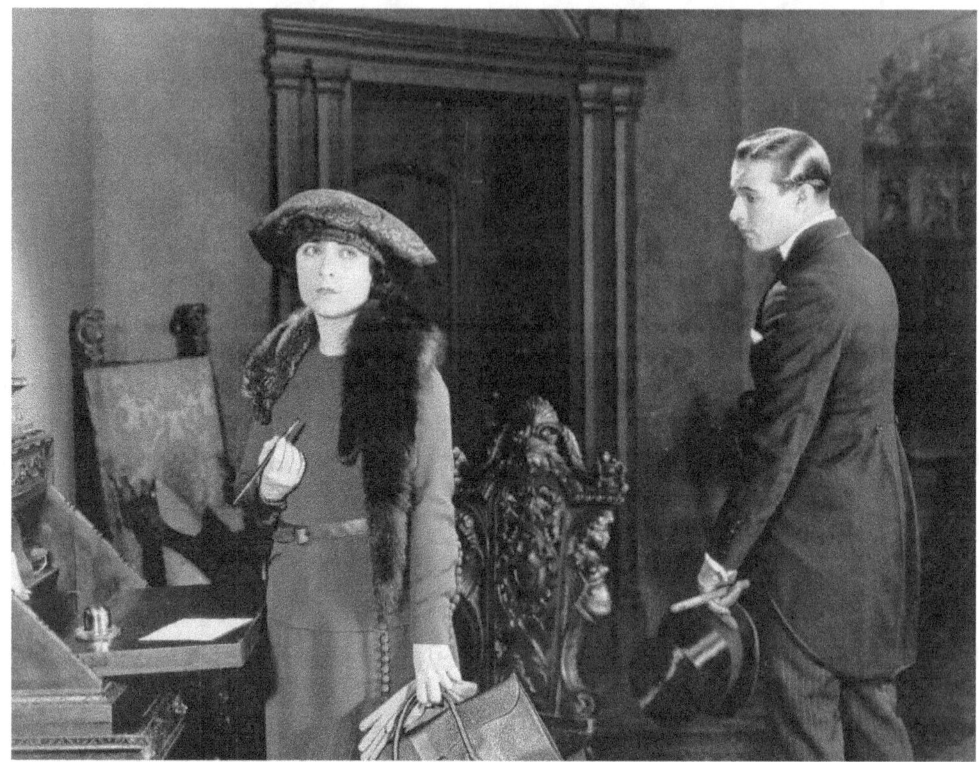

Once to Every Woman with Dorothy Phillips. (Robert S. Birchard collection)

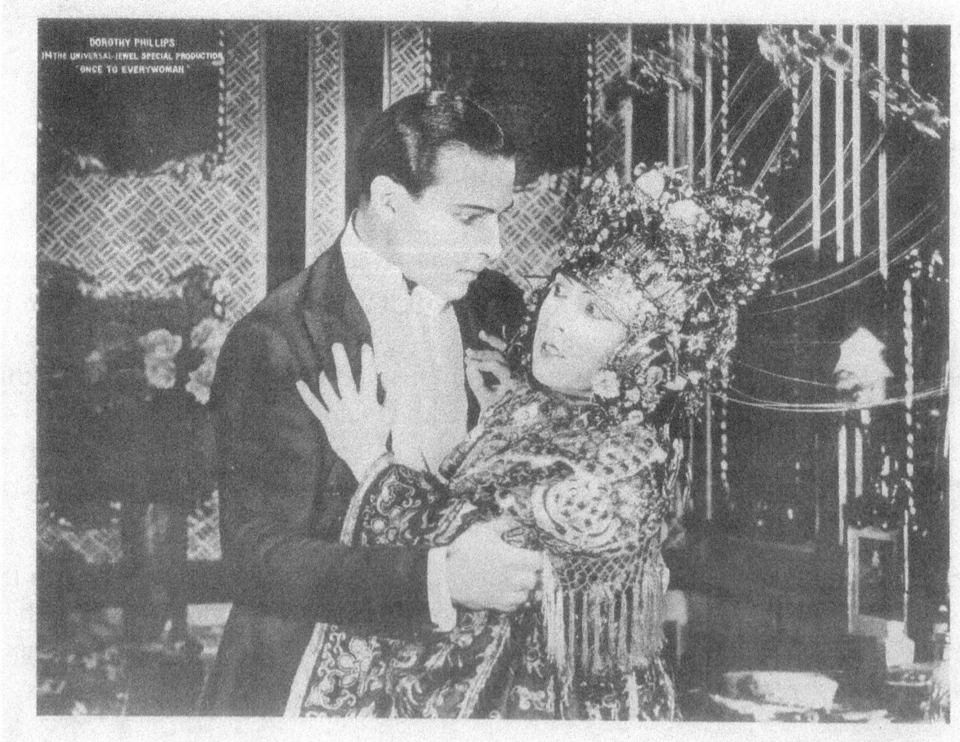

Lobby card from *Once to Every Woman* (Author's collection)

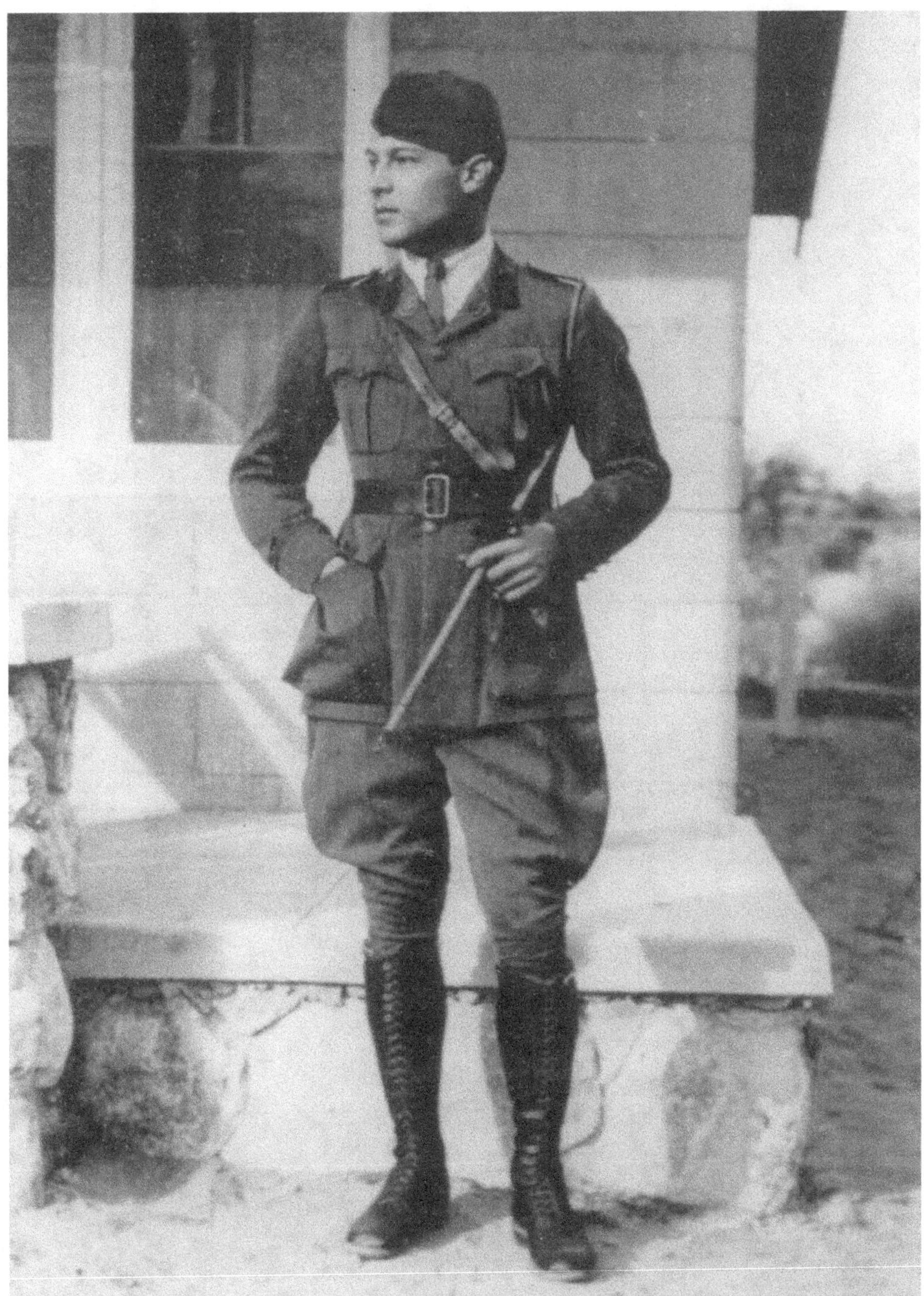

Rudolph Valentino's love of dressing for every part, ready to head out for a canter in Palm Springs *circa* 1920. (Kristen Burkhart collection)

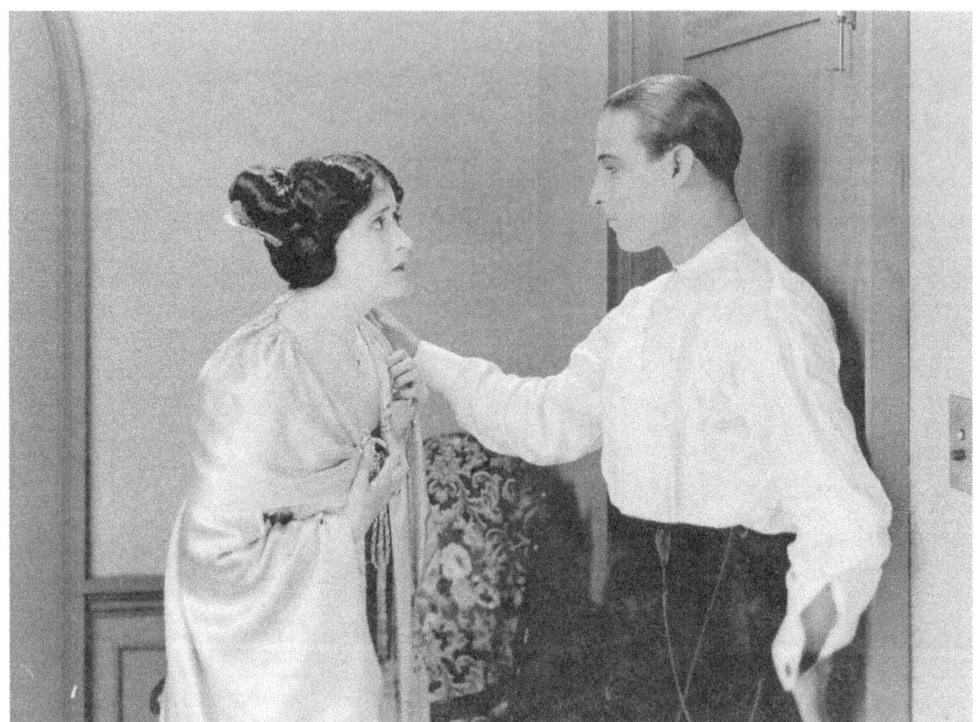

Feigning reassurance in *The Eyes of Youth.* (Author's collection)

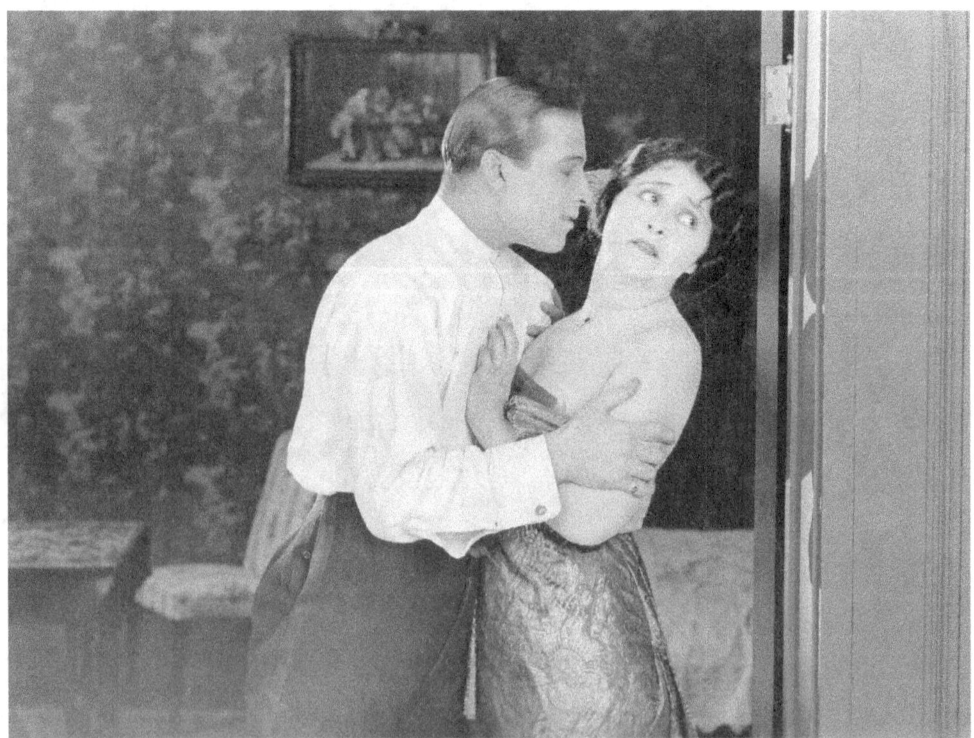

Menacing Clara Kimball Young in *The Eyes of Youth*, this film would prove to be both a life and career changer. (Robert S. Birchard collection)

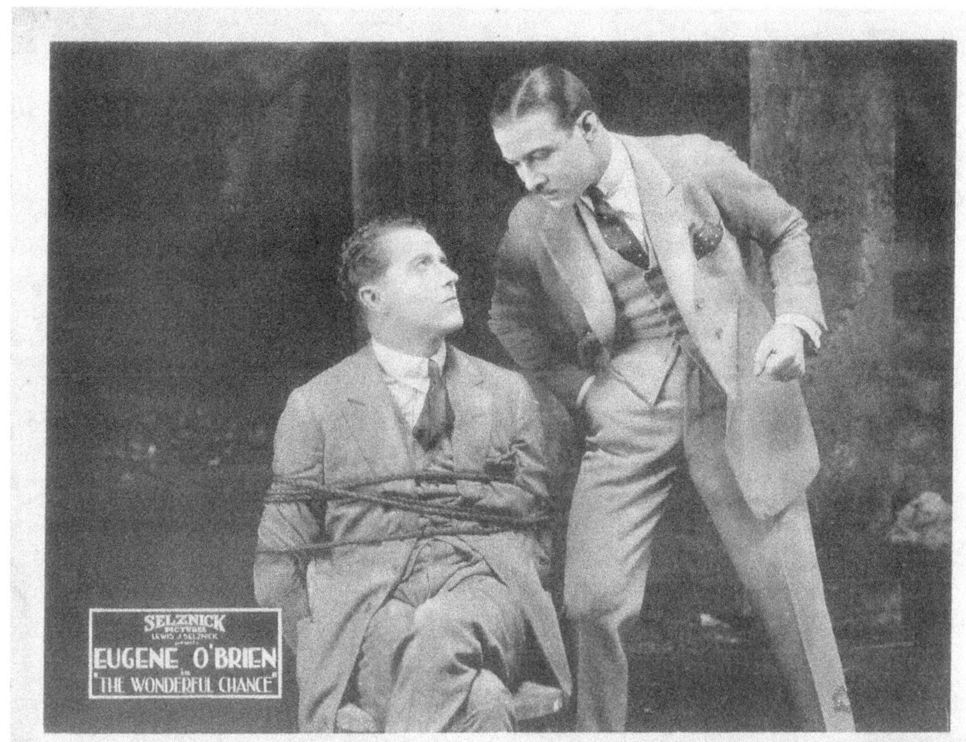

Lobby card for *The Wonderful Chance* (Michael Hawks collection)

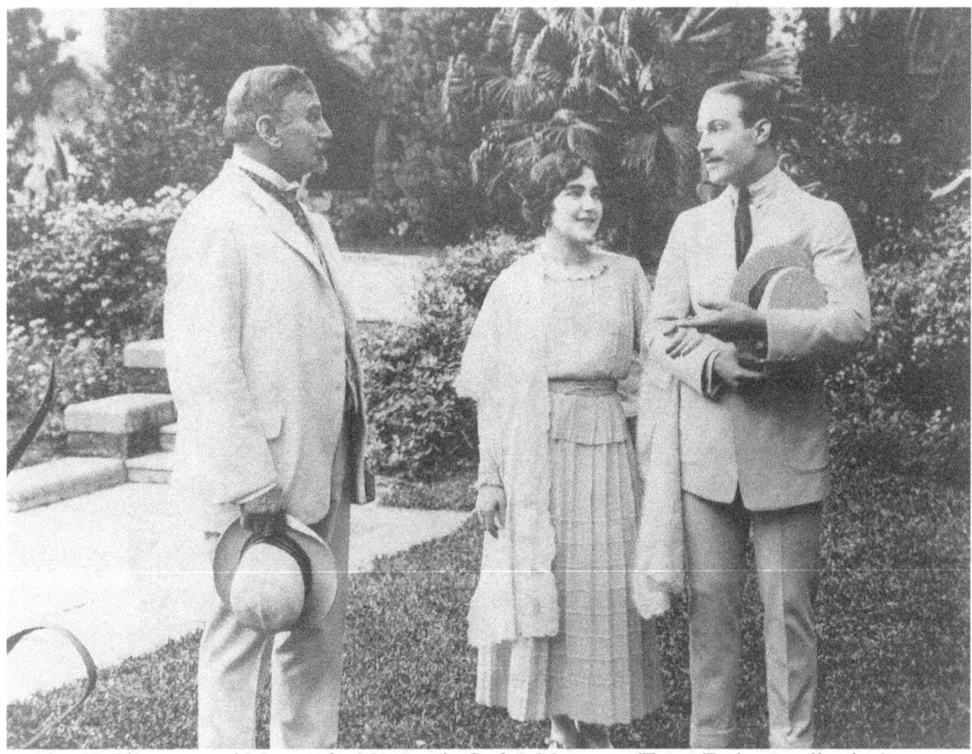
Alex K. Shannon and Marguerite Namara in *Stolen Moments*. (Tracy Terhune collection)

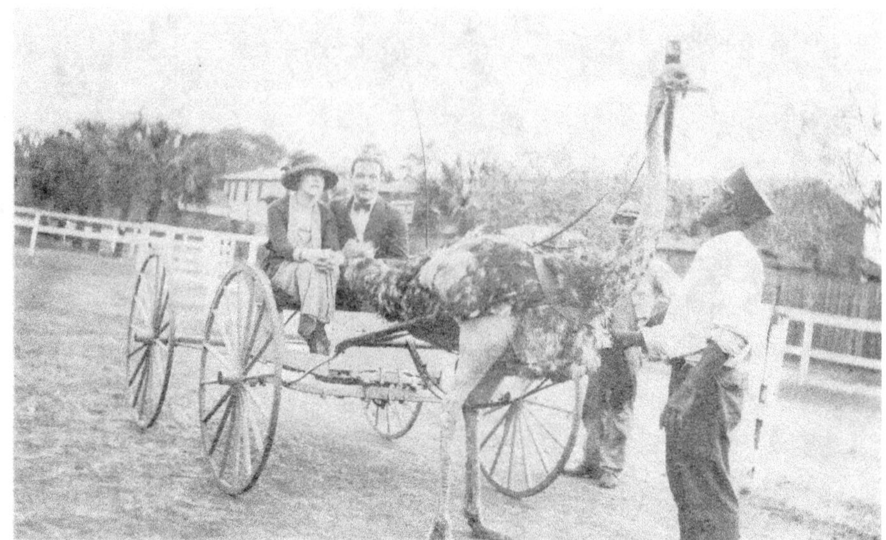

Visiting an ostrich farm during the filming of *Stolen Moments* with Marguerite Namara.
(Author's collection)

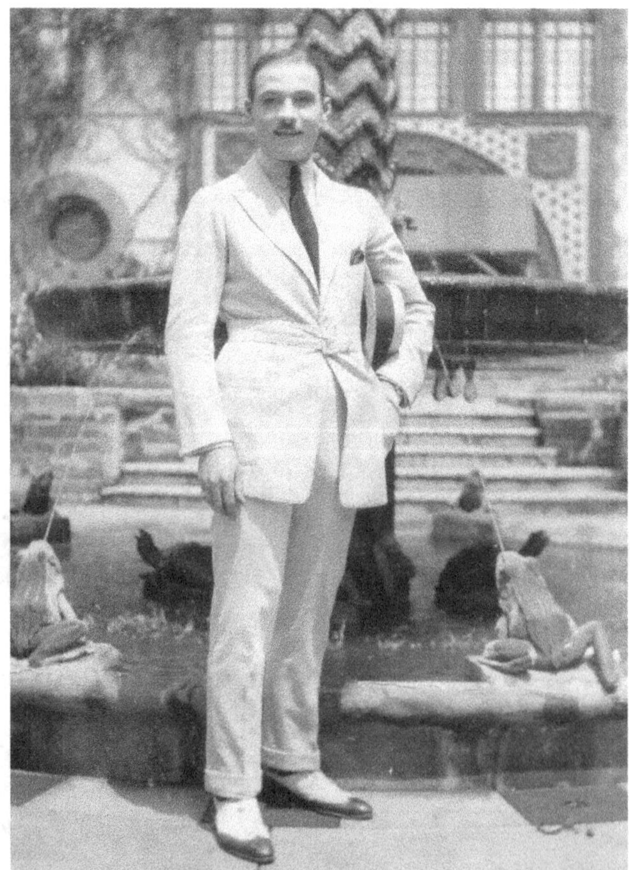

Posing in front of the frog fountain at the Hotel Ponce de León
filming *Stolen Moments*.
(Author's collection)

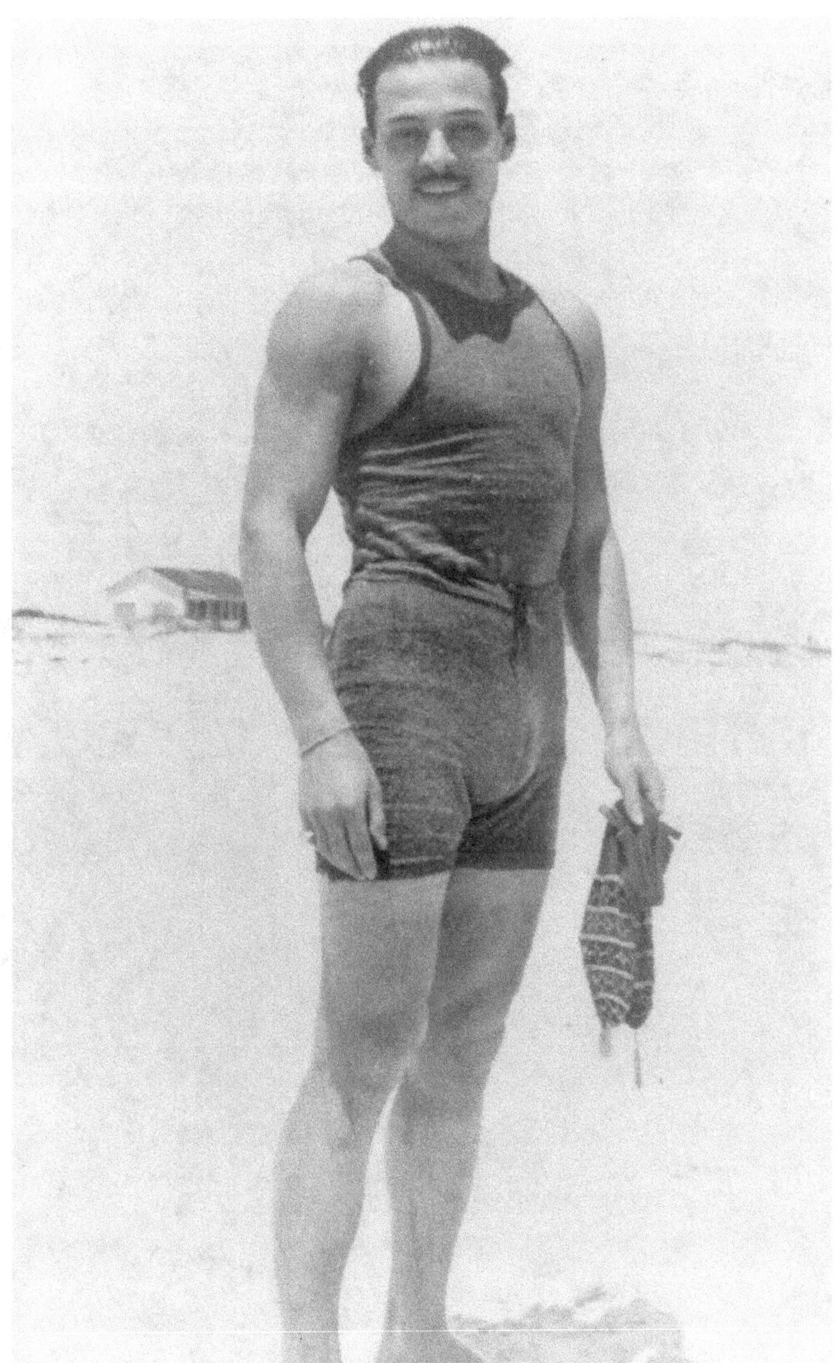

On the beach during filming *Stolen Moments*.
(Tracy Terhune collection)

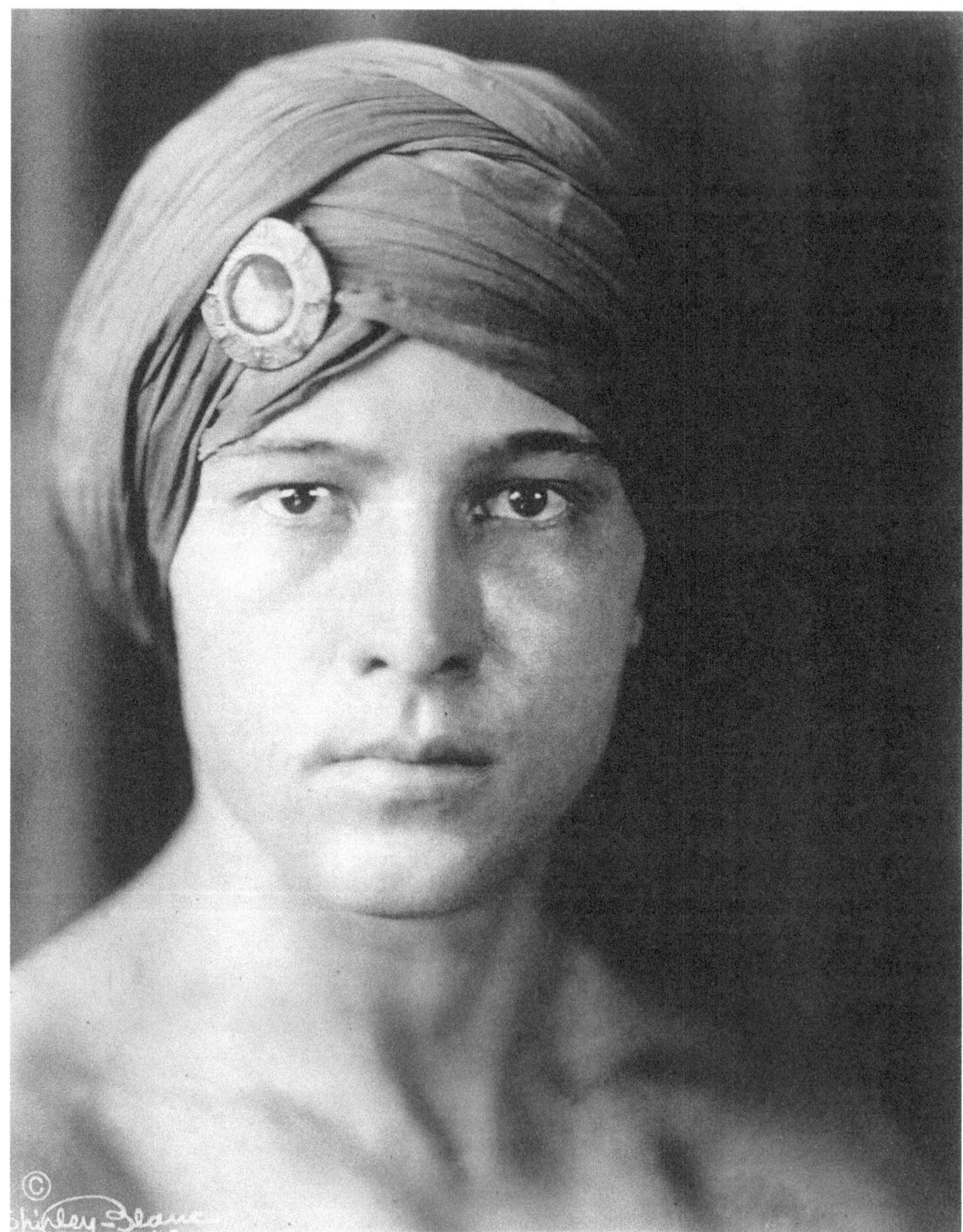

Unretouched portrait by Shirley Sloane *circa* 1920. (Author's collection)

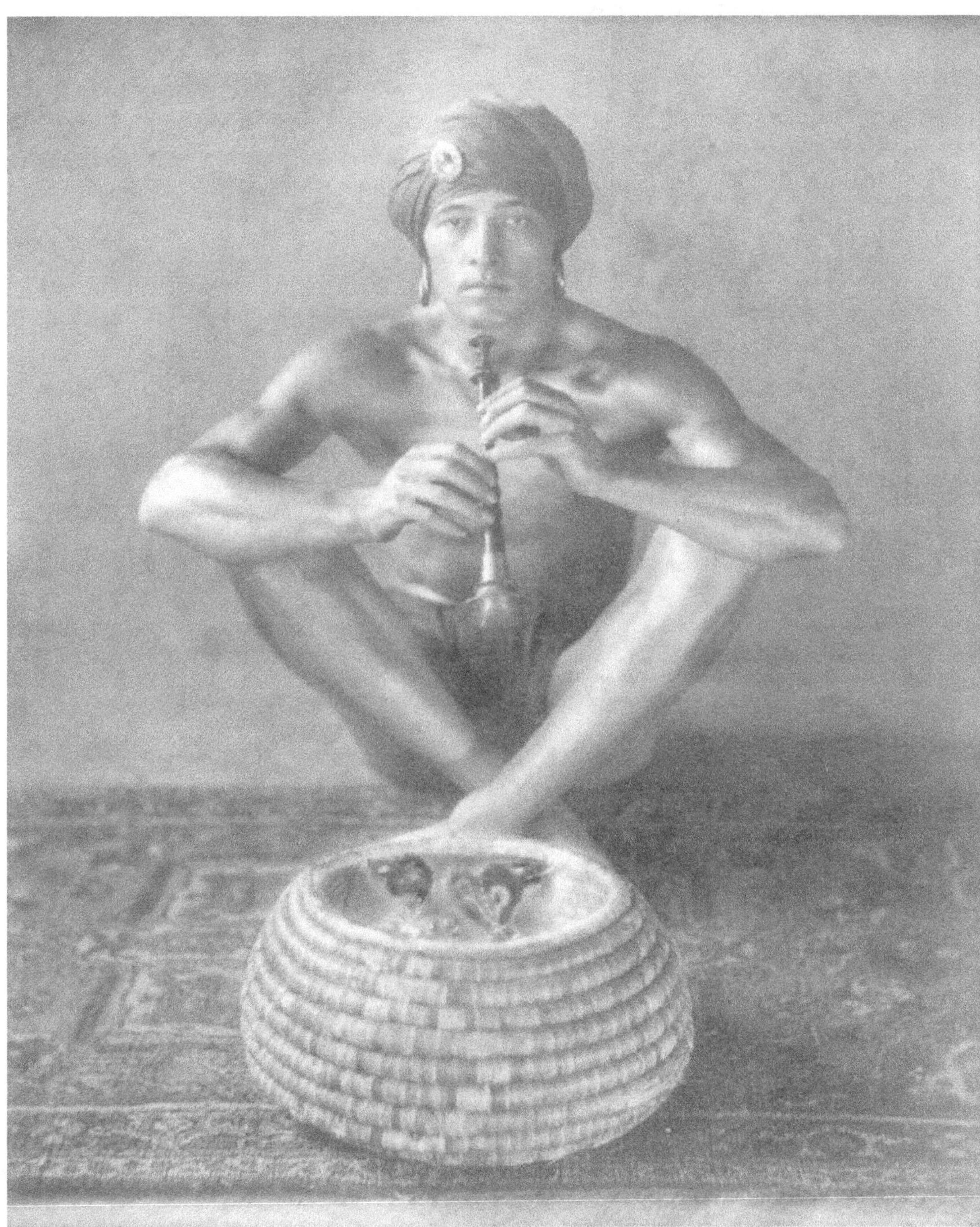

Rudolph Valentino was in no danger, photographer Shirley Sloane painted in the cobra heads afterwards.
This portrait does show of his physique quite nicely.
(Author's collection)

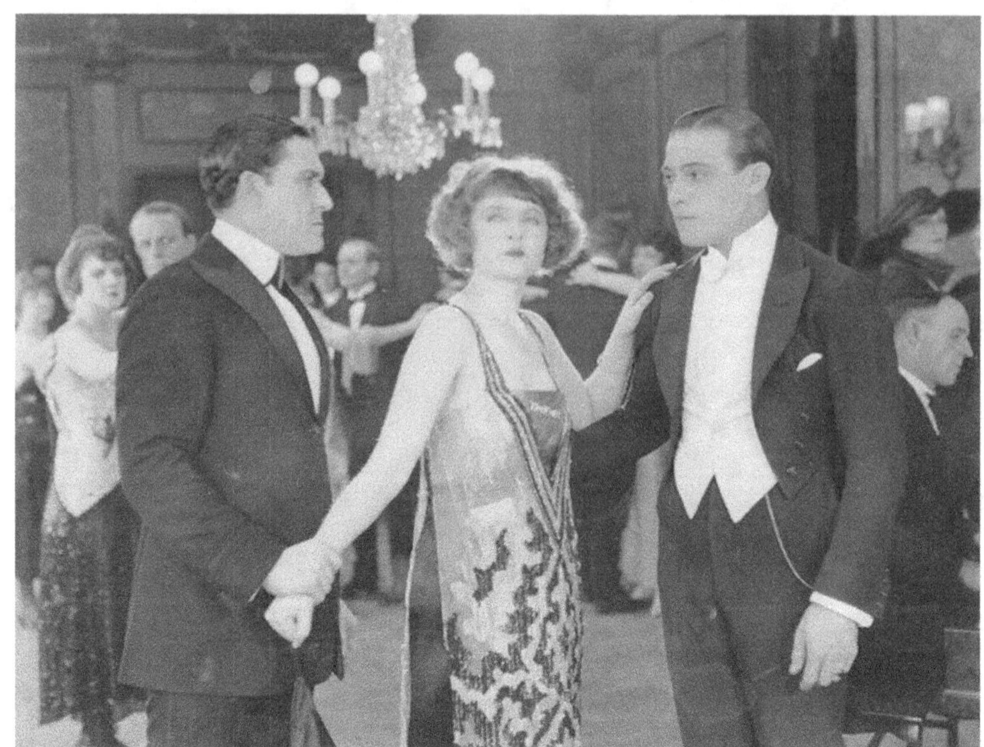

Valentino only had little more than bit part in the Metro film *The Cheater* with May Allison.
He soon would be starring in Metro's most ambitious and prestigious production.
(Author's collection)

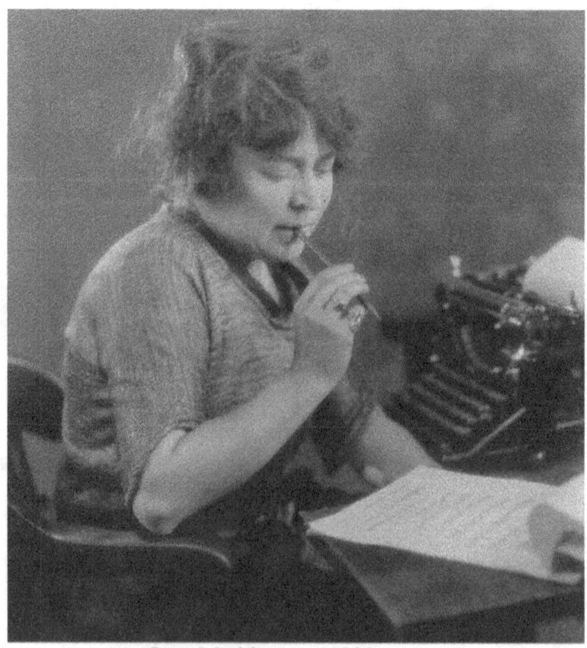

June Mathis *circa* 1920.
Her influence on Rudolph Valentino's life
and career cannot be underestimated.
(Marc Wannamaker/Bison Archives)

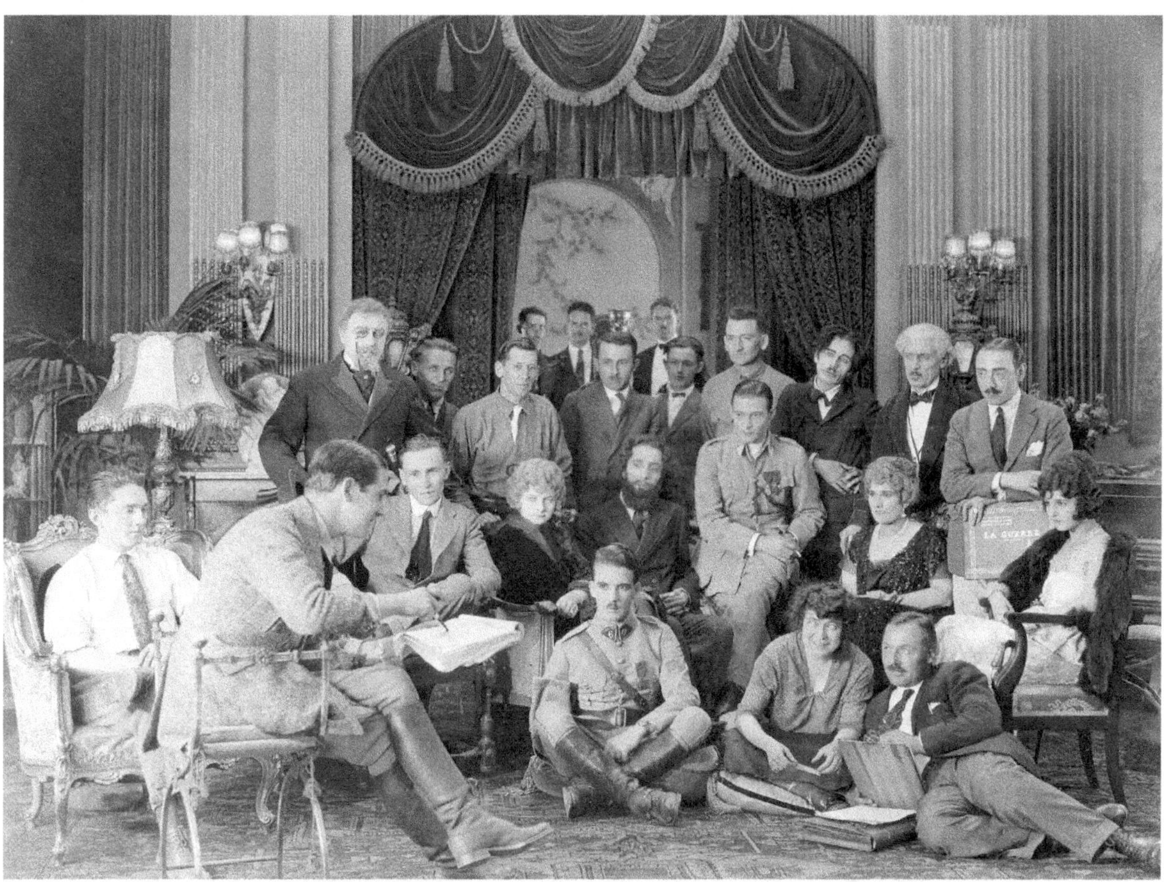

It would seem Rex Ingram and June Mathis are having a private joke
for this publicity portrait. Cameraman John Seitz seated next to Ingram's left.
The rest of the cast and crew seems to lack enthusiasm to sit for the camera.
(Author's collection)

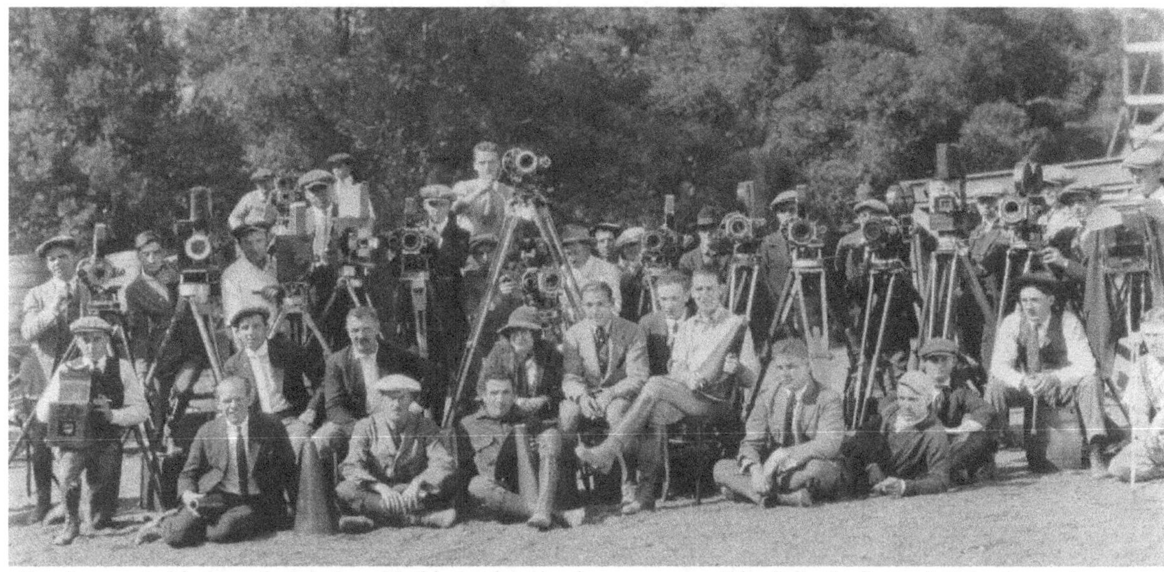

Rex Ingram (with megaphone), June Mathis (under tripod), cameraman John Seitz (in flat cap) Valentino and camera crew during shooting *The Four Horsemen of the Apocalypse* (1921). Impressive number of cameras in use.
(Bison Archives/Marc Wanamaker)

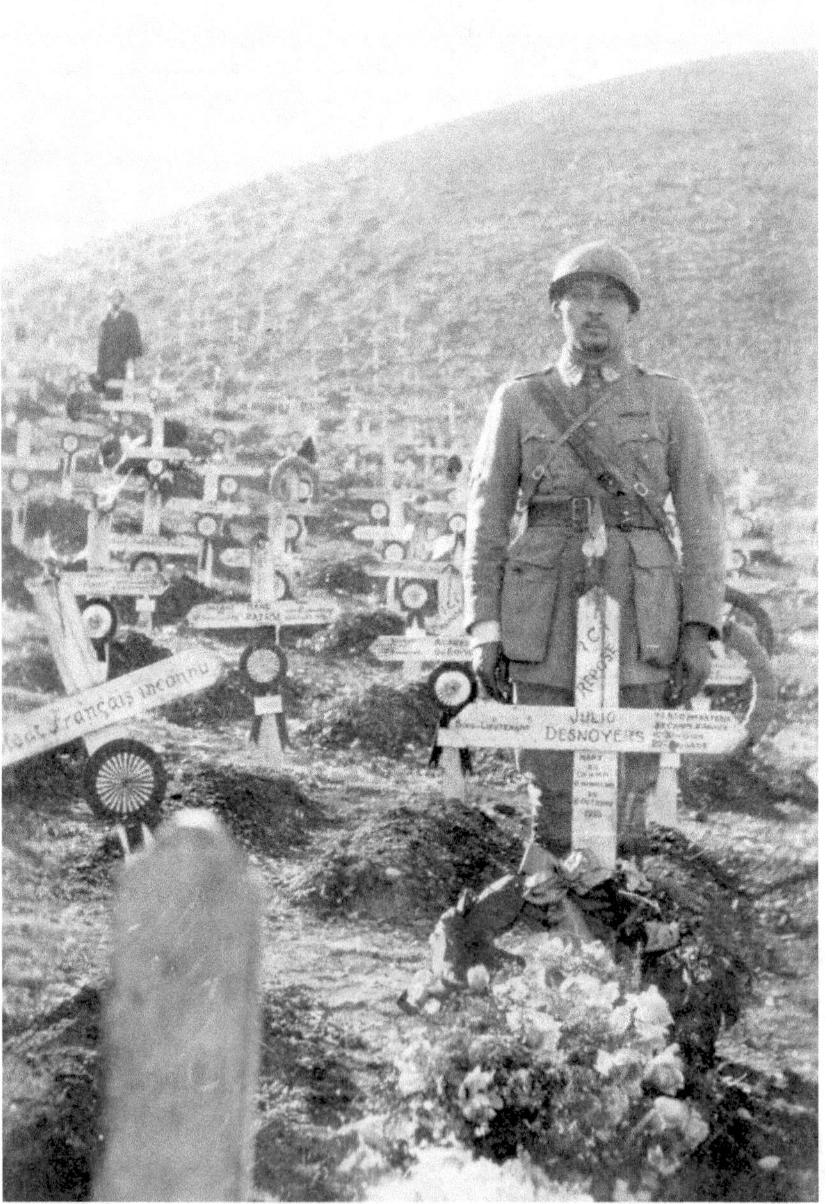

Rudolph Valentino poses at his character's gravesite for a macabre gag shot.
Nigel de Brulier can be seen in the background.
This snapshot is from Valentino's personal collection.
(Author's collection)

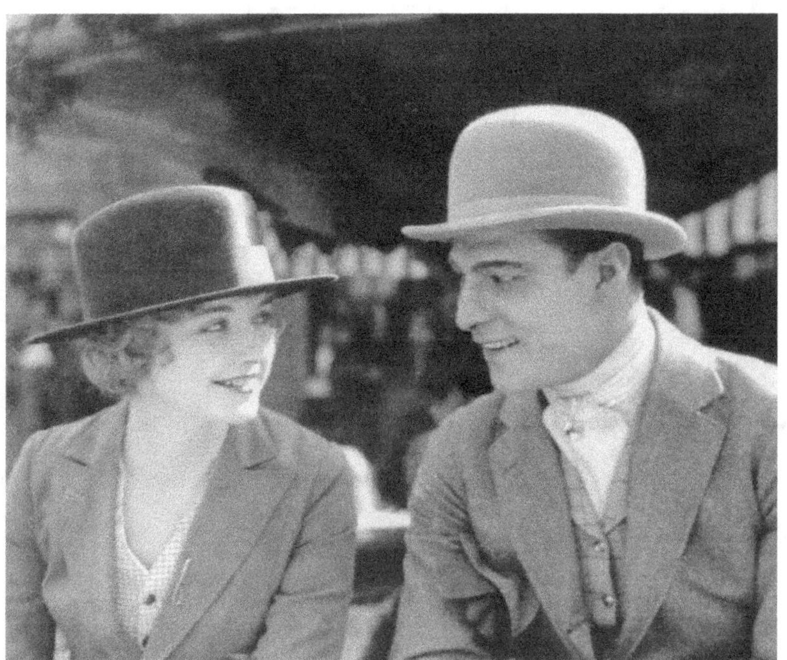

In between scenes in Four Horsemen of the Apocalypse with Alice Terry.
Paul Ivano who also worked on the film, took this snapshot.
(Francis Laccasin collection courtesy Flicker Alley and Lobster Films)

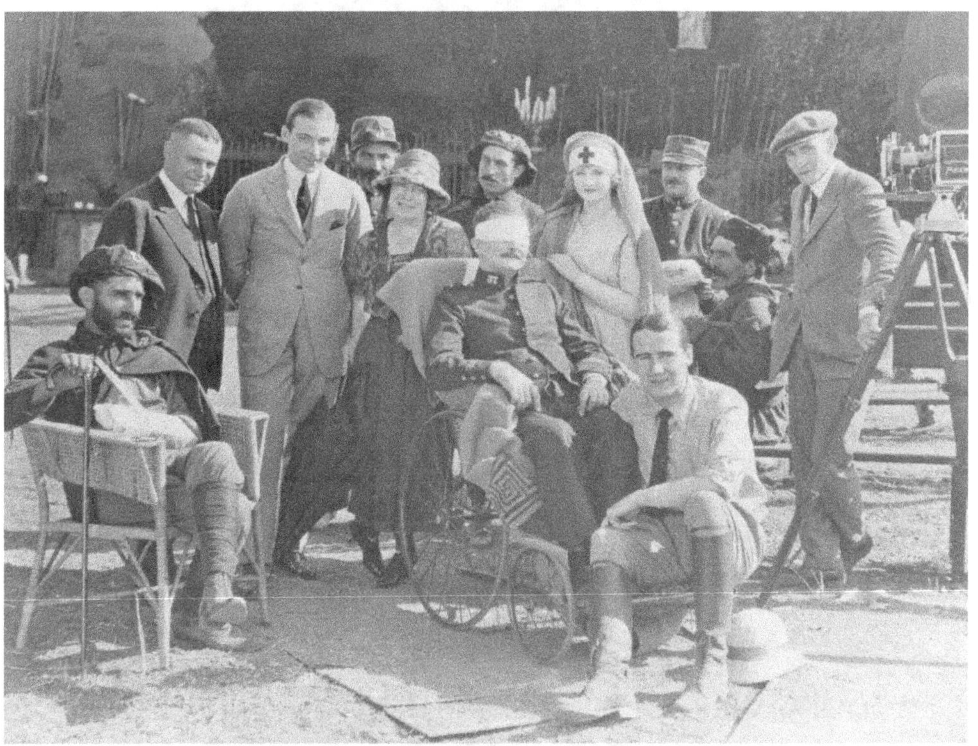

Producer Maxwell Karger (to Valentino's right) visits the set. June Mathis,
Alice Terry, Rex Ingram in front of John Sainpolis, John Seitz in flat cap next to the camera.
(Author's collection)

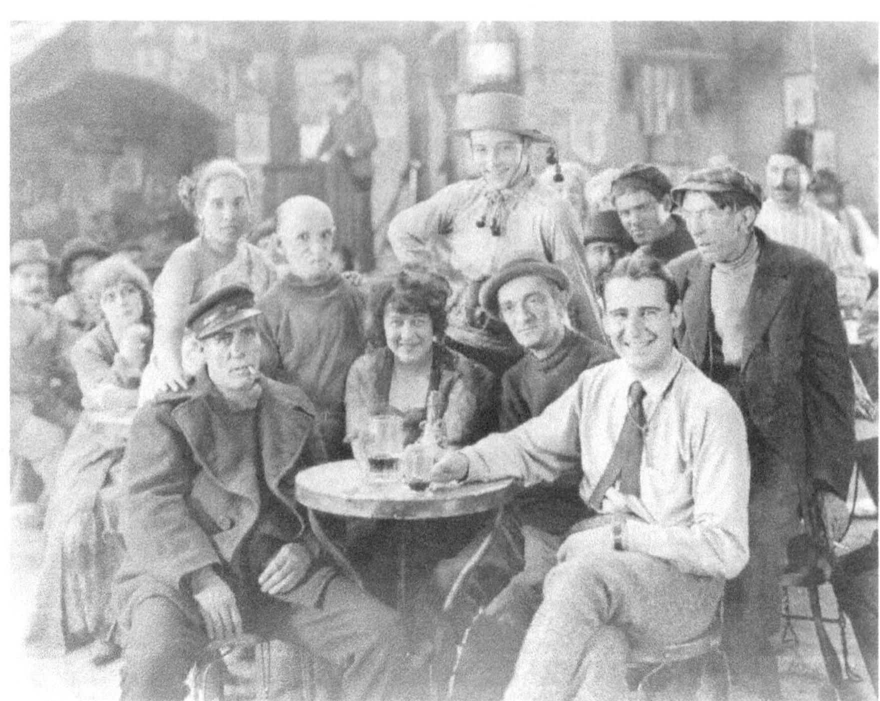

June Mathis joins Valentino and Rex Ingram on the tango set for a gag shot with some of the more colorful regulars of the Boca.
(Independent Visions collection)

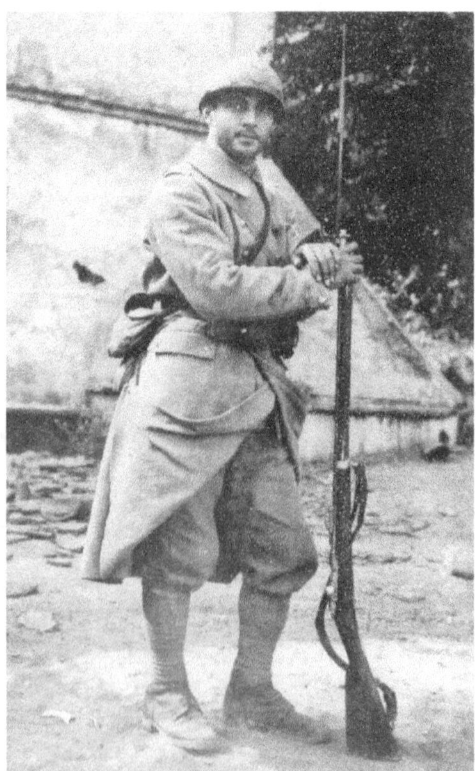

A relaxed Valentino poses on the set of
The Four Horsemen of the Apocalypse
(Kristen Burkhart collection)

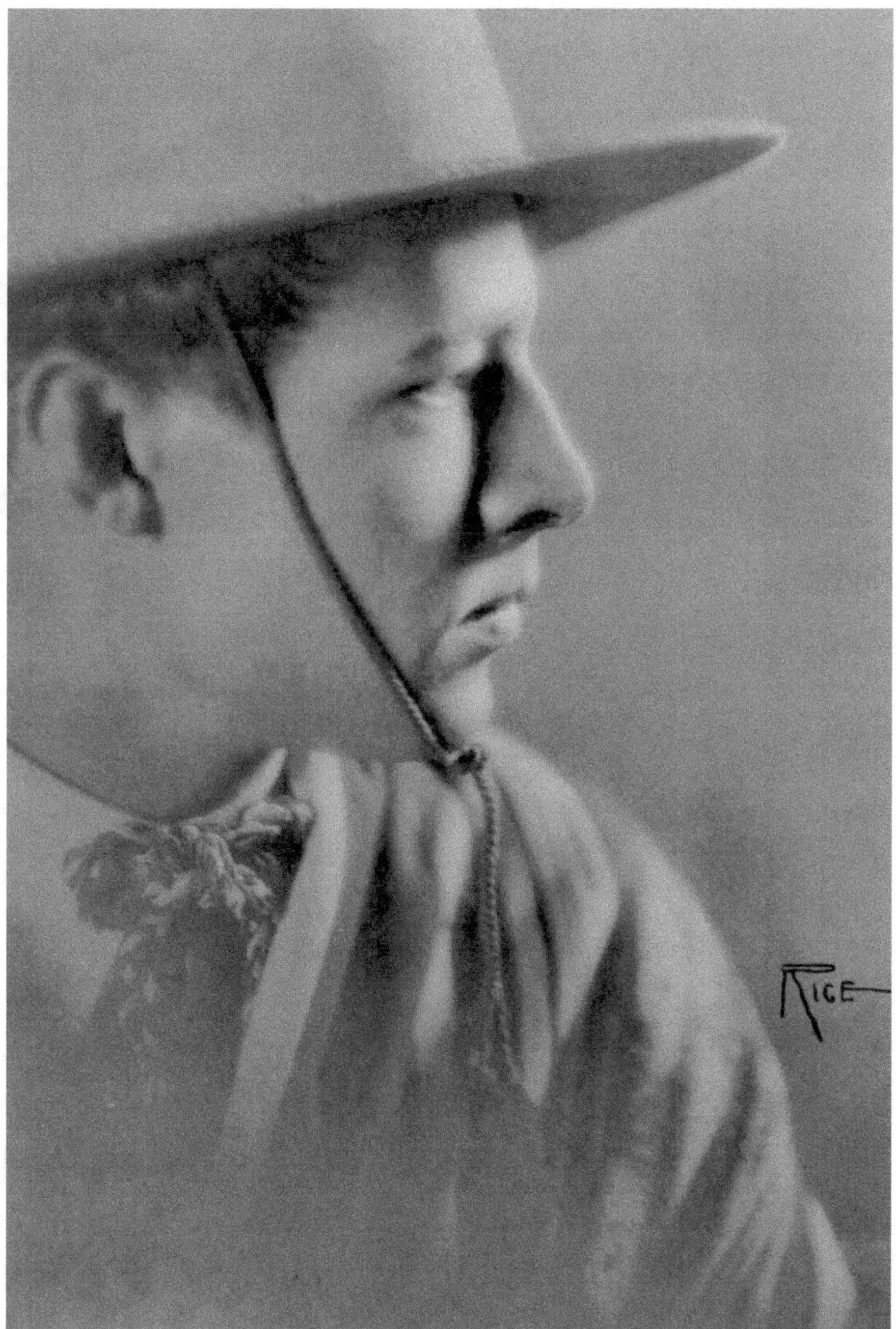

Dramatic profile portrait by Arthur Rice. (Author's collection)

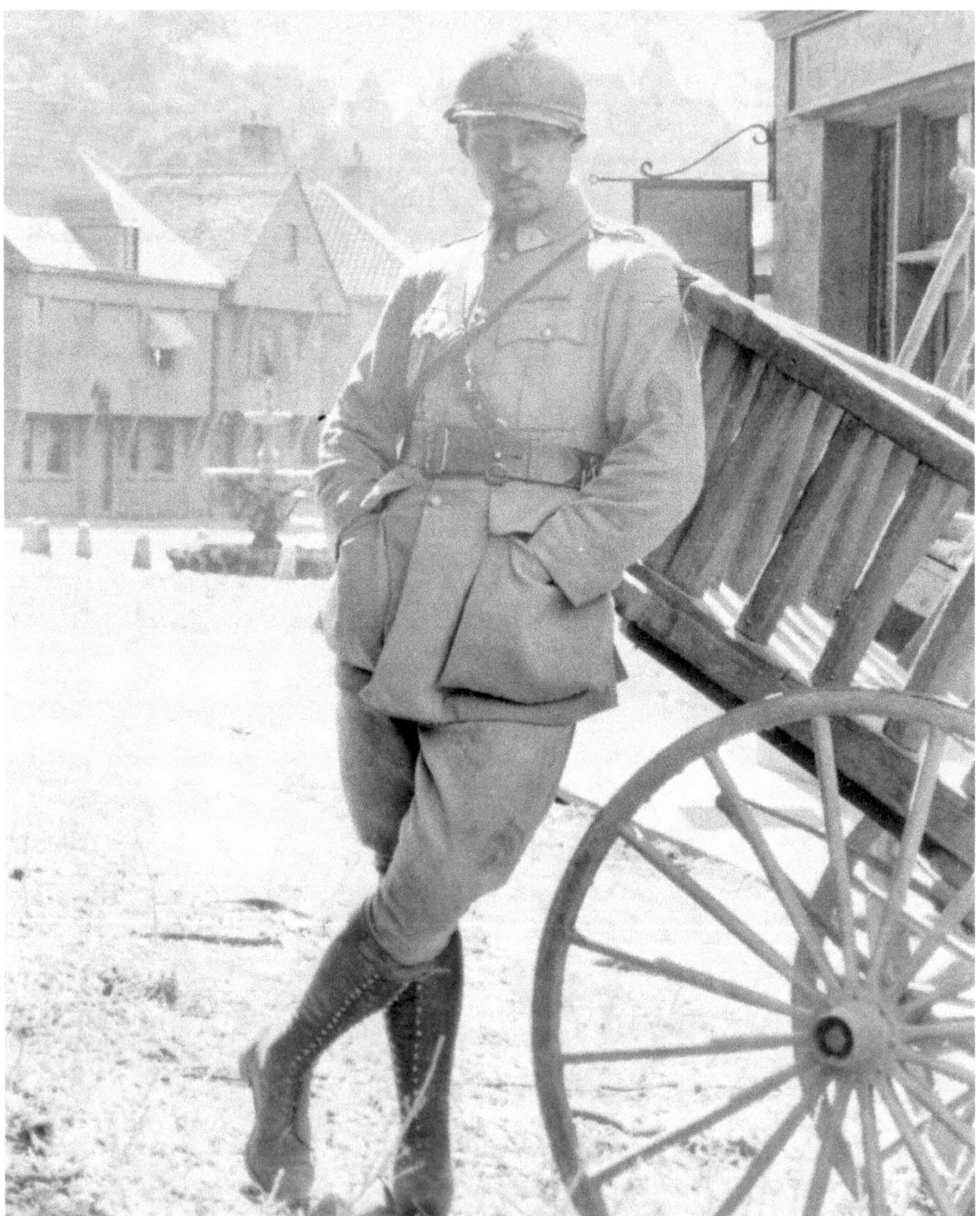

Valentino in costume for the finale of the film on the set of the village of Villeblanche.
(Author's collection)

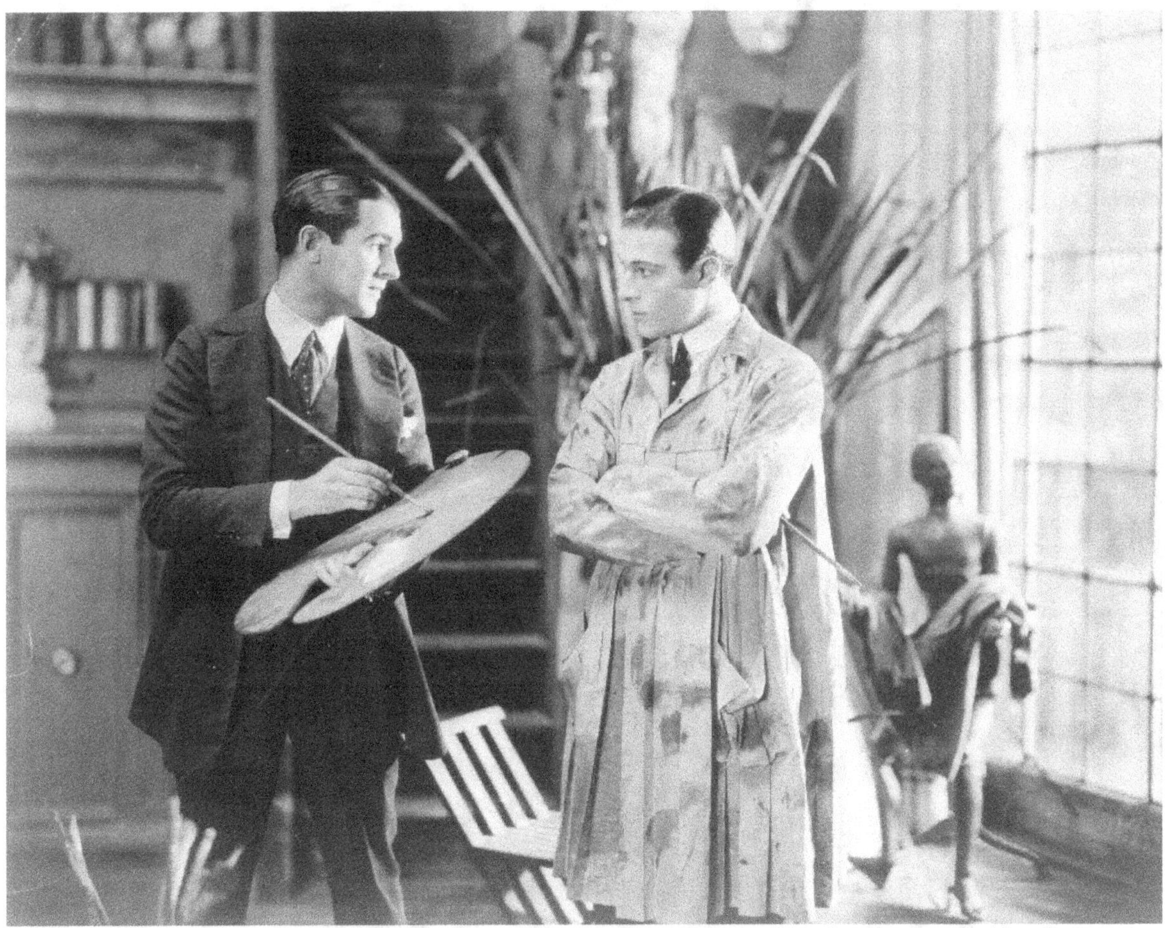

Rex Ingram, an artist in his own right, instructs Valentino in the proper use of brush and palette for his role as Julio. Not discounting Valentino's natural acting talent; he was nurtured by both Ingram and Mathis which resulted in nothing less than spectacular results.
(Author's collection)

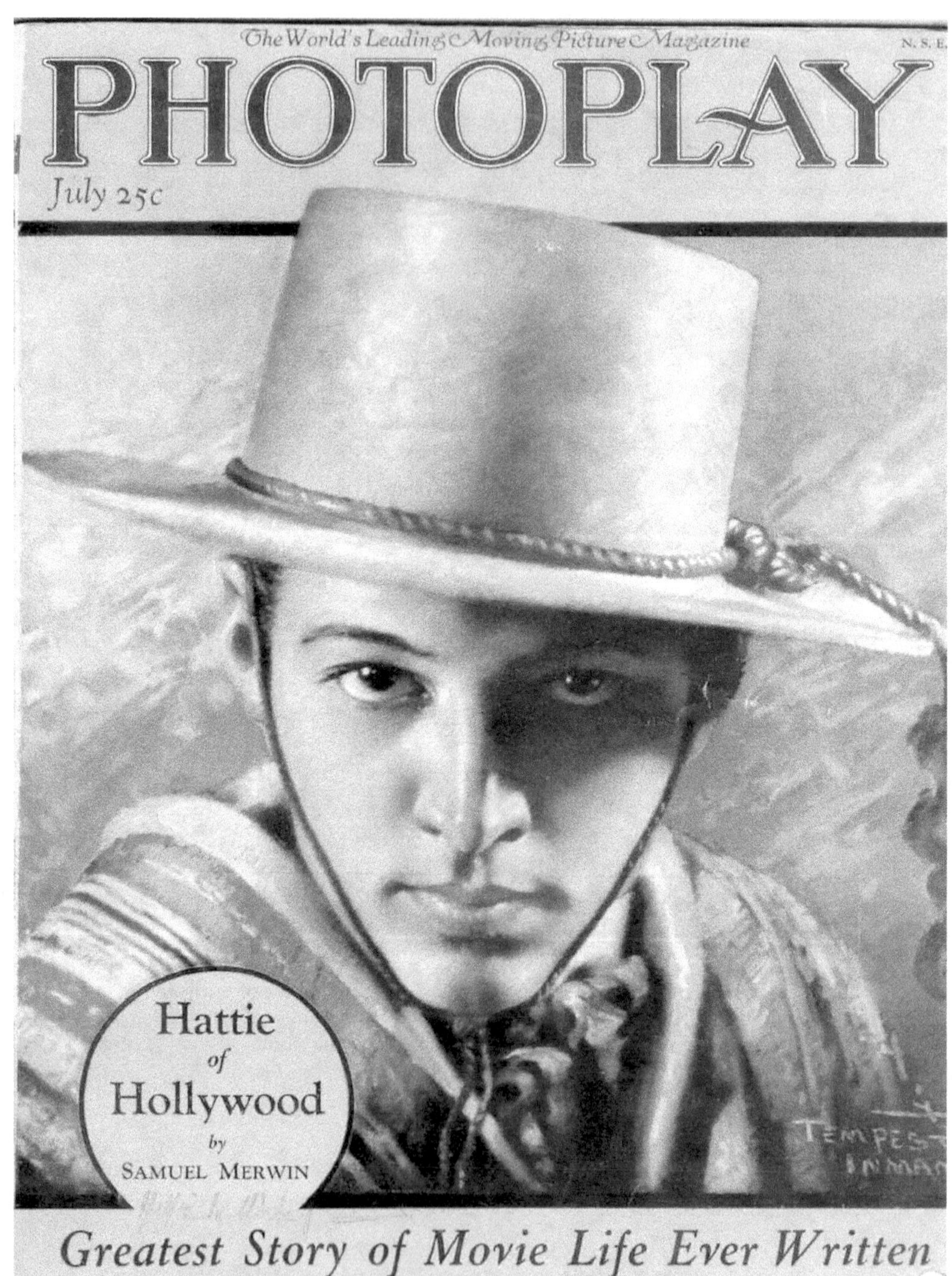

Valentino's first appearance on a magazine cover.
Painting is based on a portrait taken by Arthur Rice. (Author's collection)

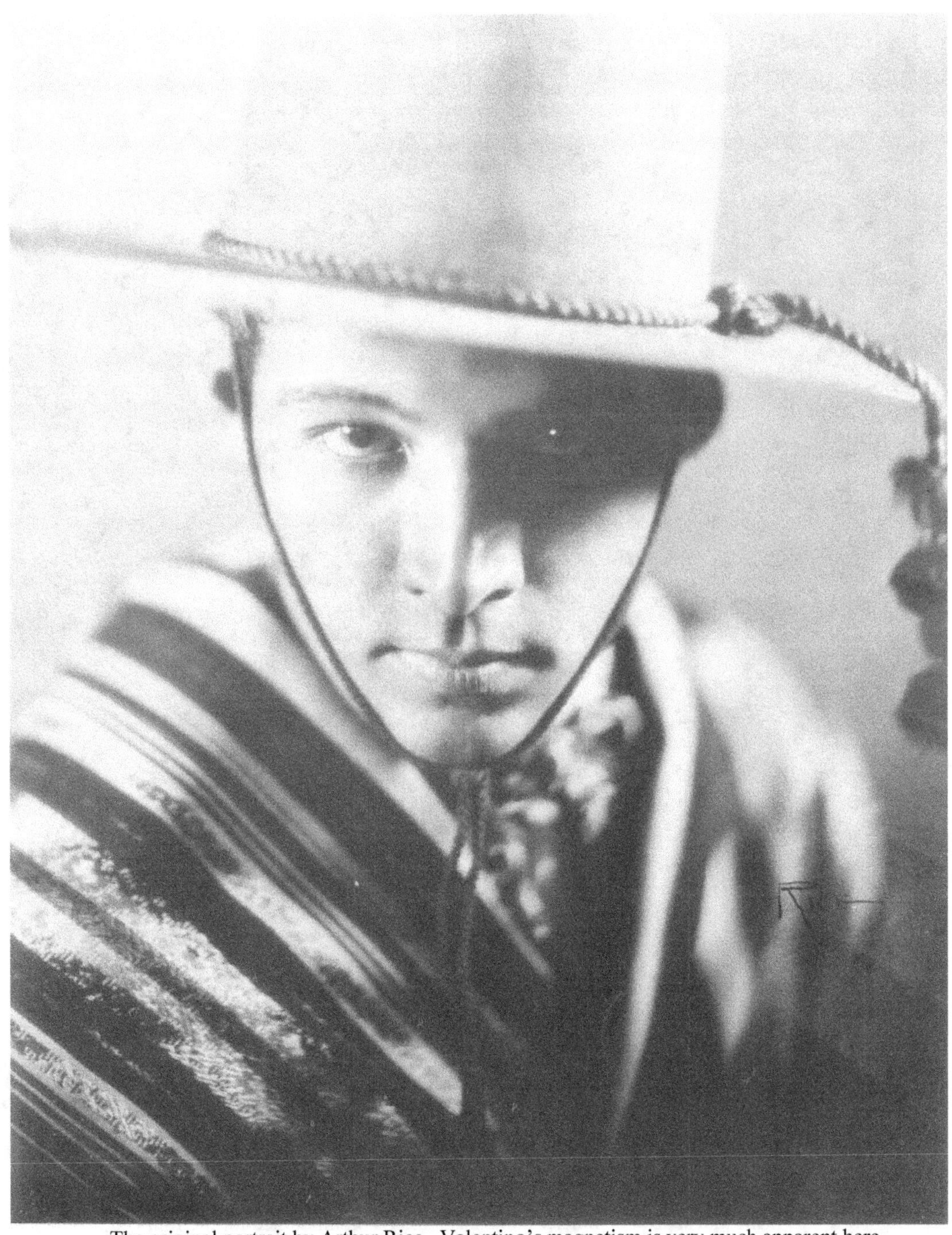

The original portrait by Arthur Rice. Valentino's magnetism is very much apparent here. (Author's collection)

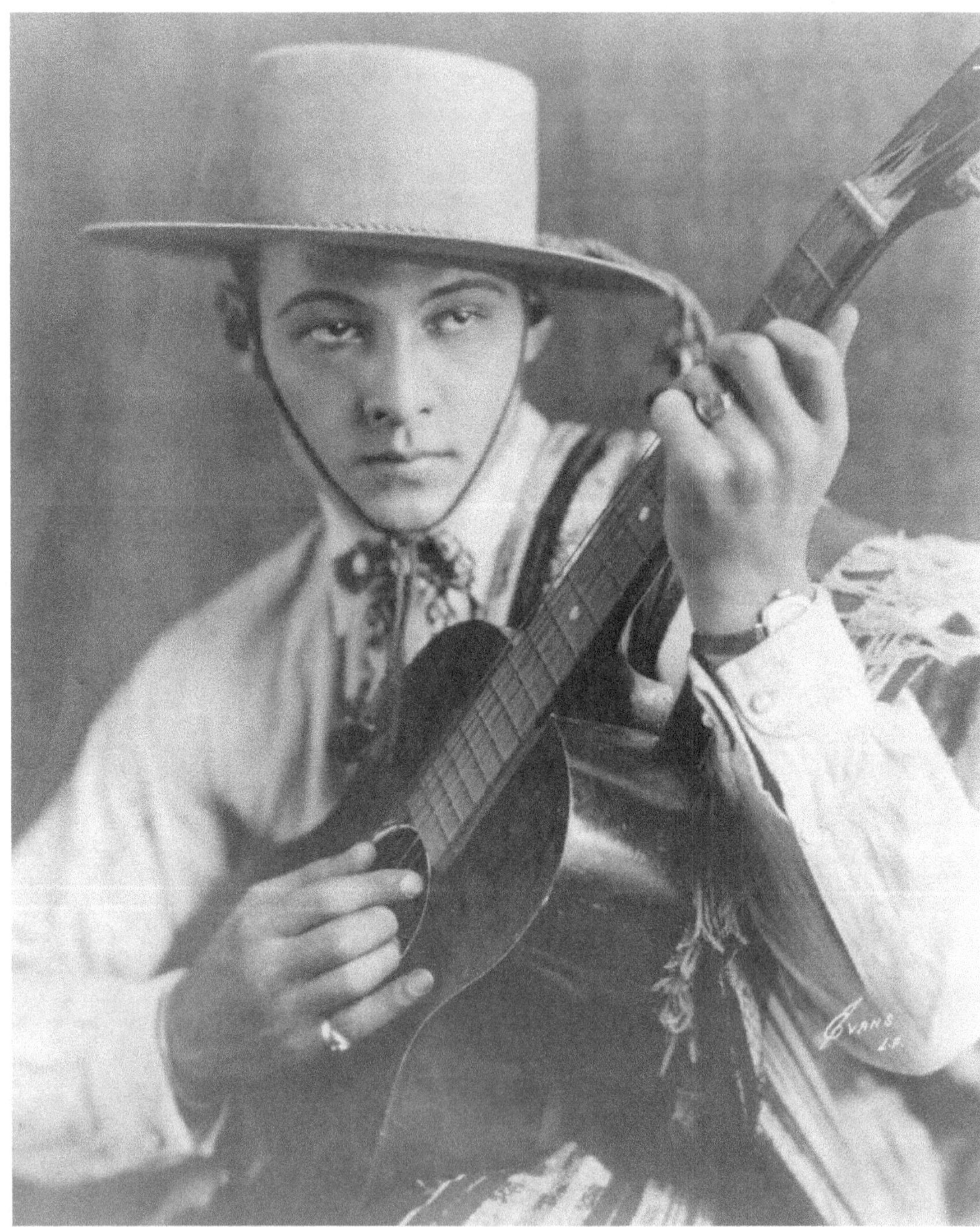

One of a series of publicity photos Valentino commissioned for the film
by Evans Studio. (Author's collection)

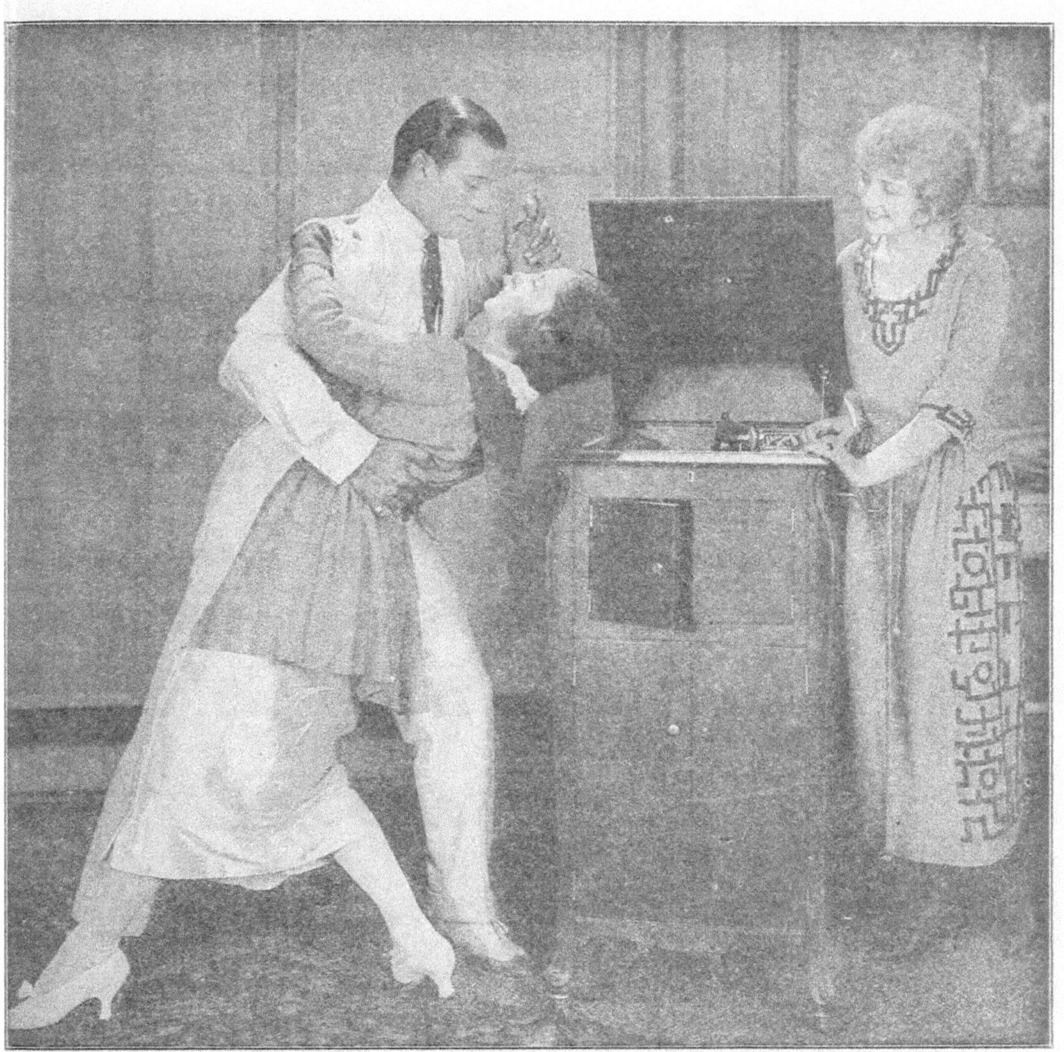

Try This with Your Victrola

It's the trot of the Four Horsemen. Incidentally the latest step of Rudolph Valentino toward screen fame.

By Charles Carter

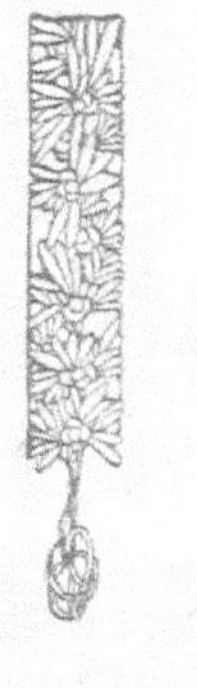

THE FOUR HORSEMEN OF THE APOCALYPSE" will set the pace for syncopation. The Ibañes novel when unreeled will introduce a new dance originated and executed by Rudolph Valentino, who might be said to be putting his best foot forward toward film fame.

Valentino already has been seen in "Eyes of Youth" with Clara Kimball Young, in "Ambition" with Dorothy Phillips, and in "The Cheater" with May Allison. But in "The Four Horsemen" he reverts to the occupation of dancing which employed him at Rector's with Bonnie Glass, at the Winter Garden, and on the Keith vaudeville circuit. Incidentally, he plays the vivid rôle of *Julio*, for which he seems born. *Julio*, you may recall, was a dancer, a romantic devil, and handsome in a foreign way.

Valentino was born in Tarnto, Italy. His father was a captain in the Italian cavalry. Rudolph hearkened to paternal advice and spent four years at the Royal Military College of Agriculture at Genoa, graduating with a plowman's degree. At the age of eighteen he came to the United States, intending to make a furrow for himself as a Western rancher. He tarried too long in New York, however, where he met a number of theatrical people. Although he had never taken a dancing lesson in his Italian life, he was considered an excellent "find" by Bonnie Glass, who engaged him as her partner.

The series of tango photographs with Valentino and Alice Terry were used in magazine advertisements designed to sell Victrolas. Also, by implication, RCA Victrola recordings of tangos. (Author's collection)

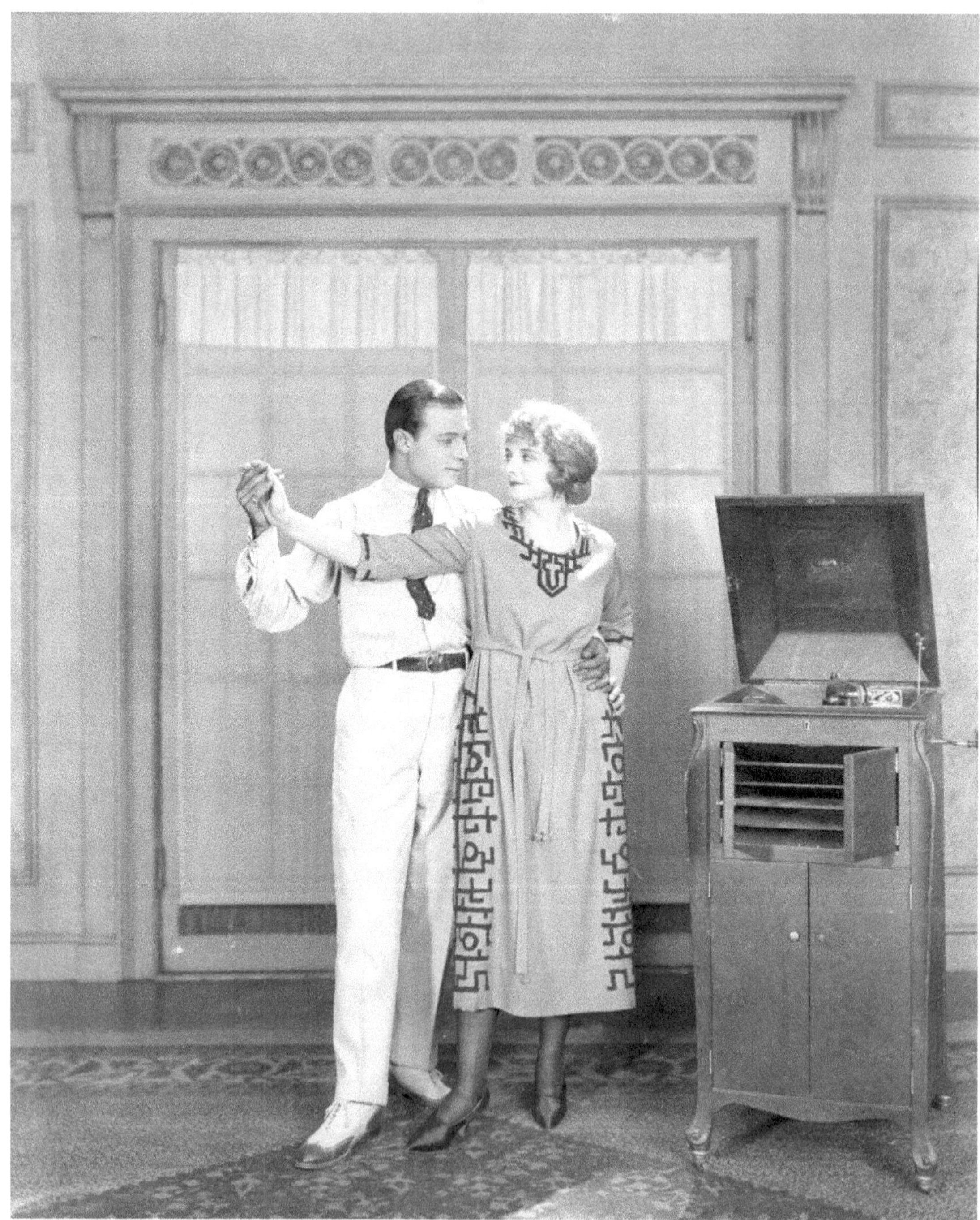

Valentino and Alice Terry's rapport can be gauged in this photo posed to advertise the Victrola on their left. (Author's collection)

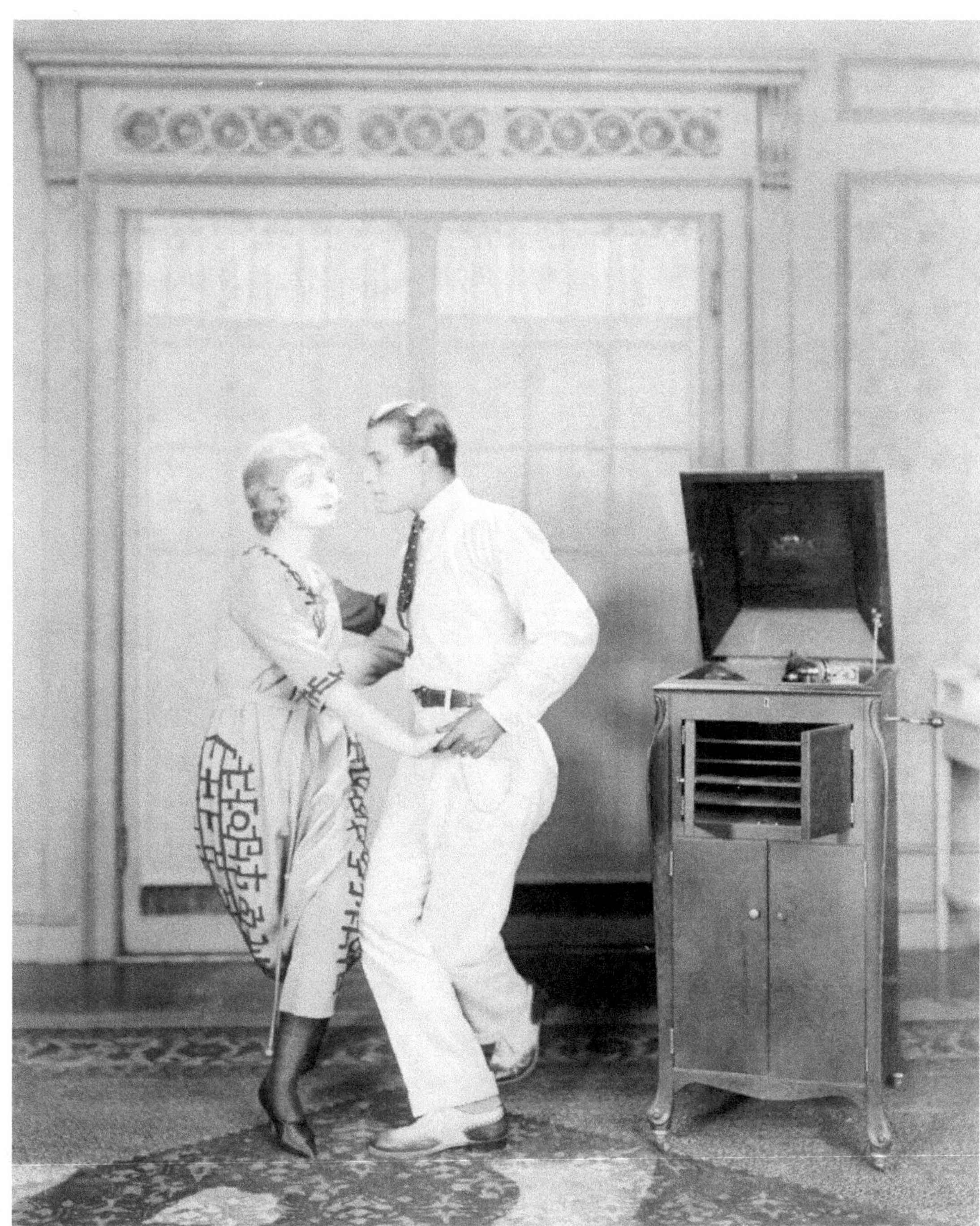

Another photo not used for the advertisements.
Alice Terry has locked eyes with Rudolph Valentino taking the lead.
(Author's collection)

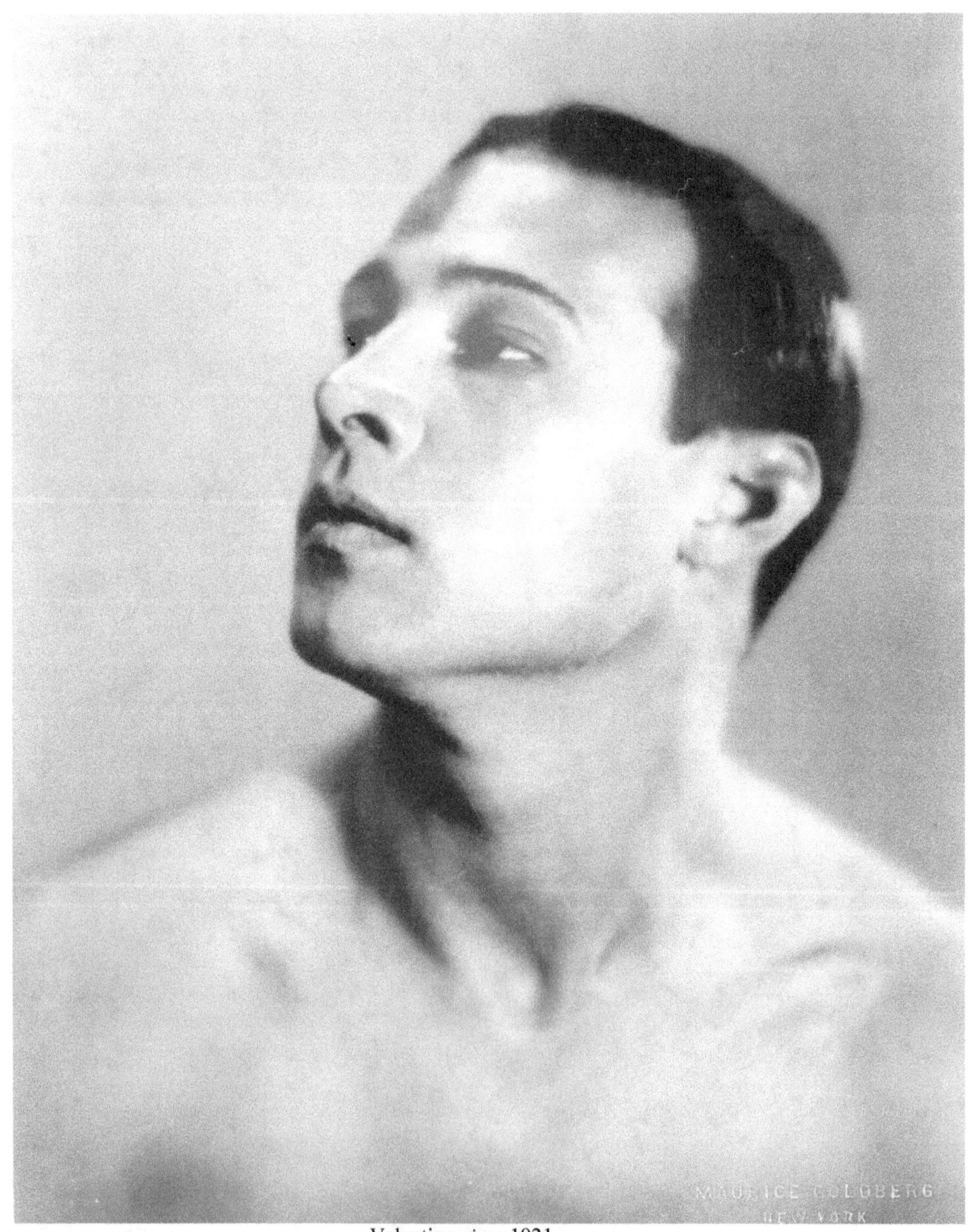

Valentino *circa* 1921
(Margaret Herrick Library; Academy of Motion Picture Arts and Sciences)

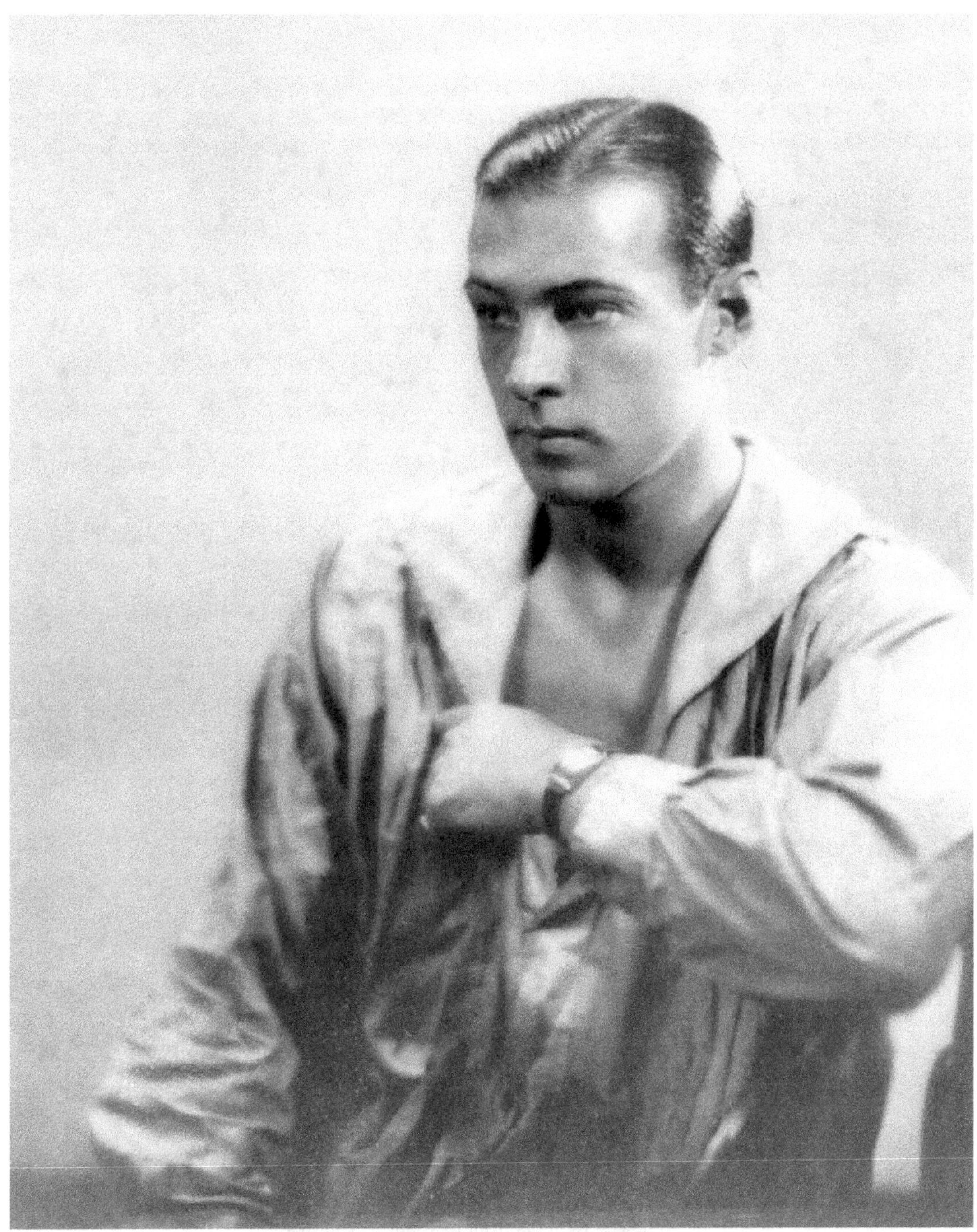

A portrait study *circa* 1921 by Maurice Goldberg.
(Author's collection)

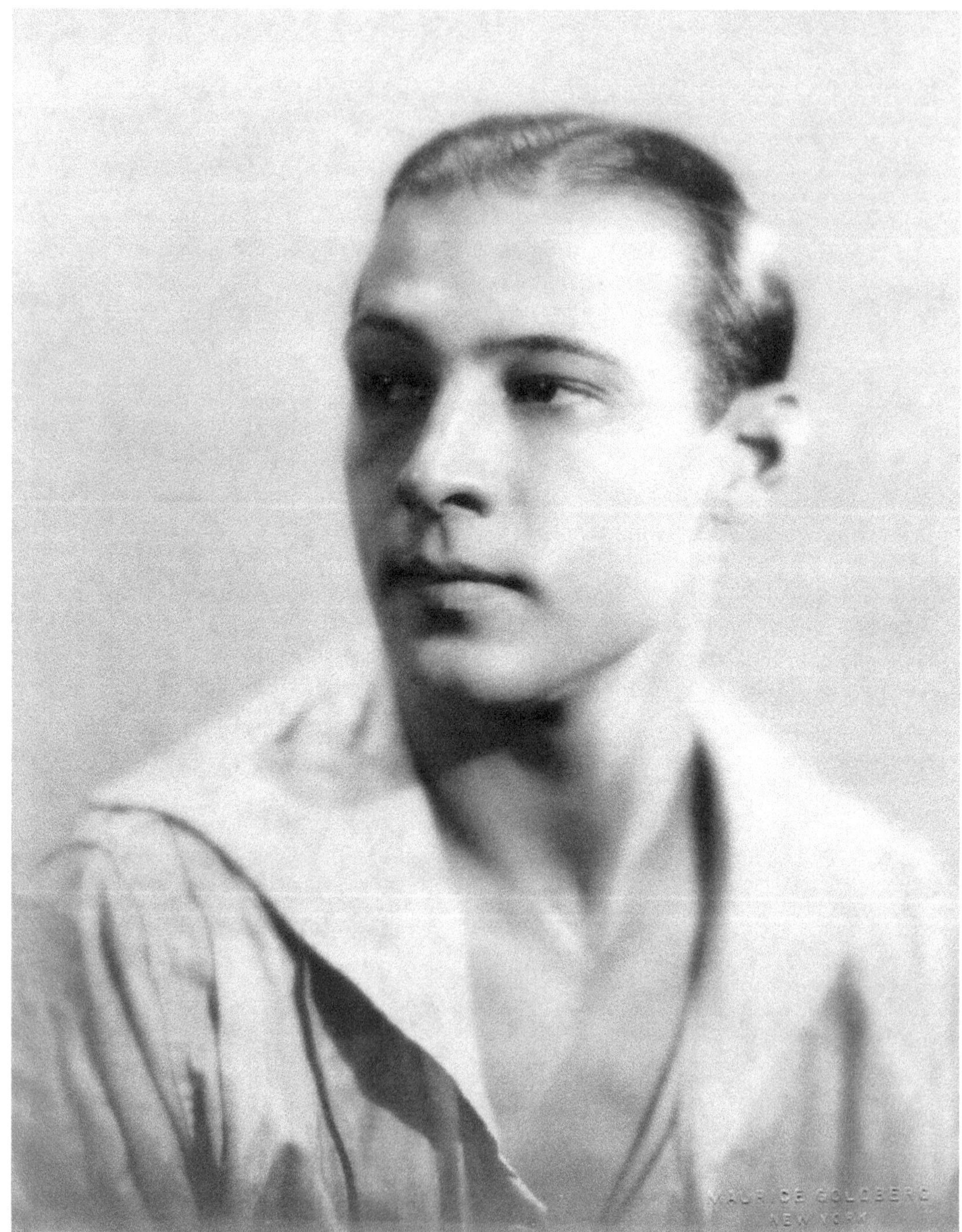

Another striking portrait by Maurice Goldberg.
(Author's collection)

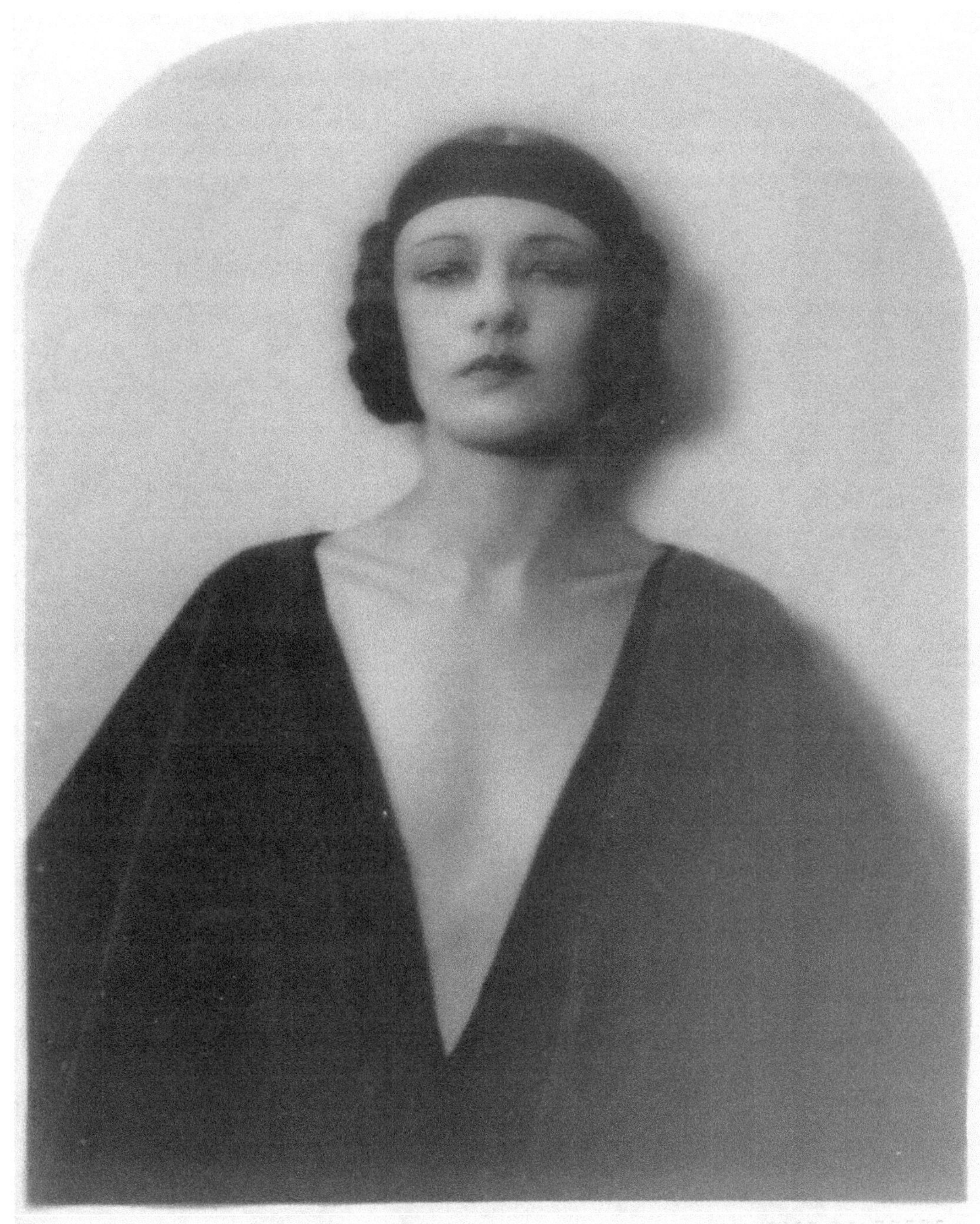

Natacha also sat for Maurice Goldberg, her haughty look here belied a real warmth.
(Author's collection)

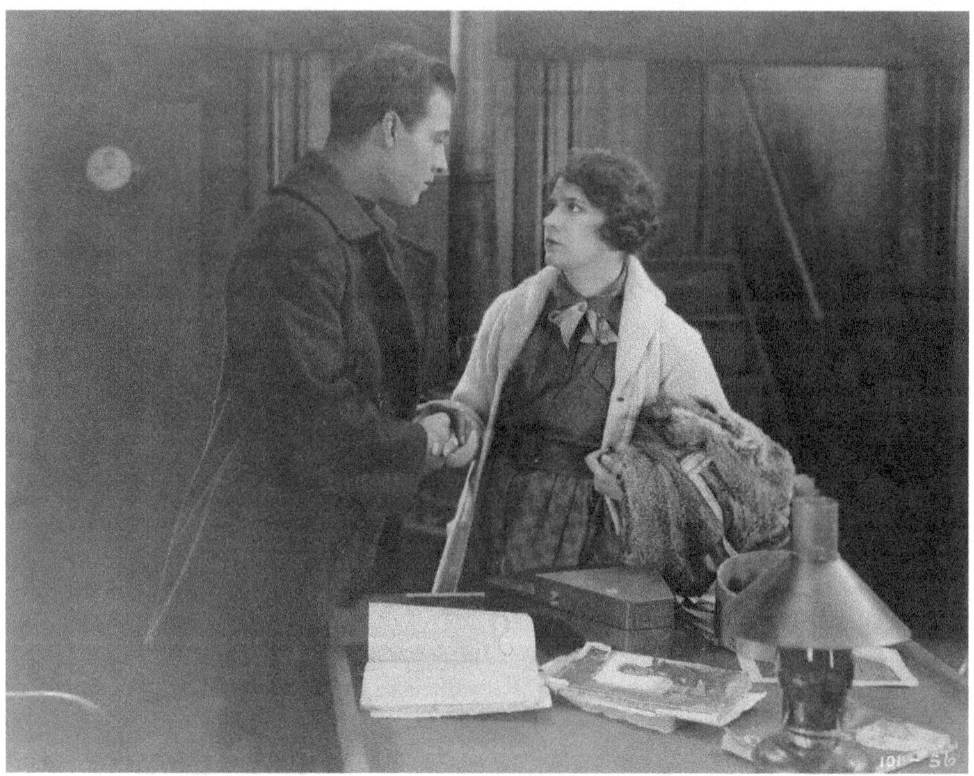

Valentino with Alice Lake in *Uncharted Seas*. (Author's collection)

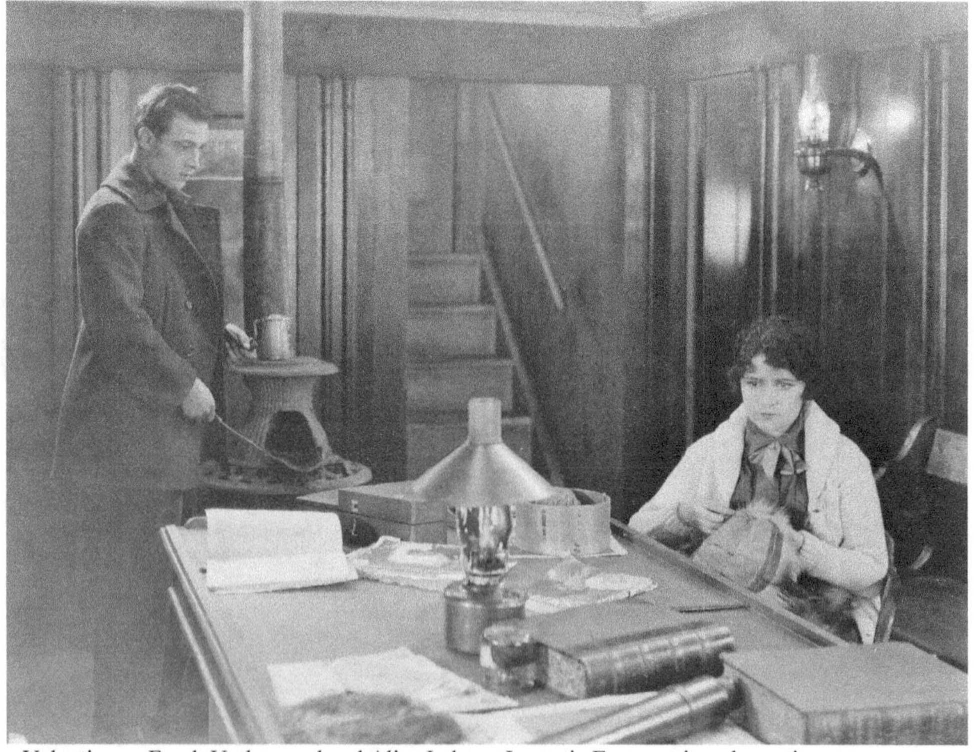

Valentino as Frank Underwood and Alice Lake as Lucretia Eastman in a dramatic moment in *Uncharted Seas*. (Author's collection)

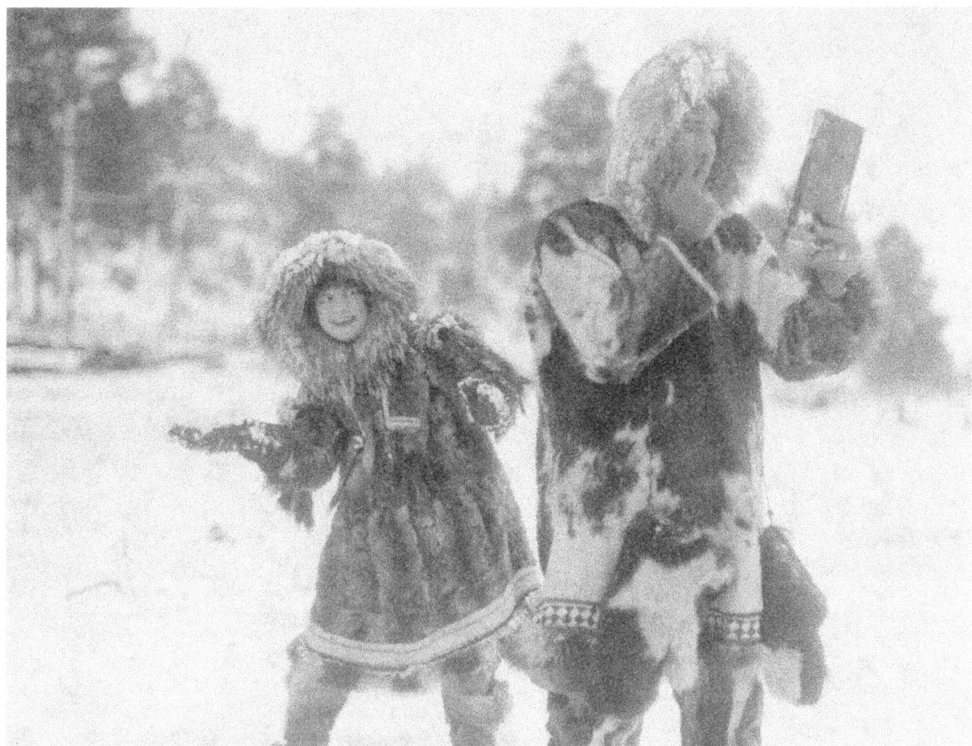

A playful Alice Lake prepares to paste Valentino with a snowball on location in Flagstaff, Arizona. (Author's collection)

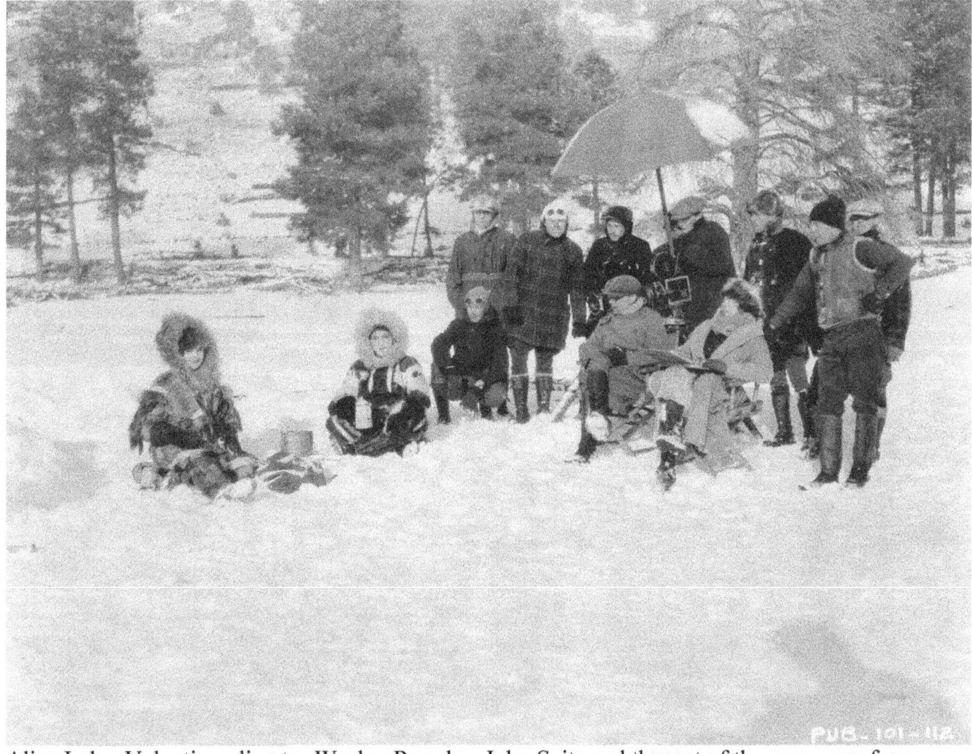

Alice Lake, Valentino, director Wesley Ruggles, John Seitz and the rest of the crew pose for a group shot on location in Flagstaff, Arizona during the filming of *Uncharted Seas*. (Margaret Herrick Library; Academy of Motion Picture Arts and Sciences)

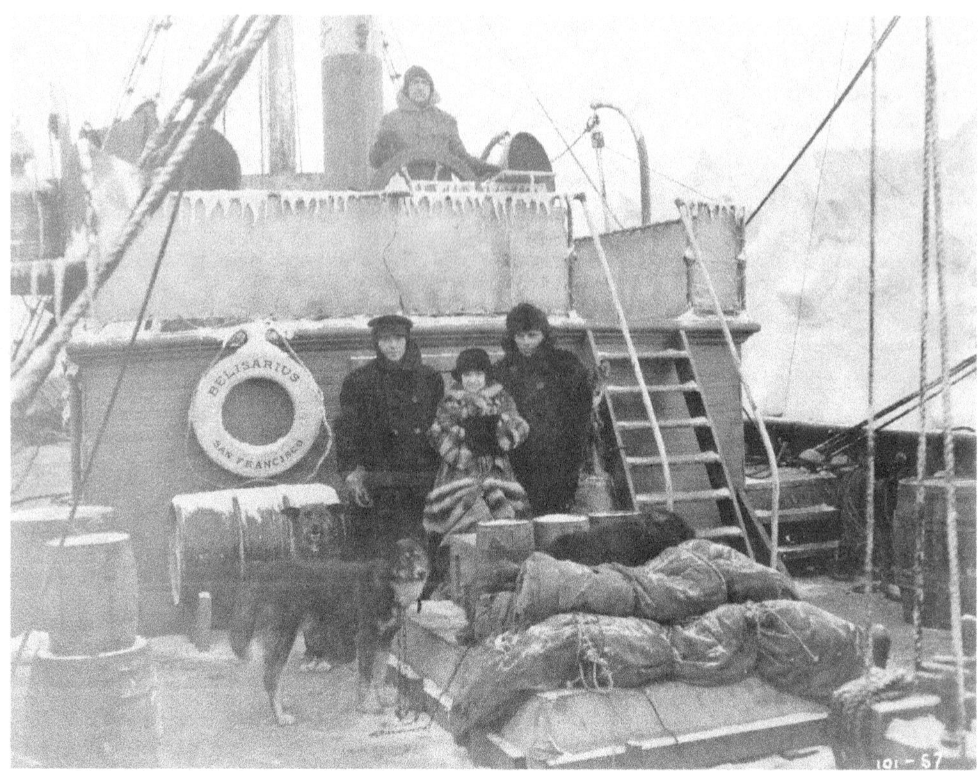

Valentino, Alice Lake and Wesley Ruggles pose on the set of the ship Belisarius with some of the sled dogs. (Author's collection)

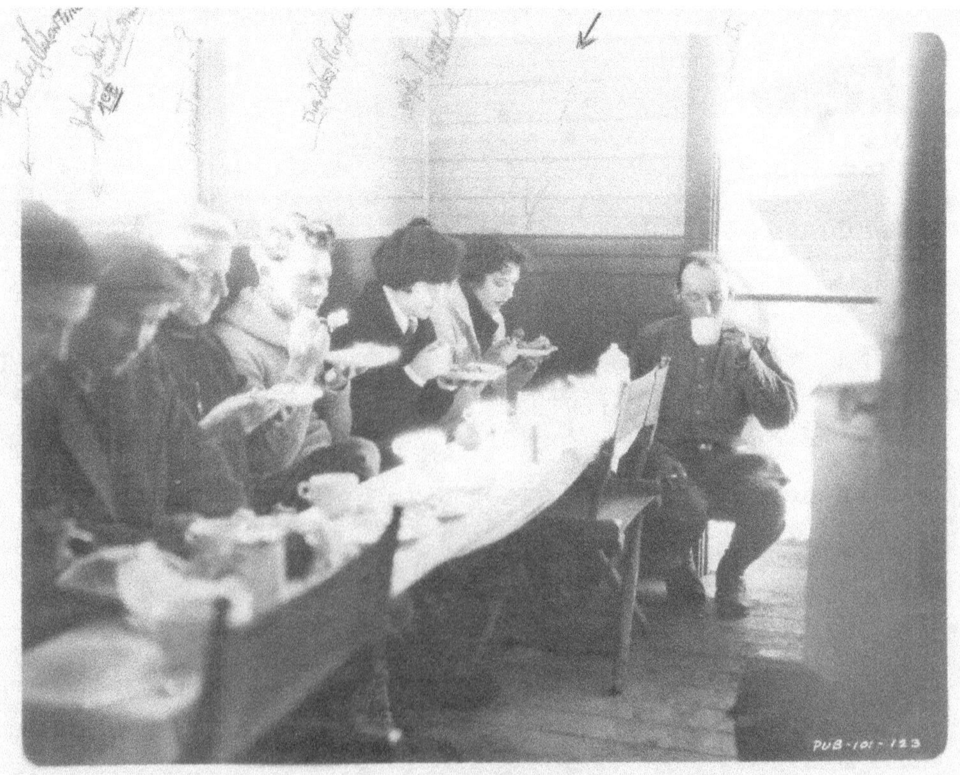

Cast and crew share a meal on location in Flagstaff, AZ. Valentino can be glimpsed far left. John Seitz, unknown, Wesley Ruggles, Mrs. Wesley Ruggles, Alice Lake and unknown. (Margaret Herrick Library; Academy of Motion Picture Arts and Sciences)

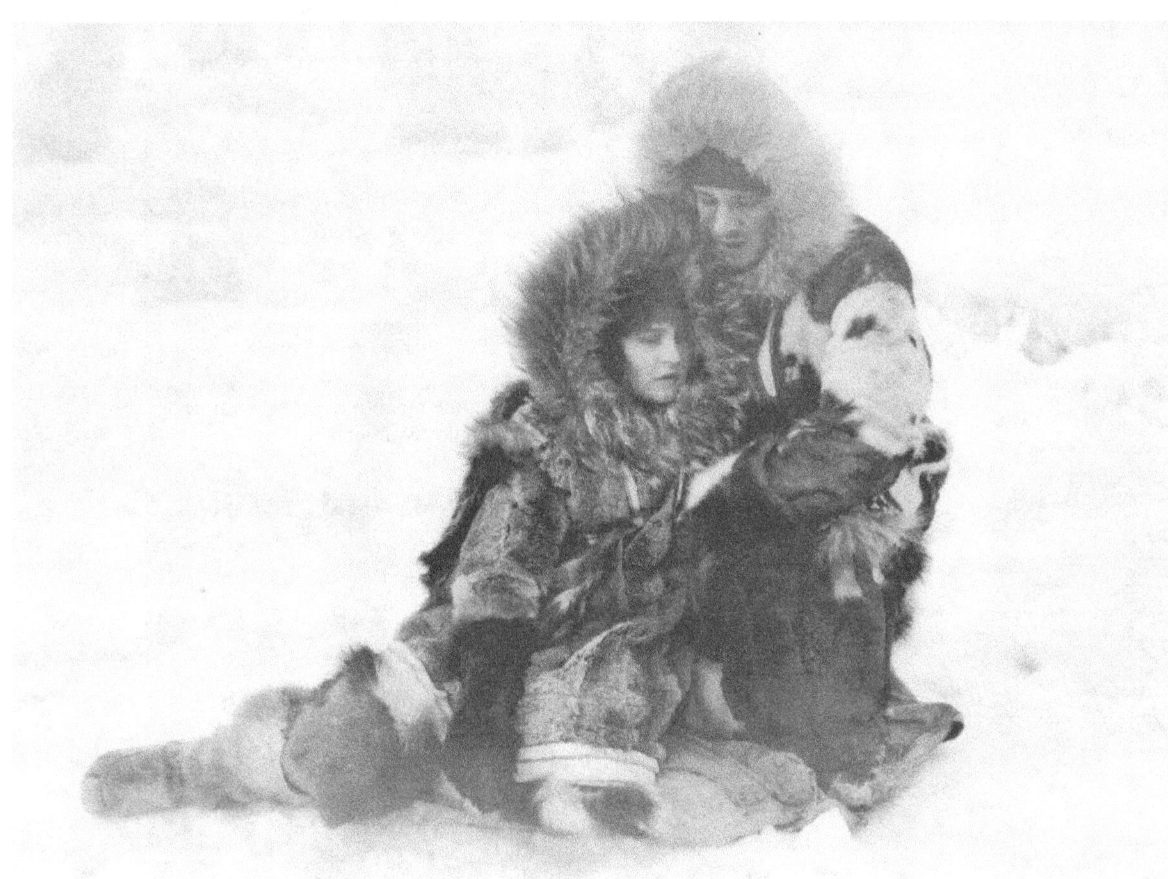

Valentino and Alice Lake in trouble in the adventure/romance *Uncharted Seas*. (Author's collection)

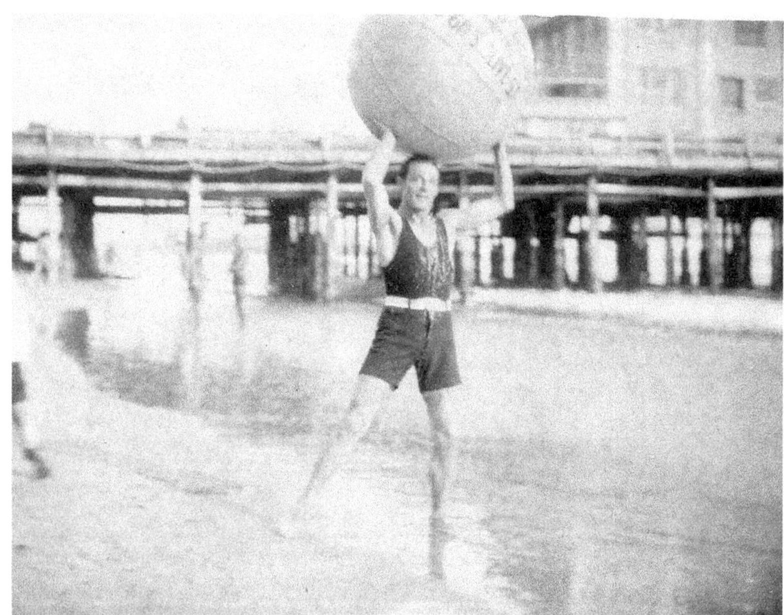

After the wintery Flagstaff, Valentino enjoyed some much-needed beach time at the Santa Monica Pier. Here he is utterly drenched.
(Tracy Terhune collection)

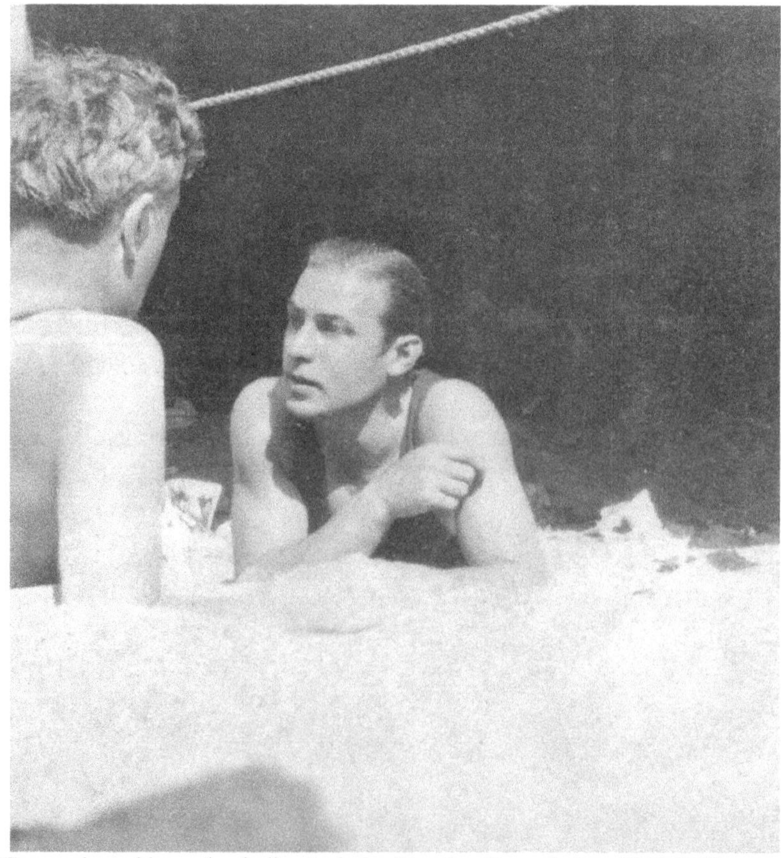

Conversing with good pal, director/actor Douglas Gerrard *circa* 1920-1921.
(Author's collection)

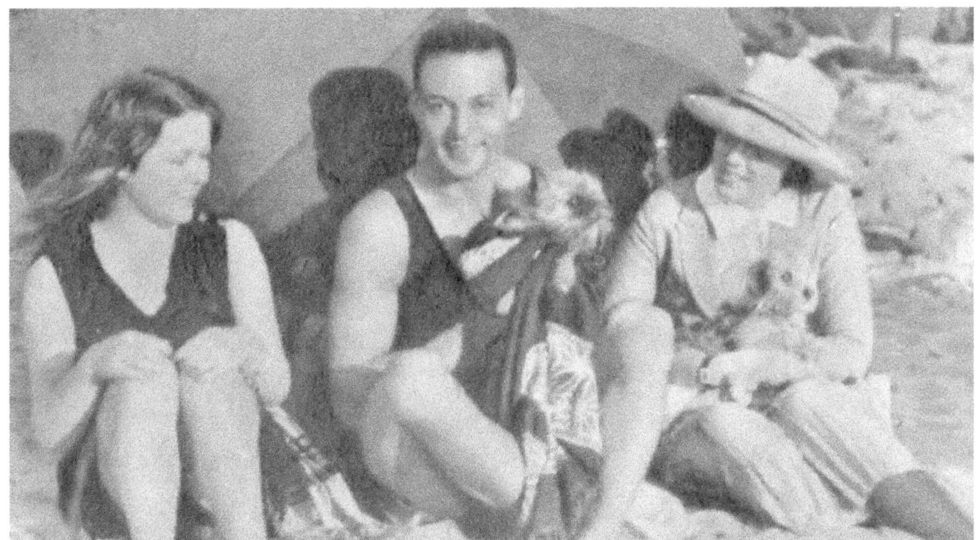

At the Crystal Pier in Santa Monica with Rudy sandwiched between Mrs. Mahlon Hamilton and Gertrude Selby. Sadly, the names of the dogs are lost to history.
(Author's collection)

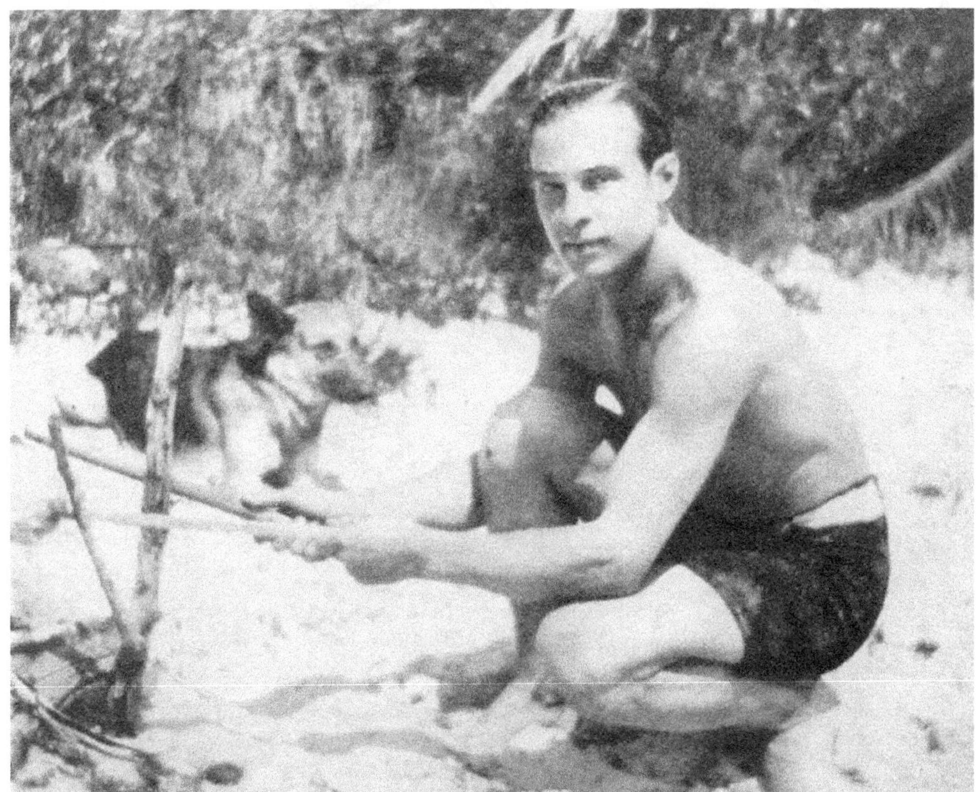

Valentino and Sheik enjoying an informal campfire cookout on the beach *circa* 1920-21.
(Author's collection)

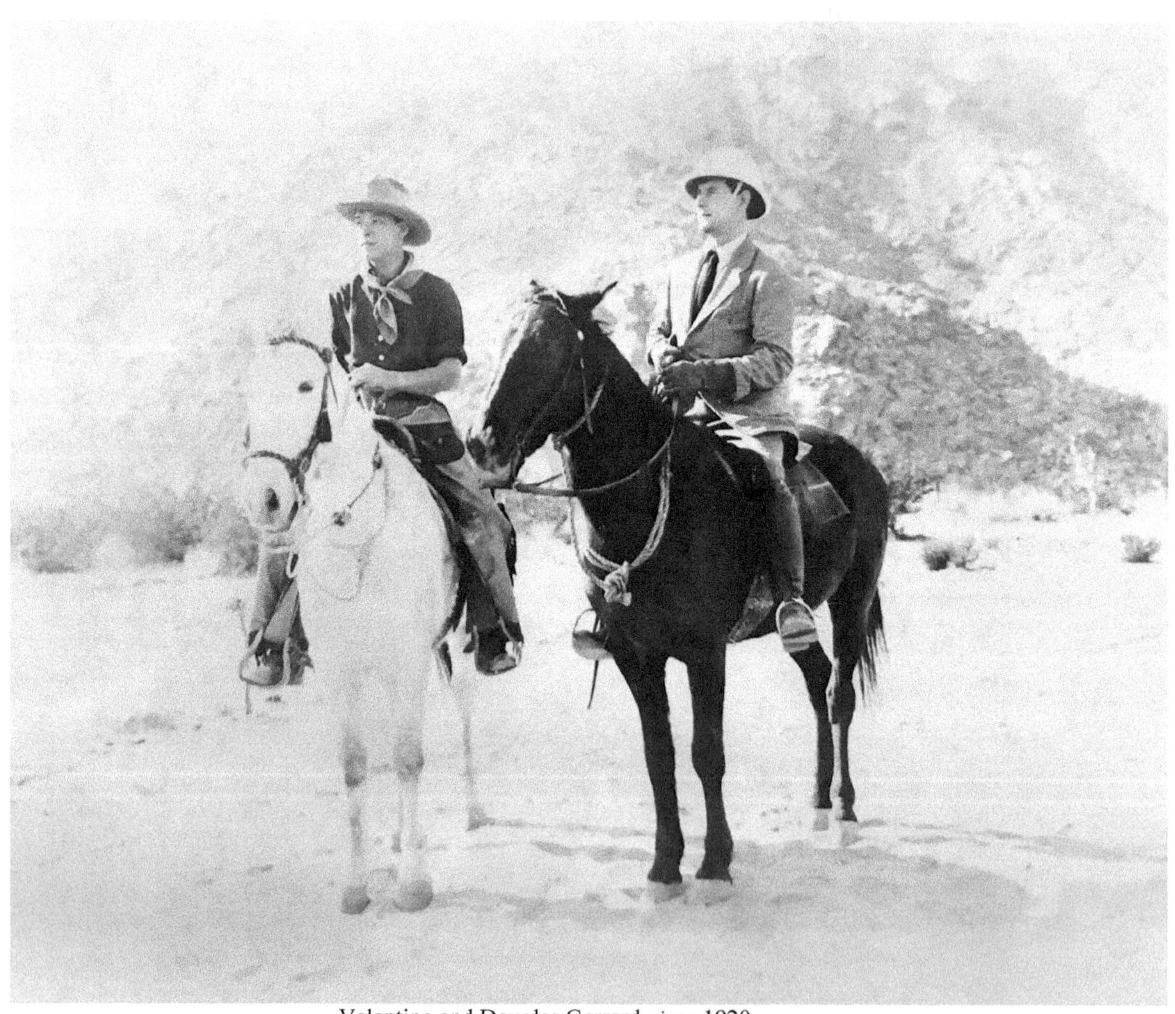

Valentino and Douglas Gerrard *circa* 1920.
(Author's collection)

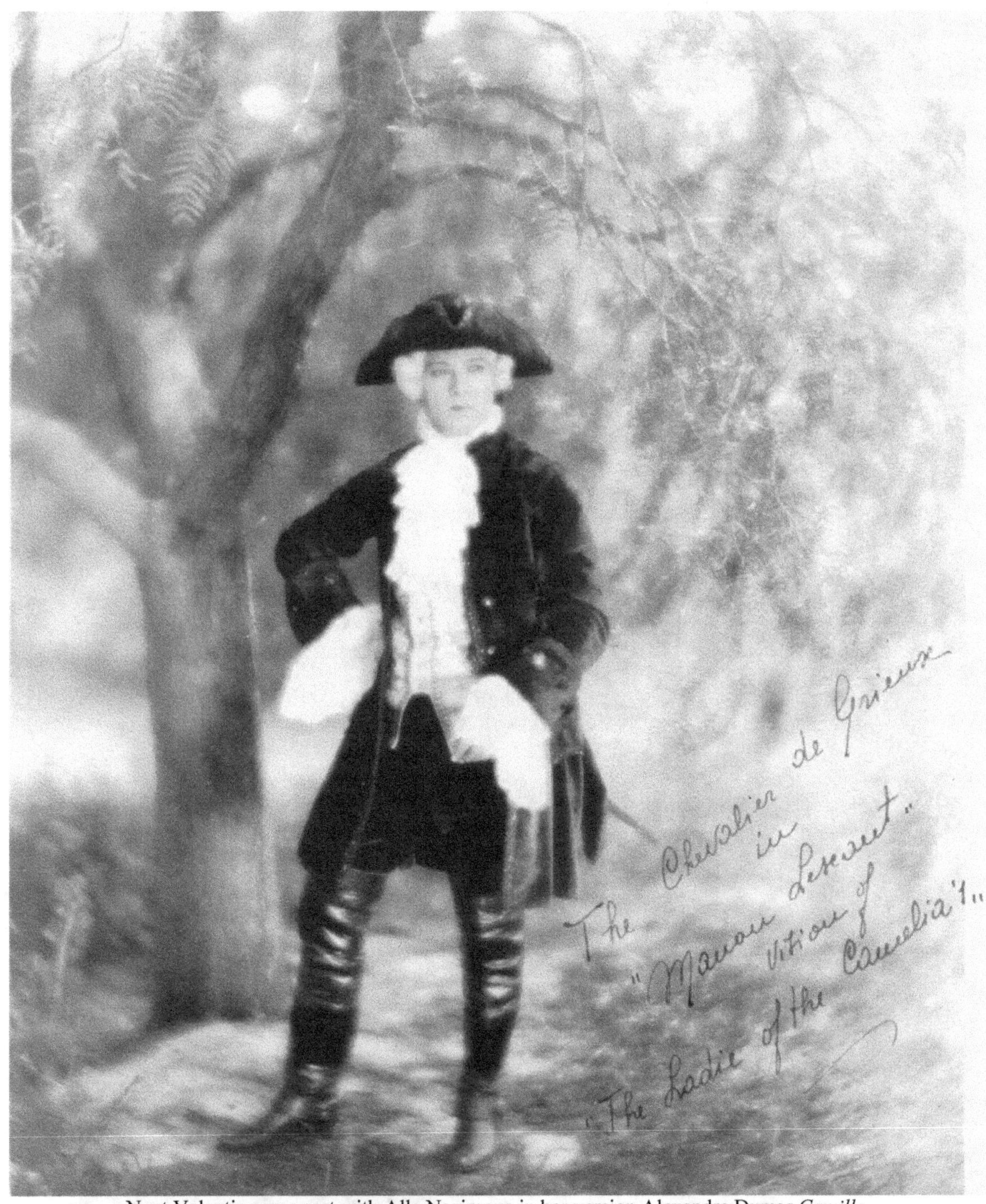

Next Valentino was cast with Alla Nazimova in her version Alexandre Dumas *Camille*.
Valentino's life would change during filming, smitten with his own beloved Natacha Rambova.
The inscription on this photograph is in Valentino's own hand in his traditional green ink.
(Author's collection)

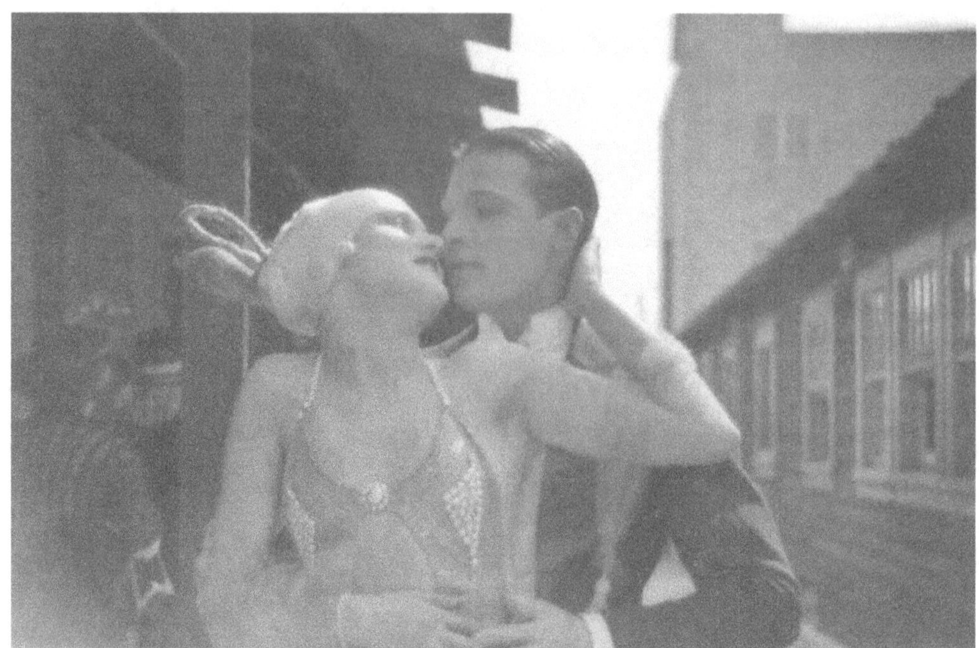

Valentino and Consuelo Flowerton clowning for Paul Ivano's camera during filming of the casino sequence in *Camille*. (Francis Laccasin collection courtesy Flicker Alley and Lobster Films)

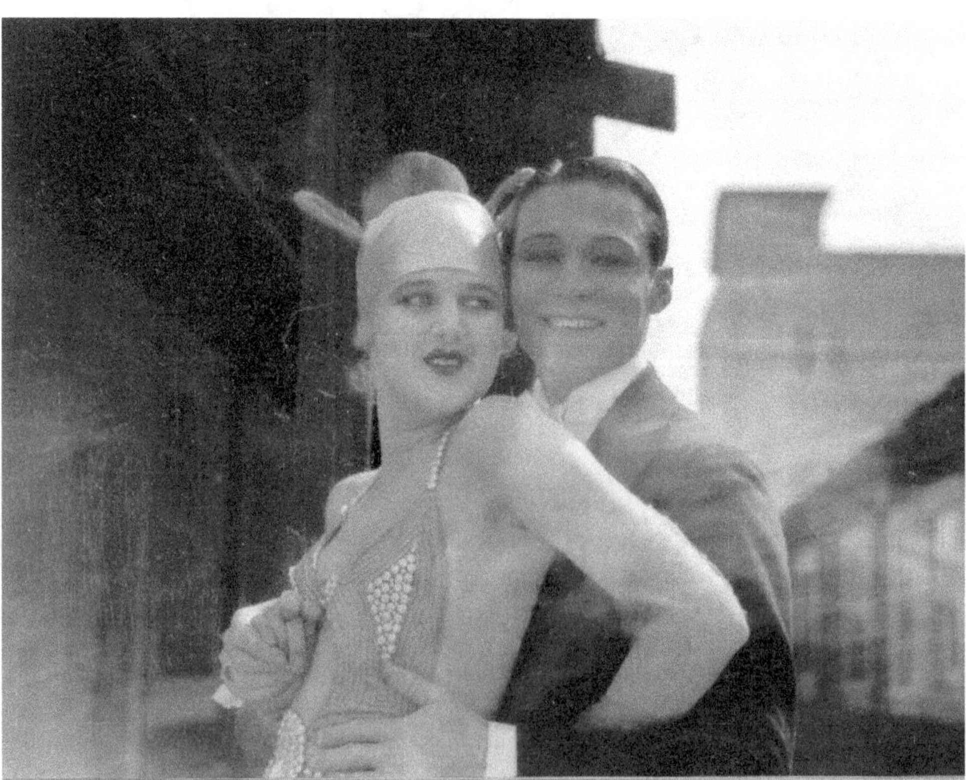

The most natural smile, enjoying life to the fullest and on the brink of great stardom for Rudolph Valentino. (Francis Laccasin collection courtesy Flicker Alley and Lobster Films)

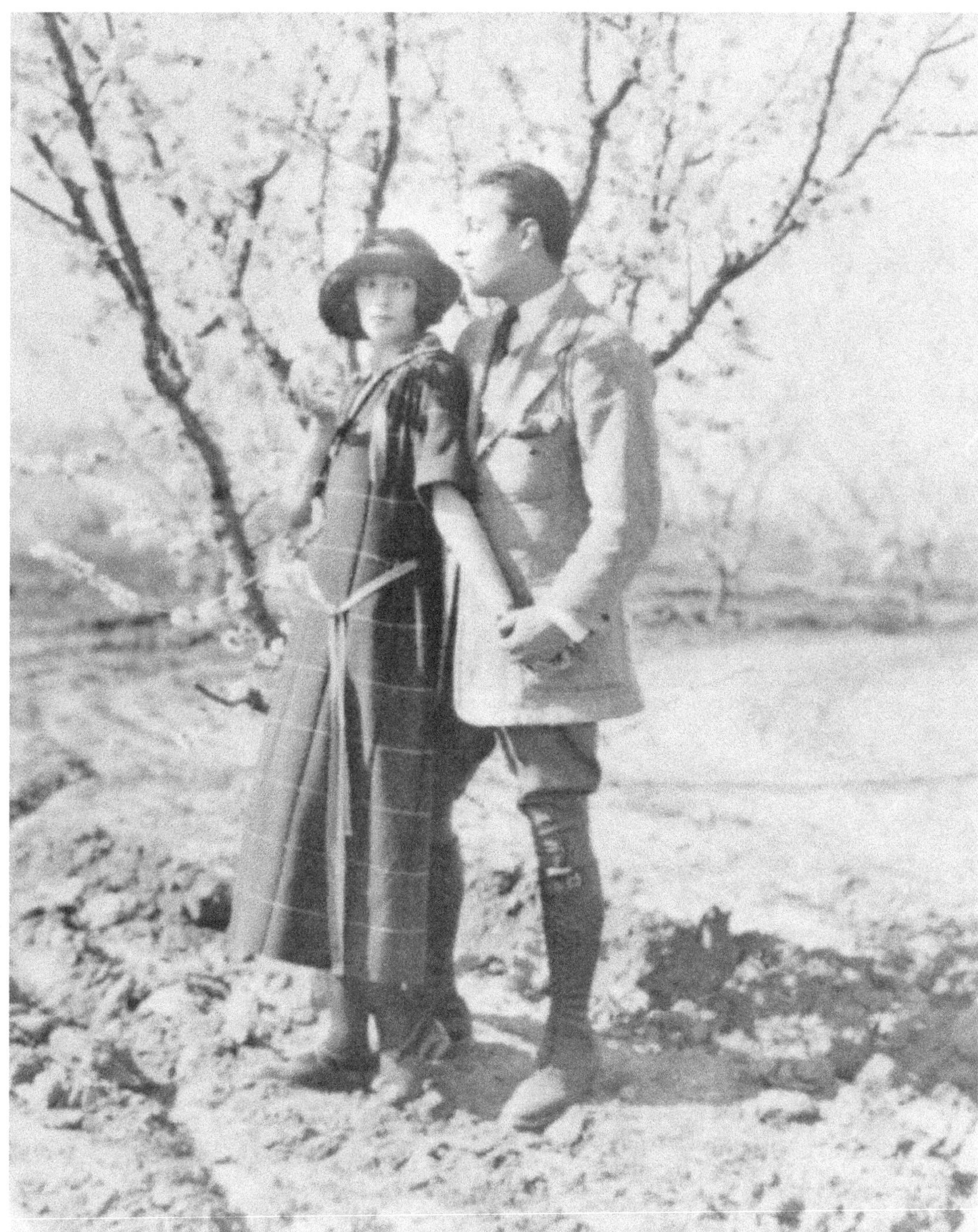

Posing with Natacha Rambova during filming of *Camille*. (Author's collection)

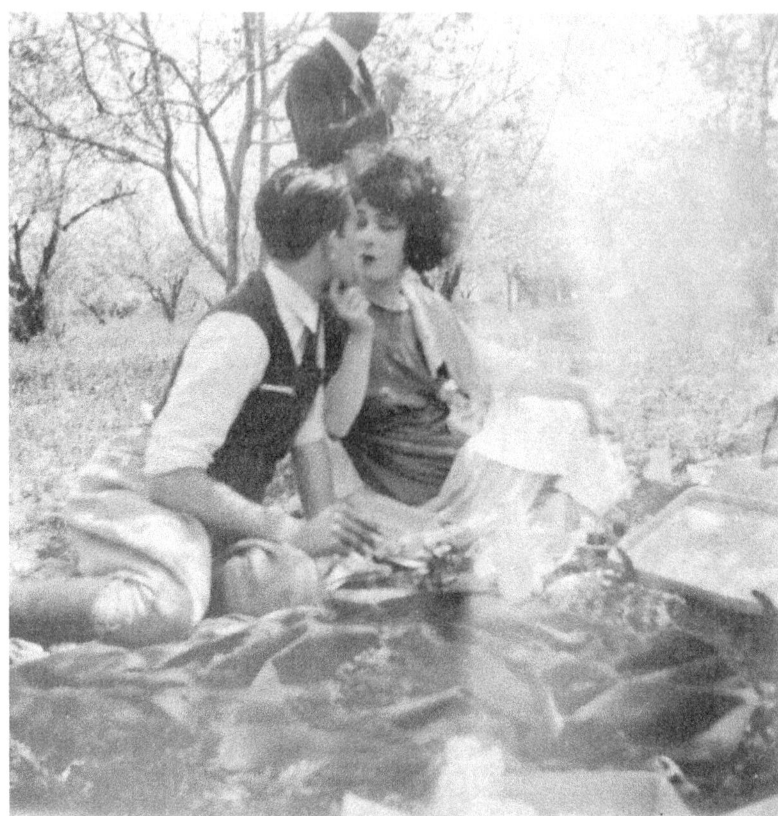

Nazimova and Paul Ivano also enjoyed the romance in the air during the making of *Camille*. This photo was likely taken by Valentino during a lunch time picnic. (Jeff Carrier collection)

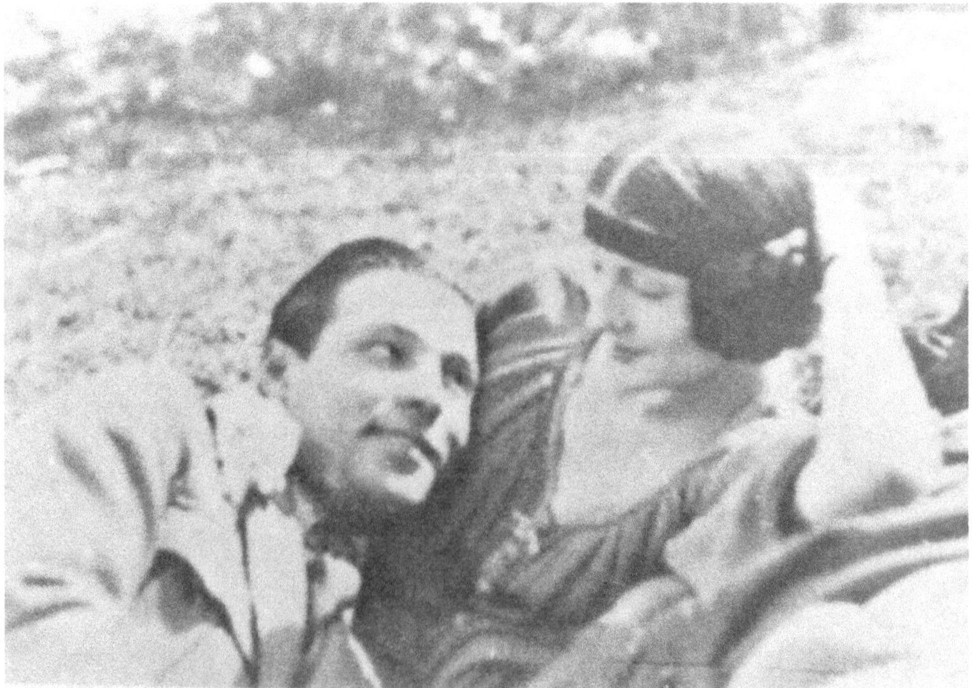

Valentino with eyes only for Natacha on location. (Michael Morris collection)

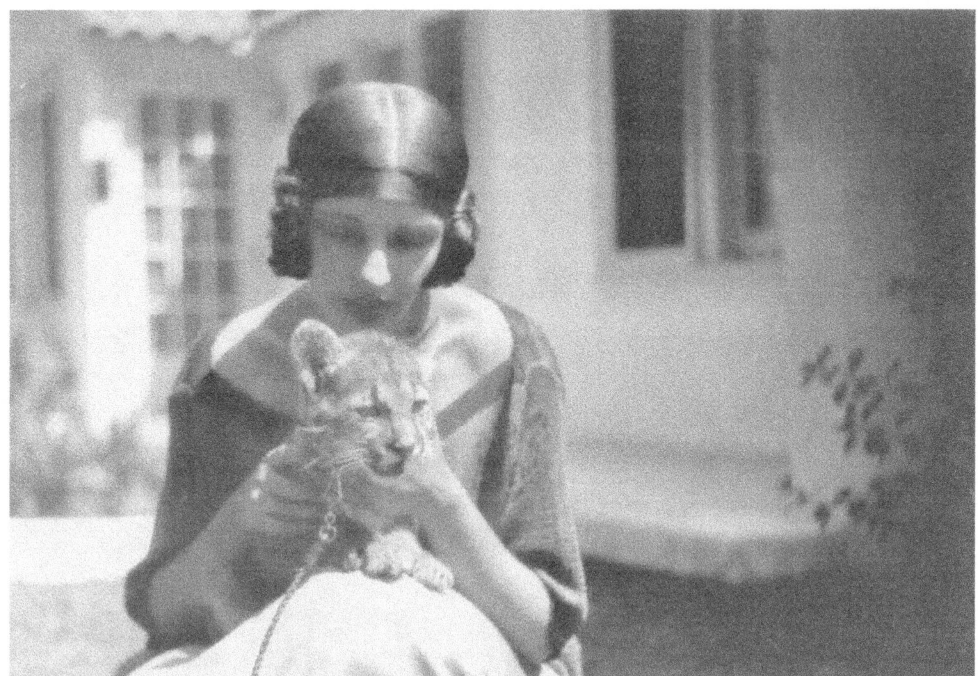

Natacha outside her bungalow on Sunset Blvd. with her lion cub Zela.
(Francis Laccasin collection courtesy Flicker Alley and Lobster Films)

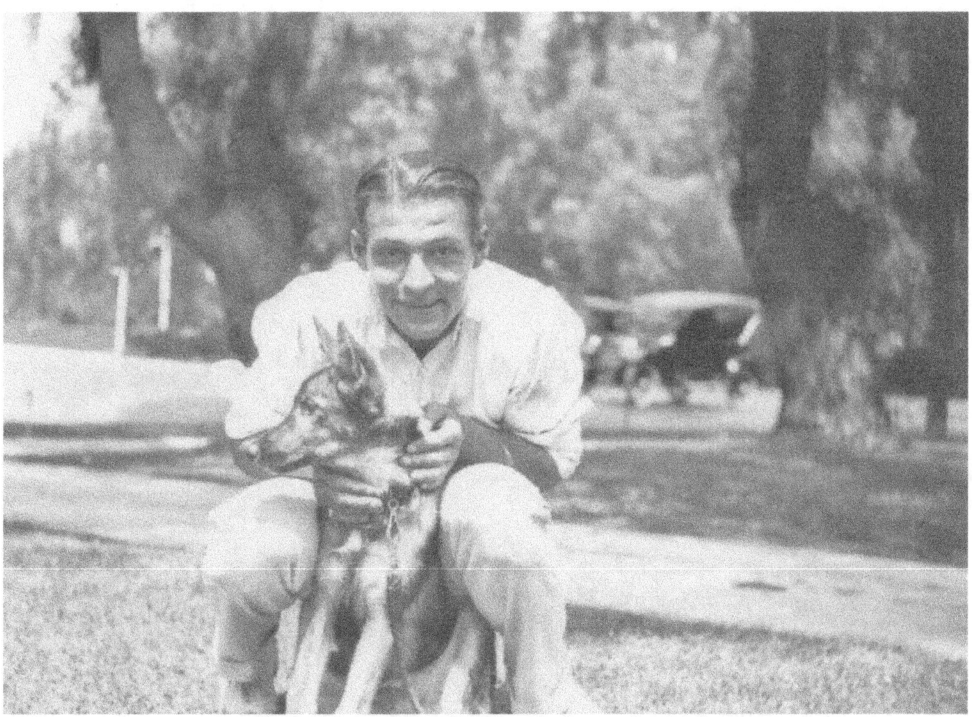

Valentino and Natacha shared a love of animals.
(Francis Laccasin collection courtesy Flicker Alley and Lobster Films)

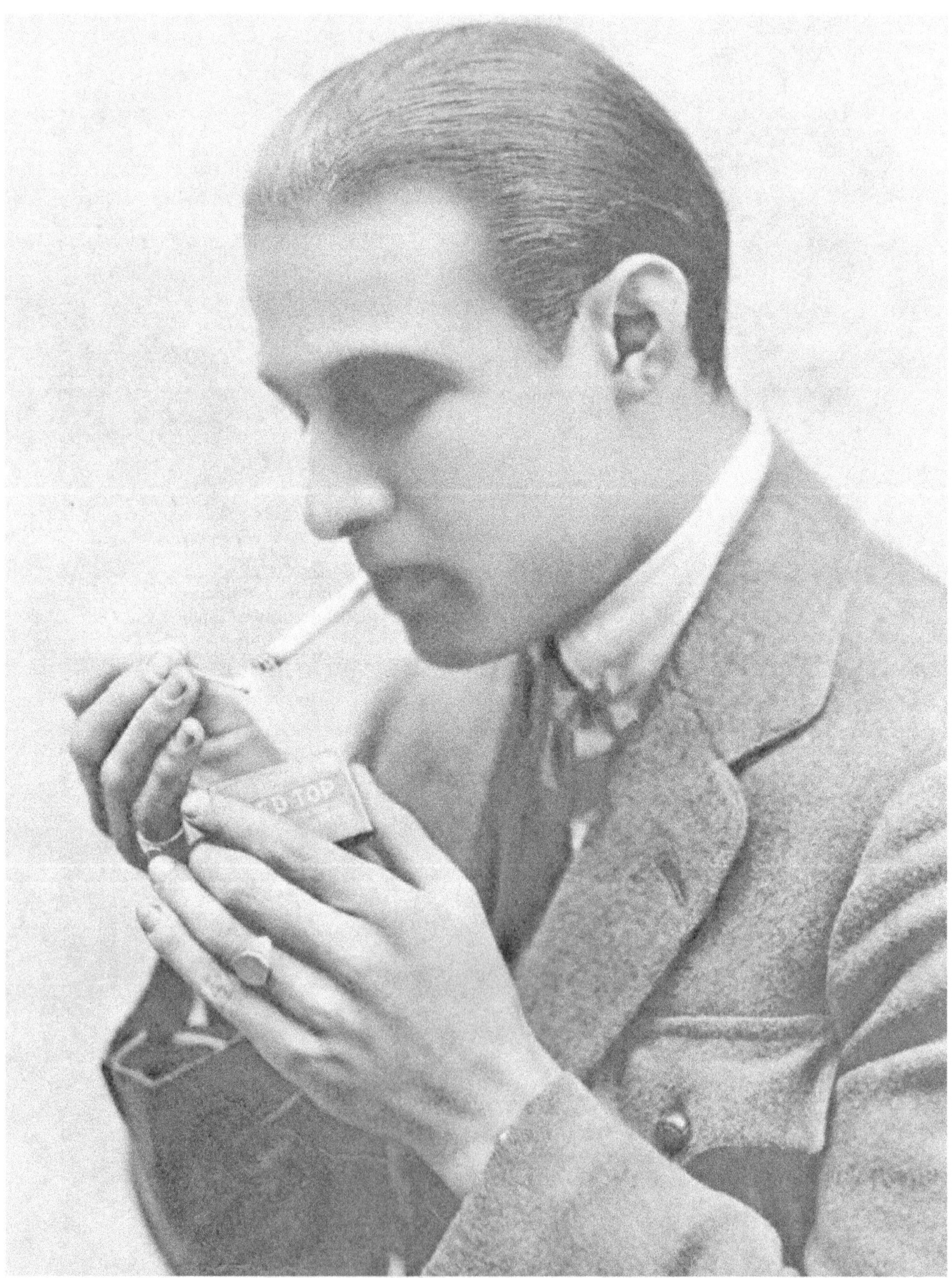

Portrait circa 1920. Valentino valued his good health, yet smoked like a proverbial chimney.
(Author's collection)

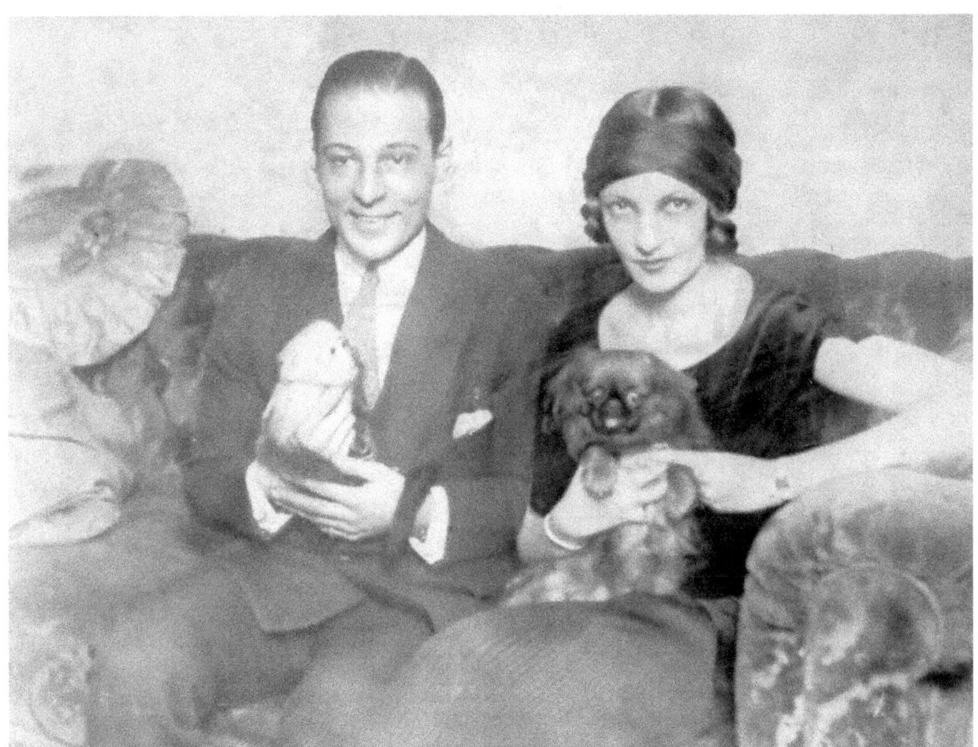

Valentino and Natacha Rambova with their pet monkey and one of her Pekinese puppies inside the tatty Sunset Blvd. bungalow.
Natacha claimed one could do wonders with throw pillows, they had little money for expensive furniture.
That all would come later. (Author's collection)

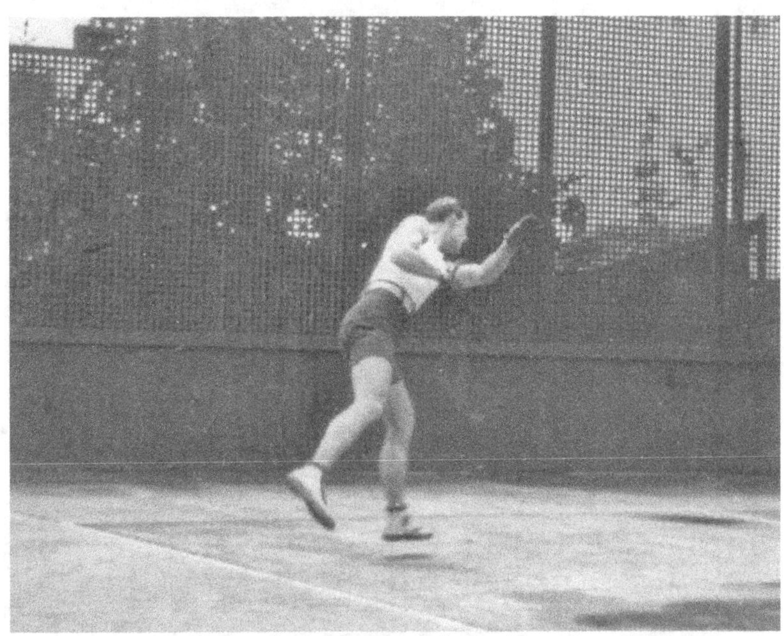

Valentino playing handball at Nazimova's. Paul Ivano recalled later that
Valentino was very competitive and "anxious to shine" in playing the game.
He took great pride in exceling at it.
(Tracy Terhune collection)

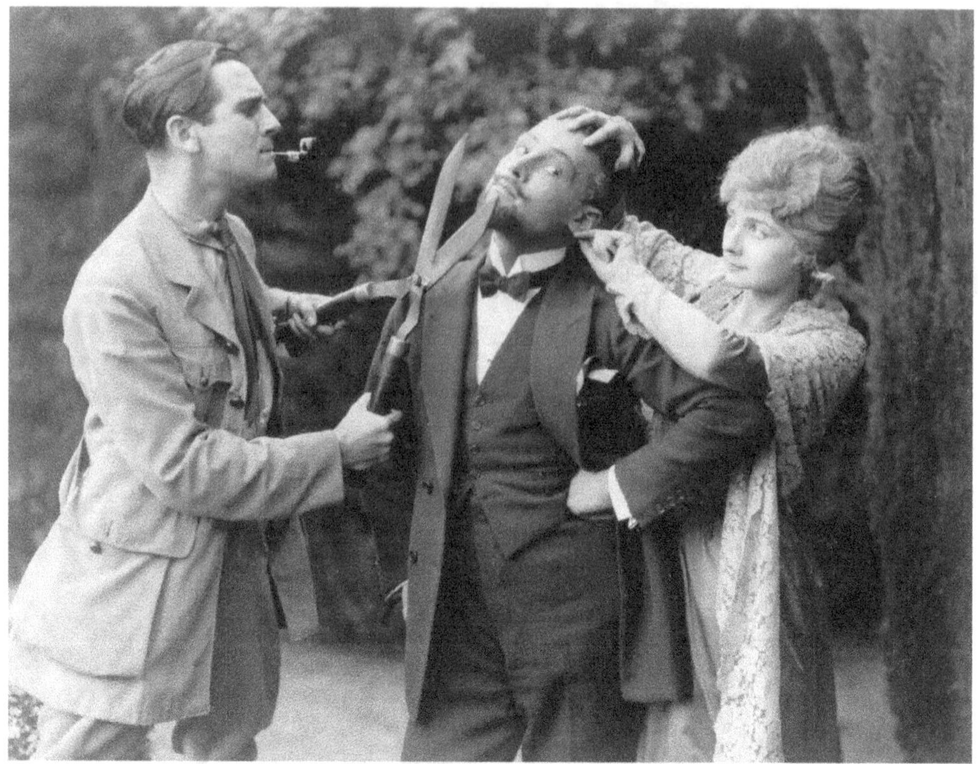

Next assigned to play again with Alice Terry under the direction of her now husband
Rex Ingram in *The Conquering Power*. (Margaret Herrick Library; Academy of Motion Picture Arts and Sciences)

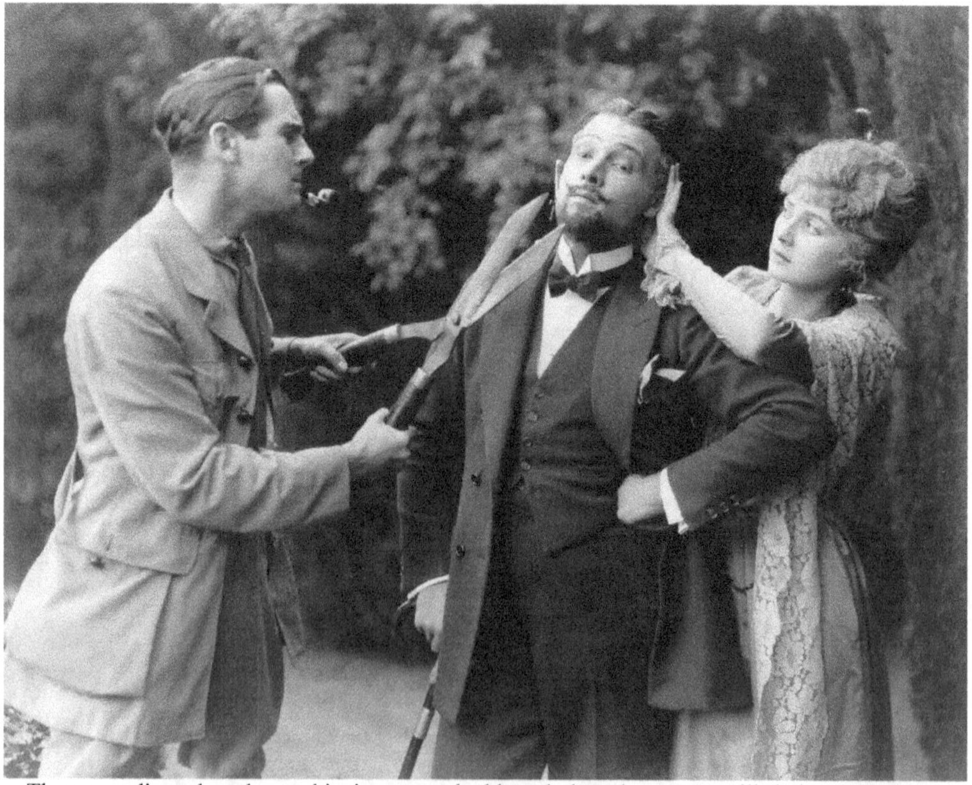

There was discord on the set this time around, although these humorous stills belay that notion.
(Margaret Herrick Library; Academy of Motion Picture Arts and Sciences)

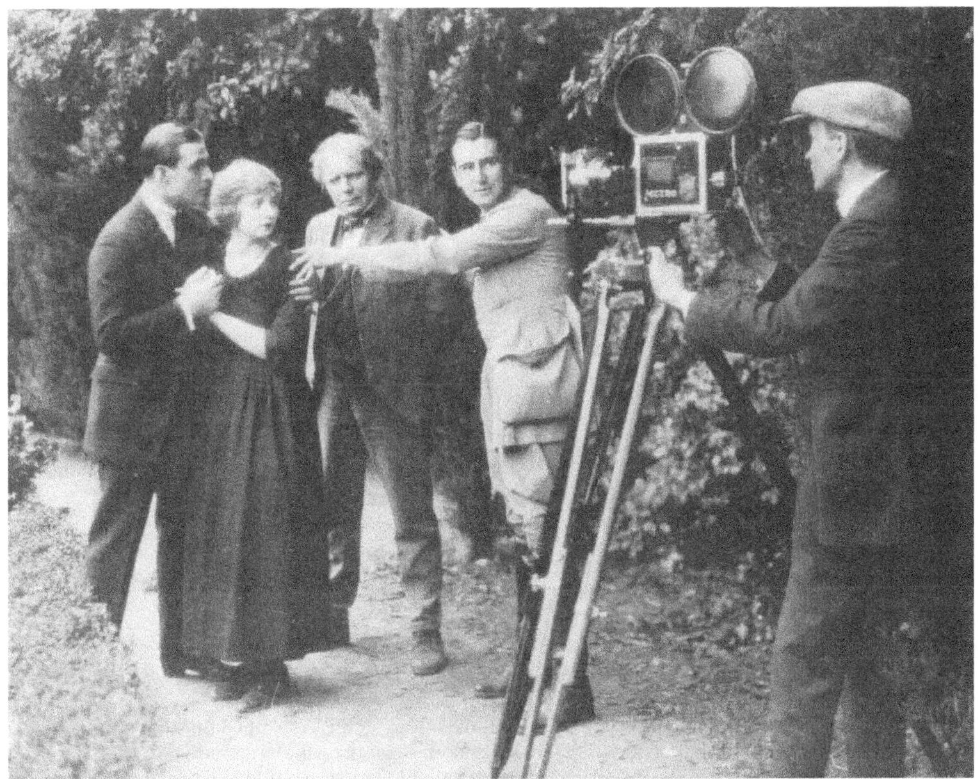

Rex Ingram directs Ralph Lewis, Alice Terry and Valentino while John Seitz mans the camera. (Kristen Burkhart collection)

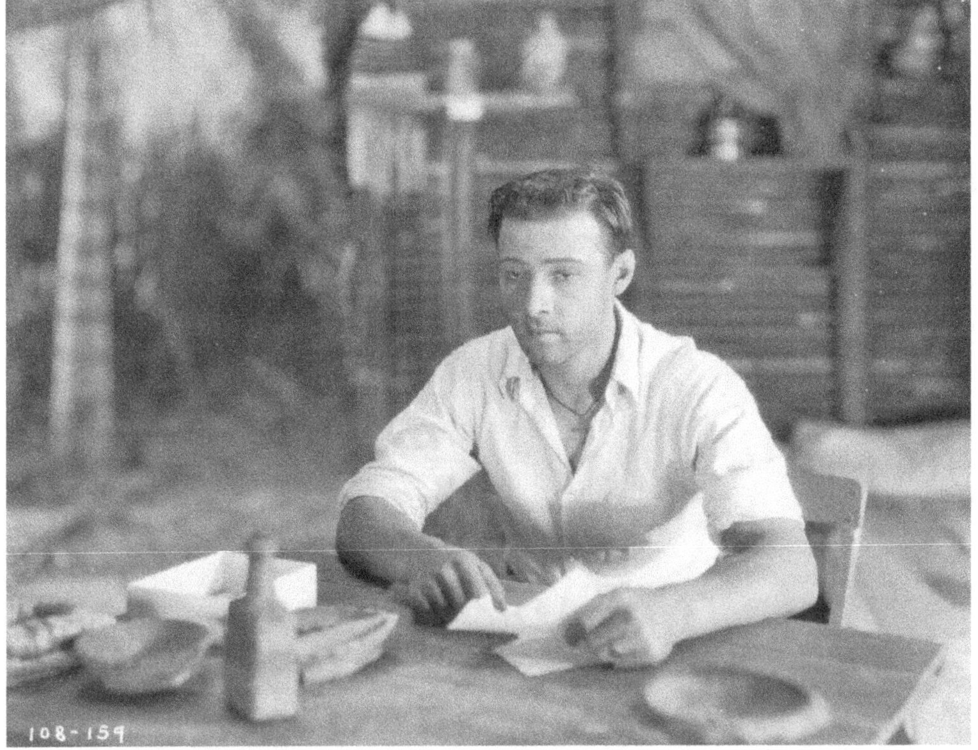

Valentino in a scene from *The Conquering Power*. (Author's collection)

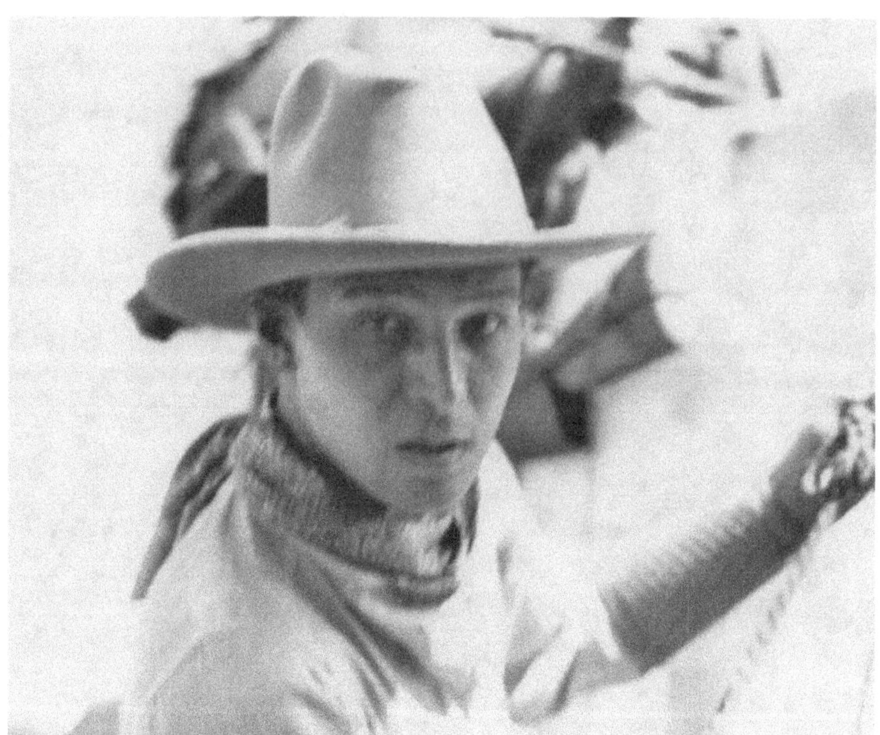

Valentino is caught by surprise by Paul Ivano's ever present camera.
Ivano, in his memoirs, recalled that Valentino enjoyed dressing up in cowboy gear
"… chaps and a Western hat and a handkershief (sic) around his neck."
(Francis Laccasin collection courtesy Flicker Alley and Lobster Films)

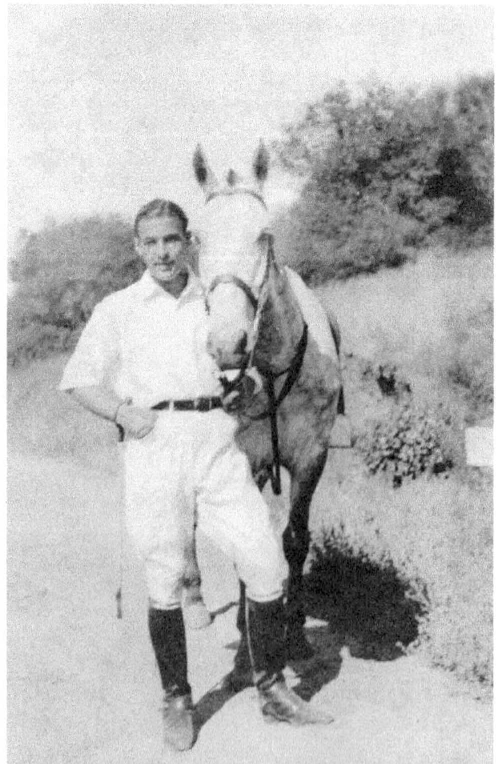

Valentino and horse posing for a snapshot *circa* 1920.
(Gloria Bowman collection)

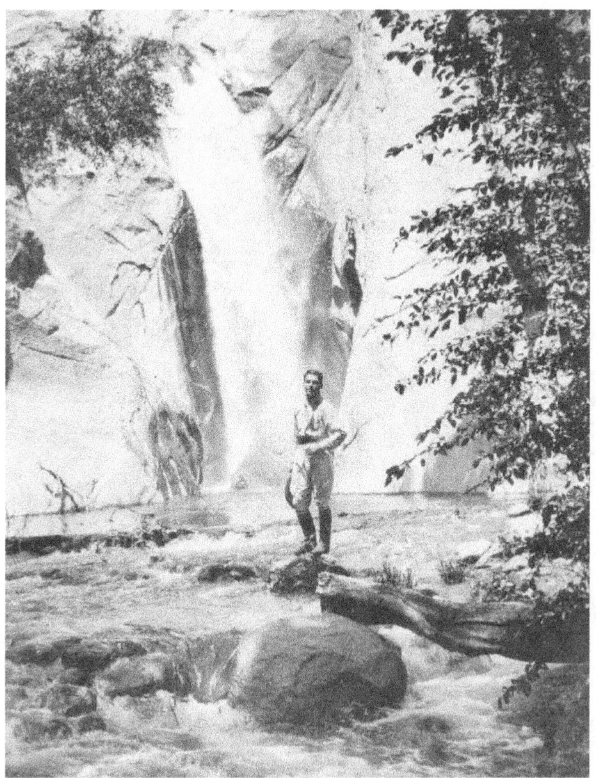

Posing in front of the Tahquitz Falls, Palm Springs.
(Tracy Terhune collection)

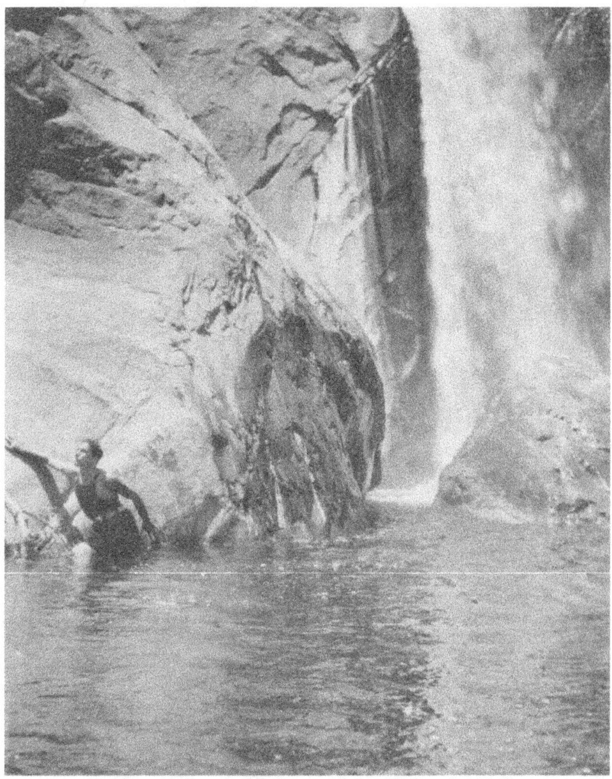

Taking a dip at the base of the Tahquitz Falls.
(Craig MacPherson collection)

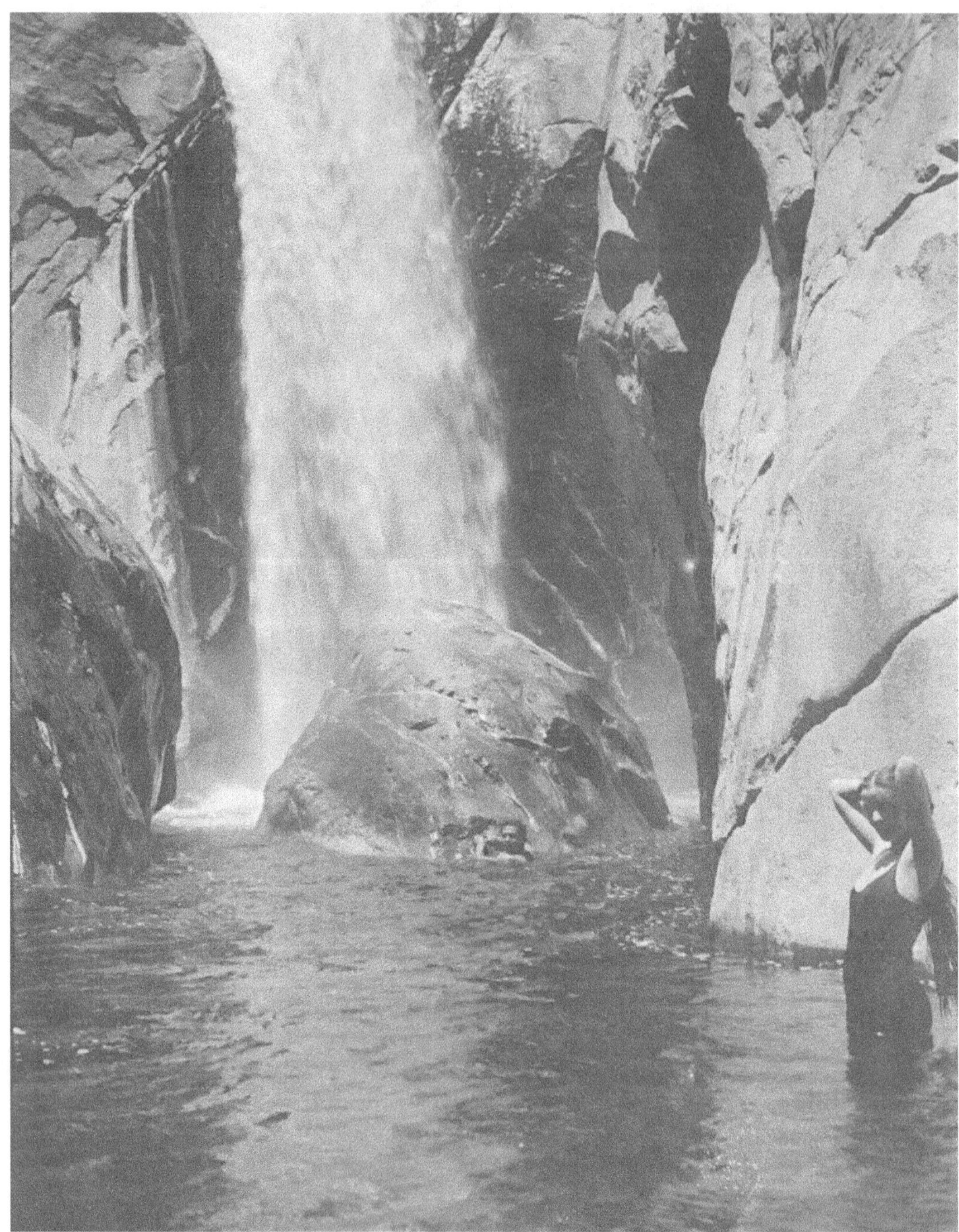

Natacha and Rudy enjoying a swim at the base of the Tahquitz Falls in Palm Springs.
Their friend Paul Ivano took this snapshot. (Valentino Family collection)

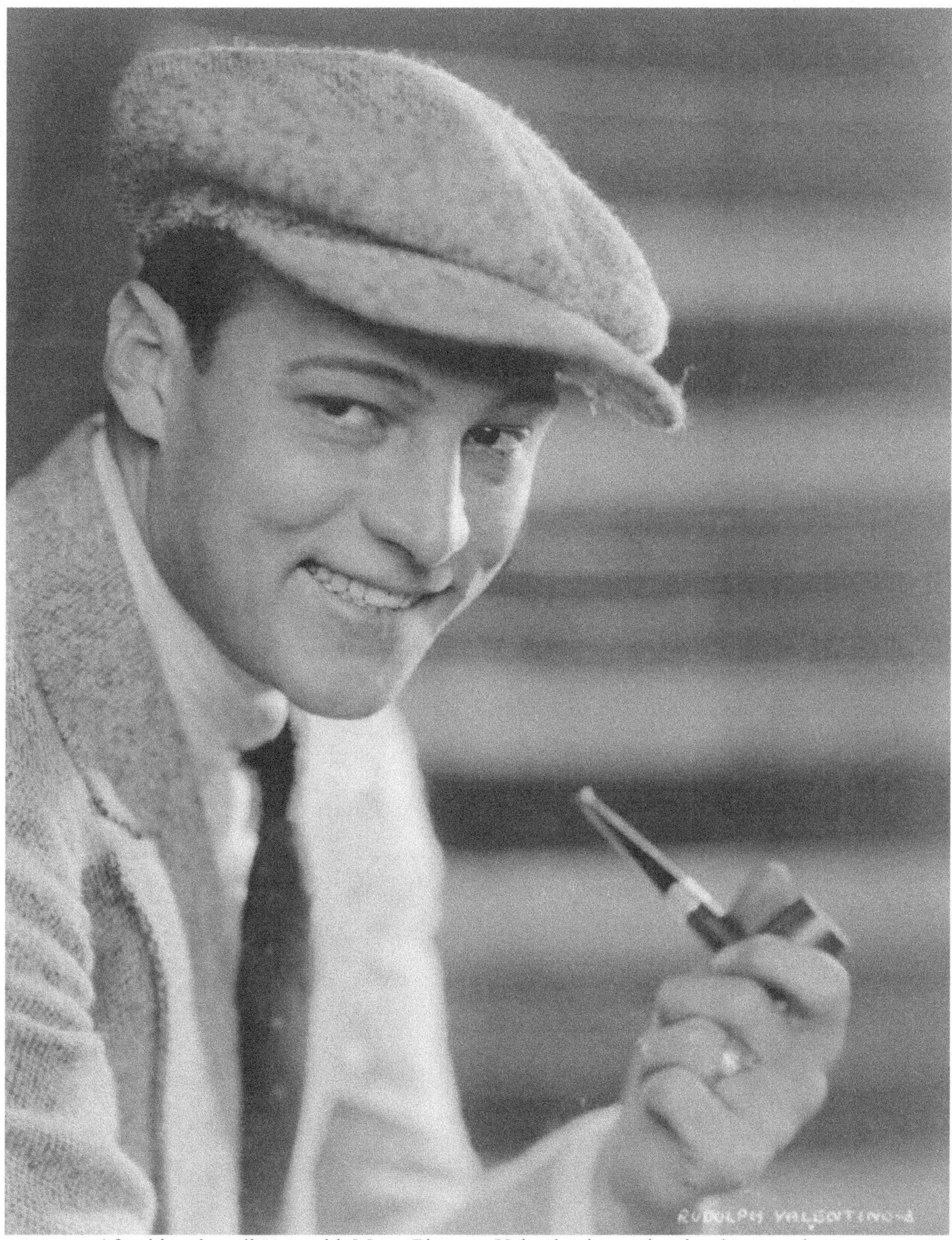

After his salary dispute with Metro Pictures, Valentino jumped at the chance and joined Famous Players Lasky to appear in the hottest and raciest picture of the year, *The Sheik.* (Author's collection)

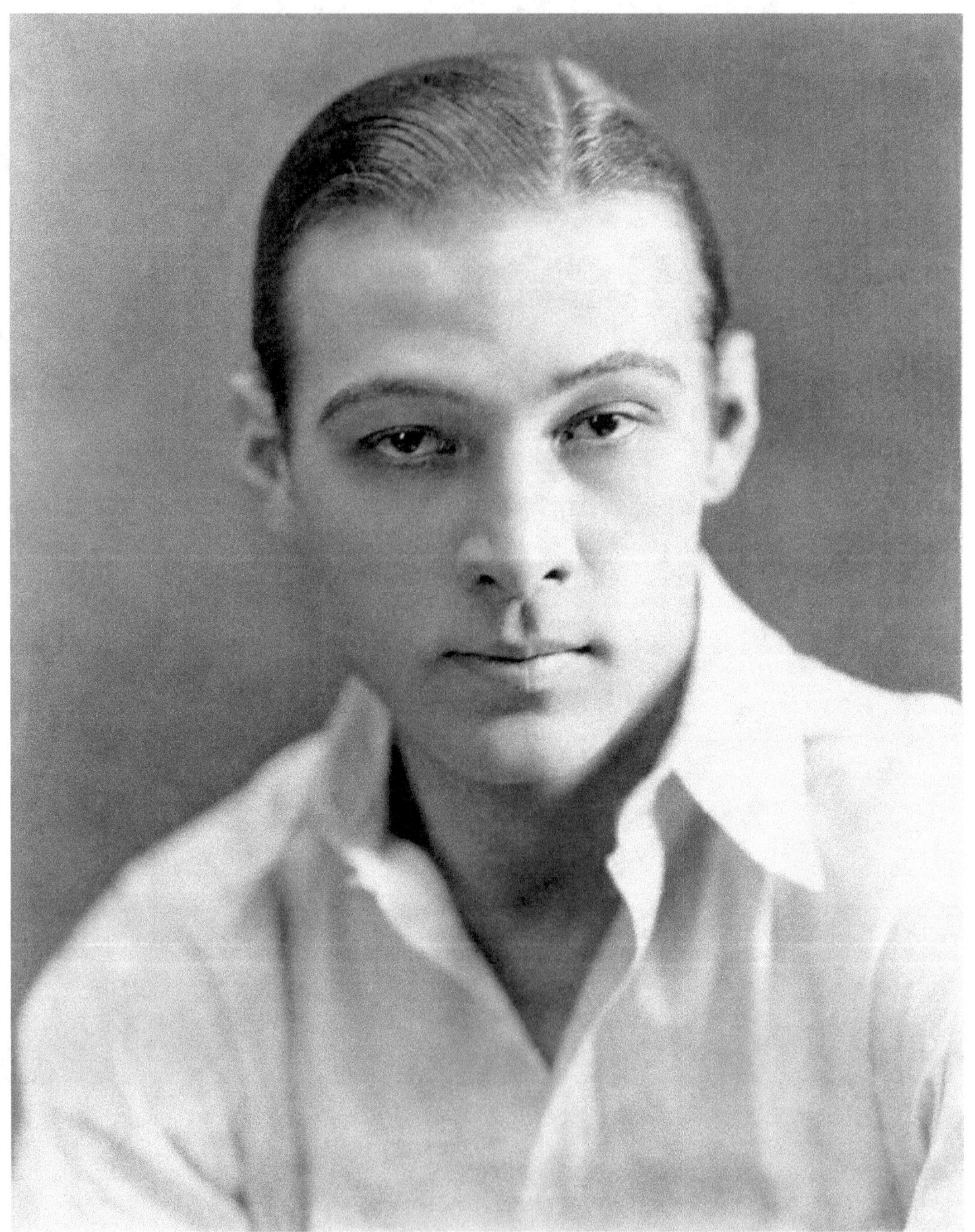

One of the first things the studio did was to send Valentino to the photographer's studio for a series of publicity portraits, anticipating the demand.
(Author's collection)

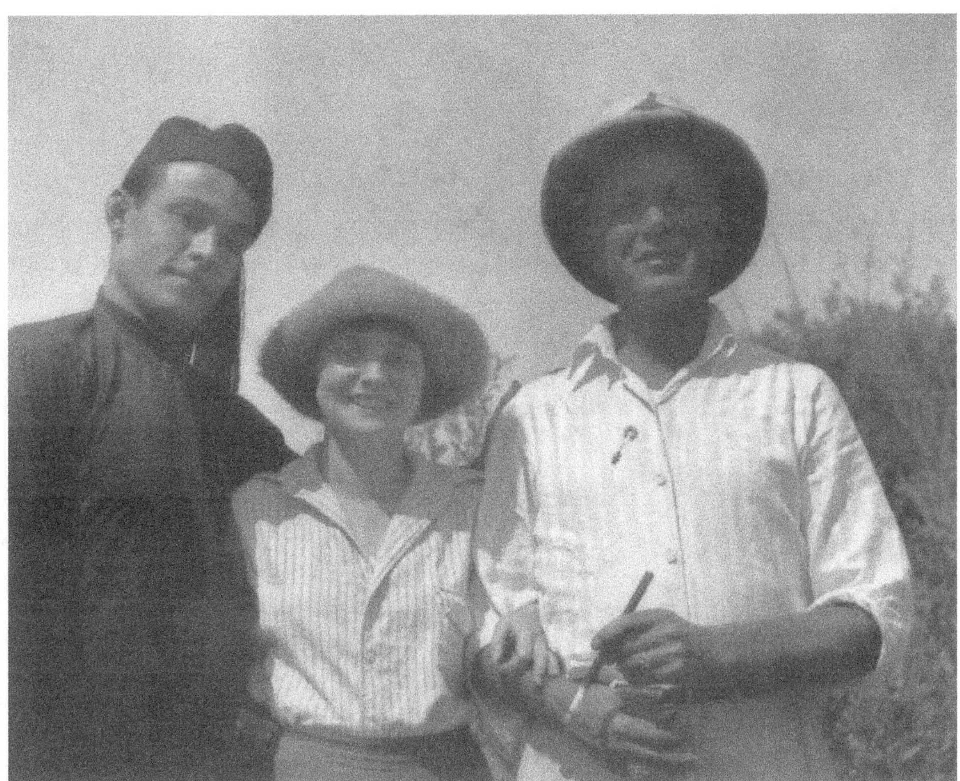

Shortly after signing his contract, Valentino was sent on location to start filming. Here he is with Agnes Ayres and director George Melford.

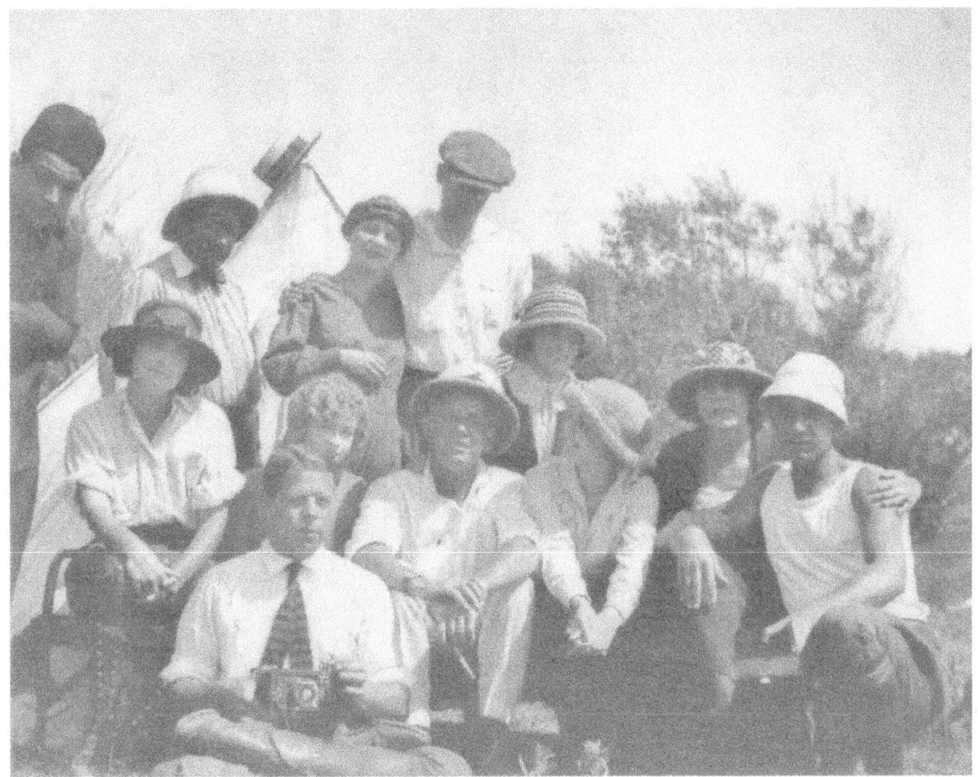

The camaraderie of cast and crew was evident as they bonded on location. (Francis Laccasin collection courtesy Flicker Alley and Lobster Films)

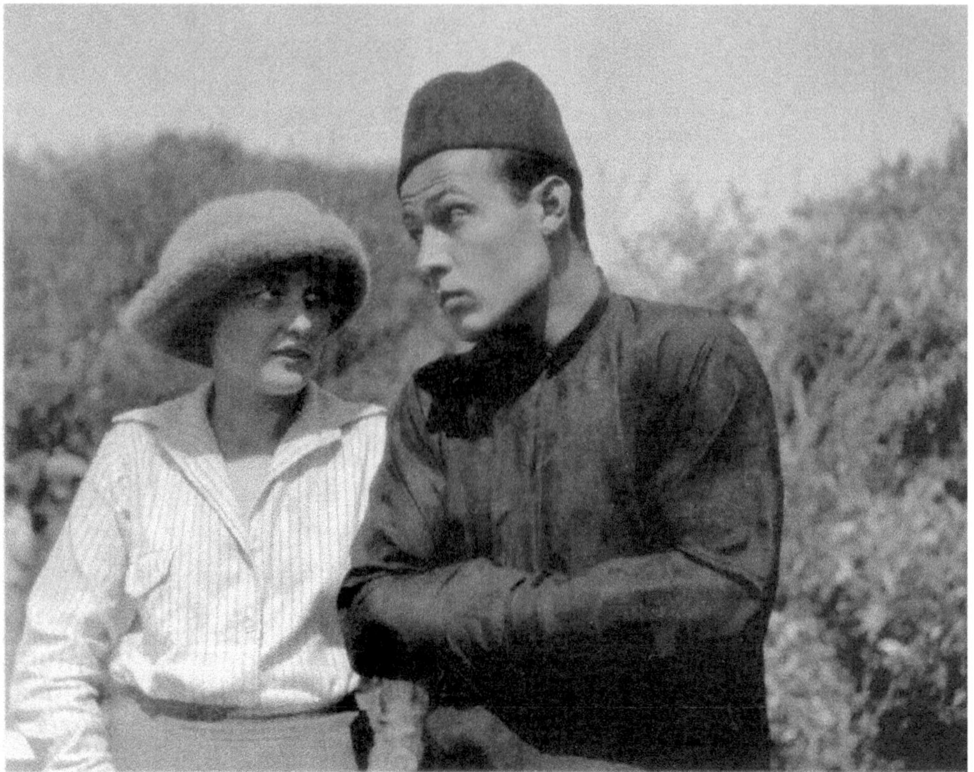

Clowning with a dubious Agnes Ayres. Valentino is able to indulge in silk pajamas.
(Francis Laccasin collection courtesy Flicker Alley and Lobster Films)

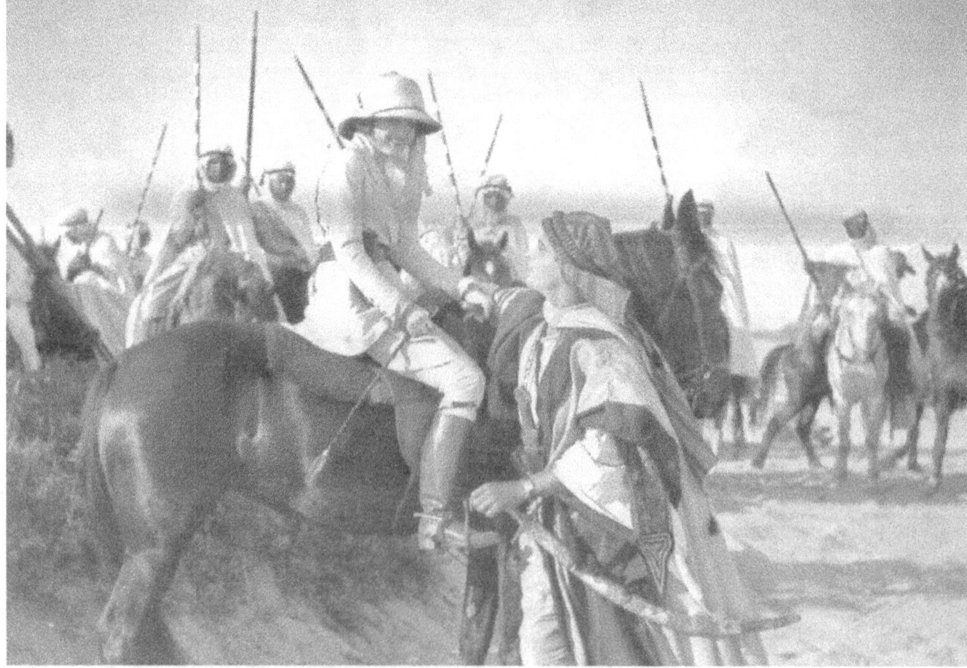

The co-stars enjoying a chat during filming of the famous abduction sequence in *The Sheik.*
(Francis Laccasin collection courtesy Flicker Alley and Lobster Films)

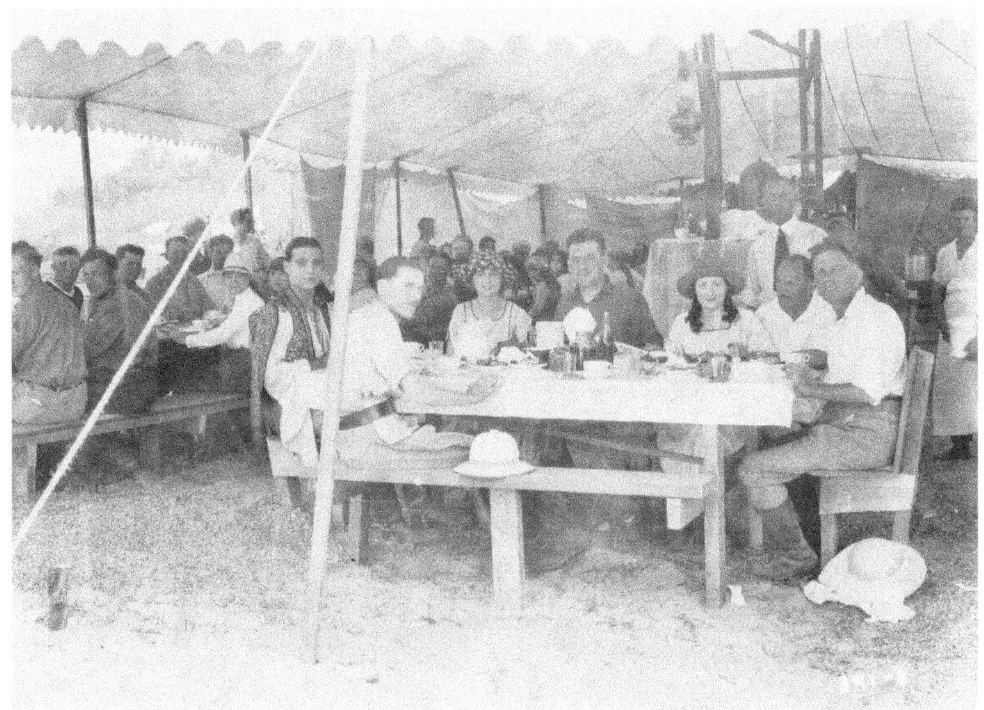

Cast and crew in the mess tent on location. (L-R) Valentino, Rudolph Bylek in the foreground, Agnes Ayres, Water Long, unknown , unknown, and George Melford.
(Author's collection)

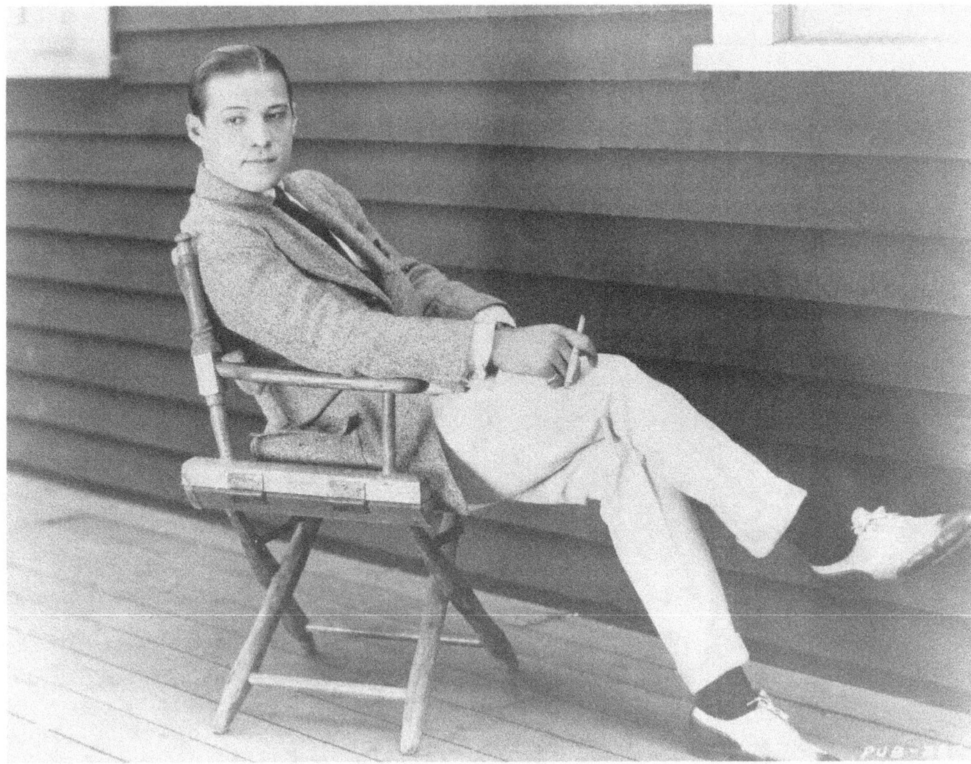

An immaculate dresser in private life, Valentino posing for publicity during filming of *The Sheik*.
(Author's collection)

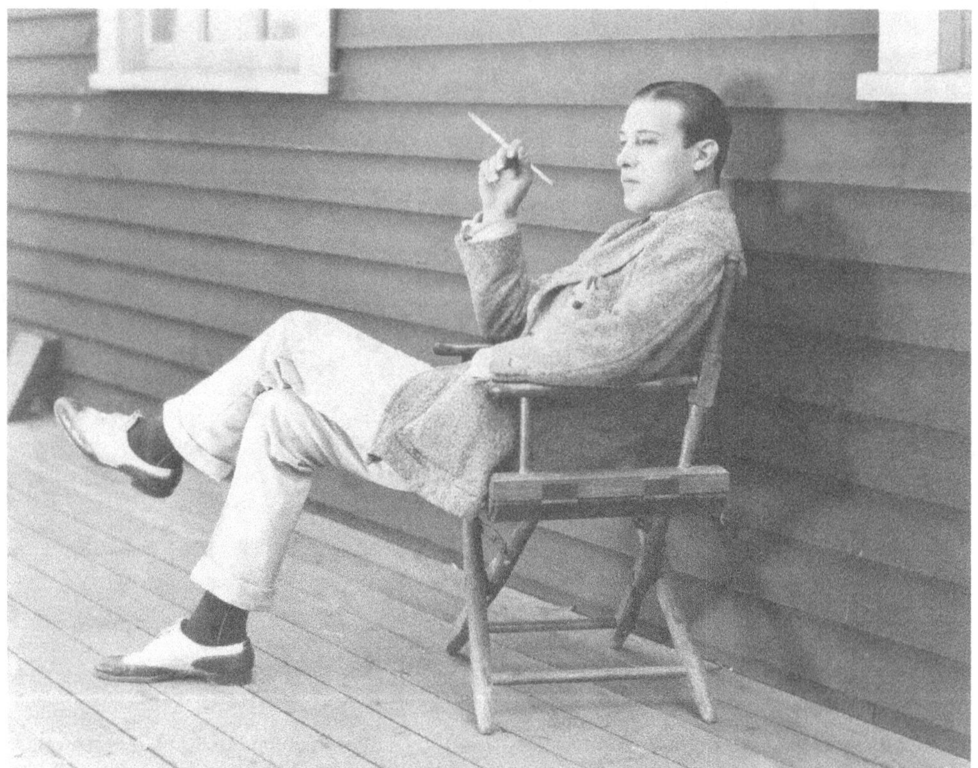

Another pose on the backlot casual elegance. (Author's collection)

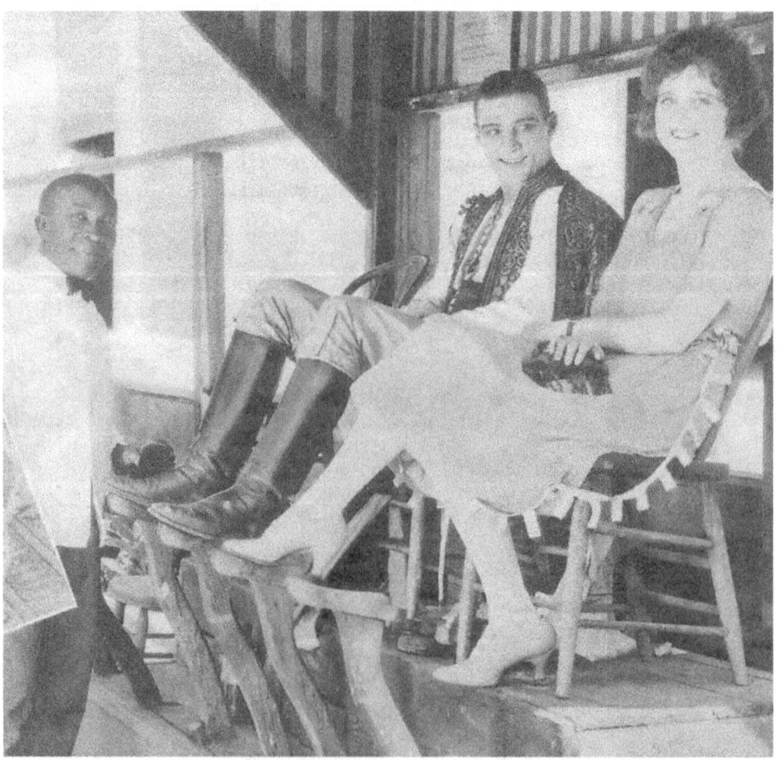

Valentino and Agnes Ayres getting a shoeshine from Oscar Smith.
Oscar, the bootblack for Lasky Studios was as famous at the stars he served.
He also appeared in small parts in films as needed. (Author's collection)

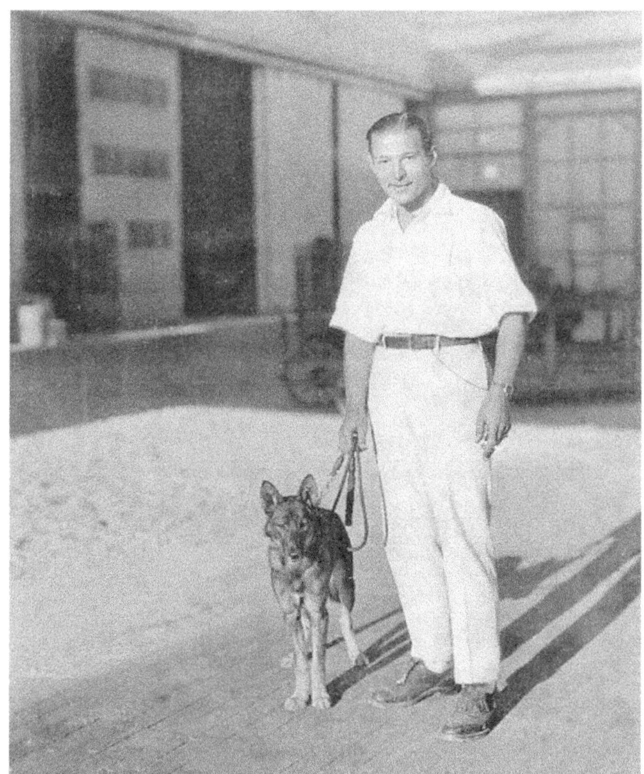

Taking Sheik for a walk around the studio. (Author's collection)

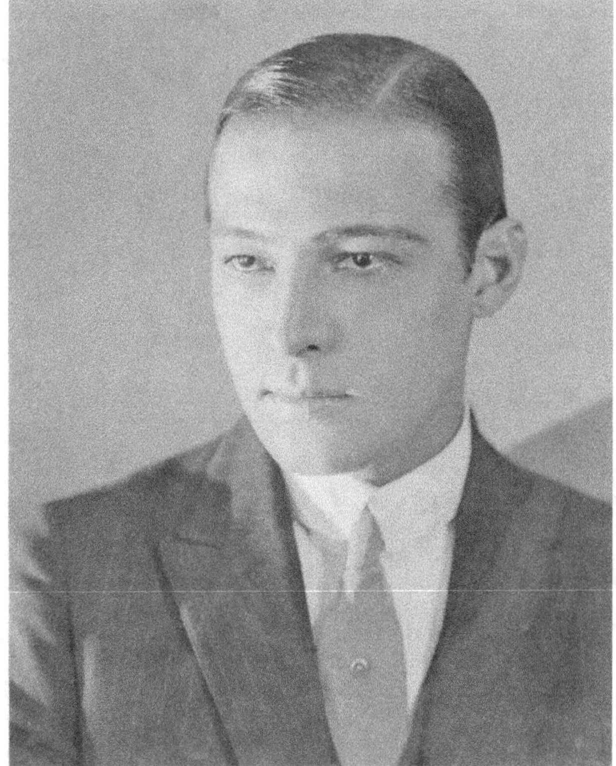

Valentino circa 1921, portrait by Donald Biddle Keyes.
(Author's collection)

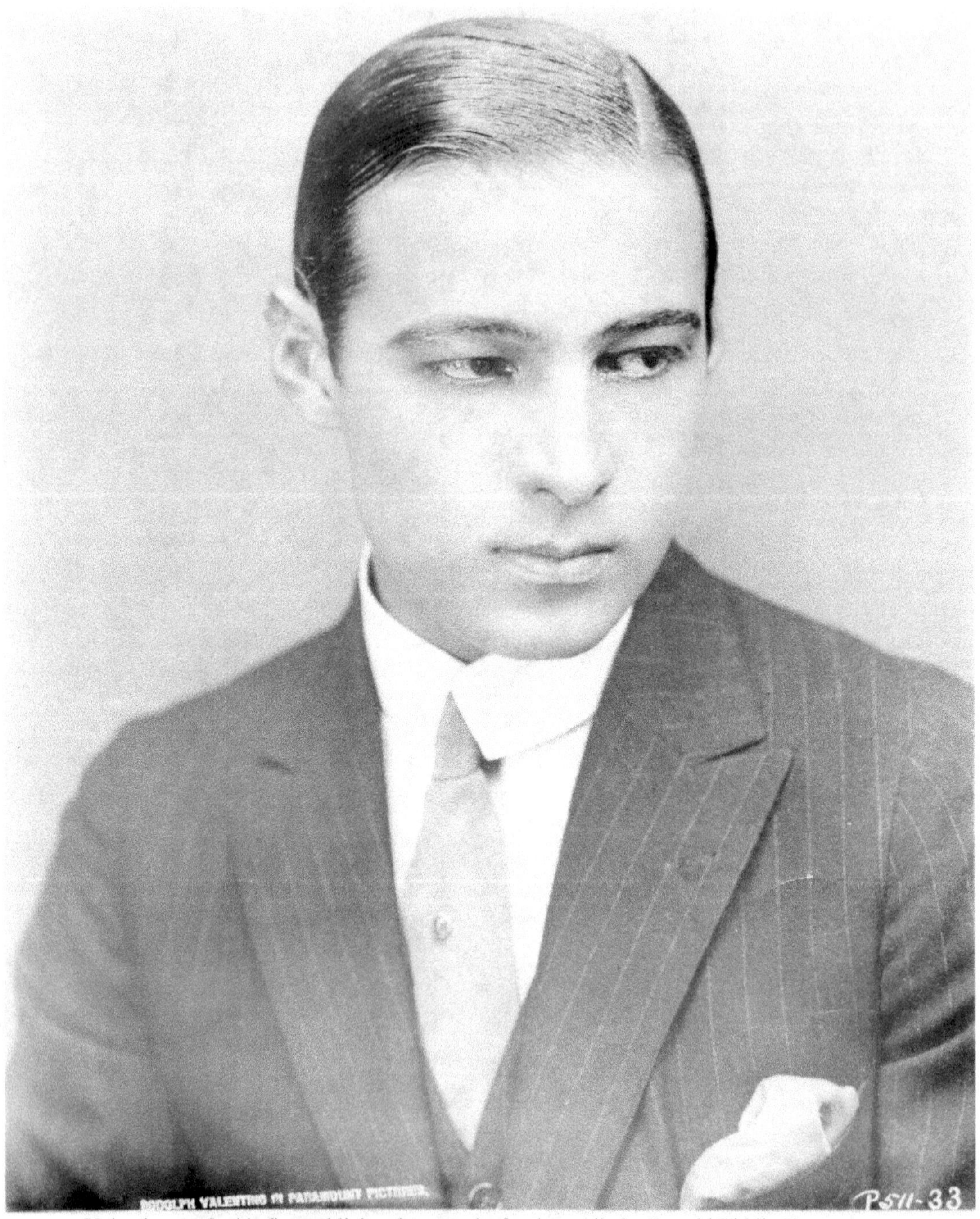

Valentino sat for his first publicity photographs for the studio by Donald Biddle Keyes.
Keyes captured in Valentino a sense of shyness and vulnerability.
(Author's collection)

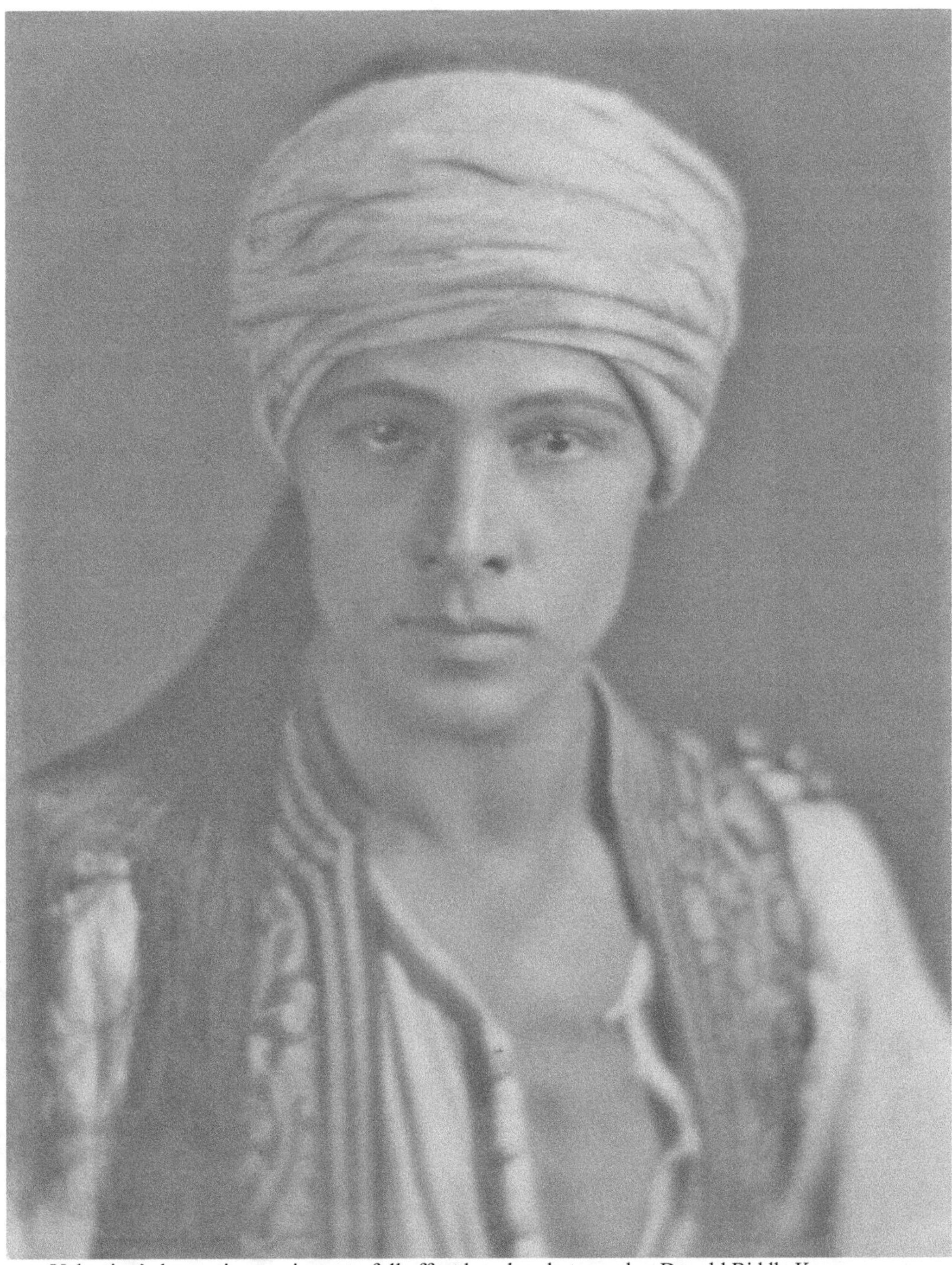

Valentino's hypnotic gaze is put to full effect here by photographer Donald Biddle Keyes. (Author's collection).

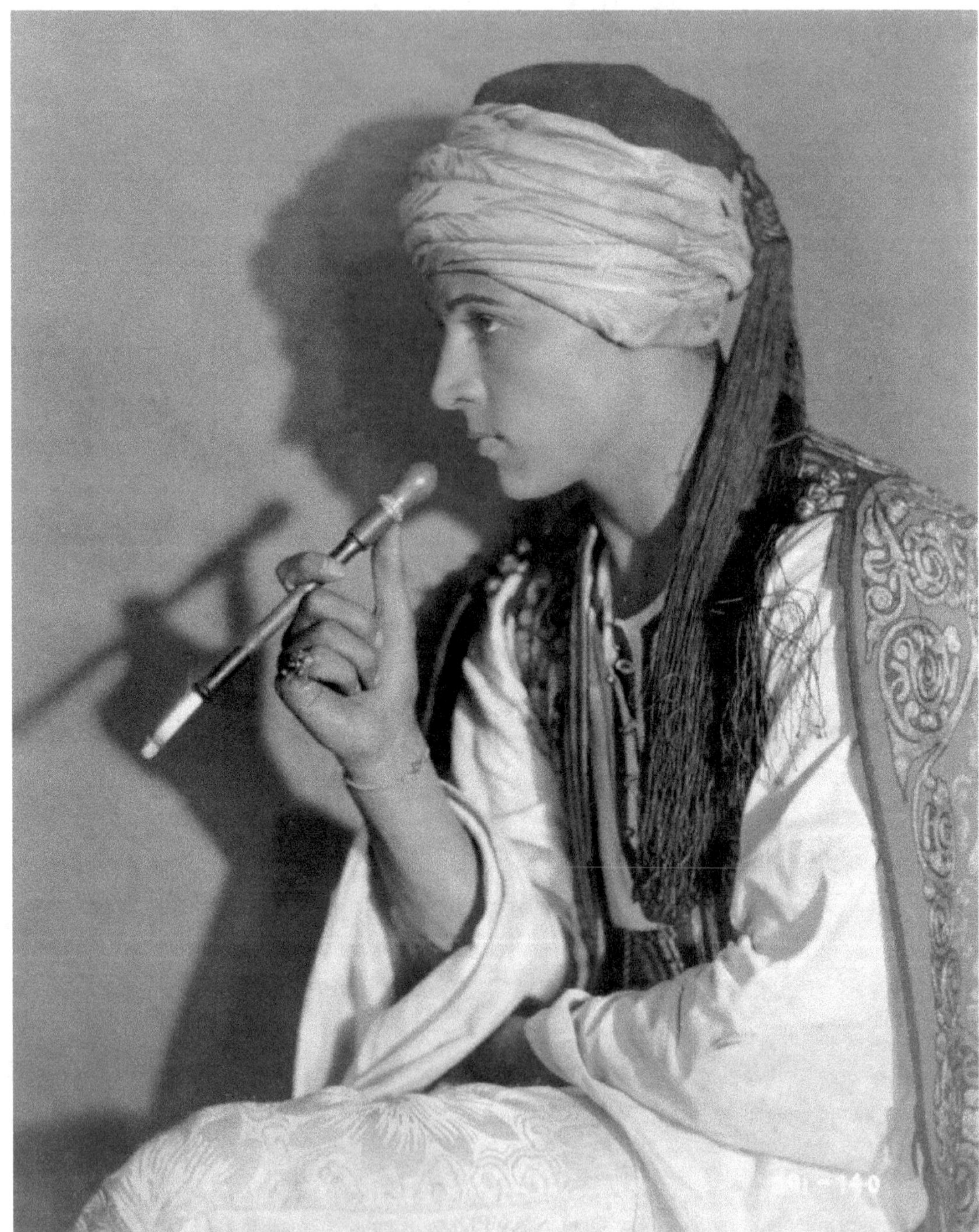

This portrait shows off the beautiful silken fabrics Valentino wore in his role as *The Sheik*. (Author's collection)

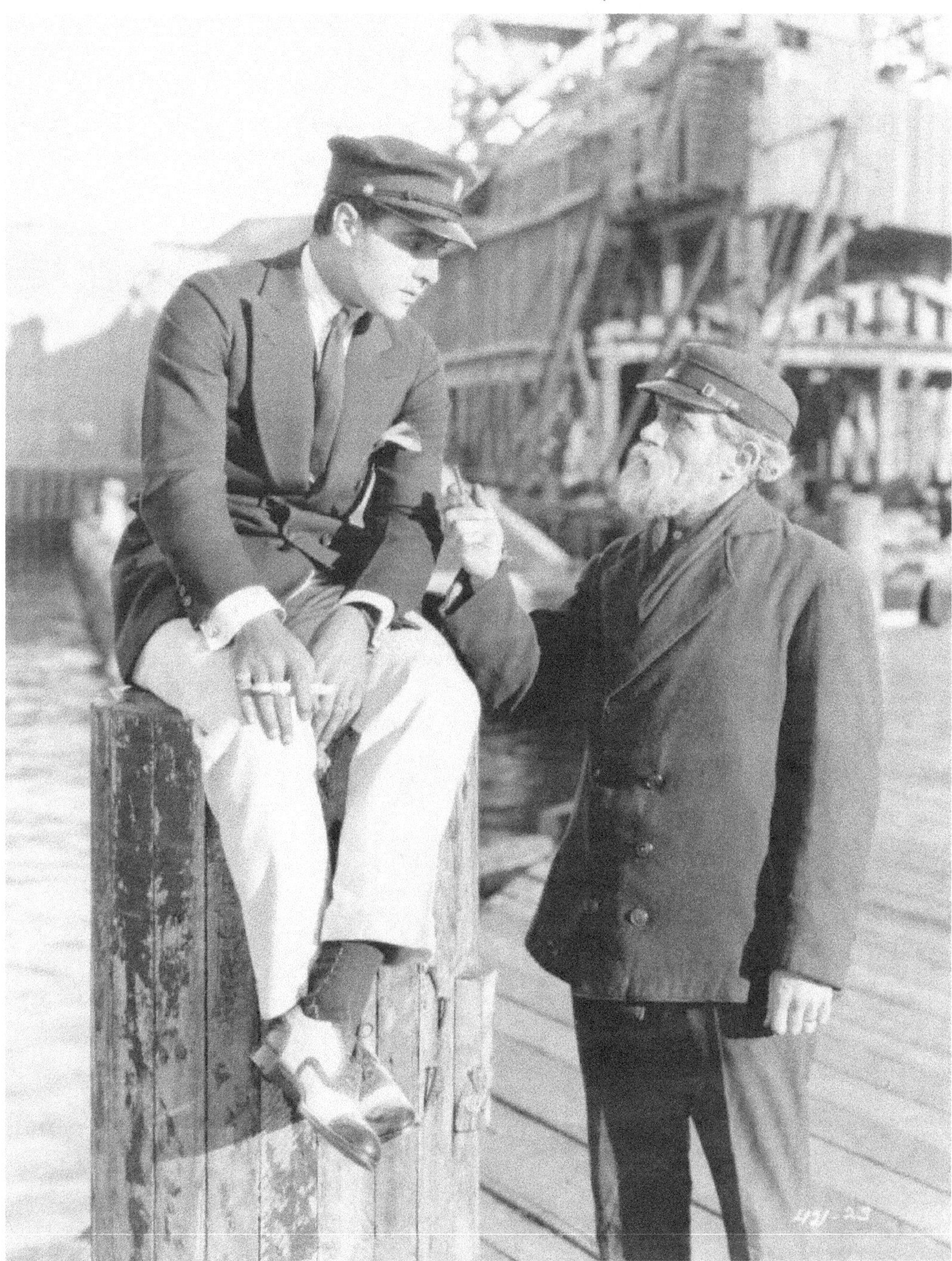

Valentino traveled to San Francisco for location shooting on his next film, *Moran of the Lady Letty*. (Author's collection)

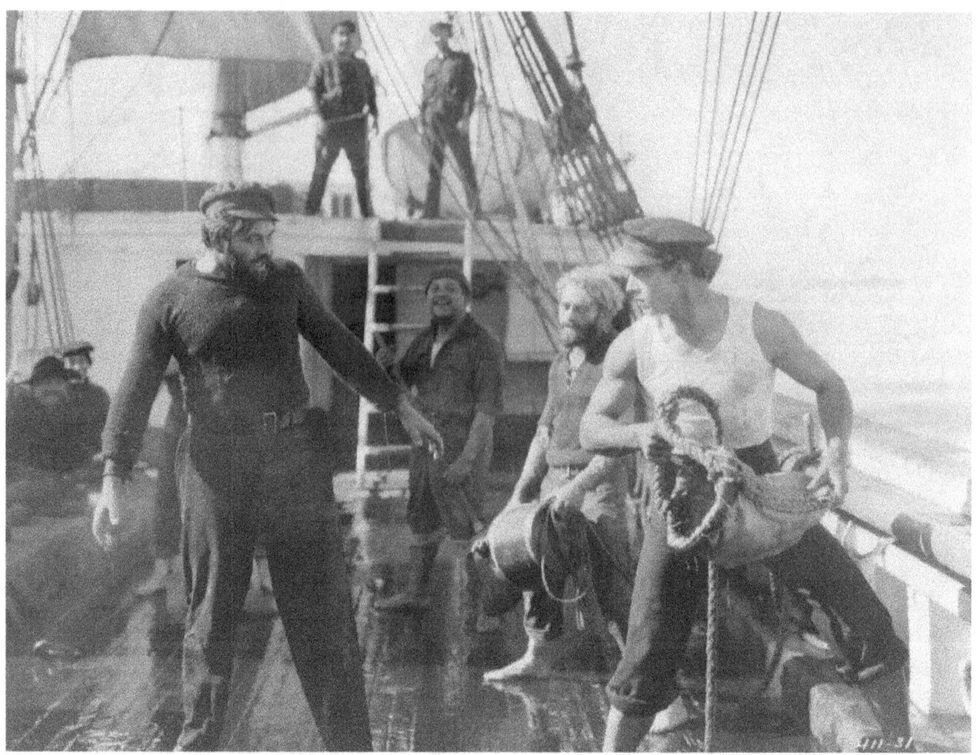

Valentino played another exotic type somewhat closer to home, Ramon Laredo.
He got a chance to wear street clothes and show off his muscular form. (Author's collection)

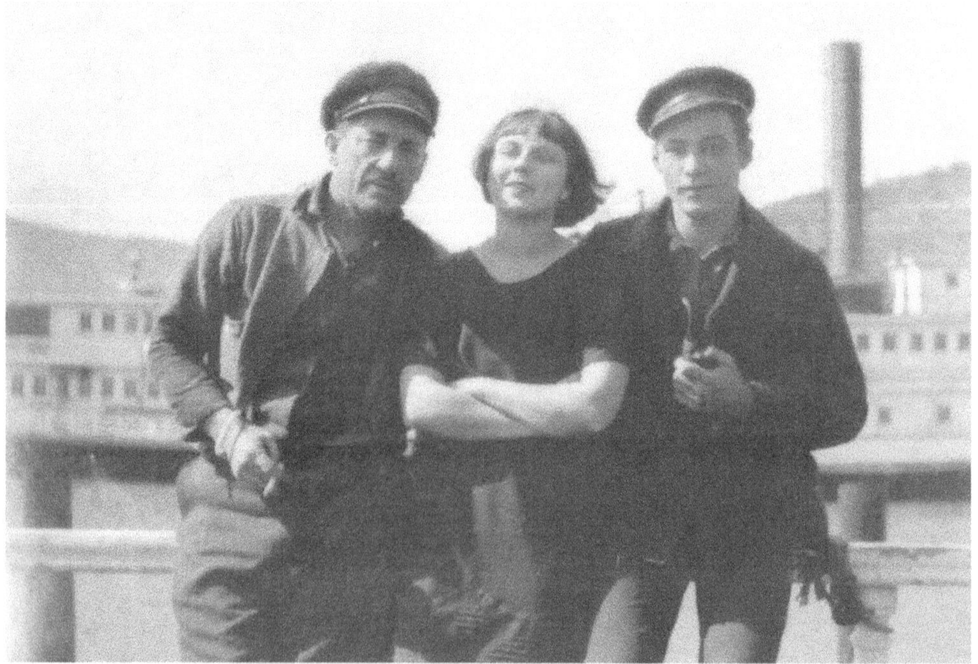

Walter Long, Dorothy Dalton and Valentino on location in San Francisco.
(Francis Laccasin collection courtesy Flicker Alley and Lobster Films)

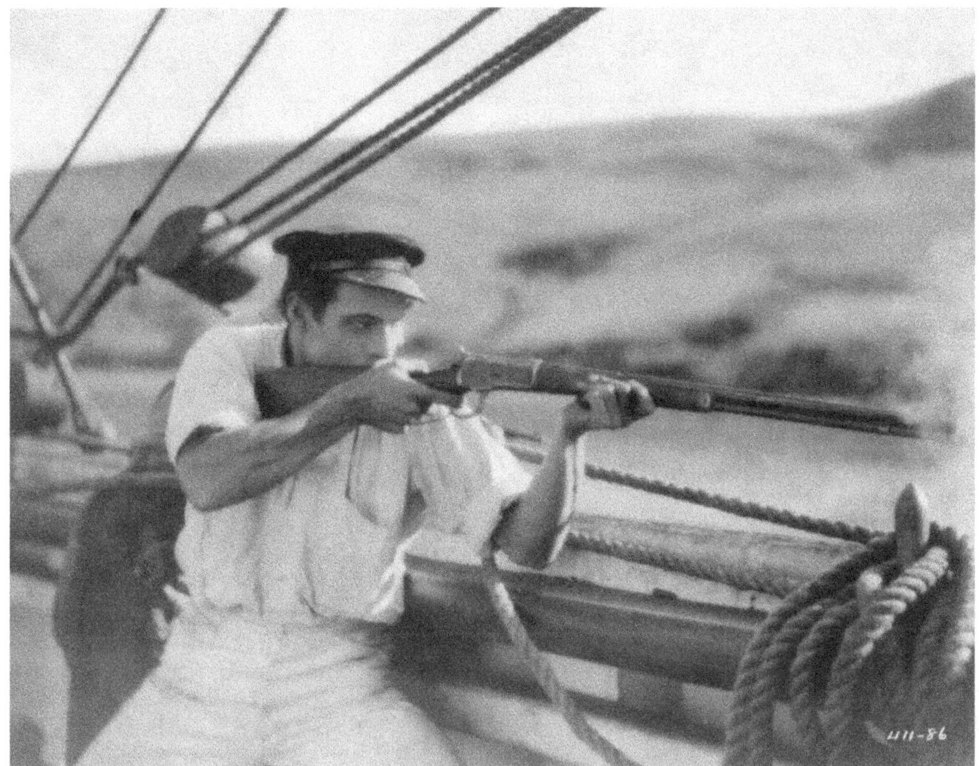

Valentino relished the action in the film. (Author's collection)

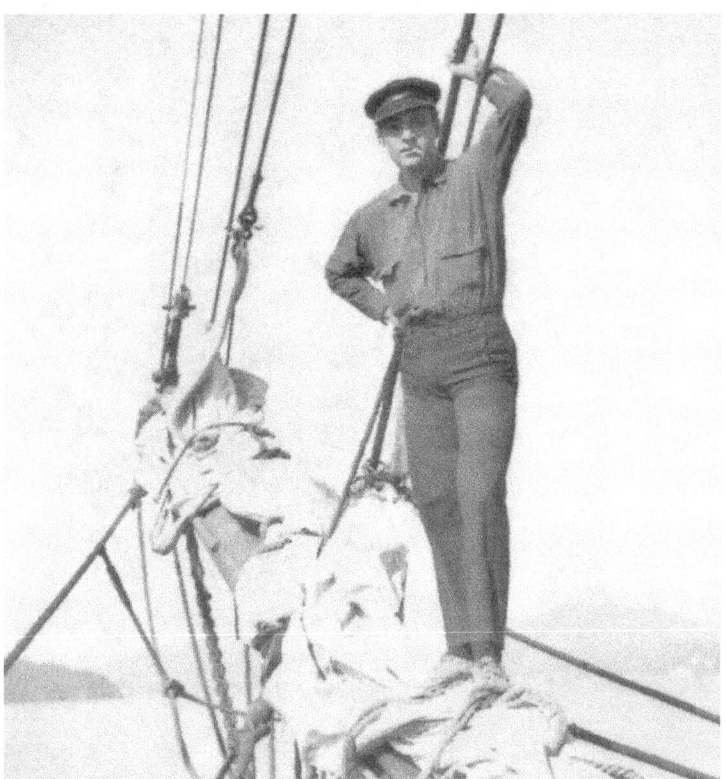

Valentino relaxing for Paul Ivano's camera on San Francisco Bay
filming *Moran of the Lady Letty*.
(Francis Laccasin collection courtesy Flicker Alley and Lobster Films)

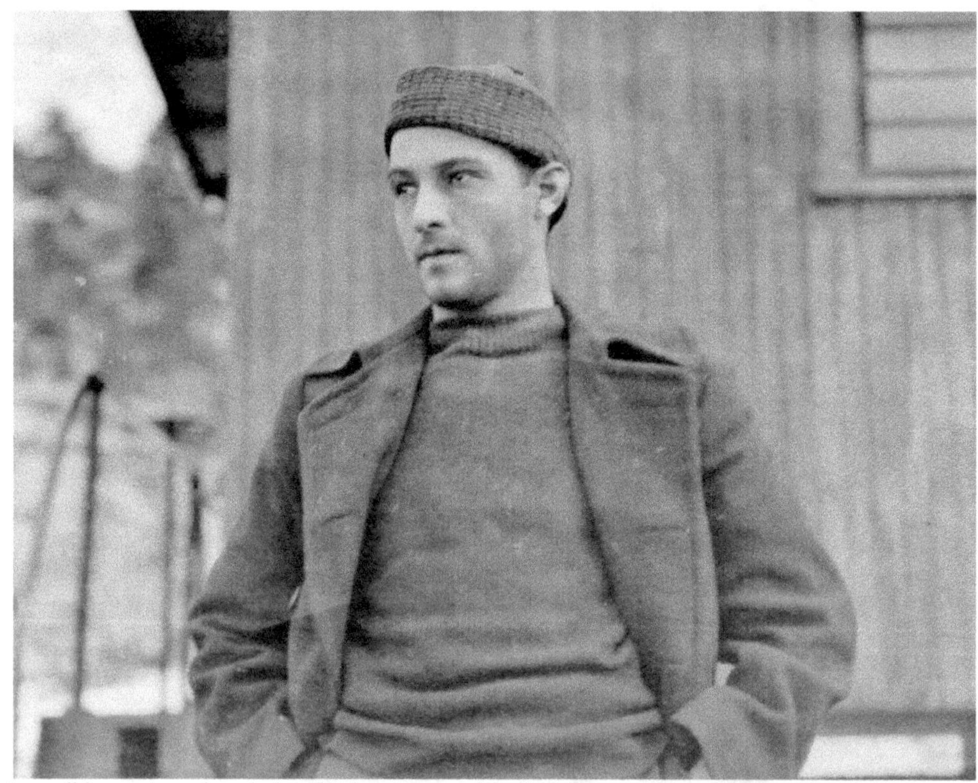

A candid snapshot taken during filming *Moran of the Lady Letty*. (Kristen Burkhardt collection)

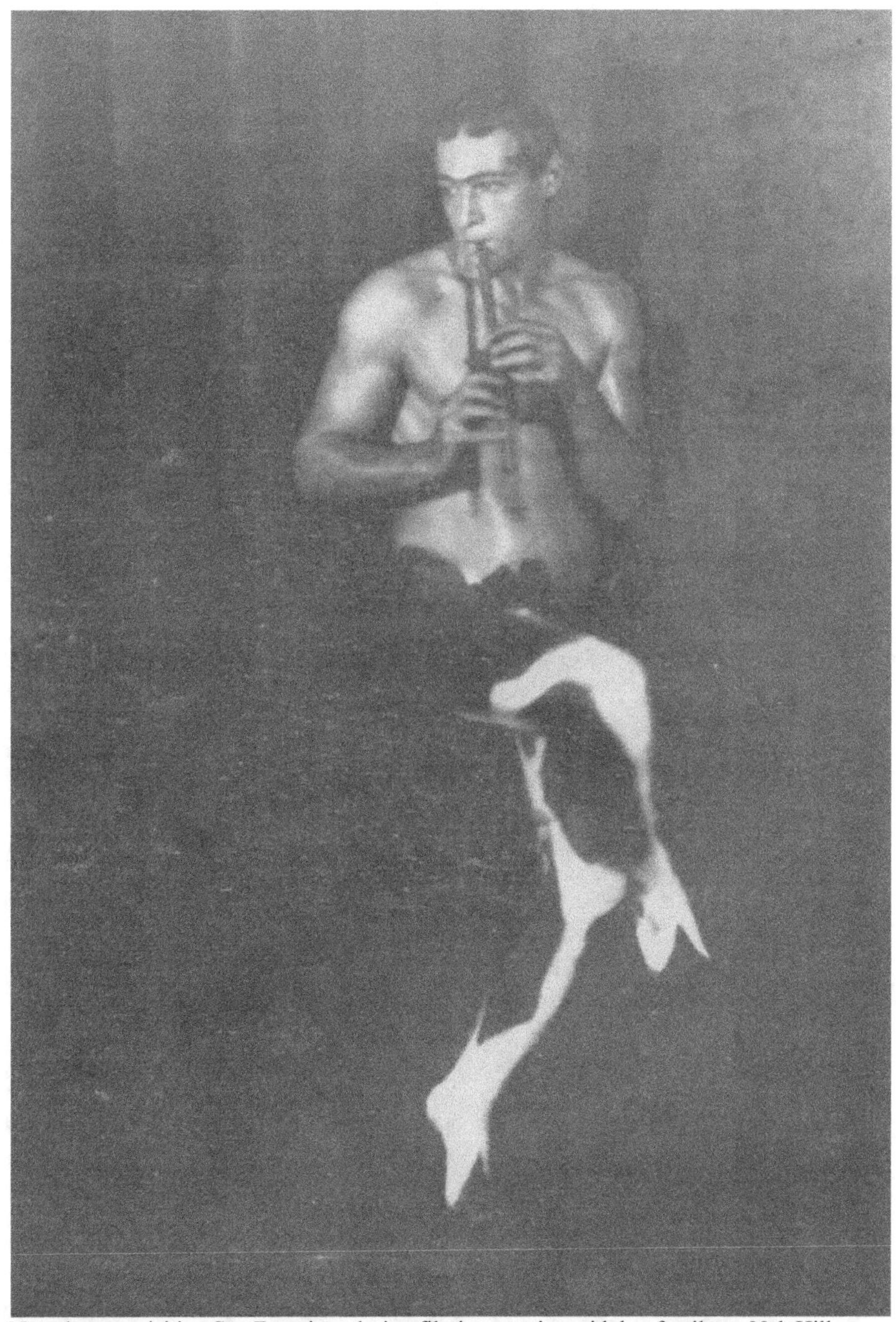

Natacha was visiting San Francisco during filming, staying with her family on Nob Hill. During her visit, she persuaded Valentino to pose for local photographer Helen MacGregor. (Author's collection)

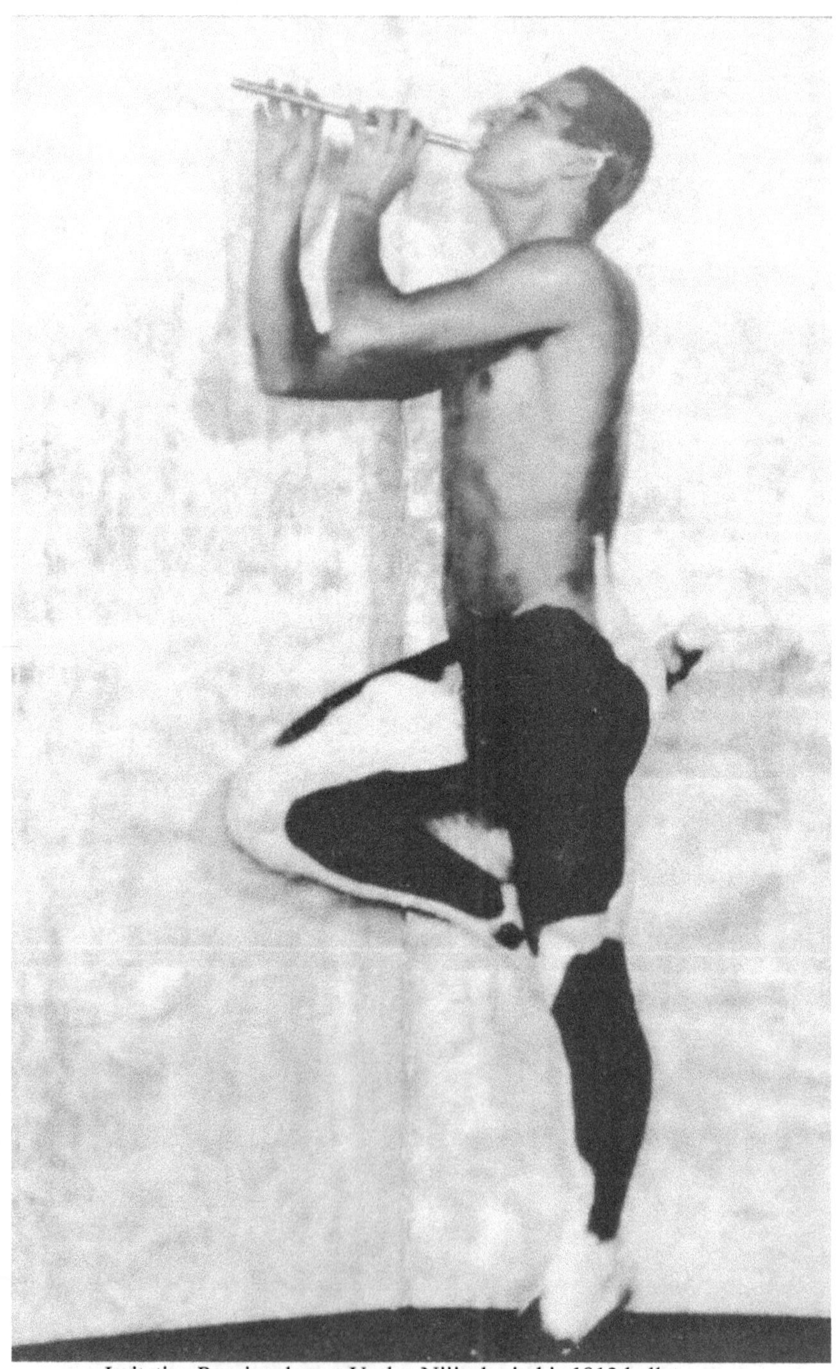

Imitating Russian dancer Vaslav Nijinsky in his 1913 ballet
L'après-midi d'un faune. Wearing little more than grease paint and
a loincloth these scandalous photos would soon come back to haunt him.
(Margaret Herrick Library; Academy of Motion Picture Arts and Sciences)

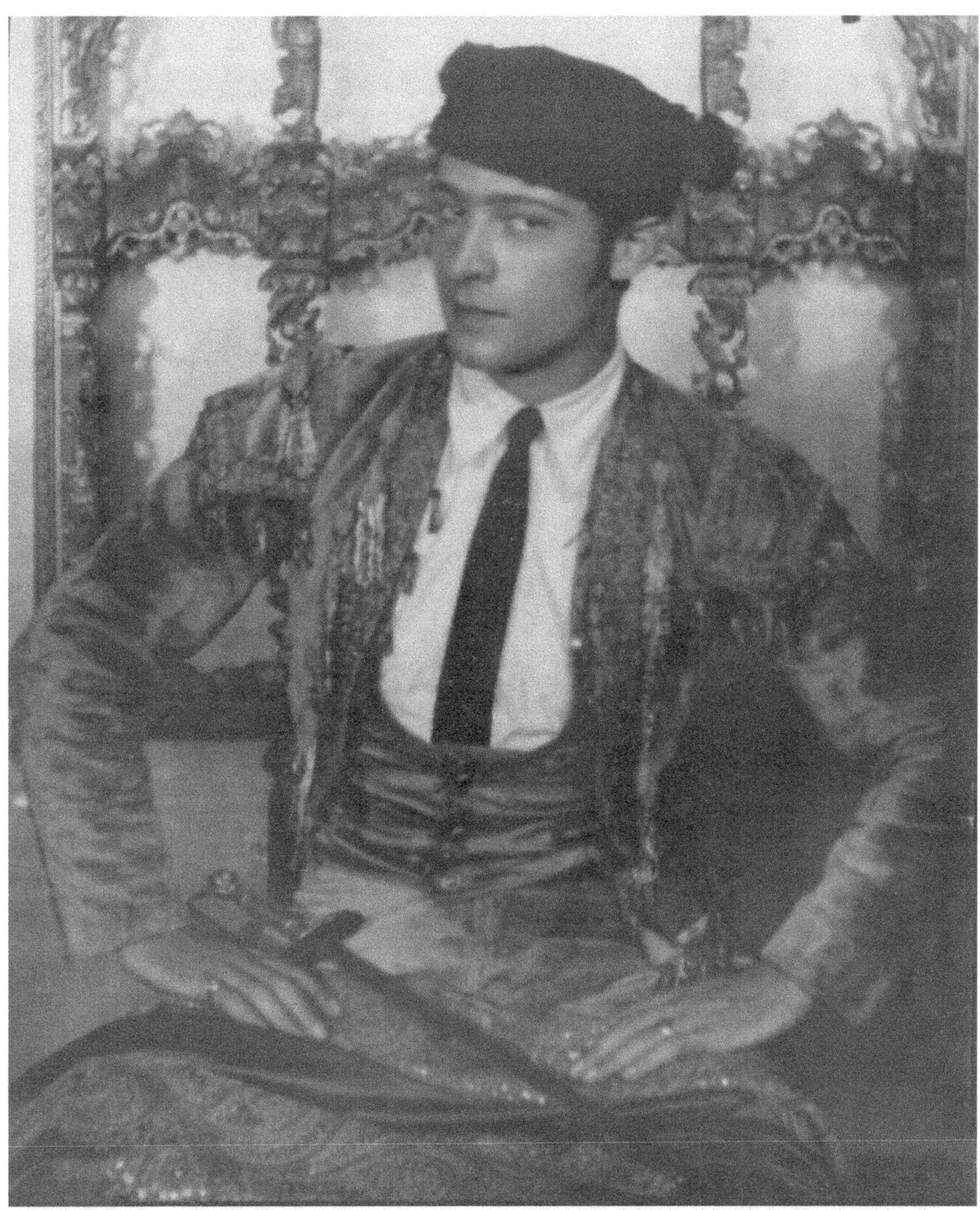

Valentino also posed for MacGregor's lens in costume as a toreador anticipating his role in *Blood and Sand.* Valentino was looking forward to his role and working with June Mathis once again. (Independent Visions collection)

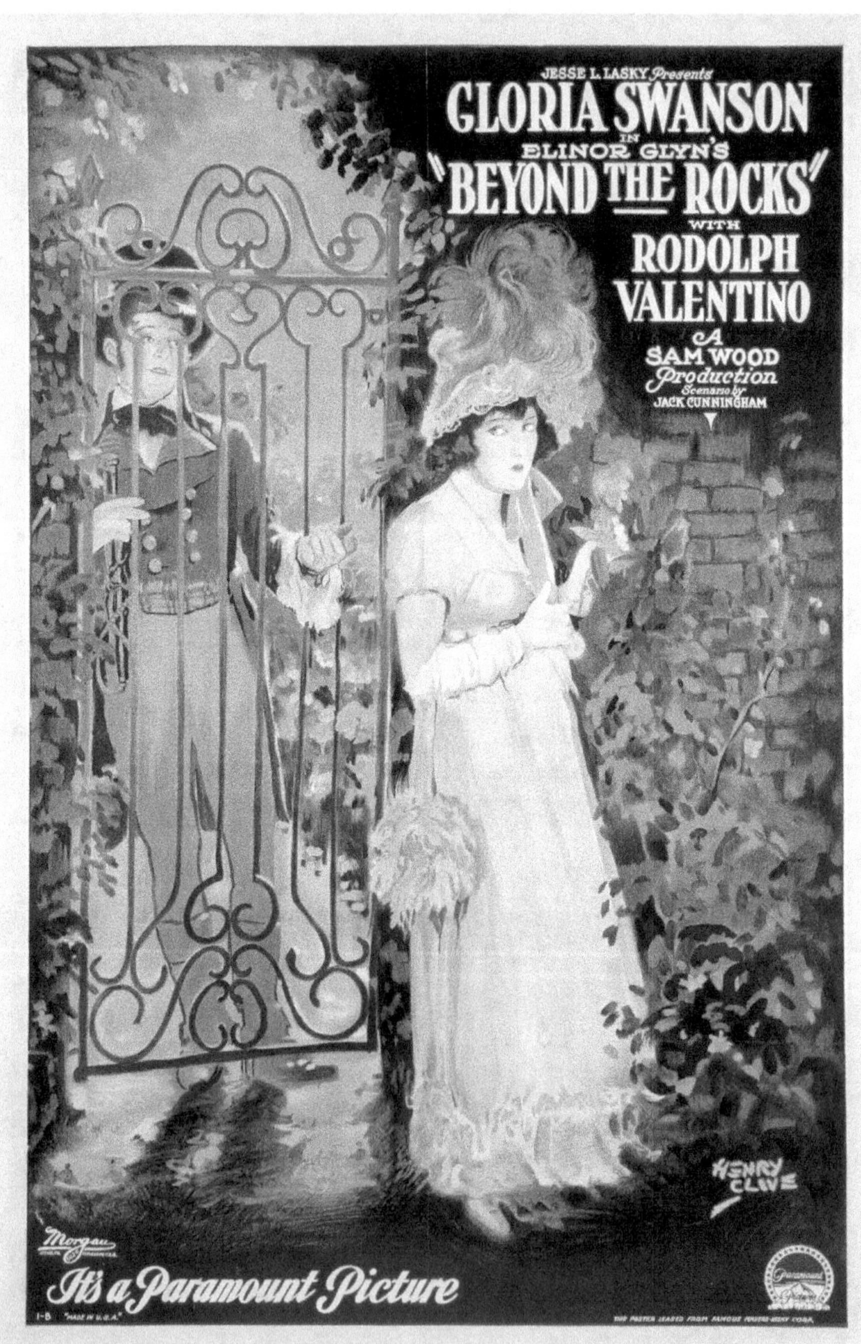

Beyond the Rocks was the last film in which Valentino was billed as a featured player. (Courtesy Milestone Films)

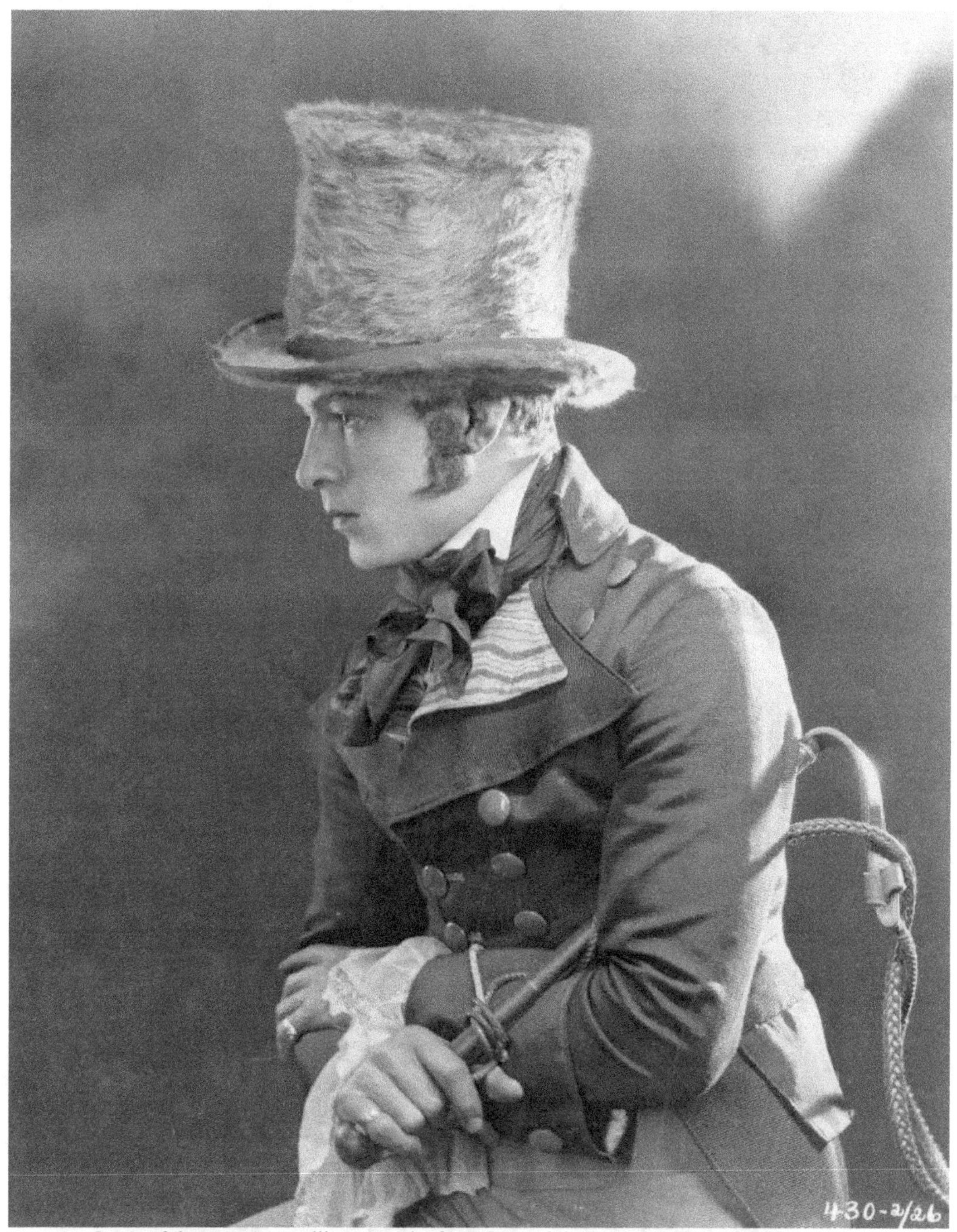

Some of the most compelling portraits from *Beyond the Rocks* are Valentino in the fantasy/flashback sequences as a highwayman. (Author's collection)

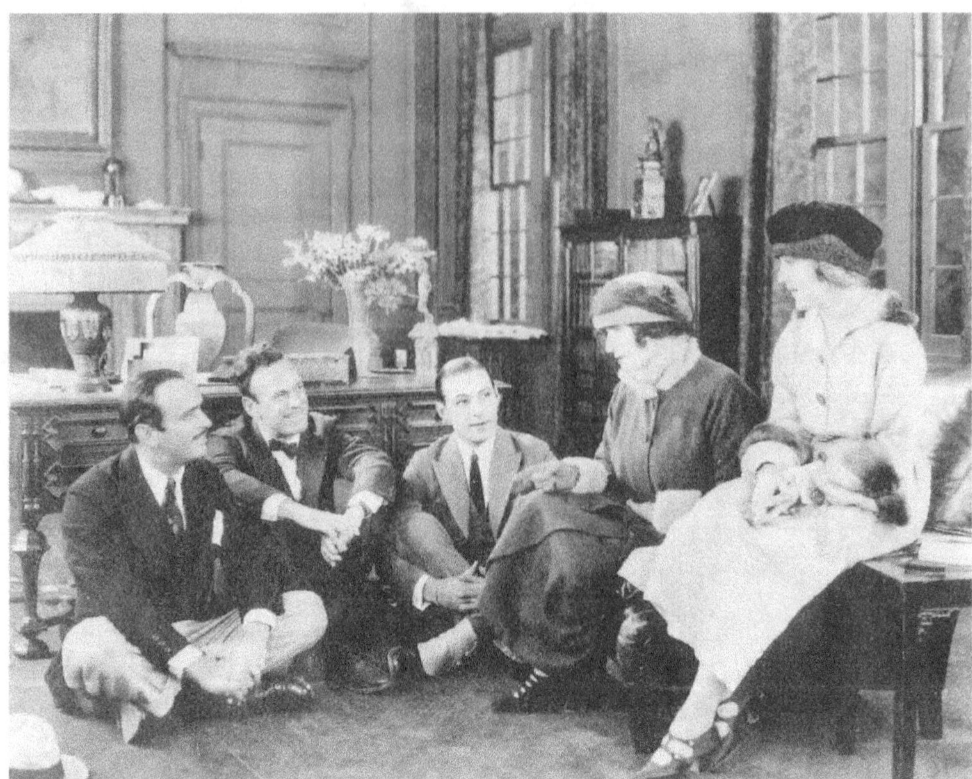

The presence of author Elinor Glyn ensured visits of Hollywood Royalty to the set.
Pictured here, Douglas Fairbanks, director Sam Wood, Valentino, Elinor Glyn and Mary Pickford.
(Tracey Goessel collection)

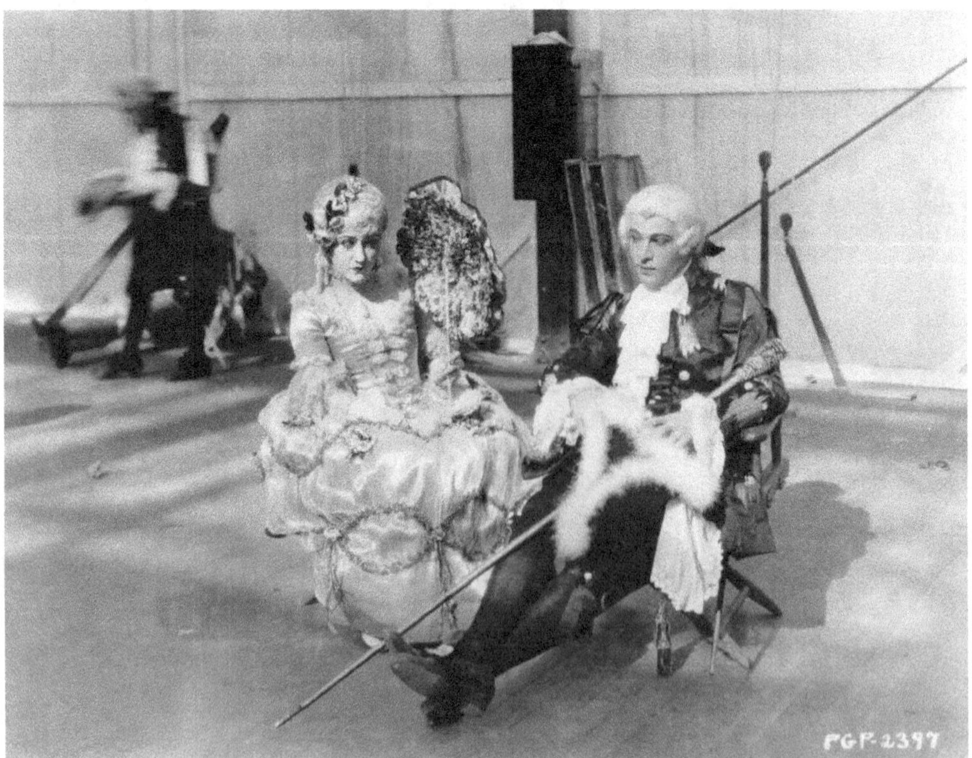

Gloria Swanson and Rudolph Valentino relaxing between scenes during filming of *Beyond the Rocks*.
(Author's collection)

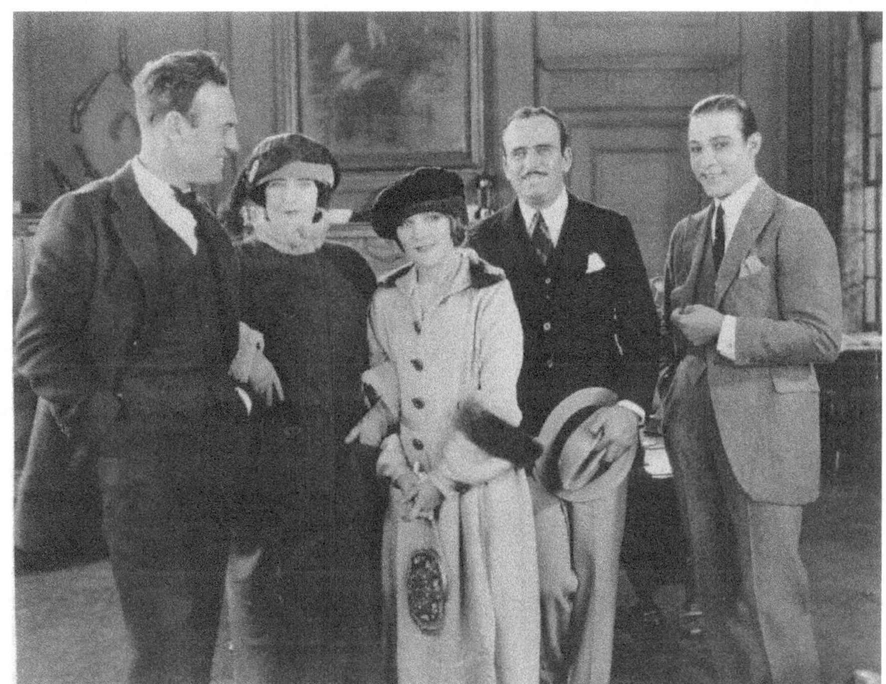

Everyone wanted to be seen with Elinor Glyn *and* Valentino. Mary Pickford and Douglas Fairbanks pay a call.
(Tracey Goessel collection)

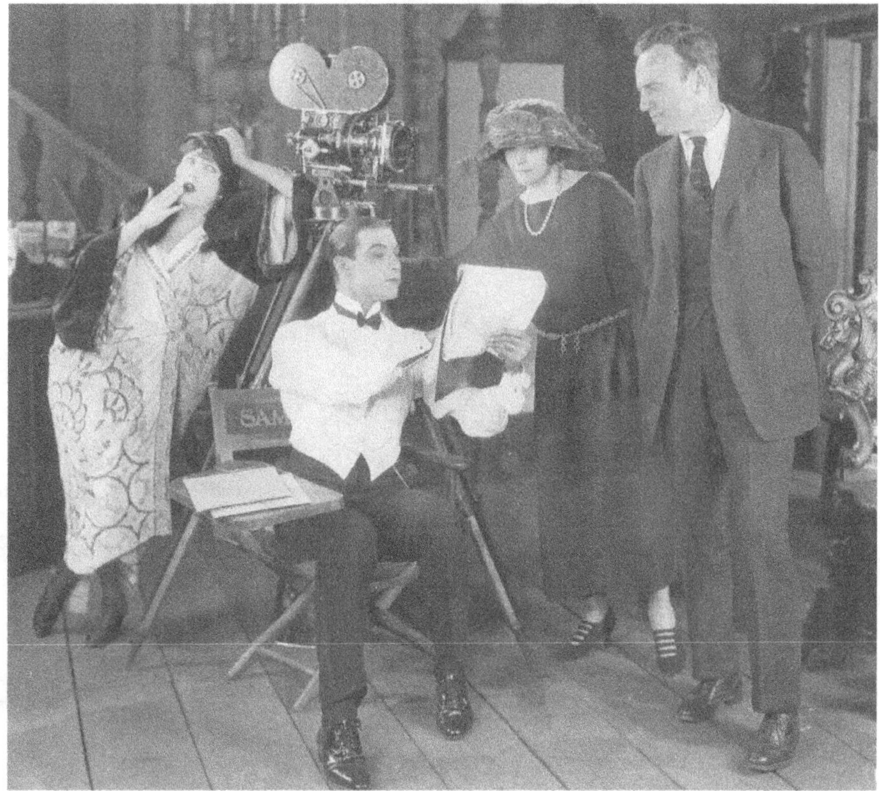

Glyn's visit may have halted production, it looks like everyone enjoyed themselves
in the numerous "gag" shots for publicity.
(Author's collection)

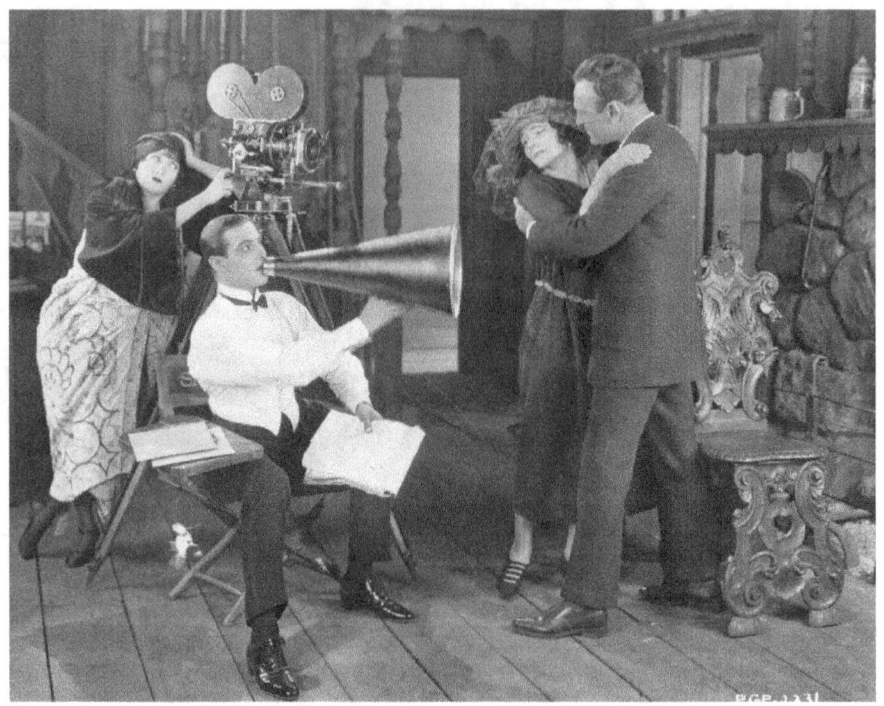

Gloria Swanson waits impatiently while Valentino
tries his hand at directing Sam Wood and Elinor Glyn in a love scene.
(Author's collection)

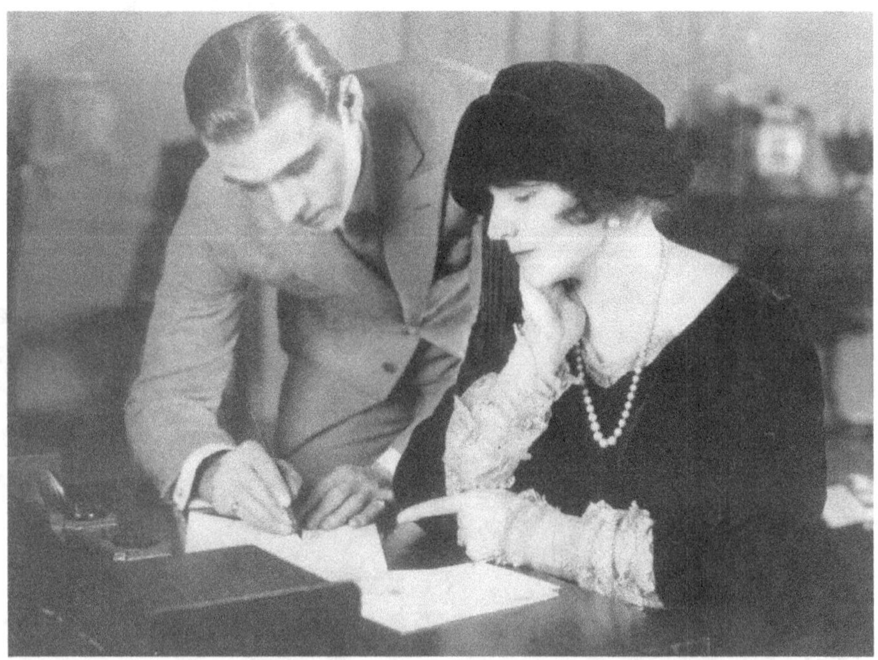

Valentino and Elinor Glyn comparing notes. (Author's collection)

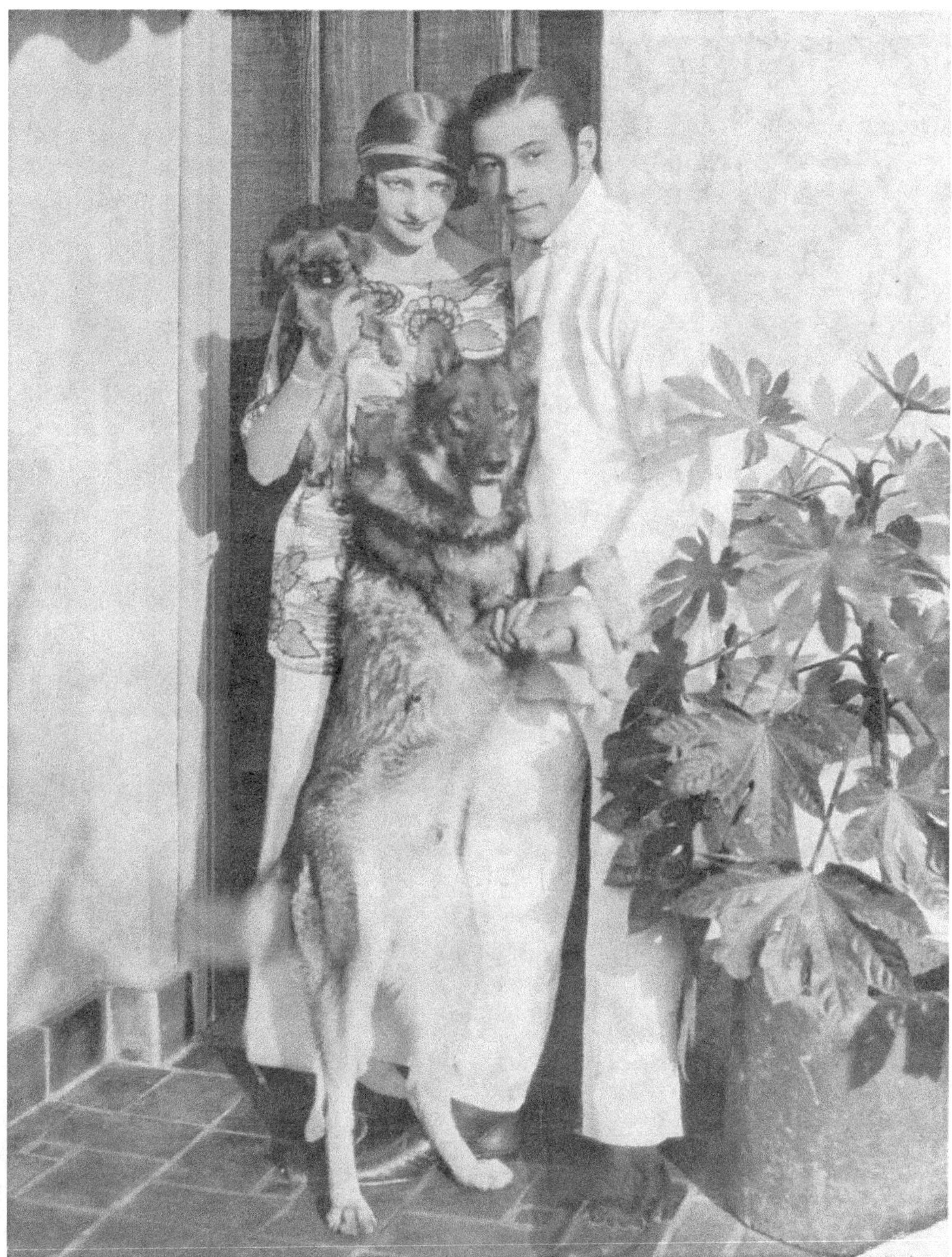

The pair settled in at Whitley Heights, happy with their beloved animals.
A rare smile from Natacha, the peaceful homelife did not last long.
(Author's collection)

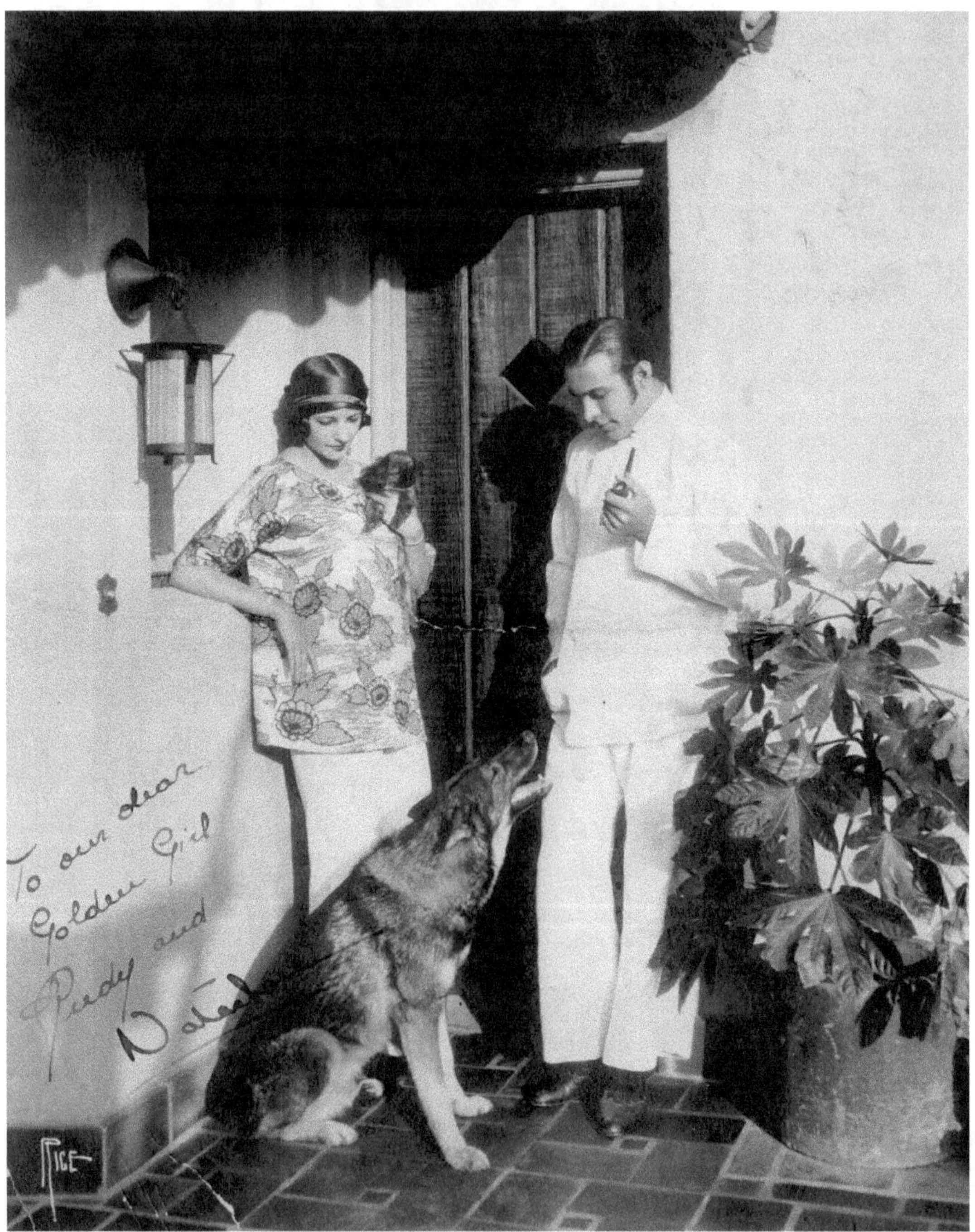

Photograph inscribed to their friend Cora McGeachy. Natacha seen here in slacks. (Private collection)

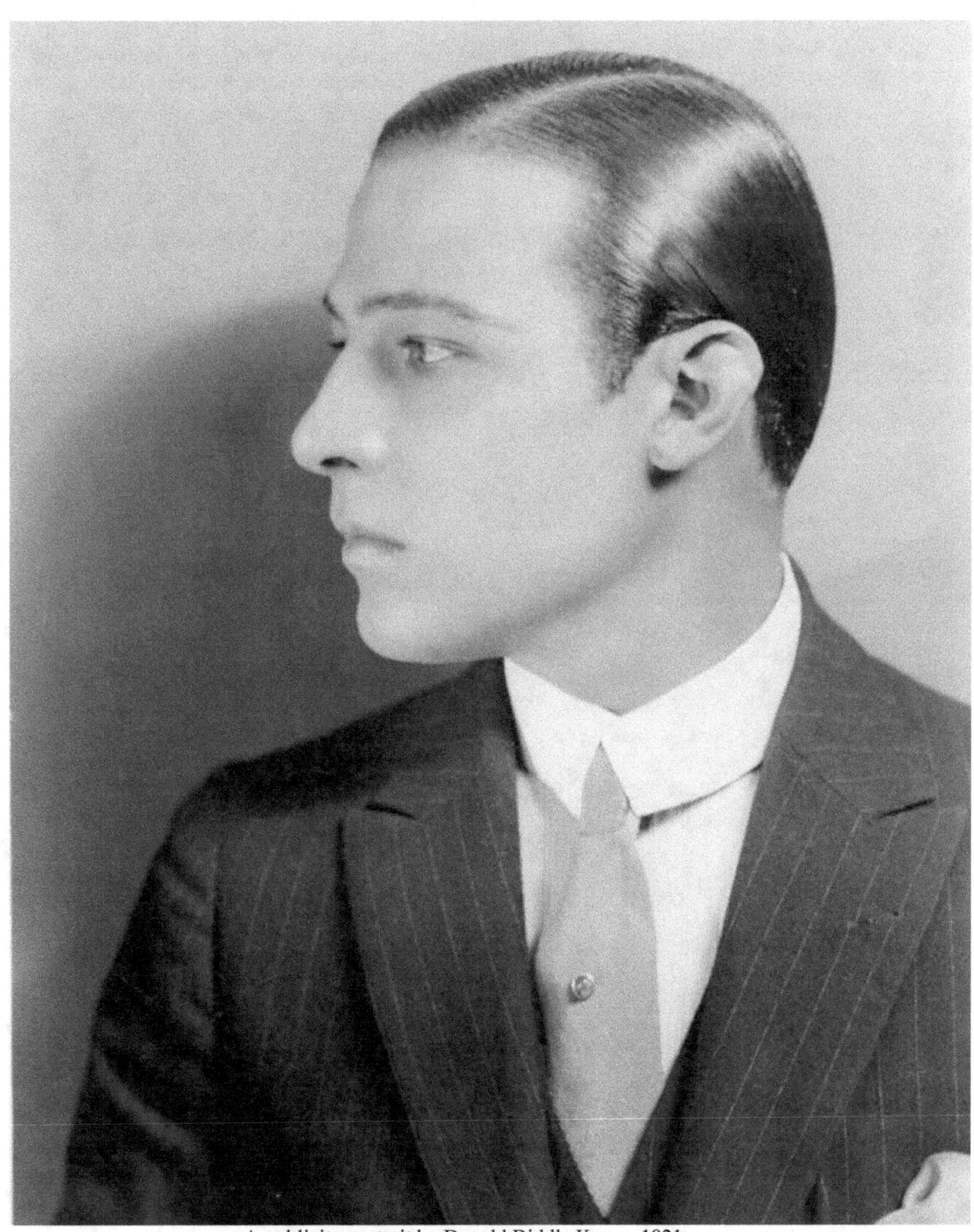

A publicity portrait by Donald Biddle Keyes, 1921.
(Author's collection)

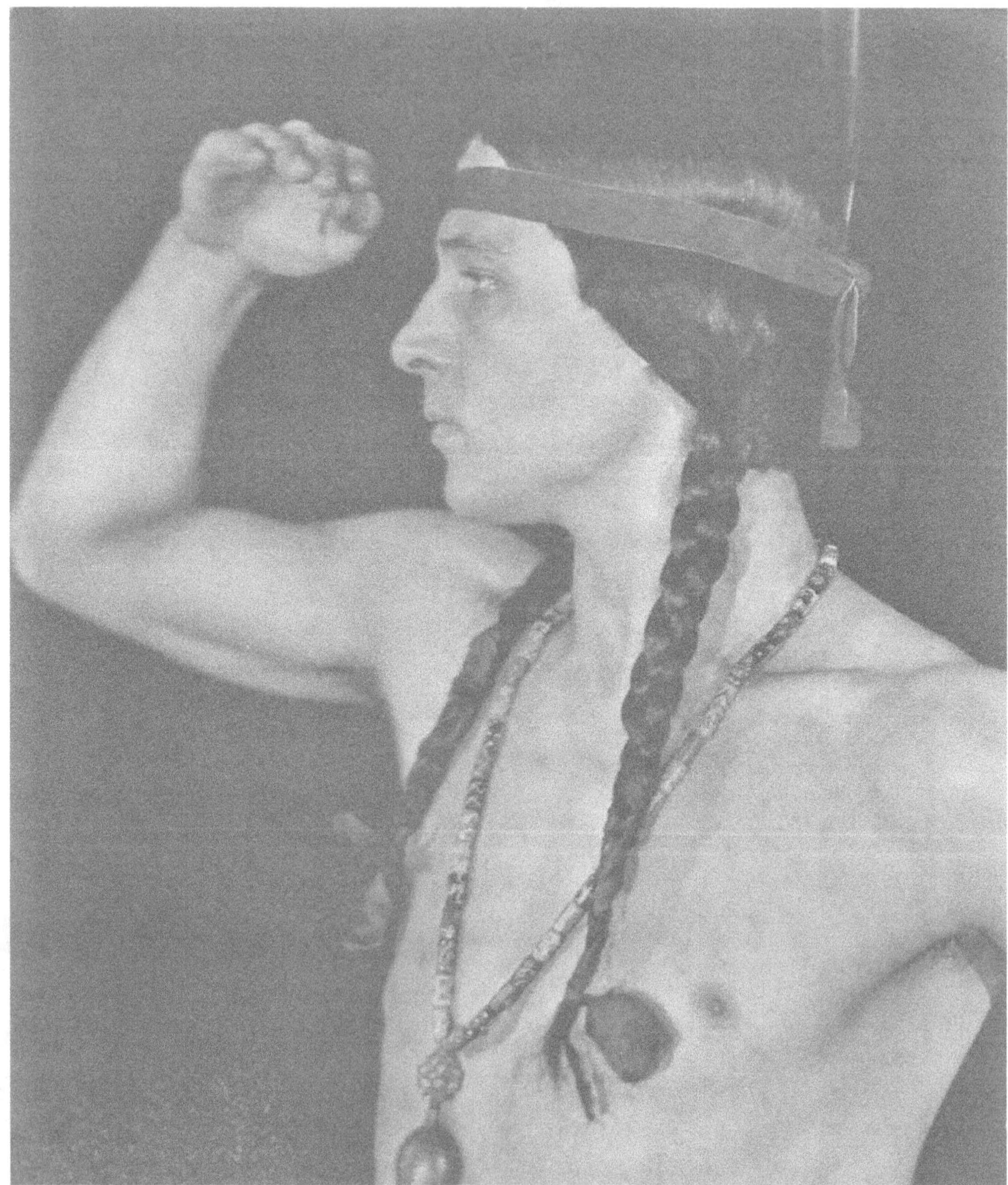

Valentino posed for photographer Russell Ball in a series of portraits in native American garb.
Natacha recalled they were an homage to his spirit guide Black Feather. Valentino clad in a loincloth,
with bow and quiver of arrows, in a near state of complete undress.
While he may have posed in all seriousness in a quest to play a Native American in a film,
these photos resulted in more fodder for the movie going flapper's delight.
(Author's collection)

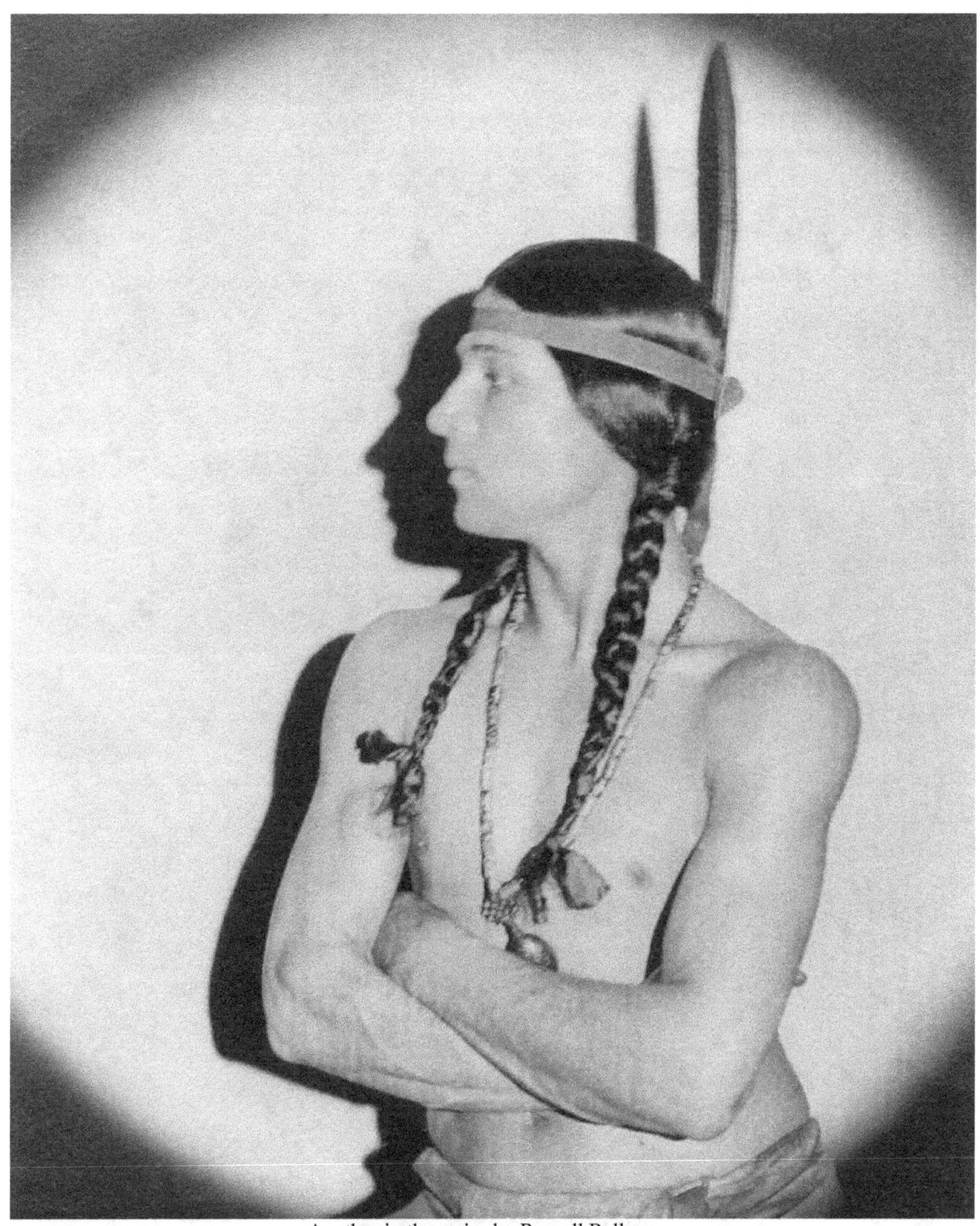

Another in the series by Russell Ball.
(Tracy Terhune collection)

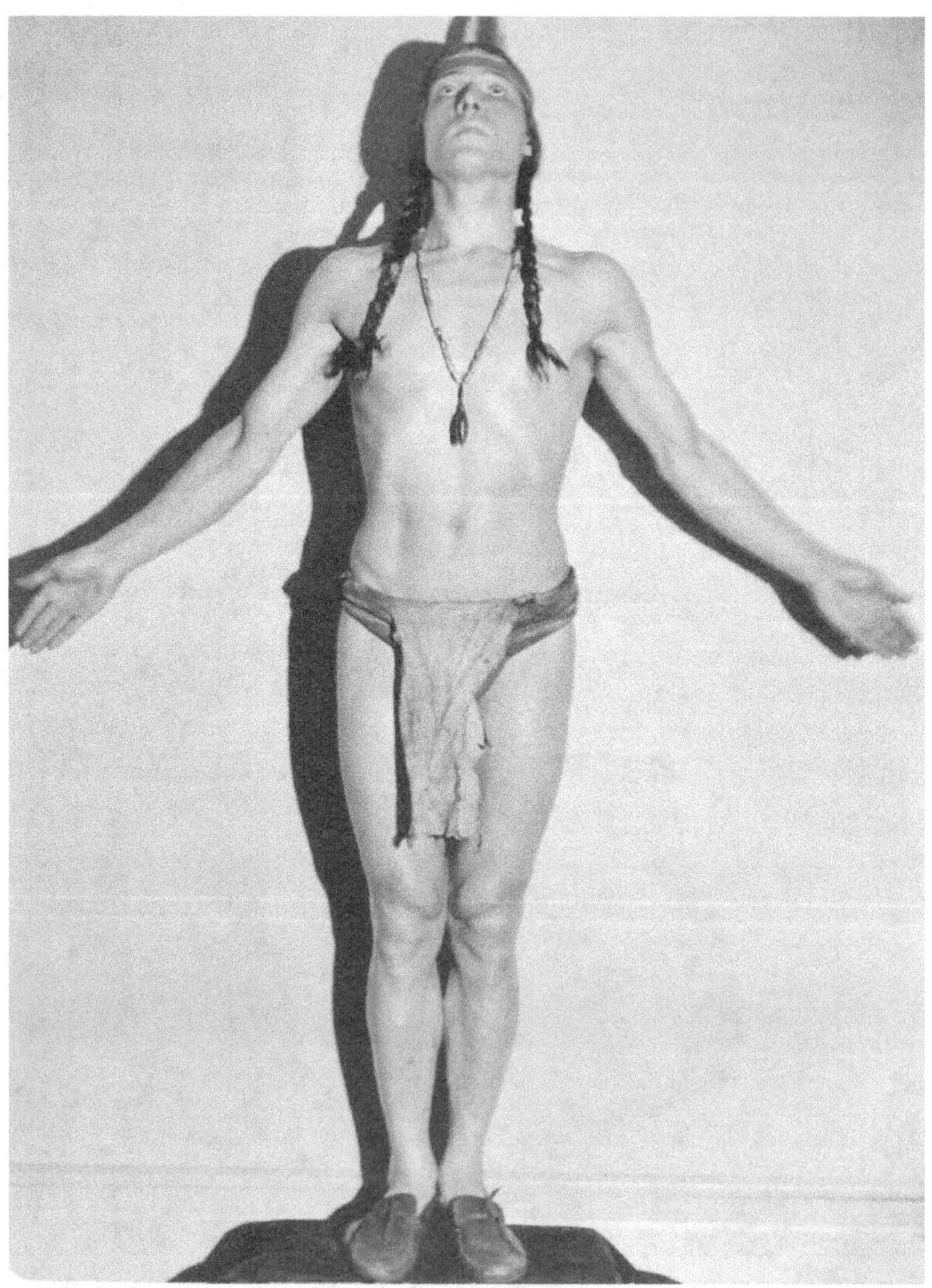

Valentino invoking similar pathos as the famed painting *End of the Trail* by James Earl Fraser.
(Tracy Terhune collection)

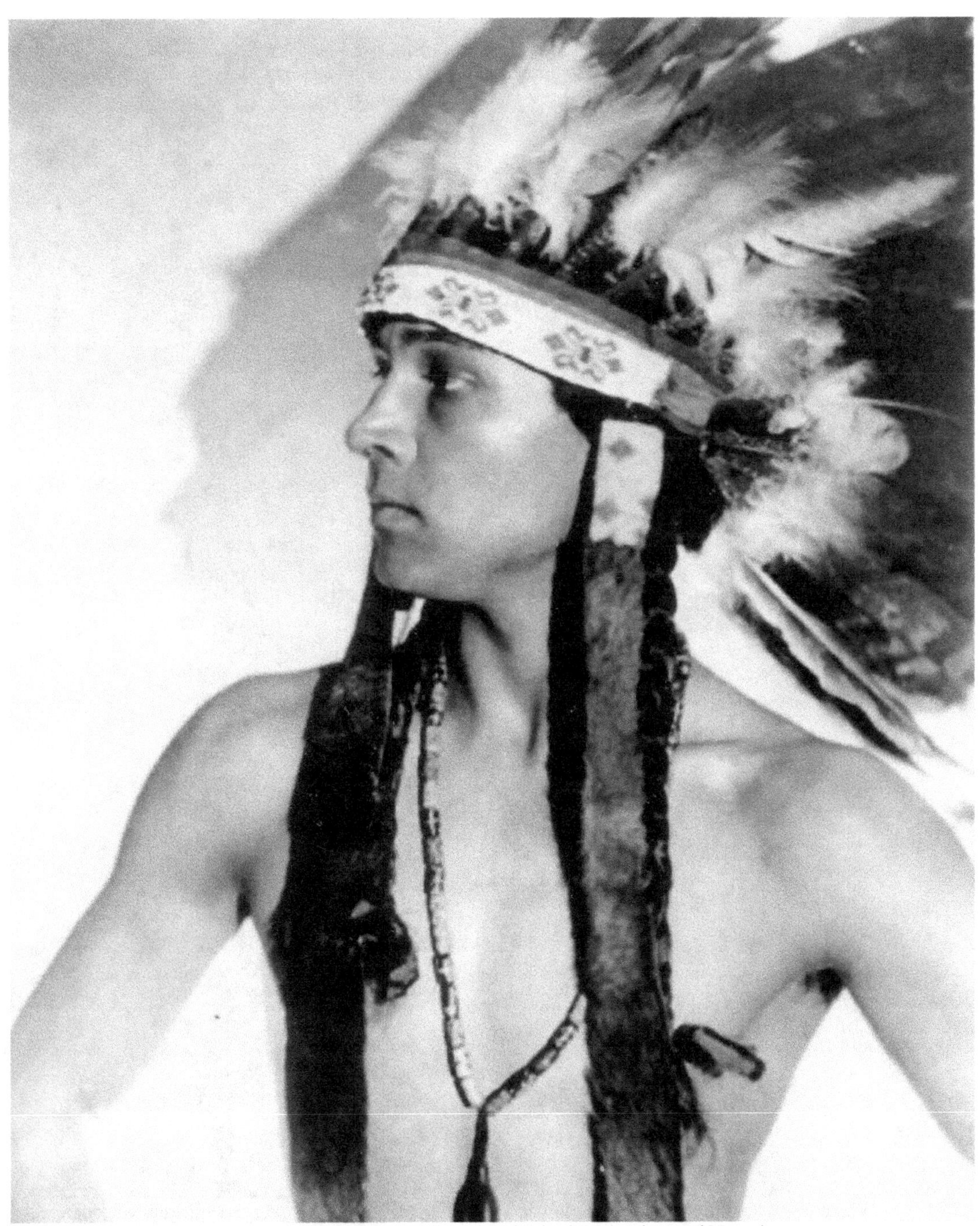

Russell Ball was a favored photographer for both Valentino and Natacha.
(Author's collection)

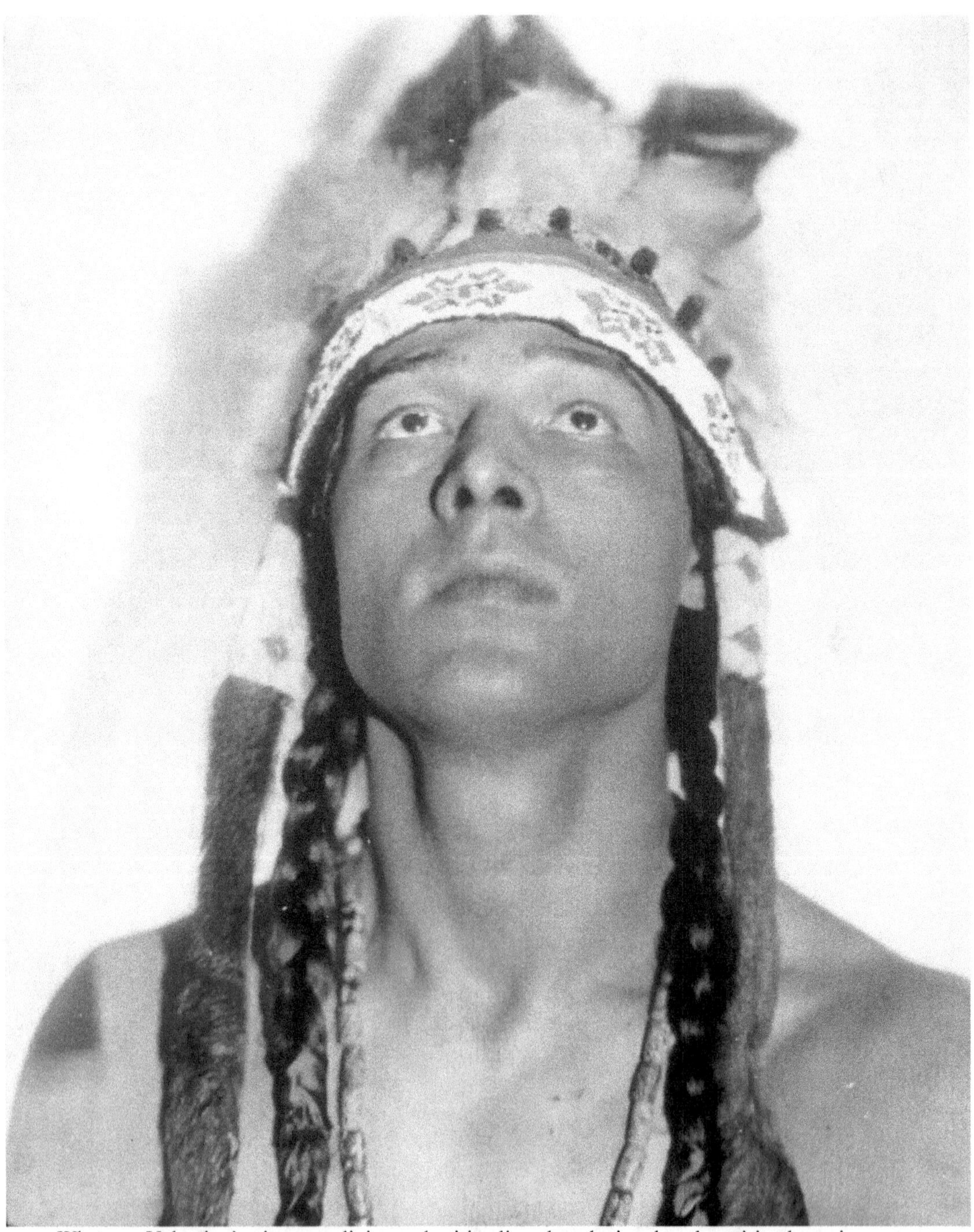

Whatever Valentino's view on religion and spiritualism, here he invokes the spiritual warrior.
(Author's collection)

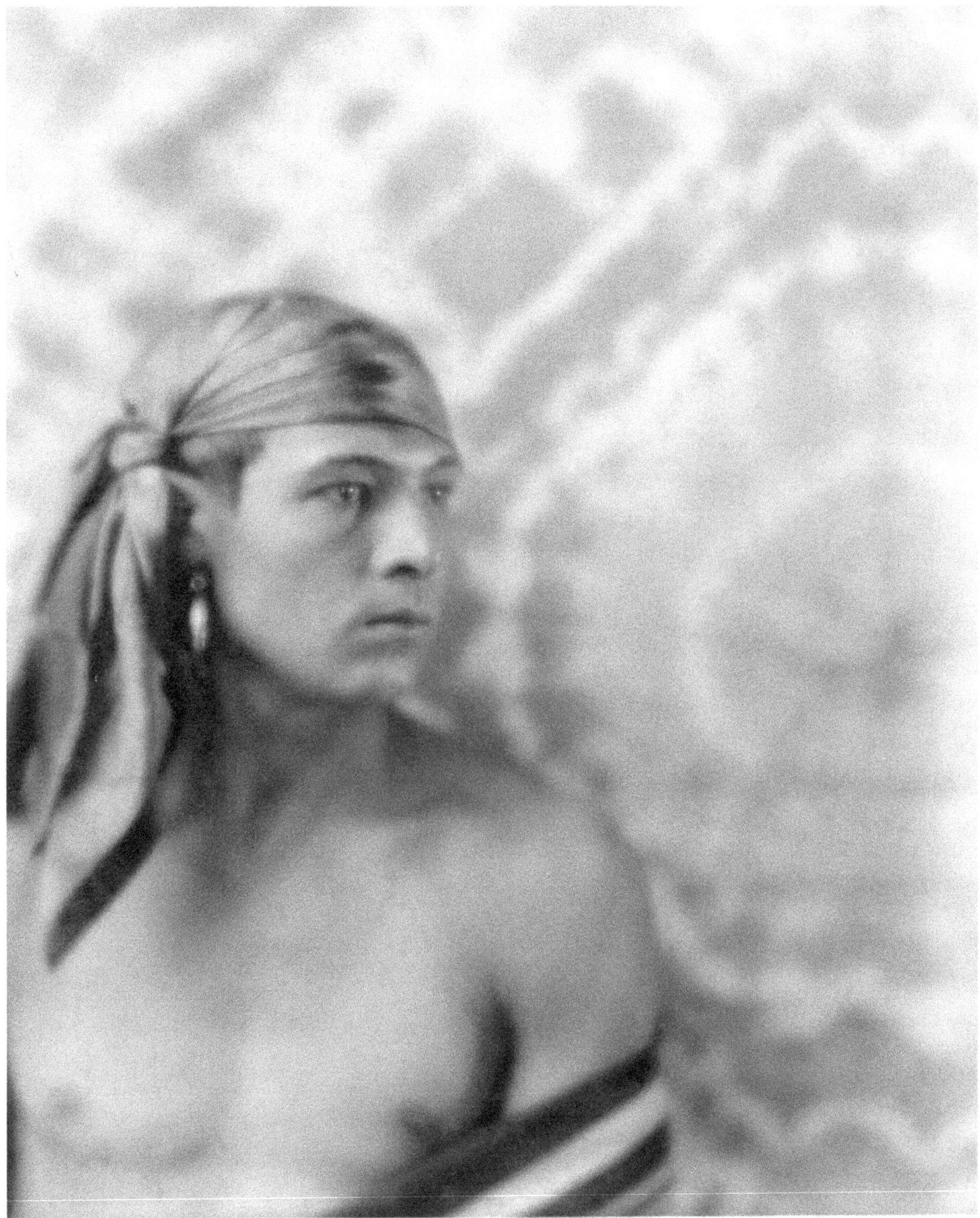

This portrait remains unidentified. It is likely another Donald Biddle Keyes portrait.
Perhaps dating when Valentino was making *Blood and Sand.*
(Author's collection)

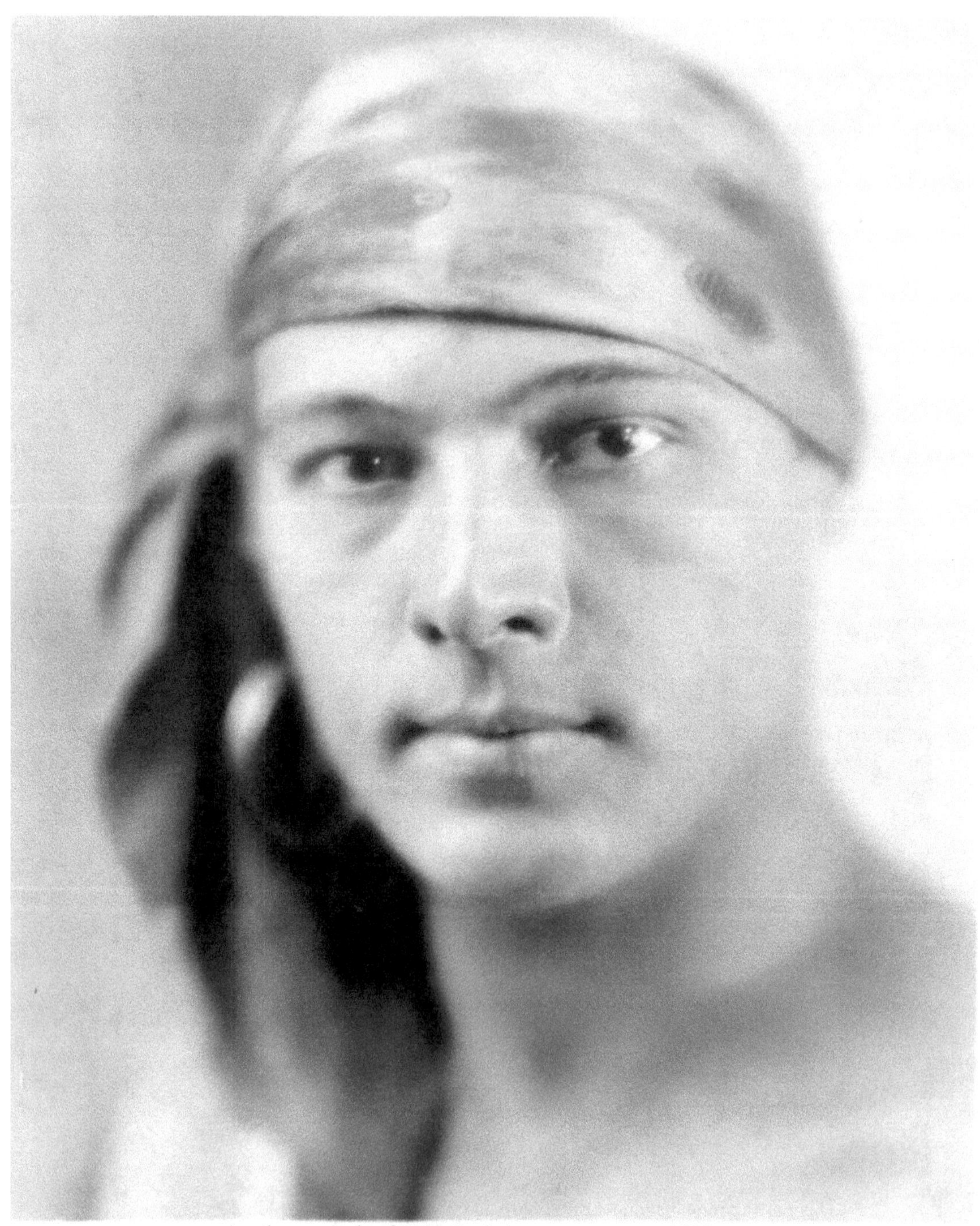

Another example of Valentino's intense gaze *circa* 1922
(Author's collection)

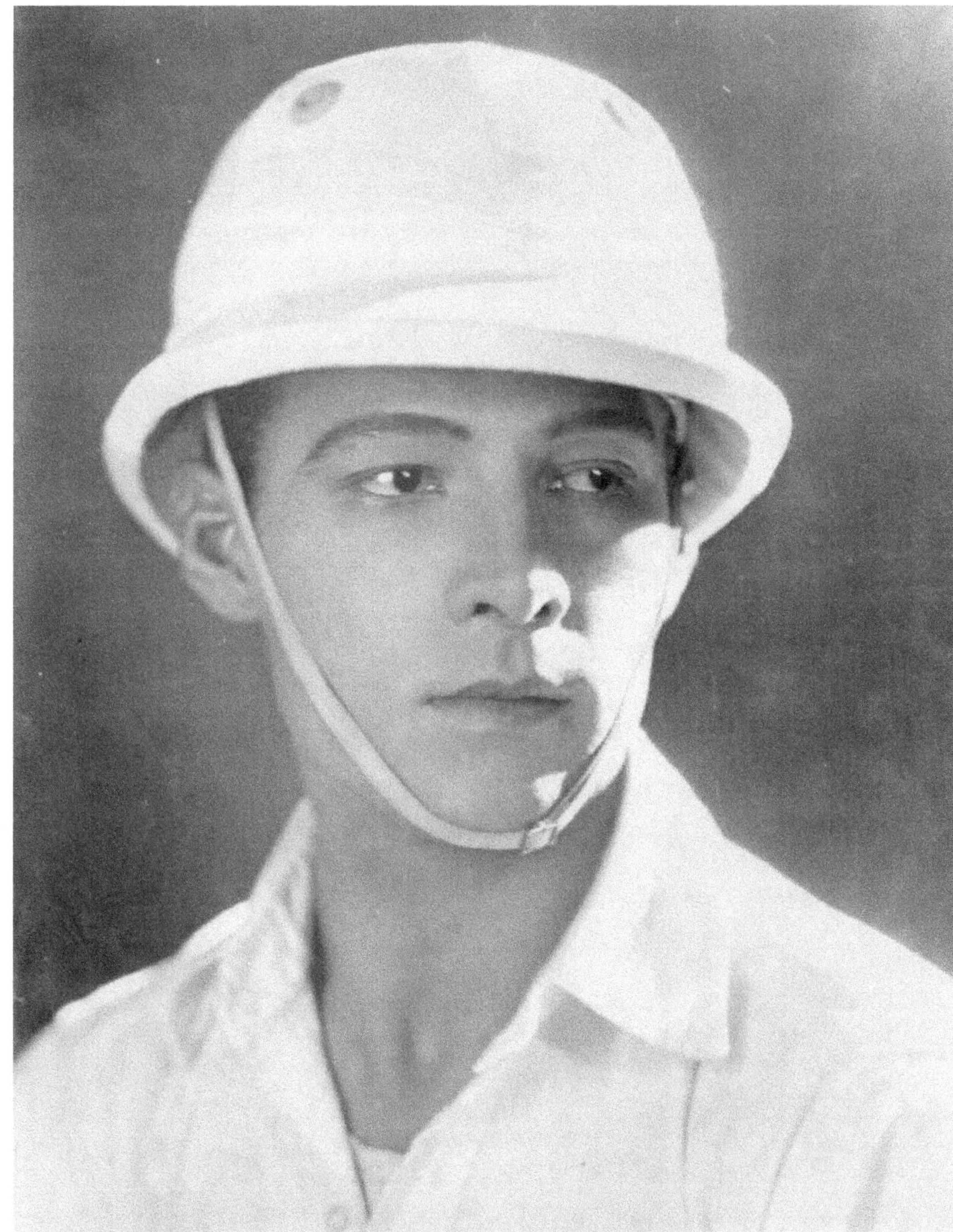

Donald Biddle Keyes publicity portrait for *Beyond the Rocks*.
(Author's collection)

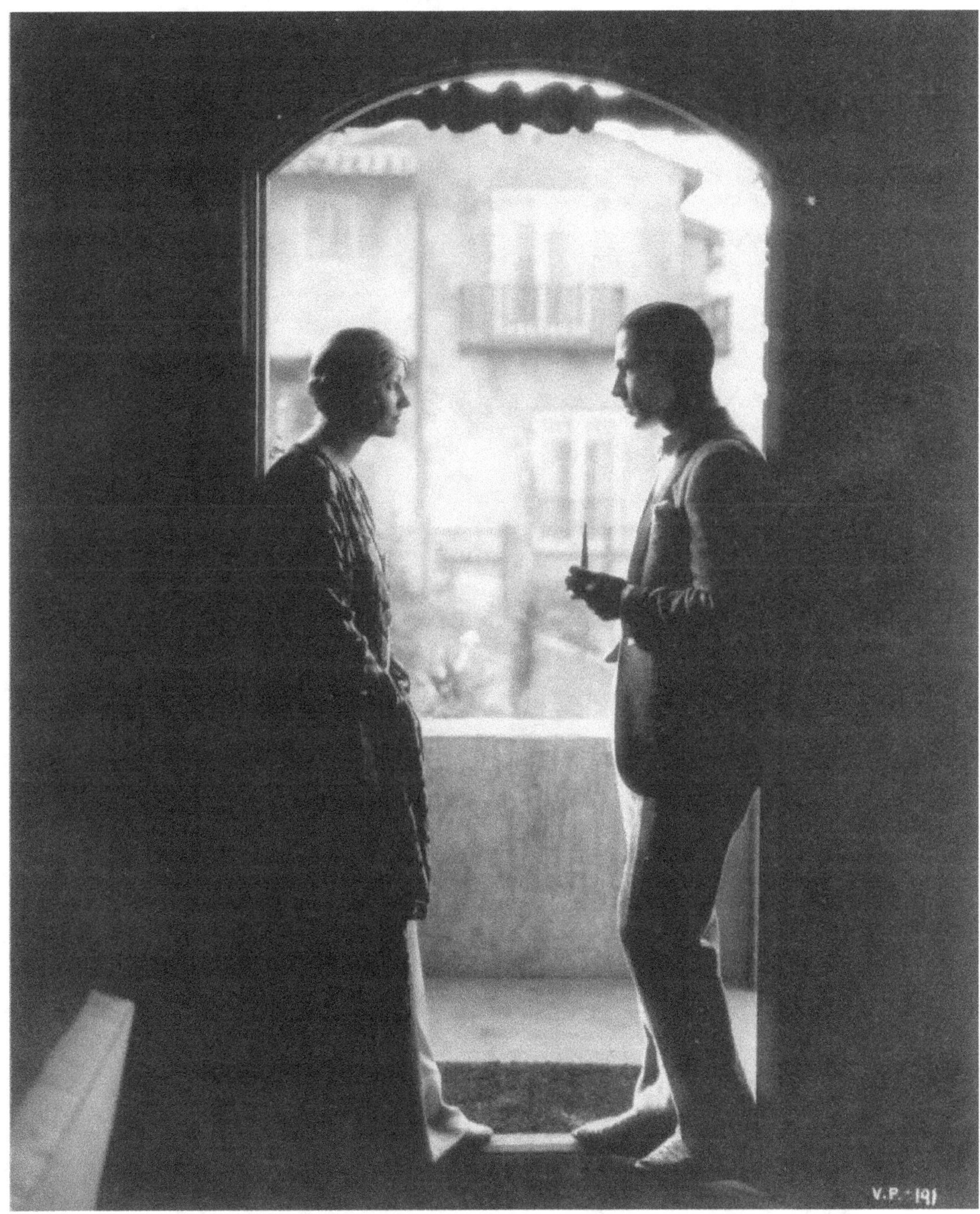
V.P. 191

I saw a slender, boyish, athletic-looking Adonis, with dark, fervent eyes of romance and a frank, honest smile that completely won my heart.

—Natacha Rambova, 1926

Valentino's status had now changed. *Beyond the Rocks* was Valentino's first film under his new contract and the last in which he was billed as a co-star. Cinematographer Osmond Borradaile recalled that women would flock around Valentino while on location and the crew had to chase them off the set. "Rudy was too much of a gentleman—or a star—to resent the constant invasion to his privacy. But like me, he felt the need to escape the constraints of studio production whenever possible." Swanson recalled that Valentino was relaxed and happy during the shoot, and candid shots taken on the set bear this out. Valentino also appeared to enjoy visits to the set by the eccentric author of *Beyond the Rocks*, Madame Elinor Glyn.

It was around this time that Valentino also met and befriended Robert Florey. Florey joined the band of close male friends who enjoyed Valentino's confidences and who would provide moral support for him in the times of trouble which were to come.

Immediately after completing the shoot for *Beyond the Rocks*, Valentino began filming *Blood and Sand*. This production, shot on the Famous Players-Lasky backlot and at the Lasky Ranch, was helmed by Fred Niblo and co-starred Lila Lee and Nita Naldi. Valentino prepared for *Blood and Sand* by taking lessons in bullfighting from a retired matador and by reading the Ibáñez novel in Spanish, immersing himself in the character. Natacha recalled that he so immersed himself in the role of the illiterate peasant, he adopted rough and slovenly ways in the course of his attempts to meld with the character. The lengthy shoot concluded filming shortly after Valentino's 27th birthday.

With *Blood and Sand* completed, Valentino and Natacha decided on a quick break in Palm Springs. Both enjoyed the desert and had made friends with Dr. Florilla White and Mrs. Freeman, the woman who ran the inn where they loved to stay. Palm Springs allowed them both time to decompress from the stress of studio and public life. Valentino, in particular, enjoyed joining Florilla White and friends on trail rides. He also enjoyed hiking in the canyon and swims in the Tahquitz Canyon River. While in Palm Springs, the two decided to marry.

Although Valentino's divorce from Jean Acker was not yet final, the couple believed they could skirt the legalities if they married in Mexico. On Saturday, May 13, 1922, accompanied by friends Douglas Gerrard, Paul Ivano, and Alla Nazimova, they drove from El Centro to Mexicali and went straight to the home of Otto Moller, the alcalde. The entire town turned out for the hasty nuptials and impromptu wedding party. After the wedding dinner, the happy couple returned to Palm Springs for their honeymoon. Waters would not be calm for long.

Scarcely four days later, Cecil B. DeMille sent a telegram to Adolph Zukor in New York that the District Attorney was preparing to prosecute Valentino for bigamy. Cecil B. DeMille assured Adolph Zukor he was doing what he could to straighten things out, but felt he should let Zukor know "and be prepared in case storm breaks."[14] Valentino indeed received news that the State of California had recognized his Mexican marriage and that he had been charged with bigamy. Attorneys at Paramount advised the couple to separate. Natacha was hustled

[14] Telegram, to Adolph Zukor from Cecil B. DeMille, May 17, 1922. (Margaret Herrick Library)

onto a train bound for the east coast and her family's estate in the Adirondacks, Foxlair. Valentino returned to the Whitley Heights house, alone, frustrated and more than a little concerned about Natacha, his future and their future.

He turned himself in and was briefly jailed. Bail was set at $10,000. Famous Players-Lasky, still smarting and fresh off the dual publicity disasters dealt them by the Arbuckle manslaughter trials and the William Desmond Taylor murder, refused to provide the funds for Valentino's bail. Instead, the studio allowed its hottest star to cool his heels in jail. Douglas Gerrard sprang to action and contacted friends, including San Francisco's chief of police, Daniel J. O'Brien (father of actor George O'Brien), and June Mathis for help. Fellow Paramount star Thomas Meighan paid most of the bail and Valentino was released. Meighan later recalled that Valentino "seemed like a good enough fellow."

At Whitley Heights friends rallied around him, providing companionship and advice while his legal troubles were sorted out. They organized dinners and outings, and spent time trying to distract Valentino both from the upcoming trial and from his loneliness. Telegrams and letters crisscrossed the country between the lovelorn Valentino and an equally heartbroken Natacha. They shared amorous conversations via daily long-distance telephone calls between Hollywood and upstate New York. This limited contact provided some consolation, but what the pair really desired was to be allowed to be man and wife.

Thanks to testimony presented by witnesses, including Douglas Gerrard, the charges of bigamy were dismissed for lack of any evidence that the couple was cohabitating. But before Valentino could head east to be with Natacha, he had to film *The Young Rajah*. The scenario was adapted by his friend and mentor, June Mathis, but the shoot was not a happy experience for him. He was emotionally exhausted from the trial, the separation from Natacha, and the feeling that Famous Players-Lasky had not played fair with him. He complained that he had been promised *Blood and Sand* would be filmed in Europe but was instead filmed cheaply on the Lasky backlot. *The Young Rajah* was also filmed with a tight budget. Helmed by Phil Rosen, not one of their top-flight directors, Valentino took little comfort in working again with June Mathis. Valentino disliked the film, felt the material was beneath him, and grumbled throughout the entire shoot.

His discontent was relegated to the background when he departed for New York and Natacha. Douglas Gerrard traveled with him across the country. In order to escape the press (and to Natacha's amusement), Valentino donned a false beard and glasses. They spent happy days at Foxlair, hiking, swimming, hunting, and playing poker. It was during this extended stay with Natacha's family that Valentino got to know his future in-laws, cosmetics magnate Richard Hudnut (nicknamed "Uncle Dickie") and Winifred Hudnut (nicknamed "Muzzie"). Uncle Dickie was still not 100% convinced that Valentino was a suitable partner for his step-daughter, nor was he entirely won over by Valentino's charms. By the end of the visit, Uncle Dickie was charmed and fully in Valentino's camp.

When *Blood and Sand* was released in September 1922, the two returned to New York City. Valentino moved into the Hotel des Artistes on W. 67th St. and Natacha roomed with her aunt Teresa Werner just around the corner on Central Park West. Publicly the pair needed to be discreet, but they were able to spend many evenings at Valentino's favorite New York haunts, dining on the simple Italian fare he loved.

Blood and Sand was a smash hit. Valentino, still peevish with his employer, decided to go on strike for more control over his films, better scenarios, and higher production standards.

The studio, though still scandal-shy, knew his value; it offered a new contract and the princely sum of $7,000 a week. Valentino, never a canny businessman, refused. The studio, in turn, exercised its rights under his contract and filed for an injunction to bar him from performing on film, on stage or, indeed, in any venue. The injunction was granted. As his debts mounted, Valentino was prevented from earning a living.

Then, in the winter of 1922, Valentino met S. George Ullman. It was at this time, according to Ullman, that he presented his idea of the Mineralava Dance Tour to the Valentinos. However, with the injunction in place Valentino was unable to perform in theaters. In the years to come, George Ullman would become one of the most important figures in Valentino's life: business manager, close friend, and, ultimately, executor of his estate.

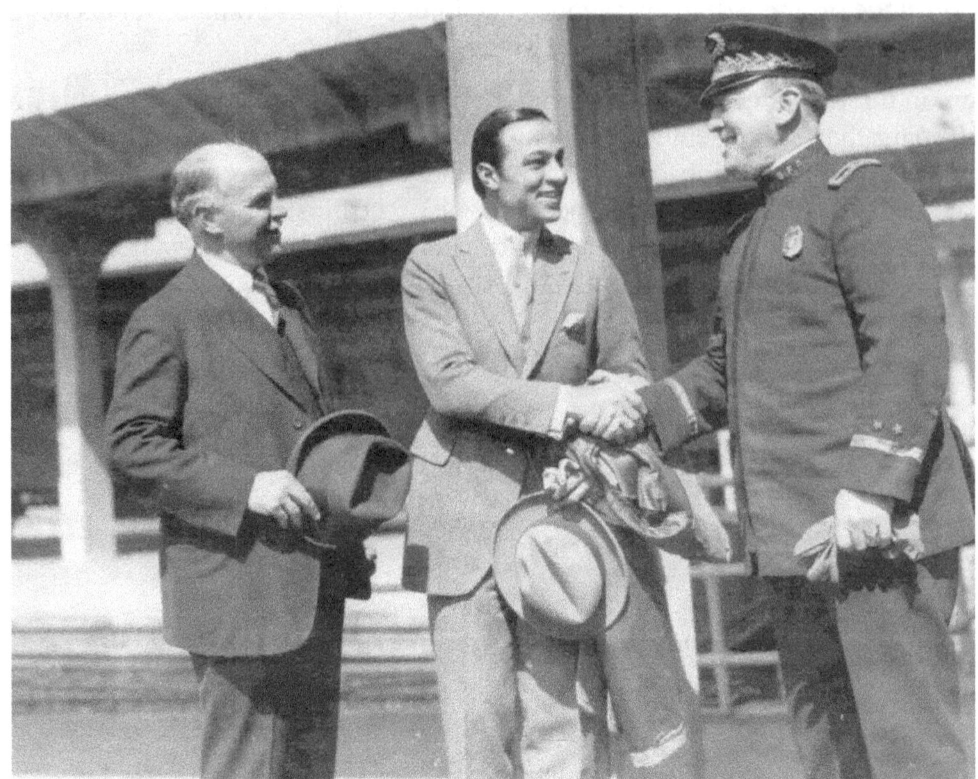

Valentino enjoyed a sojourn north to San Francisco in May 1922.
He was met at the 3rd Street Station by Mayor James Rolph and Chief of Police Daniel O'Brien.
(Author's collection)

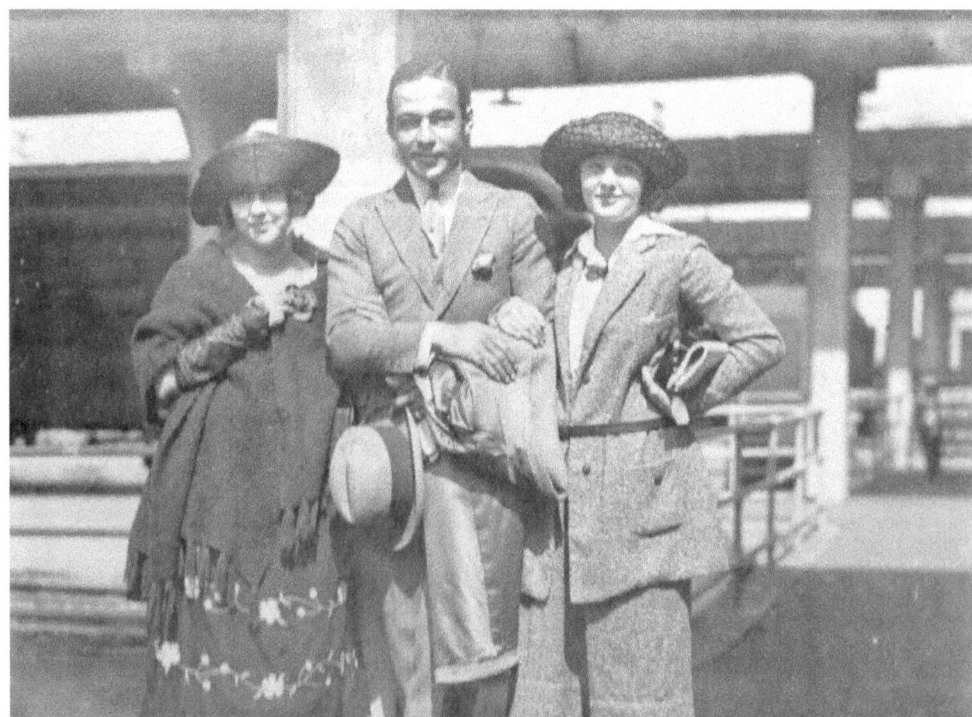

Unknown, Valentino and Ivy Crane Lombard at the San Francisco train station.
(Author's collection)

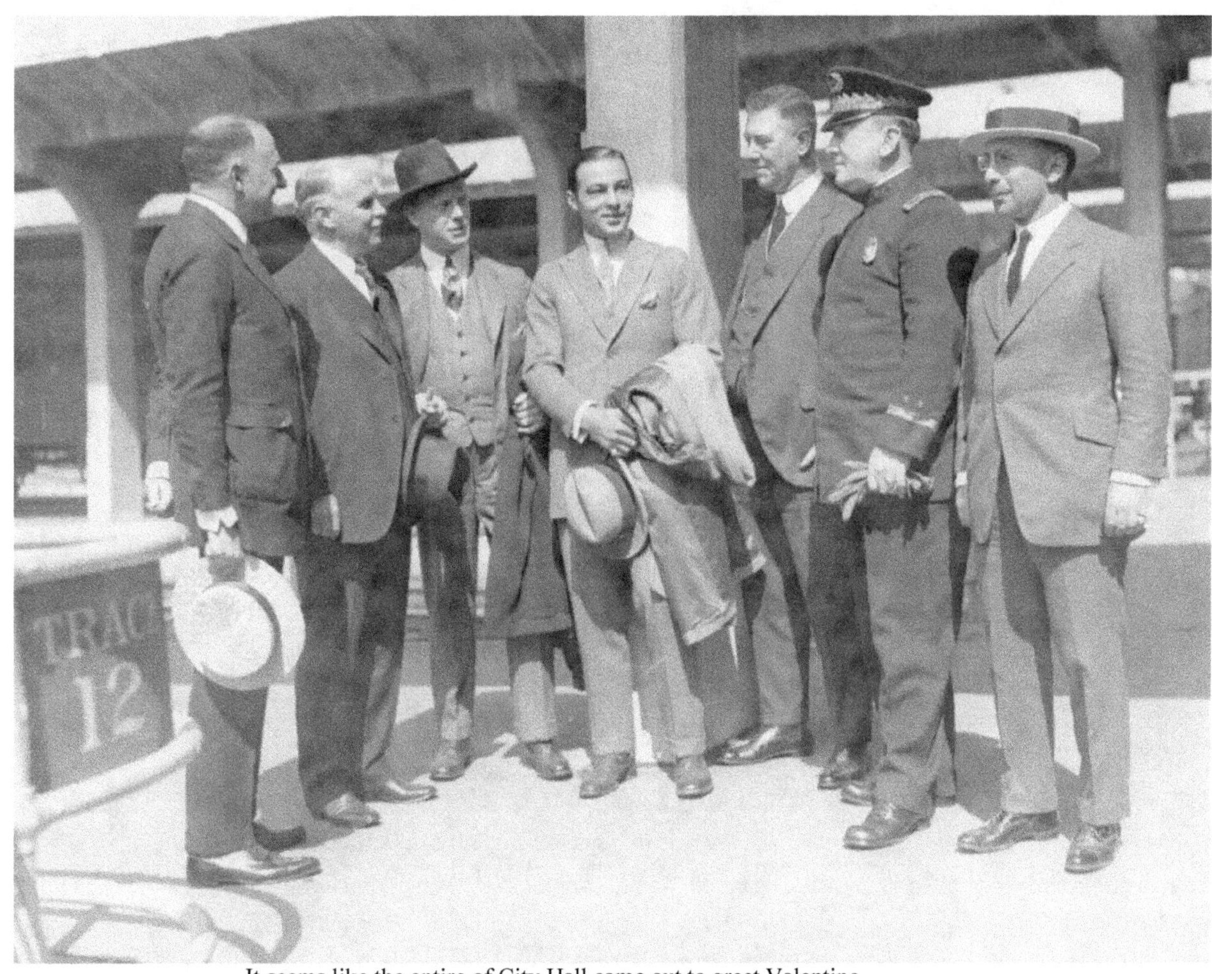

It seems like the entire of City Hall came out to greet Valentino.
Valentino and Mayor James Rolph traveled south to San Jose and attended a local rodeo.
(Author's collection)

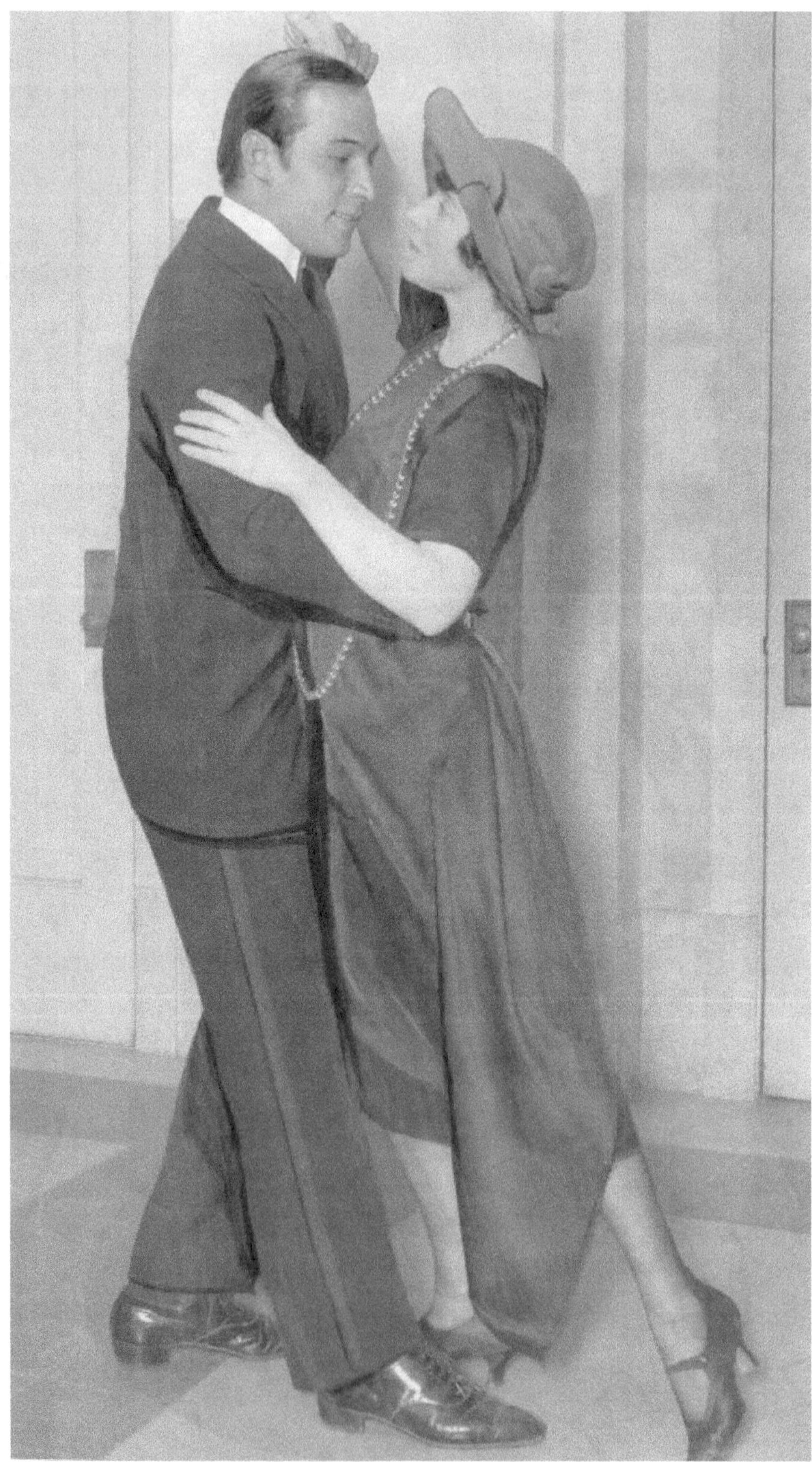

In preparation for a Veterans Benefit in San Francisco,
Valentino rehearses a tango with friend and socialite Ivy Crane Lombard.
(Author's collection)

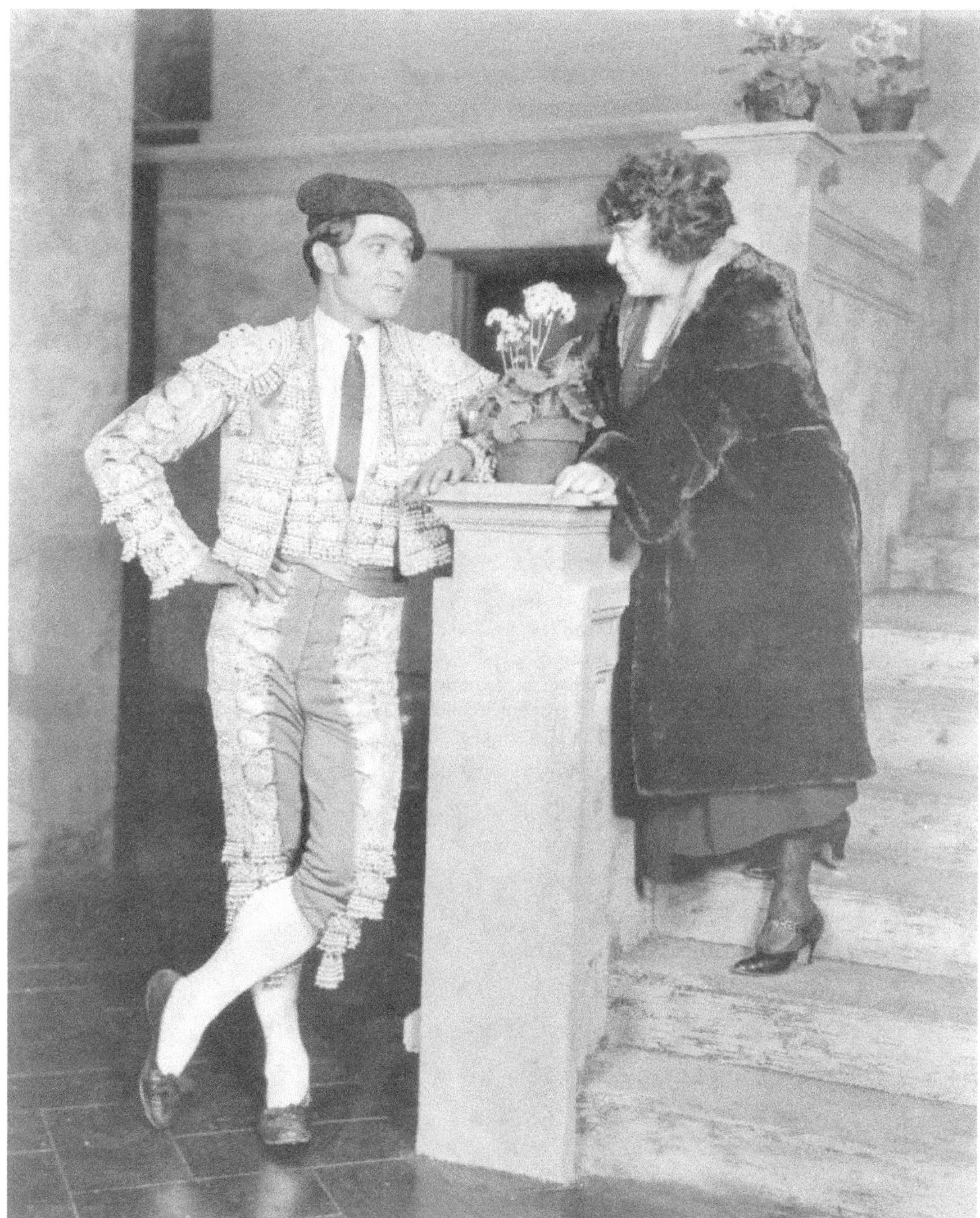

June Mathis, author of the scenario for *Blood and Sand* pays a visit to her dear friend.
(Author's collection)

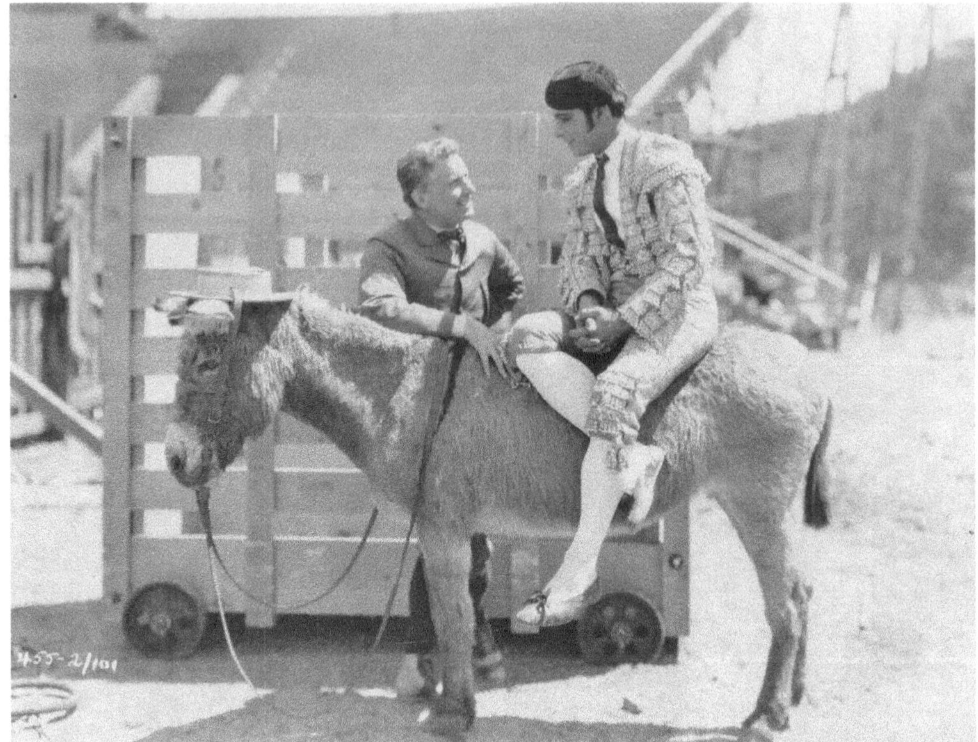

Fred Niblo and Valentino hold an impromptu conference with an obliging donkey.
(Author's collection)

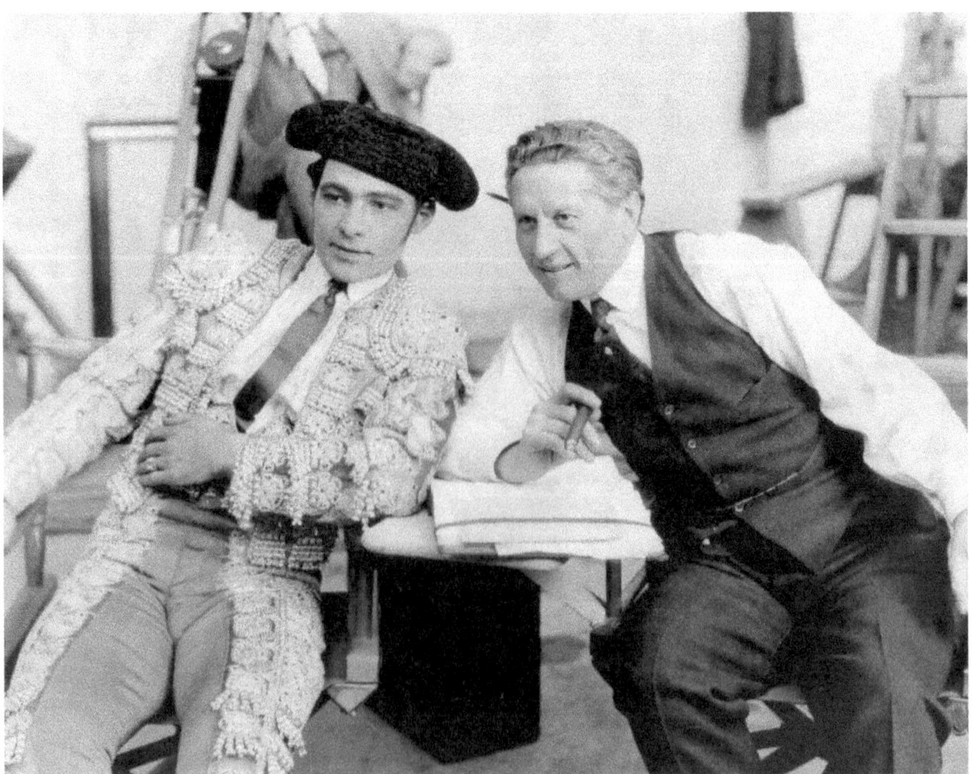

Valentino and Fred Niblo are enjoying a moment together between scenes.
(Kevin Brownlow collection)

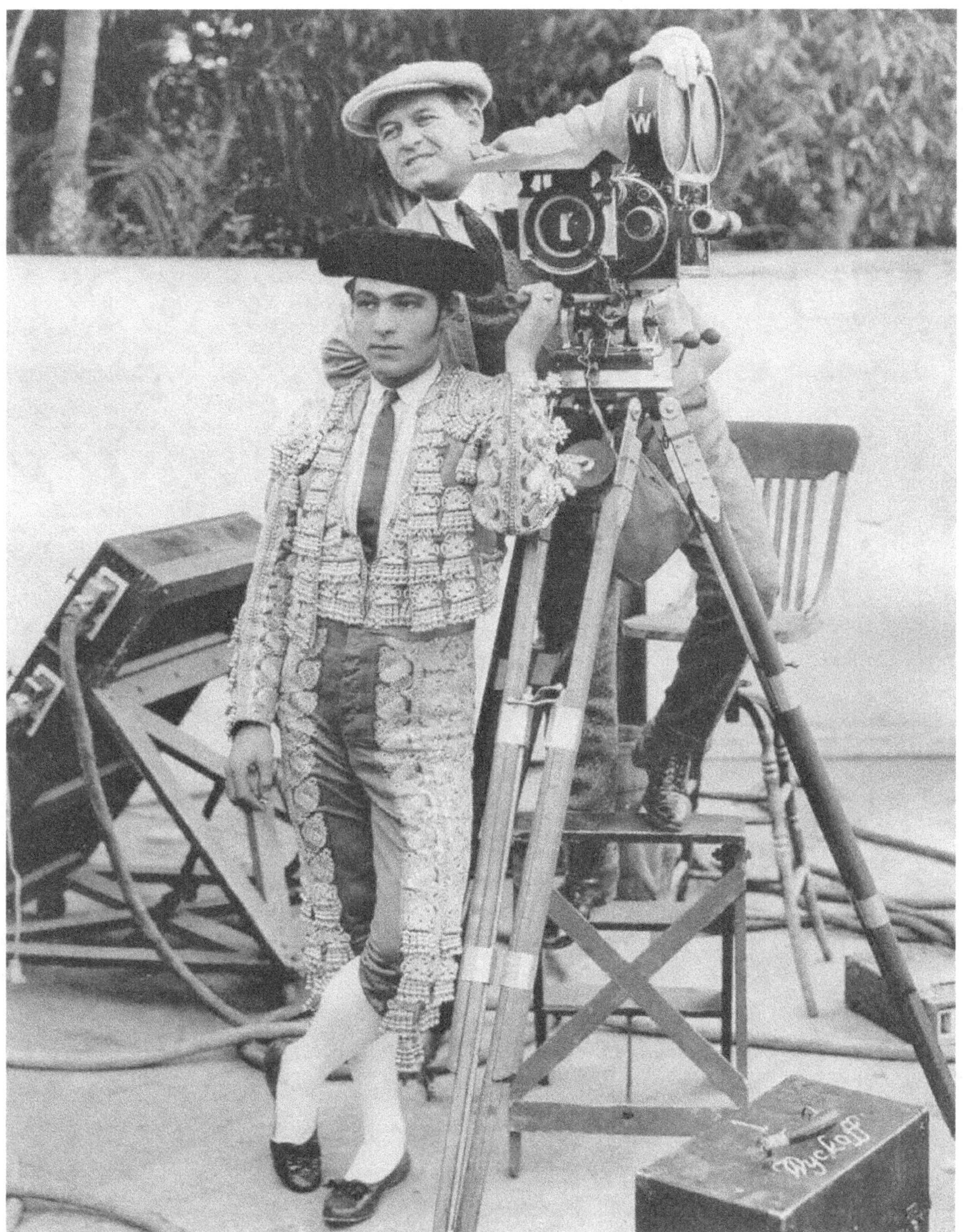

Valentino and cameraman Alvin Wyckoff waiting during a setup.
Wycoff was a legendary lensman, as skilled in the art of lighting a scene as was John Seitz.
(Author's collection)

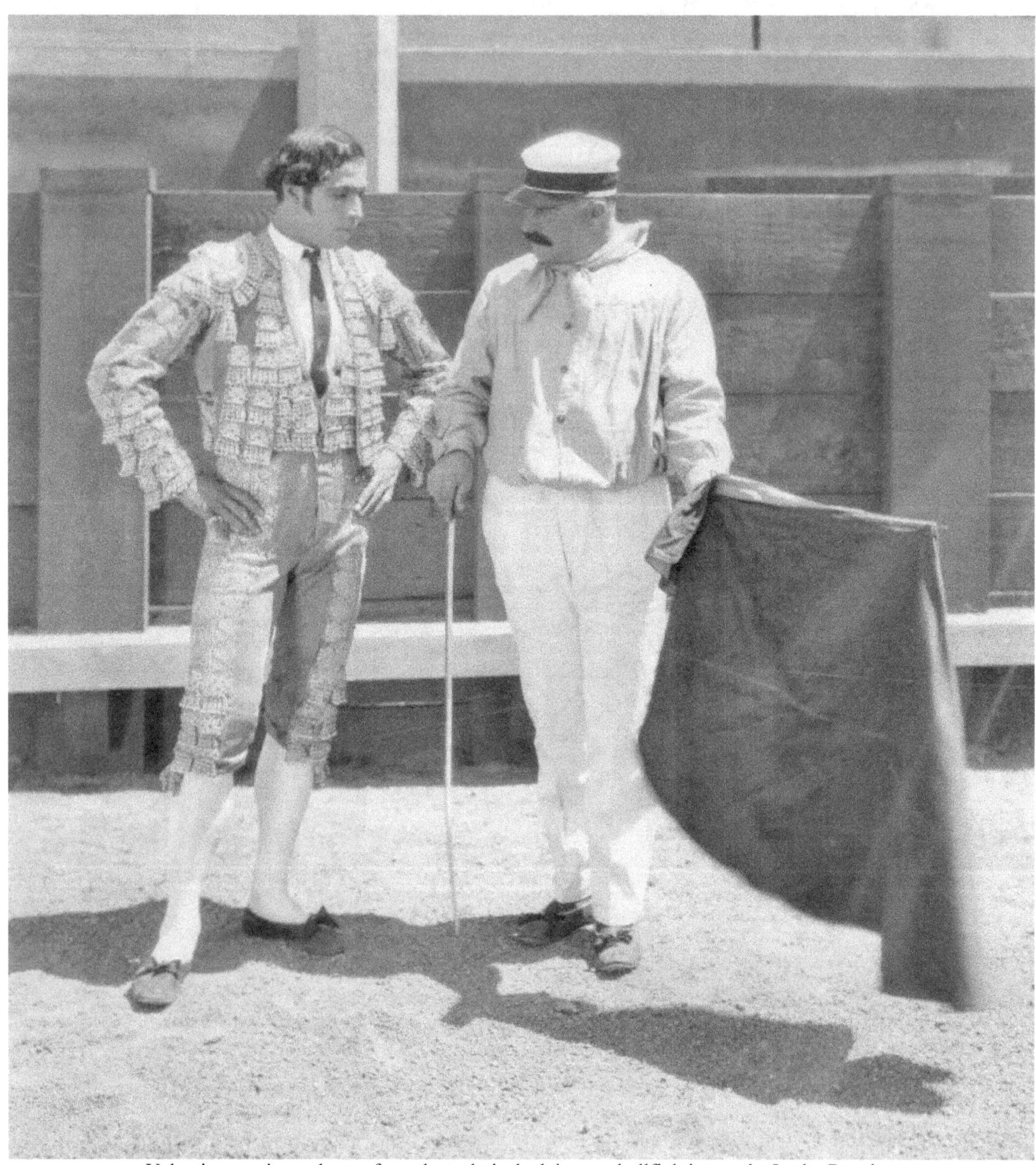

Valentino receives a lesson from the technical advisor on bullfighting as the Lasky Ranch.
(Author's collection)

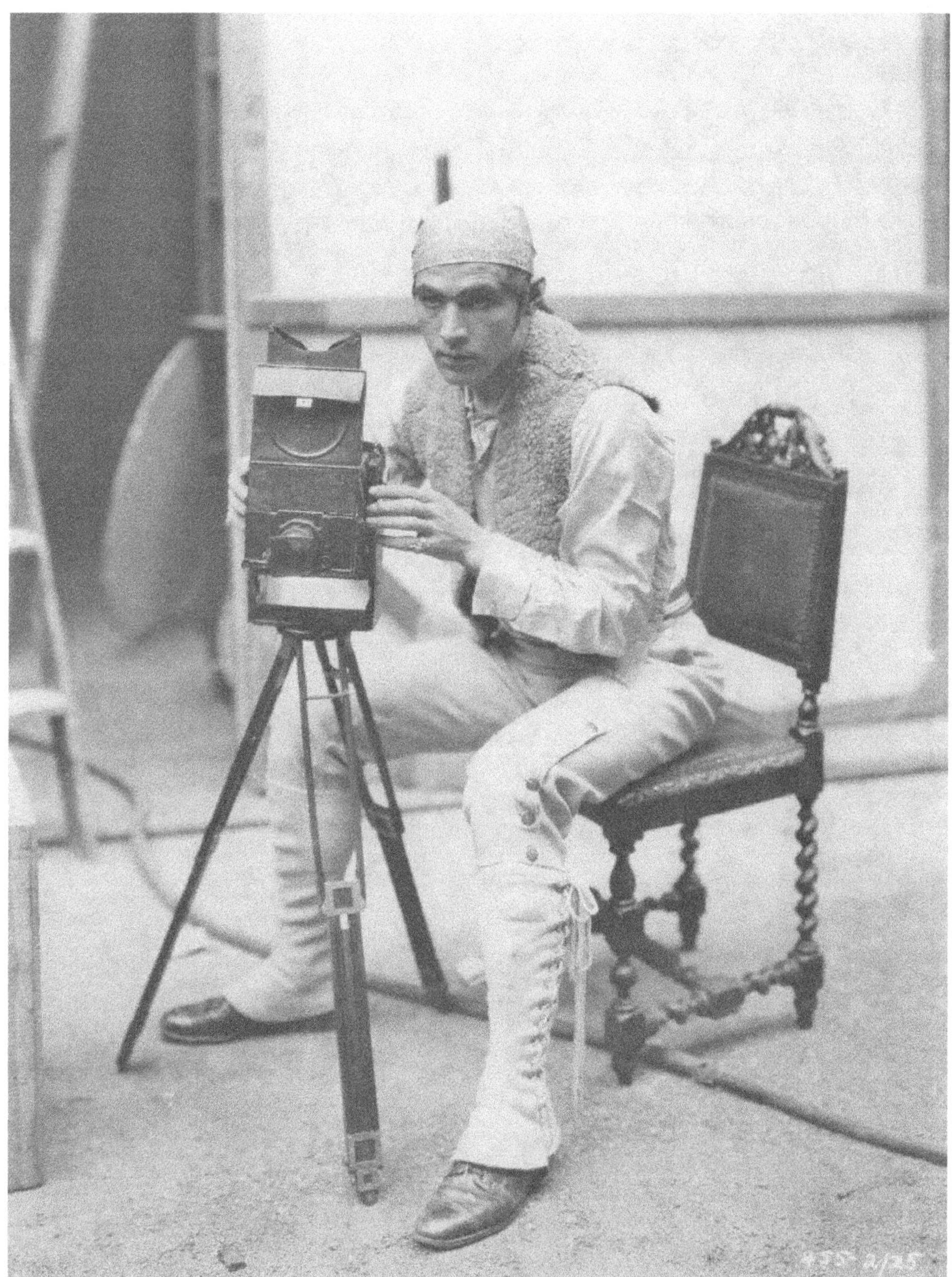

Valentino indulged his hobby as an amateur photographer during *Blood and Sand.*
(Author's collection)

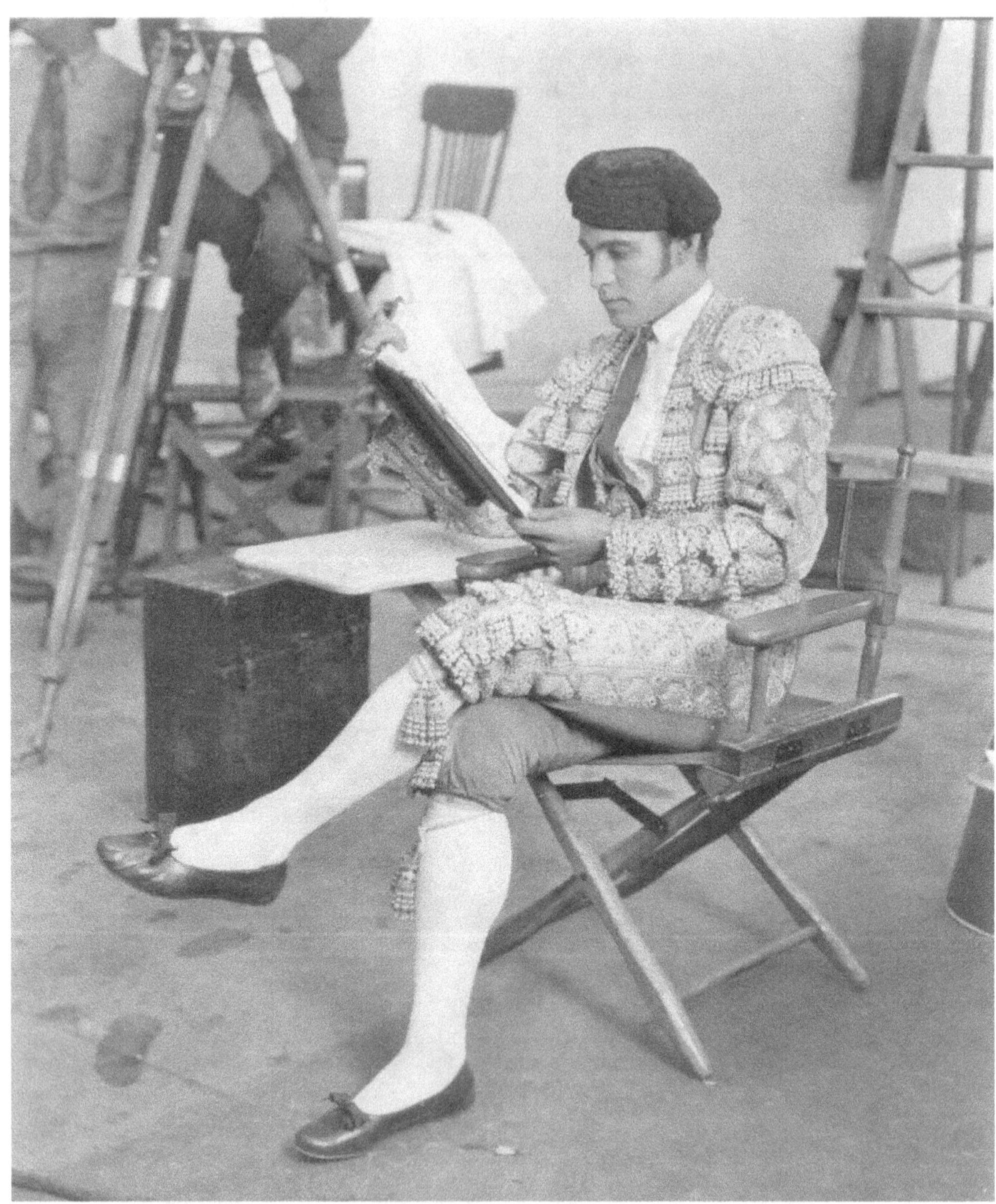

Valentino studies the scenario for his upcoming scene in *Blood and Sand*.
(Kevin Brownlow collection)

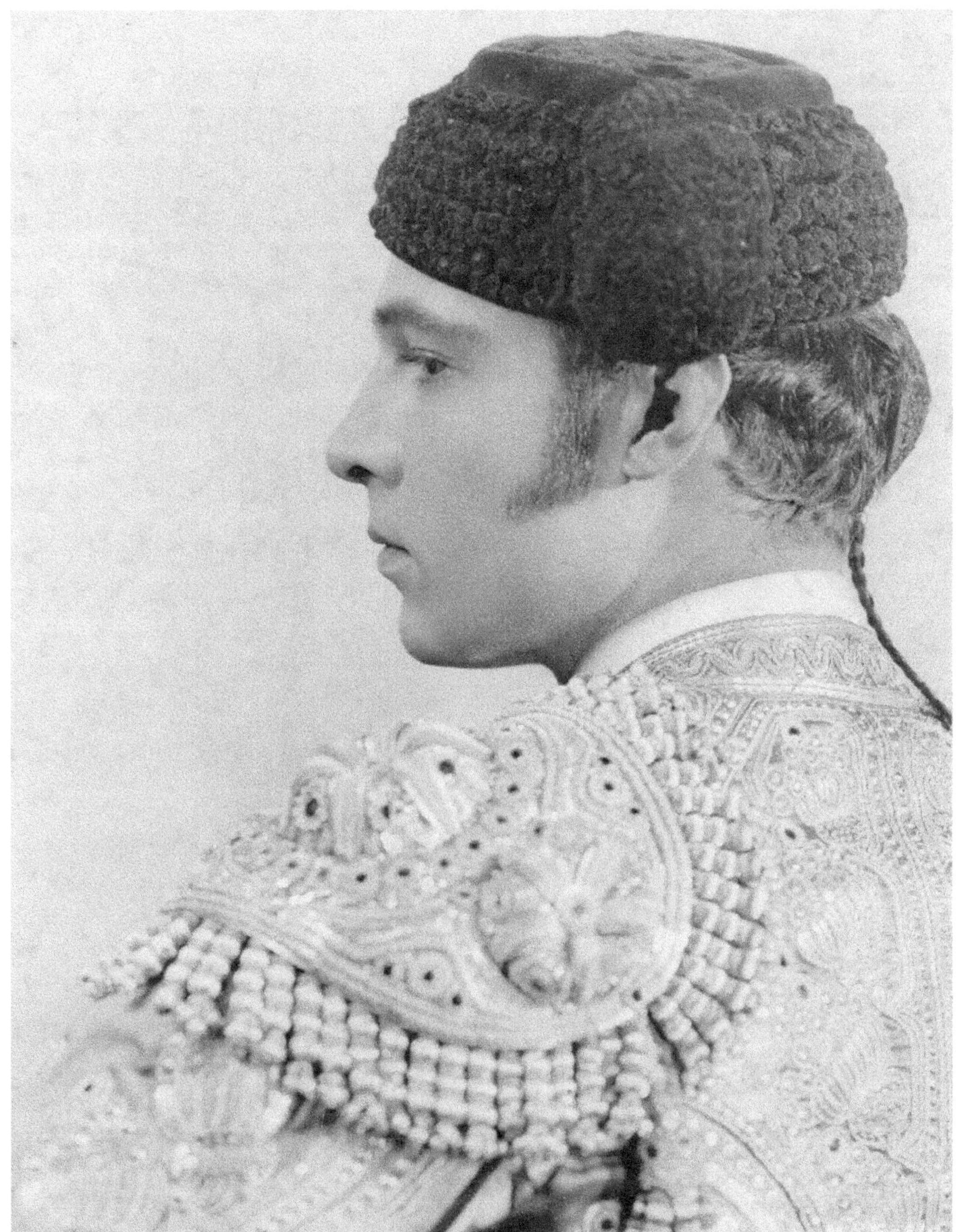

Valentino as Gallardo portrait by Donald Biddle Keyes.
(Author's collection)

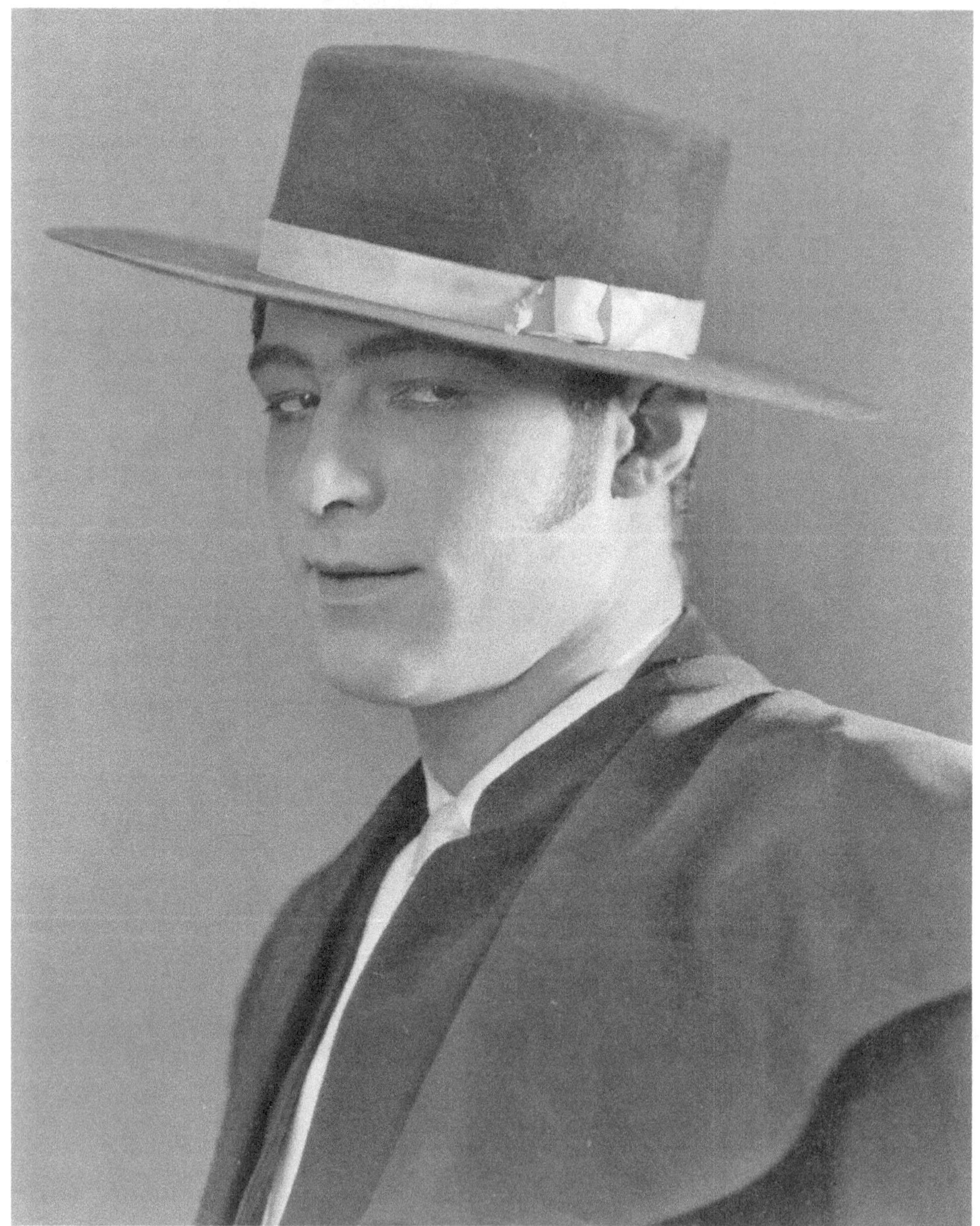

Valentino as Juan Gallardo by Donald Biddle Keyes
(Author's collection)

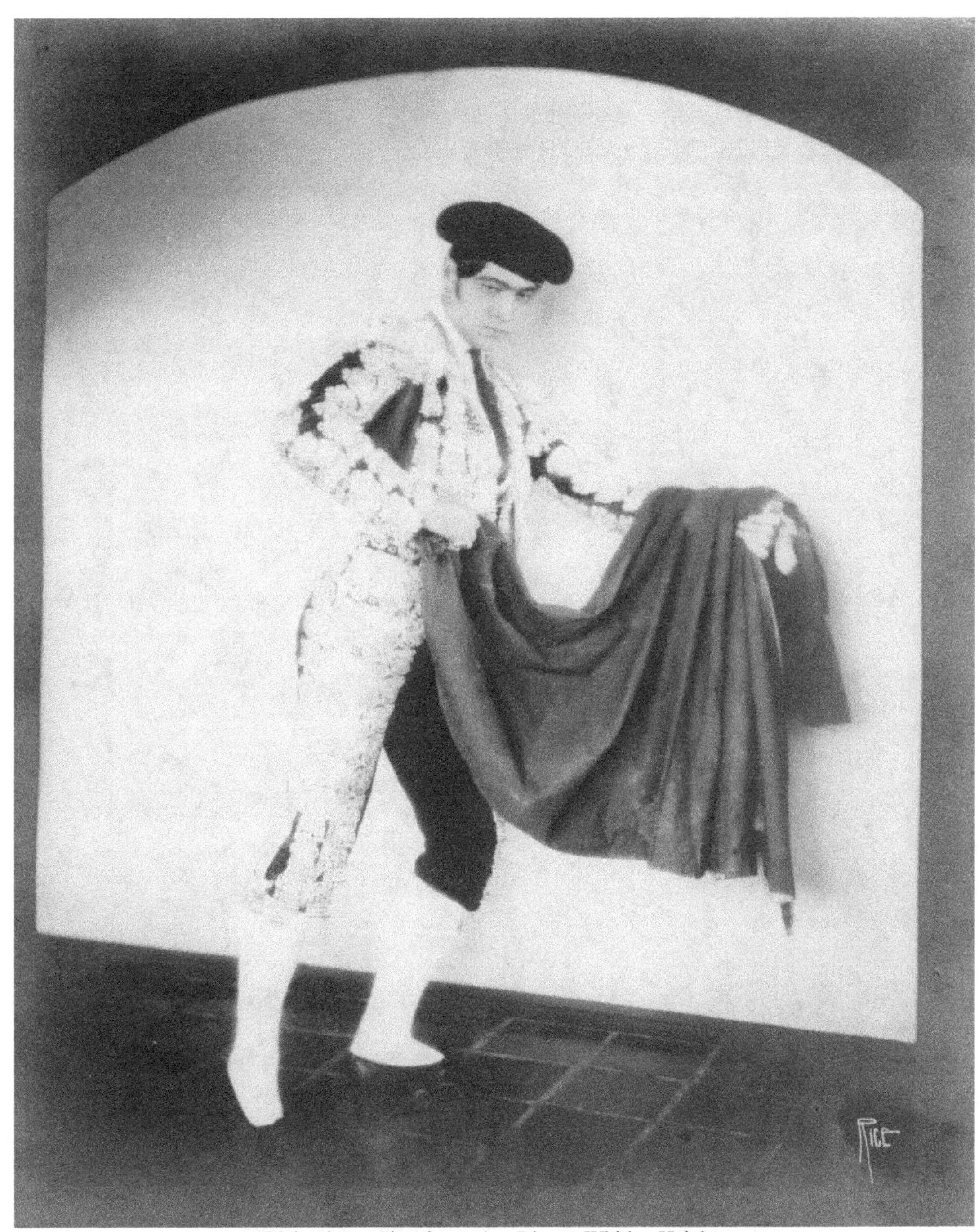

Valentino posing for Arthur Rice at Whitley Heights
(Author's collection)

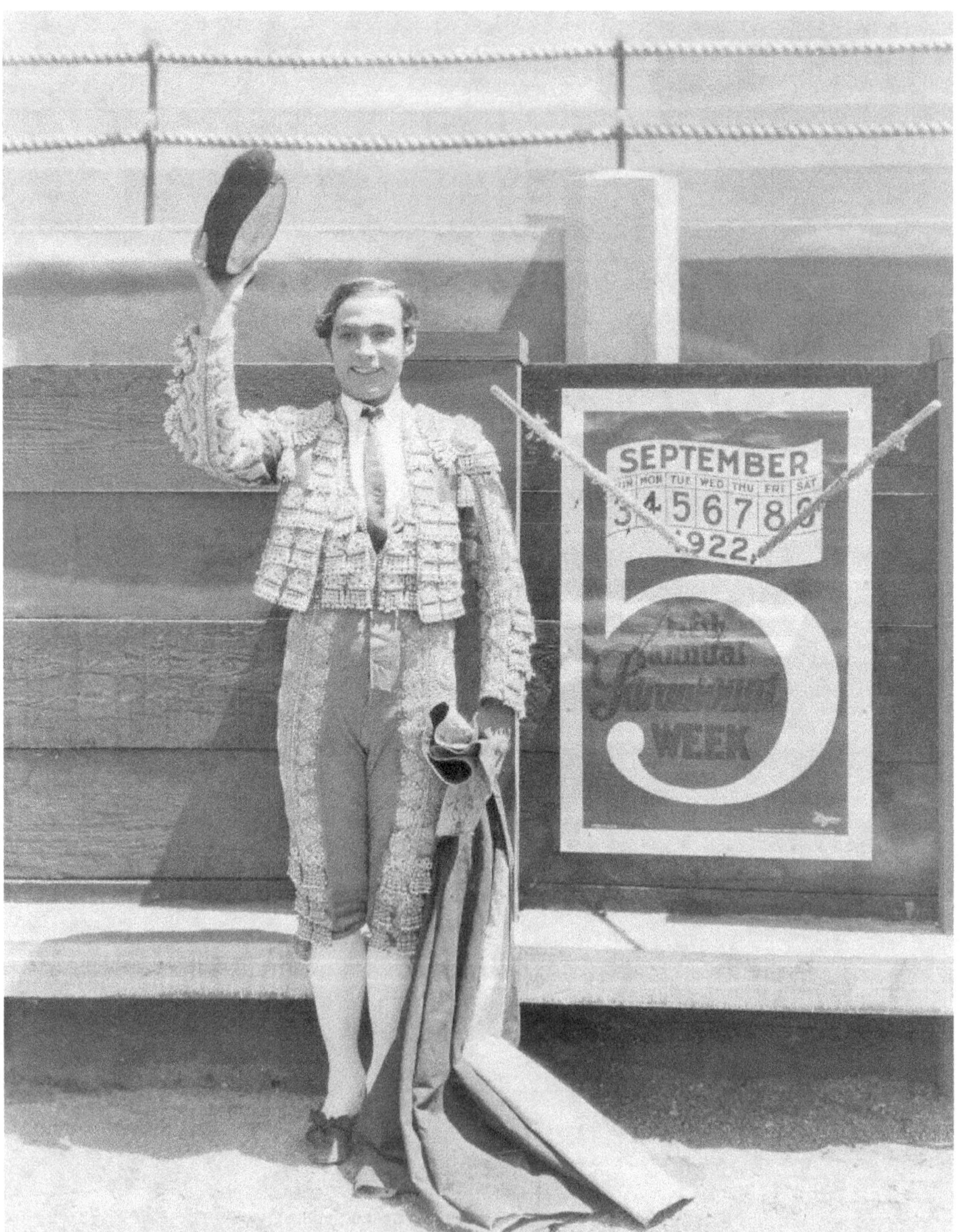

Valentino posing to promote the Paramount Week anniversary.
He will be on strike just after the celebration begins.
(Author's collection)

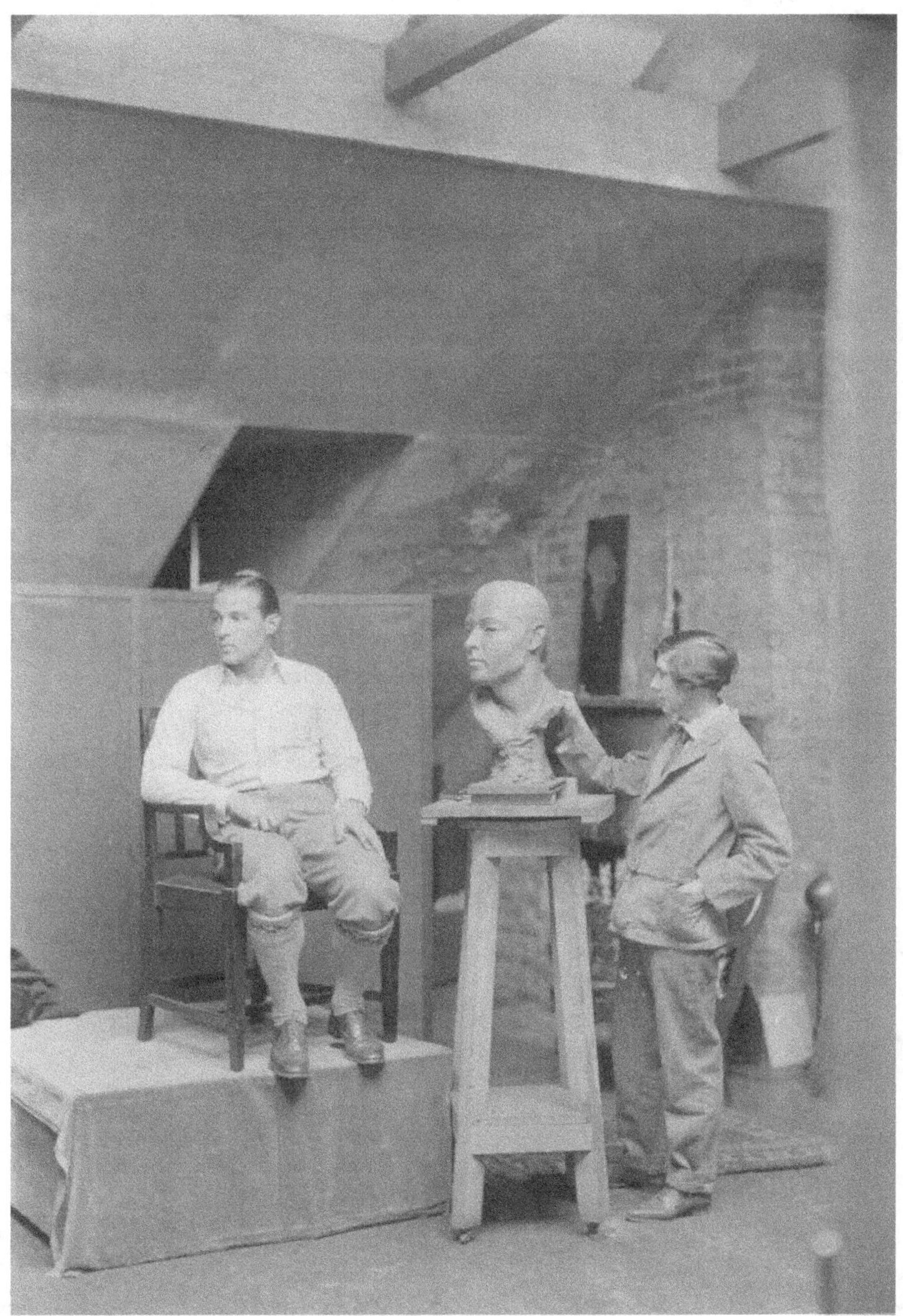

Valentino posing for his likeness, immortalized.
The artist and the whereabouts of the bust are unknown.
(Author's collection)

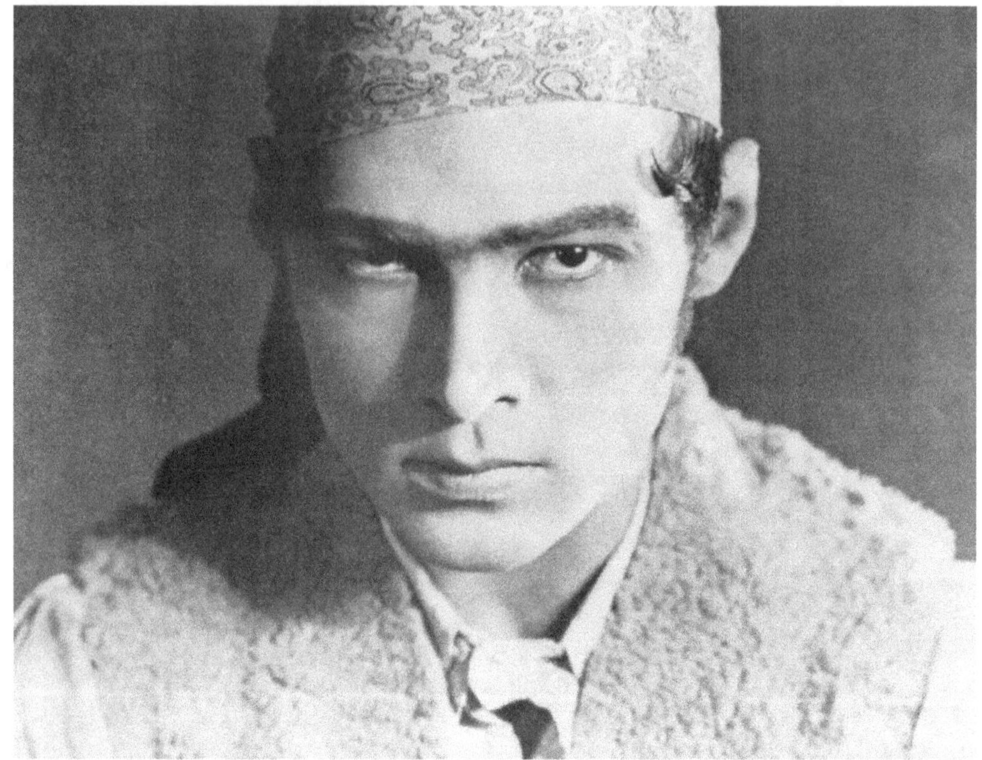

Valentino's intense gaze fascinated audiences.
(Author's collection)

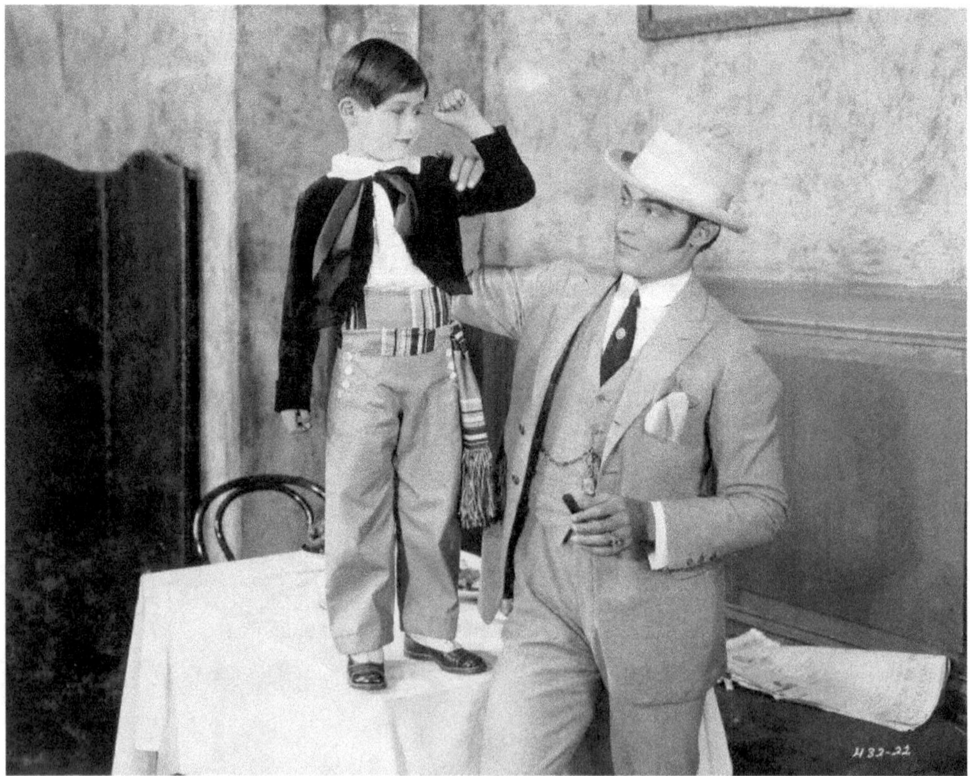

Valentino had a special rapport with any children cast in his films.
(Tracy Terhune collection)

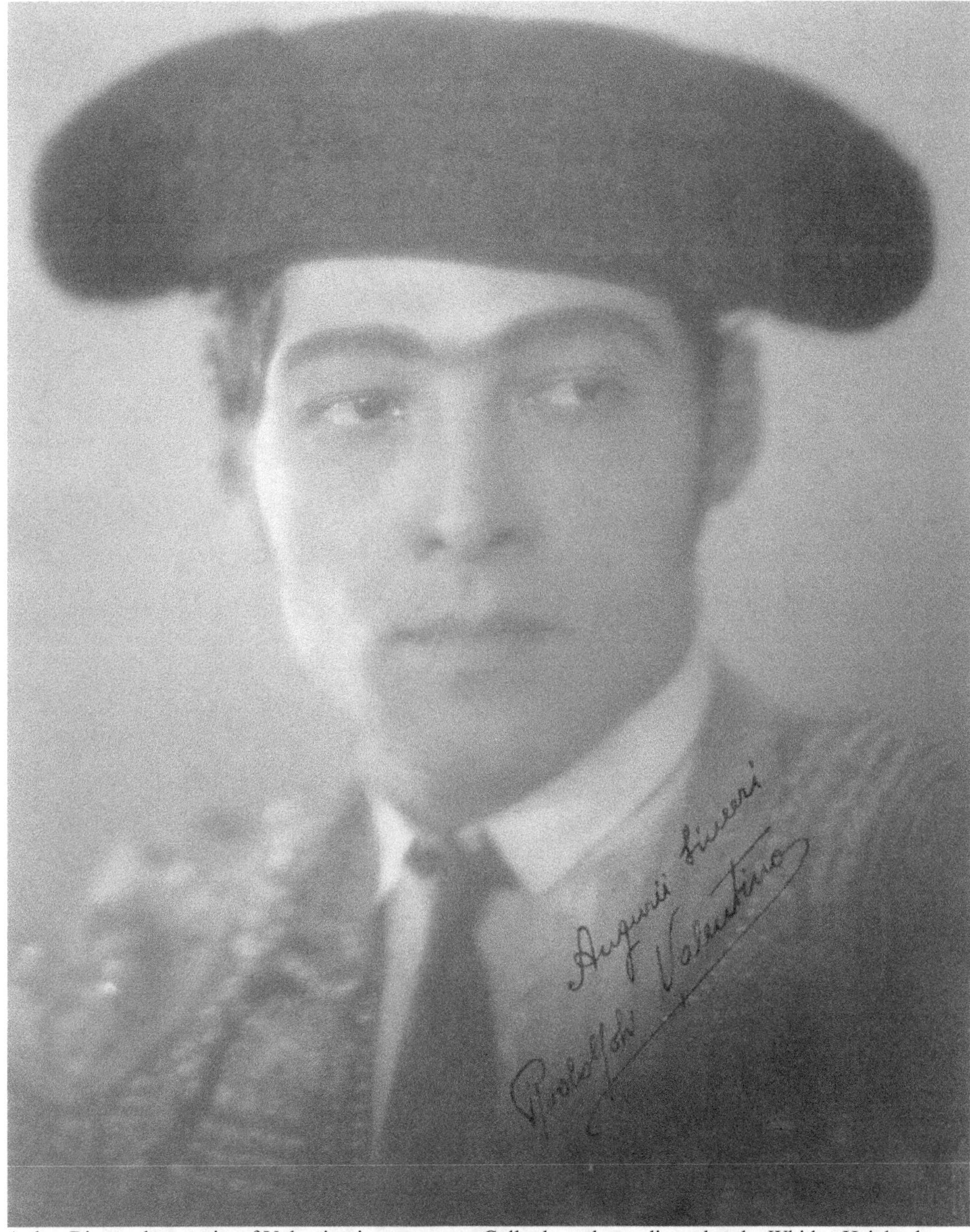

Arthur Rice took portraits of Valentino in costume as Gallardo at the studio and at the Whitley Heights house. These were the last sitting Valentino and Natacha had with Arthur Rice, he died soon afterwards. (Author's collection)

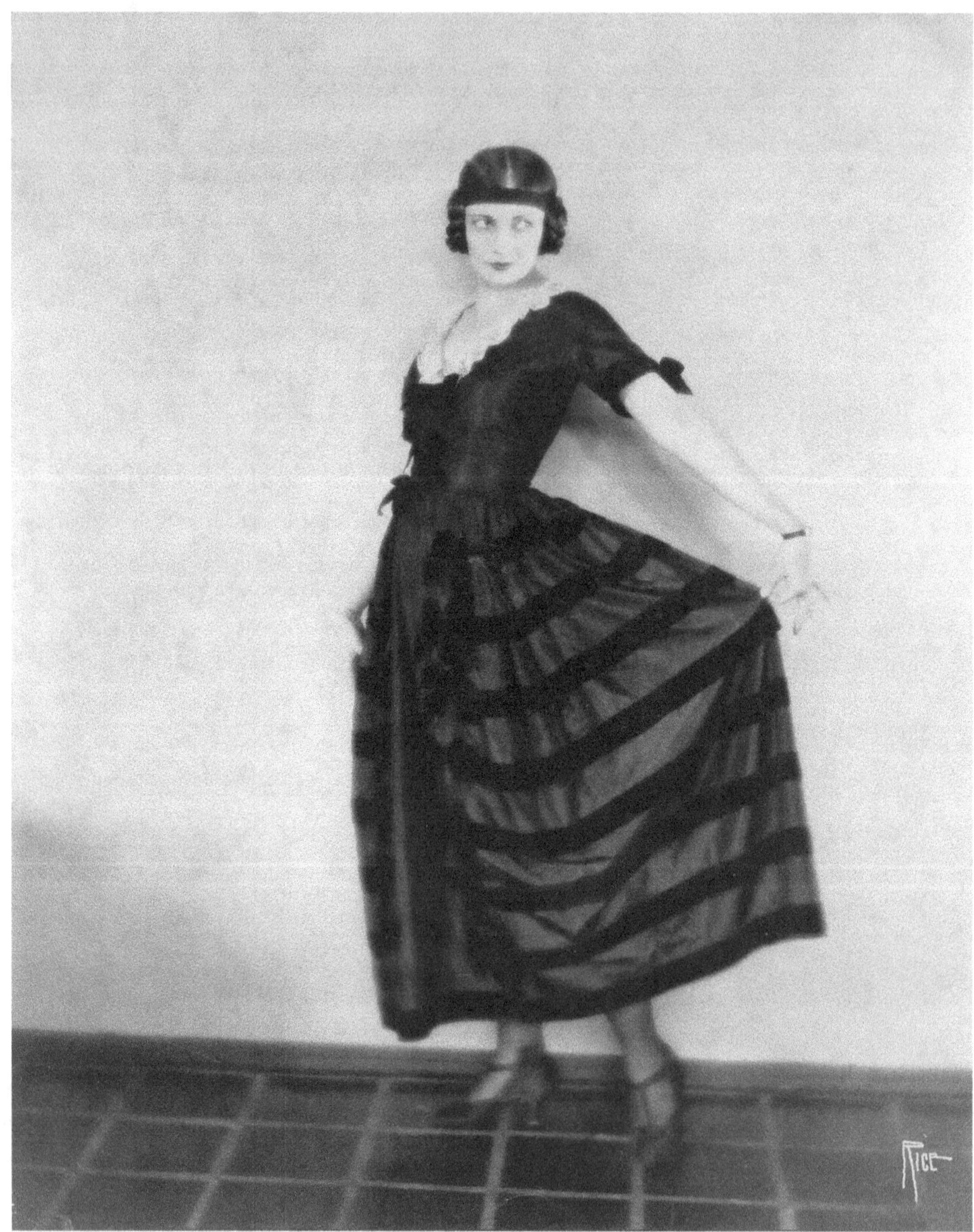

Natacha also posed at their home in Whitley Heights.
(Author's collection)

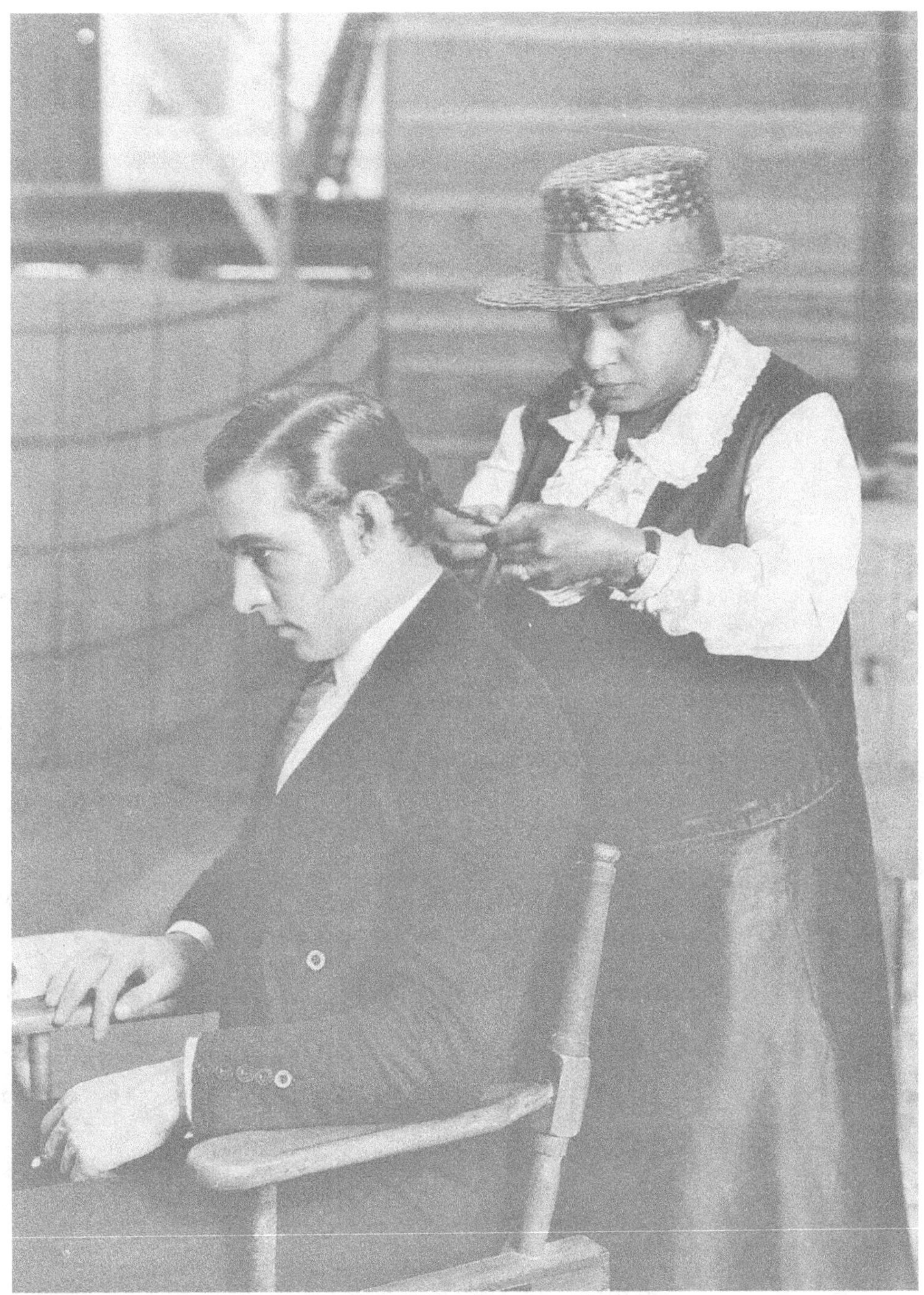

Valentino has his pigtail braided by Hattie Wilson Tabourne. Hattie had a seven-year contract with the studio, just like a movie star. She not only did Valentino's hair dressing, but Gloria Swanson, Pola Negri and every other star on the lot. (Author's collection)

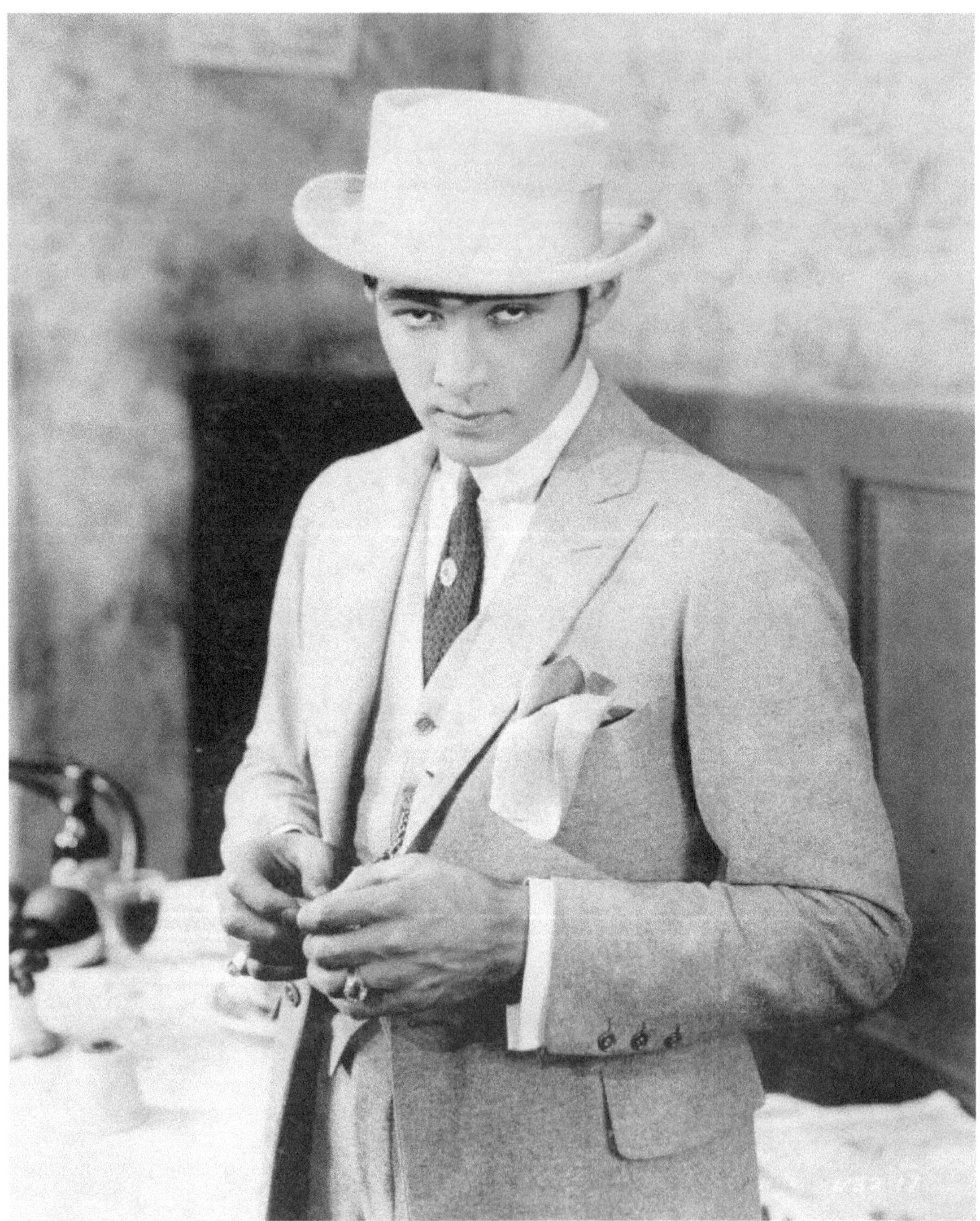

Valentino telegraphing sexual desire and vulnerability as only he could.
(Author's collection)

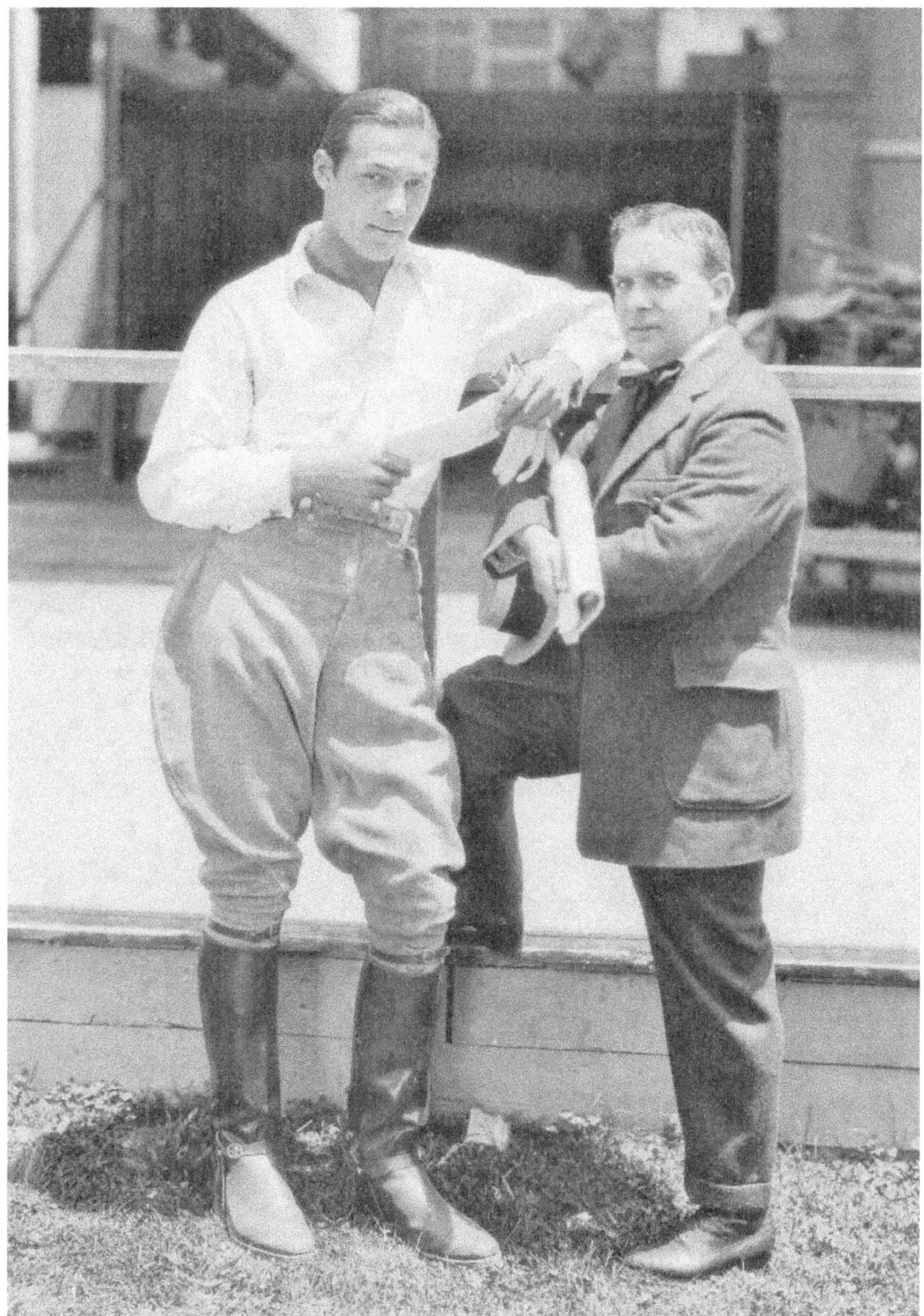

Valentino posing with Mexican journalist Jose Maria Sanchez Garcia while filming *The Young Rajah*. (Margaret Herrick Library; Academy of Motion Picture Arts and Sciences)

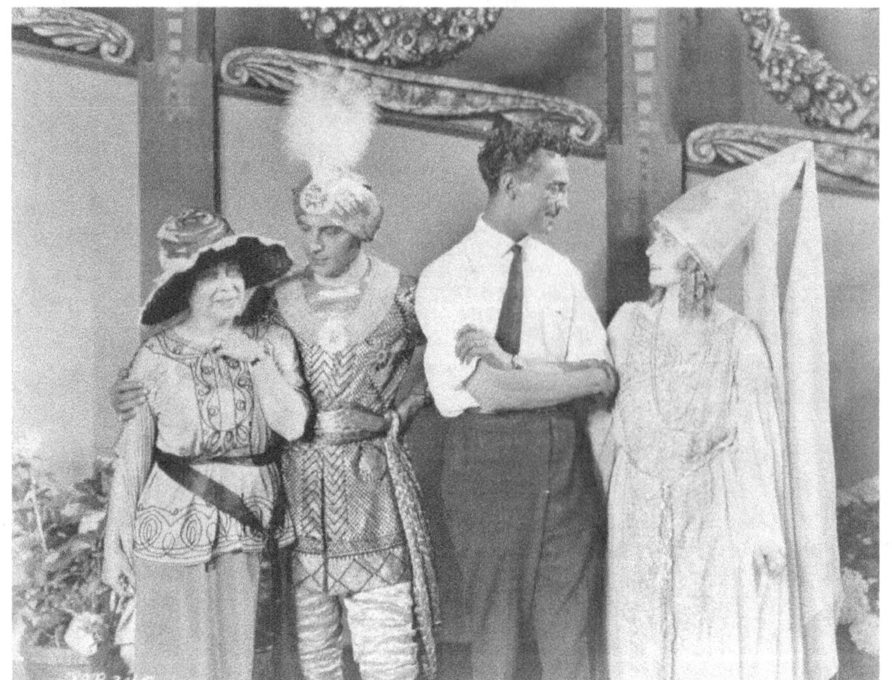

June Mathis, Valentino, director Phil Rosen and Wanda Hawley on the set of *The Young Rajah.*
(Margaret Herrick Library; Academy of Motion Picture Arts and Sciences)

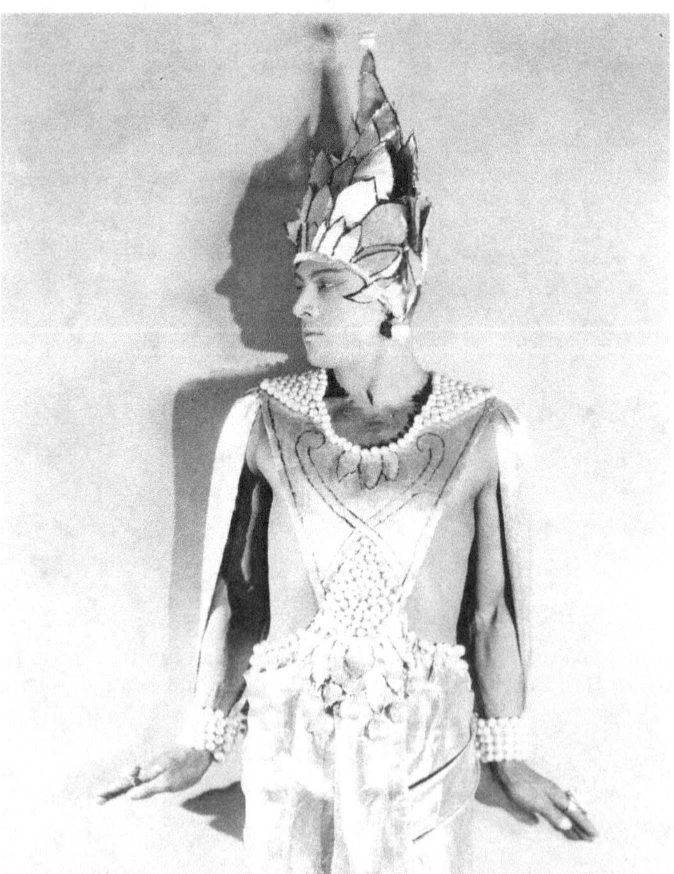

He did not seem to mind posing for publicity stills in which
he was garbed in outrageous costumes.
(Author's collection)

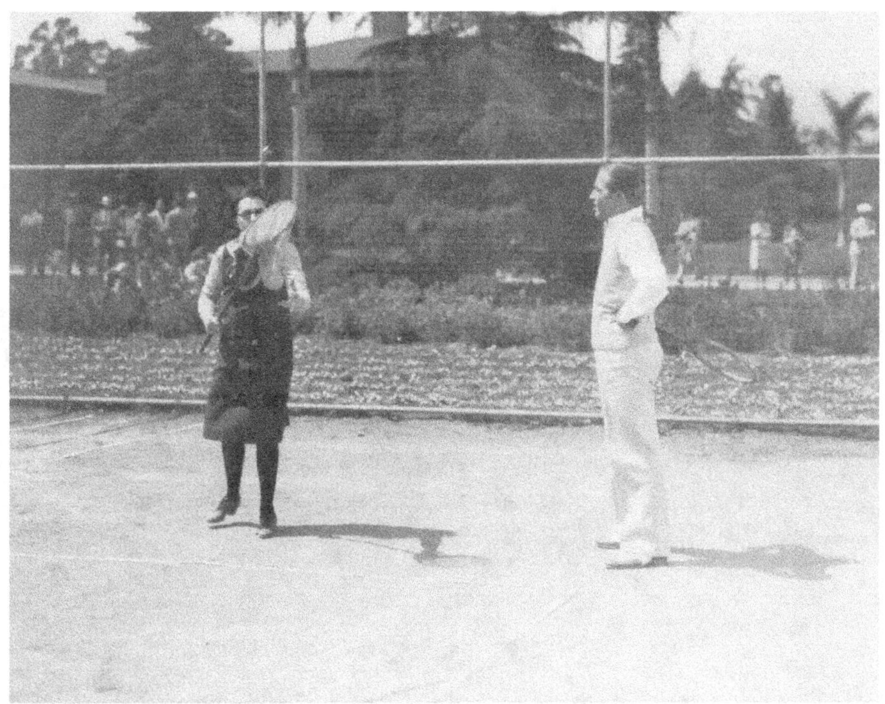

Future co-star Bebe Daniels and Valentino pair up for mixed-doubles at a charity event in Hollywood in 1922.
(Author's collection)

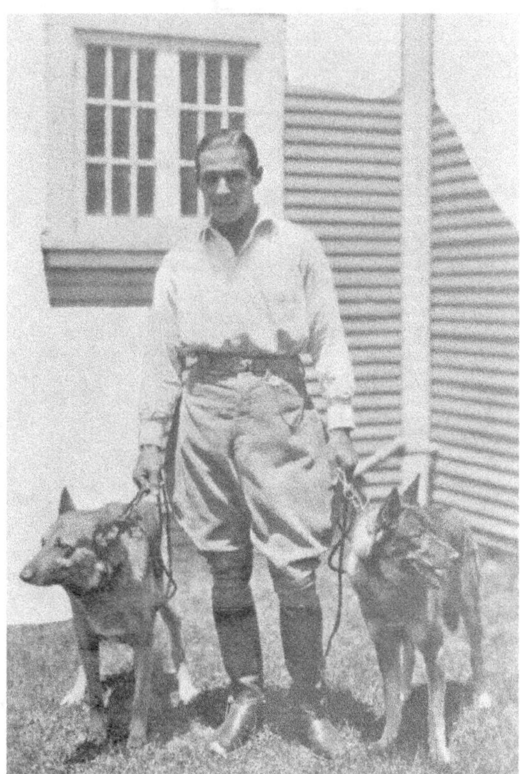

Valentino walking Sheik and Marquis at the studio.
(Author's collection)

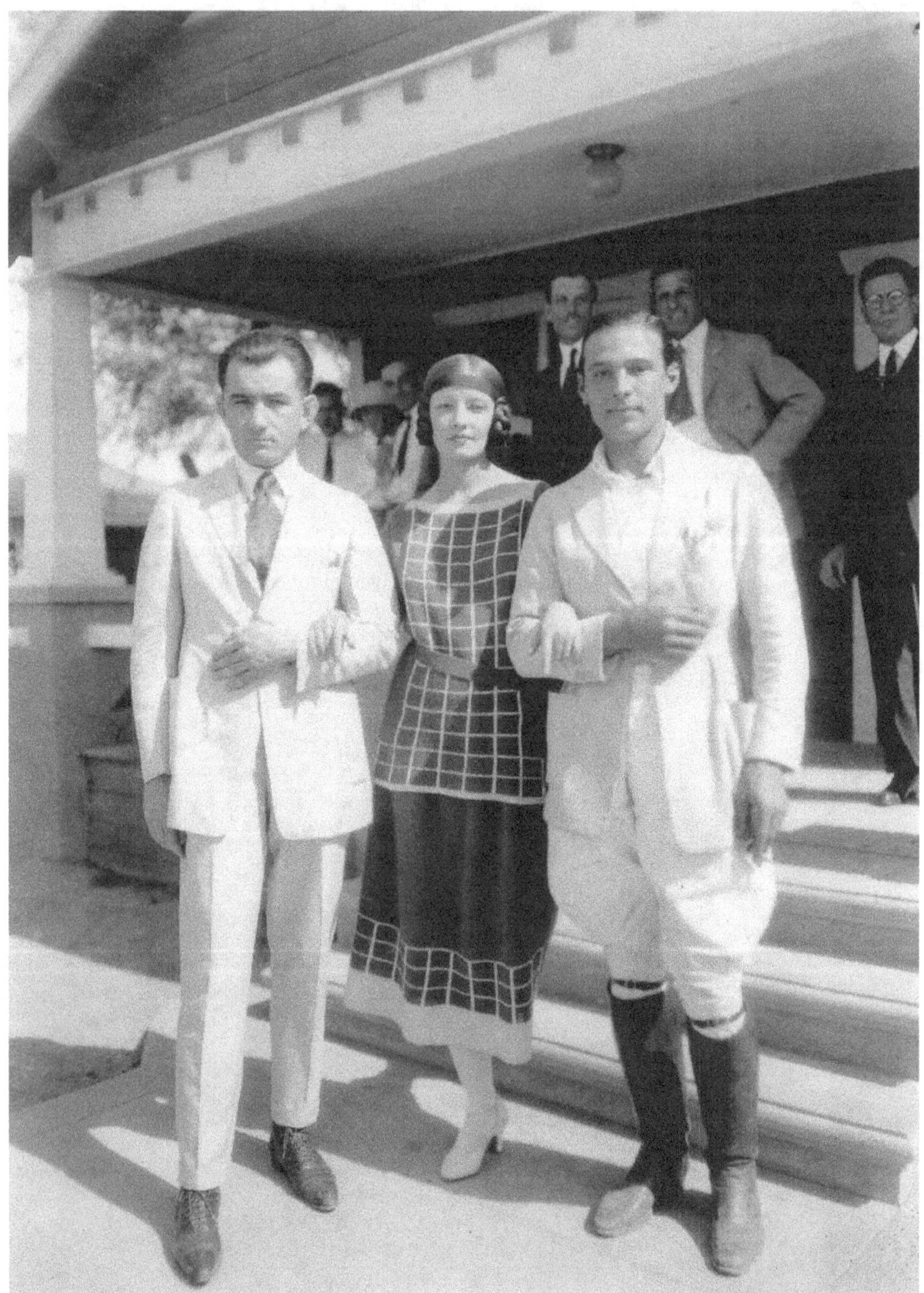

Natacha and Valentino while taking a break in Palm Springs traveled impulsively to Mexicali, Mexico to get married. Their honeymoon idyll did not last very long. (Margaret Herrick Library; Academy of Motion Picture Arts and Sciences)

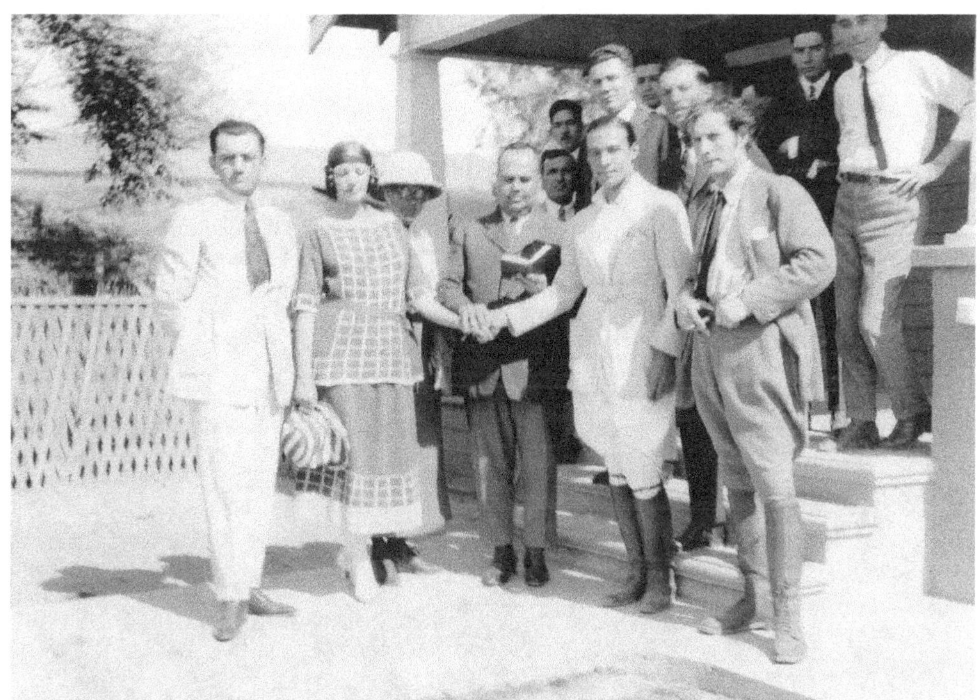

The wedding party poses after the ceremony. Unknown, Natacha, Dr. Florilla White, Otto Moller the Magistrate of Mexicali, Valentino and Douglas Gerrard. (Margaret Herrick Library; Academy of Motion Picture Arts and Sciences)

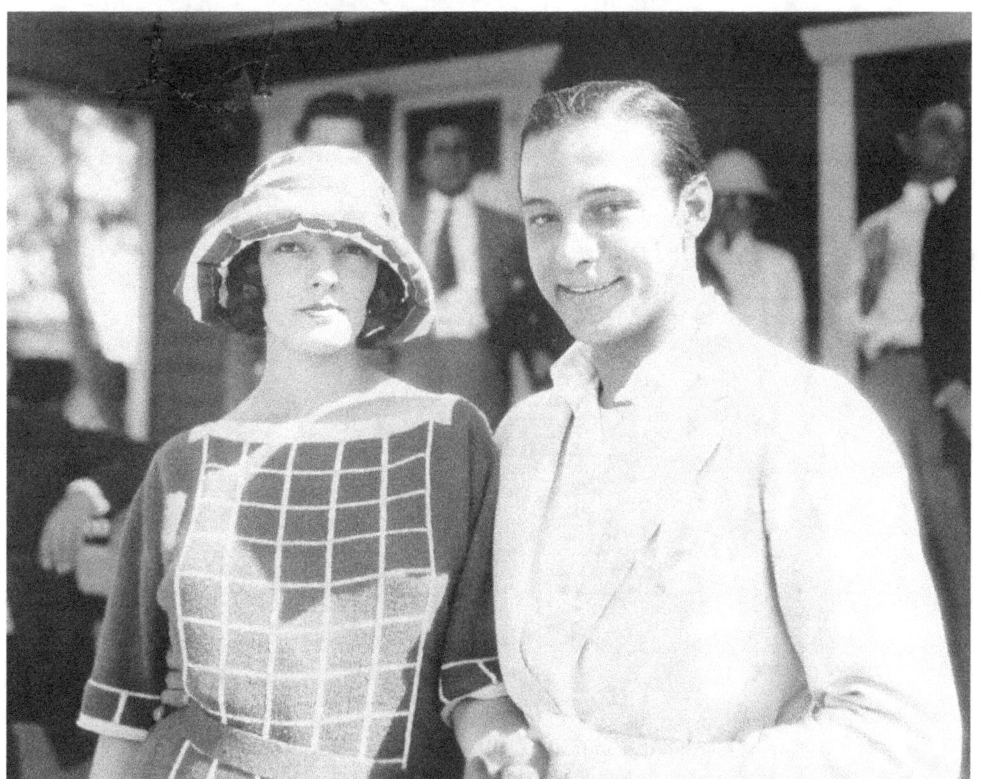

Valentino rarely looked happier than on this day. (Author's collection)

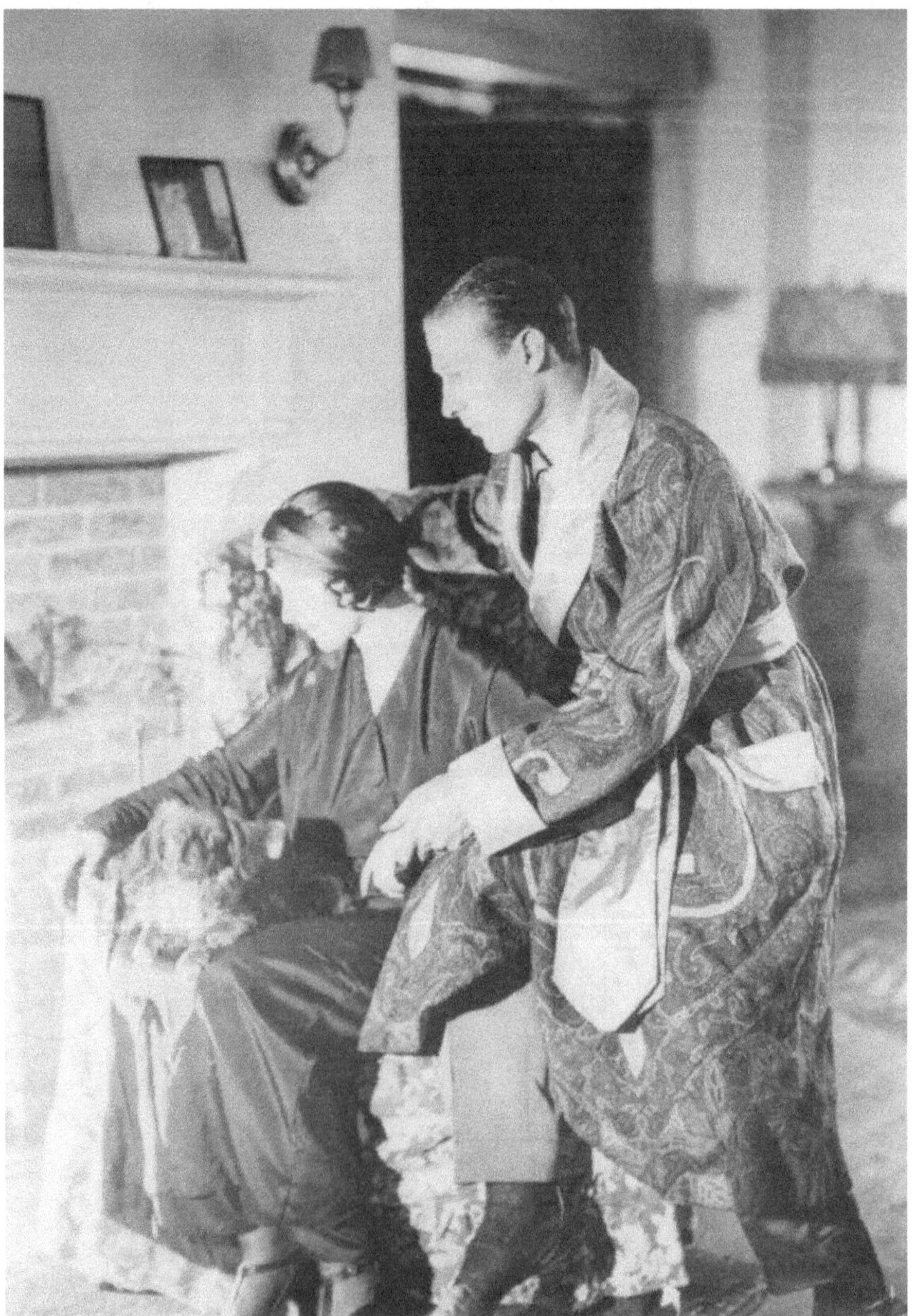
The Valentinos sat for Russell Ball for an additional series of portraits.
A picture of marital bliss until the California divorce laws came in to play.
(Michael Morris collection)

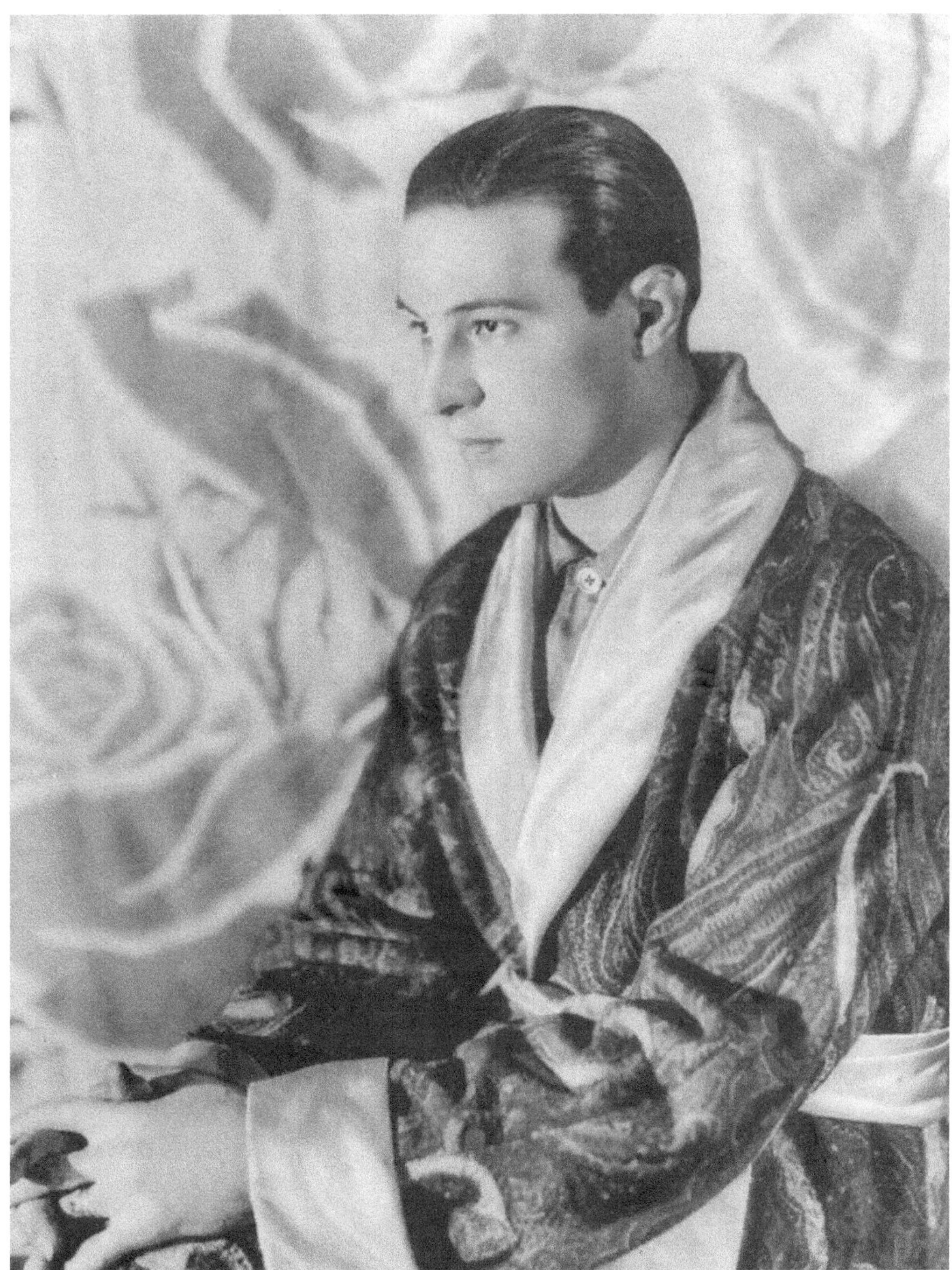

Valentino *circa* 1923, portrait by Russell Ball (Author's collection)

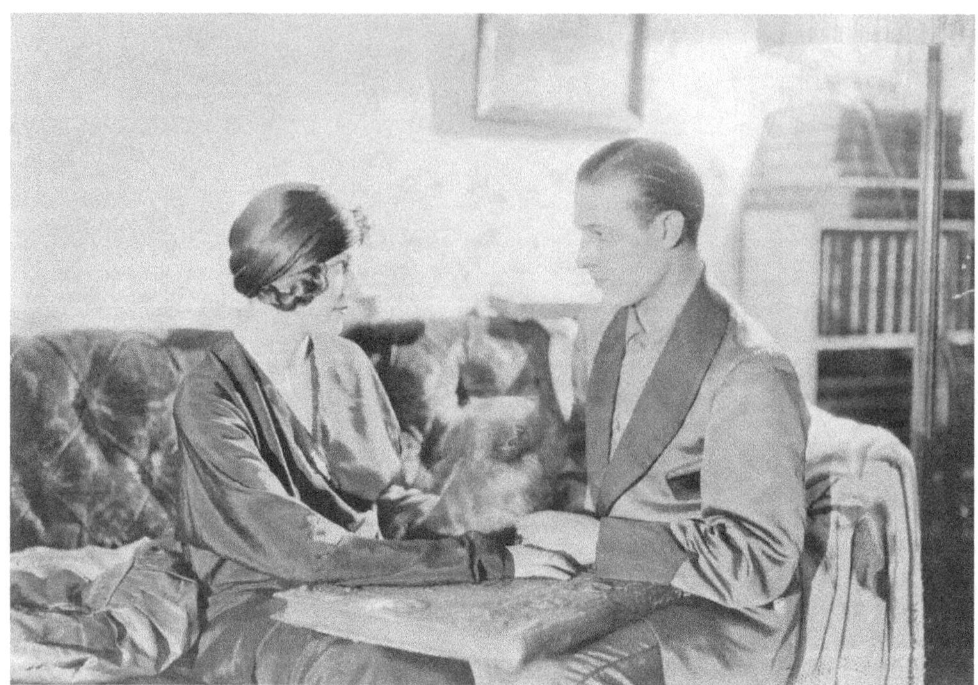
The pair shared a love of animals of which there is little doubt that helped cement their affection.
Natacha helped design their furniture for Whitley Heights.
This was their tatty old couch from the Sunset Blvd. bungalow.
(Author's collection)

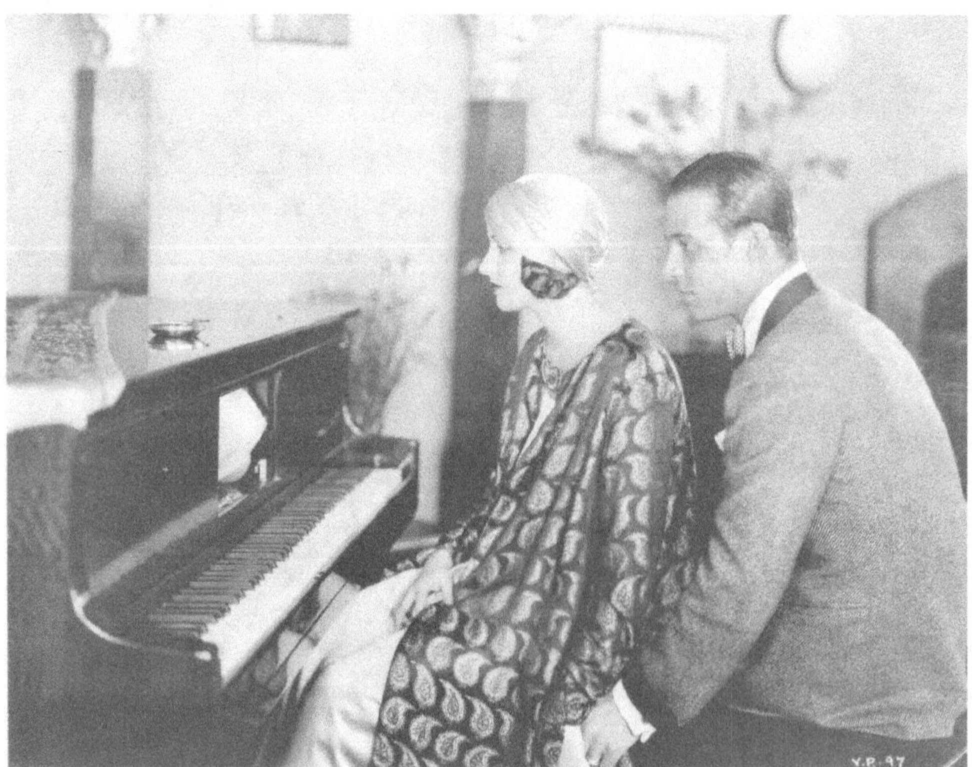
While neither could play, they had the most up to date player piano. (Author's collection)

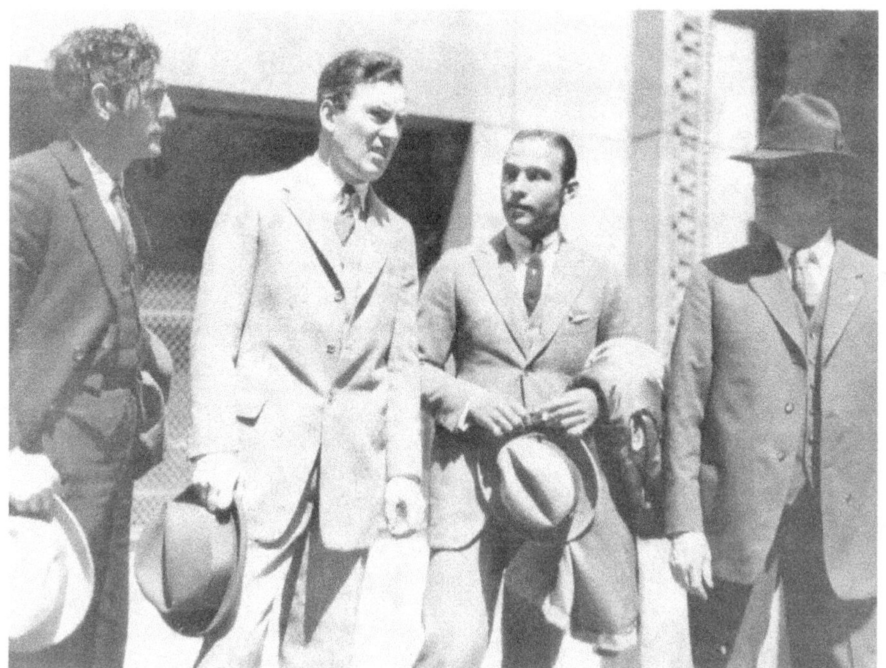

Having been arrested for bigamy, Douglas Gerrard and June Mathis moved heaven and earth to drum up bail money. Douglas Gerrard, Thomas Meighan, Valentino and counsel W.I. Gilbert exiting the courthouse after bail had been posted.
(Author's collection)

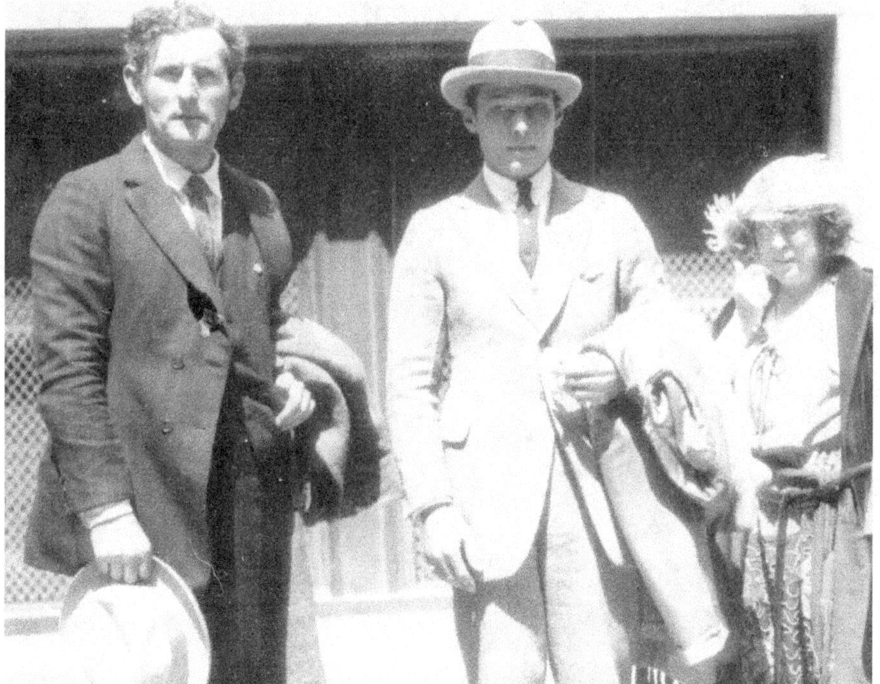

Douglas Gerrard, Valentino and June Mathis outside the courthouse.
(Author's collection)

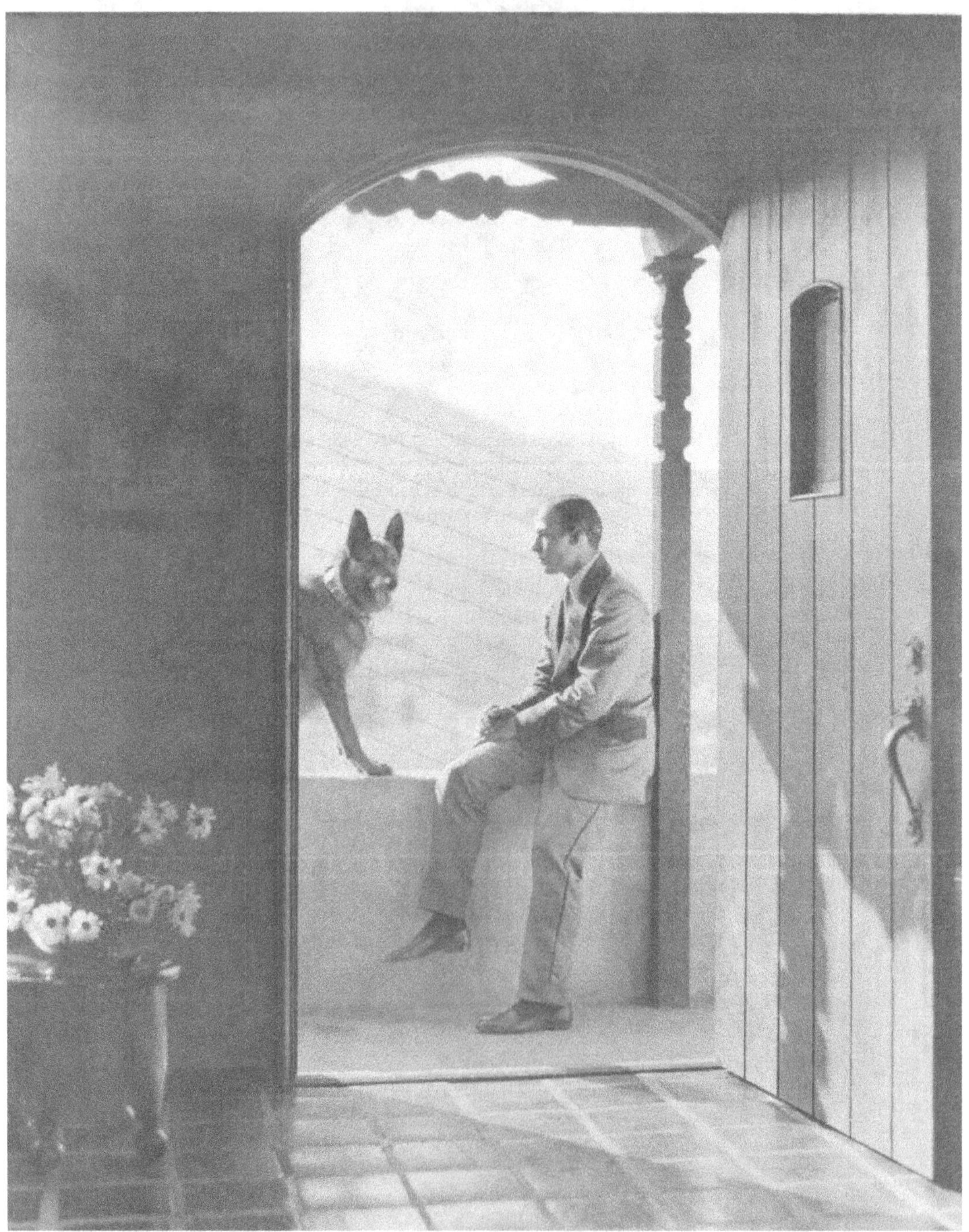

After the bigamy charges were filed, Natacha fled to the East coast to hide out.
Valentino went on the offensive and posed for a series of lonely photographs at Whitley Heights.
(Author's collection)

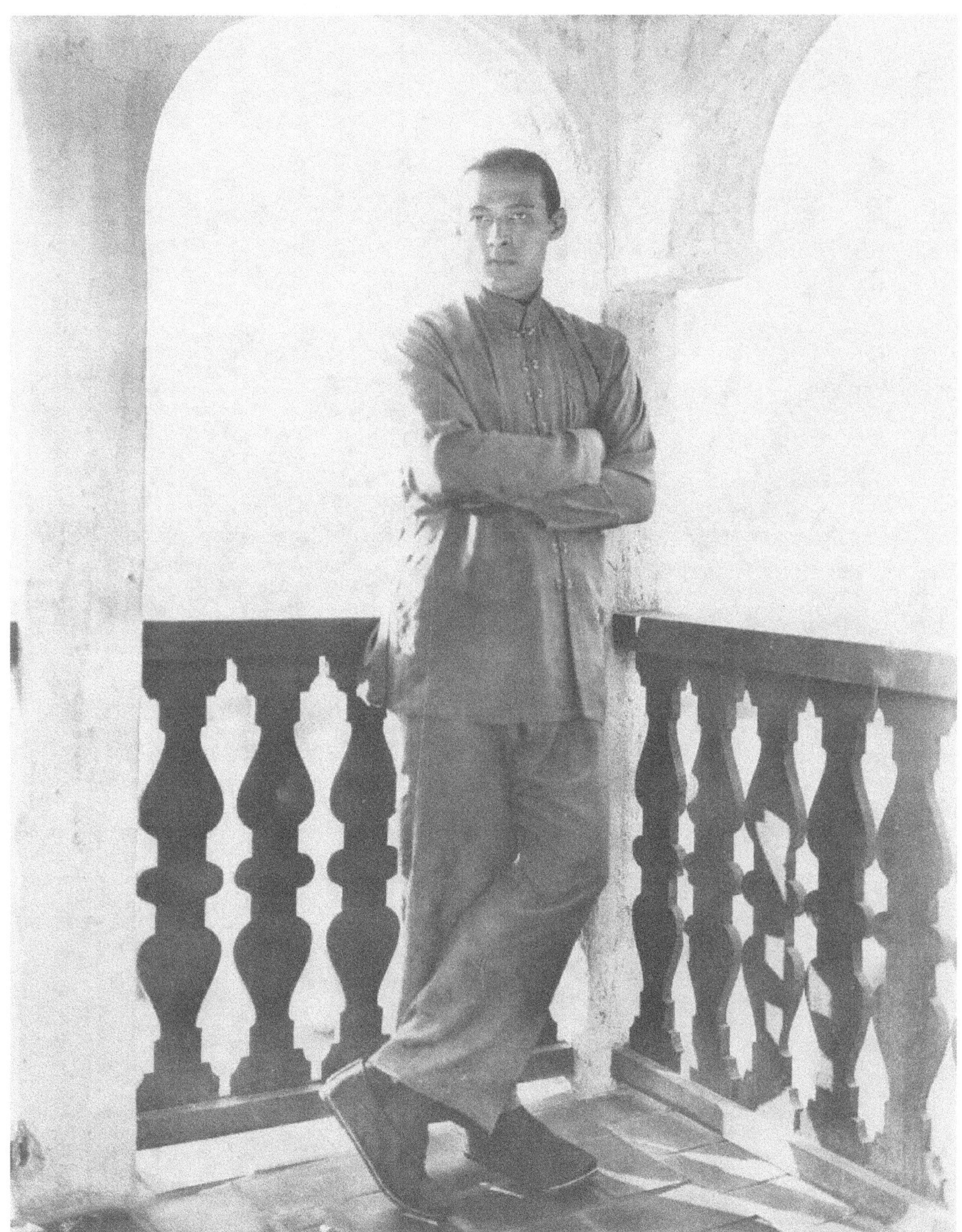

Valentino alone, defiant and angry wanting nothing more than to be with Natacha.
(Author's collection)

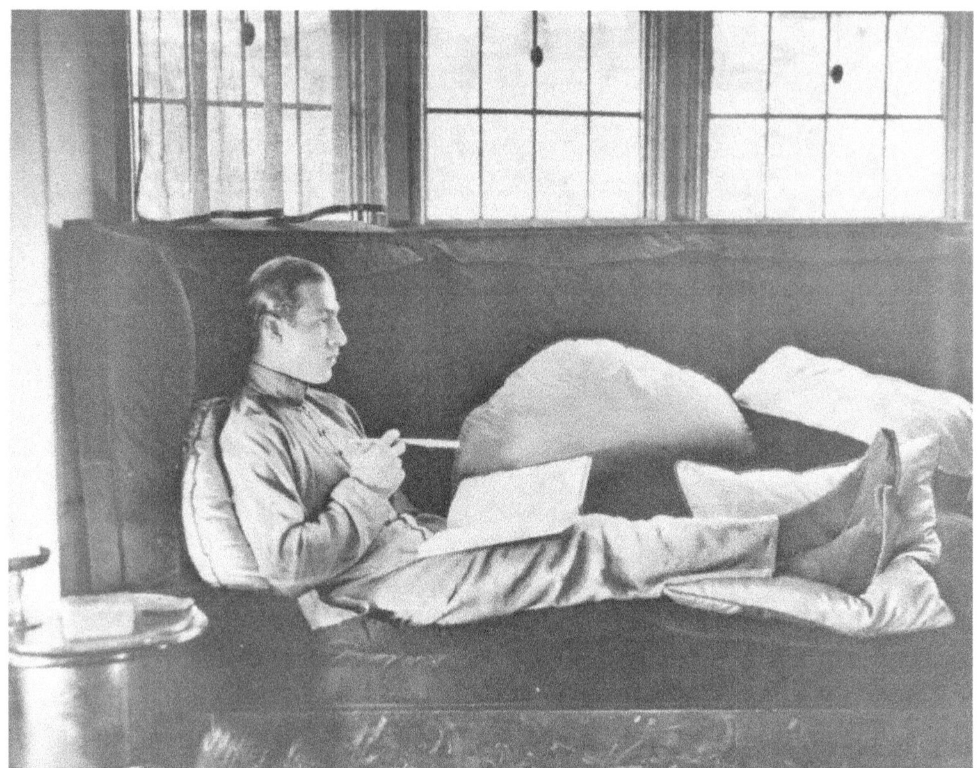

A pensive Valentino captured by James Abbe. (Author's collection)

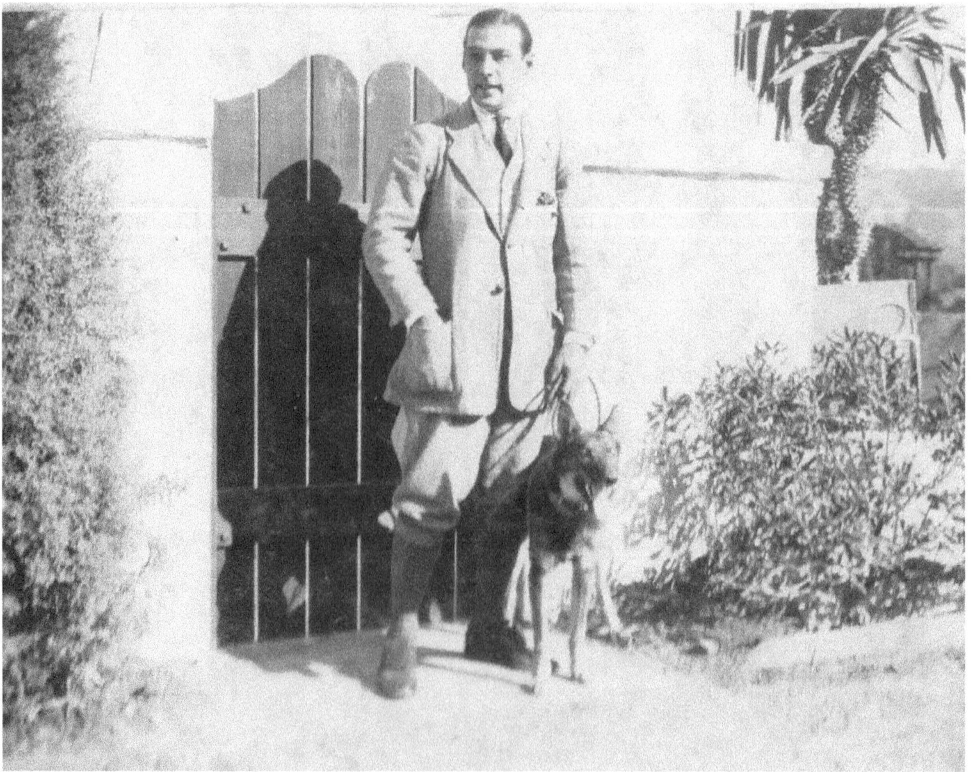

Walking with Sheik outside the Whitley Heights house. (Author's collection)

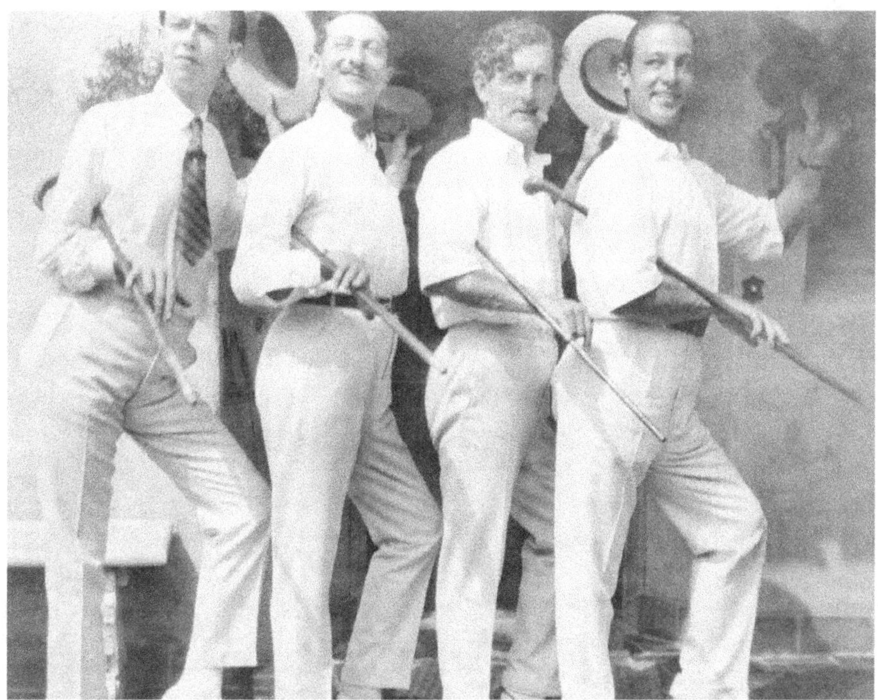

Valentino's friends rallied around him to keep him company and entertained.
They spent afternoons clowning for Paul Ivano's camera at Whitley Heights.
Robert Florey, Jean di Limur, Douglas Gerrard and Valentino as debonair chorus boys.
(Paul Lamastra collection)

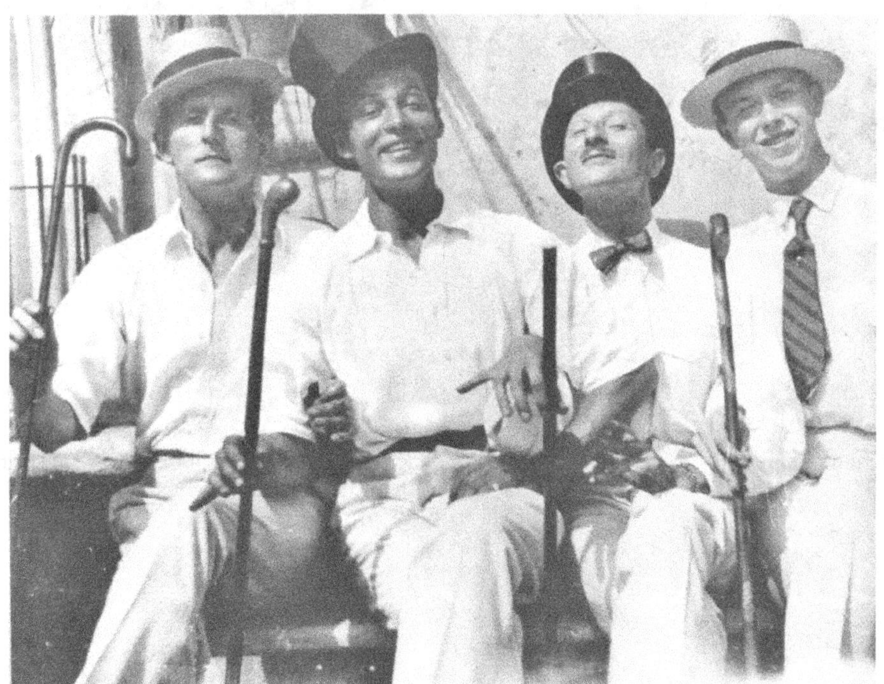

Valentino enjoyed spending time and clowning with his friends.
While Natacha was gone, it is clear his support group meant a great deal to him.
(Author's collection)

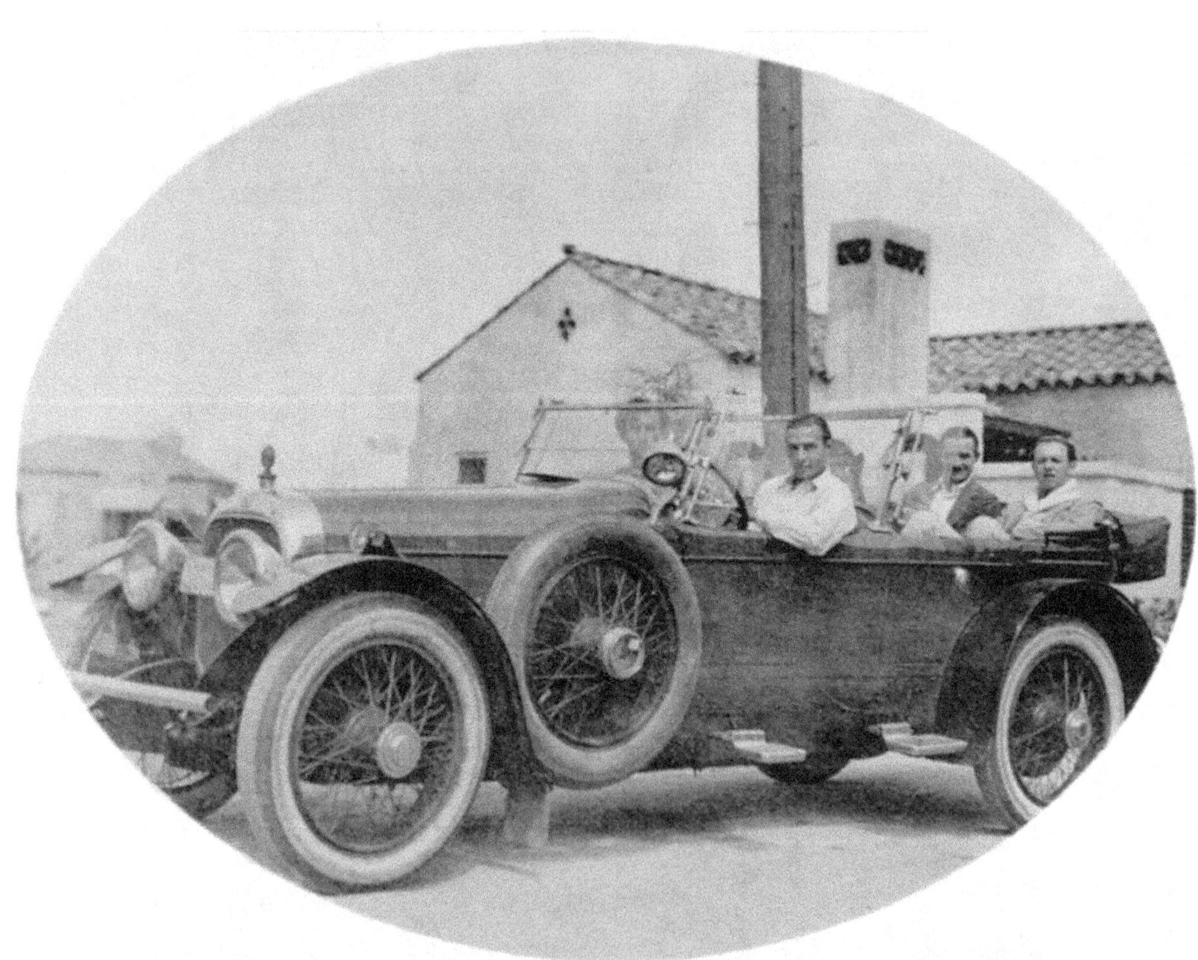

Douglas Gerrard and Valentino (front seat) Carl Weiderman and Robert Florey (back seat) posing in Valentino's almost completely restored 1915 Cadillac. Valentino prided himself on his mechanical instincts and he loved this car, which was a wreck when he bought it.
(Private collection)

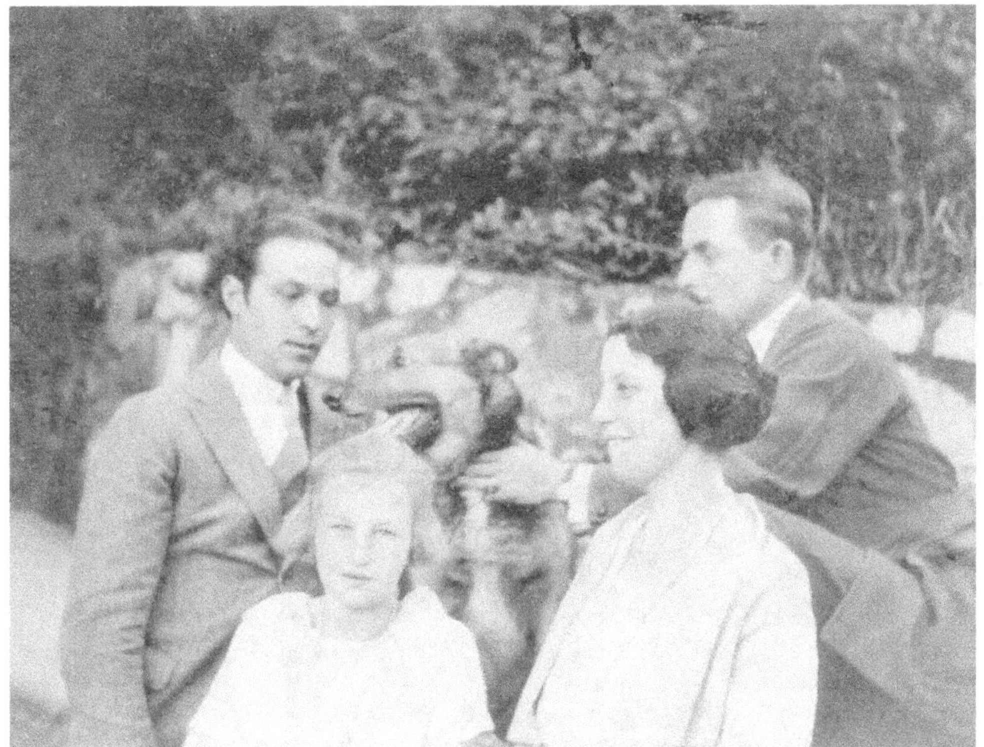

Valentino with Marquis, Mr. and Mrs. Carl Weiderman and their daughter. (Author's collection)

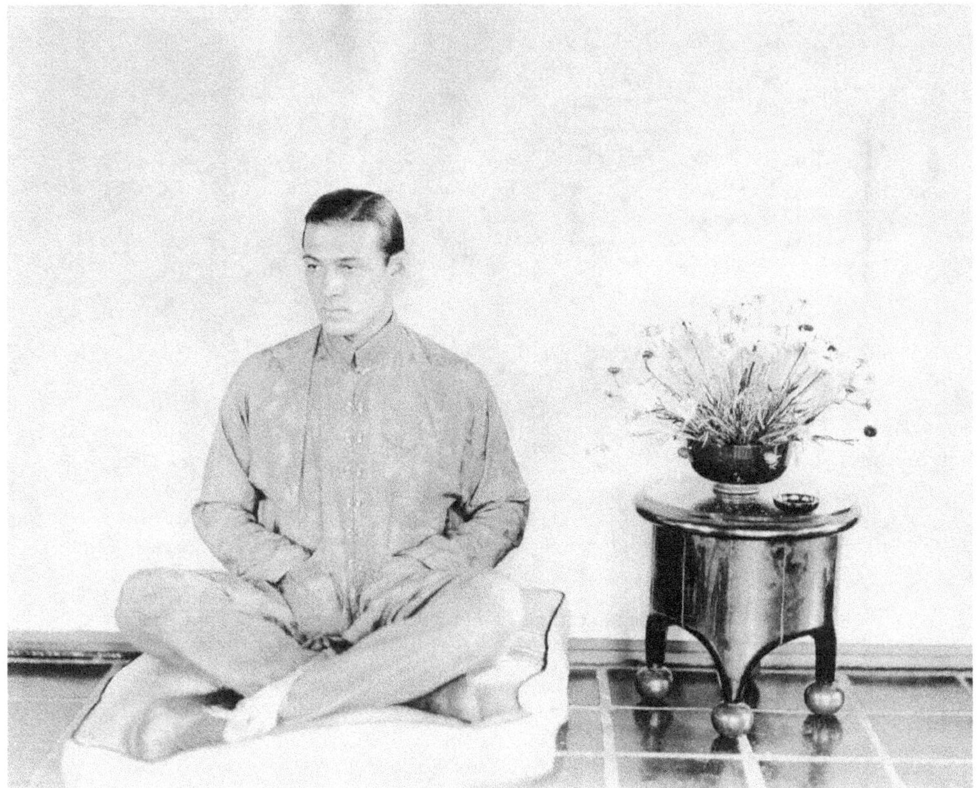

Valentino exhibiting loneliness at Whitley Heights. (Author's collection)

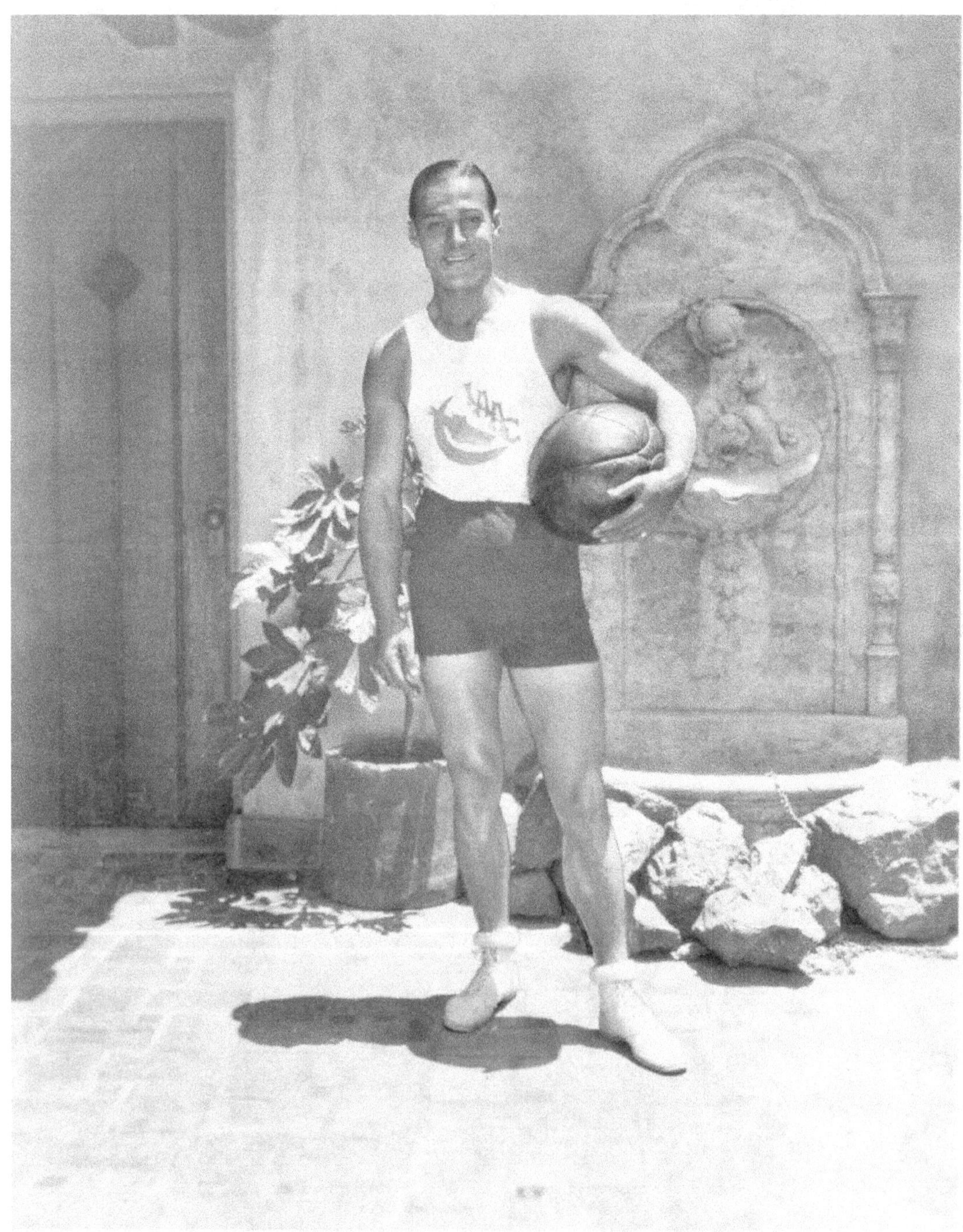

Valentino took great pride in keeping fit. He loved all manner of outdoor sports and he worked hard to keep his physique in shape.
(Author's collection)

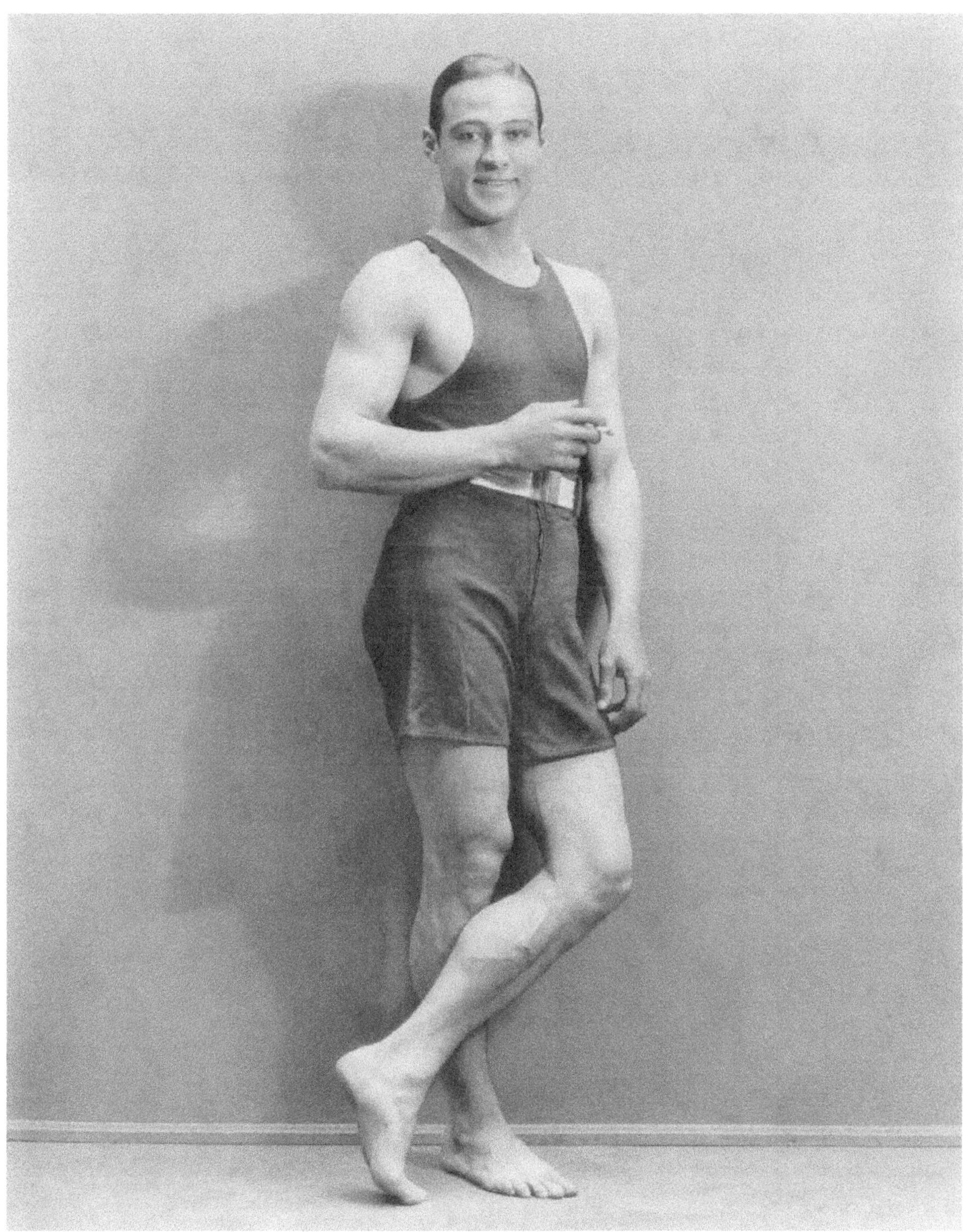

Valentino's obvious pride in his physique.
Relaxed and ever-present cigarette, his only true vice where his health was concerned.
(Michael and Virginia Back collection)

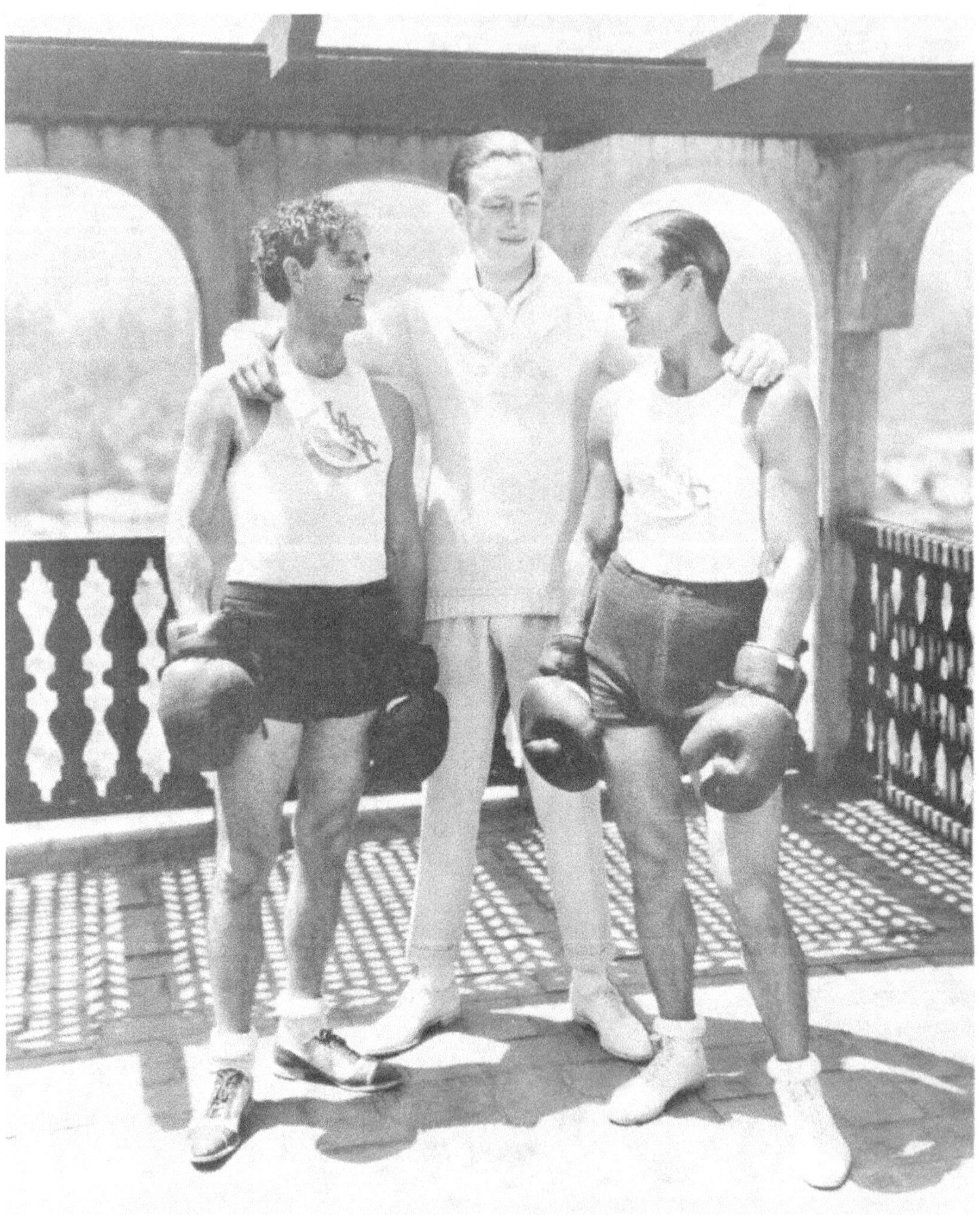

Valentino posed for home movies and with his pals Douglas Gerrard and Robert Florey at Whitley Heights. (Author's collection)

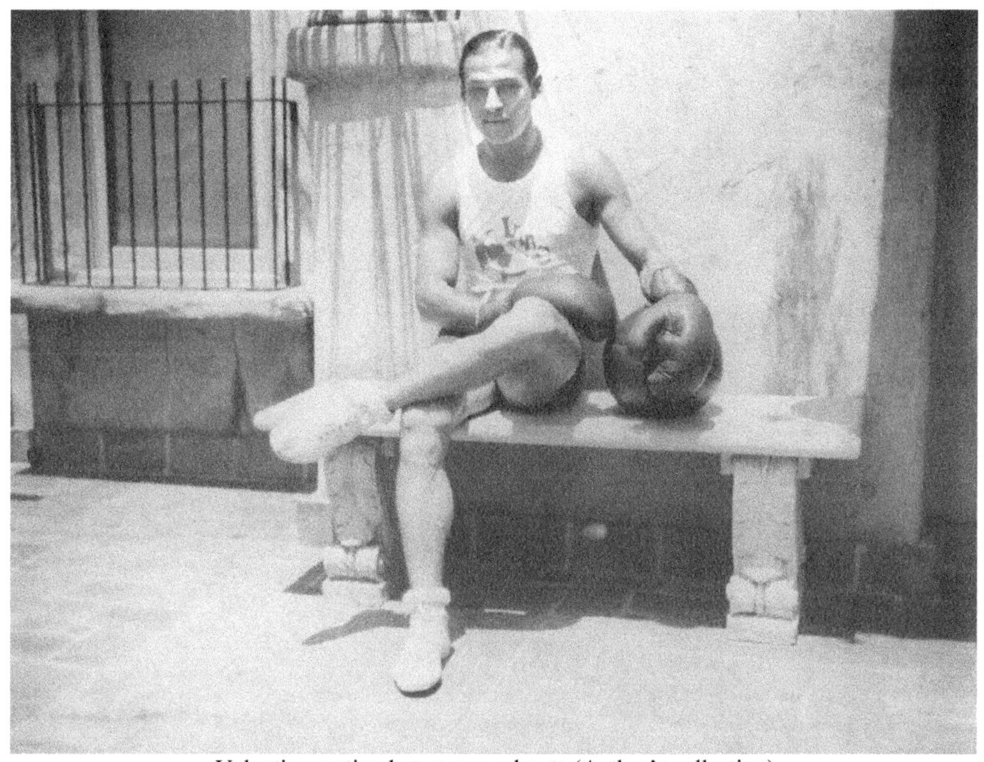

Valentino resting between workouts (Author's collection)

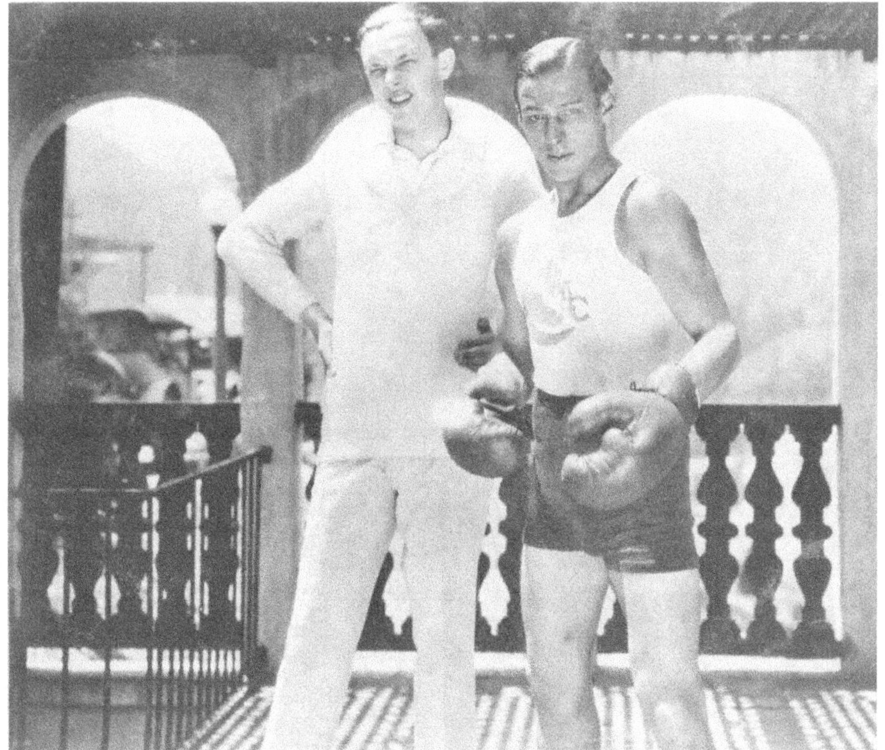

Robert Florey is ready to referee a match between Valentino and Douglas Gerrard. (Author's collection)

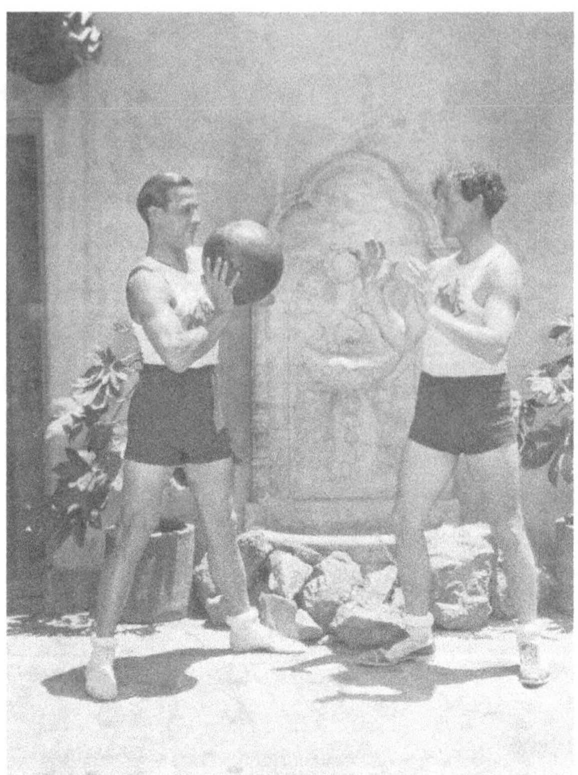

Valentino and Douglas Gerrard workout with a medicine ball.
(Author's collection)

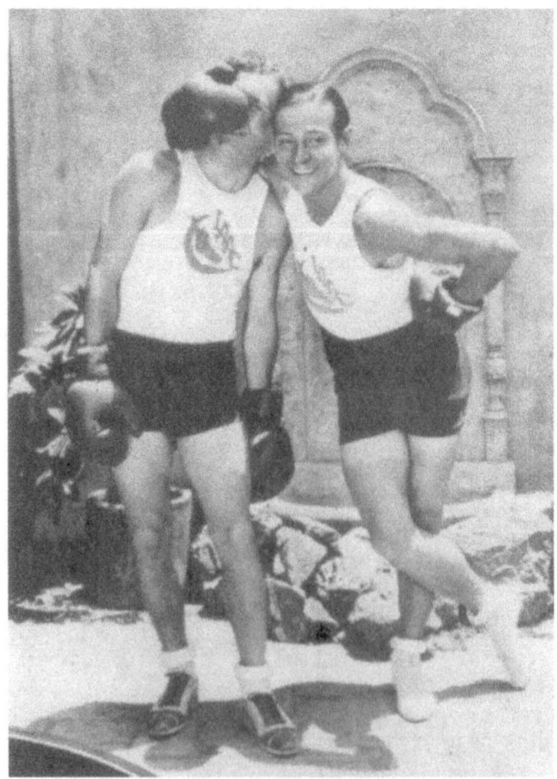

Valentino and Douglas Gerrard clown for the camera.
(Author's collection)

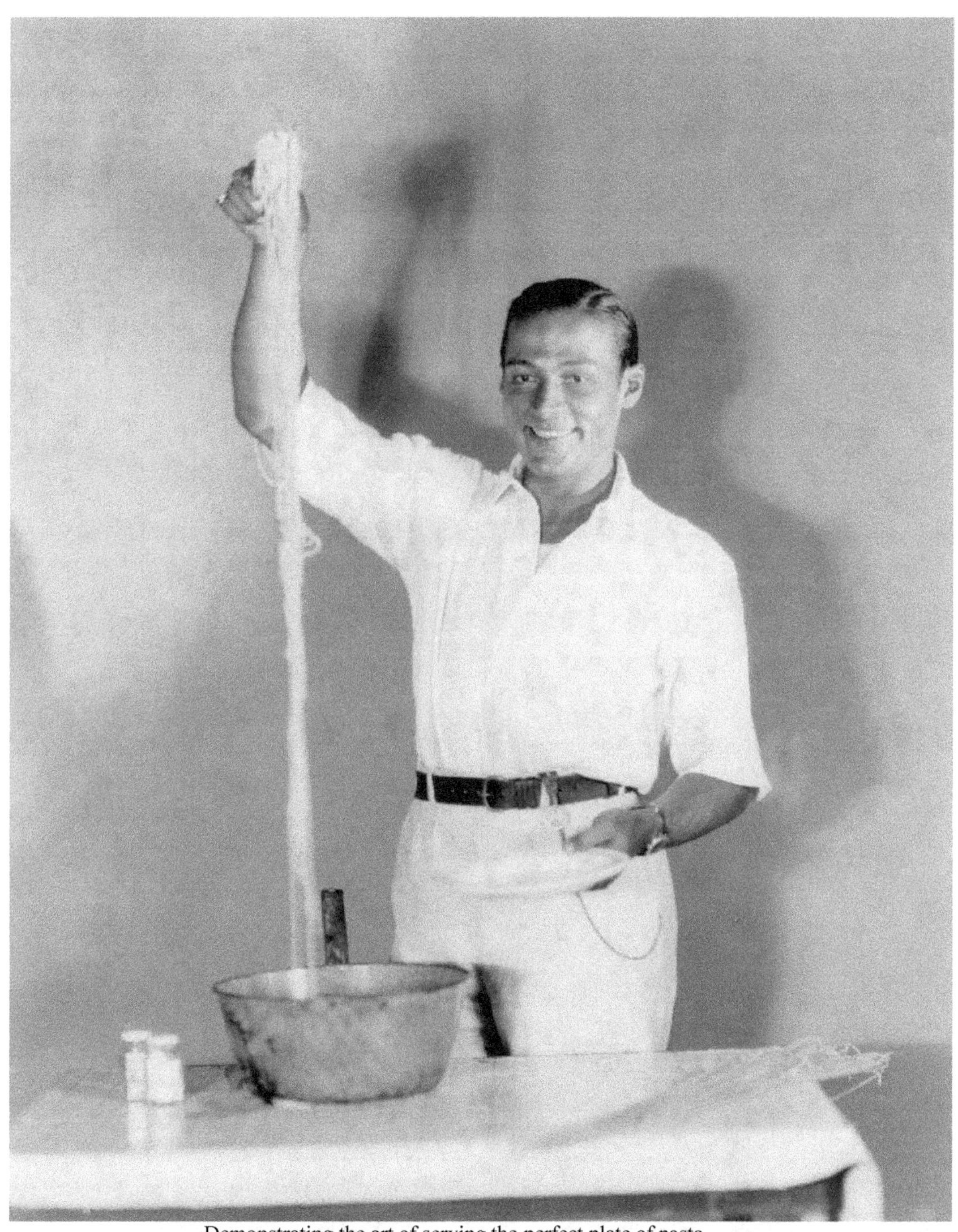

Demonstrating the art of serving the perfect plate of pasta.
Paul Ivano recalled Valentino always served spaghetti that was six feet long.
(Author's collection)

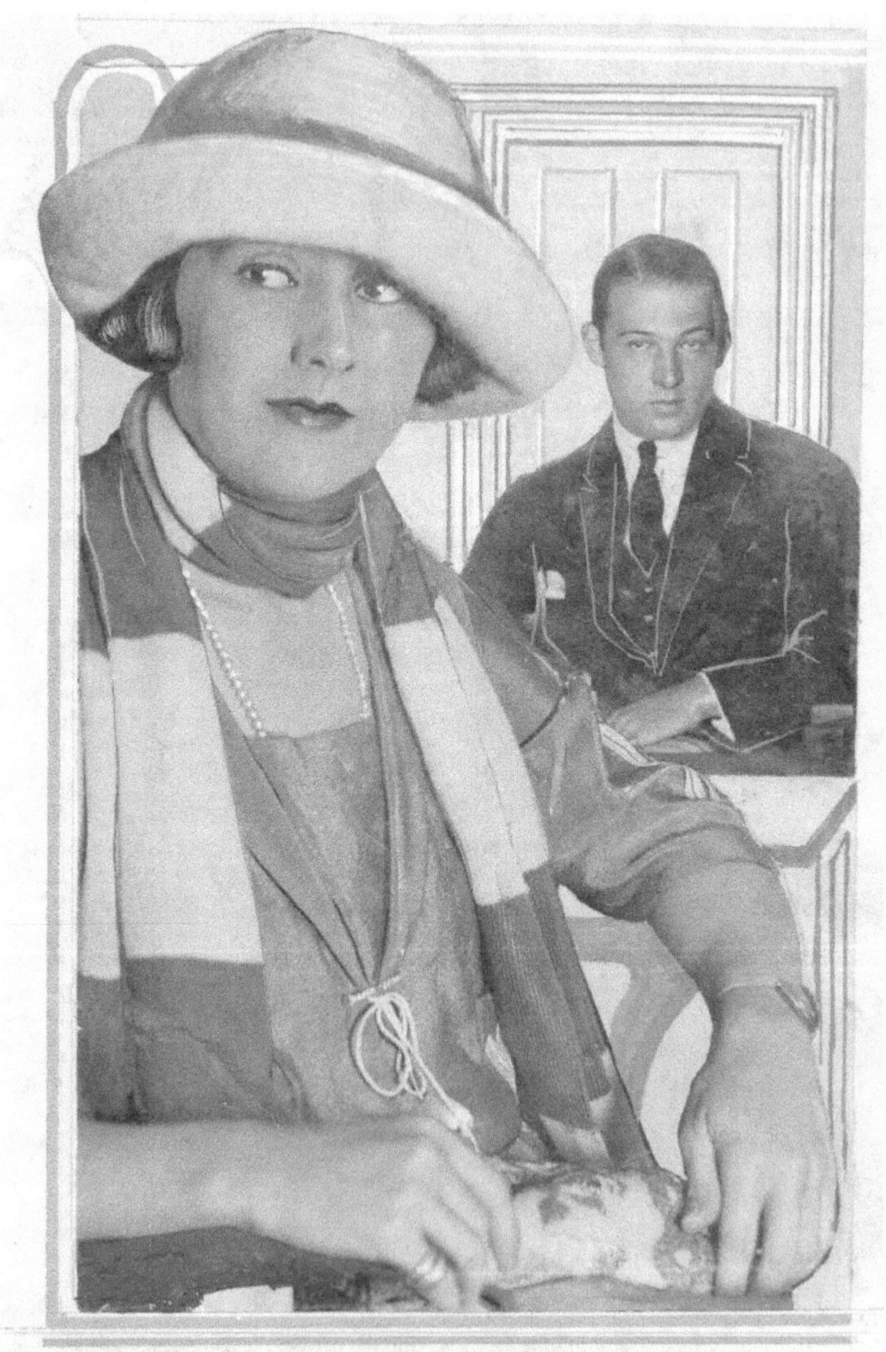

The bigamy trial began and his name and face were in the papers.
In this case, he was not sure about the adage “any publicity is good publicity.”
Plenty of new coverage for Jean Acker, which she did enjoy.
This image is a mock-up published in the newspapers at the time.
(Author’s collection)

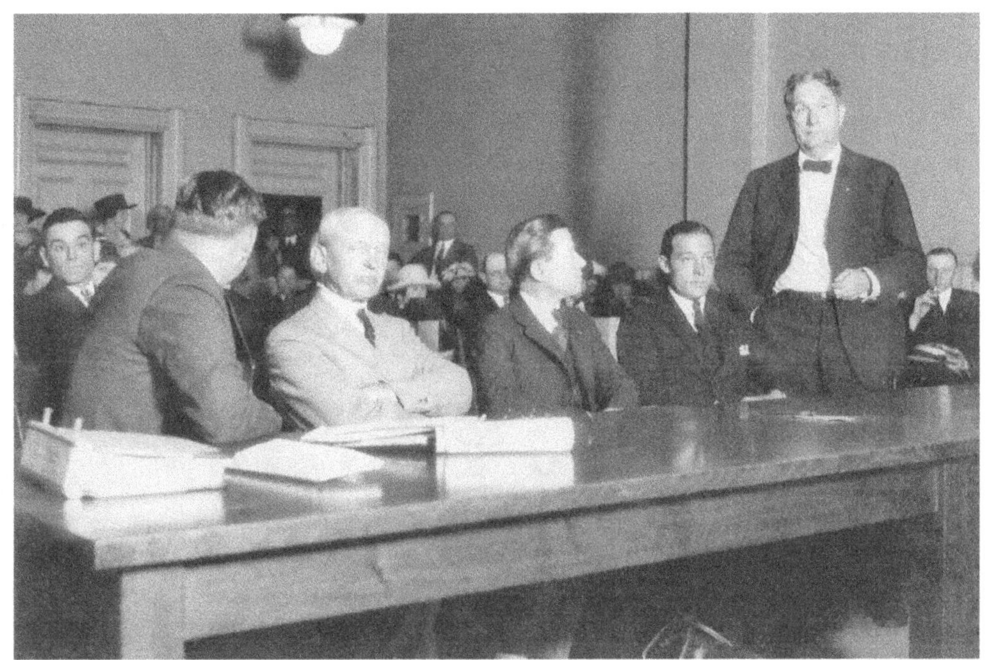

A very nervous Valentino seated in court with his legal counsel.
(Michael and Virginia Back collection)

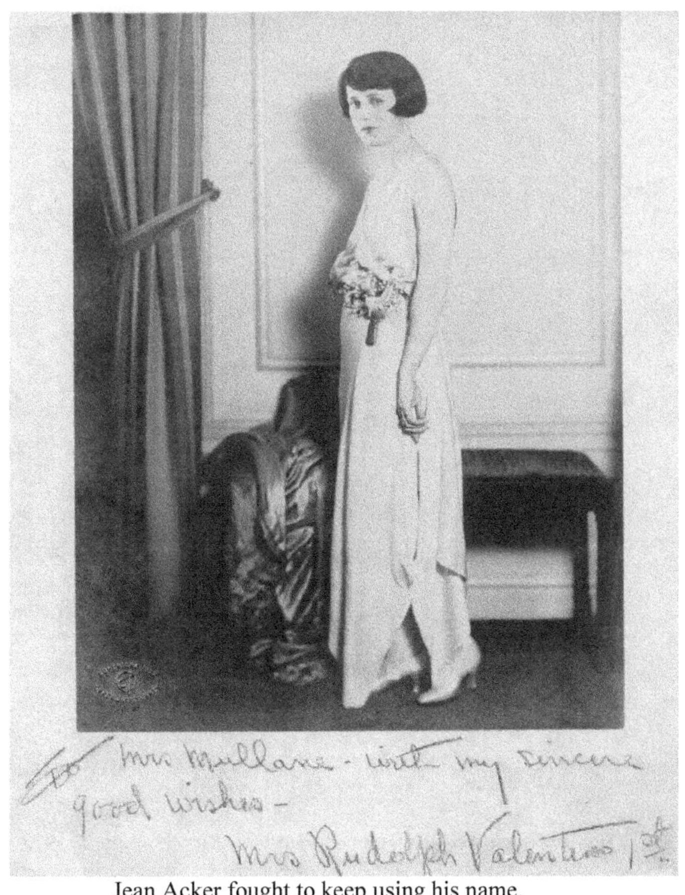

Jean Acker fought to keep using his name.
She shamelessly tried to capitalize on his fame for years to come.
(Author's collection)

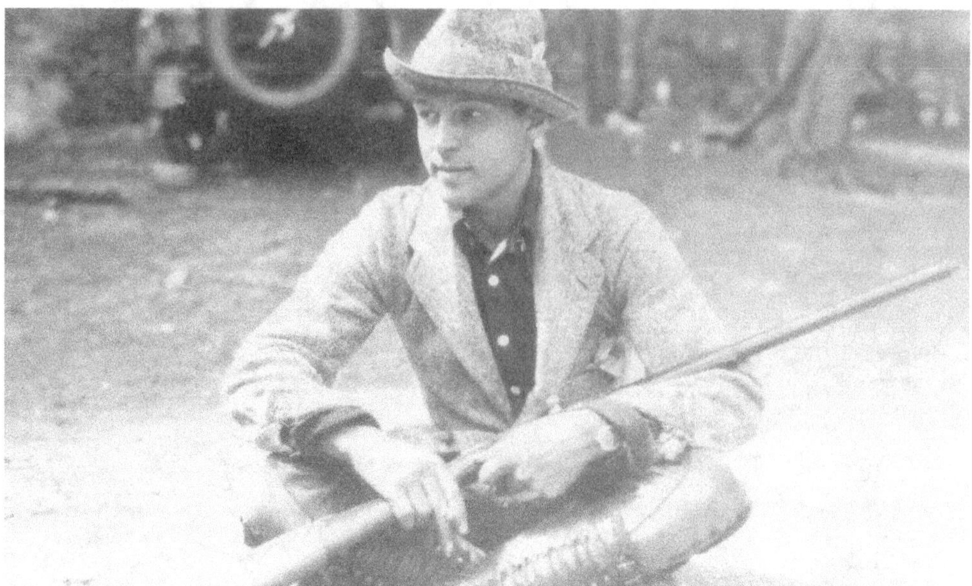

Valentino traveled to New York and spent time at Foxlair in the Adirondack mountains. There he indulged in shooting and riding, and most importantly, time with Natacha. (Author's collection)

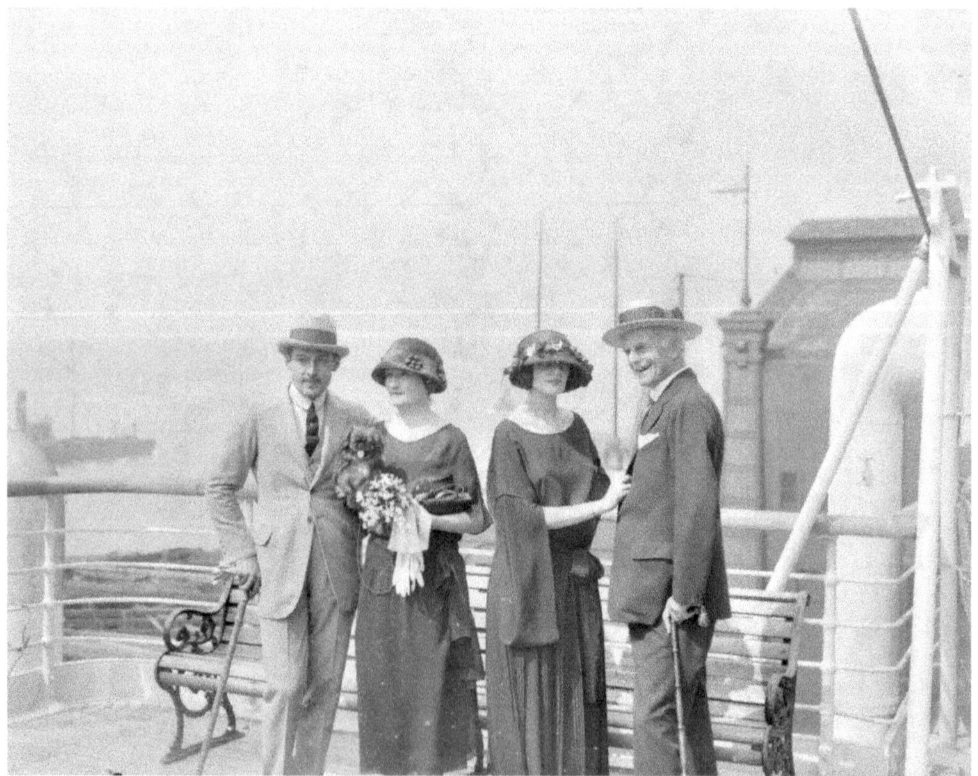

Valentino seeing off Natacha and Mr. and Mrs. Hudnut in 1922. (Author's collection)

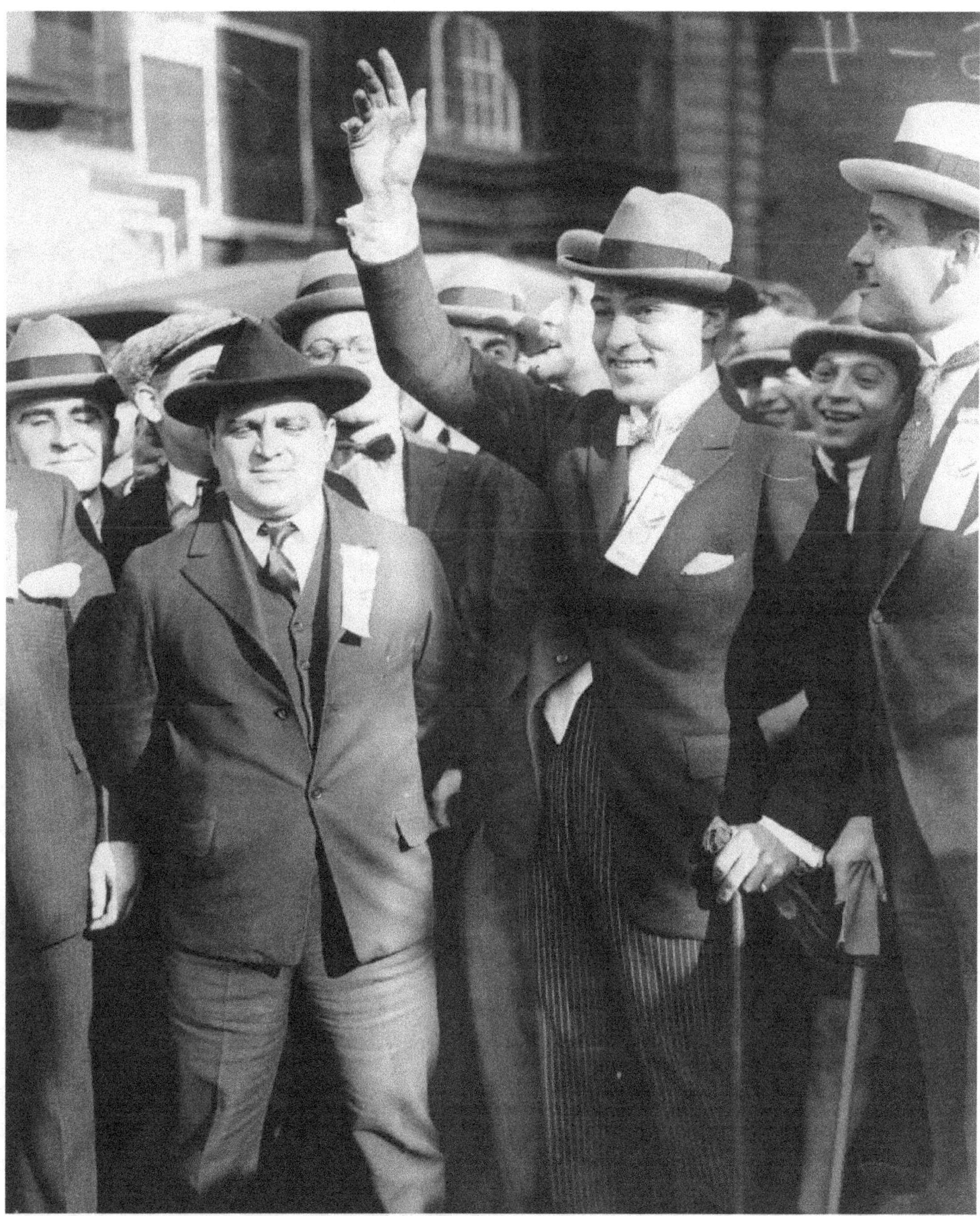

Alderman Fiorello La Guardia at the Columbus Day celebrations in New York, October 1922.
(Author's collection)

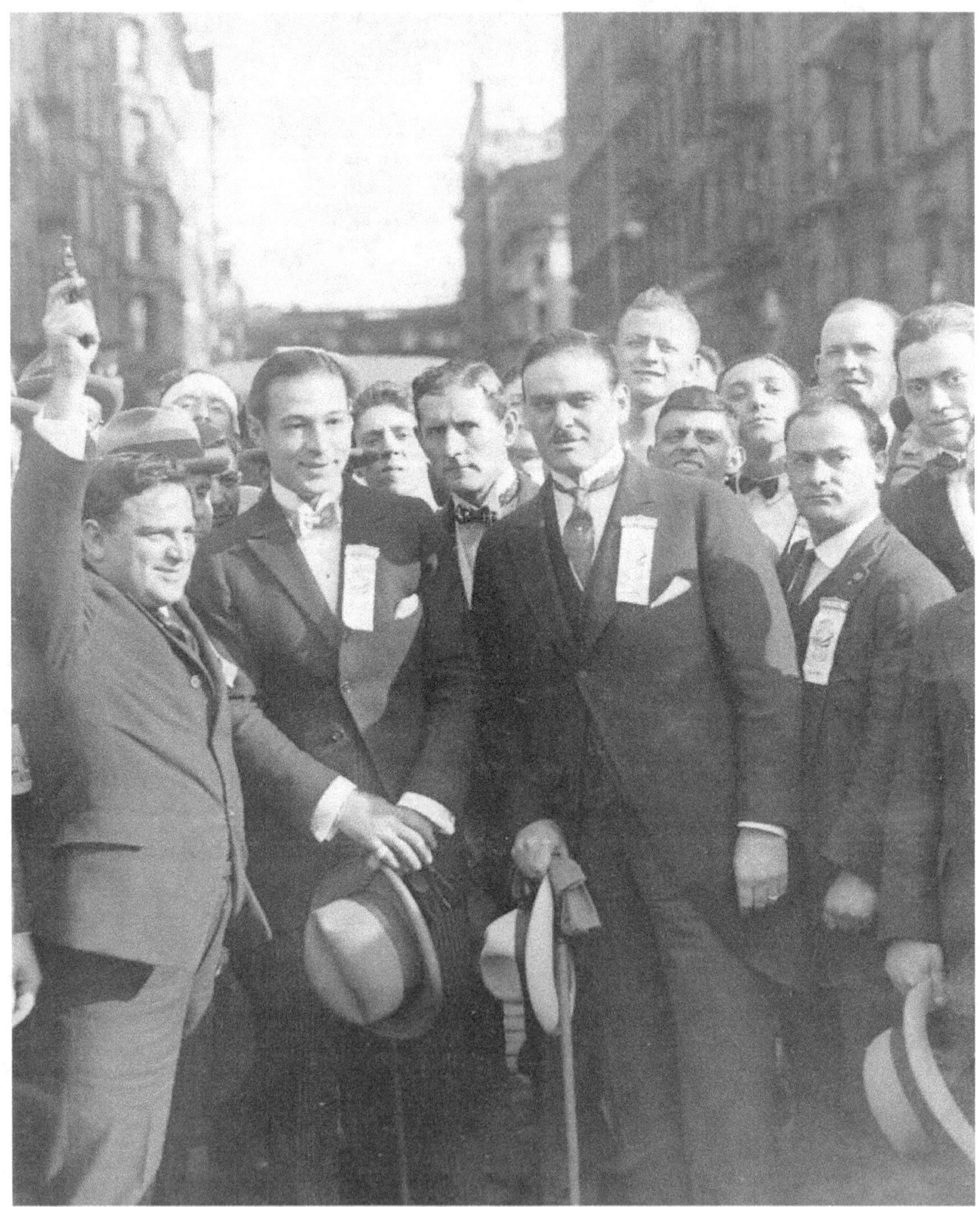

Fiorello La Guardia is about to fire the starting pistol for the annual marathon.
Seen behind Valentino is Douglas Gerrard and to Valentino's left is Frank Menello.
(San Francisco History Center)

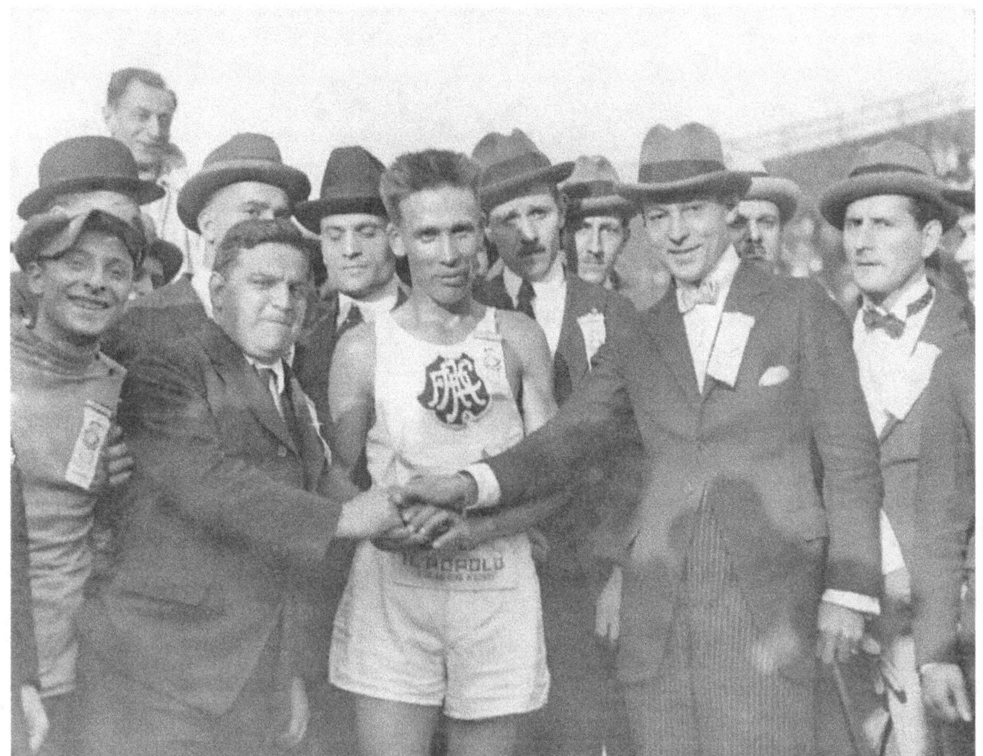

Fiorello La Guardia and Valentino congratulate the Columbus Day marathon winner Willie Ritola.
(Author's collection)

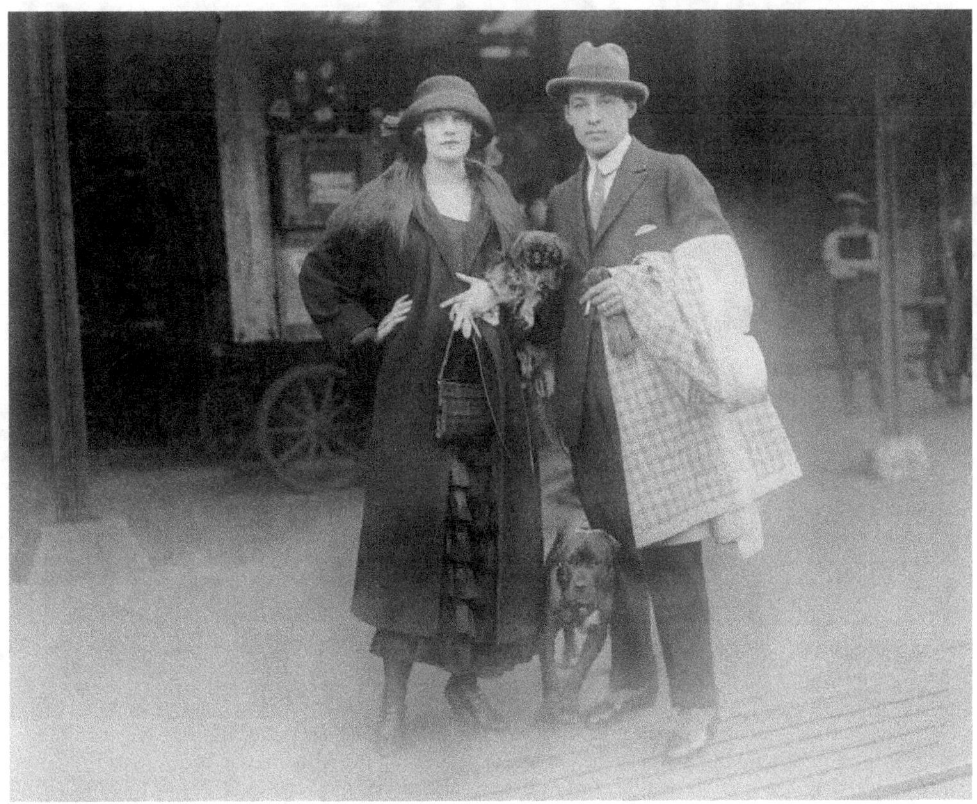

Natacha Rambova and Valentino in 1922
(Franz Kunst collection)

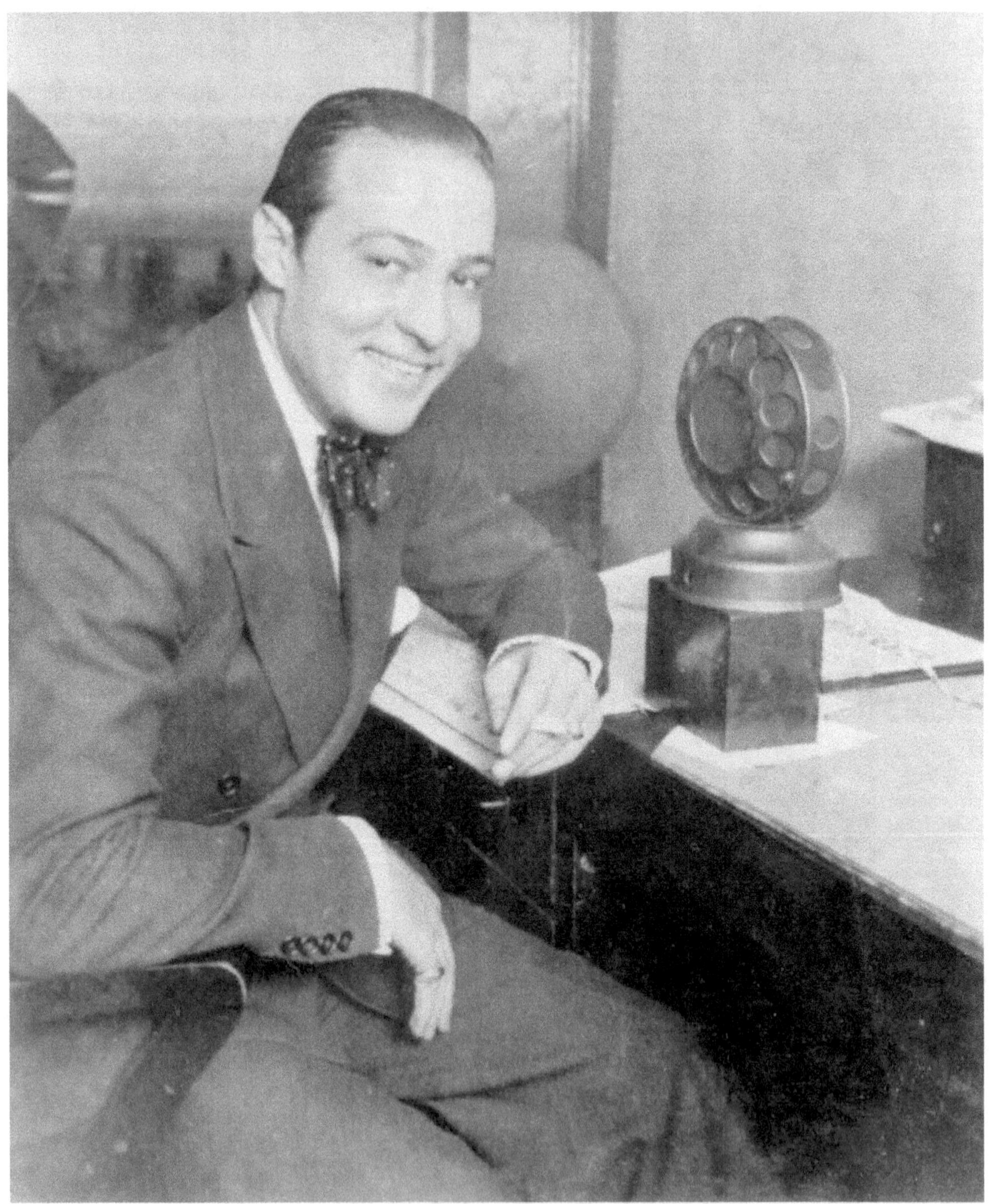

Valentino tried his hand at radio to plead his case for making better films in New York, and later, across the United States during the Mineralava Tour.
(Author's collection)

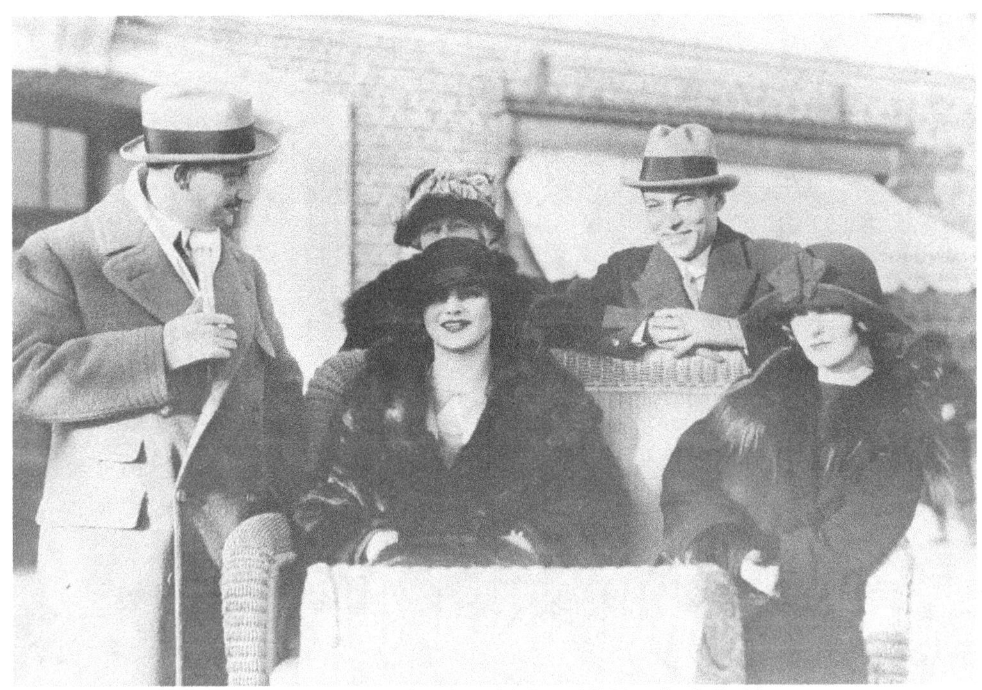

On the Boardwalk in Atlantic City with Ben Ali Haggin, Julia Hoyt, Natacha and Teresa Werner next to Valentino
(Author's collection)

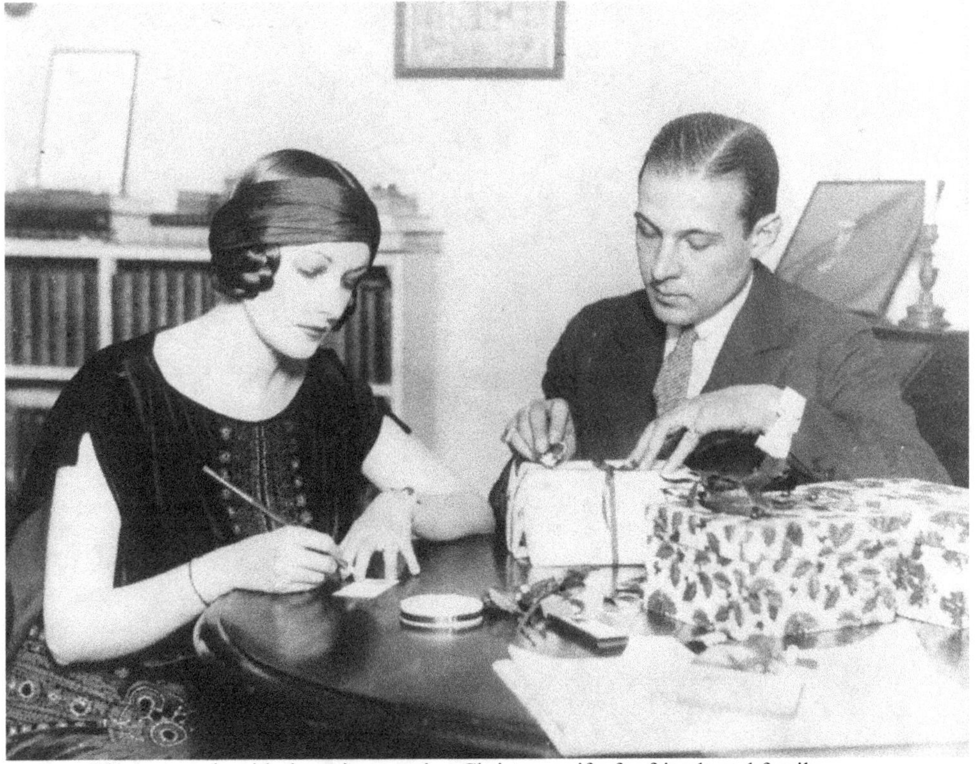

The year ends with the pair wrapping Christmas gifts for friends and family.
(Author's collection)

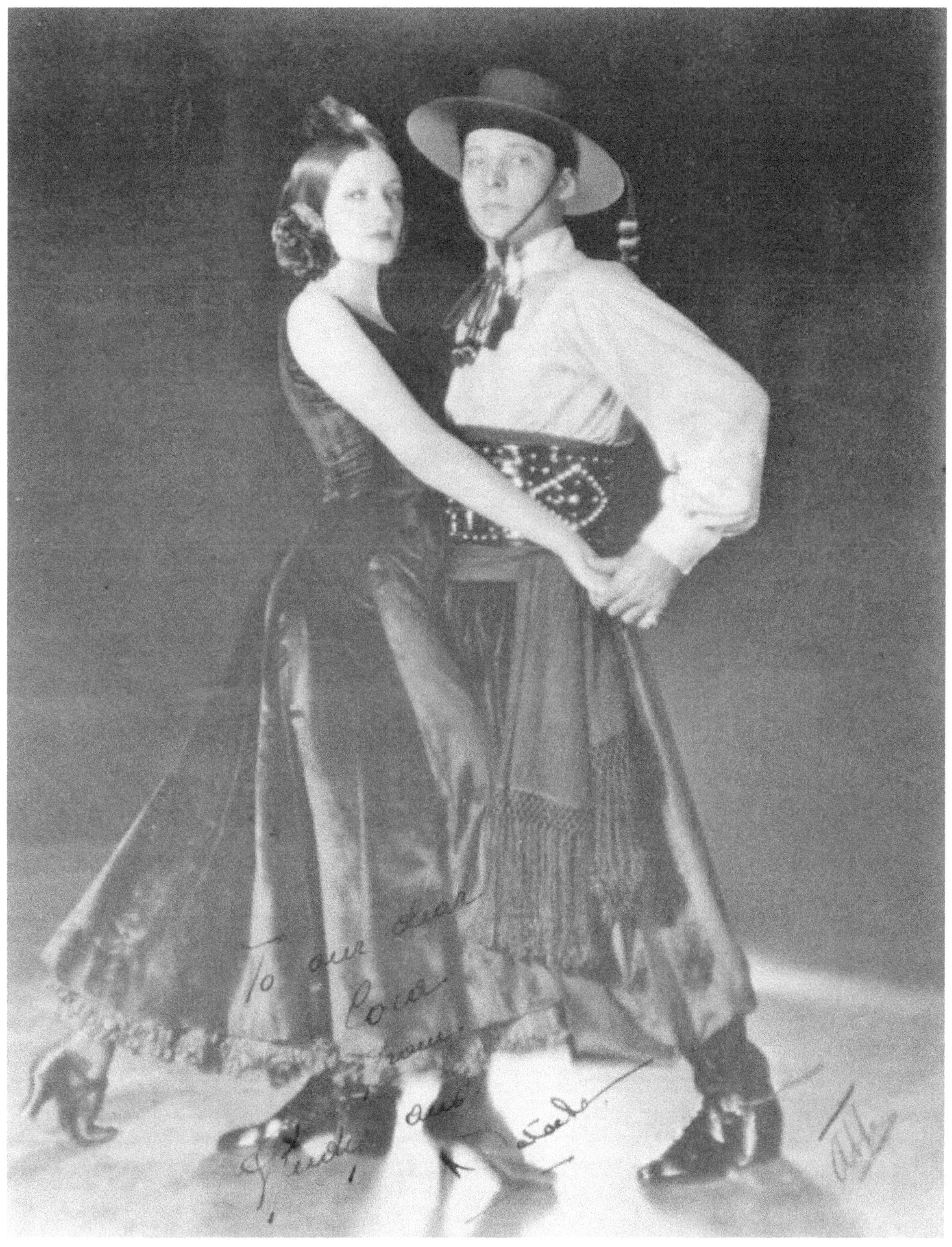
To our dear
Cora

Swamped as it was beneath silly advertising, and ridiculed by newspapers and wise-crackers, the dancing tour they made together should not be forgotten. I do not think a more beautiful nor more perfect dancing has ever been seen in this country than the dancing of those two when they loved each other.

—Adela Rogers St. John, 1929

With the Famous Players-Lasky injunction still in place, Valentino was unable to work. Then, as now, litigation was an expensive business, and he had borrowed heavily to pay his attorneys and fund his luxurious lifestyle. He was still unemployed, still unmarried, and his debts were mounting each day. As his attorneys worked to settle the suit, Valentino bided his time in New York. He was not entirely unoccupied, for he was, among other things, experimenting with writing poetry.

In January 1923, the Appellate Court modified Lasky's injunction and struck out the clause restraining Valentino from engaging in "any other business of any kind or class whatsoever." He was still restricted from accepting employment as an actor by appearing in theaters, film, or on the speaking stage, but his attorney announced that he had been offered an engagement dancing in restaurants for $6,000 per week, and $5,000 to sing or speak into phonographs. He also had been invited to write for the press and to author books on dancing, projects which would bring him "many thousands of dollars."

S. George Ullman headed the advertising division of the Mineralava Beauty Clay Company; a cosmetics firm that produced face powders and other skin-care products. In late 1922 he had approached Valentino with a proposal to combine local beauty contests with exhibition dancing by Valentino and Rambova in an advertising campaign for Mineralava's products. Valentino turned the offer down.

Valentino and Natacha were invited to be on the board for the 1923 Actors' Fund Benefit and to dance for the benefit show at the Century Theater in New York City. The lineup was a who's-who of the New York theater world. The two danced (as Mr. Rudolph Valentino and Miss Winifred Hudnut immediately after Will Rogers performed; they danced "the original tango" from *The Four Horsemen of the Apocalypse*, accompanied by "Mr. Valentino's Own Tango Orchestra." They were a huge success, and at the conclusion of their performance the pair "answered no less than twenty encores" while Valentino was greeted by "several hundred girls" outside the stage door. The box office receipts for the evening of entertainment raised a whopping $25,000 for the Actors' Fund.

On January 25, 1923, there was a brief announcement in the New York papers that Rudolph Valentino and Winifred Hudnut would embark on a "two-a-day" exhibition dance tour on the B.F. Keith dance circuit, for a reported salary of $6,000 per week. They would appear in armories, hotel ballrooms, tents, tea dances, and other nontheatrical venues. Saddled with burgeoning legal expenses, as well as the cost of the Whitley Heights house, Valentino desperately needed the work. They danced for Keith from the end of February to mid-March. During that engagement, he reconsidered George Ullman's proposal for the Mineralava Tour, and, after much discussion with Natacha, decided to sign with Ullman. The two signed a contract with sports promoter Jack Curley to handle publicity and arrange venues during the tour, which began in Omaha, Nebraska on March 17, 1923. Natacha was later enraged by the ridiculous press Curley drummed up for their engagement in her home town, Salt Lake City. Relations between the two parties soon deteriorated.

While the couple danced in Chicago, the final divorce decree from Jean Acker was entered on March 13. Joyously, they planned to remarry, but the law in Illinois required still more waiting time. Therefore, on March 14, 1923, Valentino, Rambova, George Ullman, Teresa Werner, Valentino's friend Michael Romano, and his attorney Mr. Arthur Butler Graham, along with Mrs. Graham, motored across the Illinois border to Crown Point, Indiana and to the Lake County Courthouse for a civil ceremony. Curiously, no news photographs of the wedding party are known to exist.

With no time for even a brief honeymoon, the Valentinos returned to Chicago to embark on the Mineralava Tour. The scheduled route covered the United States in a demanding schedule of nearly 100 stops. They rode in a private Pullman train car nicknamed "The Colonial," lavishly furnished in a style to which the Valentinos had become accustomed. They traveled with full retinue, including a valet and cook, a personal secretary, the Valentino Tango Orchestra, George Ullman, Valentino's friend Robert Florey, a flock of press agents, many trunks, two police dogs, and a Pekingese. Over four months, the train crisscrossed the United States, from the cool vistas of Seattle to humid Atlanta.

It was a grind. In several cities they danced in two or three different venues, giving multiple performances daily, seven days a week. Valentino was not just hawking Mineralava preparations; he was, in fact, promoting himself. The public may not have been convinced that his campaign for better pictures was worthwhile, but if nothing else, the tour made it abundantly clear that he was a draw. No matter the weather, he lured droves of flappers and sheiks to the performances.

The publicity campaign for each town preceded the tour's arrival by a week. Beauty contest hopefuls had to submit a photograph and give age, height, weight, eye color, hair color, and shoe size. An additional lure was a promise that the winner would appear in one of Valentino's future films. Local papers in most cities were swamped with entries. The winner of each local contest would then advance to the final pageant, to be held at Madison Square Garden in November later that year.

Tickets were sold in advance for both the main event and the public dance that followed, and they weren't cheap: the average for the tea dansants was $3.00 (plus tax) and the Grand Ball tickets ranged from $1.00 to $3.00 (plus tax). The program in each town followed the same tight schedule. The doors would open and a local band and the Valentino Tango Orchestra would play music for a half an hour. Then came the dancing contest, followed by the beauty contest. The Valentinos would finally take the stage and dance the famous "Four Horsemen" tango and "other special dances by Mr. Valentino." The pair were on stage for twenty to thirty minutes, dancing and speaking extemporaneously to promote Mineralava products.

After the advertising, the Valentinos would bestow a loving cup on the dance contest winner and award the beauty contest winner either a trophy or a pair of dolls, doppelgangers of the Valentinos. The couple then left the stage and a public dance promptly started. The pair would quickly be ushered back to The Colonial and—after a search for stowaways—head for the next stop.

As time permitted, Valentino visited hospitals and orphanages in different cities, to the delight of the doctors, nurses, and patients. Local Italian groups were thrilled, and welcomed Valentino when he was able to make time for visits during the scheduled stops. The stop in Atlanta was notable in that the journalist who interviewed Valentino was Peggy Marsh, later better known as Margaret Mitchell, author of Gone With the Wind.

In the middle of the tour, on May 14, 1923, Valentino recorded two songs for Brunswick Records: El Relicario and The Kashmiri Song. Upon hearing the results, his only comment was, "There goes my opera career." These two records are all that survives of Valentino's voice recordings. As far as we know, nothing of any of his radio work exists. In 1922-1923 not many households had crystal sets and radio stations did not yet record acetates to preserve shows. Later recordings, done in 1926 to promote *The Son of the Sheik*, also do not survive.

Once the tour concluded the Valentinos returned to New York and made the business relationship with George Ullman official. The lawsuit with Famous Players-Lasky was settled, and Valentino's new contract with Lasky was signed in mid-July. He would be paid a hefty $7,500 a week, with his next two films to be shot in New York at Paramount's Astoria Studios. On paper, at least, Valentino finally got some of the artistic control he fought for, and Paramount offered him a choice between two good properties: *Captain Blood* by Rafael Sabatini or *Monsieur Beaucaire* by Booth Tarkington. Valentino chose *Monsieur Beaucaire* as his next film. He and Natacha then embarked for Europe, for a much-needed vacation and a long-overdue honeymoon.

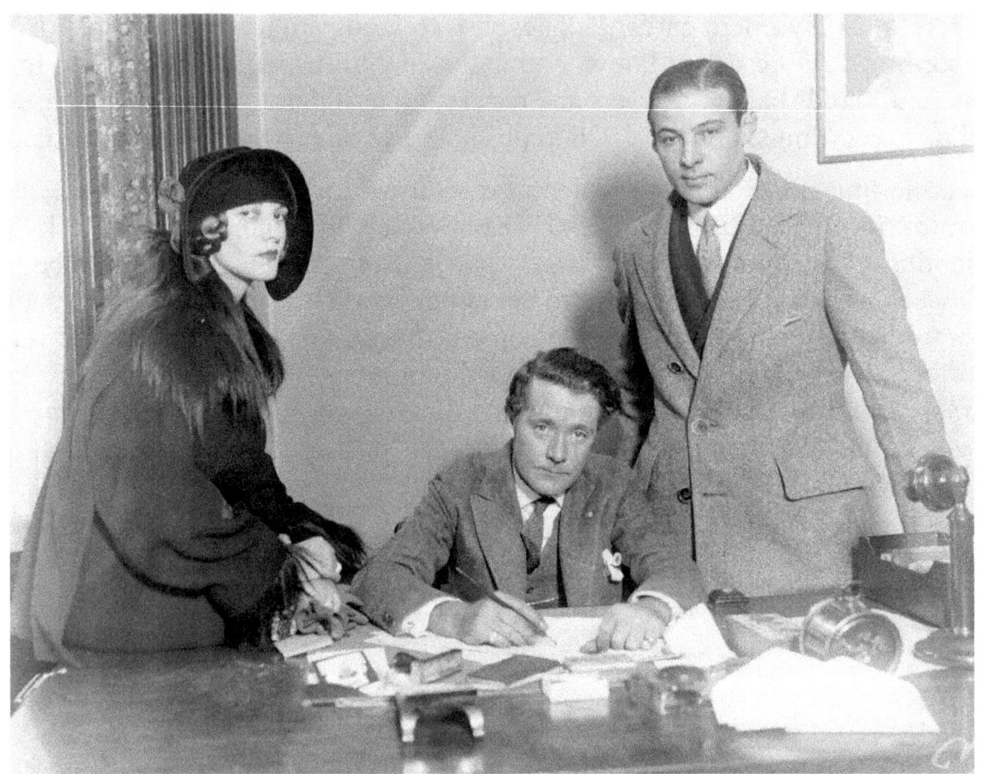

Natacha Rambova, producer George Le Guerre and Valentino
discuss details of the upcoming Actors Fund Benefit. (Author's collection)

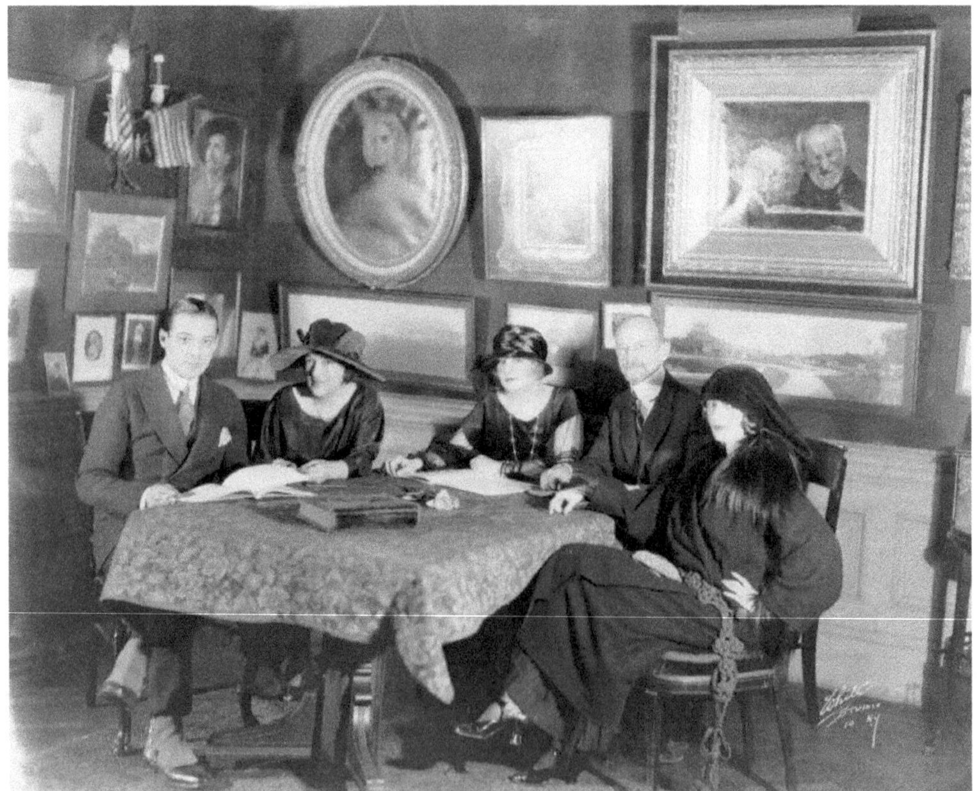

The Valentinos with Blanche Bates, Nora Bayes and Daniel Frohman, in Frohman's office.
(Author's collection)

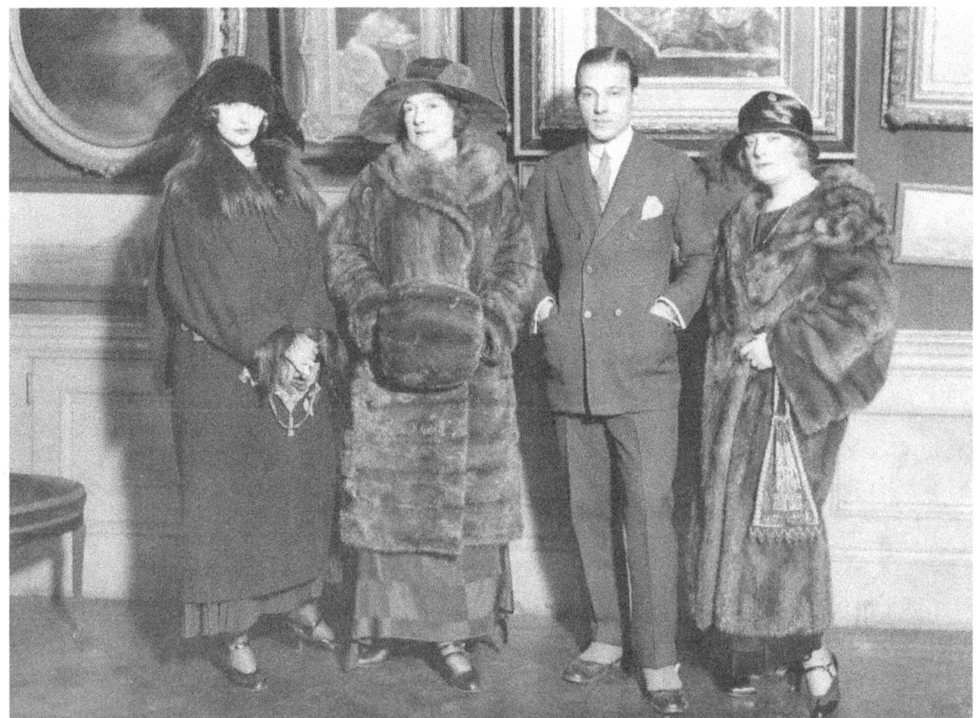

Natacha Rambova, Blanche Bates, Valentino and Nora Bayes,
The Actors Fund Benefit Committee. (Author's collection)

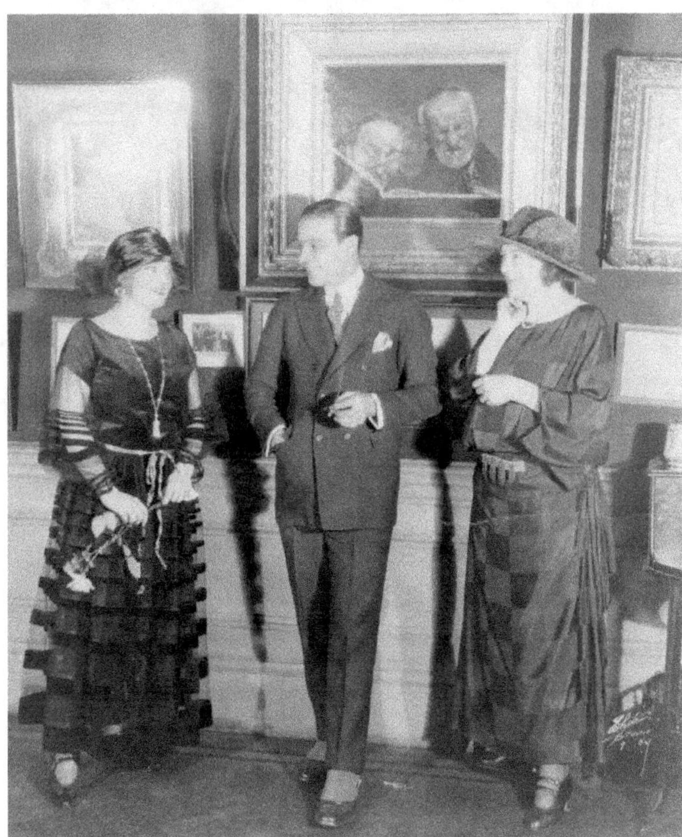

Valentino charms Nora Bayes and Blanche Bates
(San Francisco History Center)

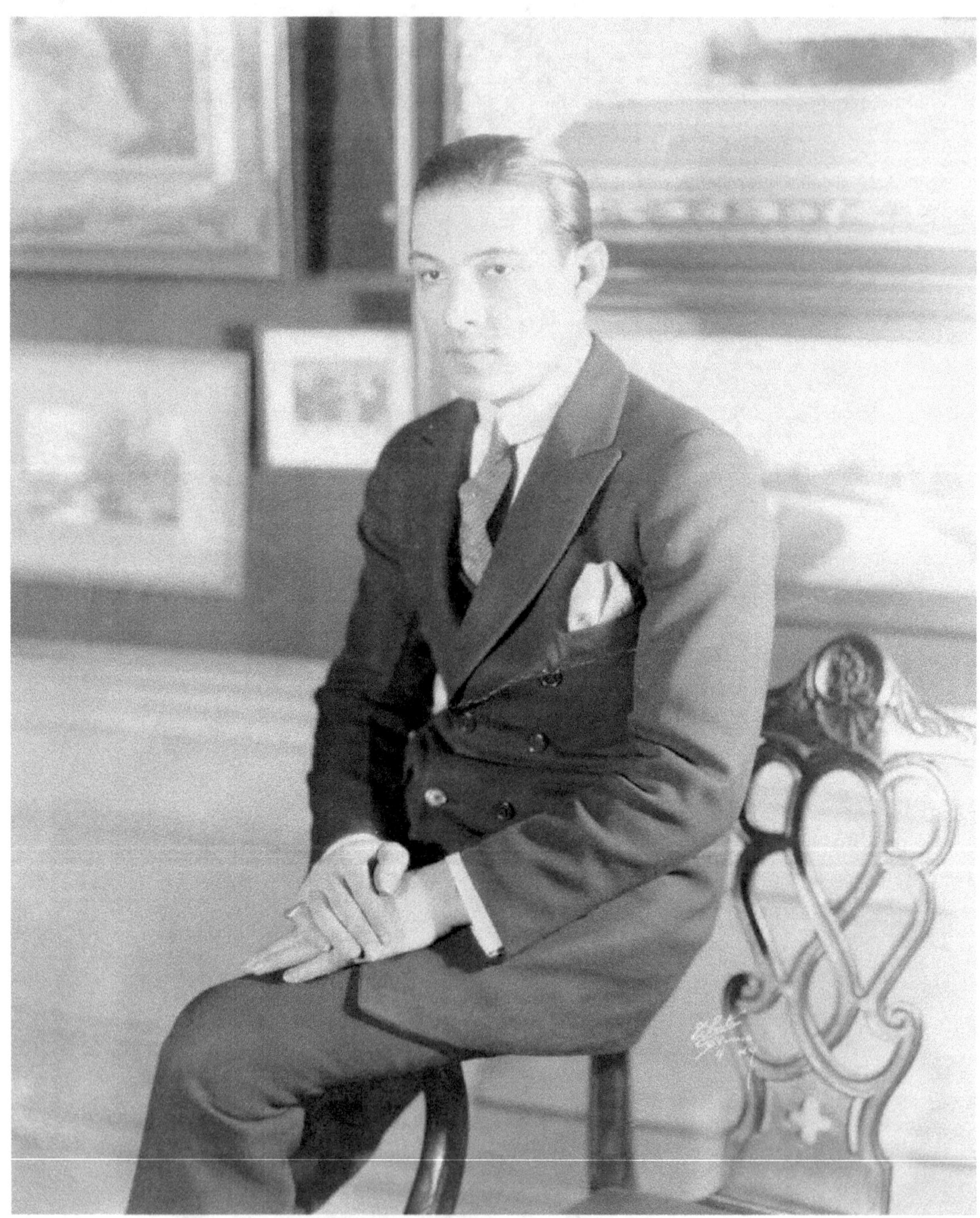

Valentino posed for famed Broadway photographer White Studios in Daniel Frohman's office. (Author's collection)

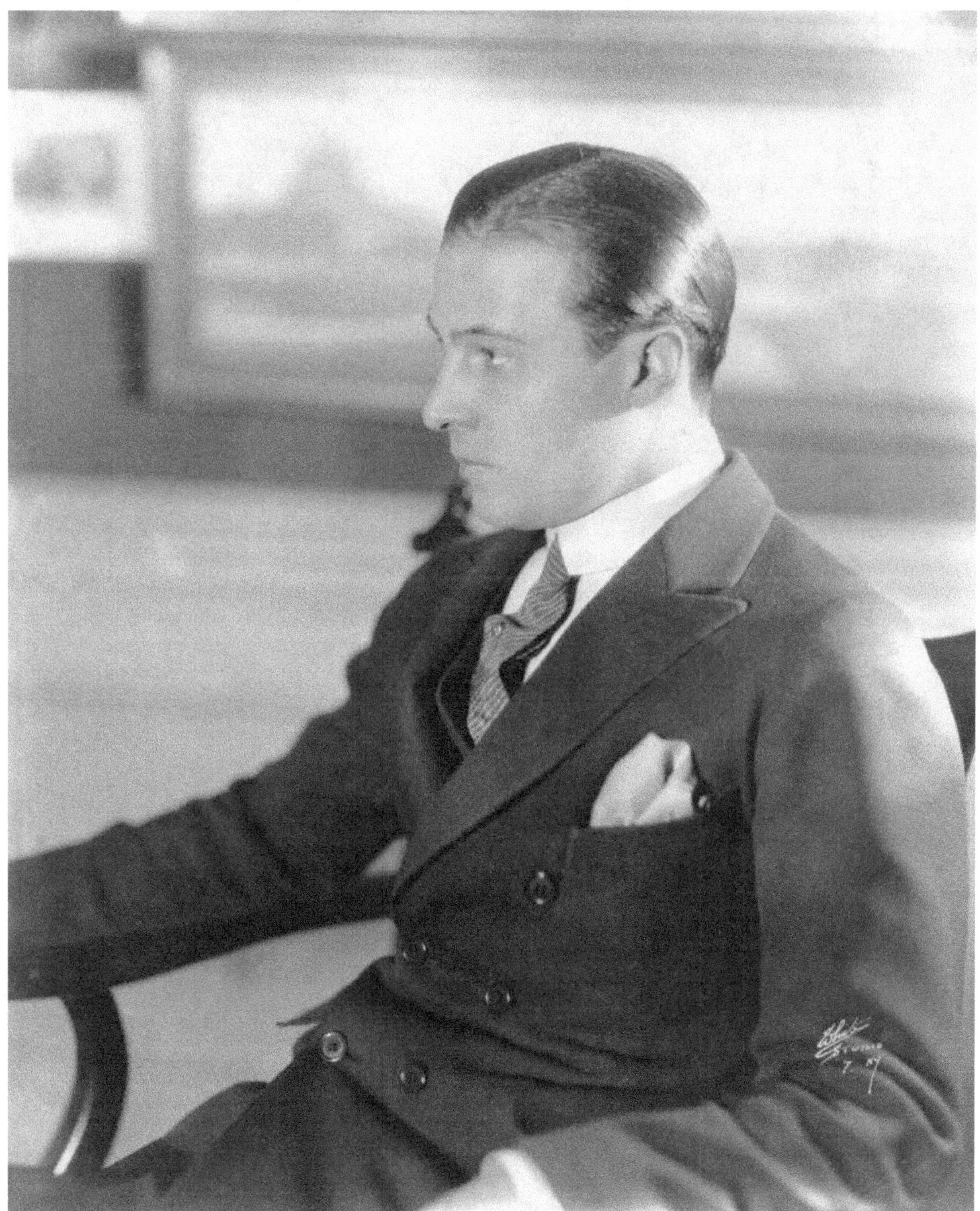

Valentino's famous profile. (Author's collection)

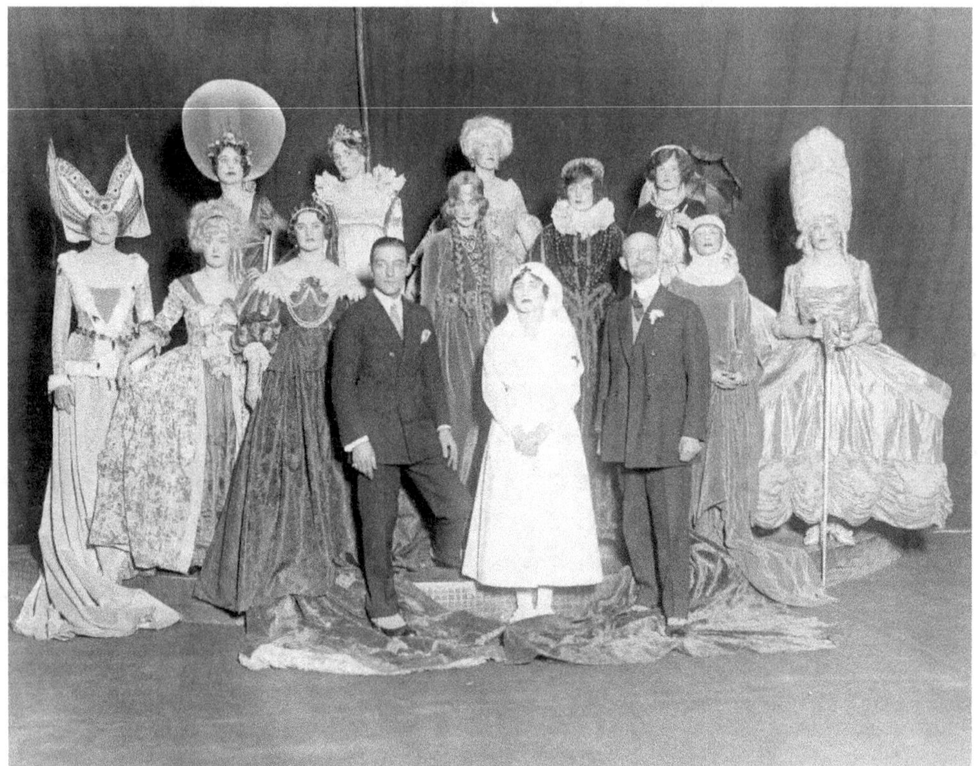

Valentino and Daniel Frohman posing with some of the New York social butterflies who are in costume for the Actors Fund Benefit. (Tracy Terhune collection)

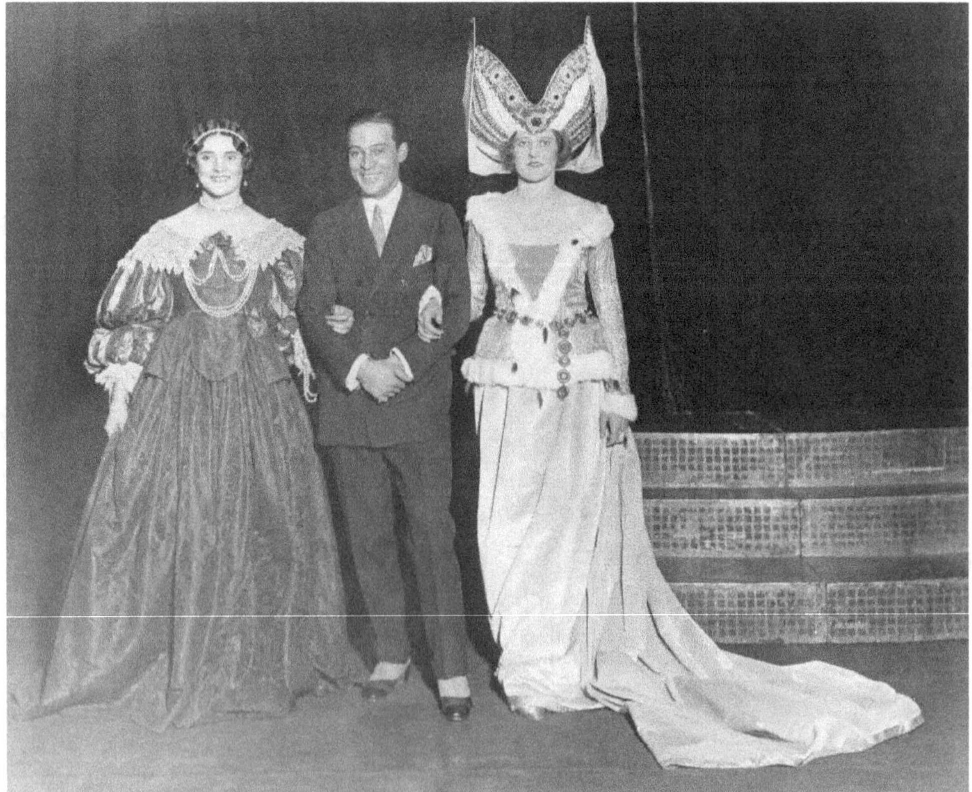

Aiding the actors and actresses in the benefit for the Actors Fund were a number of society girls. L-R Miss Barbara Brokaw, Valentino and Miss Isabella Rockefeller."
(Tracy Terhune collection)

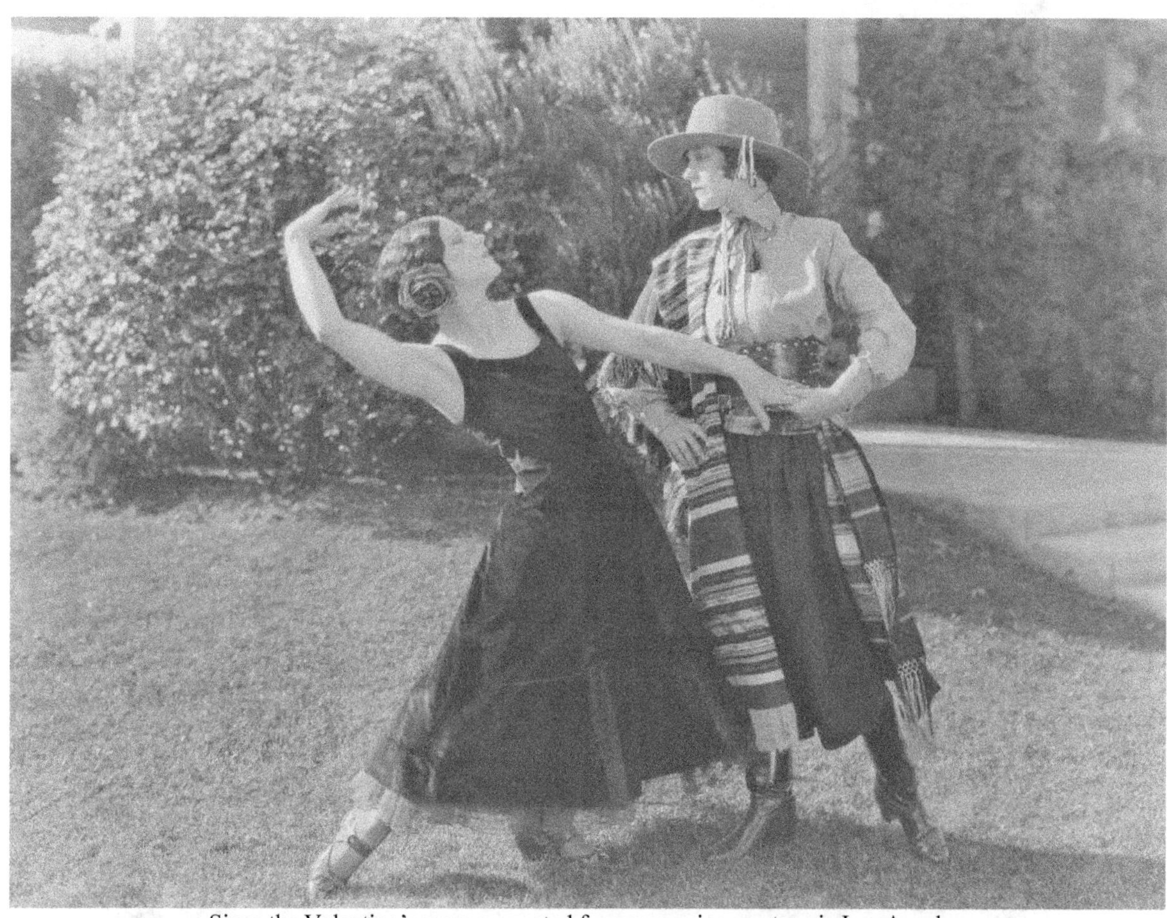

Since the Valentino's were prevented from appearing on stage in Los Angeles, sisters Viola Dana and Shirley Mason took the stage for the Los Angeles Actors Fund Benefit. Imitation, in this case, was the sincerest form of flattery. (Author's collection)

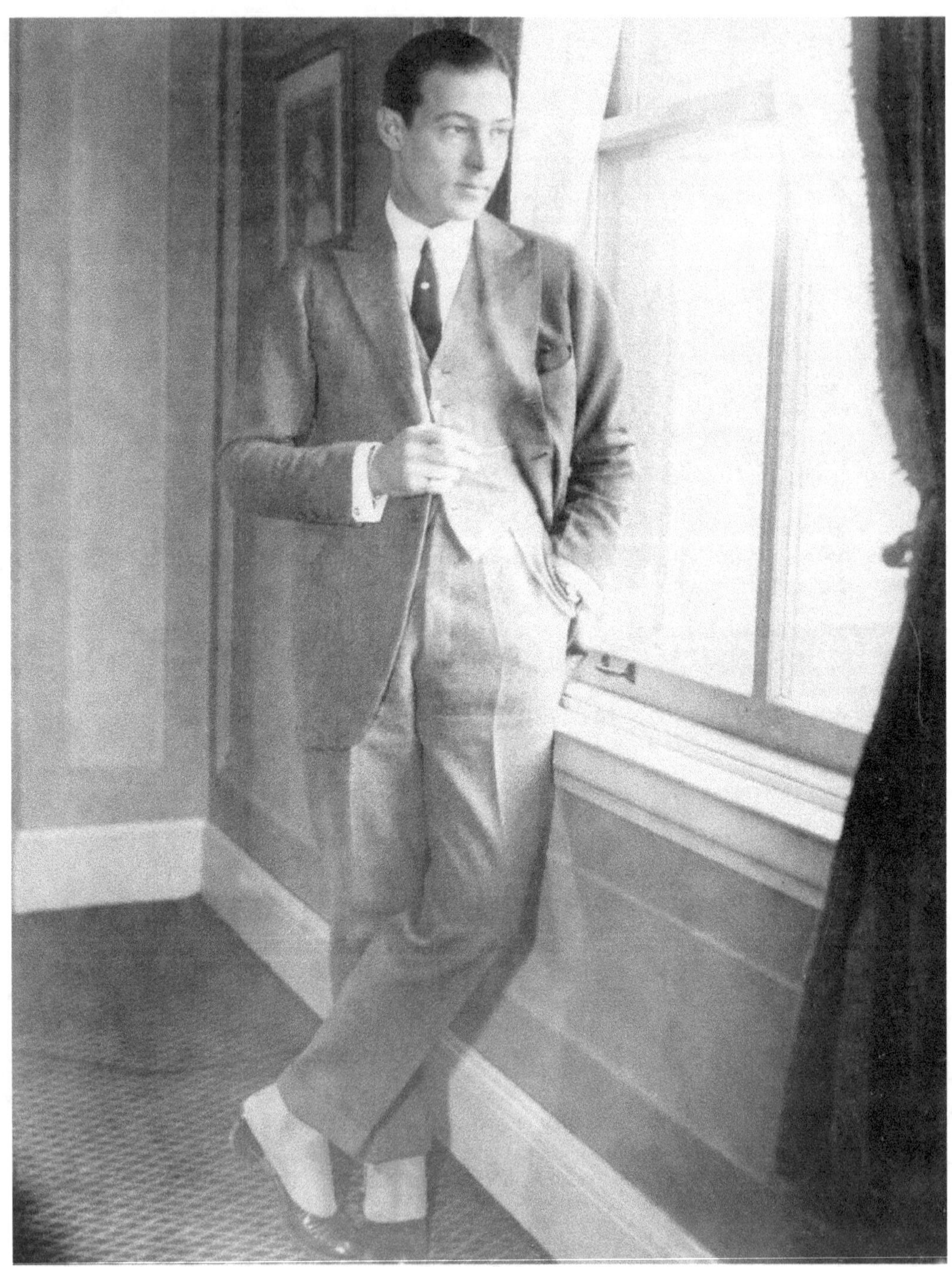

A pensive Valentino in his hotel suite in Detroit.
This early stop on the exhibition tour would prove to be an unhappy one.
(Author's collection)

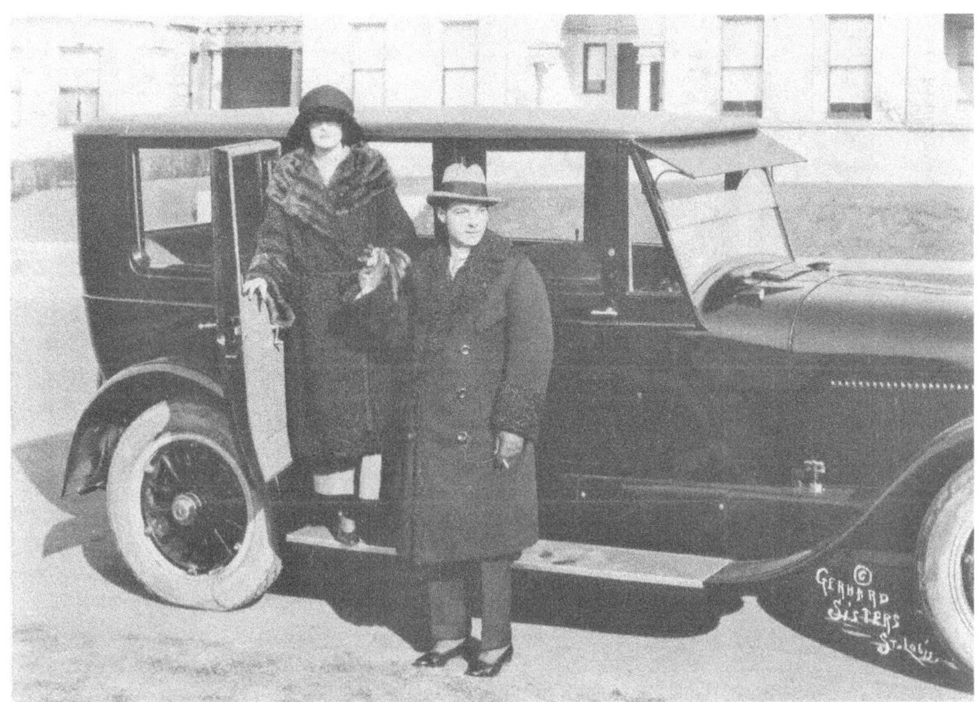

The Valentinos arrive in St. Louis, Missouri. (Library of Congress)

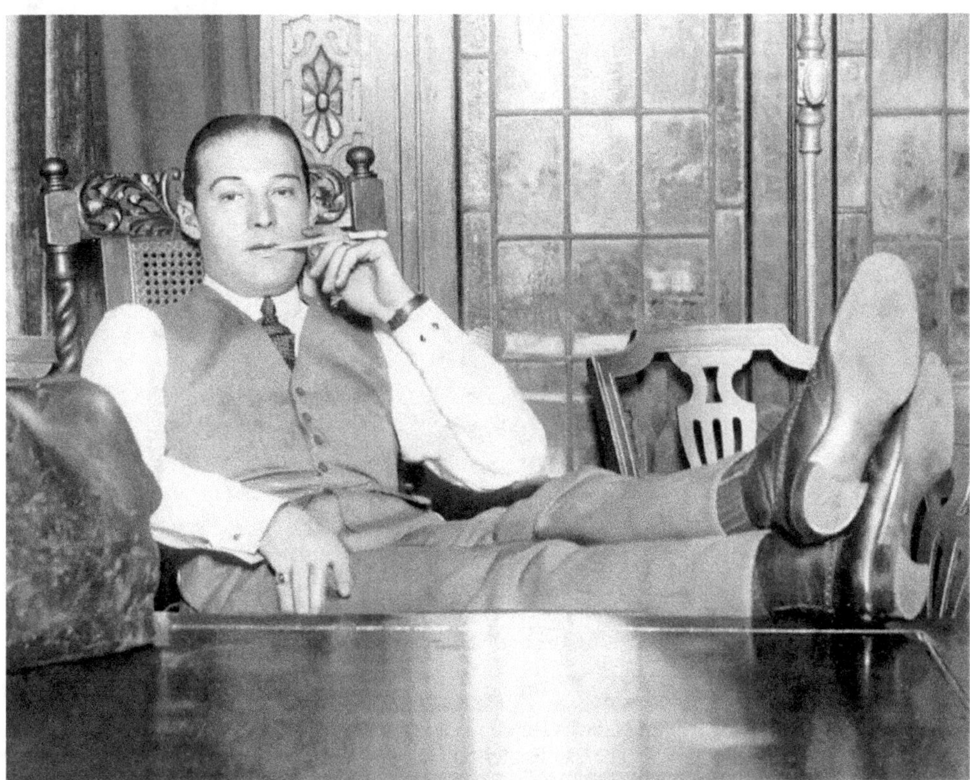

Valentino at the Blackstone Hotel in Chicago, about to start dancing at the Marigold.
(Author's collection)

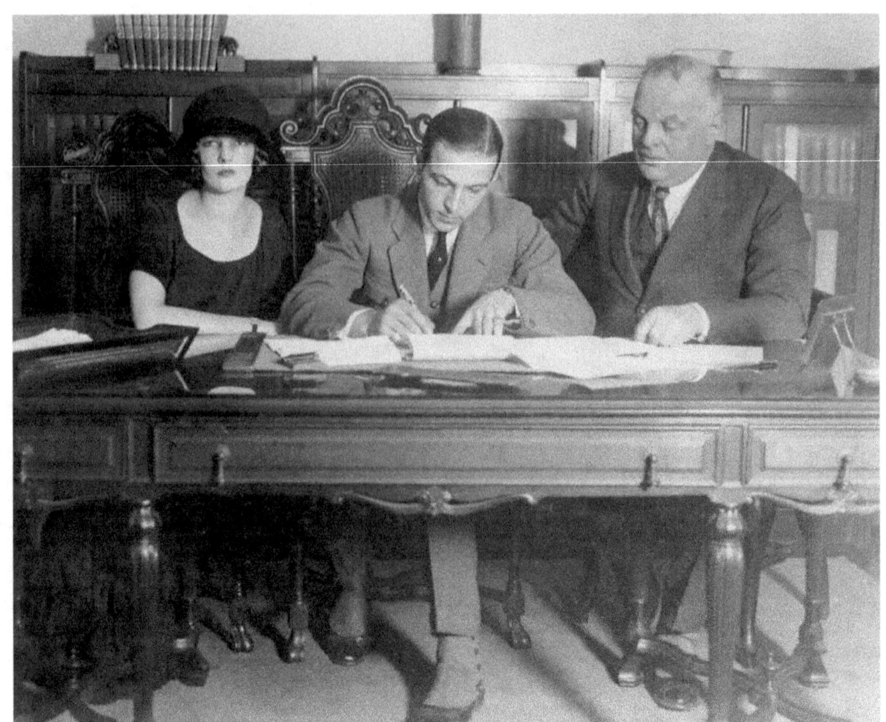

Valentino executes the contract with promotor Jack Curley who would be handling the publicity for the Mineralava Tour. Natacha Rambova's apparent uneasiness would prove prescient. (Author's collection)

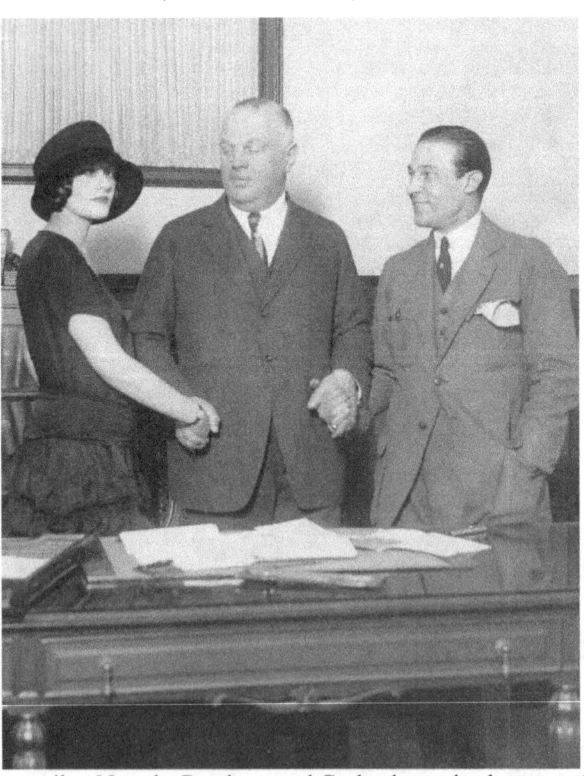

Ever amiable, Valentino smiles. Natacha Rambova and Curley have sized one another up correctly. (The San Francisco History Center)

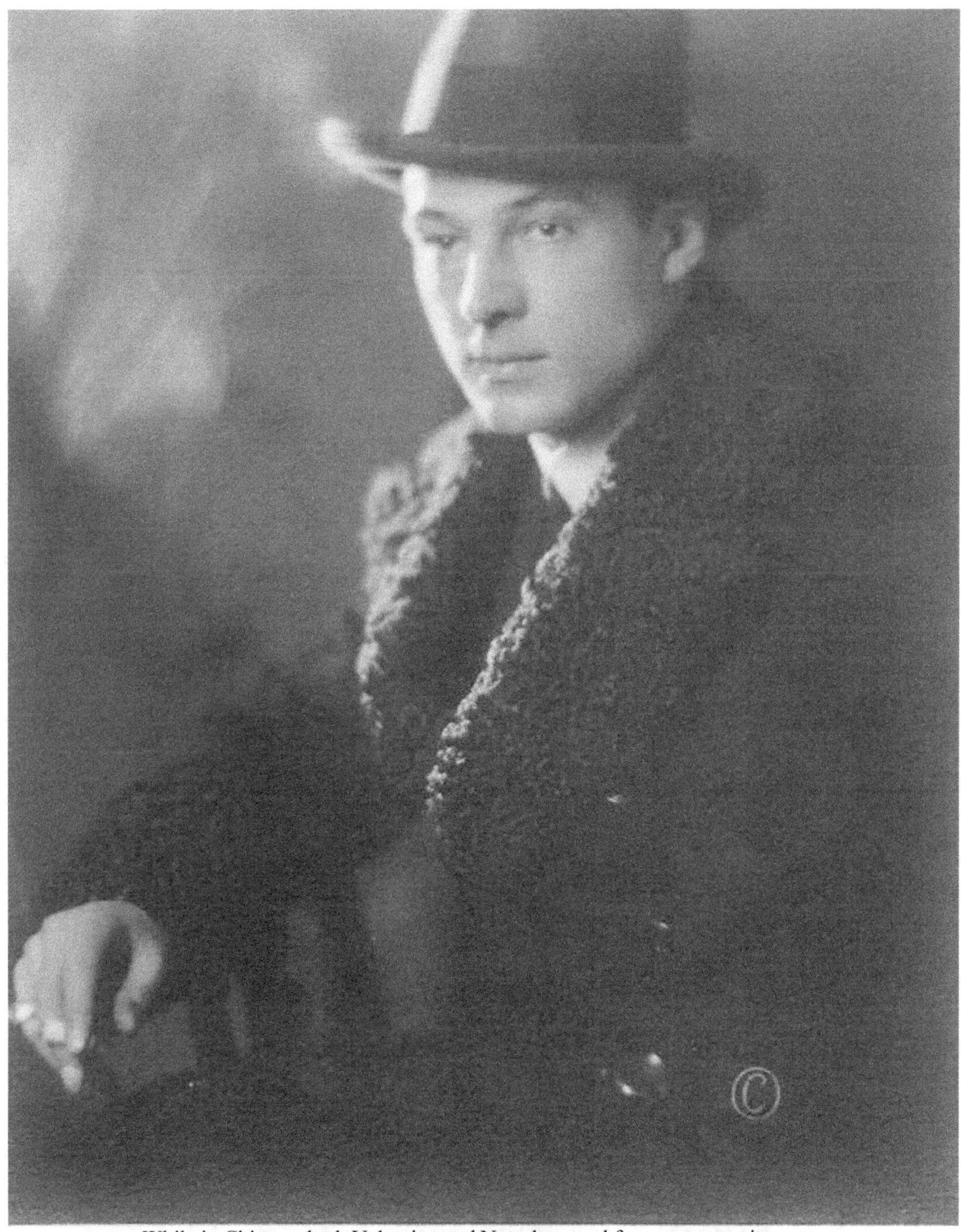

While in Chicago, both Valentino and Natacha posed for many portraits.
Valentino posed for Mabel Sykes, whom he soon declared to be his favorite photographer.
She became a close and trusted friend whom he visited every subsequent trip through Chicago.
(Author's collection)

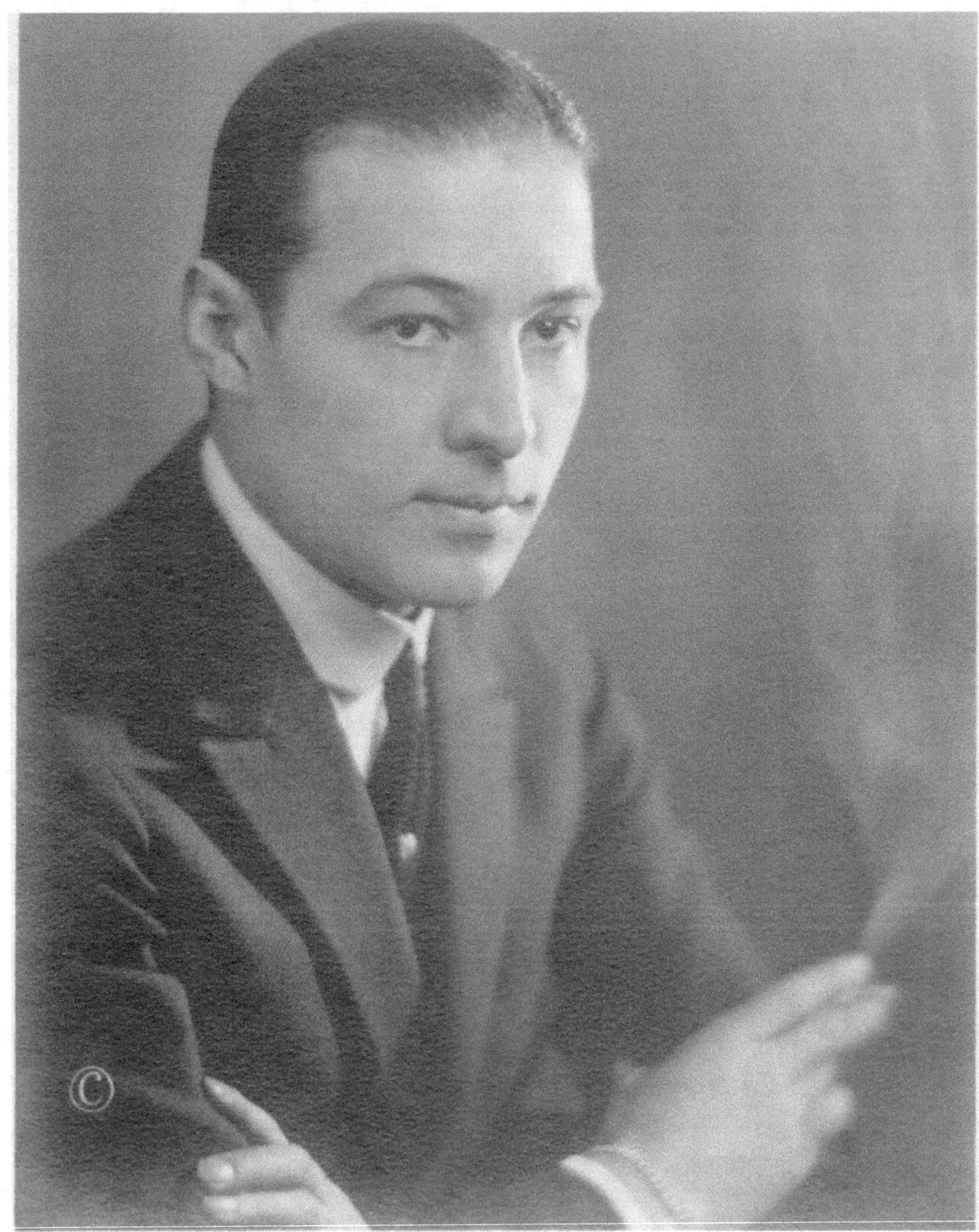

Mabel Sykes portrait 1923
(Author's collection)

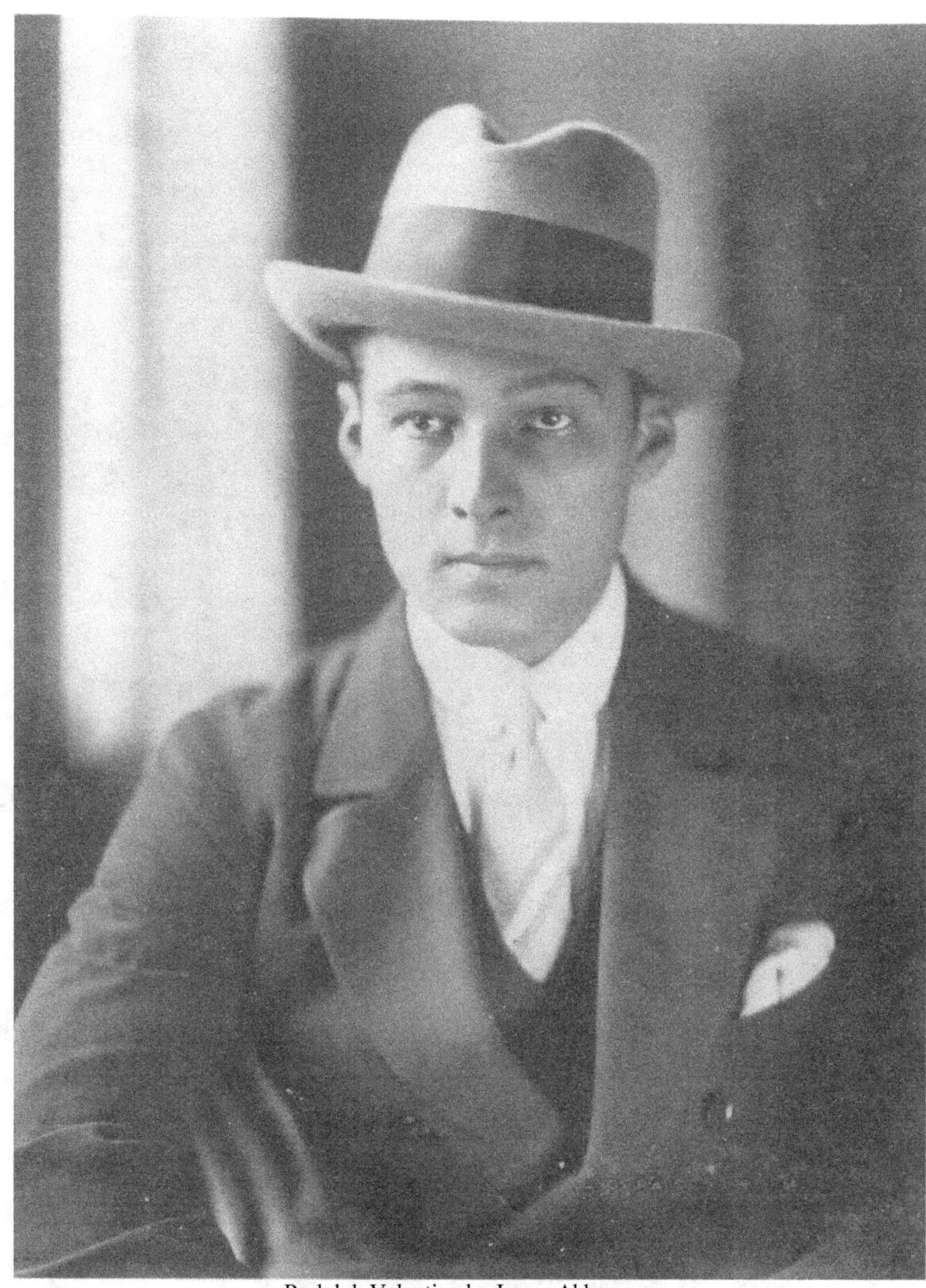

Rudolph Valentino by James Abbe
(Author's collection)

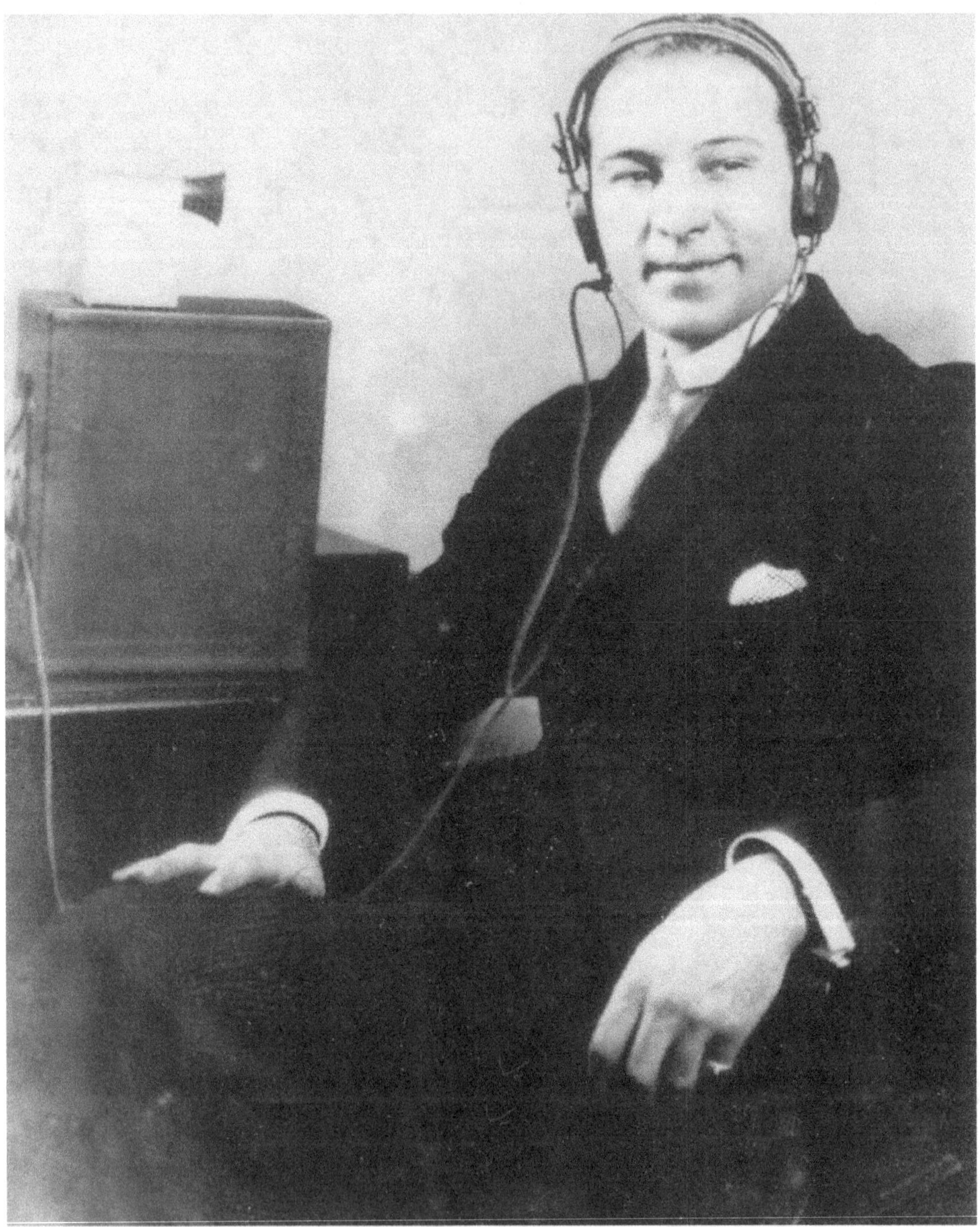

Valentino loved anything mechanical, enjoys listening to a crystal radio set during the Mineralava Tour. (Author's collection)

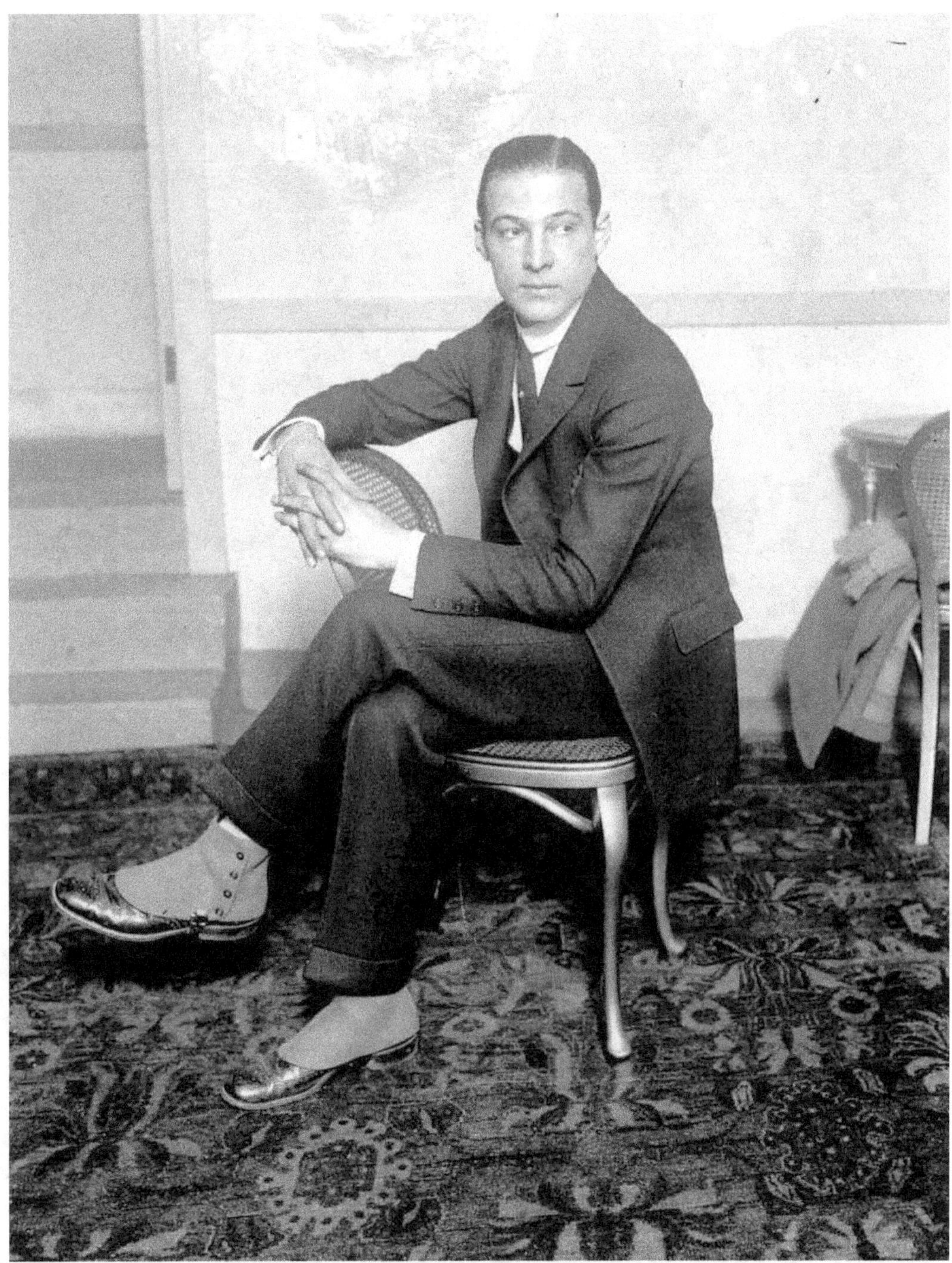

Valentino relaxing backstage in Chicago. The days of rest and relaxing would soon be a distant memory with the whistle stop tour beginning in a few weeks. (Author's collection)

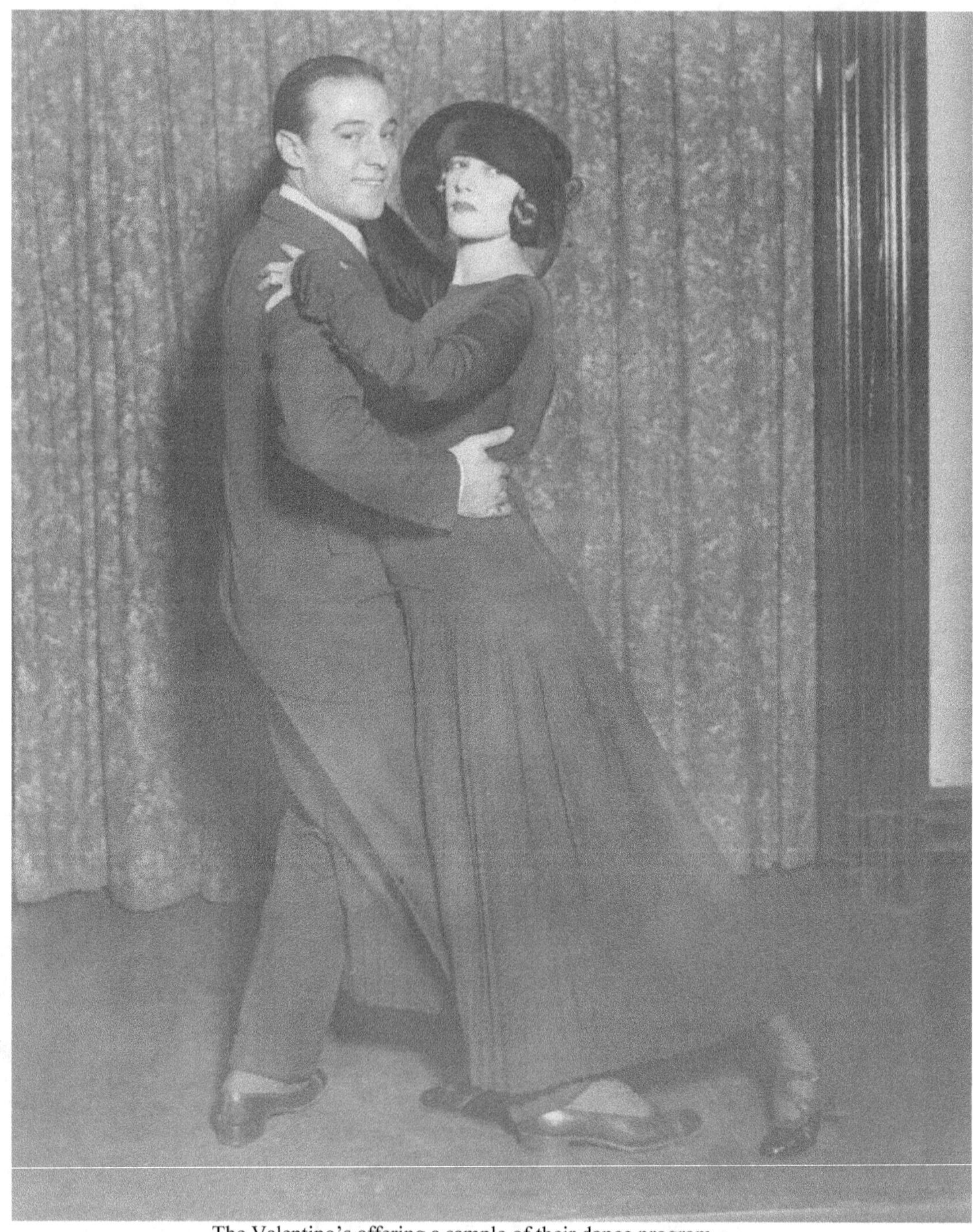

The Valentino's offering a sample of their dance program.
To say Valentino looks to be a very happy man is an understatement. (Gloria Bowman collection)

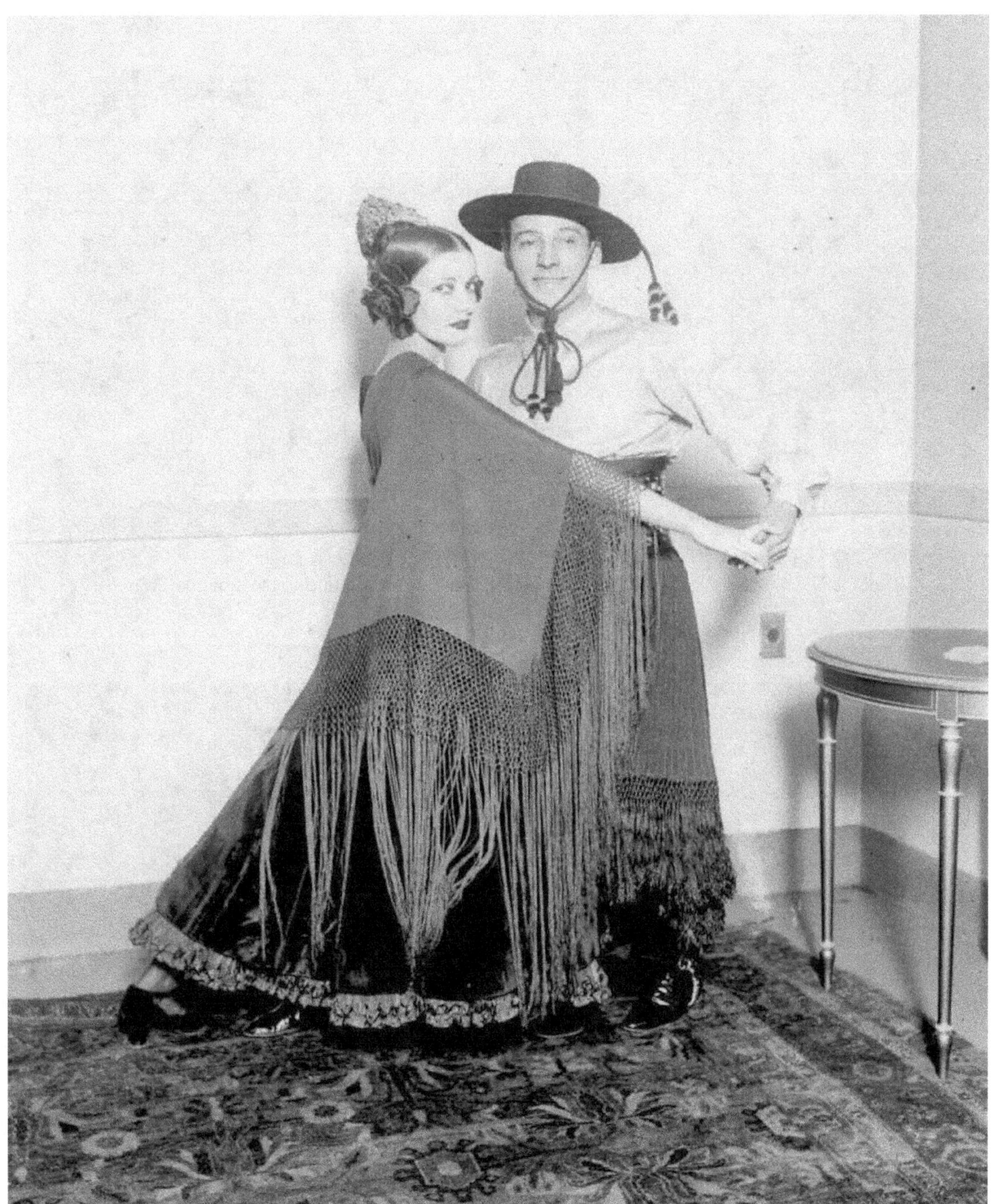

Rehearsing backstage for the news cameras. Natacha's reserved personality is on full display.
(Author's collection)

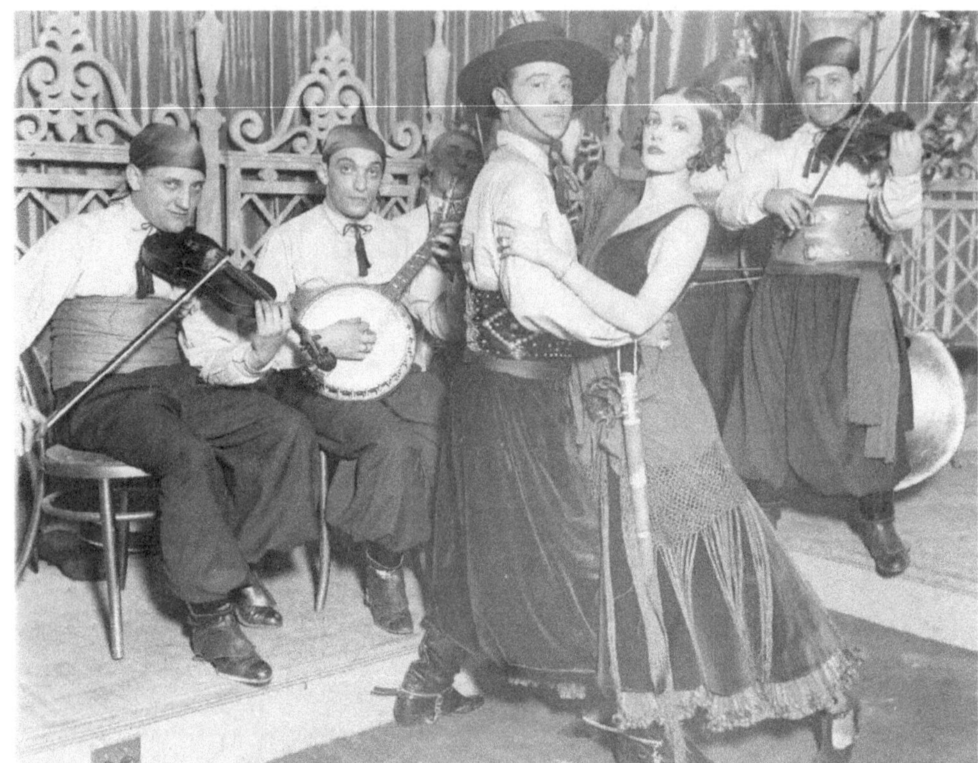

Rudolph Valentino and Natacha Rambova performing in Chicago during the month of March 1923.
(Tracy Terhune collection)

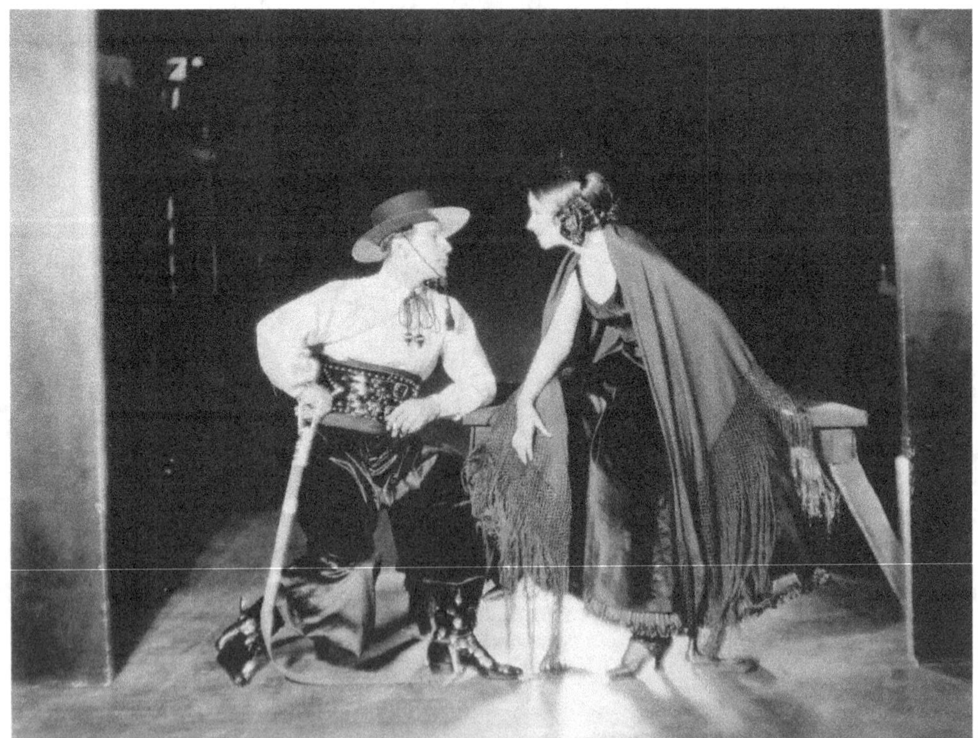

They posed for a series of dramatic portraits for the tour by photographer James Abbe.
(Margaret Herrick Library; Academy of Motion Picture Arts and Sciences)

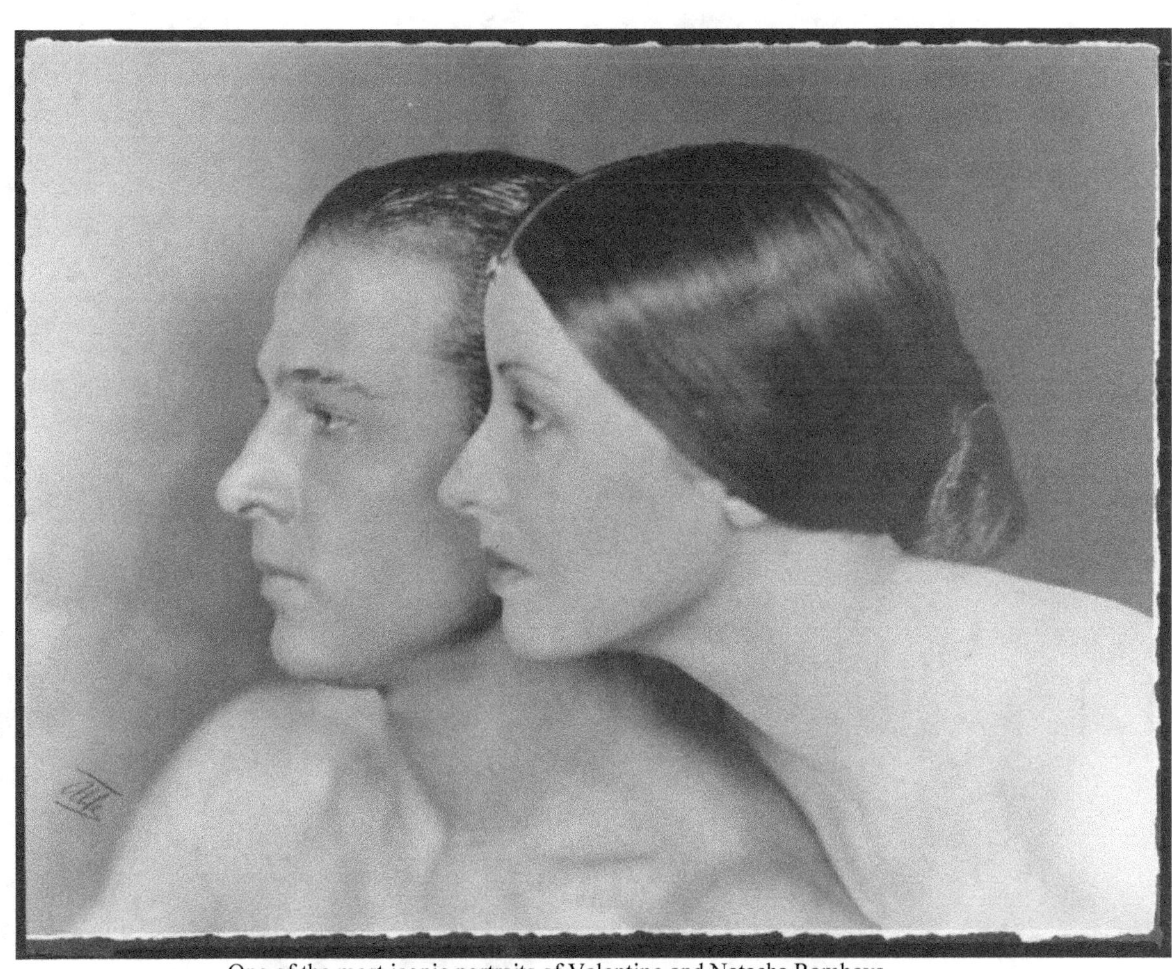

One of the most iconic portraits of Valentino and Natacha Rambova
(Author's collection)

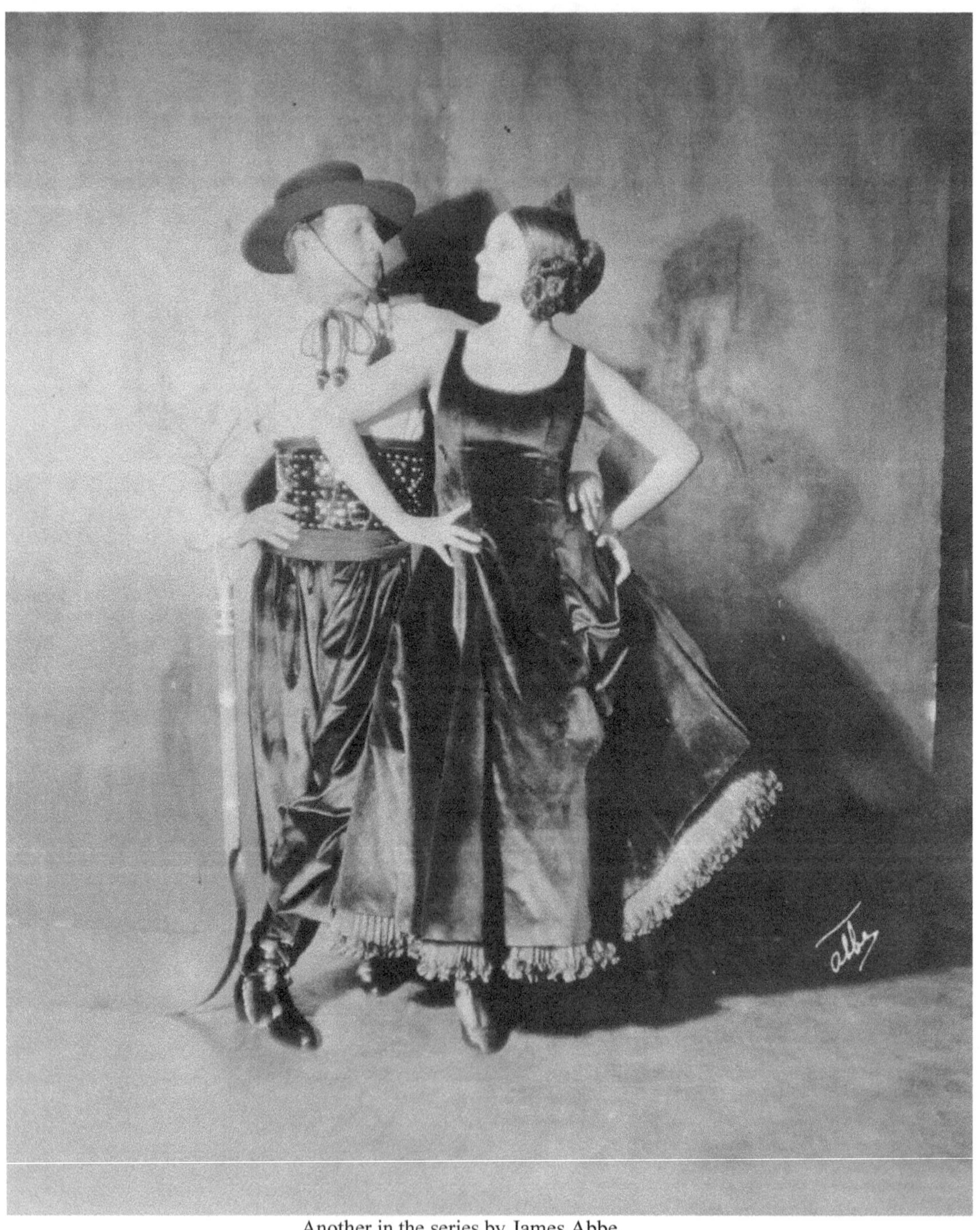

Another in the series by James Abbe.
(Author's collection)

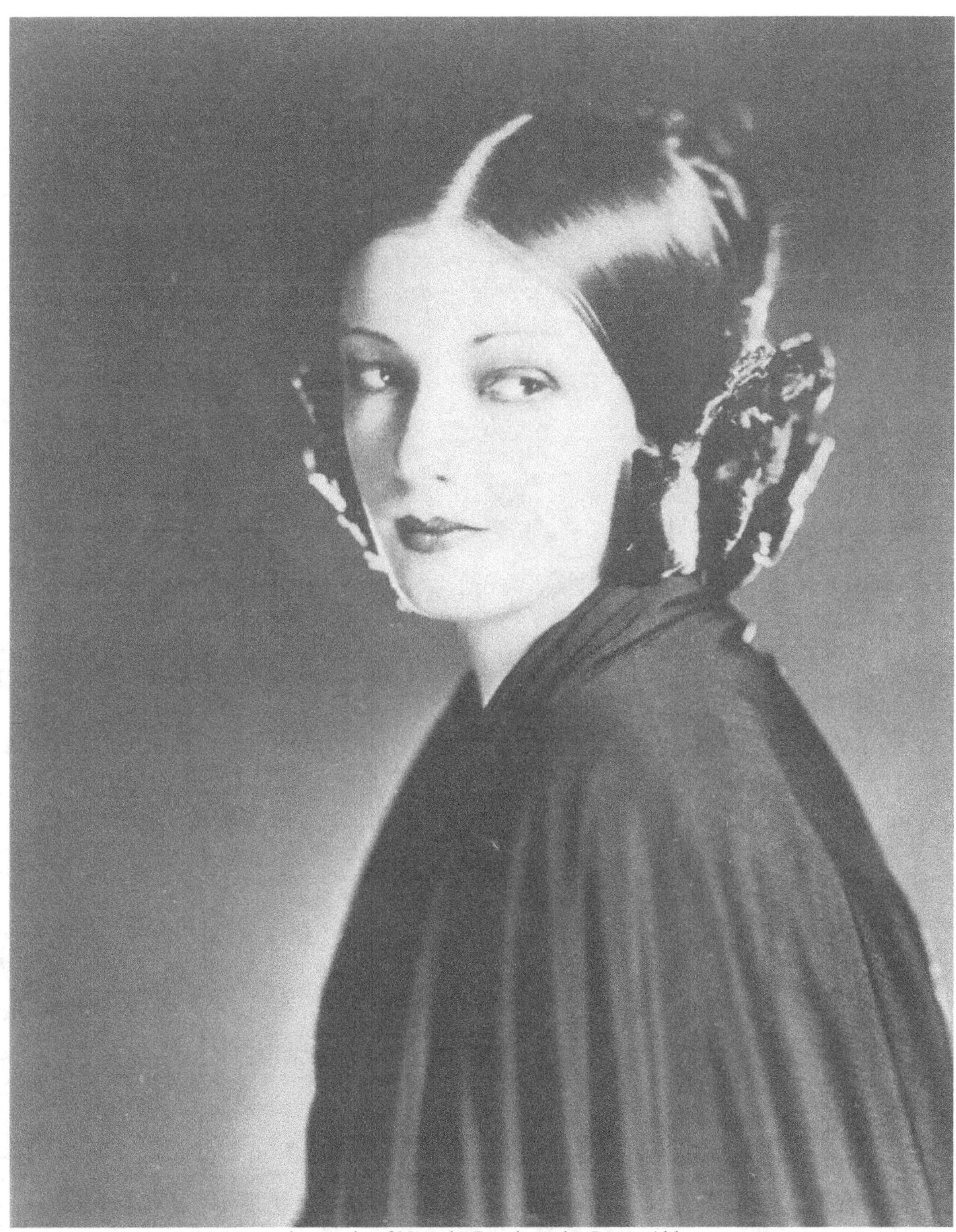

A stunning study of Natacha Rambova by James Abbe
(Author's collection)

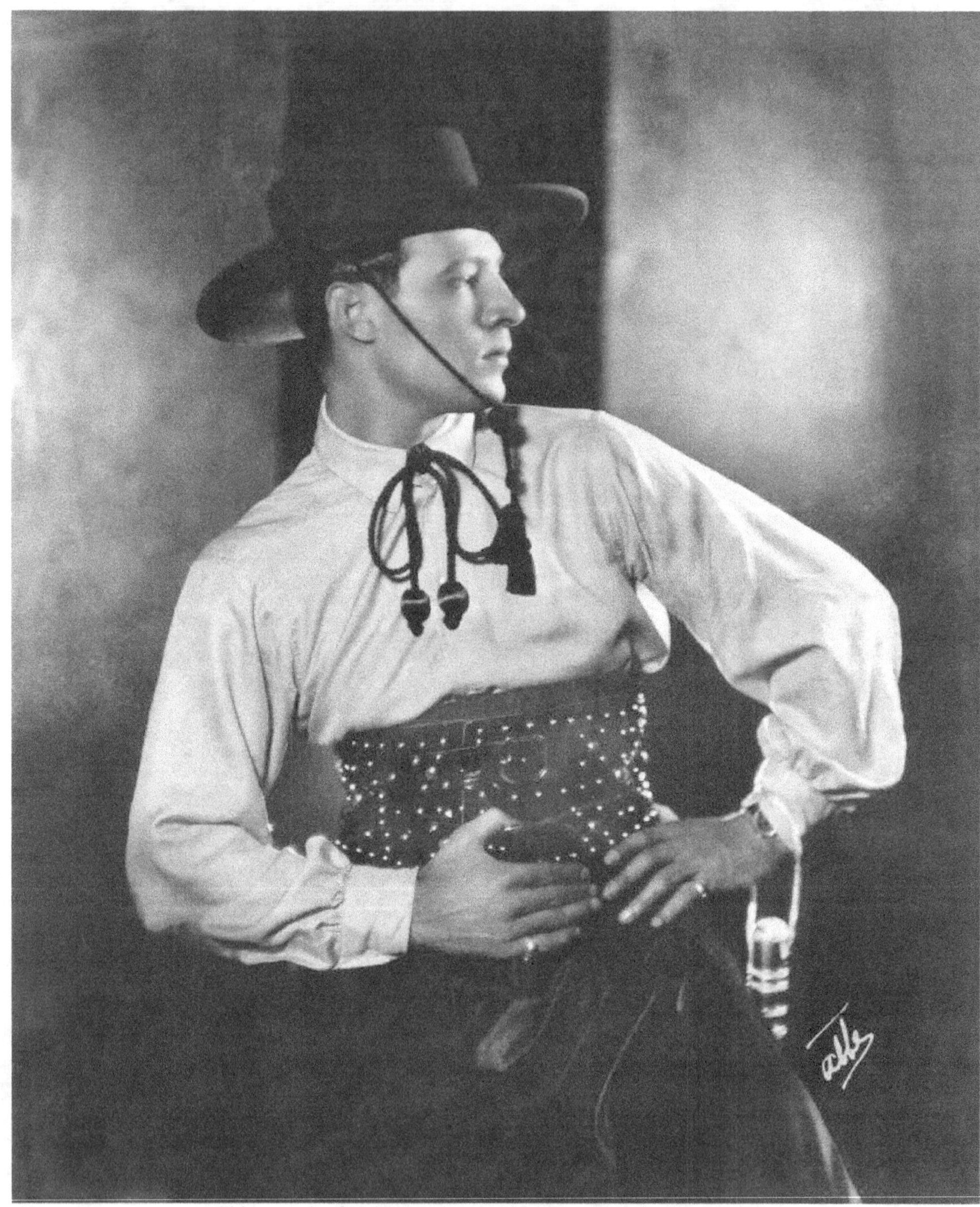

This portrait of Valentino was used in promotional material by the Mineralava company. (Author's collection)

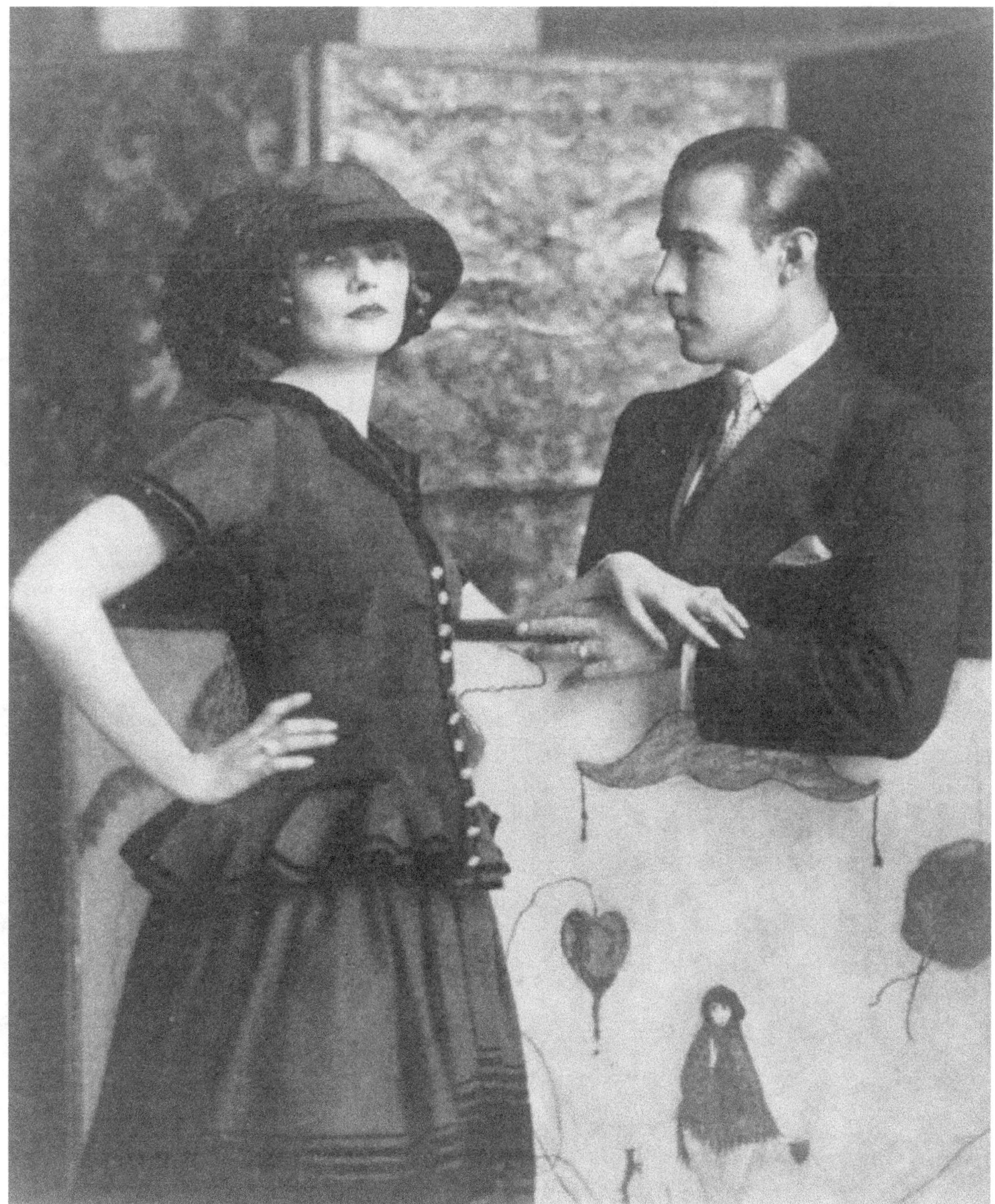

The pair were also photographed by Edward Steichen.
(Author's collection)

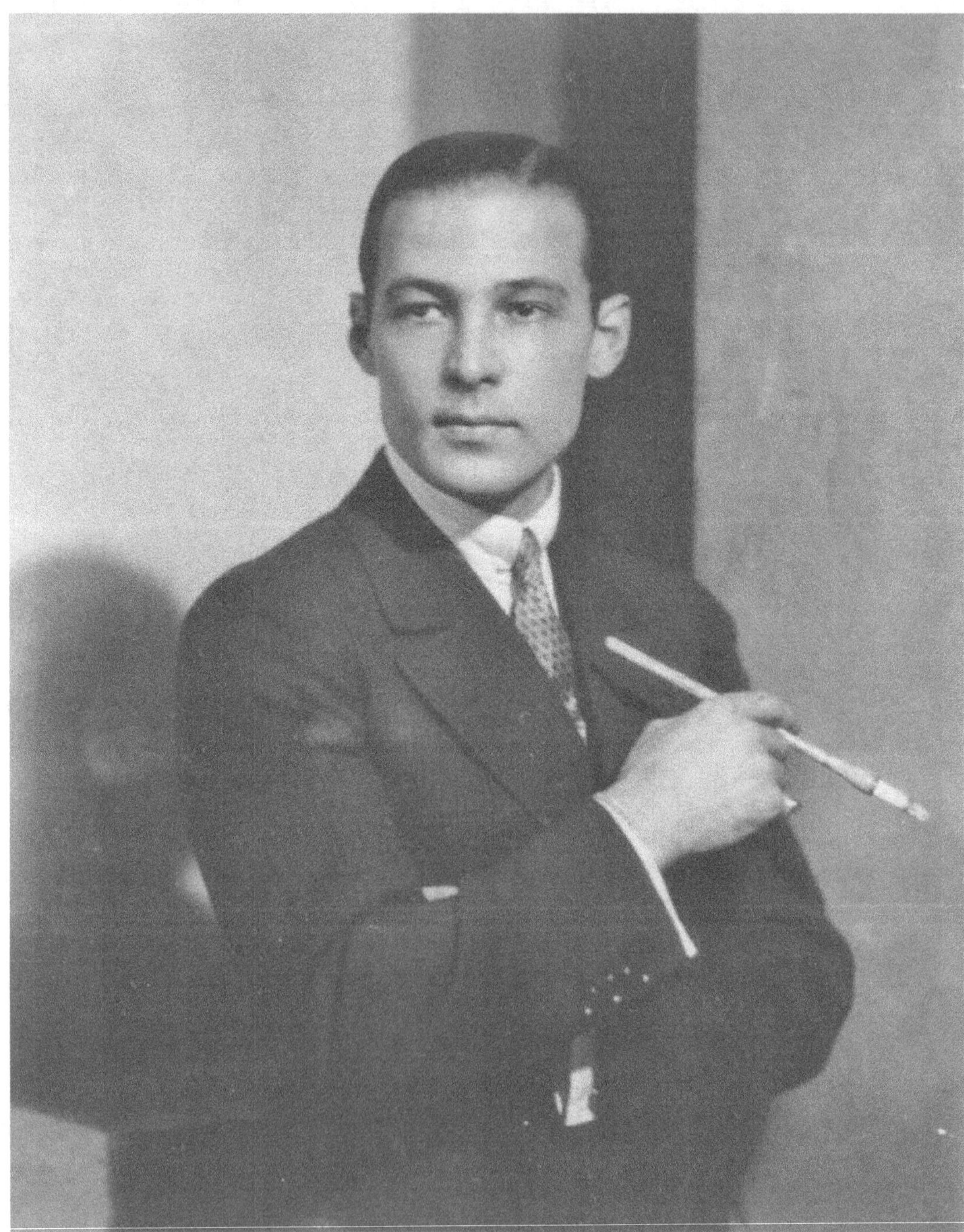

Valentino by Edward Steichen.
(Author's collection)

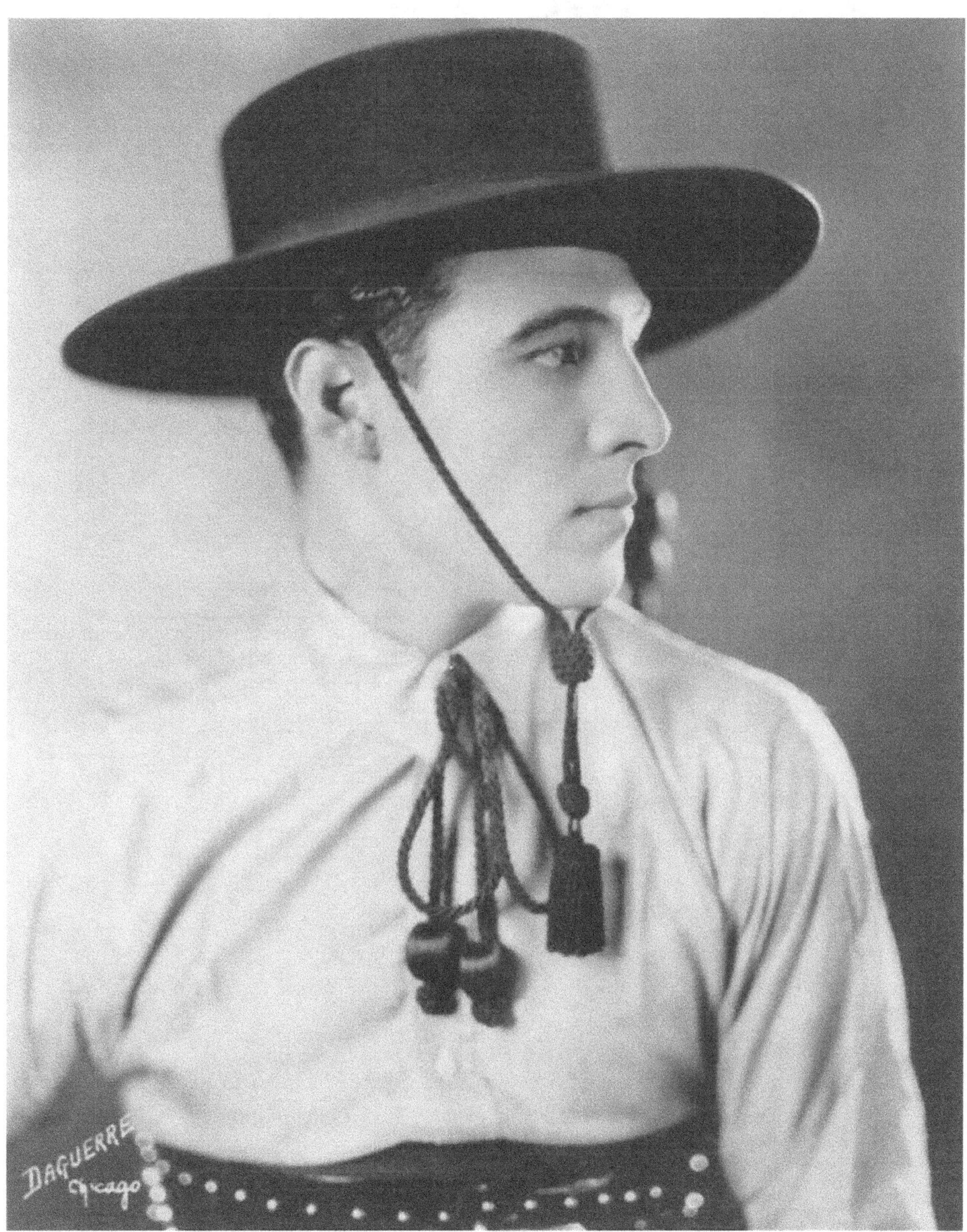

Valentino and Natacha also posed for dance photographer Daguerre while in Chicago.
This is a previously unpublished portrait.
(Author's collection)

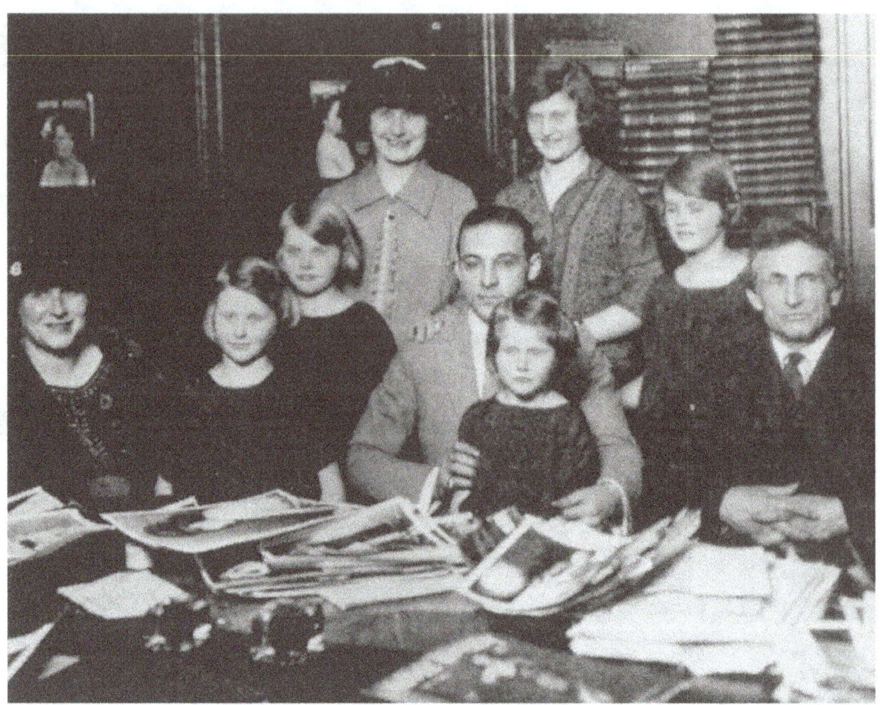

Rudolph Valentino meets with publisher Bernarr MacFadden and is contracted to pen a series of articles to be serialized in *Movie Weekly Magazine* chronicling his trip to Europe.
MacFadden also will publish Valentino's book of poetry *Day Dreams*.
(Author's collection)

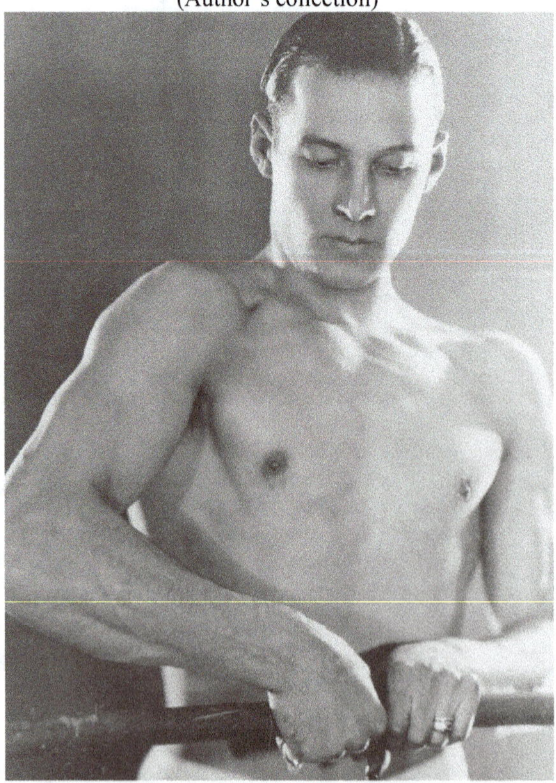

One of the series of fitness photos for Valentino's book *How You Can Keep Fit* (1923).
(Author's collection)

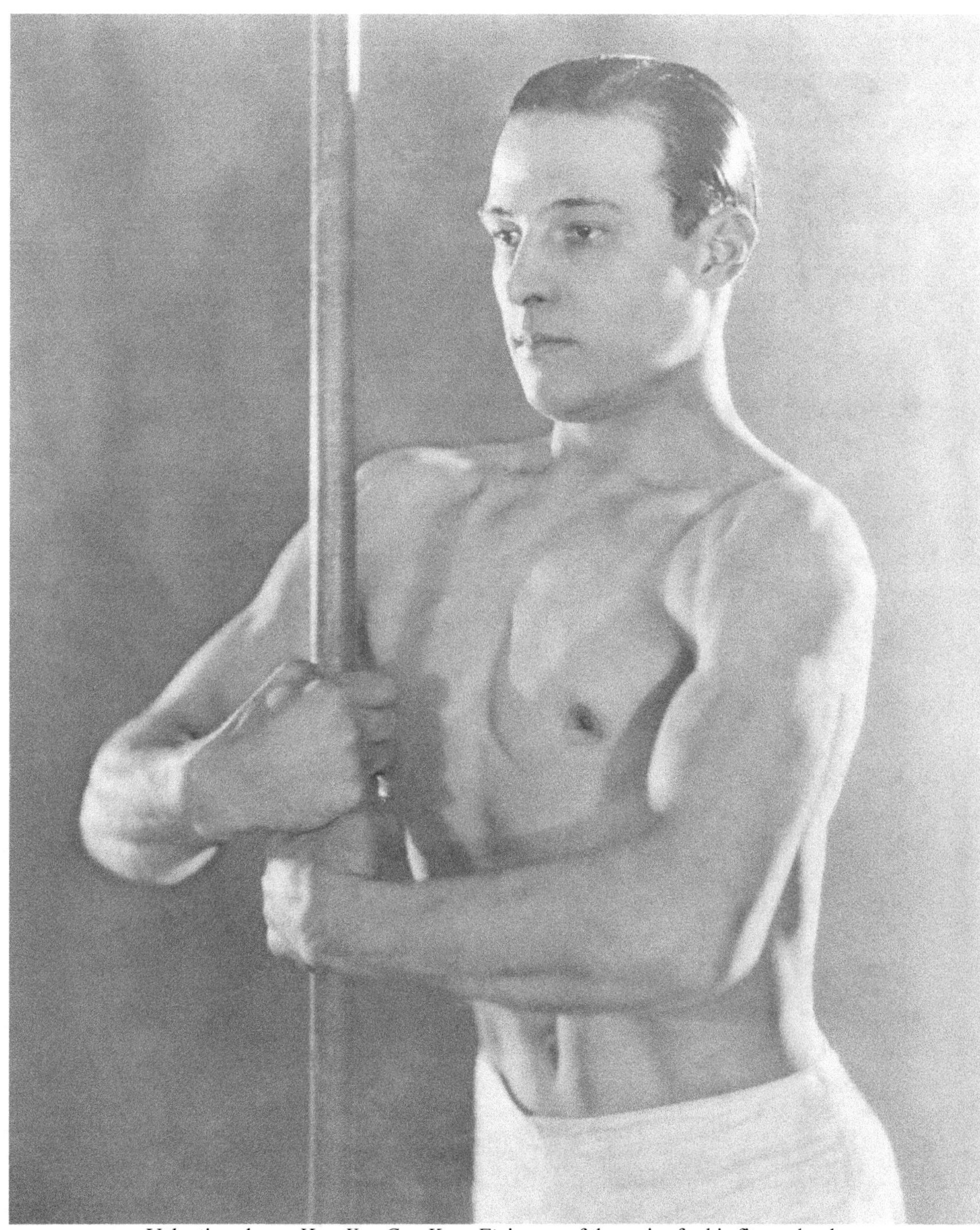

Valentino shows *How You Can Keep Fit* in one of the series for his fitness book.
(Author's collection)

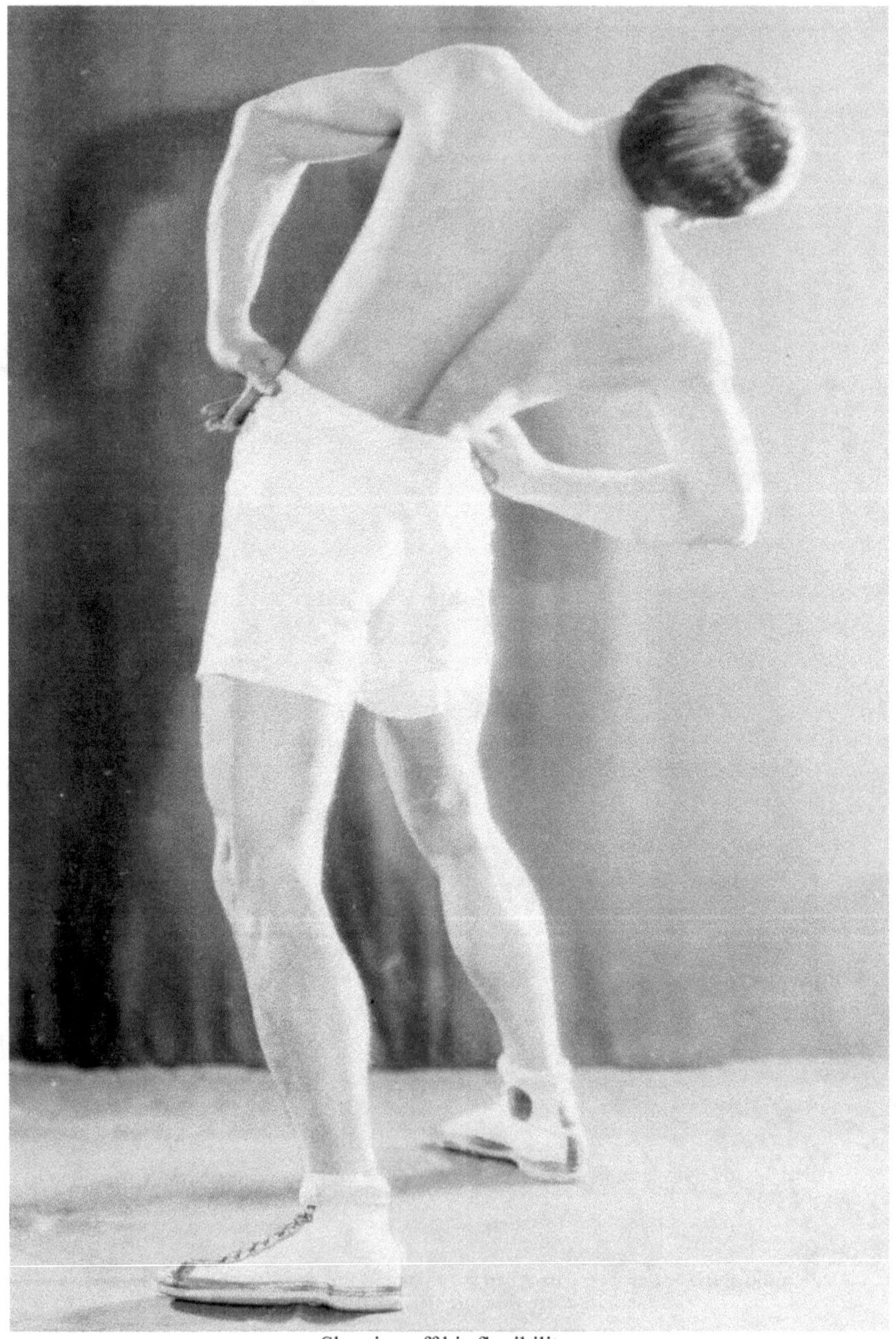

Showing off his flexibility.
(Author's collection)

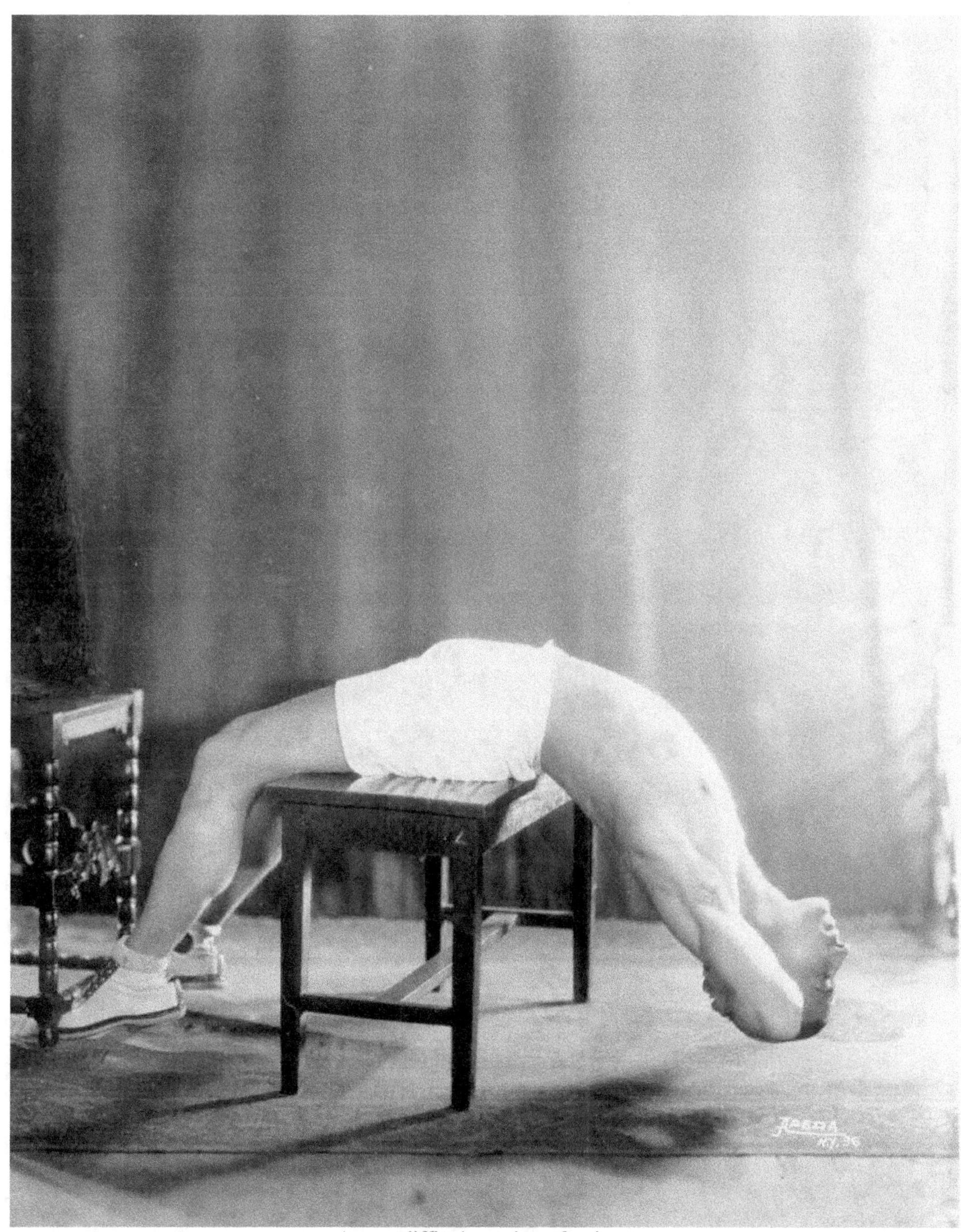

A very difficult version of a sit-up.
(Author's collection)

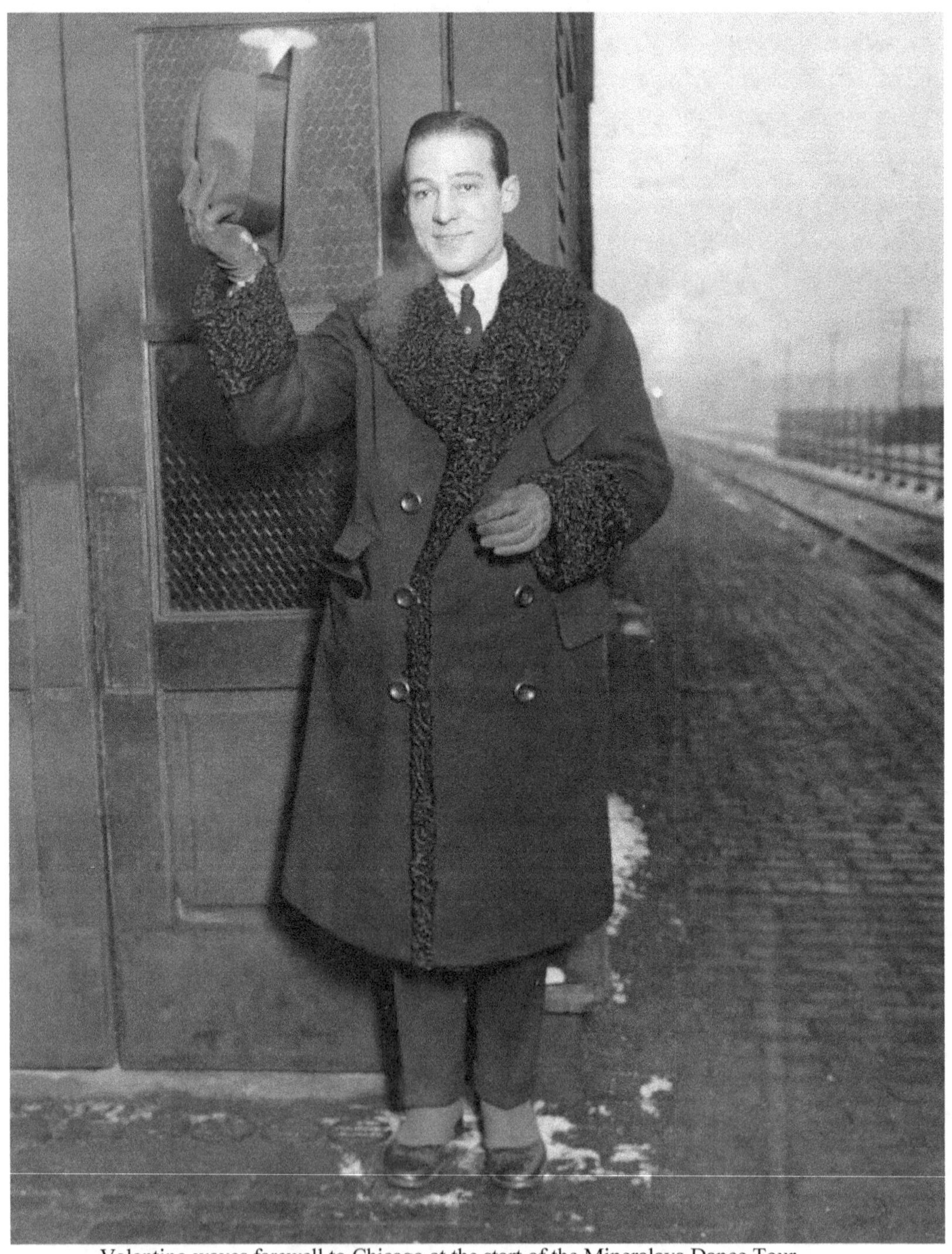

Valentino waves farewell to Chicago at the start of the Mineralava Dance Tour.
(San Francisco History Center)

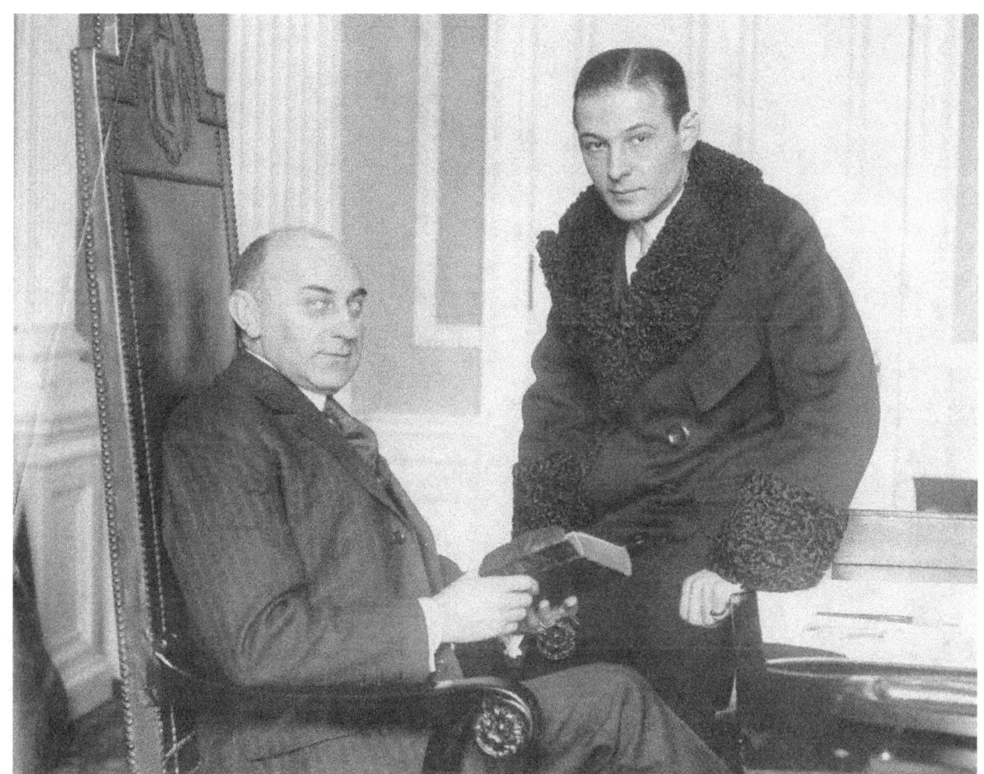

Valentino visits with former Governor Cox in Ohio.
(author's collection)

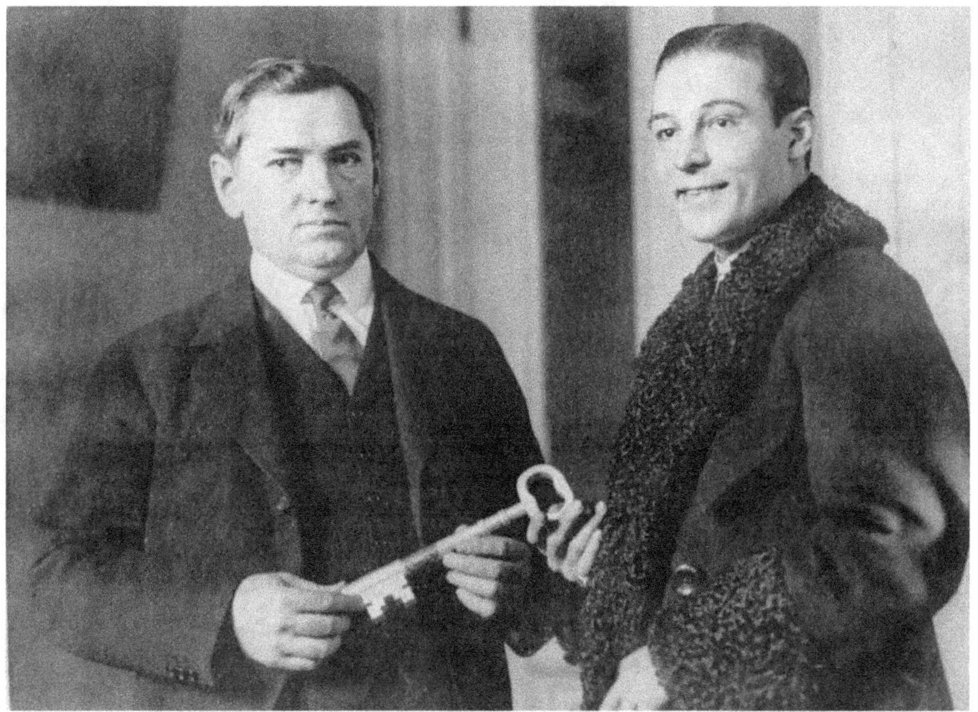

Valentino receiving the key to the city of Boston. (San Francisco History Center)

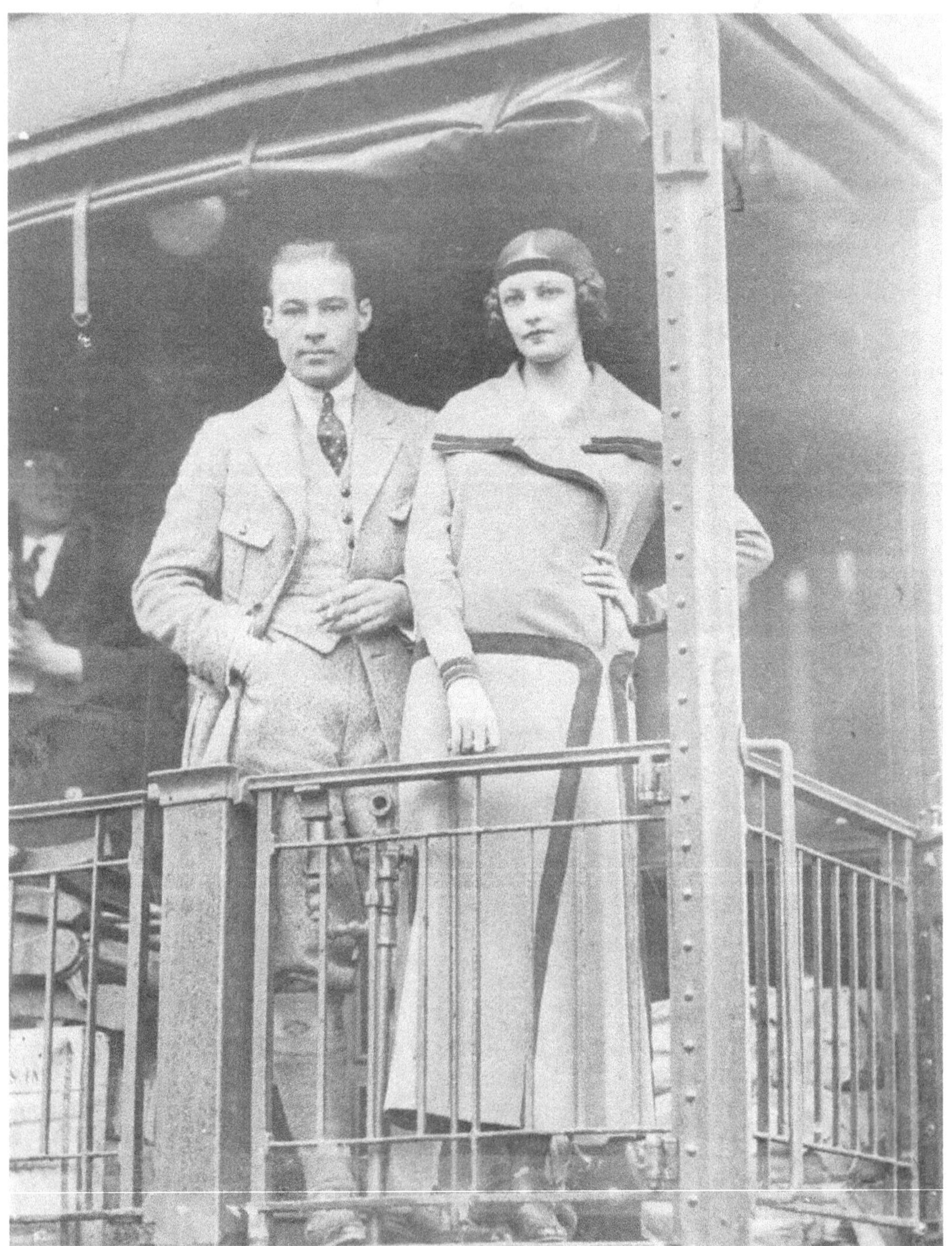

Rudolph Valentino and Natacha Rambova on their Pullman car The Colonial.
The grueling effects of the tour is etched on their faces.
(Author's collection)

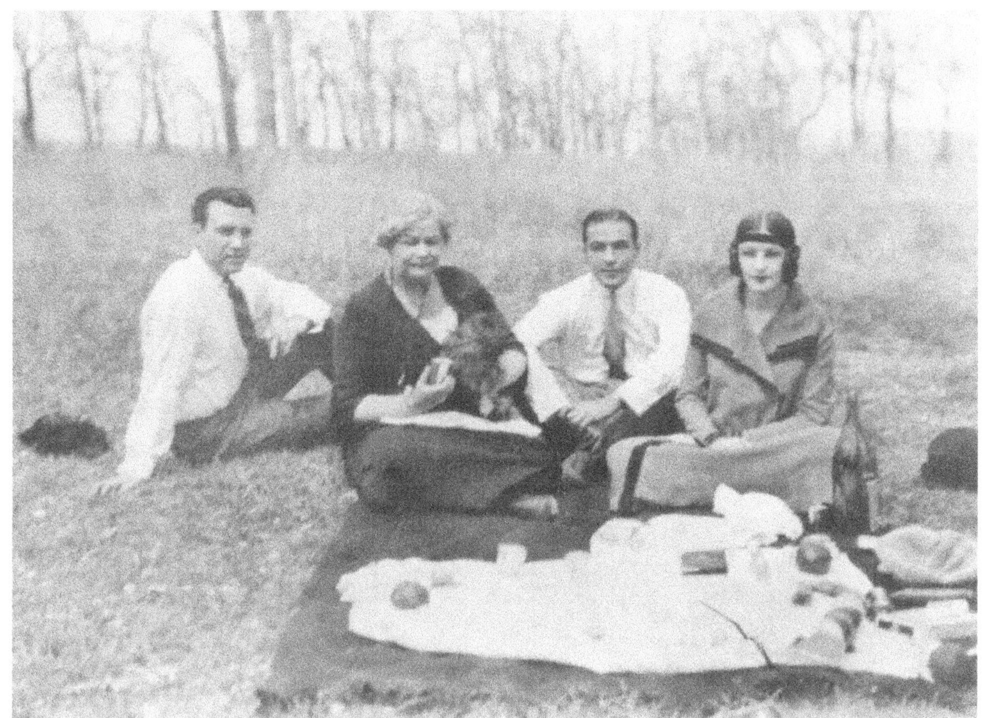

S. George Ullman, Teresa Werner, Valentino and Natacha enjoying a rural picnic during the tour. (Michael Morris collection)

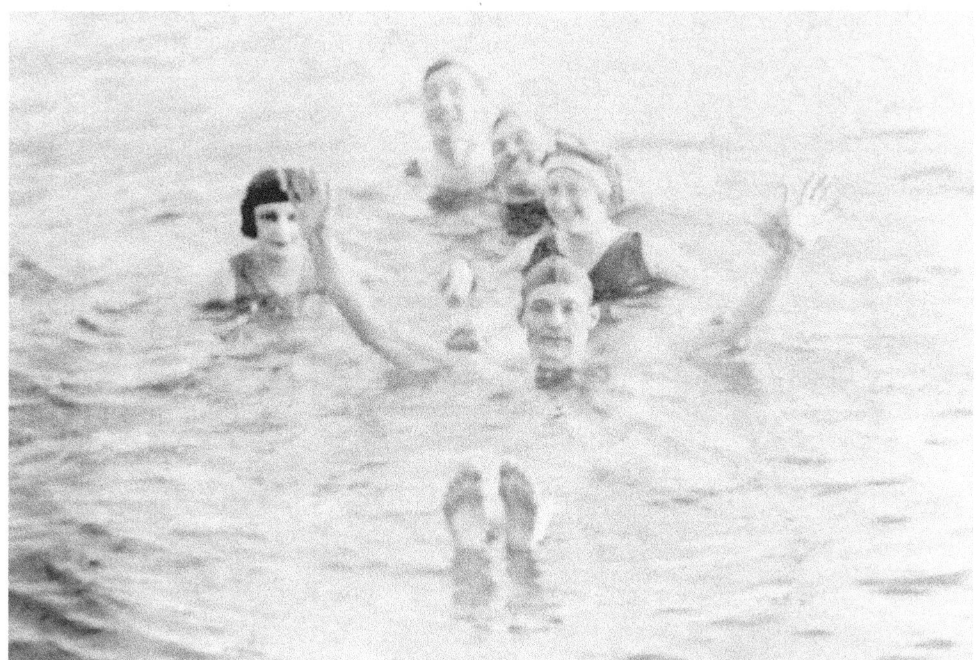

Valentino, Natacha and friends floating in the great Salt Lake. (Michael Morris collection)

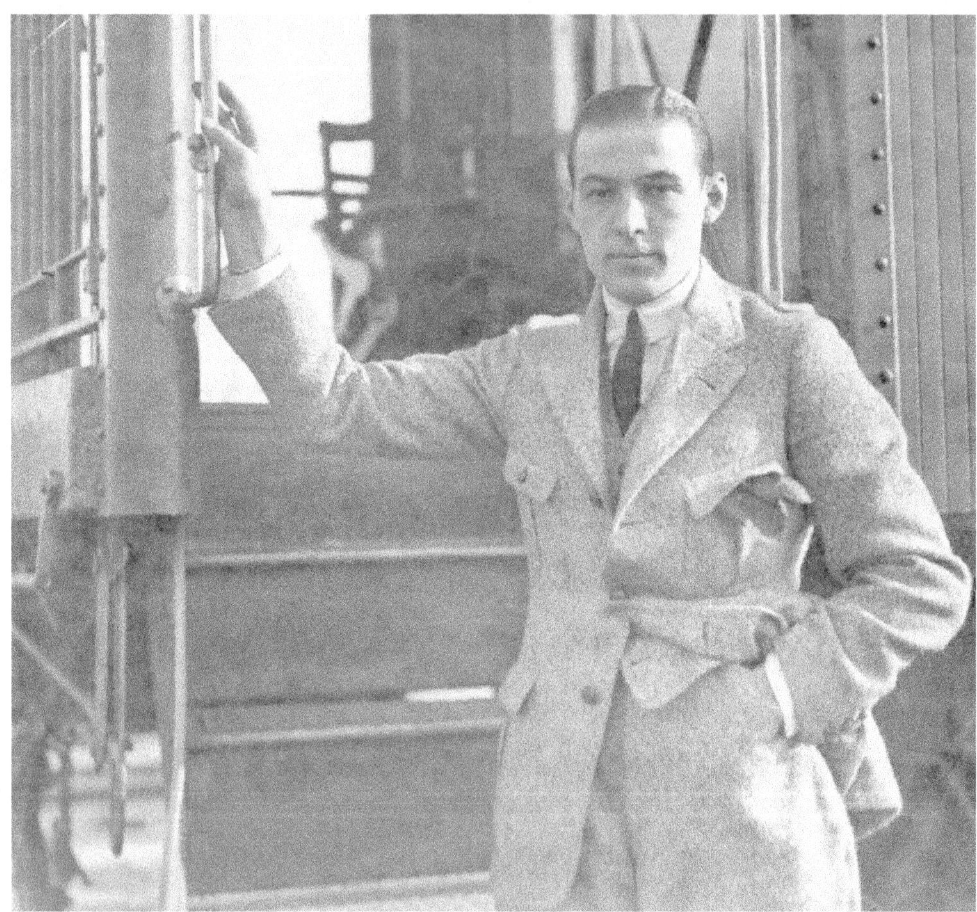

Valentino posting outside The Colonial, the lavish Pullman car at a stop in Oklahoma.
(Author's collection)

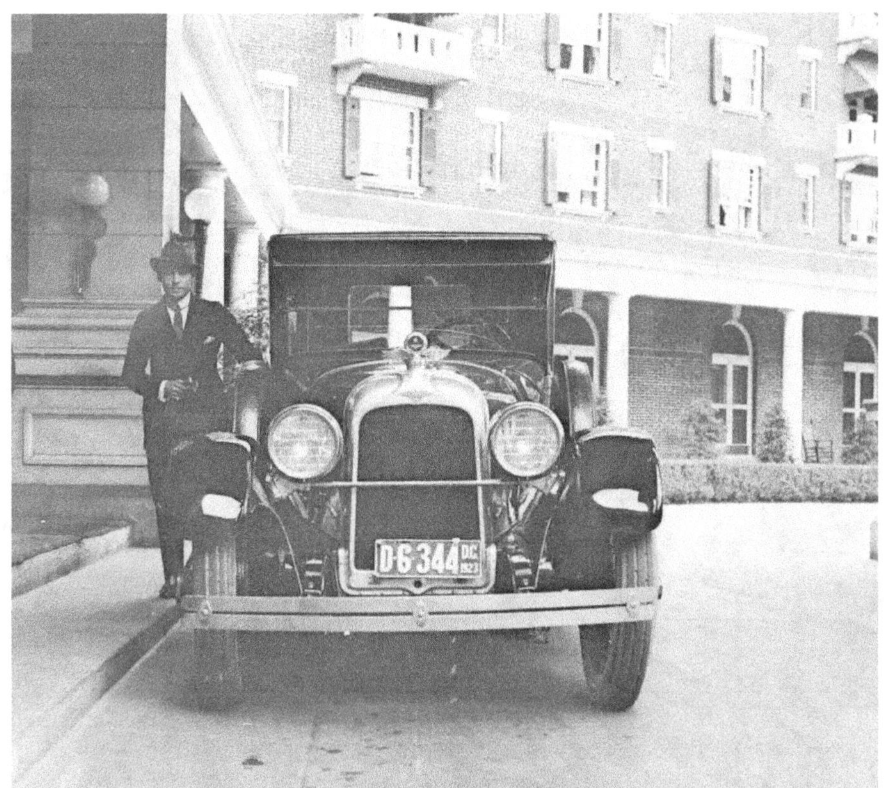

Valentino in Washington D.C. at the Wardman Park Hotel. (Library of Congress)

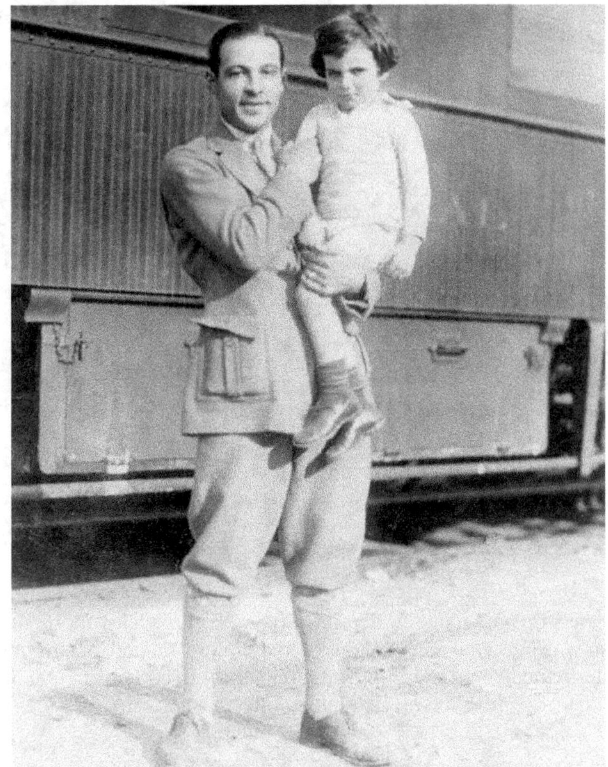

Valentino made friends with George Ullman's boy Daniel Ullman.
(Author's collection)

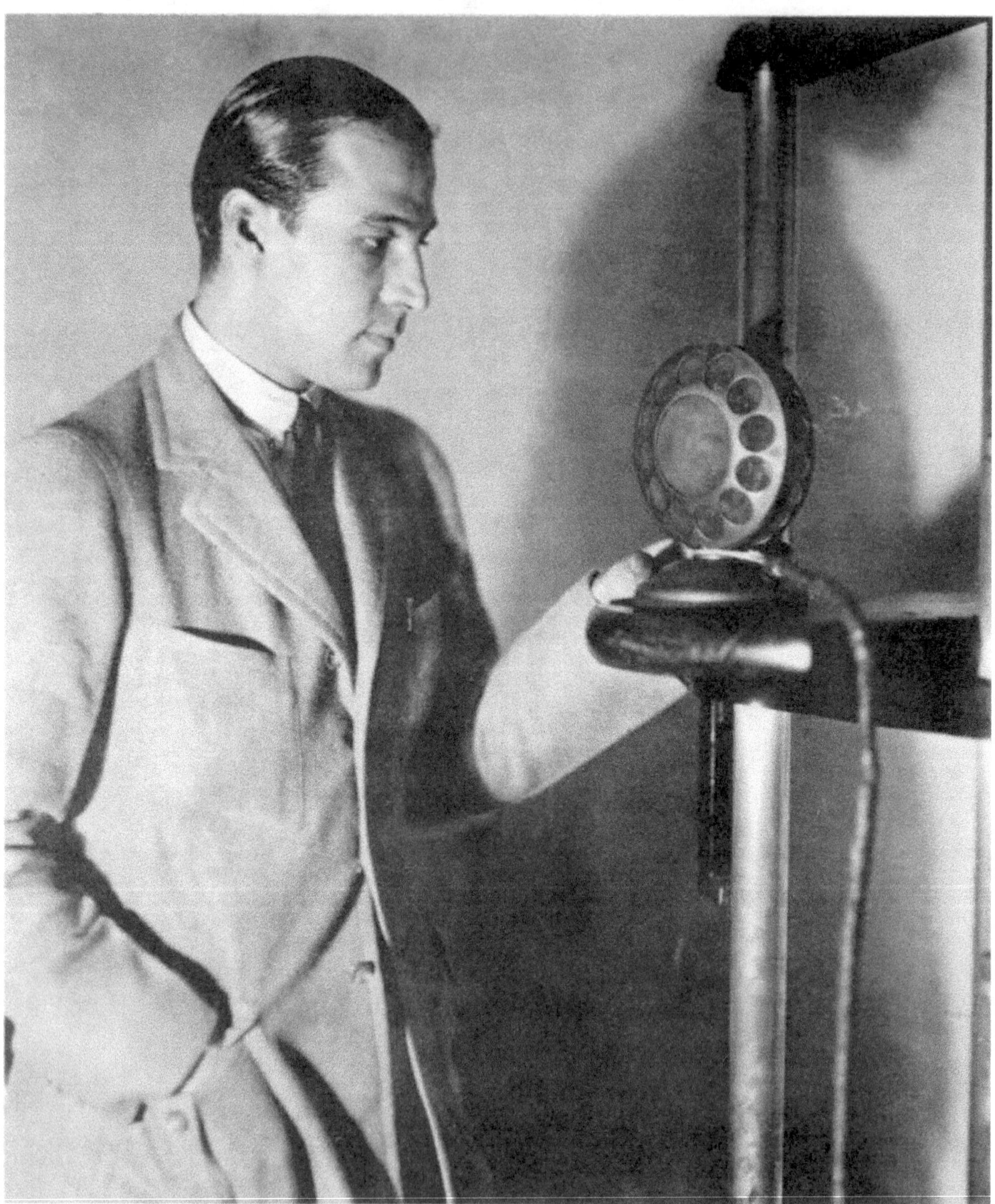

During the stop on Atlanta, Valentino did a radio broadcast for the local station.
He also was interviewed by Peggy Marsh of the Atlanta Constitution Journal.
She is better remembered today as Margaret Mitchell, author of *Gone with the Wind.*
(Author's collection)

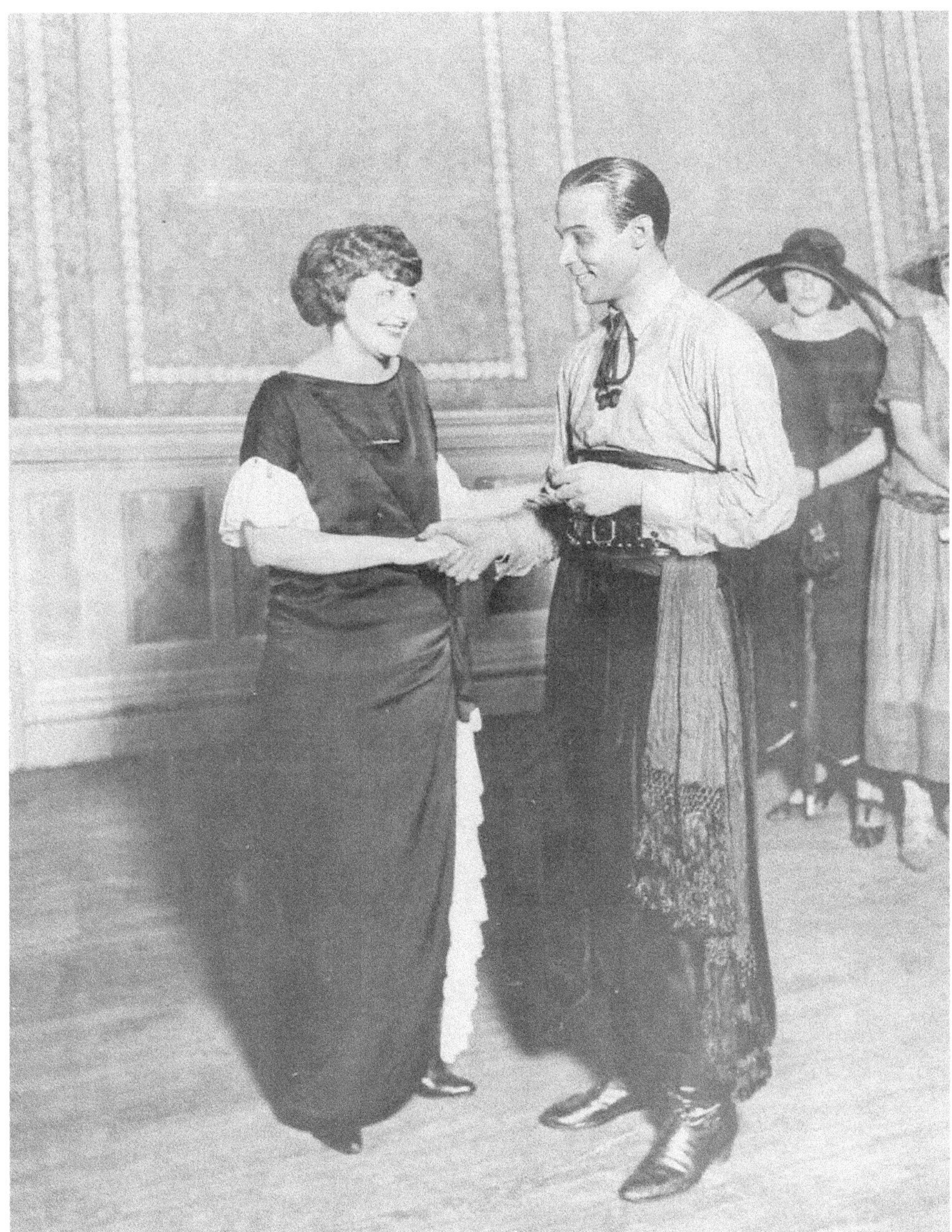

Valentino meets with and congratulates the Atlanta contest winner S. Geraldine Byfield.
(Gloria Bowman collection)

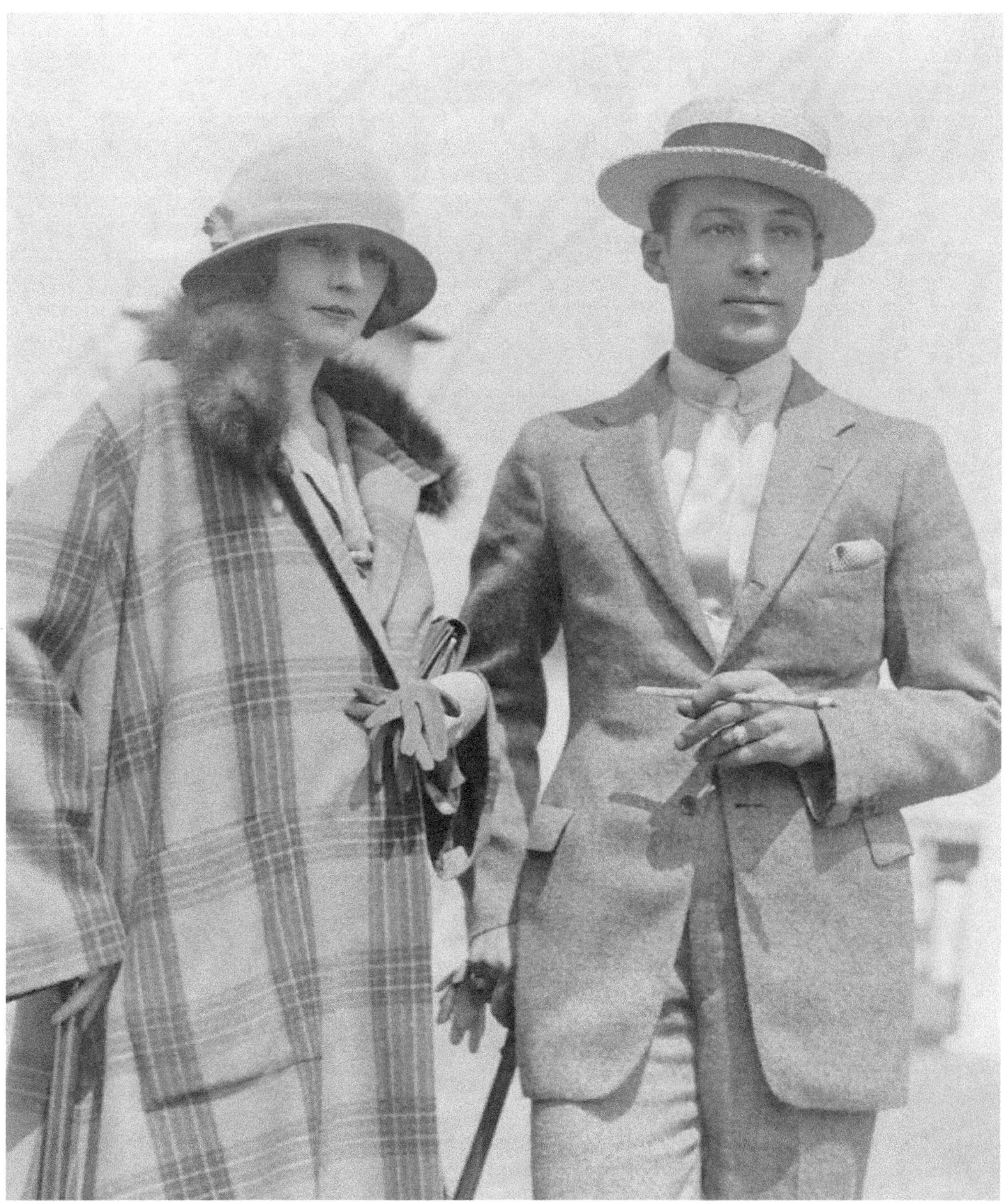

. . . and now I am tired. I want to rest. Out there on the boundless, unfathomable waters, under the free and riding moon, I may be, not Valentino, the actor, but a tired dreamer, going home . . . that is a sweet thought to me.

—Rudolph Valentino, 1923

The Valentinos were worn out. The Mineralava Tour, their marital and legal woes, and the ongoing litigation with Famous Players-Lasky had made for an exhausting and emotionally draining year. With George Ullman now handling their business affairs, they finally felt free to enjoy themselves, and they were exhilarated by the prospect of experiencing Europe together and enjoying some privacy. Before sailing in late July, Valentino contracted with publisher and fitness guru Bernarr MacFadden to keep a travel diary for later serialization in *Movie Weekly Magazine*.

They boarded the RMS Aquitania, obligingly posing for photographs and mugging for the newsreels. Fellow passengers Mr. and Mrs. George Arliss provided pleasant company and conversation on the voyage, and the two couples promised to meet while in London. After an excited welcome to the city by the press and the public, the pair dined with a number of titled gentry and Valentino paid visits to Savile Row's most famous tailors. Natacha deferred her fashion expenditures, preferring to wait until they reached Paris. Her shopping in Britain was confined to the three pedigreed Pekingese puppies she purchased at the kennels of Mrs. Ashton Cross.

On August 16 the pair flew with friend Robert Florey across the English Channel and were greeted by enthusiastic fans at Paris's Le Bourget Airport. In town they met magazine publisher and theater producer Jacques Herbetot, who would become a close friend. Herbetot organized outings in Paris and arranged posh dinners, introducing the Valentinos to Parisian society. While Natacha visited the salon of the famed French couturier Paul Poiret, Valentino shopped for cars and expensive cameras. A dedicated shutterbug, he purchased expensive still and movie cameras from Debrie. He also ordered a touring car from luxury automobile manufacturer Avions Voisin, which (perhaps foolishly) loaned the Valentinos a car to use for travel to the Riviera and to Italy. They drove to Normandy with Herbetot for the Grand Prix, but missed the races due to inclement weather. Back in Paris, Valentino continued socializing with new friends and touring the city while Natacha purchased more clothing suitable for traveling on the open road. Their next stop was the Riviera, for a visit to Natacha's family.

They arrived in Juan les Pins not without incident. Natacha was a poor traveler, suffering not only from the poor roads but from her husband's penchant for reckless speed. "Every car that Rudy saw ahead of him on the road was to him a special invitation to prove our (automotive) superiority." They also narrowly avoided an accident on a mountain pass, although Natacha claimed that Valentino credited the miracle to the munificence of his spirit guide, Black Feather. They remained at the Hudnut chateau in Juan les Pins for ten days to relax, refuel, and recover from the road trip. Valentino played with the dogs, took photographs and home movies, and rented a boat to cruise the Mediterranean Sea at high speed.

Teresa Werner, Natacha, Rudy, and a myriad of trunks then journeyed from France to Italy. The roads were dusty and pitted with holes and ruts, but Valentino was on a mission to make a triumphant return to his home country. On the way, Natacha suffered every bump, not always in silence. Her Aunt Teresa was more of a trouper and handled Valentino's erratic and dangerous driving with aplomb. Adding to Natacha's distress were the hotel accommodations, which were not up to their posh standards.

The travelers stopped in Genoa, and Valentino relived happy memories during a nostalgic visit to Istituto di Agraria de Sant'Illario. Milan afforded a tender reunion with sister Maria, who, Natacha noted, looked much like her older brother. For her part, the provincial Maria was shocked by her brother's sophisticated and heavily rouged wife. The party then motored south to Rome, where they were again received by fans in the style to which they'd now become accustomed. They toured Rome's antiquities and met German actor Emil Jannings, then in Rome filming *Quo Vadis*.

In Rome, Natacha decided she'd had enough traveling and took the train back to the comforts and peace of Nice. Sister Maria joined Rudy and Aunt Teresa on the journey further southward to visit Alberto and his family.

In Campobasso, Valentino shared a happy reunion with his brother and his sister-in-law Ada. He also met for the first time his nine-year-old nephew, Jean. It was a joyful introduction: Valentino adored children and loved spoiling his nephew. Jean, in turn, adored his uncle. Valentino and a cousin visited his uncle's estate in Carostino where as children they had spent happy summers. From there he motored south to Taranto and to his childhood home in Castellaneta. He was recognized and remembered by some of the locals as a bit of a ne'er-do-well. He visited his place of birth and also made an emotional pilgrimage to the grave of the sister he never knew, Bice.

The visit to Castellaneta reminded him of how far he had come. This was no longer home; he'd long ago surpassed the small-town jealousies. He was eager to return to Nice, to Natacha, and, ultimately, to America and his career.

Back in New York, Valentino was scheduled to judge the final beauty contest at Madison Square Garden for the Mineralava Tour. The panel of judges also included Mark Hellinger, Gilda Gray, Beniamino Gigli, Christopher Morley, Winsor McCay, Edmund Pizella, and conductor Hugo Riesenfeld. Valentino presented the trophies to the five finalists and crowned the winner, eighteen-year-old Miss Norma Niblock of Toronto.

With their obligations to Mineralava completed, the Valentinos returned to Europe to spend Christmas with Natacha's family in Juan les Pins. The two were determined to have an old-fashioned holiday, and the Hudnuts arranged to have an enormous tree brought in from a neighboring estate. Natacha brought a trunk full of decorations and the tree was traditionally festooned with ornaments and candles.

Valentino eagerly participated in the tree-trimming. While lighting the candles he noticed an unlit stray. Reaching back to light it, he accidentally set a paper snowflake alight; within moments the entire tree was ablaze. Almost everyone panicked. The fire was finally doused by pouring water from the balcony above, whereupon the family began to lament the loss of all the lovely gifts. Fortunately, Aunt Teresa had exercised calm in the storm and moved the gifts to safety. Filthy with smoke and ash, all gratefully retired to celebrate their Christmas by imbibing champagne until the wee hours.

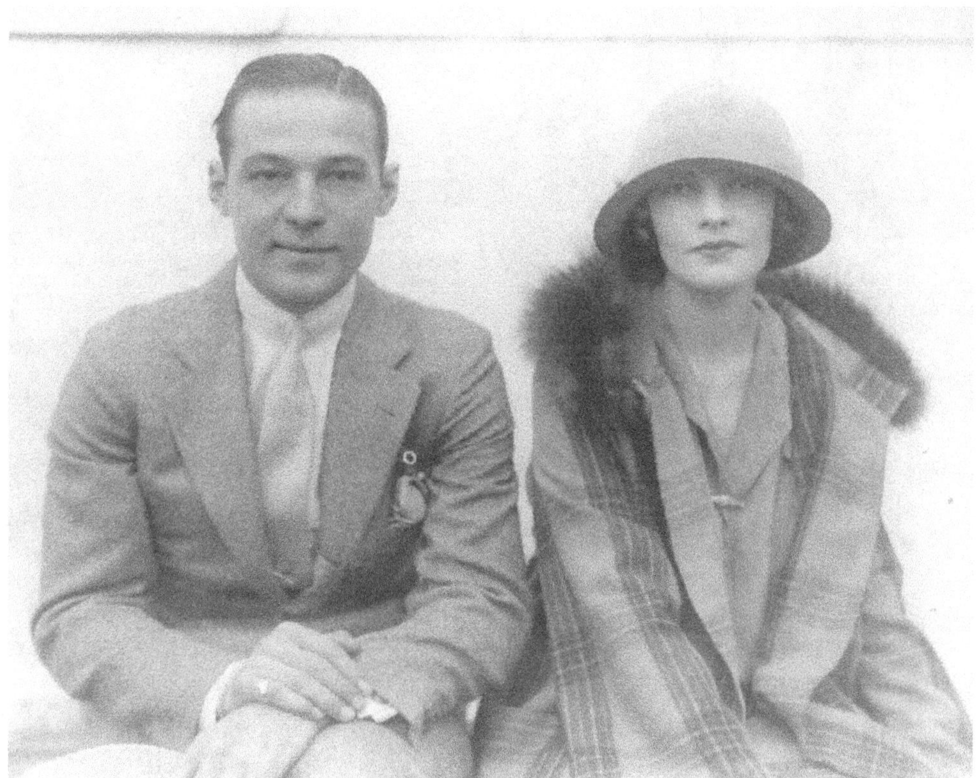

Rudolph Valentino and Natacha Rambova about to embark on a vacation in Europe.
(Craig MacPherson collection)

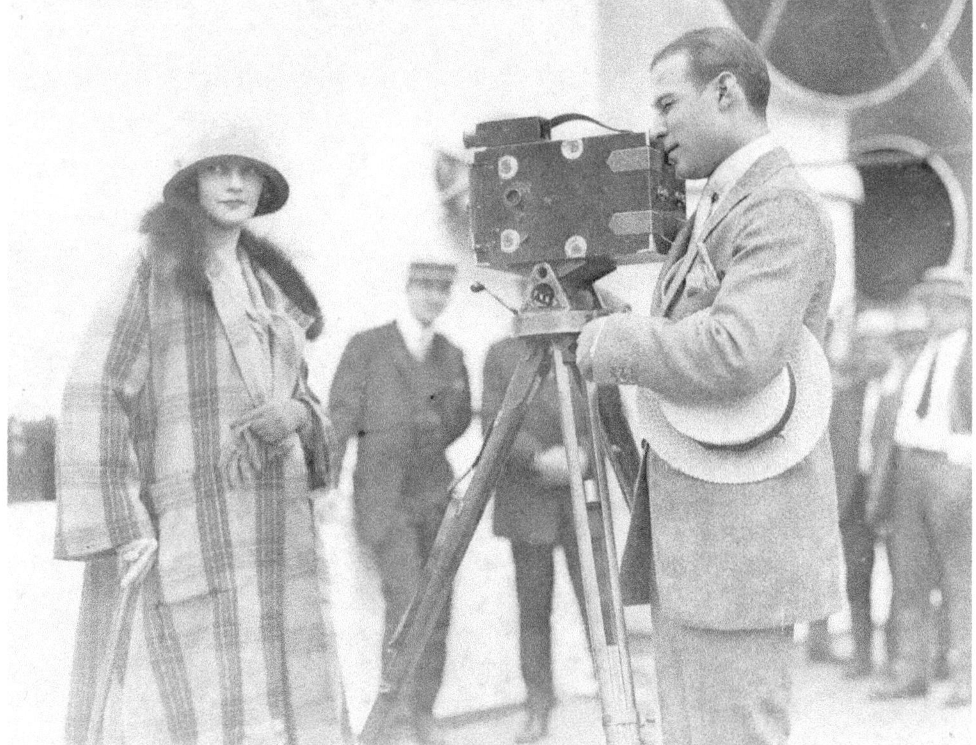

Valentino shows off his skills as a cameraman by taking over
the newsreel camera to capture a bemused Natacha.
(Author's collection)

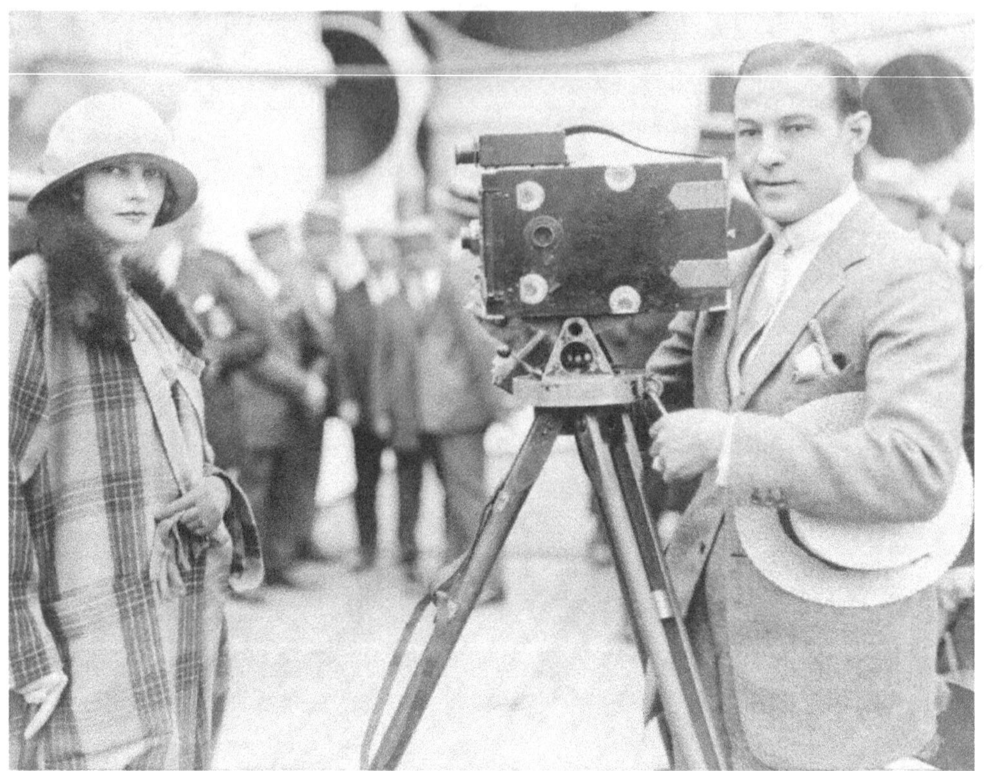

Another candid for the newspapers.
Valentino's cigarette holder jauntily peeking out from his breast pocket.
(Author's collection)

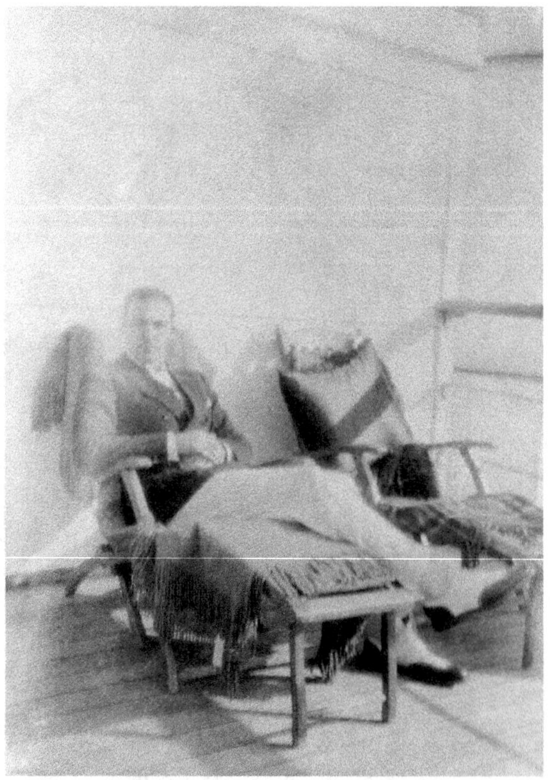

At sea, Valentino relaxing on the *Aquitania*.
(Author's collection)

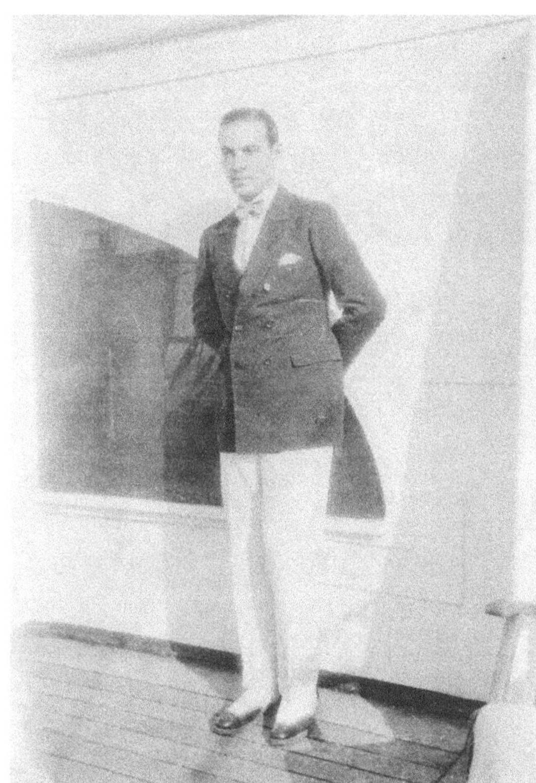

Valentino is uncharacteristically serious
posing for this snapshot.
(Author's collection)

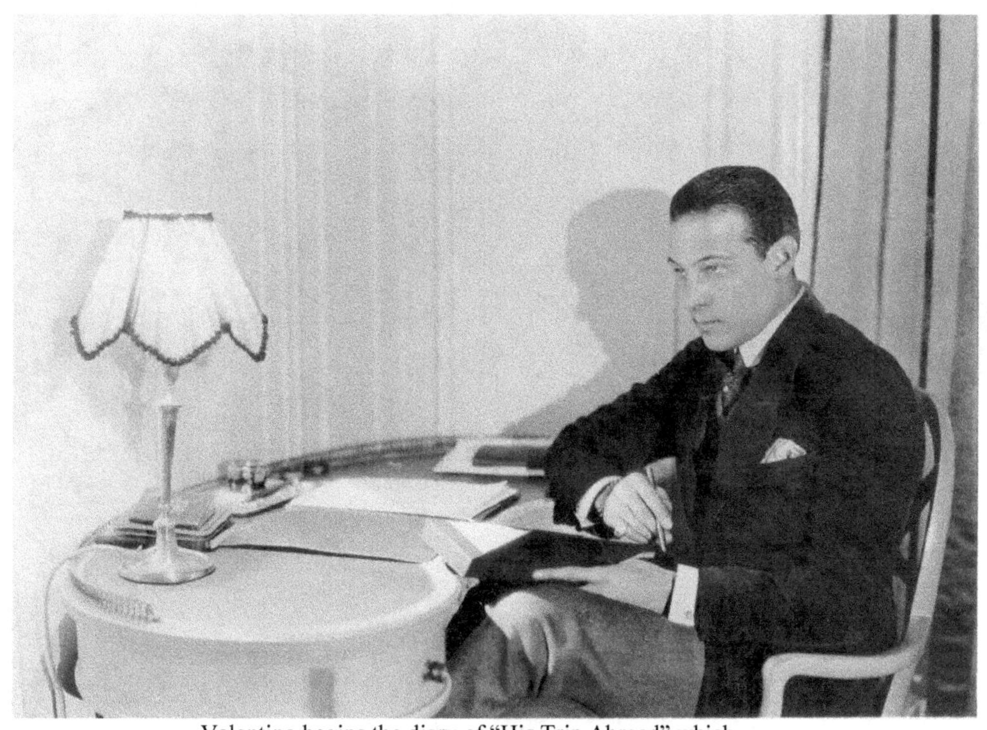

Valentino begins the diary of "His Trip Abroad" which
would later be serialized in Movie Weekly Magazine.
(Author's collection)

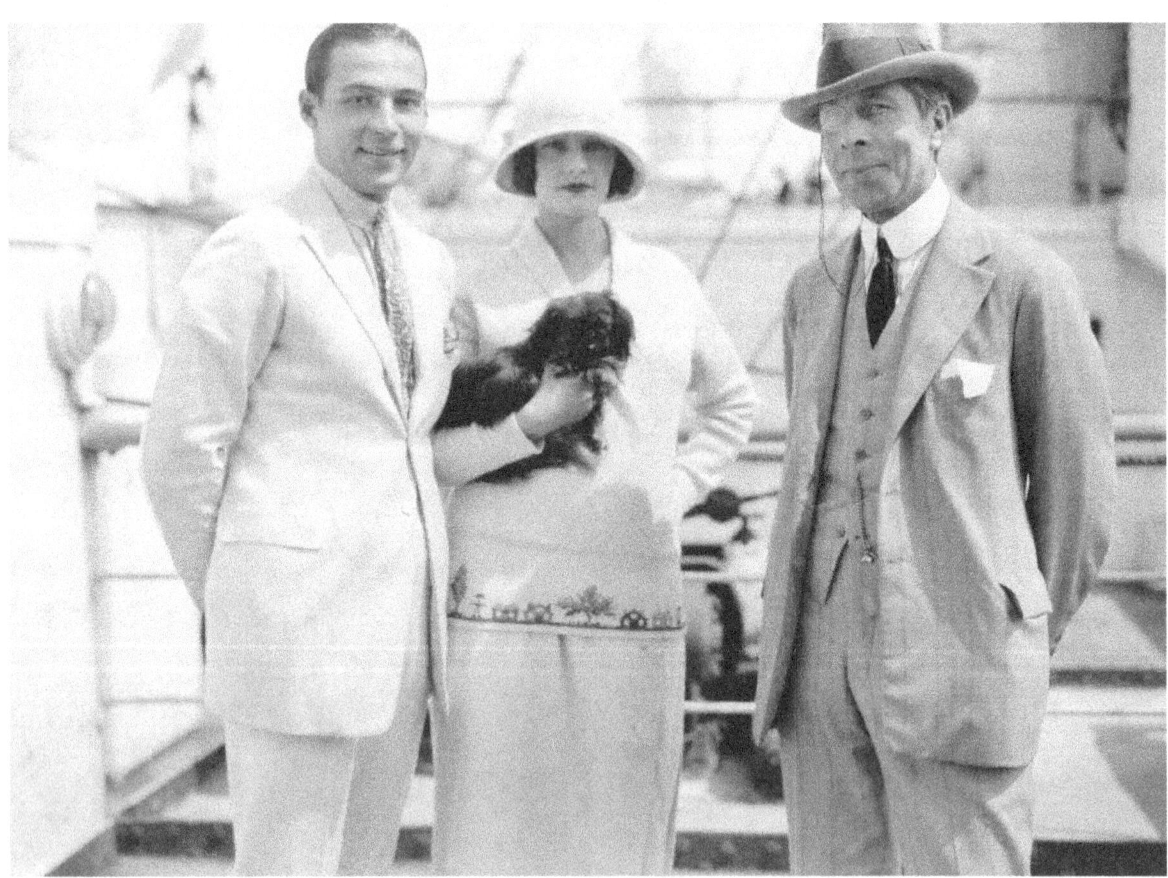

Valentino and Natacha enjoyed hobnobbing with fellow famous passengers.
Seen here Mr. George Arliss. (Craig MacPherson collection)

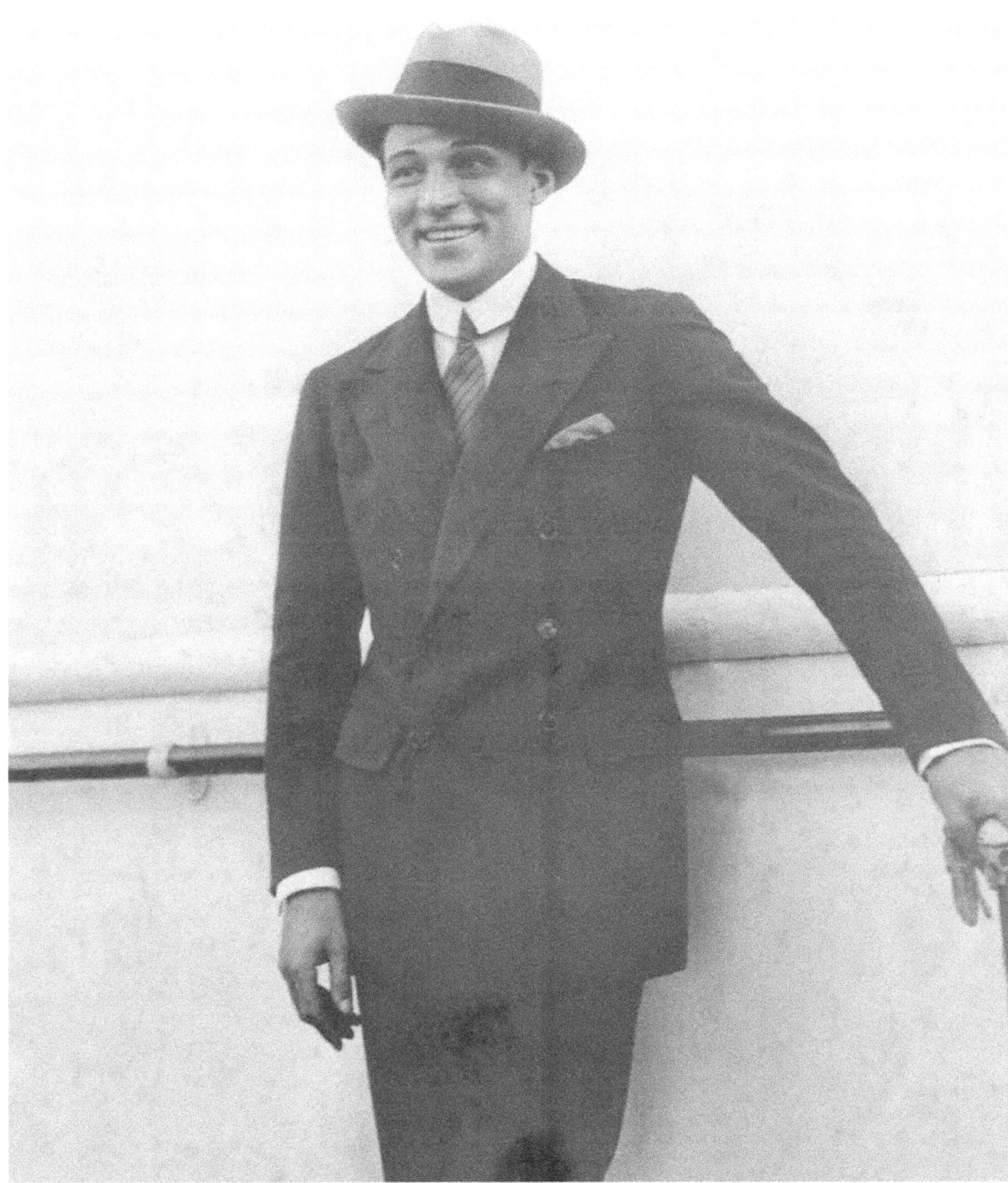

Valentino posing for eager newsmen upon arrival in Southampton.
(Author's collection)

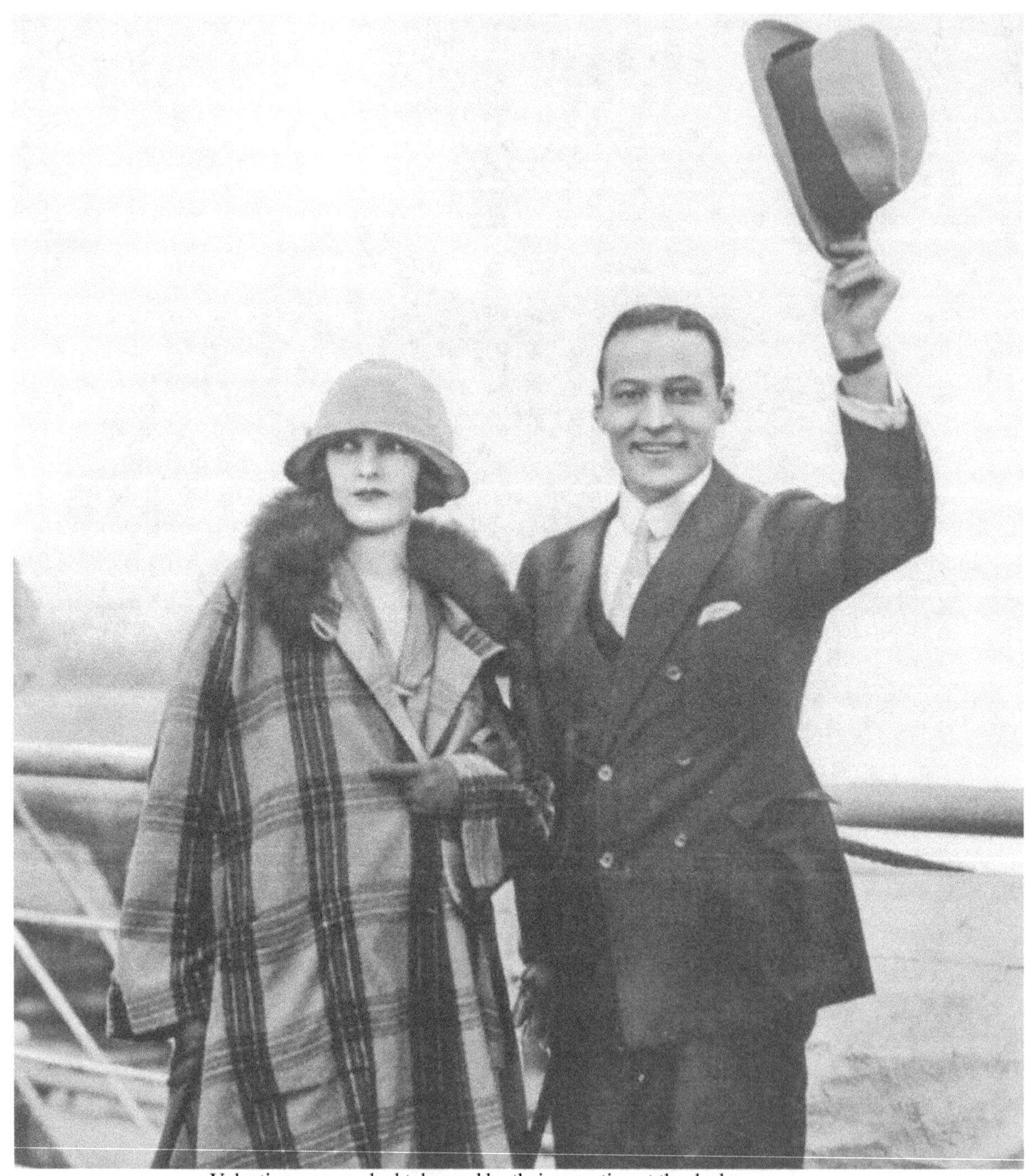

Valentino was, no doubt, buoyed by their reception at the docks.
This was small potatoes once he saw how the city of London would greet him.
(Caroline Rupprecht collection)

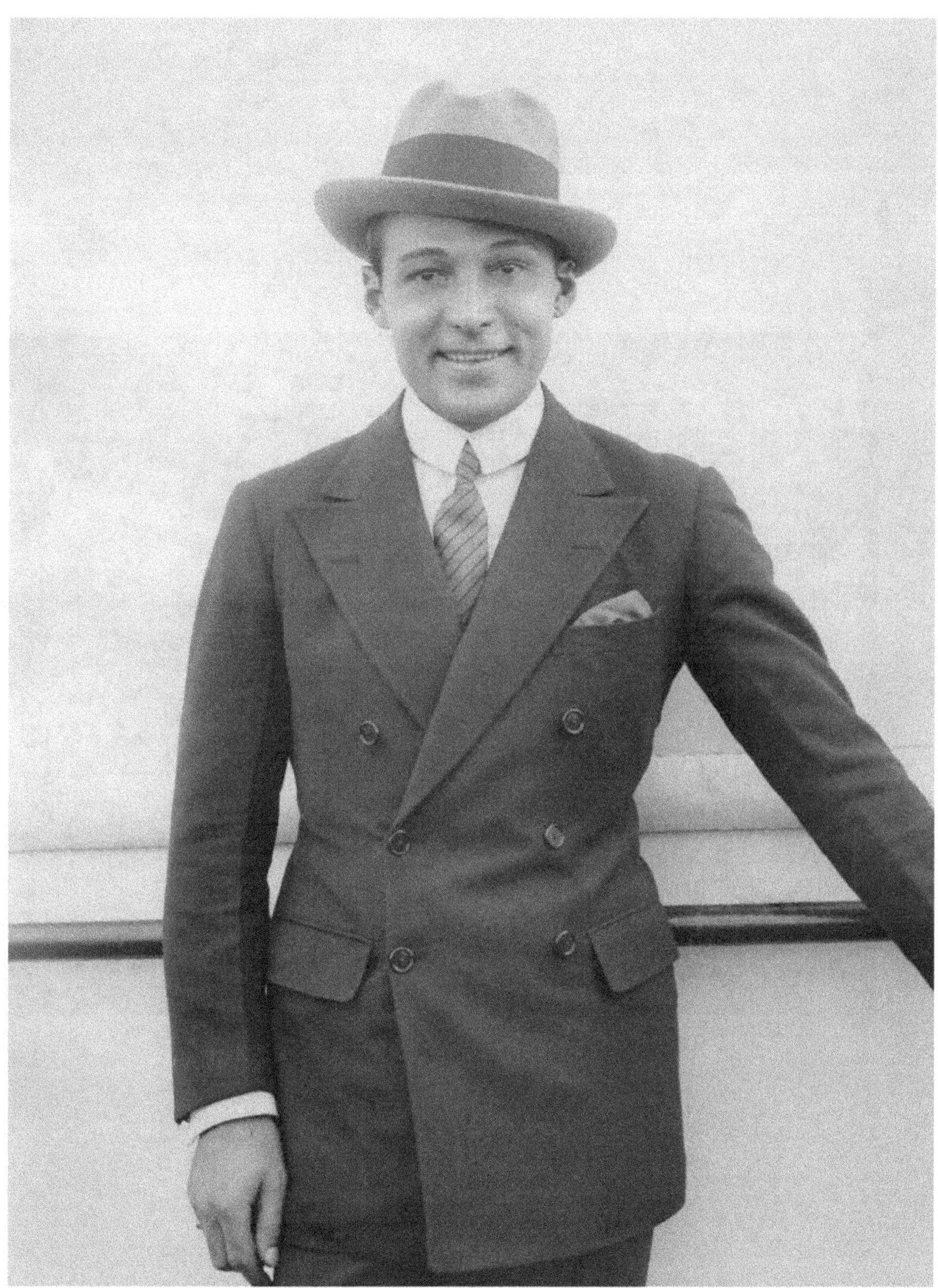

Obliging the photographers once more before disembarking. (Author's collection)

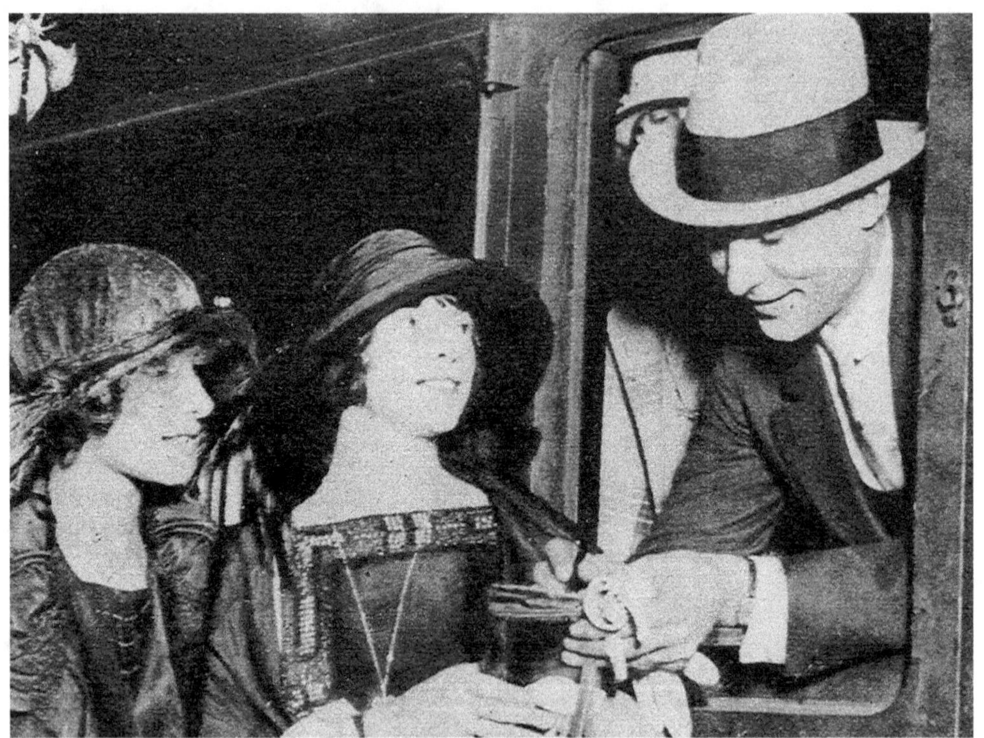

Valentino's arrival in London, met by fans in the station signing autographs.
(Author's collection)

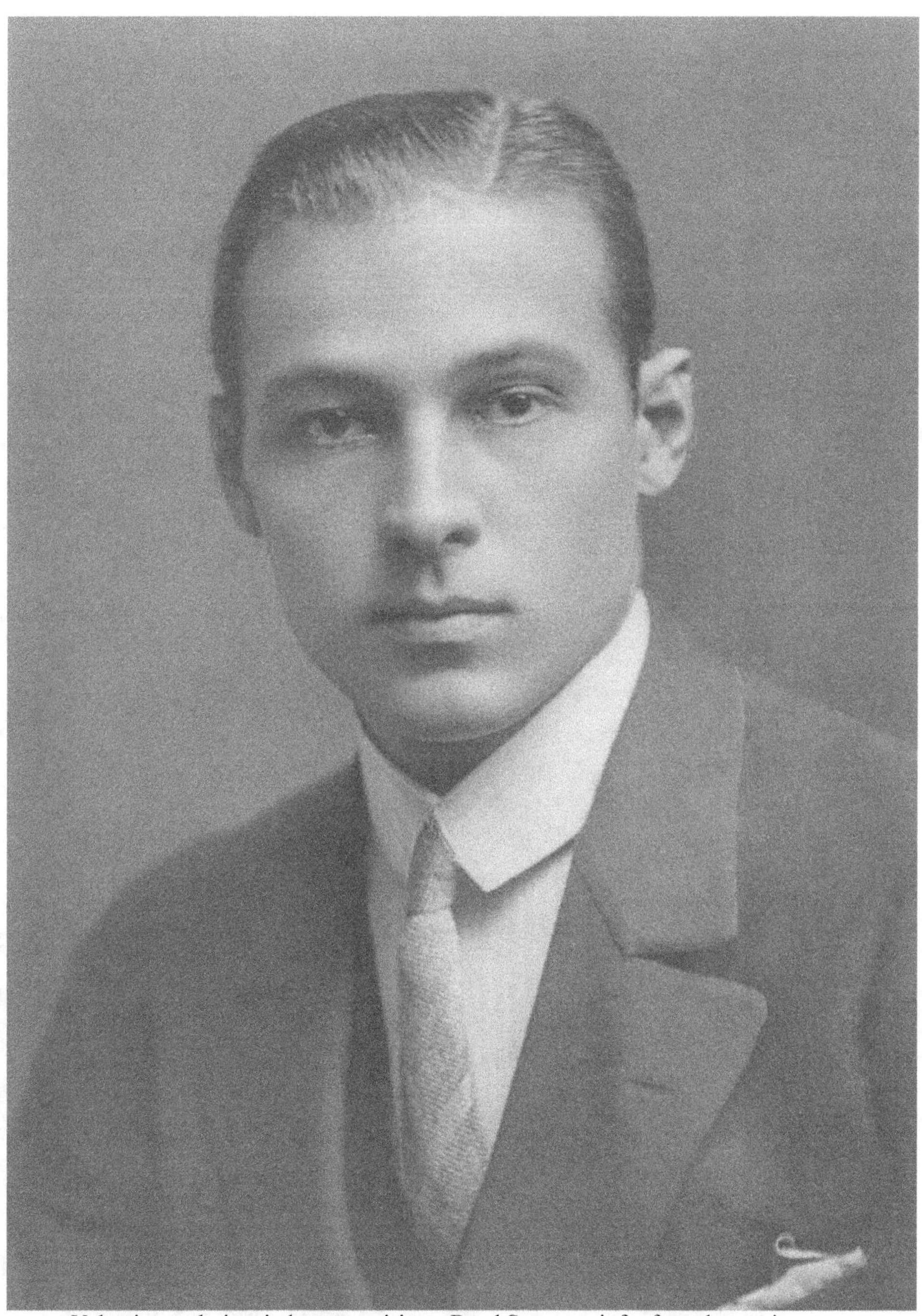

Valentino took time in between visits to Bond Street to sit for formal portraits.
Wykham of London.
(Author's collection)

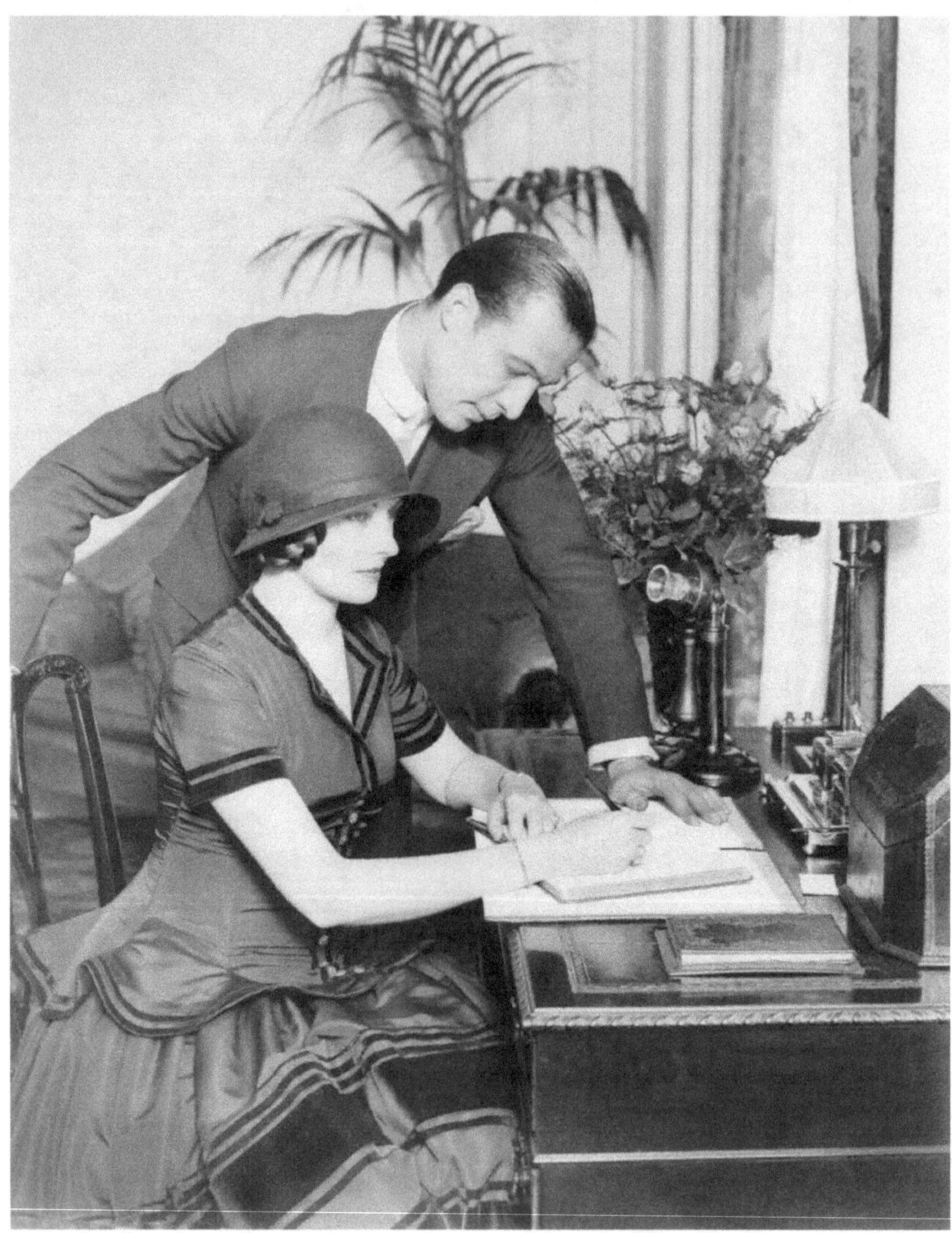

In London, the pair meet the unceasing demands of autographs, press visits and social engagements. They both would shop for animals, Natacha for Pekinese dogs, Valentino for Crabbet Arabians. (Author's collection)

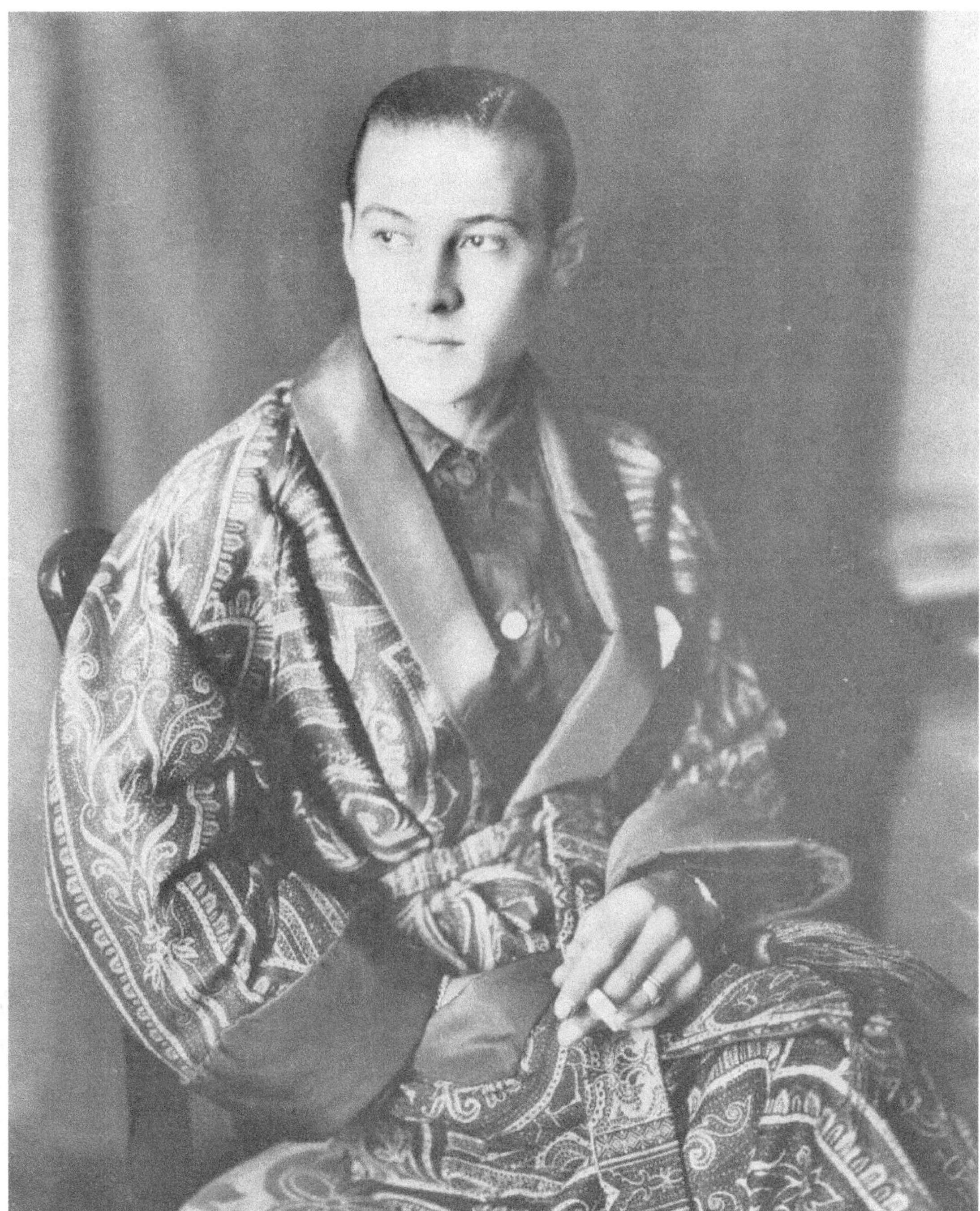

A thoughtful Valentino poses in London. (Author's collection)

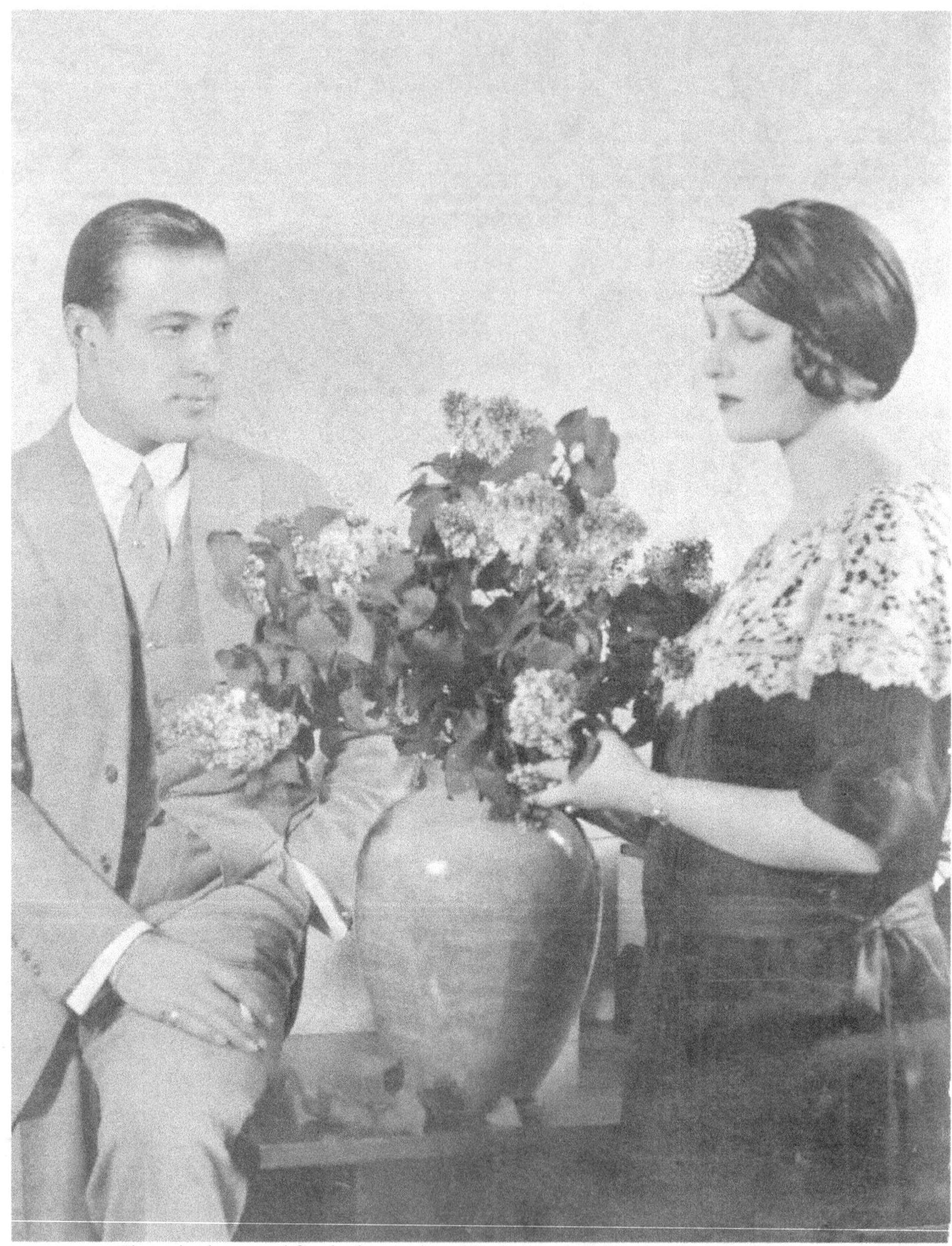

The pair also posed for dual portraits while in London. (Author's collection)

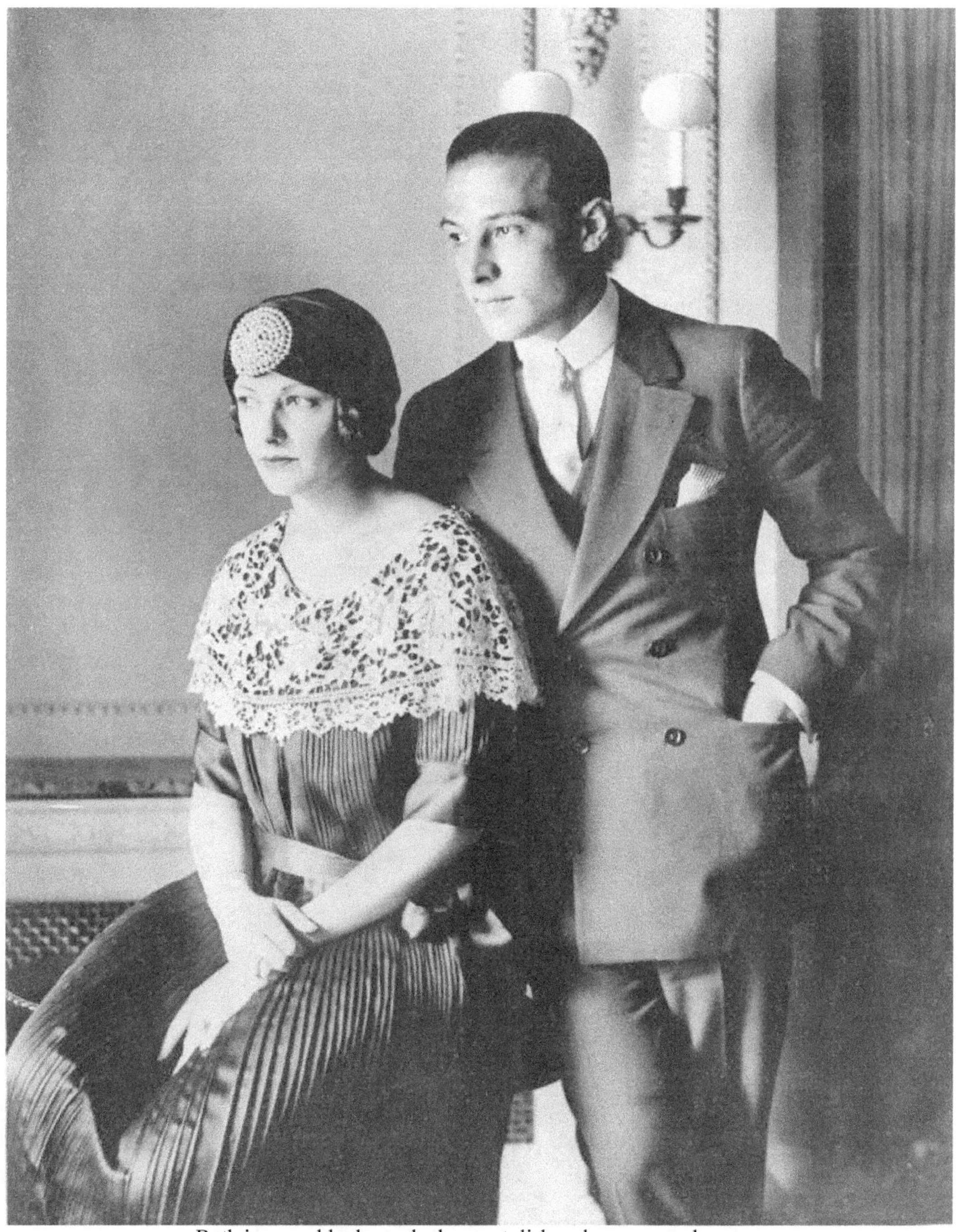

Both impeccably dressed, always stylish and camera ready.
Natacha would soon be visiting couturiers in Paris for the latest in fashion.
(San Francisco History Center)

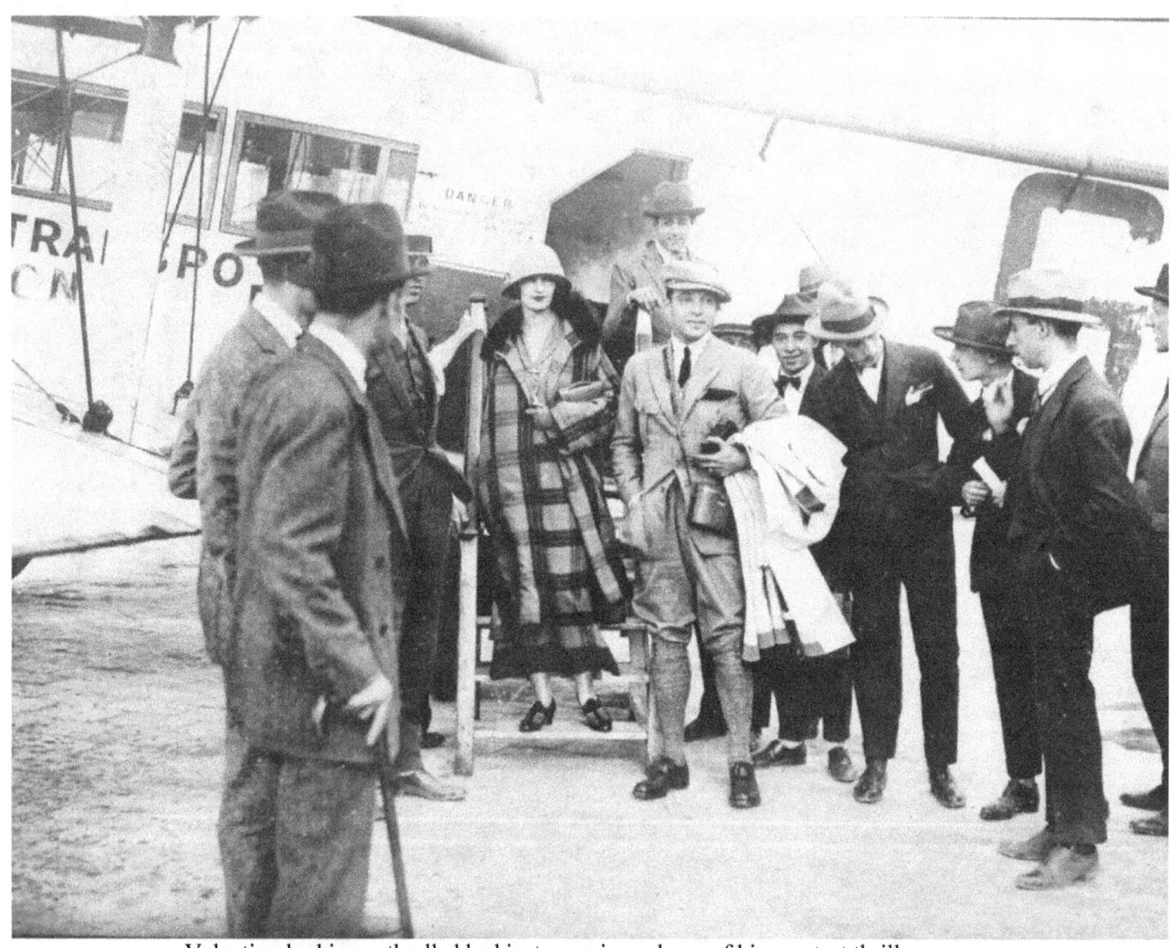

Valentino looking enthralled had just experienced one of his greatest thrills,
crossing the English Channel by aerial transport.
The pair arrive at Le Bourget just outside of Paris.
(San Francisco History Center)

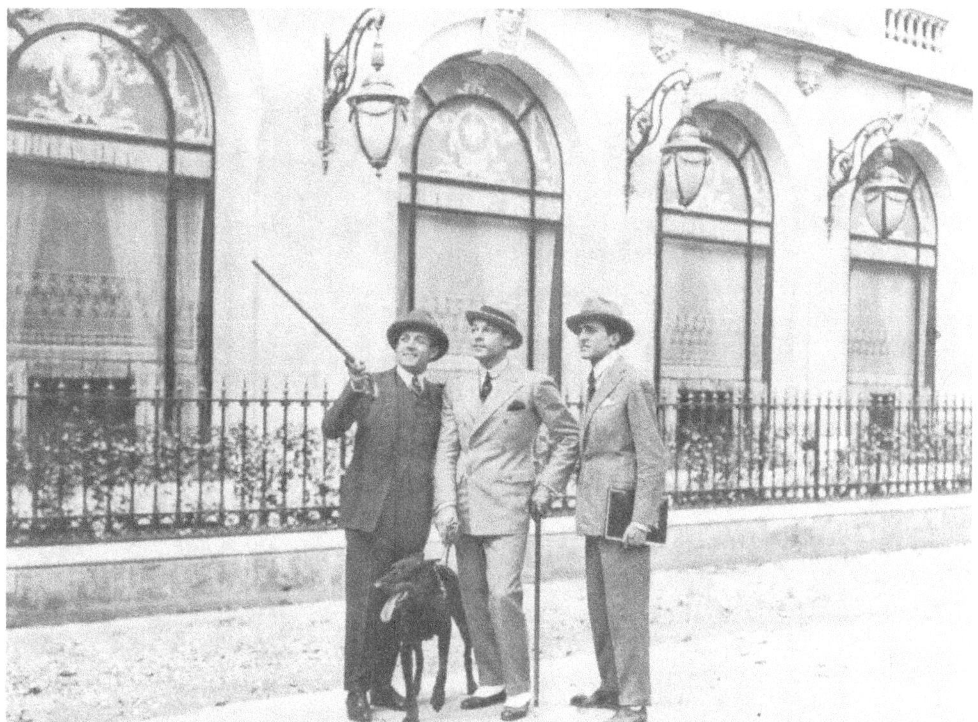

Director Rene Clair points out something of interest to Valentino and Andre Daven in Paris.
(Author's collection)

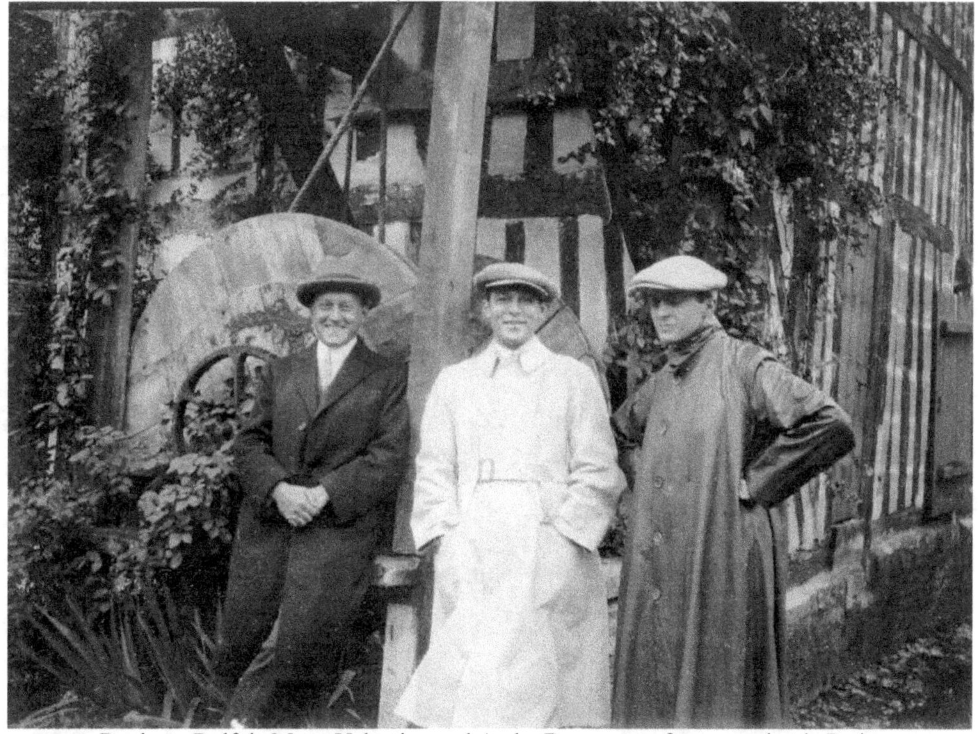

Producer Rolf de Mare, Valentino and Andre Daven pose for a snapshot in Paris.
(Dansmuseet collection)

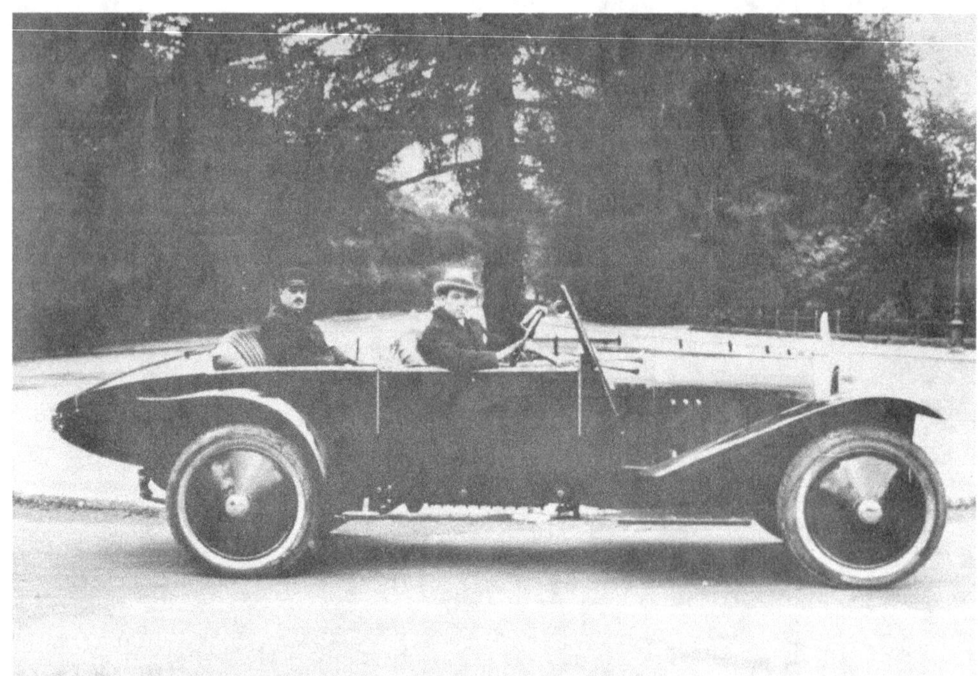

While in Paris Valentino spent some time shopping for cars.
He would soon be driving to Italy and rented an Avion-Voisin for the trip.
He is seen here driving a Voisin C5 in the Bois du Boulogne. (Author's collection)

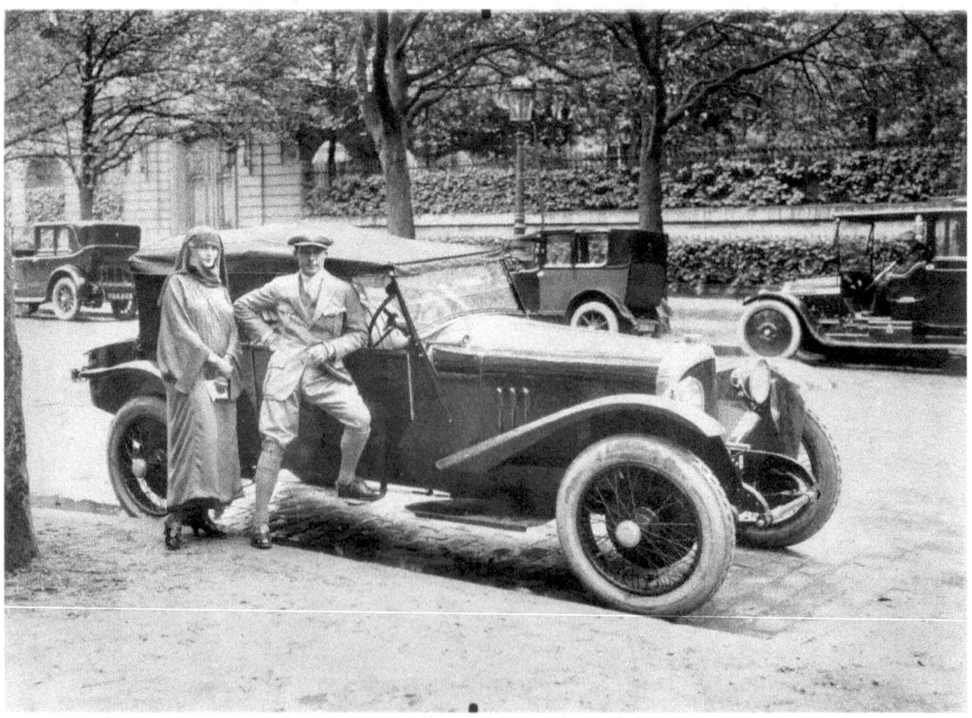

The Valentino soon to depart on a perilous journey through France and on to Italy.
Valentino in snazzy plus fours and Natacha Rambova in a very chic Paul Poiret designed driving ensemble.
Natacha and Auntie Teresa would not have a pleasant journey thanks to Valentino's
reckless speeding on dangerous roads and his nearsightedness.
(Wisconsin Center for Film and Theater Research)

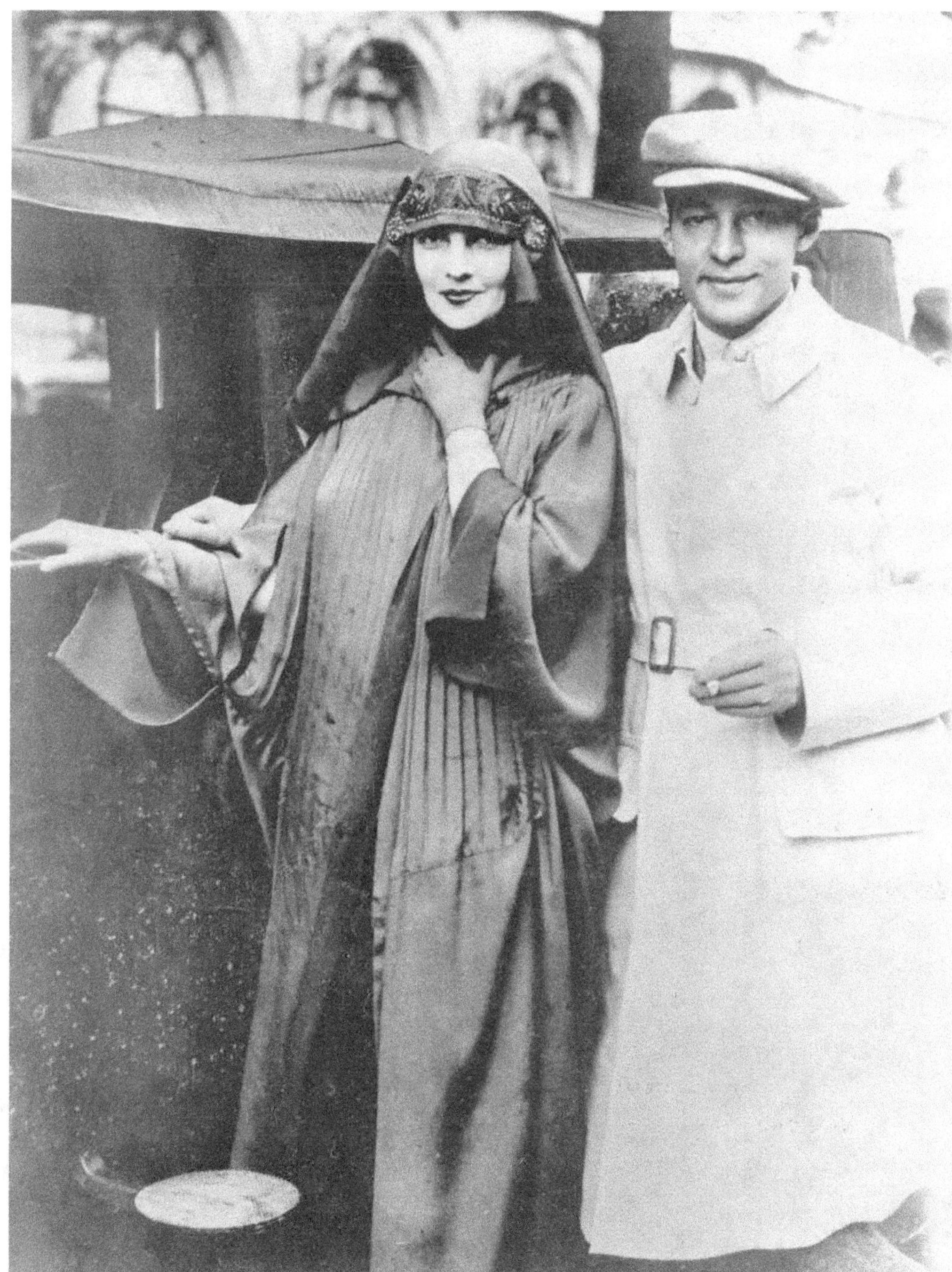

The Valentinos looks ready to embrace whatever may come.
A rare smile for Natacha, their happiness together is fully on display.
(San Francisco History Center)

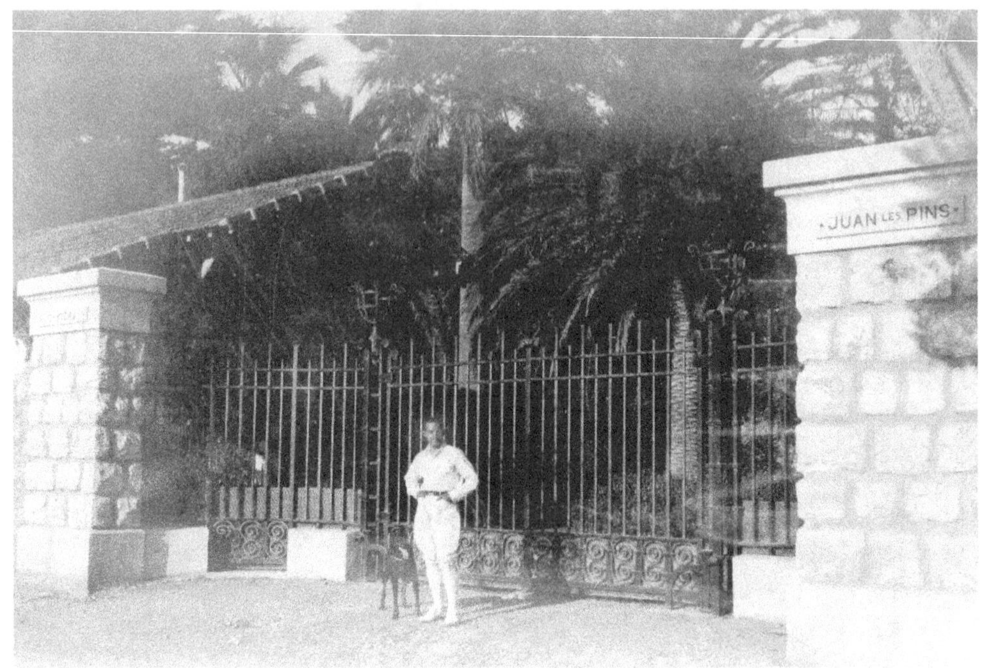

Valentino and Kabar outside the entrance gates to Juan les Pins.
(Tracy Terhune collection)

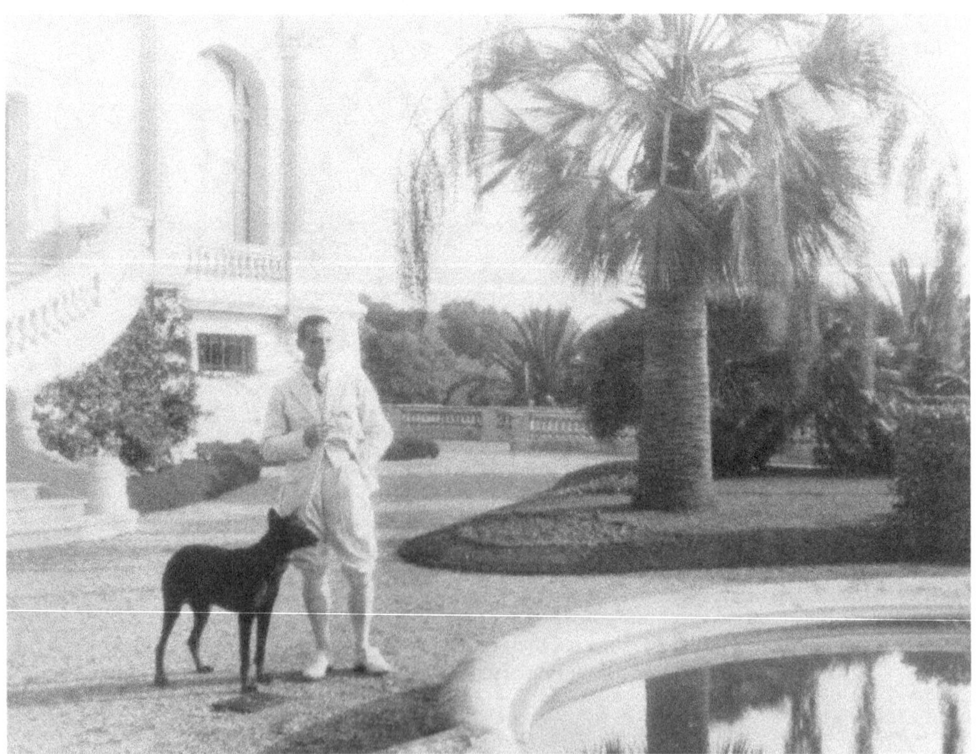

Valentino and Kabar in the garden of Juan les Pins.
(Michael Morris collection)

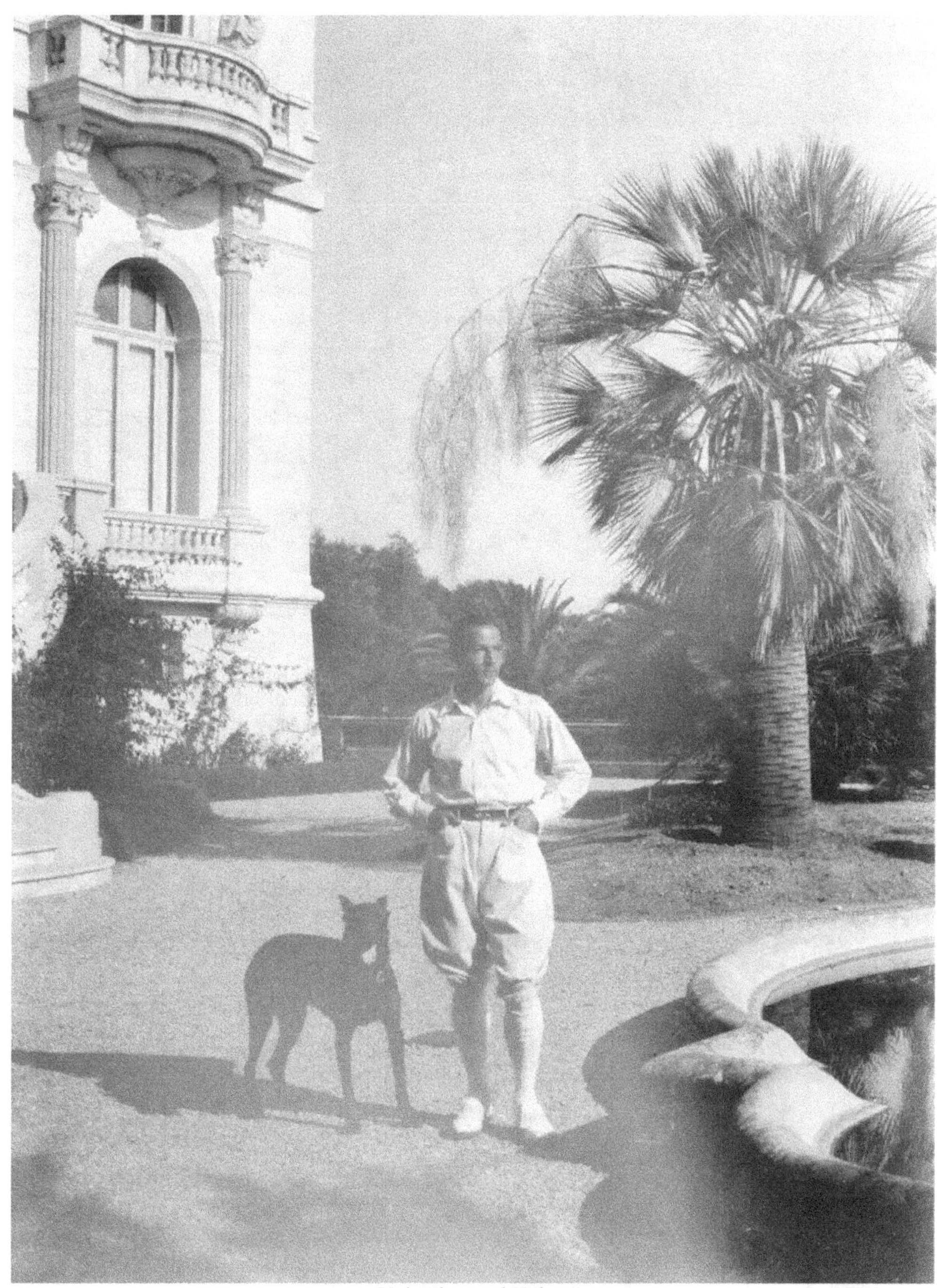

Valentino and Kabar.
(Author's collection)

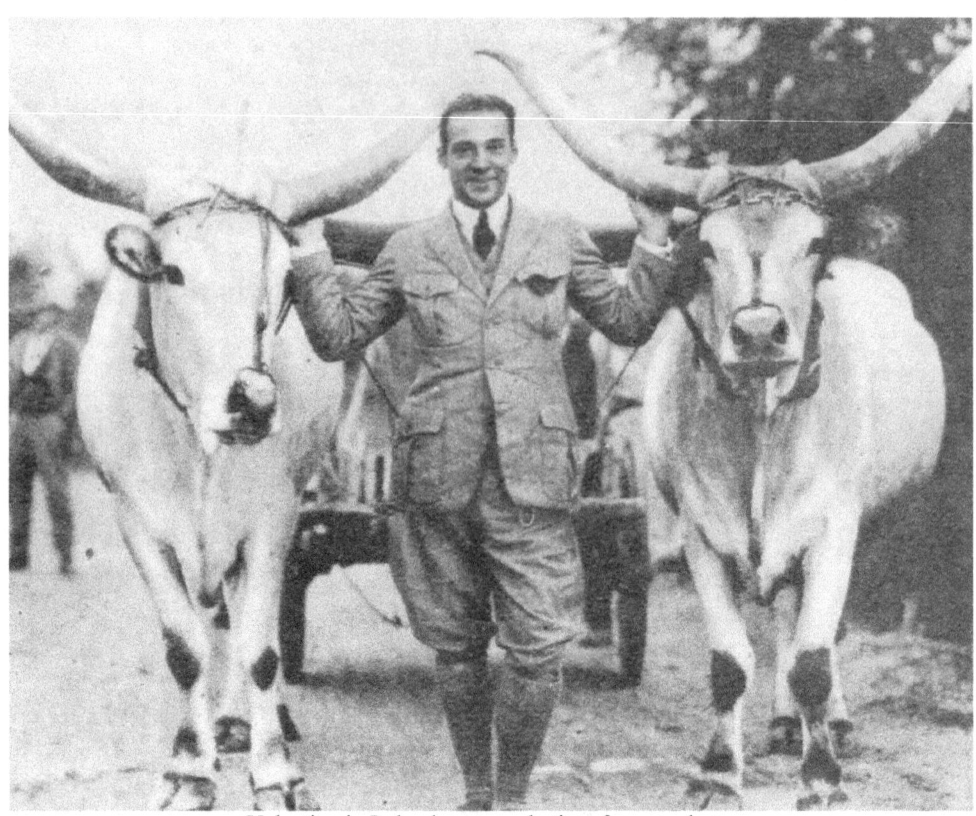

Valentino in Italy always made time for snapshots.
Harking back to his agricultural school roots, posing with some oxen.
(Author's collection)

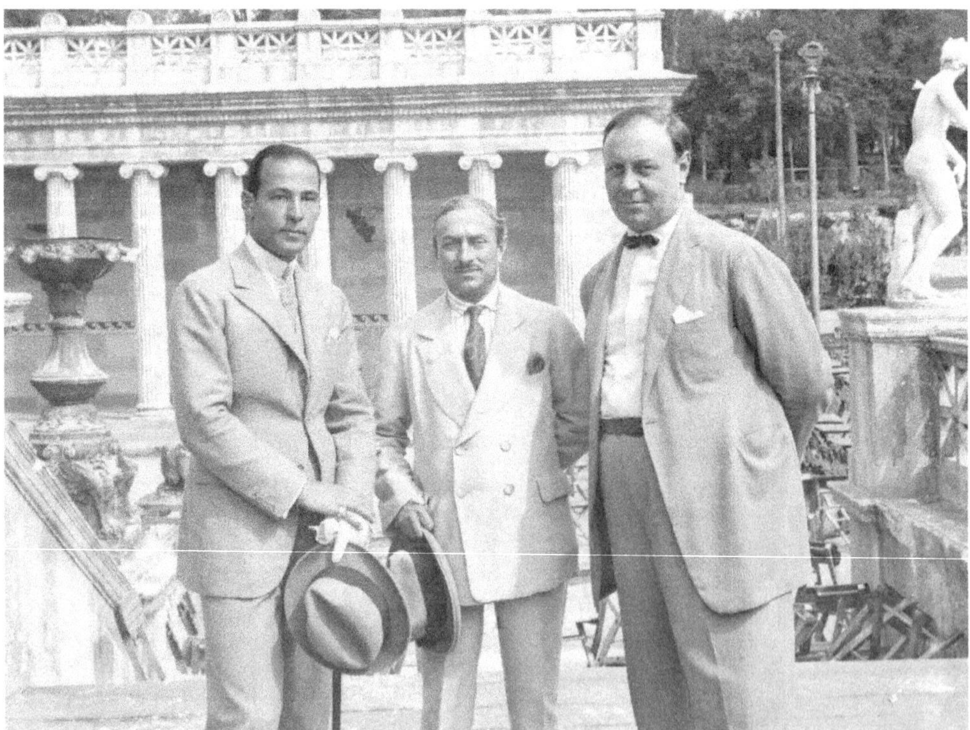

Valentino visiting with Commendatore Ambrozio and German actor Emil Jannings in Rome.
Jannings was making *Quo Vadis*.
(Craig MacPherson collection)

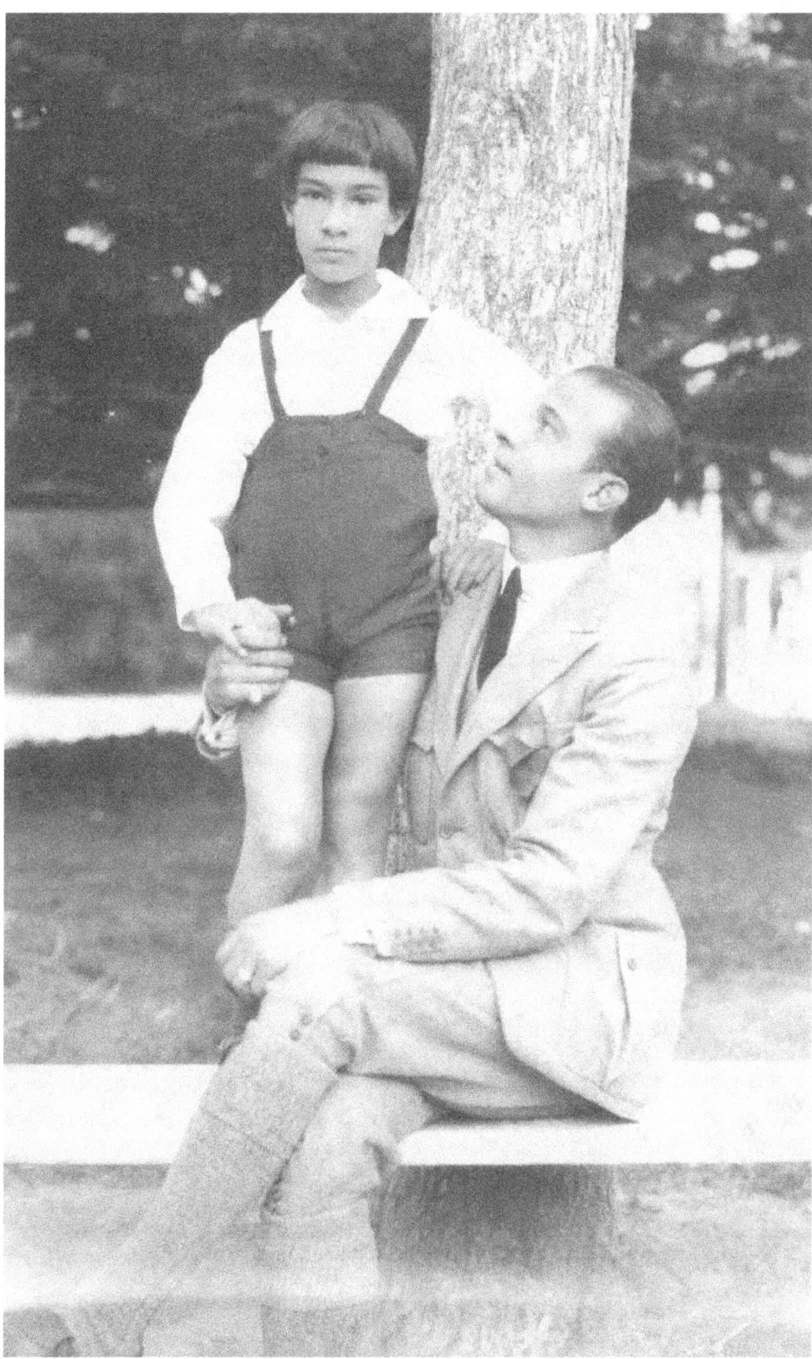

In Rome came the sweetest part of the journey, the reunion with his family.
Valentino doting on nephew Jean Guglielmi.
They took to one another instantly.
(Author's collection)

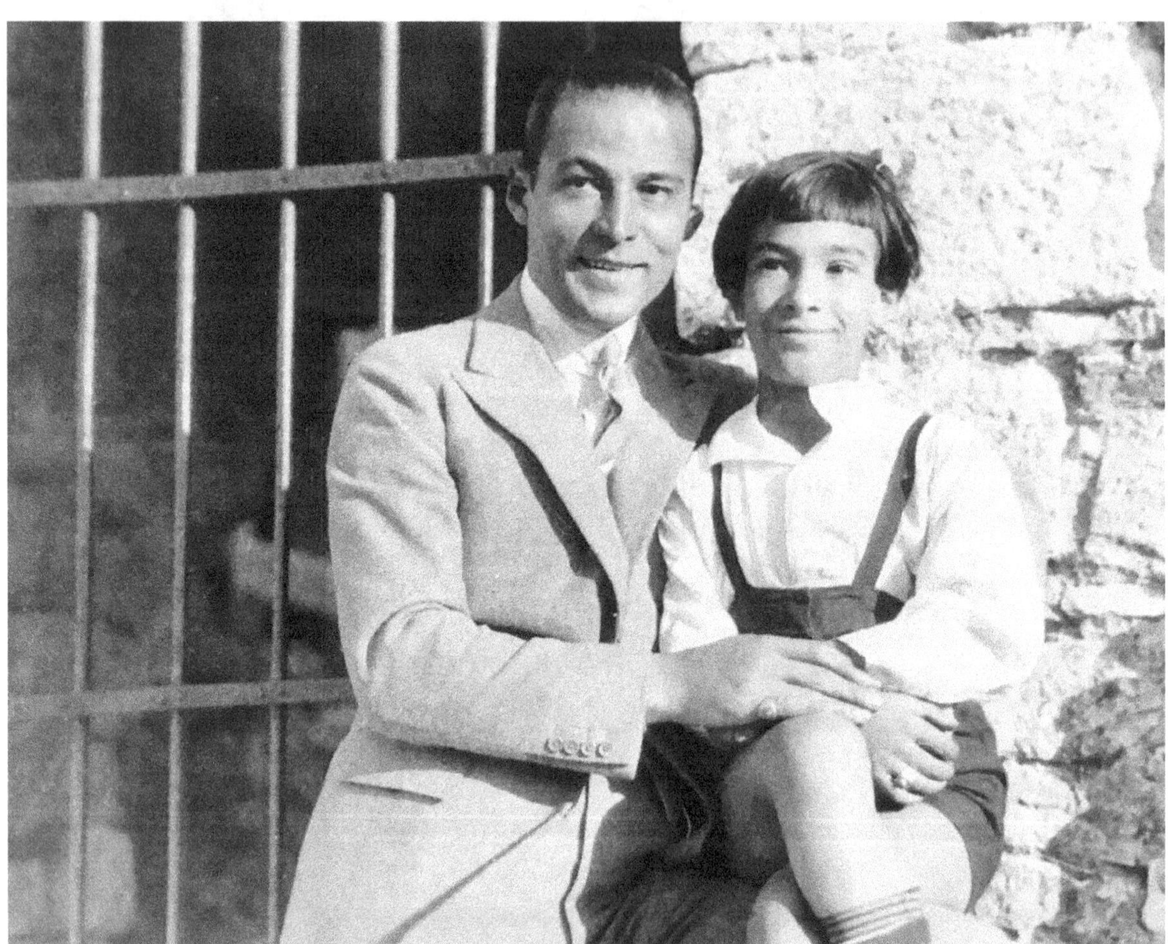

While in Rome the family visited the ancient wonder the Colosseum.
(Author's collection)

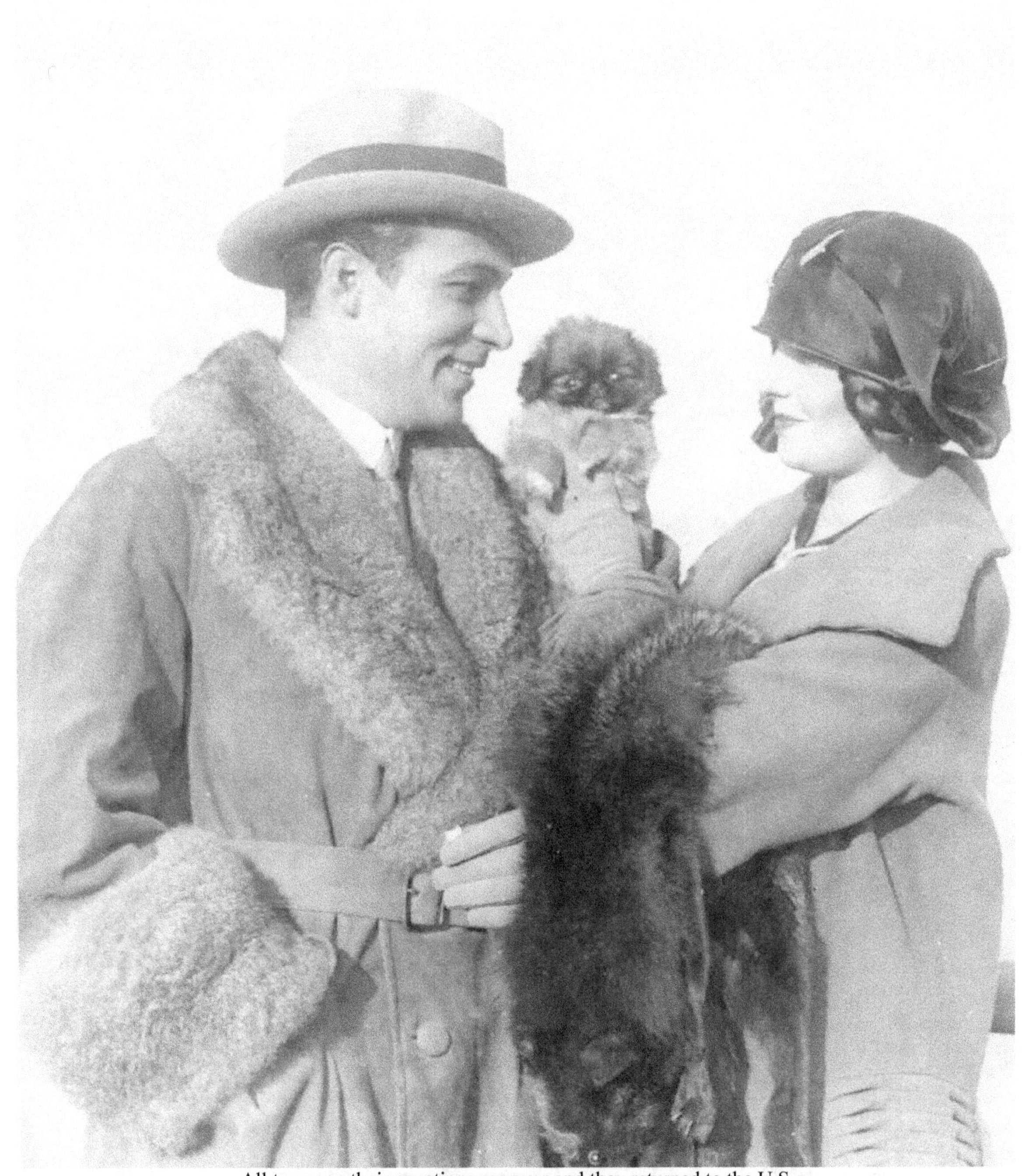

All too soon their vacation was over and they returned to the U.S.
(Author's collection)

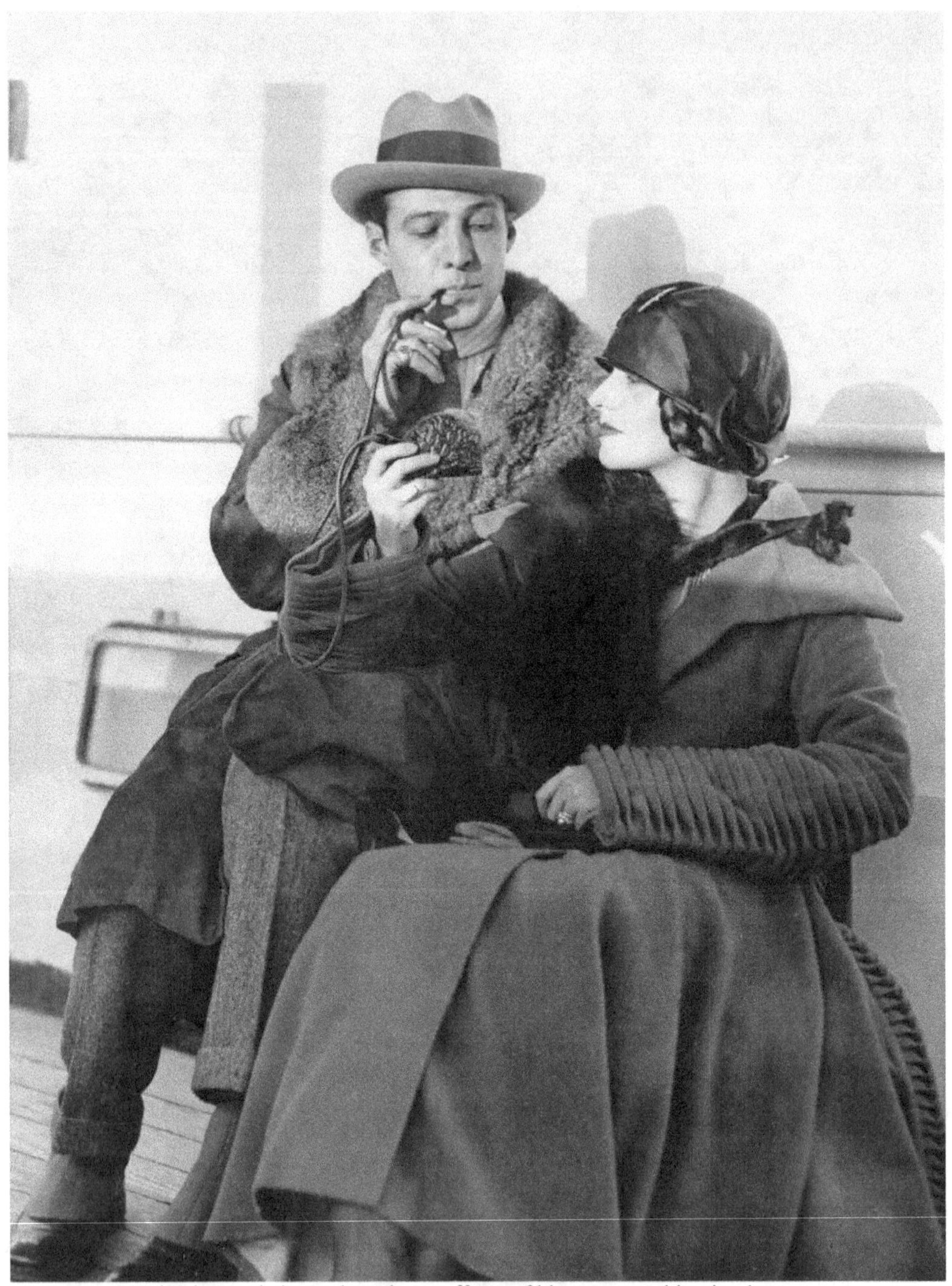

Valentino, a chain smoker, shows off one of his many smoking implements.
(Author's collection)

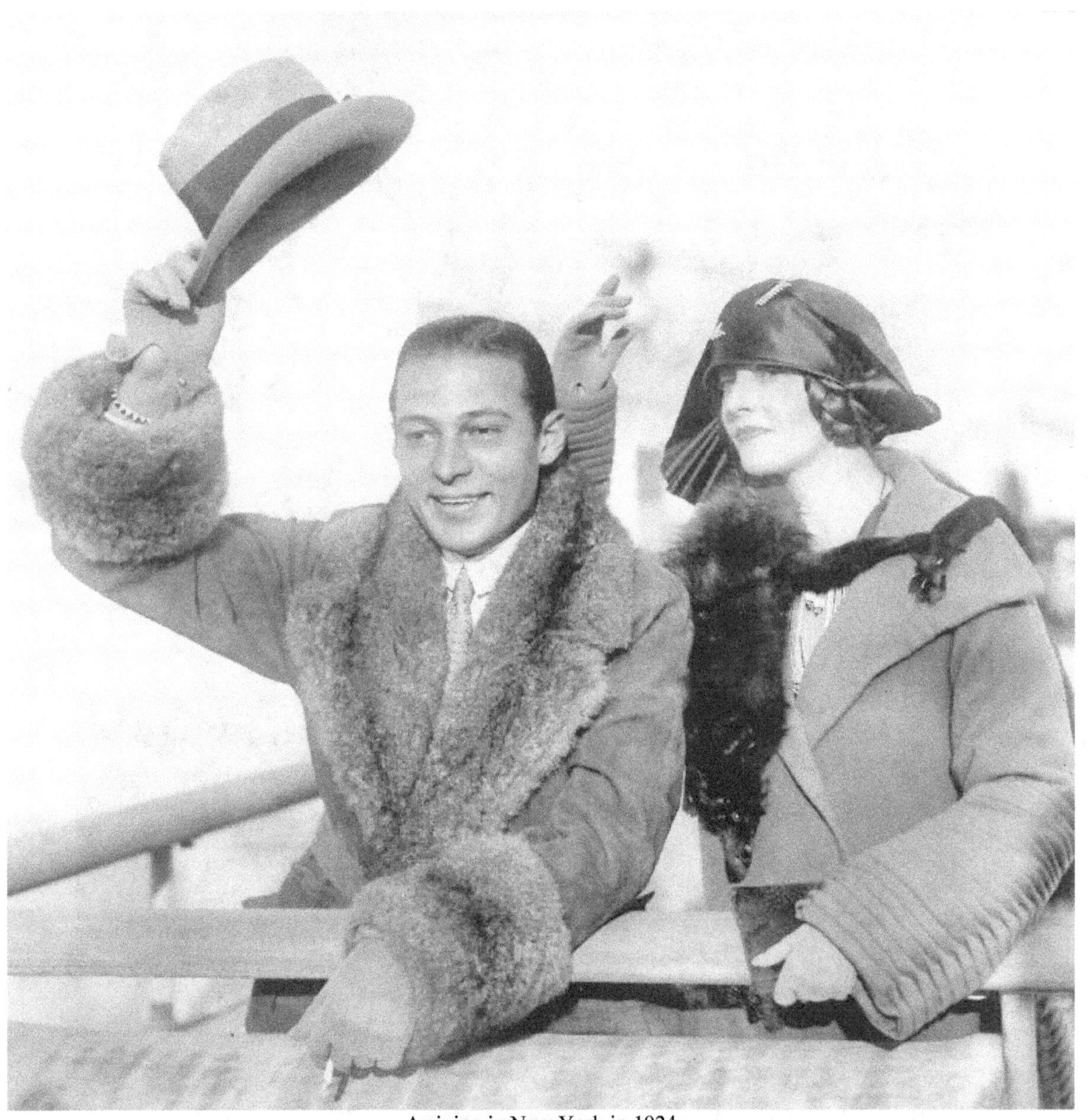

Arriving in New York in 1924.
The sleeves on Natacha's stylish coat remain envy inducing, even today.
(Author's collection)

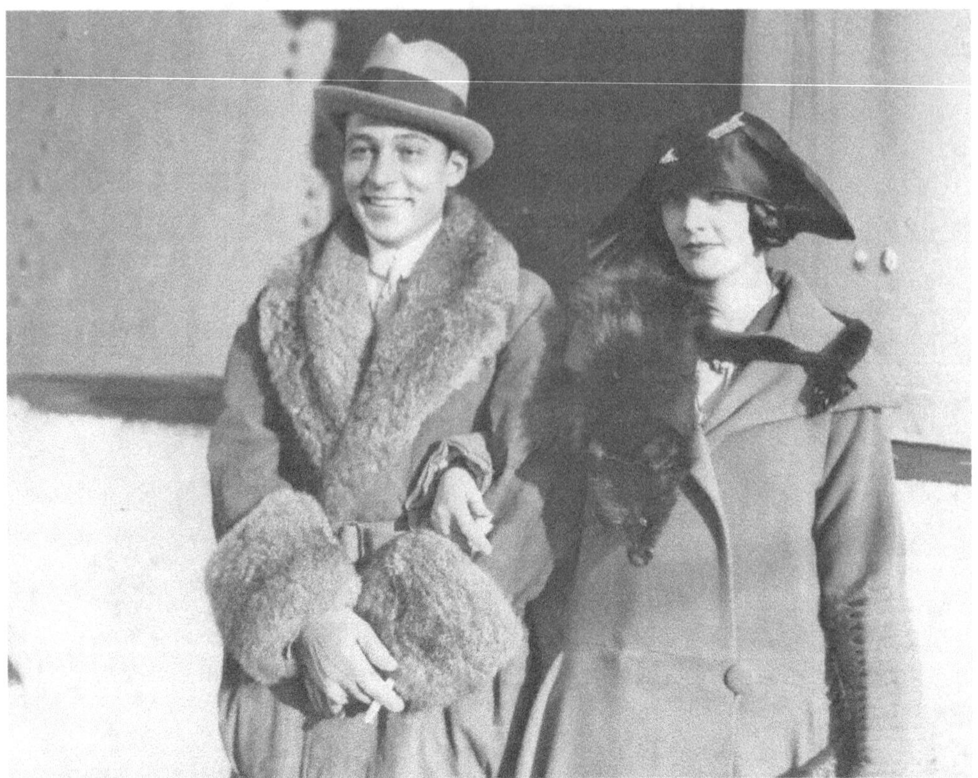

Valentino always looked so happy with Natacha on his arm.
He was particularly happy knowing he would soon be before the cameras again.
(Author's collection)

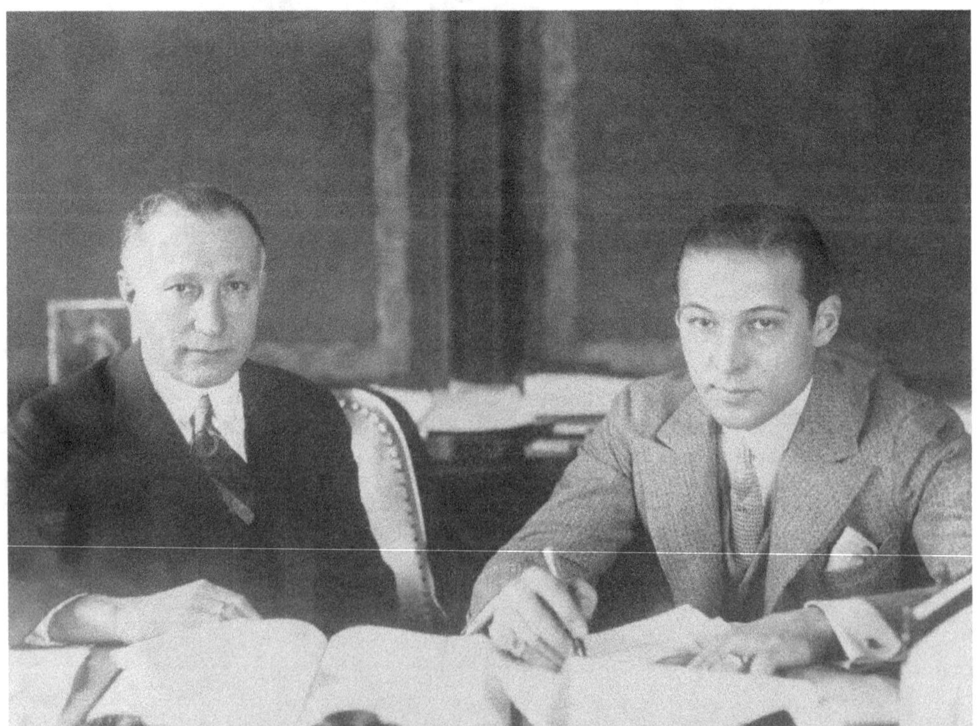

Valentino with studio head Adolph Zukor signs for two additional pictures for Paramount Studios.
Both will be shot at Paramount's Astoria Studios on Long Island.
(Author's collection)

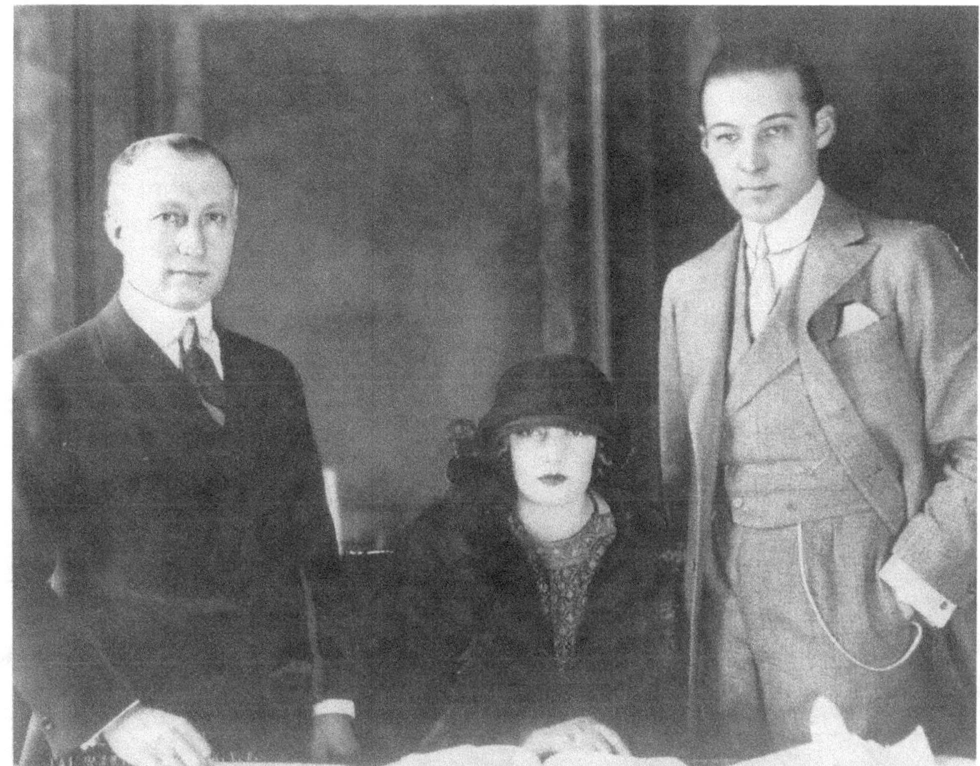

Adolph Zukor, Natacha and Valentino pose in Paramount's offices for the ceremony ending their legal squabbles. (Craig MacPherson collection)

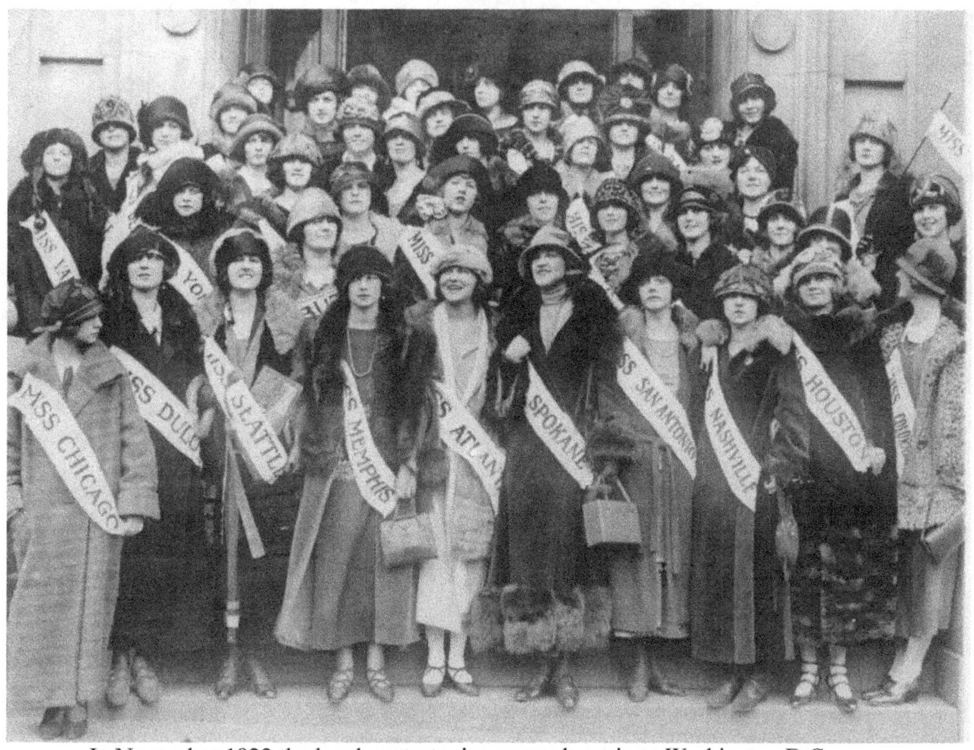

In November 1923 the local contest winners made a trip to Washington D.C. The grand finale contest at Madison Square Gardens was only a few days away. (Author's collection)

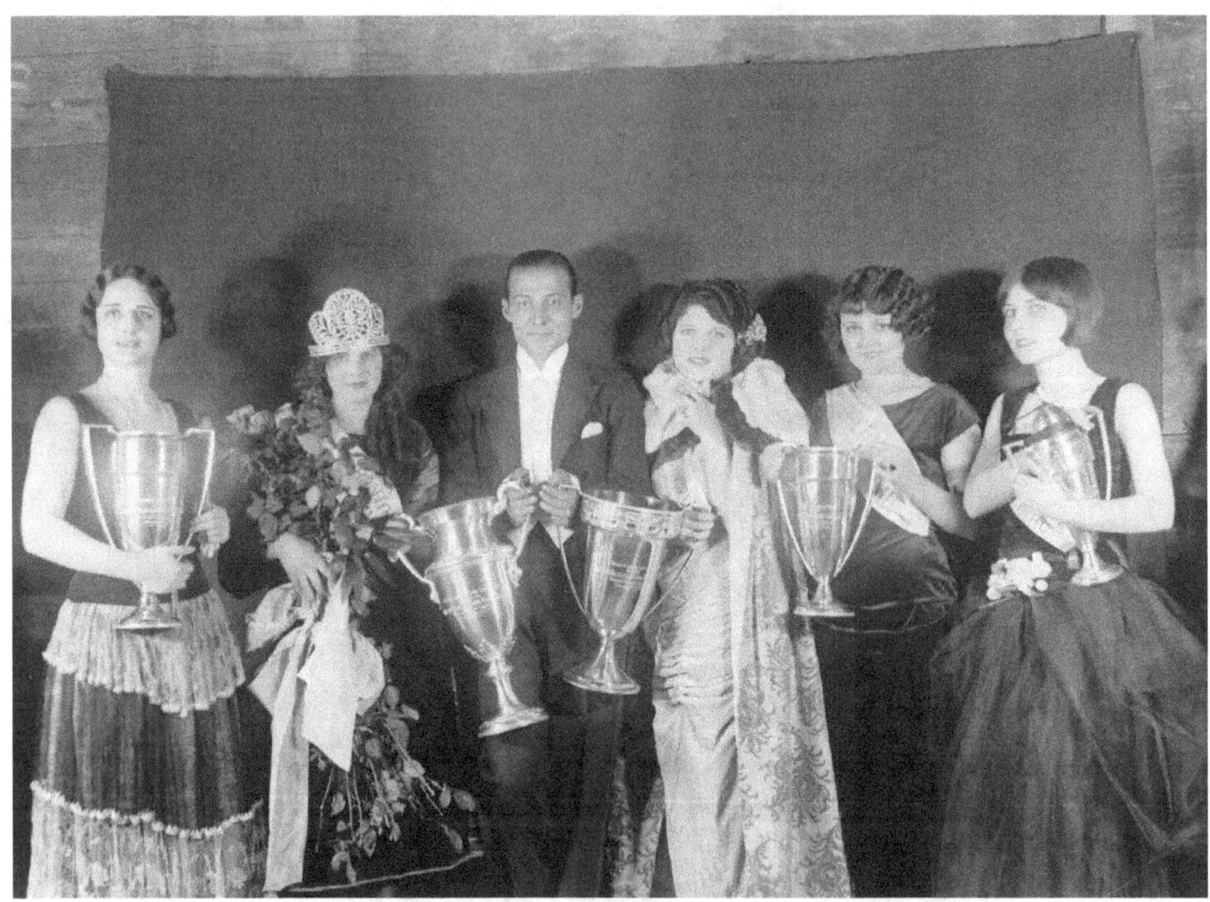

Valentino posing with the winner and runners up of the Mineralava Beauty Contest.
(L-R) Ms. Rebe Shilsom (Miss New York, 3rd place), Miss Norma Niblock (Miss Toronto, 1st place), Valentino, Miss Eugenie Gilbert (Miss Los Angeles, 2nd place), Miss Mildred Adams (Miss Baltimore, 4th place) and Miss Gloria Heller (Miss Witchita, 5th place). Only Miss Gilbert had any kind of success in films. Natacha, well and truly done with Mineralava, was a no-show at the finals.
(San Francisco History Center)

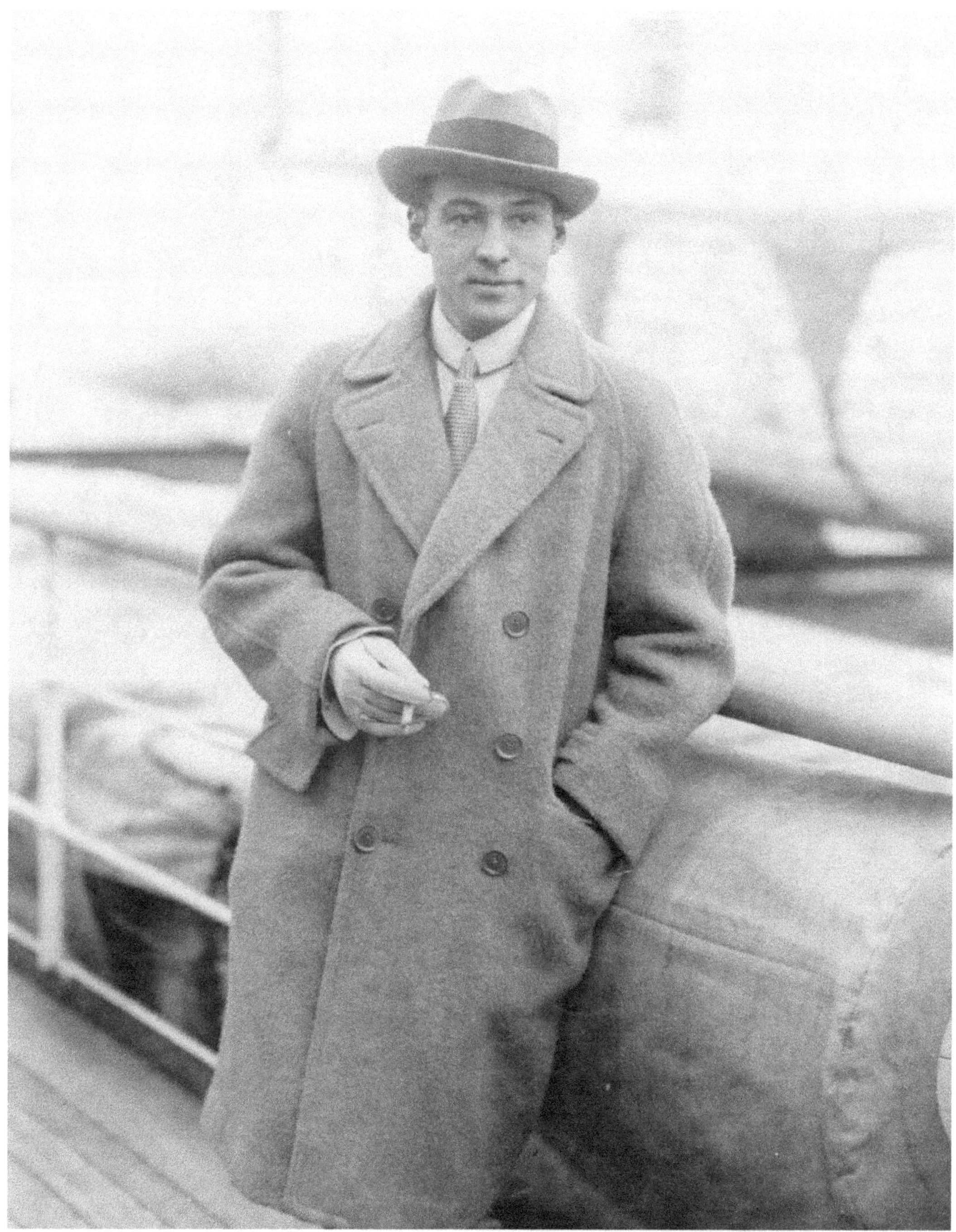

With business in New York concluded and delays in the production of his new film,
Valentino sails for Europe without Natacha. She will join him at Juan les Pins for Christmas.
(Author's collection)

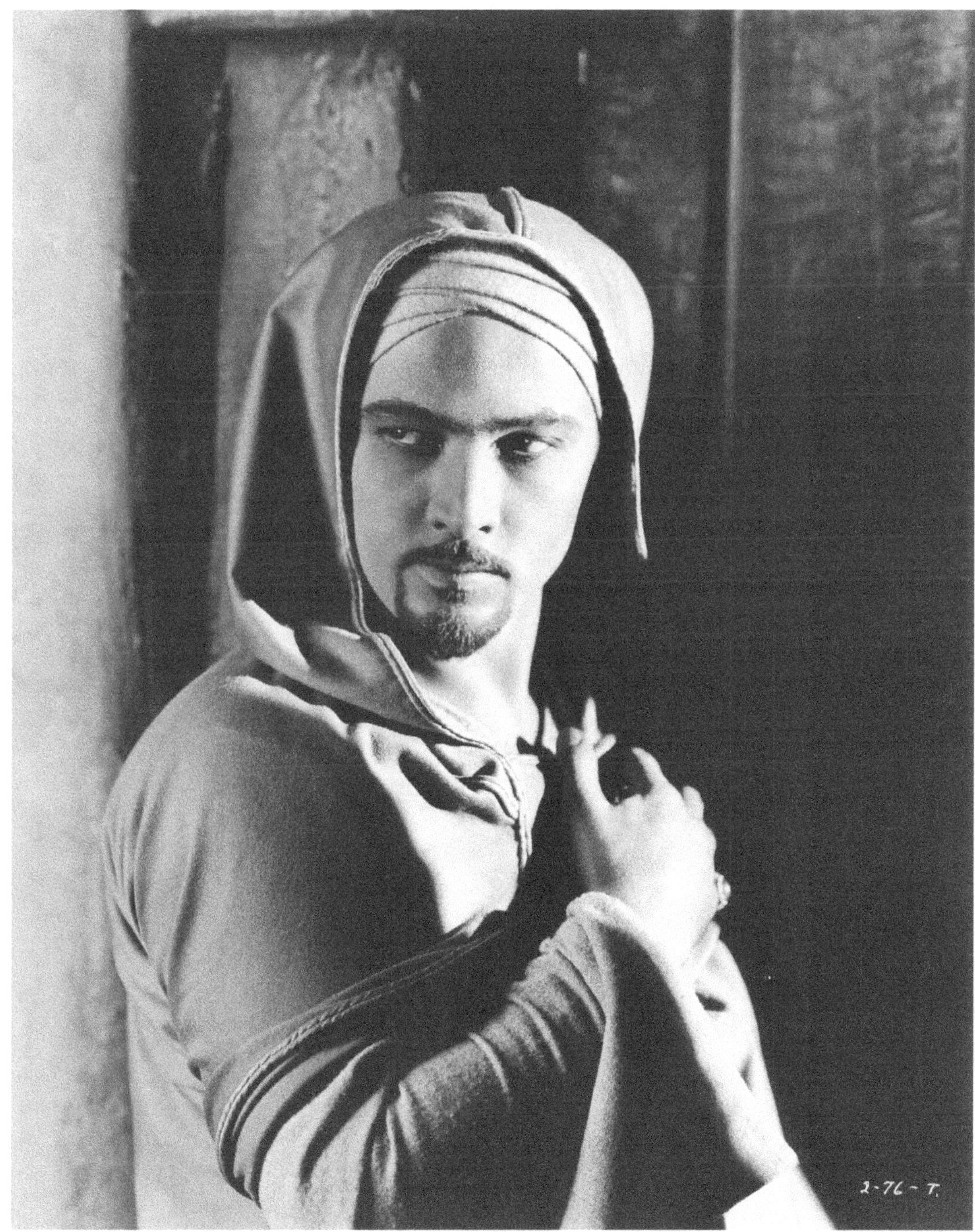
2-76-T.

The sincerity of my motivation has been ridiculed. It seems impossible for some people to believe that a player would stand out for good productions.

—Rudolph Valentino, 1924

The happy couple celebrated New Year's Eve with a little too much vigor, and their departure for New York on New Year's Day was uneventful, since both were reportedly nursing hangovers. After the unsettled and unhappy 1923, it is no wonder the two needed to celebrate. 1924 looked promising. They had a new film contract, the expectation of artistic freedom, and nothing but happiness on their horizon.

In New York Valentino saw an exhibition by the Spanish court painter Federico Beltran Masses. He was impressed, and soon contacted Beltran Masses to commission a series of portraits. The artist would join them in Hollywood in the summer of 1925.

In February 1924, he began filming *Monsieur Beaucaire* at Paramount's Astoria Studios. Morning exercise consisted of daily fencing lessons, running, and boxing. Exercise complete, Valentino appeared on the set, bewigged and costumed, and ready to work. Both the studio and the press expected him to be temperamental and were pleasantly surprised to find him studious, hard-working, and amiable.

The same imperious behavior was expected of Natacha, but though not as personable as Valentino, she proved approachable and assiduous. The actress Lois Wilson recalled a happy set, with Valentino behaving like an older brother. *Monsieur Beaucaire* provided Valentino with a new challenge: comedy. He relished the fencing scenes, but they were as much action as the script allowed. And to everyone's surprise, he proved to be a deft comic actor. It was a talent he would not be given much opportunity to display.

His next scheduled film was *A Sainted Devil*, directed by Joseph Henabery. The story was set in Spain, and Valentino's character ran the gamut from lovesick swain, to rough-and-tumble gaucho, to drunkard. The film boasted three leading ladies: Helena D'Algy, Dagmar Godowsky, and popular co-star Nita Naldi, performing another vamp role. Valentino enjoyed himself during the filming and spent countless off-camera hours shooting home movies of the goings-on. He also lugged a Graflex camera about, taking still photos of Nita Naldi and Joseph Henabery. Henabery recalled that the Valentinos rushed through filming, as they were anxious to leave Famous Players-Lasky to begin work for their own production company.

The Valentinos would be producing their next film for Ritz-Carlton Productions which was formed by J.D. Williams (formerly of rival studio First National). Rudolph Valentino was their first and, ultimately, only star client. It was for Ritz-Carlton that Valentino hoped to realize his dreams of quality film productions.

Once filming on *A Sainted Devil* was completed, the Valentinos eagerly began preparations for their first independent production, *The Scarlet Power*, later renamed *The Hooded Falcon*. Natacha wrote the scenario and hoped to research the film while in Spain and to collect antiques for use in the film. They also hoped to scout locations, as their plans included location filming at the Alhambra palaces in the ancient Spanish city of Granada. June Mathis was brought in to doctor the script once Natacha got the basics laid out. They were devastated when J.D. Williams informed them that the budget would not allow location shooting. He further advised them he had purchased Martin Brown's stage play, *Cobra*, with Valentino in mind.

In the summer of 1924, the Valentinos left for a prolonged European vacation. Valentino picked up his customized Avions Voisin convertible and drove it proudly to Juan les Pins to meet with Natacha's family. In preparation for *The Hooded Falcon* he stopped shaving and was soon seen sporting a moustache and goatee.

Valentino brought a print of *Monsieur Beaucaire* to screen at the chateau. The chateau's electrical wiring proved not up to the task—fuses were blown many times over in an attempt to run the film. Alberto, Ada, and Maria also visited the chateau. The renowned Hollywood photographer James Abbe visited and shot portraits of Valentino posing in his Voisin, chatting with his brother, and with his new dog, a Doberman Pinscher named Kabar. Valentino and Natacha also posed in the chateau's garden, where Natacha modeled her recent haute couture purchases.

Valentino enjoyed boating on this visit to the Riviera. Natacha's mother recalled, "It was a beautiful sight to see him standing at the wheel, bareheaded, in his black bathing suit, the white spray dashing up his face." He also enjoyed taking home movies with his new cameras and memorializing each new place with still photographs.

They were joined by Nita Naldi, who had traveled to Paris for *Hooded Falcon* costume fittings and journeyed with them to Spain. Laden with luggage and cameras, they took the train to Madrid and proceeded to overspend the $40,000 budget allotted for props. Valentino wired home to George Ullman for more funds.

Valentino was always an avid tourist who tried to see as much as he could each day. They were disappointed to find the Museo del Prado closed, so they scoured antique shops instead. They next visited Seville and witnessed a bullfight. Both he and Natacha were avowed animal lovers, yet became engrossed in the spectacle; Valentino proclaimed that bullfighting was his next career. In the excitement he'd forgotten to take a single photograph.

In Seville they also visited the Alcazar castle, and Valentino made up for the lack of bullfight photos by spending countless hours composing shots in the early morning, at noon, and in the evening. When he was not photographing, he was spending tremendous amounts of cash on armor, arms, and antique guns and rifles. They then traveled on to the Alhambra palaces in Granada, where they again photographed the sights and purchased more antiques.

From Spain they returned to France, where they explored a semi-ruined castle. The ever enthusiastic and impulsive Valentino decided to purchase the property on the spot, but saner heads prevailed and the dank castle remained unsold. There remained a last stop in Paris for more costume fittings before boarding the SS Leviathan for New York.

Back home, the press had a field day with Valentino's newly grown whiskers. Photographed with Natacha or posing alone wearing his goatee and a winning smile, the star's new look made the pages of every metropolitan newspaper across the country. One account told of a bevy of flappers who demanded, "Come out from behind that foliage Rudolph! We know you." "I can't, it's grown on," responded the Sheik. The reddish-brown growth on chin and lips gave Valentino a decidedly more exotic cast, but it was not a look he cared for. "Don't want it—too much trouble. But, can't help it. New picture you know. After that, back to the barber shop."

By the time the party reached Chicago, war had been declared on the goatee. Mobs of fans met the California Limited in Los Angeles, along with reporters, newsreel cameras, and the vice mayor of Los Angeles, who carried a straight razor on behalf of the Barbers of America. It was quite the publicity stunt and Valentino played along for the cameras, laughing all the while. The goatee garnered so much attention that Photoplay printed a withering comment on his fashion influence: a cartoon in which Douglas Fairbanks, Charlie Chaplin, William S. Hart, Pola Negri, and even little Jackie Coogan all sported facial hair.

During a meeting in New York with J.D. Williams, the Valentinos learned that he had financed *The Hooded Falcon* and *Cobra* with backing from Famous Players-Lasky, the studio they had struggled so hard to be free of. They were furious. They were further incensed to learn that both films would be shot in Hollywood, as it was more expeditious and economical to do so. Resentfully, they departed for their Hollywood home with Nita Naldi in tow. Also traveling were new cars, the antiquities, gifts for friends, and costumes for *The Hooded Falcon*.

During the trip the Valentinos finally read June Mathis's scenario for *The Hooded Falcon* and were not happy. George Ullman was handed the unenviable task of telling Mathis so. Natacha commented, "As it was the usual procedure to credit all disagreeable things to my account, this instance was not an exception." Mathis, offended, refused to have anything further to do with the pair.

The Valentinos returned to their Whitley Heights home thinking they would begin work on *The Hooded Falcon*, but J.D. Williams had more bad news for them. Ongoing problems with the script and budget would force yet another postponement. Williams brought up the idea of filming *Cobra* instead, and the Valentinos reluctantly agreed to begin work on the inferior property after the holidays.

They soon added a new employee to their staff. Police officer Luther Mahoney had once been assigned to accompany Valentino in New York, and later left the force and moved his family to Hollywood to take a job as an assistant to art director William Cameron Menzies. Valentino and Natacha were surprised to find Luther working at the studio and immediately hired him away from Menzies to become his jack-of-all-trades handyman.

The Christmas season was then upon them, and it was time to find special gifts. Valentino purchased an ornate electric train set for George Ullman's son Daniel. He gifted Natacha with a moonstone wristwatch encrusted with diamonds. Luther Mahoney later told of taking Natacha's design for her husband's Christmas gift to Brock & Co. in Los Angeles. On Christmas Day 1924, Natacha placed the platinum "slave" bracelet on Valentino's wrist. He never removed it.

It would be their last happy Christmas together.

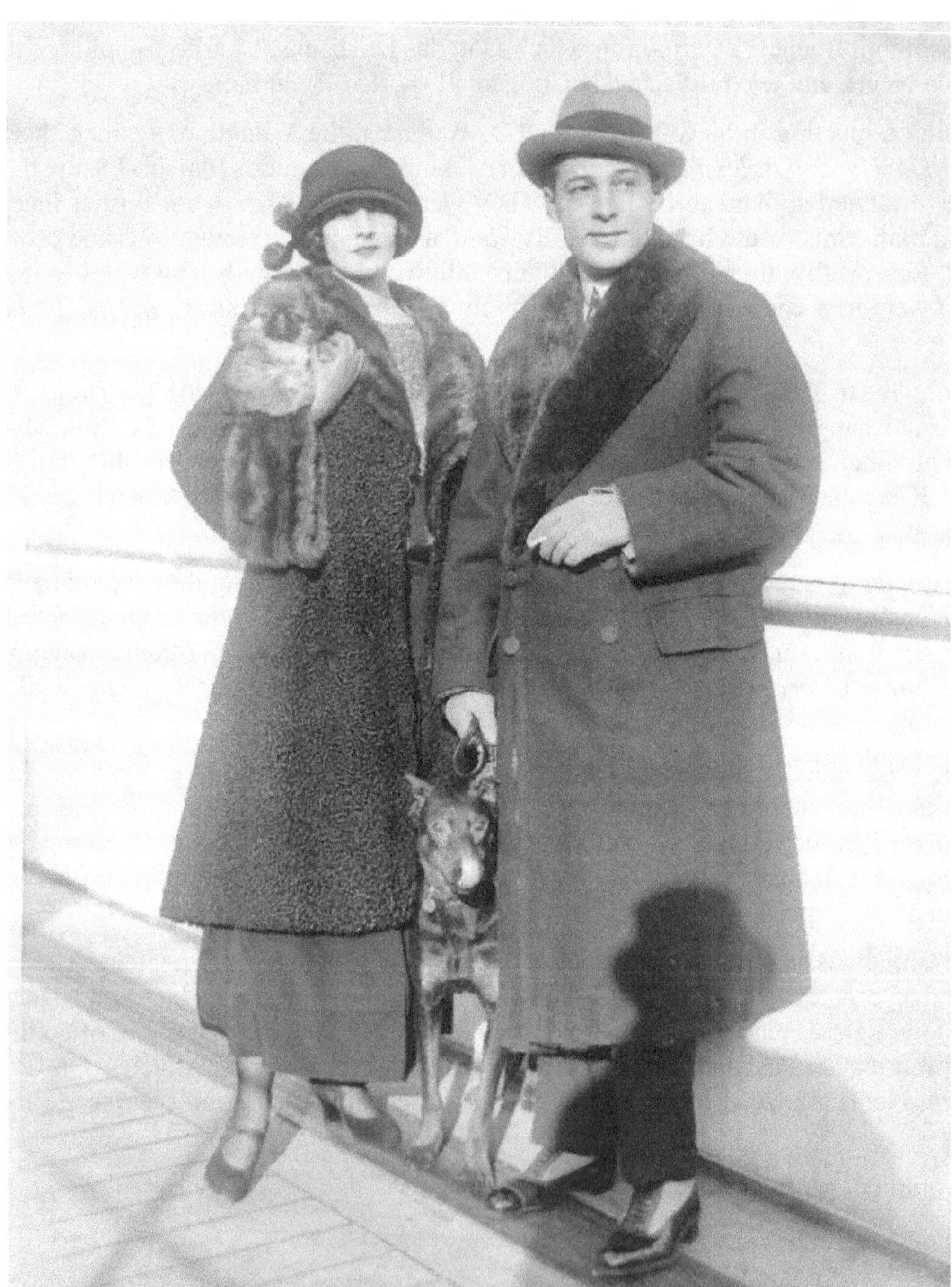

Natacha and Valentino posing for the news photographers. (San Francisco History Center)

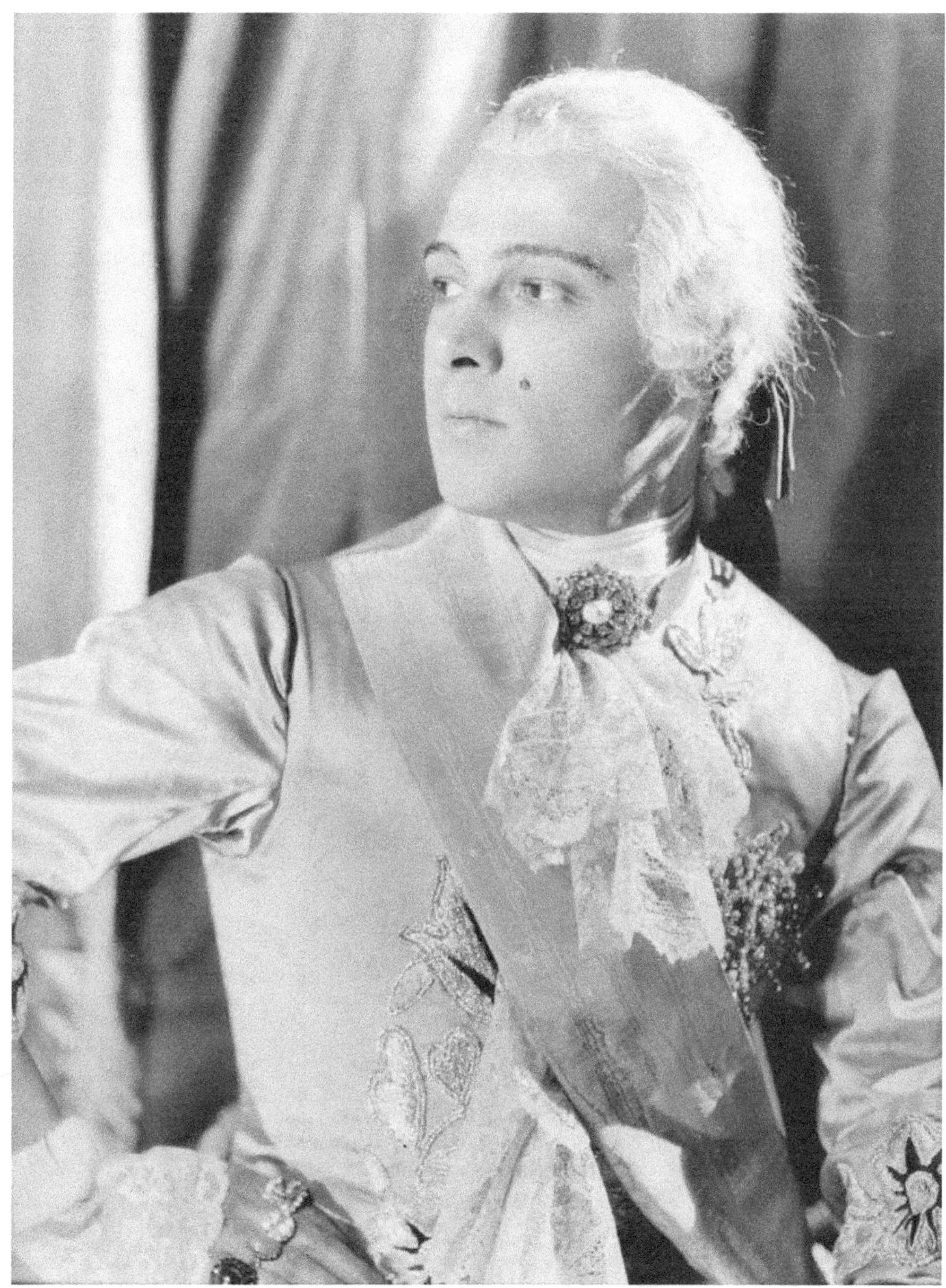

Valentino adored dressing up in costume.
This publicity portrait was one of a series taken of all the stars of the film by Russell Ball.
(Author's collection)

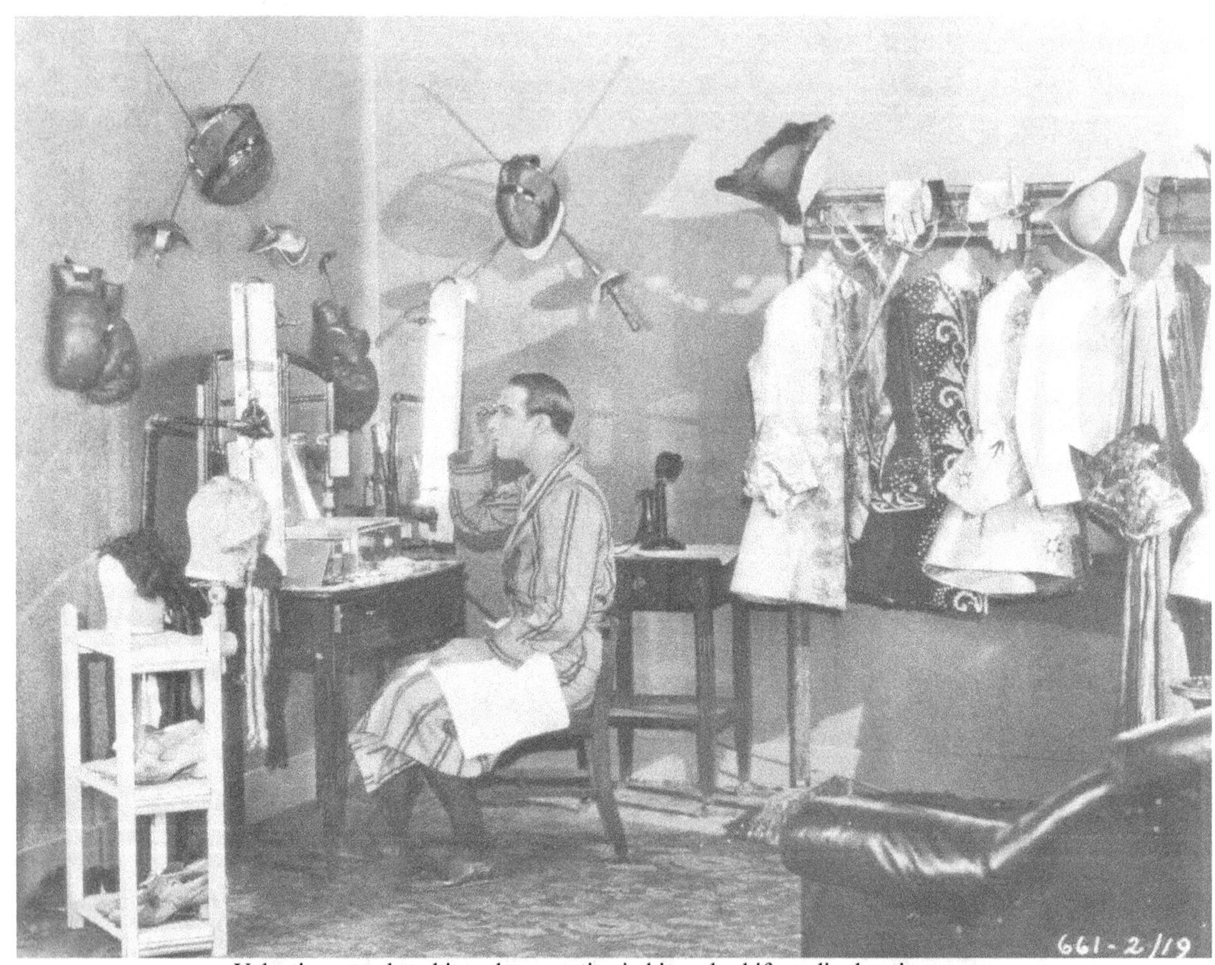

Valentino attends to his makeup routine in his makeshift studio dressing room.
He is surrounded by his costumes for the film and decorated with his fencing gear.
(Barb Nichols collection)

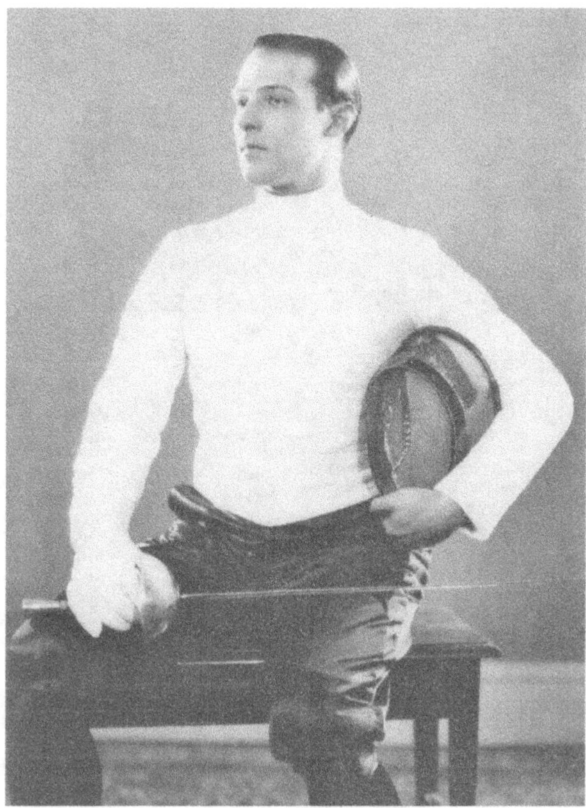

Valentino had long practiced fencing as a means to keep fit.
He enjoyed using the skills in *Monsieur Beaucaire*.
(Author's collection)

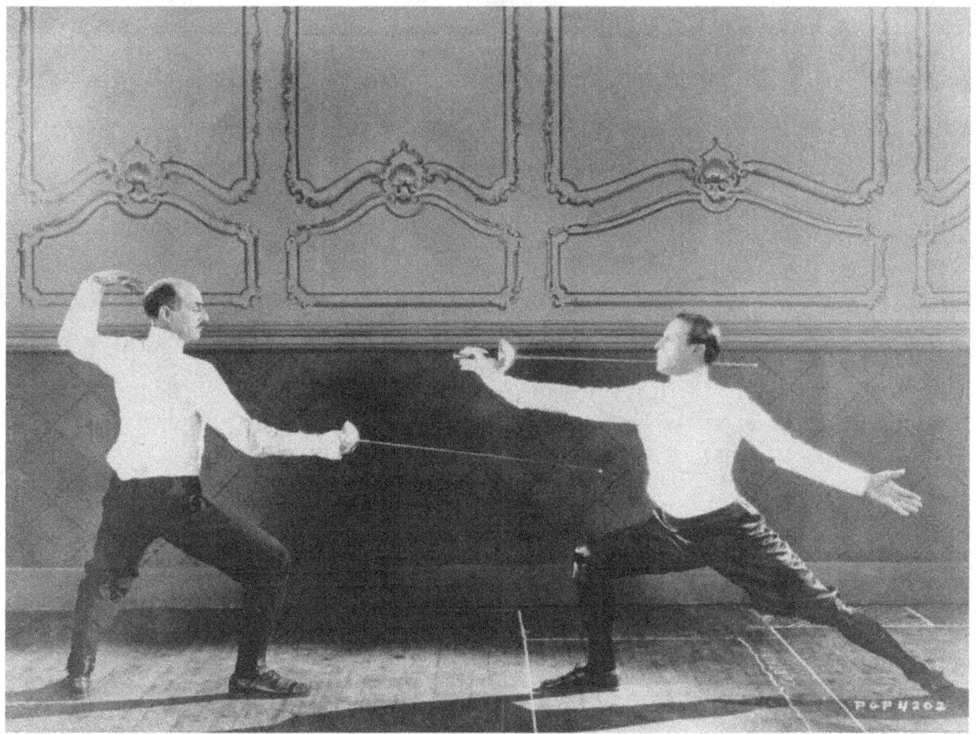

Valentino's natural grace and ease as a former dancer assisted him and enhanced his fencing.
Shown here practicing with instructor Martínez Castelló
(Michael Morris collection)

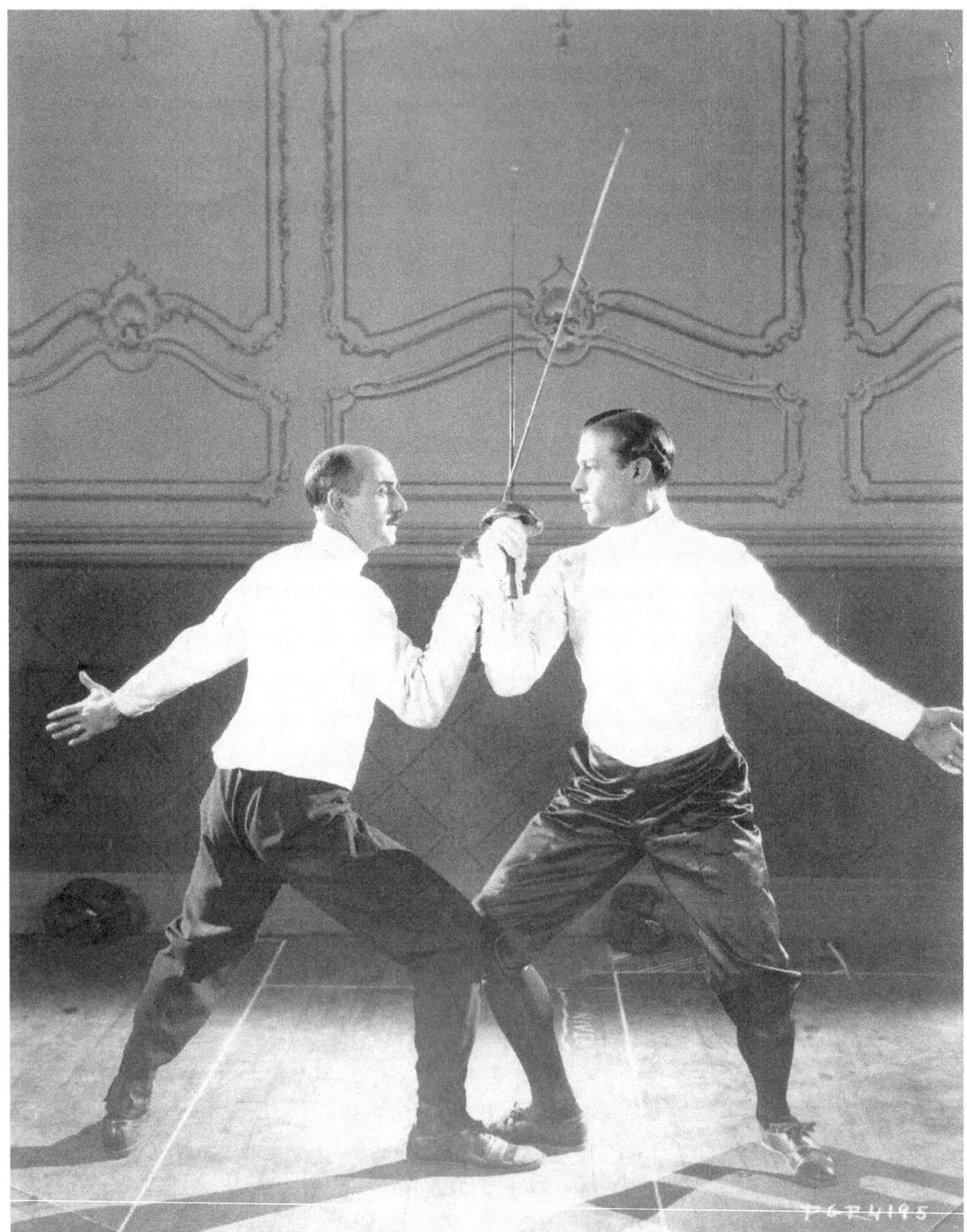

Crossing swords with his instructor Martínez Castelló.
(Author's collection)

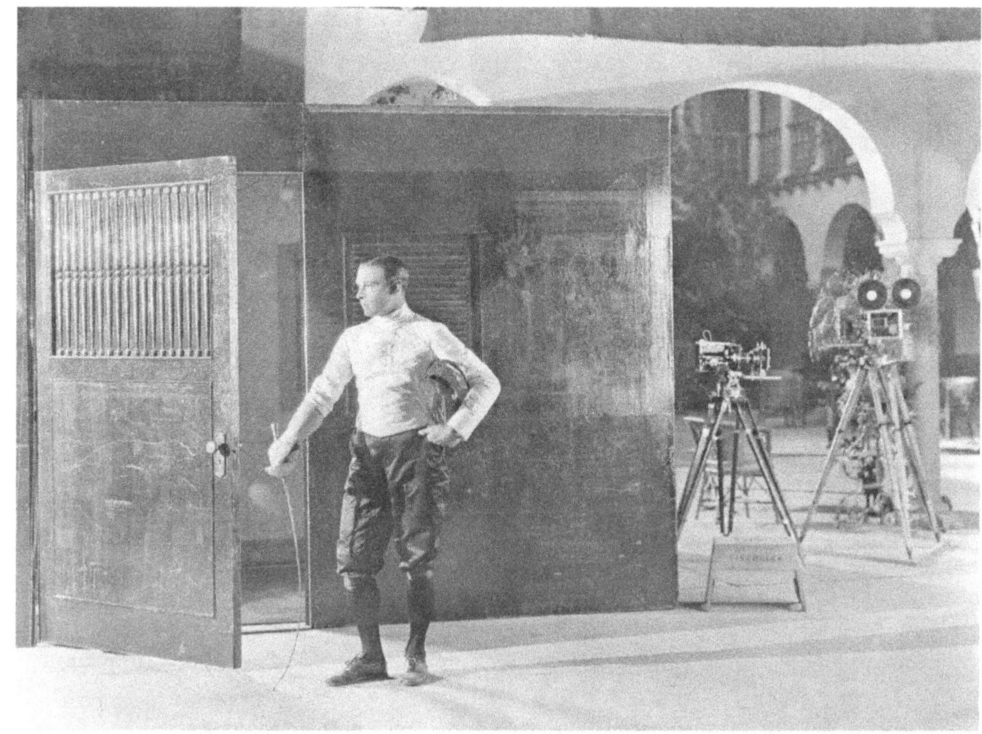

Valentino posing outside his portable dressing room on the set of *A Sainted Devil* before he begins his workout.
(Independent Visions collection)

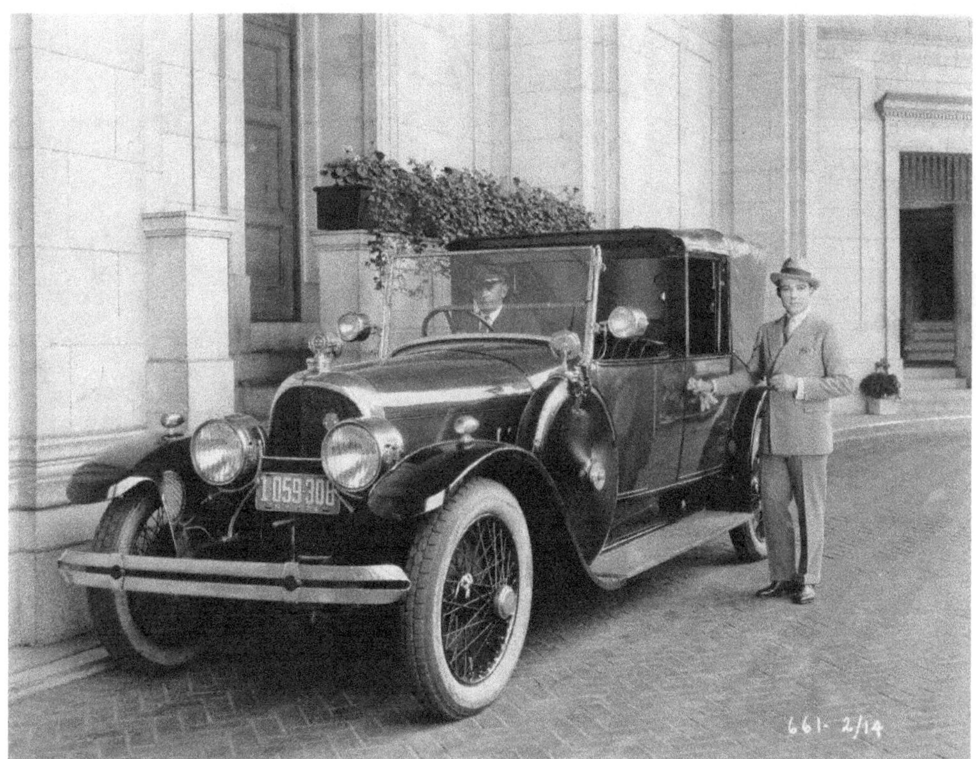

Valentino leaving the Park Avenue apartment to commute to Astoria Studios on Long Island to work on *A Sainted Devil*.
(Author's collection)

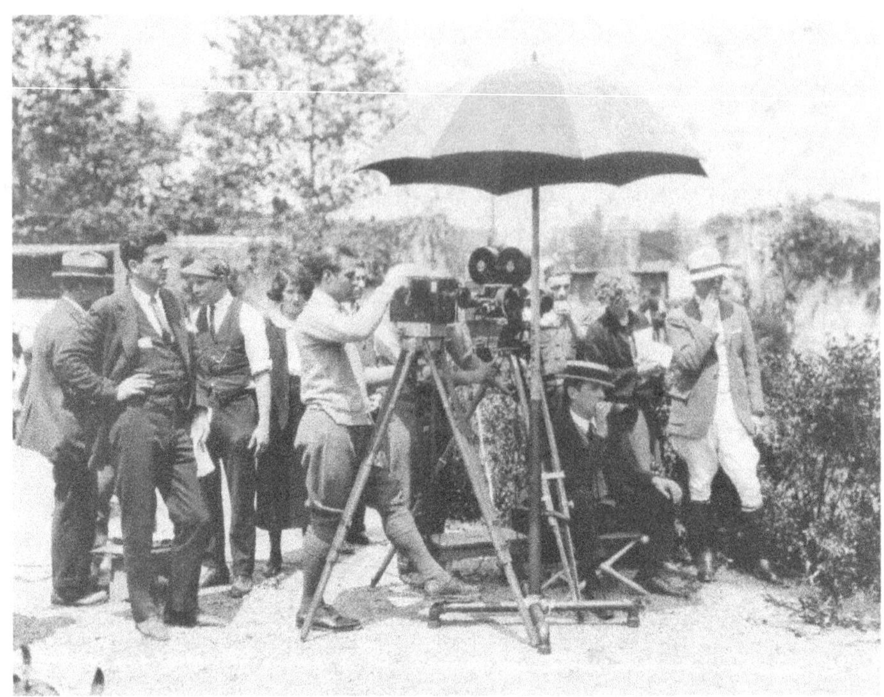

Valentino also enjoyed taking some movies with his own equipment.
He had already expressed a desire to move on to directing.
Director Joseph Henabery seated in boater with megaphone
(Author's collection)

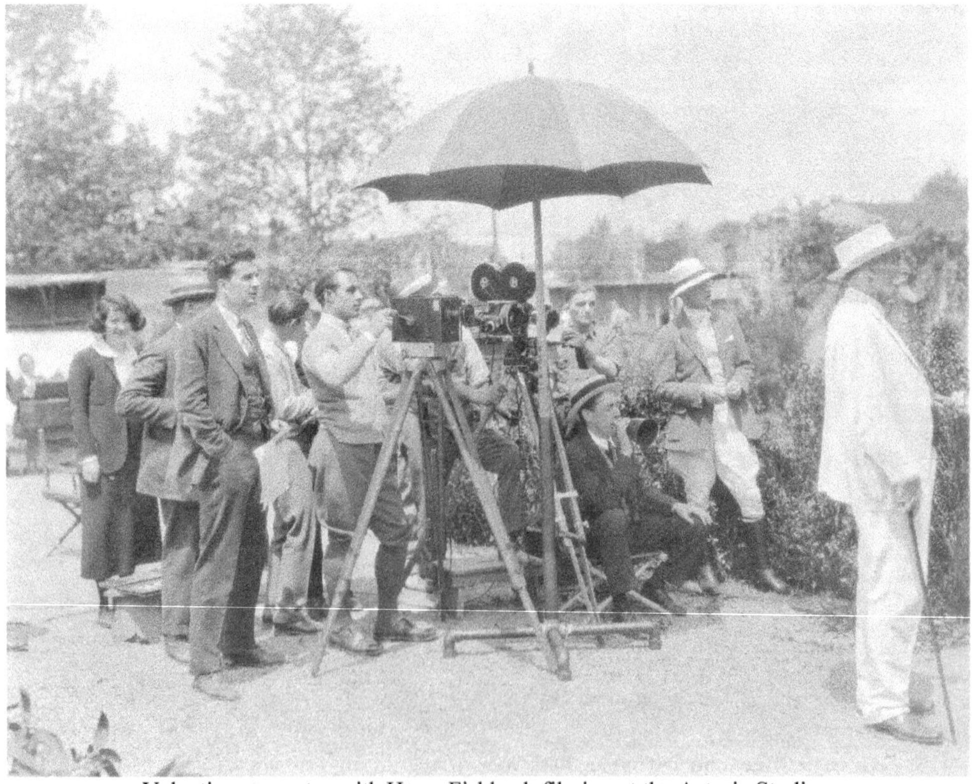

Valentino competes with Harry Fishbeck filming at the Astoria Studios.
Joseph Henabery and L. Rogers Lytton who played Don Balthasar is standing at extreme right.
(Author's collection)

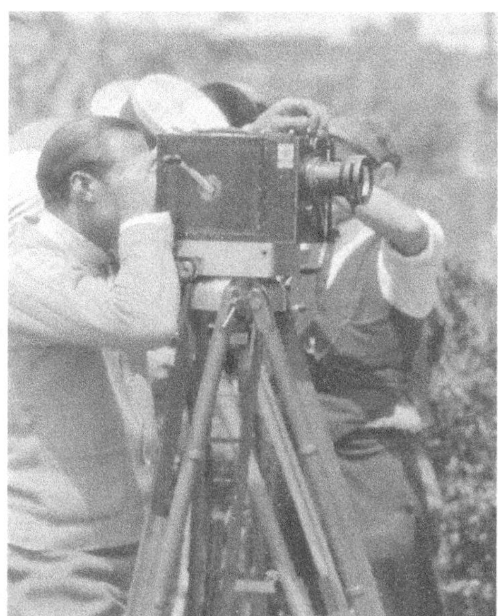

A cropped detail of Valentino focusing on a scene.
Harry Fishbeck (blocked by Valentino) is setting up a shot.
(Author's collection)

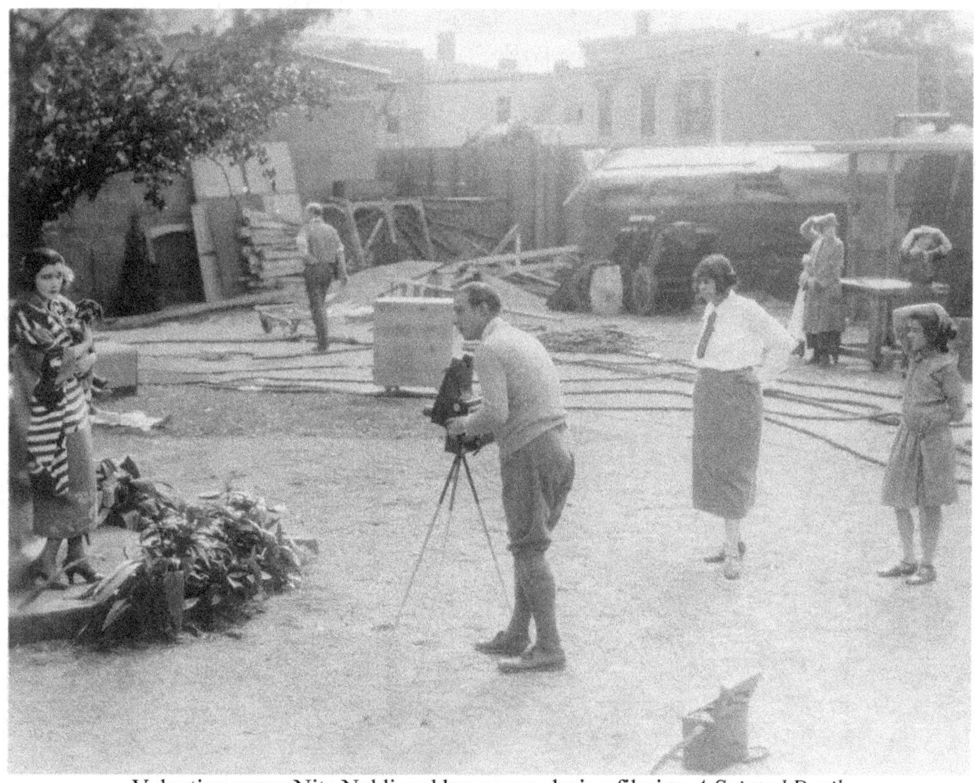

Valentino snaps Nita Naldi and her puppy during filming *A Sainted Devil*.
Note the close proximity to the locals over the studio fence.
(Author's collection)

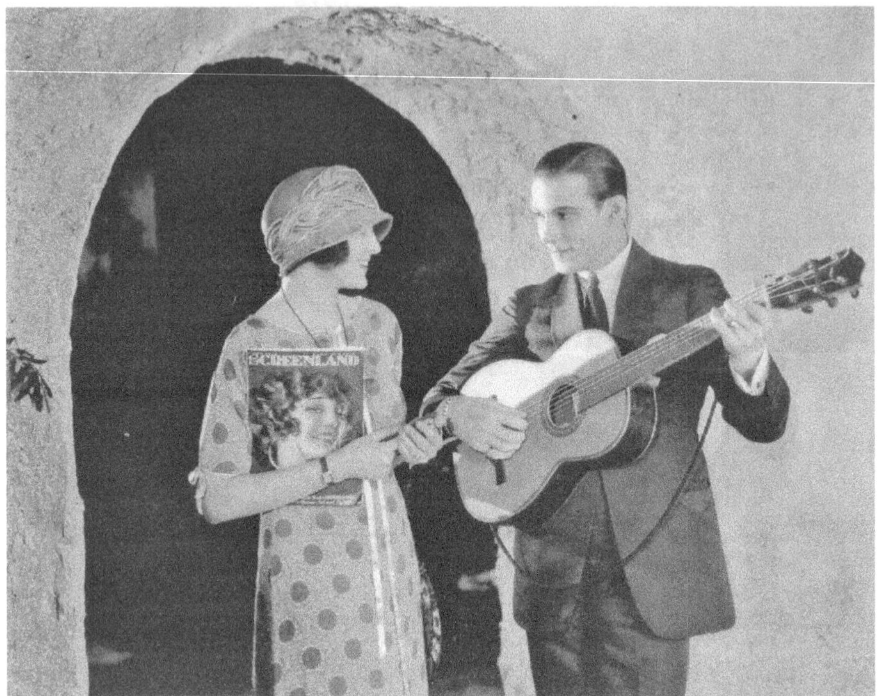

Valentino serenades visitor Billie Dove on special assignment from Screenland Magazine.
(Kevin Brownlow collection)

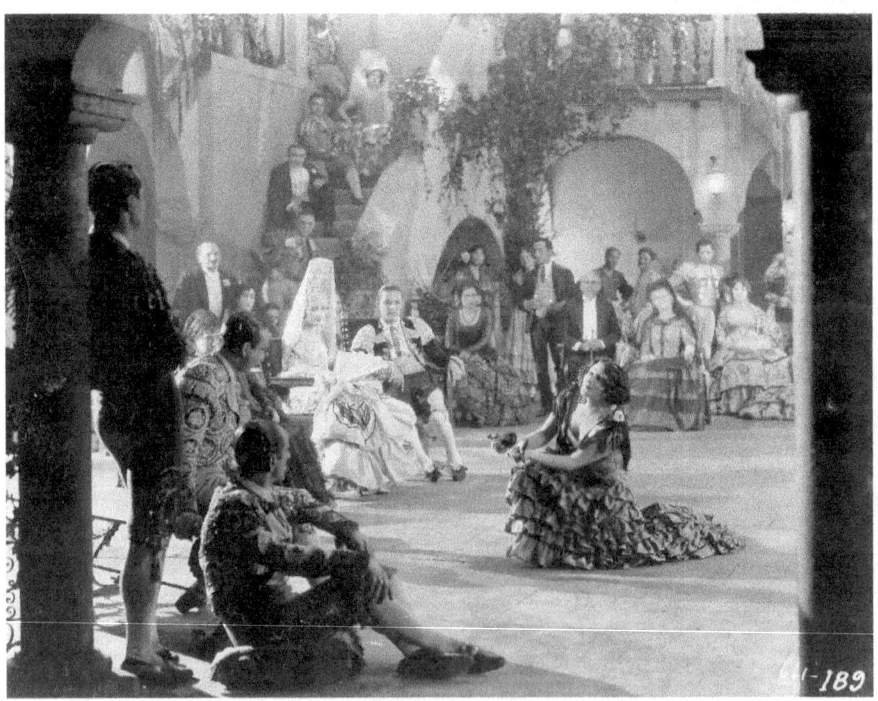

A scene from A Sainted Devil showing off cameraman
Harry Fishbeck's deep focus and use of lighting.
(Author's collection)

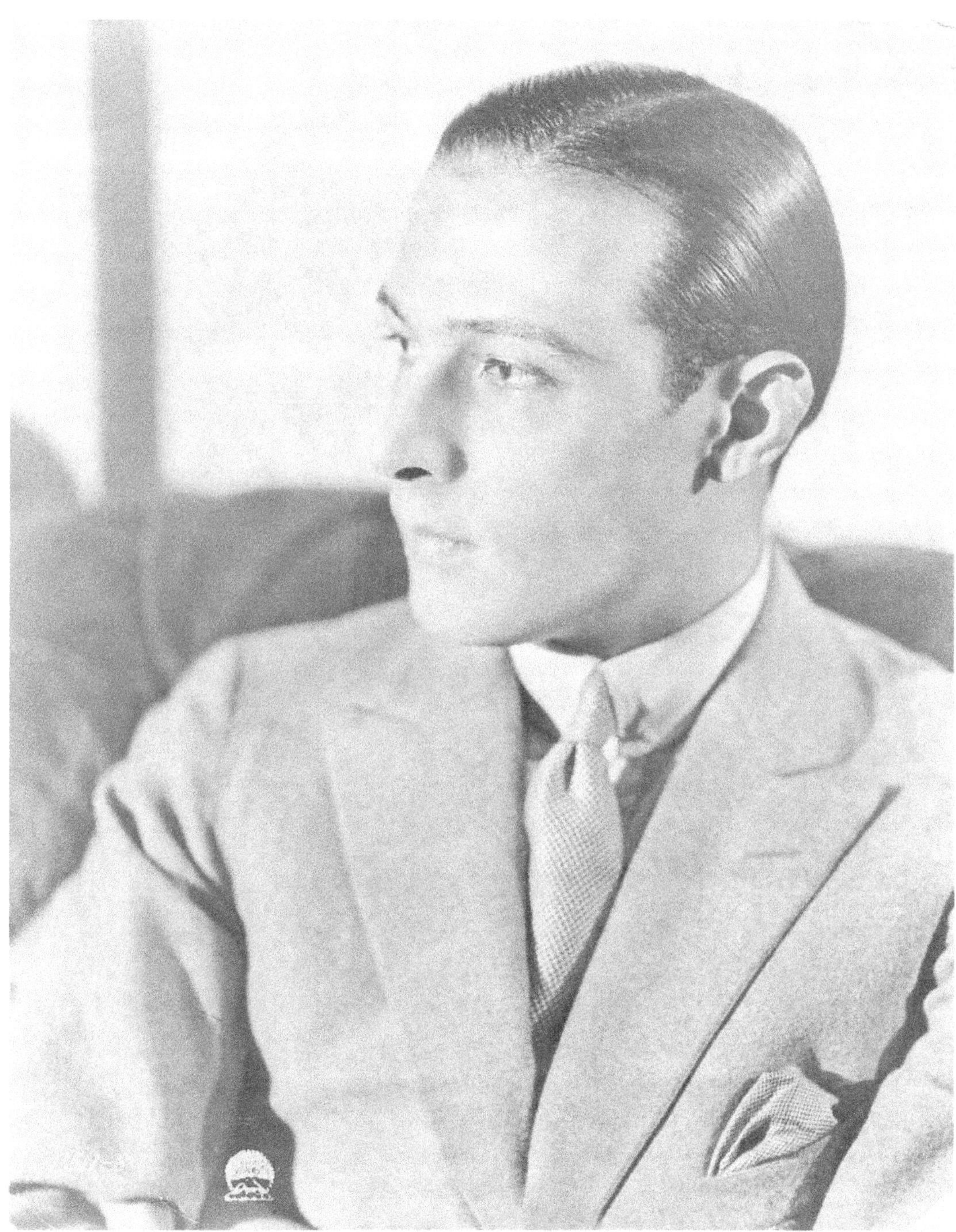

Russell Ball did his last portrait studies of Valentino as he completed his obligations for Paramount. (Author's collection)

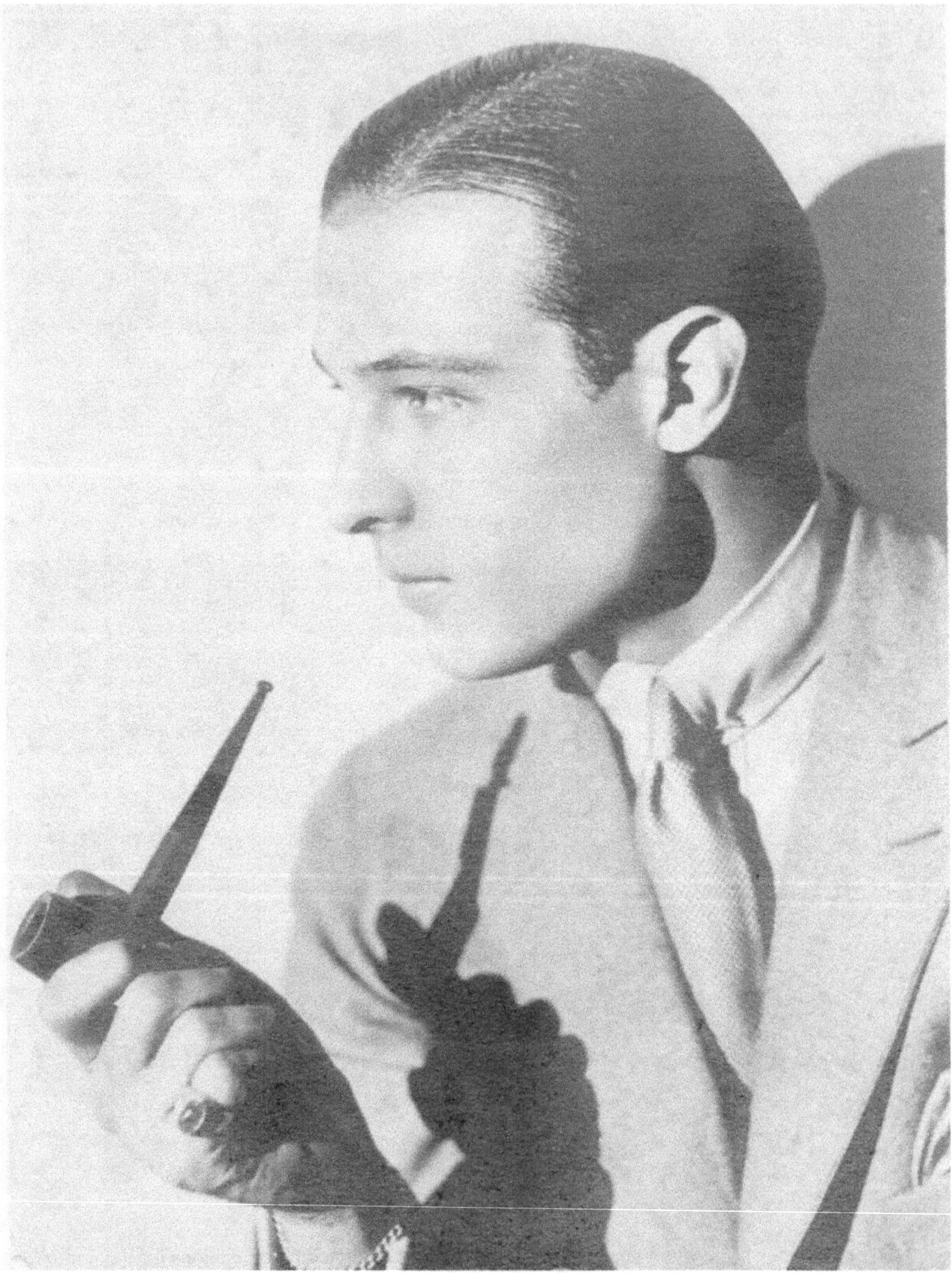

Valentino would soon leave for an extended vacation to Europe to shop for costumes for his next film. He assumed he was independent at last and free to make *The Hooded Falcon.* (Author's collection)

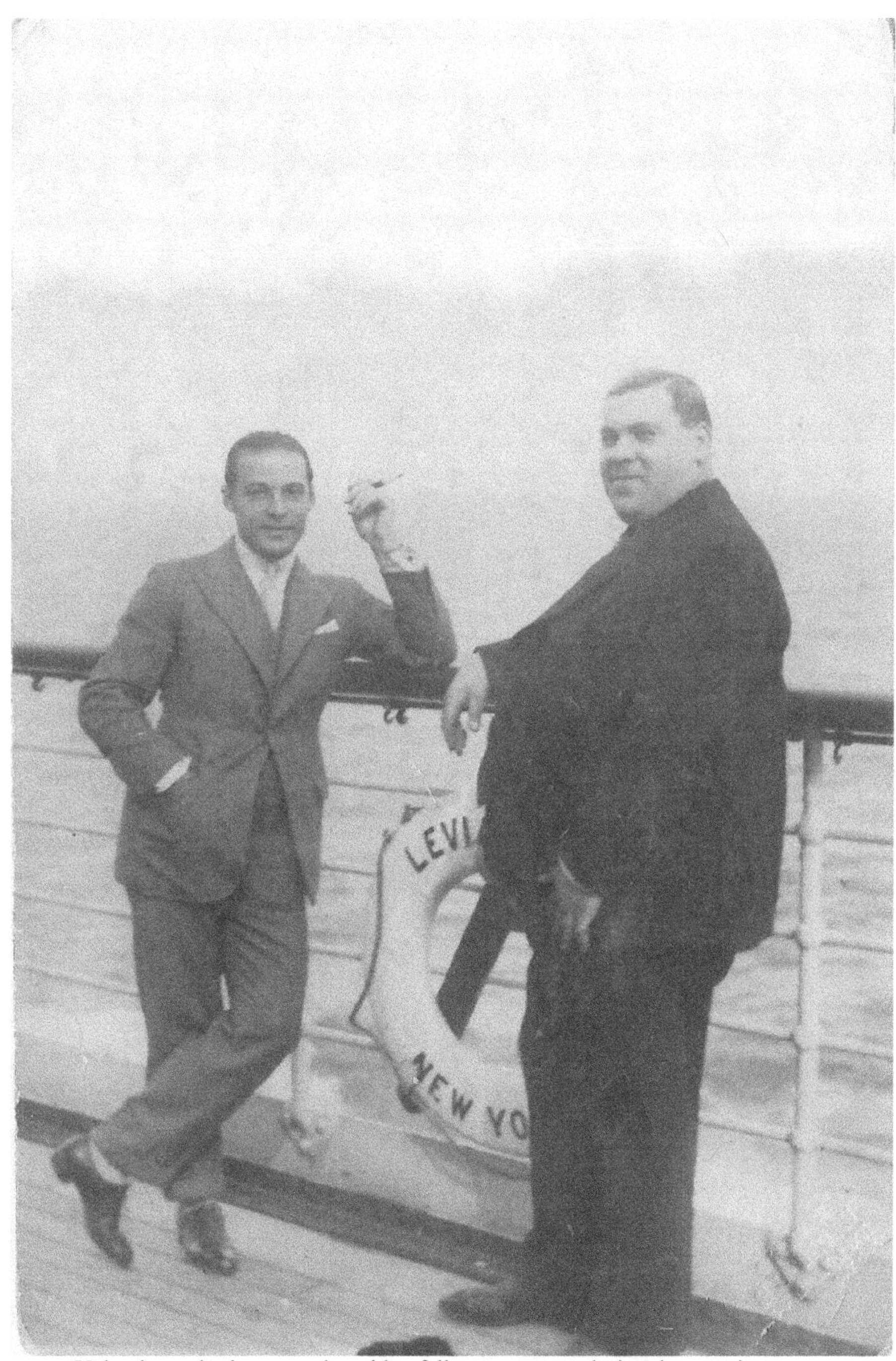

Valentino enjoying a smoke with a fellow passenger during the crossing.
(John Neil collection)

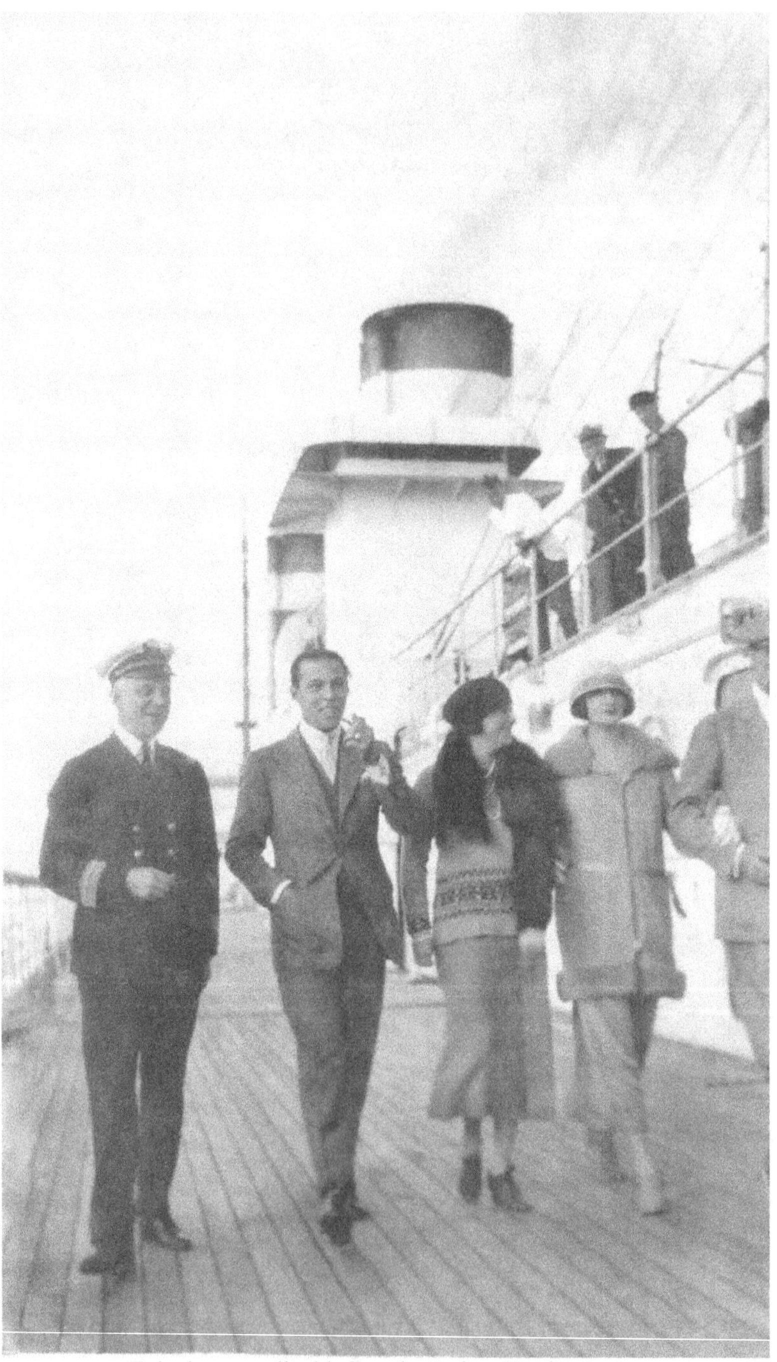

Enjoying a stroll with Captain Herbert Hartley.
(Craig MacPherson collection)

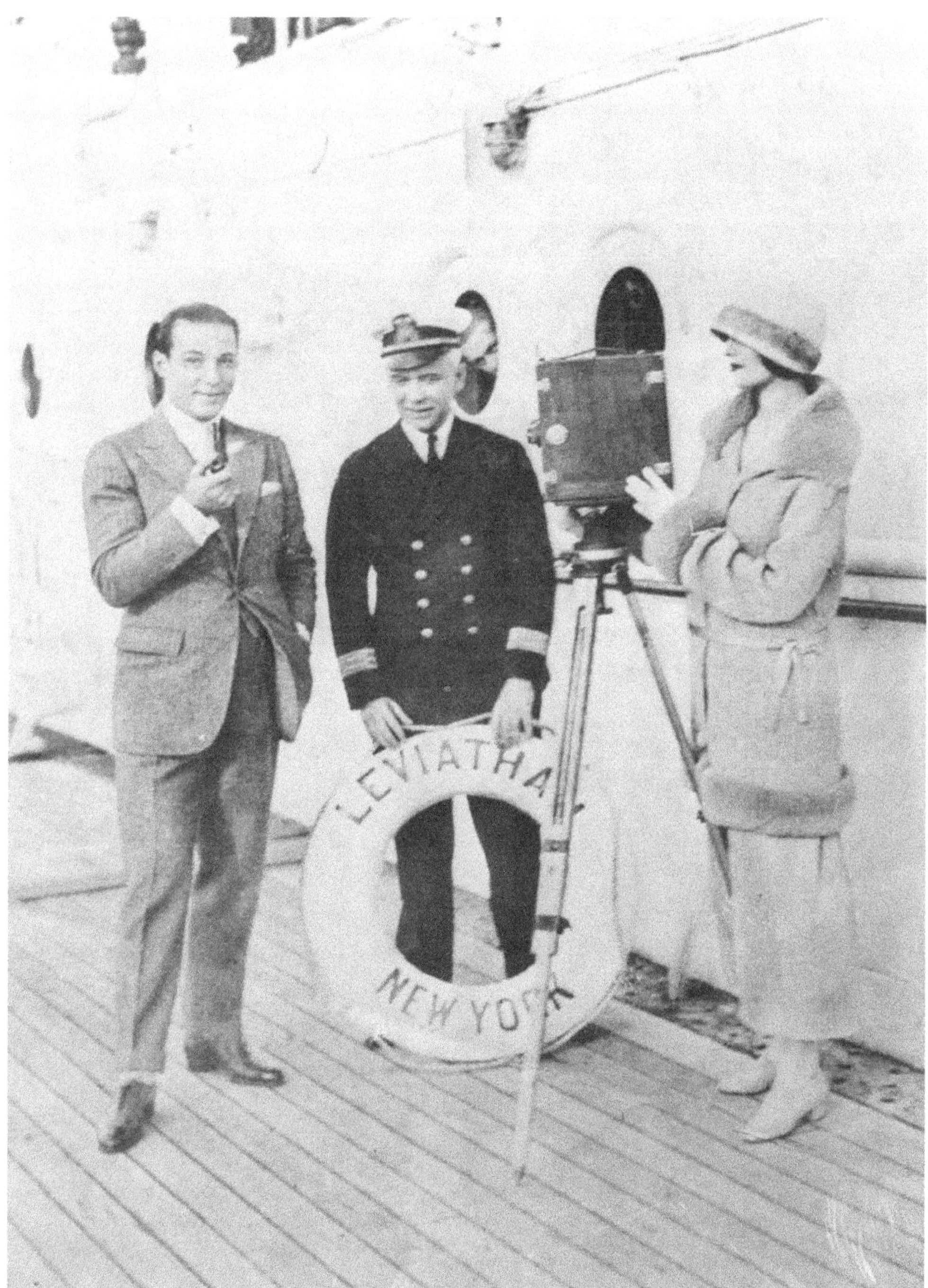

Valentino and Natacha Rambova pose with Captain Herbert Hartley of the Leviathan
(Author's collection)

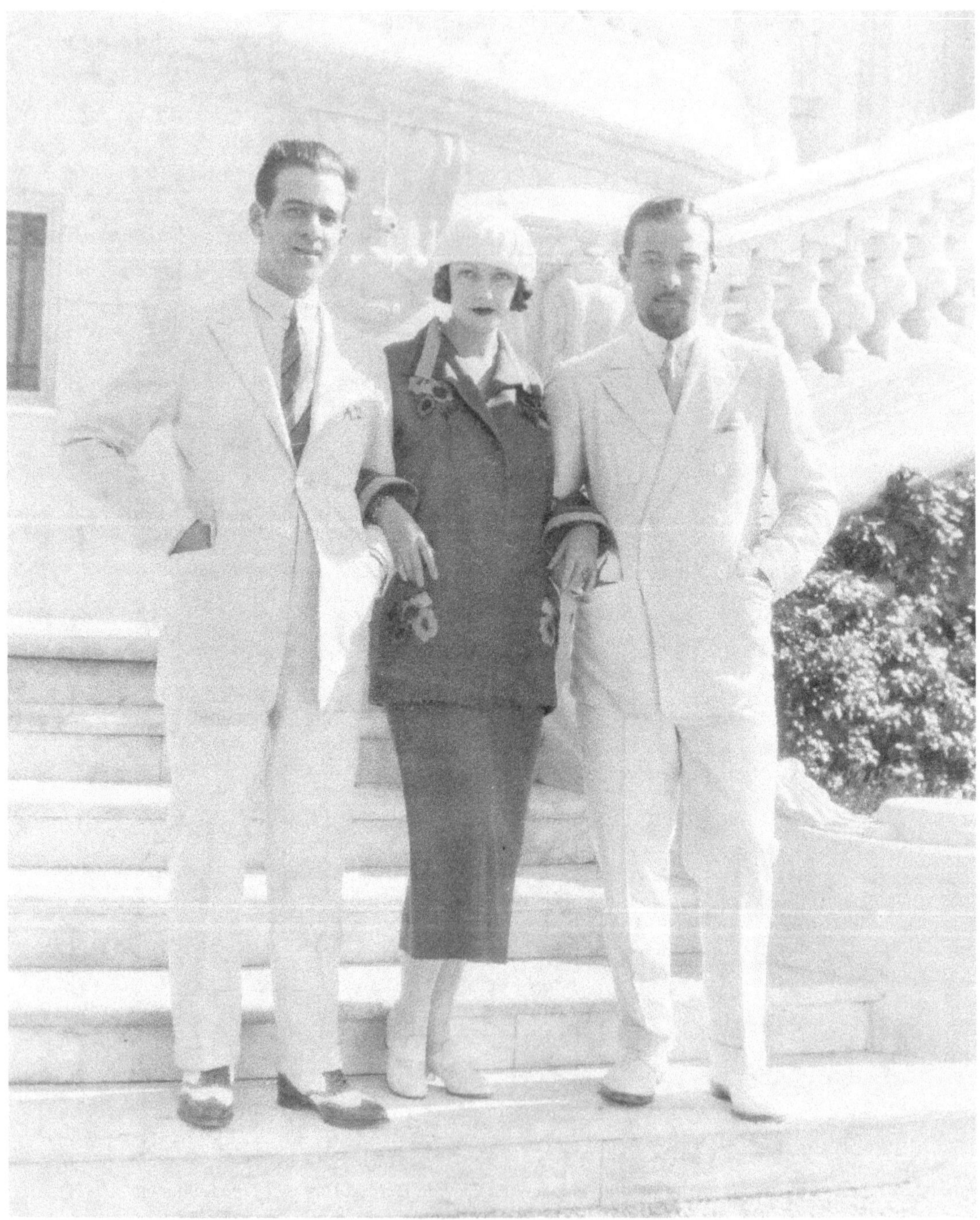

Summer in France, Valentino got to spend time with his family.
Brother Alberto and sister Maria visited Juan les Pins. This would be the only time Natacha and Alberto met.
(Author's collection)

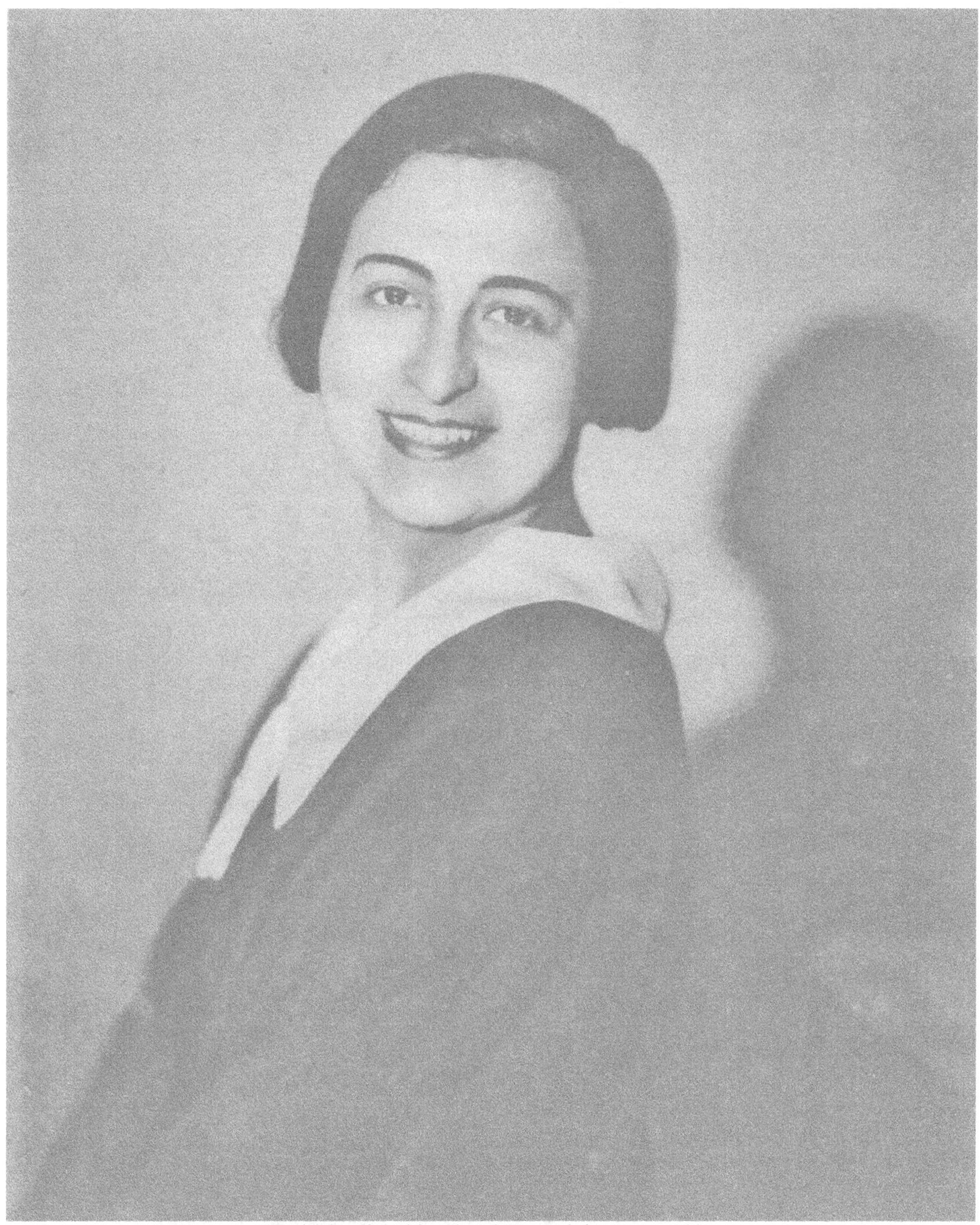

Maria Guglielmi in a lovely portrait by James Abbe.
Abbe was visiting Juan les Pins and took many portraits of the family during this trip.
Movie Weekly Magazine published the portrait indicating Maria would come to Hollywood to make pictures.
This never happened.
(Author's collection)

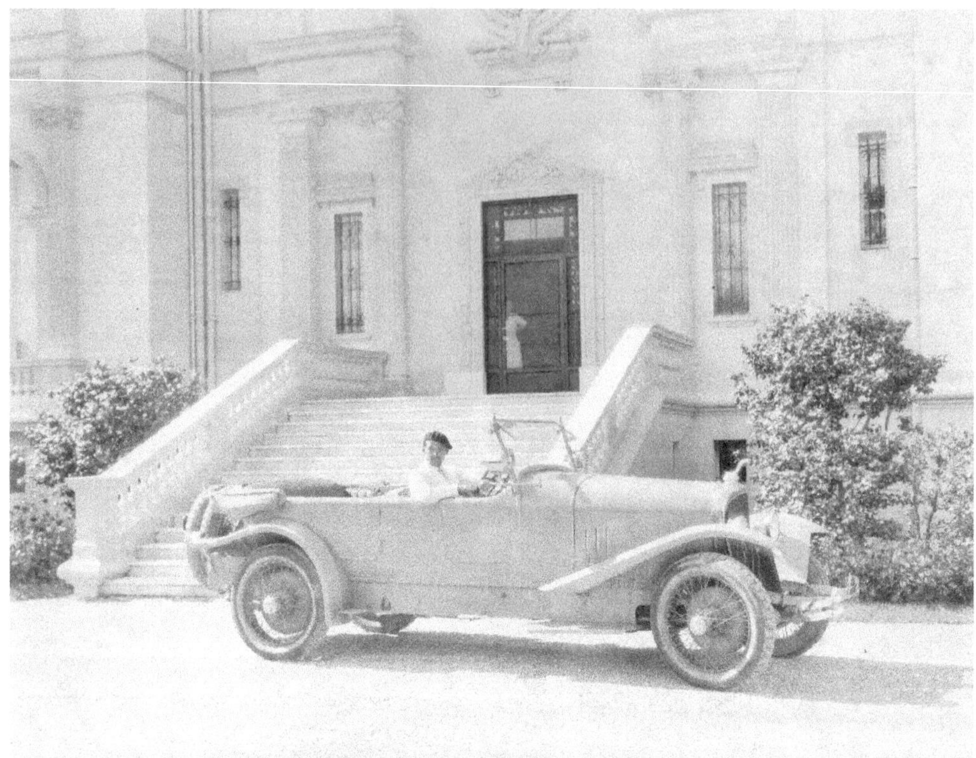

Valentino in a jaunty French beret shows off his new Avion Voisin.
(Author's collection)

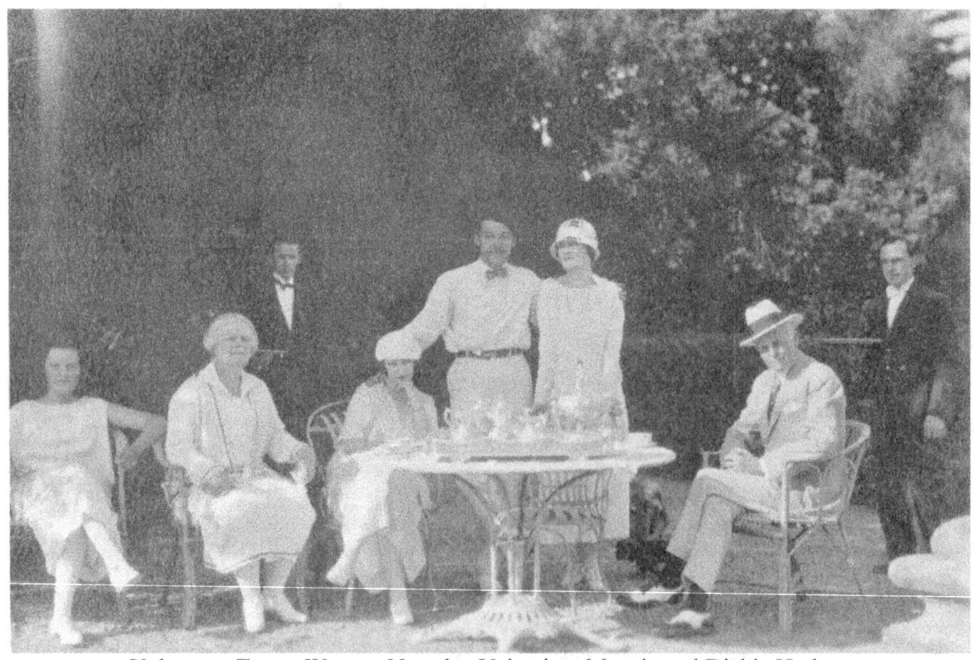

Unknown, Teresa Werner, Natacha, Valentino, Muzzie and Dickie Hudnut
flanked by staff at Juan les Pins.
Natacha looks thoughtful, Valentino looks happy.
(Michael Morris collection)

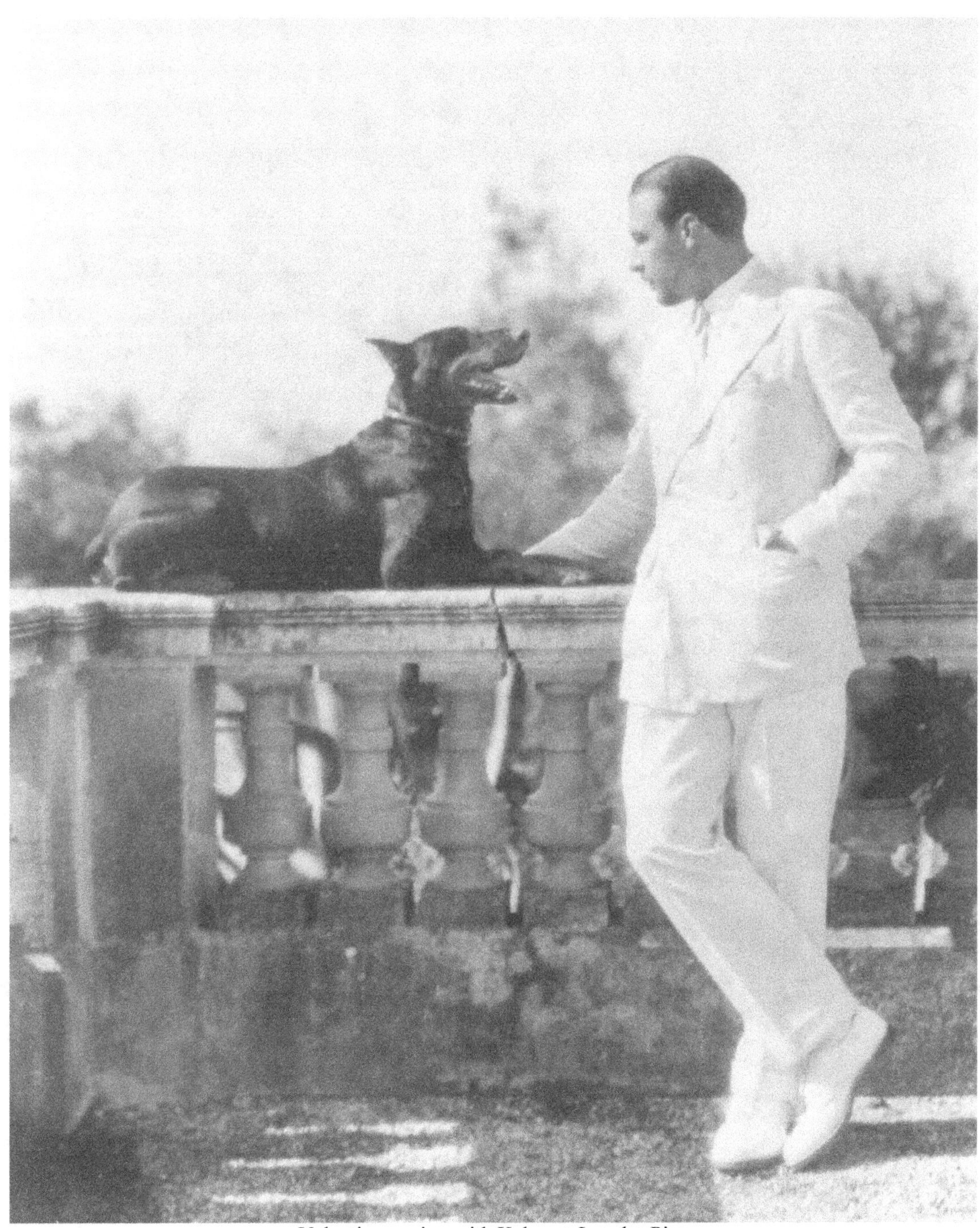

Valentino posing with Kabar at Juan les Pins.
(Author's collection)

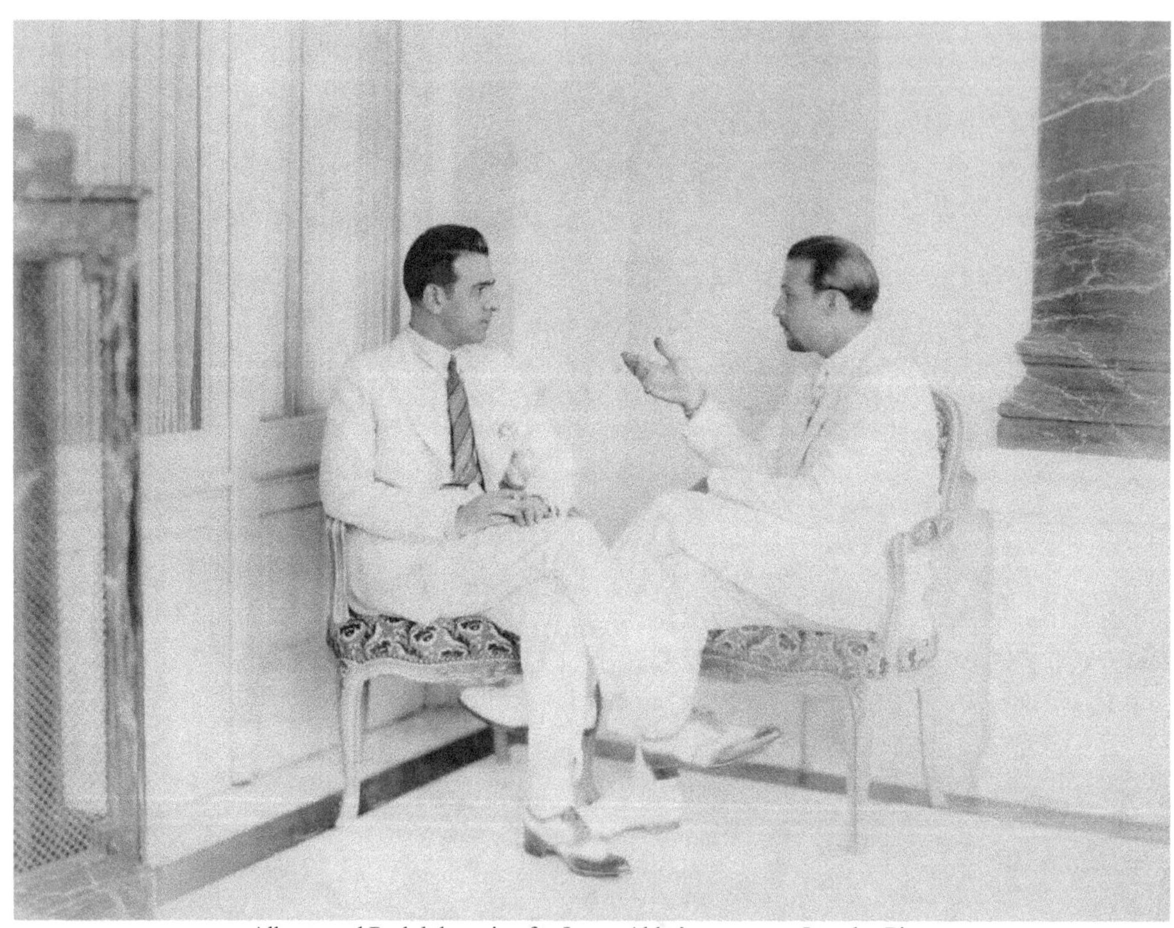

Alberto and Rudolph posing for James Abbe's camera at Juan les Pins.
(Author's collection)

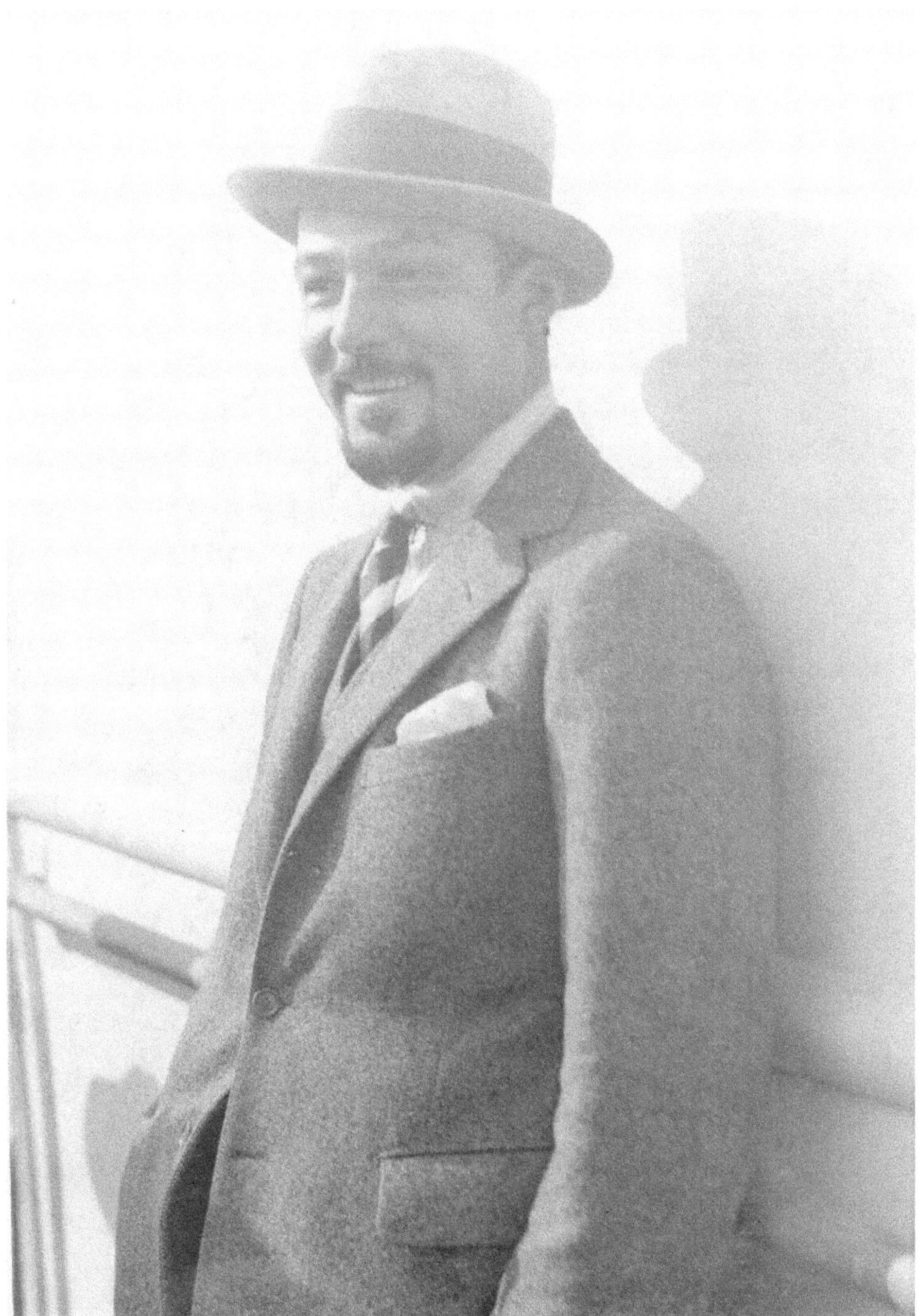

Valentino returning to the U.S. with a goatee was cause for much comment.
(Author's collection)

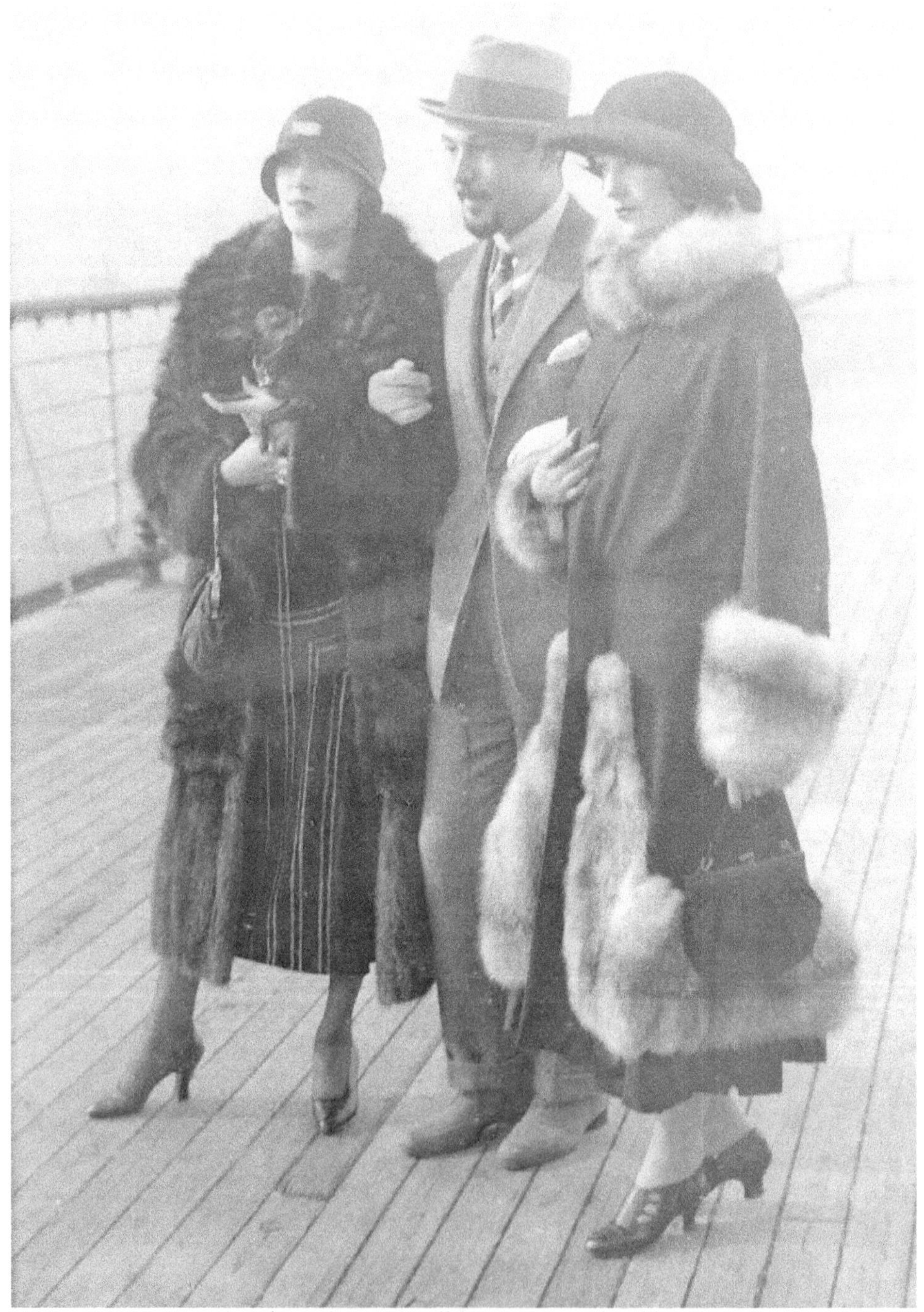

The return trip was, by all accounts, an enjoyable one.
Nita Naldi made crossing back with the pair bound for Hollywood.
(Author's collection)

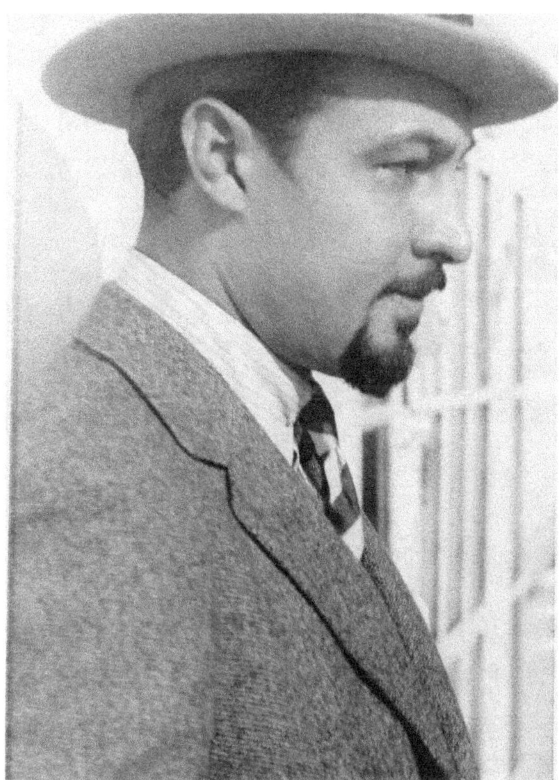

Valentino's scar, for once, not retouched out.
(Author's collection)

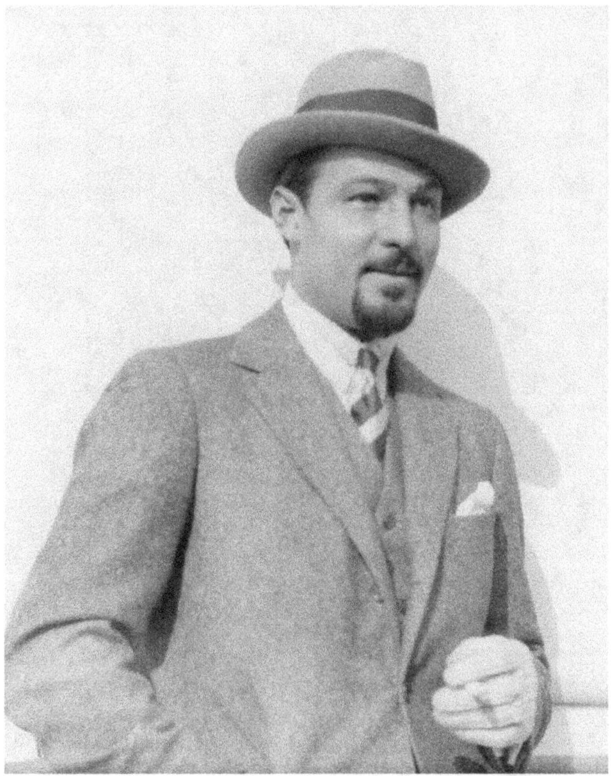

Valentino posed for the press as long as they needed.
(Author's collection)

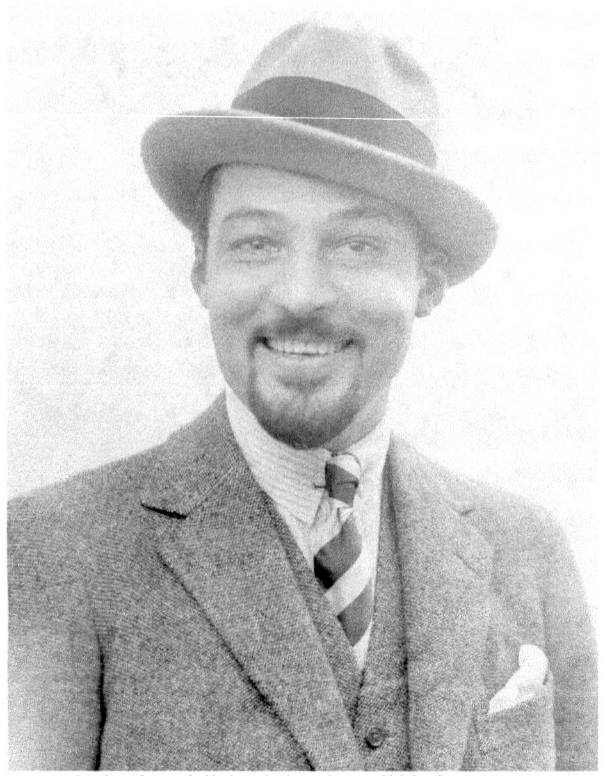

Valentino, delighted showing off his facial hair
and his winning smile.
(Author's collection)

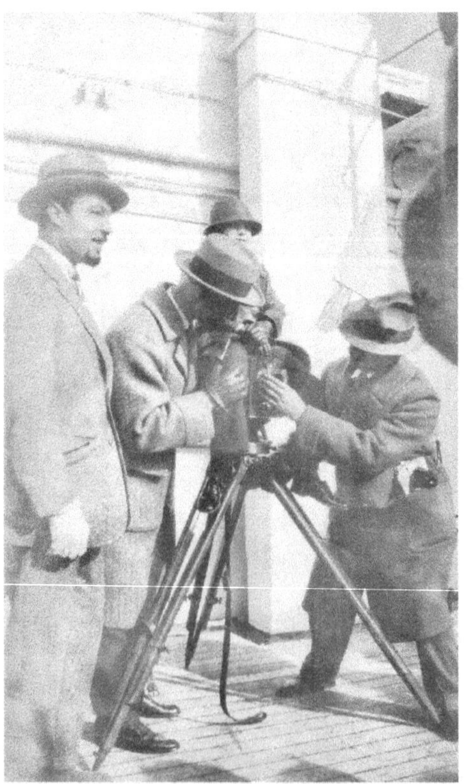

Valentino was not the only celebrity on board,
Jackie Coogan (sitting on the camera) was a passenger.
(Craig MacPherson collection)

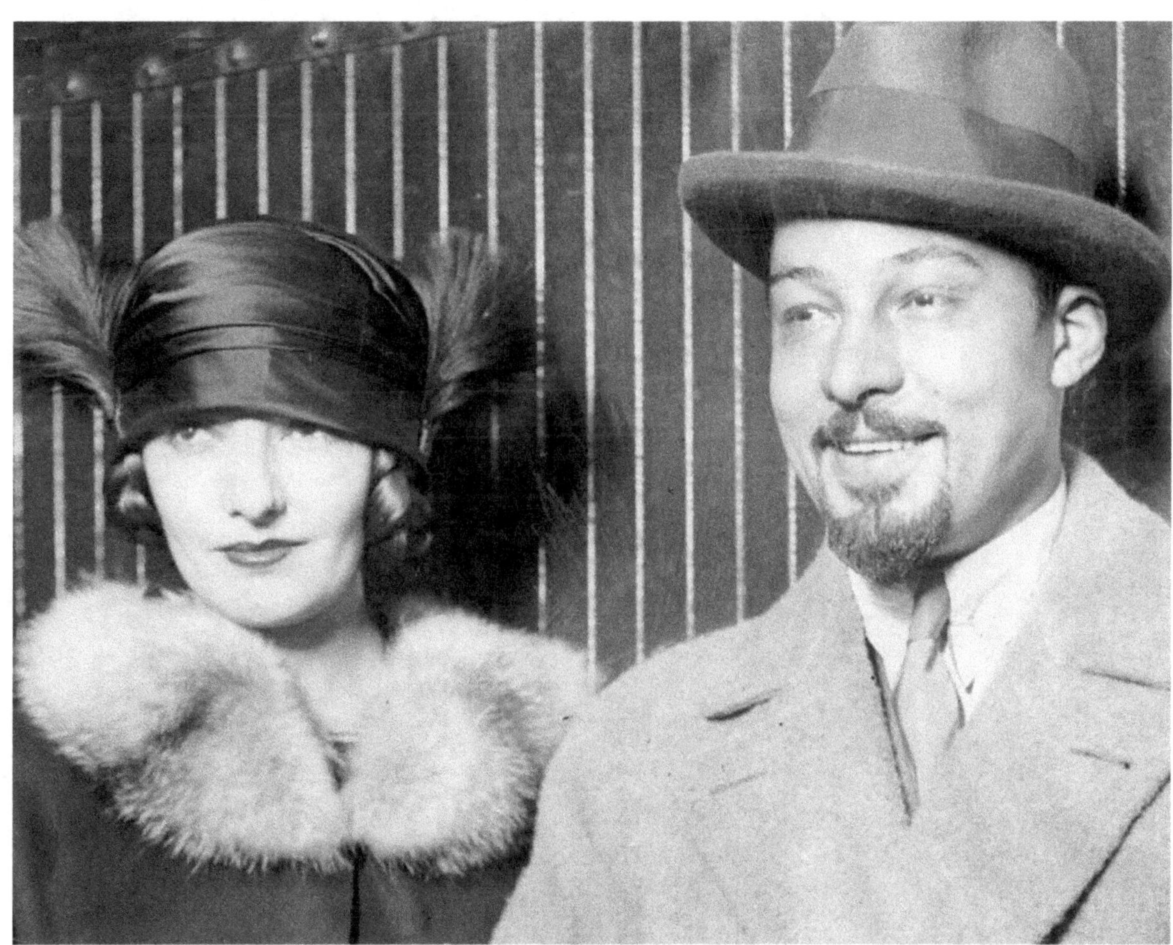

Arriving in Chicago in 1924
(Author's collection)

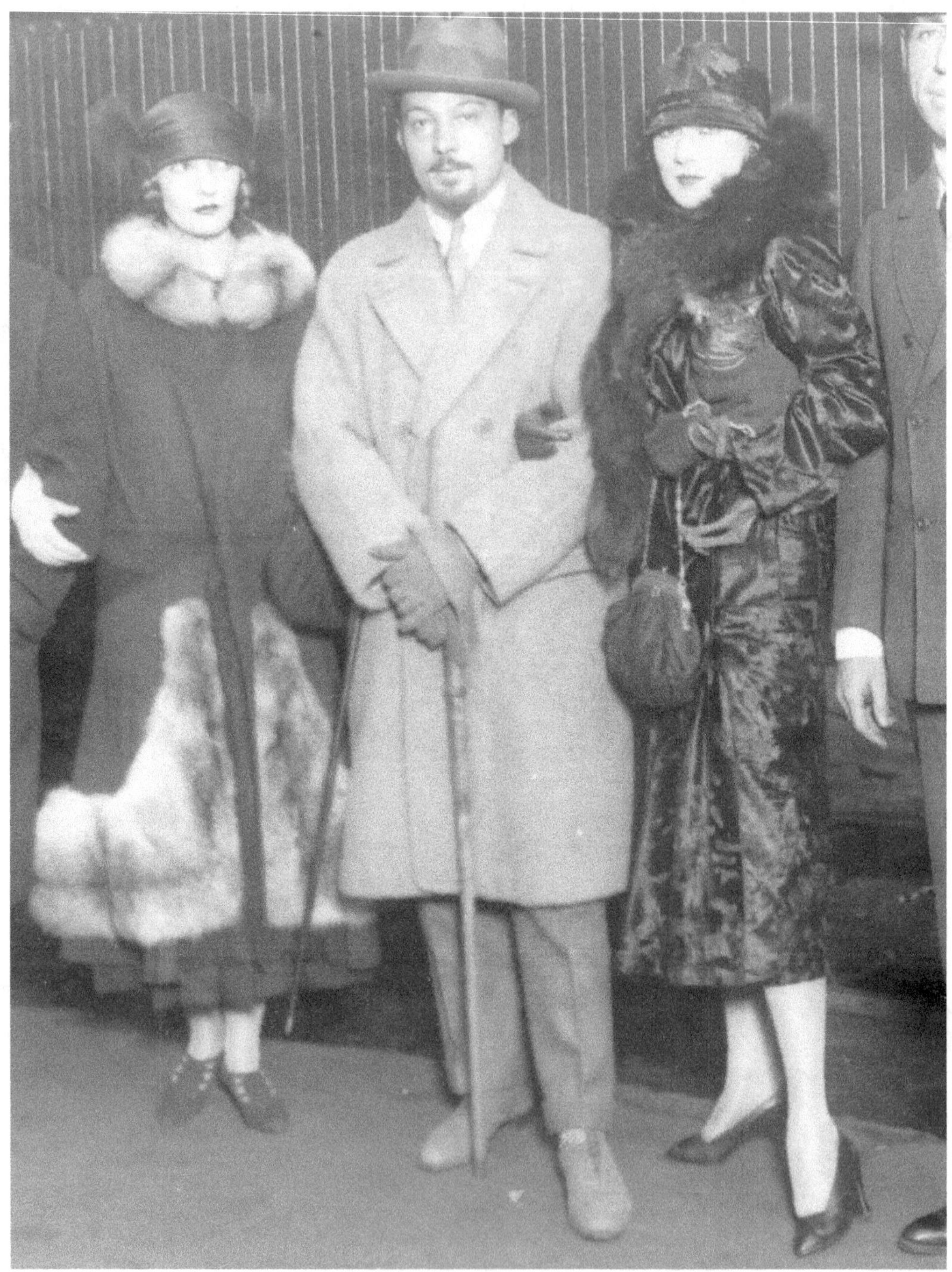

Natacha, Rudy and Nita Naldi posing in Chicago enroute to L.A.
(Author's collection)

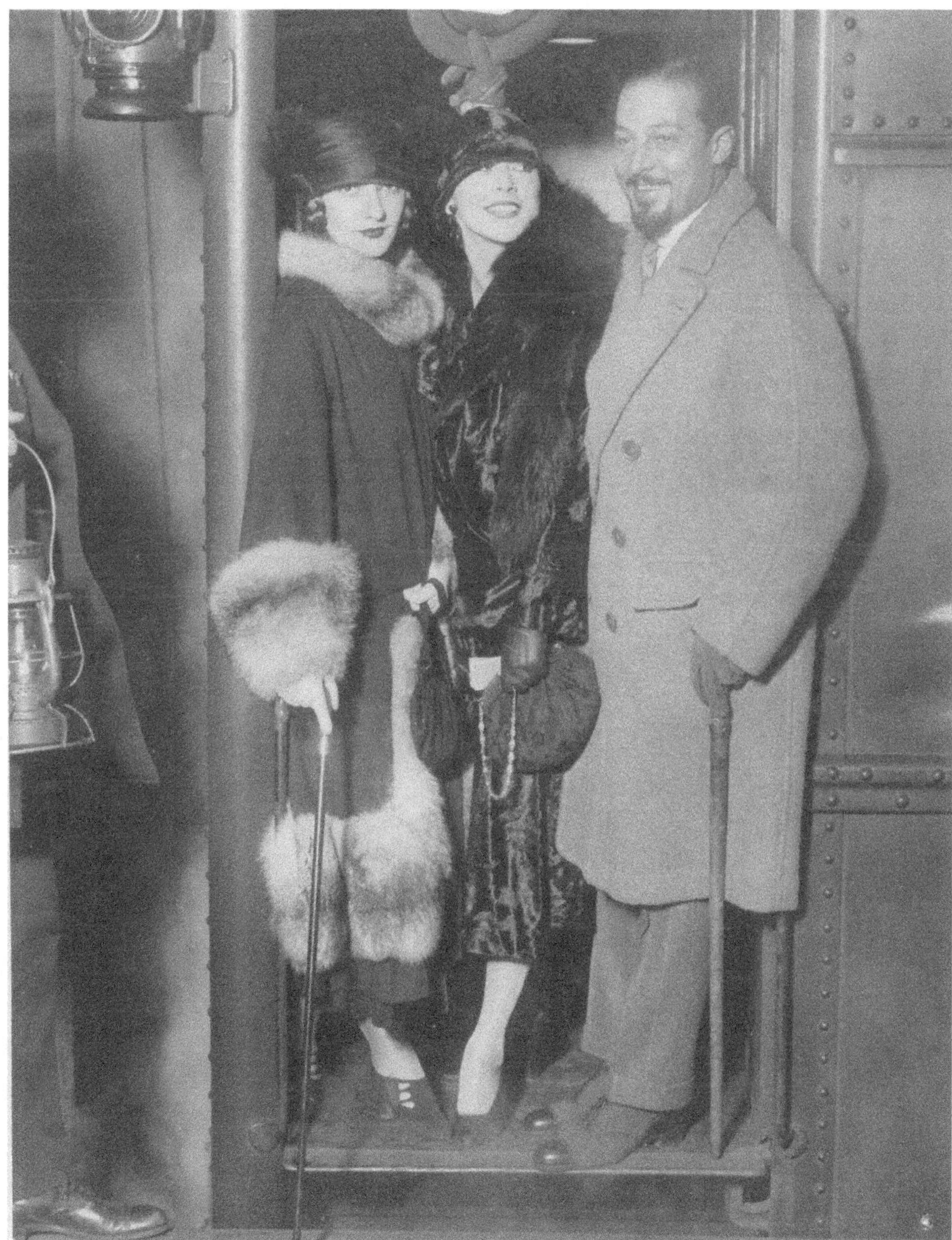

Chicago 1924.
(Author's collection)

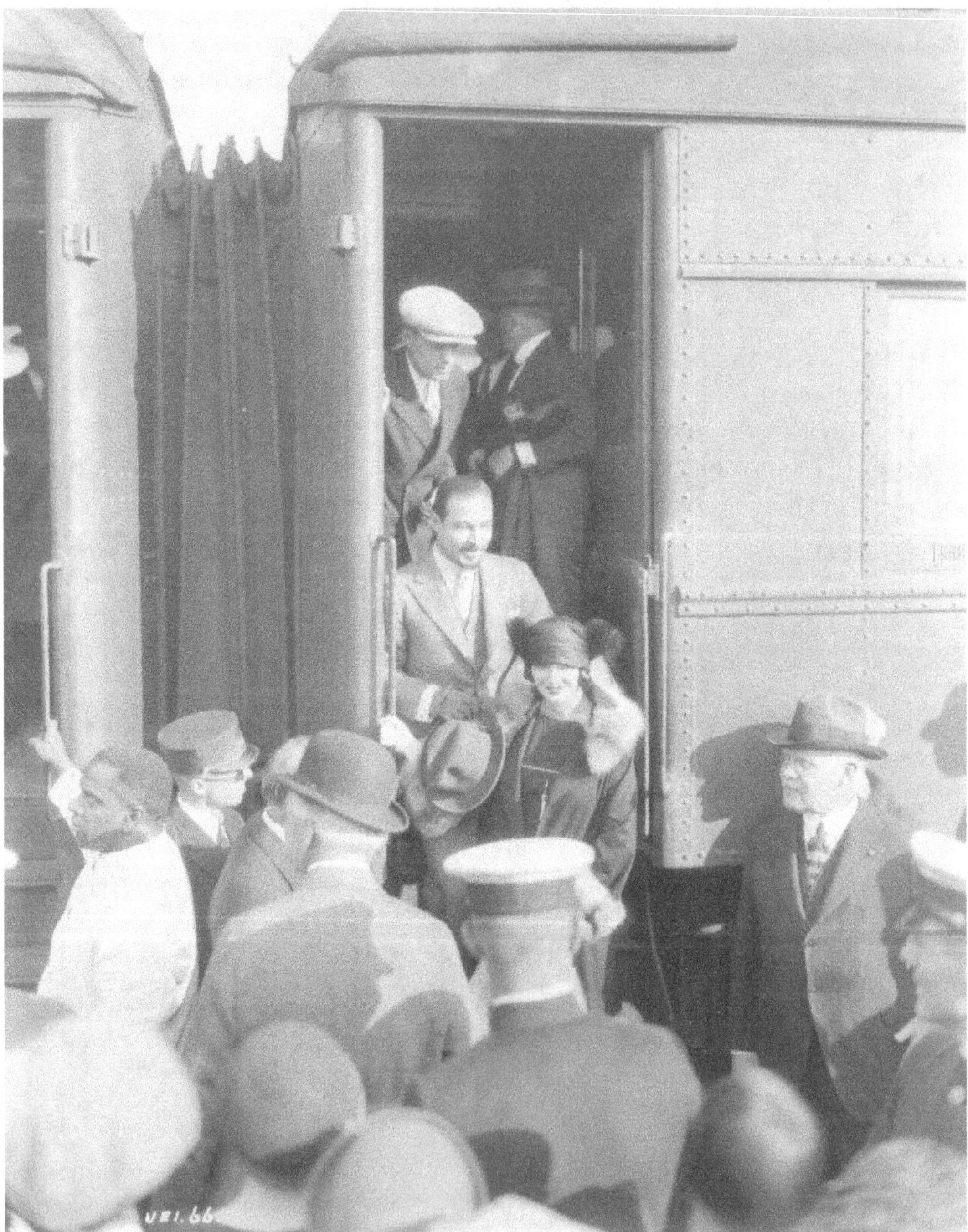

Natacha Rambova and Rudolph Valentino are greeted at the Pasadena Southern Pacific rail station. Acting Mayor Boyle Workman is waiting to greet them (on the right). (Author's collection)

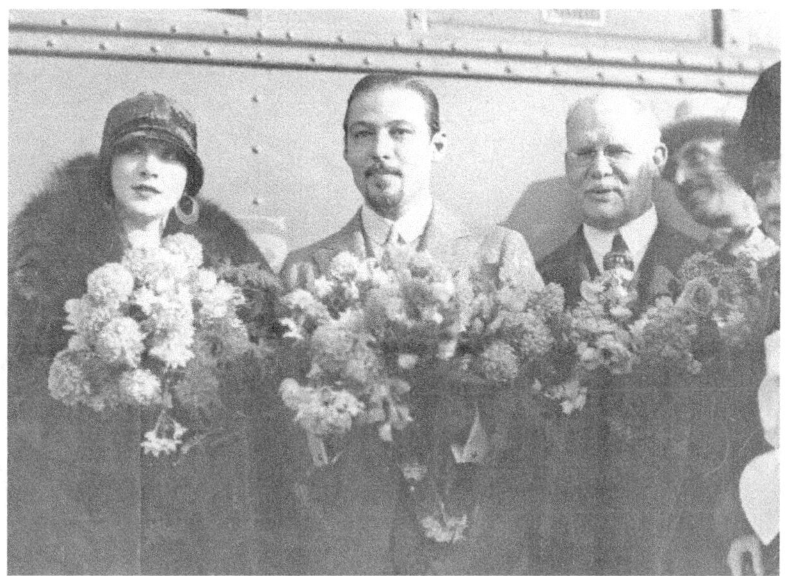

Nita Naldi and Valentino are greeted by acting Mayor Boyle Workman.
(Author's collection)

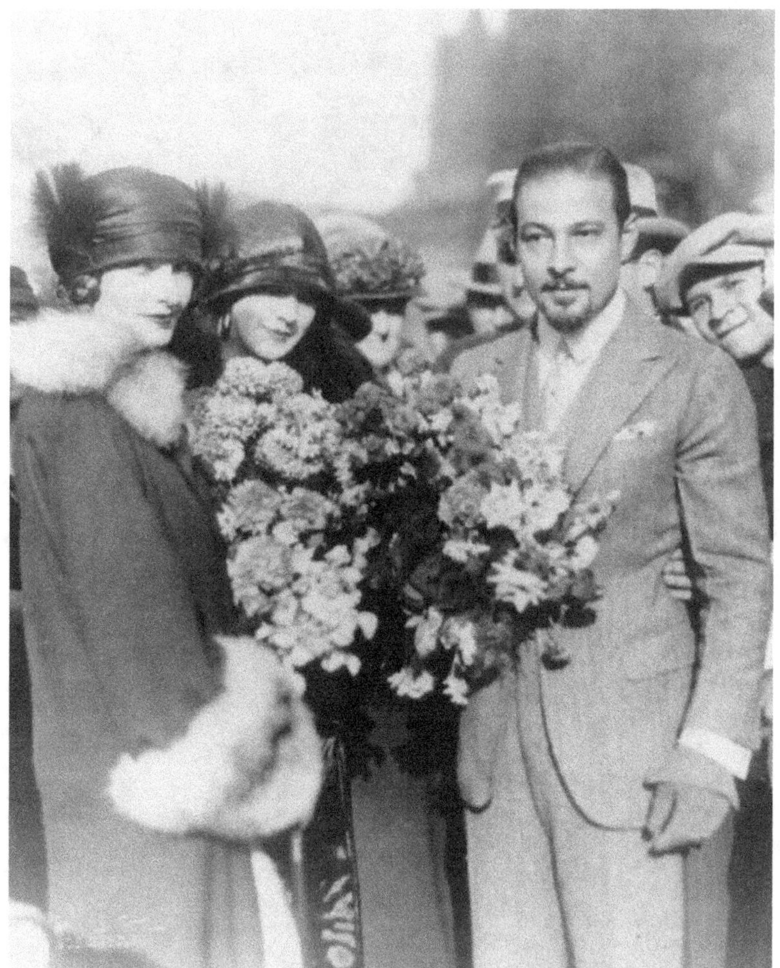

Their arrival in Los Angeles was a press agent's dream.
(Author's collection)

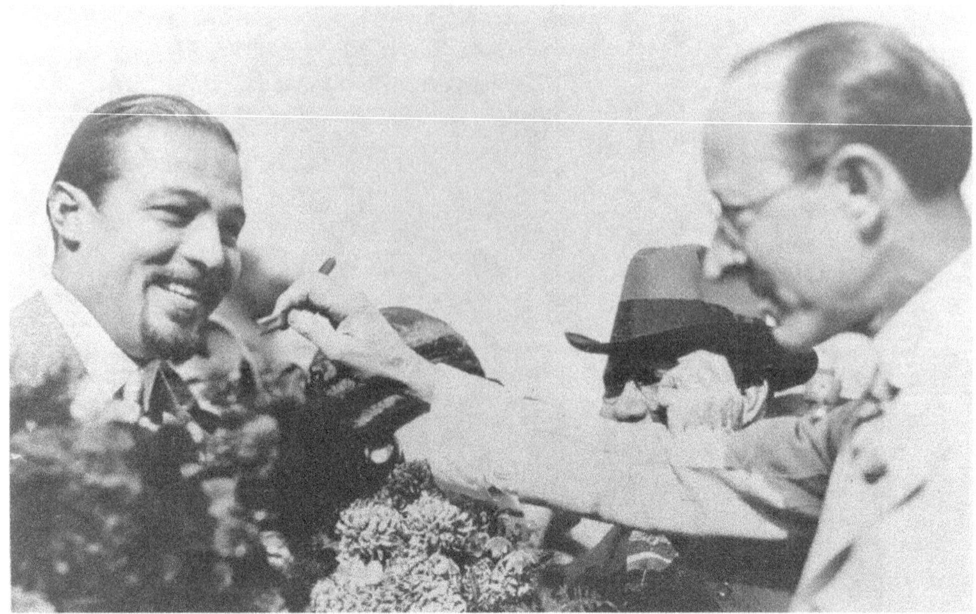

Valentino's publicist arranged for a local barber to meet Valentino with a razor in hand. Mayor Workman and Nita Naldi share in with the laughs. (Author's collection)

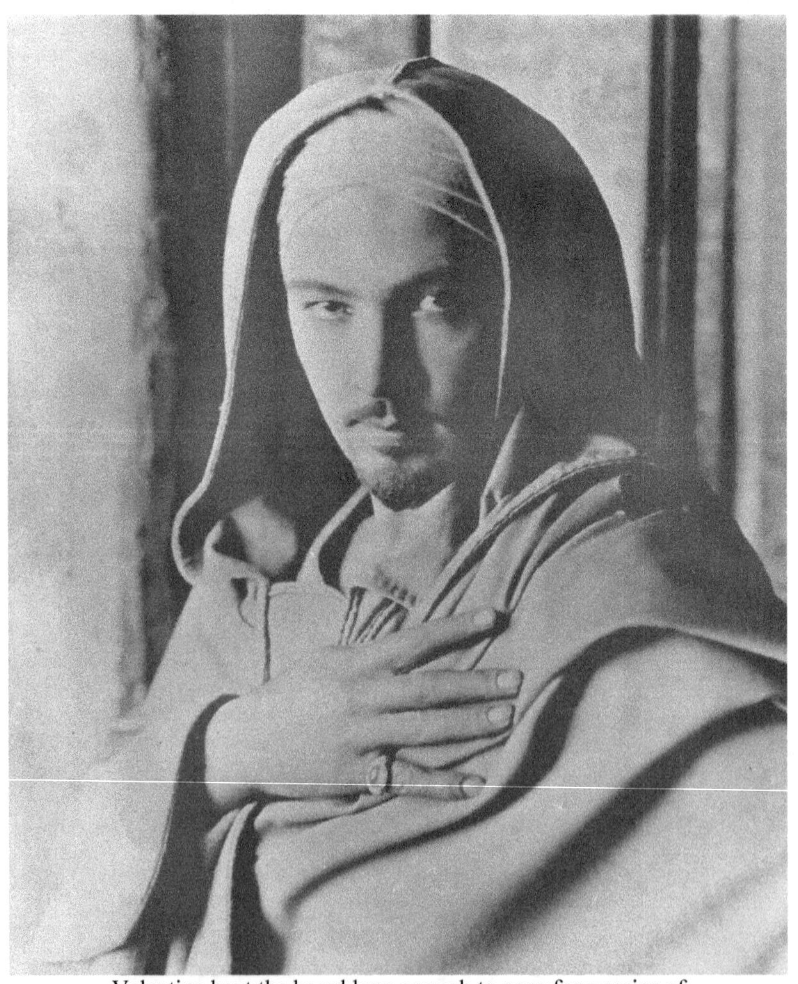

Valentino kept the beard long enough to pose for a series of costume test shots in preparation for *The Hooded Falcon*. (Author's collection)

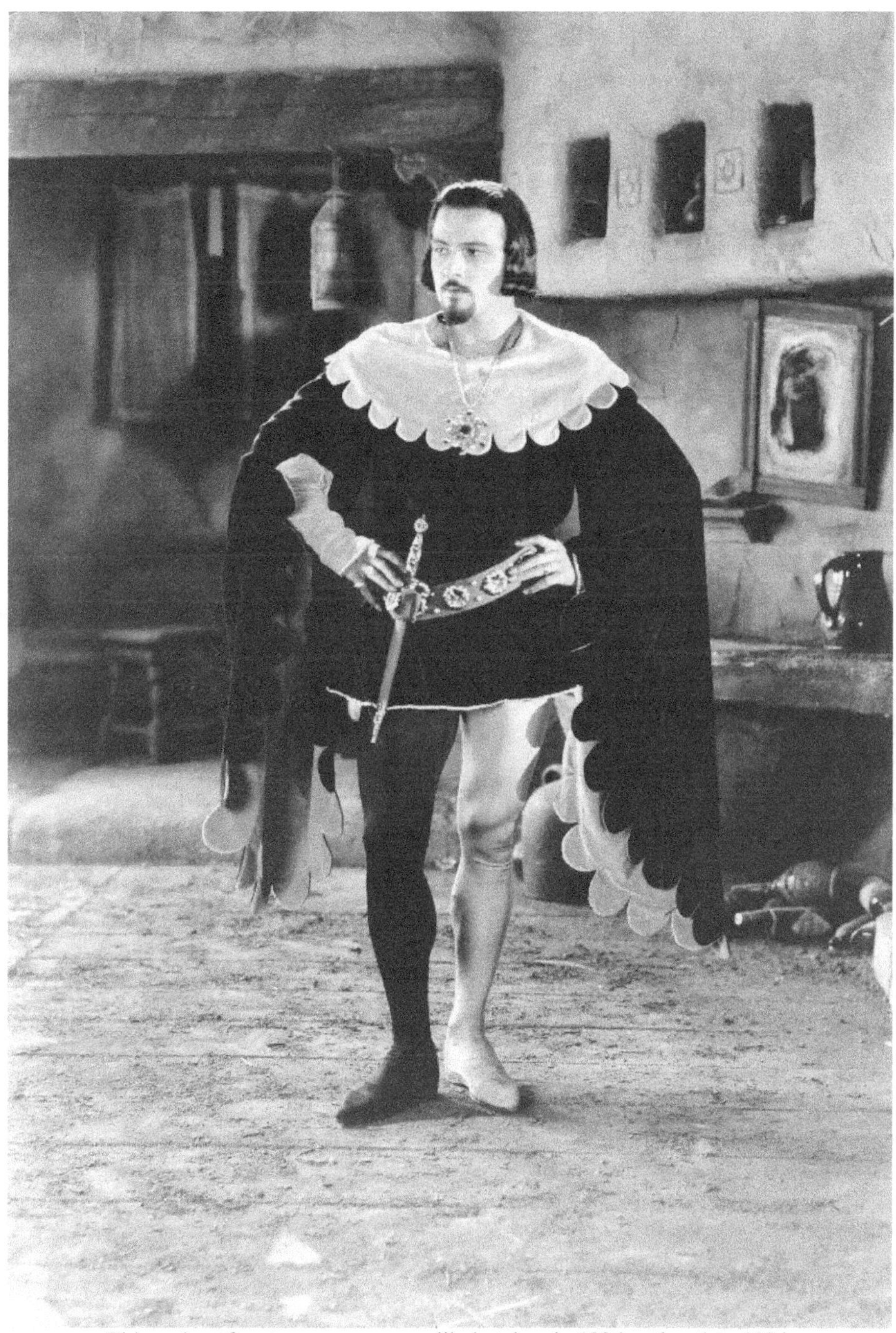

This series of costume poses were likely taken in 1926, rather than 1924.
This is a costume created by Gilbert Adrian.
(Author's collection)

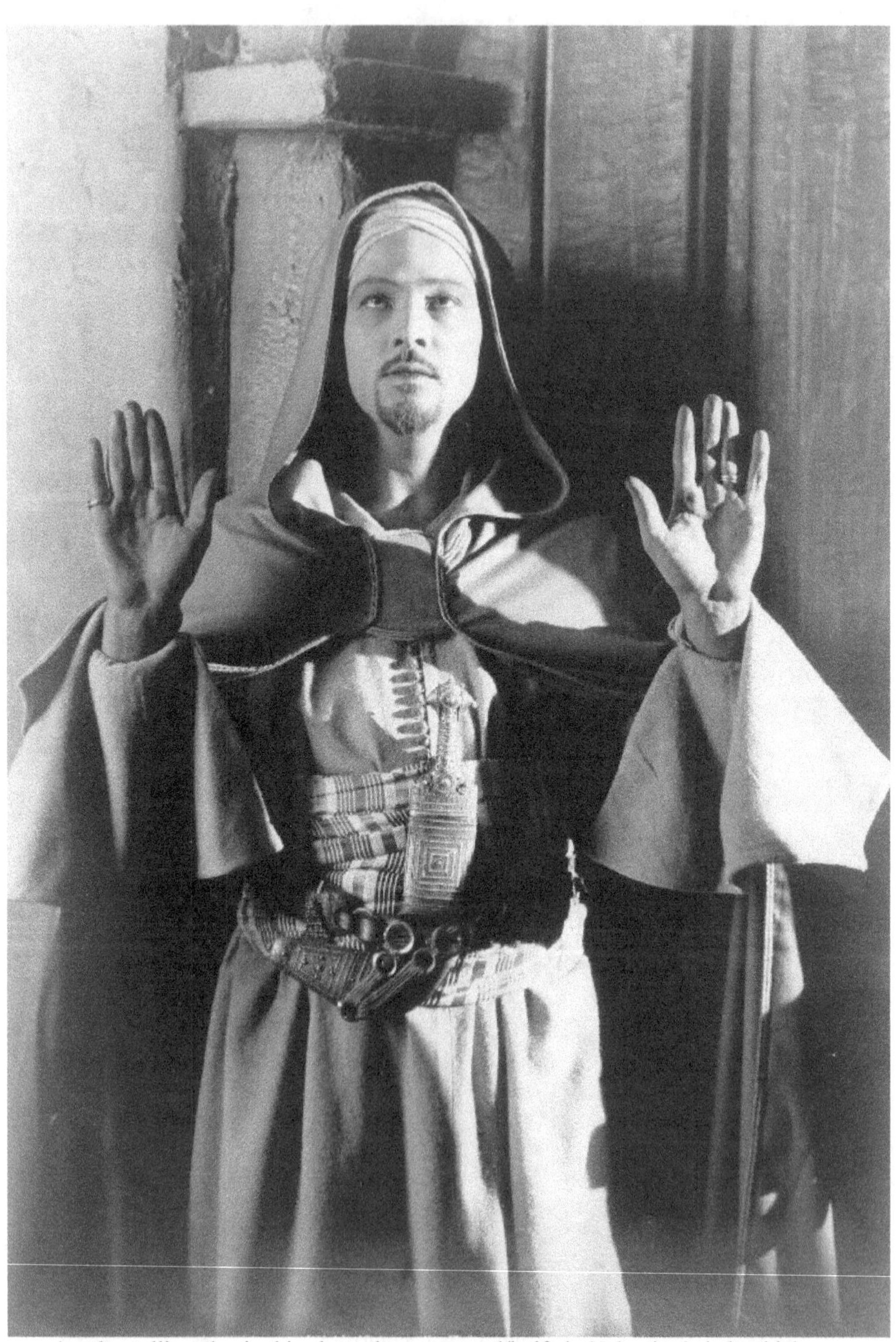

Another telling clue in this photo shows a sword/knife in Valentino's belt which was used in *The Son of the Sheik.*
(Author's collection)

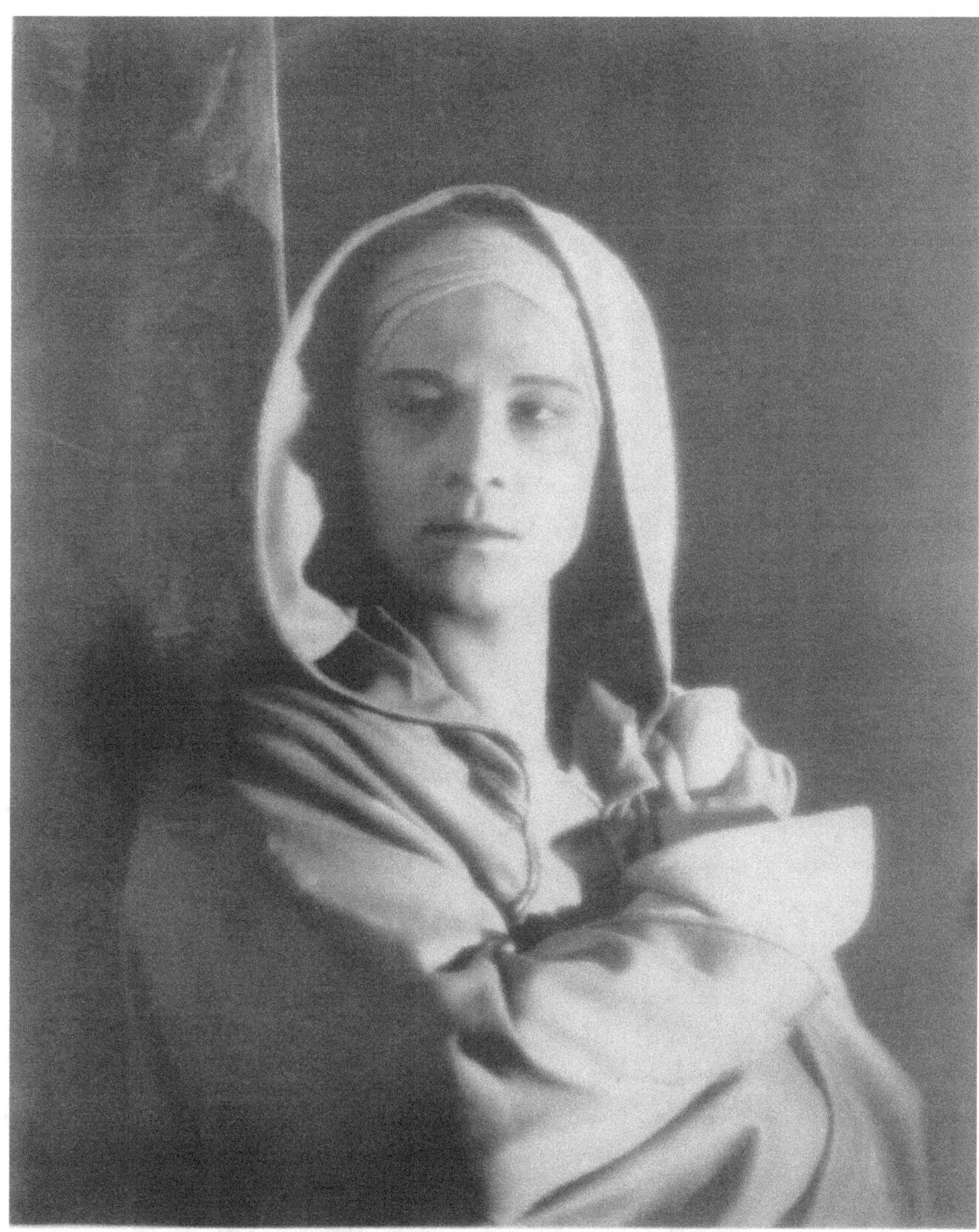

Valentino posed for photographer Nealson Smith in this series of portraits
to test out his look as the moor in *The Hooded Falcon.*
(Author's collection)

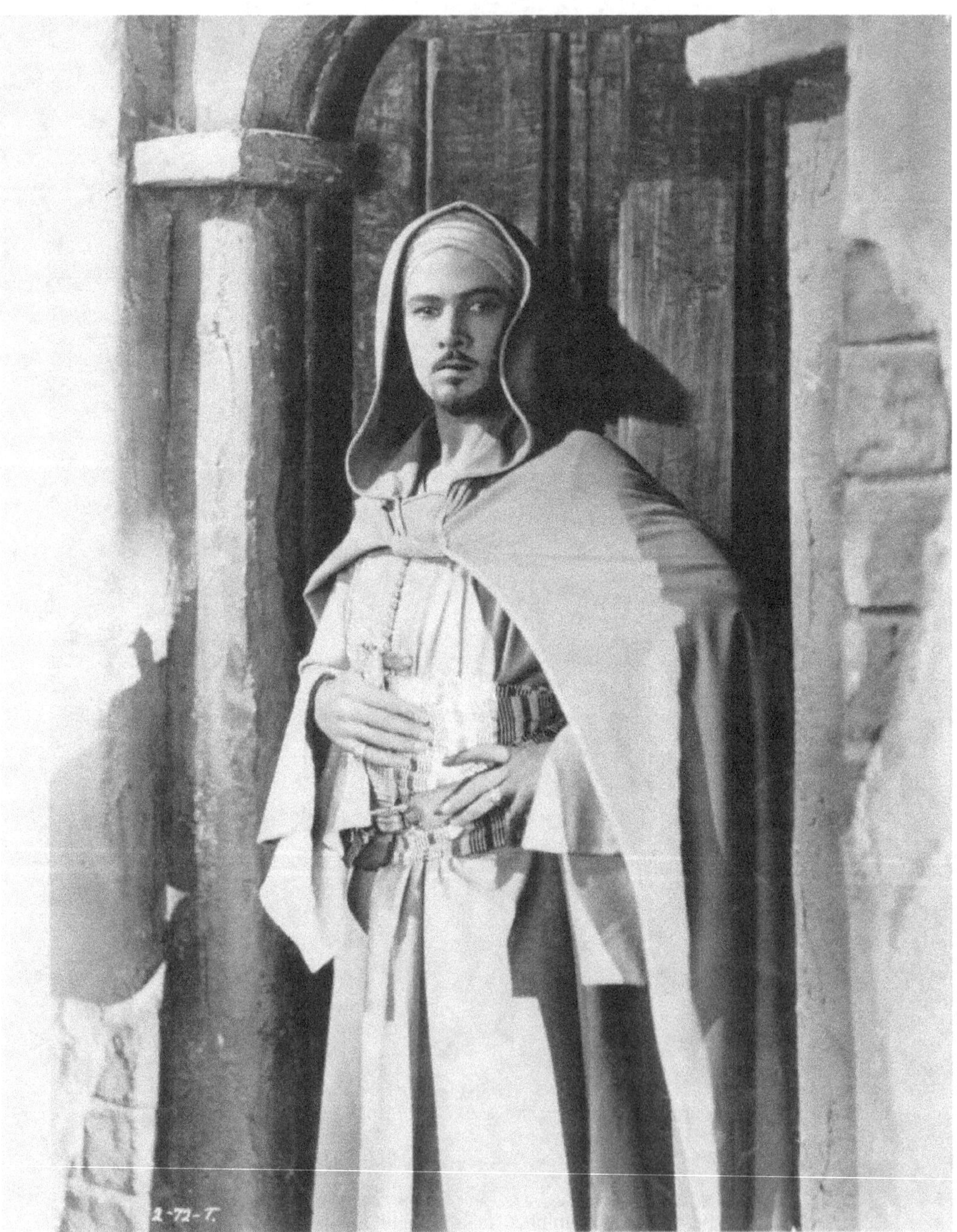

This time with a false beard. The still code in the left corner is a clue this series were taken after Valentino had moved to United Artists. The "T" indicates this is a test.
(Author's collection)

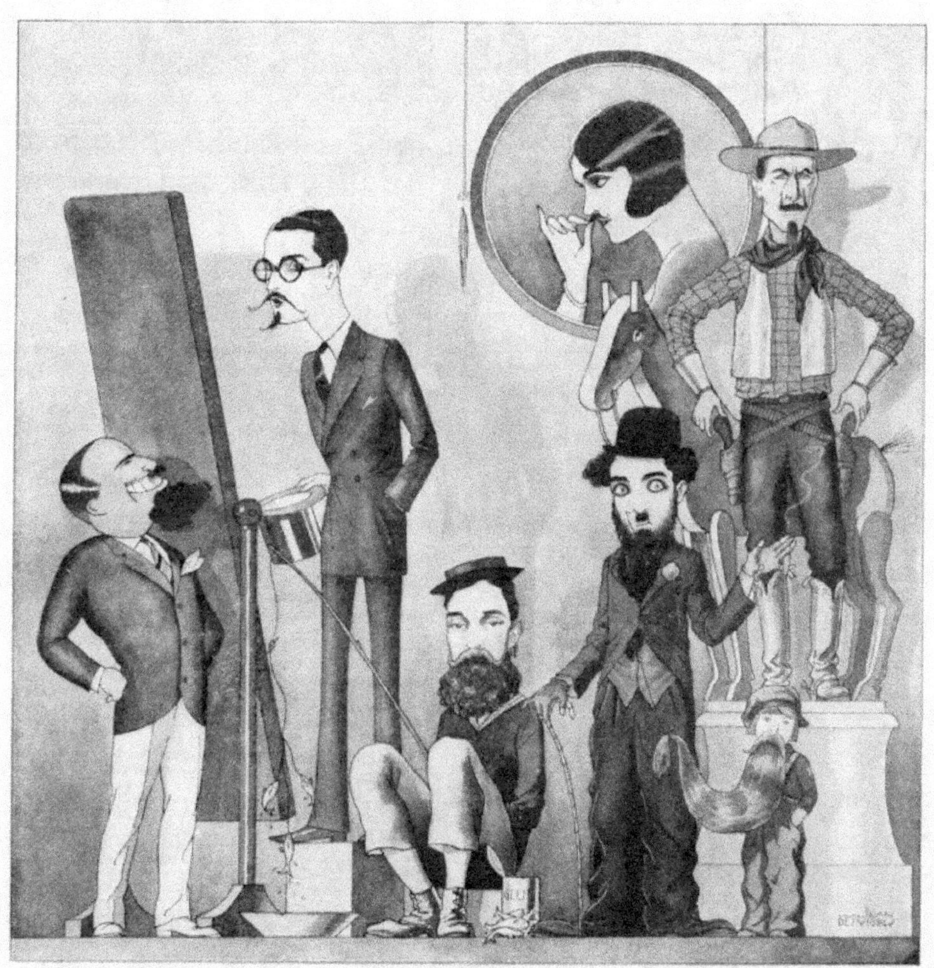

What!!! Valentino???

By Margaret Caroline Wells

I opened once a paper and I tell you what was in.
It was Rudolph Valentino with a beard upon his chin.
My heart stopped off from beating and I fainted dead away.
And I never want to come to life until the judgment day.

If I had seen dear Rudolph with a wart upon his nose,
I wouldn't been a bit surprised, for that's where a big wart grows.
But as an aid to beauty, they make of him a freak
He'd better see a barber and be the same old sheik

For Pete's sake what could make him leave them grow so wild and free?
If that's the style on deserts, or perhaps in gay Paree,
I hope he goes back over and stays across the sea.
We want our Valentino just as he used to be.

The Lord tore up the pattern and threw away the plan,
So we know there never could be just such another man.
Why he went and got himself bewhiskered, I can't tell,
But if he doesn't shave 'em off, we'll all raise —.

72

Photoplay Magazine ribbed Valentino in their February 1925 issue.
Douglas Fairbanks, Harold Lloyd, Buster Keaton, Pola Negri, William S. Hart and Jackie Coogan.
(Author's collection)

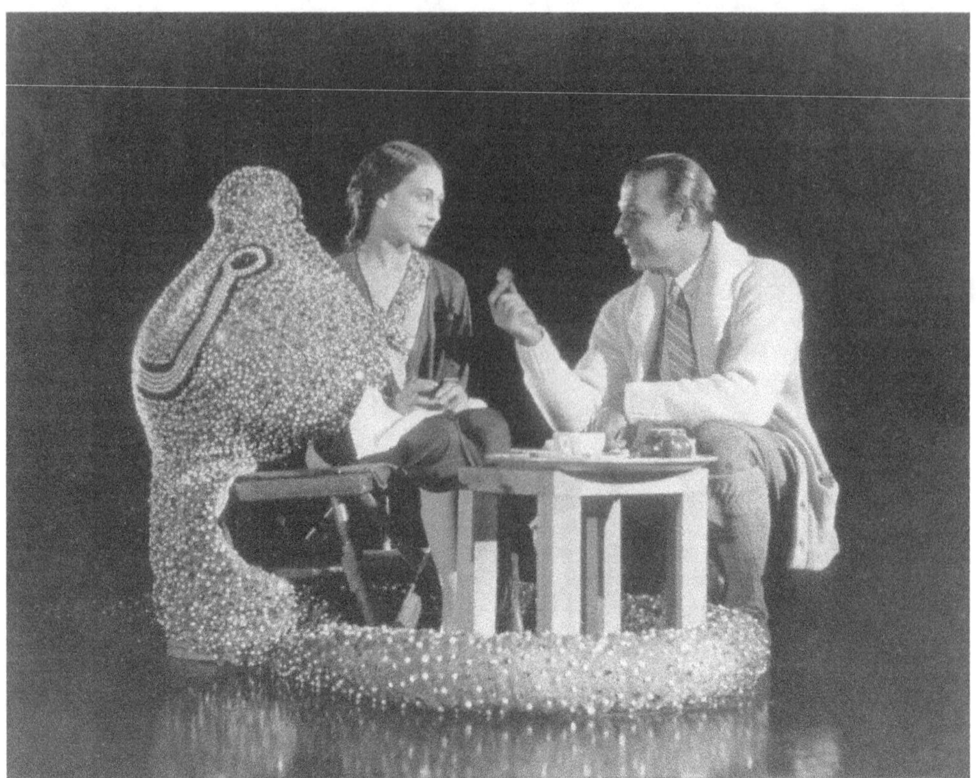

Ever the gentleman, Valentino shares coffee and cookies with the Cobra Dancer.
(Tracy Terhune collection)

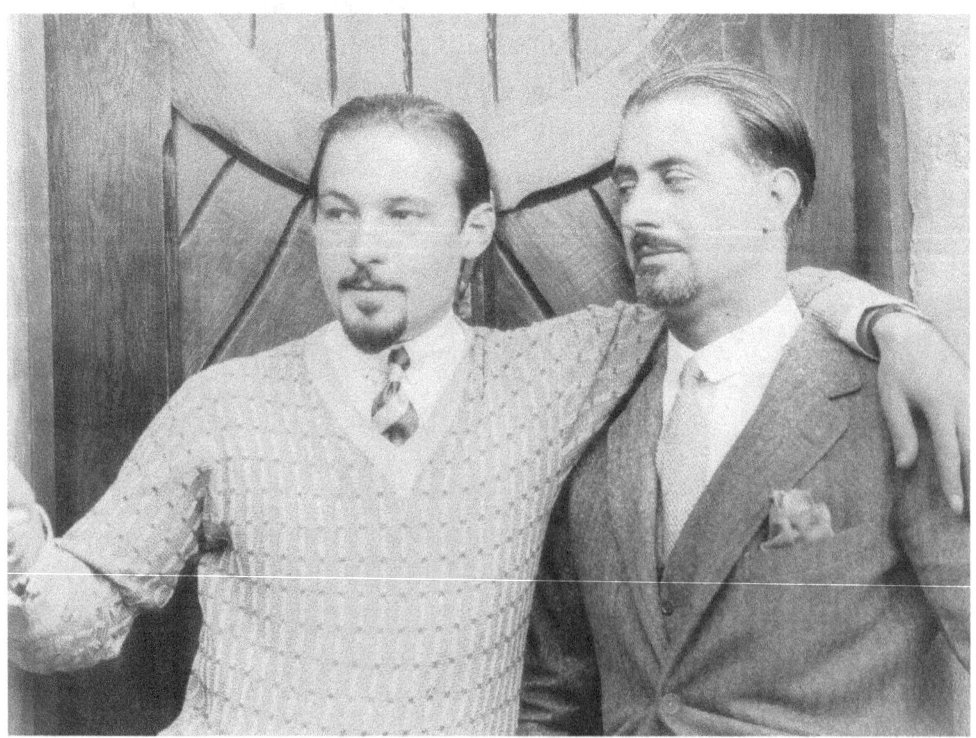

Valentino and his good friend Mario Carillo.
(Michael and Virginia Back collection)

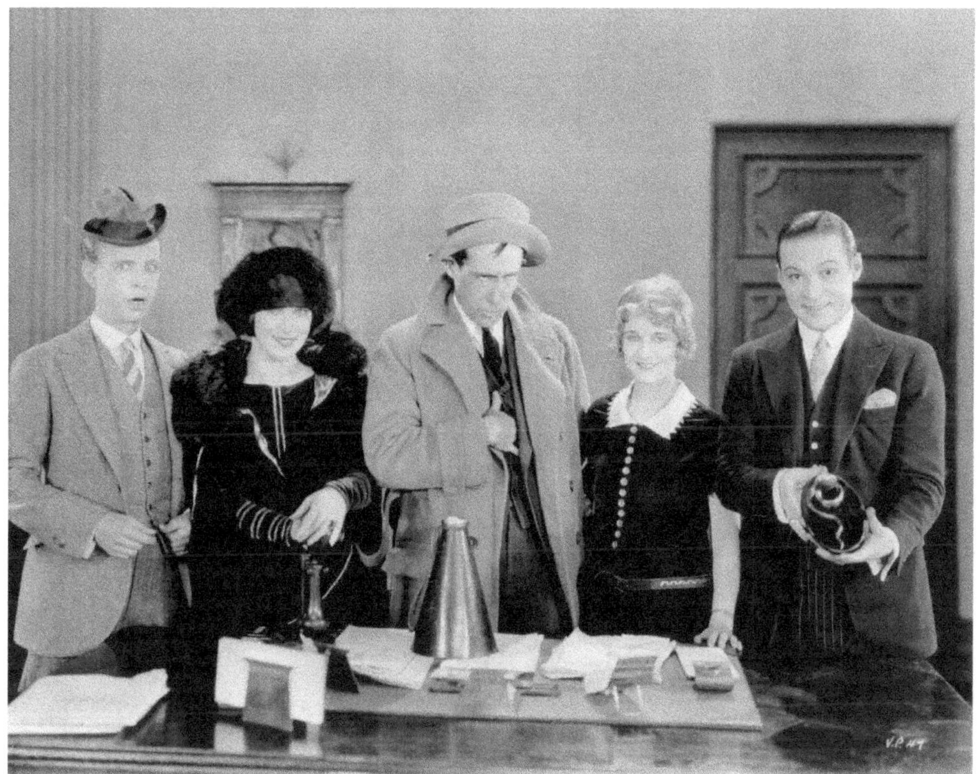

While Valentino was going through some personal turmoil during filming of *Cobra*, it did not prevent him from clowning around with his colleagues. (Author's collection)

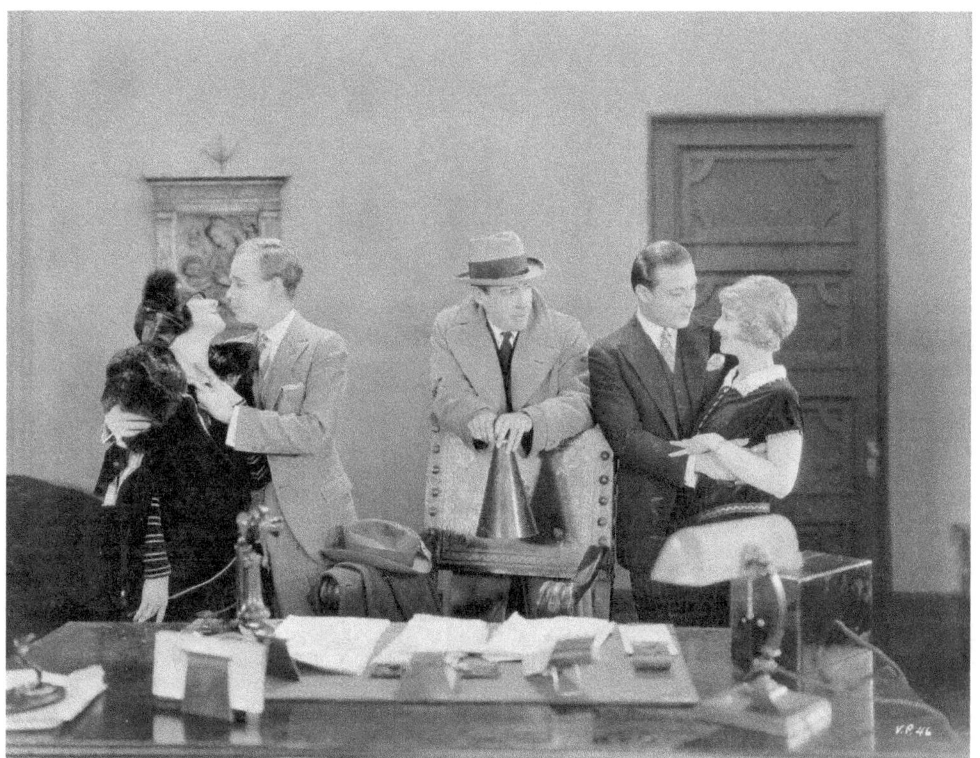

Nita Naldi, Casson Ferguson, director Joseph Henabery, Valentino and Gertrude Olmstead. (Robert Lanier collection)

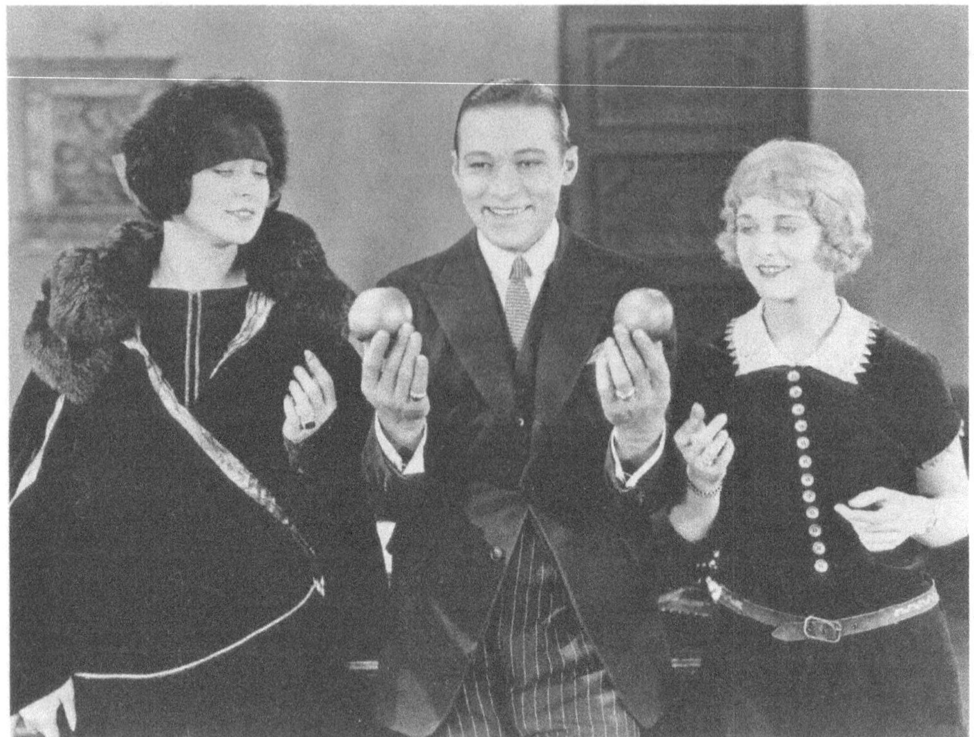

Valentino presents his co-stars with their Golden Apple Awards.
(Author's collection)

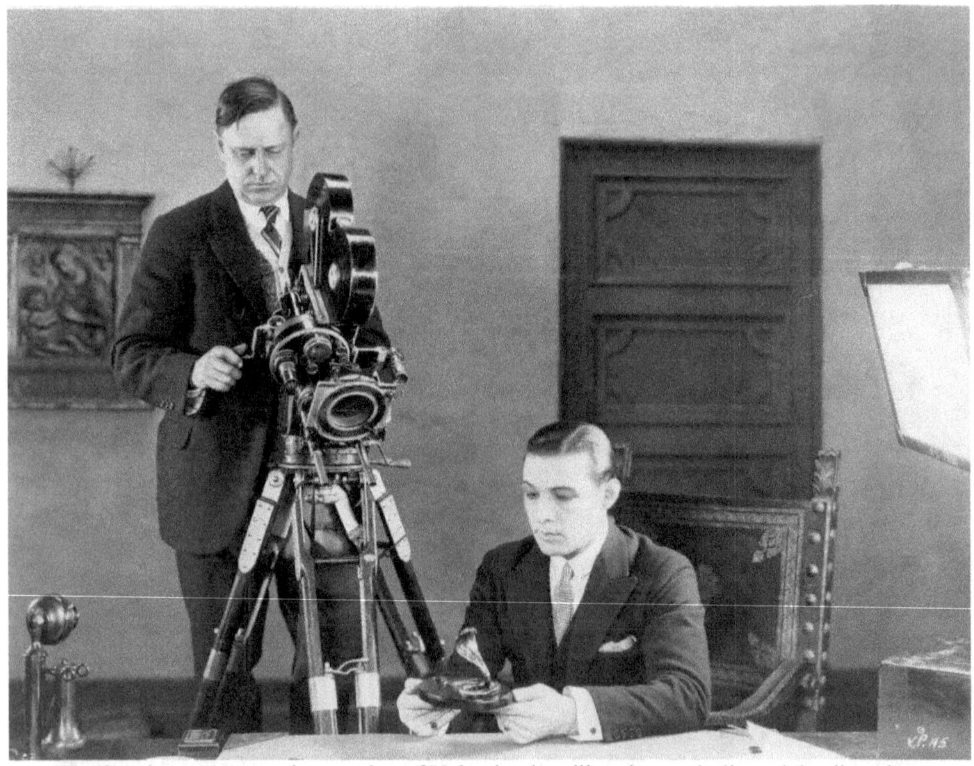

Dev Jennings sets up a closeup shot of Valentino handling the symbolic and deadly cobra.
(Author's collection)

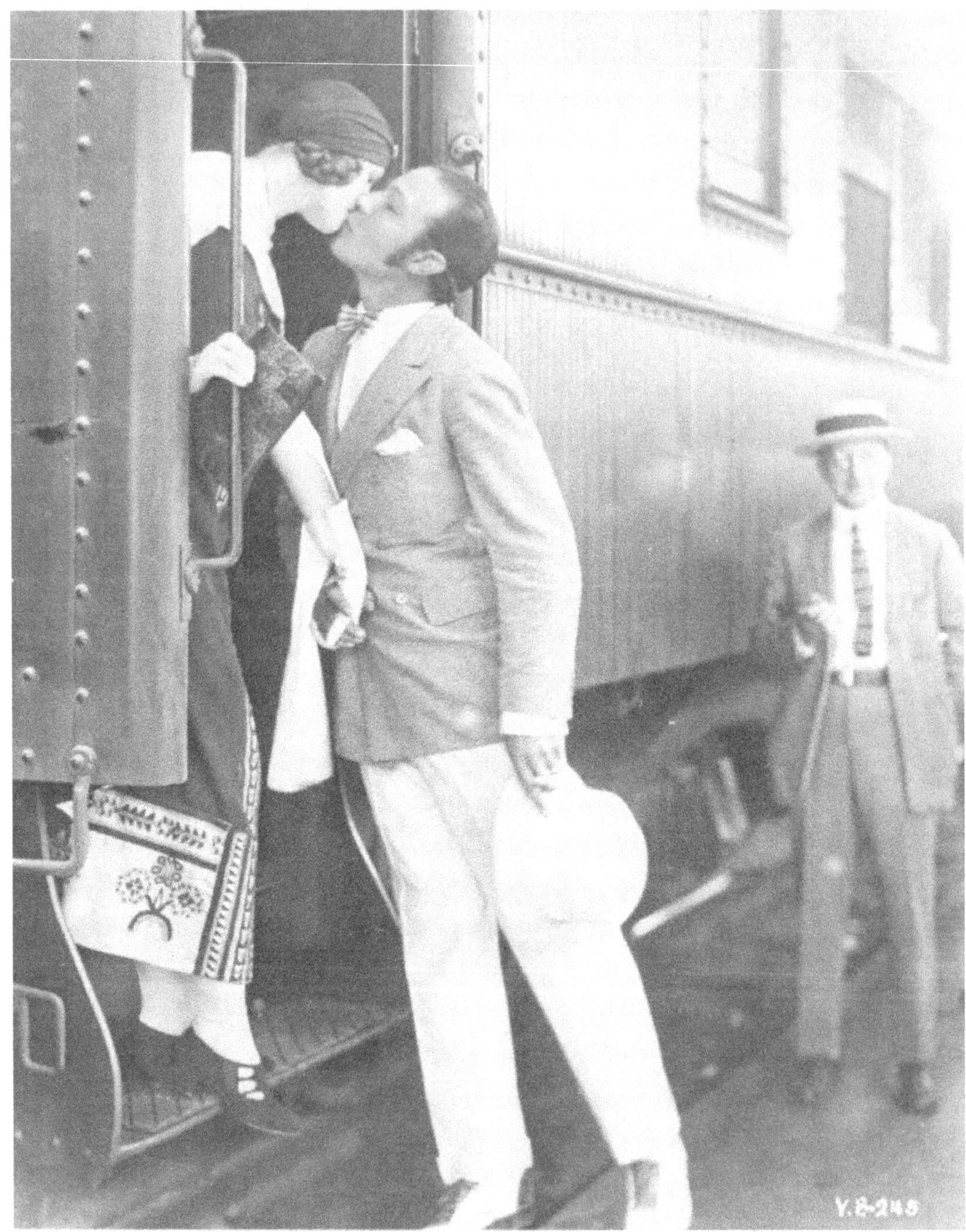

I am sure this marital holiday will be a good thing for us both.

—Natacha Rambova

Natacha was uninterested in *Cobra* and delegated set design for the production to William Cameron Menzies. She focused on problems with *The Hooded Falcon* and on the Whitley Heights house, working with Luther Mahoney. Valentino continued his fitness regime, rising early to train at the studio with a few rounds of boxing, running, fencing, and throwing a medicine ball.

George Ullman was de facto production manager during the filming of *Cobra*. He later claimed he let the reins slip and Natacha took over, but in truth she was largely absent from the production. The shoot was not an entirely happy or comfortable one; Natacha was not present, Valentino was glum, and Joseph Henabery suffered from a lung infection and complained of the freezing soundstages. There were a few pleasures: A flashback sequence allowed Valentino to indulge his love of costume, and Valentino's friend Mario Carillo was given a small part, with the two able to enjoy the occasional morning trail ride when the shooting schedule permitted.

The shoot was visited by several celebrities, including Knute Rockne, composer Rudolph Friml, and famed violinist Mischa Elman. Valentino, as always, obligingly posed for photographs. He also gallantly poured hot coffee for the young actress who portrayed the film's eponymous *Cobra*, clad in little more than a sheath costume and a cobra-like hood on the freezing soundstage.

During the filming of *Cobra*, the Valentinos decided to purchase a new home in exclusive Beverly Hills. They soon found a compact Spanish-style home on eight hillside acres that they christened Falcon Lair, and Luther Mahoney was tasked with getting the house in shape for the new owners. They also took part in Hollywood's social whirl, although Natacha later related that both did so with empty hearts. After *Cobra* completed filming, they retreated to their beloved Palm Springs. Ullman continued to prepare for *The Hooded Falcon*, and Mahoney continued readying Falcon Lair.

Ullman soon called the vacationers with devastating news. J.D. Williams had canceled their contract and dissolved Ritz-Carlton Productions. $150,000 had been frittered away on the as-yet not produced *Hooded Falcon*, and Williams wanted nothing further to do with either of the Valentinos. Natacha immediately left Palm Springs for Hollywood to consult with Ullman, who was negotiating with Joseph Schenck of United Artists. Natacha agreed with Ullman's course of action and returned to Palm Springs. Ullman completed the deal and Valentino was welcomed into the select group of artist-moguls. He would produce his own films under their banner. United Artists hosted a splendid welcome dinner for President Hiram Abrahms at the Ambassador Hotel which the Valentinos attended.

After some indecision, Valentino's first picture for his own production company, Rudolph Valentino Productions, was *The Eagle*, a Douglas Fairbanks style tale of derring-do set in imperial Russia. The film co-starred Hungarian beauty Vilma Banky, and Clarence Brown was set to direct. Lubitsch's frequent collaborator, Hans Kraly, wrote the script, which leavened the physical adventure and romance with comedic flourishes. Valentino and Brown got along famously; Brown was a graduate of Tennessee Tech and Valentino was an inveterate tinkerer, so the two had much to talk about between takes. Valentino took a special shine to Brown's young daughter, Adrienne, as she did to him. The two stars of the film became good friends despite language differences, and the film set was graced with other high-profile visitors, including Douglas Fairbanks, Erich von Stroheim, and Marion Davies.

While filming for *The Eagle* went swimmingly, all was not well on the home front. George Ullman and Luther Mahoney clashed. Tension between Valentino and Natacha grew. Mahoney noted that private detectives were following Natacha at the behest of persons unknown, but he suspected Ullman. Natacha was unhappy and Valentino was suspicious, and it appeared to Mahoney that Ullman was taking every opportunity to drive a wedge between the pair.

The Hooded Falcon was irrevocably off the table with the dissolution of Ritz-Carlton, Natacha began work on her own project, *What Price Beauty?* The film was financed by Valentino and supervised by Ullman. It starred their friend Nita Naldi and featured a small part for a pretty young Venice High School graduate, Myrna Williams—later better known as Myrna Loy.

Natacha felt adrift and it showed in her attitude. She spent her free time at the studio and suddenly made it plain she was no longer interested in moving into Falcon Lair. Relations between the two became increasingly tense, according to Ullman. There were rumors of Natacha having an affair. Her determination not to have children only added to the stress and perhaps caused the ultimate split between the pair.

A particular trial was an exhibition for Federico Beltran Masses held at the Ambassador Hotel. Natacha initially refused to attend; she and Valentino fought until she gave in. They arrived hours late. Valentino was edgy and upset, while Natacha surveyed the ballroom calmly. Problems between the Valentinos aside, the evening was well attended. Federico Beltran Masses, decked out in his medal-encrusted court uniform, acquired a new friend and patron in William Randolph Hearst, who commissioned the painter to capture Marion Davies on canvas.

The Eagle was still in production and the problems between the two became public. They announced a separation to the press, and Natacha boarded a train to the East Coast, accompanied by George Ullman and Teresa Werner. Newsreel cameras were at the train station to capture what would be their final kiss. Although Valentino played for the camera, he was heartbroken. He threw himself into his physically demanding role, performing most of his own stunts, even spraining a wrist during a horseback sequence.

After Natacha's departure, the two immediately began sniping at each other in the press, with the arguments becoming increasingly bitter and accusatory. Valentino retreated to the companionship of his friends and squired Vilma Banky to the premiere of her film, *The Dark Angel*. When Falcon Lair was ready for habitation, Valentino moved in alone. His unhappiness manifested itself in increased recklessness on horseback and behind the wheel of his car. He was stopped for speeding and had several accidents, after which he dutifully paid his traffic fines and went on his not-so-merry way. He took some delight in decorating his new home as a man's castle, with antique armor and firearms. That he chose to retain Natacha's art deco designed bedroom set shows he was not quite over her. That said, he did not always occupy it alone after their parting and final divorce decree.

The Eagle completed and in release, he set out on a press junket to promote the film. His first stop was the premiere in New York City in early November. His date for the evening was journalist Beulah Livingstone, whom he took to dinner afterward at his favorite Italian eatery, Villa Penza. Natacha was also in New York but they did not meet, although Valentino did pay a visit to Mrs. Hudnut. Convinced that the relationship was irreparably broken, the two decided to end the marriage. In mid-November, he and his friend, Manuel Reachi, sailed for Southampton on the Leviathan to establish residence in Paris for a divorce.

The crossing was uneventful, although Reachi later related that Valentino pined for Natacha and spoke of little else. They attended the London premiere of *The Eagle* at the Marble Arch Pavilion, where some of the besieging fans were willing to offer £5 (£200 today) for seats. Valentino had to escape through the back entrance of the theatre, using the fire escape, while thousands of fans brought Oxford Street to a standstill. While in London he stayed at George Arliss's house in Westbourne Grove, which would one day become the headquarters of the Valentino Memorial Guild.

Valentino being Valentino, he stayed in London just long enough to order a fashionable new wardrobe. In early December he and Reachi traveled to Paris, checking in at the upscale Plaza Athénée and making the rounds of nightclubs and parties. Valentino's old friend Mae Murray also made an appearance. It is rumored that she and Valentino had a brief affair while in Paris, although she always denied it. Valentino and Reachi next went to Berlin and met director F.W. Murnau at the UFA studio complex.

He returned to London in time for the holiday and met brother Alberto, sister Maria, and Alberto's family. The family celebrated Christmas together for the first time since they were children.

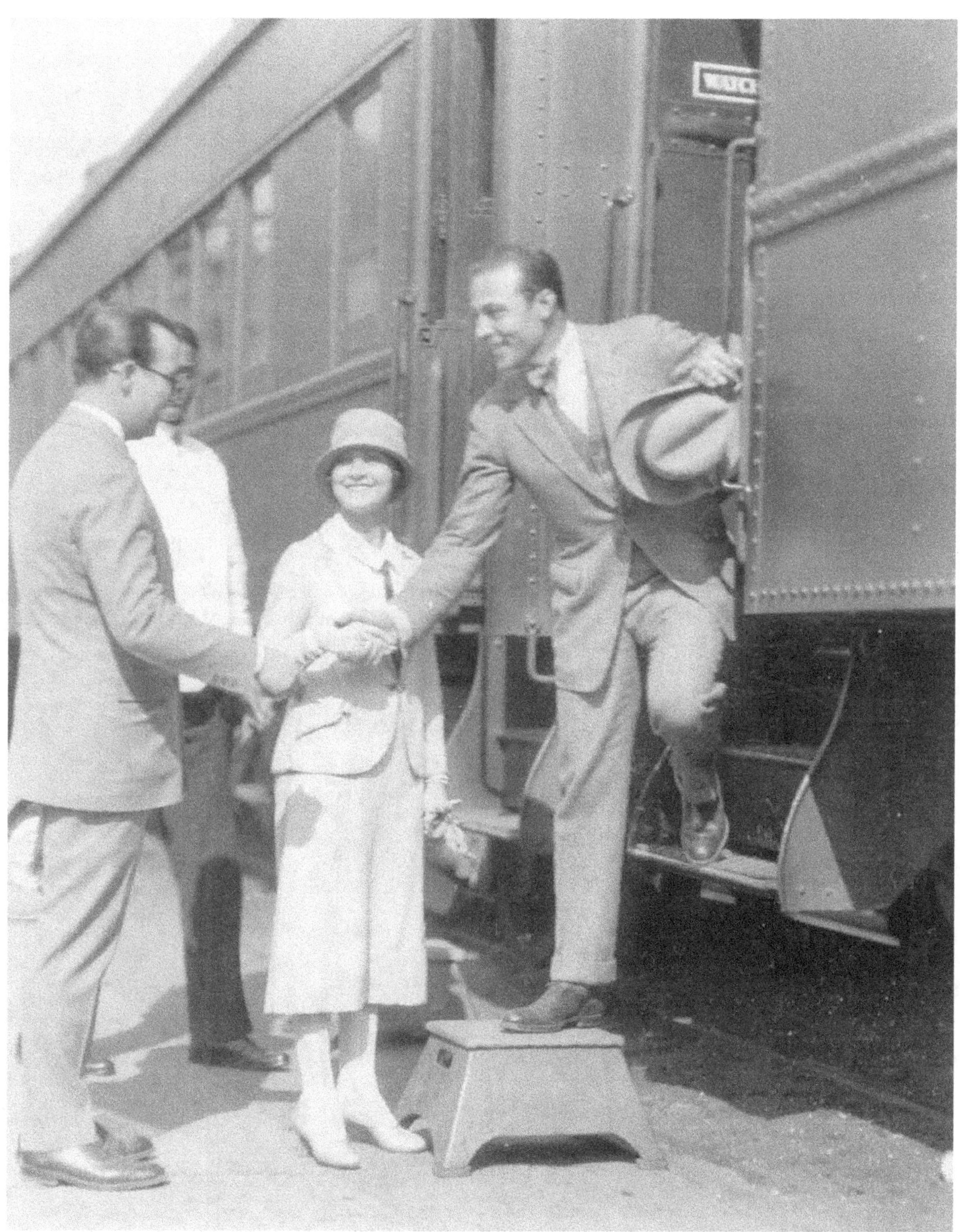

Valentino is welcomed home by Mr. and Mrs. S. George Ullman.
(Author's collection)

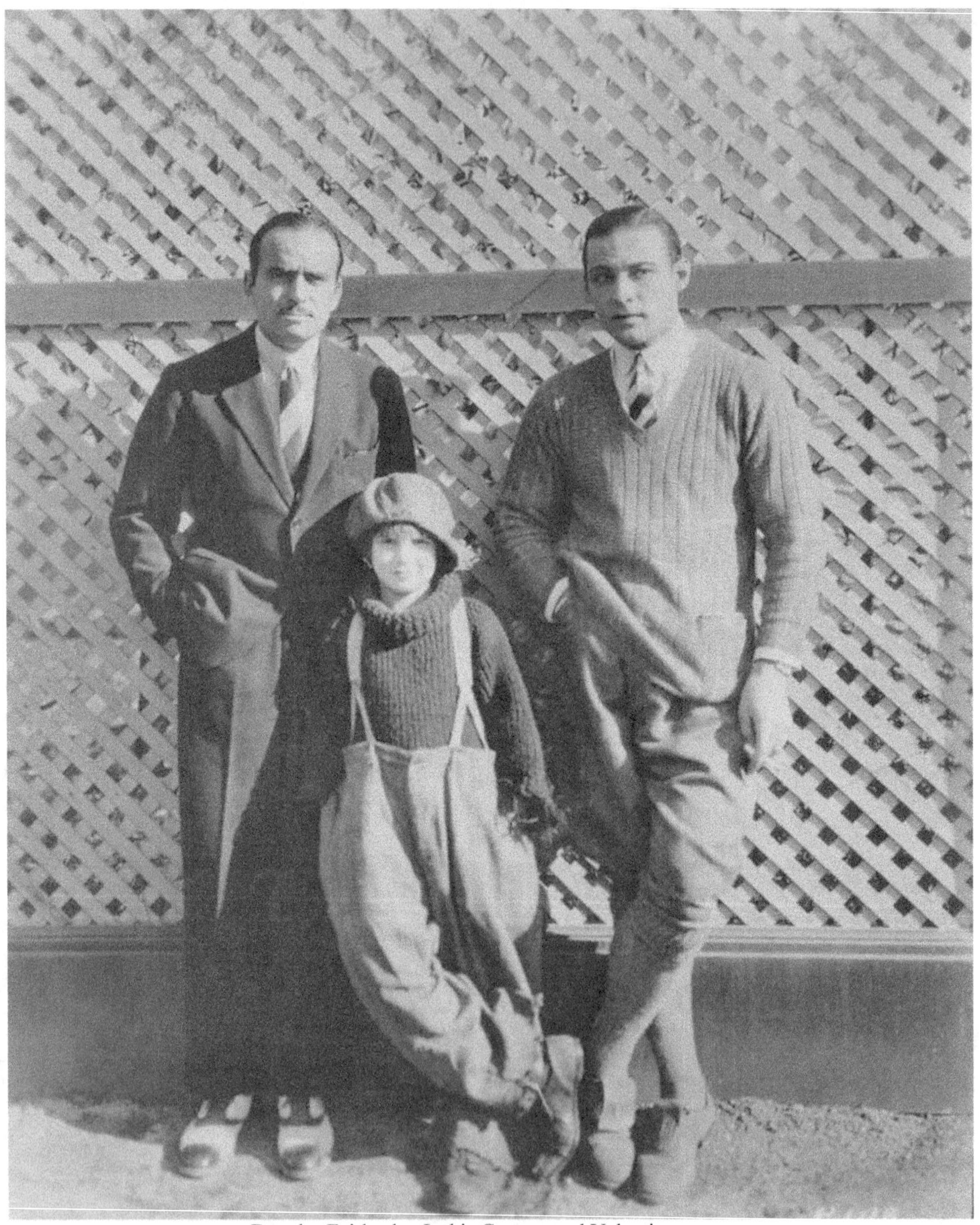

Douglas Fairbanks, Jackie Coogan and Valentino
posing for a candid publicity photo at the United Artists studio in 1925.
(Author's collection)

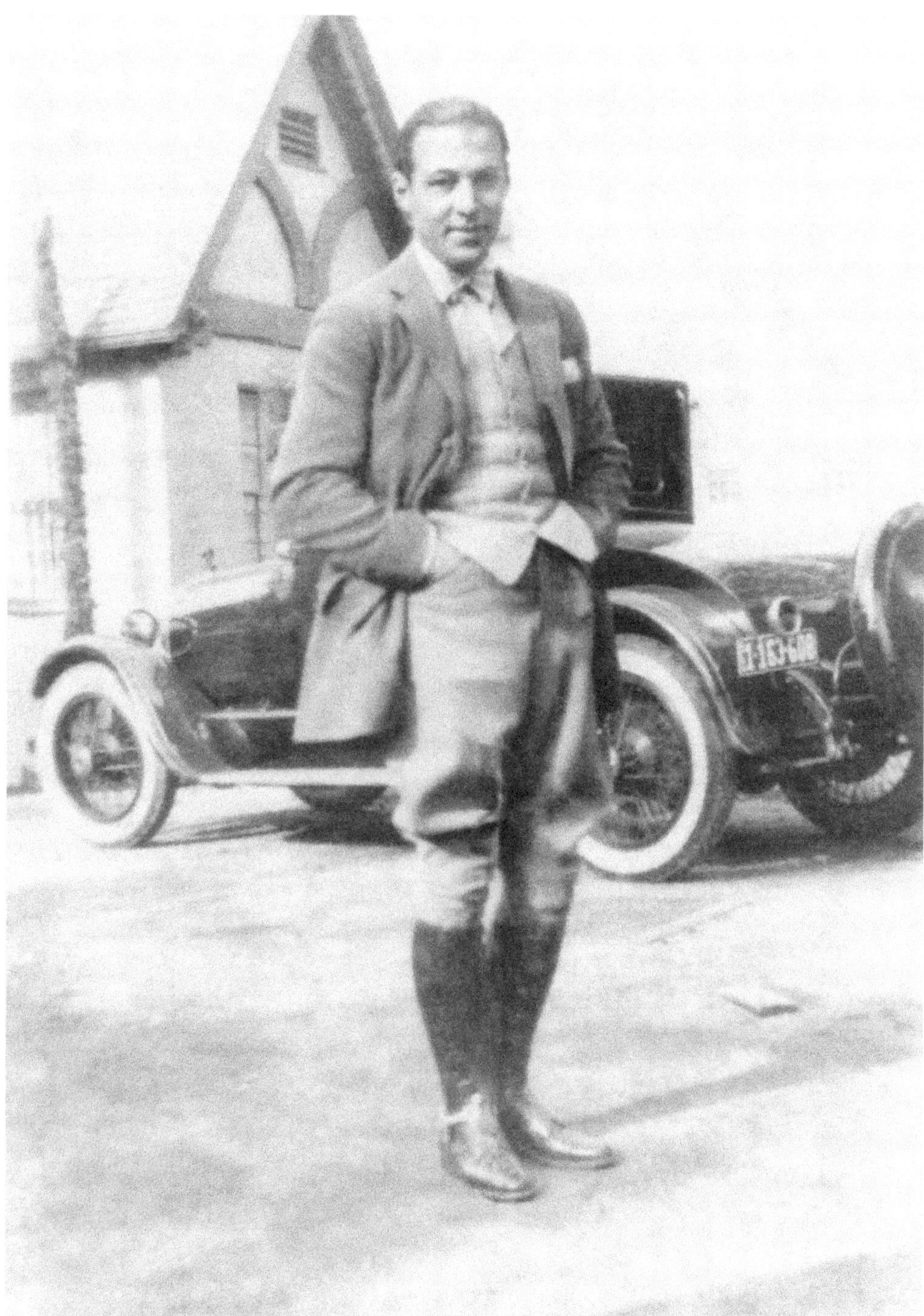

Posing for a snapshot outside his private studio bungalow with his Franklin Coupe.
(Author's collection)

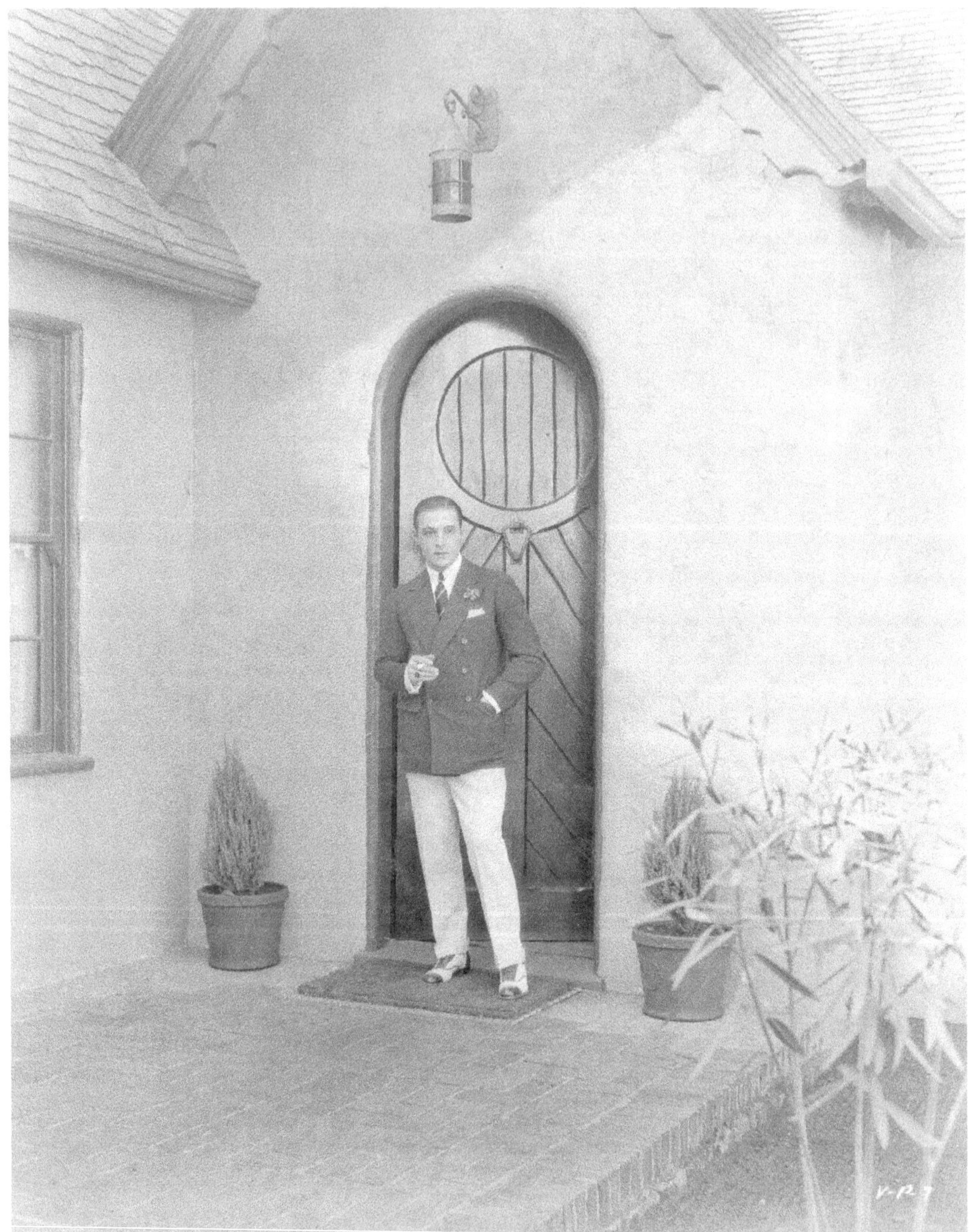

A natty Valentino posing in front of his bungalow.
(Author's collection)

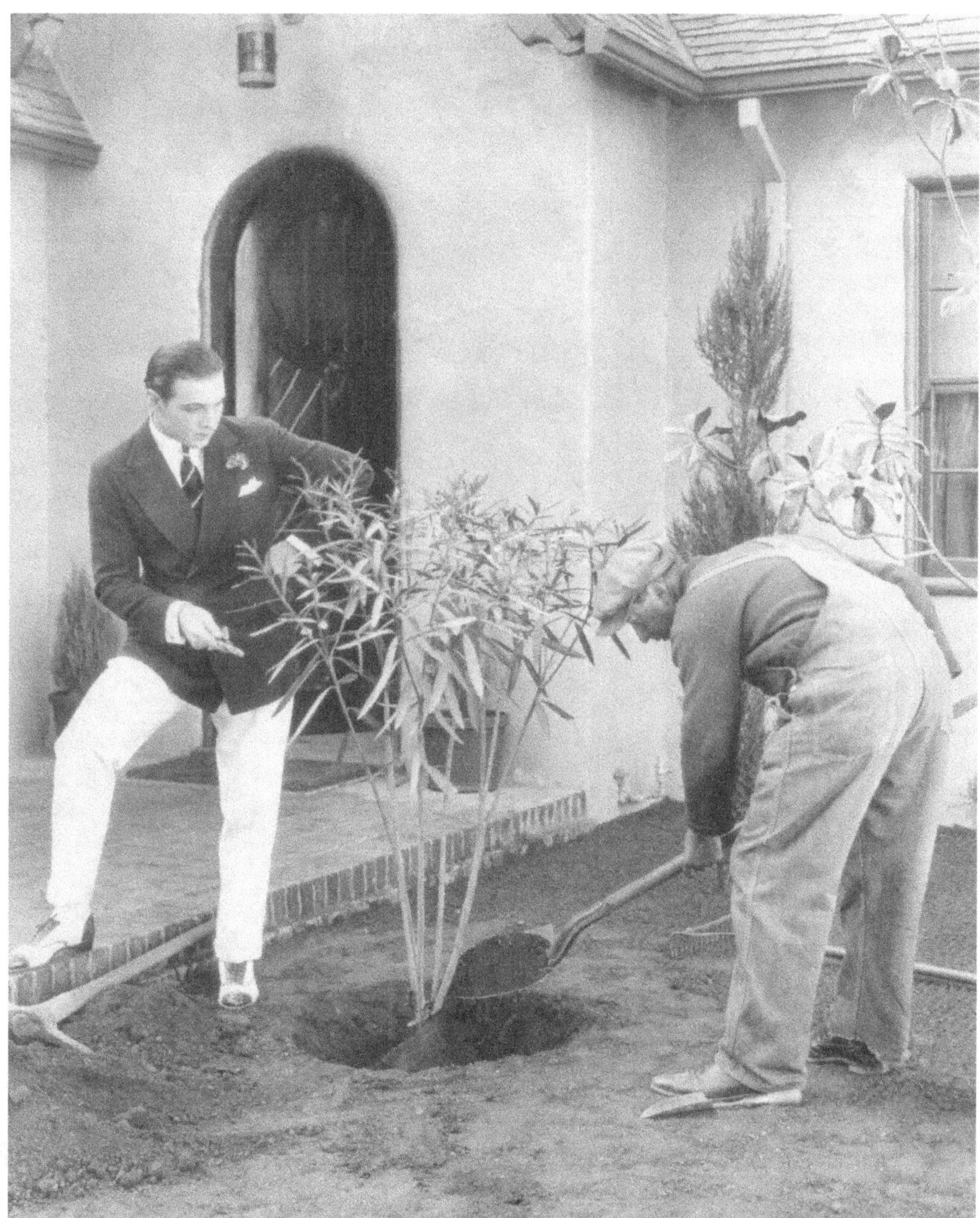

Valentino taking care not to get his hands dirty.
(Author's collection)

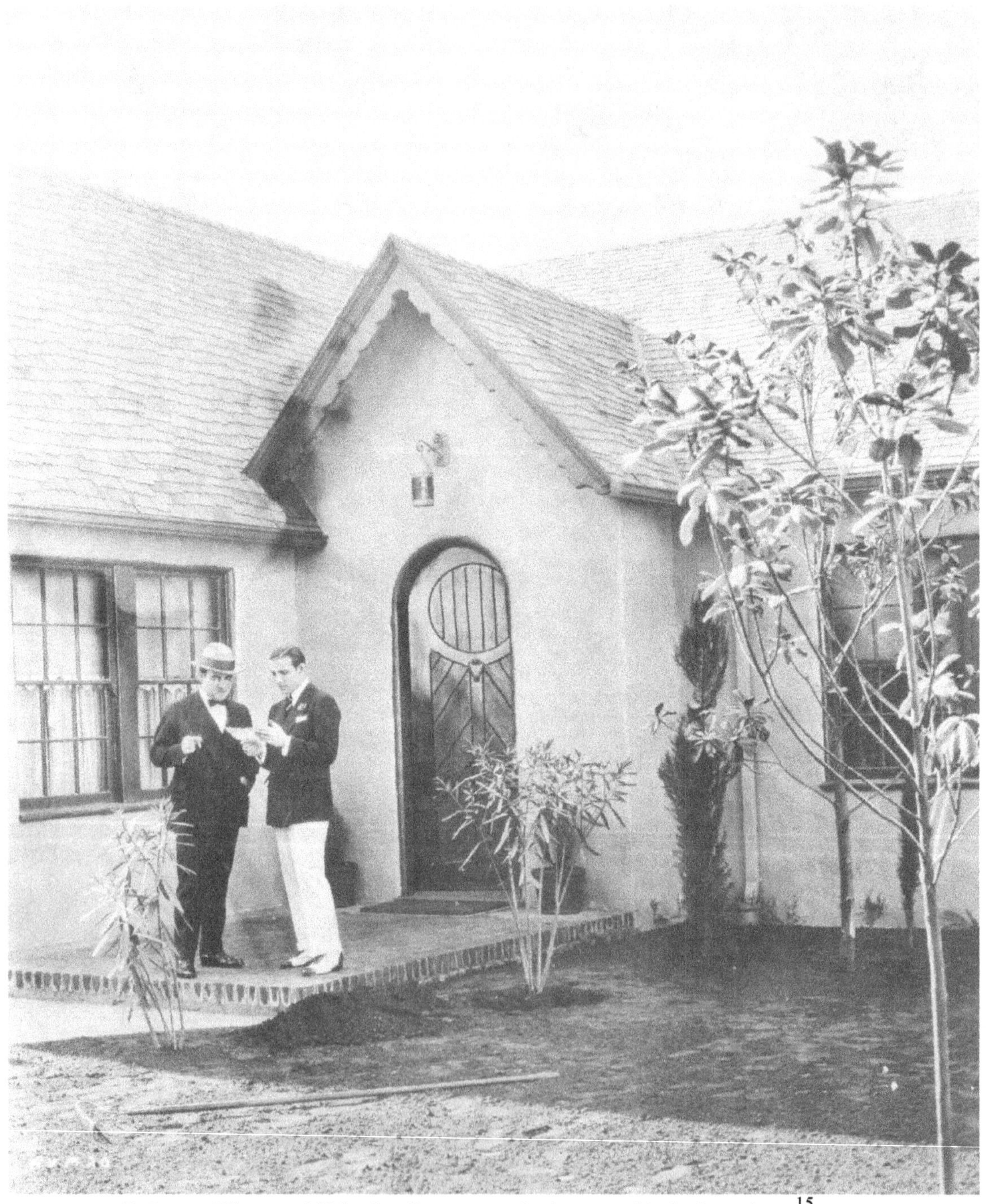

S. George Ullman and Valentino discuss some business outside the bungalow. [15]

[15] The rake in the foreground indicates this was just after Valentino planted the tree just to his left. This was part of a series of photographs taken as publicity and used in the book *Reforesters of America* by Mabel L. Mills (1925). Many stars like Mary Pickford and Douglas Fairbanks also posed planting trees.

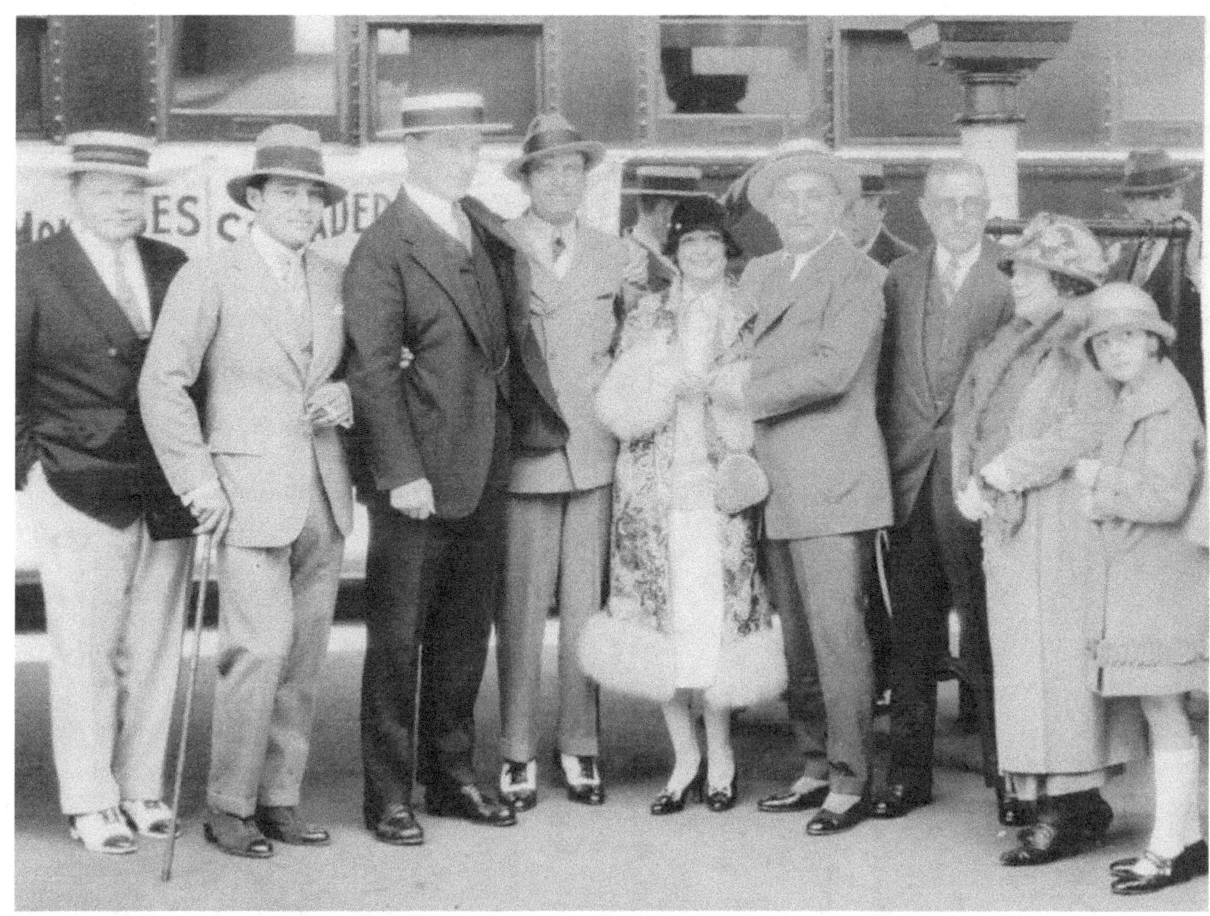

Joseph Schenck and Norma Talmadge get the royal welcome back to Hollywood. Roscoe Arbuckle, Valentino, William S. Hart, Douglas Fairbanks (on tip-toe), Norma and Joe, unknown, Charlotte and Gwen Pickford. (Tonia Salom collection)

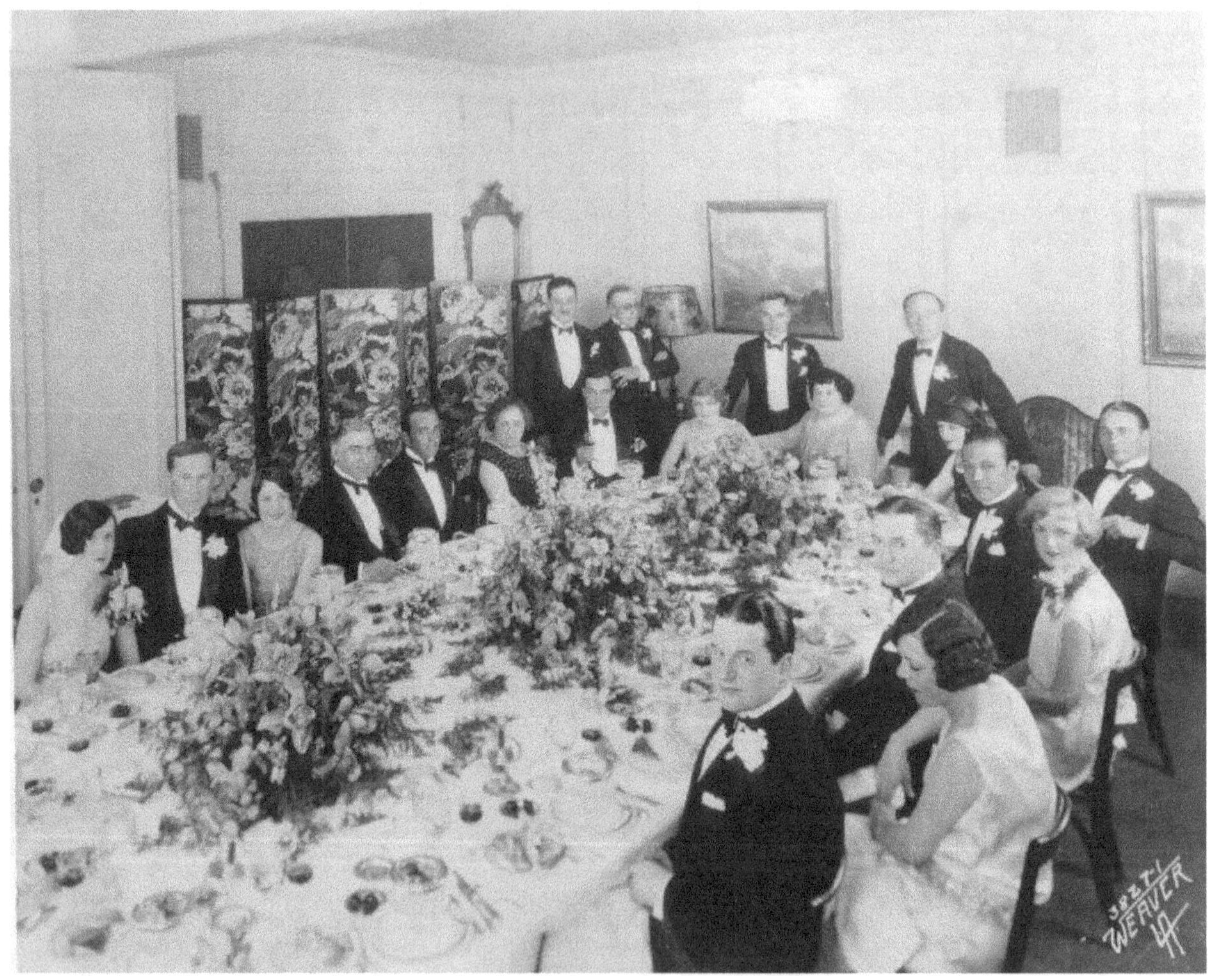

A gathering of United Artists often incorrectly identified as a party to welcome Valentino to United Artists. Joseph Schenck hosted the dinner for Hiram Abrahms which was a dual celebration for Mary Pickford's birthday.[16]
(Author's collection)

[16] Pictured around the table, Natalie Talmadge, William S. Hart, NormaTalmadge, Hiram Abrahms, Douglas Fairbanks, Margaret Talmadge, Buster Keaton, Allan Forrest (standing), R.W. MacFarlane (standing), Mary Pickford, Charles Chaplin (standing), Charlotte Pickford, Joseph Schenck (standing), Natacha Rambova, Sydney Chaplin, Valentino, Constance Talmadge, John W. Considine, Lottie Pickford, and Arthur Kelly.

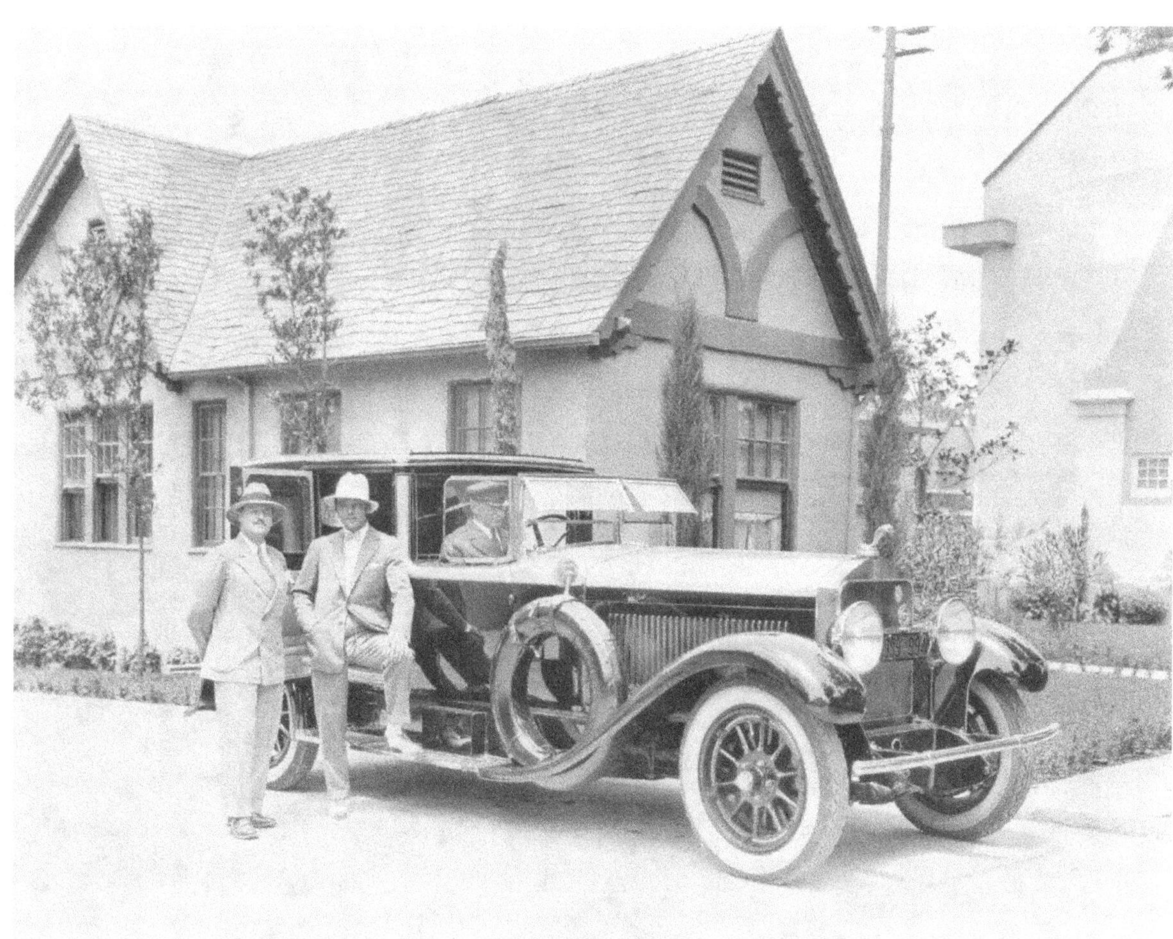

New toys for Valentino, a bungalow and his new Isotta-Fraschini.
(Author's collection)

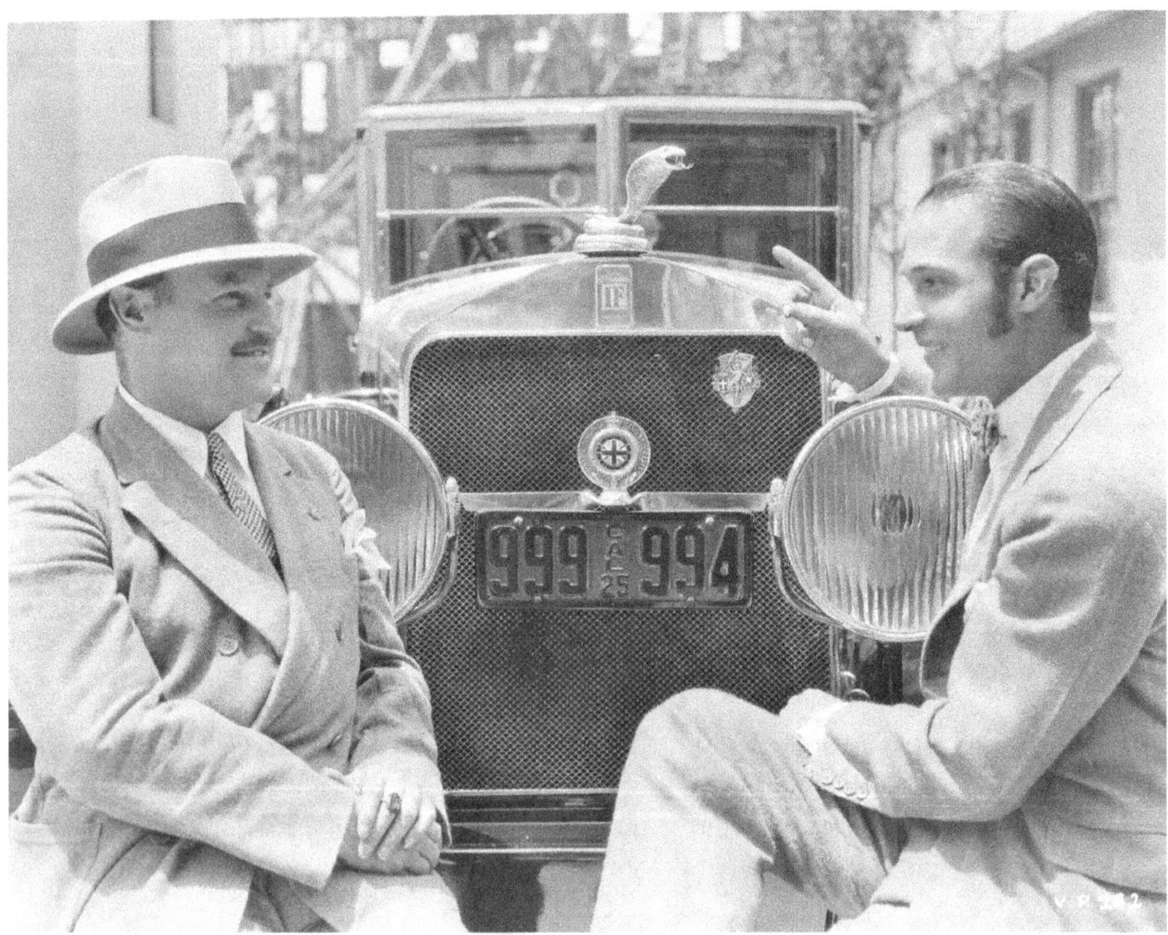

Valentino's Isotta-Fraschini was a source of pride and status. A huge vehicle, Valentino sometimes lost control of in his need for speed. Here he is showing off the Cobra car mascot to Federico Beltran Masses. (Author's collection)

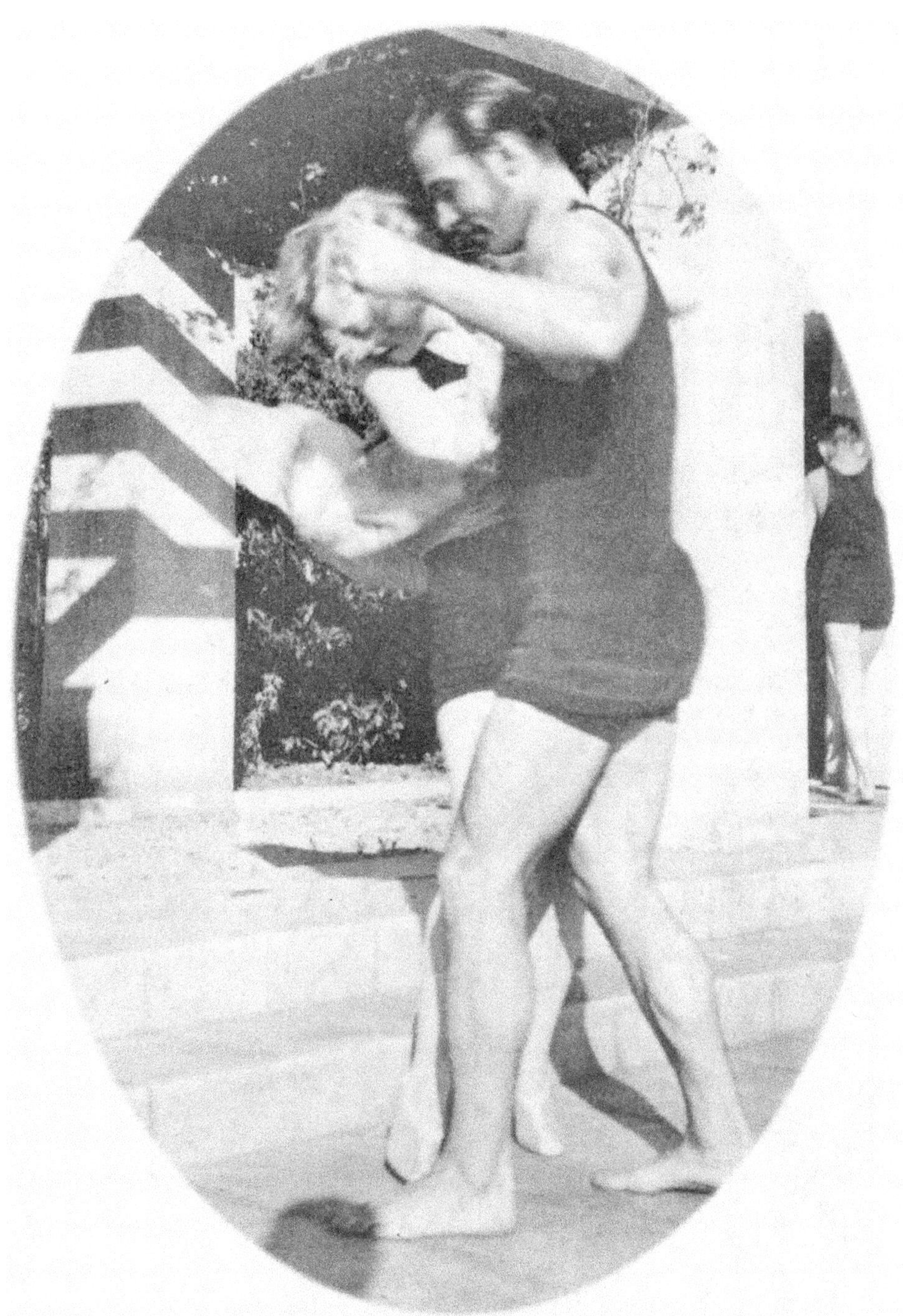

Valentino visiting Marion Davies
and dancing an impromptu tango poolside.
(Author's collection)

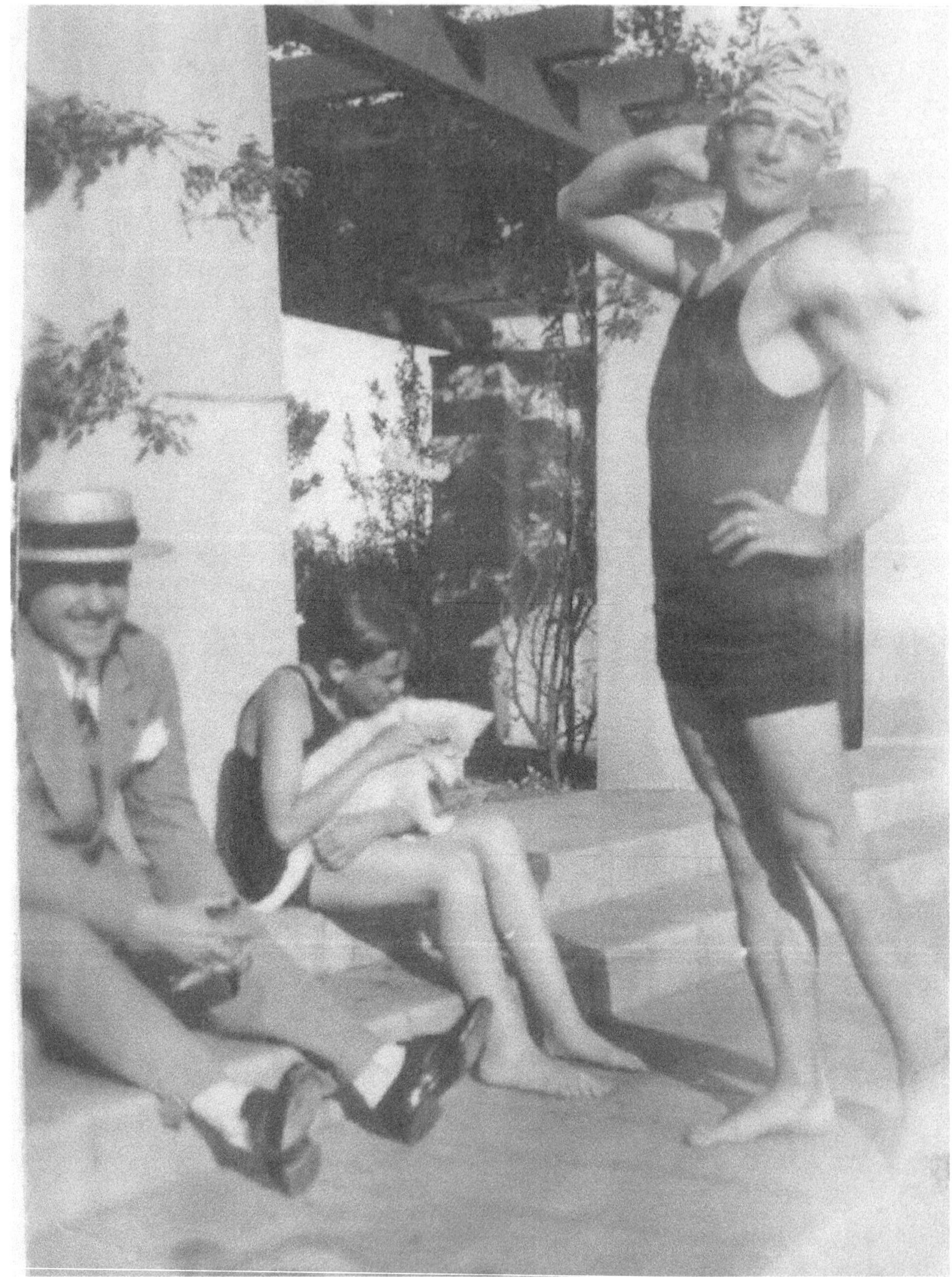

Federico Beltran Masses, Charles Lederer (nephew of Marion Davies)
and Valentino enjoying an afternoon
by the pool. (Tonia Salom collection)

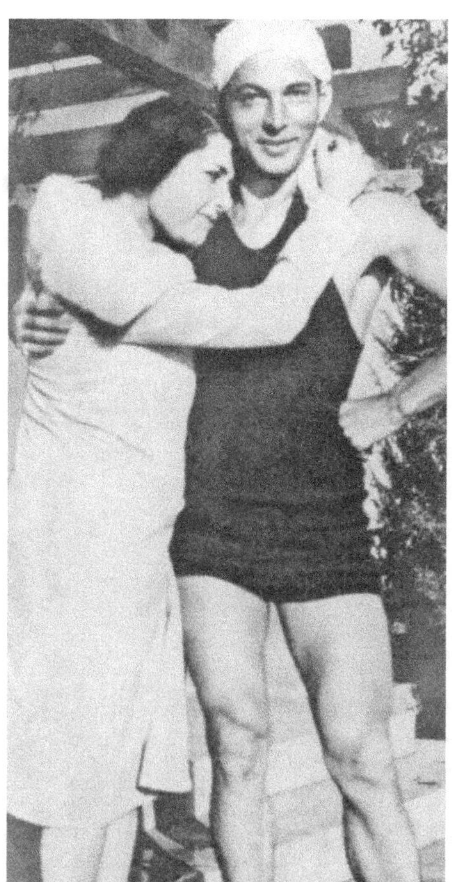

Valentino with Louella Parsons.
(Michael Morris collection)

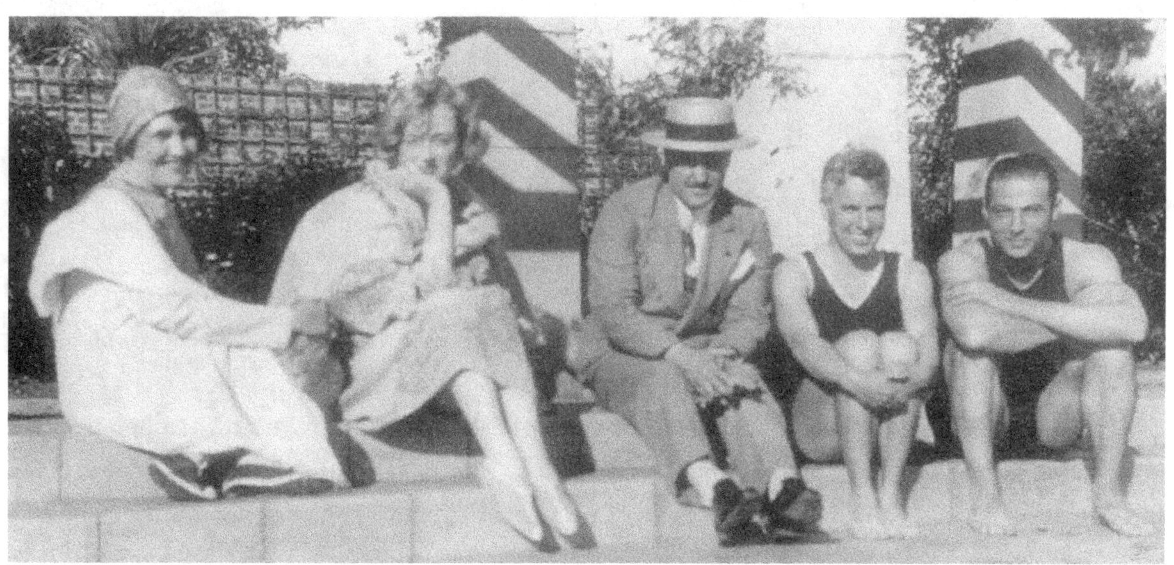

Louella Parsons, Marion Davies, Federico Beltran Masses, Charles Chaplin and Valentino enjoying an afternoon at Marion's pool. (Tonia Salom collection)

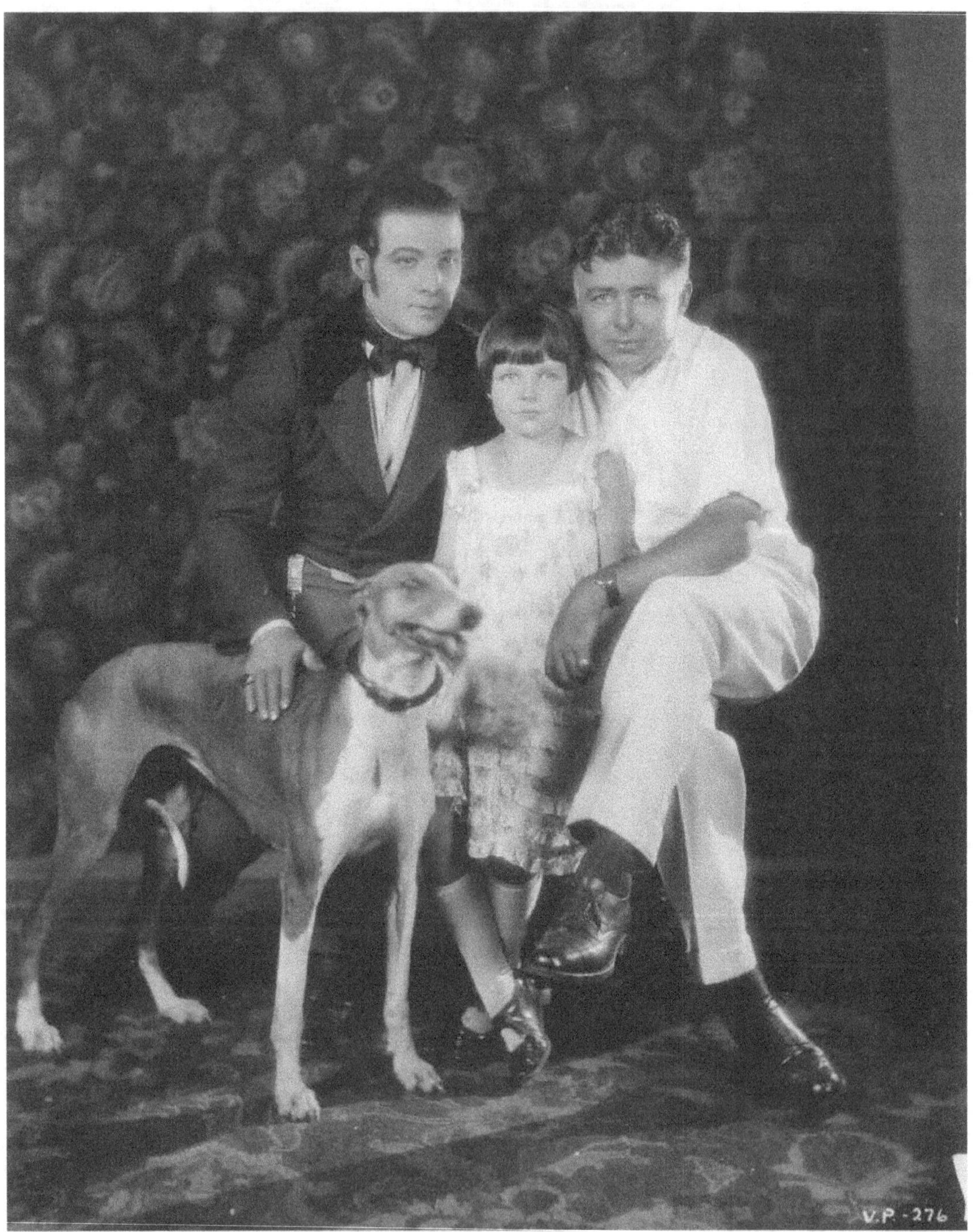

Valentino, his Spanish Greyhound Mirza, Adrienne Brown
and her father Clarence Brown pose for a portrait by Nealson Smith.
(Author's collection)

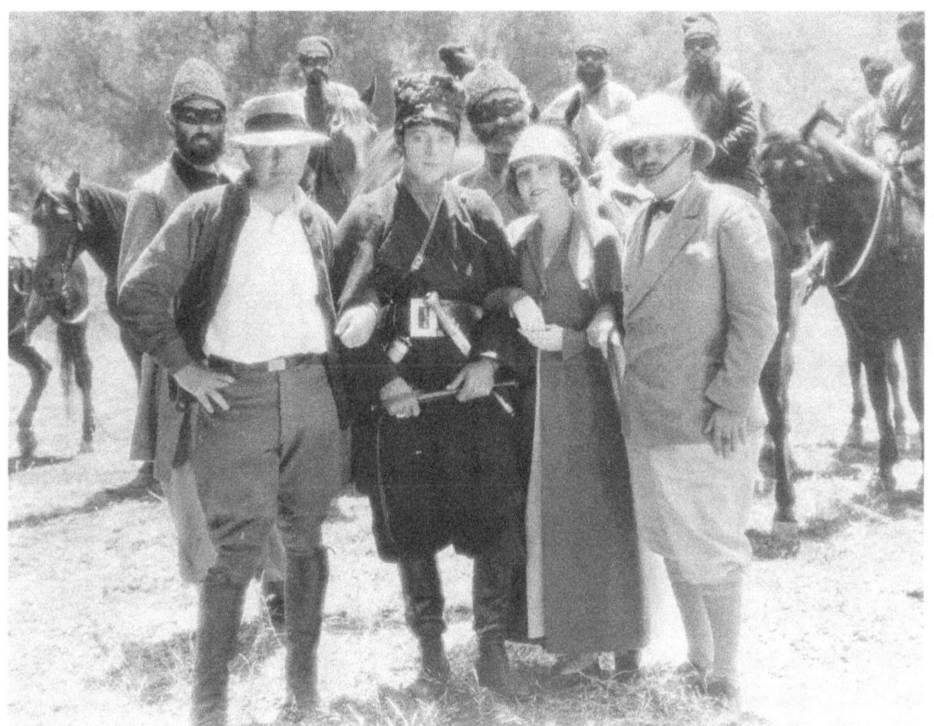

Clarence Brown, Valentino, Vilma Banky
and Federico Beltran Masses pose on location in Griffith Park.
(Author's collection)

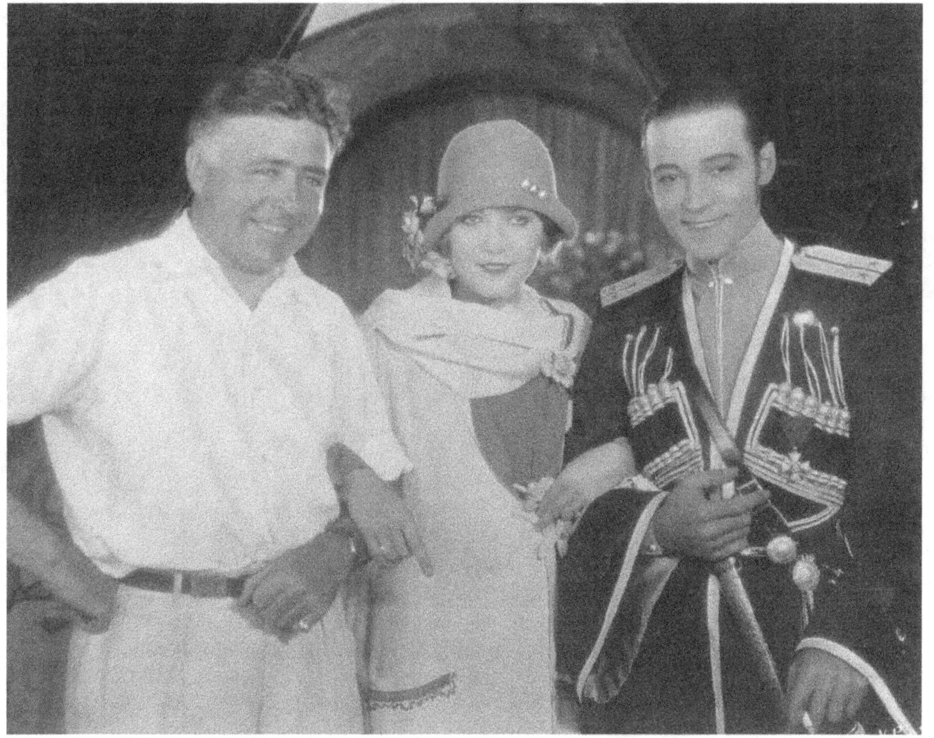

Vilma Banky pays a visit on her off day. (Author's collection)

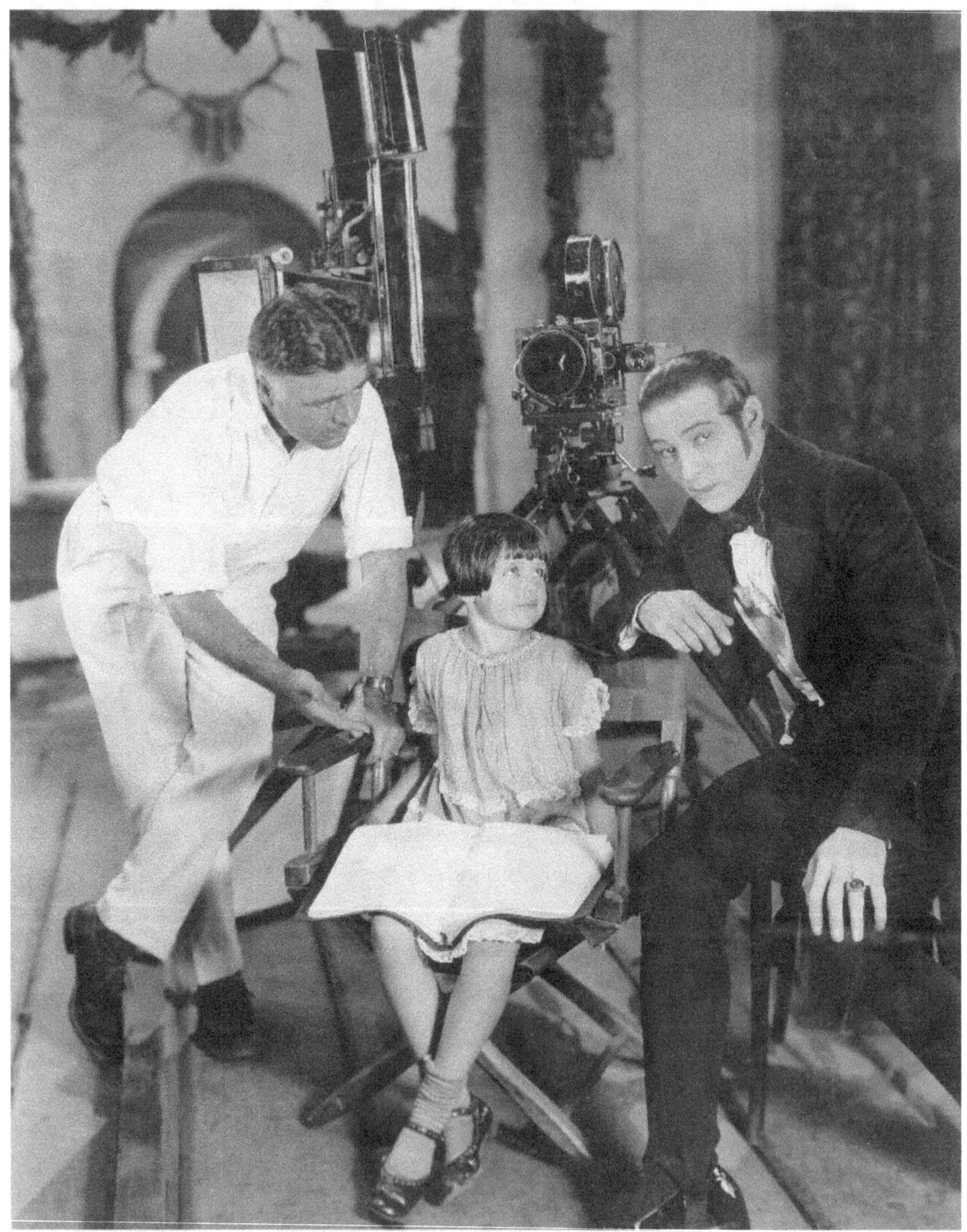

Clarence Brown, Adrienne Brown and Valentino on the set of *The Eagle*.
Her expressive face says everything about her feelings for Valentino.
(Author's collection)

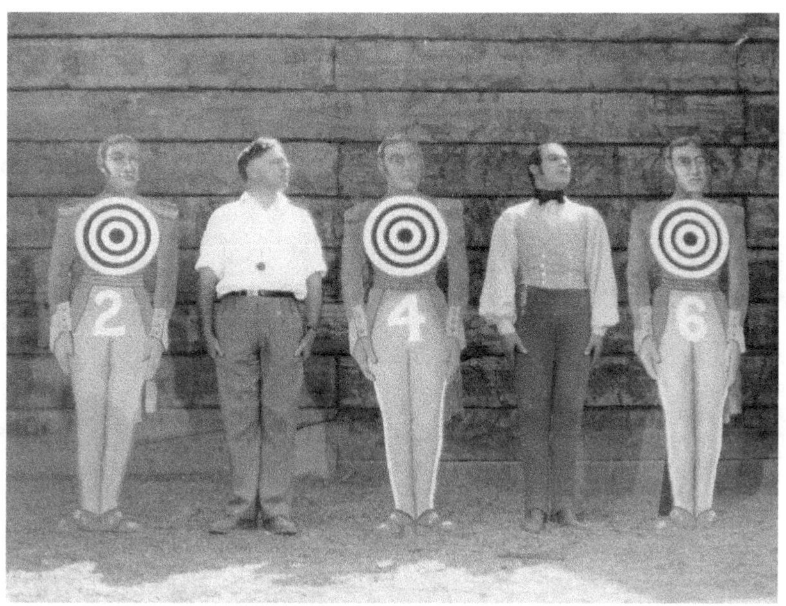

Valentino and Clarence Brown pose for a gag shot
on the set of *The Eagle*.
(Author's collection)

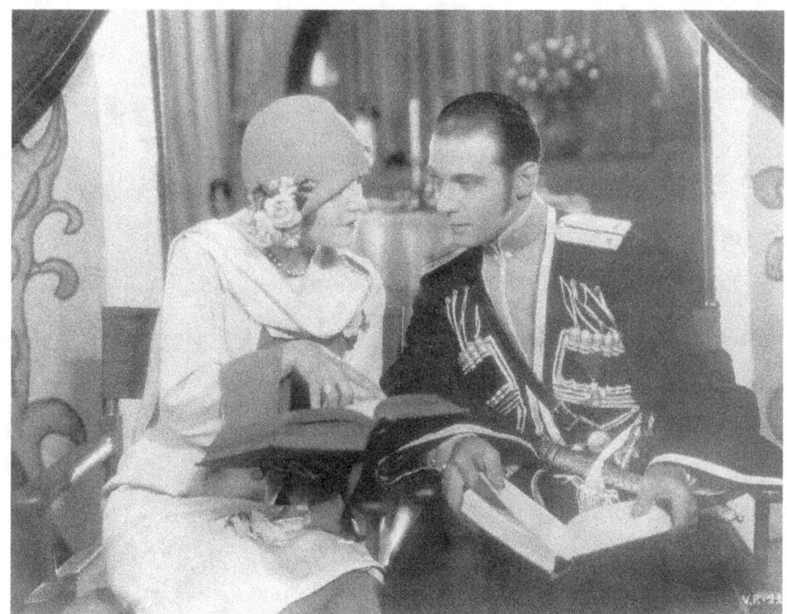

Vilma Banky and Valentino try to find a common language.
(Author's collection)

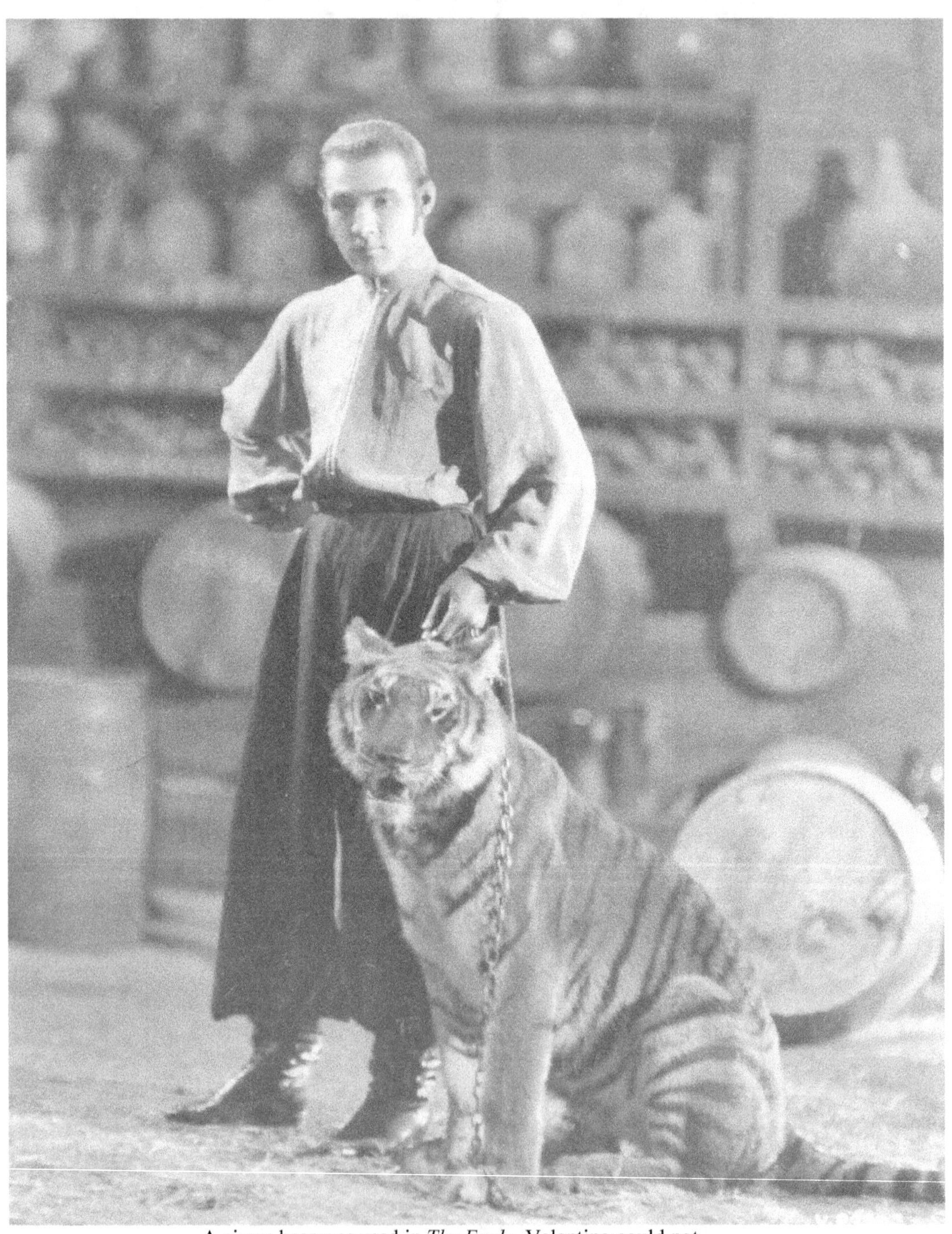

A circus bear was used in *The Eagle*, Valentino could not
resist the opportunity to commemorate the occasion to pose with a visiting tiger.
His experience with the Natacha's pet lion cub, Zela, clearly came in handy.
(Author's collection)

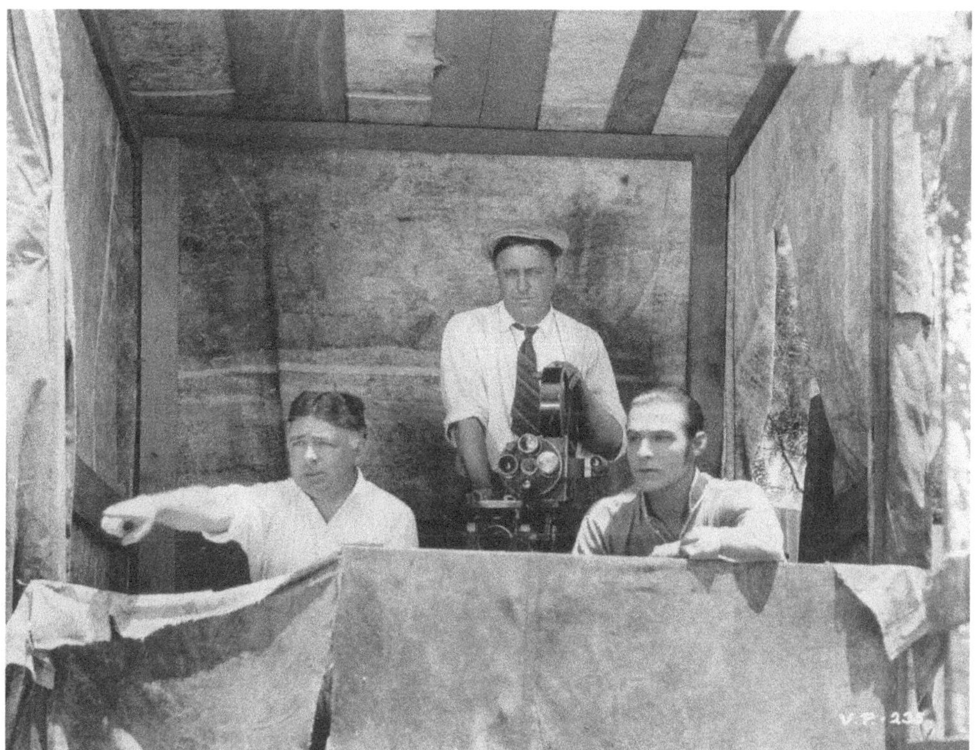

Clarence Brown, Dev Jennings and Valentino watching the action
behind the scenes. A rare moment of the film when Valentino was not in front of the camera.
(Author's collection)

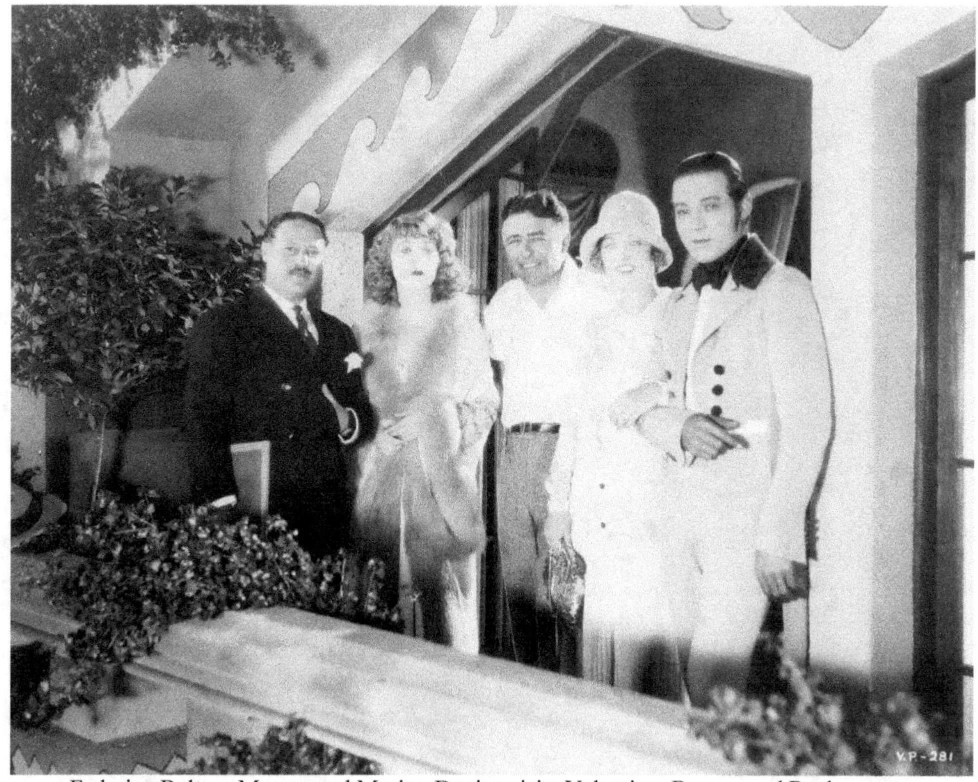

Federico Beltran Masses and Marion Davies visits Valentino, Brown, and Banky.
(Author's collection)

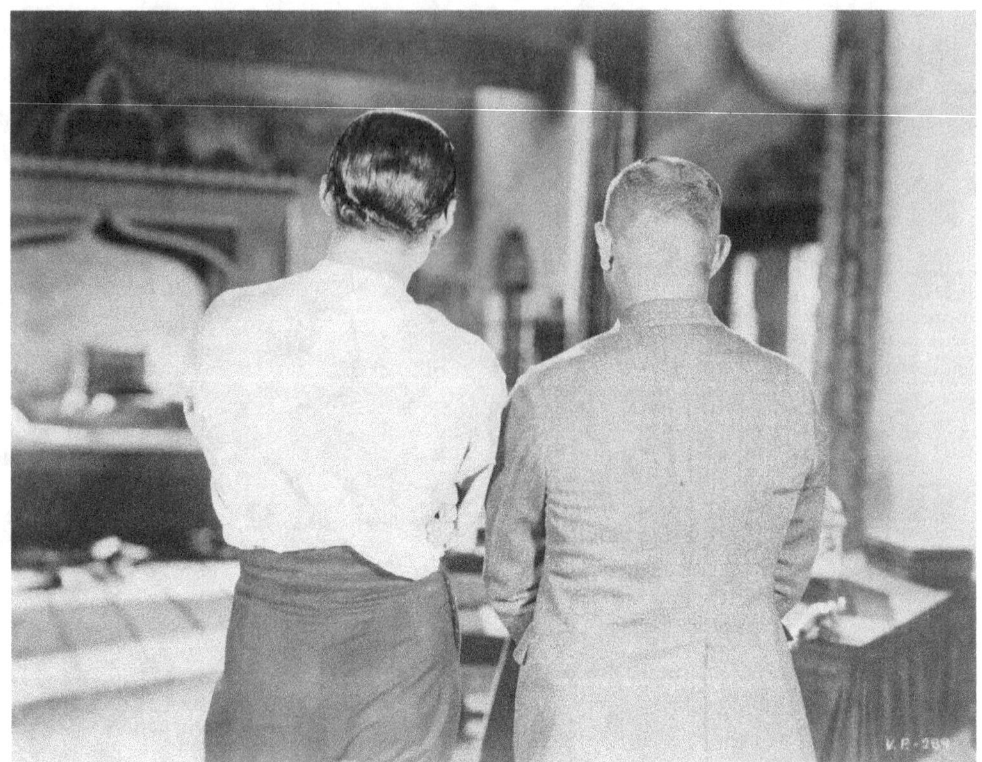

Among visitors were maverick director and actor Erich von Stroheim.
Von Stroheim and Valentino posed for this witty study by Nealson Smith.
(Author's collection)

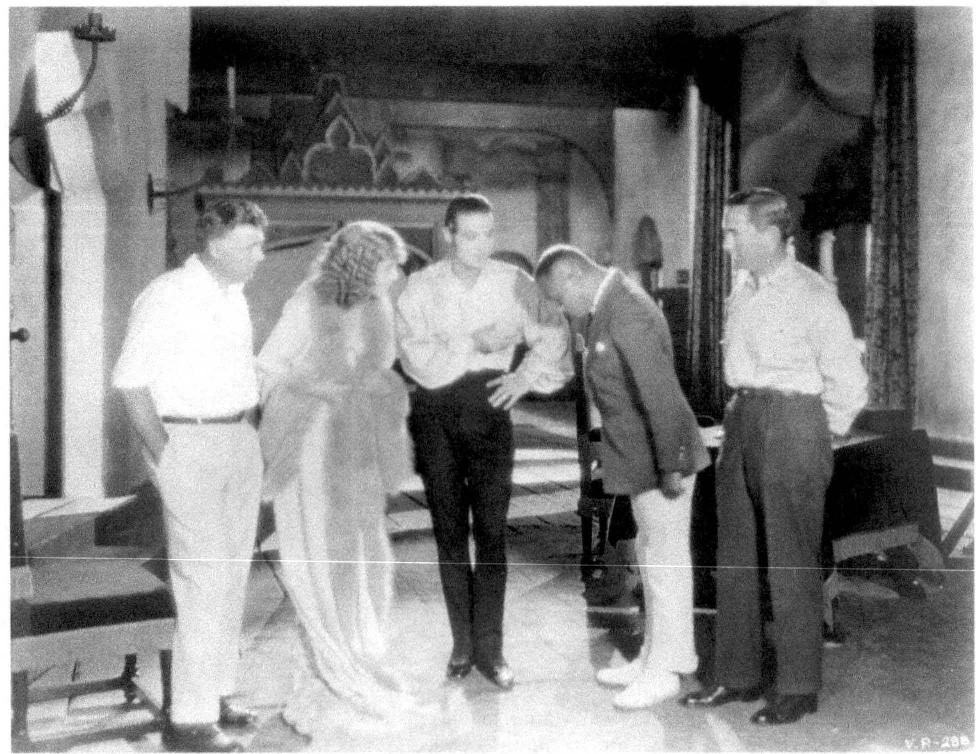

Clarence Brown, Vilma Banky, Valentino, von Stroheim and producer John Considine.
(Author's collection)

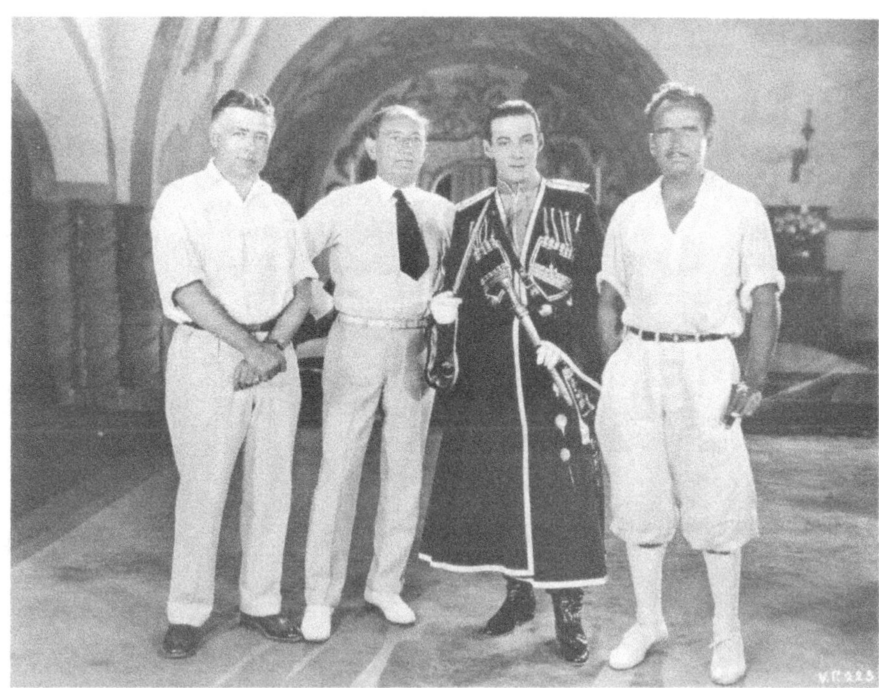

Joseph Schenck and an unusually dour Douglas Fairbanks
visiting the set of *The Eagle*.
(Author's collection)

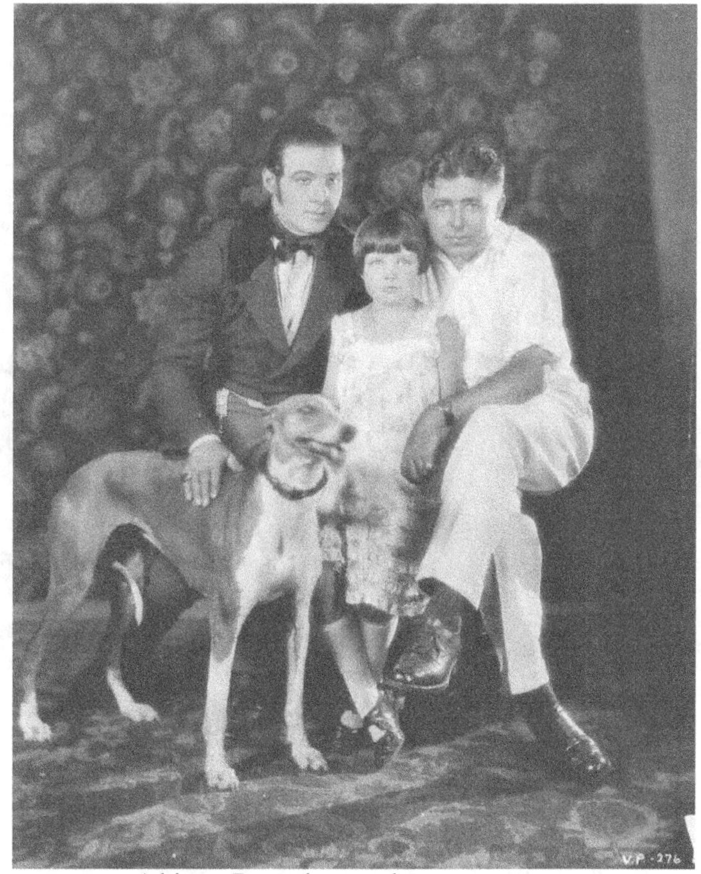

Adrienne Brown between her two men.
(Author's collection)

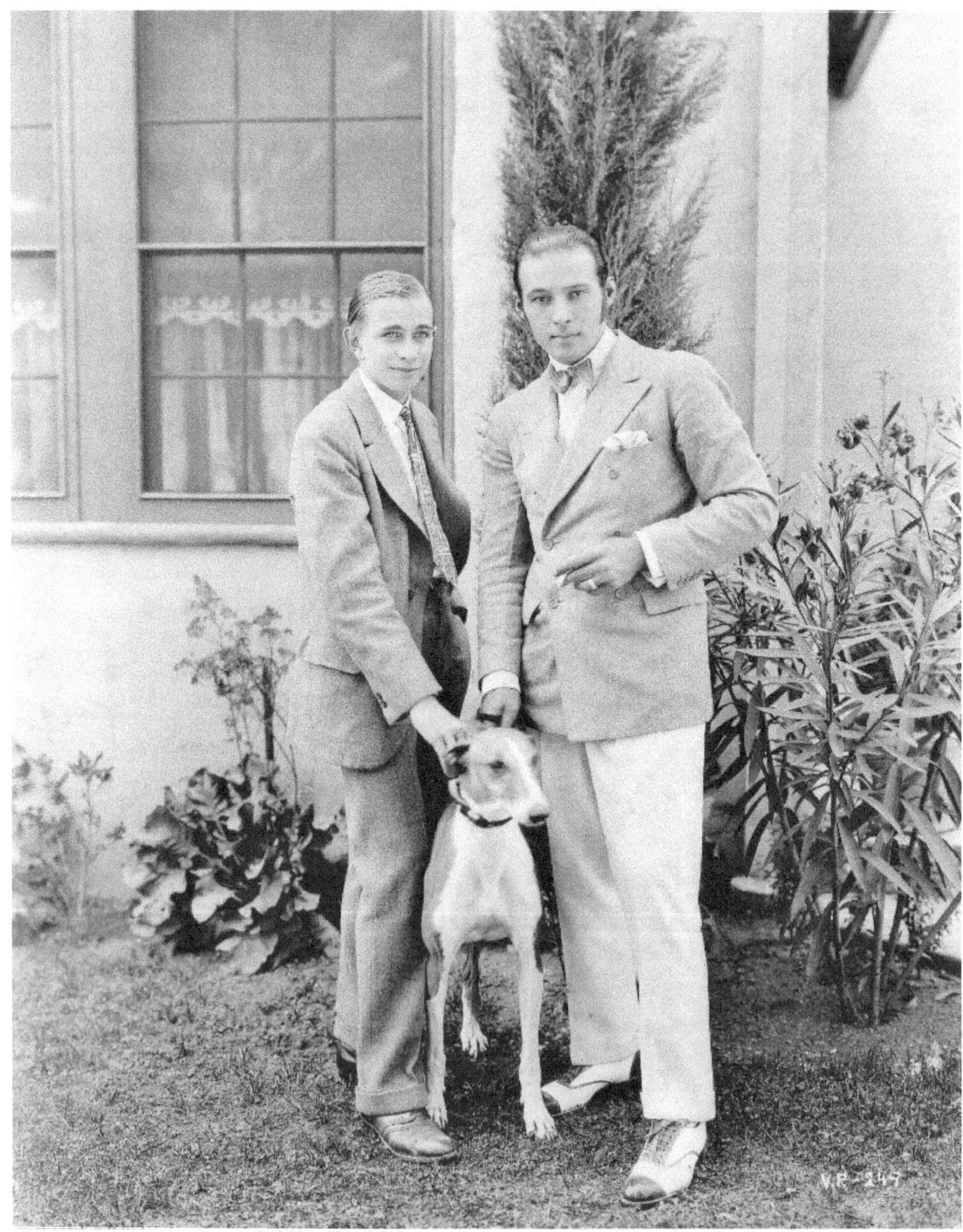

Valentino and Mirza posing with fan Horace Wade.
(Margaret Herrick Library; Academy of Motion Picture Arts and Sciences)

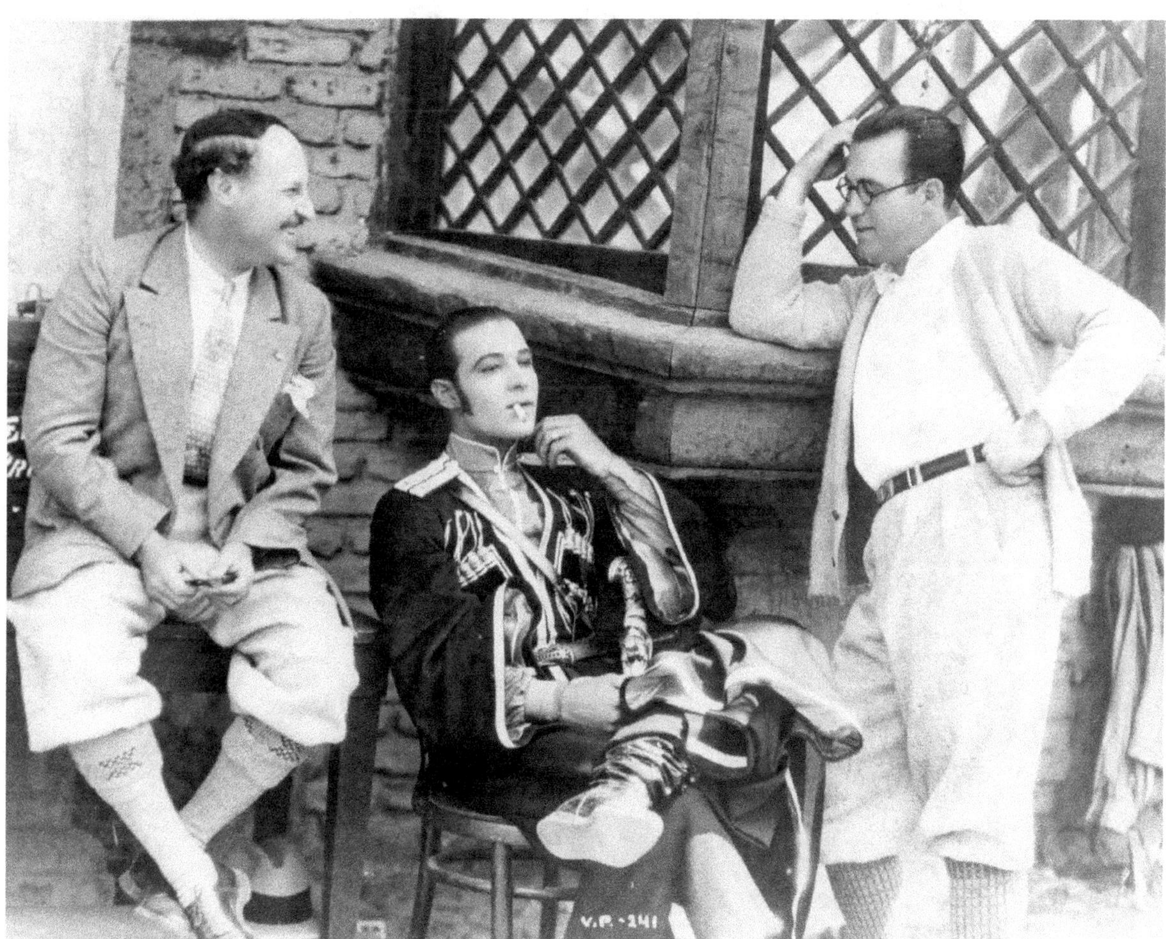

Federico Beltran Masses, Valentino and George Ullman while making *The Eagle*.
(Author's collection)

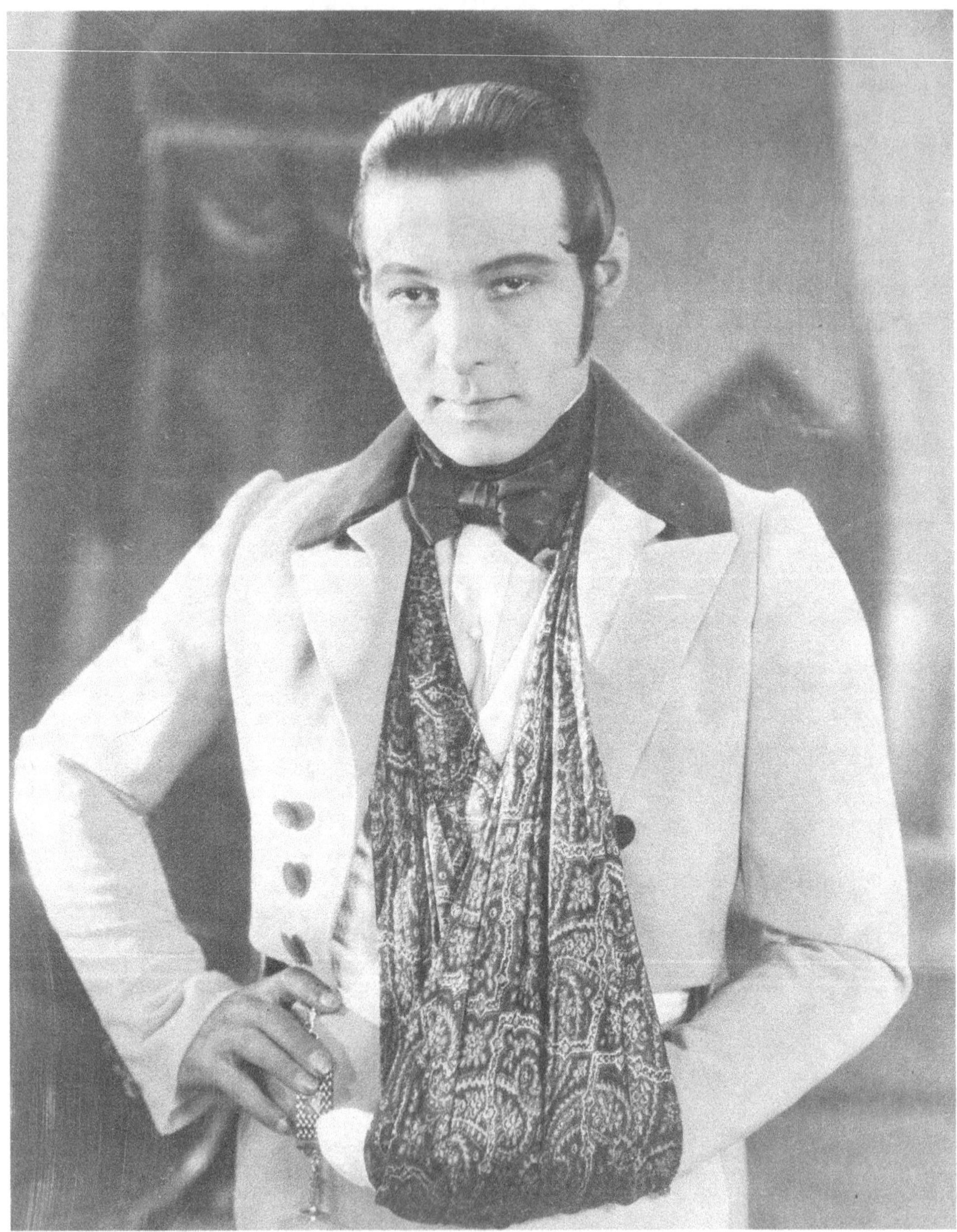

Valentino took great pride in doing his own stunts and riding in *The Eagle*.
This injury was the result of a mishap during filming. Valentino said he was none the worse for wear.
(Author's collection)

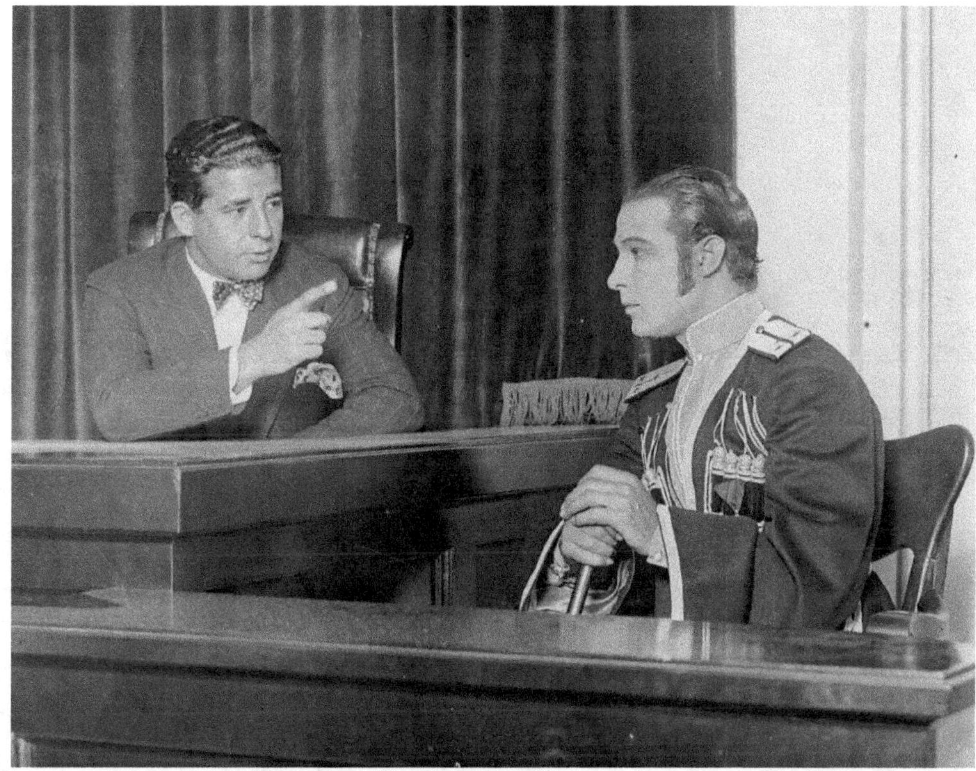

Valentino was a notoriously reckless driver. Here he is in traffic court, in costume while filming *The Eagle*. Traffic Court Judge Mancuso poses for a posed still admonishing Valentino. (Author's collection)

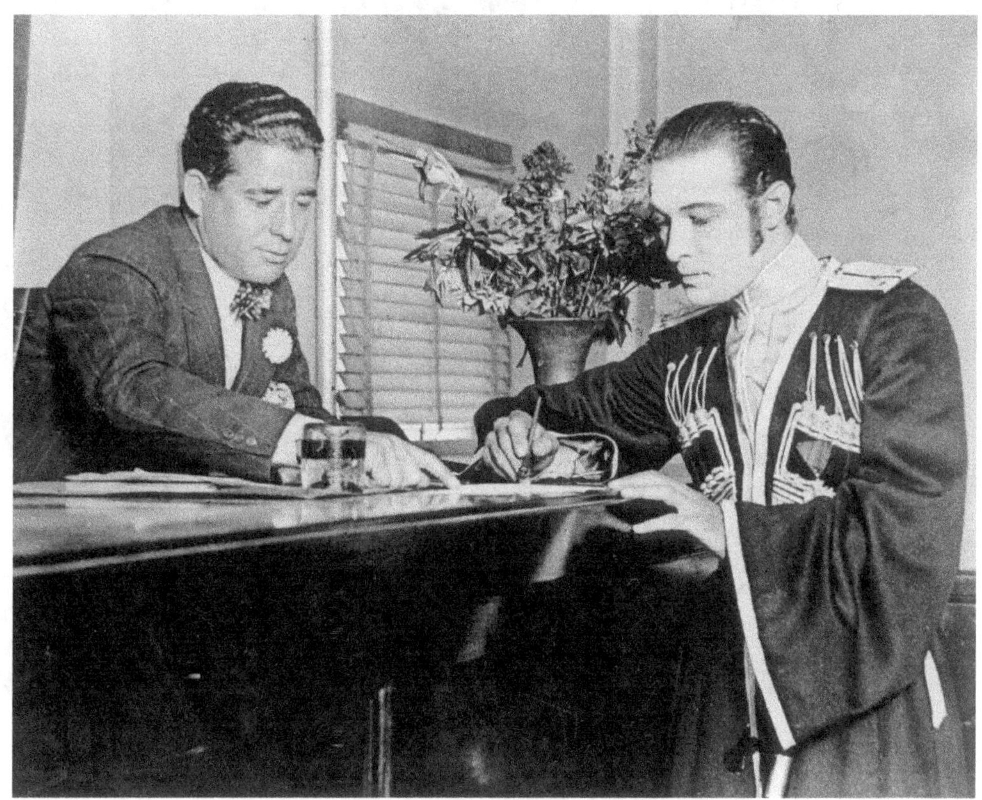

Valentino signs his citation and pays his traffic fine. (Tracy Terhune collection)

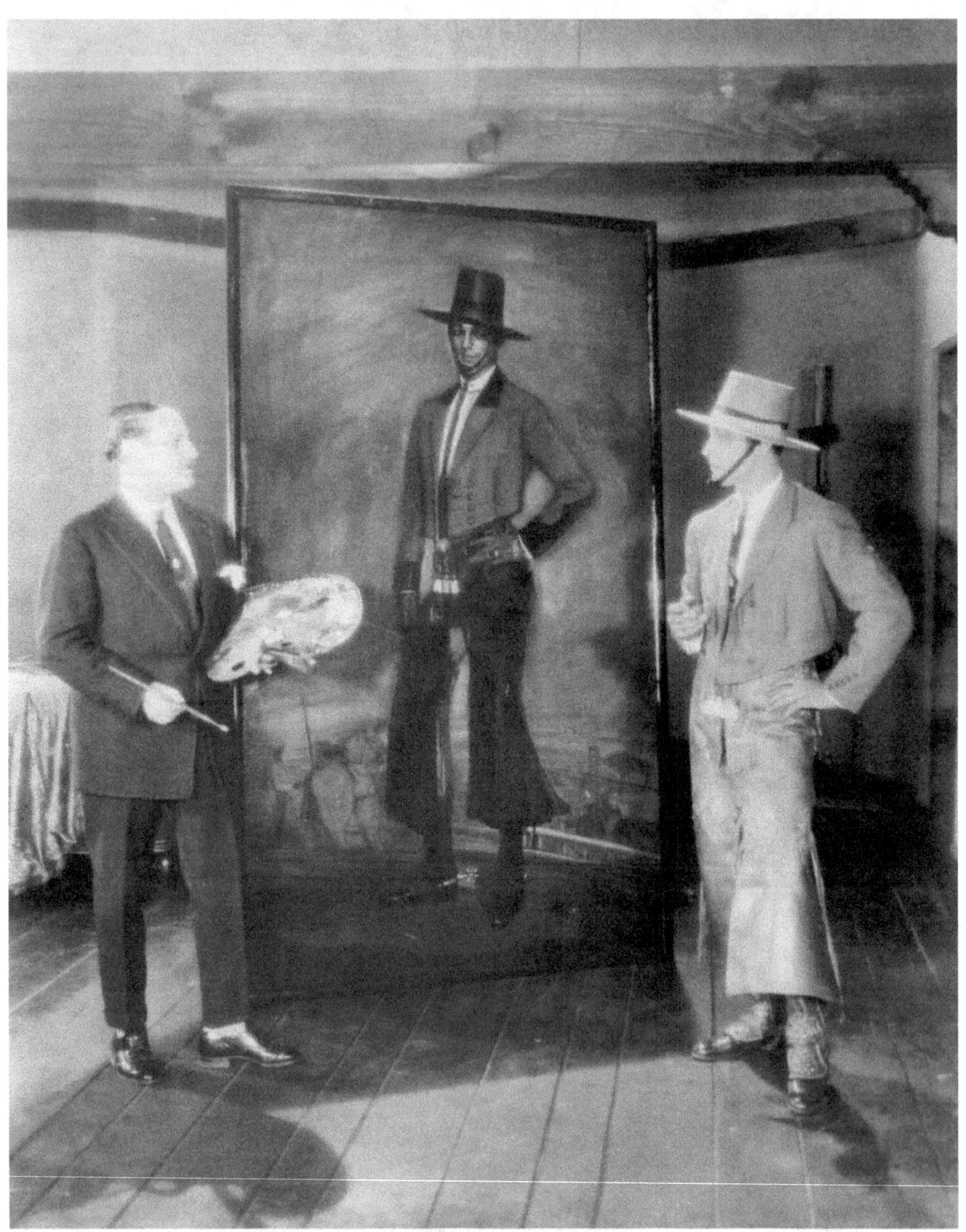

Valentino posing for Federico Beltran Masses.
(Author's collection)

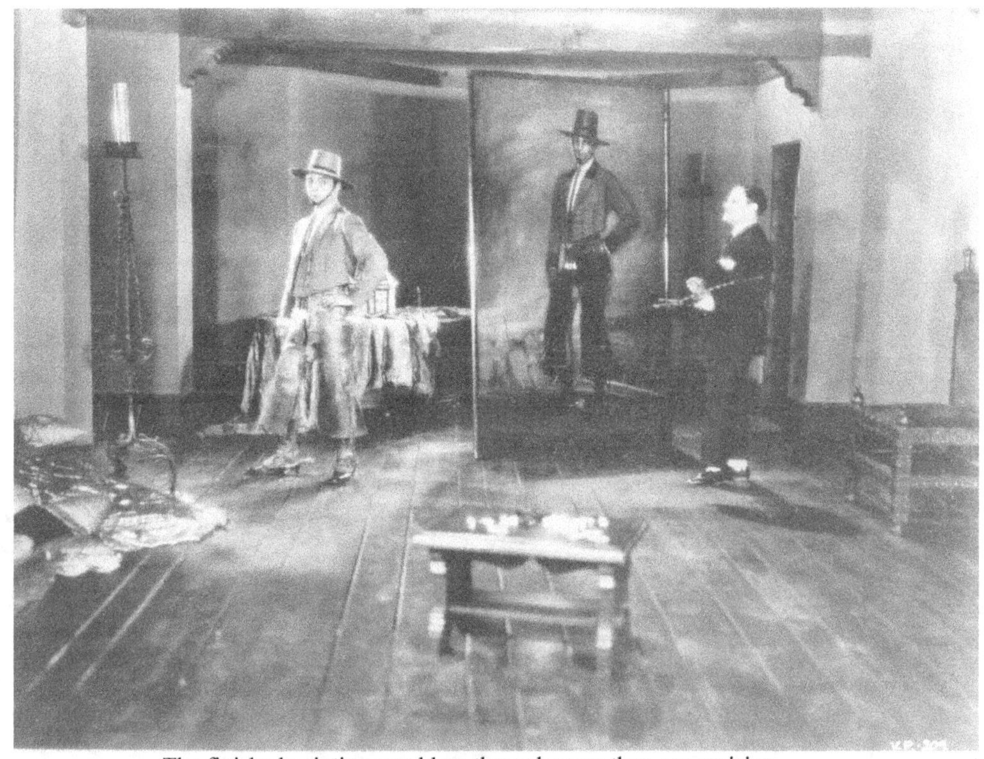

The finished painting would go through more than one revision
before the painting was hung in the library.
(Author's collection)

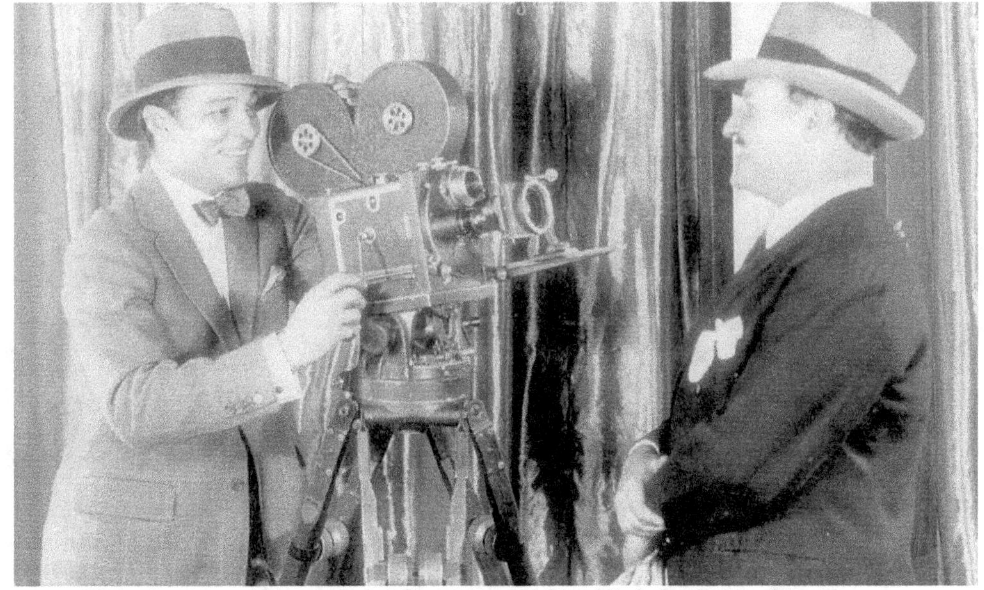

Valentino mans the camera and films his good friend Federico Beltran Masses.
(Tonia Salom collection)

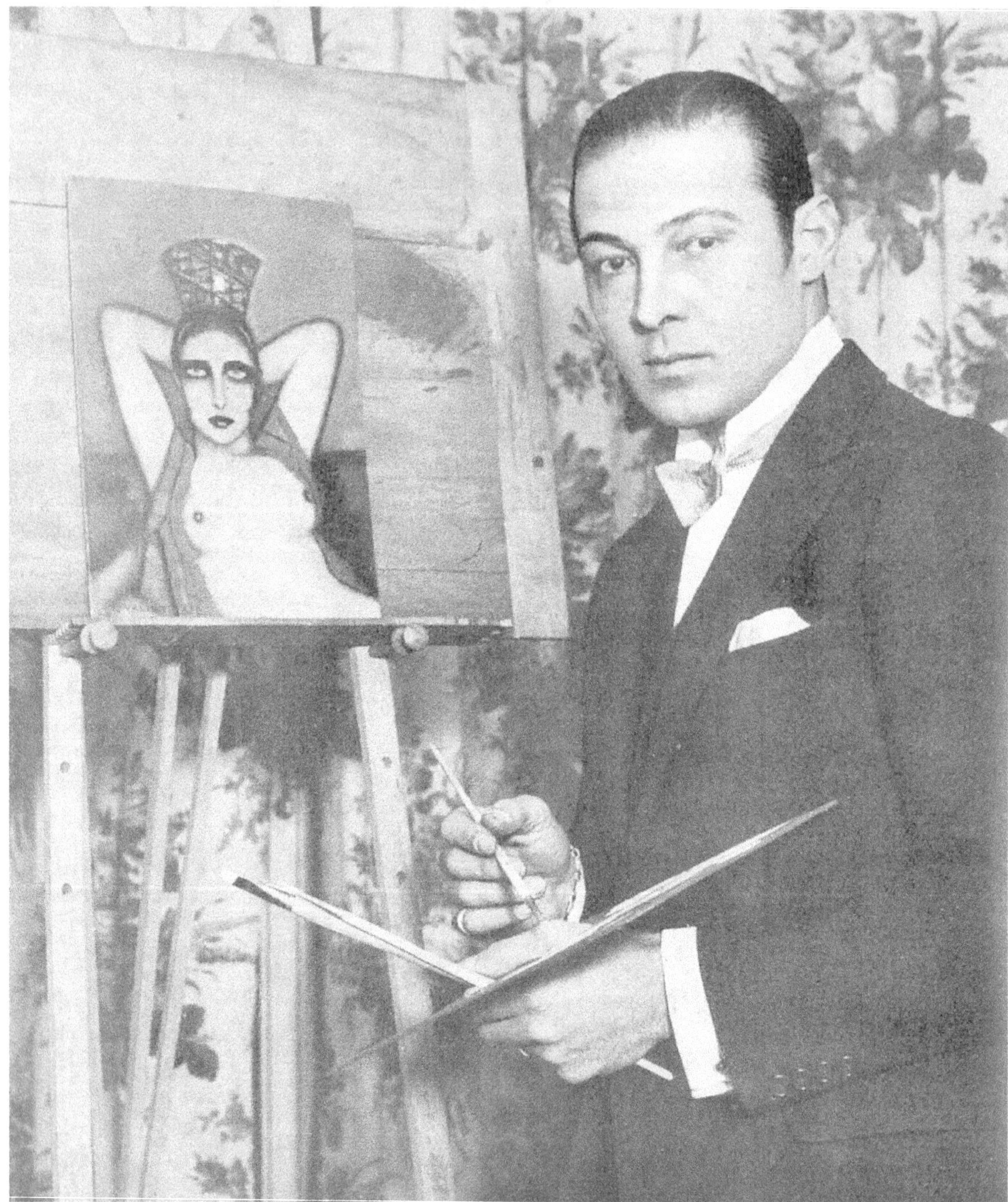

Valentino's burgeoning friendship with Federico Beltran Masses inspired Valentino to take up painting.
Here he is shown copying a detail of Beltran Masses portrait Senorita Gaditana.
Valentino's signature on the canvas/board can be glimpsed in the lower left.
The original Beltran Masses painting hung in Valentino's bedroom at Falcon Lair.
(Author's collection)

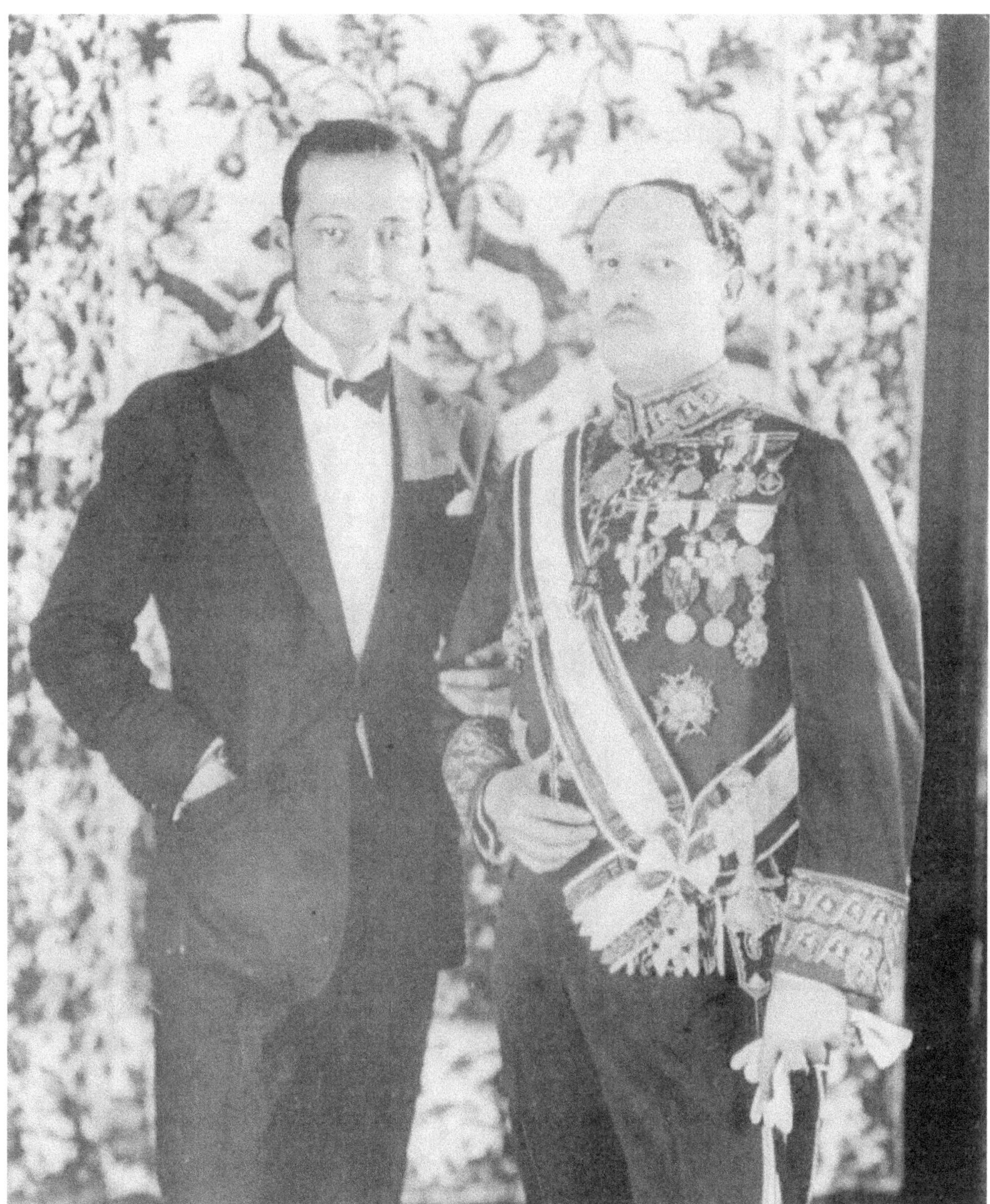

Valentino and Federico Beltran Masses pose at the Ambassador Hotel for the gala exhibition of some of his work.
(Tonia Salom collection)

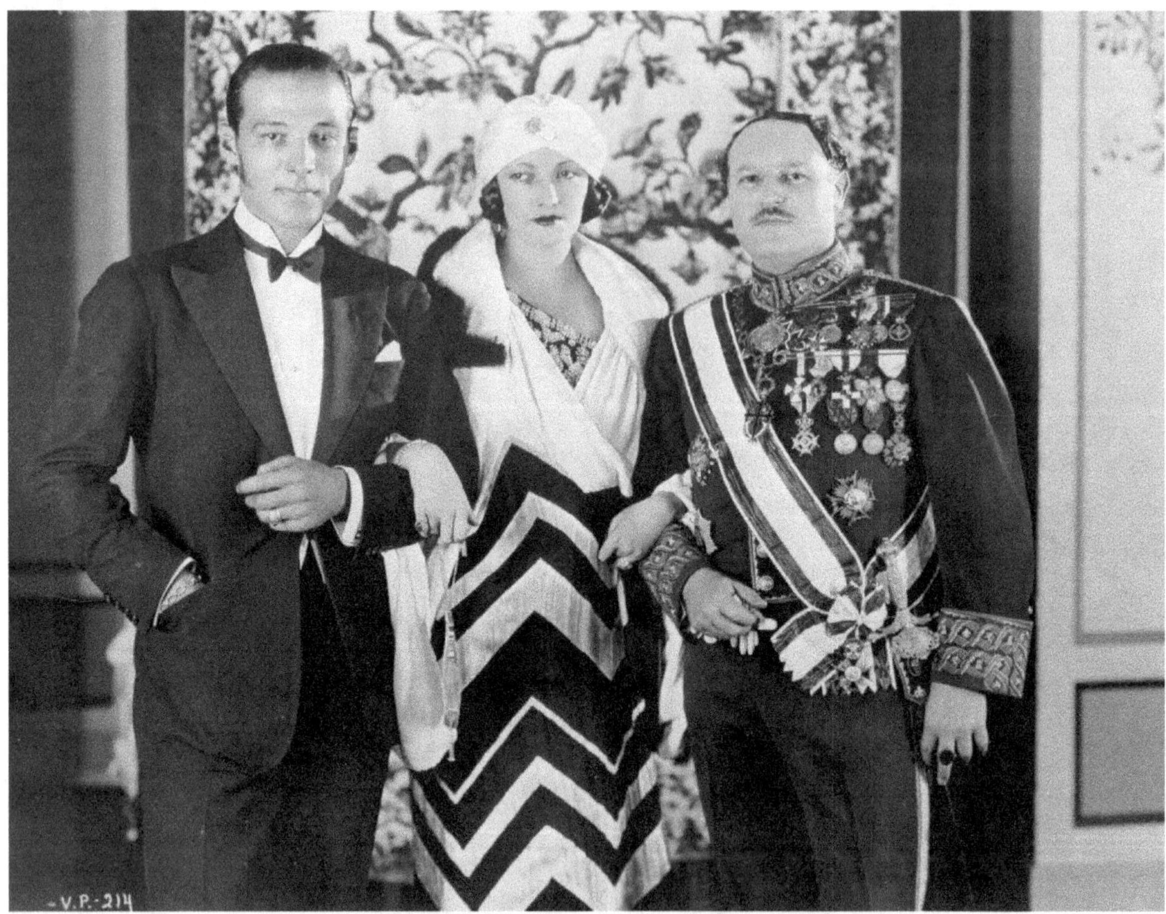

Valentino, Natacha and Federico Beltran Masses pose at the Ambassador Hotel. (Author's collection)

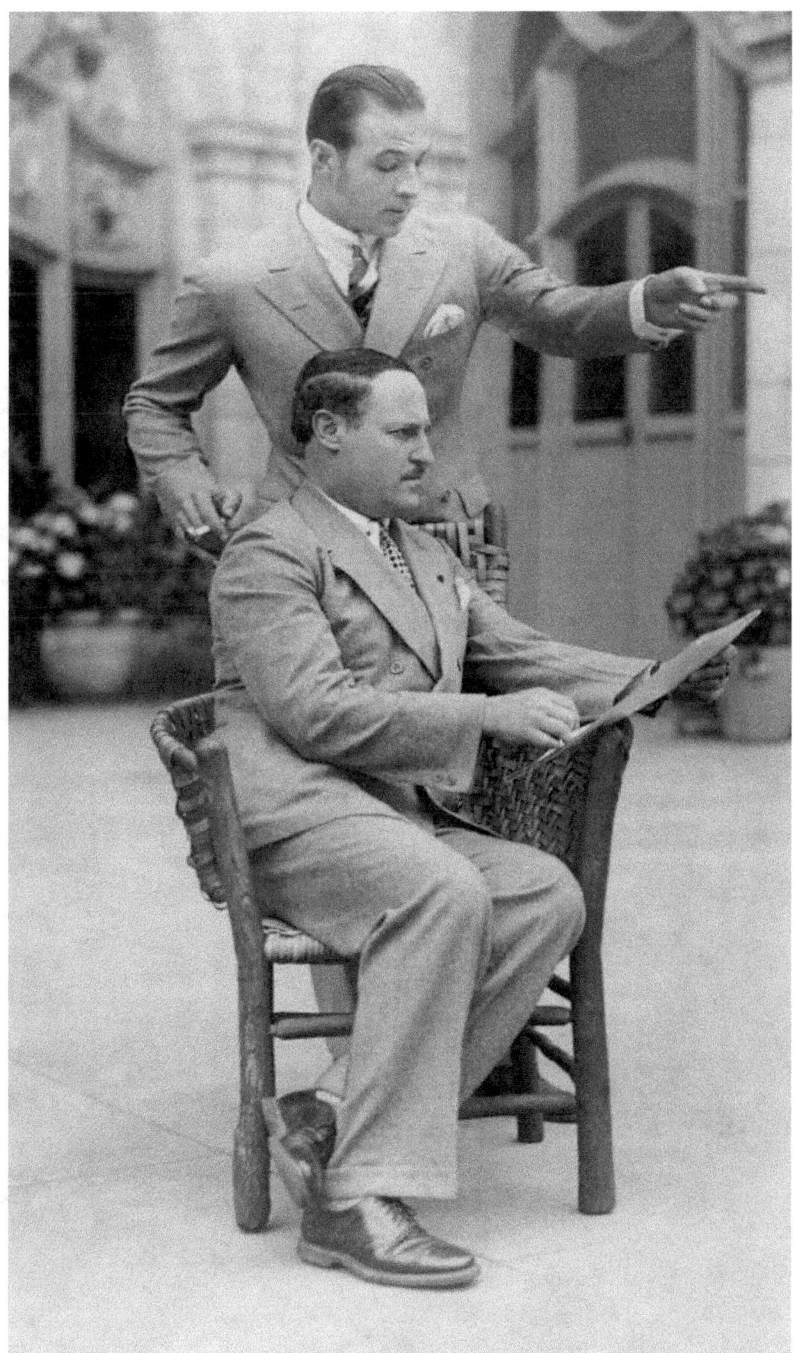

Valentino points to a worthy subject for Federico Beltran Masses' sketch pad.
(Author's collection)

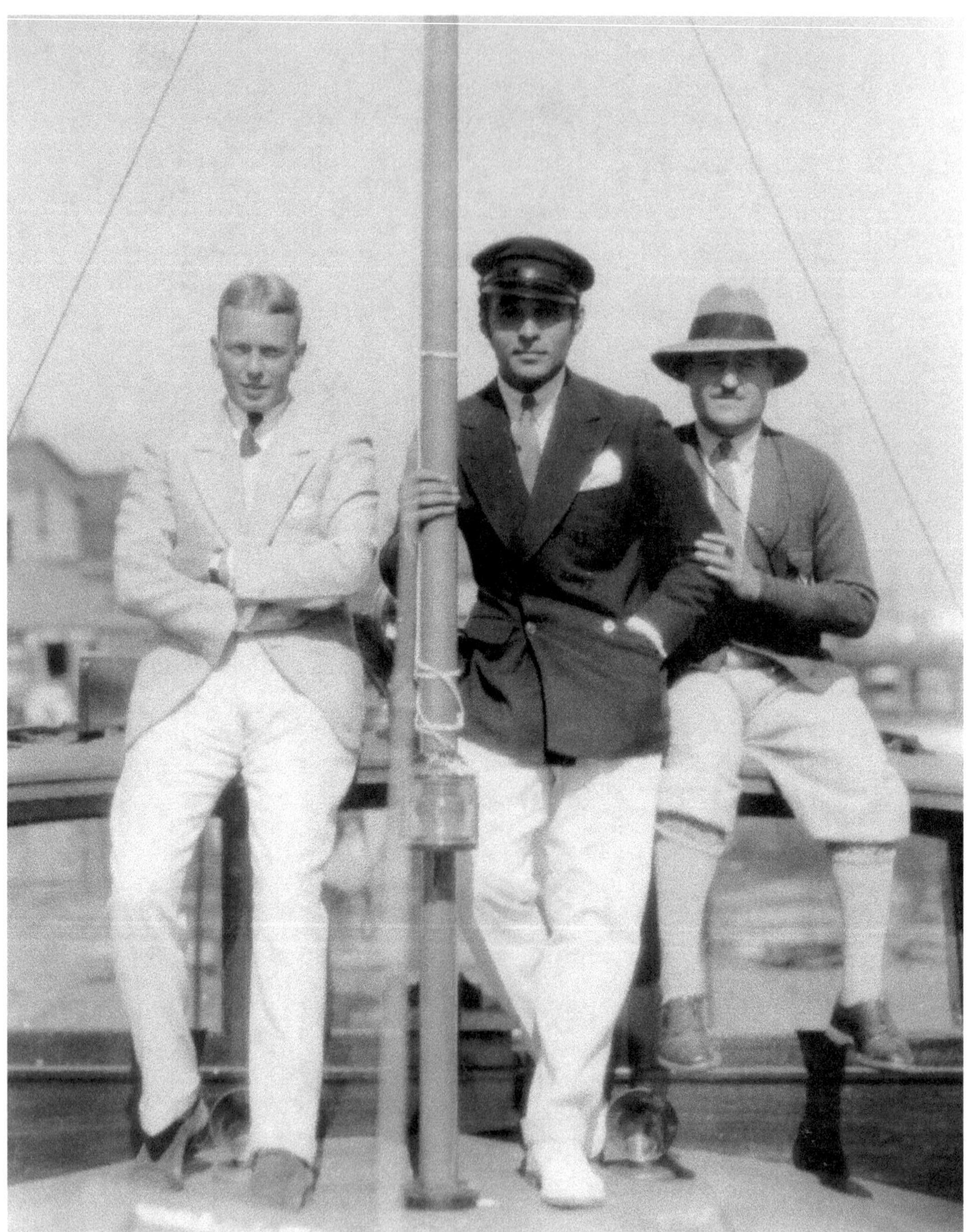

Unknown friend, Valentino and Federico Beltran Masses on board the Phoenix 1925.
(Author's collection)

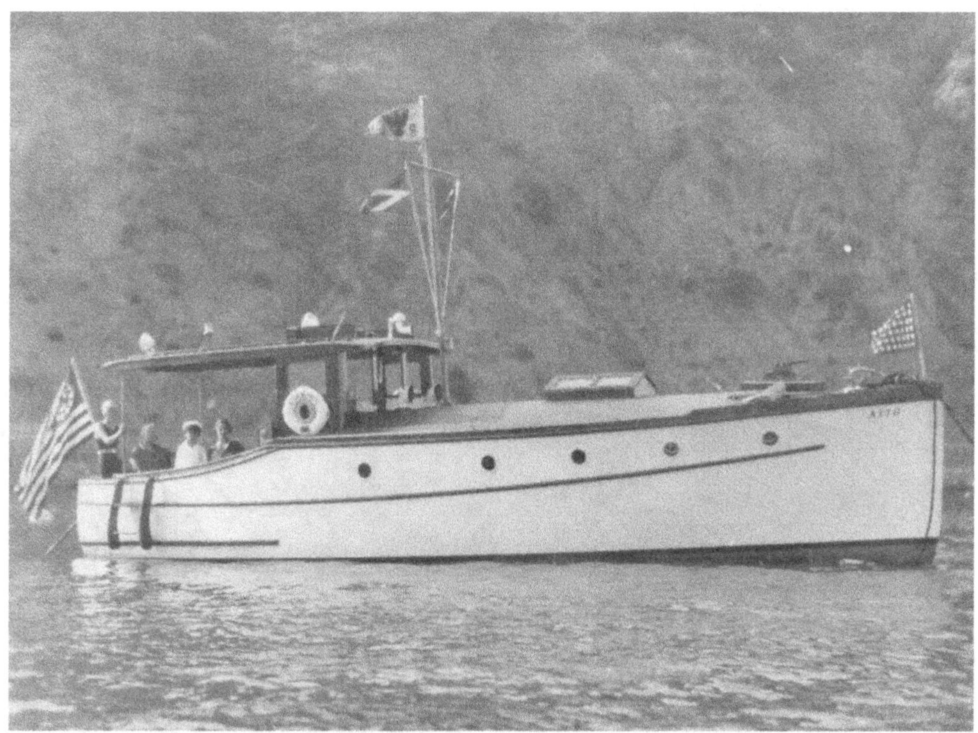

Snapshot of the Phoenix off Catalina Island. This photograph was taken by Valentino and preserved in one of his personal scrapbooks. (Author's collection)

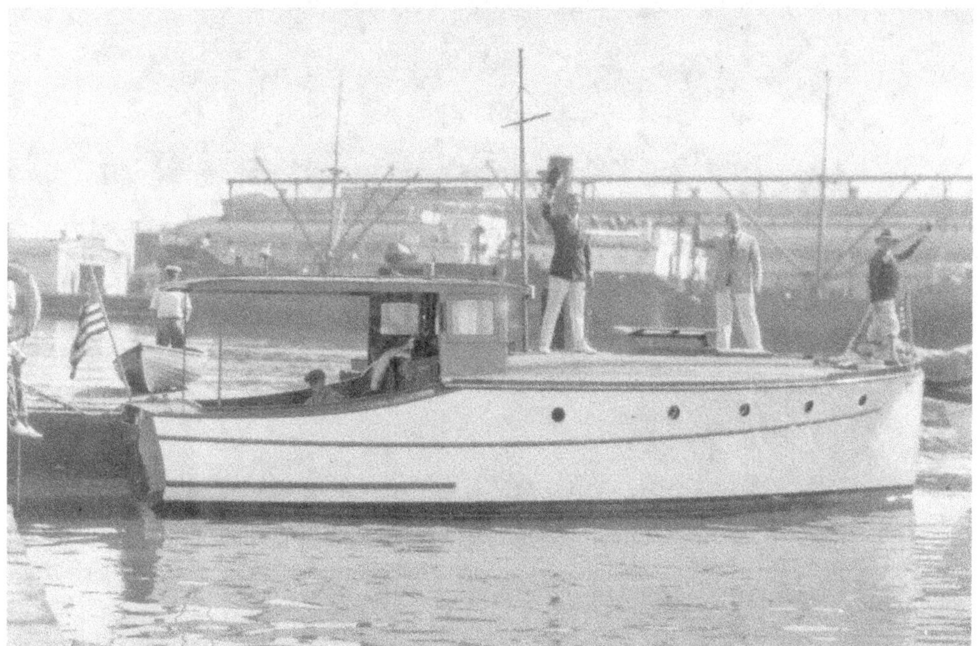

Valentino, Enrique de Menses and Federico Beltran Masses departing on an afternoon pleasure cruise. (Tracy Terhune collection)

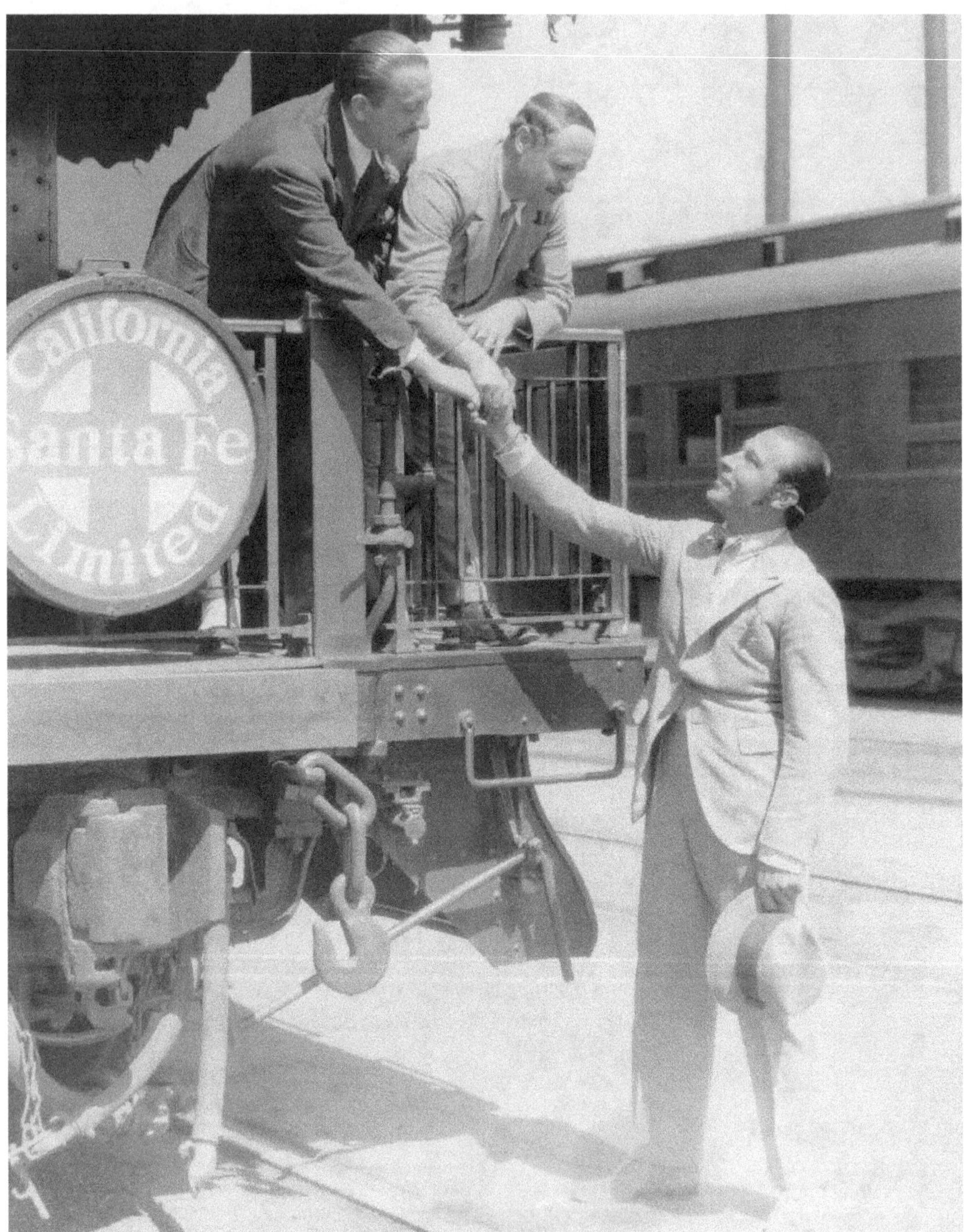

Valentino, Federico Beltran Masses greeting Mexican author Enrique de Menses
at the Pasadena train station.
(San Francisco History Center)

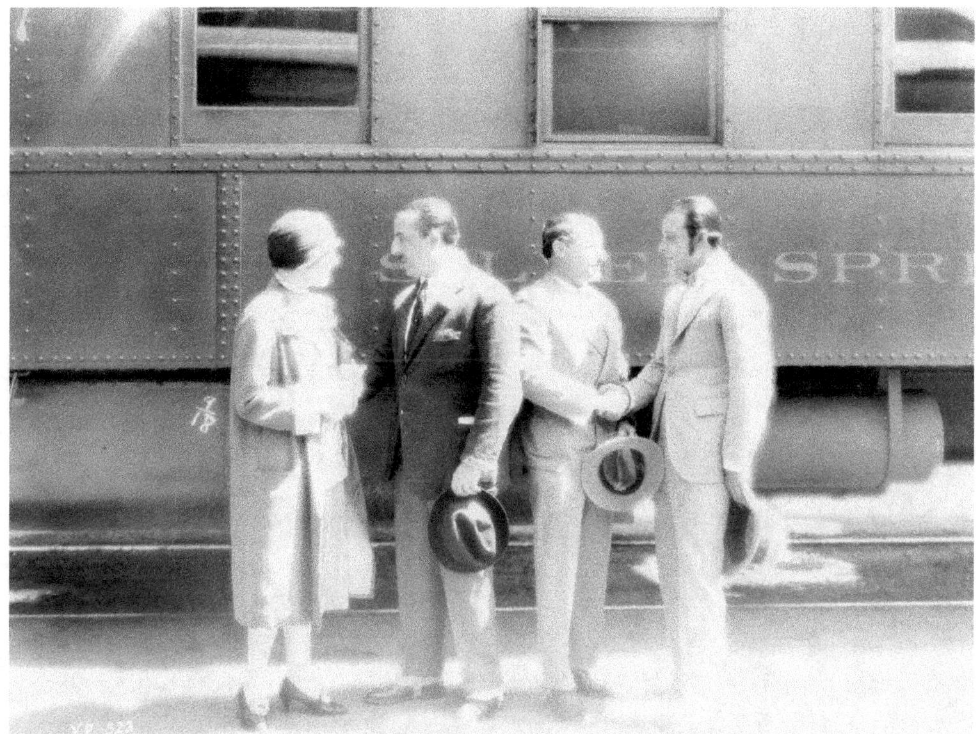

Vilma Banky, Enrique de Menses, Beltran Masses and Valentino.
(Author's collection)

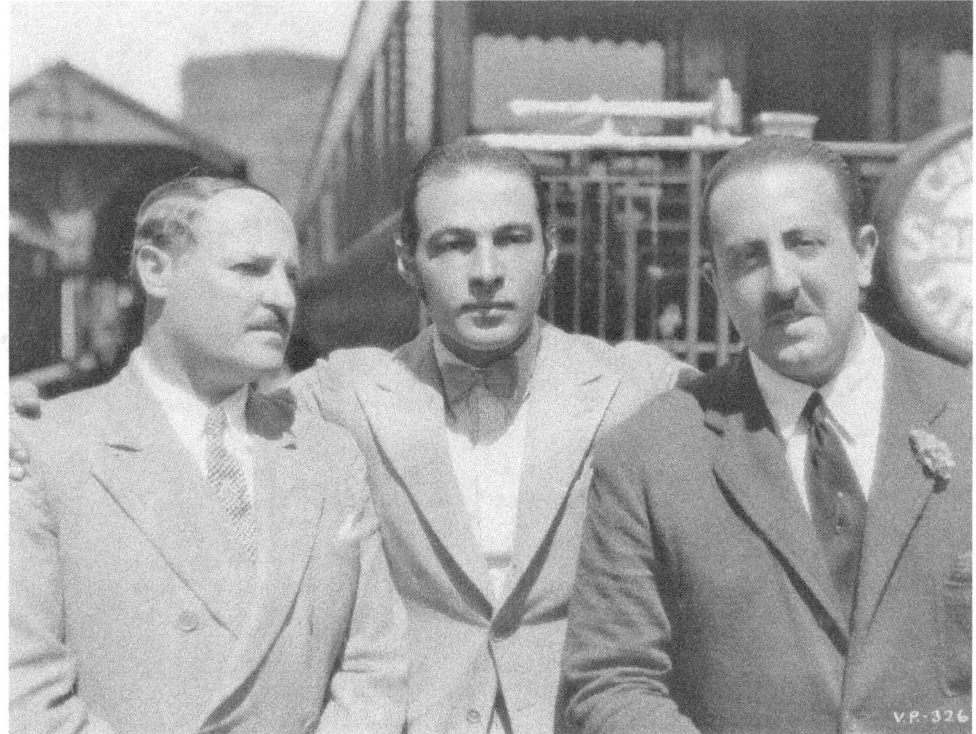

The trio of friends pose for another photograph. (Author's collection)

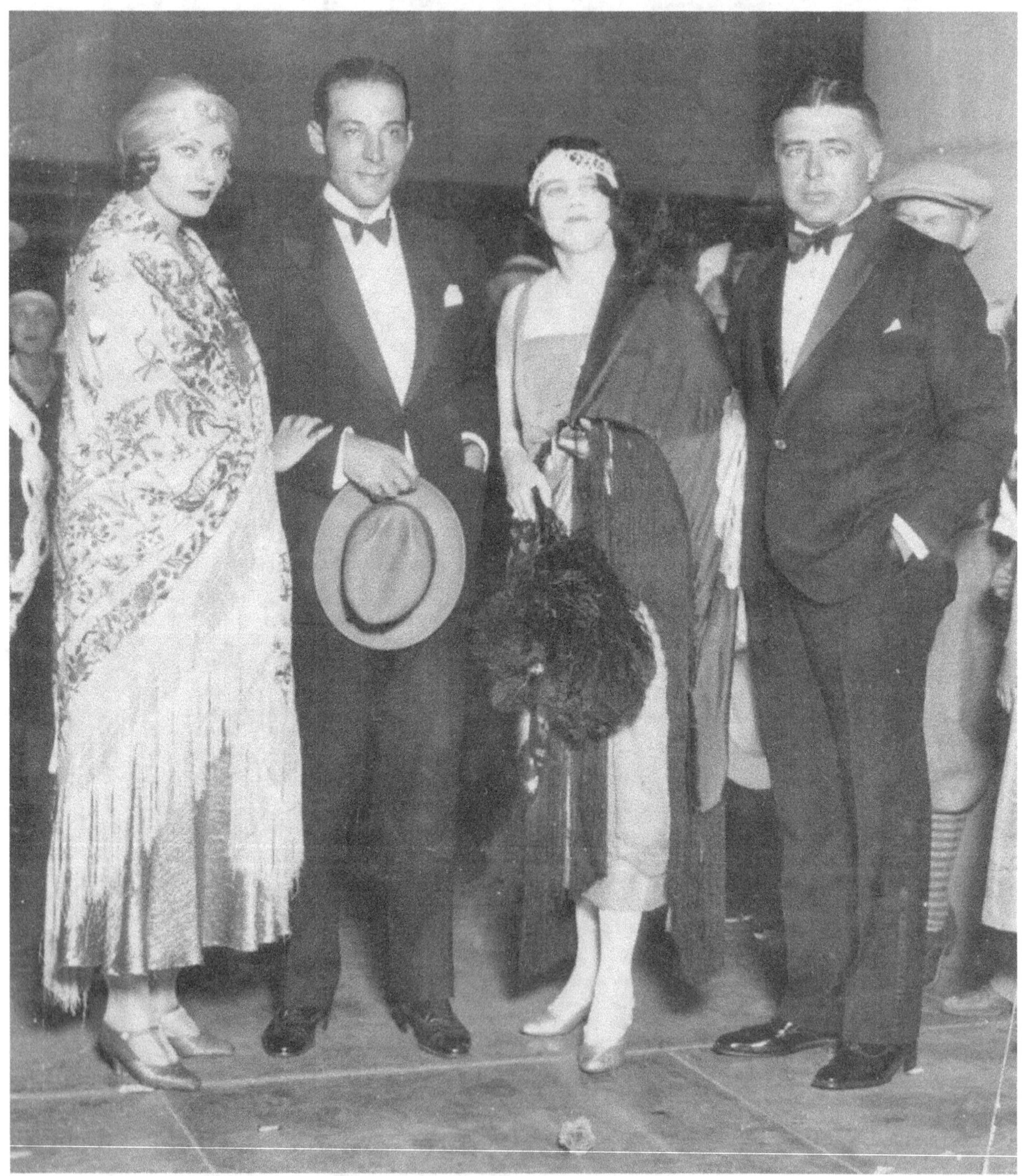

The Valentinos and Mr. and Mrs. Clarence Brown (Ona Wilson) attending a party.
(Author's collection)

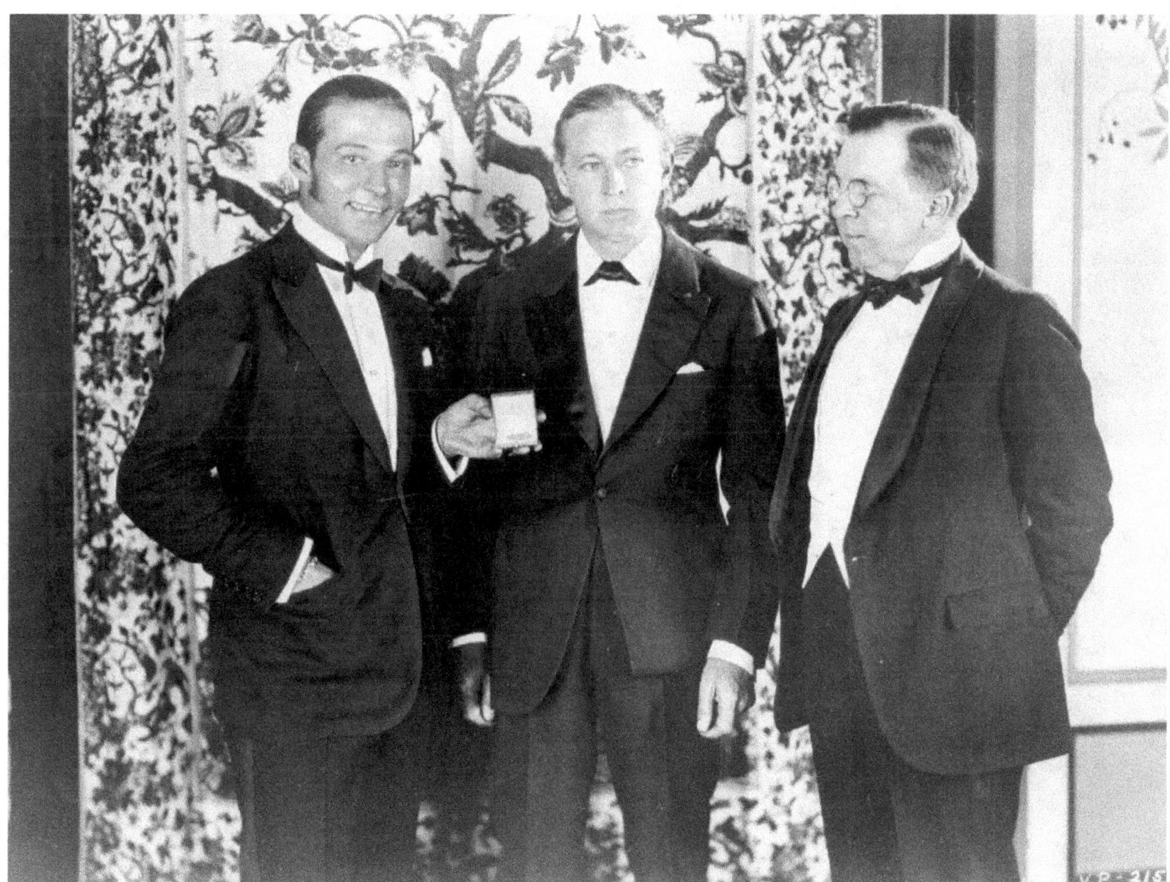

Valentino predated the founding of the Academy of Motion Picture Arts and Sciences by a couple of years. Here he is awarding the Rudolph Valentino Medal for Screen Acting to John Barrymore for 1924 with Hiram Abrahms. Barrymore was accorded this honor for his film *Beau Brummell.* The award was only given in 1925.
The whereabouts of the medal today are a mystery.
(Author's collection)

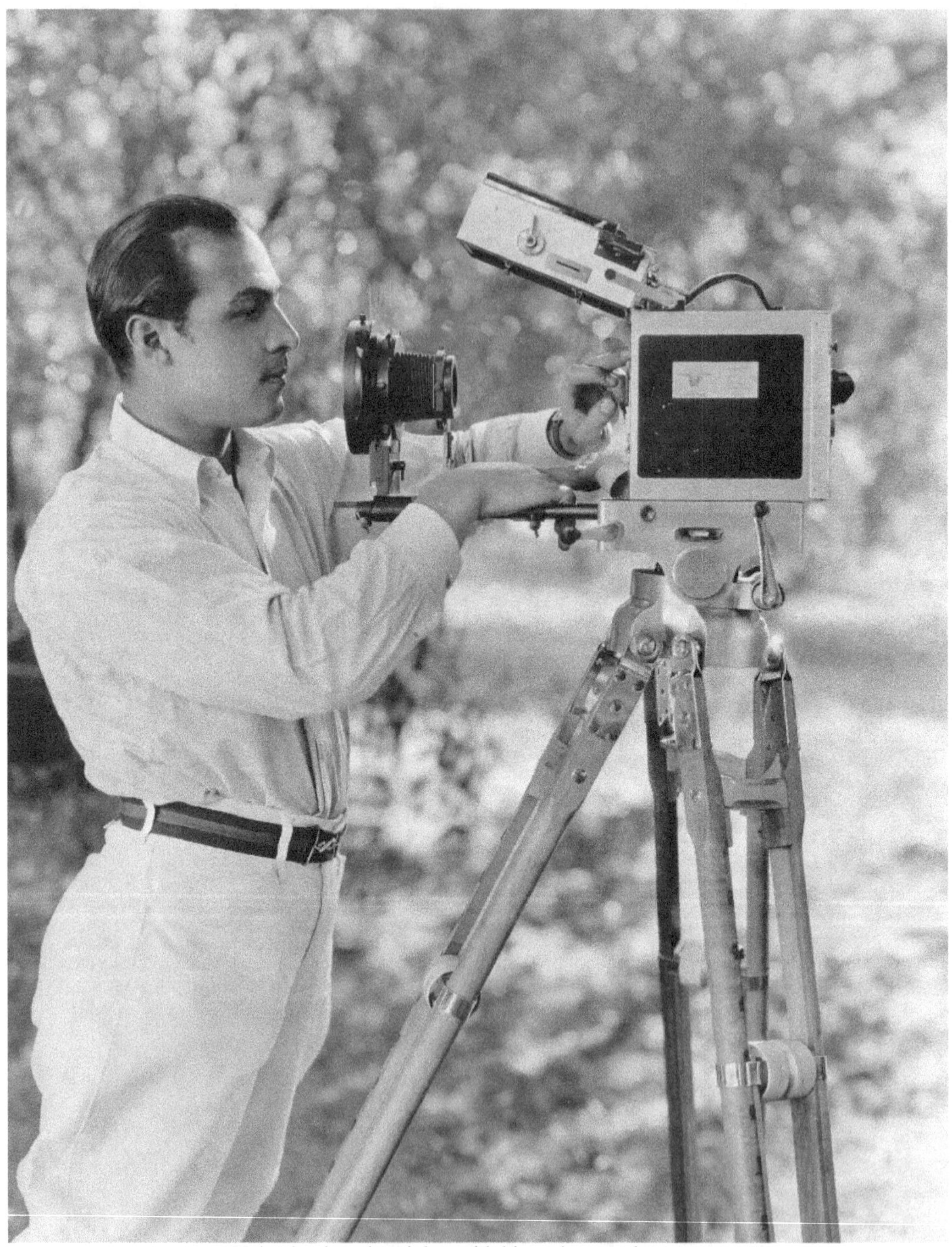

Valentino loved to tinker with his gadgets and cameras.
Early on he may have only had a Kodak Brownie, with fame and fortune,
he only used the best gear, in this case a French made Debrie movie camera.
(Author's collection)

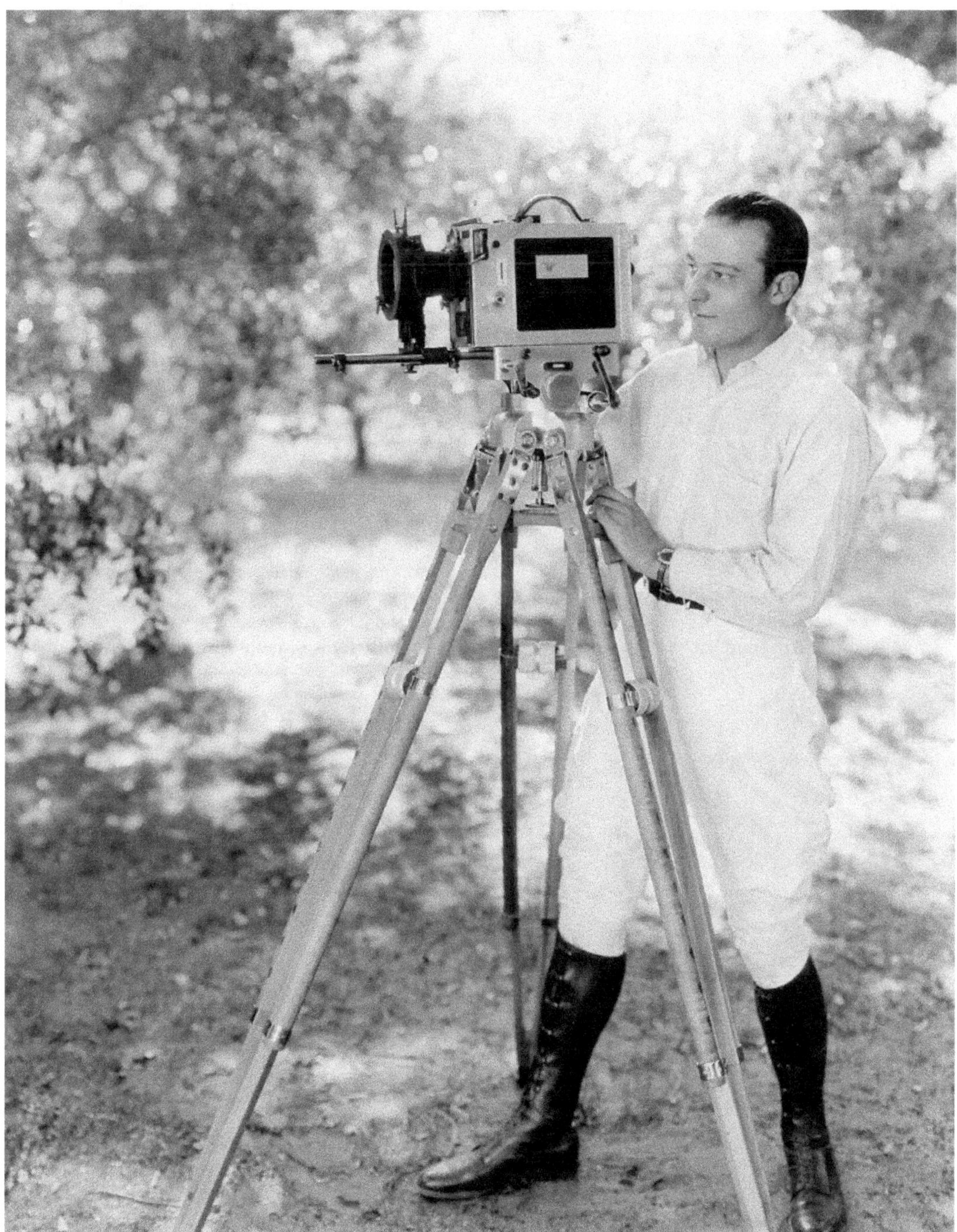

Valentino loved this hobby, and loved the freedom his visits to Palm Springs afforded him in the way of privacy to be himself.
(Author's collection)

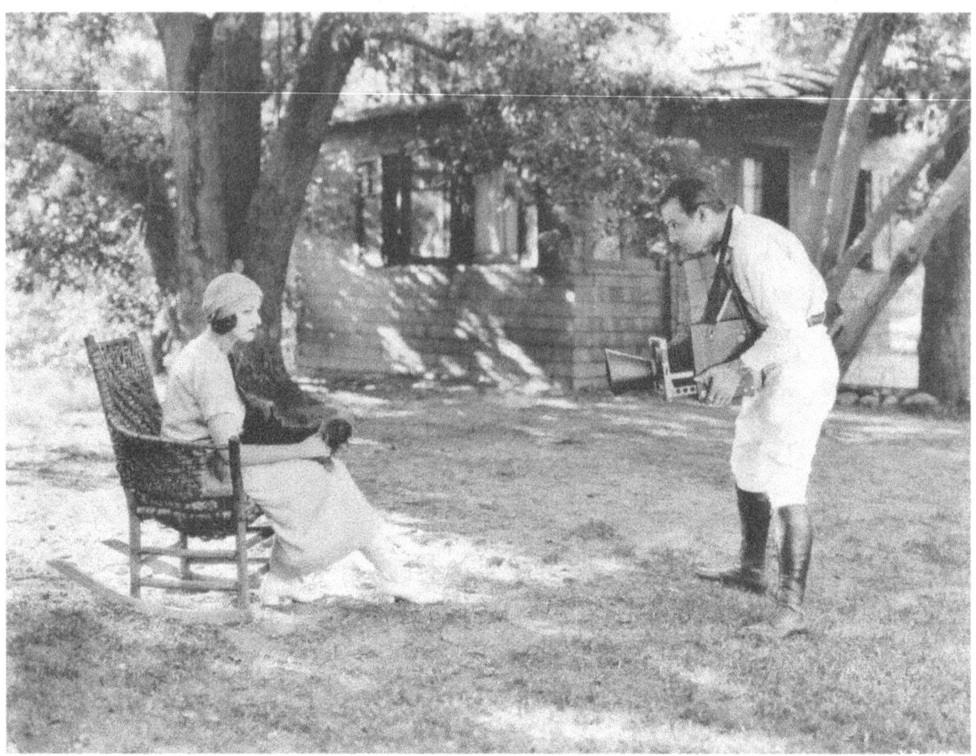

Never were Valentino and Natacha
more relaxed and happy than when enjoying the rustic pleasures of the California desert.
(Author's collection)

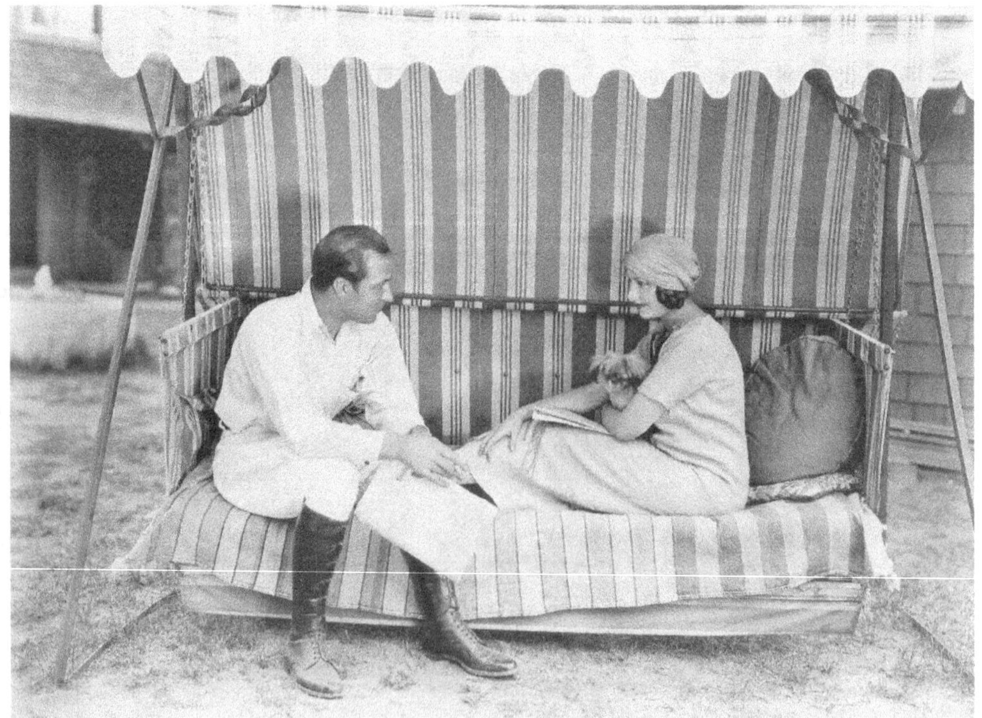

Even though these stills are posed for publicity,
you can see how relaxed and happy they were. (Brad Frick collection)

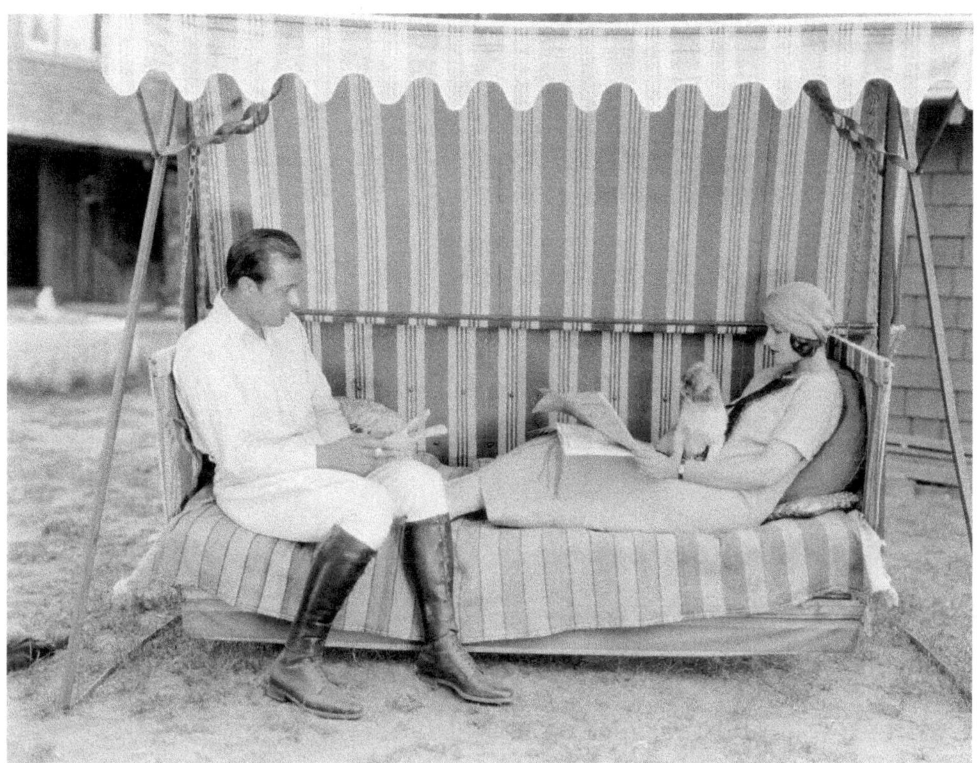

Valentino planned to purchase his own property in Palm Springs, sadly this never came to be.
(Author's collection)

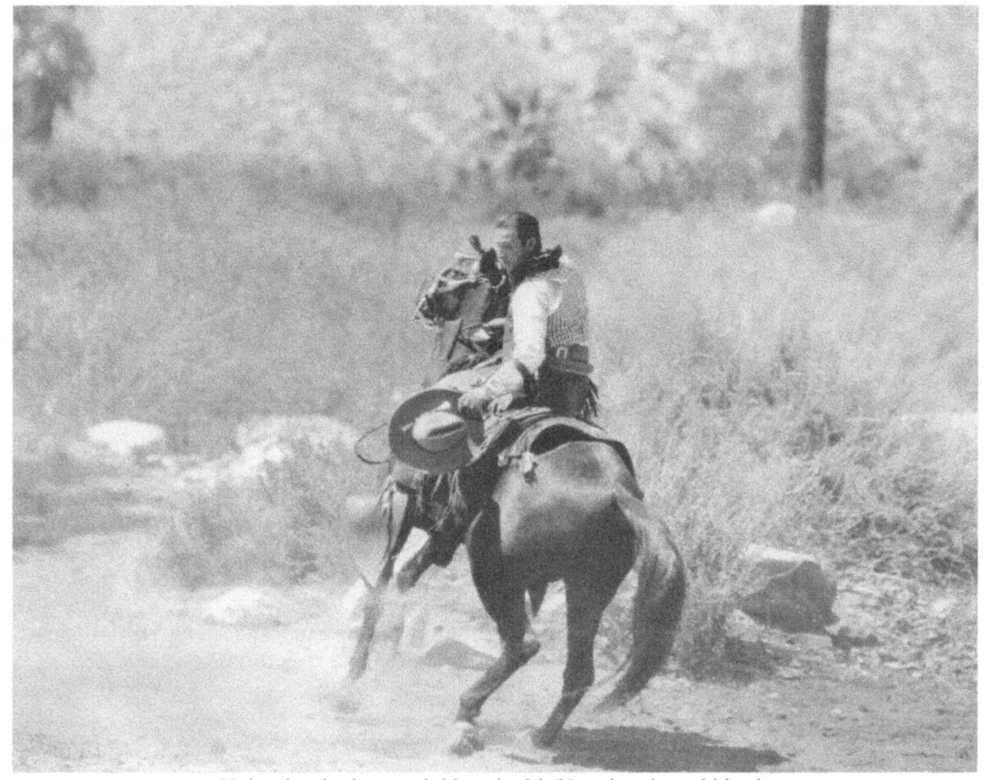

Valentino had a special bond with Yaqui and used him in both *The Eagle* and *The Son of the Sheik.*
(Author's collection)

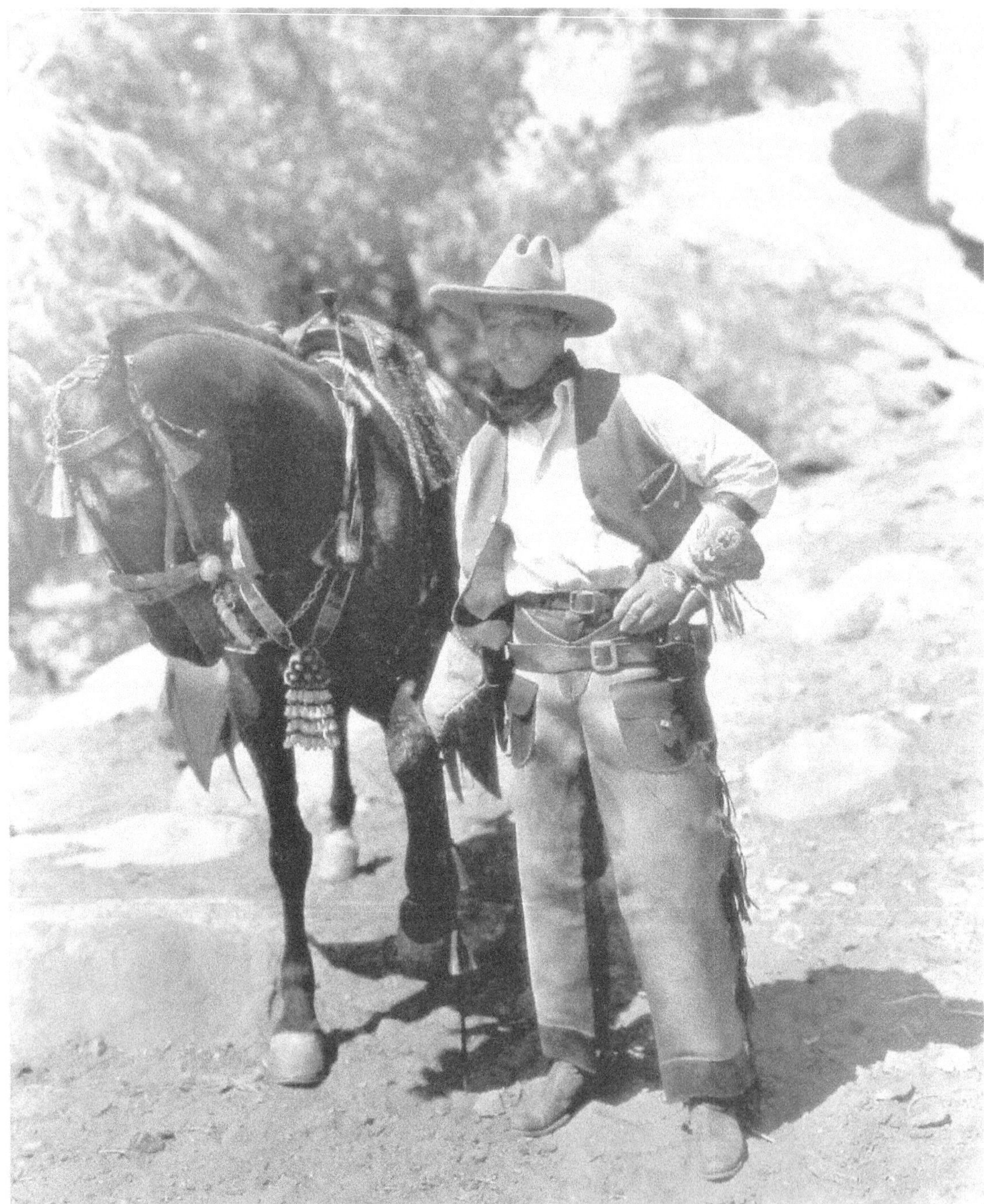

Valentino loved nothing better than tacking up his horse and himself in western garb and riding hell-for-leather in Beverly Hills and, in this case, Palm Springs. (Author's collection)

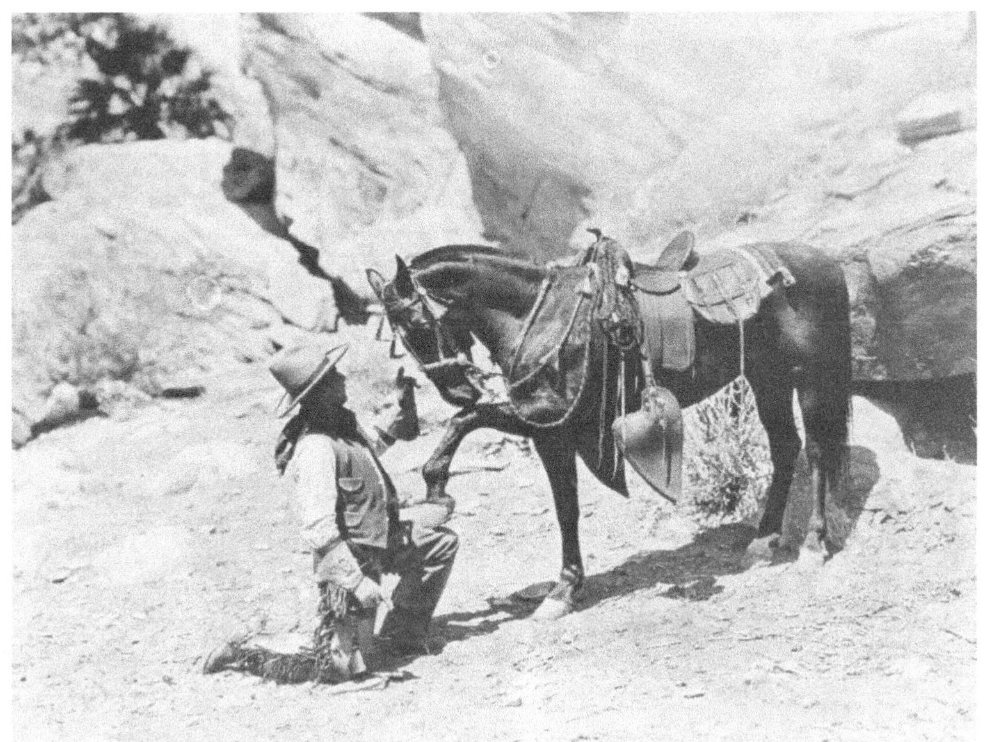

Valentino was an accomplished equestrian and he also worked closely training his horses and his dogs. (Author's collection)

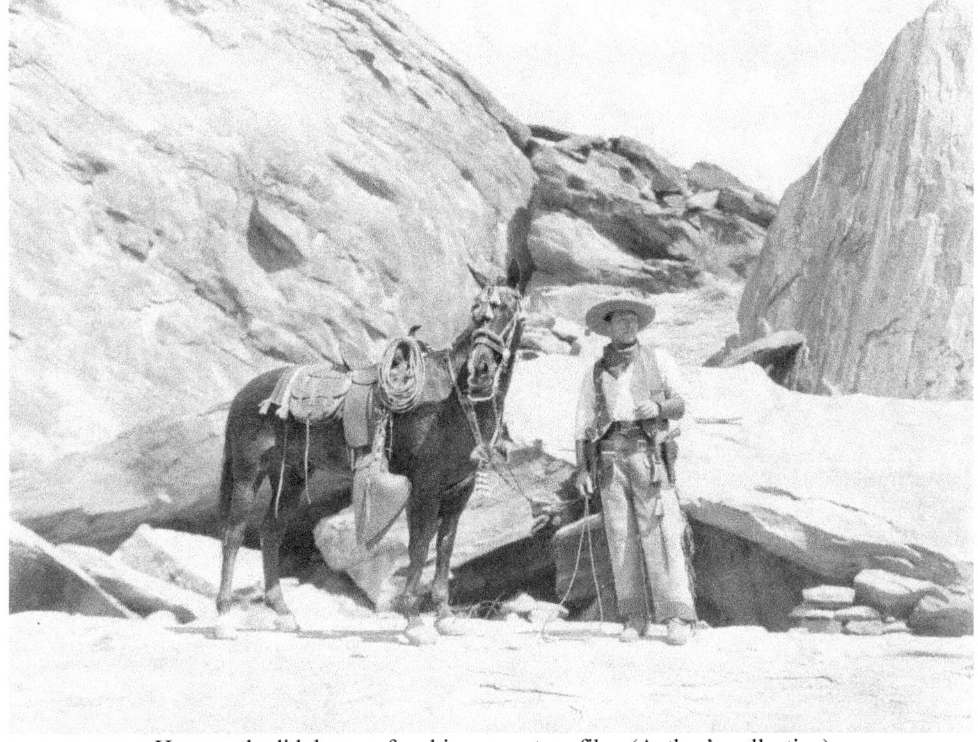

He secretly did dream of making a western film. (Author's collection)

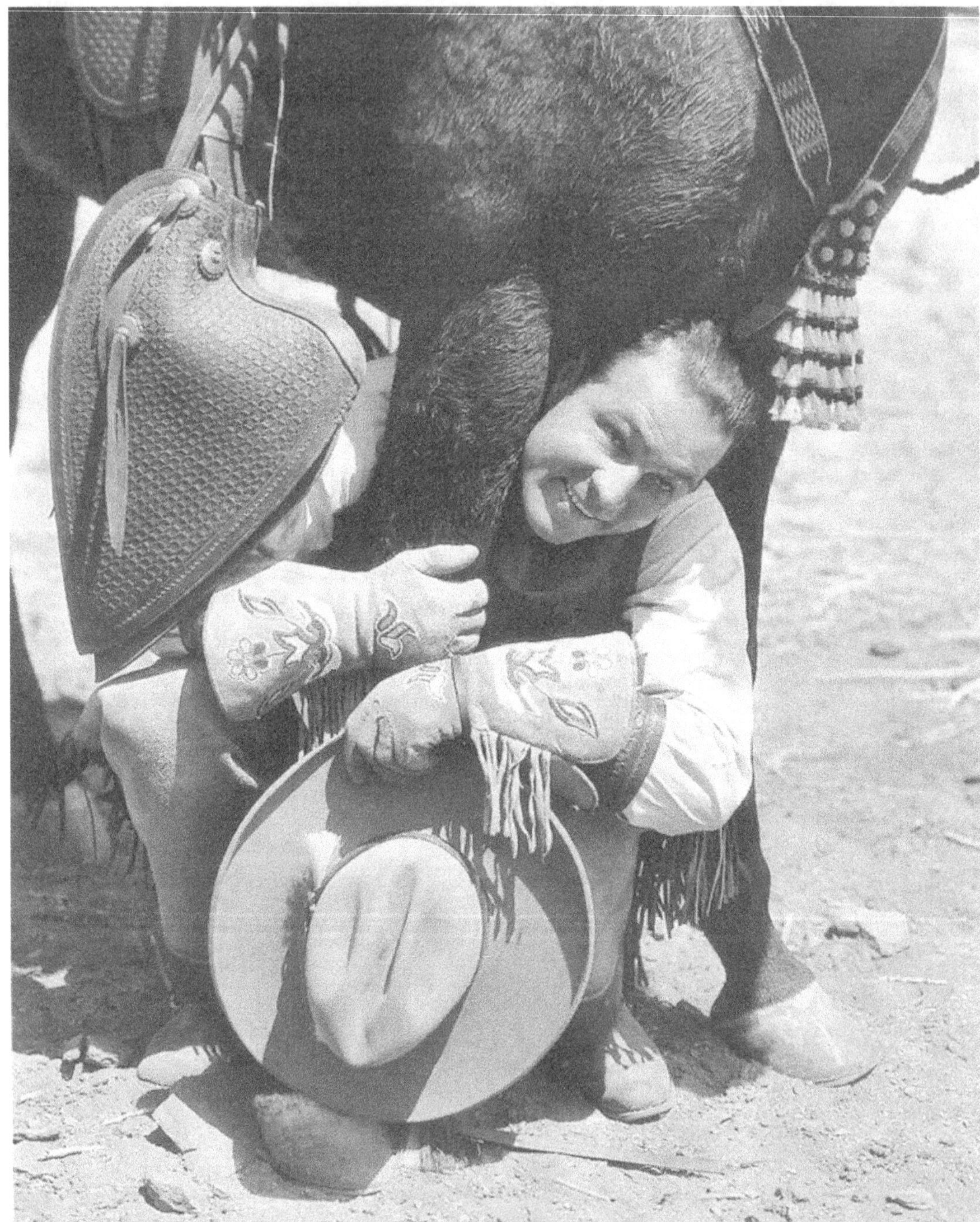

Valentino was really never happier spending time with his animals, or his cars.
(Author's collection)

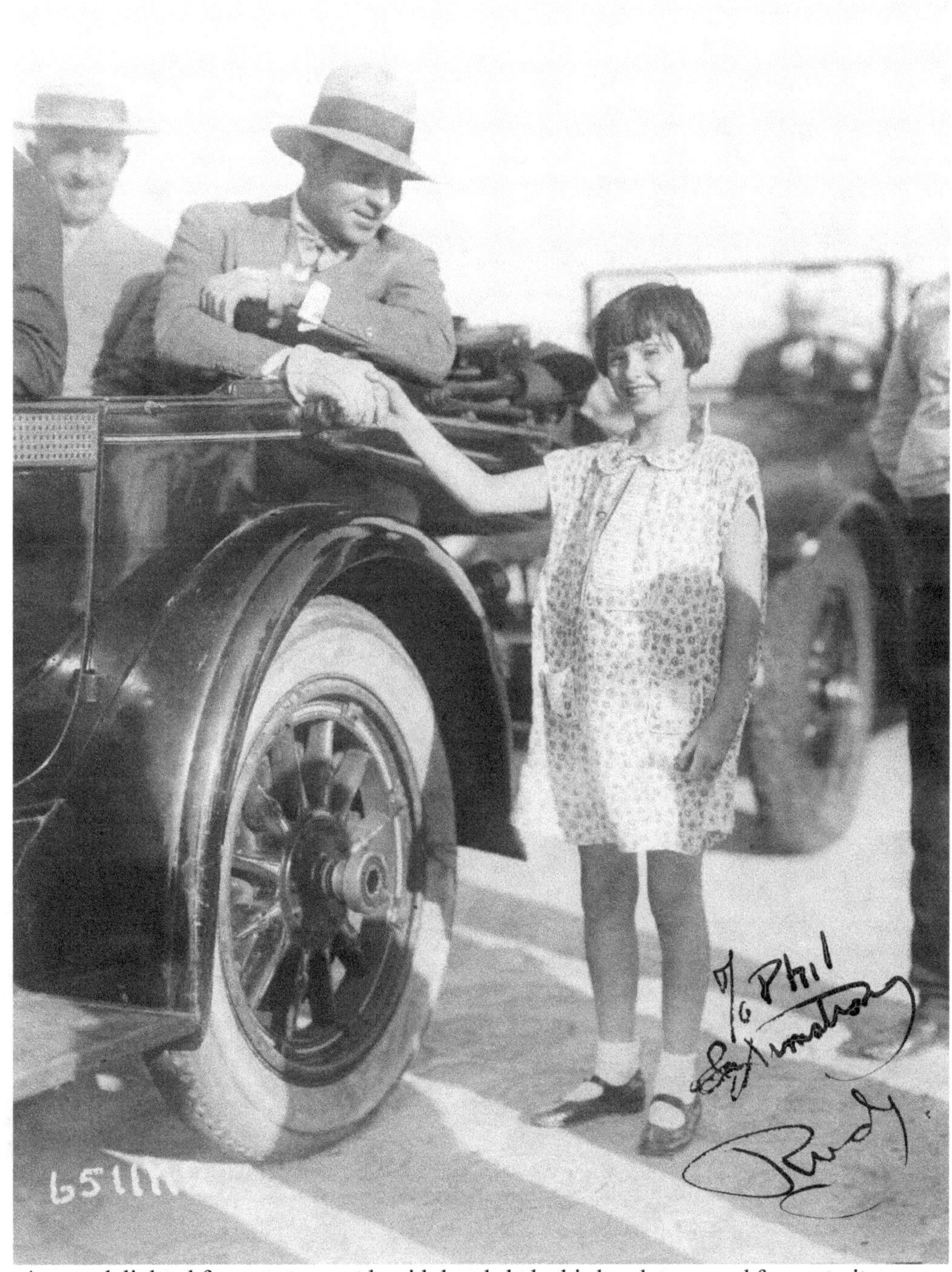

A very delighted fan gets to meet her idol and shake his hand preserved for posterity.
This is believed to be taken sometime in 1925. The signature in the corner is not Valentino's hand.
(Author's collection)

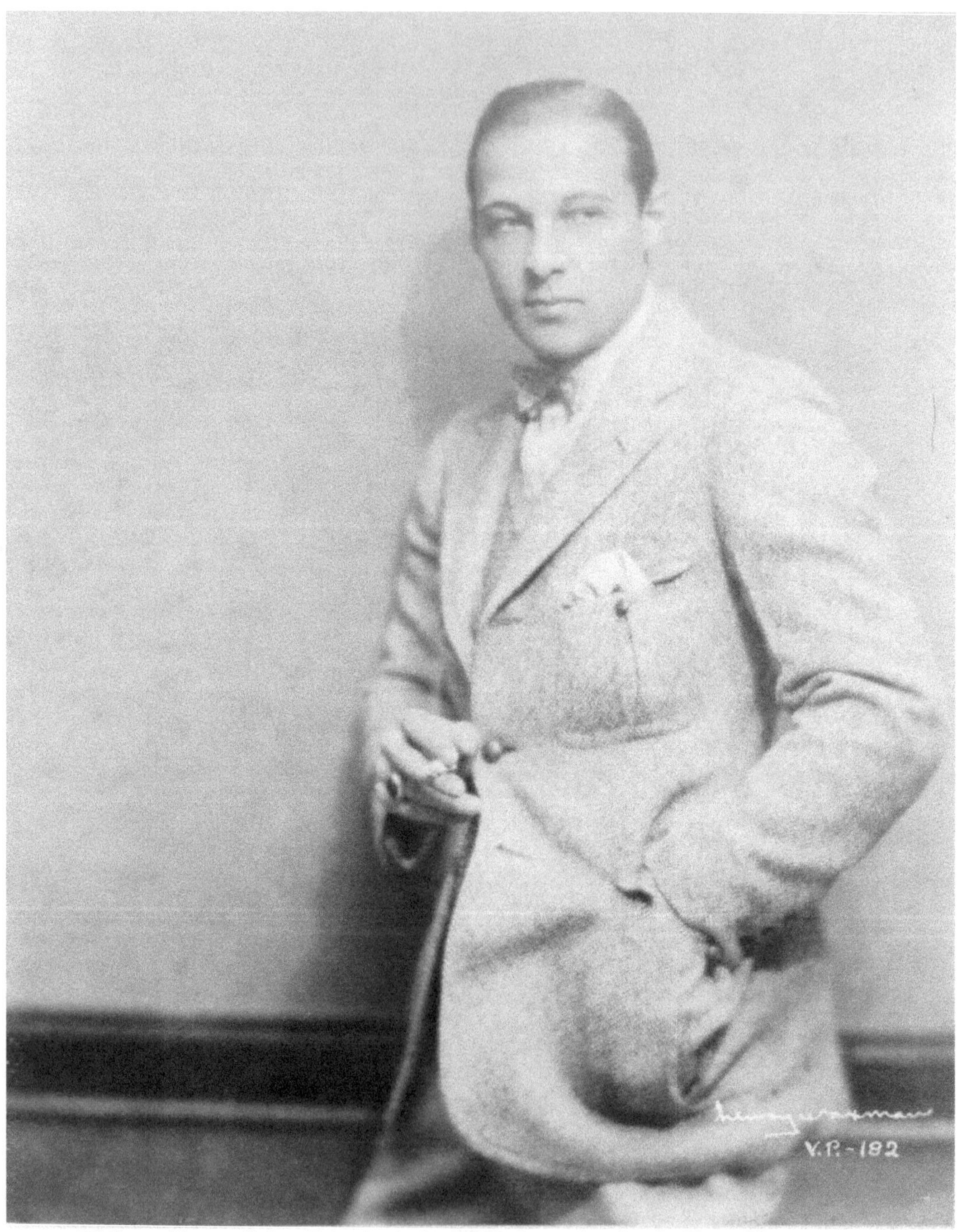

While working on *Cobra*, Valentino had a series of portraits taken by Henry Waxman.
(Author's collection)

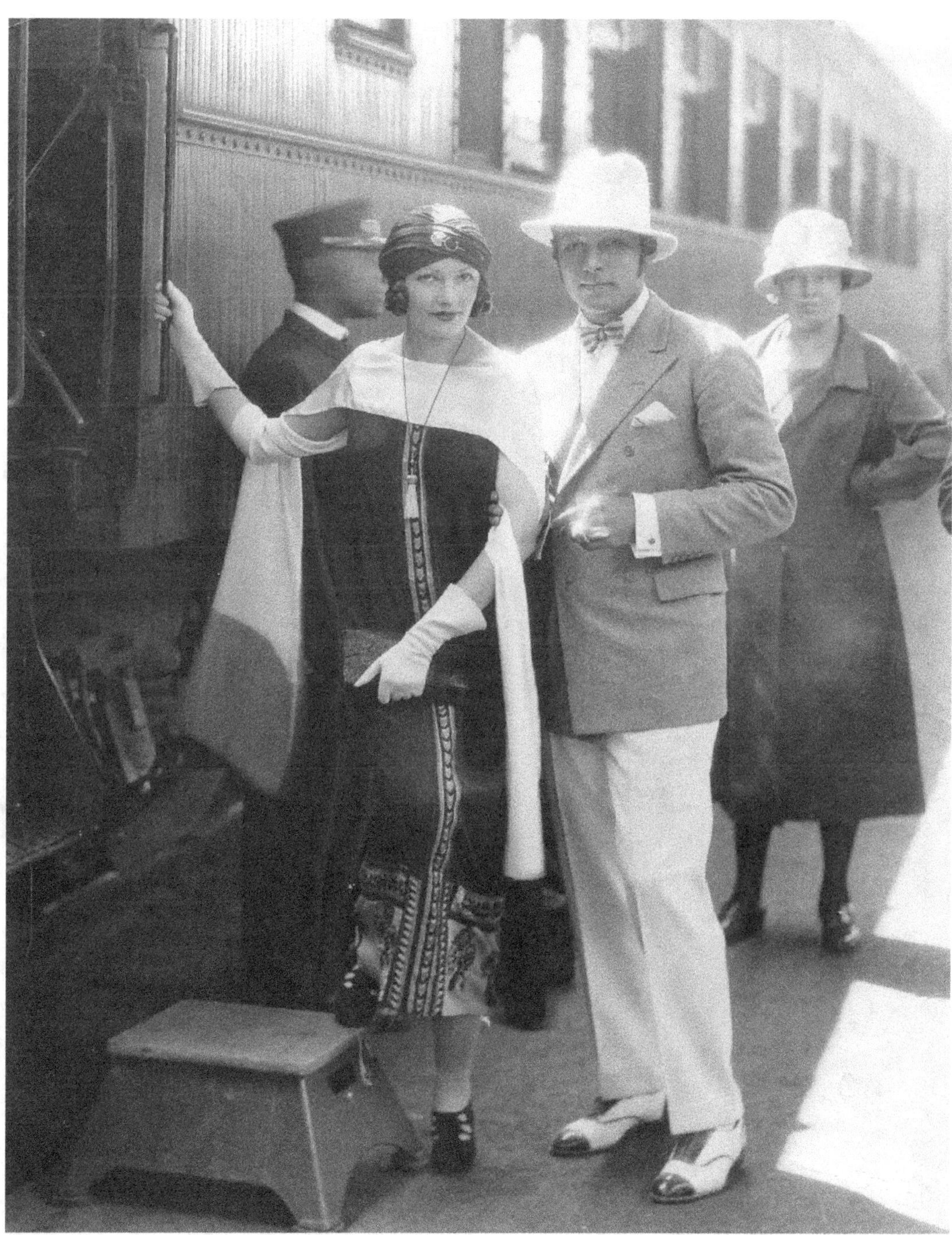

When these photos were originally taken, no mention of divorce was made. Natacha was going to New York for her film *What Price Beauty*, Rudy stayed in Hollywood to work on *The Eagle*. (Author's collection)

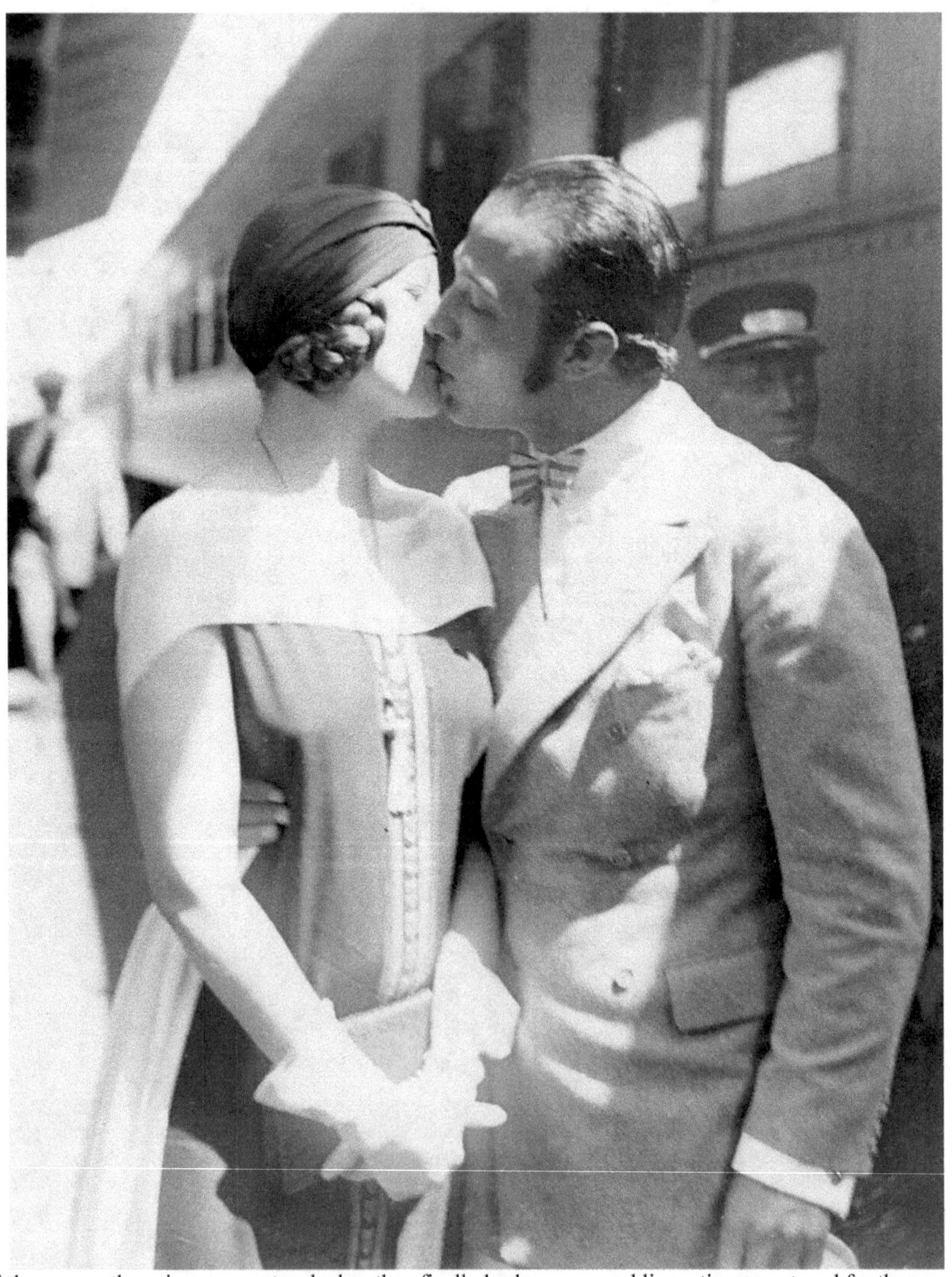

Behind the scenes, the pair grew apart and when they finally broke, a very public parting was staged for the press. The personal battle between the pair was soon being waged in the press.
(Author's collection)

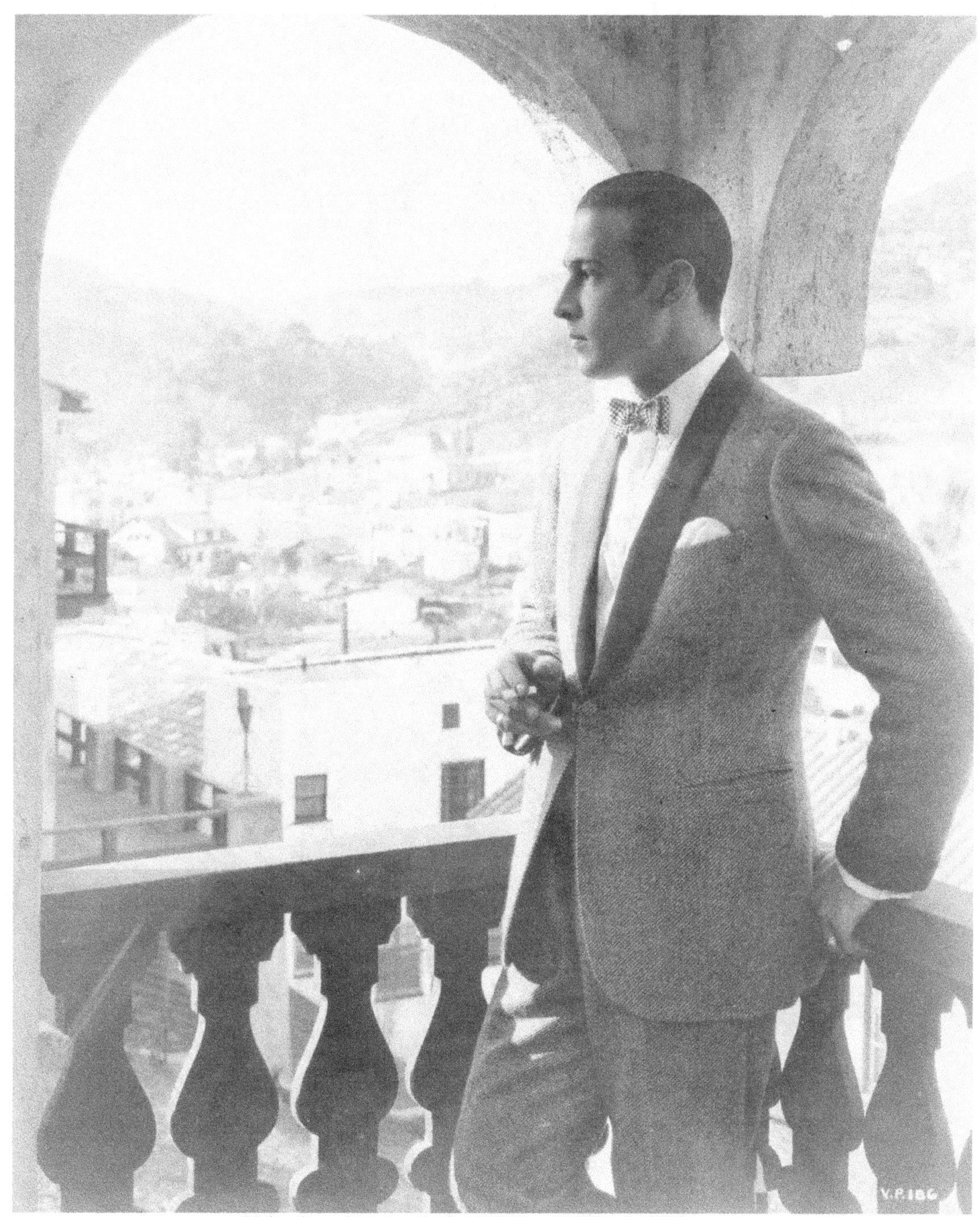

Valentino photographed at Whitley Heights in 1925.
(Author's collection)

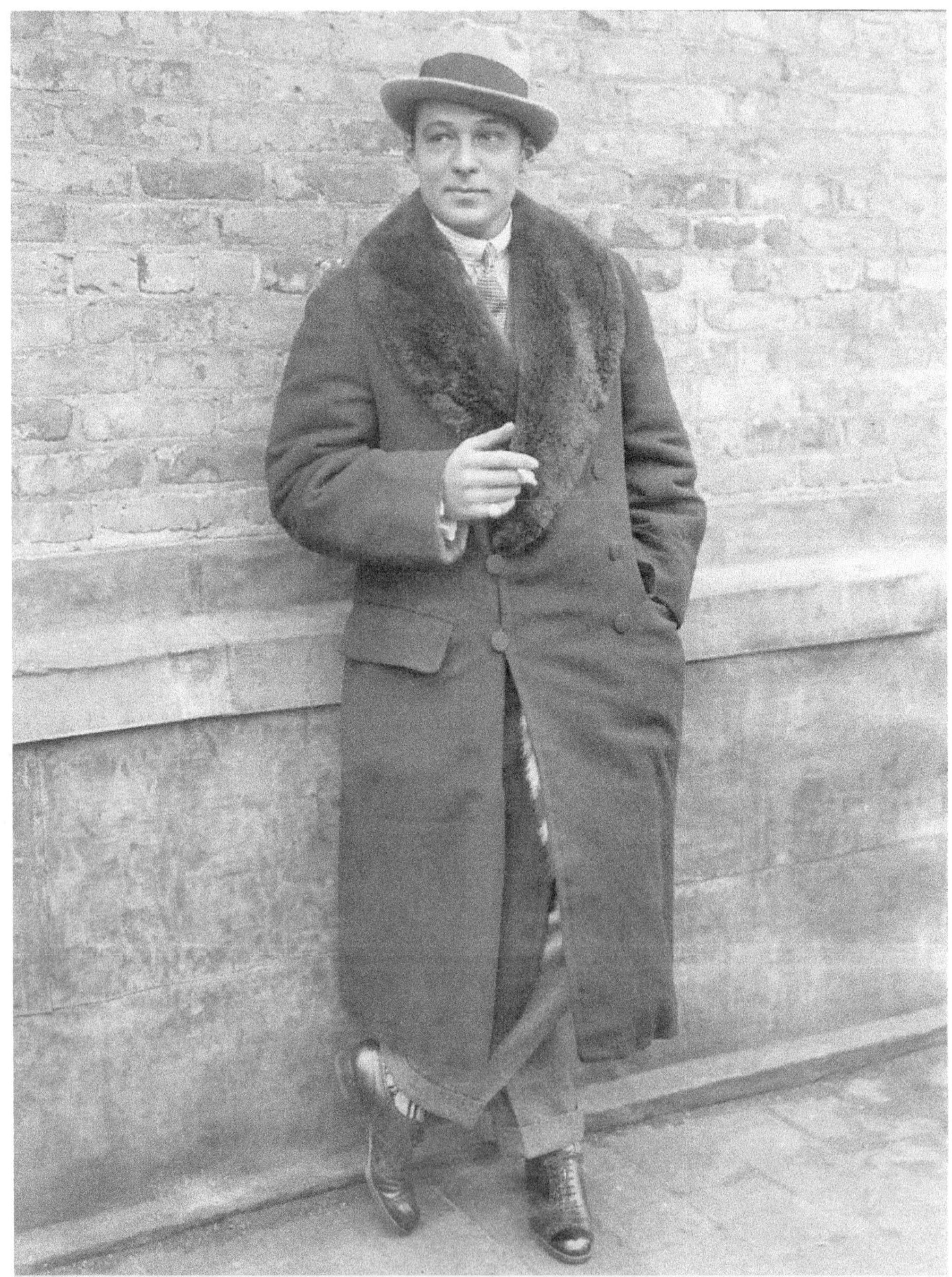

Valentino caught on the street in New York in late 1925.
(Author's collection)

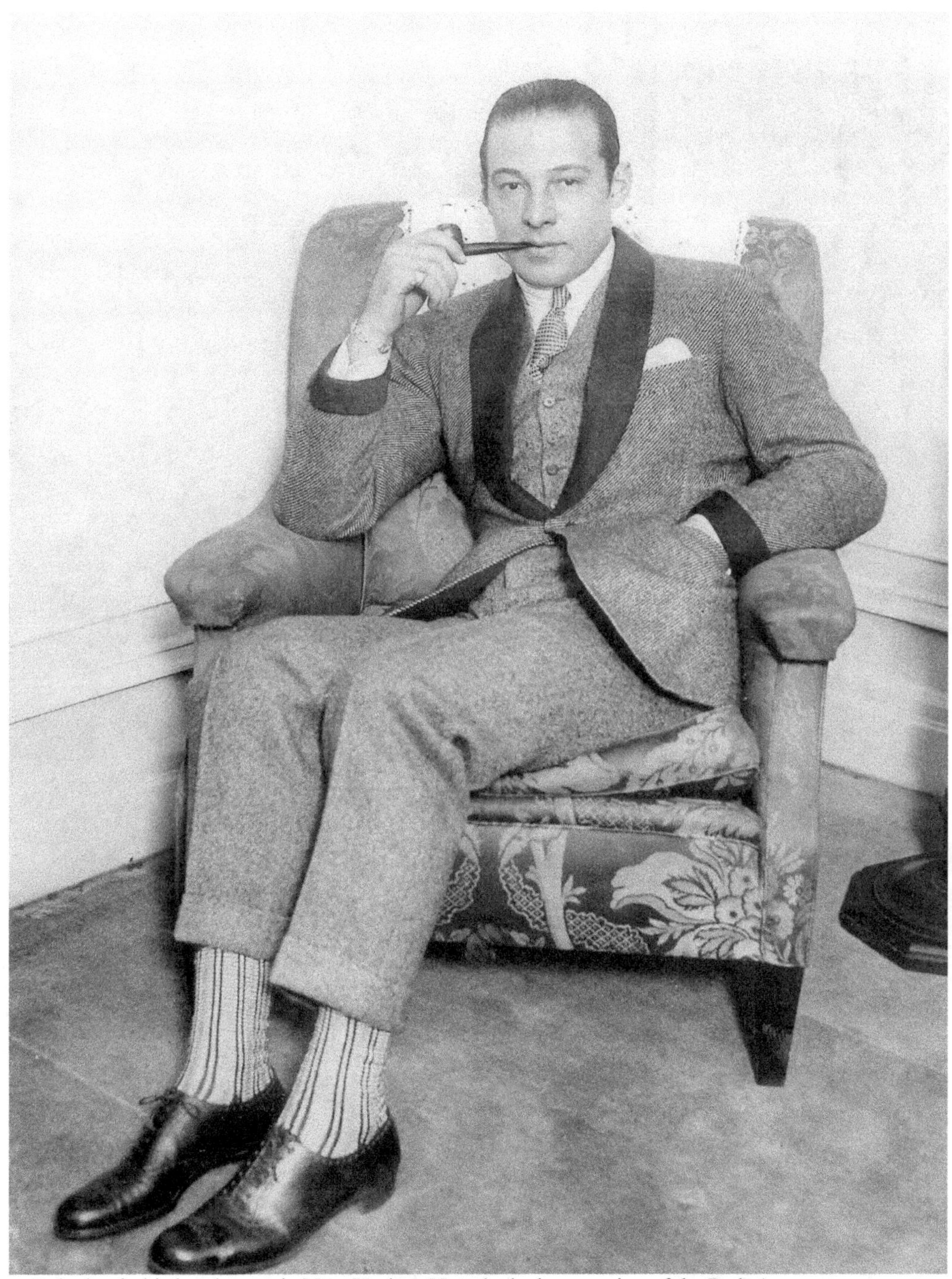

Relaxing in his hotel room in New York as Natacha had possession of the Park Avenue apartment. Valentino was in town to attend the premiere of *The Eagle* before embarking to Europe. (Author's collection)

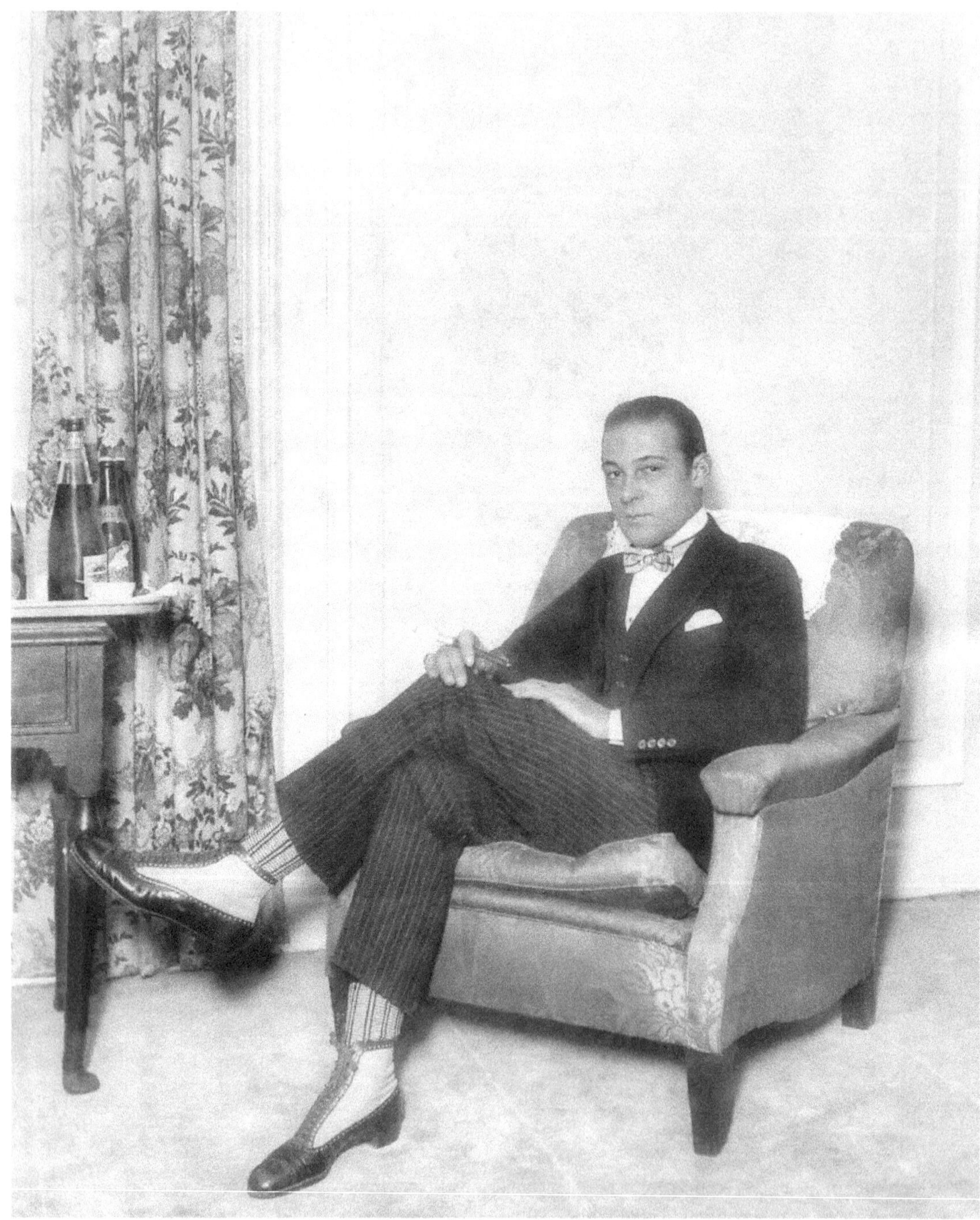

Valentino resting in New York at his hotel. Utterly stylish footwear and socks.
(Caroline Rupprecht collection)

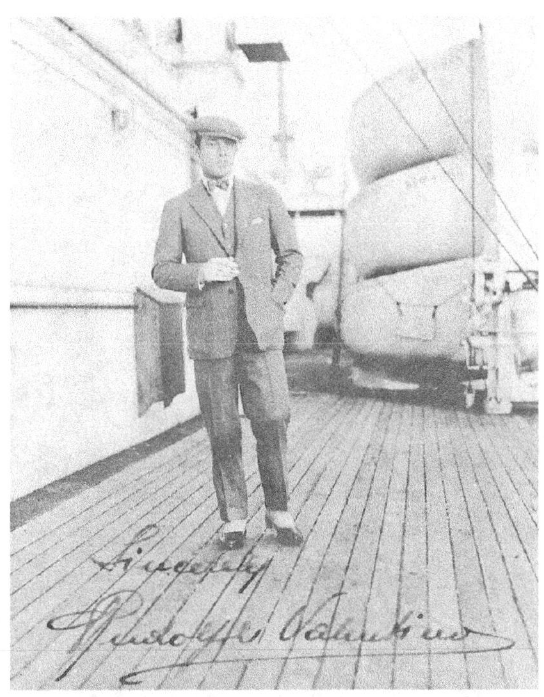

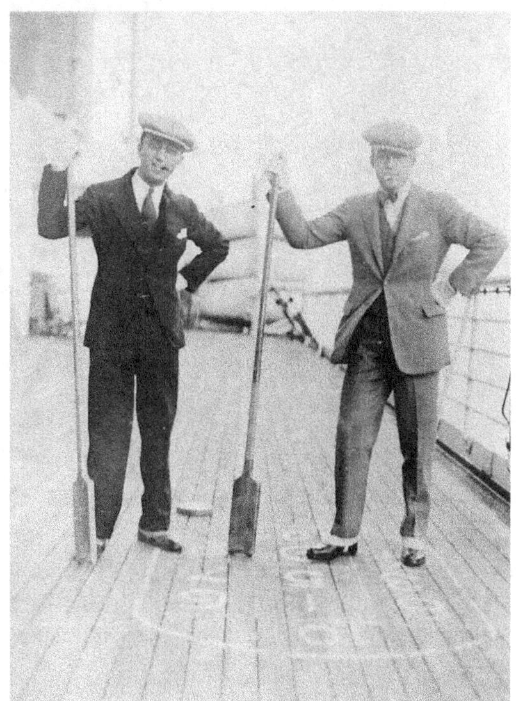

Valentino and Manuel Reachi set sail for Europe.
(Author's collection)

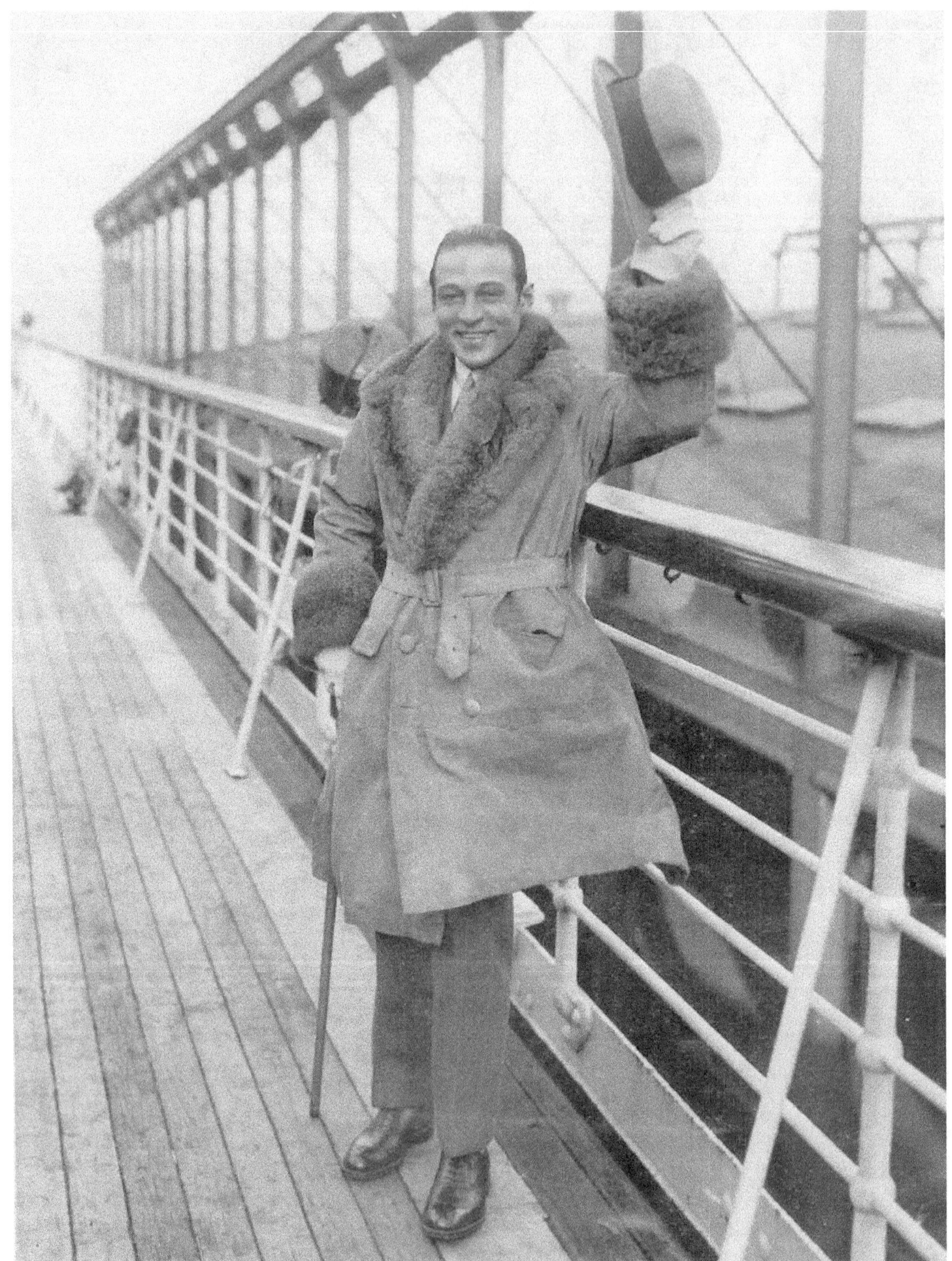

Valentino arrives at Southampton for the last time.
(Author's collection)

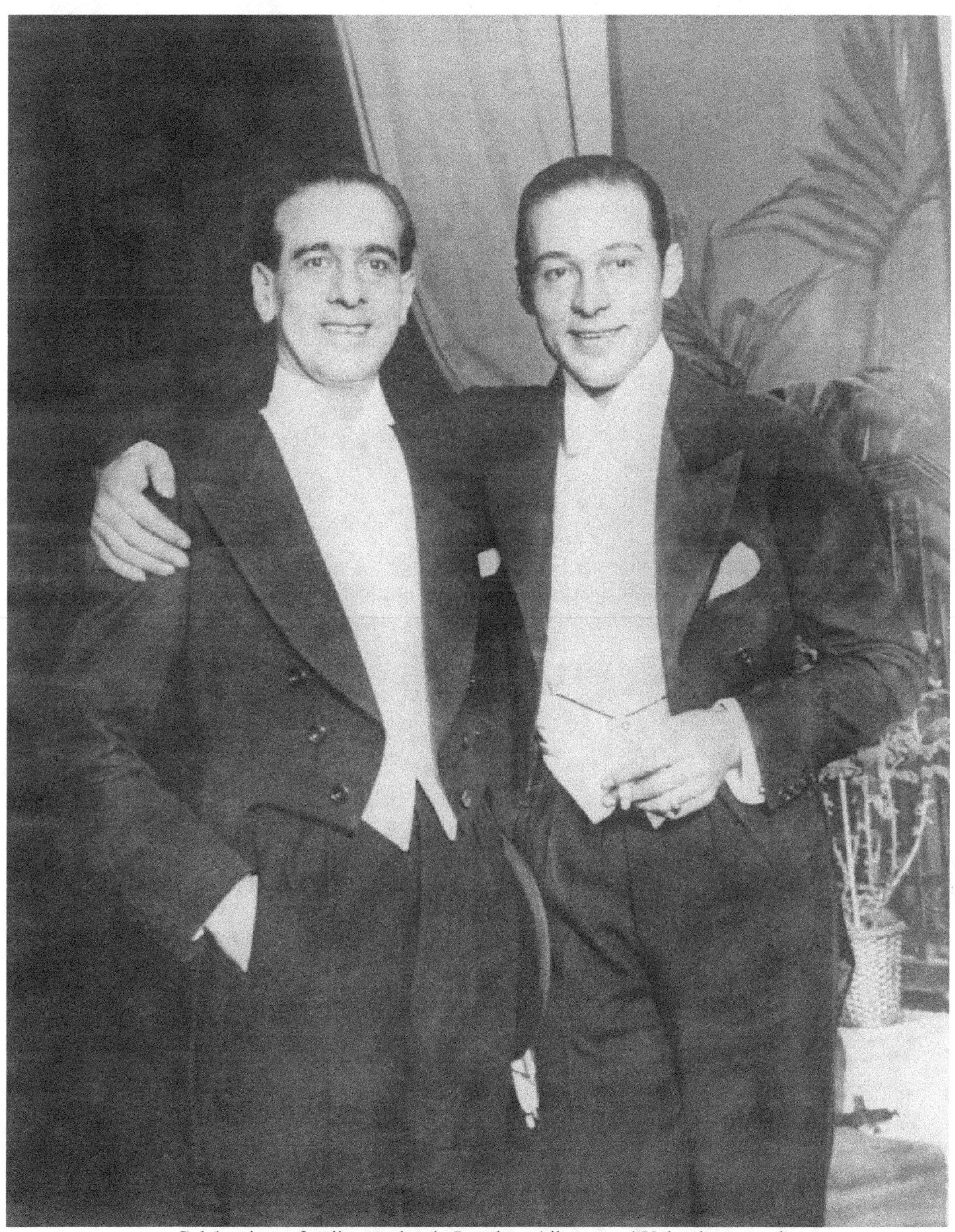

Celebrating a family reunion in London, Alberto and Valentino attend the premiere of *The Eagle* at the Marble Arch Pavilion. (Author's collection)

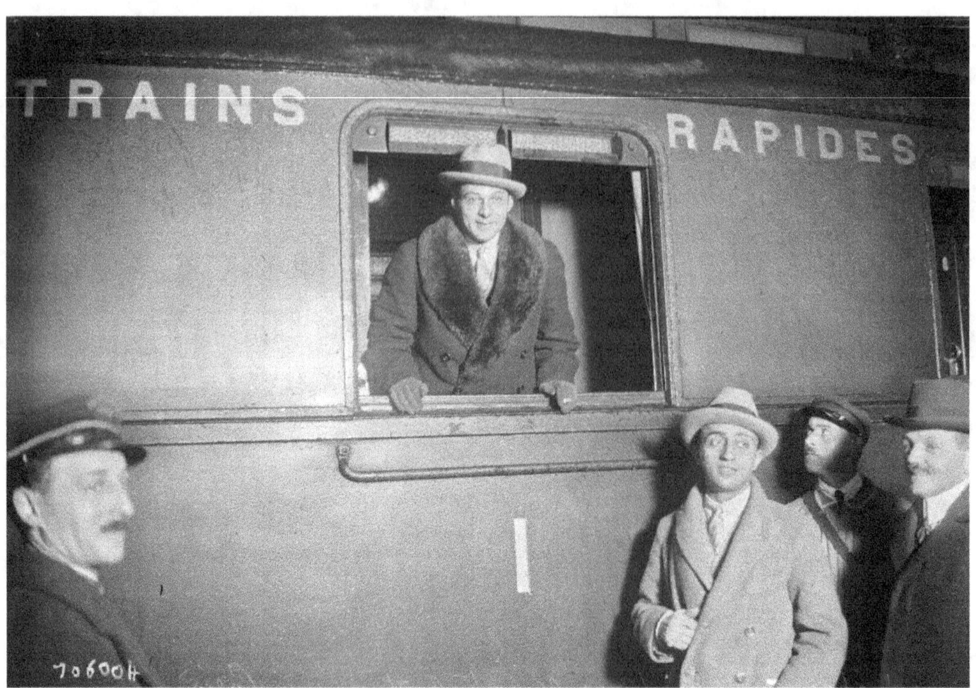

Valentino and Manuel Reachi arrive in Paris and are met by throngs of people and police.
(Bibliothèque Nationale de France)

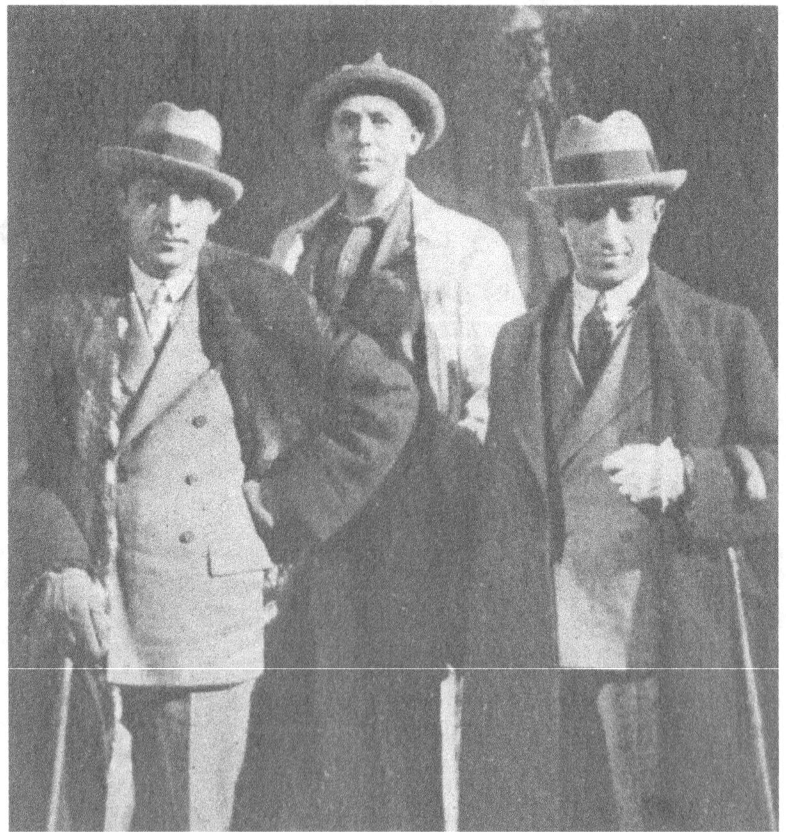

Valentino and Manuel Reachi visiting F.W. Murnau at the UFA studios.
(Author's collection)

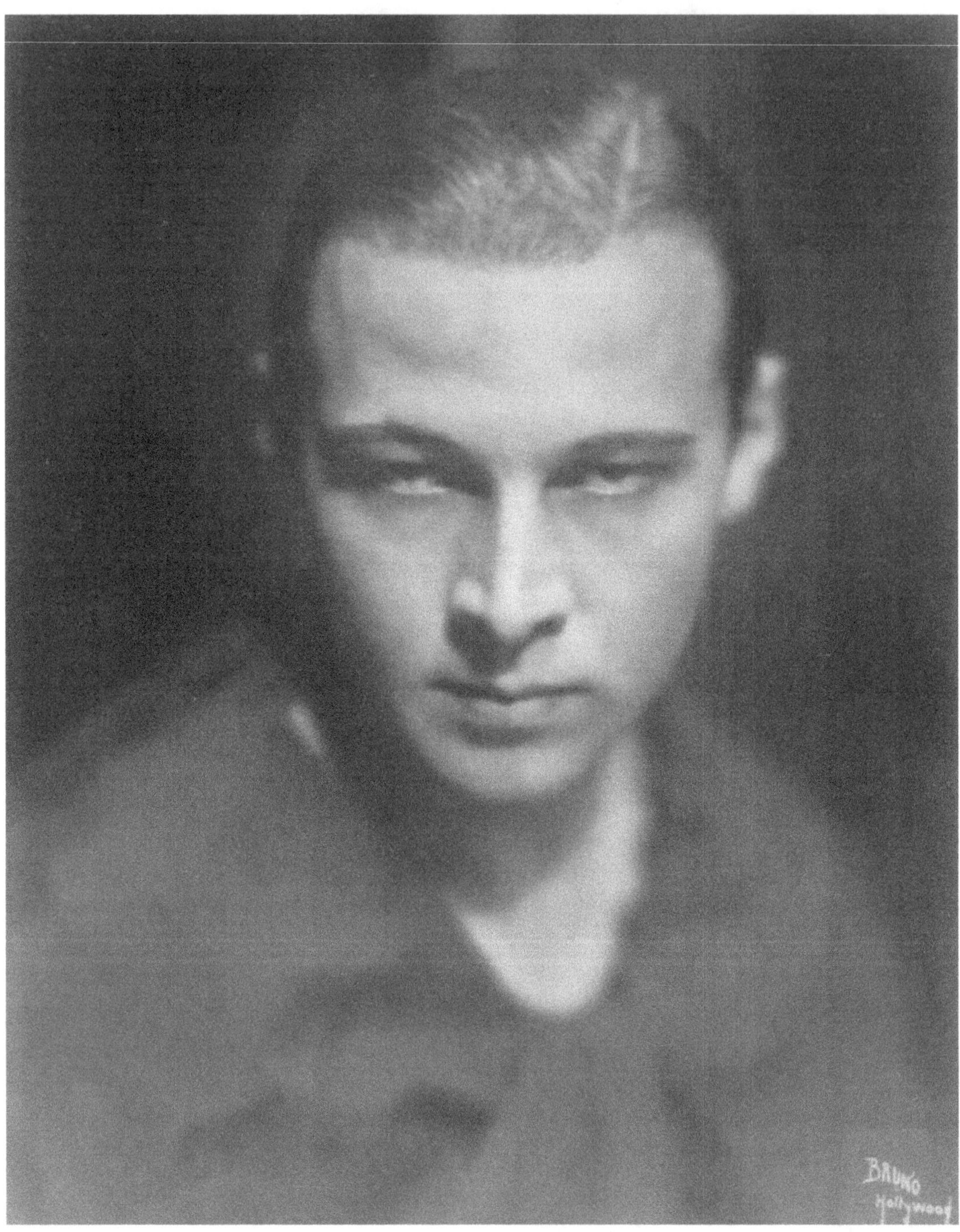
BRUNO
Hollywood

I cross the ocean a free man. That closes a chapter in my life. It only remains to turn the page and begin anew

—Rudolph Valentino, 1926

Before returning to America, Valentino traveled to Juan les Pins to say farewell to the Hudnuts. He, Alberto, Ada, and nephew Jean then embarked on the Leviathan to New York. There they arranged for the contents of the Park Avenue apartment to be packed and freighted to California. They also took a side trip to Washington D.C.

In Hollywood, the Guglielmi clan was treated to a whirlwind of activities, activities as varied as riding in the hills surrounding Falcon Lair and enjoying afternoon swims at the home of Valentino's newest love interest, Pola Negri. He had been introduced to the temperamental Polish star by Marion Davies, and by all accounts it was a memorable first meeting. Negri was tempestuous, self-absorbed, dramatic, and passionate in her pursuit of Valentino. In early February 1926, the two motored north toward San Francisco together in his Isotta Fraschini and were seen dining in the California coastal towns of Santa Barbara and Monterey, although Negri was apparently absent in San Francisco. On the return trip, Valentino's habitual speeding and poor eyesight got him in trouble—he crashed the Isotta Fraschini at a rail crossing.

His next film was *The Son of the Sheik*, directed by George Fitzmaurice, in which he was reteamed with the exquisite Vilma Banky. Shot on the backlot and on location in Yuma, Arizona, The Son of the Sheik had everything the first film lacked: beautiful sets by William Cameron Menzies, rich silken costumes garnished with jeweled daggers, careful production values, and a generous budget. Valentino delighted in the physicality of his role and enjoyed parading around unrecognized and unhindered in full makeup as the elder Sheik Ahmed. Despite his pleasure in the role, he was not feeling well during the shoot. He complained of stomach troubles and consumed large quantities of bicarbonate of soda, which did little to ease his discomfort.

Shooting completed, Valentino and Negri continued to spend time together on the weekends, both on Valentino's yacht, the Phoenix, and at parties. The two won a dancing and costume contest at the Biltmore Hotel; judging from photographs taken at the event, Valentino's physical attraction to Negri was quite apparent. In late June, Negri and Valentino served as maid of honor and best man at Mae Murray's wedding to Prince David M'divani at the Church of the Good Shepherd in Beverly Hills. A breakfast reception, hosted by Valentino, was held at the Ambassador Hotel.

The Son of the Sheik premiered to great acclaim at Sid Grauman's Million Dollar Theater in Los Angeles, and it was clear from the film's reception that United Artists had a hit on its hands. Valentino was very pleased with the film as well as with the public's reaction. Before departing for the East Coast premiere in New York, he signed a new three-picture contract with John Considine; his next picture, then being developed, would be based on the life of the artist Benvenuto Cellini and was to be photographed by the celebrated cameraman Charles Rosher. Valentino and Ullman then traveled to San Francisco, where he hosted a press party at the Fairmont Hotel and visited old friends and old haunts. He also met with San Francisco's popular mayor, "Sunny" Jim Rolph, and was given a beautiful black Cocker Spaniel that he admired. Privately, he was still complaining of stomach problems.

His next stop was Chicago. While there, Valentino was enraged by an article in the Chicago Tribune, entitled "Pink Powder Puffs," which attacked his masculinity. He publicly challenged the anonymous author to a boxing match, but needless to say, the craven author did not respond. Valentino sat for a few final portraits with photographer Mabel Sykes and then departed for New York feeling angry, ill, and tired.

In New York, he stayed in a suite of rooms at the Ambassador Hotel and met with his good friend Jack Dempsey and Estelle Taylor (Mrs. Dempsey). Still reacting to the "Pink Powder Puffs" article, he posed for newsreels boxing with Dempsey and sportswriter Buck O'Neil. In the newsreels he appeared good humored, but underneath, the veiled accusations in the article still stung, and Valentino seethed.

On July 24, Alberto, Ada, and Jean departed New York for their return trip to Italy. The family posed together for final photographs on the SS Paris before the ship sailed.

Single once again, Valentino was seen with several women, including his ex-wife Jean Acker and Ziegfeld Follies beauty Marion Benda, and was regularly spotted in nightspots around Manhattan. When quizzed about his relationship with Pola Negri and whether they would marry, he diplomatically responded, "ask the lady." Although he did not feel well, he continued to burn the candle at both ends.

On August 15 in his hotel room, Valentino was stricken with agonizing abdominal pains. His valet called George Ullman, who arrived at the suite to find him doubled over in pain and spitting up blood. Doctors were called and he was rushed to the Polyclinic Hospital in a private ambulance. X-rays confirmed a large perforated ulcer in the abdominal cavity surrounded by other ulcerated areas. There was infection in the abdominal cavity, which would spread rapidly without surgery. Emergency surgery was duly performed several hours later and the abdominal cavity was cleansed and closed. He was taken to a private room. When he woke, he was feverish and vomiting blood, groaning in pain.

Four days passed, and Valentino was still in agonizing pain. He remained feverish and was unable to eat. As his strength ebbed, he was fed via injections of vitamins. On the morning of the 20th he awoke in great pain and had difficulty breathing; he was given morphine and he went back to sleep. Later, when the attending physician arrived to check Rudy's dressings and the drains, he smiled. For the first time since the 15th, he was not in pain. But his condition worsened dramatically in the space of a few hours. The doctors took further X-rays and confirmed their worst fears: pleurisy and peritonitis had set in, and all hope for recovery was lost. Crowds had gathered outside the hospital, eager for any news of the stricken star.

On the evening of August 22 his trial really began. His feverish temperature held steady, his breathing was labored, he moaned in pain, and he was finally advised of the gravity of his condition. He agreed to see a Catholic priest and made confession. He was given absolution but was too weak to take communion.

Early in the morning of August 23 Valentino was given more morphine to ease his discomfort. As the sun rose, the heat and humidity became oppressive and the crowd that had gathered outside the hospital could be heard from the open window. Dr. Meeker tried to close the window blinds, but in one of his last lucid moments, Valentino stopped him. His final hours, however, were spent in an unconscious state. Nothing more could be done, except wait for the inevitable. George Ullman waited in the hospital corridor, weeping. Priests administered extreme unction.

Just before noon on August 23, the doctor sponged the sweat from his face and neck. The priests knelt at the foot of his bed, praying. His eyes fluttered open for the briefest moment; then his head fell back onto the pillow. He died at ten minutes after the noon hour.

Valentino's body was transferred to the Frank E. Campbell Funeral Church for preparation. Crowds surged on the streets and surrounded the funeral home. It was decided to allow fans a glimpse of the star as he lay in state. The stories of the crowds and the mayhem of the days leading up to Valentino's New York funeral at St. Malachy's Church are well documented.

Alberto Guglielmi, shocked and grieving, returned to New York and was met by George Ullman and Frank Menillo. The bronze casket containing the body was sent by rail to California for burial, with Alberto, Menillo, Pola Negri, Frank E. Campbell and Ullman and his wife accompanying it. Alberto later recalled many touching scenes that took place in different towns during Rudolph Valentino's sad, final journey. People from all walks of life, young and old, greeted the train at various stops along the way to pay their respects.

The funeral mass on the morning of September 7, 1926, was held at the Church of the Good Shepherd in Beverly Hills. He was entombed later that afternoon at Hollywood Memorial Park in a crypt that originally belonged to June Mathis. His grave is a place of pilgrimage for Valentino fans to this day.

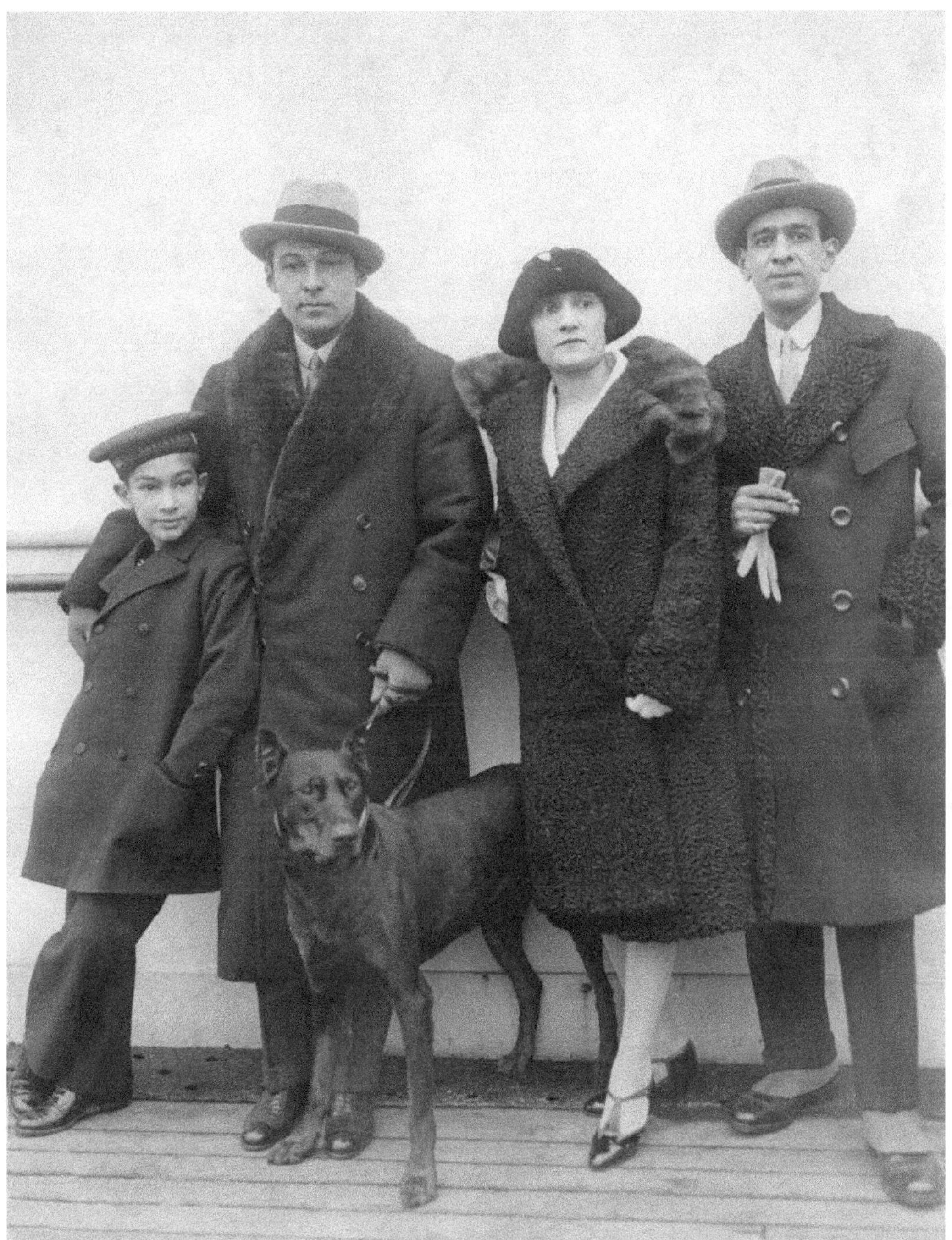

The Guglielmi clan arrive in New York, January 1926.
(Author's collection)

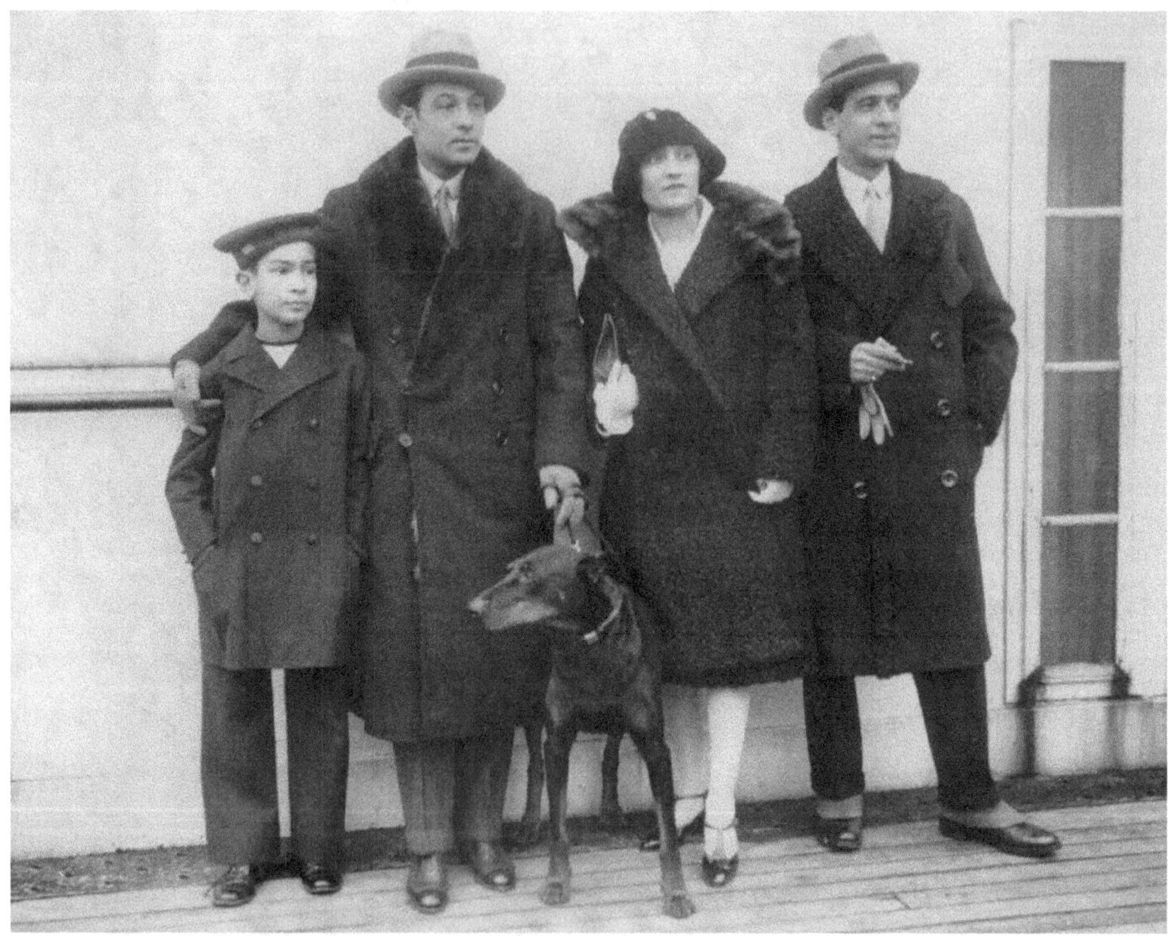

Valentino, Alberto, Ada and nephew Jean experience their first taste experiencing what it is to travel with someone who is world famous. (Author's collection)

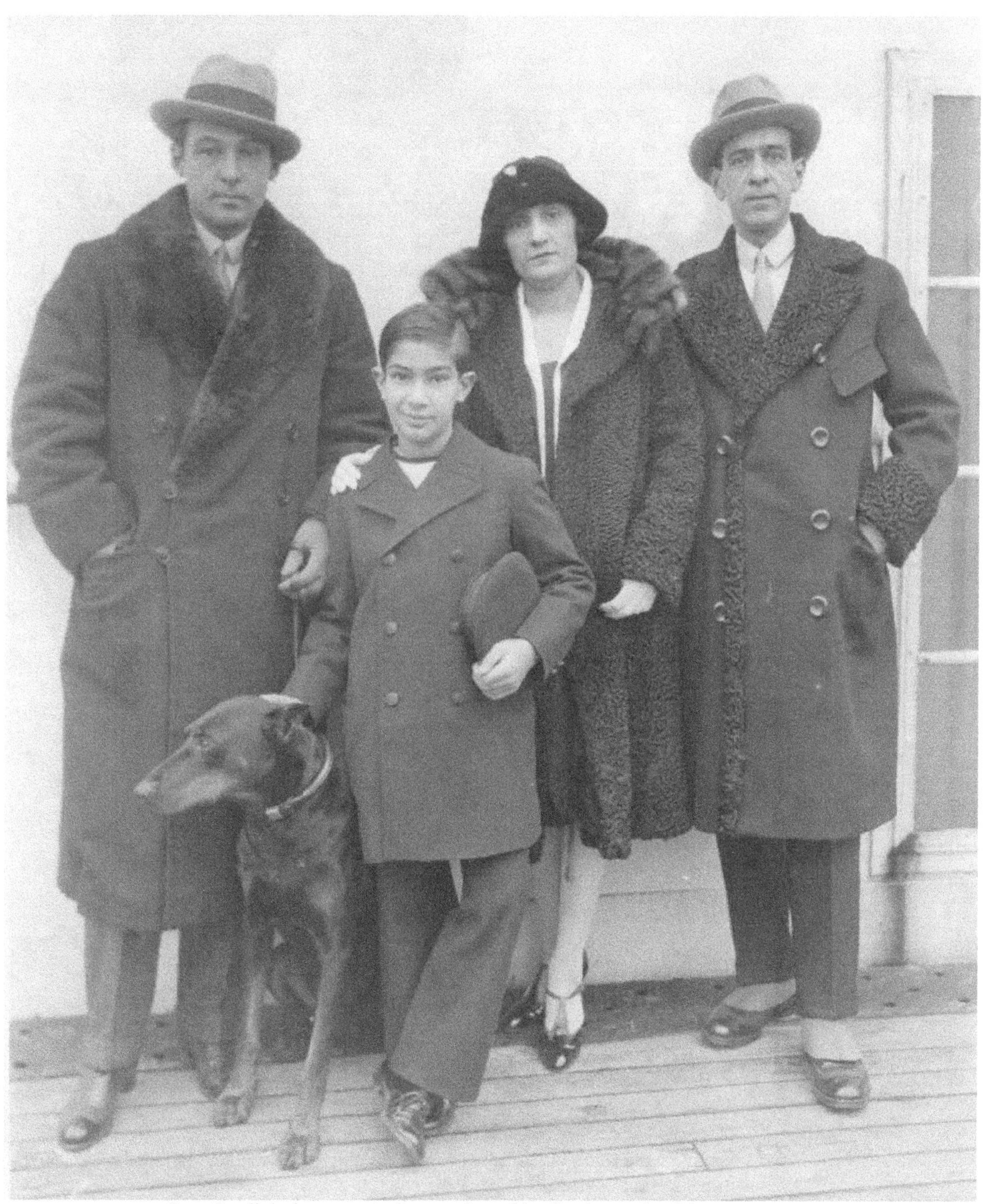

Jean Guglielmi appears to be nonplussed by the demands of the press.
(Author's collection)

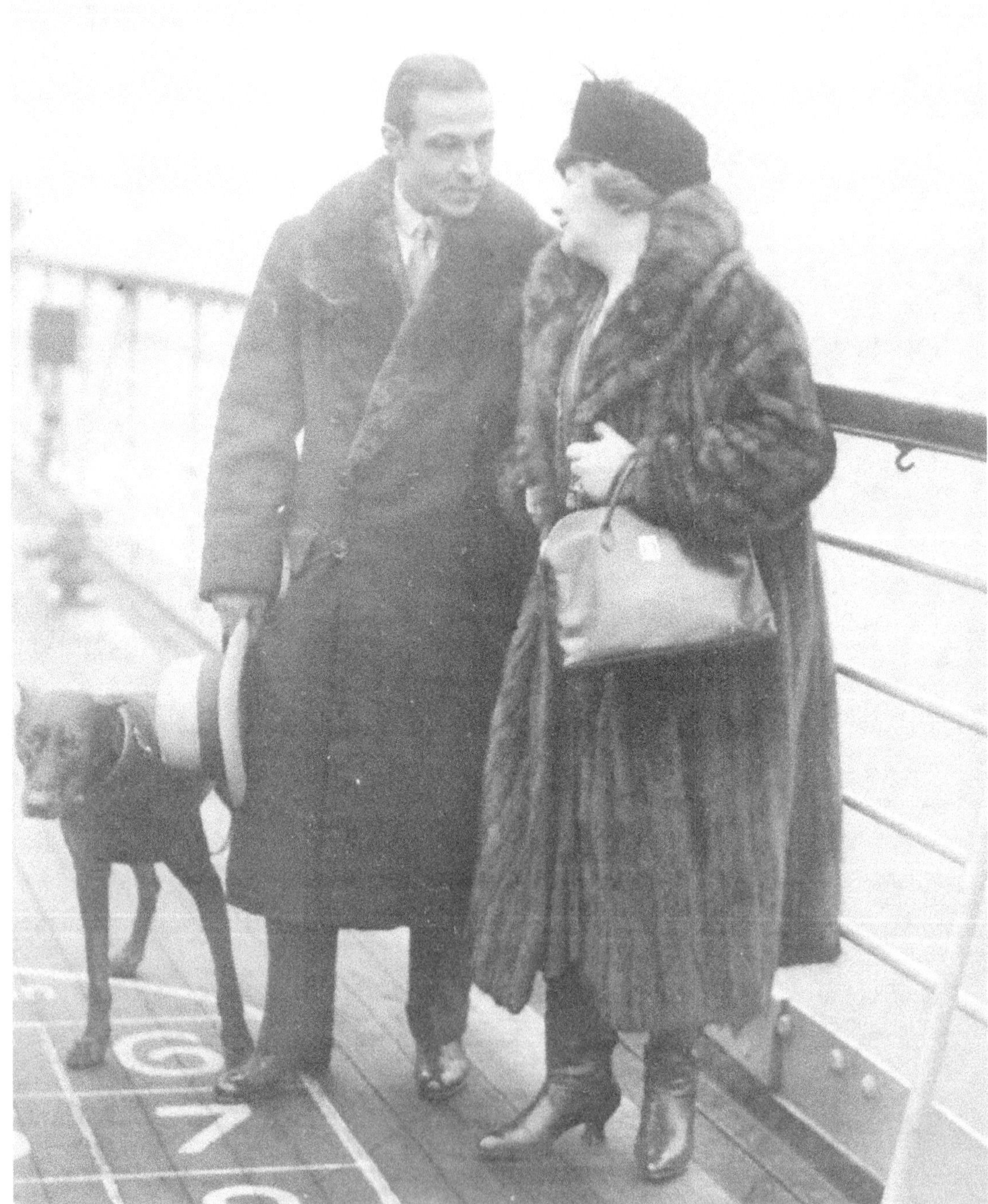

Sophie Tucker and Valentino were pals from at least 1922. Valentino was a fan, and Sophie reciprocated. On this trip Valentino's friendship helped Tucker during a time of mourning. (Author's collection)

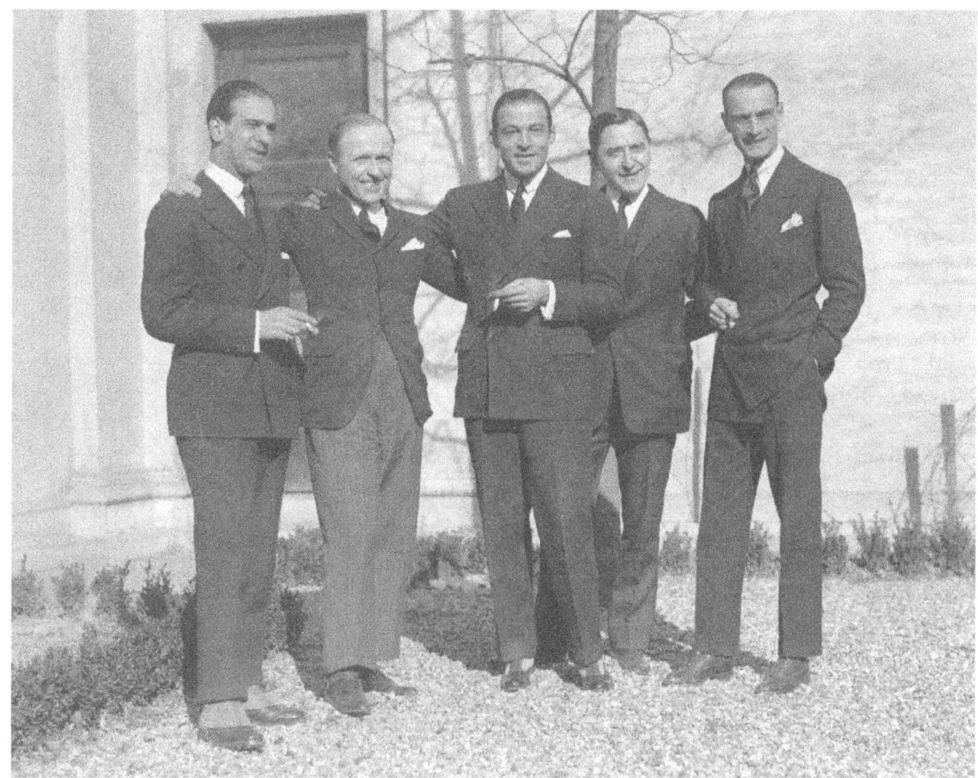

Alberto Guglielmi and Valentino pay a visit to the Italian Consulate in Washington, D.C. Conte Delfino di Villanova, Romelo Angelone, and Luciano Mascia complete the party. (Library of Congress)

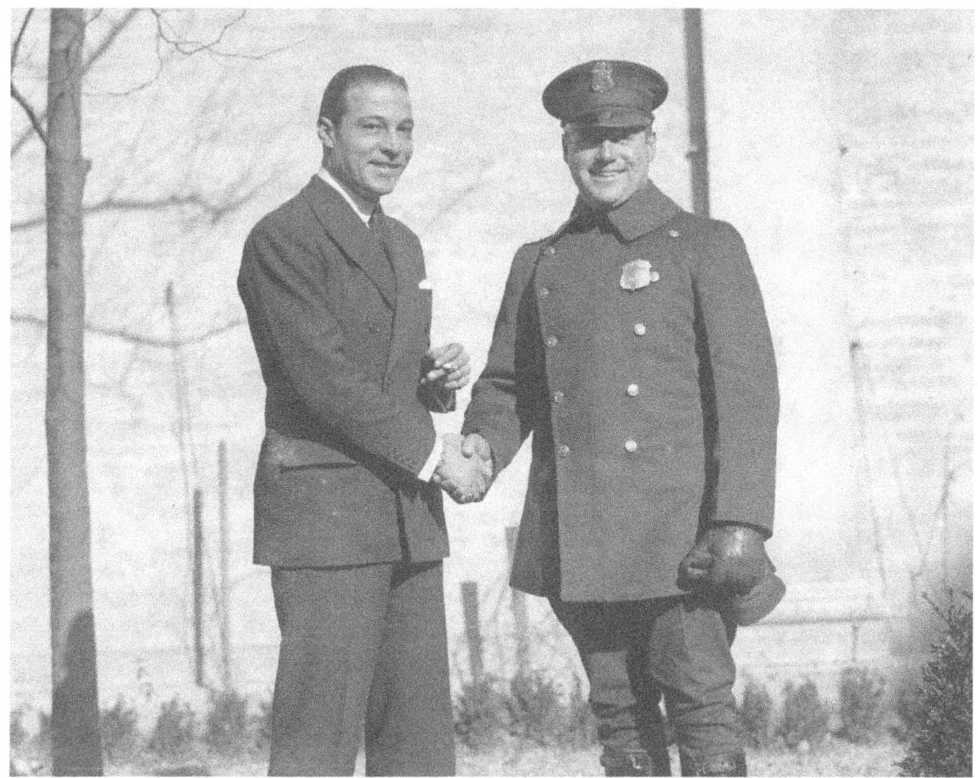

Valentino and Washington, D.C. Policeman B.J. Beckman. (Library of Congress)

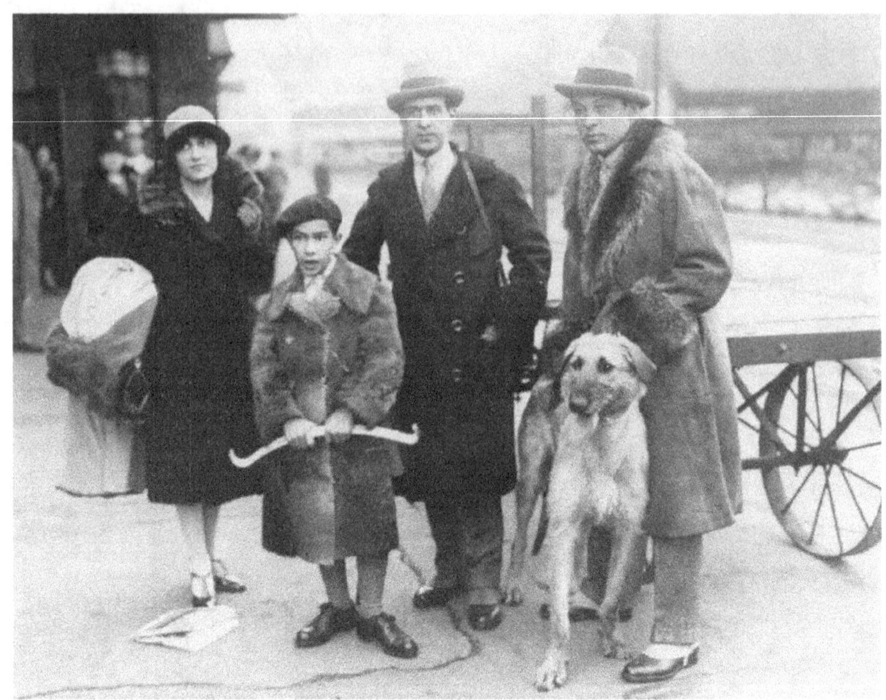

En route to California, the family takes a stroll at a station to stretch their legs and walk the dog, Centaur Pendragon. (Author's collection)

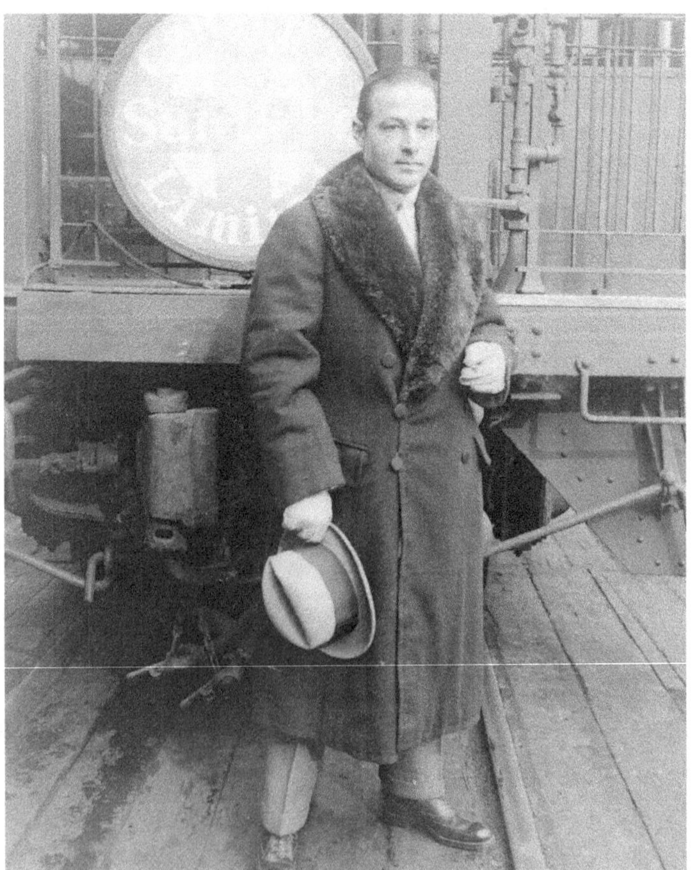

Posing in front of the Santa Fe Limited *en route* to Los Angeles. (San Francisco History Center, San Francisco Public Library)

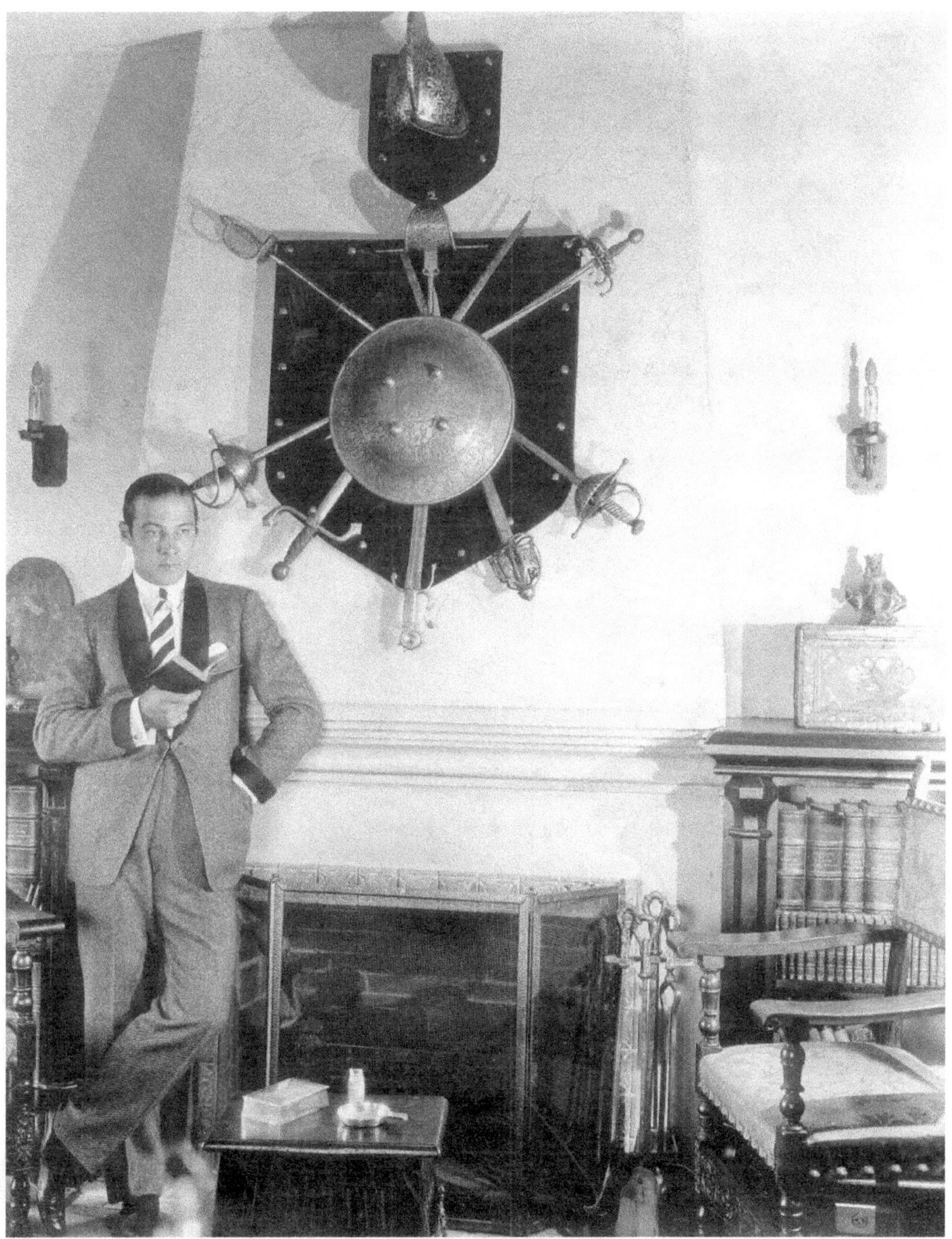

Rudolph Valentino as country squire at the living room in Falcon Lair.
(Author's collection)

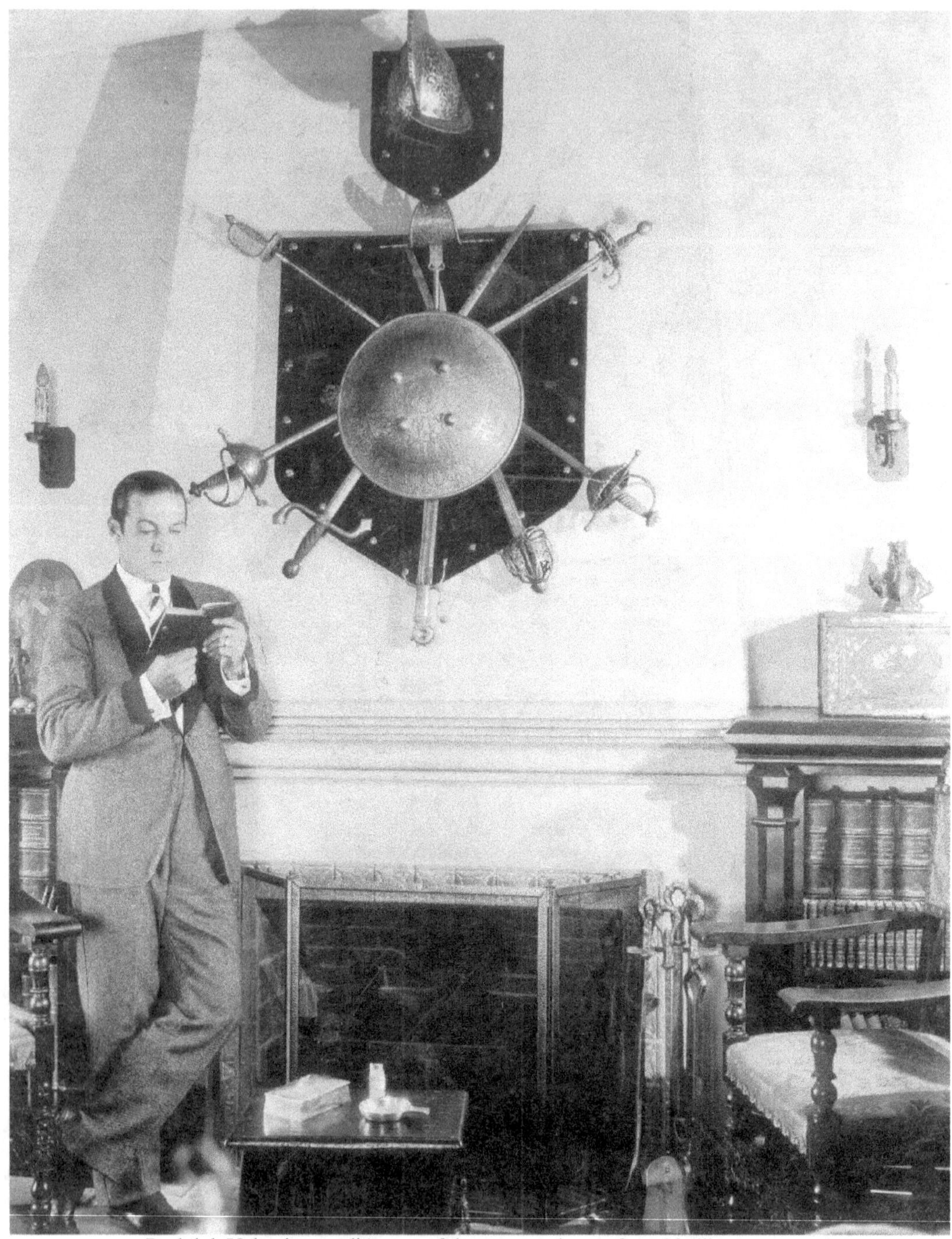

Rudolph Valentino reading one of the many volumes from his library.
(Michael and Virginia Back collection)

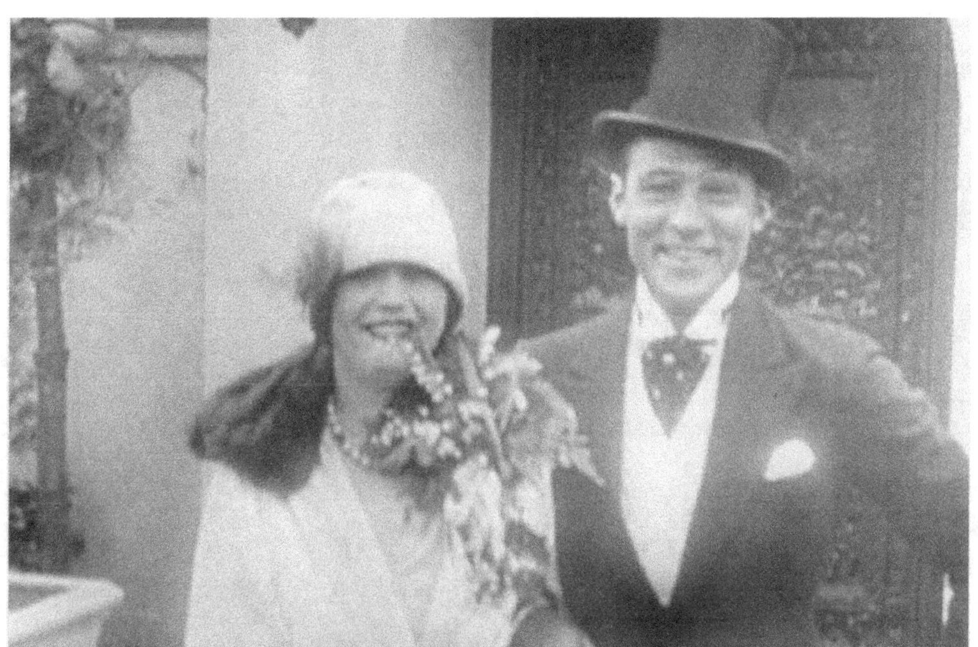

Pola Negri and Valentino at Falcon Lair
on the way to host Mae Murray and Prince David M'divani's wedding breakfast
(Author's collection)

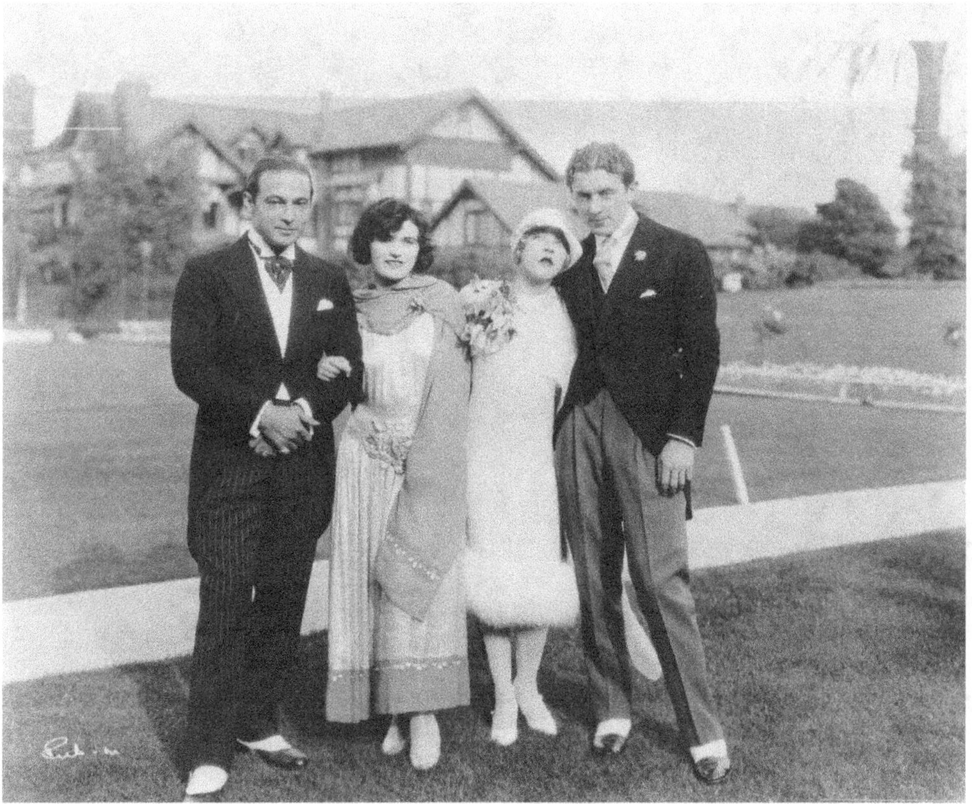

Best Man, Maid of Honor, Bride and Bridegroom, east Garden Ambassador Hotel.
(Allen Ellenberger collection)

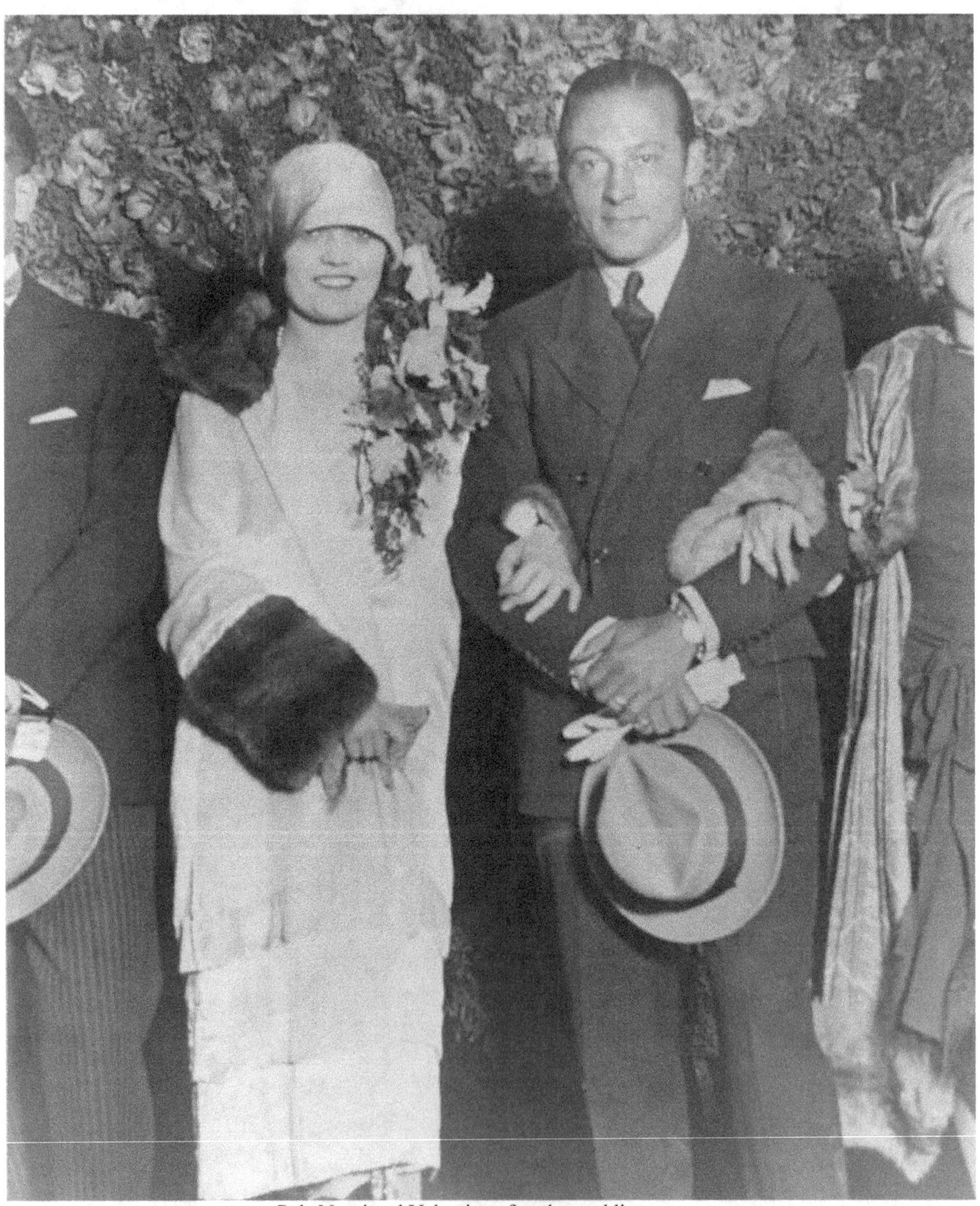

Pola Negri and Valentino after the wedding.
Valentino is still wearing a wedding ring and the slave bracelet watch which was a gift from Natacha. (Author's collection)

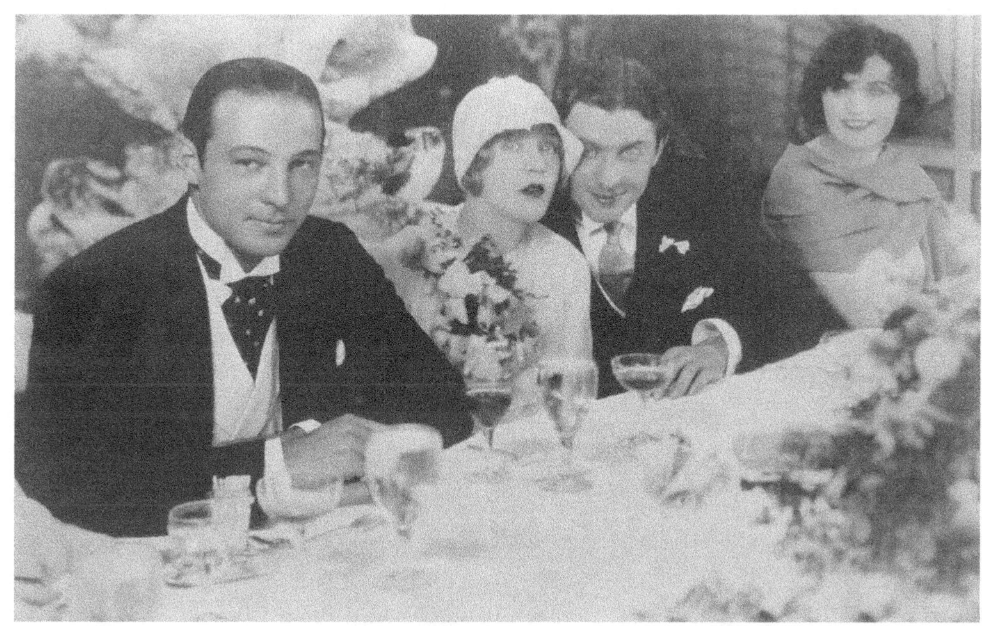

Valentino, Mae Murray, David M'divani, and Pola Negri at the wedding breakfast.
(Author's collection)

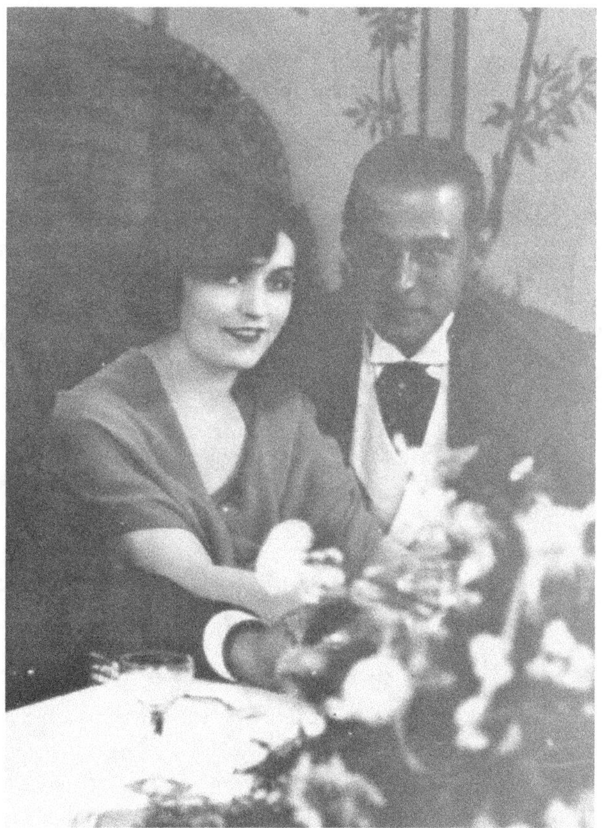

Pola and Rudy at the wedding breakfast.
(Author's collection)

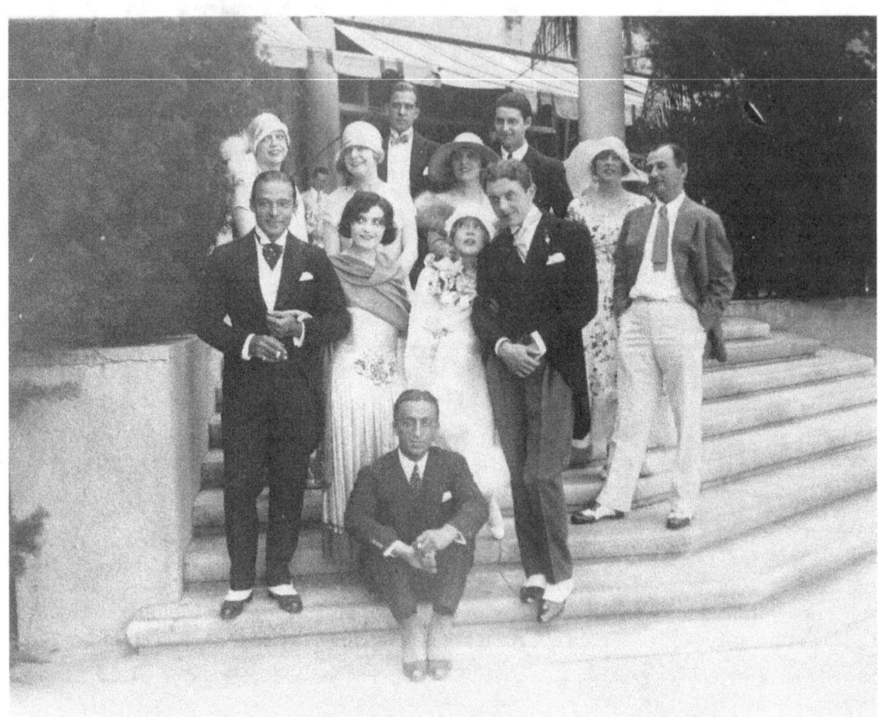

The wedding party and guests in the east Garden at the Ambassador Hotel.
(seated front) Manuel Reachi, Valentino, Pola Negri, Mae Murray, David M'divani,
Elizabeth Stack, Kathleen Williams, Agnes Ayres, Claire Windsor, unknown,
(fourth row) Alberto Valentino, Serge M'divani. (Author's collection)

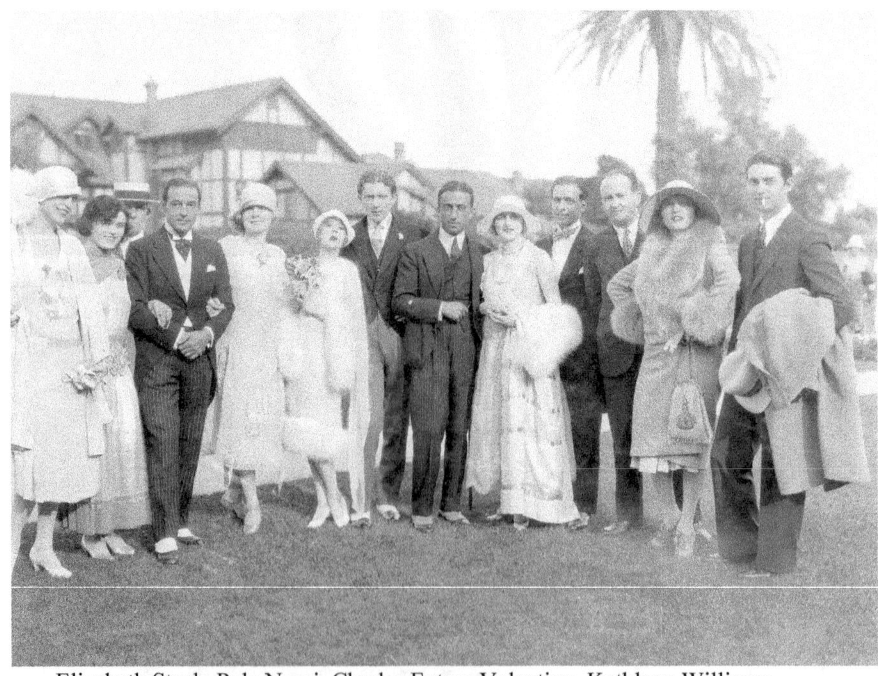

Elizabeth Stack, Pola Negri, Charles Eyton, Valentino, Kathleen Williams,
Mae Murray, David M'divani, Manuel Reachi, Agnes Ayres, Alberto Valentino, Balthazar Cue,
Marguerite Namara, and M. Lord, East Garden at the Ambassador Hotel.. (Author's collection)

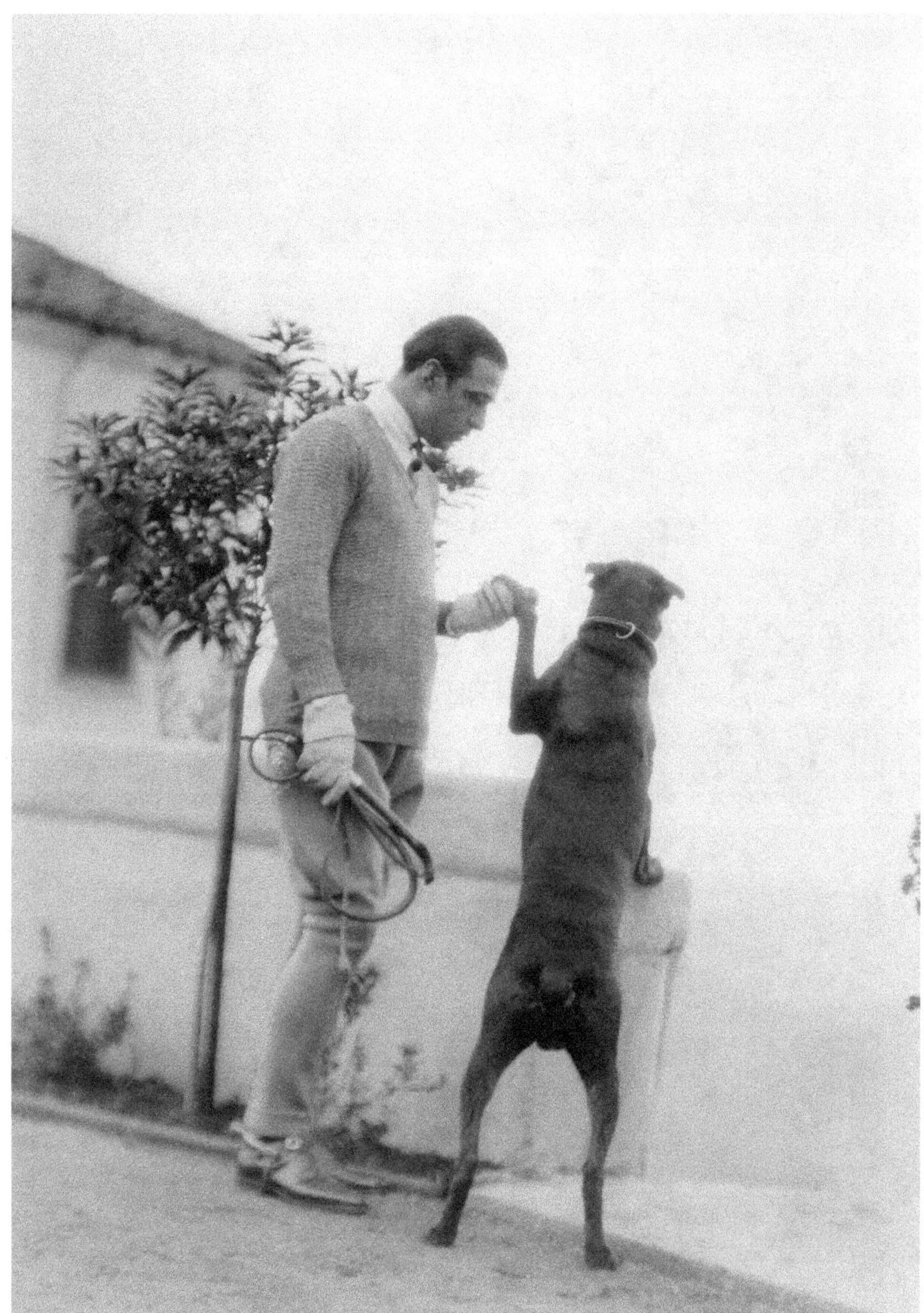

Rudy and Kabar at Falcon Lair. (Author's collection)

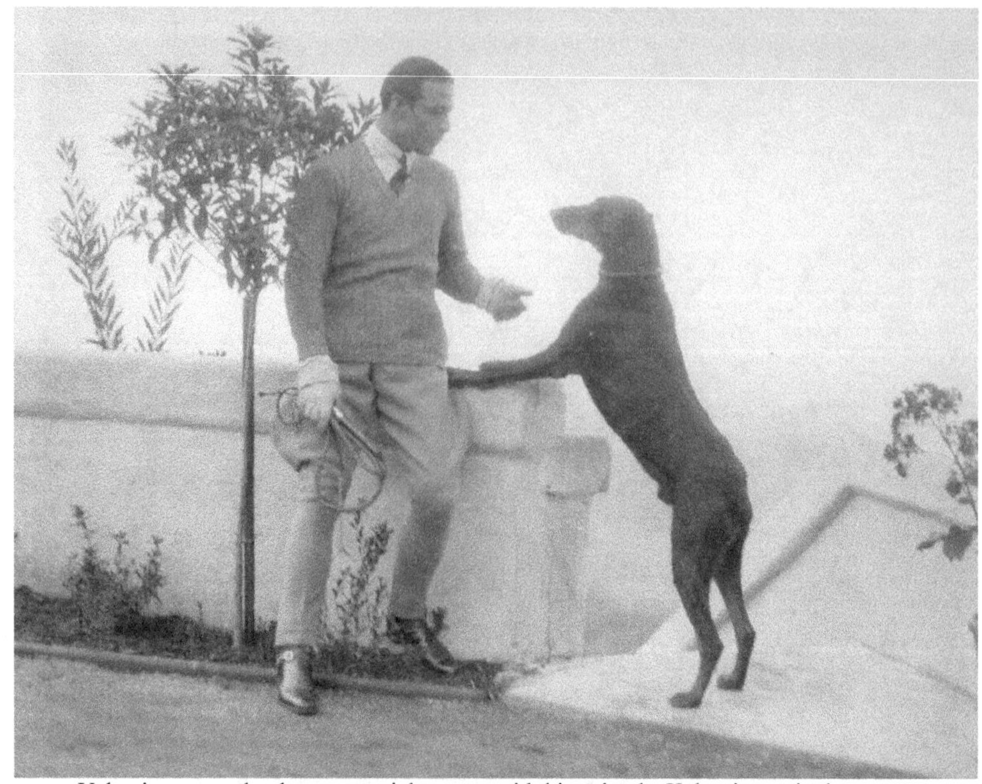

Valentino seemed to have a special rapport with his animals, Kabar in particular. (Author's collection)

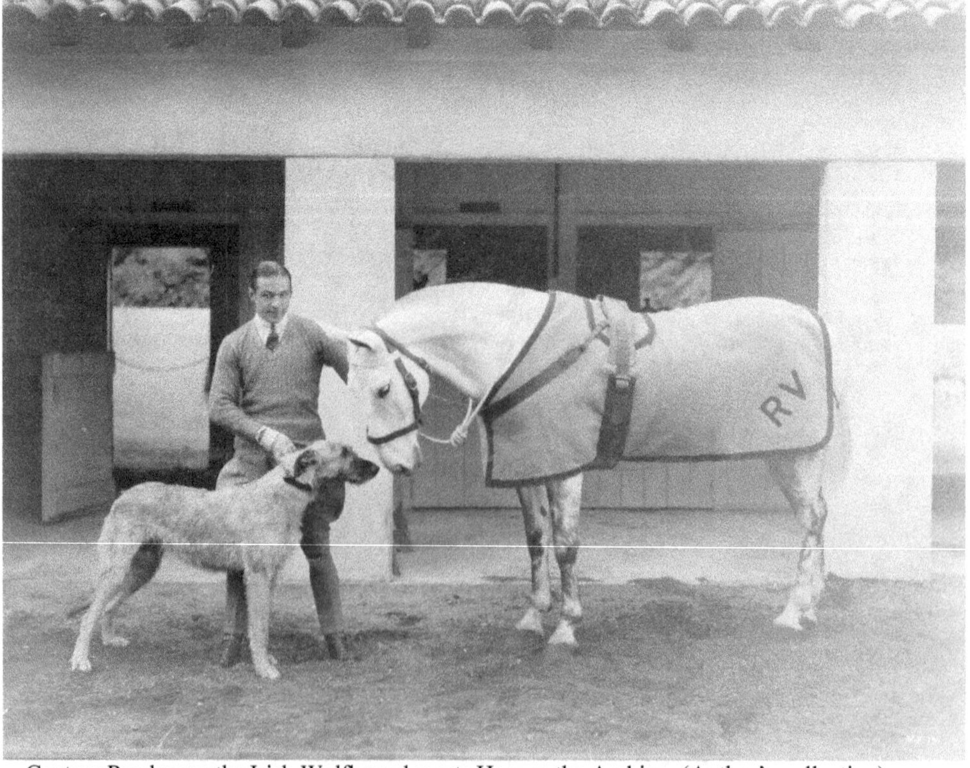

Centaur Pendragon the Irish Wolfhound meets Haroun the Arabian. (Author's collection)

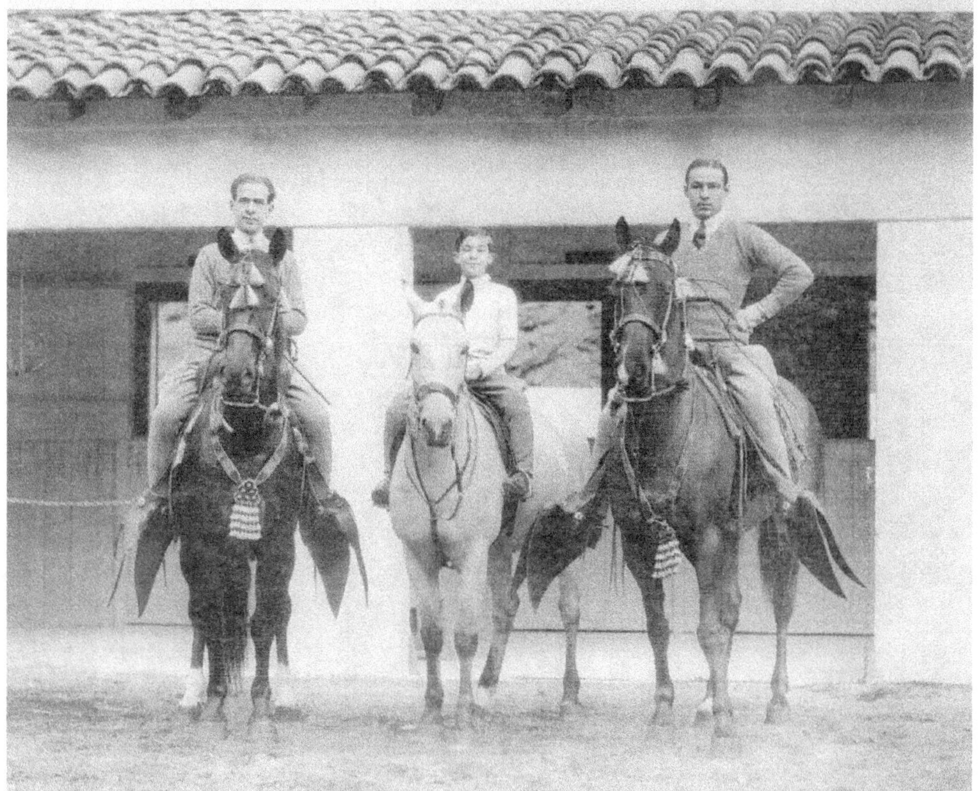

Alberto, Jean and Rudy at the stables in 1926. (Stella Grace collection)

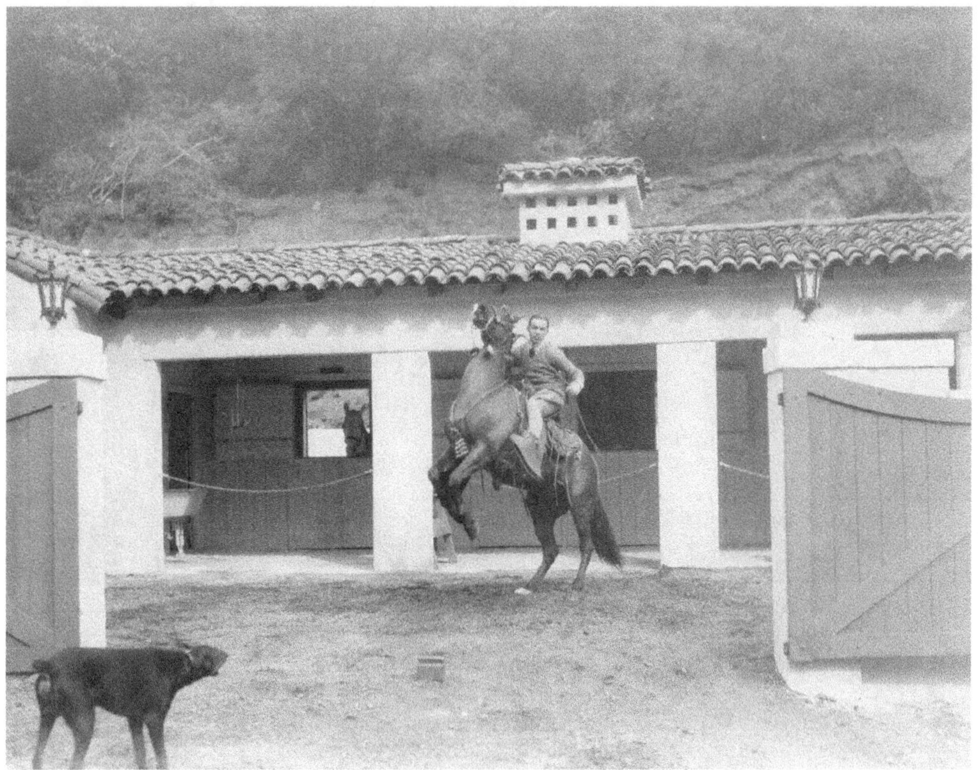

Valentino showing off his equestrian skills at the Falcon Lair stables.
Kabar is in the foreground. (Author's collection)

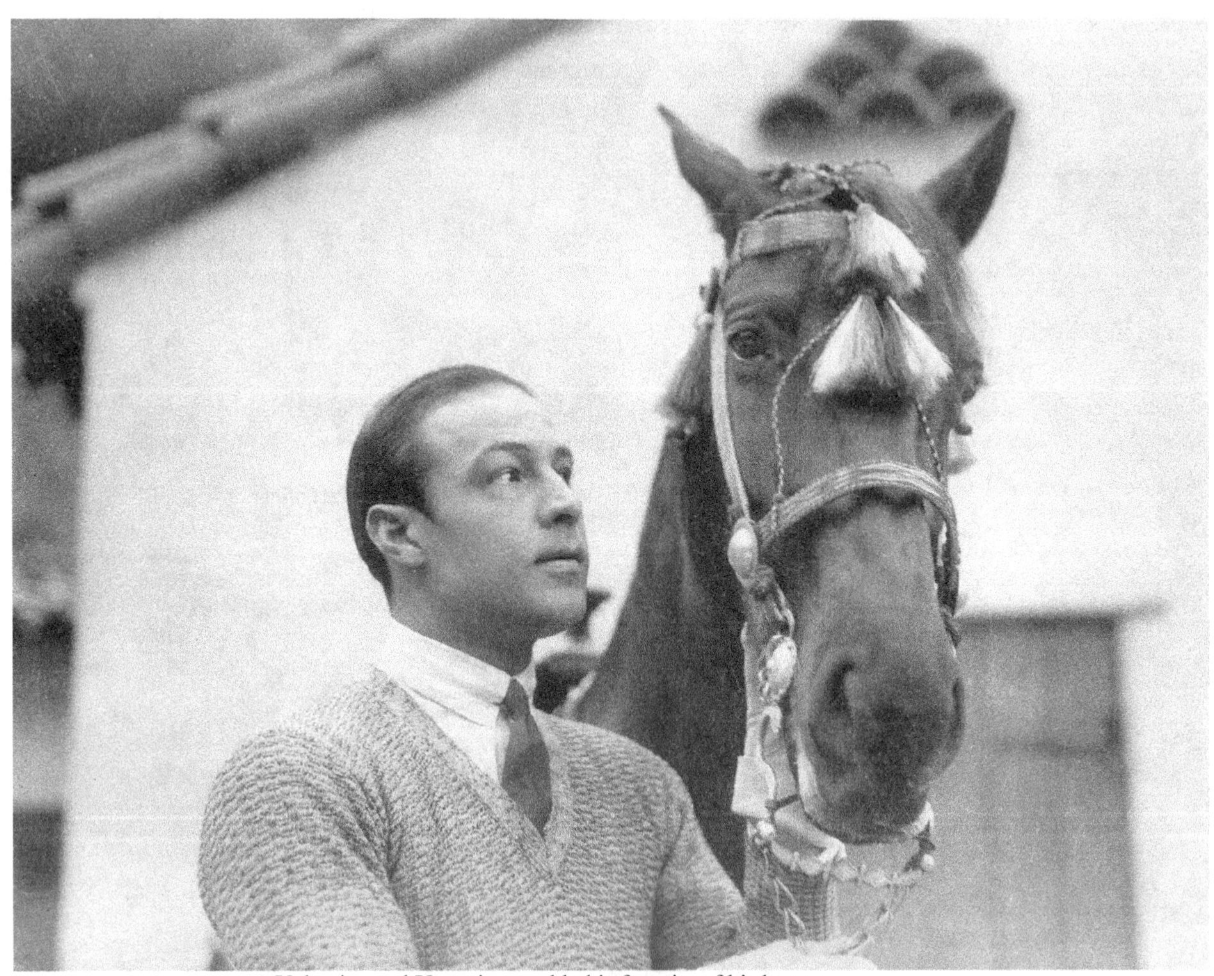

Valentino and Yacqui, arguably his favorite of his horses.
(Caroline Rupprecht collection)

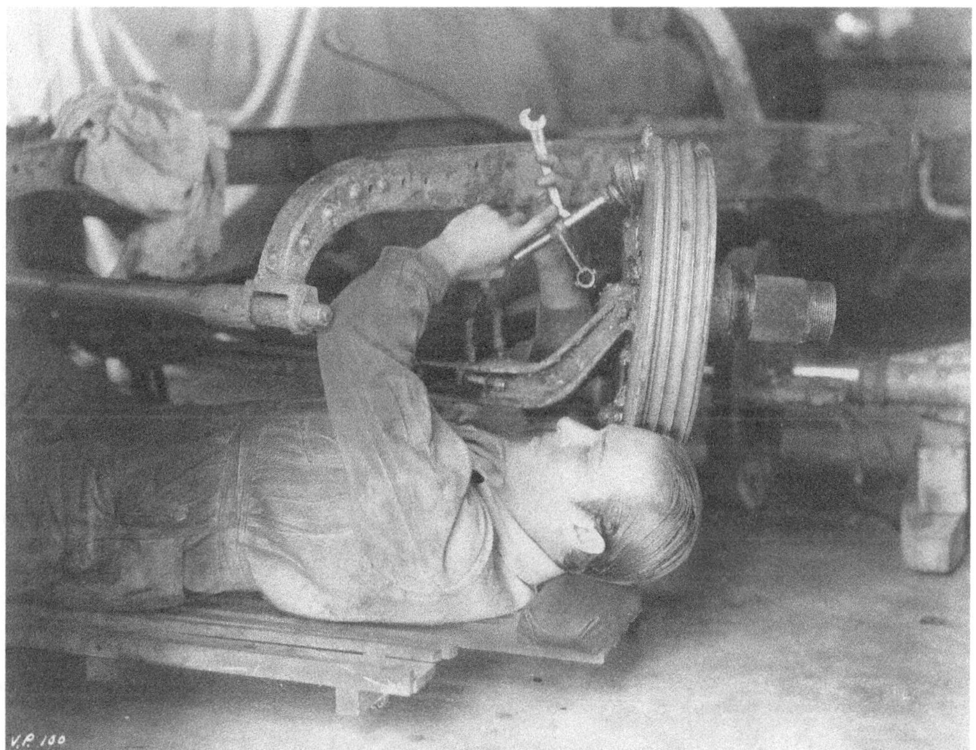

Valentino enjoyed tinkering with his cars. (Paula Hinton collection)

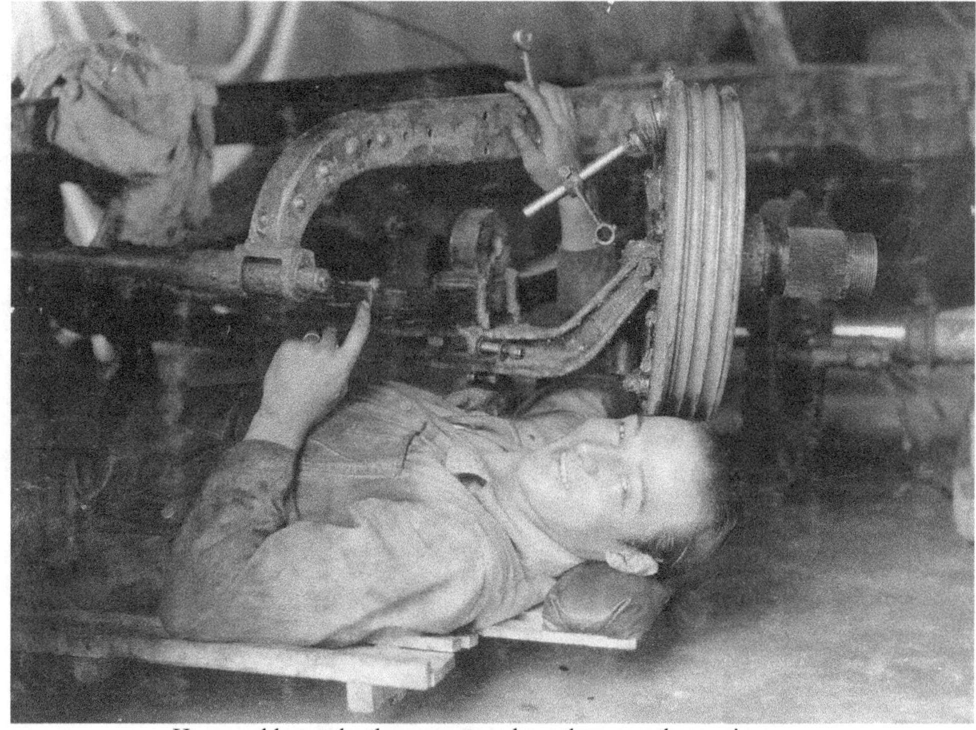

He was able to take them apart, and put them together again.
(Author's collection)

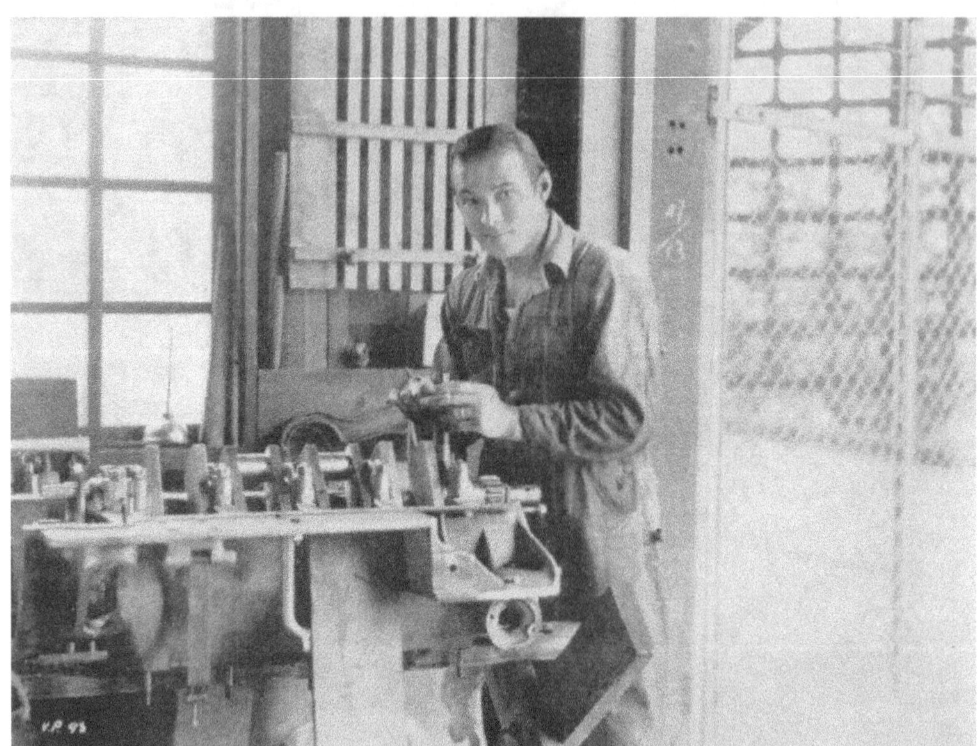
Valentino in his working garage at Falcon Lair. (Author's collection)

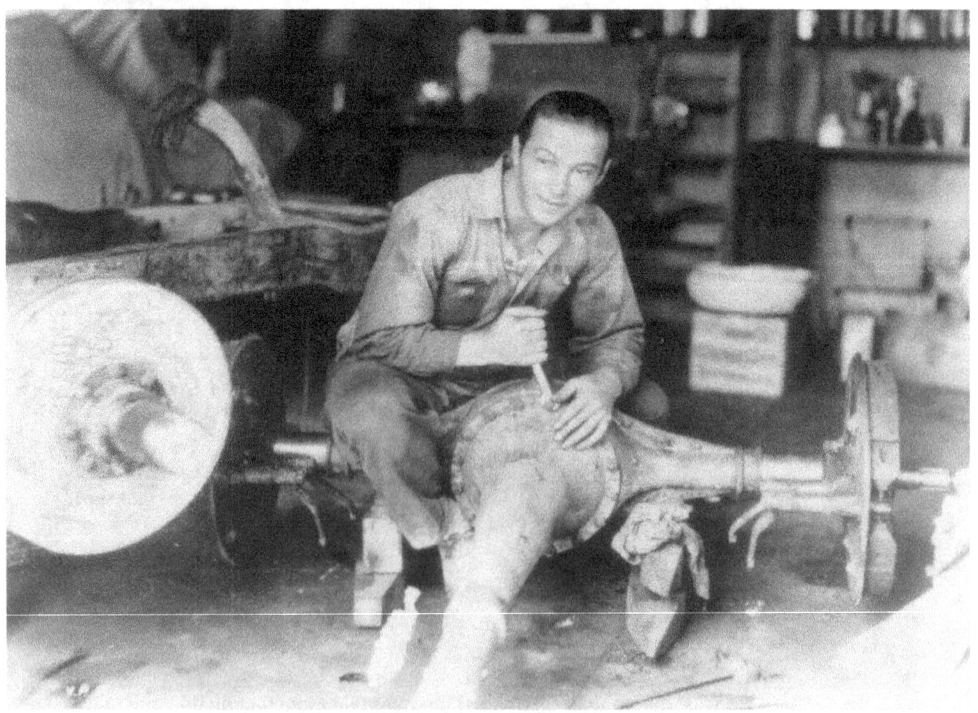
Valentino celebrated his 31st birthday working on his cars.
(Barb Nichols collection)

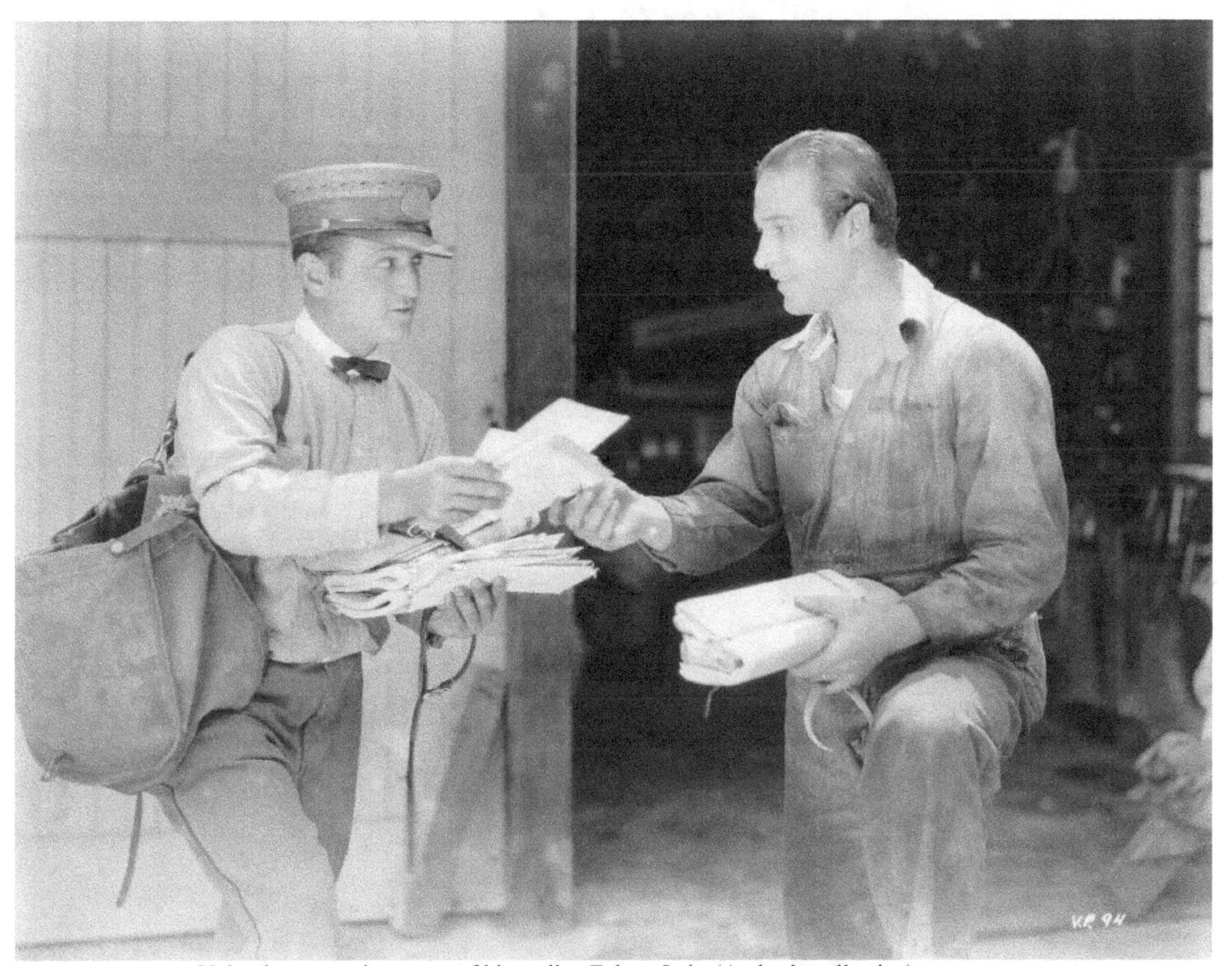

Valentino accepting some of his mail at Falcon Lair. (Author's collection)

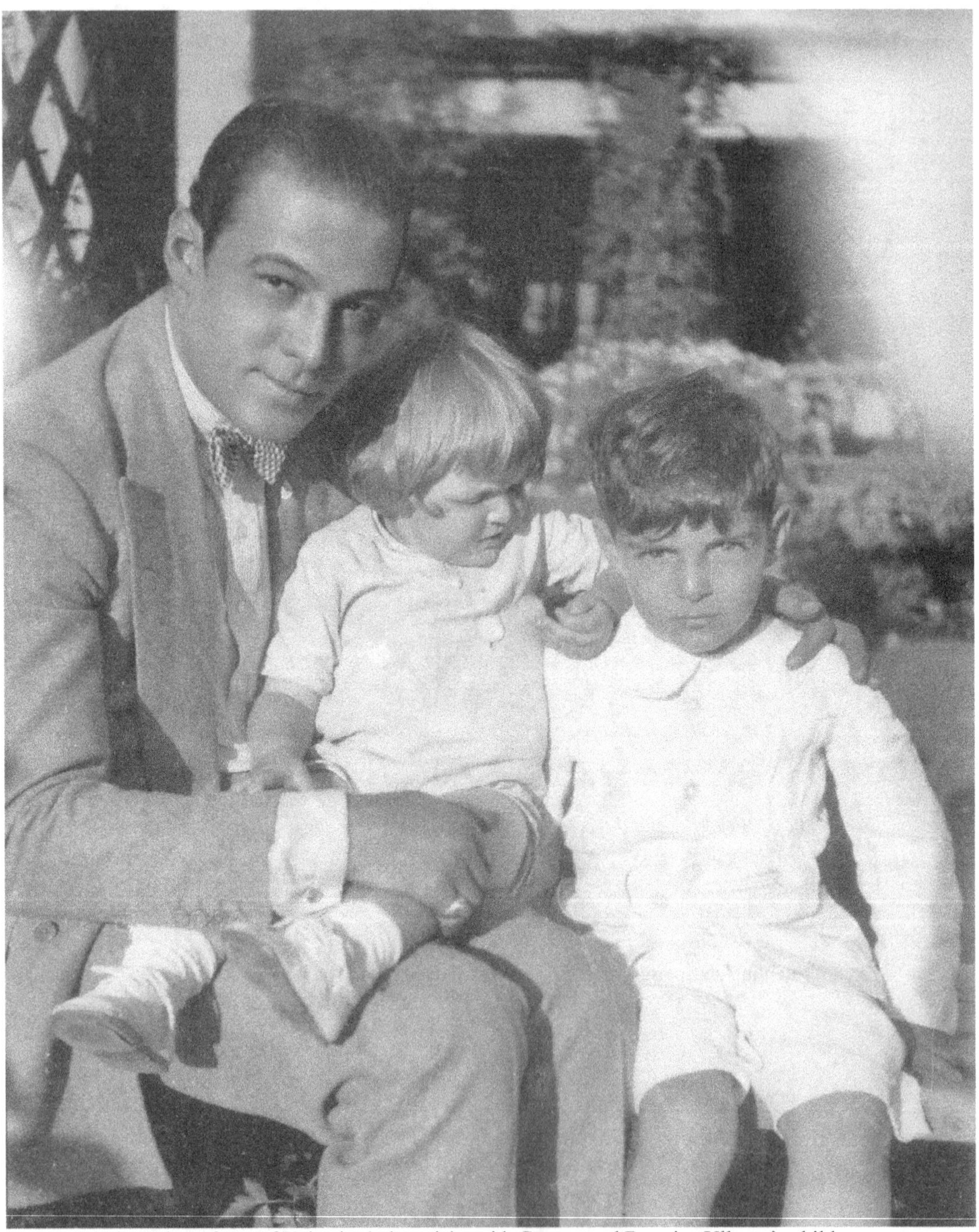

Snapshot of one of Valentino's last visits with George and Beatrice Ullman's children.
Valentino loved them as if they were his own, Robert and Daniel.
(Author's collection)

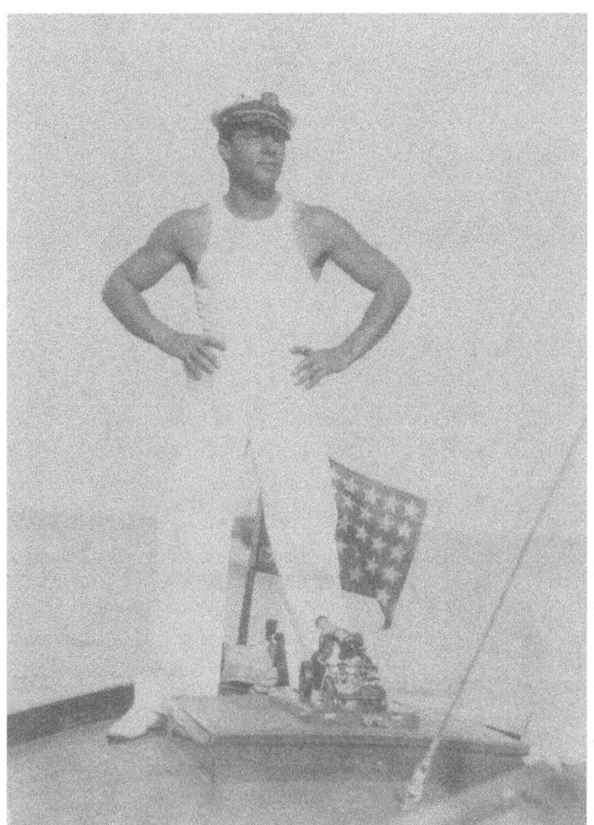

Valentino purchased a small yacht named the *Phoenix*.
He relished playing captain.
(Author's collection)

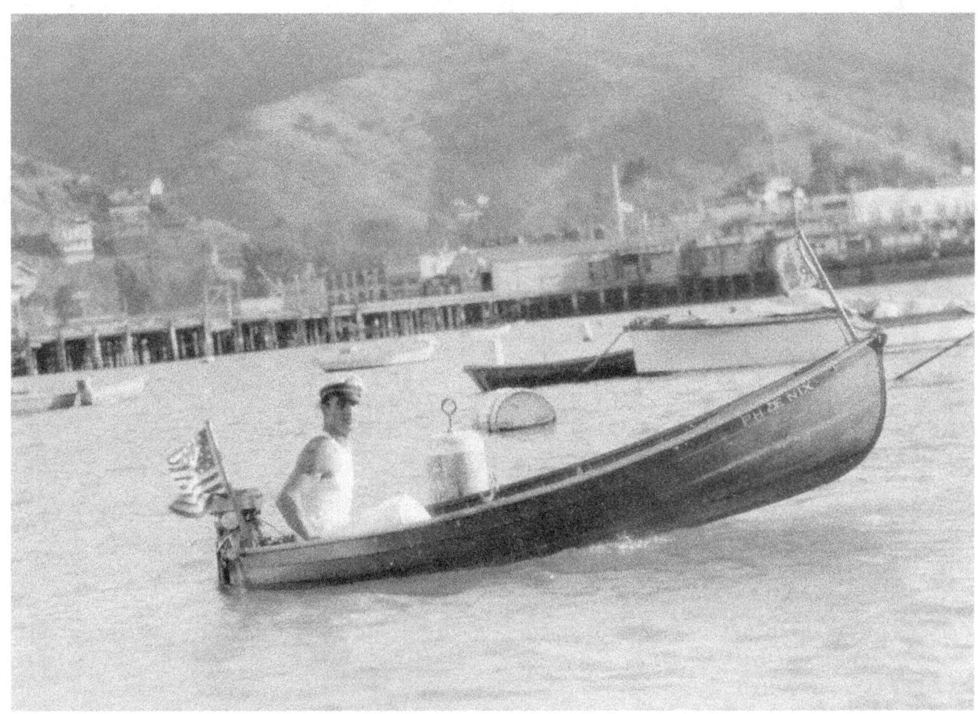

Valentino piloting the dinghy. Note the "R" flag on the bow.
(Author's collection)

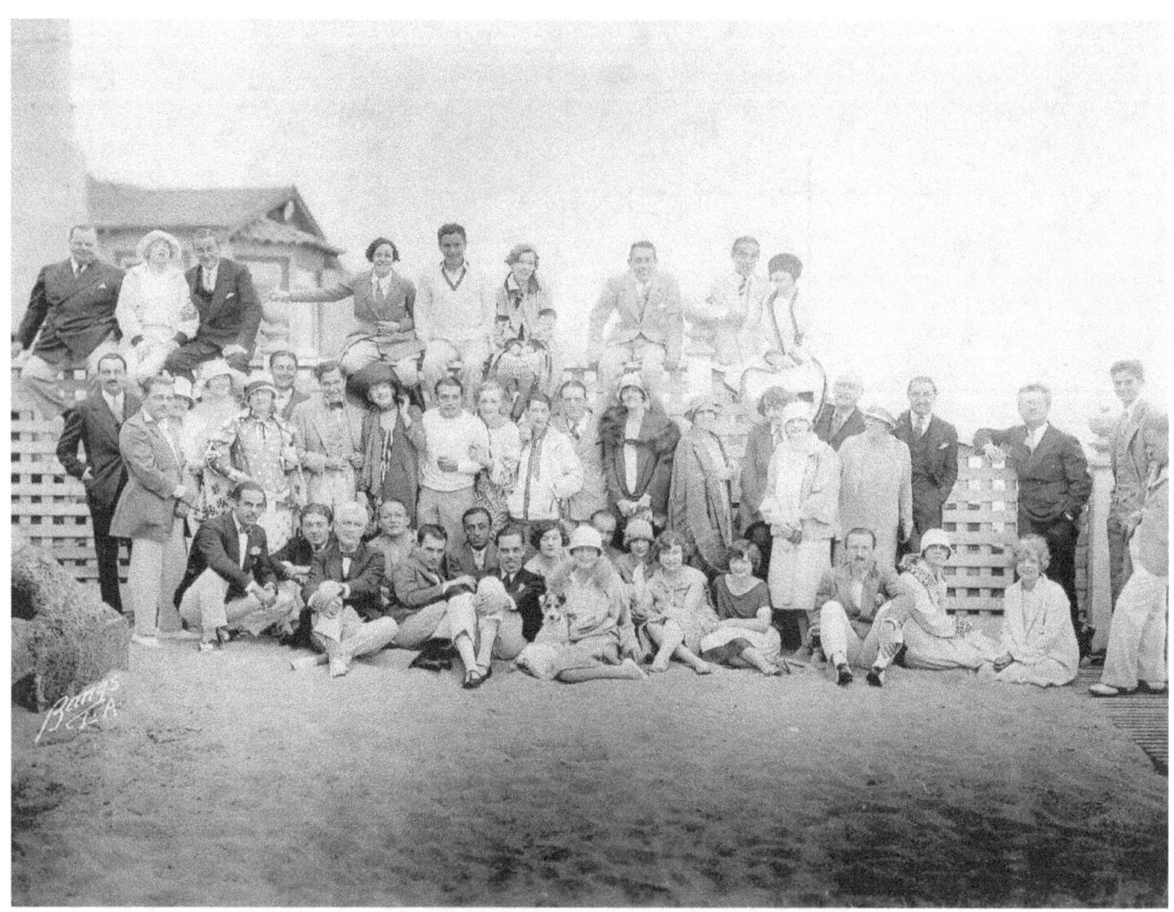

Valentino and Pola Negri attended a party at Norma Talmadge's beach house in Santa Monica. Practically all of Hollywood was there. (Author's collection)

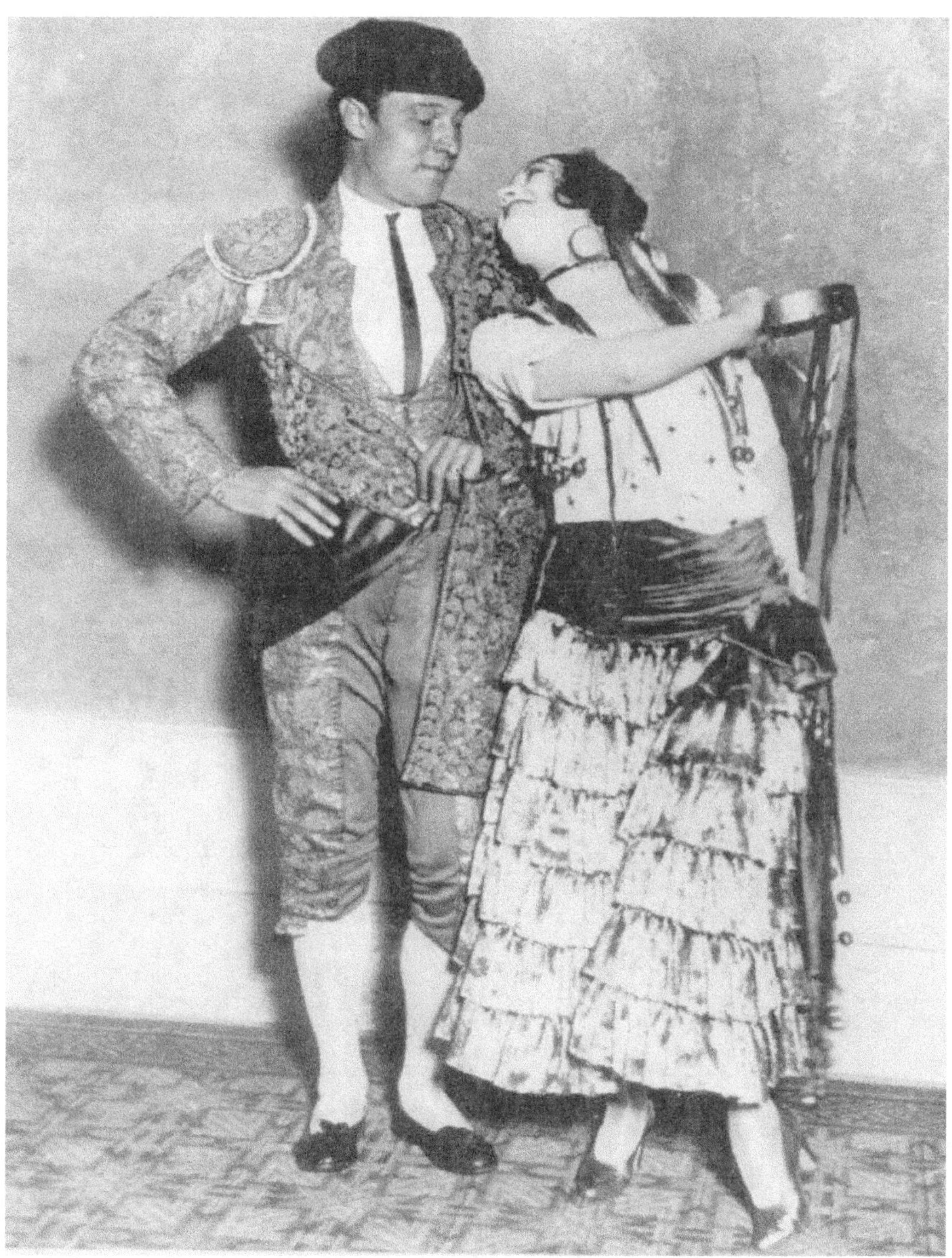

Valentino and Negri were seen about town, here they attended and won a dancing/costume contest at the Biltmore Hotel. Their romance burned both hot and cold. Though divorced, Valentino still wears his wedding ring. (Author's collection)

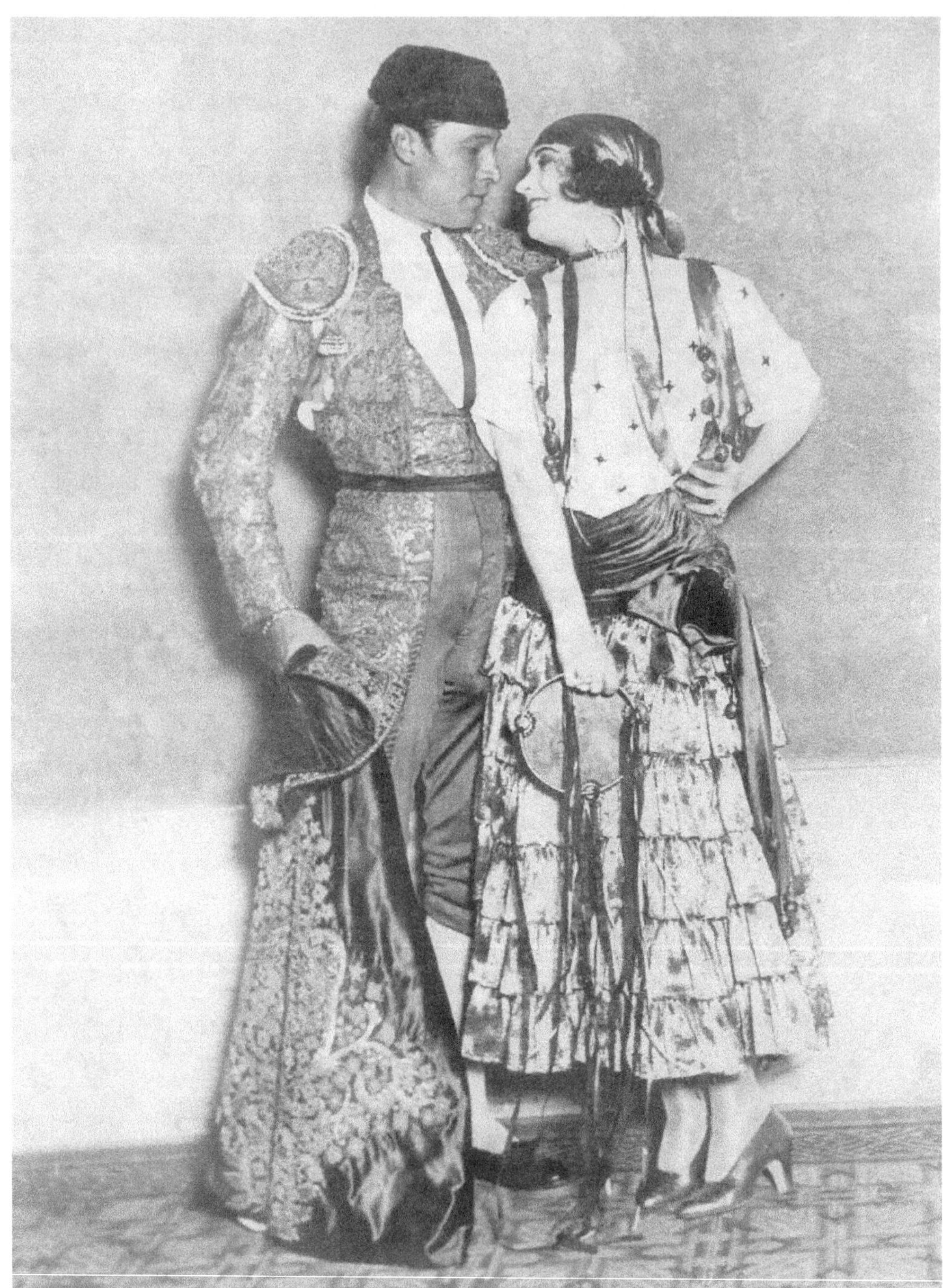

Valentino costumed as Juan Gallardo in *Blood and Sand* and Pola Negri costumed as Marina in *The Spanish Dancer* a film they could have made together in 1923. (Author's collection)

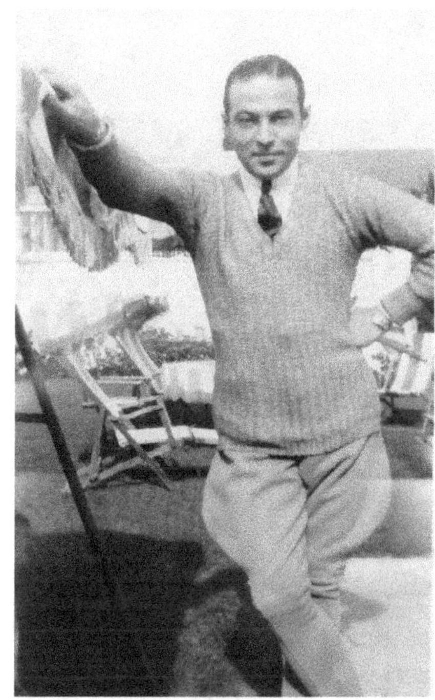

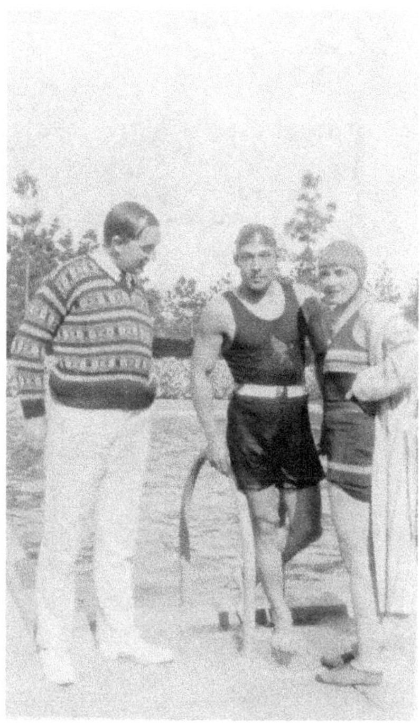

Falcon Lair lacked a swimming pool, Pola Negri was able to provide one.

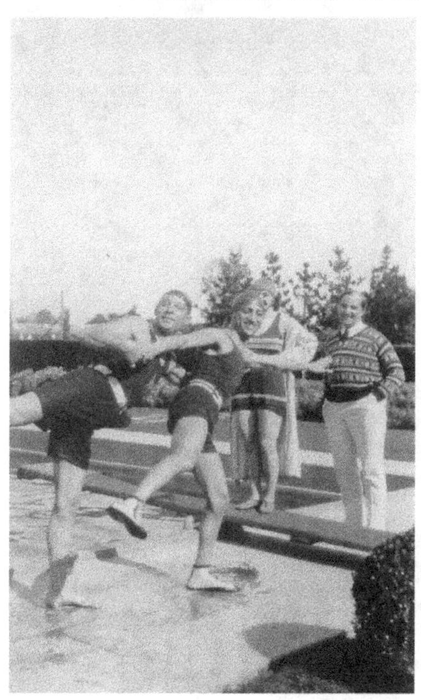

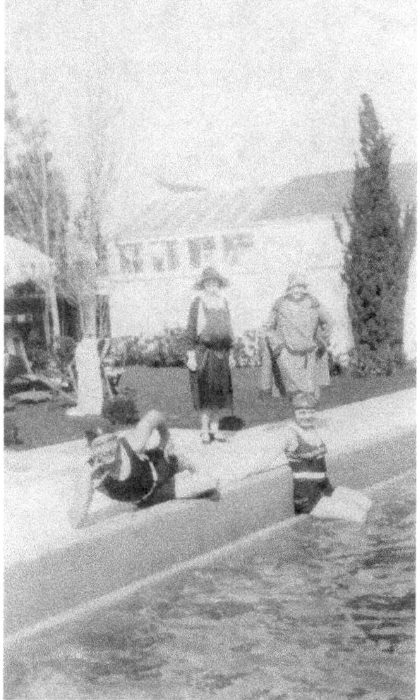

Pola Negri, Manuel Reachi, Agnes Ayres, and Leopold Brodzinski
can be seen in these snapshots. (Craig MacPherson collection)

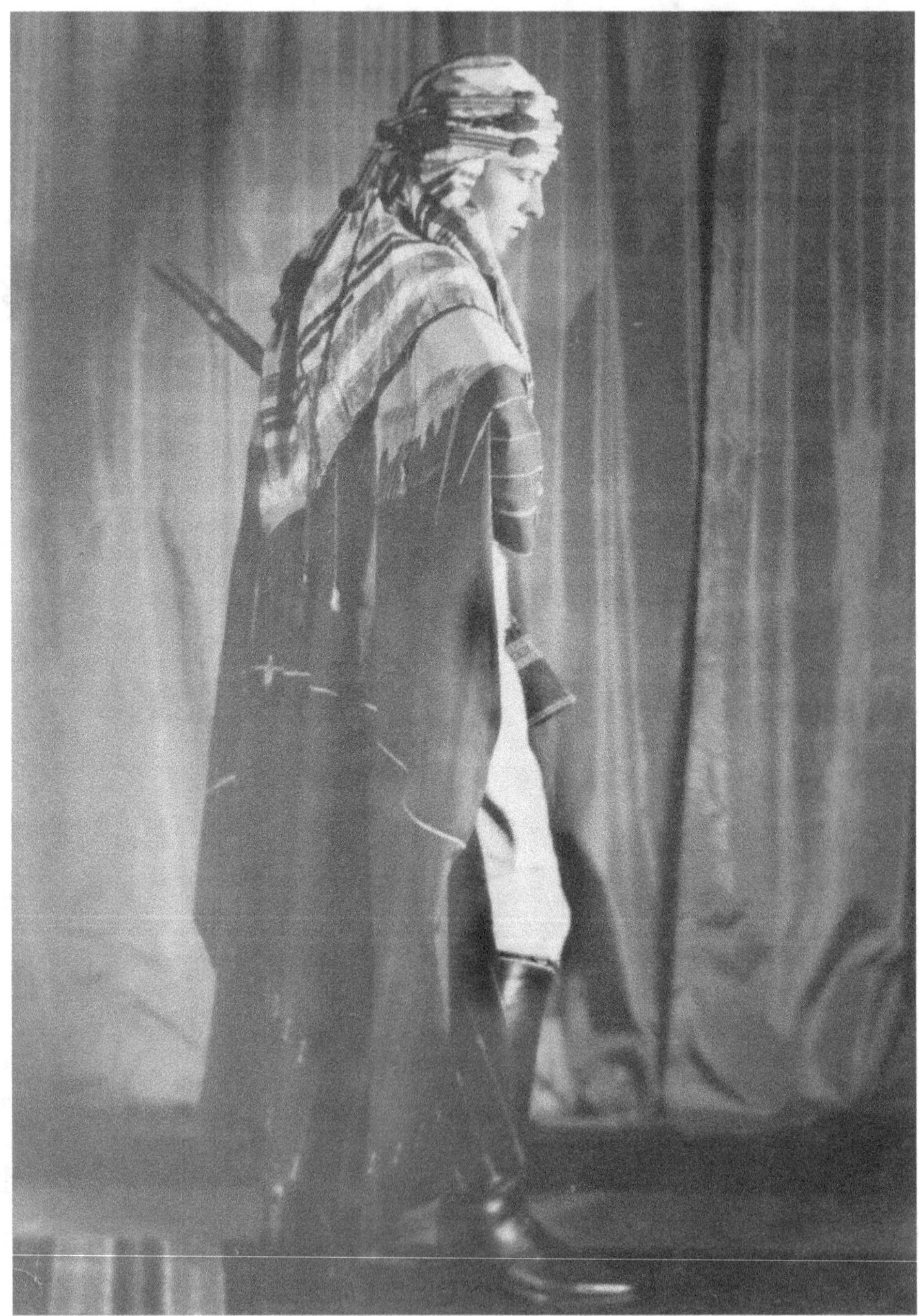

Portrait study by Harold Dean Carsey, photographed at Falcon Lair.
(Author's collection)

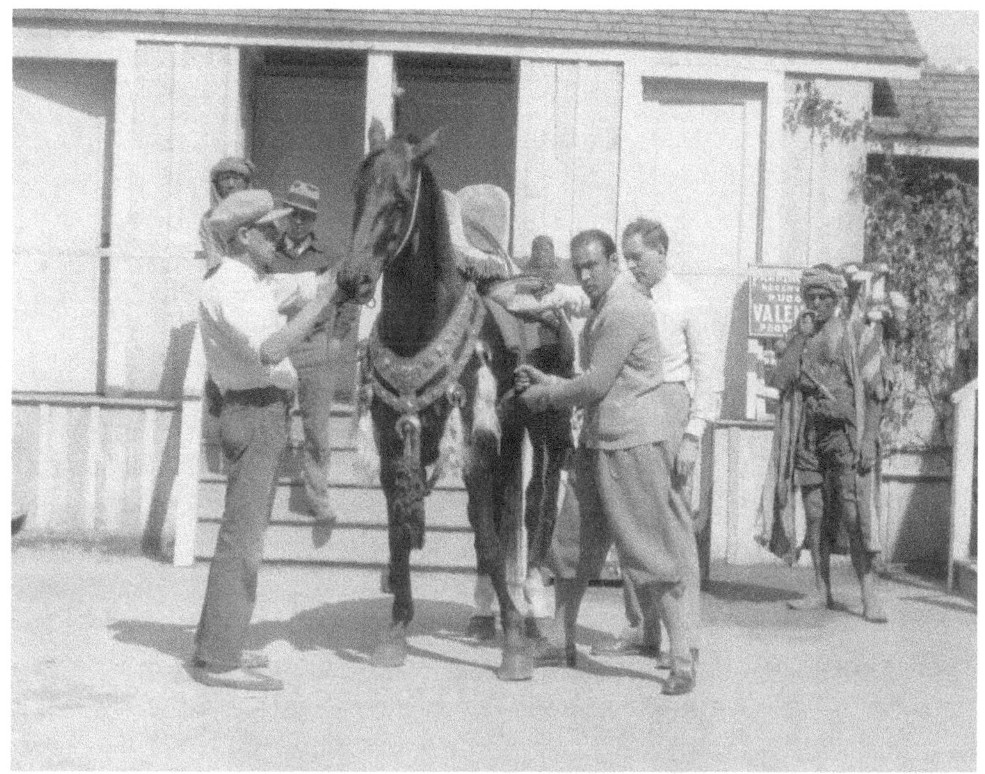

Getting ready for the day of shooting, Valentino personally tacks up his horse Yacqui.
(Craig MacPherson collection)

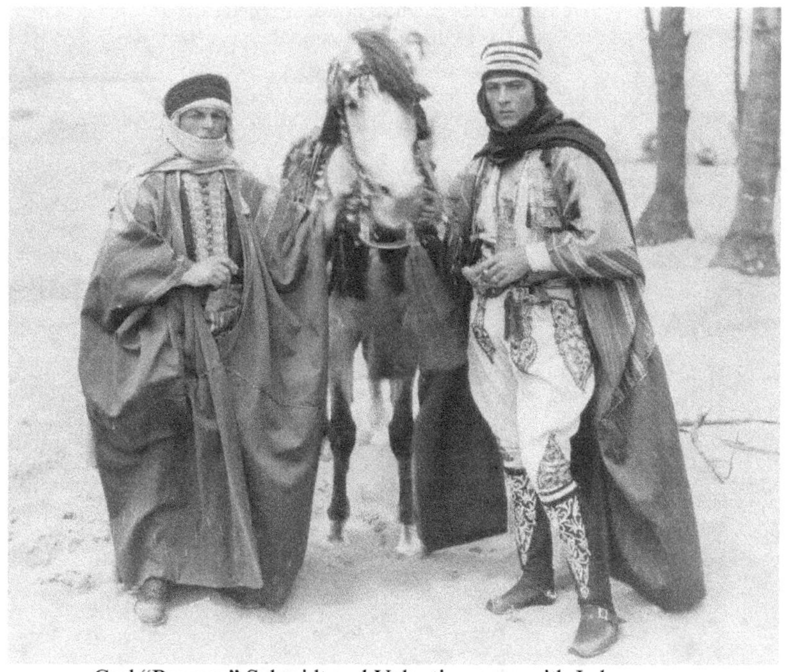

Carl "Raswan" Schmidt and Valentino pose with Jadaan
on location in the Yuma, AZ desert. (Author's collection)

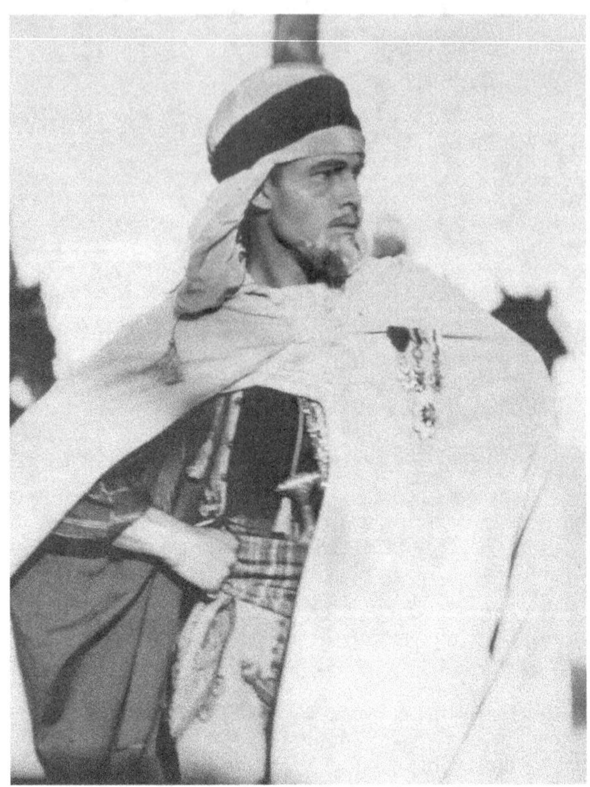

Valentino delighted in wandering the studio
made up as the elder Sheik Ahmed.
He further delighted in not being recognized.
(Author's collection)

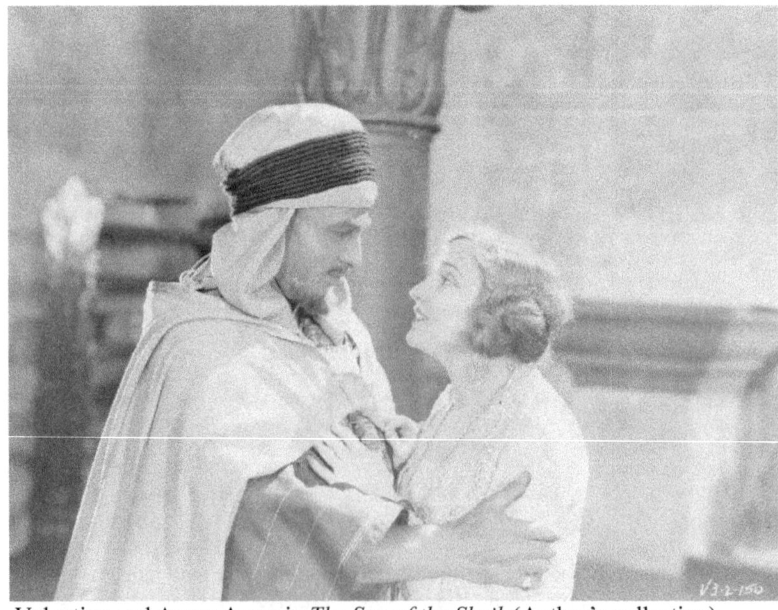

Valentino and Agnes Ayres in *The Son of the Sheik* (Author's collection)

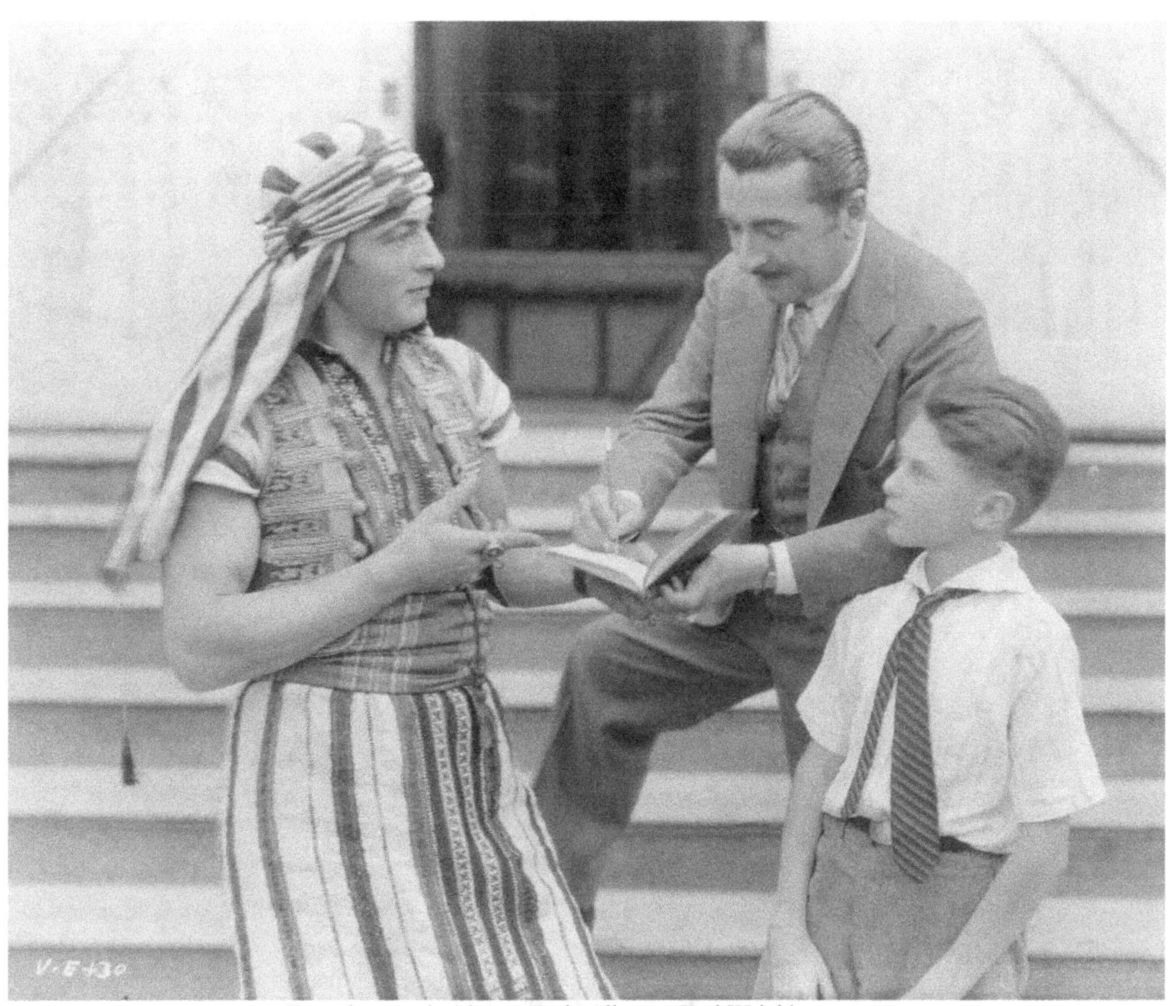

Famed young local autograph collector, Paul Wrinkle,
nabbing a signatures from Valentino and George Fitzmaurice. (Author's collection)

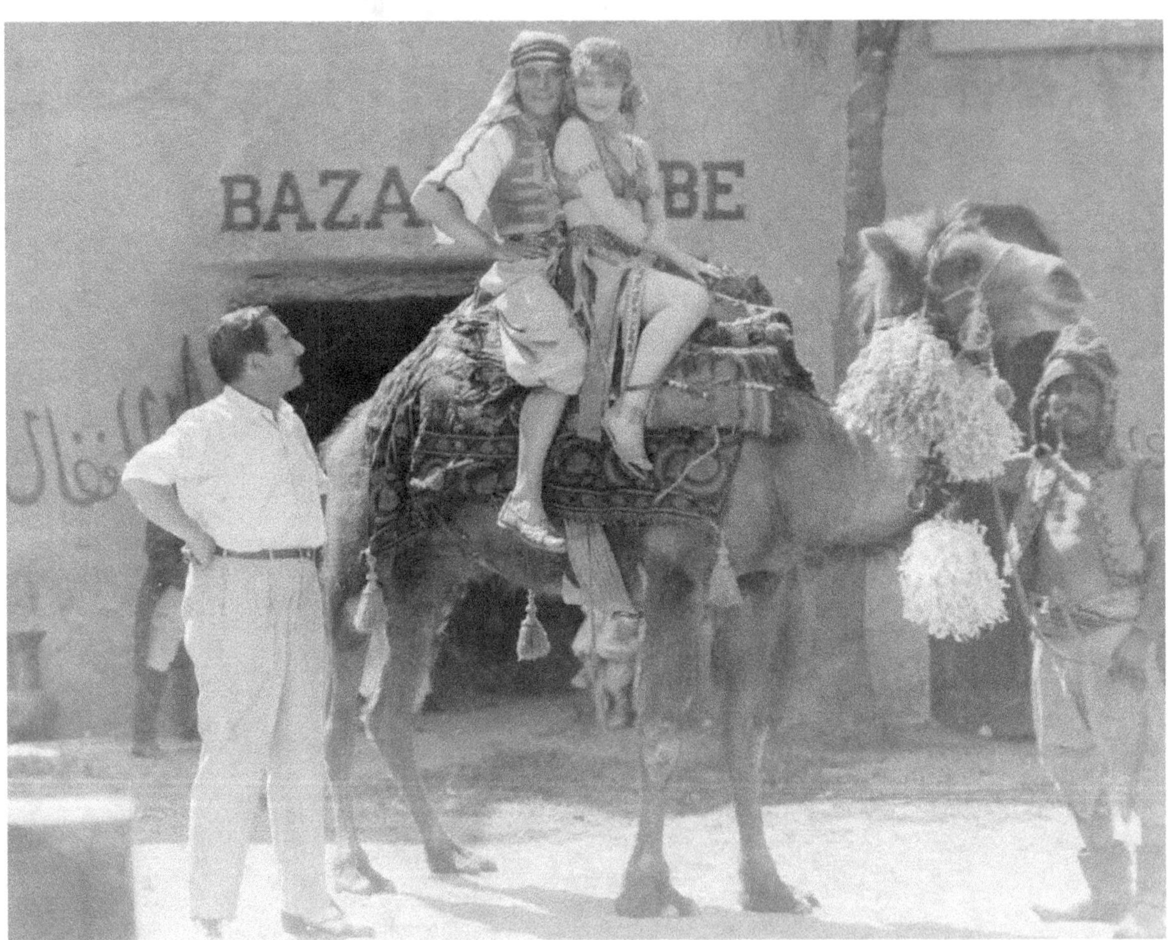

Posing for publicity on the Touggourt street set with George Fitzmaurice, Vilma Banky and unknown extra. (Author's collection)

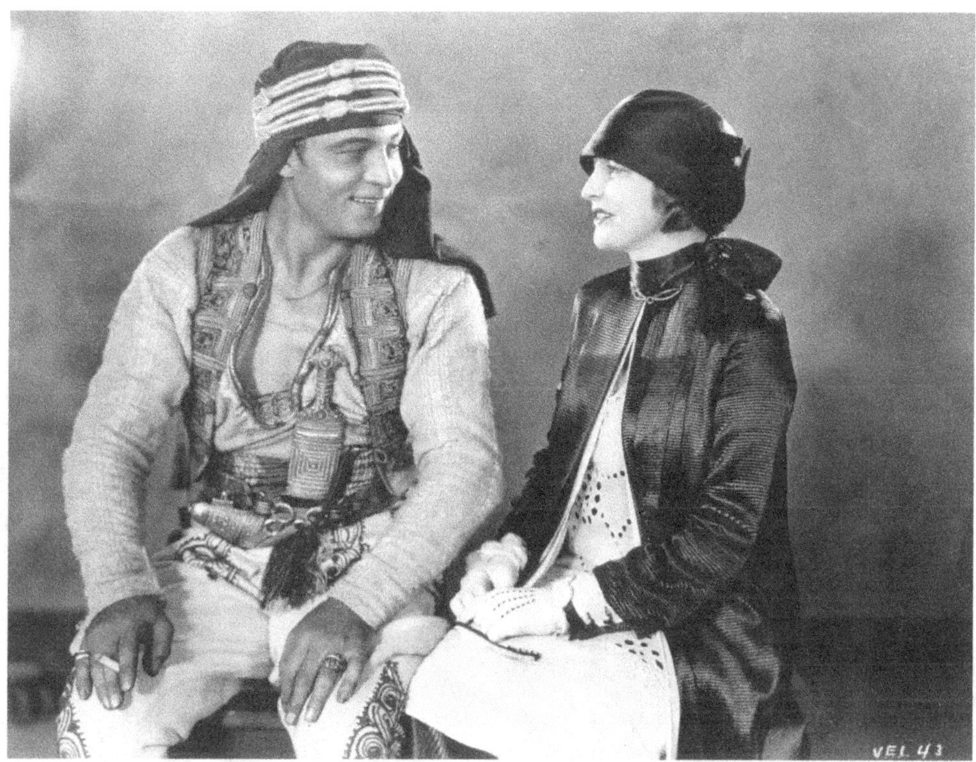

Valentino enjoying a visit with his co-star Agnes Ayres. (Author's collection)

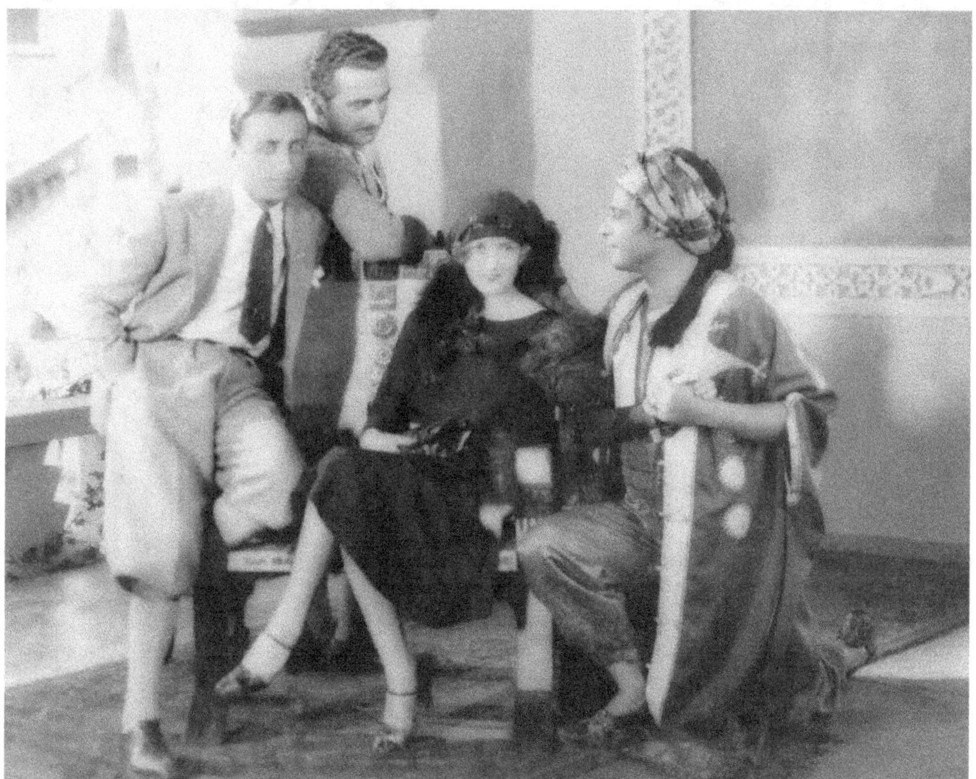

Constance Talmadge also took time to pay a visit to the set with Valentino, Manuel Reachi, and George Fitzmaurice. (Author's collection)

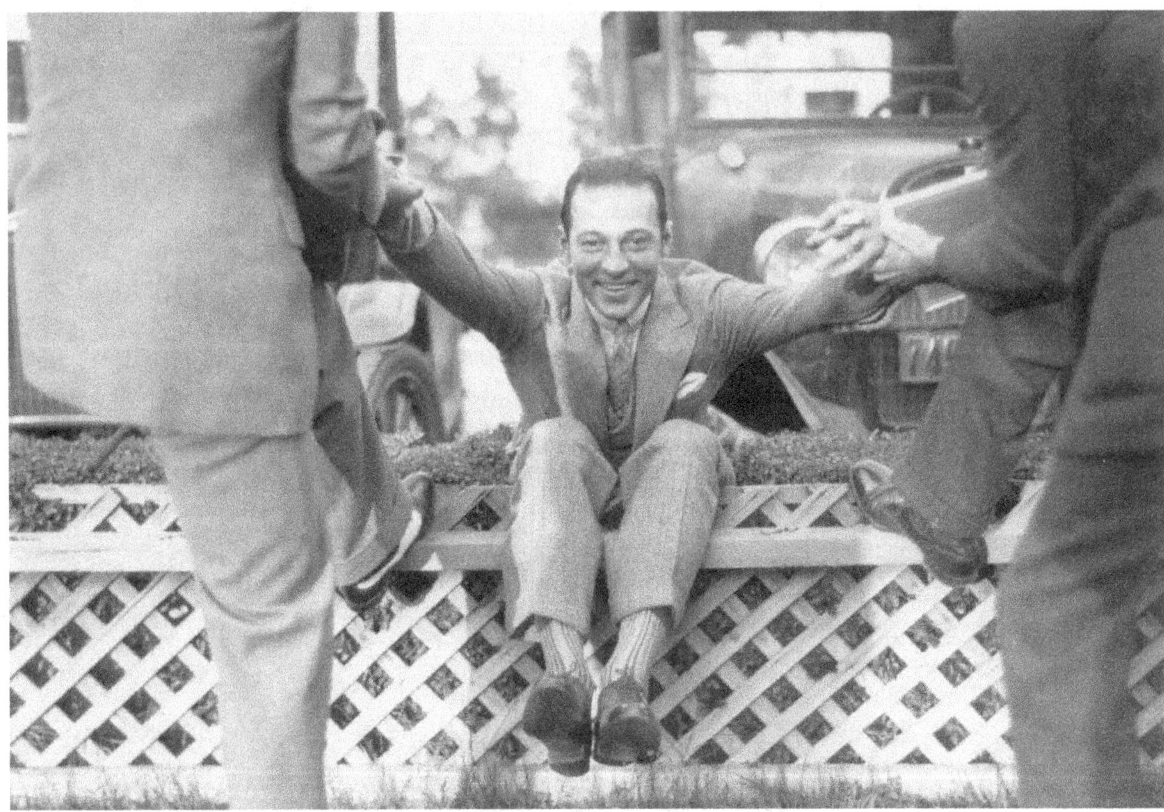

Valentino and a couple of unknown pals clowning around on the United Artist studio lot.
Valentino with his ever-present cigarette.
(Michael and Virginia Back collection)

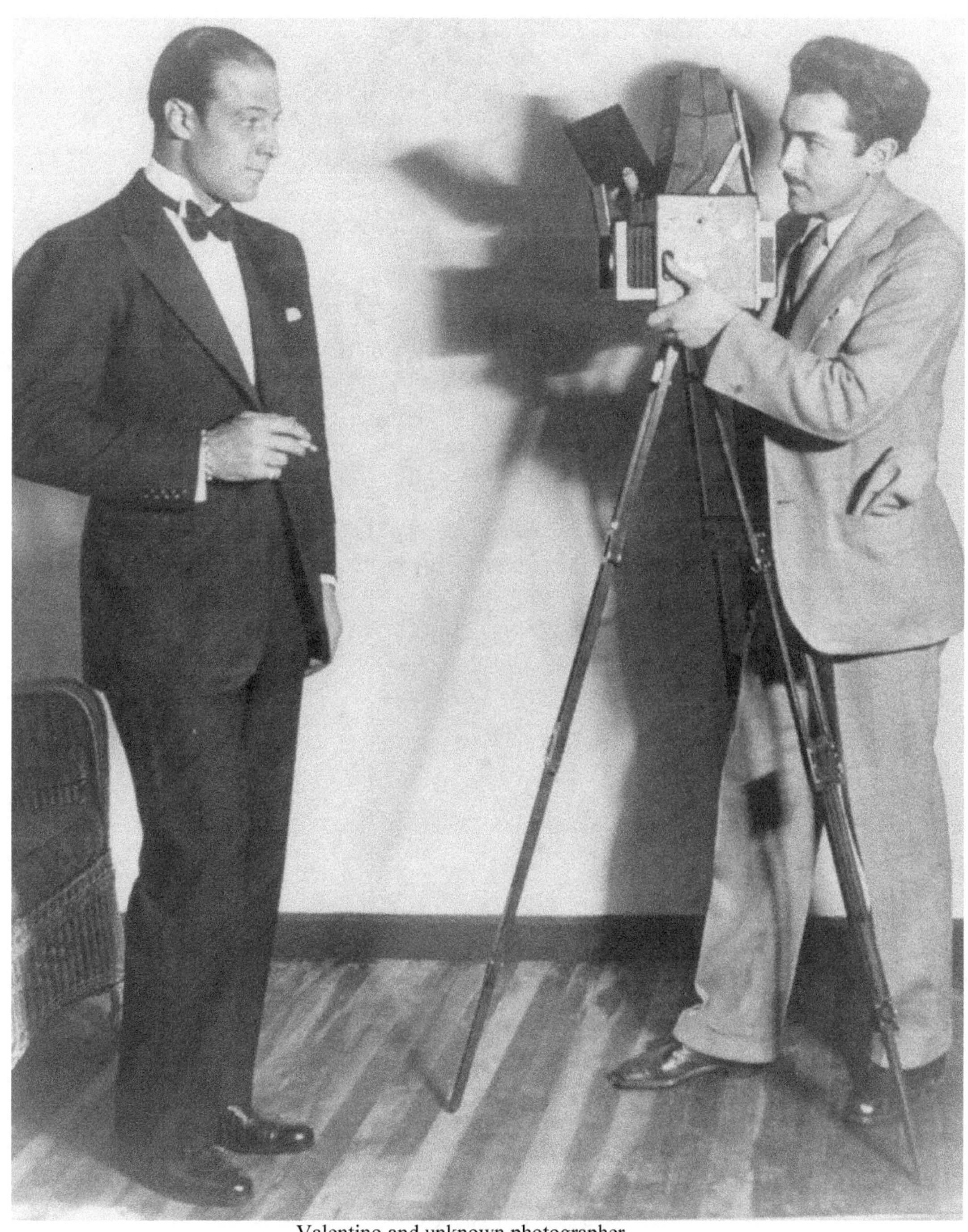

Valentino and unknown photographer.
Valentino, naturally, looks like a million dollars, the photographer, not so much.
(Author's collection)

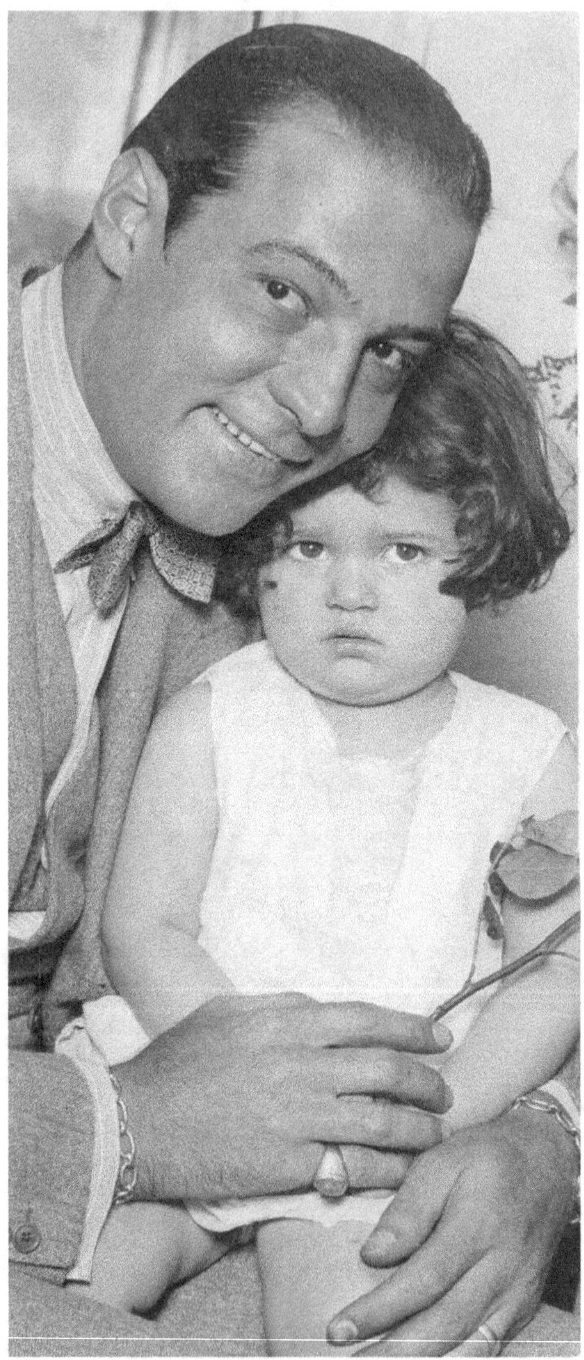

Valentino posing with Gloria Corea at his suite in
The Fairmont Hotel in San Francisco.
(Author's collection)

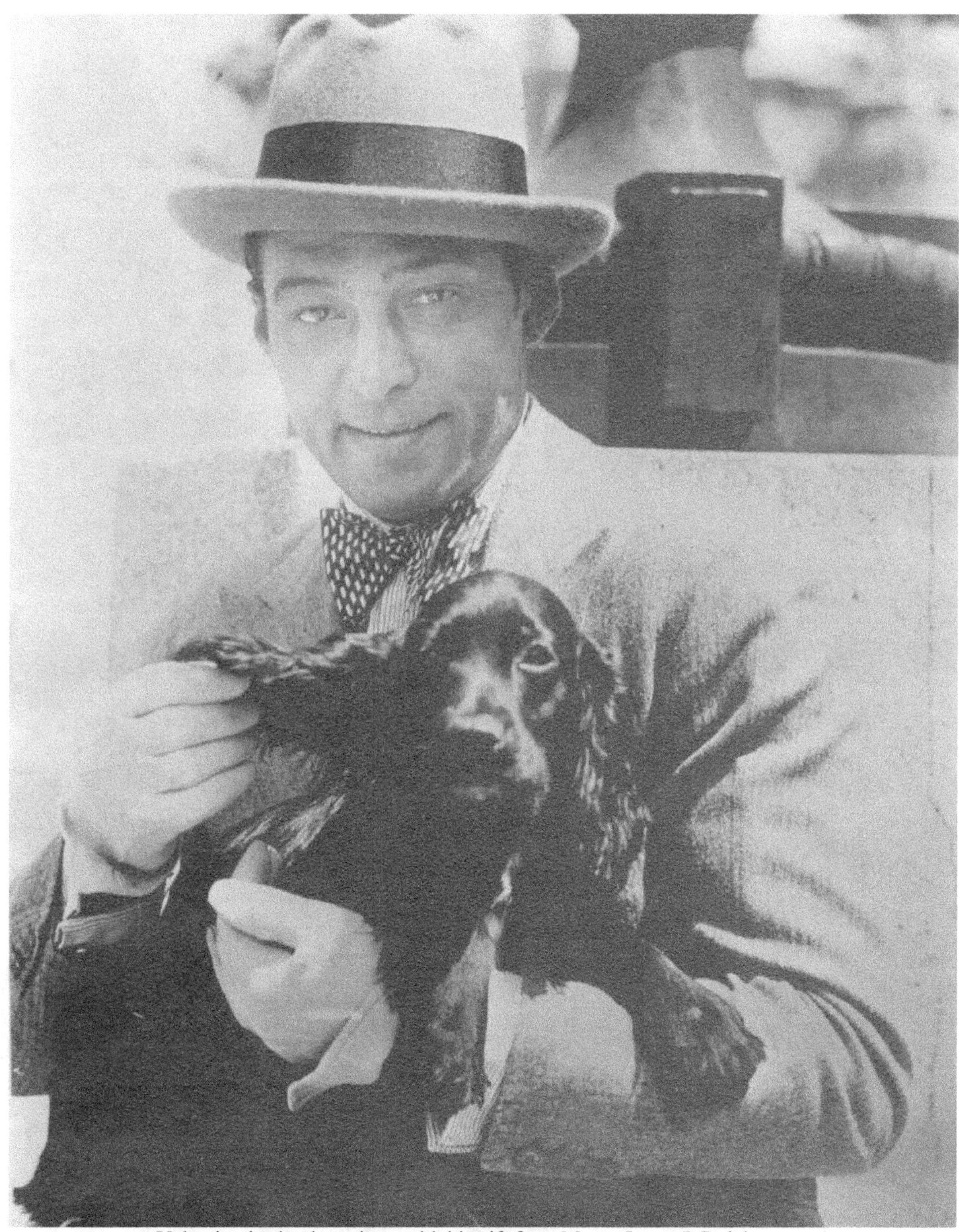

Valentino is clearly smitten with his gift from Mayor James J. Rolph.
The Mayor bred spaniels and dubbed this one 'Mission Rudy."
(Author's collection)

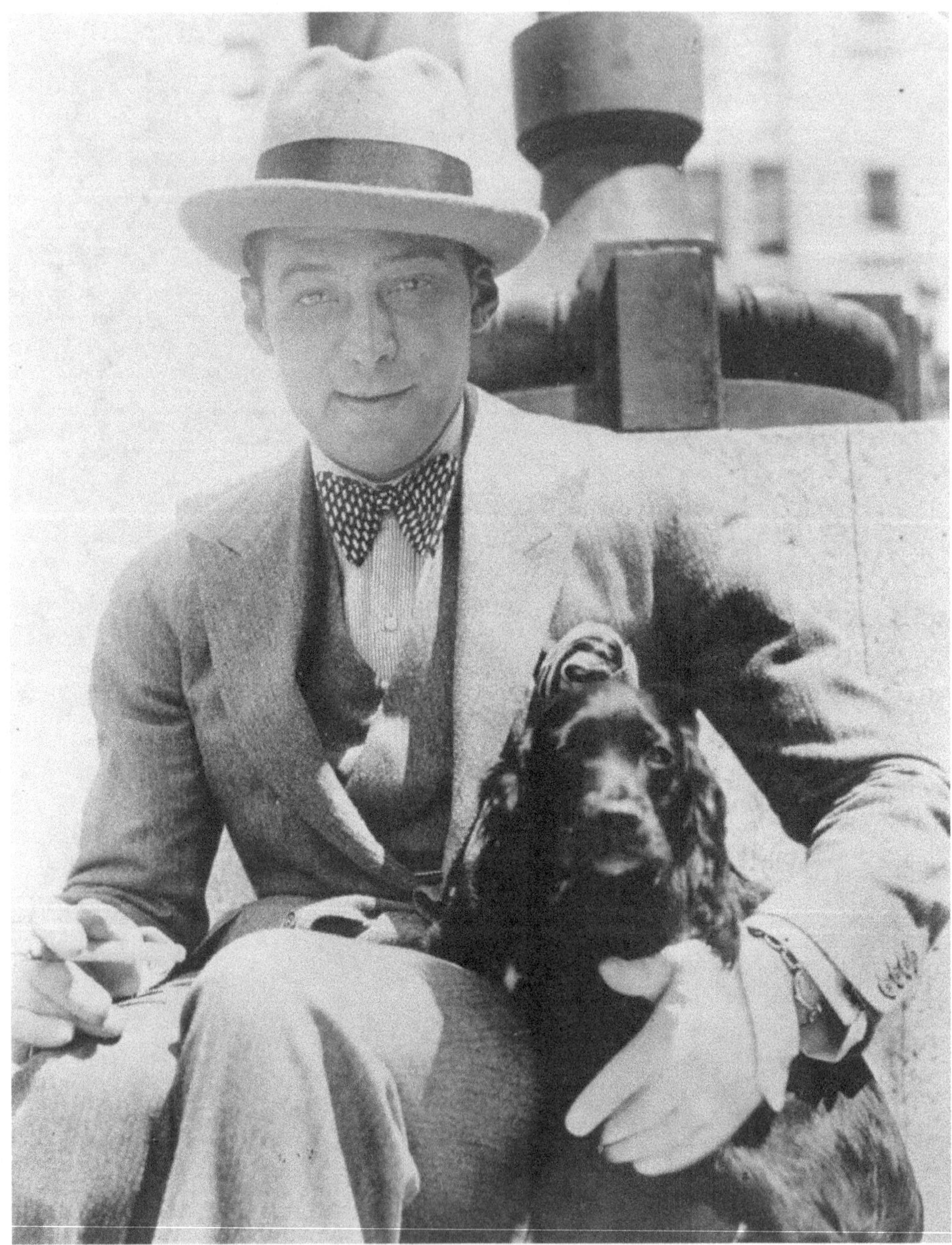

Valentino and "Mission Rudy" posing in front of the Fairmont Hotel in San Francisco.
(Author's collection)

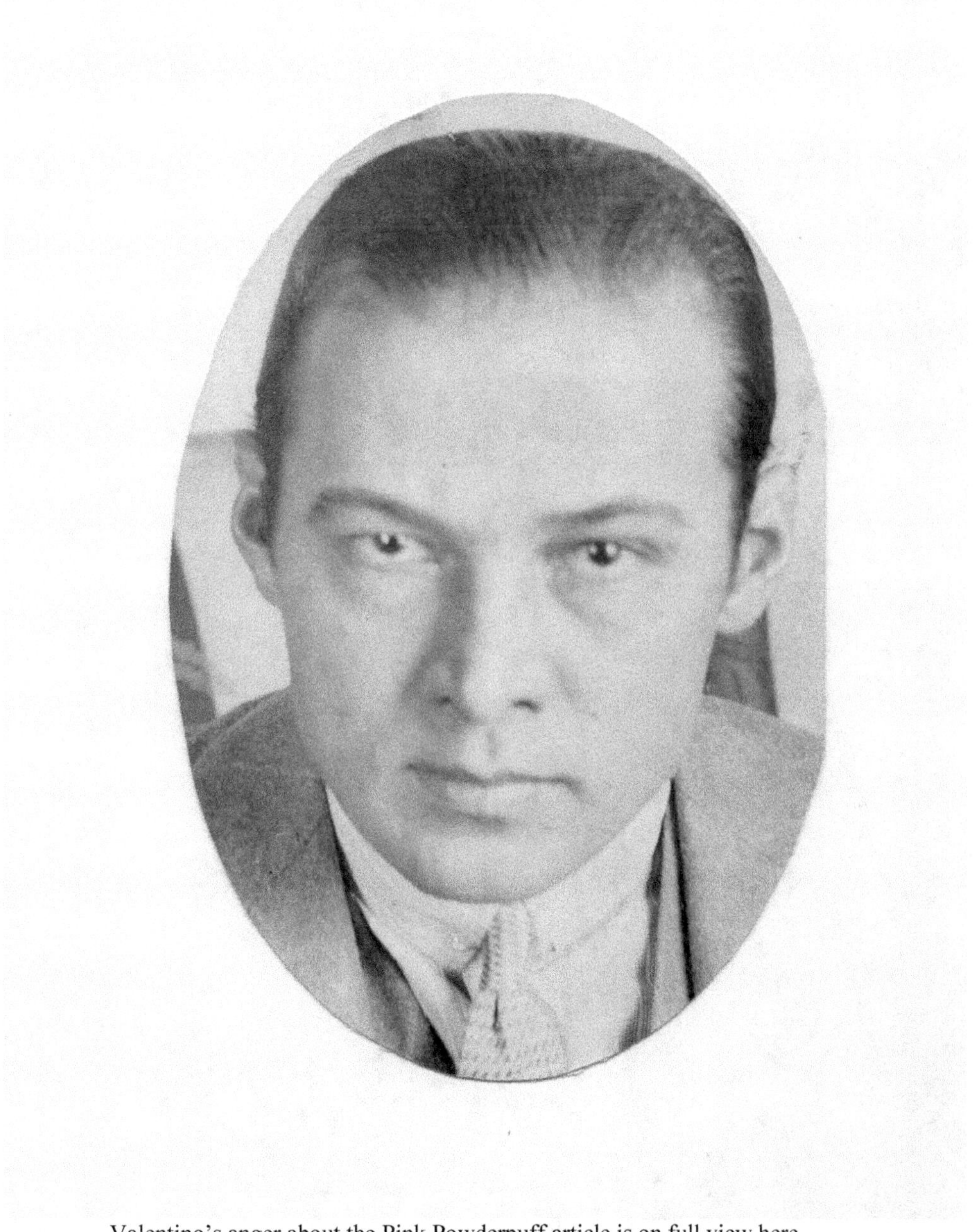

Valentino's anger about the Pink Powderpuff article is on full view here.
(Author's collection)

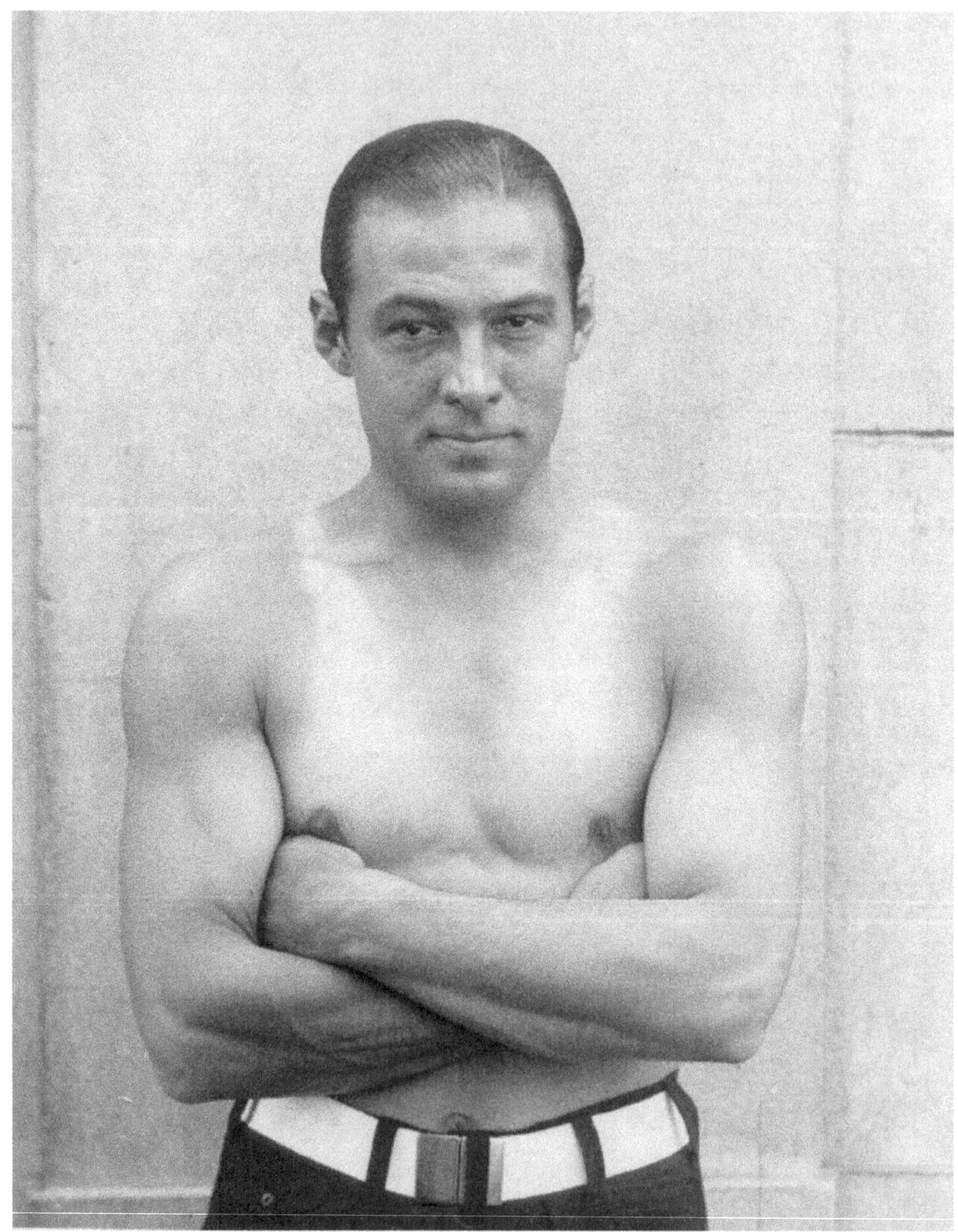

In the wake of the scurrilous "Pink Powder Puff" editorial in Chicago, an angry Valentino shows off his physique. His direct gaze tells you he meant business. (Michael and Virginia Back collection)

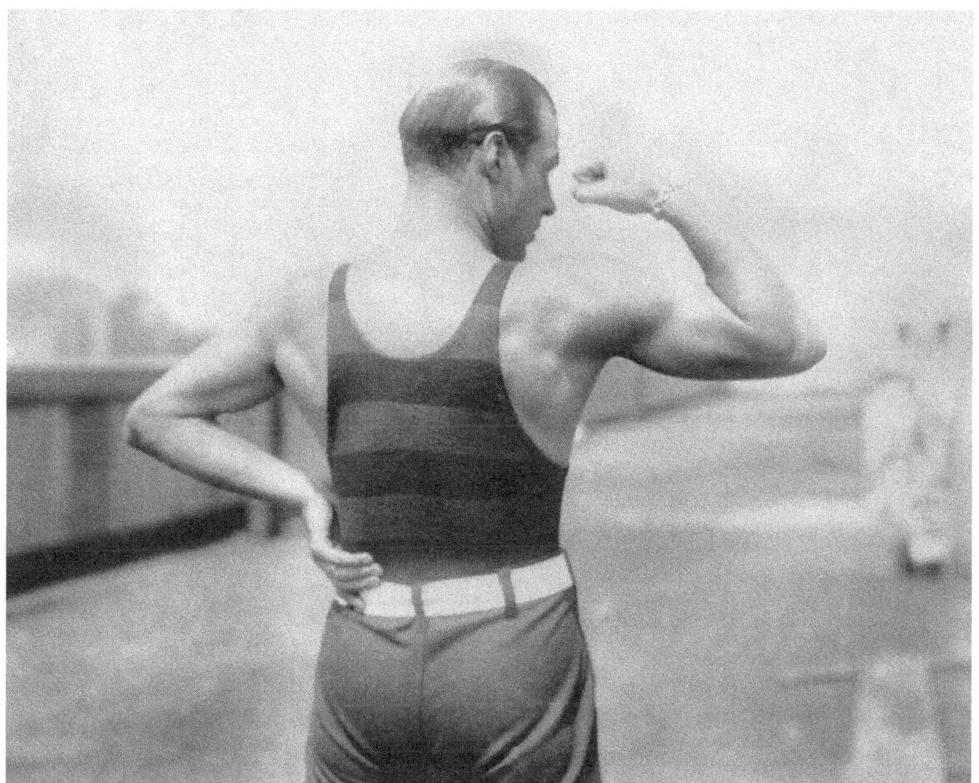

Valentino took the opportunity to flex his muscles for emphasis.
(The San Francisco History Center)

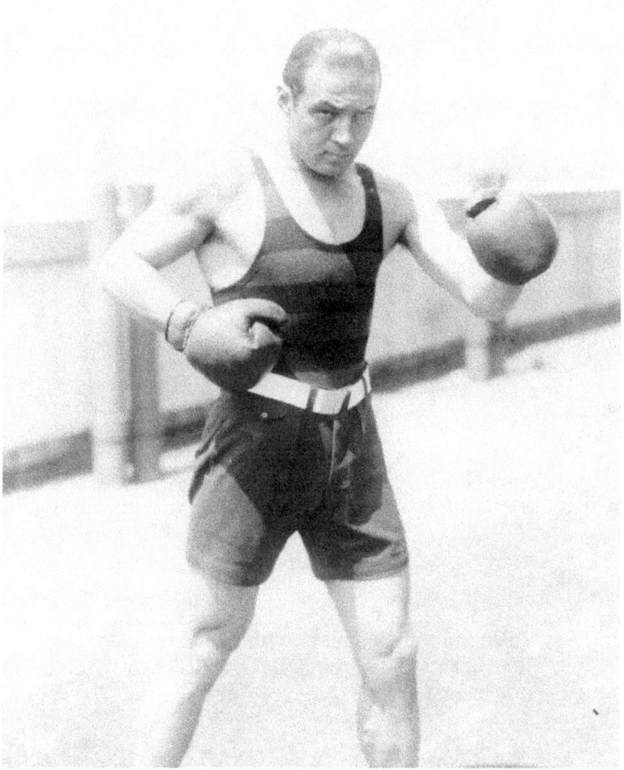

Valentino's anger and torment are plainly visible.
(Author's collection)

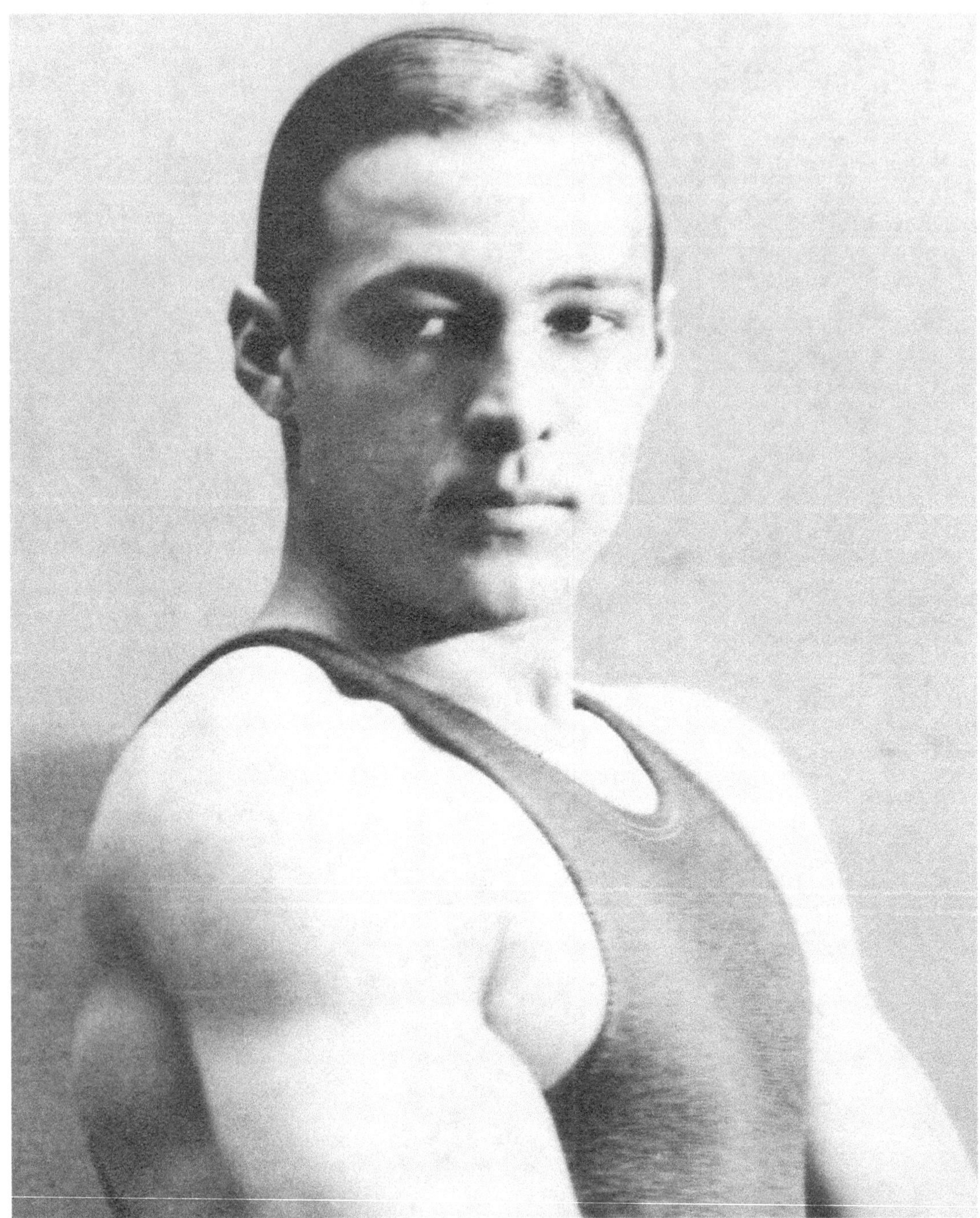

Valentino showing his determination to fight.
(Michael and Virginia Back collection)

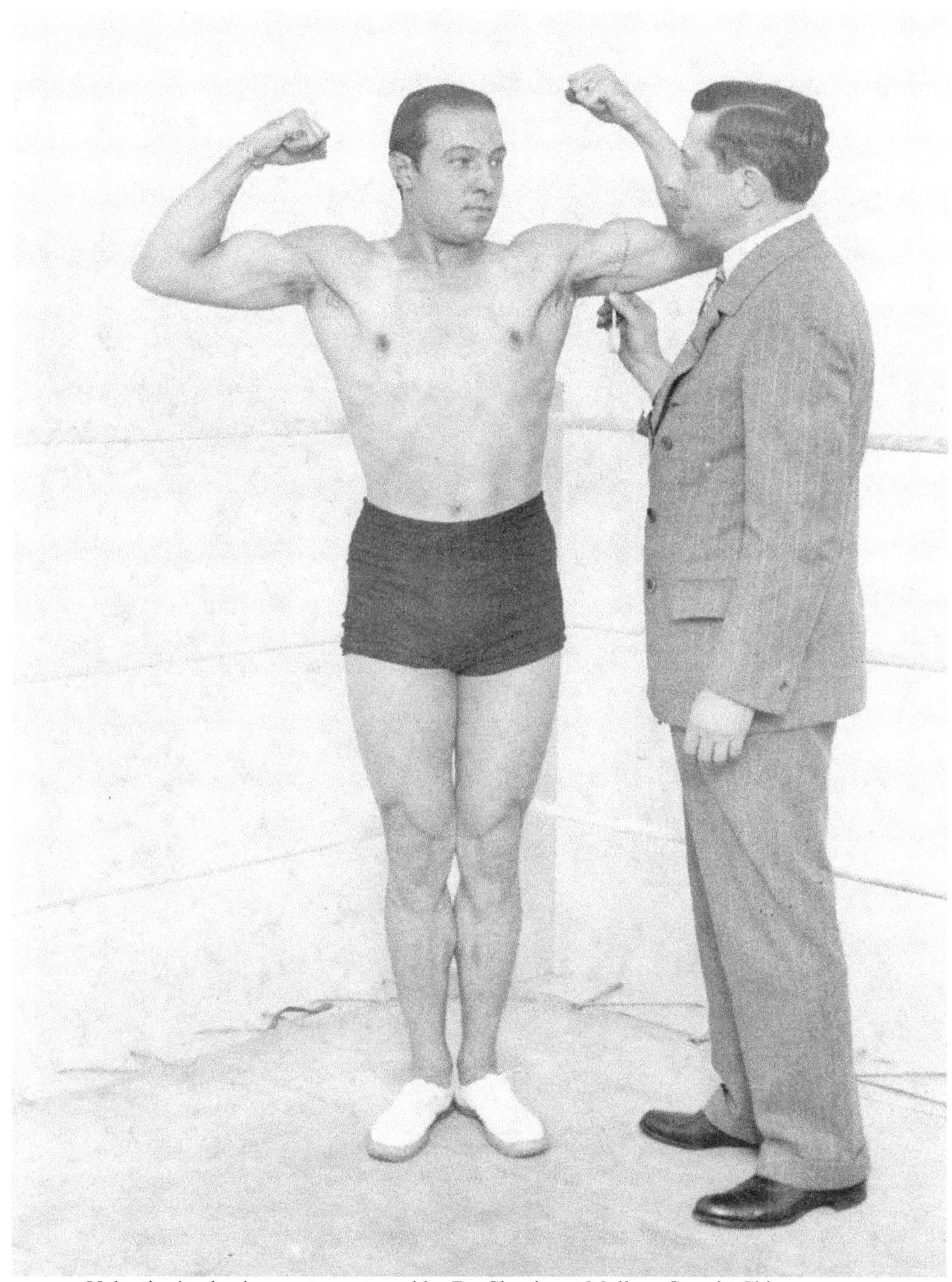

Valentino's physique gets measured by Dr. Shapiro at Mullens Gym in Chicago.
(Author's collection)

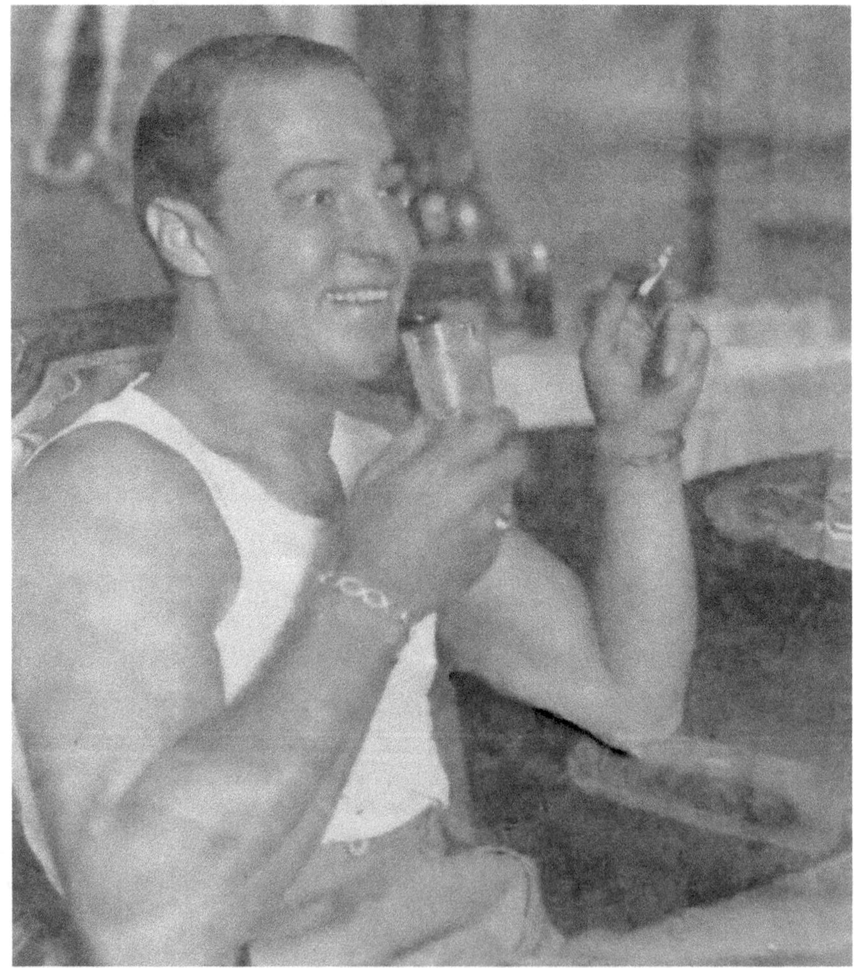

Valentino relaxing and enjoying a cool drink in a sweltering Chicago, July 1926.
(Stella Grace collection)

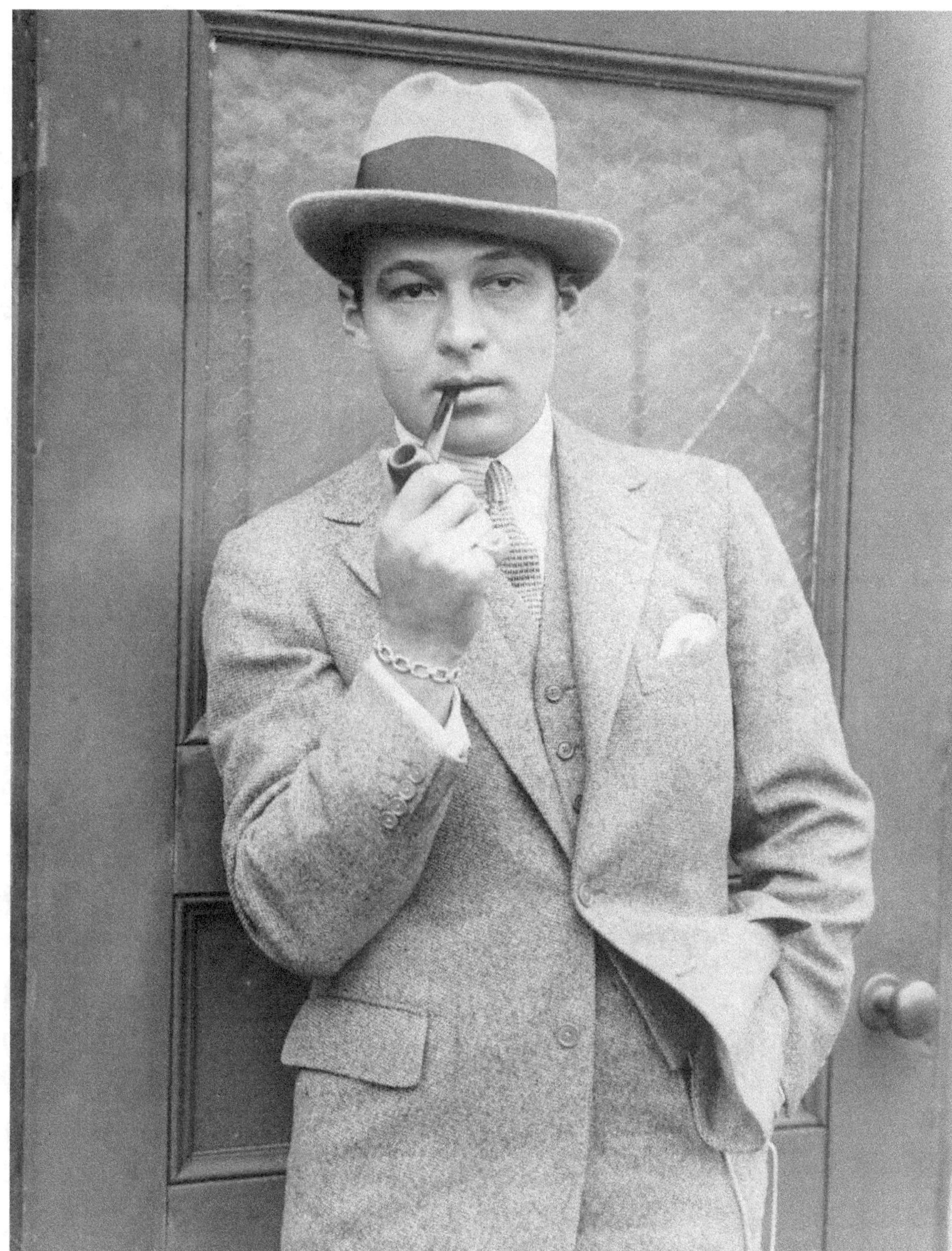

His eyes sad, his countenance exhausted, Valentino departs Chicago for New York to promote *The Son of the Sheik*. (The San Francisco History Center)

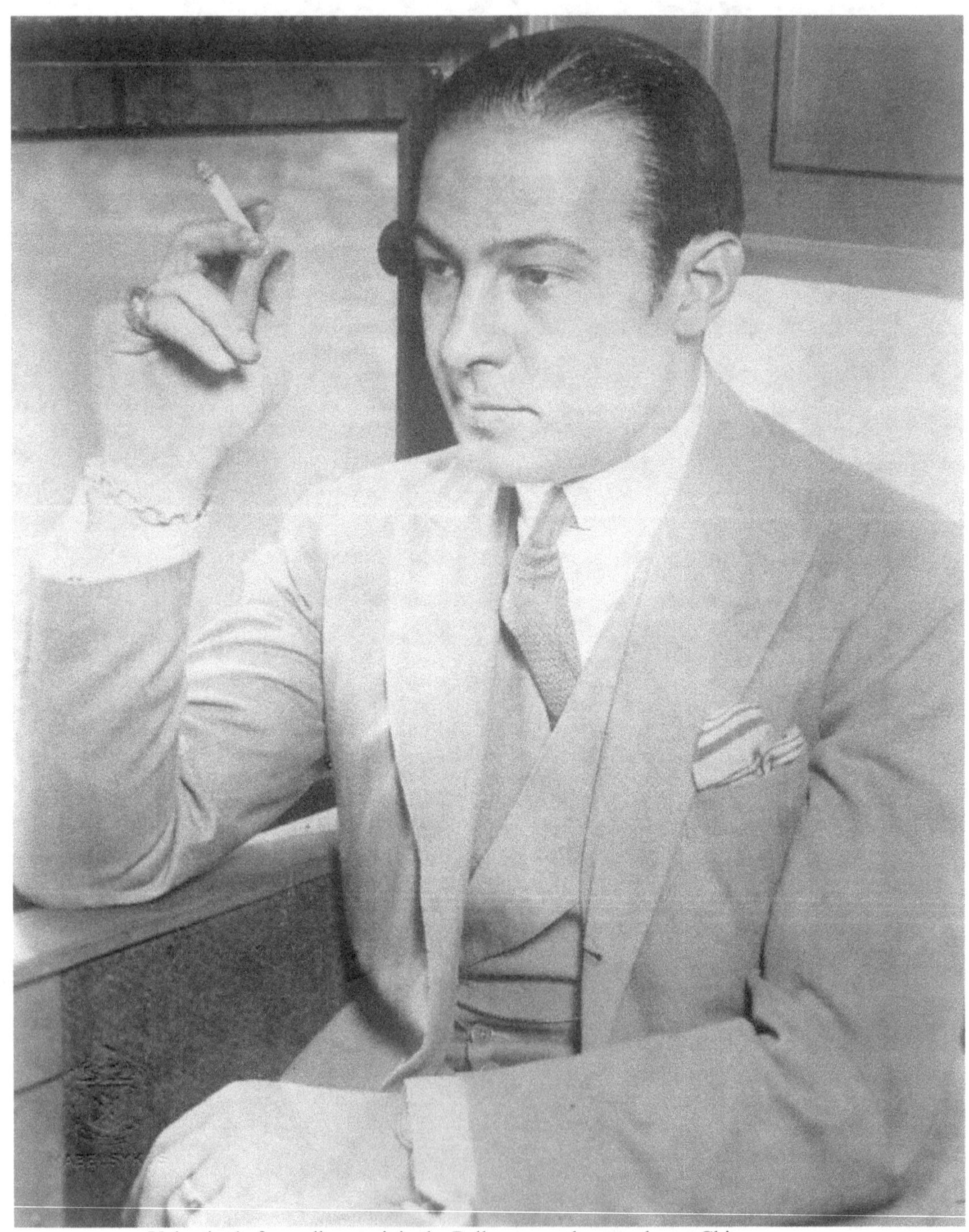

Valentino's farewell portrait in the Pullman car about to depart Chicago.
This is the last portrait taken of him by Mabel Sykes.
(Author's collection)

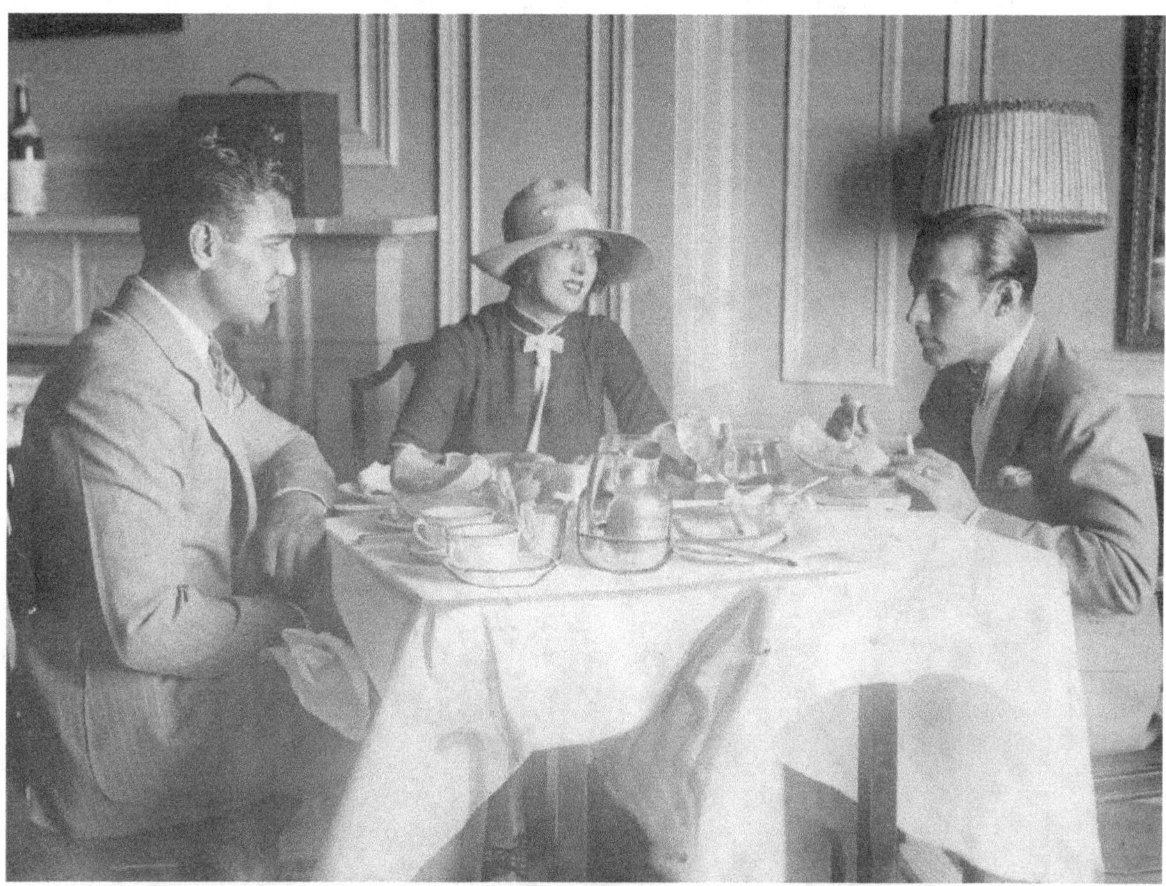

Valentino is seen breakfasting with good pal Jack Dempsey and Estelle Taylor (Mrs. Dempsey) in Valentino's hotel suite in New York. Taylor had just been signed to appear with Valentino in his next film. (Author's collection)

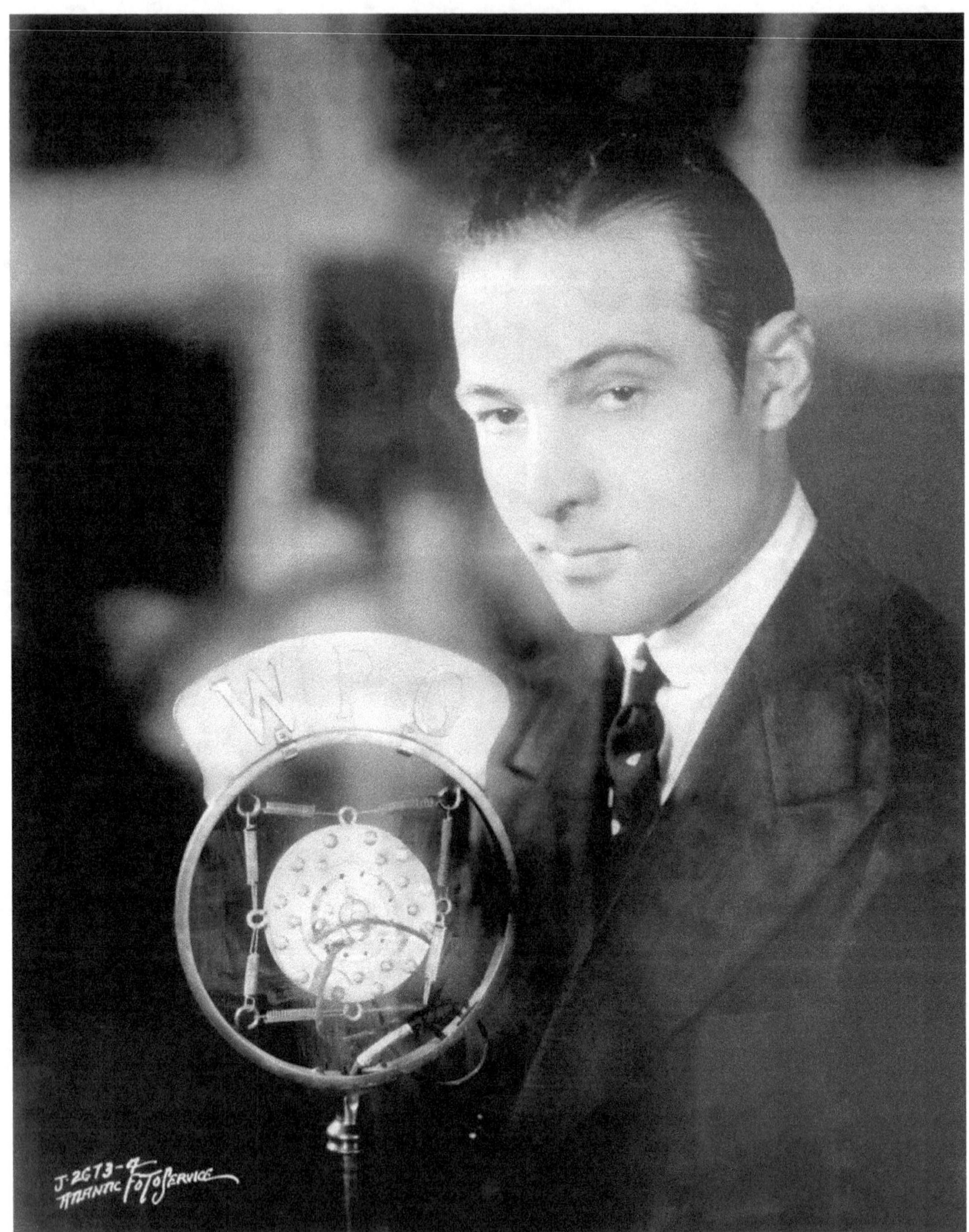

Valentino in Atlantic City, 1926.
(Author's collection)

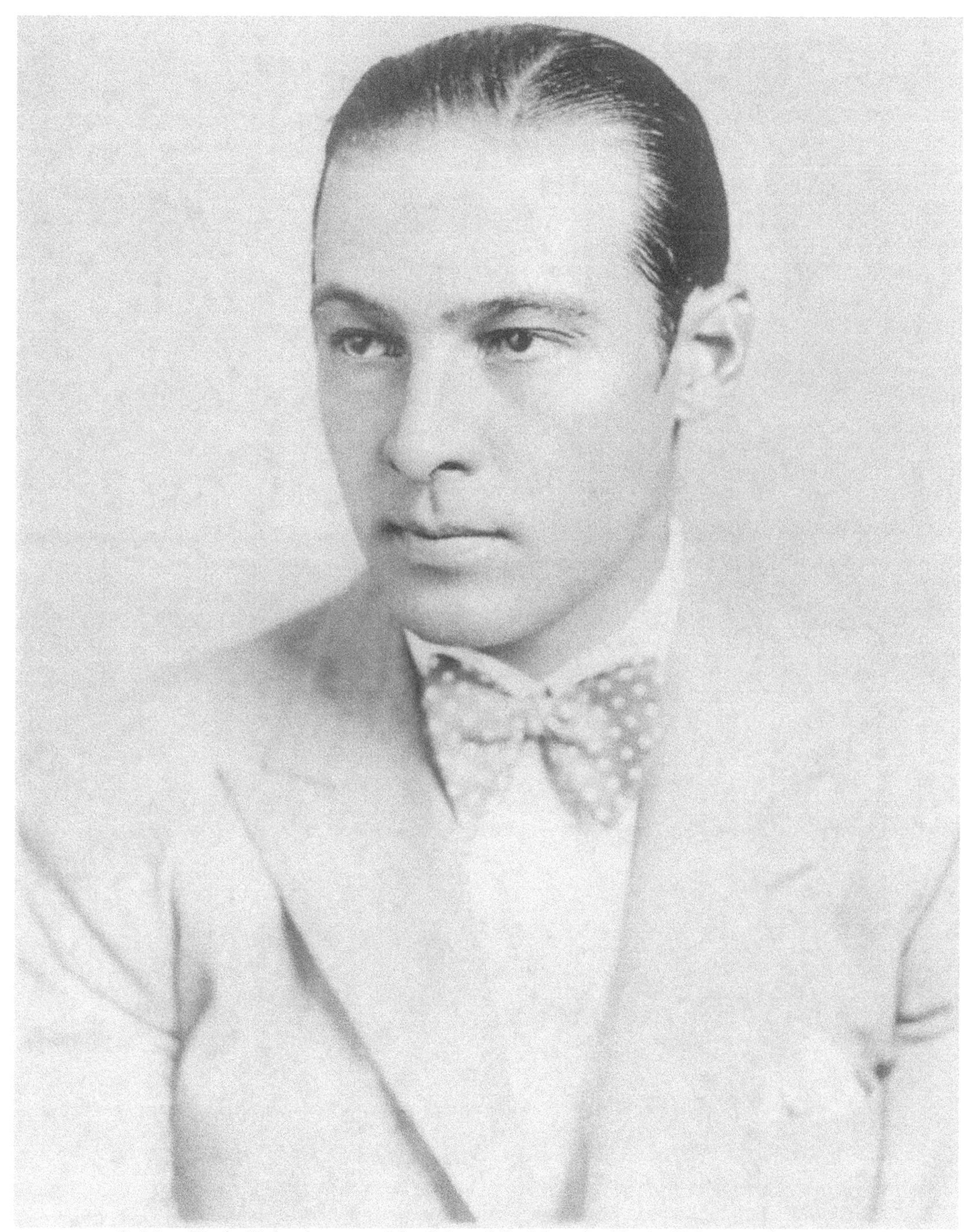

In New York, Valentino posed for Edward Steichen for Vanity Fair magazine.
(Author's collection)

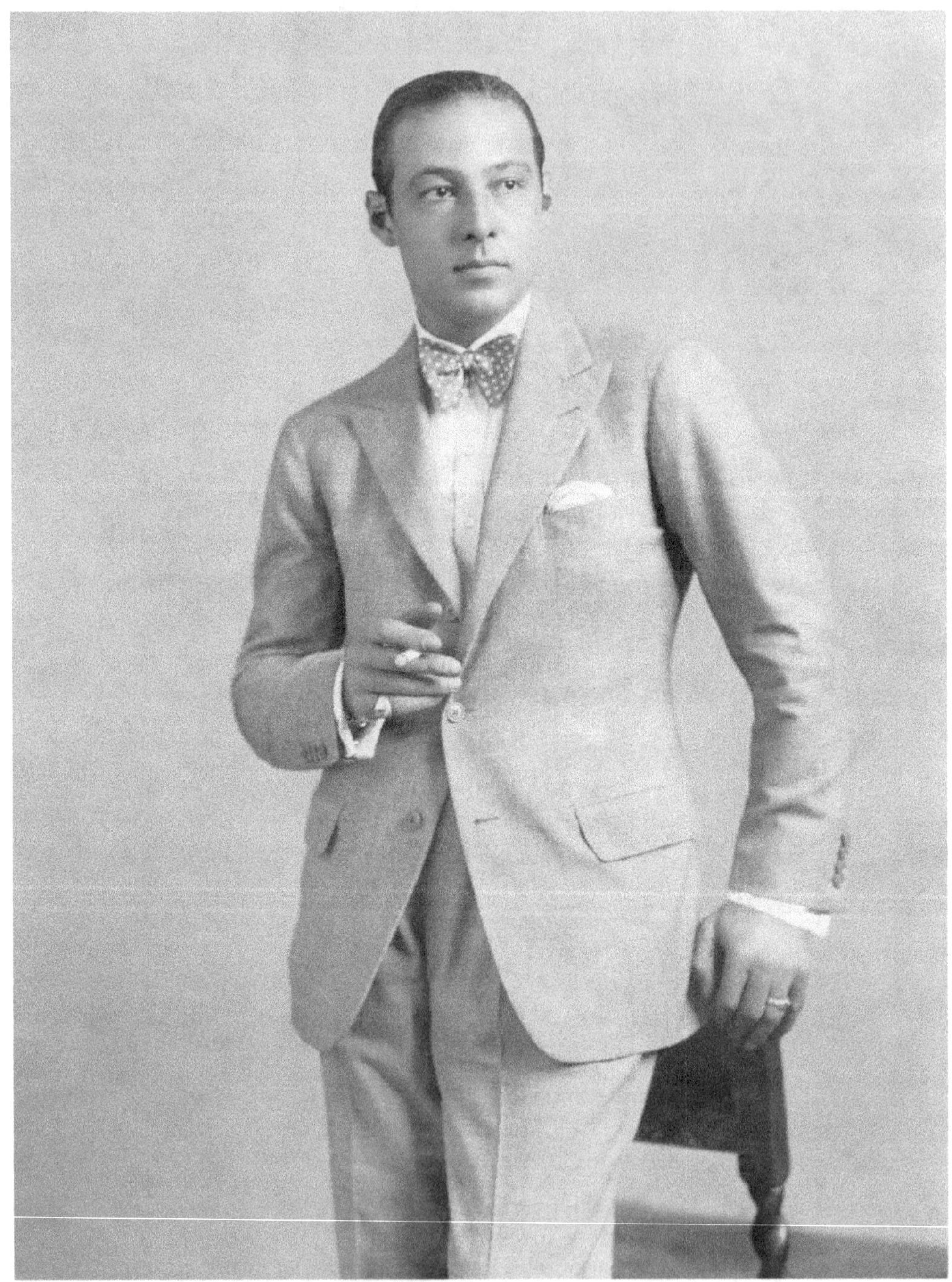

Steichen's lens could not hide Valentino's stress nor his illness.
(Caroline Rupprecht collection)

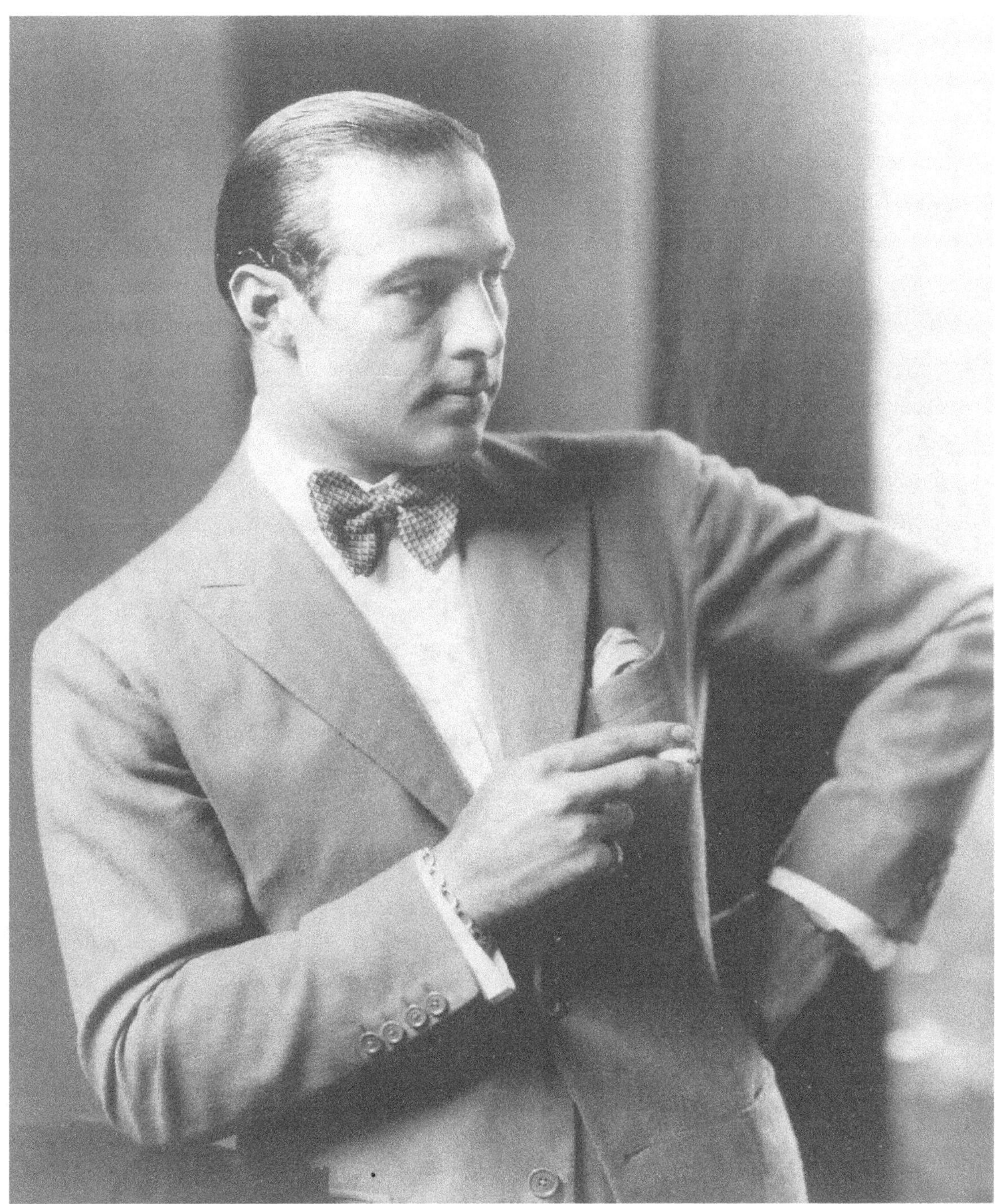

A final Steichen portrait which was published in Vanity Fair.
(Author's collection)

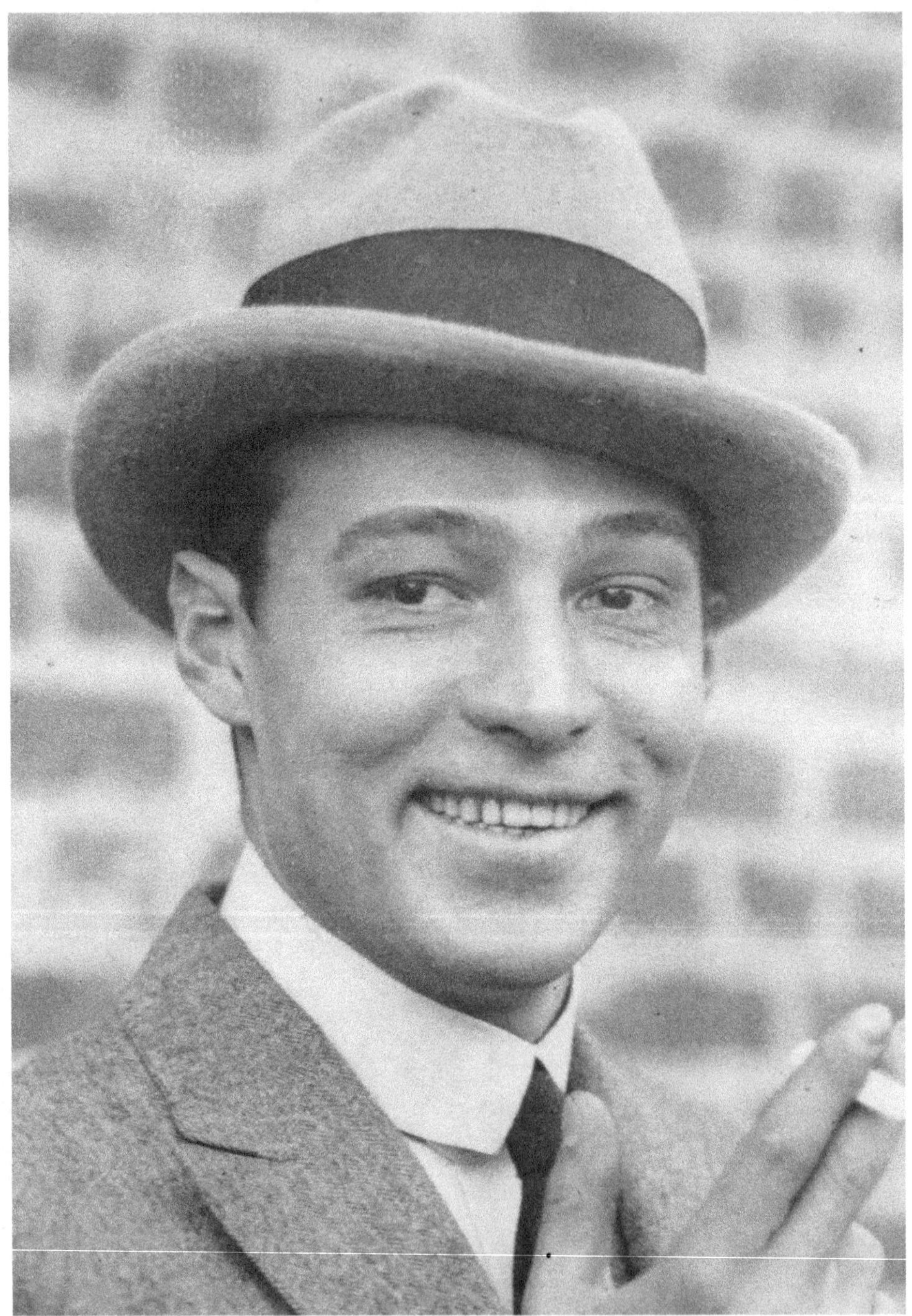

Valentino captured in a candid moment in New York, 1926.
(Author's collection)

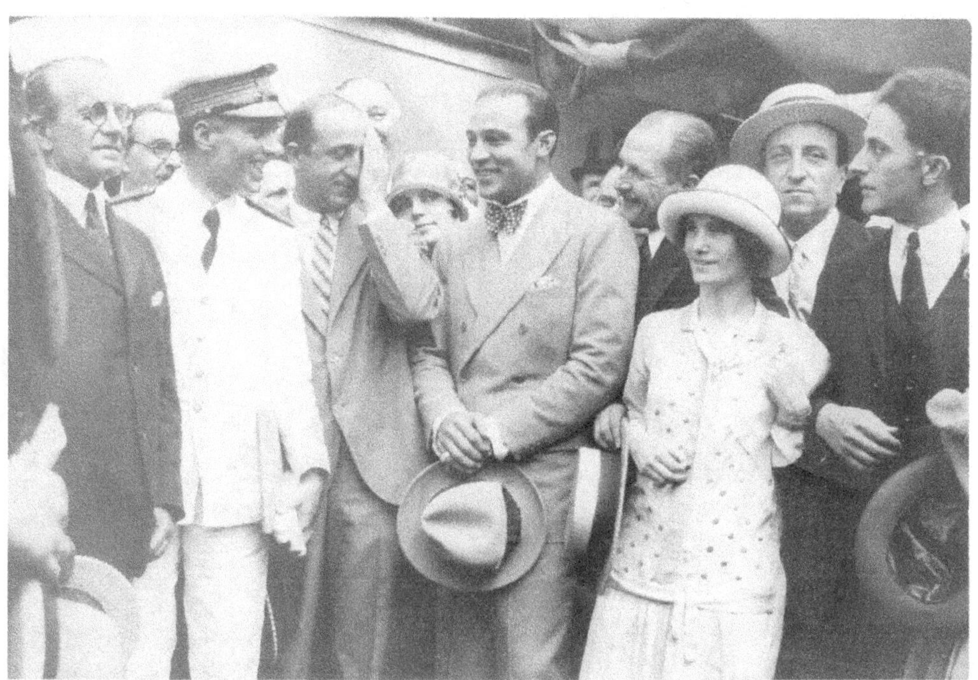

Valentino boards the S.S. Conte Biancamana to visit with Gen. Umberto Nobile.
(Author's collection)

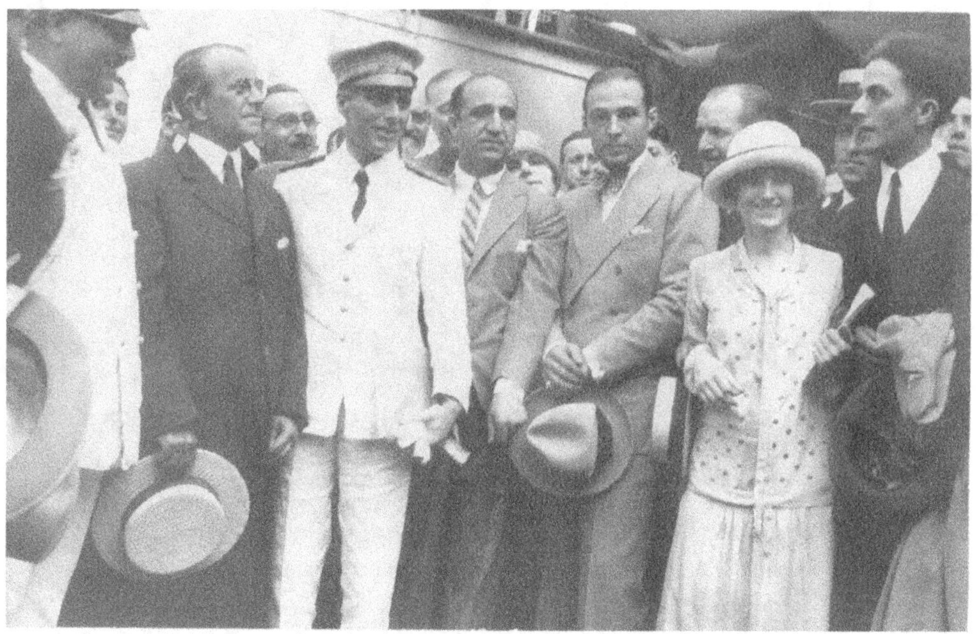

General Nobile was a famed aviator, aeronautical engineer and Arctic explorer.
Of course, Valentino, proud Italian that he was, could not resist welcoming him to New York.
(Author's collection)

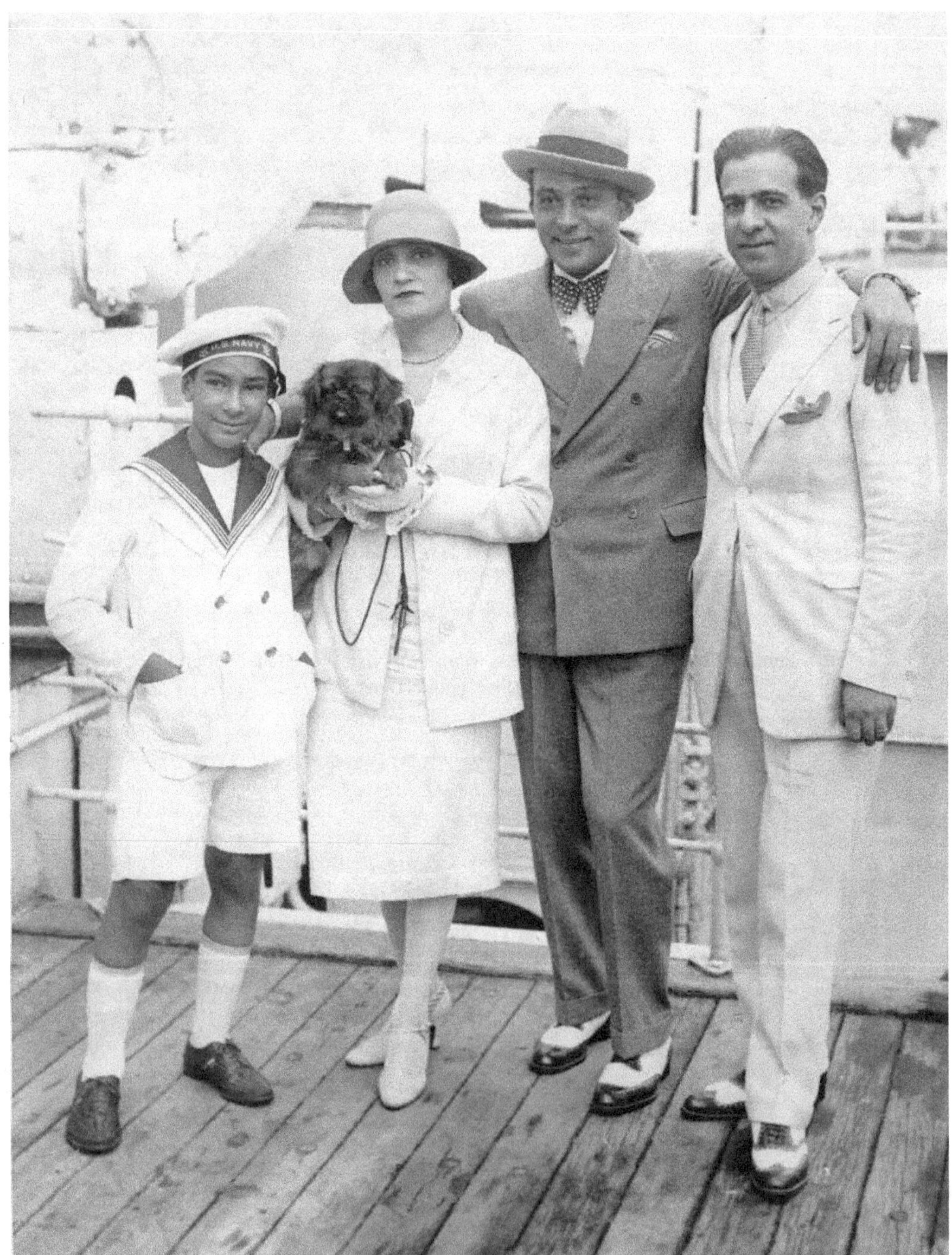

Valentino posed for a final family portrait for the news cameras on July 24, 1926.
This was their final goodbye.
(The San Francisco History Center)

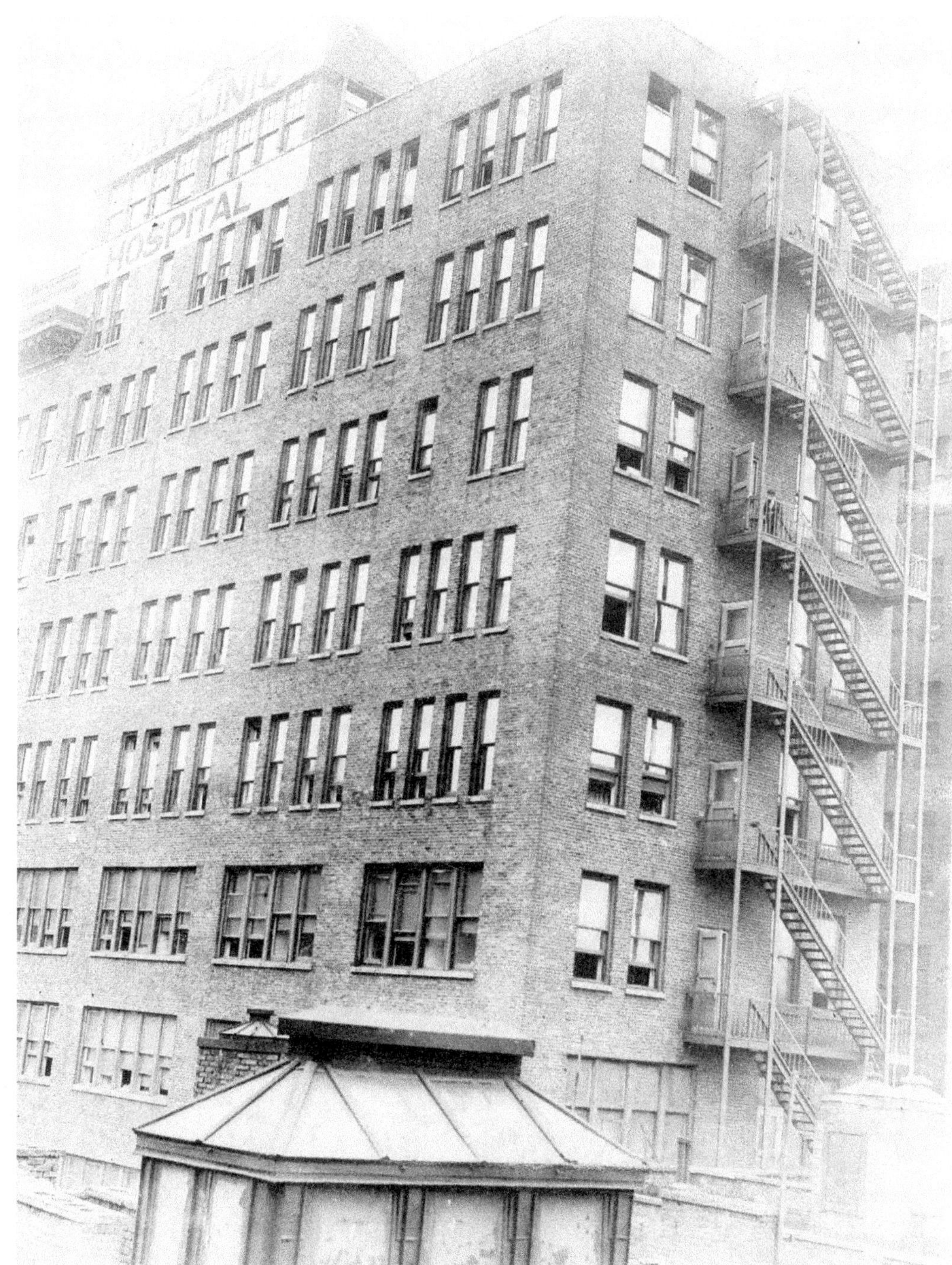

The Polyclinic Hospital where Valentino was taken for treatment.
(Author's collection)

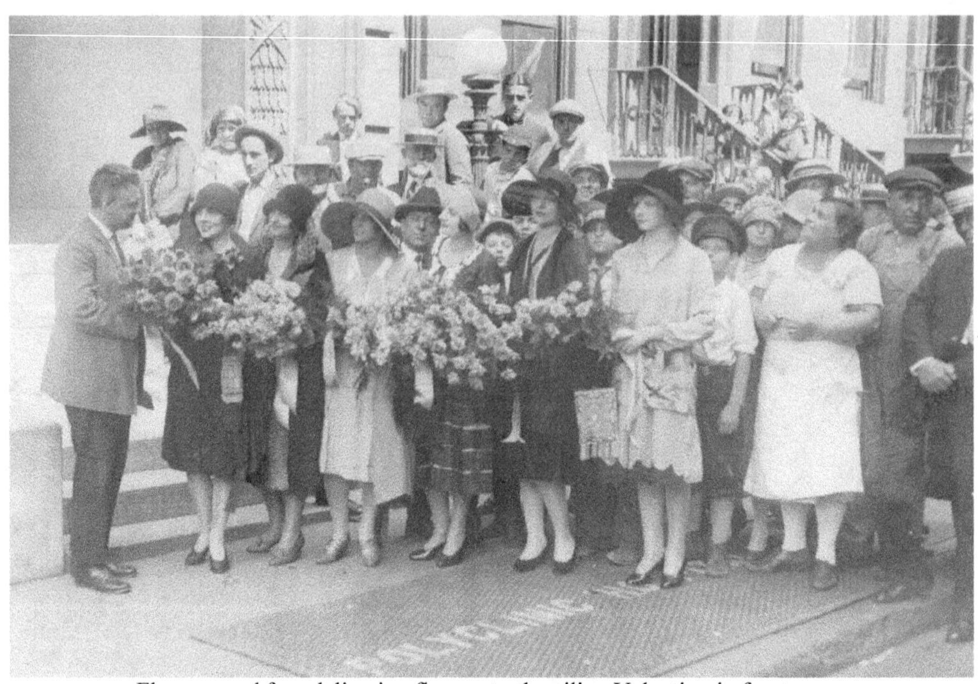
Flappers and fans delivering flowers to the ailing Valentino in front of the Polyclinic Hospital.
(Tracy Terhune collection)

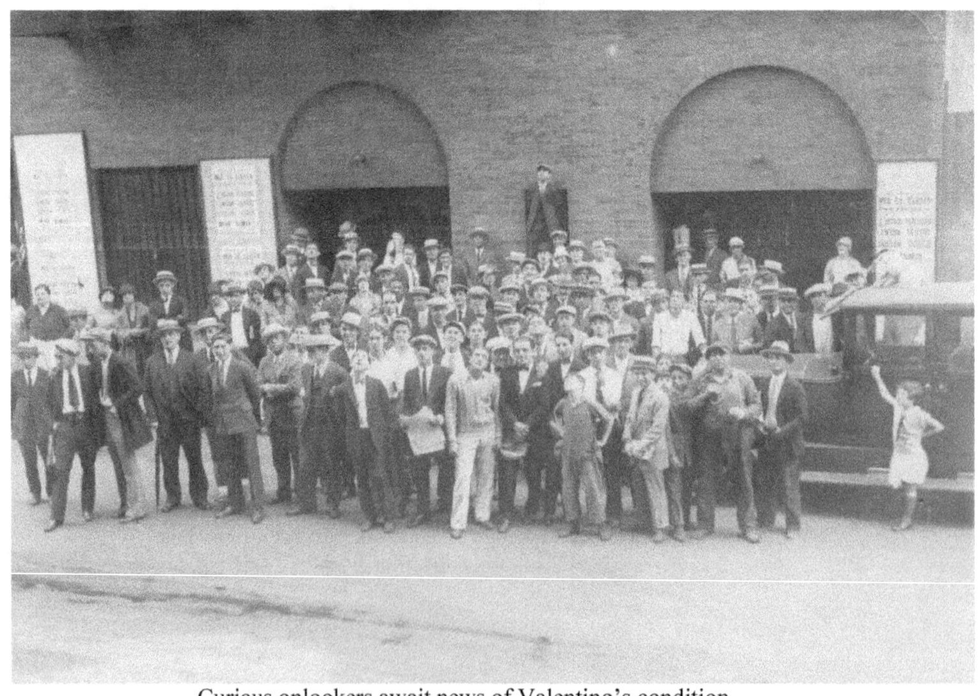
Curious onlookers await news of Valentino's condition across the street from the hospital.
(Tracy Terhune collection)

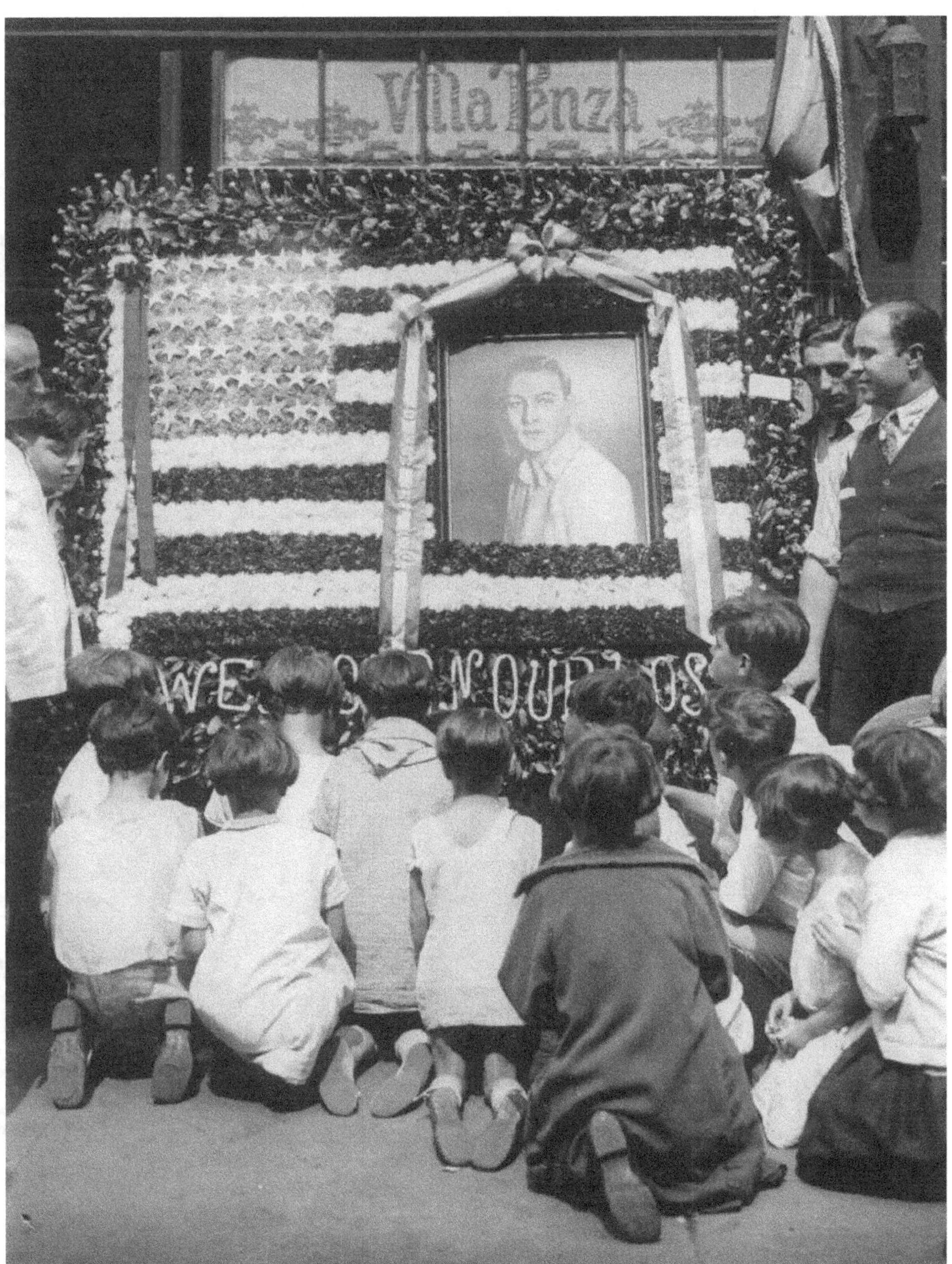

One of Valentino's favorite Italian restaurants in New York's Little Italy, Villa Penza.
Their tribute to their friend the screen idol after his passing.
(Tracy Terhune collection)

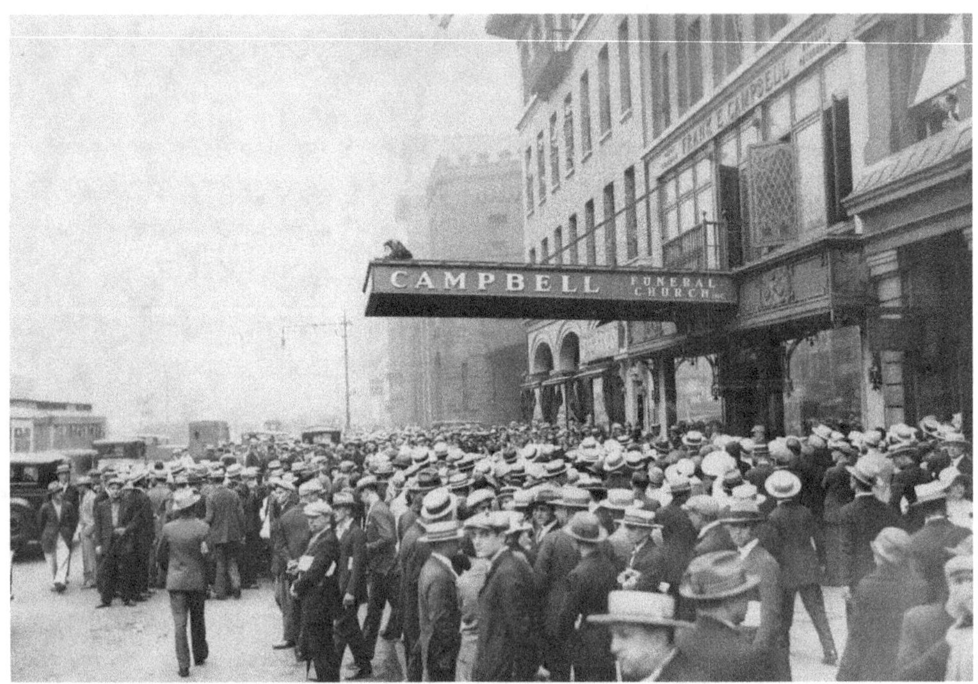

Contrary to modern belief, the crowds were not solely made up of anxious flappers.
(Tracy Terhune collection)

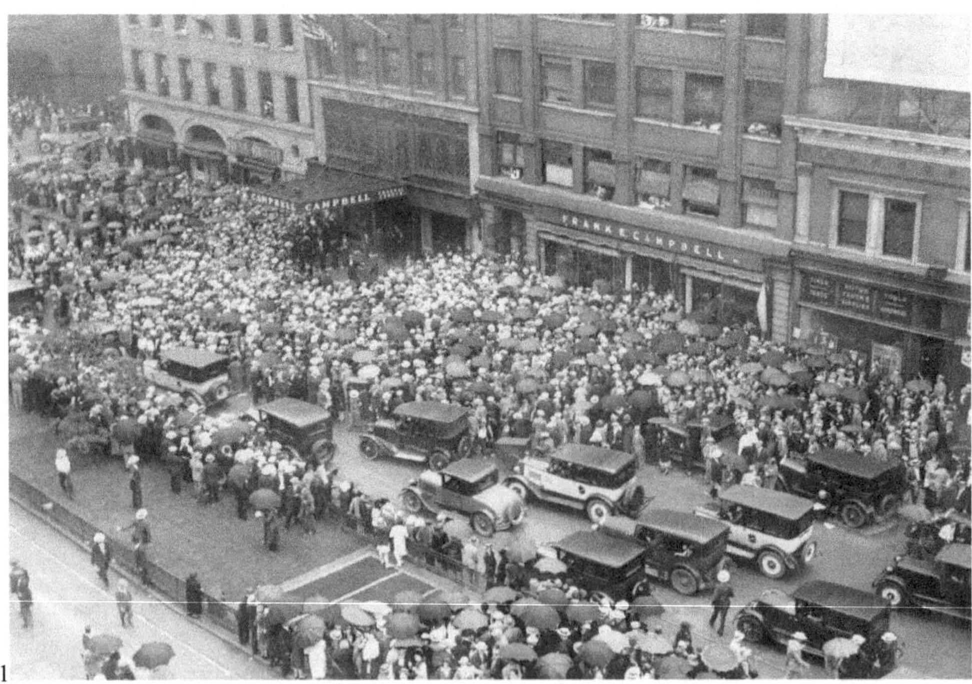

1

The crowds overwhelm Campbell's Funeral Church awaiting their final glimpse of Valentino.
(Tracy Terhune collection)

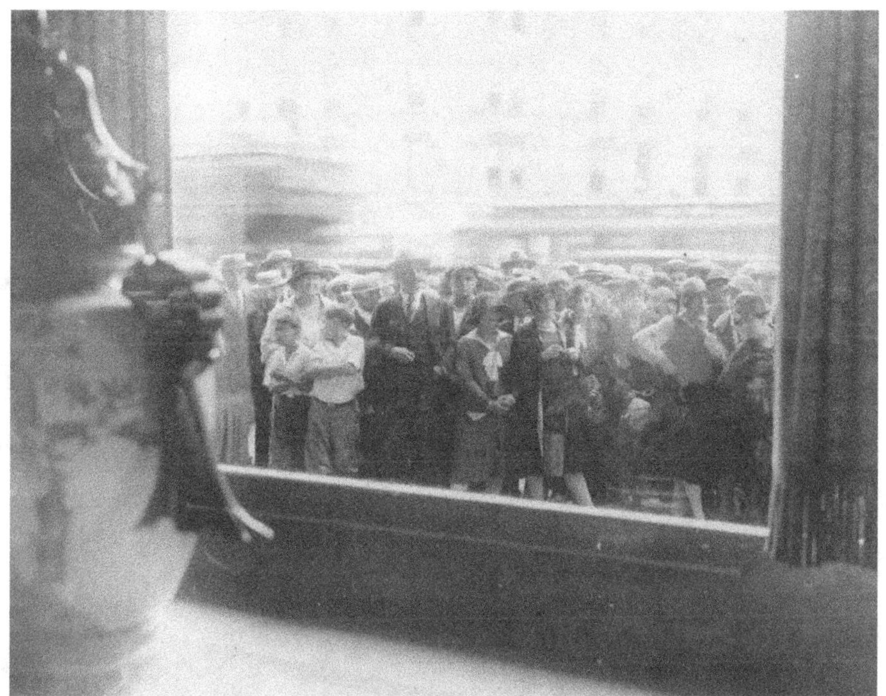

Part of the vast crowd pictured outside Campbell Funeral Parlors from inside Campbell's.
(Author's collection)

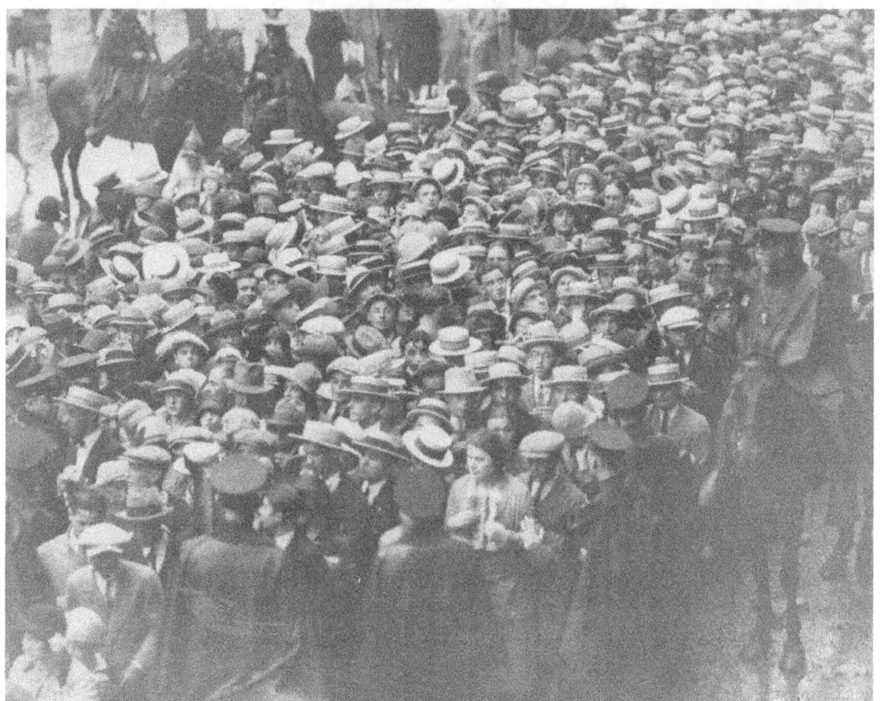

Note the majority of men in the photo.
Hundred(s) were injured during a stampede for the doors.
(Author's collection)

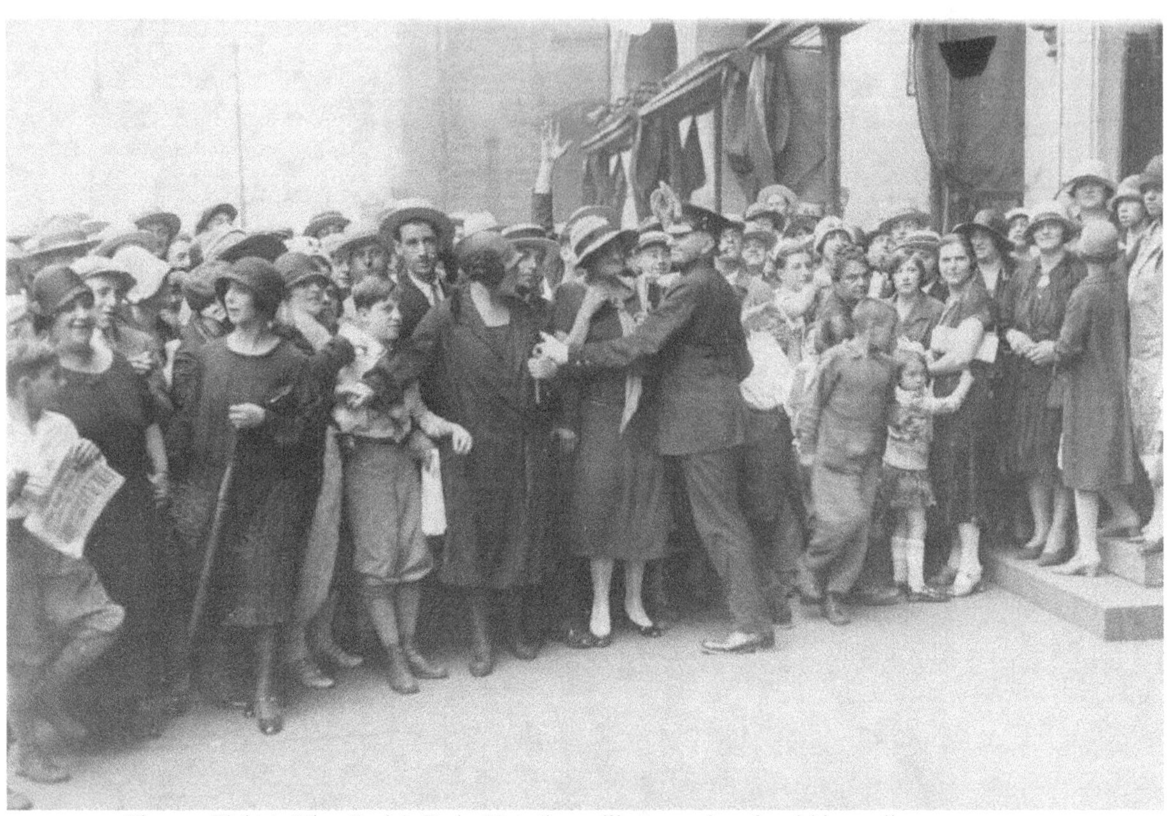

Throngs Fight to View Rudy's Body. Note the smiling crowd, and smirking policeman.
While the mob behavior was horrifying in newsreels, in this case, this was posed for the cameras.
(Author's collection)

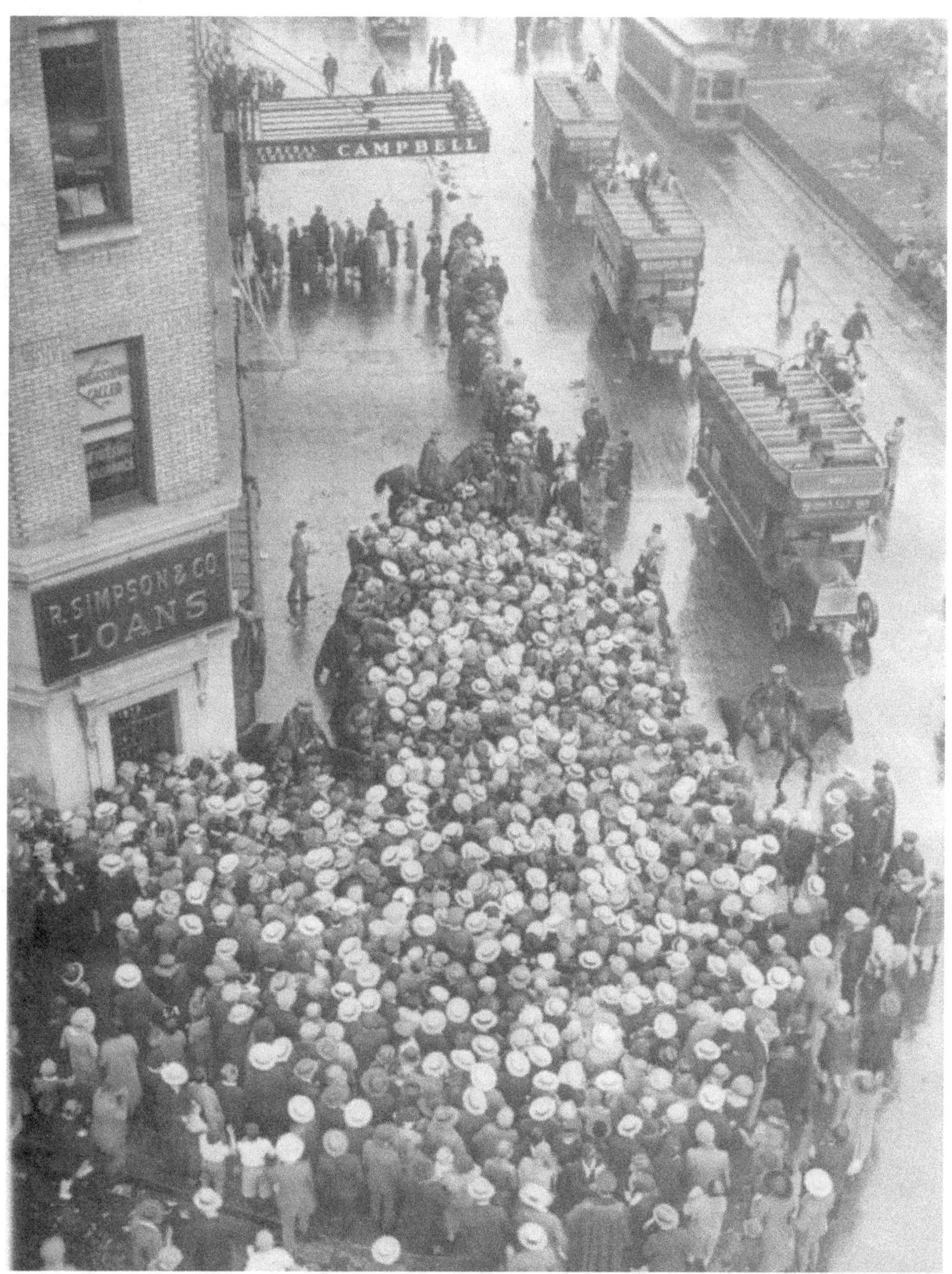

Mounted Police winnow down the crowd into a more manageable line to enter Campbell's.
(Author's collection)

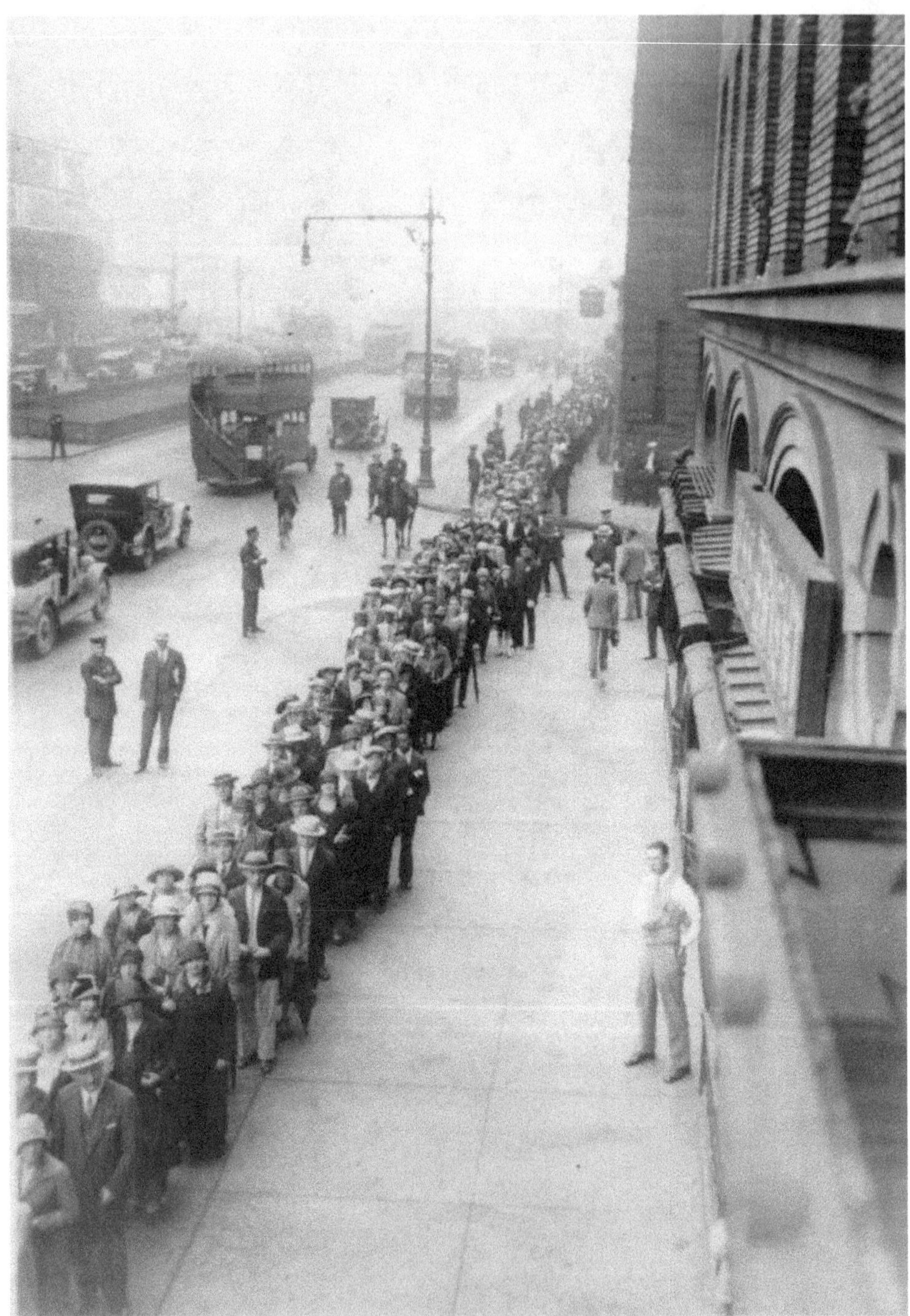

A view of the line heading up Broadway.
(Author's collection)

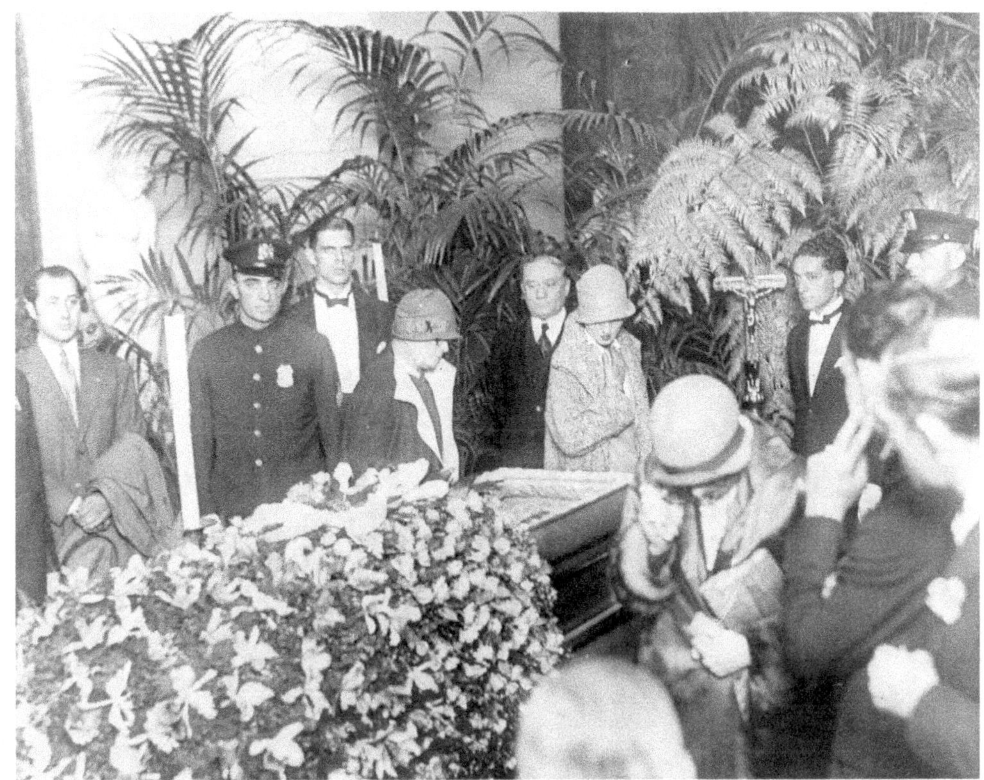

A rare view from inside Campbell's as crowds file past.
Frank Campbell is center, Jean Acker and Acker's mother is to Campbell's right.
(Author's collection)

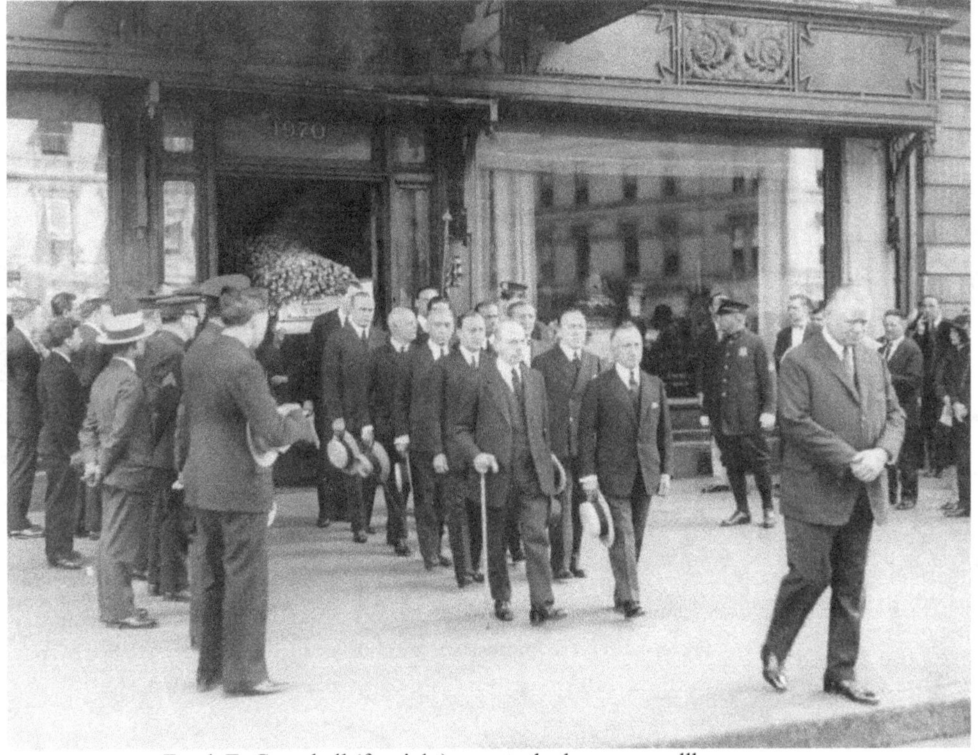

Frank E. Campbell (far right) escorts the honorary pallbearers
and Valentino's casket out to the awaiting hearse. (Tracy Terhune collection)

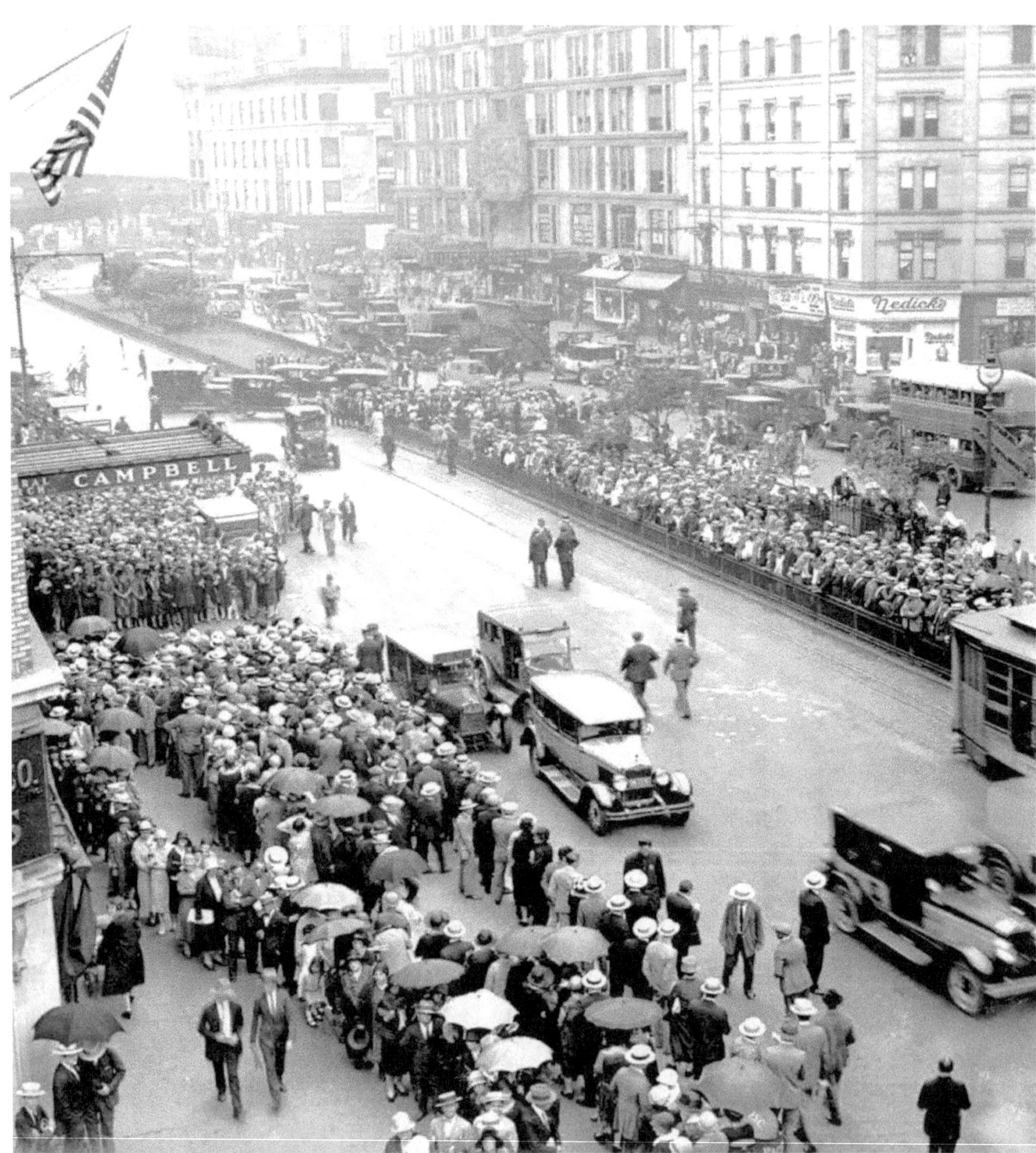

The crowds were impressive. (Author's collection)

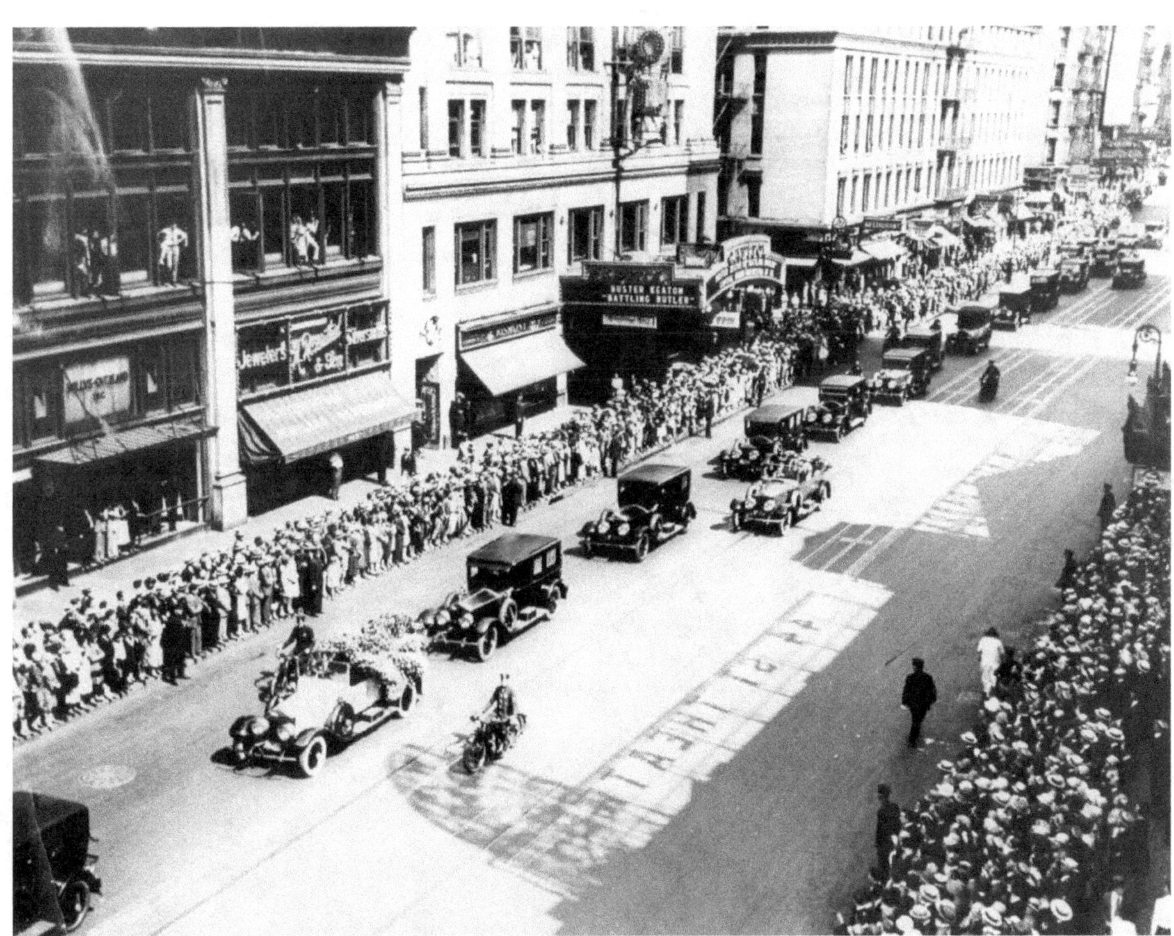

Crowds line 44th Street to pay their final respects as Valentino's funeral cortege makes its way to St. Malachy's for the Solemn High Funeral Mass.
(Author's collection)

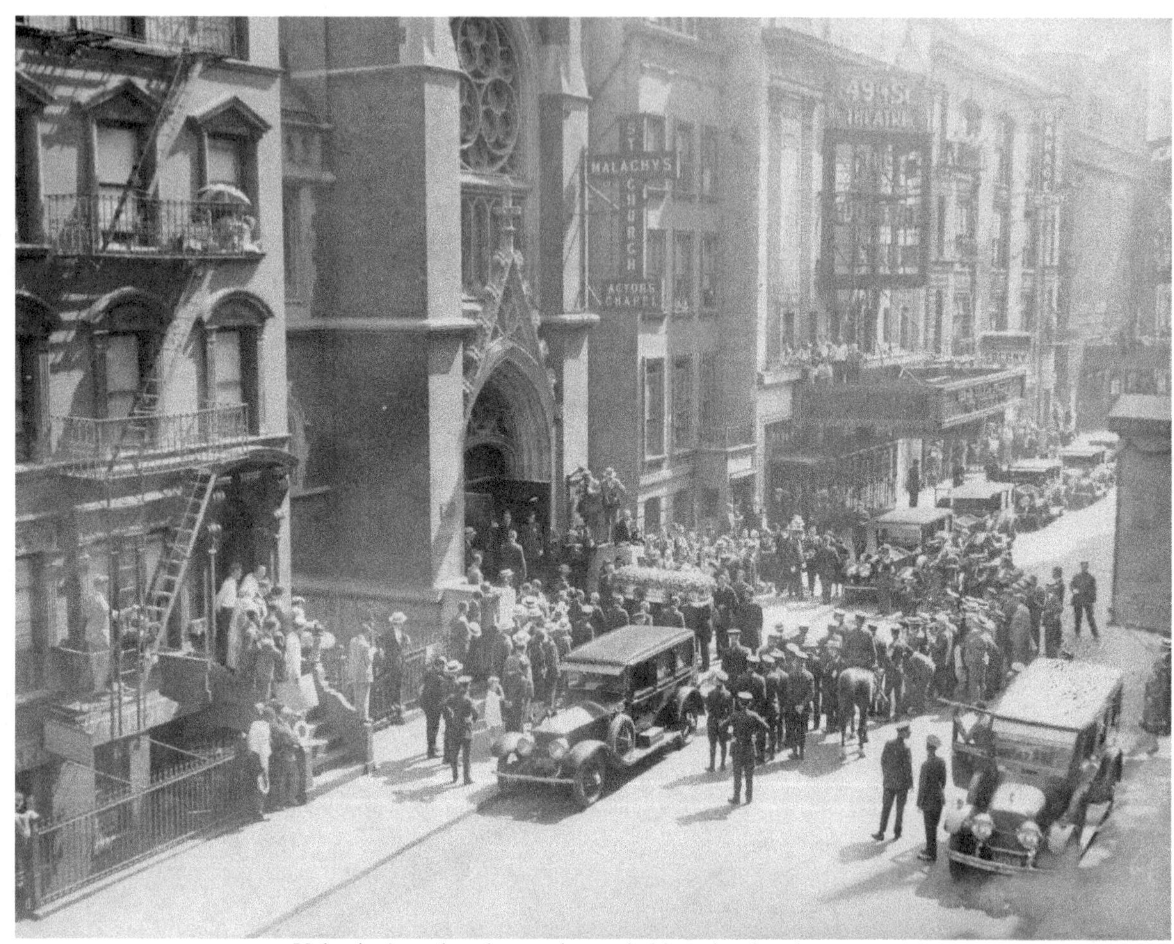

Valentino’s casket about to be carried into the church.
(Author’s collection)

Solemn High Funeral Mass
for Rudolph Valentino
St. Malachy's Church
West 49th Street
between Broadway and 8th Avenue
Monday August 30th 1926 at 11 A.M.

This card must be presented
for admission to the Church
it is also necessary for passage
of Automobile through Police Traffic Lines

Invitation to Valentino's funeral mass. (Author's collection)

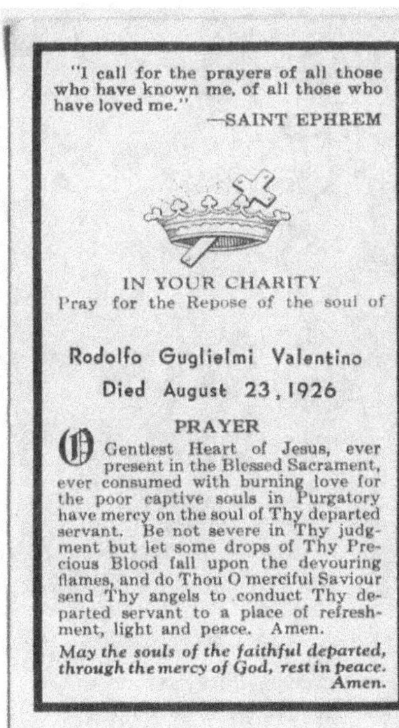

"I call for the prayers of all those who have known me, of all those who have loved me."
—SAINT EPHREM

IN YOUR CHARITY
Pray for the Repose of the soul of

Rodolfo Guglielmi Valentino
Died August 23, 1926

PRAYER

O Gentlest Heart of Jesus, ever present in the Blessed Sacrament, ever consumed with burning love for the poor captive souls in Purgatory have mercy on the soul of Thy departed servant. Be not severe in Thy judgment but let some drops of Thy Precious Blood fall upon the devouring flames, and do Thou O merciful Saviour send Thy angels to conduct Thy departed servant to a place of refreshment, light and peace. Amen.

May the souls of the faithful departed, through the mercy of God, rest in peace. Amen.

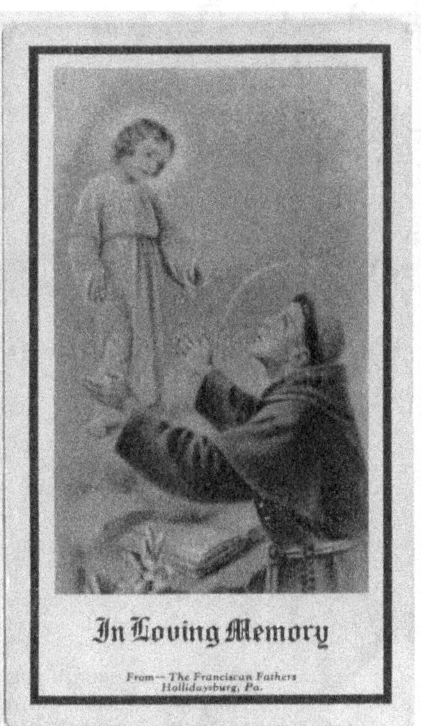

Funeral prayer card from the New York services. (Author's collection)

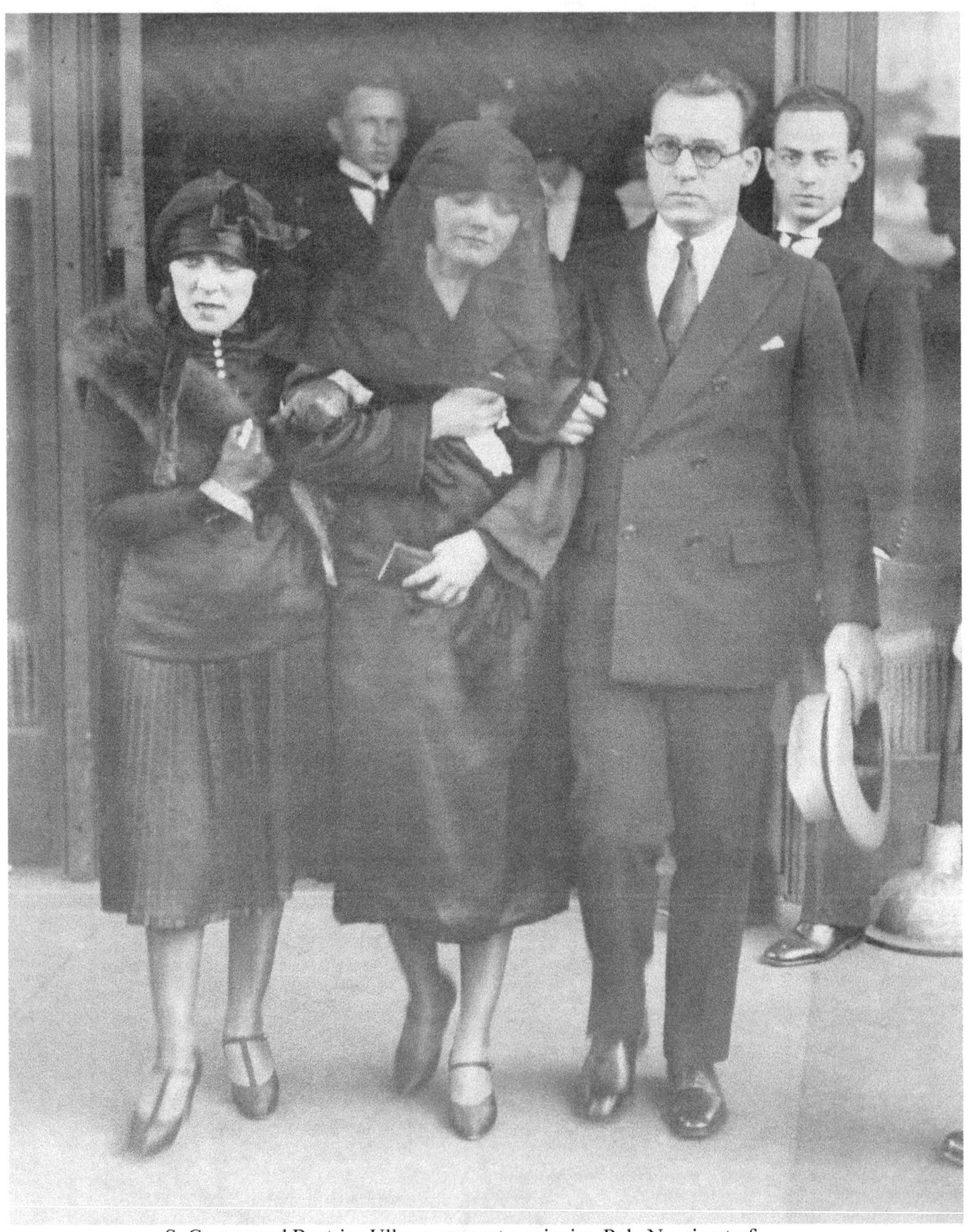

S. George and Beatrice Ullman support a grieving Pola Negri out of St. Malachy's Funeral Church after Valentino's funeral mass. Beatrice Ullman looks like she's had quite enough of the press. (Author's collection)

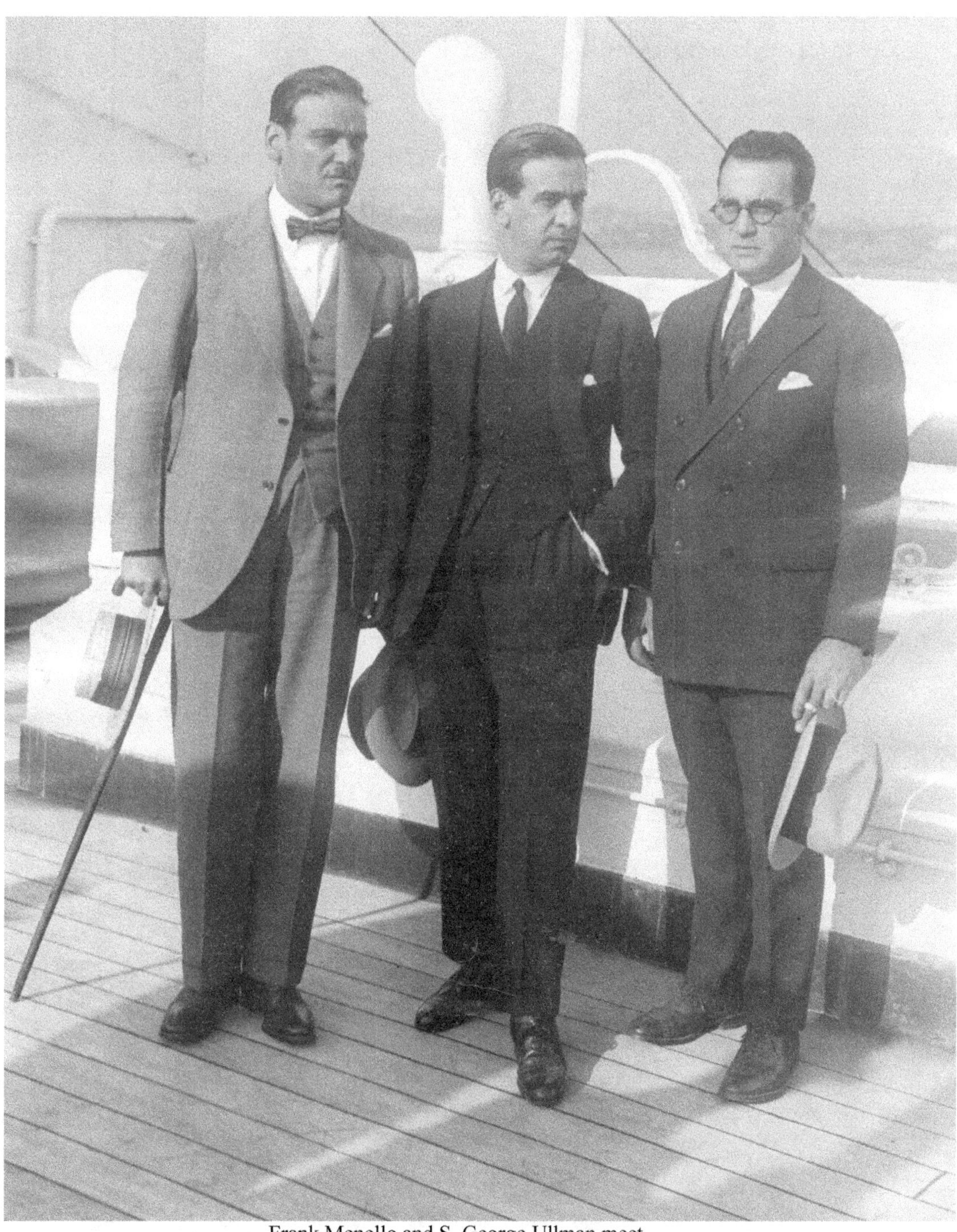

Frank Menello and S. George Ullman meet
a stricken Alberto Guglielmi who returned to New York on the RMS Homeric.
(Author's collection)

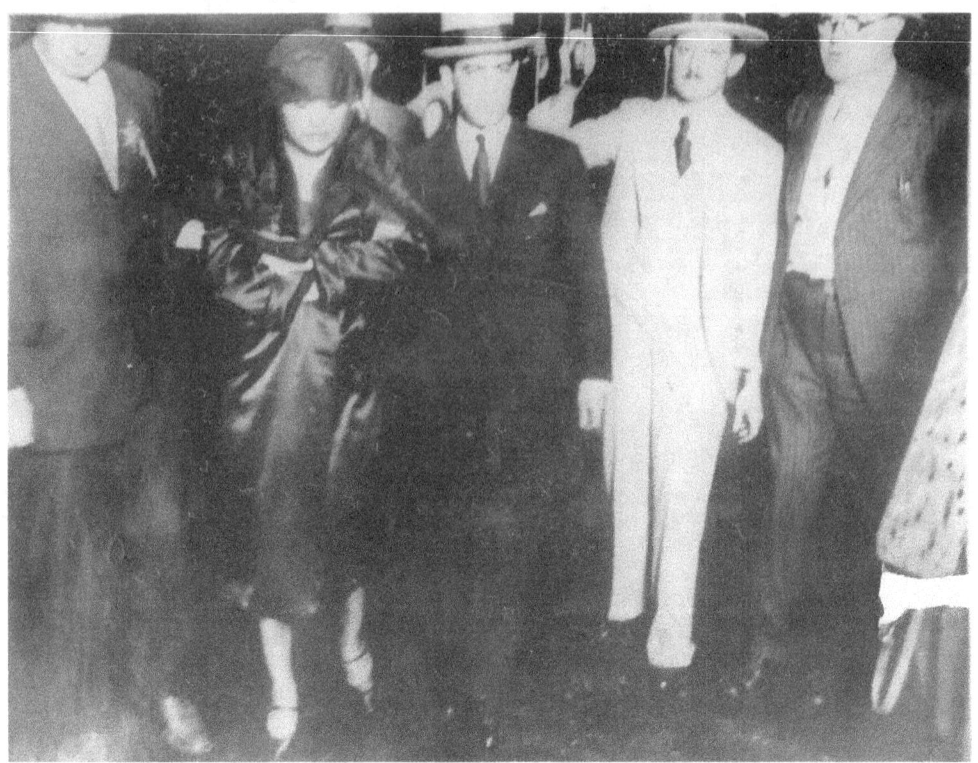

Pola Negri, Alberto, and George Ullman in Chicago accompanying Valentino's body. Alberto later recalled the many simple and touching tributes from fans and fellow Italians along the route. (Author's collection)

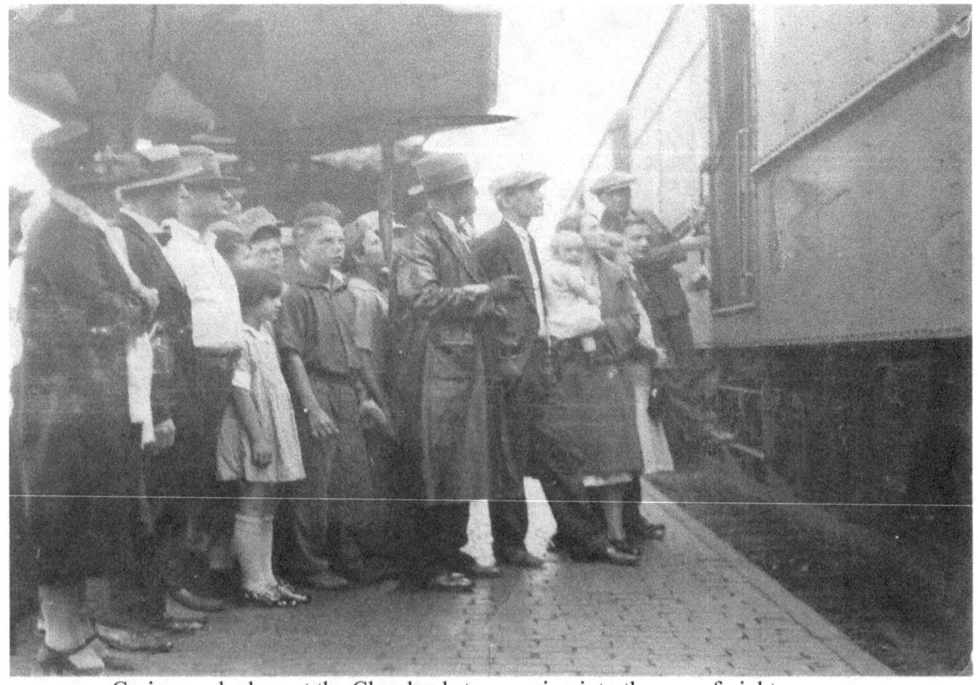

Curious onlookers at the Cleveland stop peering into the open freight car bearing Valentino's sarcophagus. (Author's collection)

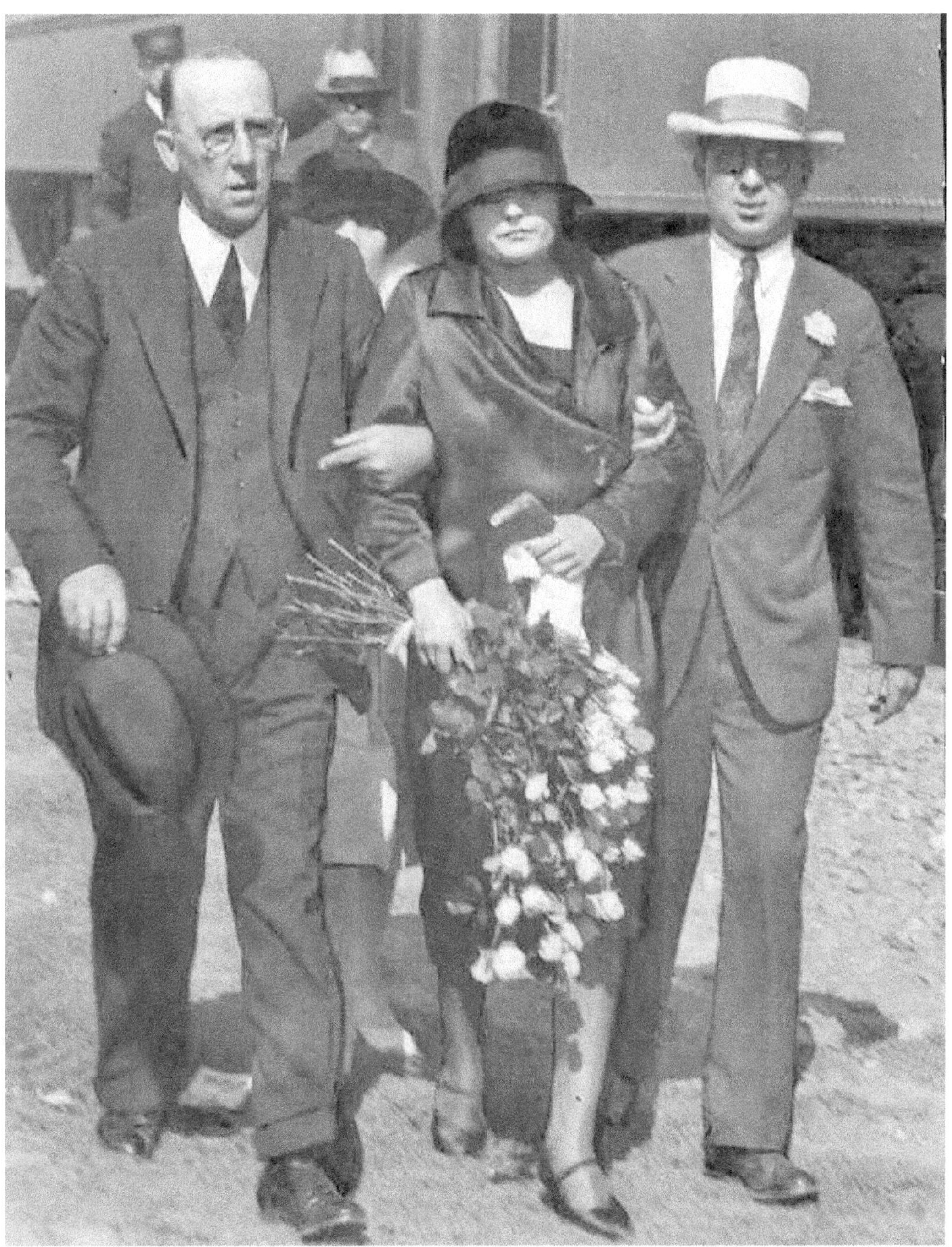

Pola Negri arrives in Pasadena, seen here with her doctor, who later proved to be no doctor at all. (Michael and Virginia Back collection)

Solemn Requiem High Mass
will be celebrated in the
Church of the Good Shepherd
Beverly Hills
for the repose of the soul of
Rudolph Valentino
on Tuesday morning, September seventh
at ten o'clock

ADMITTANCE BY CARD

Invitation to Valentino's Mass.
(Author's collection)

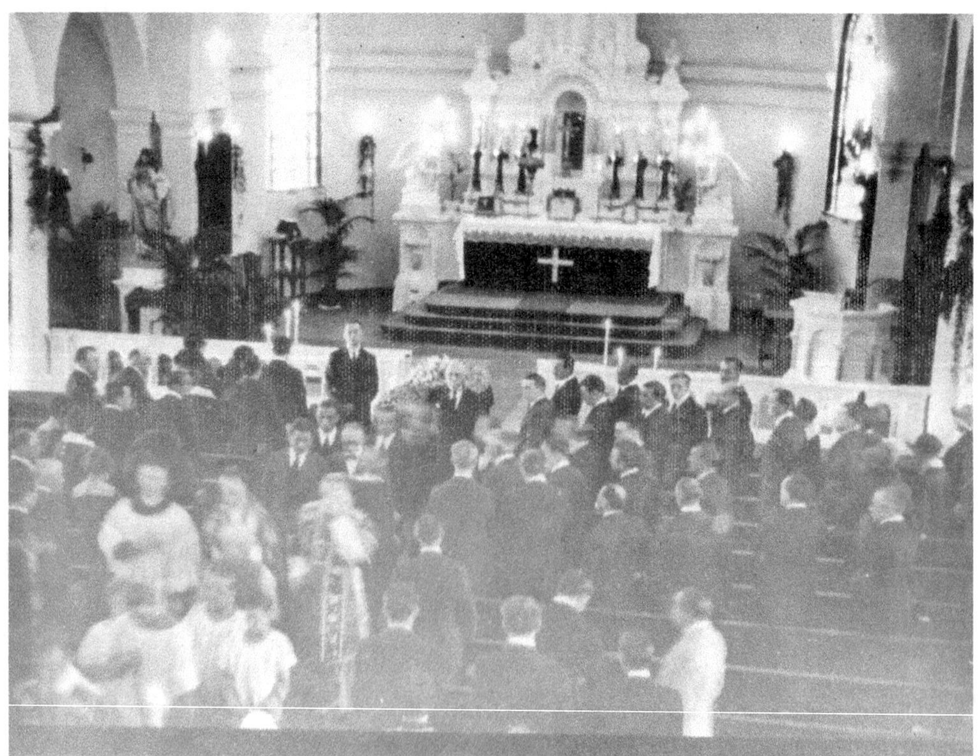

A rare view inside the Church of the Good Shepherd at the end of Valentino's funeral mass, September 7, 1926 (San Francisco History Center)

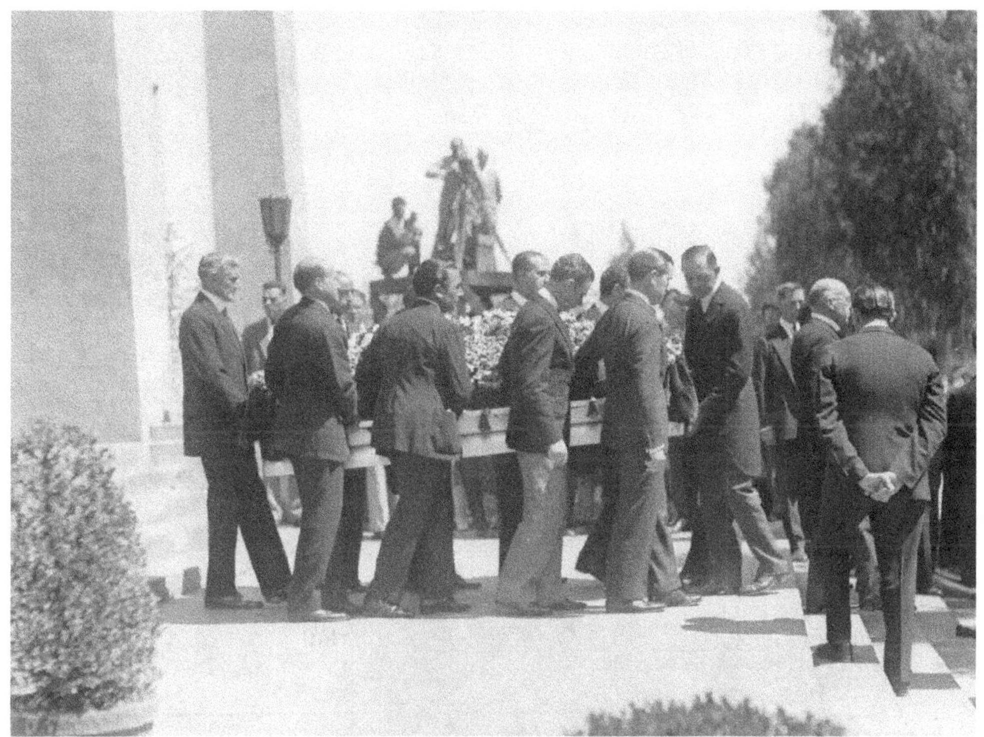

Valentino's flower-laden casket is carried out of The Church of the Good Shepherd before his final journey to Hollywood Memorial Park for internment. (Tracy Terhune collection)

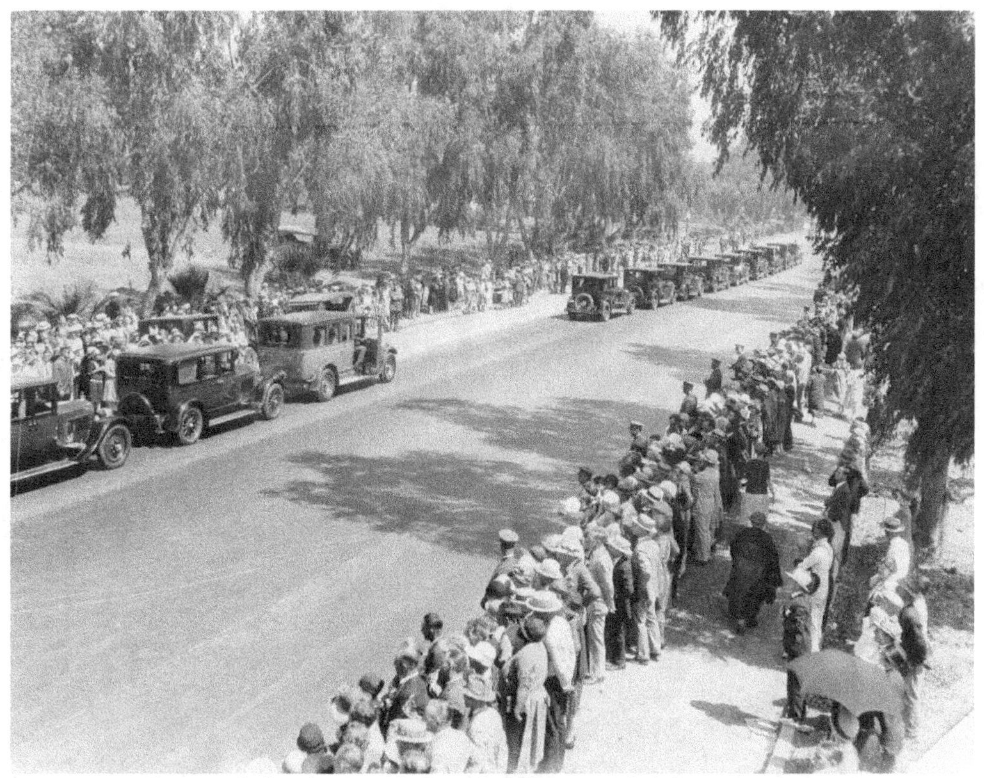

The crowds line the street in Beverly Hills to pay their last respects along the route for Valentino's final journey. (Tracy Terhune collection)

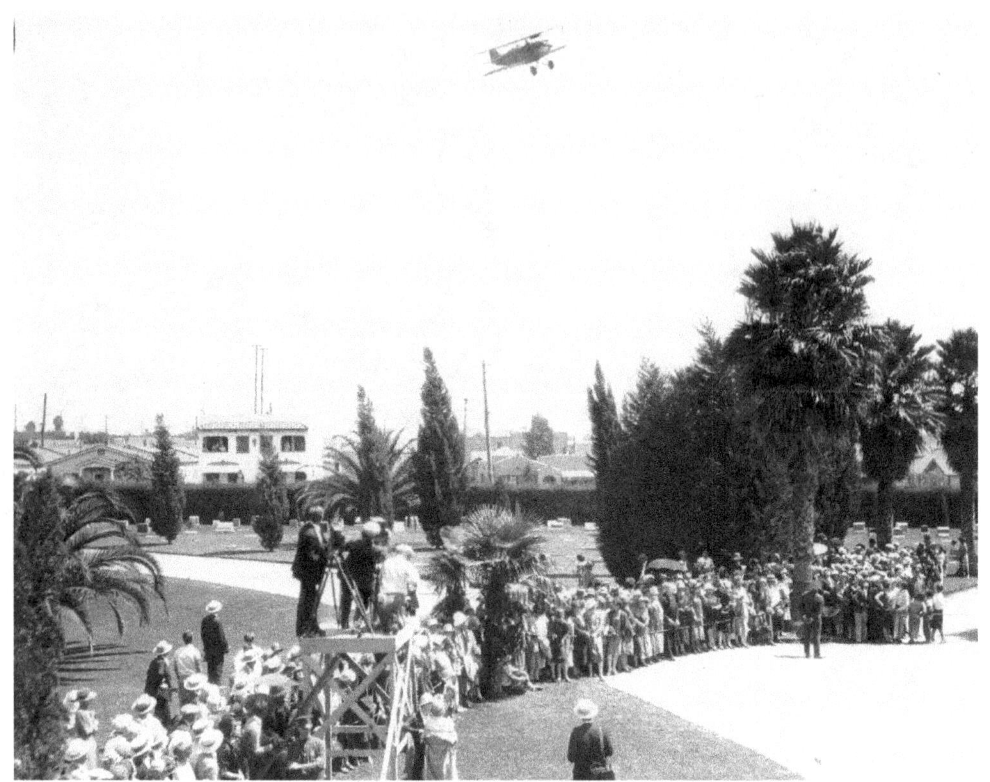

Pilot is about to drop rose petals along Valentino's final route.
(Michael and Virginia Back collection)

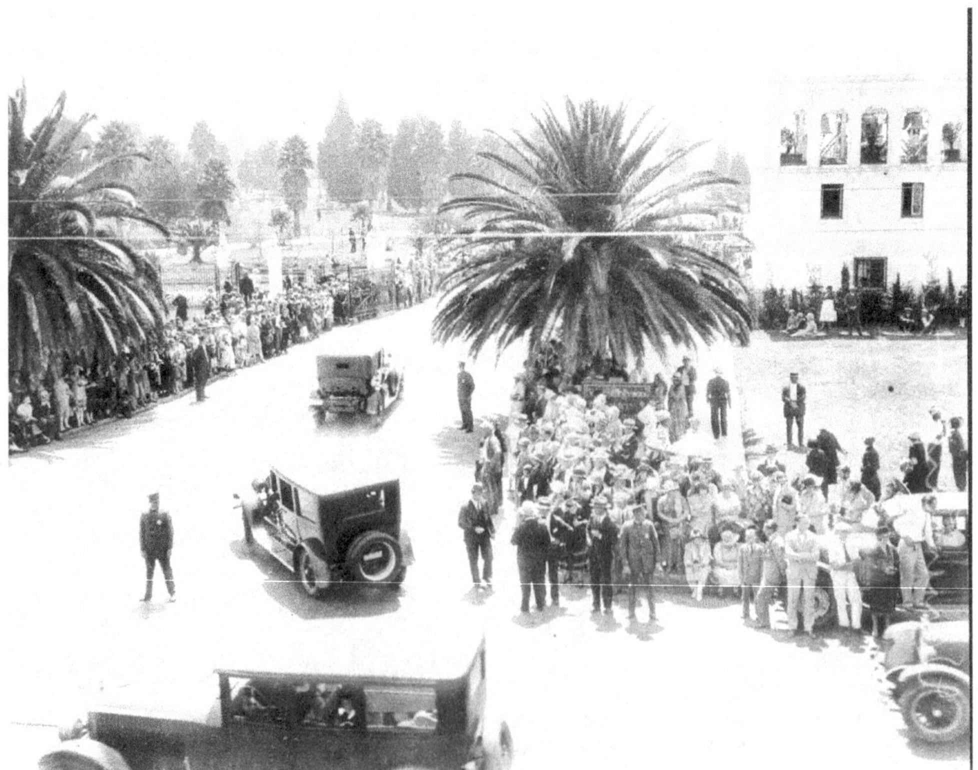

The Funeral Cortege enters Hollywood Cemetery (Tracy Terhune collection)

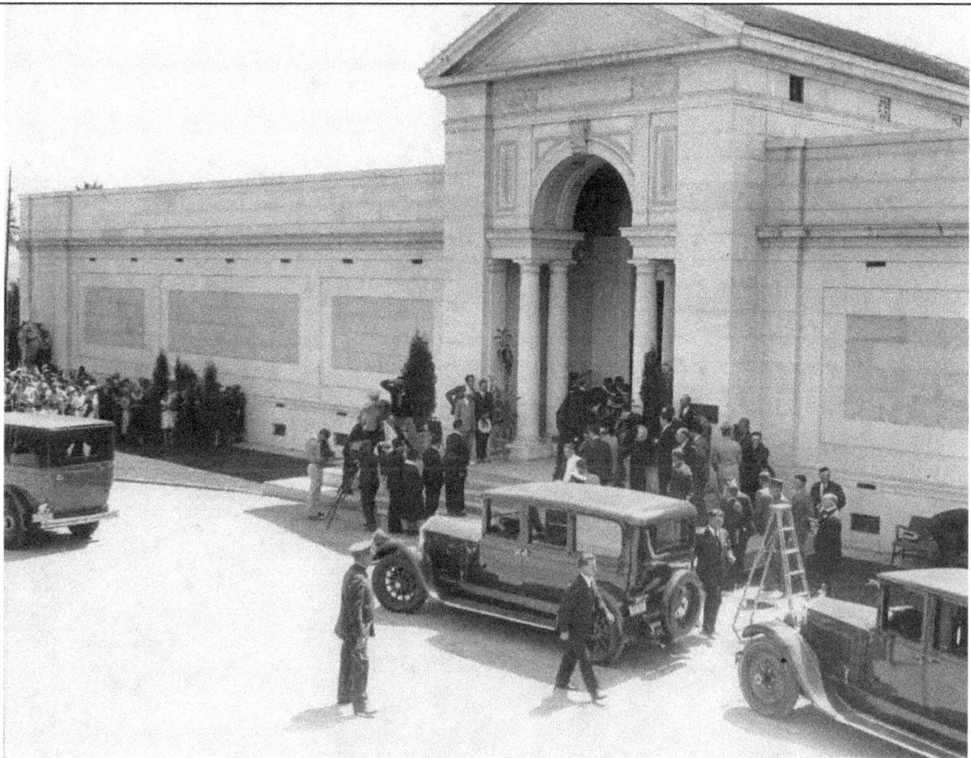

Just outside the Cathedral Mausoleum before final internment. (Tracy Terhune collection)

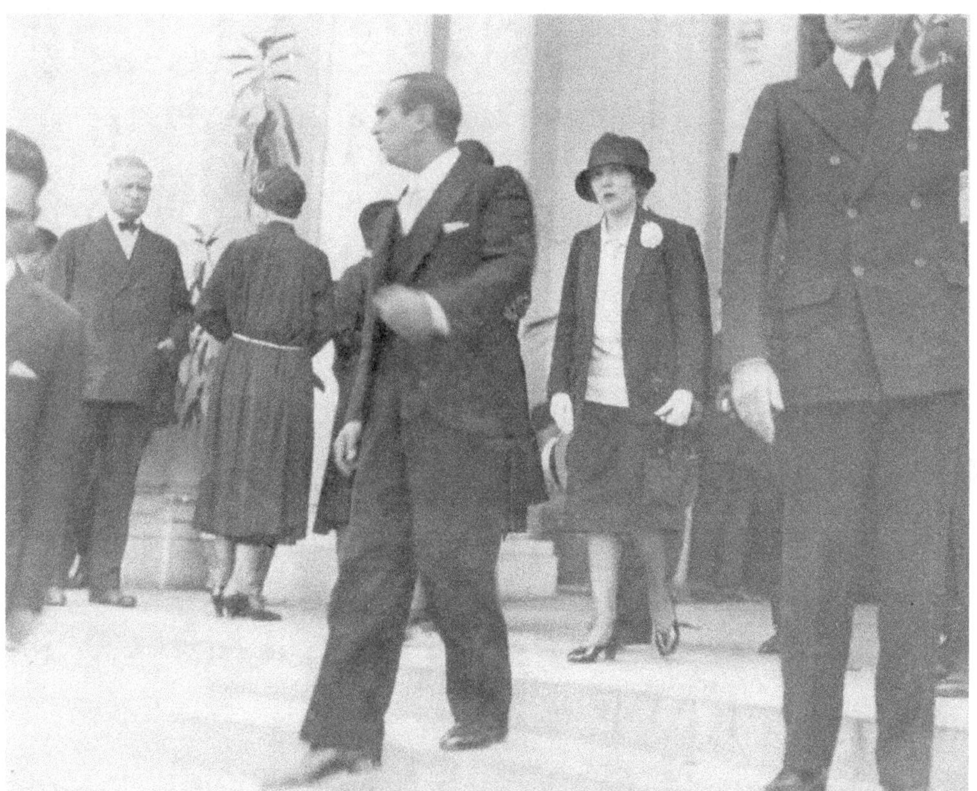

Douglas Fairbanks and a distraught Mary Pickford exit the Cathedral Mausoleum at Hollywood Cemetery. Frank E. Campbell can be seen on the left. (Tracy Terhune collection)

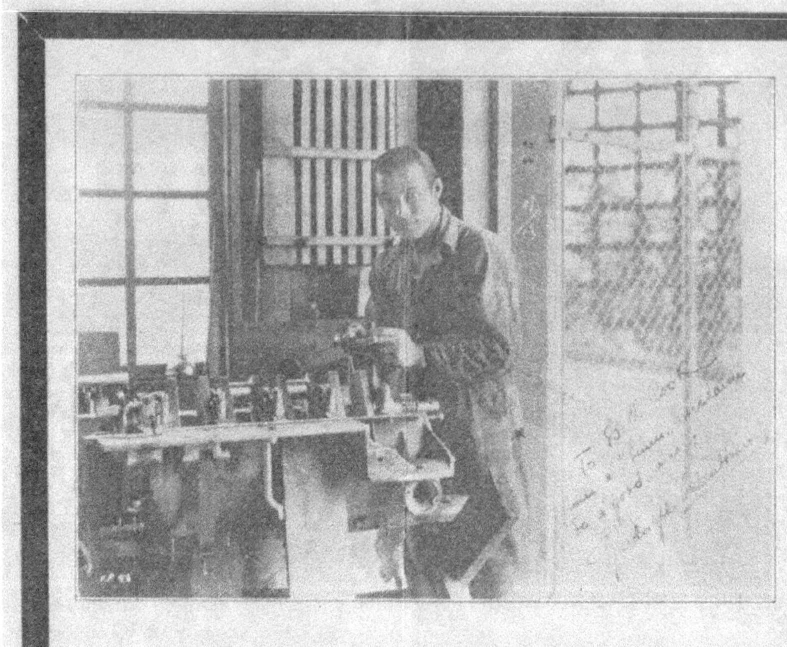

A Tribute to a Man and a Mechanic

RUDOLPH VALENTINO—perhaps the most loved of moving picture stars—a star because he played the part of the perfect lover, and played each part better than anyone before him had done. But because he did play these parts, many people had the idea that he was not a REAL MAN.

He was. He was just like you and me and all of us in many of the things he loved to do. Rudolph enjoyed, perhaps more than anything else, working on his fine cars—he loved to hear the soft purr of a perfectly running engine, and to feel the thrill of knowing that his hands and his skill kept his cars running so smoothly. It might interest you to know, too, that he thought very well of B. W. Cooke "JOB-WAY" training.

He was an athlete as well. Boxing, running and outdoor sports took their share of his time, keeping him always in fine physical condition.

Yes, Rudolph Valentino was a REAL MAN, and a Mechanic.

A tribute from Popular Automotive News Magazine.
(Author's collection)

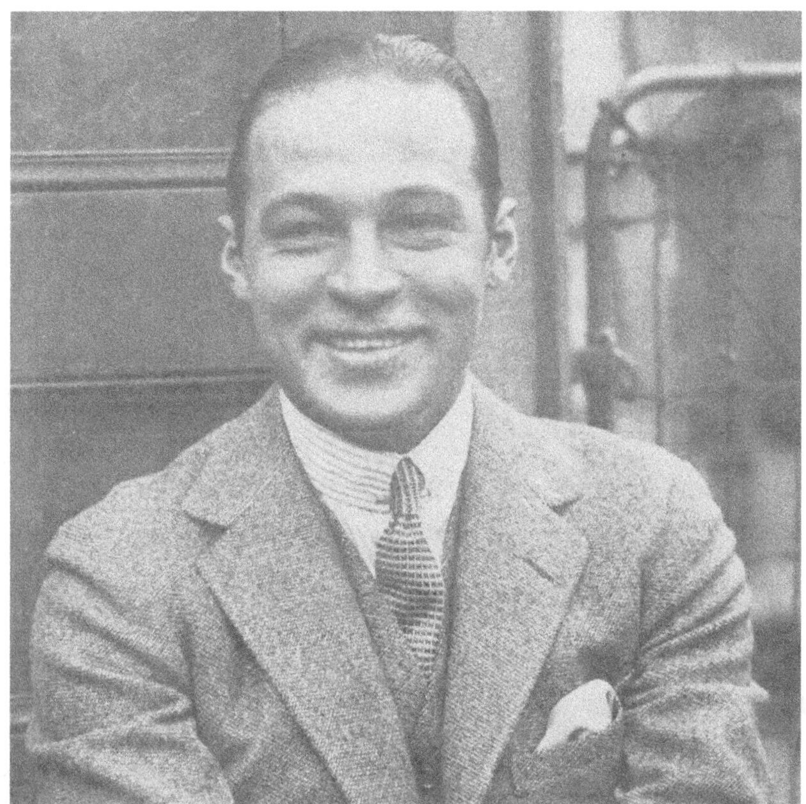

A last smile in Chicago. (Author's collection)

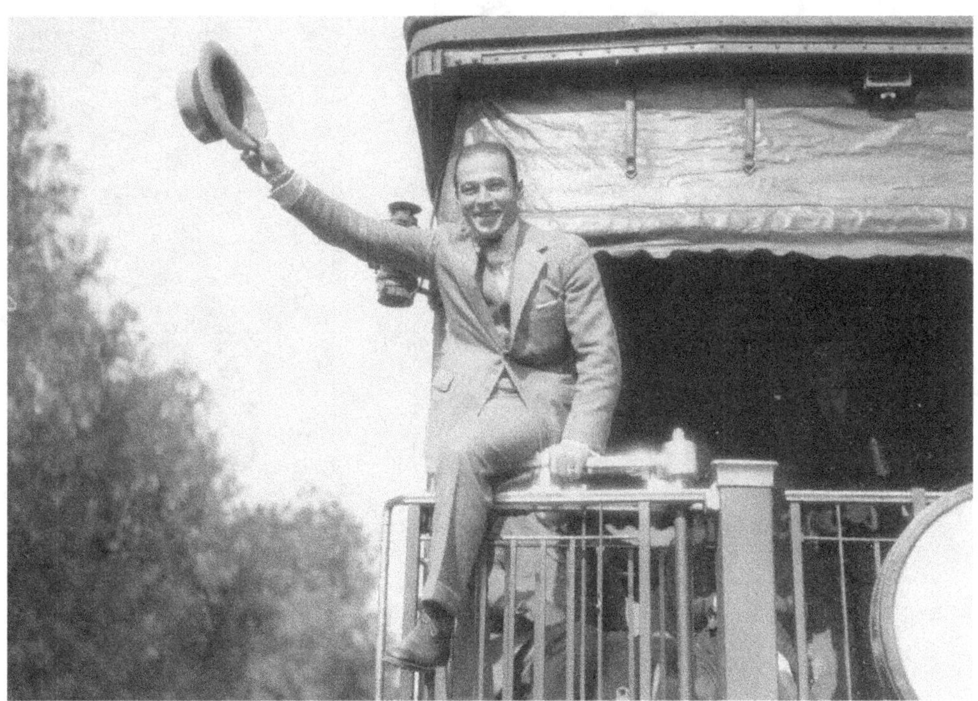

A jubilant Valentino *en route* to New York for the last time.
(Michael and Virginia Back collection)

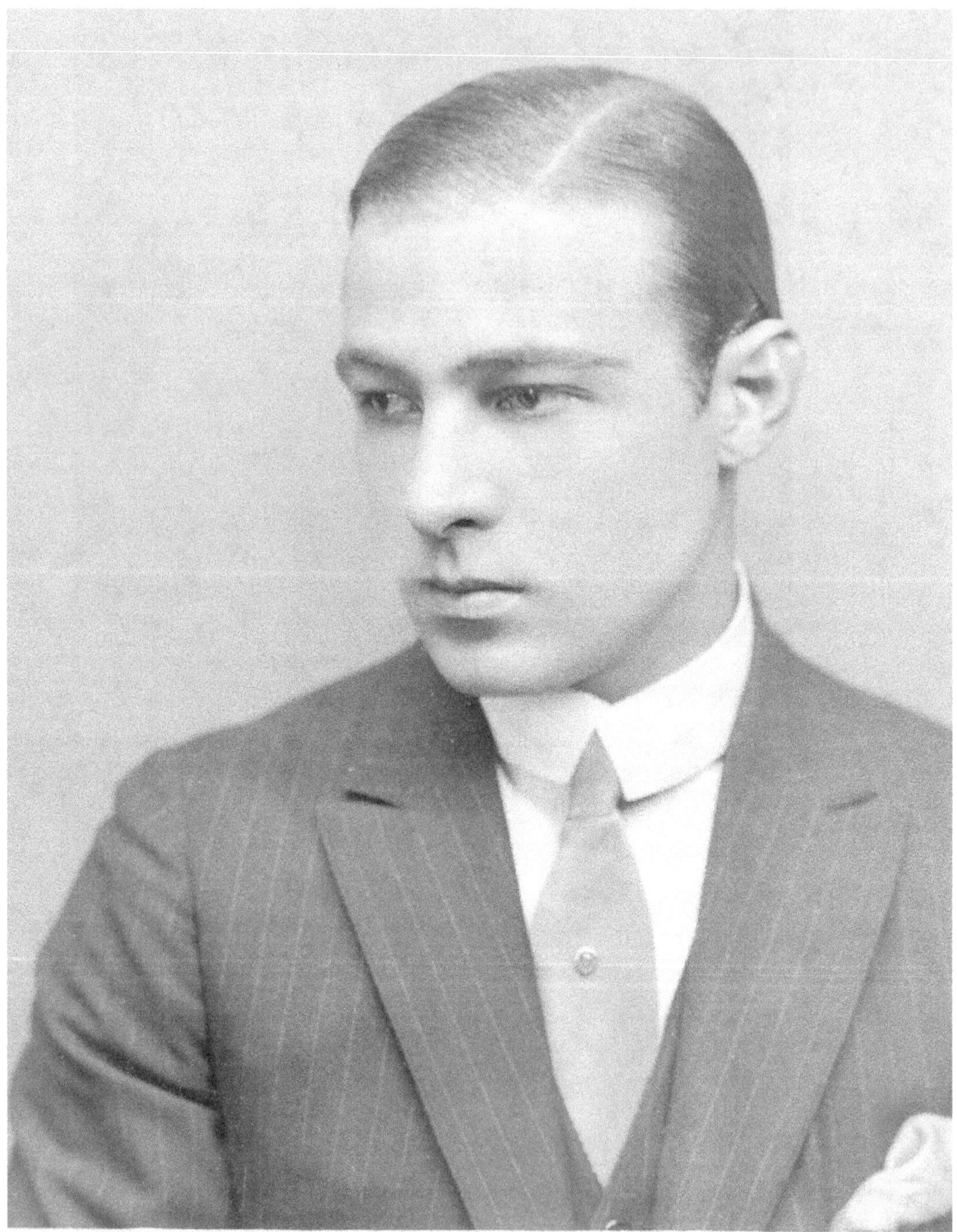

A favorite portrait of Rudolph Valentino taken in 1921 by Donald Biddle Keyes
(Author's collection)

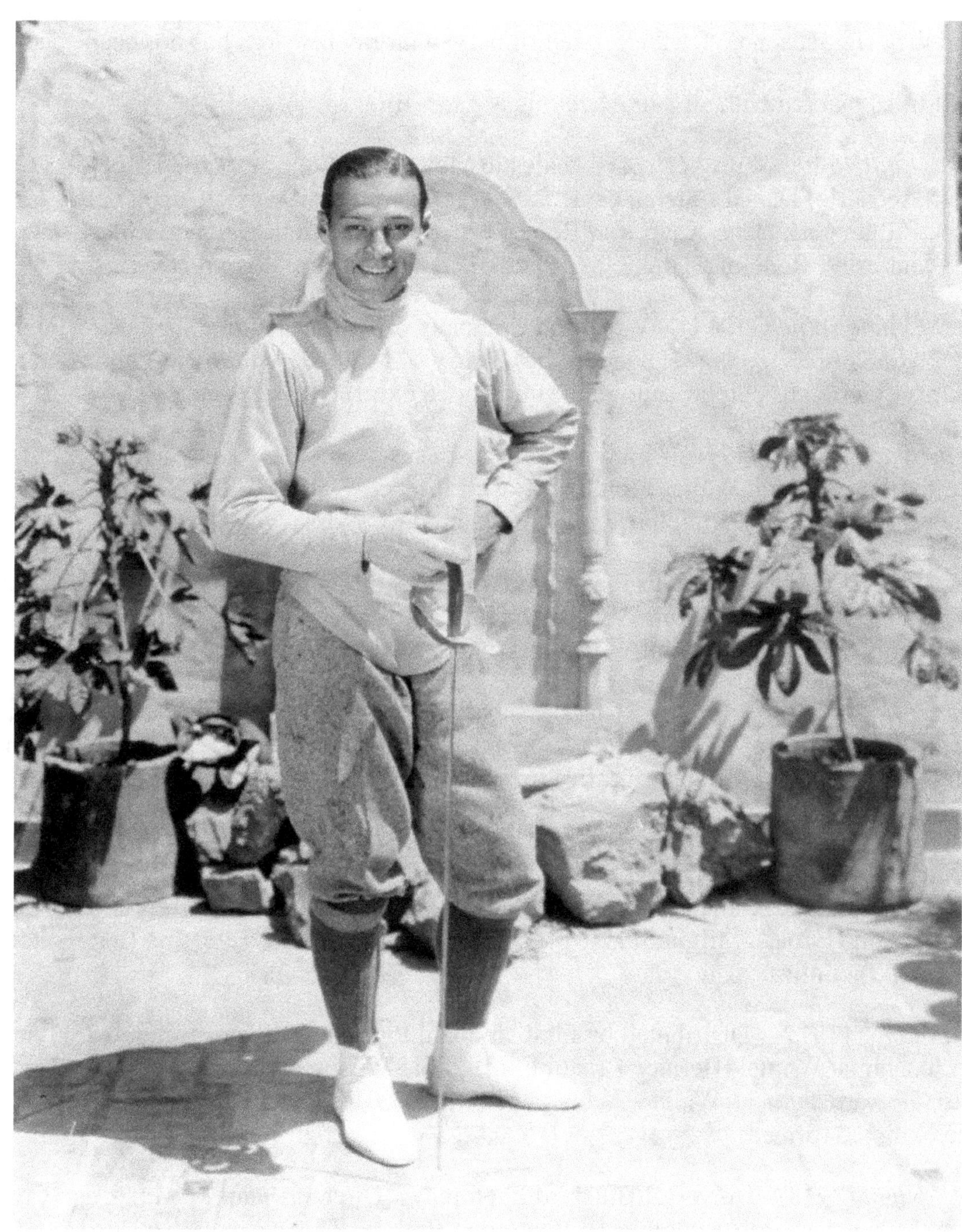

Some of the films commonly listed as part of Valentino's filmography simply cannot be verified. In particular, the first three films from 1914 and 1916 are likely errors in what has been passed down through interviews and erroneous sources. Diligent effort has been made to find the original source for these three films. So far my research has not been successful.

All titles marked with an * indicate this is a lost film.

*The Battle of the Sexes** (1914) – Majestic Motion Picture Company. Director: D.W. Griffith, scenario: Daniel Carson, camera: G.W. Bitzer. Cast: Donald Crisp (Frank Andrews), Lillian Gish (Jane Andrews), Robert Harron (John Andrews), and Mary Alden (Mrs. Frank Andrews). Rodolpho Guglielmi (uncredited dance extra) *unconfirmed*

*My Official Wife** (1914) – Vitagraph Company of America. Director: James Young. Cast: Clara Kimball Young (Helene Marie), Harry T. Morely (Arthur B. Lennox), Earle Williams (Sacha). Rodolpho Guglielmi (uncredited extra) *unconfirmed*

*The Quest of Life**(1916) – Famous Players-Lasky. Director: Ashley Miller, scenario: Ashley Miller, camera: Walter Stradling. Cast: Florence Walton (Ellen Young), Julian L'Estrange (Alec Mapelton). Rudolph Valentino (uncredited extra) *unconfirmed*

*Seventeen** (1916) – Famous Players-Lasky. Director: Robert G. Vignola. Cast: Louise Huff (Lola Pratt), Jack Pickford (William S. Baxter), Madge Evans (Jane Baxter(, Walter Hiers (George Cooper). Rudolph Valentino (uncredited extra) confirmed

*The Foolish Virgin** (1916) – Clara Kimball Young Production Company. Director: Albert Capellani, camera: Jacques Monteran, Hal Young & George Peters. Cast: Clara Kimball Young (Mary Adams), Conway Tearle (Jim Anthony). Rudolph Valentino (uncredited extra) unconfirmed

Patria (1917) – Pathe. Director: George Fitzmaurice, et al., scenario: J.B. Clymer and Charles W. Goddard, camera: Levi Bacon, et al. Cast: Irene Castle (Patria/Elaine), Warner Oland (Baron Huroki), Milton Sills (Cpt. Donald Parr). Rudolph Valentino (uncredited extra in Chapter 3) confirmed

*Alimony** (1917) - Distributed by First National Pictures. Director Emmett J. Flynn. Cast: Josephine Whittel (Bernice Bristol Flint) ; Lois Wilson (Marjorie Lansing) , George Fisher (Howard Turner), Wallace Worsley (John Flint). Rudolph Valentino appears as a dance extra. confirmed

All Night (1918) - Universal/Bluebird Photoplays. Director: Paul Powell. Cast: Carmel Myers (Elizabeth Lane), Rudolpho di Valentina (Richard Thayer), Charles Dorian (William Harcourt), Mary Warren (Maude Harcourt), William Dyer (Bradford) Wadsworth Harris (Colonel Lane), Jack Hull (Butler)

A Society Sensation (1918) – Universal/Bluebird Photoplays. Director Paul Powell. Cast: Carmel Myers (Margaret Parmelee), Lidia Titus (Mrs. Jones), Alfred Allen (Capt. Parmelee), ZaSu Pitts (Mary), Fred Kelsey (Jim), Harold Goodwin (Tommy), Rodolpho De Valentina (Dick Bradley)

A Married Virgin (1918)- Produced by Maxwell Productions. Director: Joseph Maxwell; Screenwriter: Hayden Talbot. Cast: Vera Sisson (Mary McMillan); Frank Newburg (Douglas McKee); Edward Jobsen (Fiske McMillan; Kathleen Kirkham (Mrs. Spencer McMillan); Lillian Leighton (Anne Mullin); Rodolfo di Valentina (Count Roberto di San Fraccini). Note: This film was produced in 1918 and not released until later, it was reissued in 1920 under the new title *Frivolous Wives*.

A Delicious Little Devil (1919) – Produced by Universal Pictures. Director: Robert Z. Leonard, Scenario: Harvey Thew; Camerman: Allan Zeigler. Cast: Mae Murray (Mary McGuire), Harry Rattenbury (Patrick McGuire), Richard Cummings (Uncle Barney), Ivor MacFadden (Percy), Betram Grassby (Duke de Sauterne), Edward Jobson (Michael Calhoun), Rudolpho De Valentina (Jimmie Calhoun).

Virtuous Sinners (1919) – Pioneer Films. Director: Emmett J. Flynn. Cast: Norman Kerry (Hamilton Jones), Wanda Hawley (Dawn Emerson), Henry Holden (Eli Barker), David Kirby (Stool Pigeon), Bert Woodruff (Bert McGregor), Valentino appears as an extra.

*The Big Little Person** (1919) – Universal Pictures. Director: Robert Z. Leonard, Scenario: Bess Meredyth. Cast: Mae Murray (Arathea Manning), Clarissa Selwynne (Mrs. Manning), Rodolphe De Valentina (Arthur Endicott), Allan Sears (Gerald Staples), Mrs. Bertram Grassby (Marion Beemis)

A Rogue's Romance *(1919) - Vitagraph Corporation. Director: James Young, Scenario: James Young, Cameraman: Max Dupont. Cast: Earle Williams (Jules Marier/Picard), Katherine Adams (Helen Deprenay), Maude George (Jeanne Deprenay), Sid Franklin (Burgomaster), Brinsley Shaw (Henri Duval), Rudolph Valentino (an Apache dancer)

*The Homebreaker** (1919) – Thomas Ince Production, distributed by Paramount. Director: Victor Schertzinger, Camera John S. Stumar. Cast: Dorothy Dalton (Mary Marbury), Douglas MacLean (Raymond Abbot), Edwin Stevens (Jonas Abbott), Beverly Travers (Marcia), Nora Johnson (Lois Abbott), Valentino is an uncredited dance extra.

*Out of Luck/Nobody Home** (1919) – New Art Film Co (distributed by Paramount). Director: Elmer Clifton, Camermen: John Leezer and Lee Garmes. Cast: Dorothy Gish (Frances Wadsworth), Ralph Graves (Malcolm Dale), Vivien Montrose (Florence Wellington), Vera McGinnis (Mollie Rourke), George Fawcett (Rockaway Smith), Rudolph Valentine (Maurice Renard)

The Eyes of Youth (1919) - Garson Production. Distributed by Equity Pictures Corporation. Eyes of Youth by Max Marcin and Charles Guernon. Scenario and directed by Albert Parker. Cast:Vincent Serrano (A Disciple); Clara Kimbell Young (Gina Ashling); Edmond Lowe (Peter Judson); Sam Sothern (Asa Ashling); Gareth Hughes (Kenneth Ashling); Pauline Starke (Rita Ashling); Ralph Lewis (Robert Goring); Milton Sills (Louis Anthony); William Courtleigh (Peter De Salvo); Rudolph Valentino (Clarence Morgan "A cabaret Parasite"); and Norman Selby (Dick Brodnell)

Isle of Love/An Adventuress (1920) – Republic. Director: Fred J. Balshofer Scenario: Charles Taylor, Cameraman: Tony Gaudio. Cast: Julian Eltinge (Jack Perry/Mam'sell Fedora), Alma Francis (Eunice), Fred Covert (Lyn Brook/Thelma), Virgina Rappe (Zana), Leo

White (Price Albert), Rodolpho De Valentina (Jacques Rudanyi). This film began production as Under the Rhine, was shelved and no released until later under the title *Isle of Love* and later another reissue as *An Adventuress*.

*Passion's Playground** (1920) – Katherine McDonald Pictures/First National. Director: J.A. Barry. Cast: Katherine MacDonald (Mary Grant), Norman Kerry (Prince Vanno Della Robbia), Nell Craig (Marie Grant), Rudolphe Valentine (Prince Angelo Della Robbia)

*The Cheater** (1920) – Metro Pictures. Director: Henry Otto. Cast: May Allison (Lilly Meany), King Baggot (Lord Asgarby), Frank Currier (Peg Meany), Valentino is an extra.

*Once to Every Woman** (1920) Universal. Director: Allen Holubar. Cast: Dorothy Phillips (Aurora Meredith), Margaret Mann (Mothe Meredith), Emily Chichester (Patience Meredith), Rodolfo do Valentino (Juliantino Visconti)

The Wonderful Chance (1920) – Selznick Pictures Corporation. Director: George Archainbaud. Cast: Eugene O'Brien (Lord Birmingham/Swagger Barlow), Tom Blake (Red Duggan), Joe Flanagan (Haggerty), Warren Cook (Parker Winston), Martha Mansfield (Peggy Winton), Rudolph De Valentino (Joe Klingsby)

Stolen Moments (1920) – American Cinema Corporation. Direcror: James Vincent. Cast: Marguerite Namara (Vera Blaine), Walter Chapin (Richard Huntly), Alex K. Shannon (Campos Salles), Gene Gauthier (Alvarez Salles), Rudolph Valentine (Jose Dalmarez)

The Four Horsemen of the Apocalypse (1920) - Metro Pictures. Director: Rex Ingram; Cameramen: John Seitz; Assistant Cameramen: Starrett Ford, Walter Mayo; Assistant Directors: Joseph Calder, Amos Myers; Adaptation: June Mathis; Editor: Grant Whytock; Art Director: Walter Mayo; Art Titler: Jack W. Robson; Costumes: Unknown; Musical Score: Louis F. Gottschalk. Cast: Rudolph Valentino (Julio Desnoyers); Alice Terry (Marguerite Laurier); Pomeroy Cameron (The Centaur); Joseph Swickard (Marcelo Desnoyers); Alan Hale (Karl von Hartrott); Nigel de Brulier (Tchernoff); Bridgetta Clark (Dona Luisa); Mabel van Buren (Elena); Beatrice Dominguez (Tango Dancer). Based on Vicente Blasco Ibanez' novel The Four Horsemen of the Apocalypse.

*Uncharted Seas** (1920) - distributed by Metro Pictures. Director: Wesley Ruggles; Cameraman: John Seitz; Screenwriter: George Edward Jenks; Editor: Unknown; Art Director: John Holden. Cast: Rudolph Valentino (Frank Underwood); Alice Lake (Lucretia Eastman); Carl Gerard (Senator Eastman). Based on John Henry Wilson's story The Uncharted Seas published in Munsey's Magazine, September 1920.

Camille (1920) - Nazimova Productions/Metro Pictures. Director: Ray C. Smallwood; Cameraman: Rudolph Bergquist; Screenwriter: June Mathis; Art Director: Natacha Rambova; Editor: Unknown. Cast: Alla Nazimova (Camille); Rudolph Valentino (Armand). Based on Alexandre Dumas' play and novel La Dame Aux Camelias.

The Conquering Power (1920) - Metro Pictures. Producer/Director: Rex Ingram; Cameraman: John Seitz; Adaption: June Mathis; Editor: Unknown. Cast: Rudolph Valentino (Charles Grandet); Alice Terry (Eugenie Grandet); Eric Mayne (Victor Grandet); Ralph Lewis (Pere Grandet). Based on Honore de Balzac's novel Eugene Grandet.

The Sheik (1921) - Famous Players-Lasky/Paramount. Director: George Melford; Cameraman: William Marshall; Screenwriter: Monte Katterjohn; Editor: Unknown; Art Direction: Unknown. Cast: Rudolph Valentino (Ahmed Ben Hassan); Agnes Ayres (Lady Diana); Adolph Menjou (Raoul de Saint Hubert); Walter Long (Omair). Based on E.M. Hull's novel The Sheik.

Moran of the Lady Letty (1922) - distributed by Famous Players-Lasky/Paramount. Director: George Melford; Cameraman: William Marshall; Screenwriter: Monte Katterjohn; Editor: Unknown; Art Direction: Unknown. Cast: Rudolph Valentino (Ramon Laredo); Dorothy Dalton (Moran); Charles Brinly (Captain Sternerson); Walter Long (Captain Kitchell). Based on Frank Norris's novel of the same name.

Beyond the Rocks (1922) - Famous Players-Lasky/Paramount. Director: Sam Wood; Cameraman: Alfred Gilks; Adapter: Jack Cunningham; Editor: Unknown; Art Direction: Unknown. Cast: Gloria Swanson (Theodora Fitzgerald); Rudolph Valentino (Lord Bracondale); Edythe Chapman (Lady Bracondale); Alec B. Tranis (Captain Fitzgerald). Based on Elinor Glyn's novel Beyond the Rocks.

Blood and Sand (1922) - Famous Players-Lasky/Paramount. Director: Fred Niblo; Cameraman: Alvin Wyckoff; Adaptor: June Mathis; Editor: Dorothy Arzner; Art Direction: Unknown. Cast: Rudolph Valentino (Juan Gallardo); Lila Lee (Carmen); Nita Naldi (Dona Sol); George Fied (El Nacoional); Walter Long (Plumitas the Bandit). Based on Vicente Blasco Ibanez's novel Blood and Sand.

The Young Rajah (1923) - Famous Players-Lasky/Paramount. Director: Philip Rosen; Cameraman: James C. Van Trees; Adaption/Screenwriter: June Mathis; Editor: Unknown; Art Direction: Unknown; Costumes: Natacha Rambova. Cast: Rudolph Valentino (Amos Judd); Wanda Hawley (Molly Cabot); Jack Giddings (Austin Slade); Joseph Swickard (Narada). Based on John Ames Mitchell's novel Amos Judd. Extant in a partial print. A complete print of this film is believed to be lost.

Rudolph Valentino and His 88 American Beauties (1923)- Selznick Pictures.

Monsieur Beaucaire (1924) - Famous Players-Lasky/Paramount. Director: Sidney Olcott; Cameraman: Harry Fishbeck; Adaptor: Forrest Halsey; Editor: Patricia Rooney; Art Director: Natacha Rambova; Costume Designer: Unknown. Cast: Rudolph Valentino (Duc de Chartres/Beaucaire); Bebe Daniels (Princesse Henriette); Lowell Sherman (King of France); Lois Wilson (Queen of France); Doris Kenyon (Lady Mary); Ian McLaren (Duke of Winterset). Based on Booth Tarkington's novel Monsieur Beaucaire.

*A Sainted Devil** (1924) - Famous Players-Lasky/Paramount. Director: Joseph Henabery; Cameraman: Harry Fishbeck; Adaption: Forrest Halsey; Editor: Unknown; Art Direction: Unknown; Dress Designer: Unknown. Cast: Rudolph Valentino (Don Alonzo de Castro); Nita Naldi (Carlotta); Helen D'Algy (Julietta Valdez); Dagmar Godowsky (Dona Florencia). Based on Rex Beach's Rope's End published in Cosmopolitan, May, 1913. This film is believed to be lost. Only a few brief moments of footage are known to exist.

Cobra (1925) - Ritz-Carlton Productions/Paramount. Director: Joseph Henabery; Cameramen: J.D. Jennings, Harry Fishbeck; Screenwriter: Anthony Coldeways; Editor: unknown; Art Direction: William Cameron Menzies; Dress Designer: Gilbert Adrian. Cast: Rudolph

Valentino (Count Torriani); Nita Naldi (Elise Van Zile); Casson Fergusson (Jack Dorning); Gertrude Olmstead (Mary Drake). Adapted from Martin Brown's play Cobra

The Eagle (1925) - United Artists. Director: Clarence Brown; Cameramen: George Barnes, Dev Jennings; Titles: George Marion, Jr.; Screenwriter: Hans Kraly; Editor: Hal C. Kern; Art Director: William Cameron Menzies; Costumes: Gilbert Adrian. Cast: Rudolph Valentino (Vladimir Dubrovsky); Vilma Banky (Mascha Troekouroff); Louise Dresser (Empress Catherine the Great); Albert Conti (General Kuschka). Based on Pushkin's novel Dubrovsky.

The Son of the Sheik (1926) - United Artists. Director: George Fitzmaurice; Cameraman: George Barnes; Titles: George Marion, Jr.; Adaption by: Frances Marion, Fred de Gresac; Editor: Hal C. Kern; and Art Director: William Cameron Menzies. Cast: Rudolph Valentino (Ahmed/Old Sheik); Vilma Banky (Yasmin); George Fawcett (Andre); Agnes Ayres (Diana); Montague Love (Gabah the Moor). Based on E.M. Hull's novel The Sons of the Sheik

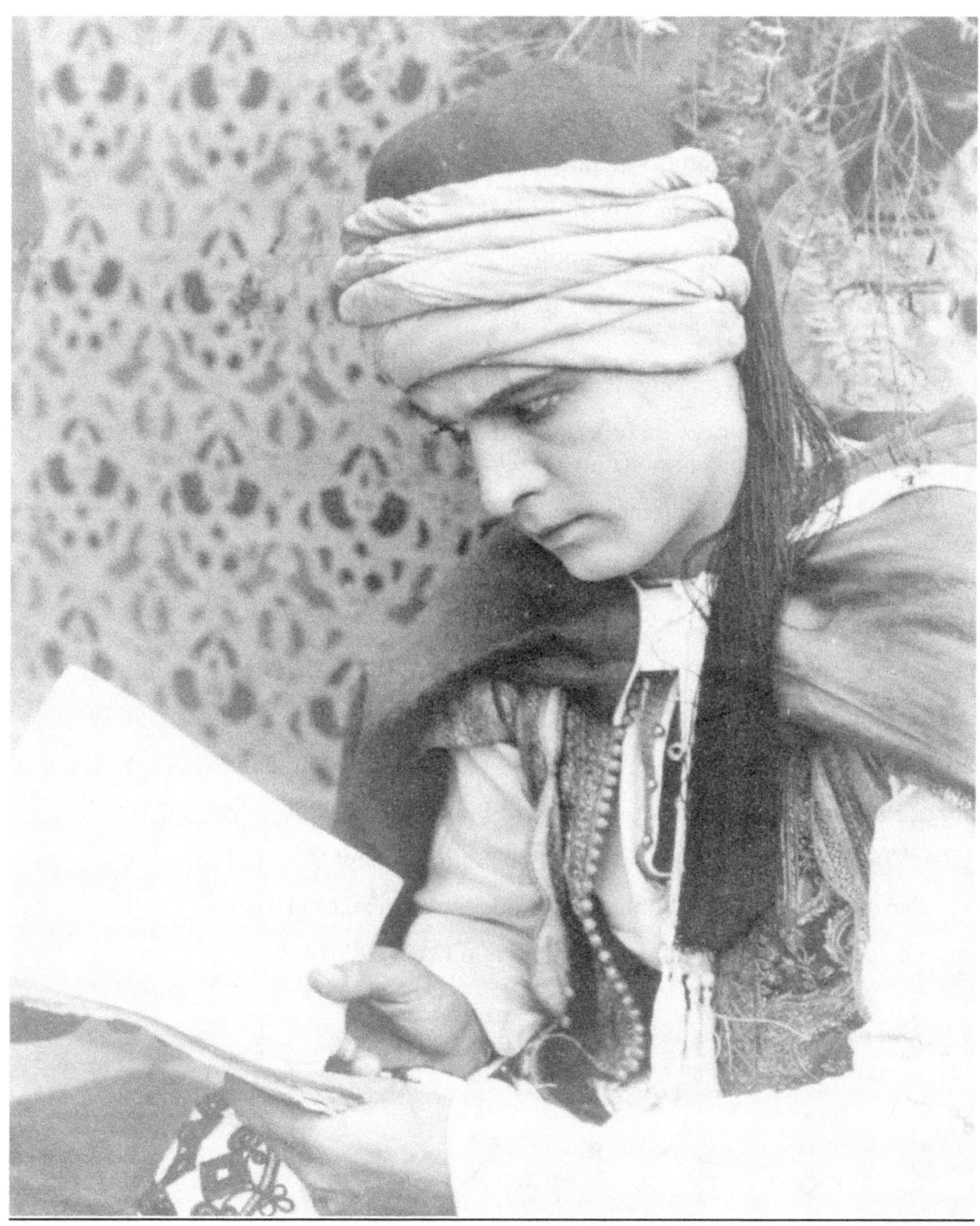

Books

Anon., Rudolph Valentino Sa Vie - Ses Films - Ses Aventures, Les Publications Jean-Pascal (Paris, France) (1926)

Anon., The Life and Loves of Rudolph Valentino (1926)

DeRecqueville, Jeanne, Rudolph Valentino, Empire Editions (Paris) (1977)

Ellenberger, Allan, The Valentino Mystique, McFarland (2005)

Florey, Robert, Rudolph Valentino, Anthologie du Cinema, (1969)

Leider, Emily Wortis, Dark Lover: The Life and Death of Rudolph Valentino, Farrar, Straus and Giroux (US) (2003)

Livingstone, Beulah, Remember Valentino (1938)

Miredi, Antonio and Morone, Chicca Guglielmi, Rodolfo Valentino Una Mitologia Per Immagini, Libreria Petrini Torino (Italy) (1996)

Morris, Michael, Madame Valentino: The Many Lives of Natacha Rambova, Abbeville Press (1991)

Rambova, Natacha, Rudy: An Intimate Portrait of Rudolph Valentino by His Wife, Hutchinson & Co. Ltd. (London) (1926)

Scagnetti, Jack, The Intimate Life of Rudolph Valentino, Jonathan David Publishers (1975)

Shulman, Irving, Valentino, Trident Press, division of Simon and Schuster (1967)

Ullman, S. George, Valentino as I Knew Him, Macy-Masius Publishers (1926)

Valentino, Rudolph, Day Dreams, MacFadden Publications, New York (1923)

How You Can Keep Fit, MacFadden Publications, New York (1923)

My Private Diary, Occult Publishing Company (Chicago) (1929)

Walker, Alexander, Rudolph Valentino, Stein and Day (1976)

Magazines

Filmjournalin
Mon Cine
Motion Picture
Motion Picture Classic
Movie Weekly
Moving Picture World
Photoplay
Picture Play
Screenland
Shadowland
Theatre Magazine
Time
Vanity Fair
Variety

Newspapers

Chicago Herald Tribune
Los Angeles Herald Examiner
Los Angeles Times
San Francisco Call and Post
San Francisco Chronicle
San Francisco Examiner
New York Daily News
New York Times
Washington Post

Online Sources

Newspaperarchive.com
Proquest
Internet Archive
Ancestry.com

www.ingramcontent.com/pod-product-compliance
Lightning Source LLC
LaVergne TN
LVHW061235100826
845148LV00008B/961

9780578472249